Handbook of Research on Strategic Management of Interaction, Presence, and Participation in Online Courses

Lydia Kyei-Blankson
Illinois State University, USA

Joseph Blankson
Ohio Northern University, USA

Esther Ntuli
Idaho State University, USA

Cynthia Agyeman
Ohio University, USA

A volume in the Advances in Educational
Technologies and Instructional Design (AETID)
Book Series

Information Science
REFERENCE
An Imprint of IGI Global

Published in the United States of America by
    Information Science Reference (an imprint of IGI Global)
    701 E. Chocolate Avenue
    Hershey PA, USA 17033
    Tel: 717-533-8845
    Fax: 717-533-8661
    E-mail: cust@igi-global.com
    Web site: http://www.igi-global.com

Library of Congress Cataloging-in-Publication Data

Library of Congress Cataloging-in-Publication Data

Names: Kyei-Blankson, Lydia, editor of compilation.
Title: Handbook of research on strategic management of interaction, presence,
  and participation in online courses / Lydia Kyei-Blankson, Joseph
Blankson, Esther Ntuli, and Cynthia Agyeman, editors.
Description: Hershey, PA : Information Science Reference, [2016] | Includes
  bibliographical references and index.
Identifiers: LCCN 2015032772| ISBN 9781466695825 (hardcover) | ISBN
  9781466695832 (ebook)
Subjects: LCSH: Education, Higher--Computer-assisted instruction--Evaluation.
  | Web-based instruction--Evaluation.
Classification: LCC LB2395.7 .H244 2016 | DDC 378.1/7344678--dc23 LC record available at http://lccn.loc.
gov/2015032772

This book is published in the IGI Global book series Advances in Educational Technologies and Instructional Design (AE-TID) (ISSN: 2326-8905; eISSN: 2326-8913)

British Cataloguing in Publication Data
A Cataloguing in Publication record for this book is available from the British Library.

For electronic access to this publication, please contact: eresources@igi-global.com.

Advances in Educational Technologies and Instructional Design (AETID) Book Series

Lawrence A. Tomei
Robert Morris University, USA

ISSN: 2326-8905
EISSN: 2326-8913

MISSION

Education has undergone, and continues to undergo, immense changes in the way it is enacted and distributed to both child and adult learners. From distance education, Massive-Open-Online-Courses (MOOCs), and electronic tablets in the classroom, technology is now an integral part of the educational experience and is also affecting the way educators communicate information to students.

The **Advances in Educational Technologies & Instructional Design (AETID) Book Series** is a resource where researchers, students, administrators, and educators alike can find the most updated research and theories regarding technology's integration within education and its effect on teaching as a practice.

COVERAGE

- K-12 Educational Technologies
- Social Media Effects on Education
- Higher Education Technologies
- Instructional Design Models
- Hybrid Learning
- Curriculum Development
- Collaboration Tools
- Educational Telecommunications
- Classroom Response Systems
- E-Learning

IGI Global is currently accepting manuscripts for publication within this series. To submit a proposal for a volume in this series, please contact our Acquisition Editors at Acquisitions@igi-global.com or visit: http://www.igi-global.com/publish/.

Titles in this Series

For a list of additional titles in this series, please visit: www.igi-global.com

Intelligent Design of Interactive Multimedia Listening Software
Vehbi Turel (Bingol University, Turkey)
Information Science Reference • copyright 2015 • 449pp • H/C (ISBN: 9781466684997) • US $215.00 (our price)

Utilizing Virtual and Personal Learning Environments for Optimal Learning
Krista Terry (Appalachian State University, USA) and Amy Cheney (Appalachian State University, USA)
Information Science Reference • copyright 2016 • 376pp • H/C (ISBN: 9781466688476) • US $185.00 (our price)

Handbook of Research on Individual Differences in Computer-Assisted Language Learning
Mehrak Rahimi (Shahid Rajaee Teacher Training University, Iran)
Information Science Reference • copyright 2015 • 556pp • H/C (ISBN: 9781466685192) • US $325.00 (our price)

Fuzzy Logic-Based Modeling in Collaborative and Blended Learning
Sofia J. Hadjileontiadou (Hellenic Open University, Greece) Sofia B. Dias (Universidade de Lisboa, Portugal)
José A. Diniz (Universidade de Lisboa, Portugal) and Leontios J. Hadjileontiadis (Aristotle University of Thessaloniki, Greece)
Information Science Reference • copyright 2015 • 520pp • H/C (ISBN: 9781466687059) • US $195.00 (our price)

Handbook of Research on Educational Technology Integration and Active Learning
Jared Keengwe (University of North Dakota, USA)
Information Science Reference • copyright 2015 • 435pp • H/C (ISBN: 9781466683631) • US $305.00 (our price)

Psychological and Pedagogical Considerations in Digital Textbook Use and Development
Elena Railean (University of European Studies, Republic of Moldova & Academy of Sciences of Moldova, Republic of Moldova)
Information Science Reference • copyright 2015 • 295pp • H/C (ISBN: 9781466683006) • US $175.00 (our price)

Macro-Level Learning through Massive Open Online Courses (MOOCs) Strategies and Predictions for the Future
Elspeth McKay (RMIT University, Australia) and John Lenarcic (RMIT University, Australia)
Information Science Reference • copyright 2015 • 307pp • H/C (ISBN: 9781466683242) • US $200.00 (our price)

Implementation and Critical Assessment of the Flipped Classroom Experience
Abigail G. Scheg (Elizabeth City State University, USA)
Information Science Reference • copyright 2015 • 333pp • H/C (ISBN: 9781466674646) • US $175.00 (our price)

www.igi-global.com

701 E. Chocolate Ave., Hershey, PA 17033
Order online at www.igi-global.com or call 717-533-8845 x100
To place a standing order for titles released in this series, contact: cust@igi-global.com
Mon-Fri 8:00 am - 5:00 pm (est) or fax 24 hours a day 717-533-8661

List of Contributors

Table of Contents

Section 1
Theoretical Applications and Research Basis for Interaction, Presence, and Participation in Online Courses

Genevieve Marie Johnson, Curtin University, Australia
Audrey Cooke, Curtin University, Australia

Cindy Stewart, University of Houston – Downtown, USA
Travis Crone, University of Houston – Downtown, USA

Judi Simmons Estes, Park University, USA

David Starr-Glass, University of New York in Prague, Czech Republic

Arianne J Rourke, University of New South Wales
Annabelle Lewer-Fletcher, University of New South Wales

Section 2
Practical Applications and Strategies for Ensuring Interaction, Presence, and
Participation in Online Courses

Detailed Table of Contents

Section 1
Theoretical Applications and Research Basis for Interaction, Presence, and Participation in Online Courses

Chapter 1

    Genevieve Marie Johnson, Curtin University, Australia
    Audrey Cooke, Curtin University, Australia

Ecological theory conceptualized the student as surrounded by a series of environmental systems and the processes of learning as interaction between the student (i.e., bioecology) and the systems (i.e., microsystem, exosystem and macrosystem). This chapter synthesizes the literature and proposes an ecological model of student interaction in online learning environments. Specifically, learner-learner, learner-instructor and learner-content interactions occur in the microsystem and are mediated by the interface subsystem. Student microsystemic interactions influence and are influenced by the instructional design exosystem. The macrosystem reflects the indirect influence of university culture on all aspects of the microsystem, exosystem and interface subsystem. The chronosystem captures the effect of time on the student and on all ecological systems (e.g., students mature and university culture evolves)

Chapter 2

    Cindy Stewart, University of Houston – Downtown, USA
    Travis Crone, University of Houston – Downtown, USA

This chapter provides an overview of the major motivation theories, and examines how the ARCS-V model applies motivational theory to instructional design. The chapter also provides a cognitive framework to support aspects of the ARCS-V model. Special attention is given to course design and instructional practices aimed at reducing online student attrition and improving academic performance. Additionally, the chapter reviews research examining the utility of the ARCS-V model, as well as recommendations for implementation within the online modality.

Chapter 3

The premise of this chapter is that higher education online faculty have a pivotal role in student retention; faculty participation is key to student engagement and engaged students tend to complete courses in which they are enrolled. However, frequently faculty members are unaware of the impact their active participation and visibility has on student engagement and retention. In addition, online courses are an important source of revenue for many institutions of higher education and attrition results in loss of revenue. Given that faculty have a pivotal role in retention, institutions of higher education can benefit fiscally from guiding and supporting online faculty in strategies of student engagement and retention. Faculty support is needed during the process of change inherent in faculty adapting to teaching online, through providing on-going faculty professional development and by creating a teaching culture inclusive of informal scholarly investigations related to instructional effectiveness in online course delivery.

Participation is actively encouraged and promoted in online distance learning environments because it is associated with effective learning behaviors and with overall learner satisfaction. Participation is easily observed and measured; indeed, it is often seen as "making visible" underlying behaviors and dynamics at both the individual and group level. The reality, however, is that the ease with which participation can be assessed is in stark contrast with the complexity that surrounds its role in the productive distance online learning environments. This chapter explores the multiplicity of meanings, definitions, and attributions associated with participation. It attempts to make sense of this complexity, to consider a broader framework that makes a connection between participation and learning outcomes, and to examine the ways in which individual learning styles and national culture assumptions impact and mediate student participation in online learning contexts.

Chapter 5

In higher education in recent years the educational value of blog journals for facilitating student engagement, reflection and learning has been emphasized (Chu, Kwan, & Warning, 2012; Ellison & Wu, 2008; Richardson, 2005; Yang, 2009). According to Williams and Jacobs (2004), blogs are seen as a 'transformative educational tool', which assists in the development of 'reflective and critical thinking skills' (Joshi & Chugh, 2009). This chapter critically analyzes the reflective and collaborative value of two different systems of blog journaling used by postgraduate student to reflect on their arts industry internships. Firstly Blogger (https://www.blogger.com), used between 2008 and 2012 and secondly, journal blogging in the Learning Management System (LMS) of Moodle (2014) are critiqued in terms their ability to promote student engagement, reflection, connection and collaboration. There is particular emphasis on how recent blog journals (2014) reflect how students' confidence, awareness and understandings evolve as they develop professional expertise.

Social Presence theory seeks to explain how people present themselves as being "there" and "real" while using a communication medium. Most studies on social presence focus on how students present themselves and/or are perceived as being "there" and "real" in computer-mediated environments. However, to date, very few studies have focused on how instructors establish and maintain their own social presence in online learning environments. The following study explored the phenomenon of instructor social presence in accelerated online courses. The results suggest that the construct of presence is more complicated than previously thought and that future studies should employ multiple methods to further explore the concept of instructor social presence.

This chapter provides a case study example using cross-case analysis (Merriam, 2001) of digital mentoring within an online Master's level literacy course at a large public university in the Southwest United States. Two mentors provided individualized video conference sessions, using Blackboard Collaborate™ to 28 students (mentees). Data included written reflections from students as well as transcripts from selected videoconference sessions. Structured synchronous mentoring sessions provided a predictable framework for students and mentors alike. This chapter provides an analysis of the students' perceptions of the conferences, the types of discourse patterns and language analysis of the conferences, as well as description of themes and trends across the data. Suggestions on the usefulness of the conferences as well as the structure of mentoring sessions are described in the chapter. Established and emerging models of mentorship and e-development are outlined and utilized to frame the analyses and future research directions.

Integrating the principles of adult education in online environment -an environment which empowers the engagement of learners and their active participation, promotes interaction and immediacy between educator and learners, as well as between learners themselves, and improves learning outcomes- is a very important task. In this task the role of the educator is crucially important and simultaneously very complicated and demanding, as the integration of adult education principles in an online environment is not an easy issue and forms a big challenge for each online educator of adults. This chapter focuses on building interaction in adults' online courses by integrating the principles of adult education in an online environment, and presents one case study on training e-educators of adults. This case study concerns a one-month intensive seminar addressed to e-educators who teach adult courses, demonstrating that online interaction is both possible and effective by integrating the adult education principles in online educational environment.

Chapter 9

Juhong Christie Liu, James Madison University, USA
Elaine Roberts Kaye, James Madison University, USA

Online learning readiness is fundamental to student successful participation, presence, and interaction in online courses. Effective facilitation of these key components depends on sound instructional design. In self-directed online environments, learner-content interaction and scaffolding self-regulated learning have been found of primary importance to generate meaningful learning. To provide a solution to the challenges of interoperability of various functions in synchronous online learning environments, this chapter presents a case study about the design and development of a self-paced orientation to help students acquire online learning readiness. Learner-content interaction is strategically utilized in the design to scaffold self-regulated learning. The results of the case study demonstrate that this orientation positively prepares students to be ready for learning in a synchronous online environment. The approach can be of practical use to individuals and groups.

Chapter 10

Olivia P. Morris, Online Learning, Chicago, USA

This chapter discusses findings from a study of five faculty and 33 students from micro- and macroeconomics sections of online economics courses over the course of a semester. The study investigated faculty choice of web-based technologies for interaction and students' perceptions of such technologies. The objectives of the study were twofold. First, the author investigated faculty choice of web-based technologies for three major types of online interactions (learner–instructor, learner–content, and learner–learner). Second, the author examined student perceptions of technologies and recorded recommendations. Results from two online surveys of faculty and students at 2- and 4-year colleges showed strong agreement with perceptions of Moore, Drouin, Rhode, and Gardner. Faculty and students reported learner–learner interactions as the least important of the three interaction types. Although the discussion board was most effective for all three types of interactions, students from this sample did not prefer more learner–learner discussions.

Section 2
Practical Applications and Strategies for Ensuring Interaction, Presence, and Participation in Online Courses

B. Jean Mandernach, Grand Canyon University, USA
Rick Holbeck, Grand Canyon University, USA
Ted Cross, Grand Canyon University, USA

There are a plethora of best practices highlighting strategies to personalize the online learning experience, promote interaction and establish teaching presence. Despite this knowledge, a gap remains between online instructors' pedagogical knowledge and teaching behaviors. This discrepancy is largely a function of time. With a wide range of instructional tasks to complete, faculty struggle to balance all the demands of the online classroom. To maximize student success and satisfaction, it is essential that faculty effectively manage their time to engage in instructional behaviors with the greatest impact. This chapter overviews strategies to help online instructors: 1) create an efficient online classroom; 2) manage teaching time more effectively; and 3) prioritize their time investment to promote interaction, presence and participation.

Michelle Kilburn, Southeast Missouri State University, USA
Martha Henckell, Southeast Missouri State University, USA
David Starrett, Southeast Missouri State University, USA

The purpose of this chapter is to provide readers with strategies and techniques to enhance social interaction/presence within the online learning environment. A discussion of current definitions and the importance of social media will be discussed, as well as examples for use in the online classroom. Proven effective and interactive instructional components (i.e., instructor response time, video lecturing, and pedagogical considerations) are included as best practices and quality assurance guidelines. Topics in this chapter include types of social media tools available, examples of appropriate use in higher education, and recommended strategies to assist faculty in identifying the best tool to match the pedagogical goal. With a wide variety of experiences and knowledge regarding the topic, the authors provide unique perspectives including: teaching in the online environment, instructional design, oversight of online programs, technology training/user services, quality assurance, and faculty/student support.

Sang Chan, Weber State University, USA
Devshikha Bose, Boise State University, USA

Online learning will continue to be one of the popular modes of instruction offered by higher education institutions to accommodate different learning needs. Student engagement is critical to the success of online learning. Students should be engaged cognitively, emotionally, and behaviorally. This chapter discusses design considerations for online courses to promote student-instructor, student-student, and student-content interactions to engage students cognitively, emotionally, and behaviorally. The chapter also discusses the application of flow theory, specifically, in the design of instruction to engage students during their interaction with course content.

Online learning in higher education has rapidly grown in recent years and has become the norm. However, pedagogical aspects on online learning environments are still developing. This chapter focuses on one foundational aspect of online and blended learning known as presence. First, the concept of presence in online learning is described i.e. teaching presence, social presence, and cognitive presence. Secondly, strategies for ensuring presence are discussed from different angles: course design, course instructors and course facilitators, and course participants. Thirdly, the implications for future research are outlined. This chapter enhances the research on the Community of Inquiry (CoI) framework a useful guide to the design of learning experiences that support learners' critical reflection and engagement within collaborative online learning environments.

This chapter explores online learning and the pedagogical techniques needed to create an effective learning environment. In addition, it emphasizes the advances in contemporary online learning tracing its difficult beginning and the progress made due to advances made in technology especially the World Wide Web and the Internet. The chapter also discusses the importance of immediacy in online learning, and its ability to allow students to learn from anywhere and at any time. Student problems include lack of access to the technology, readiness to work online, and the erroneous impression that they know the technology more than the instructor. Interaction includes the effective application of scenarios of student and content, interaction between instructor and students, and the interaction between students which help promote social presence. We strongly believe the application of the afore-mentioned strategies will ensure successful development and implementations of an effective online course.

Effective online instruction requires understanding not only interaction but also how to facilitate interaction through technology (Moore & Kearsley, 2012). Specifically, Moore and Kearsley (2012) categorize these types of interactions as "learner with content, interaction with instruction [or] interaction with other learners" (p. 132). This chapter examines each of these interaction types and suggests ways to incorporate them into online learning environments (OLEs). The chapter provides techniques and approaches that will be beneficial to both instructional design practitioners and online instructors. It seeks to assuage some of the concerns that faculty have about OLEs and provides ideas and activities that can be implemented by course designers or instructors in OLE projects.

Advances in technology have increased opportunities for students to participate in online courses. While some instructors are beginning their careers teaching only online courses, others are discovering a need to teach sections of courses online after they have enjoyed a long career teaching in a traditional classroom. In either situation, it is important for instructors to recognize that students in online learning environments require the use of different strategies for encouraging engagement and participation in class. In this chapter, the author describes the challenges that students and instructors face specifically in the online learning environment as well as strategies for success, including how to maximize the impact of students' experiences and prior knowledge, using multiple platforms to deliver information, discouraging procrastination, setting clear expectations, encouraging individuality, capitalizing on diversity, and providing and utilizing helpful resources.

With the increase demand for distance education, institutions of higher education are actively exploring opportunities to weave self, subject and students for web based distance education. The pedagogical skills necessary to create effective active learning opportunities are explored throughout this chapter as well as lessons learned from research. The authors used vignettes to position effective course design and implementation aligned with both Bloom's Taxonomy and the SAMR (Substitution, Augmentation, Modification, Redefinition) model to enhance online learning environments. Learning objectives and course goals provided direction for developing task for social presence, cognitive presence and a collaborative stance in authentic online learning.

In the 21st century, online education provides an alternative instructional medium for teachers and students in United States educational systems and the world at large. Technology transforms how, when, and where students can learn, as well as the trends and use of instructional tools by students and teachers in the teaching-learning process. Online learning has developed during the past two decades to support traditional face-to-face classroom instruction and provides an opportunity for students to "interact with faculty and peers about substantive matters" (National Survey of Student Engagement, 2007, p. 7). The increase in minority students within U.S. schools has created a rise in socio-cultural, personal histories, educational, religious, and language/linguistic differences within the virtual classroom, requiring online instructors who teach in these contexts to be prepared to meet students' diverse needs. Despite the increase in online instruction, many questions remain unanswered with regards to how one group of minorities, particularly, English learners, adjust to instructional processes and teacher presence in an online learning environment. This chapter addresses the role of teacher presence in multicultural and online education, potential challenges of online learning for English learners, and teacher presence in multicultural online education.

Chapter 20

This chapter provides academic researchers and teachers with access to a unique pedagogical approach to teaching film online with a detailed exhibition of strategies and technological tools that have proven to encourage and ensure interaction, presence, and participation in an asynchronous online setting. With a persistent comparative eye toward both F2F and asynchronous online versions of the course, the chapter reveals both the content and the infrastructure as it is currently delivered to 100 students, detailing how each component works, and the advantages and disadvantages of delivering such a course online.

Foreword

Online learners come to our courses in many forms, but to succeed they must be engaged learners capable of quality online interaction and participation. An emerging research base tells us that they must also possess—or develop—a solid online presence. While we have known for some time that an exclusively teacher centric, content driven approach does not work well for many online learners, we haven't yet fully resolved how best to address this issue.

This volume seeks to provide insight into these complex issues via an interdisciplinary dialogue intended to assist instructors considering how to effectively integrate social presence into their online courses. Through research and practical experiences teaching online, chapter authors document the importance of interaction, participation, and social presences even as they identify concrete ideas to scaffold quality, rigorous online learning using these methods. Similarly, those considering the efficacy of online instruction or of building and curating their own online presence will find evidence here to spark their own thinking.

In its totality, this volume seek to assist educators to improve the online learning experience without sacrificing rigor or quality. The evidence offered here suggests that the integration of purposeful interaction, participation, and social presence activities can assist us to do so.

In summary, this volume makes a valuable contribution to the literature on course development and delivery to improve instruction, learning, and satisfaction in online courses. The chapters that make up this volume serve as a valuable resource for stakeholders interested in improving online learning. Those who teach or plan to teach online will find this interdisciplinary volume useful as will those interested in conducting research further exploring issues of interaction, presence, and participation in online courses. Specifically, those looking to make the case for the necessity of active learner engagement in the online learning course will find ample evidence here to support their future research efforts.

Beverly B. Ray
Idaho State University, USA

Preface

Online learning is ubiquitous in higher education. The number of students taking online courses offered by higher education institutions continues to increase. The increase in enrollment is largely driven by the demand for easy access to engaging course materials and web resources that address diverse learner needs especially among nontraditional students. While enrollment in online education continues to expand, concerns regarding rigor and comparability to traditional course outcomes persist. Unlike in traditional learning environments, the concepts of interaction, presence, and participation in the online courses can be challenging.

In order to ensure effective and significant outcomes, attention needs to be paid to the levels of interaction, presence, and participation in online courses as proposed by the two distance education learning theories of Transactional Distance (Moore, 1993) and Community of Inquiry (Garrison, Anderson, & Archer, 2000). According to the Moore's theory of Transactional Distance, the three levels of interaction key to effective teaching and learning in online environments are learner-instructor, learner-learner, and learner-content interaction. The Community of Inquiry theoretical framework on the other hand establishes the need for presence, which has been described as the degree to which one feels connected to the learning community. The three types of presence deemed essential to learning are namely social presence, cognitive presence, and teaching presence. In essence the two theories of distance education postulate the need for considerations of the existence of elements of structure, dialogue, self-directedness, a sense of membership, collaboration, meaning-making, and instructor immediacy in the design, implementation, and delivery of online courses.

Researchers have suggested the need for continued inquiry into best practices, strategies, and approaches that help address the challenges of ensuring interaction, presence, and participation in online education to meet students' diverse learning needs. The objective of this book is to provide educators with access to information regarding theoretical foundations, empirical or research-based tips, practical pedagogical strategies, and appropriate technological tools for encouraging, individually and in combination, the important elements of interaction and presence in online courses to ensure student learning, satisfaction, and participation in online courses. In addition, this book is intended for course designers who help develop and design online courses. Finally, the proposed publication is meant for researchers with an agenda in examining interaction, presence, and participation in online courses. More broadly, the publication contributes significantly to the literature on course development and delivery techniques that help improve instruction, learning, and satisfaction in online courses. From the research presented through this scholarly endeavor, course designers, instructors, and researchers will gain a deeper understanding of how elements of interaction and presence ensure optimal participation and quality online learning experiences.

ORGANIZATION OF THE BOOK

This book is comprised of 20 chapters that are organized into two main sections: *Theoretical Applications and Research Basis for Interaction, Presence, and Participation in Online Courses* and *Practical Applications and Strategies for Ensuring Interaction, Presence, and Participation in Online Courses*. Each chapter is authored or co-authored by a best practice educator in higher education settings and discusses research-based evidence strategies for successful participation, interaction, problem-solving and developing presence in online learning environments.

A brief description of each of the chapters follows:

In Chapter 1, the literature on the ecological model and its application to student interaction in online learning environments is discussed. The author focuses on the importance of considering the interface in the design and delivery of online courses as the interface is important in the mediation of the three levels of interaction: learner-learner, learner-instructor and learner-content interactions. The macro and microsystems or environments in which online learning occurs are presented.

Chapter 2 first provides an overview of the major motivation theories, and then follows up with an examination of the research on the application of motivational theory and the ARCS-V model to instructional design. Special attention is given to discussing course design and instructional strategies for tackling issues of academic performance and attrition in online environments.

In Chapter 3, the important role faculty play in the design and delivery of instruction in online learning environment and the effect on student engagement and retention is presented. In this chapter, emphasis is placed on how faculty participation and visibility in the online course is central to students' motivation to "stick" with learning online. The author of this chapter echoes the need for on-going faculty professional development and support as suggested in past research.

Chapter 4 switches from a focus on the online instructor to a focus on the online student and participation in online environments. In this chapter, the author explores the meanings, definitions, and attributions associated with student participation in online courses. The author also offers a viewpoint on how students' individual learning styles influence participation.

Chapter 5 discusses past literature on the use of a specific educational medium, reflective blog journals, for building critical thinking, collaboration, interaction, and engagement among students in online courses. A description of how reflective blog journals were used in a postgraduate online course to help develop professional expertise among students is presented.

Chapter 6 presents a mixed methods study on how instructors established their own social presence in an accelerated online course and the effect of this strategy on student learning. The author of this chapter cautions readers on the complexity of designing and implementing online courses with the construct of presence in mind.

In Chapter 7, the outcomes from a case study on the use of individualized structured synchronous video conference sessions in an online literacy course for graduate students are presented. The study's data included student written reflections and session transcripts. Suggestions on the usefulness of and how to design online mentoring sessions to promote presence, interaction, and engagement online are discussed.

Chapter 8 presents another case study on training educators of adult learners in online environments. In this chapter, the authors highlight the principles of adult education and its application in online learning for promoting engagement, active participation, interaction, and immediacy among educators and learners.

Chapter 9 presents solutions to the challenges faculty face in synchronous online learning environments. In this chapter, readers are exposed to findings from a case study on the design and development of a self-paced orientation to develop student readiness. The results of the case study demonstrate how this orientation positively prepared students to be ready for learning in a synchronous online environment.

Chapter 10 discusses the findings from a study on online economics courses. The objectives of the study were twofold: To investigate faculty choice of web-based technologies for implementing the three major types of online interaction in the courses and to examine student perception and recommendations regarding such technologies. The results from this investigation suggest that discussion boards are most effective for promoting all three types of interaction in online learning environments.

Chapter 11 highlights a number of best practices and time management strategies for promoting interaction and presence online to maximize student success and satisfaction. The strategies shared in the chapter are helpful for creating an efficient online classroom while managing teaching time effectively to ensure interaction, presence and participation.

In Chapter 12, the authors provide a list of practical strategies and techniques that can be applied to enhance interaction and social presence within the online learning environments. Specifically, the authors focus on how this can be done while using social media and other collaborative technological tools applicable in online learning.

Chapter 13 discusses different tips and strategies necessary for enhancing student engagement in online environments. The authors point out the importance of having instructors design and deliver courses that engage their students in the cognitive, affective, and behavioral domains of online learning by promoting all the three levels of interaction of learner-content, learner-instructor, and learner-learner interactions. In the process, the authors propose the application of flow theory in the design and implementation of online courses.

Chapter 14 focuses on the Community of Inquiry (CoI) framework and describes the construct of presence. Strategies for ensuring presence through course design to promote learners' critical reflection and engagement are presented. Also presented are techniques for establishing presence from the perspective of the course instructors, facilitators, and course participants.

In Chapter 15, the authors explore pedagogical techniques needed to design and teach courses effectively in online learning environments. The authors emphasize the importance of interaction and immediacy in online learning and the share applications and strategies that ensure successful development and implementation of effective online courses.

In Chapter 16, the authors remind readers that effective online instruction requires an understanding of not only interaction but also of how to facilitate interaction through the use or application of technology in the online course. The authors of this chapter examine the different types of interaction and suggest ways faculty could work on incorporating each of these types of interaction in their online courses.

Chapter 17 offers different strategies for encouraging and maximizing student engagement and participation for both novice and experienced instructors who are beginning their teaching careers online. In this chapter, the author describes the challenges faculty might face in their quest to teach online for the first time and offers best practices for discouraging procrastination, setting clear expectations, encouraging individuality, capitalizing on diversity, and providing and utilizing helpful resources for online students.

Chapter 18 presents a number of vignettes that demonstrate how to design, position, and implement effective online courses aligned with both Bloom's Taxonomy and the Substitution, Augmentation, Modification, Redefinition (SAMR) model. The purpose of this chapter is to provide direction for developing the task for social presence, cognitive presence and a collaborative stance in authentic online learning environments.

In Chapter 19, the authors address the dearth of research on establishing the importance of teaching presence for the integration of multicultural online education with specific focus on English language learners. The study highlights the role of teaching presence in multicultural and online education, the merits and demerits of English language learners in online learning, and best practices for teaching multicultural education online.

Chapter 20 provides readers with information on pedagogical approaches, strategies, and tools for teaching film style to students in a way that encourages and ensures interaction, presence, and participation in an asynchronous online setting. The author draws from the experience of twenty years of traditional course teaching and from five years of teaching online. The chapter openly confronts questions of instructional quality, academic rigor, assessment, interaction, and the parity of teaching online as against teaching face-to-face.

In general, the chapters presented in this book highlight the importance of designing and delivering interactive and engaging online courses while holding important the concepts of interaction and presence. As previously stated, having present the elements of interaction and presence encourages participation and significant learning in online environments. Again, the chapters highlight advances in instructional design practices, the role of faculty, faculty training and development, and appropriate technological tools and resources essential for the design and delivery of effective courses in online learning environments.

Lydia Kyei-Blankson
Illinois State University, USA

Joseph Blankson
Ohio Northern University, USA

Esther Ntuli
Idaho State University, USA

Cynthia Agyeman
Ohio University, USA

REFERENCES

Garrison, D. R., Anderson, T., & Archer, W. (2000). Critical inquiry in a text-based environment: Computer conferencing in higher education. *The Internet and Higher Education, 2*(2/3), 87–105.

Moore, M. (1993). Theory of transactional distance. In D. Keegan (Ed.), *Theoretical principles of distance education* (pp. 22–38). New York: Routledge.

Acknowledgment

The editors would like to express their deepest gratitude to all individuals for their immense contributions without which this book would not have become a reality. To begin with, we would like to thank all our contributing authors for submitting such informative and provocative chapters and their relentless desire to revise their chapters based on the reviews. We are grateful to Dr. Beverly Ray, *Idaho State University, USA,* for writing an insightful foreword to this book.

We also wish to acknowledge the reviewers for taking the time to provide constructive comments and suggestions to make this book more coherent and readable. Most of the authors also served as reviewers and we highly appreciate their double task.

In addition, we are thankful to our editor, Rachel Ginder at the IGI Global, for her support and mostly for keeping us on schedule. Finally, we are most grateful to our families for their continued patience and encouragement throughout this project. Thank you!

Section 1
Theoretical Applications and Research Basis for Interaction, Presence, and Participation in Online Courses

Chapter 1
An Ecological Model of Student Interaction in Online Learning Environments

Genevieve Marie Johnson
Curtin University, Australia

Audrey Cooke
Curtin University, Australia

ABSTRACT

Ecological theory conceptualized the student as surrounded by a series of environmental systems and the processes of learning as interaction between the student (i.e., bioecology) and the systems (i.e., microsystem, exosystem and macrosystem). This chapter synthesizes the literature and proposes an ecological model of student interaction in online learning environments. Specifically, learner-learner, learner-instructor and learner-content interactions occur in the microsystem and are mediated by the interface subsystem. Student microsystemic interactions influence and are influenced by the instructional design exosystem. The macrosystem reflects the indirect influence of university culture on all aspects of the microsystem, exosystem and interface subsystem. The chronosystem captures the effect of time on the student and on all ecological systems (e.g., students mature and university culture evolves)

THEORETICAL FOUNDATIONS

According to Johnson (2014), educational theory serves two critical functions. "First, it provides a vocabulary and a conceptual framework for interpreting observations of teaching and learning. Second, it suggests solutions to improve teaching and learning under a range of circumstances including, recently, interactive online environments" (p. 298). White, Collins and Frederiksen (2011) noted that theory construction is the central goal of science "where theories are coherent bodies of concepts, laws and models, which account for a wide range of observations and enable humans to predict, control and explain what happens as events occur" (p. 42).

In 1989, Moore proposed three types of student interaction in distance education; learner-learner, learner-instructor and learner-content. *Learner-learner interaction* is "between one

DOI: 10.4018/978-1-4666-9582-5.ch001

learner and other learners, alone or in group settings, with or without the real-time presence of an instructor" (p. 4). During *learner-instructor interaction*, the teacher seeks "to stimulate or at least maintain the student's interest in what is to be taught, to motivate the student to learn, to enhance and maintain the learner's interest, including self-direction and self-motivation" (p. 2). *Learner-content interaction* "is the process of intellectually interacting with the content that results in changes in the learner's understanding, the learner's perspective, or the cognitive structures of the learner's mind" (p. 2). More recent terminology as submitted by Garrison (2011) for roughly equivalent latent constructs includes *social presence* (i.e., learner-learner interaction), *teacher presence* (learner-instructor interaction) and *cognitive presence* (learner-content interaction). Moore encouraged educators to "organize programs to ensure maximum effectiveness of each type of interaction, and ensure they provide the type of interaction most suitable for various teaching tasks of different subject areas, and for learners at different stages of development" (p. 5). Anderson (2003a) suggested that a high level of one type of interaction may be sufficient to support student learning, although "it is impossible to determine with certainty which exact combination of human and nonhuman interaction is necessary for effective instruction with any group of learners or for the teaching of any subject domain" (Anderson, 2003b, p. 130).

In 1994, given the growing popularity of online courses in distance education, Hillman, Willis and Gunawardena added the concept of *learner-interface interaction* to Moore's (1989) typology. At the most fundamental level, successful online learning is based upon the student's ability to interact with hardware and software and, obviously, have reliable internet connectivity. The four types of online interaction (i.e., learner-learner, learner-instructor, learner-content and learner-interface) provide a conceptual framework for examining

student interaction in online learning environments. Essentially, satisfying and instructionally-effective interaction is built upon a foundation of congruence or perceived congruence between individual student characterises and elements of the learning environment. In this regard, ecological theoretical models are particularly well-suited to conceptual organization and exploration of interaction in online learning environments (Johnson, 2010a, 2010b, 2014). While applied professions may not readily embrace theoretical models, no human behaviour can be understood without a conceptual blueprint of assumptions that guide instructional and managerial processes.

Ecological Theoretical Models

Ecological models of human learning and development situate the person within a system of relationships affected by multiple levels of the surrounding environment (Bronfenbrenner, 1977). Bronfenbrenner (1989) organized the contexts of human development into five nested environmental systems, with bidirectional influences within and between systems. The *microsystem* refers to direct environments and includes teachers, peers and family. The *mesosystem* is comprised of connections between direct environments (e.g., family support for school learning). The *exosystem* includes environmental settings that indirectly affect the person (e.g., infrastructures of instructional support). The *macrosystem* reflects overarching social ideologies and cultural values (e.g., the value of digital literacy). The *chronosystem* highlights the effect of time on the individual (e.g., cognitive maturation) and on all systems (e.g., new applications of digital technology). Bronfenbrenner (2005) subsequently proposed the *bioecology*, that is, the person's own biology is conceptualized as a dimension of the microsystem that interacts with all other aspects of the microsystem. Such an ecological framework provides "a unified but highly differentiated conceptual scheme for describing and interrelating structures and processes in both the immediate and more remote environment as it shapes the course of human development" (Bronfenbrenner, 1979, p. 11).

Ecological systems theory (Bronfenbrenner, 1977, 1979) emerged prior to the digital revolution and the impact of then available technology (e.g., analogue television) was conceptually situated in the microsystem. Given the continuously increasing complexity and availability of digital technology, Johnson and Puplampu (2008) proposed the *ecological techno-subsystem*, a dimension of the microsystem which includes direct interaction with living (e.g., peers) and nonliving (e.g., hardware) elements of communication, information and recreation digital technologies. From an ecological perspective and presented in Figure 1, the techno-subsystem mediates bidirectional interaction between the person and the microsystem.

Apparent from Figure 1, ecological conceptual models typically place the individual in the center of a series of nested environmental systems with bidirectional influence between individual bioecological characteristics and the microsystem, although bioecology changes over time due to biological processes and environmental experiences (i.e., the chronosystem). Ecological systems theory provides a conceptual framework for synthesis of the extensive literature relevant to student interaction in online environments. Review of such literature establishes the ecological nature of e-learning and provides the building

Figure 1. The ecological techno-subsystem (Johnson & Puplumpu, 2008)

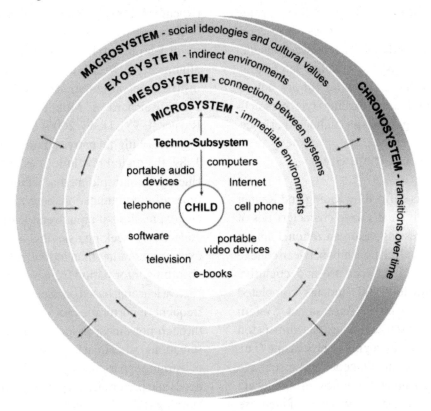

blocks for the subsequently presented ecological model of student interaction in online learning environments.

Bioecology: Student Characteristics and Online Interaction

In online and traditional learning environments, student characteristics affect learning outcomes (Johnson, 2005, 2008a). The exact mechanisms of such causal relationships are difficult, if not impossible, to precisely describe because human learning is enormously complex and controlled by a wide range of student and environmental variables. Indeed, Vygotsky (1997) claimed that the educational process is active on at least three levels: "the student is active, the teacher is active, and the environment created between them is an active one" (p. 54). In constructing an ecological model of student interaction in online learning environments, it is necessary to consider research which establishes relationships between student biological characteristics and online interaction. Such student variables include, but are not restricted to, cognitive and learning style, personality, attitude, demographics and online experience.

Cognitive and Learning Style

Cognitive style is defined by Riding and Rayner (1998) as an individual's fixed characteristics of information processing and organization. Johnson (2008b) established relationships between college student patterns of internet use and cognitive style. Approximately 400 students completed four modified Cognitive Assessment System (CAS) subtests, each assessing one dimension of the PASS model of cognitive processing (i.e., planning, attention, simultaneous and successive processing). Students also completed a rating scale that determined the extent and nature of their use of the internet. Reportedly, "CAS subtest scores were greater for individuals who frequently, as opposed to infrequently, used the Internet, both in general and with respect to specific applications such as online communication" (p. 2103). Further, "college students who reported frequently using search engines scored significantly higher on the measure of metacognition (i.e., planning) than students who infrequently used the same cultural artifact" (p. 2104). From an ecological perspective, such research confirms that student bioecology (e.g., cognitive architecture) is influenced by microsystemic online interaction.

Similar to the construct of cognitive style, *learning style* refers to "characteristic cognitive, affective, and psychological behaviors that serve as relatively stable indicators of how learners perceive, interact with, and respond to the learning environment" (Keefe, 1979, p. 4). "Each person's style is a combination of various biological and experiential variables that contribute to learning" (Rochford, 2003, p. 667). A considerable body of literature has addressed the instructional utility of learning style, most often recommending alignment between student learning style and instructional presentation (Felder & Brent, 2005; Jones, Reichard, & Mokhtari, 2003; Riding & Rayner, 1998). Dede (2005) described the learning style of digital natives (individuals born after 1989, the digital revolution) as characterized by fluency in multiple media, valuing each for the types of communication, activities, experiences and expressions it empowers; learning based on collectively seeking, sieving and synthesizing experiences rather than individually locating and absorbing information from a single best source; "active learning based on experience that includes frequent opportunities for reflection; expression through non-linear associational webs of representations rather than linear stories; and co-design of learning experiences personalized to individual needs and preferences" (p. 10). The bioecological learning style of the current generation of university students influences and has been influenced by online environments (Johnson, 2007b)

Personality and Attitude

In additional to the bioecological characteristics of cognitive and learning style, personality and attitude affect student interaction in online environments. Johnson (2006a) assessed the relationship between a range of personality and attitudinal variables and student satisfaction with cooperative online study groups. Approximately 100 university students permitted their course marks to be used for research purposes and completed a questionnaire that assessed individual difference variables such as locus of control (e.g., planning ahead makes things turn out better), obsessive-compulsive tendencies (e.g., I check and double check my work), achievement anxiety (e.g., nervousness while I am taking an exam hinders me from doing well), academic self-esteem (e.g., I am a good student) as well as personal interpretations of the online study group experience. Reportedly, students did not perceive the benefits of online study groups equally, but such evaluation was not associated with academic achievement. For example, students with the highest internal locus of control and the highest perception of peer support were most likely to rate the online study groups as effective. Students with the highest academic self-esteem expressed the perception that the online study groups enhanced their achievement. Students with the lowest orientation to cooperative learning expressed the perception that the online study groups were not helpful in mastering course content. Student bioecological personality characteristics influence student satisfaction with learner-learner online interaction.

The personality dimension of introversion-extroversive has been linked to student satisfaction in online learning environments (MacGregor, 2002). Extroverts tend to focus on the outer world of people and external events while introverts "focus on their own inner world of ideas and experiences" (Myers, 1993, p.4). Soles and Moller (2002) proposed that synchronous online communication is best suited to extroverts while asynchronous

online communication is best suited to introverts. Daughenbaugh, Daughenbaugh, Surry and Islam (2002) compared student satisfaction in online and traditional introductory computer science courses in terms of a range of personality characteristics including introversion-extroversion. Reportedly, "the data indicated that students rated as extroverts, rather than introverts, showed a stronger preference for the ways in which information is presented in online courses" (p. 72). Extroverts enjoyed synchronous and asynchronous communication. Introverts, on the other hand, rarely engaged in synchronous chat and asynchronous discussion although some use of email was noted. In contrast, Johnson and Johnson (2006) reported that students who stated a preference for synchronous over asynchronous online discussion, or vice versa, were not significantly different with respect to the personality variable introversion-extroversion. Apparently, student personality characteristics are differentially manifest in various online learning environments; a conceptual model is required to explain the complexity of student interaction in online learning environments.

Demographics and Online Experience

According to Huang and Yang (2014) and reflecting ecological theoretical assumptions, "the cyber lifestyle of the student" (p. 5) encompasses learning preferences, age, access to technology and level of self-direction; the technological and pedagogical learning environment; and the overall environment that is determined by culture, the government and society. Student demographic characteristics such as gender and age have been implicated in emerging technology up-take including comfort with instructional applications of digital technology (Hargittai, 2010; Joiner, Gavin, Duffield, Brosnan, Crook et al., 2005). Jones, Ramanau, Cross and Healing (2010) concluded that while there were strong age-related variations, it was simplistic to describe university students as a single generation. "The generation is not homogenous in its use and appreciation of new technologies and there are significant variations amongst students that lie within the Net generation age band" (p. 773). Romero, Guitert, Sangra and Bullen (2013) found limited differences in the characteristics of Net generation and the non-Net generation e-students. They concluded the differences were based on the use of digital technologies rather than age; the Net generation used technology more for social activities and the non-Net generation used a more limited range of software.

Experience with software reportedly mediates student satisfaction with e-learning (Sharpe & Greg, 2005). Rodriquez, Ooms, Montanez and Yan (2005) surveyed 700 professional and graduate students and reported that "comfort with technology was related to satisfaction with online course experience which was related to perceived quality; motivation to learn more about technology was also related to satisfaction of online learning experience" (p. 1). Johnson and Howell (2005) compared two groups of students: 1) those whose use of online learning tools was required, in some cases, and optional, in other cases and 2) those whose use of online learning tools was entirely optional. All students made pre- and post-course ratings of the perceived value of instructional technology. Reportedly, students required to use online learning tools showed a greater overall change in attitude toward technology and made greater use of optional online course material relative to students whose use was optional. Similarly, university students discussed two cases studies synchronously and two case studies asynchronously (Johnson & Johnson, 2006). At the end of the course, approximately 40% of the students indicted that they preferred synchronous chat and 60% indicted that they preferred asynchronous discussion. Students who most enjoyed chat as opposed to discussion had more internet experience than students who expressed the alternate preference. "Given the fast-paced and highly interactive nature of realtime CMC [computer mediated communication], Internet experience may have created a level of user familiarity and corresponding comfort that facilitated student appreciate of synchronous CMC" (p. 5). A conceptual model is required to explain the complex relationships between student online experience and interaction in online learning environments.

The Microsystem: Direct Student Interaction in Online Learning Environments

From an ecological perspective, student bioecology (e.g., learning style, personality and age) interacts directly with elements in the microsystem. In online learning environments, direct interaction in the microsystem includes learner-learner, learner-instructor and learner-content interaction. Traditionally, the teacher is often identified as the single most important variable in the learning environment (Johnson, 2006b), although peers and learning resources also impact on student achievement and satisfaction (Johnson, 2011). Synthesis of research relevant to ecological theory construction may reasonably include e-teachers, e-peers and e-learning materials and resources.

E-Teachers, E-Tutors and E-Moderators

Because online learning environments are considerably more learner-centered than most traditional university instructional contexts, terms such as *e-tutor* and *e-moderator* are interchangeable with the term *e-teacher* (McPherson & Nunes, 2004). Goold, Coldwell and Craig (2010) defined the role of the e-tutor as essentially social, pedagogical, technical and organizational. The role of the e-moderator is not simply the provision of learning resources but, rather, the successful facilitation of online interaction and adequate student support (Lewis & Price, 2007). In addition to e-teachers, software supports student learning. For example, *eTeacher*, an intelligent agent, "uses the information contained in the student profile to proactively assist the student by suggesting him/her personalized courses of action that will help him/her during the learning process" (Schiaffino, Garcia, & Amandi, 2008, p. 1744). Similarly, *e-Tutor* is an intelligent language tutoring program that "provides error-specific feedback; that is, it not only marks errors, but informs the user of the specific type of error [and] … offers help, clickable from the same screen" (Sanders, 2012, p. 581). The distinction between human and nonhuman student support, obvious in traditional university environments, is less apparent in online environments. An interactive conceptual framework specific to online learning environments is required.

There is general agreement that human e-teachers and e-tutors are essential as mechanisms of e-student support and encouragement. "An online teacher must create a coherent learning experience for students with whom they may not meet face-to-face and, therefore, must develop new support strategies that maintain motivation and encourage interaction" (Bennett, 2004, p. 231). In a survey based on Moore's (1989) typology of learner interaction, Johnson (2011) reported that the majority university students in a blended learning environment expressed the perception that interaction with their teachers contributed more to their learning than interaction with instructional content or with other students. In a comprehensive study of over two thousand e-learners, Paechter, Maier and Macher (2010) reported that "students' assessments of the instructor's expertise in e-learning, and her/his counseling and support were the best predictors for learning achievement and course satisfaction" (p. 222). Young (2006) identified that seven e-teacher characteristics that explained 86.2% of the variability in student perception of online teacher effectiveness in higher education: adapting to student needs, using meaningful examples, motivating students to do their best, facilitating the course effectively, delivering a valuable course, communicating effectively, and showing concern for student learning. "In open-ended comments,

the students wrote that effective teachers are visibly and actively involved in the learning, work hard to establish trusting relationships, and provide a structured, yet flexible classroom environment" (p. 65). In this regard, direct e-student interactions include both human (i.e., teachers and peers) and non-human (i.e., resources and software) aspect of the microsystem.

E-Peers and Online Peer Collaborative Learning

While Johnson (2011) reported that a minority of university students (11.6%) in a blended learning environment expressed the perception that learner-learner interaction was more important to their learning that instructor and content interaction, online instructional practice emphasizes collaborative peer-based interaction (Garrison, 2011). Pan, Xu, Wang, Zhang, Ling and Lin (2014) concluded that interpersonal relationships enabled and encouraged through social networking increased the frequency of sharing and seeking knowledge in online learning environments. Ma and Yuen (2011) identified the need to connect with peers, to maintain connections, and to promote a feeling of belonging within the peer group as contributors to the prevalence of online learning interactions. Ma and Chan (2014) found that college students who perceived themselves as successful in relationships, had higher self-esteem and were optimistic were most likely to share knowledge online. However, Swan and Shih (2005) reported that student perception of e-teacher social presence "was a more influential factor in determining student satisfaction than the perceived presence of peers" (p. 115).

Online peer collaboration is encouraged and supported by highly interactive Web 2.0 technologies (e.g., blogs and wikis; Bejjar & Boujelbene, 2014). University students reportedly enjoyed peer-based microblogging (e.g., twitter), although learning benefits were not established (Inghilterra & Ravatua-Smith, 2014). Nonetheless, e-student enjoyment, satisfaction and motivation are essential to engagement in the processes of e-learning which is linked with course completion (Paechter et al., 2010). Ensuring meaningful student participation and quality postings in online discussion forums is facilitated by e-teacher modeling, scaffolding and feedback (Miyazoe & Anderson, 2010). Cheng, Paré, Collimore and Joordens (2011) concluded that students who voluntarily engaged in online discussion with peers achieved better examination results than those who did not, although the direction of causation is subject to speculation. Swan and Shih (2005) reported that the perceived social presence of e-peers accounted for 13% of the variance in e-student perception of achievement. An ecological model of interaction in online learning environments would explain variation in student needs and preferences in terms of unique e-student bioecologies interacting with elements of unique microsystems at a specific point in time (i.e., chronosystem).

E-Learning Material and Resources

The potential of learner-content interaction in online learning environments may not consistently be actualized, perhaps because traditional classroom practice is assumed to generalize to online learning environments (Scheg, 2014). According to Littlejohn, Falconer and McGill (2008), e-learning materials and resources are made available to students for a variety of reasons including being: easily found or sourced, appropriately priced, in accessible formats, easily understood, from a trustworthy site, suitable for more than one purpose, compatible with other resources, suitable for the context of the course, engaging to students and usable within several learning models. Herrington, Reeves and Oliver (2006) argued for synergies among the learner, task and technology to create innovative and immersive e-learning environments. "The most widely accepted model of online higher education appears to be one of reductionism, whereby learning management systems facilitate the design of easily digested packets of information, usually assessed by discrete stand-alone tests and academic assignments" (p. 233). In contrast, *authentic learning* refers to a pedagogical approach that situates learning tasks in the context of potential and real use. "It offers an alternative instructional model based upon sound principles for the design and implementation of complex and realistic learning tasks" (Herrington, Reeves, & Oliver, 2014, p. 401).

In reviewing the literature, Lust, Juarez Collazo, Elen and Clarebout (2012) concluded that students benefit from using e-learning materials and resources. Rufer and Adams (2013) found that an interactive reusable learning object was successful in increasing student understanding of required content. Reportedly, 92.5% of students demonstrated mastery of new content, an increase from 75% without the learning object. Supporting ecological theoretical assumptions, such increase in learning may be the consequence of "providing learning approaches that are congruent with a variety of cognitive learning styles and increased interaction and reflection" (p. 113). In blended learning environments, Lust, Elen and Clarebout (2013) identified four types of student-users of online instructional tools and materials. The first group, referred to as *no-users*, only accessed the recorded lectures provided online; the second group, referred to as *selective users*, limited their use to tools that connected to their face-to-face environment (i.e., lectures and slides provided online and the activities required for the face-to-face sessions); the third group, *intensive superficial users*, used more tools but were passive in their use; and the final group, *intensive active users*, used all tools and actively participated online. Johnson (2005) conducted a study in which academic achievement was correlated with first-year university student use of online instructional tools and materials. Curvilinear relationships emerged. That is, low achieving students had the lowest level of online presence; average achieving students had the highest level of online presence, and high achieving students had moderate levels of online presence. From an ecological perspective, interaction in online learning environments is a function of the e-learner's unique bioecology interacting with elements of a specific microsystem (e.g. resources and materials). Microsystemic interactions over time explain student learning outcomes. Online microsystemic interactions, however, differ markedly from interactions in traditional classrooms and lecture theaters because online interactions are mediated by the *interface subsystem*.

The Interface Subsystem: The Digital Interface and Student Online Interaction

In ecological models, the microsystem encompasses direct interactions between the environment and the individual (Bronfenbrenner, 1977, 1979, 1989, 1995, 2005). Johnson and Puplampu (2008) proposed the *ecological techno-subsystem*, a dimension of the microsystem which includes digital technology with which the child directly interacts. The term *subsystem*, as opposed to system, is used because, since individuals interact directly with the technology, such interactions must be situated in the microsystem. In applying ecological theory to online learning interactions, the *interface subsystem* is proposed because all direct interactions are mediated by hardware, software, internet connectivity, and the university learning management system (LMS). The interface is a subsystem because it is a collection of digital elements relatively distinct from other microsystemic elements.

Hardware, Software and Connectivity

At the most fundamental level, online learning is influenced, if not controlled, by the quality of hardware, software and internet connectivity available to e-learners. "Younger generations of students are trending away from computer use because desktops, and even laptops, are too unwieldy, location-centric, and thus inconvenient" (Pursell, 2009, p. 1219). In 2008, Kennedy, Judd, Churchward, Gray and Krause reported that approximately 96% of Australian first-year university students reported owning a mobile phone, 89.5% reported owning a desktop computer and 63.2% a laptop computer. Nagler and Ebner (2009) found ubiquitous use of Wikipedia, YouTube and social networking sites among undergraduate university students. Reportedly, students used a limited range of specific internet applications and only one-third of students used their mobile phones for school work. From an ecological theoretical perspective, Johnson (2012) reported that first-year university students were not unanimously connected across all microsystemic learning environments; approximately 10% of students indicated that they did not use the internet at home and approximately 12% indicated that they did not use the internet at university.

In rural and remote communities reliable high speed connectivity is not consistently available which affects the feasibility of online learning in such regions (Johnson & Oliver, 2014). Fortunately, mobile phone technology has improved remote access to internet applications and LMS apps such as Blackboard Mobile Learn are increasingly available to students (iTunes, 2014). Such ubiquitous connectivity has resulted in the next generation of e-learning, often referred to as mobile learning or m-learning (Cochrane & Bateman, 2010). *M-learning* is defined as "the provision of education and training on PDAs/palmtops/handhelds, smartphones and mobile phones" (Rismark, Sølvberg, Strømme, & Hokstad 2007, p. 1). Learners with diverse bioecological backgrounds benefit from mobile technologies which emphasize interactivity and oral communication (Litchfield, Dyson, Lawrence, & Zmijewska, 2007). Supporting ecological theoretical assumptions, Hargittai (2010) found "considerable variation ... even among fully wired college students when it comes to understanding various aspects of Internet use" and suggested that "differentiated contexts of uses and experiences may explain these variations" (p. 108). Further supporting the ecology of interaction in online learning environments, Bullen, Morgan, Belfer and Qayyum (2008) observed that student use of the internet at university was the consequence of "the student and instructor dynamic within a course or program, the technical requirements of the discipline, and the affordances that a tool provided within a given context" (p. 10).

Learning and Course Management Systems

An LMS or course management system (CMS) refers to the "infrastructure that delivers and manages instructional content, identifies and assesses individual and organizational learning or training goals, tracks the progress towards meeting those goals, and collects and presents data for supervising the learning process of an organization as a whole" (Watson & Watson, 2007, p. 28). The LMS adopted by a university (e.g., Moodle or BlackBoard) as well as other digital resources (e.g., Apple teaching apps) highlight the primacy of the ecological interface subsystem on student interaction in online learning environments (Johnson & Davies, 2014; Zhao & Johnson, 2012). Adeyinka and Mutula (2010) proposed the Course Management System Success Model which highlights the importance of the technical infrastructure including hardware, software and support for teachers and students. Similarly, Pollard, Gupta and Satzinger (2010) suggested that contemporary approaches to LMS development are extending user focus by adopting a service-oriented view which emphasizes the importance of user (i.e., teachers and students) LMS and CMS support. Specific online tools available in LMS (e.g., web-conferencing, blogs and discussion forums) facilitate learner-learner and learner-instructor interaction (Garcia-Valcarcel, 2010). Other tools commonly available in LMS and CMS are particularly well-suited to learner-content interaction included auto-marked practice quizzes (Johnson, 2006c) and the essay test tool which requires teacher marking (Johnson & Davies, 2012). From an ecological perspective, the LMS, CMS and other instructional software are situated in the microsystemic interface subsystem because the e-learner is in direct contact with those technologies. However, decisions concerning the selection and use of specific LMS/CMS tools and other software occur outside the microsystem. The *ecological exosystem* encompasses indirect influences on the individual; such influences affect elements of the microsystem which, in turn, affect the individual (Johnson & Puplampu, 2008). In the context of online learning environments, the exosystem includes, most notably, elements of instructional design.

The Exosystem: Instructional Design and Online Student Interaction

Instructional design is a general term used to refer to all decisions and subsequent development of student learning experiences (Reiser & Dempsey, 2012). From an ecological perspective, instructional design processes correspond with the exosystem because they indirectly affect the e-learner. Kemp (1985) conceptualized instructional design as a continuous cycle that requires constant planning, design, development and assessment to insure effective instruction (Morrison, Ross, Kemp, & Kalman, 2010). Such a dynamic orientation to instructional design is compatible with an ecological model of student interaction in online learning environments and includes the development of learning objectives, content sequencing, instructional strategies and delivery, student assignments and assessment, and continuous course improvement processes.

Learning Objectives and Content Sequencing

From an ecological perspective and in the context of pre-instructional decisions situated in the exosystem, learning objectives (i.e., the knowledge and skills required of the e-learner) are identified and delineated prior to microsystem student interaction in the online learning environment. In post-secondary institutions, learning objectives emerge from a variety of sources including university-prescribed graduate attributes (Barrie, 2007), statutory and regulatory professional certification frameworks, the expertise of instructional faculty, and various committees and groups (McKimm & Swanwick, 2009). Learning objectives reflect theoretical assumptions which typically include student learning outcomes expressed as the capacity to create, evaluate, analyze, apply, understand and remember (Anderson & Krathwohl, 2001). Because learning objectives inform, if not determine, all aspects of instructional design, such objectives exert considerable influence on elements of the microsystem. For example, university graduate attributes often include the ability to work collegially in teams and, as such, may influence the nature and extent of learner-learner collaborative activities in online learning environments. Higher order thinking such as the ability to evaluate the appropriateness of professional decisions may result in learner-learner and learner-instructor online asynchronous discussion of clinical case studies. Defining technical terms may be achieved by exosystemic instructional design decisions to use specific learning objects for drill and practice (i.e., learner-content interaction).

Curriculum content sequencing involves managing a learning route to help students achieve learning objectives (Morrison et al., 2010). In traditional classrooms, course content and associated learning objectives are often sequenced using a textbook and a syllabus where content is linear and students have limited choice; individual interests and preference are largely ignored (Chen, Liu, & Chang, 2006). In contrast, LMS tools and learning objects allow for increased selectiveness in sequence composition of instructional activities (Chi, 2009). Relative to traditional paper-based and lecture class formats, digital repositories have enormous storage capacity, collectively develop over time, and afford individualized sequencing of e-learning activities. McCalla (2004) promoted an ecological approach to e-learning systems by "attaching models of learners to the learning objects they interact with, and then mining these models for patterns that are useful for various purposes" (p. 2). Using techniques inspired by collaborative filtering, Champaign and Cohen (2010) proposed an intelligent tutoring system for determining the sequencing of content of highly successful e-students which could be shared with subsequent students and proposed as effective sequencing of instructional activities.

Instructional Strategies and Instructional Delivery

Further to specifying learning objectives and sequencing learning content, exosystemic instructional design involves the development of strategies to facilitate student learning (Morrison et al., 2010). Online instructional strategies typically include some combination of discussions forums, e-lectures, videos, self-directed learning, mentorship, collaborative learning, and individual and group assignments. Online discussion includes peer and/or teacher interaction and can occur in real-time or delayed-time, although student learning is more apparent in asynchronous than synchronous online forums (Johnson, 2008c). Learner-instructor and learner-learner mentorship may occur via email, discussion boards, and in LMS chat rooms. Self-directed learning is commonly expressed as learner-content interaction and involves reading and interacting with learning objects such as games and auto-marked quizzes (Johnson, 2006c). Lectures are usually relatively brief in online learning environments and tied to concepts rather than time and location, as is the case in traditional classes. Collaborative learning is supported by many tools (e.g., wikis) and reflects learner-learner interaction particularly in relation to assignment completion (Richardson, 2010). From an ecological perspective, students should be provided with a variety of instructional opportunities for all three types of interaction and encouraged to make selections that are compatible with, but also extend, their individual bioecological capabilities. This may be best achieved by a combination of required and selected e-learning events and experiences.

With respect to instructional delivery, online environments are uniquely advantaged by freedom from the constraints of time and place. Instruction can be delivered or, perhaps more aptly, *learning can occur* at any time and under a range of conditions that accommodate individual student differences. It is this very feature of e-learning, however, that blurs the distinction between learner-learner, learner-instructor and learner-content interaction. For example, podcasts or recorded mini-lectures are often distributed throughout instructional materials; student viewing of such brief videos might be conceptualized as learner-instructor as well as learner-content interaction. Students can read and respond to asynchronous communication (e.g., email and discussion board postings) at any time and such interaction involves both peer and teacher interaction (Johnson, 2008c). While some students participate in e-lectures in real time, many students choose to view the recorded lecture (Richardson, 2010). Thus, for some students, e-lectures may be classified as learner-instructor interaction; for other students, e-lectures may be classified as learner-content interaction. In online environments, the distinction between learner-person and learner-content interaction is not necessarily or consistently obvious. An ecological model of student interaction in online learning environments is required.

Student Assignments and Assessment

In higher education, assessment strategies and processes have a profound impact on student learning and satisfaction with university experiences (Klenowski, 2011). Indeed, "university grades are of considerable consequence in terms of subsequent student employment and educational opportunities" (Johnson, 2014, p. 2). From an ecological perspective, exosystemic instructional design includes conceptualization and development of assessment tasks used to motivate and evaluate student mastery of the learning objectives. Such evaluative strategies often include both formative assessment (i.e., not directly contributing to final course grade but used to inform instructional practice and student learning needs) and summative assessment (i.e., directly contributing to final course grade; Morrison et al., 2010). Online learning environments support a range of assessment strategies including: student archived written contributions to chatrooms and discussion boards concerned with, for example, case study analysis; review and application of learning content or professional issues; selected-response tests which can be auto-marked as well as constructed-response tests which require teacher marking; individual and group multimedia projects; entries into cumulative e-portfolios; as well as more traditional text-based essays and assignments (Gaytan & McEwan, 2007).

Relative to traditional student assessment, online learning environments supported dynamic, creative and student-centered approaches to evaluation. For example, Johnson and Broadly (2012) described a case in which 30 brief weekly assignments each contributed 2% to 5% to the final university course grade. Ten of the assignments were auto-marked e-quizzes; ten assignments were student-generated questions posted in an online forum; and ten were student-generated answers to the posted questions. Reportedly, "students expressed collective agreement that the weekly online quizzes were useful and that posting weekly questions and answers facilitated mastery of required learning content" (p. 86). Johnson and Davies (2012) reported a case study in which the Blackboard essay test tool was used to evaluate university e-student learning. To promote learning as well as maintain the integrity of test results, constructed-response items were randomly selected from a large pool of questions and the time available to complete the tests was limited. Overall, e-students evaluated the use of the online constructed-response tests positively and e-lecturers were particularly positive about the benefits of such as approach to online assessment citing ease of test management including submission, provision of feedback and grading. Student and teacher feedback, easily collected in online learning environments, provides a mechanism for continuous course and program improvement, an essential aspect of instructional design (Kemp, 1985; Morrison et al, 2010).

Continuous Course Improvement

Although a variety of theoretical paradigms of continuous quality improvement exist, Rubenstein and colleagues (2014) identified three essential features: 1) systematic data guided activities, 2) iterative development and testing and 3) designing with local conditions in mind. Kemp's (1985) systemic approach to instructional design reflects a continuous cycle of iterative planning, redesign, development and assessment. Feedback from e-students and e-teachers including student retention rates and final grades are mechanisms by which instructional design (e.g., content sequencing, instructional strategies, instructional delivery and student evaluation) is continuously improved to increasingly meet the needs of e-students. Additionally, patterns of student interactions with

LMS tools and learning objects can be identified and linked with retention rates and final grades (Champaign & Cohen, 2010). García, Romero, Ventura and de Castro (2006) present a cyclical methodology for the continuous improvement of e-learning courses using an interactive data mining processes without parameters. "Unlike other data mining approaches applied to education, which focus on the student, this method is aimed at professors and how to help them improve the structure and contents of an e-learning course by making recommendations" (p. 887). From an ecological perspective, course planning and revisions flow between the direct microsystemic instructional online environment and indirect exosystemic instructional design. Simultaneously, the instructional design exosystem affects and is affected by the university *macrosystem*.

The Macrosystem: University Culture and Online Student Interaction

"The macrosystem can be thought of as the social blueprint of a given culture, subculture, or broad social context and consists of the overarching pattern of values, belief systems, lifestyles, opportunities, customs, and resources embedded therein" (Johnson, 2008, p. 3). The macrosystem of a specific university is embodied in the cultural, political, social and economic climate of the local community as well as that of the nation as a whole and, increasingly, international forces. Jones and Goodfellow (2012) stated that "the university in a digital age is renegotiating its boundaries in new networks that destabilize traditional and taken-for-granted understandings of what a university is and does" (p. 63). Macrosystemic university culture is manifest in the provision of online learning opportunities and associated support for students, teachers and instructional designers. Such learning opportunities and support exert influence on the exosystem, microsystem and interface subsystem which then impacts on student interaction in online learning environments.

Online Learning Opportunities

Student interaction in online learning environments is contingent upon opportunities for online interaction; such opportunities reflect university values and culture. Fully-online university programs have rapidly increased in popularity (Kahu Stephens, Leach, & Zepke, 2013). Open Universities Australia experienced a doubling of enrolments in four years with more than 55,000 students enrolled in 170 programs (Maslen, 2012). More than 70% of USA universities offer fully-online programs (Lederman, 2013). With more than one-quarter of a million students in 23 countries, the UK Open University "has become a record breaker on the iTunes U service, which provides a digital library of materials for university students and staff" (John, 2011, paragraph 3). Compared to on-campus university programs, fully-online programs are flexible and convenient and, thereby, attractive to non-traditional students (Kim, Kwon & Cho 2011), although the distinction between traditional and non-traditional university students is eroding (Bell 2012). Correspondingly, since on-campus students increasingly study online (Allen & Seaman 2013), the distinction between on-campus and online students may also be eroding. From an ecological perspective, the erosion of categorical differences between traditional learners and e-learners reflects increased and improved online learning opportunities caused by student demand which influences macrosystemic university culture.

Support for Online Learning

The more that university culture values e-learning, the more the university will provide online infrastructures to support e-students, e-teachers and e-course developers. Such online infrastructures include traditional types of student support (e.g., financial aid, admissions, registration and personal counseling) as well as technical helplines, LMS support, online library services, student portals and e-tutor training (Davies, Little, & Stewart, 2008). "One of the biggest gaps in online education is institutions' inability to provide time- and location-independent access to a complete array of student support services" (LaPadula, 2003, p. 120). Nonetheless, meta-analytic data supports the effectiveness of online asynchronous student support (Carey, Scott-Sheldon, Elliott, Bolles, & Carey, 2009). In quest of improved student retention rates, some universities adopt an inclusive and collaborative approach to online student services which are equally valued by both traditional and e-students (Crawley, 2012). Such an inclusive approach is apparent in Simpson's (2013) organization of university support for e-learning: academic and non-academic support; enrollment, induction and preparatory support; course design support; and staff development. Macrosystemic university culture provides strategic planning to ensure the up-take of emerging instructional technology and that such technology is adopted on the basis of established benefits with appropriate infrastructures of support (Nawaz & Khan, 2012). For example, Bennett, Bishop, Delgarno, Waycott and Kennedy (2012) indicated that the use of specific tools created "technical challenges associated with the fact that many of the tools were new and still under development, and also because the institutions involved had not yet developed systems to support Web 2.0 tools" (p. 532). The quality of student interaction in online environments (learner-learner, learner-instructor, learner-content and learner-interface) is influenced by the quality of support for online learning. Macrosystemic university support of e-learning evolves over time in response to socio-historical events.

The Chronosystem: The Effect of Time on Student Online Interaction

"Although not one of the four system layers per se, the chronosystem represents a time-based dimension that influences the operation of all levels of the ecological systems" (Johnson, 2008, p. 3). The chronosystem includes student changes across years of study with accumulating microsystemic experiences; such change may be conceptualized as student maturation. The chronosystem also includes the sociohistorical dimension of the university macrosystem; universities evolve over time and such evolution influences exosystemic instructional design which influences student interaction in online learning environments. From an ecological perspective, the chronosystem acknowledges the effect of time on all systems and on student bioecology. In the context of university e-learning, the effect of time on student online interaction is perhaps most apparent in student maturation and learning (e.g., increased competence with digital learning tools) and university evolution (e.g., increased e-learning opportunities).

Student Maturation and Learning

University students differ from each other on a wide range of bioecological characteristics (e.g., demographics, learning style and personality). Over time, each individual university student changes and matures in response to biological processes as well as environmental experiences which include formal and informal learning (Johnson, 2014). For example, there are differences between undergraduate and graduate students and between mature and traditional first-year entrants (Johnson, 2012). Student bioecological maturational and experiential processes unfold within the context of the microsystem but are the consequence of the chronosystemic passages of time (Johnson, 2008). For some students, university learning may be their first exposure to instructional applications of technology and, in the context of intensive and prolonged interaction in online learning environments, students develop increased competence with e-learning tools (Hargittai, 2010; Huang & Yang, 2014). Equally, with each passing semester, students mature in their study strategies and orientation to learning (Johnson & Davies, 2014). Student-centered open learning environments require students to "assume responsibility for both identifying and monitoring individual learning goals and selecting and utilizing means to support their learning" (Hannafin, Hill, & Land, 2014, p. 642). In this regard, the ecological chronosystem includes both gradual change (e.g., learning) and abrupt life events (e.g., starting university) which modify student bioecology. The maturing bioecology impacts on the quality of all microsystemic interactions (learner-learner, learner-instructor, learner-content and learner-interface) but not necessarily in a linear fashion. Mature students with family commitments may ration study time in ways that decrease some forms (e.g., learner-learner) and increase other forms (learner-content) of interaction.

University Evolution

Over time, universities have evolved to value students who cannot physically attend classes and to value instructional applications of technology. Such evolution is manifest in the extent to which universities offer fully-online programs and programs (Lederman 2013) and in the popularity of blended learning (Garrison, 2011). Since information and communication is currently more accessible than at any time in human history (Baron, 2009), a radical transformation of higher education is occurring. As with any radical transformation, change is not uniform and ideology precedes practical considerations. This is particularly apparent in the expectation that lecturers, professors and instructors have the capacity to design effective online courses despite, in most case, lack of training and minimal institutional support

(Beaudoin, 2013). In reality, most teaching faculty are self-taught, not only in the mechanics of a course design but also in teaching online. Means, Johnson and Graff (2013), concluded that lack of faculty skill and instructional design knowledge "is a problem that will require innovative and creative solutions to address" (p. 63). Ecological theoretical assumptions provide a template for comprehensive, innovative and creative solutions to providing required support to busy people who often work in isolation – that is, higher education teaching faculty.

Easy and inexpensive access to knowledge may be paving the way for a transformation to *Open Education*. Hodgkinson-Williams (2014) presented three forms of Open Education; Open Textbooks, Open Educational Resources and Massive Open Online Courses (MOOC). Reportedly, and consistent with ecological theoretical assumptions, five factors will influence the development and implementation of these forms of Open Education; technical, legal, cultural, pedagogical and financial. While the university was once described as an ivory tower, a new metaphor is emerging as the institution becomes more embedded in society. "Universities, governments, and industries are now described as the DNA strands of a triple helix, forming the dynamic building blocks of the knowledge economy" (Malone, 2011). As universities evolve in response to sociohistorical changes, the structures and processes of student interaction in online learning environments correspondingly evolve. Indeed, the distinction between online learning environments and online work environments is already eroding (Reddy, 2011). An ecological model of e-student interactions is fluid and responsive to microsystemic changes driven by macrosystemic university culture and chronosystemic sociohistorical conditions.

An Ecological Model of Student Interaction in Online Learning Environments

Based upon synthesis of existing theory, research and practice, Figure 2 presents an ecological model of student interaction in online learning environments. In keeping with original ecological models (Bronfenbrenner, 1977, 1979, 1989, 1995, 2005) and more recent ecological e-learning models (Champaign & Cohen, 2010; Johnson, 2008; Johnson, 2010b, 2014; McCalla, 2004), the individual e-learner is situated in the center of a series of nested environmental systems. As with all ecological models, the proposed model of student interaction in online learning environments is learner-centered. From an ecological perspective, each e-learner is unique in terms of a wide range of personal, physical, psychological and cognitive characteristics. The term *bioecology* is preferred over terms such as *the individual* because bioecology emphasized that each learner is a unique combination of genetic predispositions influenced by microsystemic experience over chronosystemic time. Each unique student influences and is influenced by direct and indirect interactions with all environmental systems (i.e., microsystem, interface subsystem, exosystem and macrosystem). All systems and all e-learners change as a function of time (i.e., chronosystem).

Further depicted in Figure 2 and in obvious contrast to traditional teaching models, the interface subsystem mediates all student interaction in online learning environments. Without internet connectivity, hardware and software, there is no interaction because the learner cannot access the online learning environment. Conceptual inclusion of the proposed interface subsystem emphasizes the fundamental importance and never-to-be-

Figure 2. An ecological model of student interaction in online learning environments

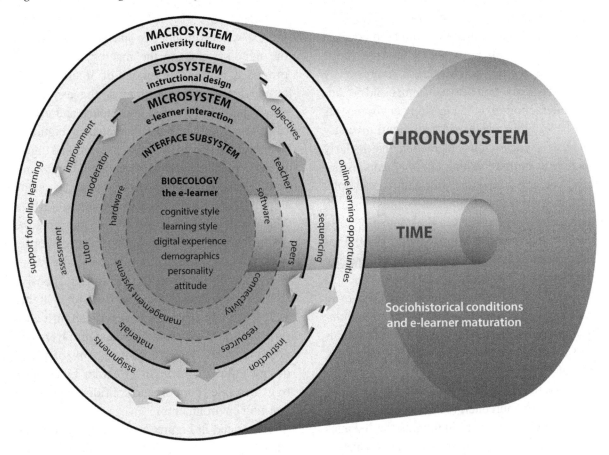

overlooked e-learner dependency on technology. While most academics, administrators and professionals rarely experience a systems crash and can readily access improved technologies, this is not the case for individuals in remote communities and emerging economies (Johnson & Oliver, 2014; Reddy, 2011). Chronosystemic sociohistorical changes have increased global concern for teaching and learning (Malone, 2011). From an ecological theoretical perspective and at the most fundamental level, e-learning is contingent upon a viable interface subsystem.

Graphically illustrated in Figure 2, the interface is a subsystem of the microsystem. The ecological microsystem, to review, includes all direct interactions between the individual and the environment (Johnson, 2014). In an online environment, the e-learner directly interacts with other e-learners,

e-teachers and e-resources. However, because all direct microsystemic interactions occur online, they must, necessarily and obviously, be mediated by technology (Hillman et al., 1994). It could be argued that no online interaction is direct and this may be true if direct interaction requires the capacity to physically touch the peer, teacher and learning resources. We choose to argue, in contrast, that the digital revolution has changed the nature of human-environment interaction and that such change has improved the quality of the human experience. The most relevant example of that improved quality of human experience is the exponential growth of e-learning across educational and professional sectors (Kahu et al., 2013). E-learning has resulted in increased learning (Johnson, 2007b) and increased learners (John, 2011).

Summarized and presented in Figure 2, via unique interface subsystems, each individual e-learner bioecology engages in direct interaction with some combination of peers, tutors, teachers, moderators, resources and materials. As previously stated, the distinction between human and nonhuman interaction in online learning environments may be less apparent than in traditional university classes. Asynchronous interaction, particularly popular in online learning environments, is not easily categorized as interaction with, for example, instructors or resources (e.g., e-lectures). Indeed, such distinction emerged in the context of early forms of distance education (Moore, 1989). Precise description of interaction in online learning environments may be compromised by concepts and corresponding vocabulary borrowed from traditional learning environments. The circular systems presented in Figure 2 are conceptualized as fluid and descriptors are explanations, not definitions.

Ecological models typically include the *mesosystem* (Bronfenbrenner, 1977, 1979, 1989, 1995, 2005). The mesosystem highlights the linkages between elements of the microsystem (Johnson, 2008). For example, the mesosystem includes interaction between home and school environments which are both elements of the microsystem. Consequently, unlike the microsystem, exosystem and macrosystem, the mesosystem does not include any specific elements. Instead, the mesosystem is most often depicted as a series of bidirectional arrows of influence situated as a band between the microsystem and the exosystem (see Figure 1). Apparent in Figure 2, the proposed ecological model of student interaction in online learning environments does not include a mesosystem. We reason that elements within other systems (e.g., exosystem and macrosystem) also exert within-system influence. In this regard, we contribute to the development of ecological systems theory by removing the mesosystem, adding the interface subsystem and emphasizing interaction within and between all systems.

Consistent with original ecological models (Bronfenbrenner, 1977, 1979, 1989, 1995, 2005), the exosystem influences and is influenced by the microsystem and the macrosystem. In the proposed ecological model of interaction in online learning environments, the exosystem specifically captures the importance and impact of instructional design. Illustrated in Figure 2, instructional design includes instructional objectives, sequencing, delivery, student assignments and evaluation, and processes of continuous quality improvement (Kemp, 1985; Morrison et al., 2010). Macrosystemic university values determine the quality of instructional design; in turn, the impact of instructional design modifies university values over time. Since instructional design is responsive to learner and teacher characteristics (e.g., digital skill level), the microsystem exerts an influence on exosystemic instructional design. Over time and via microsystemic changes, instructional design indirectly changes e-learner bioecology (e.g., increased comfort and confidence in online learning environments).

Illustrated in Figure 2, the macrosystem and chronosystem exert a powerful, albeit indirect, influence on student interaction in online learning environments. In the proposed ecological model, the macrosystem is composed of university culture (e.g., values, traditions, procedures, processes and infrastructures). University values are manifest in the availability and quality of online learning opportunities and associated support including elements of the interface subsystem (e.g., LMS). Universities employ and support instructional designers, graphic artists, video production teams, web designers, curriculum project managers, technicians and e-teachers. Universities provide learning opportunities to students including blended and fully-online courses and, increasingly, adopt open approaches to knowledge sharing such as MOOCs (Hodgkinson-Williams, 2014). Macrosystemic university culture evolves over time and, depicted in Figure 2 as the chronosystem, time affects all aspects of student interaction in online learning environments. E-learner bioecology matures in response to biological growth processes (e.g., cognitive development) and environmental experiences (e.g., increased ability to learn in online environments). The interface subsystems changes over time with improved hardware, software and connectivity. The microsystem changes as e-learners, e-teachers and e-resources improve over time. The proposed ecological model of interaction in online learning environments is a unifying theoretical framework for guiding policy, research and practice to improve student learning in online environments. Such a theoretical model is particularly useful to those who are increasingly expected to function as instructional designers, -- that is, most instructors in higher education.

REFERENCES

Adeyinka, T., & Mutula, S. (2010). A proposed model for evaluating the success of WebCT course content management system. *Computers in Human Behavior*, 26(6), 1795–1805. doi:10.1016/j.chb.2010.07.007

Allen, E., & Seaman, J. (2013). *Changing course: Ten years of tracking online education in the United States*. Babson Survey Research Group and Quahog Research Group. Retrieved from http://www.onlinelearningsurvey.com/reports/changingcourse.pdf

Anderson, L. W., & Krathwohl, D. R. (Eds.). (2001). *A taxonomy for learning, teaching, and assessing: A revision of Bloom's taxonomy of educational objectives*. New York: Longman.

Anderson, T. (2003a). Getting the right mix again: An updated and theoretical rationale for interaction. *International Review of Open and Distance Learning, 4*. Retrieved from http://www.irrodl.org/content/v4.2/anderson.html

Anderson, T. (2003b). Modes of interaction in distance education: Recent developments and research questions. In M. G. Moore & W. G. Anderson (Eds.), *Handbook of distance education* (pp. 129–144). Mahwah, NJ: Lawrence Erlbaum.

Baron, D. E. (2009). *A better pencil: Readers, writers, and the digital revolution*. New York: Oxford University Press.

Barrie, S. C. (2007). A conceptual framework for the teaching and learning of generic graduate attributes. *Studies in Higher Education*, 32(4), 439–458. doi:10.1080/03075070701476100

Beaudoin, M. F. (2013). The evolving role of the instructor in the digital age. In Y. Kats (Ed.), *Learning Management Systems and Instructional Design: Best Practices in Online Education* (pp. 233–247). Hershey, PA: IGI Global. doi:10.4018/978-1-4666-3930-0.ch012

Bejjar, M. A., & Boujelbene, Y. (2014). E-Learning and Web 2.0: A couple of the 21st Century advancements in higher education. In J. Pelet (Ed.), *E-learning 2.0 technologies and web applications in higher education* (pp. 1–21). Hershey, PA: IGI Global.

Bell, S. (2012). Nontraditional students are the new majority. *Library Journal*. Retrieved from http://lj.libraryjournal.com/2012/03/opinion/nontraditional-students-are-the-new-majority-from-the-bell-tower/

Bennett, S., Bishop, A., Dalgarno, B., Waycott, J., & Kennedy, G. (2012). Implementing Web 2.0 technologies in higher education: A collective case study. *Computers & Education*, 59(2), 524–534. doi:10.1016/j.compedu.2011.12.022

Bennett, S., & Lockyer, L. (2004). Becoming an online teacher: Adapting to a changed environment for teaching and learning in higher education. *Educational Media International*, 41(3), 231–248. doi:10.1080/09523980410001680842

Bronfenbrenner, U. (1977). Toward an experimental ecology of human development. *The American Psychologist, 32*(7), 513–531. doi:10.1037/0003-066X.32.7.513

Bronfenbrenner, U. (1979). *The ecology of human development: Experiments by nature and design.* Cambridge, MA: Harvard University Press.

Bronfenbrenner, U. (1989). Ecological systems theory. *Annals of Child Development, 6,* 187–24.

Bronfenbrenner, U. (1995). Developmental ecology through space and time: A future perspective. In P. Moen & G. H. Elder Jr., (Eds.), *Examining lives in context: Perspectives on the ecology of human development* (pp. 619–647). Washington, DC: American Psychological Association. doi:10.1037/10176-018

Bronfenbrenner, U. (2005). *Making human beings human: Bioecological perspectives of human development.* Thousand Oaks, CA: Sage.

Bullen, M., Morgan, T., Belfer, K., & Qayyum, A. (2008). The digital learner at BCIT and implications for an e-strategy. In *Proceedings of the 2008 Research Workshop of the European Distance Education Network (EDEN) Researching and promoting access to education and training: The role of distance education and e-learning in technology-enhanced environment.* Retrieved from http://www.box.net/shared/fxqyutottt

Carey, K. B., Scott-Sheldon, L. A., Elliott, J. C., Bolles, J. R., & Carey, M. P. (2009). Computer delivered interventions to reduce college student drinking: A meta-analysis. *Addiction (Abingdon, England), 104*(11), 1807–1819. doi:10.1111/j.1360-0443.2009.02691.x PMID:19744139

Champaign, J., & Cohen, R. (2010). A model for content sequencing in intelligent tutoring systems based on the ecological approach and its validation through simulated students. In *Proceedings of the Ninth Florida Artificial Intelligence Research Symposium.* Daytona Beach, FL: Academic Press.

Chen, C.-M., Liu, C.-Y., & Chang, M.-H. (2006). Personalized curriculum sequencing utilizing modified item response theory for web-based instruction. *Expert Systems with Applications, 30*(2), 378–396. doi:10.1016/j.eswa.2005.07.029

Cheng, C. K., Paré, D. E., Collimore, L. M., & Joordens, S. (2011). Assessing the effectiveness of a voluntary online discussion forum on improving students' course performance. *Computers & Education, 56*(1), 253–261. doi:10.1016/j.compedu.2010.07.024

Chi, Y. L. (2009). Ontology-based curriculum content sequencing system with semantic rules. *Expert Systems with Applications, 36*(4), 7838–7847. doi:10.1016/j.eswa.2008.11.048

Cobb, S. C. (2009). Social presence and online learning: A current view from a research perspective. *Journal of Interactive Online Learning, 8*(3), 241–254.

Cochrane, T., & Bateman, R. (2010). Smartphones give you wings: Pedagogical affordances of mobile 2.0. *Australasian Journal of Educational Technology, 26*(1), 1–14.

Crawley, A. (2012). *Supporting online students: A practical guide to planning, implementing, and evaluating services.* San Francisco: John Wiley & Sons.

Daughenbaugh, R., Daughenbaugh, D., Surry, D., & Islam, M. (2002). Personality type and online versus in-class course satisfaction. *EDUCAUSE Quarterly, 3,* 71–72.

Davies, A., Little, P., & Stewart, B. (2008). Developing and infrastructure for online learning. In T. Anderson (Ed.), *The theory and practice of online learning* (pp. 121–142). Athabasca University Press.

Dede, C. (2005). Planning for neomillennial learning styles. *EDUCAUSE Quarterly, 28*(1), 7–12.

Felder, R. M., & Brent, R. (2005). Understanding student differences. *The Journal of Engineering Education, 94*(1), 57–72. doi:10.1002/j.2168-9830.2005.tb00829.x

García, E., Romero, C., Ventura, S., & de Castro, C. (2006). Using rules discovery for the continuous improvement of e-learning courses. In *Intelligent Data Engineering and Automated Learning–IDEAL 2006* (pp. 887–895). Berlin: Springer. doi:10.1007/11875581_106

Garcia-Valcarcel, A. (2010). Integrating ICT into the teaching-learning process. *British Journal of Educational Technology, 41*(5), E75–E77. doi:10.1111/j.1467-8535.2009.00988.x

Garrison, D. R. (2011). *E-learning in the 21ˢᵗ century: A framework for research and practice.* New York: Taylor and Francis.

Gaytan, J., & McEwen, B. C. (2007). Effective online instructional and assessment strategies. *American Journal of Distance Education, 21*(3), 117–132. doi:10.1080/08923640701341653

Goold, A., Coldwell, J., & Craig, A. (2010). An examination of the role of the e-tutor. *Australasian Journal of Educational Technology, 26*(5), 704–716.

Hannafin, M. J., Hill, J. R., Land, S. M., & Lee, E. (2014). Student-centered, open learning environments: Research, theory, and practice. In J. M. Spector, M. D. Merrill, J. Elen, & M. J. Bishop (Eds.), *Handbook of Research on Educational Communications and Technology* (pp. 641–651). New York: Springer. doi:10.1007/978-1-4614-3185-5_51

Hargittai, E. (2010). Digital na(t)ives? Variation in internet skills and uses among members of the "Net Generation.". *Sociological Inquiry, 80*(1), 92–113. doi:10.1111/j.1475-682X.2009.00317.x

Herrington, J., Reeves, T., & Oliver, R. (2014). Authentic learning environments. In J. M. Spector, M. D. Merrill, J. Ellen, & M. J. Bishop (Eds.), *Handbook of research on educational communications and technology* (4th ed., pp. 401–412). New York: Springer. doi:10.1007/978-1-4614-3185-5_32

Herrington, J., Reeves, T. C., & Oliver, R. (2006). Authentic tasks online: A synergy among learner, task, and technology. *Distance Education, 27*(2), 233–247. doi:10.1080/01587910600789639

Hillman, D. C., Willis, D. J., & Gunawardena, C. N. (1994). Learner-interface in distance education: An extension of contemporary models and strategies for practitioners. *American Journal of Distance Education, 8*(2), 31–42. doi:10.1080/08923649409526853

Hodgkinson-Williams, C. (2014, June). *Degrees of ease: Adoption of OER, Open Textbooks and MOOCs in the Global South.* Paper presented at the 2ⁿᵈ Regional Symposium on Open Educational Resources: Beyond Advocacy, Research and Policy, Penang. Retrieved from https://open.uct.ac.za/handle/11427/1188

Huang, R., & Yang, J. (2014). The framework and method for understanding the new generation of learners. In R. Huang, Kinshuk, & N. Chen (Eds.), The new development of technology enhanced learning (pp. 3-25). Berlin: Springer. doi:10.1007/978-3-642-38291-8_1

Hunter, S. B., Ober, A. J., Paddock, S. M., Hunt, P. E., & Levan, D. (2014). Continuous Quality Improvement (CQI) in addiction treatment settings: Design and intervention protocol of a group randomized pilot study. *Addiction Science and Clinical Practice, 9*(4), 1–11. PMID:24467770

Inghilterra, X., & Ravatua-Smith, W. S. (2014). Online learning communities: Use of micro blogging for knowledge construction. In J. Pelet (Ed.), *E-learning 2.0 technologies and web applications in higher education* (pp. 107–128). Hershey, PA: IGI Global. doi:10.4018/978-1-4666-4876-0.ch006

iTunes. (2014). *Blackboard Mobile Learn™ by Blackboard Inc.* Retrieved from https://itunes.apple.com/au/app/blackboard-mobile-learn/id376413870?mt=8

John, M. (2011). Going to Harvard from your bedroom. *BBC News Business.* Retrieved from http://www.bbc.co.uk/news/business-12766562

Johnson, E. S. (2008). Ecological systems and complexity theory: Toward an alternative model of accountability in education. *Complicity: An International Journal of Complexity and Education, 5*(1), 1–10.

Johnson, G. (2011). Learning style and interaction preference: Application of Moore's typology. In S.-M. Barton, J. Hedberg, & K. Suzuki (Eds.), *Proceedings of global learn asia pacific* (pp. 1445–1450). AACE.

Johnson, G. (2012). Internet use among first-year university students: Computer versus mobile phone activities across home, school and community contexts. In *Proceedings of World Conference on Educational Multimedia, Hypermedia and Telecommunications 2012* (pp. 2637-2642). Chesapeake, VA: AACE.

Johnson, G., & Davies, S. (2012). Unsupervised online constructed-response tests: Maximising student learning and results integrity. In M. Brown, M. Harnett, & T. Steward (Eds.), Future challenges, sustainable futures. Proceedings ascillite Wellington 2012 (pp. 400–408). Available at http://www.ascilite2012.org/images/custom/johnson,_genevieve_-_unsupervised_online_constructed_response.pdf

Johnson, G. M. (2005). Student alienation, academic achievement, and WebCT use. *Journal of Educational Technology & Society, 8,* 179–189.

Johnson, G. M. (2006a). College student psycho-educational functioning and satisfaction with online study groups. *Educational Psychology, 26*(5), 677–688. doi:10.1080/01443410500390848

Johnson, G. M. (2006b). Perception of classroom climate, use of WebCT, and academic achievement. *Journal of Computing in Higher Education, 17*(2), 25–46. doi:10.1007/BF03032697

Johnson, G. M. (2006c). Optional online quizzes: College student use and relationship to achievement. *Canadian Journal of Learning & Technology, 32,* 105–118.

Johnson, G. M. (2007a). Learning style under two web-based study conditions. *Educational Psychology, 27*(5), 617–634. doi:10.1080/01443410701309159

Johnson, G. M. (2007b). Restricted versus unrestricted learning: Synthesis of recent meta-analyses. *AACE Journal, 15,* 267–278.

Johnson, G. M. (2008a). Online study tools: College student preference versus impact on achievement. *Computers in Human Behavior, 24*(3), 930–939. doi:10.1016/j.chb.2007.02.012

Johnson, G. M. (2008b). Cognitive processing differences between frequent and infrequent Internet users. *Computers in Human Behavior, 24*(5), 2094–2106. doi:10.1016/j.chb.2007.10.001

Johnson, G. M. (2008c). The relative learning benefits of synchronous and asynchronous text-based discussion. *British Journal of Educational Technology, 39,* 166–169.

Johnson, G. M. (2010a). Internet use and child development: The techno-microsystem. [AS B]. *Australian Journal of Educational and Developmental Psychology, 10,* 32–43.

Johnson, G. M. (2010b). Internet use and child development: Validation of the ecological techno-subsystem. *Journal of Educational Technology & Society, 13*, 176–185.

Johnson, G. M. (2014). The ecology of interactive learning environments: Situating traditional theory. *Interactive Learning Environments, 22*(3), 298–308. doi:10.1080/10494820.2011.649768

Johnson, G. M., & Broadley, T. (2012). Web-based active learning and frequent feedback: Engaging first-year university students. In A. Herrington, J. Schrape, & K. Singh (Eds.), *Engaging students with learning technologies* (pp. 77-96). Perth, Australia: Curtin University. Available at http://espace.library. curtin.edu.au/R/?func=dbin-jumpfull&object_id=187378&local_base=GEN01-ERA02

Johnson, G. M., & Davies, S. M. (2014). Self-regulated learning in digital environments: Theory, research, praxis. *British Journal of Research, 1*(2), 1–14.

Johnson, G. M., & Howell, A. J. (2005). Attitude toward instructional technology following required vs. optional WebCT usage. *Journal of Technology and Teacher Education, 13*, 643–654.

Johnson, G. M., & Johnson, J. A. (2006). *Personality, internet experience, and e-communication preference*. Paper presented at the Annual Conference of the International Association for Development of the Information Society, Murcia, Spain. (ERIC Document Reproduction No. ED494002). Available at http://files.eric.ed.gov/fulltext/ED494002.pdf

Johnson, G. M., & Oliver, R. (2014). Small screen technology use among Indigenous boarding school adolescents from remote regions of Western Australia. *Australian Journal of Indigenous Education, 43*(2), 75–84. doi:10.1017/jie.2014.15

Johnson, G. M., & Puplampu, P. (2008). Internet use during childhood and the ecological techno-subsystem. *Canadian Journal of Learning and Technology, 34*, 19–28.

Joiner, R., Gavin, J., Duffield, J., Brosnan, M., Crook, C., Durndell, A., & Lovatt, P. et al. (2005). Gender, internet identification, and Internet anxiety: Correlates of internet use. *Cyberpsychology & Behavior, 8*(4), 371–378. doi:10.1089/cpb.2005.8.371 PMID:16092894

Jones, C., & Goodfellow, R. (2012). The digital university: Discourse, theory, and evidence. *International Journal of Learning and Media, 4*(3-4), 59–63. doi:10.1162/IJLM_a_00103

Jones, C., Ramanau, R., Cross, S., & Healing, G. (2010). Net generation or digital natives: Is there a distinct new generation entering university? *Computers & Education, 54*(3), 722–732. doi:10.1016/j.compedu.2009.09.022

Jones, C., Reichard, C., & Mokhtari, K. (2003). Are students' learning styles discipline specific? *Community College Journal of Research and Practice, 27*(5), 363–375. doi:10.1080/713838162

Kahu, E. R., Stephens, C., Leach, L., & Zepke, N. (2013). The engagement of mature distance students. *Higher Education Research & Development, 32*(5), 1–14. doi:10.1080/07294360.2013.777036

Keefe, J. W. (1979). Learning style: An overview. In J. W. Keefe (Ed.), *Student learning styles: Diagnosing and prescribing programs* (pp. 1–17). Reston, VA: National Association of Secondary School Principals.

Kemp, J. E. (1985). *The instructional design process*. New York: Harper and Row.

Kennedy, G. E., Judd, T. S., Churchward, A., Gray, K., & Krause, K.-L. (2008). First year students' experiences with technology: Are they really digital natives? *Australasian Journal of Educational Technology, 24*(1), 108–122.

Kim, J., Kwon, Y., & Cho, D. (2011). Investigating factors that influence social presence and learning outcomes in distance higher education. *Computers & Education, 57*(2), 1512–1520. doi:10.1016/j.compedu.2011.02.005

Klenowski, V. (2011). Assessment for learning in the accountability era: Queensland, Australia. *Studies in Educational Evaluation, 37*(1), 78–83. doi:10.1016/j.stueduc.2011.03.003

LaPadula, M. (2003). A comprehensive look at online student support services for distance learners. *American Journal of Distance Education, 17*(2), 119–128. doi:10.1207/S15389286AJDE1702_4

Lederman, D. (2013). Growth for online learning. *Inside Higher Ed.* Retrieved from http://www.insidehighered.com/news/2013/01/08/survey-finds-online-enrollments-slow-continue-grow

Lewis, P. A., & Price, S. (2007). Distance education and the integration of e-learning in a graduate program. *Journal of Continuing Education in Nursing, 38*(3), 139–143. doi:10.3928/00220124-20070501-08 PMID:17542173

Litchfield, A., Dyson, L., Lawrence, E., & Zmijewska, A. (2007). Directions for m-learning research to enhance active learning. In ICT: Providing choices for learners and learning. *Proceedings Ascilite Singapore 2007.* Retrieved from http://www.ascilite.org.au/conferences/singapore07/procs/litchfield.pd

Littlejohn, A., Falconer, I., & McGill, L. (2008). Characterising effective eLearning resources. *Computers & Education, 50*(3), 757–771. doi:10.1016/j.compedu.2006.08.004

Lust, G., Elen, J., & Clarebout, G. (2013). Students' tool-use within a web enhanced course: Explanatory mechanisms of students' tool-use pattern. *Computers in Human Behavior, 29*(5), 2013–2021. doi:10.1016/j.chb.2013.03.014

Lust, G., Juarez Collazo, N. A., Elen, J., & Clarebout, G. (2012). Content management systems: Enriched learning opportunities for all? *Computers in Human Behavior, 28*(3), 795–808. doi:10.1016/j.chb.2011.12.009

Ma, W. W., & Chan, C. K. (2014, December). Online knowledge sharing and psychological well-being among Chinese college students. In C. K. Chan, K. M. Chan, W. L. Chan, H. L. Chui, C. W. Fong, H. Fung, ... Tong, K. W. (Eds.), Communication and education: New media, knowledge practices, and multiliteracies. Hong Kong: HKAECT. Retrieved from http://stu.hksyu.edu/~wkma/ref/Ma_Chan_2014_hkaect_pp77-86.pdf

Ma, W. W., & Yuen, A. H. (2011). Understanding online knowledge sharing: An interpersonal relationship perspective. *Computers & Education, 56*(1), 210–219. doi:10.1016/j.compedu.2010.08.004

MacGregor, C. J. (2002). Personality differences between online and face-to-face students. *Journal of Continuing Higher Education, 50*(3), 14–23. doi:10.1080/07377366.2002.10401201

Malone, D. M. (2011). Forward. In B. Göransson & C. Brundenius (Eds.), *Universities in transition: The changing role and challenges for academic institutions* (pp. v–vi). Ottawa: Springer.

Martínez-Torres, M. R., Toral, S. L., & Barrero, F. (2011). Identification of the design variables of eLearning tools. *Interacting with Computers, 23*(3), 279–288. doi:10.1016/j.intcom.2011.04.004

Maslen, G. (2012). Digital campus changes the game. *The AGE National*. Retrieved from http://www.theage.com.au/national/education/digital-campus-changes-the-game-20120604-1zrtd.html

McCalla, G. (2004). The ecological approach to the design of e-learning environments: Purpose-based capture and use of information about learners. *Journal of Interactive Media in Education*, *7*(1), 1–23.

McKimm, J., & Swanwick, T. (2009). Setting learning objectives. *British Journal of Hospital Medicine*, *70*(7), 406–409. doi:10.12968/hmed.2009.70.7.43125 PMID:19584784

McPherson, M. A., & Nunes, J. M. B. (2004). The role of tutors as an integral part of online learning support. *European Journal of Open and Distance Learning*. Retrieved from http://www.eurodl.org/materials/contrib/2004/Maggie_MsP.html

Means, T., Johnson, D., & Graff, R. (2013). Lessons learned from a course management system review at the University of Florida. In Y. Kats (Ed.), *Learning Management Systems and Instructional Design: Best Practices in Online Education* (pp. 55–71). Hershey, PA: IGI Global. doi:10.4018/978-1-4666-3930-0.ch004

Miyazoe, T., & Anderson, T. (2010). Learning outcomes and students' perceptions of online writing: Simultaneous implementation of a forum, blog, and wiki in an EFL blended learning setting. *System*, *38*(2), 185–199. doi:10.1016/j.system.2010.03.006

Moore, M. G. (1989). Three types of interaction. *American Journal of Distance Education*, *3*(2), 1–6. doi:10.1080/08923648909526659

Morrison, G. R., Ross, S. M., Kemp, J. E., & Kalman, H. (2010). *Designing effective instruction*. Hoboken, NJ: John Wiley & Sons.

Myers, I. B. (1993). *Introduction to type*. Palo Alto, CA: Consulting Psychologists Press.

Nagler, W., & Ebner, M. (2009). Is your university ready for the Ne(x)t-Generation? In J. Luca, & E. Weippl (Eds.), *Proceedings of 21st world conference on educational multimedia, hypermedia and telecommunications* (pp. 4344–4351). Honolulu, HI: Academic Press.

Nawaz, A., & Khan, M. Z. (2012). Issues of technical support for e-learning systems in higher education institutions. *International Journal of Modern Education and Computer Science*, *4*(2), 38–44. doi:10.5815/ijmecs.2012.02.06

Paechter, M., Maier, B., & Macher, D. (2010). Students' expectations of and experiences in e-learning: Their relation to learning achievements and course satisfaction. *Computers & Education*, *54*(1), 222–229. doi:10.1016/j.compedu.2009.08.005

Pan, Y., Xu, Y. C., Wang, X., Zhang, C., Ling, H., & Lin, J. (2014). Integrating social networking support for dyadic knowledge exchange: A study in a virtual community of practice. *Information & Management*, *52*(1), 61–70. doi:10.1016/j.im.2014.10.001

Pollard, C., Gupta, D., & Satzinger, J. (2010). Teaching systems development: A compelling case for integrating the SDLC with the ITSM life-cycle. *Information Systems Management*, *27*(2), 113–122. doi:10.1080/10580531003684959

Pursell, D. P. (2009). Adapting to student learning styles: Engaging students with cell phone technology in organic chemistry instruction. *Journal of Chemical Education*, *86*(10), 1219–1222. doi:10.1021/ed086p1219

Reddy, P. (2011). The evolving role of universities in economic development: The case of university–industry linkages. In B. Göransson & C. Brundenius (Eds.), *Universities in transition: The changing role and challenges for academic institutions* (pp. 25–51). Ottawa: Springer. doi:10.1007/978-1-4419-7509-6_3

Reiser, R. A., & Dempsey, J. V. (2012). *Trends and issues in instructional design and technology.* Boston: Pearson.

Richardson, W. W. H. (2010). *Blogs, wikis, podcasts, and other powerful web tools for classrooms.* Thousand Oaks, CA: Corwin Press.

Riding, R., & Rayner, S. (1998). *Cognitive styles and learning strategies: Understanding style differences in learning and behaviour.* London: David Fulton.

Rismark, M., Sølvberg, A. M., Strømme, A., & Hokstad, L. M. (2007). Using mobile phones to prepare for university lectures: Student's experiences. *The Turkish Online Journal of Educational Technology, 6*(4), Article 9. Retrieved from http://www.tojet.net/articles/649.pdf

Rochford, R. (2003). Assessing learning styles to improve the quality of performance of community college students in developmental writing programs: A pilot study. *Community College Journal of Research and Practice, 27*(8), 665–677. doi:10.1080/713838240

Rodriquez, M. C., Ooms, A., Montanez, M., & Yan, Y. L. (2005). *Perceptions of online learning quality given comfort with technology, motivation to learn technology skills, satisfaction, and online learning experience.* Paper presented at the Annual Meeting of the American Educational Research Association. Montreal, Canada. (ERIC Document Reproduction Service No. ED491688).

Romero, M., Guitert, M., Sangrà, A., & Bullen, M. (2013). Do UOC students fit in the Net Generation profile? An approach to their habits in ICT use. *International Review of Research in Open and Distance Learning, 14*(3), 158–181.

Rubenstein, L., Khodyakov, D., Hempel, S., Danz, M., Salem-Schatz, M., Foy, R., & Shekelle, P. et al. (2014). How can we recognize continuous quality improvement? *International Journal for Quality in Health Care, 26*(1), 6–15. doi:10.1093/intqhc/mzt085 PMID:24311732

Rufer, R., & Adams, R. H. (2013). Deep learning through Reusable Learning Objects in an MBA Program. *Journal of Educational Technology Systems, 42*(2), 107–120. doi:10.2190/ET.42.2.c

Sanders, R. H. (2012). E-Tutor. *The Computer Assisted Language Instruction Consortium, 29*(3), 580–587.

Scheg, A. G. (2014). *Reforming teacher education for online pedagogy development.* Hershey, PA: IGI Global. doi:10.4018/978-1-4666-5055-8

Schiaffino, S., Garcia, P., & Amandi, A. (2008). eTeacher: Providing personalised assistance to e-learning students. *Computers & Education, 51*(4), 1744–1754. doi:10.1016/j.compedu.2008.05.008

Sharpe, R., & Greg, B. (2005). The student experience of e-learning in higher education: A review of the literature. *Brookes eJournal of Learning and Teaching, 1.* Retrieved from http://www.brookes.ac.uk/publications/bejlt/volume1issue3/academic/sharpe_benfield.html

Simpson, O. (2013). *Supporting students in online, open and distance learning.* New York: Routledge.

Soles, C., & Moller, L. (2002). Myers Briggs type preferences in distance learning education. *International Journal of Educational Technology, 2.* Retrieved from http://education.illinois.edu/ijet/v2n2/soles/index.html

Swan, K., & Shih, L. F. (2005). On the nature and development of social presence in online course discussions. *Journal of Asynchronous Learning Networks, 9*(3), 115–136.

Vygotsky, L. S. (1997). The collected works of L. S. Vygotsky, Vol. 4: The history of the development of higher mental functions (M. J. Hall, Translator; R. W. Reiber, Ed.). New York: Plenum Press.

Watson, W. R., & Watson, S. L. (2007). What are Learning Management Systems, What are they not, and what should they become? *TechTrends, 51*(2), 28–34. doi:10.1007/s11528-007-0023-y

White, B. Y., Collins, A., & Frederiksen, J. R. (2011). The nature of scientific meta-knowledge. In M. S. Khine & I. Saleh (Eds.), *Dynamic modeling: Cognitive tool for scientific enquiry* (pp. 41–76). London: Springer.

Young, S. (2006). Student views of effective online teaching in higher education. *American Journal of Distance Education*, 20(2), 65–77. doi:10.1207/s15389286ajde2002_2

Zhao, P., & Johnson, G. (2012). A theoretical framework of self-regulated learning with web-based technologies. In Proceedings of Global TIME 2012 (pp. 163–168). AACE. Retrieved from http://www.editlib.org/p/39417

ADDITIONAL READING

Allen, B. S., Otto, R. G., & Hoffman, B. (2003). Media as lived environments: The ecological psychology of educational technology. In D. H. Jonassen & M. P. Driscoll (Eds.), *Handbook of research for educational communications and technology: A Project of the Association for Educational Communications and Technology (AECT Series)* (pp. 215–241). Mahwah, NJ: Lawrence Erlbaum.

Berkes, F., Colding, J., & Folke, C. (Eds.). (2002). *Navigating social-ecological systems: Building resilience for complexity and change.* New York: Cambridge University Press. doi:10.1017/CBO9780511541957

Bronfenbrenner, U. (1992). *Ecological systems theory.* London: Jessica Kingsley Publishers.

Davey, G. (1989). *Ecological learning theory.* Florence, KY: Taylor & Frances/Routledge.

Johnson, G. M. (1991). Ecological theory and conventional science: Irreconcilable differences? *Canadian Journal of Special Education*, 7, 153–163.

KEY TERMS AND DEFINITIONS

Bioecology: The biological constitution of an individual such as personality and memory capacity.

Chronosystem: The effect of time on all ecological systems, for example, attitudes toward the rights of students of ethnic minority status to receive a university education have changed over time and such changed attitudes have impacted on student learning opportunities.

Ecological Systems Theory: A conceptual model that interpreted human behavior as the consequence of complex interactions between the individual and aspects of the environment.

Exosystem: An aspect of the environment that includes indirect interactions, for example, the parent's work environment may indirectly influence university student achievement via parental job stress.

Interface-Subsystem: A subsystem of the ecological microsystem in which direct interaction with technology occurs, for example, a learning management system displayed on a computer screen.

Learner-Content Interaction: Interaction between a student and the content to be learned including reading a textbook and completing activities.

Learner-Interface Interaction: Interaction between a student and the digital interface that mediates all interactions in the online instructional context, for example, a learning management system displayed on a computer screen.

Learner-Learner Interaction: Interaction between students including talking, listening, viewing, emailing and posting in discussion boards.

Learner-Teacher Interaction: Interaction between a student and a teacher including talking, listening, viewing, emailing and posting in discussion boards.

Macrosystem: An aspect of the environment that effects indirect interactions, for example, cultural and social attitudes affect university funding which may indirectly affect student services which may indirectly affect student academic achievement.

Mesosystem: Connections between elements of the microsystem, for example, university recruitment sessions in which parents are at university demonstrate a connection between home and school.

Microsystem: An aspect of the environment that includes direct person-environment interactions, for example, the person interacts directly with others and objects at home and school.

Techno-Microsystem: A reorganization of the ecological microsystem in which direct interaction with technology occurs, for example, human interaction with computers and television in home, school and community environments.

Techno-Subsystem: A subsystem of the ecological microsystem in which direct interaction with technology occurs, for example, human interaction with computers and television.

Chapter 2
Maintaining Motivation in Online Students:
An Examination of the ARCS–V Motivation Model

Cindy Stewart
University of Houston – Downtown, USA

Travis Crone
University of Houston – Downtown, USA

ABSTRACT

This chapter provides an overview of the major motivation theories, and examines how the ARCS-V model applies motivational theory to instructional design. The chapter also provides a cognitive framework to support aspects of the ARCS-V model. Special attention is given to course design and instructional practices aimed at reducing online student attrition and improving academic performance. Additionally, the chapter reviews research examining the utility of the ARCS-V model, as well as recommendations for implementation within the online modality.

INTRODUCTION

Educational technology improvements, availability of high-speed Internet access, increases in non-traditional student enrollment, and decreases in state funding are related to growth and sustained enrollment in online courses (Means, Toyama, Murphy, Bakia, & Jones, 2010). Growth in online offerings has outpaced the scholarship of online teaching and learning and consequently, and use of evidence-based instructional practices

are haphazard. This chapter aims to describe the prevalence of online education, with particular attention given to higher education, as well as summarize the ways in which grand motivation theories have been applied to online teaching and learning.

Online courses are those in which 80% or more of the content is delivered online, either synchronously or asynchronously (Allen & Seaman, 2013). Online courses are offered in K-12 education, but are more common in higher education (Means et

DOI: 10.4018/978-1-4666-9582-5.ch002

al., 2010). Recent data estimates that one million K-12 students participated in online courses (Zandberg & Lewis, 2008); whereas, approximately 6.7 million university students were enrolled in at least one online course in the United States (Allen & Seaman, 2013). Moreover, longitudinal growth in online enrollments has been fairly stable. For more than ten years, universities have experienced double-digit growth in online education per year; only recently have online enrollments dropped to 9.3 percent (Allen & Seaman, 2013). Although overall enrollments may be showing a slight decline, university online enrollment growth exceeds growth of the larger student body. To illustrate, between 2002 and 2011 the compound annual growth rate in online education was 17.3 percent, whereas, the compound growth rate was 2.6 percent for the higher education student body (Allen & Seaman, 2013). A plateau in online enrollments is expected, but is yet to be seen.

There are several factors attributed to the growth of online education in the United States. An increasing number of students are graduating from high school, which increases the number of students qualified to enroll in colleges and universities (Allen & Seaman, 2013). The economic downturn in recent years is speculated to have increased enrollments as education improves individuals' opportunities to gain meaningful employment (Allen & Seaman, 2010; 2013). Advances in technologies, Web resources, and learning management systems can be credited with long-term enrollment growth (Means et al., 2010), as well as decreased tuition costs and other associated student expenses (Lips, 2010). Finally, student demand for online education has dramatically increased online offerings (Allen & Seaman, 2007) as universities clamber to meet students' needs for the flexibility afforded by online education (Means et al., 2010; Stewart, Bachman, & Johnson, 2010a).

Cost is a chief benefit of online education. Decreased space and facility requirements, in addition to increased student access make online education cost effective for universities (Bowen, Chingos, Lack, & Nygren, 2012; Parsad & Lewis, 2008), while costs associated with commuting and residential housing make it less expensive for students (Rickard, 2010). Reduced costs are not associated with inferior education. In fact, national data demonstrating the equivalence in learning outcome mastery further strengthens the argument for growth in online education (Russell, 2005). Bernard and colleagues (2014), in a meta-analytic study found online and face-to-face learning to be comparable; yet in an earlier investigation, Bernard and colleagues (2004) found a slight advantage for online students' mastery of course content in comparison to face-to-face students. These data coupled with the cost effectiveness of online instruction make online education appealing to students and universities leaders alike.

Faculty, however, have not shared the same enthusiasm for online education with their academic leaders. Both faculty and academic leadership recognize that online instruction requires more time and effort than face-to-face instruction (Allen & Seamen, 2013; Shea, 2007a; Stewart, Bachman, & Johnson, 2010b), but faculty members have additional concerns that inhibit their involvement. Some faculty members believe that the course content in their fields is not compatible with online education (Yang & Cornelius, 2005). Faculty also cite that they are inadequately trained to develop and/or deliver online courses (Panowski, 2004). Moreover, experienced online educators voice that they are not adequately compensated for their additional time and effort (Shea, 2007a: Stewart et al., 2010b). Perhaps most troubling is that faculty members often report that online education is of poorer quality than traditional education (Allen & Seaman, 2013; Stewart et al., 2010b). In fact, the most commonly cited cause of faculty refusal to participate in online education is related to the value and legitimacy of this delivery mode (Stewart et al., 2010b; Yang & Cornelius, 2005), and faculty acceptance has not improved significantly in the past decade (Allen & Seaman, 2011; 2013).

On average, approximately 30 percent of faculty members consider online and face-to-face instruction equivalent (Allen & Seamen, 2013). Even in universities that offer online courses and fully online degree programs, less than 40 percent of faculty accept the value and legitimacy of online education, with fewer finding the delivery modes comparable at universities offering online courses only (18%), followed by universities with only face-to-face courses (10%). Stewart and colleagues (2010b) found that faculty with greater online teaching experience were more likely to value the merits of online education, but independent of experience, the majority believed face-to-face education was superior. Lack of faculty acceptance is recognized as the most significant barrier to the growth of online education (Mullenberg & Berge, 2001; Shea, 2007b).

Given that national data demonstrate that online and face-to-face learning outcome mastery are equivalent (Bernard, Borokhovski, & Tamim, 2014; Means et al., 2010; Russell, 2005), it may be difficult to understand why faculty remain resolute in their contention that online education is inferior to conventional teaching and learning. Perhaps faculty members' experiences with online education are not accurately portrayed in these meta-analytic studies. There are several factors related to the quality of student learning that may, in part, assist in explaining faculty's disapproval of online education. Means and colleagues' national study (2010) as well as Russell's meta-analytic study (2005), neither examined student persistence nor the academic rigor of the learning outcomes measured. These studies reported aggregate differences between delivery modes in student achievement of learning outcomes. Quality of higher education is most commonly defined by student retention, grades, and graduation rates (Mitchell, 2010).

Another widespread reason for faculty reticence toward online education is high attrition rates for students enrolled in online classes, which is typically six to seven times greater than that of students enrolled in comparable face-to-face courses (Crosling, Heagney & Thomas, 2009). Student persistence is a significant problem in online education (Boston, Ice, & Gibson, 2011), with significantly more students in face-to-face courses persisting than online students (Bowden, 2008; Hart, 2012; Park, Perry, & Edwards, 2011; Rovai, 2003). Much has been written about persistence as it relates to conventional education, but much less is known about how well those research findings translate to online education (Harter & Szurminski, 2001). Student, instructional, and institutional factors have interrelated effects on persistence (Rovai, 2003), but few studies have examined the interaction of these factors on online student attrition.

Retention, at the course-level, is a prerequisite for student mastery of learning outcomes. Students' course grades reflect their successes or failures at accomplishing their instructors' learning outcomes for the course as measured by the assigned learning assessments. Learning outcomes vary in their expectations of skills and knowledge. Bloom and colleagues (1956) developed a classification system with six levels of learning, advancing from basic knowledge of terminology and concepts to higher order thought. Typically, lower level university courses focus on mastery of lower level knowledge and skills, while upper level courses require more complex thought (Taft, Perkowski, & Martin, 2011). In order to achieve the higher levels of Bloom's taxonomy, increased faculty-to-student communication is required, and class sizes tend to be reduced to facilitate greater interaction (Taft et al., 2011). However, this practice of reduced class size in upper level online courses is not universal across colleges and universities. In fact, in a review of the literature examining online student learning, online courses typically exceeded 30 students, and were characterized by little faculty-to-student interaction (Schutt, Allen, & Laumakis, 2009; Taft et al., 2011). Moreover, studies show that larger online courses rarely include or assess higher level learning outcomes (Burress, Billings, Brownrigg, Skiba, & Connors, 2009; Taft et al., 2011), and are associated with decreased student learning (Bernard et al., 2004; Bonnel, Ludwig, & Smith, 2008; Schutt et al., 2009; Taft et al., 2011). Faculty members' reluctance to engage in online instruction could be a consequence of increased student attrition and a combination of reduced academic rigor necessitated by large class size, as well as decreased student learning.

There are a number of student-centered variables that make online learning more challenging. For instance, online education is alluring to the growing non-traditional student population (Aud et al., 2011; Wladis, Hachey, & Conway, 2015). Non-traditional students are described as those students who have one or more of the following characteristics: delayed enrollment in college, attend college part-time, work full-time, are financially independent, have dependents other than a spouse, or single parent (Provansnik & Planty, 2008). Currently, non-traditional students comprise more than half of the university student population, and are the fastest growing student population (Choy, 2002). Online education provides students with greater access to higher education (Allen & Seaman, 2011; 2013), flexibility in terms of location and class time (Pontes, Haskit, Pontes, Lewis, & Siefring, 2010; Stewart et al., 2010a), as well as affordability (Lips, 2010). However, a number of variables that classify a student as non-traditional also increase that student's risk for attrition (Adelman, 2006; Horn, Cataldi, & Skilor, 2005), and academic failure. For example, part-time enrollment is associated with increased attrition (Aragon & Johnson, 2008), and students with work and family obligations are more apt to drop online courses and less likely to complete their degrees (Jaggars & Xu, 2010), as are students with small children (Wladis et al., 2015). Some non-traditional students report that they prefer face-to-face instruction, but are forced to enroll in online courses due to work schedules,

time constraints related to childcare, or costs associated with commuting to campus (Stewart et al., 2010b).

University academic leaders believe that online education is necessary for sustained institutional growth (Allen & Seaman, 2013). Faculty are reticent to participate in online instruction because many consider it subpar in comparison to face-to-face instruction, despite national data that demonstrates the delivery modes equivalence. Non-traditional students are overrepresented in online courses, which compounds the likelihood that they will withdraw or potentially fail. Given these complexities, it is essential to identify and implement instructional strategies to improve online students' potential for success. This chapter will present theory as well as practical applications of theory aimed at improving student retention and achievement in online courses. Specifically, this chapter will present major theories of motivation, as well as their collective application to online course design and delivery using Keller's (1987; 2008) ARCS-V model. The chapter will conclude with recommendations for implementation of the ARCS-V motivational design model within the online modality, as well as a discussion of future directions.

BACKGROUND

Motivation can be broadly described as a drive to engage in a particular behavior (Ryan & Deci, 2000b). Contemporary motivation theories examine how an individual's goals, beliefs, and values drive behavior (Eccles & Wigfield, 2002; Ozturk, 2012). Modern motivation theories rely less on reward and punishment as motivators of learning, and rather examine the social-cognitive aspects of motivation (Wigfield, Eccles, Roeser, & Schiefele, 2009). There are several theories of motivation that apply to education, which explicate an individual's drive to learn. Learning, however, is an internal process that is not directly observable and therefore can be difficult to assess. Thus, researchers interested in investigating learning typically examine behaviors that result from learning such as achievement on a test, production of a behavior, and the ability to apply a concept. Motivation theorists are also interested in the continuance of a behavior over time. For example, motivation theorists might also investigate how a learner elects to behave (choice), the length of time taken to initiate a new behavior (latency), the persistence of a behavior, the intensity with which a behavior is performed, and finally, the thoughts and feelings that accompany a behavior (Graham & Weiner, 1996).

Goal Setting Theory

Locke and Latham (1990) developed a motivation theory, which states that individuals purposefully engage in behaviors that accomplish goals. Goal setting involves creating a series of sub-goals aimed at achieving a desired result (Locke & Latham, 2002). As it relates to learner motivation, goals serve to direct students' attention and effort toward goal-relevant activities and away from irrelevant tasks (Ozurk, 2012). Nevertheless, not all goals effectively motivate behavior or improve outcomes. Locke and Latham (2006) found that challenging goals motivate students because they require greater achievement in comparison to goals that are simple. Moreover, specific goals improve task performance over vague goals, and attainable goals increase performance more than impossible goals (Locke & Latham, 2002; 2006). Several reasons may cause students' goals to be deemed impossible: past failures, the effort is considerably greater than the cost of success, the belief that outcomes are outside of their control (external locus of control), and conflicting goals. The attainability of a goal is related to students' perceptions of their abilities to perform a task (Locke & Latham, 2006), as well as their performance (Donovan & Williams, 2003). In addition,

students who are lacking requisite knowledge or skills may be less likely to set high goals because the effort to achieve the goal will be too great, particularly if cost and effort are not inequitable.

Students who set challenging and specific goals are more motivated and committed to learning, and they are more satisfied with their performance than their low goal setting peers (Locke & Latham, 2002; 2006). Personal satisfaction is achieved when students are able to observe growth in knowledge and skills that result from personal effort. In addition, students who set difficult and specific goals persist longer and perform better, increasing their confidence and satisfaction (Latham & Brown, 2006; Locke & Latham, 2006). In fact, students who set challenging, specific goals have been found to have higher GPAs and enhanced metacognition (Latham & Brown, 2006).

Expectancy-Value Theory

Contemporary Expectancy-Value theory is based on the original works of Atkinson (1957), Battle (1965), and more recently Wigfield and Eccles (1992). From this perspective, an individual's expectation for success and the value placed on success for a given task motivate learning (Wigfield & Eccles, 2000). Specifically, students' choice of tasks, performance, and persistence are predicted by their expectation for success (Eccles et al., 1983). Students with an expectation of success are more apt to elect to participate, engage, and persist in learning (Wigfield & Eccles, 2000). Expectations related to a specific task are most commonly assessed, but can include students' perceptions of their proximal abilities to perform a task, as well as their expectations for future success at a given task (Eccles et al., 1983).

Eccles and Wigfield (2002) describe that expectations for success are determined primarily by past achievements; however, values are influenced by the task itself, personal goals, beliefs about self-competence, and cost. Tasks that are inherently interesting, useful, aid in accomplishing goals, and require a reasonable amount of time and effort increase the value students place on those tasks (Wigfield & Cambia, 2010). Similarly, students' values are greatly influenced by others, and tasks communicated as boring, pointless, or too difficult will likely discourage students' value of the task (Wigfield, Eccles, Roeser, & Schiefele, 2009). Parents, peers, and educators shape students' expectations for success through socialization, coaching, and feedback on performance.

Self-Efficacy and Self-Regulated Learning Theory

Bandura, Zimmerman, Pintrich, and others have amassed decades of research exploring the interrelations among perceived ability, goal-directed behavior, and learning. Self-efficacy relates to an individual's perception that he/she can organize and execute a behavior, as well as an exercise control over outcomes (Bandura, 1989). Students' self-appraisals of their ability to break a task into its discrete part, perform the task in part and whole, and personally influence their success or failure at the task are essential components of self-efficacy from the social-cognitive perspective (Pintrich, Smith, Garcia, & McKeachie, 1993). Bandura (1989) contends that self-efficacy is a multidimensional construct that includes strength (ranging from positive to negative self-efficacy), generality (efficacy in many or few situations), and complexity (efficacy for tasks that vary in level of difficulty). To illustrate, students may have positive self-efficacy in most simple tasks such as taking open-book quizzes, but have poor self-efficacy in a few tasks considered very difficult such as writing long research papers. Students who are efficacious are more motivated to elect to participate in a task (Bandura, 2001), set goals (Eccles & Wigfield, 2002), persist (Bandura, 1997; 2001), and achieve (Bandura, 2001; Domlyei, 2001) than are their less efficacious peers.

Self-efficacious students are also more apt to self-regulate their learning (Zimmerman, Ban-

dura, & Martinez-Pons, 1992). Self-regulated learning refers to the extent to which students are metacognitively, motivationally, and behaviorally proactive in their learning (Zimmerman, 1986), and can be considered as both a strategy and an event. The self-regulated learning process includes setting challenging goals, using appropriate learning strategies, monitoring and assessing learning, and persisting through challenging tasks (Bandura, 2001; Bandura & Cervone, 1986; Zimmerman, 1989). Regulating behaviors are strategies put forth by the student to accomplish learning goals, but these behaviors are also events in that they occur before a learning task, during a learning task, and following a task (Pintrich, 2000; Zimmerman, 2000). Self-regulation extends beyond the immediate learning environment to include ways in which students enlist social and academic support, in addition to regulating emotions such as frustration (Zimmerman et al., 1992). Self-regulated learning is associated with increased persistence, achievement responsibility (Zimmerman, 2006), (Komarraju & Nadler, 2013; Zimmerman, 2008), and academic performance (Zimmerman & Schunk, 2001; Zimmerman & Kitsantas, 2005).

Self-efficacy and self-regulated learning, although distinct concepts, are highly related (Zimmerman, 2008), such that students develop self-regulated learning efficacy, a students' perceived abilities to regulate various forms of learning such as studying, conducting research, and strategy use (Kitsantas & Zimmerman, 2009). Efficacious self-regulated students take greater responsibility for their learning and perform better in coursework (Kitsantas & Zimmerman, 2009). Moreover, students who are efficacious about their self-regulated learning are more likely to brave challenging tasks, sustain effort, and increase effort if necessary for success; whereas, students with low efficacy about their self-regulated learning are more apt to give up when tasks are too difficult and concentrate on their personal deficiencies and failures (Dormyei, 2001).

Self-Determination Theory

Self-determination theory examines the extent to which an individual's behavior is volitionally endorsed (i.e., self-determined), rather than motivated by some external source (Deci & Ryan, 1991; Ryan & Deci, 2000a). Deci and colleagues argue that behaviors are motivated by three universal human needs: autonomy, competency, and connectedness (Deci & Ryan, 1991; Deci, Vallerand, Pelletier, & Ryan, 1991; Ryan & Deci, 2000a). Autonomy concerns an individual's ability to choose tasks and set personal goals, competence refers to an individual's belief that he/she can perform a task, and relatedness involves developing satisfying relationships (Stone, Deci, & Ryan, 2009). These inherent needs provide the framework for active pursuit of goals and the internalization of the regulated activities required to attain those goals (Deci et al., 1991).

However, internalization varies between and within individuals and is a function of the social context (Deci & Ryan, 1991; Deci et al., 1992). Behaviors performed because of an external, tangible consequence (e.g., reward or punishment) are externally regulated, and differ slightly from behaviors performed to avoid guilt or shame, known as introjected regulation (Deci & Ryan, 1991; Deci et a., 1992). Identified regulatory behaviors are those willingly performed because of their utility; whereas, fully internalized behaviors (i.e., integrated regulation) are performed because they are integrated into an individual's values and identity (Deci et al., 1992). Finally, behaviors that are intrinsically regulated are preformed because they are inherently valued (Ryan & Deci, 2000b). The process of advancing from external to internal regulation relates to motivation.

Most theories consider motivation a unitary construct that quantitatively differs in amount or degree. Self-determination theory views motivation as qualitatively different and progressing from amotivation to intrinsic motivation (Deci & Ryan, 2008). Amotivation describes a behavior performed without intent because it has little value, there is little chance for success, and will not lead to a desired outcome (Ryan, 1995; Ryan & Deci, 2000b). Extrinsic motivation describes a behavior that is motivated by an external outcome and includes external, introjected, identified, and integrated regulation. Intrinsic motivation describes a behavior performed because it is inherently interesting, satisfying, and enjoyable and typifies intrinsic regulation (Ryan & Deci, 2000b).

Although motivation is an internal phenomenon, social contexts affect, implicitly and explicitly, individuals' cognitions, emotions, and reactions (Ryan & Deci, 2003; Ryan & Niemiec, 2009). Educational environments can do much to support or undermine internalization and motivation. Classrooms that provide students with opportunities to meet their needs for autonomy, competence, and relatedness enhance students' self-determination and encourage intrinsic motivation. Specifically, tasks that are interesting, engaging, and facilitate growth in knowledge increase intrinsic motivation (Bachman & Stewart, 2011; Tsai, Kunter, Ludtke, Trautwein, & Ryan, 2008). In contrast, external factors such as deadlines, testing, and controlling language increase extrinsic motivation (Vansteenkiste, Simons, Lens, Sheldon, & Deci, 2004; Vansteenkiste, Lens, & Deci, 2006).

Considerable evidence has demonstrated that self-determined students are more intrinsically motivated, persist more, and achieve goals more often than their less self-determined peers (Bachman & Stewart, 2011; Deci et al., 1991; Pintrich & DeGroot, 1990; Stewart et al., 2010a; Vansteenkiste et al., 2004). Moreover, research shows that intrinsically motivated students have improved performance, persistence, and creativity (Deci & Ryan, 1991; Sheldon, Ryan, Rawsthorne, & Ilardi, 1997; Reeve, Deci, & Ryan, 2004). Other studies demonstrate that intrinsically motivated students are more engaged (Connell & Wellborn, 1991; Vansteenkiste et al., 2006), have higher achievement (Miserandino, 1996; Reeve, Deci, & Ryan,

2004), higher order learning (Grolnick & Ryan, 1987), reduced attrition (Johnson, Stewart, & Bachman, 2013; Vallernad & Bissonnette, 1992; Vansteenkiste et al., 2004), improved concentration (Standage, Duda, & Ntoumanis, 2005), sustained effort (Johnson et al., 2013; Ntoumanis, 2000), and greater course satisfaction (Babb, Stewart, & Bachman, 2010).

ARCS-V MOTIVATIONAL DESIGN MODEL

Notably, the grand motivation theories have common characteristics. For example, Goal Setting theory, Self-Efficacy theory, and Self-Determination theory emphasize the importance of students' setting personal goals. Expectancy-Value theory and Self-Determination theory assert that autonomous choices improve student outcomes. Students' perceived competence is primary to Expectancy-Value theory, Self-Efficacy theory, and Self-Determination theory. Moreover, task value is an essential component of Goal Setting theory, Expectancy-Value theory, and Self-Determination theory, and regulated learning behaviors are aspects associated with both Self-Efficacy theory and Self-Determination theory.

Recognizing the commonalities among motivation theories, each using slightly different terminology to describe similar constructs, each making slightly different recommendations for best practices, Keller (1983) developed a motivation theory that encompasses many of the theories previously described, yet aimed at implementation through instructional design. Keller clustered grand motivational theories based on shared attributes and determined that there were five aspects common among them: attention, relevance, confidence, satisfaction, and volition. These broadly defined aspects encapsulate much of the grand motivational theories (Table 1).

Attention

Among psychologists and educational psychologists, attention is typically viewed from an Information Processing perspective. Schneider and Shiffrin (1977) posit that attention can be both controlled and automatic processes, meaning that attention can be controlled by an individual and fixated on a target (typically only very few targets at any given moment). However, with training, attention can be deployed automatically to targets that have become noteworthy as demanding immediate attention. Automated attention can be initiated and sustained regardless of memory load or other stimuli that are simultaneously receiving attention (Schneider & Shiffrin, 1977). The process of automating attention requires significant training, but through repeat exposure, individuals become sensitized to attend to target stimuli, which allows individuals to selectively attend to some stimuli while ignoring others (Schneider & Shiffrin, 1977).

Similarly, Keller (1983) describes attention within the instructional design context, as the ability to direct and manage students' concentration on tasks. However, Keller (1987) recognizes that motivation is a prerequisite for students to direct or sustain attention. Thus, the attention component of his theory includes motivational and cognitive aspects. Keller (1983; 1987) contends that instructional design should cue students to attend to stimuli related to learning outcomes. Presumably, with frequent presentation of cues, students can be trained to automate attention to cues related to learning objectives or goals. Moreover, the attention component involves capturing students' interest in a task or course content. There is ample cognitive psychological research to support this assertion. Several classic studies demonstrate that attention is affected by stimulus characteristics. For example, Postman, Bruner, and McGinnies (1948) discovered that out of the infinite stimuli

Table 1. ARCS-V motivational model components and related theoretical constructs

ARCS-V Component	ARCS-V Component Description	Related Theoretical Concept	Related Motivation Theories
Attention	Capture students' interest; stimulate curiosity in a learning activity	Direct students' attention to goal relevant activities Students value interesting tasks Use appropriate learning strategies Choose tasks that are interesting	Goal Setting theory Expectancy-Value theory Self-Efficacy theory Self-Determination theory
Relevance	Describe how learning activity meets students' needs and accomplishes goals	Direct students' attention to goal relevant activities Students value tasks that accomplish their goals Self-regulate learning to accomplish goals Allow students to develop their own goals to increase autonomous motivation	Goal Setting theory Expectancy-Value theory Self-Efficacy theory Self-Determination theory
Confidence	Help students believe that they can succeed and control their success	Accomplishing challenging goals increases students' confidence Confidence influences expectations Students' appraisals that they are able to perform a task successfully Self-assess learning Self-regulate learning	Goal Setting theory Expectancy-Value theory Self-Efficacy theory Self-Determination theory
Satisfaction	Highlight past successes, reward students' effort and growth in knowledge and skills	Explicate effort to cost ratio Set challenging, specific goals Develop satisfying relationships	Goal Setting theory Self-Determination theory
Volition	Direct students toward goal achievement and describe typical effort required to accomplish goals	Set challenging, specific goals Redirect students away from goal-irrelevant tasks Students' appraisals that they can break tasks into its discrete parts Regulate learning environment Seek social support Students develop personal learning goals	Goal Setting theory Self-Efficacy theory Self-Determination theory

that an individual could attend to, stimuli related to one's interests, needs, and values receive selective attention. In addition, their study showed that words related to participants' values were recognized more quickly than other words. Likewise, Kelly (1955) posited that individuals use social constructs as a tool for filtering relevant from irrelevant stimuli to preferentially attend. Personal meaningfulness influences not only individuals' attention to visual stimuli, but auditory stimuli as well. Moray (1959) found that personally relevant stimuli were attended to, even when participants were encouraged to ignore certain stimuli. In this phenomenon, referred to as the "cocktail party effect," attention is drawn to person-centered information such that neutral information becomes selectively attended to when it is included with personally applicable information (Gray, Ambady, Lowenthal, & Deldin, 2004). Taken together, these investigations show the interrelatedness of attention and relevance.

Relevance

Keller's notion of relevance is supported by decades of experimental research, as well as recent neuroscientific findings. He describes relevance as tasks and/or course content that is personally useful and applicable (Keller, 1983; 1987). Keller (1987) argues that instructional design should clarify how content and tasks are relevant to students' goals and lives, thereby increasing students' motivation to engage, persist, and master the course material. There are two paradigms that aid in understanding the importance of personal relevance in motivation and learning.

Gray and colleagues (2004) examined selective attention (i.e., the ability to direct one's attention on a target), comparing target stimuli with personally relevant stimuli. In all experimental conditions, participants selectively attended to personally relevant information, even when instructed to ignore that information and attend to a specific target (Gray et al., 2004). In addition, there was greater parietal cortex activation for personally relevant stimuli in comparison to target stimuli (Gray et al., 2004). The parietal cortex is the location within the brain that initiates sensory enhancement of the biasing source, in this instance, personally relevant information (Behrmann, Geng, & Shomstein, 2004). Thus, personally relevant stimuli trigger a reaction within the brain that fixates attention preferentially on those stimuli in lieu of other stimuli.

Personally relevant information has social, historical, and cultural significance that is deeply rooted in an individual's mind. In fact, the self serves as a guide in cognitive processes in that self-relevant information receives greater attention and elicits affective responses more so than other types of information (Cunningham, Brebner, Quinn, & Turk, 2014). Consequently, self-relevant information is preferentially represented, encoded, stored, and later retrieved from memory, a phenomenon known as the self-reference effect (Rogers, Kuiper, & Kirker, 1977; Turk, Cunningham, & Macrae, 2011). Specific areas of the brain responsible for encoding self-relevant information have been identified (Klein, 2012), and there is a clear memory advantage for self-relevant memories over semantic memories (Rogers et al., 1977; Symons & Johnson, 1997). Given that information related to self is stored more efficiently and with greater

capacity (Turk et al., 2011), it follows that this information is accumulated in a rich and accessible framework wherein incoming personally relevant information can be easily incorporated and stored (Klein & Loftus, 1988). Furthermore, cues that highlight self-relevance have a similar effect on affective arousal, attention, elaborative encoding, and improved retrieval (Van den Bos, Cunningham, & Turk, 2010). Implementation of Keller's *relevance* aspect frames course content and tasks in a way that emphasizes personal relevance, thereby enhancing cognitive processes.

Confidence

Keller (1983; 1987) claims that confidence is the belief that one controls his/her success and that success is possible. The degree to which individuals perceive life events as caused by their own actions versus fate is known as locus of control (Bandura, 1986; Rotter, 1966). Students with an internal locus of control attribute academic success to their own effort and ability, whereas students with an external locus of control attribute success to luck or an easy task. Students with an internal locus of control have higher academic achievement than students with an external locus of control (Choi, 2013; Kirkpatrick, Stant, Downes, & Gaither, 2008), and are more likely to persist when content is difficult to master (Choi, 2013; Dollinger, 2000; Kirkpatrick et al., 2008). Locus of control is malleable and educational intervention can assist students with external loci of control to adopt internal loci (Kirkpatrick et al., 2008; Noel, Forsythe, & Kelly, 1987), in addition to improving academic performance (Kirkpatrick et al., 2008).

Most self-concept theorists argue that individuals are motivated to enhance and maintain positive self-perceptions, which is known as "self-enhancement" (Alport, 1937; Rogers, 1959). Although individuals have a tendency to self-enhance (Taylor & Brown, 1988), not all information stored about self is positive, and conflict can arise between how an individual views him/herself versus feedback received from others (John & Robbins, 1994). In such instances, research points to individuals ignoring or minimizing feedback that conflicts with self-perceptions and maintaining steadfast adherence toward self-enhancement (Taylor & Brown, 1988). Yet, others argue that self-concept is a socially defined construct that develops through a complex negotiation between the ideal self (who a person wishes to be) and the actual self (who an individual really is) with the actual self defined by social consensus (Mead, 1934).

However, in situations in which negative feedback challenges self-concept over time, schemas about the self evolve to accommodate that negative feedback (Piaget, 2003). Negative self-concepts can lead to a self-diminishment bias, or the tendency of an individual to underestimate one's abilities (Campbell & Fehr, 1990). In such instances personal evaluations are negatively skewed, leaving the individual feeling incapable of doing tasks that others believe he/she is capable of performing. Negative feedback can also affect an individual's sense of control over outcomes (Abramson, Seligman, & Teasdale, 1978). Behavioral experiments of learning demonstrate that pervasive and consistent negative feedback results in a perceived loss of control, and eventually learned helplessness, referring to the belief that no amount of effort will lead to success (Abramson et al., 1978). Attributing behavioral consequences to external causes removes ownership of success and failure. While attributing failures to external sources, such as bad luck may aid in self-enhancement, it also prevents internalization of success.

Accepting responsibility for outcomes does not breed confidence single-handedly; confidence is achieved by trusting in one's potential for success. Definitions of success vary. Some consider perfectionism, characterized by obsessive mistake avoidance and the tendency to set extremely high standards, success (Hewitt & Flett, 1991; Suddarth & Slaney, 2001); while others evaluate success by performing comparisons between self and others

(Covington, 1984). In addition, success might differ for those who define it as an event rather than a process (Dweck, 1986). Students who adopt a view of success that is based on a process orientation, as well as a mastery orientation (Ames, 1992; Ames & Archer, 1988) perform better in educational settings (Ames, 1992; Linnenbrink-Garcia et al., 2012; O'Keefe, Ben-Eliyahu, & Linnenbrink-Garcia, 2013).

In accord with a mastery orientation approach, Keller (1983; 1987) and others recommend that learning environments should: focus on the learning process, be cooperative rather than competitive, and emphasize the development of competencies and growth in knowledge and skills. Students who similarly adopt a mastery orientation place greater value on learning (Plante, O'Keefe, & Theoret, 2013; Pintrich, 2003), are more likely to be intrinsically motivated rather than extrinsically motivated (O'Keefe et al., 2013), and motivation is sustained over time and across different contexts (Fryer & Elliot, 2007; O'Keefe et al., 2013)

Satisfaction

Investigations of satisfaction typically assess an individual's level of satisfaction with people, situations, and events external to the self. In educational settings research examining satisfaction most commonly assesses students' satisfaction with their professors' instruction and/or their overall courses (Babb et al., 2010). However, satisfaction with instruction and/or courses is influenced by students' satisfaction with their learning, which is an internal construct. Factors such as self-concept, locus of control, self-efficacy, and goal orientation affect students' levels of satisfaction. For example, Choi (2013) found that students with internal loci of control were significantly more satisfied with their courses than students with external loci of control. This finding is consistent with previous research that shows that students who take responsibility for their educational outcomes have a greater sense of accomplishment from their achievements (Kirkpatrick et al., 2008; Sagone & De Caroli, 2014). Moreover, Choi (2013) found that students' course satisfaction was predictive of their academic performance, over and above self-efficacy and locus of control. Certainly, these constructs are interrelated, but little research has examined the predictive power of course satisfaction on performance outcomes. Satisfaction is related to intrinsic motivation, which in turn, is related to improved achievement (Ryan & Deci, 2000b). Regrettably, Choi (2013) did not assess the mediating effect of motivation orientation on academic performance.

Other individual differences, such as self-efficacy, affect satisfaction, even with difficult tasks. Individuals with high self-efficacy that are given challenging tasks see the benefit in mastering them. In contrast, those with low self-efficacy approach challenges as undeserved opportunities to fail (Judge & Bono, 2001; Locke, McClear, & Knight, 1996). Cognitions about personal ability and the task impact satisfaction before the task is attempted, let alone completed. Students with expectations for success outperform students who expect to fail (Chemers, Hu, & Garcia, 2001; Sagone & De Caroli, 2014). Efficacious students are more likely to set high goals for themselves (Chemers et al., 2001; Zimmerman et al., 1992), self-regulate learning (Cervone, Jiwani, & Wood, 1991; Ryan & Deci, 2000a; Sagone & De Caroli, 2014), perform better, and have greater satisfaction than their less efficacious peers (Bandura & Schunk, 1981; Chemers et al., 2001; Sagone & De Caroli, 2014).

Factors external to the student such as course design and instructor expectations also impact students' satisfaction. Keller (1987) contends that course design and communicated expectations can improve students' satisfaction with both their learning and the course in general. Faculty members endorsing a performance approach focus on achievement events, which minimize opportunities for students' success and decrease

students' satisfaction (O'Keefe et al., 2013). For example, a course design based on a performance approach might include a limited number of summative assessments with emphasis placed on test achievement. From this approach, faculty may encourage recitation of facts or knowledge, which can breed competition and the need for impression management among students (Maehr, 2001; Kaplan & Maehr, 2007). In situations in which a student's self-worth and perceived competence are on the line, satisfaction with learning and the course decline (Leary, 1995).

Students in performance-based courses who fail to perform well on assessments may engage in maladaptive behaviors to avoid appearing incompetent in front of their peers and professor. Rather than engaging in self-regulatory behaviors to improve performance, some students engage in self-handicapping behaviors aimed at enhancing one's perceived competence (Berglas & Jones, 1978). Self-handicapping behaviors include procrastinating, effort withdrawal, and claiming test anxiety or personal illness (Urdan & Midgley, 2001). Self-handicapping behaviors are much more common within performance based courses and are related to poorer academic performance and satisfaction (Schwinger, Wirthwein, Lemmer, & Steinmayr, 2014).

In comparison to performance-based courses, mastery-oriented courses are designed to include formative assessments that assess improvements in knowledge and competencies over time. Courses designed from a mastery approach seek to create academically and emotionally supportive learning environments (Patrick, Kaplin, & Ryan, 2011). Instructors with mastery-oriented goals for their courses communicate improvement, learning, and deeper understanding of course content (O'Keefe et al., 2013). Research shows that students in mastery-oriented courses assume mastery-oriented learning goals are more cooperative, less competitive, have higher self-worth, and greater satisfaction (O'Keefe, 2013; Patrick et al., 2011).

Volition

The concept of volition was recently added to Keller's Motivational Model, and its addition strengthens his theory in that is synthesizes and enhances the ARCS components (2008). Volition is the ability to regulate emotion, motivation, and other mental efforts (Kuhl, 1984; 1985). Most initial theorizing approached volition from a motivation perspective, examining the inter-relations among motivation, volition, and performance (Collins, 1913; James, 1902; Kuhl, 1984; 1985; Kuhl & Fuhrmann, 1998). However, some researchers argue that intrinsically motivated students require less volition because they find tasks interesting and do not require volitional strategies to persist and perform (Bembenutty, 2000; Dewitte & Lens, 2000). Moreover, research indicates that intrinsically motivated students who are required to use volitional strategies withdraw from those activities (Dewitte & Lens, 2000). When intrinsically motivated students capable of delayed gratification are forced to use volitional strategies, they become frustrated (Mischel, 1974) and endorse a performance-orientation (Bembenutty, 2000).

However, amotivated and extrinsically motivated students persist and perform better when encouraged to use volitional strategies (Dewitte & Lens, 2000; Dewitte, Siegfried, Lens, & Willy, 1999). Volitional strategies include action-based behaviors that increase self-efficacy (Bandura, 1997) and self-regulation (Baumeister, Heatherton, & Tice, 1994; Kuhl & Fuhrmann, 1998), as well as develop mastery-oriented goals (Dewitte et al., 1999; Kuhl, 1985; Vallacher & Wegner, 1985). Volitional strategies also include cognitive-based actions such as directing attention to content and tasks related to goals, elimination of cognitive and situational distractions, and management of competing goals (Dewitte et al., 1999; Kuhl, 1984; 1985).

Volitional actions such as these are believed to mediate the relationship between behavioral intentions and goal-directed behavior (Kuhl & Fuhrmann, 1998; Milne, Orbell, & Sheeran, 2002). Specifically, volition involves action planning, which requires individuals to generate mental representations of their goals, as well as the behavioral actions required to accomplish those goals (Gollwitzer, 1999; Sniehotta, Scholz, & Schwarzer, 2005). Planning helps to initiate behavioral action (Milner et al., 2002), while behavioral persistence is affected by self-efficacy as individuals examine the cost to effort ratio (Luszczynska & Schwarzer, 2003). As unexpected struggles arise or barriers to success occur, efficacious individuals will persist and increase effort when necessary. Volition also requires action control, or the ability to self-monitor, self-assess, and use alternative strategies (Baumeister et al., 1994; Sniehotta et al., 2005). Diemann and Keller (2006) recommend that instructional design can improve volition through communication of recommended control strategies that aid students' initiation and sustenance of action control processes.

SOLUTIONS AND RECOMMENDATIONS

The preponderance of theory previously presented is based on research conducted in conventional educational settings (i.e., face-to-face teaching and learning), and less in known about the applicability of motivational theories to online education. Presumably, factors that support learning and academic performance for a face-to-face student will also reinforce online student learning and performance. Yet online education is a qualitatively different experience for faculty and students, and faculty have communicated difficulties in transitioning instruction from face-to-face to the online environment. Moreover, differences between face-to-face and online students further muddy the generalizability of theories and research derived from conventional education and applied to online education. Thus an investigation of the generalizability of motivational theory and cognitive research to online teaching and learning is of prime importance, particularly considering its projected growth and impact.

Studies examining online students' motivations for enrolling in online courses typically are related to extrinsic motivations such as limited time, needed flexibility, and non-traditional student characteristics (Stewart et al., 2010a; Johnson et al., 2013), and these traits place online students at a greater risk for attrition (Nash, 2005; Stewart et al., 2010). Regardless of what initially prompts students to enroll in online courses, it is essential for students' success that they remain engaged. Maintaining student motivation has been a topic of much research in face-to-face instruction and more recently, in online education (Kyndt, Dochy, Struyven, & Cascallar, 2011; Pintrich, 2004; Visser, Plomp, Amirault, & Kuiper, 2002). Identifying instructional design practices that decrease online student attrition rates, while increasing learning, is a crucial topic of investigation (Carr, 2000). Keller (1987, 1999) argued that the most neglected facet of instructional design is student motivation. Keller and Kopp (1987) contend that ARCS-V is intended to supplement the instructional design process, by focusing course design on motivational objectives (i.e., the ARSC-V aspects).

As part of the instructional design process, faculty should first identify the instructional problem that requires remedy, such as high student attrition or poor overall performance. Once the problem has been identified, faculty should conduct a motivational analysis. For example, a faculty member may want to assess students' self-efficacy, motivation orientations, or goal orientations. Third, motivational objectives for course design should be developed to address issues noted in steps one and two. Fourth, the design phase should include a process of sequencing instructional course content. Materials should be selected and motivational messages developed that apply motivational strategies. In addition, formative feedback should be collected to determine if motivational strategies have their intended effect on motivation and course objectives, with revisions made as needed. Last, summative feedback should be gathered to examine the cumulative effect of motivational design on student outcomes (Keller, 1987).

Research on the effectiveness of the motivational design process proved effective in conventional learning environments (Cheng & Yeh, 2009; Keller, 1984; 1987); thus, Keller began to examine the applicability of the ARCS-V motivational design model to web-based courses in 2004. The ARCS-V model is associated with increased motivation and performance in face-to-face (Keller, 2008a, 2008b; Tinto, 2007), and online courses (Chang & Lehman, 2002; Huett, Kalinowski, Moller, & Huett, 2008; Pittenger & Doering, 2010), as well as decreased online student attrition (Huett et al., 2008; Visser et al., 2002). The following portion of this chapter will provide suggestions for implementing motivational design using the ARCS-V model.

Attention

One of the benefits afforded by asynchronous online courses is that learning can occur regardless of time of day or location. Even synchronous online courses can be attended remotely at a location of a student's choosing. However, not all situations and environments are conducive to student learning, and some may detract from student learning. In addition to situational and environmental distractors, characteristics of online course design can challenge students' attention. For example, courses that make use of visual stimuli, auditory stimuli, or their combination require different types of attention and cognitive processing (Fan, McCandliss, Sommer, Raz, & Posner, 2002). Research has shown that the format and location of information on a webpage impacts directed and sustained attention (Chen, 2012). In addition, students' attention can be negatively affected by stress, exhaustion due to work, and caregiving demands.

In order to combat factors that challenge students' attention, it is essential that course design direct and encourage sustained attention. To that means, Keller (1987) recommends "attention-getting" strategies, which includes the presentation of information, as well as the content itself. Research shows that attention is selectively directed toward personally relevant stimuli (Kelly, 1955; Gray et al., 2004); accordingly, it is essential for faculty to gain insight into what aspects of the course are most interesting to students. This could be accomplished by creating an Ice Breaker activity that requires students to review the chapter titles and share the chapters that seem most interesting to them and why, or by requesting that students share their motivations for enrolling in the course. If the results of these activities demonstrate that students find the content uninteresting or students report extrinsic motivations for enrolling in the course, then this data can serve to dictate how other aspects of the course should be designed to improve motivation. However, if this data shows that students are inherently interested in the course content, then the need for the volition aspect of the model may be minimized.

Another way to capture topics that are personally relevant to students and encourage introspection is to pose a few open-ended questions. For example, questions housed within survey tools or discussions that inquire about students' work, family, or other personal experiences that relate to course content can help to gauge students' current understandings, as well as identify students who could serve as scaffolds (i.e., learning supports) for students with less knowledge or experience (Stewart, Bachman, & Babb, 2009). Capitalizing on online students' interests and real-life experiences will generate greater personal interest, and consequently, improve students' attention and concentration (Gray et al., 2004).

Attention, also, can be improved by the manner in which information is presented. Stimuli novelty is associated with increased attention (Daffner et al., 2000), and therefore, use of varied instructional strategies improves students' attention. Recent studies of online students' attention spans have shown that course content displayed in the typical learning management system leads to greater distraction (Broadbent, 2002; Chen, 2012; Yen, Hu, & Ke, 2011). Specifically, Chen (2012) examined students' directed and sustained attention while varying content delivery methods. After students were given a pretest to determine their knowledge about a particular construct, they were randomly assigned to one of three experimental conditions. The first experimental group received course information via a content-page, which presented information on a webpage housed in the learning management system. The webpage included learning outcomes, course content, and hyperlinks to glossary terms. The second experimental group was presented with course content using a tutorial-simulation in which students reviewed a tutorial on a topic and then engaged in an interactive simulation. The third experimental group was presented with case studies. The case studies included hyperlinks to glossary terms. Students were required to apply the content using a series of interactive questions about the case studies. Attention data was gathered during content delivery and followed by a post-test assessing content knowledge. Results showed that students in the tutorial-simulation group had the greatest sustained attention, as well as post-group test scores (Chen, 2012). Similarly, Yen and colleagues (2011) found that interactive media displays of course content augments students' attention. Therefore, interactive course content displays, particularly those that allow for simulation activities, should be selected over the more typical concept-page presentation.

Relevance

Prior research has shown that personally relevant stimuli increase attention (Gray et al., 2004), motivation (Eccles & Wigfield, 2002), and action control (Kuhl, 1984). However, in terms of motivational design in the online modality, relevance can be thought of as strategically aligning course content and tasks with students' needs, goals, and interests. Coursework that is perceived as superfluous, unnecessarily difficult, or self-abasing will be viewed as irrelevant, which decreases motivation, self-efficacy, and self-regulation. In order to increase the relevance of online coursework, faculty should adopt and communicate mastery-oriented learning goals, which focus on growth in knowledge and competence rather than performance-based achievements. Consistent with Goal Setting theory, students should be encouraged to create their own specific, yet challenging learning goals (Locke & Latham, 2006). Keller (1987) encourages faculty to use students' goals to guide the development of cooperative activities, opportunities for personal goal fulfillment, and growth in valued knowledge and skills. For instance, faculty could provide feedback on the complexity of the students' learning goals, as well as their goal orientation, including ways to revise goals to endorse mastery-orientation. An activity of this nature would allow students to take ownership of their goals and mastery, as well as encourage opportunities to self-regulate learning based on their formative evaluative data. Information gathered through student-developed learning goals could assist faculty identify goals that commonly occur across students, so that content and tasks can be tailored to address students' learning objectives.

Creating associations between online learners' experiences and course content enhances relevance (Keller, 1987). There are several techniques that can be used to relate the familiar with the unfamiliar such as authentic tasks, problem-based learning, and case studies. Authentic tasks imitate the "ill structured challenges" and complexities of adult and professional life (Oliver & Omari, 1999; Wiggins, 1990). These tasks require students to plan (Herrington, Oliver, & Reeves, 2006; Bransford, Vye, Kinzer, & Risko, 1990), apply knowledge and competencies (Winn, 1993), reason about

their solutions through communications with faculty and classmates (Herrington et al., 2006), and revise their work after reflection (Lebow & Wager, 1994; Wiggins, 1990; Young, 1993). Although authentic tasks of this nature and complexity are rare in online courses, they are associated with increased student motivation, engagement, performance, and persistence (Herrington et al., 2003; 2006). Specifically, problem-based learning is associated with increased motivation (Hung et al., 2007; Ryan, 1993; Wood, 2003), deep learning (Polanco, Calderon, & Delgado, 2004), activation of prior knowledge and competencies (Watson, 2002; Wood, 2003), growth in broad skills and understanding (Lohman & Finkelstein, 2000; Polanco et al., 2004; Schmidt, Vermeulen, & van der Molen, 2006), improved long-term retention (Dochy, Segers, van den Bossche, & Gijbels, 2003; Wood, 2003), higher-order thought (Kuhn, 1998), and persistence (Hung et al., 2007; Reznich & Werner, 2001; Wood, 2003). Hung and colleagues (2007) claim that students who participate in problem-based learning have improved confidence because they value the competencies developed through group discussion, as well as presentations of their findings.

Confidence

Students' success in valued domains, especially those that relate to challenging goals, increases their confidence (Wigfield & Eccles, 2000). However, there are several factors that undermine students' opportunities for success such as performance-based courses (Choi, 2013), histories of failure in related content areas (Abramson et al., 1978), lack of prerequisite knowledge or skills (Stewart et al., 2010a), lack of relevant role models (Bandura, 1997), external loci of control (Kirkpatrick et al., 2008), and lack of motivational feedback (Keller, 1987). Fear of failure may be compounded for online students whom may additionally doubt their abilities to use educational technologies (Stewart et al., 2010a). In fact, Stewart and colleagues (2010a) discovered that students who are efficacious in technology are more apt to enroll in online courses than less technology efficacious students.

Nevertheless, not all students who enroll in online courses are technologically proficient. Moreover, technology efficacy does not necessarily predict students' success in using learning management systems (Stewart et al., 2010a). Therefore, faculty need to provide online students with opportunities to develop prerequisite knowledge and competencies in learning management system use at the course onset. This can be accomplished by having students complete online readiness pretests, with opportunities for remediation when necessary. Students who are found wanting in some domain should receive interactive trainings that allow for practice and skill development. Providing students with support at the beginning of the course prevents anxiety over using the learning management system, and allows students to focus their energies on course materials and tasks.

Faculty can support students' adoption of internal loci of control, self-efficacy, and self-regulation in several ways. First, express expectations for students' success without minimizing course difficulty or the effort required to succeed. Students' confidence is improved when they accomplish goals that are challenging and required sustained effort, and faculty's expectations for students color the expectations they hold for themselves (Wigfield et al., 2009). Second, clearly communicate mastery-oriented course-level goals that focus on progressive growth in knowledge and skills. In this way, faculty can serve as role models for students' endorsement of personal mastery-oriented goals. Third, Keller (1984; 1987) advocates that course design should provide ample opportunities for success. Self-assessments, reflection exercises, and resubmissions of revised drafts are examples of formative assessments that permit students' to measure their understanding and progress toward accomplishing goals. These

sorts of tasks also encourage students to assume control over their learning in that improvement is dependent on their additional efforts. Fourth, faculty should provide motivational feedback to students (Keller, 2008).

Conventional classrooms allow faculty and students to provide feedback through verbal comments, facial expressions, and other gestures. These forms of communication can be limited in asynchronous modalities; therefore, it is essential that written communications target students' confidence and motivation (Keller, 1984; Visser & Keller, 1990). To that end, communications should include the following: 1) Recognize students' efforts and past successes, for example, "You have reviewed the feedback I provided on your previous discussion, and made great strides in improving the quality of your post." 2) Provide mastery-oriented corrective feedback so that students understand how to improve over time such as, "You cited your text book, which I applaud, but I encourage you to include some outside research from academic sources in your upcoming discussion post." 3) Communicate the value in the additional effort; "Conducting outside research will deepen your understanding of this topic and prepare you to apply what you know within your future career." 4) Conclude by encouraging your students to persist; for example, "I want you to serve as a role model on the discussion board and these few changes will help you to accomplish that. Continue your efforts to grow each week."

Satisfaction

Satisfaction is inherent to the learner and influenced by the learning environment; therefore, efforts to improve students' levels of satisfaction should address both their satisfaction with their educational goals and their satisfaction with instruction and the course. Too often research examining satisfaction addresses the later rather than the former, and the two are certainly interrelated. Personal satisfaction is a function of students' loci of control. Specifically, students who assume control of their learning, when successful, internalize success and feel satisfied with their accomplishments (Sagone & De Caroli, 2014). Conversely, students with external loci of control minimize their accomplishments and their resulting satisfaction. As such, it is important for faculty to reinforce students' perceived control by providing them with opportunities to assert their autonomy, perhaps by selecting a learning activity from a set of tasks. Additionally, faculty should reinforce students' academic control (Grimes, Milea, & Woodruff, 2004; Lavendar, Nguyen-Rodriguez, & Spruijt-Metz, 2010; Perry, 2003). For example, faculty should encourage students to celebrate the results of improvement and hard work. In contrast, faculty should reframe students' comments related to external locus of control in terms of internality (Stewart & De George-Walker, 2014). Faculty members who incorporate such instructional strategies are able to reform students with external loci of control (Lavendar et al., 2010; Stewart et al., 2014). Students with internal loci of control are more efficacious, self-regulate learning, and have higher levels of satisfaction (Stewart et al., 2014).

Course design also affects students' satisfaction. Specifically, courses that allow for communication among students, in addition to communication between students and faculty improve students' satisfaction (Babb et al., 2010; Babb, Stewart, & Johnson, 2013), as do collaborative courses (O'Keefe et al., 2013; Ryan & Deci, 2000b). Ryan and Deci (2000b) claim that courses, which encourage communication and collaboration meet students' needs for relatedness. Conventional classrooms are social by nature, and it is essential that motivational design intentionally create social contexts in which knowledge can be constructed, negotiated, and internalized (Vygotsky, 1987) within the online environment (Stewart et al., 2009). Learning enjoyment is a vital aspect of intrinsic motivation (Deci & Ryan, 2008), and students who preferentially enroll

in online courses report that they enjoy online interaction with classmates and faculty more than communications that occur in face-to-face classrooms (Stewart et al., 2010a). Online learning environments, designed for supportive social interaction, facilitate intrinsic motivation, feelings of competence, and meet basic psychological needs (Ryan & Deci, 2000a). When creating venues for student-to-student interaction, faculty and instructional designers should fashion online social domains that are optimally challenging, promote feedback and discussion, and free of demeaning comments or evaluative remarks (Deci & Ryan, 2008; Ryan & Deci, 2000b). Thus, it is important for faculty to establish communication expectations and serve as models for effective communication.

Volition

Several factors can diminish online students' volition. Students who are caring for dependents or work full-time can have more distractions than students who do not have these obligations. Many characteristics that make online courses attractive to students, particularly non-traditional students, introduce competing goals, distract their attention, increase extrinsic motivations, and cause them to endorse performance-based goals. For example, an investigation of non-traditional students demonstrated that students were motivated to enroll in online courses because of work and home responsibilities, as well as the course schedule (i.e., not having required courses at various times of day), especially for parents and those who work more than 30 hours a week (Johnson et al., 2013; Stewart et al., 2010a). Additionally, non-traditional students reported that they were motivated to enroll in online courses to make timely gains toward degree completion (Stewart et al., 2010a). Extrinsic motivation factors such as these are associated with increased attrition (Lepper & Henderlong, 2000; Miltiadou & Savenye, 2003), and poorer academic performance among online students in comparison to students in conventional courses (Dutton, Dutton, & Perry, 2002; Patron & Lopez, 2011).

To reduce attrition and improve academic performance, motivational design should encourage students' volitional actions. Volition is a protective factor that combats against difficulties related to acting on intentions (Pintrich & Garcia, 1994), as well as managing distractors (Wolters, 2003). There are a number of theories that have investigated the relationship between behavioral intentions and behavioral engagement (Davis, 1989; Fishbein & Ajzen, 1975; Madden, Ellen, & Ajzen, 1992). Some argue that motivation orientation mediates the relationship between intention and engagement (Roca & Gagne, 2008; Ryan & Deci, 2000), others suggest attitudinal variables (Gibson, Harris, & Colaric, 2008; Roca & Gagne, 2008; Venkatesh & Davis, 2000), while still others point to action control (Kuhl, 1984; 1985). Based on these findings and others, Deimann and Keller (2006) acknowledge that online student characteristics and aspects of the online learning environment pose challenges to volition. Therefore, Keller and colleagues (Deimann & Keller, 2006; Kim & Keller, 2011) recommend that motivational design include volitional messages.

Volitional messages are intended to encourage intrinsic motivation (Chatzisarantis, Hagger, Smith, & Sage, 2006; Visser, Plomp, Amirault, & Kuiper, 2002), improve attitudes (Fazio & Dutton, 1997; Venkatesh & Davis, 2000), action control behaviors (Kim & Keller, 2008), and persistence (Svetkey et al., 2008). Kim and Keller (2011) advise tailoring messages based on individuals' pre-assessed motivational and volitional needs. Volitional messages, in addition to the other ARCS aspects, should additionally include statements that remind students of personal goals, direct students' attention to content and tasks that aid in goal achievement, encourage action planning, mastery orientation, self-regulated behavior, and self-monitoring, as well as provide guidance on effort required to complete the task (Kim &

Keller, 2008; 2011). Messages of this nature have been shown to be effective in improving attitudes, motivation, and behavioral engagement (Kim & Keller, 2008; 2011).

FUTURE DIRECTIONS

There is limited knowledge about how to integrate motivational and volitional messages effectively (Keller, 2005), or how these messages might differentially affect students of varying ages, motivation orientations, attitudes, etc. Kim and Keller (2011) examined the impact of volitional messages on technology use. Participants were randomly assigned to a control or experimental condition. The investigation demonstrated that motivational messages improved attitudes and increased behavioral intentions for participants in the experimental condition in comparison to those in the control condition. However, the sample included mostly women enrolled in an "Introduction to Educational Technology" course. Examining participant characteristic differences, as well as students from multiple courses, particularly courses unrelated to technology and education, could have improved the study. In an earlier study, Kim and Keller (2008) examined the effect of volitional messages on students' motivation, study habits, and achievement. Students enrolled in an archeology course were randomly assigned to one of two experimental conditions: one that received ARCS-V emails or another that received personalized ARCS-V emails, which included the student's name and personally relevant information attained through pretests. Results showed that students who received personalized ARCS-V messages experienced improved achievement over time (Kim & Keller, 2008). Although the results of this study are limited by significant achievement differences between the experimental groups, with the ARCS-V group outperforming the group that received personalized ARCS-V emails across the course.

Previous versions of the ARCS model were shown to be too time consuming for educators to implement (Keller, 1999); thus, motivational emails were intended to reduce educators' workloads (Kim & Keller, 2008). However, personalization of ARCS-V emails was also time consuming (Kim & Keller, 2008). Implementation of the ARCS-V model requires long motivational communications, and there is a negative relationship between passage length and reading comprehension (Paul & Verhulst, 2010); therefore, some students may not receive the full intervention when long communications are required. However, no research to date has examined the additive contributions of the various model aspects. If some aspects of the model are found to be equally as effective as the full ARCS-V model, then it is more efficient to disperse the shorter motivational message.

To that end, a recent investigation attempted to examine the advantage of mass motivational emails using a model that focused exclusively on the attention aspect versus the full ARCS-V model (Stewart & Crone, 2014). Results from the experiment did not demonstrate a significant reduction in student performance or attrition for the attention condition versus the ARCS-V condition. Moreover, within-instructor comparisons failed to demonstrate a significant difference between previous semesters and the intervention semester. It is important to note, however, that faculty reported that they routinely drew attention to due dates and weekly reading assignments via mass emails and course announcements. Thus, it could be that drawing attention to goal-related content and tasks is as effective as implementation of the full ARCS-V model.

Future research should examine the additive contributions of each aspect of the model by assigning participants to five experimental conditions; thus, data analyses could demonstrate the added variance accounted for in students' performance for each component of the model. In addition, the previous study did not include a control group, which could yield additional data to assess the effectiveness of the ARCS-V model. Last, future research should examine the mediating effect of the ARCS-V model on behavioral intention and behavioral engagement.

CONCLUSION

There has been a decade of significant and sustained growth in online education (Allen & Seaman, 2013). Student demand for online courses and online degree programs is high (Allen & Seaman, 2011), but faculty members remain reluctant to participate for a variety of reasons, such as high attrition and perceived inferiority in comparison to conventional education (Stewart et al., 2010b).

A number of theories, initially developed based on face-to-face instruction, have been applied to technology-based modalities. Applications of cognitive and motivational theories have shown some success in improving online students' retention and performance, yet the majority of scholarship in online teaching and learning involves evaluating techniques and trade secrets, rather than holistic theoretical testing.

The ARCS-V model attempts to summarize several popular motivational theories such as Goal Setting theory, Expectancy-Value theory, Self-Efficacy and Self-Regulation theory, and Self-Determination theory. Moreover, the theory draws on aspects of cognitive, neuroscience, and behavioral intention research. To date, investigations examining the effectiveness of the ARCS-V motivational model have been limited to single class investigations, homogeneous samples, mismatched samples, quasi-experimental paradigms that lack true control groups, and time-consuming methodologies.

The ARCS-V model shows promise in improving students' motivation orientation, mastery orientation, self-regulated behavior, as well as performance and persistence. However, additional research is needed to determine the additive contributions of the various model aspects. If future research determines that one or some aspects are equally as effective as the entire ARCS-V model, it would decrease educator workload and increase chance of procedural adherence.

REFERENCES

Abramson, L. Y., Seligman, M. E., & Teasdale, J. D. (1978). Learned helplessness in humans: Critique and reformulation. *Journal of Abnormal Psychology, 87*(1), 49–74. doi:10.1037/0021-843X.87.1.49 PMID:649856

Adelman, C. (2006). *The toolbox revisited: Paths to degree completion from high school through college.* (U.S. Department of Education, Office of Policy, Research, and Evaluation). Retrieved from: http://www.ed.gov/pubs/edpubs.html

Allen, E. I., & Seaman, J. (2007). *Blending in the extent and promise of blended education in the United States.* (Research Report No. 6). Retrieved from http://sloanconsortium.org/sites/default/files/Blending_In.pdf

Allen, E. I., & Seaman, J. (2010). *Learning on demand: Online education in the United States, 2009* (Research Report No. 7). Retrieved from: http://www.sloan-c.org/publications/survey/pdf/learningondemand.pdf

Allen, E. I., & Seaman, J. (2011). *Going the distance: Online education in the United States, 2011* (Research Report No. 8). Retrieved from: http://www.babson.edu/Academics/centers/blank-center/global-research/Documents/going-the-distance.pdf

Allen, E. I., & Seaman, J. (2013). *Changing course: Ten years of tracking online education in the United States* (Research Report No. 10). Retrieved from: http://www.onlinelearningsurvey.com/reports/changingcourse.pdf

Alport, G. W. (1937). *Personality: A psychological interpretation.* New York, NY: Holt.

Ames, C. (1992). Classrooms: Goals, structures, and student motivation. *Journal of Educational Psychology, 84*(3), 262–274. doi:10.1037/0022-0663.84.3.261

Ames, C., & Archer, J. (1988). Achievement goals in the classroom: Students' learning strategies and motivation processes. *Journal of Educational Psychology, 80*(3), 260–267. doi:10.1037/0022-0663.80.3.260

Aragon, S., & Johnson, R. (2008). Factors influencing completion and non-completion of community college online courses. *American Journal of Distance Education, 22*(3), 146–158. doi:10.1080/08923640802239962

Atkinson, J. W. (1957). Motivational determinants of risk taking behavior. *Psychological Review, 64*(6, Pt.1), 359–372. doi:10.1037/h0043445 PMID:13505972

Attewell, P., Heil, S., & Reisel, L. (2012). What is academic momentum? And does it matter? *Educational Evaluation and Policy Analysis, 34*(1), 27–44. doi:10.3102/0162373711421958

Aud, S., Hussar, W., Kena, G., Bianco, K., Frolich, L., Kemp, J., & Tahan, K. (2011). *The condition of education. (U.S. Department of Education, National Center for Educational Statistics, NCES 2011-033).* Washington, DC: U.S. Government Printing Office.

Babb, S., Stewart, C., & Bachman, C. (2010). Constructing communication in blended learning environments: Students' perceptions of good practice in hybrid courses. *Journal of Online Learning and Teaching, 6*, 735–753.

Babb, S., Stewart, C., & Johnson, R. (2013). Applying the seven principles for good practice in undergraduate education to blended learning environments. In L. Kyei-Blankson & E. Ntuli (Eds.), *Practical applications and experiences in K-20 blended learning environments.* Hershey, PA: IGI Global.

Bachman, C., & Stewart, C. (2011). Self-determination theory and web-enhanced course template development. *Teaching of Psychology, 38*(3), 180–188. doi:10.1177/0098628311411798

Bandura, A. (1986). *Social foundation of thought and action: A social cognitive theory.* Upper Saddle River, NJ: Prentice Hall.

Bandura, A. (1989). Human agency in social cognitive theory. *The American Psychologist, 44*(9), 1175–1184. doi:10.1037/0003-066X.44.9.1175 PMID:2782727

Bandura, A. (1997). *Self-efficacy: the exercise of control.* New York, NY: Freeman.

Bandura, A. (2001). Social-cognitive theory: An agentic perspective. *Annual Review of Psychology, 52*(1), 1–26. doi:10.1146/annurev.psych.52.1.1 PMID:11148297

Bandura, A., & Cervone, D. (1986). Differential engagement of self-reactive influences in cognitive motivation. *Organizational Behavior and Human Decision Processes, 38*(1), 92–113. doi:10.1016/0749-5978(86)90028-2

Bandura, A., & Schunk, D. H. (1981). Cultivating competence, self-efficacy, and intrinsic interest through proximal self-motivation. *Journal of Personality and Social Psychology, 41*(3), 586–598. doi:10.1037/0022-3514.41.3.586

Battle, E. (1965). Motivational determinants of academic task persistence. *Journal of Personality and Social Psychology, 4*, 534–632. PMID:14316982

Baumeister, R. F., Heatherton, T. F., & Tice, D. (1994). *Losing control: How and why people fail at self-regulation.* San Diego, CA: Academic Press.

Behrmann, M., Geng, J. J., & Shomstein, S. (2004). Parietal cortex and attention. *Current Opinion in Neurobiology, 14*(2), 112–217. doi:10.1016/j.conb.2004.03.012 PMID:15082327

Bembenutty, H. (2000). Sustaining motivation and academic goals: The role of academic delay of gratification. *Learning and Individual Differences, 11*(3), 233–257. doi:10.1016/S1041-6080(99)80002-8

Berglas, S., & Jones, E. E. (1978). Drug choice s a self-handicapping strategy in response to non-contingent success. *Journal of Personality and Social Psychology, 36*(4), 405–417. doi:10.1037/0022-3514.36.4.405 PMID:650387

Bernard, R. M., Abrami, P. C., Lou, Y., Evgueni, B., Wade, A., Wozney, L., & Huang, B. et al. (2004). How does distance education compare to classroom instruction? A meta-analysis of the empirical literature. *Meta-Analysis of Distance Education Studies, 10*, 63–96.

Bernard, R. M., Borokhovski, E., & Tamim, R. M. (2014). Detecting bias in meta-analyses of distance education research: Big pictures we can rely on. *Distance Education, 35*(3), 271–293. doi:10.1080/01587919.2015.957433

Bloom, B., Englehard, M. D., Furst, E. J., Hill, W. H., & Kraftwohl, D. R. (1956). *Taxonomy of educational objectives: The classification of educational goals: Handbook 1. Cognitive domain* (B. Bloom, Ed.). New York, NY: David McKay.

Bonnel, W., Ludwig, C., & Smith, J. (2008). Providing feedback in online courses: What do students want? How do we do that? In M. H. Oermann (Ed.), *Annual review of nursing education.* New York, NY: Springer.

Boston, W., Ice, P., & Gibson, A. (2011). Comprehensive assessment of student retention in online learning environments. *Online Journal of Distance Learning Administration, 4*(1).

Bowden, J. (2008). Improving feedback to students in online courses. *Nurse Researcher, 15,* 253–270.

Bowen, W. G., Chingos, M. M., Lack, K. A., & Nygren, T. I. (2012, May). *Interactive learning online at public universities: Evidence from randomized trials.* Retrieved from http://www.sr.ithaka.org/research-publications/interactive-learning-online-public-universities-evidence-randomized-trials

Bransford, J. D., Vye, N., Kinzer, C., & Risko, V. (1990). Teaching thinking and content knowledge: Toward an integrated approach. In B. Jones & L. Idol (Eds.), *Dimensions of thinking and cognitive instruction.* Hillsdale, NJ: Lawrence Erlbaum Associates.

Broadbent, B. (2002). *ABCs of e-learning: Repeating the benefits and avoiding the pitfalls.* San Francisco, CA: Jossey-Bass.

Burruss, N. M., Billings, D. M., Brownrigg, V., Skiba, D. J., & Connors, H. R. (2009). Class size as related to the sue of technology, educational practices, and outcomes in web-based nursing courses. *Journal of Professional Nursing, 25*(1), 33–41. doi:10.1016/j.profnurs.2008.06.002 PMID:19161961

Campbell, D. T., & Fehr, B. (1990). Self-esteem and perceptions of conveyed impressions: Is negative affectivity associated with greater realism? *Journal of Personality and Social Psychology, 58*(1), 122–133. doi:10.1037/0022-3514.58.1.122 PMID:2308069

Carr, S. (2000). As distance education comes of age, the challenge is keeping the students. *The Chronicle of Higher Education, 46,* A39–A41.

Cervone, D., Jiwani, N., & Wood, R. (1991). Goal setting and the differential influence of self-regulatory processes on complex decision-making performance. *Journal of Personality and Social Psychology, 61*(2), 257–266. doi:10.1037/0022-3514.61.2.257 PMID:1920065

Chang, M. M., & Lehman, J. (2002). Learning foreign language through an interactive multimedia program: An experimental student of the effects of the relevance components of the ARCS model. *CALICO Journal, 20,* 81–98.

Chatzisarantis, N. D., Hagger, M. S., Smith, B., & Sage, L. D. (2006). The influence of intrinsic motivation on execution of social behavior within the theory of planned behavior. *European Journal of Social Psychology, 36*(2), 229–237. doi:10.1002/ejsp.299

Chemers, M. M., Hu, L., & Garcia, B. F. (2001). Academic self-efficacy and first-year college student performance and adjustment. *Journal of Educational Psychology, 93*(1), 55–64. doi:10.1037/0022-0663.93.1.55

Chen, H. R. (2012). Assessment of learners' attention to e-learning by monitoring facial expressions for computer network courses. *Journal of Educational Computing, 47,* 3710385.

Cheng, Y. C., & Yeh, H. T. (2009). From concepts of motivation to its application in instructional design: Reconsidering motivation from an instructional design perspective. *British Journal of Educational Technology, 40*(4), 597–605. doi:10.1111/j.1467-8535.2008.00857.x

Choi, W. (2013). The effects of self-efficacy and internal locus of control on academic performance of students: The moderating role of class satisfaction. *Journal of Convergence Information Technology, 8*(12), 391–396. doi:10.4156/jcit.vol8.issue12.47

Choy, S. (2002). *Nontraditional undergraduates. (U.S. Department of Education, National Center for Education Statistics, NCES 2002-012)*. Washington, DC: U.S. Government Printing Office.

Collins, W. J. (1913). The place of volition in education. *International Journal of Ethics, 23*, 379–396.

Connell, J. P., & Wellborn, J. G. (1991). Competence, autonomy and relatedness: A motivational analysis of the self-system processes. In M. R. Gunnar, & L. A. Sroufe (Eds.), *Minnesota Symposium on Child Psychology*. Hillsdale, NJ: Lawrence Erlbaum.

Covington, M. V. (2000). Goal theory, motivation, and school achievement: An integrative review. *Annual Review of Psychology, 51*(1), 171–2000. doi:10.1146/annurev.psych.51.1.171 PMID:10751969

Crosling, G., & Heagney, M., & Thomas. (2009). Improving student retention in higher education: Improving teaching and learning. *Australian Universities Review, 51*, 9–18.

Cunningham, S. J., Brebner, J. L., Quinn, F., & Turk, D. J. (2014). The self-reference effect on memory in early childhood. *Child Development, 85*(2), 808–823. doi:10.1111/cdev.12144 PMID:23888928

Daffner, K. R., Mesulam, M. M., Scinto, L. F., Acar, D., Calvo, V., Faust, R., & Holcomb, P. et al. (2000). The central role of the prefrontal cortex in directing attention to novel events. *Brain, 123*(5), 927–939. doi:10.1093/brain/123.5.927 PMID:10775538

Davis, F. D. (1989). Perceived usefulness, perceived ease of use, and user acceptance of information technology. *Management Information Systems Quarterly, 13*(3), 319–339. doi:10.2307/249008

Deci, E. L., & Ryan, R. M. (1991). A motivational approach to self: Integration of personality. In R. Dienstbier (Ed.), Nebraska Symposium on Motivation: Vol. 38. *Perspectives on motivation*. Lincoln, NE: University of Nebraska Press.

Deci, E. L., & Ryan, R. M. (1992). The initiation and regulation of intrinsically motivated learning and achievement. In A. K. Boggiano & T. S. Pittman (Eds.), *Achievement and Motivation. A social developmental perspective*. New York, NY: Cambridge University Press.

Deci, E. L., & Ryan, R. M. (2008). Self-determination theory: A macro-theory of human motivation, development, and health. *Canadian Psychology, 40*(3), 182–185. doi:10.1037/a0012801

Deci, E. L., Vallerand, R. J., Pelletier, L. G., & Ryan, R. M. (1991). Motivation and education: The self-determination perspective. *Educational Psychologist, 26*(3-4), 325–346. doi:10.1080/00461520.1991.9653137

Deimann, M., & Keller, J. M. (2006). Volitional aspects of multimedia learning. *Journal of Educational Multimedia and Hypermedia, 15*, 137–158.

Dewitte, S., & Lens, W. (2000). Procrastinators lack a broad action perspective. *European Journal of Personality, 27*(2), 121–140. doi:10.1002/(SICI)1099-0984(200003/04)14:2<121::AID-PER368>3.0.CO;2-#

Dewitte, S., Siegfried, R., Lens, W., & Willy, A. (1999). Volition: Use with measure. *Learning and Individual Differences, 11*(3), 321–334. doi:10.1016/S1041-6080(99)80006-5

Dochy, F., Segers, M., van den Bossche, P., & Gijbels, D. (2003). Effects of problem based learning: A meta-analysis. *Learning and Instruction, 13*(5), 533–568. doi:10.1016/S0959-4752(02)00025-7

Dollinger, S. J. (2000). Locus of control and incidental learning: An application to college student success. *College Student Journal, 34*, 537–540.

Domyei, Z. (2001). *Motivational strategies in the language classroom.* Cambridge University Press.

Donovan, J. J., & Williams, K. J. (2003). Missing the mark: Effects of time and causal attributions on goal revision in response to goal performance discrepancies. *The Journal of Applied Psychology, 89*, 1035–1056. PMID:12814288

Dutton, J., Dutton, M., & Perry, J. (2002). How do online student differ from lecture students? *Journal of Asynchronous Learning Networks, 6*, 1–20.

Dweck, C. S. (1986). Motivaitonal processes affecting learning. *The American Psychologist, 41*(10), 1040–1048. doi:10.1037/0003-066X.41.10.1040

Eccles, J. S., Adler, T. F., Fullerman, R., Goff, S. B., Kaczala, C. M., Meece, J., & Midgley, C. (1983). Expectancies, values and academic behaviors. In J. T. Spence (Ed.), *Achievement and Achievement Motives.* San Francisco, CA: W. H. Freeman.

Eccles, J. S., & Wigfield, A. (2002). Motivational beliefs, values and goals. *Annual Review of Psychology, 53*(1), 109–132. doi:10.1146/annurev.psych.53.100901.135153 PMID:11752481

Fan, J., McCandliss, B. D., Sommer, T., Raz, M., & Posner, M. I. (2002). Testing the efficiency and independence of attentional networks. *Journal of Cognitive Neuroscience, 14*(3), 340–347. doi:10.1162/089892902317361886 PMID:11970796

Fazio, R. H., & Dunton, B. C. (1997). Categorization by race: The impact of automatic and controlled components of racial prejudice. *Journal of Experimental Social Psychology, 33*(5), 451–470. doi:10.1006/jesp.1997.1330

Fishbein, M., & Azjen, I. (1975). *Belief, attitude, intention, and behavior: An introduction to theory and research.* Reading, MA: Addison-Wesley.

Fryer, J. W., & Elliot, A. J. (2007). Stability and change in achievement goals. *Journal of Educational Psychology, 99*(4), 700–714. doi:10.1037/0022-0663.99.4.700

Gibson, S. G., Harris, M. L., & Colaric, S. M. (2008). Technology acceptance in an academic context: Faculty acceptance of online education. *Journal of Education for Business, 4*(6), 355–359. doi:10.3200/JOEB.83.6.355-359

Gollwitzer, P. M. (1999). Implementation intentions: Strong effects of simple plans. *The American Psychologist, 54*(7), 493–503. doi:10.1037/0003-066X.54.7.493

Graham, S., & Weiner, B. (1996). Theories and principles of motivation. In D. C. Berliner & R. C. Calfee (Eds.), *Handbook of educational psychology.* New York, NY: Macmillan.

Gray, H. M., Ambady, N., Lowenthal, W. T., & Deldin, P. (2004). P300 as an index of attention to self-relevant stimuli. *Journal of Experimental Social Psychology, 40*(2), 216–224. doi:10.1016/S0022-1031(03)00092-1

Grimes, P., Milea, M., & Woodruff, T. (2004). Grades--Who's to blame? Students' evaluation of teaching and locus of control. *The Journal of Economic Education, 35*(2), 125–147. doi:10.3200/JECE.35.2.129-147

Grolnick, W. S., & Ryan, R. M. (1987). Autonomy in children's learning: An experimental and individual difference investigation. *Journal of Personality and Social Psychology, 52*(5), 890–898. doi:10.1037/0022-3514.52.5.890 PMID:3585701

Hart, C. (2012). Factors associated with student persistence in an online program of study: A review of the literature. *Journal of Interactive Online Learning, 11*(1), 19–42.

Harter, J., & Szurminski, M. (2001). *PASS program (Project Assuring Student Success).* Mercy College of Northwest Ohio. Unpublished paper. Retrieved from: http://www.eric.ed.gov/ERICWebPortal/custom/portlets/recordDetails/detailmini.jsp?_nfpb=true&ERICExtSearch_SearchValue_0=ED453887&ERICExtSearch_SearchType_0=no&accno=ED453887

Herrington, J., Oliver, R., & Reeves, T. C. (2003). Patterns of engagement in authentic online learning environments. *Australasian Journal of Educational Technology, 19*, 59–71.

Herrington, J., Oliver, R., & Reeves, T. C. (2006). Authentic tasks online: A synergy among learner, task and technology. *Distance Education, 27*(2), 233–248. doi:10.1080/01587910600789639

Hewitt, P. L., & Flett, G. L. (1991). Perfectionism in the self and social contexts: Conceptualization, assessment and association with psychopathology. *Journal of Personality and Social Psychology, 60*(3), 456–470. doi:10.1037/0022-3514.60.3.456 PMID:2027080

Horn, L., Cataldi, E., & Skilor, A. (2005). *Waiting to attend college: Undergraduates who delay their postsecondary enrollment. (U.S. Department of Education, National Center for Education Statistics, NCES 2005-152).* Washington, DC: U.S. Government Printing Office.

Huett, J., Kalinowski, K., Moholer, L., & Huett, K. (2008a). Improving motivation and retention of online students through the use of the ARCS-V based emails. *American Journal of Distance Education, 22*(3), 159–176. doi:10.1080/08923640802224451

Huett, J. B., Young, J., Huett, K. C., Moller, L., & Bray, M. (2008b). Supporting the distant student: The effect of ARCS-based strategies on confidence and performance. *Quarterly Review of Distance Education, 9*, 113–126.

Hung, W., Jonassen, D. H., & Liu, R. (2007). Problem based learning. In J. Spector, J. van Merrienboer, M. Merrill, & M. Driscoll (Eds.), *Handbook of research on education communications and technology.* Mahwah, NJ: Lawrence Erlbaum.

Jaggars, S., & Xu, D. (2010) *Online learning in the Virginia community college system.* Community College Research Center, Teachers College, Columbia University. Retrieved from: http://ccrc.tc.columbia.edu/publications/online-learning-virginai.html

James, W. (1902). *The principles of psychology.* New York, NY: Holt.

John, O. P., & Robins, R. W. (1994). Accuracy and bias in self-perception: Individual differences in self-enhancement and the role of narcissism. *Journal of Personality and Social Psychology, 66*(1), 206–219. doi:10.1037/0022-3514.66.1.206 PMID:8126650

Johnson, R., Stewart, C., & Bachman, C. (2013). What drives students to complete online courses? What drives faculty to teach online? Validating a measure of motivation orientation in university students and faculty. *Interactive Learning Environments.* doi:10.1080/10494820.2013.788037

Judge, T. A., & Bono, J. E. (2001). Relations of core self-evaluations traits-self-esteem, generalized self-efficacy, locus of control, and emotional stability-with job satisfaction and job performance: A meta-analysis. *The Journal of Applied Psychology, 86*(1), 80–92. doi:10.1037/0021-9010.86.1.80 PMID:11302235

Kaplan, A., & Maehr, M. L. (2007). Achievement goals and student well-being. *Educational Psychology Review, 19*, 141–187. doi:10.1007/s10648-006-9012-5

Keller, J. M. (1983). Motivational design of instruction. In C. M. Reigeluth (Ed.), *Instructional design theories and models: An overview of their current status*. Hillsdale, NJ: Lawrence Erlbaum.

Keller, J. M. (1984). The use of ARCS model of motivation in teacher training. In K. E. Shaw (Ed.), *Aspects of educational technology* (Vol. 17). London: Kogan Page.

Keller, J. M. (1987). Development and use of the ARCS model of motivational design. *Performance and Instruction*, *26*, 1–8.

Keller, J. M. (1999). Motivational systems. In H. D. Stolovitch & E. J. Keeps (Eds.), *Handbook of human performance technology*. San Francisco, CA: Jossey-Bass.

Keller, J. M. (2005). *Course interest survey: Short form*. Florida State University, Department of Educational Psychology and Learning Systems.

Keller, J. M. (2008a). An integrative theory of motivation, volition, and performance. *Technology, Instruction, Cognition, and Learning, 6*.

Keller, J. M. (2008b). First principles of motivation to learn and e³-learning. *Distance Education*, *29*(2), 175–185. doi:10.1080/01587910802154970

Keller, J. M., & Kopp, T. W. (1987). An application of the ARCS model of motivational design. In C. M. Reigeluth (Ed.), *Instructional theories in action: Lessons illustrating selected theories and models*. Hillsdale, NJ: Lawrence Erlbaum.

Kelly, G. A. (1995). *The psychology of personal constructs*. New York, NY: Norton.

Kim, C., & Keller, J. M. (2008). Effects of motivational and volitional email messages (MVEM) with personal messages on undergraduate students' motivation, study habits and achievement. *British Journal of Educational Technology*, *39*, 36–51.

Kim, C., & Keller, J. M. (2011). Towards technology integration: The impact of motivational and volitional email messages. *Educational Technology Research and Development*, *59*(1), 91–111. doi:10.1007/s11423-010-9174-1

Kirkpatrick, M. A., Stant, K., Downes, S., & Gaither, L. (2008). Perceived locus of control and academic performance: Broadening the construct's applicability. *Journal of College Student Development*, *49*(5), 486–496. doi:10.1353/csd.0.0032

Kitsantas, A., & Zimmerman, B. J. (2009). College students' homework and academic achievement: The mediating role of self-regulatory beliefs. *Metacognition and Learning*, *4*(2), 97–110. doi:10.1007/s11409-008-9028-y

Klein, S. B. (2012). A role for the self-referential processing tasks requiring participants to imagine survival in the Savannah. *Journal of Experimental Psychology. Learning, Memory, and Cognition*, *38*(5), 1234–1242. doi:10.1037/a0027636 PMID:22409181

Klein, S. B., & Loftus, E. M. (1988). The nature of self-referent encoding: The contribution of elaborative and organizational processes. *Journal of Personality and Social Psychology*, *55*(1), 5–11. doi:10.1037/0022-3514.55.1.5

Komarraju, M., & Nadler, D. (2013). Self-efficacy and academic achievement: Why do implicit beliefs, goals, and effort regulation matter? *Learning and Individual Differences*, *25*, 67–72. doi:10.1016/j.lindif.2013.01.005

Kuhl, J. (1984). Volitional aspects of achievement motivation and learned helplessness: Toward a comprehensive theory of action control. In B. A. Maher & W. B. Maher (Eds.), *Progress in experimental personality research*. Orlando, FL: Academic Press.

Kuhl, J. (1985). Volitional mediation of cognitive behavior consistency: Self-regulatory processes and actions versus state-orientation. In J. Kuhl & J. Beckman (Eds.), *Action control: From cognition to behavior*. Berlin, Germany: Springer-Verlag. doi:10.1007/978-3-642-69746-3_6

Kuhl, J., & Furhman, A. (1998). Decomposing self-regulation and self-control: The volitional components inventory. In J. Heckhausen & S. Dweck (Eds.), *Motivation and self-regulation across the life span*. New York, NY: Cambridge University Press. doi:10.1017/CBO9780511527869.003

Kyndt, E., Dochy, F., Struyven, K., & Cascallar, E. (2011). The perception of workload and task complexity and its influence on students' approaches to learning: A study in higher education. *European Journal of Education*, *26*, 393–415.

Latham, G. P., & Brown, T. C. (2006). The effect of learning, distal, and proximal goals on MBA self-efficacy and satisfaction. *Applied Psychology*, *55*, 606–623. doi:10.1111/j.1464-0597.2006.00246.x

Lavendar, R., Nguyen-Rodriguez, S. T., & Spruijt-Metz, D. (2010). Teaching the whole student: Perceived academic control in college art instruction. *Studies in Art Education*, *51*, 198–218.

Leary, M. R. (1995). *Self-presentation: Impression management and interpersonal behavior. Social psychology series*. Madison, WI: Brown and Benchmark Publishers.

Lebow, D., & Wager, W. W. (1994). Authentic activity as a model for appropriate learning activity: Implications for emerging instructional technologies. *Canadian Journal of Educational Communication*, *23*, 231–244.

Lepper, M. R., & Henderlong, J. (2000). Turnign play into work and work into play: Twenty-five years of research on intrinsic versus extrinsic motivation. In C. Sansone & J. M. Harackiewicz (Eds.), *Intrinsic and extrinsic motivation: The search for optimal motivation and performance*. San Diego, CA: Academic Press.

Linnenbrink-Garcia, L., Middleton, M. J., Ciani, K. D., Easter, M. A., O'Keefe, P. A., & Zusho, A. (2012). The strength of the relation between performance-approach and performance-avoidance goal orientations: Theoretical, methodological and instructional implications. *Educational Psychologist*, *47*(4), 281–301. doi:10.1080/004615 20.2012.722515

Lips, D. (2010, January). *How to make higher education more affordable*. The Heritage Foundation: Leadership for America, 2785. Retrieved from: http://www.heritage.org/research/education/wm2785.cfm

Locke, E. A., & Latham, G. P. (1990). *A theory of goal setting and task performance*. Englewood Cliffs, NJ: Prentice Hall.

Locke, E. A., & Latham, G. P. (2002). Building a practically useful theory of goal setting and task motivation: A 35-year odyssey. *The American Psychologist*, *57*(9), 705–717. doi:10.1037/0003-066X.57.9.705 PMID:12237980

Locke, E. A., & Latham, G. P. (2006). New directions in goal-setting theory. *Current Directions in Psychological Science*, *15*(5), 265–268. doi:10.1111/j.1467-8721.2006.00449.x

Locke, E. A., McClear, K., & Knight, D. (1996). Self-esteem and work. *International Review of Industrial and Organizational Psychology*, *11*, 1–32.

Lohman, M. C., & Finkelstein, M. (2000). Designing groups in problem based learning to promote problem solving skills and self-directedness. *Instructional Science*, *28*(4), 291–307. doi:10.1023/A:1003927228005

Luszczynska, A., & Schwarzer, R. (2003). Planning and self-efficacy in the adoption and maintenance of breast self-examination: A longitudinal study on self-regulatory cognitions. *Psychology & Health*, *18*(1), 93–108. doi:10.1080/0887044021000019358

Madden, T. J., Ellen, P. S., & Azjen, I. (1992). A comparison for the theory of planned behavior and the theory of reasoned action. *Journal of Personality and Social Psychology, 18*(1), 3–9. doi:10.1177/0146167292181001

Maehr, M. L. (2001). Goal theory is not dead-not yet anyway: A reflection on a special issue. *Educational Psychology Review, 13*(2), 177–185. doi:10.1023/A:1009065404123

Mead, G. H. (1934). *Mind, self, and society.* Chicago, IL: University of Chicago Press.

Means, B., Toyama, Y., Murphy, R., & Baki, M. (2013). The effectiveness of online and blended learning: A meta-analysis of the empirical literature. *Teachers College Record, 115*, 47–69.

Means, B., Toyama, Y., Murphy, R., Bakia, M., & Jones, K. (2010). *Evaluation of evidence-based practices in online learning: A meta-analysis and review of online learning studies.* Retrieved from the Department of Education: http://www.ed.gov/about/offices/list/opepd/ppss/reports.html

Milne, S., Orbell, S., & Sheeran, P. (2002). Combining motivational and volitional interventions to promote exercise participation: Protection motivation theory and implementation intentions. *British Journal of Health Psychology, 7*(2), 163–184. doi:10.1348/135910702169420 PMID:14596707

Miltiadou, M., & Savenye, W. C. (2003). Applying social cognitive constructs of motivation to enhance student success in online distance education. *AACE Journal, 11*, 78–95.

Mischel, W. (1974). In L. Berkowitz (Ed.), Advances in experimental social psychology: Vol. 7. *Processes in delay of gratification.* New York, NY: Academic Press.

Miserandino, M. (1996). Children who do well in school: Individual differences in perceived competence and autonomy in above-average children. *Journal of Educational Psychology, 88*(2), 203–214. doi:10.1037/0022-0663.88.2.203

Mitchell, R. L. (2010). Approaching common ground: Defining quality in online education. *New Directions for Community Colleges, 150*(150), 89–94. doi:10.1002/cc.408

Moray, N. (1959). Attention in dichotic listening: Affective cues and the influence of instructions. *The Quarterly Journal of Experimental Psychology, 34*, 740–754.

Mullenberg, L. Y., & Berge, Z. L. (2001). Barriers to distance education: A factor analytic study. *American Journal of Distance Education, 15*(2), 7–22. doi:10.1080/08923640109527081

Nash, R. (2005). Course completion rates among distance learners: Identifying possible methods to improve retention. *Online Journal of Distance Learning Administration, 8*. Retrieved from http://www.westga.edu/%7Edistance/ojdla/winter84/nash84.htm

Noel, J. G., Forsythe, D. R., & Kelly, K. N. (1987). Improving performance of failing students by overcoming their self-serving attributional biases. *Basic and Applied Psychology, 8*(1-2), 151–162. doi:10.1080/01973533.1987.9645882

Ntoumanis, N. (2001). A prospective study of participation in optional school physical education based on self-determination theory. *Journal of Educational Psychology, 97*(3), 444–453. doi:10.1037/0022-0663.97.3.444

O'Keefe, P. A., Ben-Eliyahu, A., & Linnenbrink-Garcia, L. (2013). Shaping achievement goal orientations in a mastery-structured environment and concomitant changes in related contingencies of self-worth. *Motivation and Emotion, 37*(1), 50–64. doi:10.1007/s11031-012-9293-6

Oliver, R., & Omari, A. (1999). Using online technologies to support problem-based learning: Learners responses and perceptions. *Australasian Journal of Educational Technology, 15*, 158–179.

Ozturk, E. O. (2012). Contemporary motivation theories in educational psychology and language learning: An overview. *The International Journal of Social Sciences, 3*, 33–46.

Pankowski, P. (2004). Faculty training for online teaching. *THE Journal.* Retrieved from: http://thejournal.com/Articles/2004/09/01/Faculty-Training-for-Online-Teaching.aspx

Park, C. L., Perry, B., & Edwards, M. (2011). Minimizing attrition: Strategies for assisting students who are at risk of withdrawal. *Innovations in Education and Teaching International, 48*(1), 37–47. doi:10.1080/14703297.2010.543769

Parsad, B., & Lewis, L. (2008). *Distance education at degree-granting postsecondary institutions: 2006-2007 (U.S. Department of Education, National Center for Education Statistics, NCES 2009-044).* Washington, DC: U.S. Government Printing Office.

Patrick, H., Kaplan, A., & Ryan, A. M. (2011). Positive classroom motivational environments: Convergence between mastery goal structure and the classroom social climate. *Journal of Educational Psychology, 103*(2), 367–382. doi:10.1037/a0023311

Patron, H., & Lopez, S. (2011). Student effort, consistency, and online performance. *Journal of Educators Online, 8*, 1–11.

Paul, G., & Verhulst, S. (2010). Improving reading comprehension skills of minority adults from educationally disadvantaged backgrounds. *Journal of Adolescent & Adult Literacy, 54*(2), 131–140. doi:10.1598/JAAL.54.2.5

Perry, R. (2003). Perceived (academic) control and causal thinking in achievement settings. *Canadian Psychology, 44*(4), 312–331. doi:10.1037/h0086956

Piaget, J. (2003). Development and thinking. *Journal of Research in Science Teaching, 40*, 8–18.

Picciano, A. G., & Seaman, J. (2007). K-12 online learning. A survey of U.S. school district administrators. Boston: Sloan Consortium. Retrieved from http://www.sloan-c.org/publications/survey/K-12_06.asp

Pintrich, P. R. (2000). An achievement goal theory perspective on issues in motivation terminology, theory, and research. *Contemporary Educational Psychology, 25*(1), 92–104. doi:10.1006/ceps.1999.1017 PMID:10620384

Pintrich, P. R. (2003). A motivational science perspective on the role of student motivation in learning and teaching contexts. *Journal of Educational Psychology, 95*(4), 667–686. doi:10.1037/0022-0663.95.4.667

Pintrich, P. R. (2004). A conceptual framework for assessing motivation and self-regulated learning in college students. *Educational Psychology Review, 16*(4), 385–407. doi:10.1007/s10648-004-0006-x

Pintrich, P. R., & De Groot, V. (1990). Motivational and self-regulated learning components of classroom academic performance. *Journal of Educational Psychology, 82*(1), 33–40. doi:10.1037/0022-0663.82.1.33

Pintrich, P. R., & Garcia, T. (1994). Taking control of research on volitional control: Challenges for the future theory and research. *Learning and Individual Differences, 11*(3), 335–351. doi:10.1016/S1041-6080(99)80007-7

Pintrich, P. R., Smith, D. A., Garcia, T., & McKeachie, W. J. (1993). Reliability and predictive validity of the motivated strategies for learning questionnaire (MLSQ). *Educational and Psychological Measurement, 53*(3), 801–813. doi:10.1177/0013164493053003024

Plante, I., O'Keefe, P. A., & Theoret, M. (2013). The relation between achievement goal and expectancy-value theories in predicting achievement-related outcomes: A test of four theoretical conceptions. *Motivation and Emotion, 37*(1), 65–78. doi:10.1007/s11031-012-9282-9

Polanco, R., Calderon, P., & Delgado, F. (2004). Effects of a problem based learning program on engineering students' academic achievements in a Mexican university. *Innovations in Education, Teaching, and Instruction, 41*(2), 145–155. doi:10.1080/1470329042000208675

Pontes, M., Hasit, C., Pontes, N., Lewis, P., & Siefring, K. (2010). Variables related to undergraduate students preference for distance education classes. *Online Journal of Distance Learning Administration, 13*, 8–22.

Postman, L., Bruner, J. S., & McGinnies, E. (1948). Personal values as selective factors in perception. *Journal of Abnormal and Social Psychology, 43*(2), 142–154. doi:10.1037/h0059765 PMID:18861376

Provansnik, S., & Planty, M. (2008). *Community colleges: Supplemental to the condition of education. (U.S. Department of Education, National Center for Educational Statistics, NCES 2008-033)*. Washington, DC: U.S. Government Printing Office.

Reeve, J., Deci, E. L., & Ryan, R. M. (2004). Self-determination theory: A dialectical framework for understanding socio-cultural influences on student motivation. In D. M. McInerney & S. Van Etten (Eds.), *Big theories revisited*. Greenwich, CT: Information Age.

Reznick, C. B., & Werner, E. (2001). *Integrating technology into problem based learning small groups in a medical education setting*. Paper presented at the annual meeting of the American Educational Research Association, Seattle, WA.

Rickard, W. (2010). *The efficacy (an inevitability) of online learning in higher education*. Retrieved from http://chronicle.com/items/biz/pdf/Pearson_WP_EfficacyOfOnlineLearning.pdf

Roca, J. C., & Gagne, M. (2008). Understanding e-learning continuance intention in the workplace: A self-determination theory perspective. *Computers in Human Behavior, 24*(4), 1585–1604. doi:10.1016/j.chb.2007.06.001

Rogers, C. R. (1959). A theory of therapy, personality, and interpersonal relations, developed in the client-centered framework. In S. Koch (Ed.), *Psychology: A study of a science*. New York, NY: McGraw-Hill.

Rogers, T. B., Kuiper, N. A., & Kirker, W. S. (1977). Self-reference and the encoding of personal information. *Journal of Personality and Social Psychology, 35*(9), 677–688. doi:10.1037/0022-3514.35.9.677 PMID:909043

Rotter, J. B. (1966). Generalized expectancies for internal versus external control of reinforcement. *Psychological Monographs, 80*(1), 1–28. doi:10.1037/h0092976 PMID:5340840

Rovai, A. P. (2003). In search of higher persistence rates in distance education online programs. *Internet and Education, 6*(1), 1–16. doi:10.1016/S1096-7516(02)00158-6

Russell, G. (2005). The distancing question in online education. *Innovate, 1*(4).

Ryan, G. (1993). Student perceptions about self-directed learning in a professional course implementing problem-based learning. *Studies in Higher Education, 18*(1), 53–63. doi:10.1080/03075079312331382458

Ryan, R. M. (1995). Psychological needs and the facilitation of integrative processes. *Journal of Personality, 63*(3), 397–427. doi:10.1111/j.1467-6494.1995.tb00501.x PMID:7562360

Ryan, R. M., & Deci, E. L. (2000a). Self-determination theory and the facilitation of intrinsic motivation, social development and well-being. *The American Psychologist, 55*(1), 68–78. doi:10.1037/0003-066X.55.1.68 PMID:11392867

Ryan, R. M., & Deci, E. L. (2000b). Intrinsic and extrinsic motivations: Classic definitions and new directions. *Contemporary Educational Psychology, 25*(1), 54–67. doi:10.1006/ceps.1999.1020 PMID:10620381

Ryan, R. M., & Deci, E. L. (2003). On assimilating identities to the self: A self-determination theory perspective on internalization and integrity within cultures. In M. R. Leary & J. P. Tangney (Eds.), *Handbook on self and identity*. New York, NY: The Guilford Press.

Ryan, R. M., & Deci, E. L. (2008). Self-determination theory: A macro-theory of human motivation, development, and health. *Canadian Psychology, 49*(3), 182–185. doi:10.1037/a0012801

Ryan, R. M., & Niemiec, C. P. (2009). Self-determination theory in schools of education: Can empirically supported framework also be critical and liberating? *Theory and Research in Education, 7*(2), 263–272. doi:10.1177/1477878509104331

Sagone, E., & De Caroli, M. E. (2014). Locus of control and academic self-efficacy in university students: The effects of self-concepts. *Procedia: Social and Behavioral Sciences, 114*, 222–228. doi:10.1016/j.sbspro.2013.12.689

Schmidt, H. G., Vermelen, L., & van der Molen, H. T. (2006). Long-term effects of problem based learning: A comparison of competencies acquired by graduate of problem based and conventional medical schools. *Medical Education, 40*(6), 562–567. doi:10.1111/j.1365-2929.2006.02483.x PMID:16700772

Schneider, W., & Shiffrin, R. M. (1977). Controlled and automatic human information processing: Detection, search, and attention. *Psychological Review, 84*(1), 1–66. doi:10.1037/0033-295X.84.1.1

Schutt, M., Allen, B. S., & Laumakis, M. A. (2009). The effects of instructor immediacy behavior in online learning environments. *Quarterly Review of Distance Education, 10*, 135–148.

Schwinger, M., Wirthwein, L., Lemmer, G., & Steinmayr, R. (2014). Academic self-handicapping and achievement: A meta-analysis. *Journal of Educational Psychology, 106*(3), 744–761. doi:10.1037/a0035832

Shea, P. (2007a). Bridges and barriers to teaching online college courses: A study of experienced faculty in thirty-six colleges. *Journal of Asynchronous Learning Networks, 11*, 73–128.

Shea, P. (2007b). *Study unearths what motivated RIT faculty to teach online*. RIT Online Learning. Retrieved from: http://online.rit.edu/about/newsletter/one_article.cfm?which=99

Sheldon, K. M., Ryan, R. M., Rawsthorne, L., & Ilardi, B. (1997). Trait self and true self: Cross-role variation in the big five traits and its relations with authenticity and subjective well-being. *Journal of Personality and Social Psychology, 73*, 1380–1393. doi:10.1037/0022-3514.73.6.1380

Sniehotta, F. F., Scholz, U., & Schwarzer, R. (2005). Bridging the intention-behavior gap: Planning, self-efficacy, and action control in the adoption and maintenance of physical exercise. *Psychology & Health, 20*(2), 143–160. doi:10.1080/08870440512331317670

Standage, M., Duda, J. L., & Ntoumanis, M. (2005). A test of self-determination theory in school physical education. *The British Journal of Educational Psychology, 75*(3), 411–433. doi:10.1348/000709904X22359 PMID:16238874

Stewart, C., Bachman, C., & Babb, S. (2009). Replacing professor monologues with online dialogues: A constructivist approach to online course template design. *Journal of Online Learning and Teaching, 5*, 511–521.

Stewart, C., Bachman, C., & Johnson, R. (2010a). Students' characteristics and motivation orientations for online and traditional degree programs. *Journal of Online Learning and Teaching, 6.* Retrieved from: http://jolt.merlot.org/vol6no2/stewart_0610.htm

Stewart, C., Bachman, C., & Johnson, R. (2010b). Predictors of faculty acceptance of online education. *Journal of Online Learning and Teaching, 6*, 597–616.

Stewart, C., & Crone, T. (2014). *Examining the effectiveness of the ARCS-V motivational design model on non-traditional online students performance and persistence.* Unpublished raw data.

Stewart, M. A., & De George-Walker, L. (2014). Self-handicapping, perfectionism, locus of control and self-efficacy: A path model. *Personality and Individual Differences, 66*, 160–164. doi:10.1016/j.paid.2014.03.038

Stone, D. N., Deci, E. L., & Ryan, R. M. (2009). Beyond talk: Creating autonomous motivation through self-determination theory. *Journal of General Management, 34*, 75–91.

Suddarth, B. H., & Slaney, R. B. (2001). An investigation of the dimensions of perfectionism in college students. *Measurement & Evaluation in Counseling & Development, 34*, 157–165.

Svetkey, L. P., Stevens, V. J., Brantley, P. J., Appel, L., Hollis, J., & Vollmer, W. (2008). Comparison of strategies for sustaining weight loss: The weight loss maintenance randomized controlled trial. *Journal of the American Medical Association, 299*, 1139–1148. doi:10.1001/jama.299.10.1139 PMID:18334689

Symons, C. S., & Johnson, B. T. (1997). The self-reference effect in memory: A meta-analysis. *Psychological Bulletin, 121*(3), 371–394. doi:10.1037/0033-2909.121.3.371 PMID:9136641

Taft, S. H., Perkowski, T., & Martin, L. S. (2011). A framework for evaluating class size in online education. *The Quarterly Review of Distance Education, 12*, 181–197.

Taylor, S. E., & Brown, J. (1988). Illusion and well-being: A social psychological perspective on mental health. *Psychological Bulletin, 103*(2), 193–210. doi:10.1037/0033-2909.103.2.193 PMID:3283814

Tinto, V. (2007). Research and practice of student retention: What next? *Journal of College Student Retention, 8*(1), 1–20. doi:10.2190/4YNU-4TMB-22DJ-AN4W

Tsai, Y., Kunter, M., Ludtke, O., Trautwein, U., & Ryan, R. M. (2008). What makes lessons interesting? The role of situational and individual factors in three school subjects. *Journal of Educational Psychology, 100*(2), 460–472. doi:10.1037/0022-0663.100.2.460

Turk, D. J., Cunningham, S. J., & Macrae, C. N. (2008). Self-memory biases in explicit and incidental encoding of trait adjectives. *Consciousness and Cognition, 17*(3), 1040–1045. doi:10.1016/j.concog.2008.02.004 PMID:18395467

Urdan, T., & Midgley, C. (2001). Predictors of academic self-handicapping and achievement: Examining achievement goals, classroom goal structures, and culture. *Journal of Educational Psychology, 96*(2), 251–264. doi:10.1037/0022-0663.96.2.251

Vallacher, R. R., & Wegner, D. M. (1985). *A theory of action identification.* Erlbaum Hillsdale.

Vallerand, R. J., & Bissonnette, R. (1992). Intrinsic, extrinsic, and amotivational styles as predictors of behavior: A prospective study. *Journal of Personality*, *60*(3), 599–620. doi:10.1111/j.1467-6494.1992.tb00922.x

Van den Bos, M., Cunningham, S. J., & Turk, D. J. (2010). Mine to remember: The effects of minimal ownership on remembering and knowing. *Quarterly Journal of Experimental Psychology*, *63*, 1065–1071. doi:10.1080/17470211003770938

Vankatesh, V., & Davis, F. D. (2000). A theoretical extension of the technology acceptance model: Four longitudinal field studies. *Management Science*, *2*(2), 186–204. doi:10.1287/mnsc.46.2.186.11926

Vansteenkiste, M., Lens, W., & Deci, E. L. (2006). Intrinsic versus extrinsic goal contents in self-determination theory: Another look at the quality of academic motivation. *Educational Psychologist*, *4*(1), 19–31. doi:10.1207/s15326985ep4101_4

Vansteenkiste, M., Simons, J., Lens, W., Sheldon, K. M., & Deci, E. L. (2004). Motivating learning, performance, and persistence: The synergistic role of intrinsic goals and autonomy-support. *Journal of Personality and Social Psychology*, *87*, 246–260. doi:10.1037/0022-3514.87.2.246 PMID:15301630

Visser, J., & Keller, J. M. (1990). The clinical use of motivational messages: An inquiry into the validity of the ARCS model of motivational design. *Instructional Science*, *19*(6), 467–500. doi:10.1007/BF00119391

Visser, J., Plomp, T., Amirault, R. J., & Kuiper, R. W. (2002). Motivating students at a distance: The case of an international audience. *Educational Technology Research and Development*, *50*(2), 94–110. doi:10.1007/BF02504998

Vygotsky, L. S. (1987). Thought and word. In R. Rieber & A. Carton (Eds.), *The collected works of L. S. Vygotsky* (Vol. 1). New York, NY: Plenum Press.

Watson, G. (2002). Using technology to promote success in problem based learning courses. *Technology Source*. Retrieved from: http://technology-source.org/article/using_technology_to_promote_success_in_pbl_courses/

Wigfield, A. (1984). *Relations between ability perceptions, other achievement-related beliefs, and school performance*. Paper presented at the Annual Meeting of the American Educational Research Association, New Orleans, LA.

Wigfield, A. (1994). Expectancy-value of achievement motivation: A developmental perspective. *Educational Psychology Review*, *6*(1), 49–78. doi:10.1007/BF02209024

Wigfield, A., & Cambia, J. (2010). Students' achievement values, goal orientations, and interest: Definitions, development, and relations to achievement outcomes. *Developmental Review*, *30*(1), 1–35. doi:10.1016/j.dr.2009.12.001

Wigfield, A., & Eccles, J. (1992). The development of achievement task values: A theoretical analysis. *Developmental Review*, *12*(3), 265–310. doi:10.1016/0273-2297(92)90011-P

Wigfield, A., & Eccles, J. (2000). Expectancy-value theory of achievement motivation. *Contemporary Educational Psychology*, *25*(1), 68–81. doi:10.1006/ceps.1999.1015 PMID:10620382

Wigfield, A., Eccles, J. S., Roeser, R., & Schiefele, U. (2009). Development of achievement motivation. In W. Damon & R. M. Lerner (Eds.), *Developmental psychology: An advanced course book*. New York, NY: Wiley.

Wiggins, G. (1990). *The case for authentic assessment. (Clearinghouse on Tests, Measurement, and Evaluation, American Institutes for Research, ED328611 1990-12-00)*. Washington, DC: Government Printing Office.

Winn, W. (1993). Instructional design and situated learning: Paradox or partnership. *Educational Technology, 33*, 16–21.

Wladis, C., Hachey, A. C., & Conway, K. M. (2015). The representation of minority, female, and non-traditional STEM majors in the online environment at community colleges: A nationally representative study. *Community College Review, 43*(1), 89–114. doi:10.1177/0091552114555904

Wolters, C. (2003). Regulation of motivation: Evaluating an underemphasized aspect of self-regulated learning. *Educational Psychologist, 38*(4), 189–205. doi:10.1207/S15326985EP3804_1

Wood, D. F. (2003). ABC of learning and teaching in medicine: Problem based learning. *BMJ (Clinical Research Ed.), 326*(7384), 328–330. doi:10.1136/bmj.326.7384.328 PMID:12574050

Yang, Y., & Cornelius, L. F. (2005). Preparing instructors for quality online instruction. *Online Journal of Distance Learning Administration, 8*, 12–31.

Yen, Y. S., Hu, S. C., & Ke, T. S. (2011). The impact of learning attention on learning performance in e-learning. *T & D Journal, 112*, 1–21.

Young, M. F. (1993). Instructional design for situated learning. *Educational Technology Research and Development, 41*(1), 43–58. doi:10.1007/BF02297091

Zandberg, I., & Lewis, L. (2008). *Technology-based distance education courses for public elementary and secondary school students*. Retrieved from the National Center for Education Statistics: http://nces.ed.gov/pubs2008/2008008.pdf

Zimmerman, B. J. (1986). Development of self-regulated learning: Which are the key sub-processes? *Contemporary Educational Psychology, 11*(4), 307–313. doi:10.1016/0361-476X(86)90027-5

Zimmerman, B. J. (1989). Self-regulated learning and academic achievement: An overview. *Educational Psychologist, 25*(1), 3–17. doi:10.1207/s15326985ep2501_2

Zimmerman, B. J. (2000). Attainment of self-regulation: A social-cognitive perspective. In M. Boekaerts, P. Pintrich, & M. Zeidner (Eds.), *Handbook of self-regulation, research, and applications*. Orlando, FL: Academic Press.

Zimmerman, B. J. (2006). Enhancing students' academic responsibility and achievement: A social-cognitive self-regulatory account. In R. J. Sternberg & R. Subotnick (Eds.), *Optimizing student success in school with the other three Rs: Reasoning, resilience, and responsibility*. Greenwich, CT: Information Age.

Zimmerman, B. J. (2008). Investigating self-regulation and motivation: Historical background, methodological developments, and future prospects. *American Educational Research Journal, 45*(1), 166–183. doi:10.3102/0002831207312909

Zimmerman, B. J., Bandura, A., & Martinez-Pons, M. (1992). Self-motivation for academic attainment: The role of self-efficacy beliefs and personal goal setting. *American Educational Research Journal, 29*(3), 663–676. doi:10.3102/00028312029003663

Zimmerman, B. J., & Kitsantas, A. (2005). Homework practices and academic achievement: The mediating role of self-efficacy and perceived responsibility beliefs. *Contemporary Educational Psychology, 30*(4), 397–417. doi:10.1016/j.cedpsych.2005.05.003

Zimmerman, B. J., & Schunk, D. H. (2001). *Self-regulated learning and academic achievement: Theoretical perspectives* (2nd ed.). Mahway, NJ: Lawrence Erlbaum.

KEY TERMS AND DEFINITIONS

Attention: Ability of an individual to direct and manage focus on tasks, goals, and behaviors.

Confidence: Belief that one controls his/her success and that success is possible.

Motivation: Broadly described as a drive to engage in a particular behavior.

Online Course: Courses in which 80% or more of the content is delivered online, either synchronously or asynchronously.

Satisfaction: An individual's level of contentment and acceptance of people, situations, and events.

Self-Efficacy: An individual's perception that he/she can organize and execute a behavior, as well as an exercise control over outcomes.

Volition: The ability to regulate emotion, motivation, and other mental efforts.

Chapter 3
The Pivotal Role of Faculty in Online Student Engagement and Retention

Judi Simmons Estes
Park University, USA

ABSTRACT

The premise of this chapter is that higher education online faculty have a pivotal role in student reten-tion; faculty participation is key to student engagement and engaged students tend to complete courses in which they are enrolled. However, frequently faculty members are unaware of the impact their active participation and visibility has on student engagement and retention. In addition, online courses are an important source of revenue for many institutions of higher education and attrition results in loss of revenue. Given that faculty have a pivotal role in retention, institutions of higher education can benefit fiscally from guiding and supporting online faculty in strategies of student engagement and retention. Faculty support is needed during the process of change inherent in faculty adapting to teaching online, through providing on-going faculty professional development and by creating a teaching culture inclu-sive of informal scholarly investigations related to instructional effectiveness in online course delivery.

INTRODUCTION

The offering of online courses is a viable delivery mode for institutions of higher education and can be more effective than face-to-face learning (U.S. Department of Education, 2009). In the past ten years, the offering of online courses has grown significantly in higher education; an increasingly larger portion of degree requirements are being offered online. Institutions of higher education are finding themselves in a situation where it is fiscally necessary to respond to consumer demand. To some degree, students are customers who expect their needs be anticipated and met (Lovelock & Wirtz, 2007). For example, increasingly, college and university students want course delivery modes that fit with their busy lives; accessibility to coursework anytime and anywhere has become a criteria for selecting a degree program (Johnson, Smith, Willis, Levine & Haywood, 2011). In a 2012 survey of chief academic leaders in higher educa-tion, 69.1 percent reported that offering courses

DOI: 10.4018/978-1-4666-9582-5.ch003

online is critical to the long-term strategy of the institution (Allen & Seaman, 2013). Therefore, meeting consumer need has become an important consideration.

"For some institutions, web-based courses have been viewed as a way to attract new students, as well as to provide more convenient education options for students currently enrolled" (Lion, 2011, p. 49). At the same time as institutions of higher education are attempting to increase online course offerings to meet student demands, there is also recognition that in today's environment where higher education institutions are facing increasing budget cuts, retaining students is particularly important. Yet, attrition rates for online courses are of particular concern in the academic community (Allen & Seaman, 2013); online attrition rates are higher for online students than for students taking courses face-to-face (Angelino, Williams, & Navtig, 2007). High attrition rates result in a noticeable loss of income for institution of higher education. Even a small increase in student retention can result in a significant increase in institution revenue.

Faculty must be recognized as critical stakeholders in the process of moving courses from the brick and mortar classroom to the online classroom, not only because faculty are developing the courses to be delivered online but also because of the nature of faculty relationships with students. While faculty are known to build close relationships with students in an advising capacity, the potential for a similar relationship can unfold during course delivery that invites high student and faculty engagement. In face-to-face classes, it is common knowledge that faculty engagement has a direct impact on student engagement and retention.

The increase in online course offerings has stimulated discussions about teaching pedagogy, the quality of online course delivery, and skills to teach online. Faculty expertise and dedication have been cited as the most important factors contributing to quality online courses; however,

many faculty report feeling unprepared to teach online; teaching in a traditional classroom environment is the area for which they've been prepared (Varvel, 2007). If students want courses offered online and faculty teaching these courses have influential contact with students and engaged students tend to continue in their studies and online course offerings offer a needed revenue stream for universities, then it follows that college and universities would benefit by having highly trained faculty to teach online.

The purpose of this chapter is to: a) provide background on the relationship between student engagement and retention, b) consider course infrastructure that supports student engagement and retention, c) examine teaching strategies to engage and retain students in the online classroom, d) discuss the process of faculty development to teach online, including viewing teaching online as a scholarly endeavor.

BACKGROUND

There is a direct relationship between student engagement, student retention, and the role that faculty have in teaching an online course. Mandernach (2009) posits that student engagement depends on a number of factors, including faculty personal connections with students and the faculty creation of an active online environment. Engaged students tend to complete a course. Thus, faculty have a key role not only in retaining students in courses, but also in continued enrollment toward degree completion.

Student Engagement and Retention

The study of factors related to a student's successful integration into a collegiate environment has been considered for many years, originating with a focus on face-to-face. Recent interest in retention of college students has included students taking courses online. Patterson and McFadden

(2009) found dropout rates to be six to seven times higher in online programs than in face-to-face course delivery. Regardless of the mode of instructional delivery, face-to-face or online, student engagement is central to the learning process and retention.

Tinto's (1975) model has been used by some institutions to identify student retention strategies; suggestions regarding student integration into the academic and social environment of higher education address the importance of student engagement. While there are varying definitions for engagement; for the purpose of this chapter engagement is defined as actively participating, interacting, and collaborating among students, faculty, course content, and members of the community (Angelino, et al., 2007). Tinto (1993) also argued that simply developing a connection with others is not sufficient; students need to feel connected in ways that do not marginalize them and do provide support to feel welcomed.

Retention can be impacted by factors outside of the higher education environment, as originally described by Kember (1989) in a longitudinal study of drop-out rates in distance education; these factors included family circumstances, work responsibilities, social commitments, levels of income, gender, geographic distance from the institution. More recently Collier and Morgan (2008) explored students who are at risk for not completing a course and found they were influenced by many factors, also, such as being a first generation college student, being diagnosed with a disability, representing a lower socio economic status, being a minority, and entering school on a probationary status. Students who are socially disadvantaged may benefit the most from a sense of belonging and community (Pittman & Richmond, 2008).

The creation of a caring, supportive and welcoming environment is not just the responsibility of faculty, but needs to occur within the context of the entire university, in order to create an overall sense of belonging for each student.

Experiencing a sense of belonging is a critical component for student success, but particularly for first year students (Pearson, 2012) and first-time online students. A sense of connection can emerge when a student has a relationship with just one key person within the institution and this relationship can positively impact a student's decision to remain in college; "the single most important factor in advising students who are at-risk is helping them to feel that they are cared for by the institution" (Heisserer & Parette, 2002, p. 1). As students become engaged in to the learning process, attrition appears to decline (Angelino, et al., 2007). Opportunities for student engagement are influenced by faculty presence.

The Role of Online Faculty

The role of a teacher in an online classroom environment is not a new discussion (Cappola, Hiltz, & Rotter, 2002; Goodyear, Salmon, Spector, Steeples & Tickner, 2001; Keengwe & Kidd, 2010). The 2014 National Study on Student Engagement (NSSE) found that faculty influence students through formal and informal roles as teachers, advisors, and mentors (NSSE, 2014). In an online classroom where many opportunities are provided for students to interact with one another, the teacher, and the content, a faculty member often becomes aware of problems or questions that a student has regarding personal or student life. Given that the faculty member has a much broader view of institutional resources than a student, the faculty is in a position to direct the student to resources as needed. This type of mentoring is course-based, rather than the traditional advisor-advisee mentoring and yet can be a much needed support for student retention.

As was previously discussed, Tinto's model (1975) discusses student integration into college culture and variables influencing the attrition of students. Tinto's model considers levels of social integration and academic performance as factors influencing which students are most likely to stay in college and complete their degrees. Tinto's theory posits that attrition is more likely to occur when there is a lack of congruency between students' motivation and academic ability and the institution's academic and social characteristics. A students' commitment to their educational goals is influenced by how successful they are academically and how connected they feel socially. Faculty can be available to provide support for student's to succeed in both areas. For example, linking students with one another for peer support can be beneficial. Terrion and Leonard (2010) suggest that a peer mentor "can serve as one source of support to reduce the stress experienced by a younger and less experienced student" (p. 156) which, in turn, has the potential to reduce the attrition of the student.

Mentoring is increasingly being viewed as a tool for promoting student retention (Walker & Taub, 2001). A relationship with a mentor is likely to expand a student's awareness of resources available for coping successfully with demanding academic conditions (Evans, 2000). Faculty mentoring, during a course, can have a positive impact on students' persistence and academic achievement. While some faculty may not see this as their role, in today's environment, supporting retention success of students requires the commitment and involvement of all faculty and staff. Mentoring is one of the most effective tools that can be used to heighten the level of consciousness in working with diverse students and promoting retention (Canton & James, 2008).

Faculty positively influence student cognitive growth, development, and persistence of college; and faculty model intellectual work, promote mastery of knowledge and skills, and help students make connections between their studies and post-graduate plans (NSSE, 2014). The annual NSSE survey assesses the extent to which first and senior year, undergraduate students, are engaged in effective educational practices and experiences supporting personal development.

Students tend to decide the merits of a distance education course according to their perception of the availability and interactivity of the course faculty (Flottemesch, 2000). Thus, providing faculty teaching online with effective professional development becomes a support system for student retention; it is important that faculty establish a presence in the online classroom through which the student experience and building of an online learning community is facilitated (Murphy, Smith, & Stacey, 2002). Yet, faculty in institutions of higher education are not always aware of the importance of their presence in the online classroom. Even when aware, many faculty do not feel that they know how to increase student engagement in an online environment (Su, Bonk, Magjuka, Liu, & Lee, 2005).

COURSE INFRASTRUCTURE TO ENGAGE AND RETAIN STUDENTS

O'Brien (2002) posited that contributory factors in a student's risk of withdrawal include a lack of personal feedback from the instructor, lack of contact outside of the classroom with the instructor, inaccessibility of the instructor, and unfriendliness of faculty and staff at the institution. Ease of experience before, during, and after class, contributes to a student's retention in a course. For example, for the student who tends to procrastinate or is new to the online environment, receiving faculty contact as soon as the class roster is available and until the course is completed can be a deciding factor to being engaged and remaining in the course.

Initial Contact

Students who enroll in a class may be having their first online course experience and/or their first experience with the institution. Taking a course online for the first time can be an intimidating experience for an inexperienced college student, for a person who does not have technology confidence, or a student who is generally insecure. Therefore, reaching out to students as soon as a class roster is available (e.g., at least a week before the start of the term) can serve several purposes. It provides faculty with the opportunity to provide a self-introduction, textbook information and any other materials that will be needed for class, set the tone for the expectation for active student participation, answer initial questions, and model that the teacher of the course will also be an active participant.

This early contact can motivate students to become engaged earlier than they might otherwise do if not invited by the teacher. Early engagement minimizes difficulties the first week of class by reducing the number of students who are not clear on how to begin or have not yet purchased the necessary textbook and/or materials. It is also an opportunity for faculty to communicate their passion for a course and course content. On the other hand, sometimes problems rise before the first of class and through this initial contact students know that they can ask the teacher questions (e.g., "I was dropped from class because of a financial aid issue, what do I do?") and either receive a direct answer or be referred to someone who can answer the question. Certainly, early and on-going contact by a faculty member with each enrolled student can contribute to a student's sense of belonging and retention in a course.

Introductions

Providing students an opportunity to introduce themselves is often discussed as a first step in setting the stage for a welcoming online class environment. Providing extra credit points for contributing an initial introduction and additional points for responding to peers is one strategy for engaging students immediately and beginning the process of building community. Extra credit points can provide a grade boost as the class begins which is an incentive to participate. It is important

to provide criteria for earning points, just as for any assignment. The theory behind this strategy is that sometimes the difficult part about becoming engaged in a new course is taking that first step. Introductions provide an immediate opportunity for participation and connection with both the teacher of the course and peers.

It is important for faculty to actively participate in the process of introductions by providing an introduction that models the criteria, responding to every student's introduction, and to begin making connections between students. For example, if a student mentions that their spouse is active military and the instructor has a family member who is active military, the connection can be highlighted, as well as offering a thank-you to the spouse for his/her service. Additionally, this is a good time to acknowledge that active military sometimes have situations arise that may impact class participation and invite the student to communicate should a situation arise. Introductions can also be a time to connect students with institutional resources such as services and employees on campus. For example, if a student mentions that they want additional information about employment opportunities within their major area of study, the student could be provided with the name of a person in career counseling, a telephone number and e-mail address. Introductions is a way to establish initial connection with the student; a sense of connectedness is a decisive factor in the withdrawal of students from a course (McLean, 1999).

Discussion Thread

The asynchronous discussion thread has become a standard component of many online courses. A purpose of the discussion thread is for students to have an opportunity to engage with the course content through also engaging with peers; discussion is an opportunity to take the knowledge acquired and begin to delve deeper into the subject matter. Thus, it is important for the prompts provided for discussion invite different points of view, critical thinking, and inquiry. Simple questions with yes/no or definitive answers are not appropriate for the online discussion thread. In addition, it is important for faculty to facilitate discussions without suggesting right or wrong answers or their own particular viewpoint. Well-written discussion questions invite an examination of the depth and breadth of the subject matter.

Student participation in discussion threads depends on instructor organization and presence (Dennen, 2005). This can be done in several ways. First, faculty must ask higher level questions that stimulate critical thinking. Next, faculty can balance times of facilitating discussion while encouraging students to also take the role of facilitator. Rather than being at the center of each discussion, faculty can participate as a member of the discussion. This pedagogy is new for some faculty who are more familiar with being the "sage on the stage" rather than the "guide on the side" (King, 1993).

When students engage in discussions with each other, rather than just with the teacher, the possibilities for collaboration increase. "Through valuing devil's advocacy and critical analysis, they [students] learn to reduce the tendency toward groupthink whereby certain ideas come to be regarded as off limits, sacred, unchallengeable. They learn, to create spaces in which individual efforts are recognized" (Brookfield & Preskill, 2005, p. 33). The level of interaction of students with one another and the instructor has been shown to be a predictor of learning in online and blended courses (Rovai & Jordan, 2004). Actively engaging learners in the online learning process and facilitating meaning-making, maintains student interest and contributes to retention of students in a course.

Prompt Feedback

Chickering and Gamson (1987) identified feedback as one of seven components of effective instruction for undergraduate students. In describ-

ing the criterion "gives prompt feedback" (later amended to "incorporates assessment and prompt feedback" (Chickering & Gamson, 1999). Chickering and Gamson posited that feedback allows students to assess existing knowledge, reflect on what they have learned and what they still need to learn, and receive suggestions for improvement of future work. Other authors of research studies and best practice have also identified the importance of feedback and suggested that feedback be prompt, timely, regular, supportive, constructive, meaningful, non-threatening and helpful (Grandzol & Grandzol, 2006) and that timely and constructive feedback is valued by students who study face-to-face and online (Mancuso-Murphy, 2007). More recently, Baker (2010) found a positive correlation between teacher immediacy and student affective learning, cognition, and motivation.

On another note, nothing is more frustrating to students then not knowing their grade at any point in time during a course. Just as timely feedback to e-mails, posts, and assignments are important, posting of grades with in-depth constructive feedback is an important step in engaging students, particularly in an online course. Timely posting of grades contributes to retention through engaging the student and through connection with the teacher. Visibility of the teacher is important to engaging students in an online course and particularly as related to feedback about performance. Encouraging words, specific guidance, recognition of effort and improvement, are all ways to not only connect with a student but also to guide their development. For example, if the department in which the student is majoring follows the guidelines of the American Psychological Association (APA, 2010) for writing assignments, then informing the student that you are being strict on following those guidelines as that is an expectation for every course, then a connection is being made with the department and an investment in the student's future is also being made. Most importantly, providing feedback for meeting all criteria is also important; students want feedback regardless of the grade they are getting. Today's student is as interested in feedback as they are the grade they are receiving.

Clear and Accessible Guidelines

The clearer faculty can make expectations, the more accessible the information, the more likely it is that students will self-monitor and submit assignments that meet criteria. Deciding upon a structure that will be consistently used each week provides routine and predictability for students. For example, each week students may have readings, a presentation or video to review, discussion thread participation, a quiz, and a lessons' learned in which students are expected to synthesize the week's content and apply to real-life experiences. Routine and predictability supports students in focusing on participation rather than spending time trying to figure out performance expectations.

In a face-to-face classroom, routines and repetition of instructions are commonly provided. The same needs to occur in an online class with even more intention. Posting an announcement and sending an e-mail to students at the beginning of each week (e.g., "Welcome to Week 1) with an overview of the content and assignments for the week can help students to self-organize their time during the week. Including assignment guidelines with a checklist format can be helpful to students. This same process can be helpful at the end of the week, with a closure to the week announcement and e-mail (e.g., Closure to Week 1) summarizing an overview of the week and assignments that were due. While this may seem repetitious, accessibility is key for the online student. Students profit from this structure and begin to self-manage. Accessibility to assignments is a contributor to retention.

Open Communication

The idea behind a practice of open communication is that students feel that it is okay to approach the faculty member teaching the course with any questions or concerns; faculty present themselves as a resource to assist students as needed for information about the course or the institution. While students may be daily users of social networking and an assumption is made that they are technology literate, some students may not have the skills to do well in an online class without guidance. With this is mind, it is important to have a venue for students to have open communication including asking questions. Providing opportunities for open communication, including sharing what is and is not working for them, is an indicator of an online community that is working (Collison, Elbaum, Haavind, & Tinker, 2000). Sometimes, a problem a student is having has nothing to do with the course but something else that is going on in their school life or personal life. Being able to feel connected and knowing how and where to get assistance contribute to retention of a student in a class. Sometimes all a faculty needs to do is provide the information for the needed resource and encourage a student to seek assistance as needed.

Student learning is heavily dependent on effective teaching. Organized instruction, clear explanations, illustrative examples, and effective feedback on student work, represent aspects of teaching effectiveness that promote student comprehension and learning (NSSE, 2014). Even when all of these elements are available, there will be times when students have questions and need clarity. From a consumer driven service philosophy, it can be said that students deserve the opportunity to ask as many questions as they need to ask to gain the clarity they need. Some venues for facilitating student questions include: prominently posting contact phone numbers and e-mail for the instructor, providing an Instructors' Office inclusive of a discussion thread for student questions, and providing a tab for a Virtual Café for student discussions with peers. Even when all of these opportunities are made available to students, faculty may have to remind students of these resources and some students will not want to use the resources but will want direct contact with the teacher to ask their questions.

Course Completion Recognition

Acknowledging a student's course completion, as an accomplishment, solidifies a connection with a teacher, the content, and contributes to the student's overall positive experience and likelihood to continue enrollment at the institution. Many online students today are non-traditional. They are holding down jobs and supporting families while attending classes and they are sacrificing a lot to attend school. These students may not get recognition for all that they have accomplished. A simple acknowledgement from the faculty member who has guided their knowledge acquisition can be very meaningful.

Beyond acknowledging successful course completion, it is important for faculty to offer continued contact. Different students connect with different faculty and offering to be a future contact for students, in case they may need any assistance in navigating the terrain of student life, can be a lifeline for some students. When under stress some students tend to isolate rather than reaching out for help. A lack of connection is often a variable in a student's decision to discontinue enrollment.

Collectively, all of the little ways that faculty intentionally offer opportunities to engage students, makes a difference to individual students. It is a kind of menu approach where a particular strategy engages one student and another strategy engages another student. Each of the strategies that have been discussed has the potential to contribute to a student's overall sense of an open, emotionally safe, and inviting virtual classroom environment. . It is important to acknowledge faculty variation in knowledge of how to engage and retain students;

the online environment may offer even more of a challenge in creating a virtual sense of belonging to a college community.

TEACHING STRATEGIES FOR ENGAGEMENT AND RETENTION

Identifying strategies that will successfully engage students is a key to retention. Strategies used consistently vary among faculty; to some extent strategies chosen reflect a faculty member's personality, pedagogy, content taught, technology skills, students enrolled in a course, and online teaching experience. For example, faculty who are technologically savvy may want to have synchronous virtual office hours offered in a chat room or a method that make an auditory and visual connection. Others may phone every student at the beginning of the course, toward mid-term, and at the end of the course because they want to have personal contact. The important point is that faculty support students in feeling as though they are part of the classroom and institution and that the student is satisfied with bot the instruction within the online classroom and the overall institutional environment as represented by all of the individuals who come into contact with the student. Three strategies that are most supportive to a student's development as an online learner are: building a sense of community, providing opportunities for critical thinking, and supporting a student's self-regulated learning. Once a student experiences being a part of a classroom community, enjoys the intellectual process of critical thinking and becomes self-regulated, the student has more capacity for negotiating challenges within the online classroom and/or within the institution. Students who feel that they belong in the classroom and institutional community, are engaged in the pursuit of intellectual growth and self-regulated learning, are more resilient to the "ups and downs" that can occur during the course of degree completion.

Implement Constructivist Practices

Most faculty recognize that teaching online is not as simple as applying the same pedagogical approach as they use in the face-to-face environment. A pedagogy inclusive of how students learn and how teachers teach must be considered. Faculty in online learning classrooms represent a diverse range of pedagogical practices, but are often characterized by active learning student-centered strategies (Browne, 2005). At its best, an online environment provides students with opportunities for intense participation (Palloff & Pratt, 2005). A constructivist approach to instruction is characterized by educational learning processes that rely on student participation which works well in the online classroom (Diaz & Botenbal, 2001). Collectively, the theories of Dewey (1859-1952), Piaget (1896-1980), and Vygotsky (1896-1934) represent the basis of constructivism. Constructivism is a teaching pedagogy promoting social interaction and student engagement, as well as enhancing critical thinking, inquiry, and problem-based learning. Similar to an interactive face-to-face classroom, the online classroom is dependent on construction of knowledge by use of opportunities for reflection, social interaction, and collaboration (Chin & Williams, 2006). The idea is to provide connections student to student, student to teacher, and student to content.

In addition to engaging students in a learner-centered environment, a critical component of constructivist pedagogy is that the teacher acts in the role of facilitator of student learning. In the online learning environment faculty participation is critical and can be accomplished through creating a learning environment that fosters a learning community with opportunities for student engagement and critical thinking.

Digenti (1998) posited that student engagement in a learning community stimulates and develops cognitive and social skills. Actively engaging students is crucial to the learning process in an online class; Vygotsky (1986) emphasized the role of social process in learning, suggesting that new concepts appear first socially, and only gradually become psychological; he suggested that social models of appropriate activity enable groups of learners to do more complex activities than they could handle individually.

Students often need to experience a sense of connection to other students before being willing to share meaningful responses. When a student does not have a sense of belonging or support for building social connections, their contributions can be rote and lack substance, provided more out of a sense of obligation (Kreijns, Kirschner, & Jochems, 2003). One way of actively engaging students is through offering opportunities for collaborative and engaging learning.

Build a Sense of Community

For some faculty, teaching at a university can be a process of working alone without a lot of collaborative opportunities. When this is the case, the idea of building a classroom community, providing students with collaborative activities and cooperative learning tasks can be unfamiliar. When this is the case for face-to-face classes, then it is understandable how the concept of building a classroom community in an online class may be foreign. Yet, promoting collaboration and building community are among the strategies that have been identified to engage students in an online classroom.

Meaningful academic experiences provide students with relevant accomplishments and satisfaction that build learning communities, enhance the quality of student engagement, and decrease dropout rates (Park & Choi, 2009). To facilitate positive outcomes, instructors must move beyond content oriented online delivery and create a supportive learning environment that is sensitive to student needs (Mandernach, 2009).

Pate, Smaldino, Mayall, and Luetkehans (2009) found that creating online social communities creates an encouraging environment of shared activities resulting in deeper learning, higher final course grades, and online courses that students' rate as successful. It has long been posited that increasing the interaction between learner and teacher can lead to a sense of less transactional distance (i.e., a physical separation that results in a psychological and communicative gap) and more effective learning (Moore, 1992). College environments characterized by positive interpersonal relations promote student learning and success; students who enjoy supportive relationships with peers, advisors, faculty, and staff are better able to find assistance when needed and to learn from and with those around them (NSSE, 2014).

To become a true community of learners, community members must take time to form relationships with each other (Ryman, Hardham, Richardson & Ross, 2009). Collaborating with peers in solving problems or mastering difficult material deepens understanding and prepares students to deal with the messy, unscripted problems they encounter during and after college. Working on group projects, asking others for help with difficult material or explaining it to others, and working through course material in preparation for exams all represent collaborative learning activities (NSSE, 2014) which have the potential to build community. When a student feels like part of a community, they are more likely to be engaged, and the more engaged the more likely a student is to participate through course completion. In addition, constructivist, active learning, encourages students toward drawing upon higher level critical thinking skills.

Promote Critical Thinking

Promoting critical thinking is one strategy for assisting students to engage with the content of the course. Building a bridge between critical thinking and problem-solving strategies used in face-to-face classes to the online environment is an opportunity for faculty. For example, Shea, Li, and Pickett (2006) posited that successful facilitation of a discussion thread includes active engagement of the teacher, encouragement, reinforcing contributions, prompting critical thinking in discussions, including providing all sides of an argument. As a facilitator, within a discussion thread, faculty can point out contrasting views offered by students and the depth and breadth offered through identifying a wider view of the topic. It can be tempting for faculty to offer a personal viewpoint in a discussion thread but that hints as the "sage on the stage" approach rather than the "guide on the side."

Promoting critical thinking can occur through the structuring of every assignment, but the online weekly discussion thread is a primary vehicle for setting the expectation for critical thinking. However, opportunities for critical thinking don't automatically happen as part of a discussion thread, but happen as a result of teacher interactivity and probing students to provide additional insights. The level of teacher participation in promoting interactivity with the course content influences student levels of critical thinking (Mandernach, Forest, Bambutzke, & Manker, 2009). The asynchronous discussions provided in online courses allow for thought-filled and research-based responses more than simply sharing of personal opinions. But, students will tend to provide such insightful discussions only if modeled and encouraged by an engaged teacher. Undoubtedly, teacher facilitation of the discussion is the factor most important to stimulating critical thinking.

Critical thinking moves beyond personal opinion. Encouraging students to provide a synthesized argument based on evidence to support a position is a method for scaffolding student response toward higher level thinking (Alwehaibi, 2012). Questions requiring higher level thinking (e.g., those that go beyond recall or regurgitating information) are critical to expanding knowledge and promoting deeper learning (Marzano, Pickering, & Pollock, 2001). Open-ended question invites students to give substantive responses. An open-ended question is one that does not have a right or wrong answer; the questions serve only to stimulate thinking and are a means by which to examine a body of knowledge. For example, "Make an argument for or against teaching as a research endeavor, defending your answer with research support."

Develop Self-Regulated Learners

When students have many opportunities to be engaged in a classroom environment and have opportunities to collaborate with peers, students are also being supported in becoming self-regulated learners (SRL) and successful learners. SRL is defined as the effort put forth by students to control and monitor their motivation, concentration, and affective aspect to protect their goals (Corno, 2001). In addition, SRL refers to the degree to which students are proactive and responsible participants of their own learning process (Zimmerman, 2008). Specifically, self-regulated learners engage in a number of key self-regulatory processes including setting clear, specific, and challenging goals; using a variety of task strategies to accomplish established goals; as well as self-monitoring and self-evaluating their own progress. One potential mediator between an online learning environment and academic performance is the quality of students' self-regulatory learning processes (Lajoie & Azevedo 2006). Students who are self-regulated report higher positive motivational beliefs and seek help as necessary (Zimmerman & Kitsantas, 2005). Self-regulatory skills have been noted as being positively associated with academic achievement (Nota, Soresi, & Zimmerman 2004). In turn, successful learners tend to stay engaged. Self-regulated learners report higher self-efficacy beliefs, outcome expectations, and task interest for assignments than less self-regulated learners.

Self-regulation of learning in the online versus face-to-face learning environments can be fundamentally different as students in the online learning environment must be more autonomous and proactive in their learning given the need to initiate interaction with faculty and peers (Ally, 2004). Thus, students in the online learning environment must engage in self-regulated learning behaviors more frequently. Faculty feedback can help students take control of their learning and become self-regulated learners (Nicol, 2009) and in turn, student self-regulation and motivation can facilitate academic performance and increase positive attitudes towards learning (Chang, 2007).

Using strategies to improve students' regulated participation and help them achieve better learning effects may challenge many faculty teaching online. However, it is important fo faculty to prompt and guide students to engage in self-regulated learning (Jairam & Kiewra, 2010). While intentionally designing a course that engages and guides students to be highly engaged and subsequently successful, not all students self-regulate in the same way. For example, while providing a high amount of learner independence may work well for one student, others need more teacher direction and feedback. Offering collaborative opportunities, as discussed earlier in the chapter, has an added benefit for some students of supporting peer regulation as peers work and learn together. Another variable is that some students will use the tools and supports provided within the course design more than others. Kitsantas (2013) provides a thorough discussion and examples of how faculty can use learning management system tools and learning technologies to help students develop self-regulatory skills.

PREPARING FACULTY TO TEACH ONLINE

There is a need for preparing faculty to teach online (Almala, 2006). Some methods and techniques used in face-to-face delivery can be transferred to an online setting. However, online instruction does differ from face-to-face instruction; faculty transitioning to an online environment can encounter challenges (Paloff & Pratt, 2005). To address the needs of online students, faculty often need to acquire some new skills, roles, strategies, and techniques not needed in face-to-face course delivery (Varvel, 2007). For example, online teaching requires the instructor to shift "from being content providers to facilitators of student learning… [they] must gain comfort and proficiency in using the Web as the primary teacher-student link, and learn to teach effectively without the visual control provided by direct eye contact" (Smith, Ferguson, & Caris, 2002, p. 62).

As more faculty are needed to teach online, those who are reluctant and those who have few computer skills, will be among those who are invited to teach an online course. Faculty will have varying levels of needs (content taught) and skills and will need to be on-going learners as technology changes over time. Not all faculty will welcome this viewpoint. Faculty will have different needs in regard to professional development and training and in some cases will need substantial support. For this reason, it is necessary to take instructors' needs into consideration during planning and implementation of training programs. In order to sustain successful online programs, institutions should address the needs of online instructors in a systematic and comprehensive manner and employ different mechanisms to support instructors when teaching online.

Faculty, however, must do more than develop technological skills. In a research study, Roman, Kelsey, and Lin (2010) found that online training programs should emphasize both technological and pedagogical skill development, evaluate participants' training needs prior to the training, and provide ongoing resources and support mechanisms after the training. As was discussed

earlier, teaching online requires consideration of pedagogy as a foundation for effective online delivery of instruction.

Well-planned and well-organized instructor training programs have been identified as a prerequisite for success in an online setting. Wolf (2006) identified five features for successful training of online faculty: 1) the course was led by an instructor trained to teach online, 2) participants have computing skills, 3) participants use the course delivery system they will be teaching with, 4) participants have ongoing institutional support, and 5) participants are motivated to teach online. According to Wolf, "effective distance education programs provide ongoing faculty support in the form of mentoring, shadowing, continuing education workshops, or some combination of all these" (p. 58).

The Need for a Systemic Approach

To be most effective, the training available to faculty who teach online must be a part of an institutional professional development framework that is sustainable. A well though-out multifaceted plan, with institutionalized support systems is needed to address the needs of new and seasoned online faculty. Technology is continually advancing and tools available to engage students when teaching online are changing daily. It is critical for institutions to have internal systems to be responsive to tools that most efficiently integrate into the adopted learning management system of the institution. When institutions of higher education invest in the professional development of their online faculty, chances are they will reap on-going dividends in terms of retaining students, which may also provide a fiscal impact of sustainable and/or increased revenue from online course offerings.

Collom, Dallas, Jong, and Obexer (2001) discuss the process their university went through to develop a framework for professional development. Developing the framework was a process that involved recognizing that faculty would have varying levels of knowledge, skills, and motivation for teaching online. The resulting framework recognizes the developmental process for faculty as they grow in their knowledge, skills, and commitment to the process of teaching online.

- Help faculty to identify their strengths and gaps in knowledge in I individual development for online teaching
- Support faculty in choosing and planning a learning path to further their knowledge and skills
- Aid administrators to identify broader needs in professional development
- Assist in teaming developing integrated professional development vs. an approach that is "piecemeal"

There will always be faculty that are new to online teaching that need to be trained, but just as important are the faculty who teach online on an on-going basis who not only need to be challenged to continue developing their skill base, but also supported in having avenues for contributing what they have learned about best practice.

Faculty and the Change Process

Every faculty who has been effective in teaching a course face-to-face, cannot be expected to translate what has worked face-to-face to an online format (Su, 2005). Learning how to teach effectively on-line takes the same elements needed to learn to be effective in teaching face-to-face, including professional development, institutional support, experience, and time to be a reflective practitioner. Developing and teaching online courses require a specific sets of skills that faculty must acquire in order to be successful in the process of delivery instruction online (Howell, Saba, Lindsay, & Williams, 2004). For example, faculty who develop and teach online courses must remember that it is

pedagogy, not technology that is critical to the success of online courses (Shieh, Gummer, & Niess, 2008). Yet in a study of the Internet generation, or "Net-Gen," it was found that the students care less about "bells and whistles" than they do about good teaching (Oblinger & Oblinger, 2005). To help faculty develop and teach online courses requires that instructional guides, professional development opportunities, and instructional materials are carefully designed to address all components of the learning and teaching processes including pedagogy, course management, technology, and the social dynamics (Grant & Thornton, 2007).

Teaching a course online for the first time can be intimidating to any faculty member, adjunct or full-time. Some institutions only expect faculty to provide and organize course content, instructional strategies, and assessments for weekly delivery; typically a basic training is provided on how to deliver the course using the learning management system adopted by the institution. Another model expects faculty to also be the instructional designer of the course; the faculty member is responsible for loading the content into the learning management system and choosing the "bells and whistles" of the course; this responsibility is also one where training is typically provided by the institution. Each role offers its own challenges; one requires curricular design skills and the other technological skills. The change required of faculty can be more intense when the faculty member is expected to provide not only the instructional content but also course design. It is important to keep in mind that this change is taking place while a faculty member is still engaged in teaching other courses. Faculty members vary in their readiness to agree to accept this challenge and participate in the breadth of commitment needed to teach online, particularly initially. Keengwe and Kidd (2010) provide a thorough description of this process, well-documented by other researchers.

Rogers (2003) theorized that individual adoption rates of technological innovations, such as teaching online, can be visually represented with a bell-shaped curve grouped under five categories: a) innovators, representing 2.5% of the population; b) early adopters, representing 13.5% of the population; c) early majority, representing 34% of the population; d) late majority, e) representing 34% of the population, and laggards, representing 2.5% of the population. This visual can be helpful in understanding that faculty adjust to the idea of teaching online at their own pace; only a small percentage will be innovators or early adopters embracing the idea and value of offering coursework online. It can be expected that a small percentage may lag behind and perhaps some will never willingly participate in teaching online. The question for an institution becomes how to provide opportunities for all faculty (adjunct and full-time), providing support for the innovators and early adopters, early and late majority, and accept that there will be slow to embrace change, and a minority may never embrace the idea of teaching online. Institutional support must be viewed, not only in regard to teaching faculty how to teach online initially, but also to providing support in viewing teaching as a scholarly endeavor requiring on-going instructional assessment and course modifications.

Teaching Online as a Scholarly Endeavor

Faculty teaching and research as well as time to do both, are important issues in higher education (Umbach & Wawrzynski, 2005). Teaching as a scholarly endeavor, in this paper, refers to the practice of faculty conducting formative and summative evaluations of their instruction, seeking input from students and examining the evidence provided by student work samples (e.g., assignments, discussion threads, etc.), drawing conclusions that inform teaching, and making modifications in teaching practices accordingly. This idea is not new. Barr and Tagg (1995) spoke of a paradigm shift from a focus on teaching students to a focus on student learning.

The purpose of faculty focus on evaluating the effectiveness of their own teaching is not necessarily for documenting scholarship for annual performance reviews, tenure, or promotion, but rather for the purpose of on-going assessment of instructional effectiveness focused on increasing student learning. Typically academia has approached scholarship in a relatively narrow manner and specifically related to empirical research. While empirical research is needed and valued in the online environment, faculty investigations of instructional effectiveness are also needed to inform best practices within one's own courses.

It is not the purpose of this chapter to provide a literature review or in-depth discussion on what has become known as the Scholarship of Teaching and Learning (SoTL); qualitative and quantitative research on this topic is represented in the peer reviewed *Journal of the Scholarship of Teaching and Learning*. What is being proposed, in this chapter, is for online full-time and adjunct faculty to be supported in conducting informal research and participating in on-going dialogue about the teaching and learning process as it occurs online. "While the occurrence of e-learning has continued to increase, concerns with the quality and availability of faculty support to design and deliver such programs still exist" (Lion, 2011, p. 49). A goal of institutions of higher education must be assisting faculty with identifying strategies for data-based instructional effectiveness, both face-to-face and online.

Adopting a culture that promotes and supports informal research and dialogue on the effectiveness of instruction and implications for teaching will take time, just as it takes time for faculty to embrace technology and express a desire to teach online. In many institutions, online courses are taught by adjunct faculty, rather than full-time faculty, which is even more reason for institutional support to be provided including education on the relationship between faculty participation, student engagement, and retention.

The Need for Institutional Support

To transition successfully from a traditional classroom to a virtual environment, faculty need not only training, but also institutional support (Taylor & McQuiggan, 2008). As early as 1998, Robinson posited "The starting point for any faculty staff development strategy is support from senior leadership…" (p. 35). More recently, Lion (2011) conducted a study of 364 institutions of higher education that provide online course offerings, for the purpose of identifying types and availability of instructional professional development and support provided to faculty. While Lion found that institutions are taking steps to assist faculty in learning to teach online, it is important to note that types and amounts of support vary widely. Perhaps most importantly, Lion concluded that institutions that want to influence teaching and student learning outcomes and drive faculty performance in a specific direction, must institutionalize focused supports to help attain those outcomes.

While faculty are pivotal to the process of developing online courses, when surveyed faculty reported that their institutions are below average in providing support services for teaching online (Seaman, 2009). A teacher's understanding of structuring and facilitating interaction in an online environment requires effective professional development as a foundation for confident and competent online teaching (Cueller, 2002). The more time faculty spend trying to improve their teaching: a) the more they engage students in discussion, small-group activities, student presentations or performances, and experiential activities; b) interact with students, c) use effective teaching practices, d) have significantly higher learning expectations for their students and e) the less the faculty lecture (NSSE, 2014).

According to Umbach and Wawrzynski (2005), "faculty behaviors and attitudes affect students profoundly, which suggests that faculty members may play the single-most important role in student learning" (p. 176). How do faculty behaviors and attitudes translate to students when faculty do not want to teach an online course, but participation is required because of demand. Can faculty resistance to teaching online be mediated? For example, in a national survey of faculty working within public institutions of higher education, a large percentage (64%), of 10,720 faculty members who have taught online report that it takes more time to teach an online course than a face-to-face course; faculty rate the extra effort needed as a barrier for teaching online (Seaman, 2009). To mediate this concern, institutions can make allowances for first-time online course delivery.

While institutions of higher education typically offer a class for faculty to learn to teach online, this course tends to be focused on learning to use the particular learning management system adopted by the institution than on instructional strategies to engage students. Some institutions may offer a mentor during the first term that the faculty member actually teaches the developed course; however, the focus of the mentor tends to be on following established guidelines rather than instructional effectiveness. Beyond these initial offerings, there may or may not be professional development opportunities provided for faculty to continue to grow and develop both in pedagogy and in practice.

Professional Learning Communities

Building professional learning communities, within institutions of higher education, can provide direct and indirect support to full-time and adjunct online faculty. A professional learning community can guide faculty to focus, not just on the process of teaching, but as importantly on the process of student learning. The idea is that student outcomes inform teaching and in turn adjustments are made in teaching to positively impact student learning outcomes. This focus on students learning, in collaboration with colleagues, is central to a professional learning community.

Professional learning communities can be offered through a menu of strategies. In addition to a traditional approach of offering seminars on specific topics, developing a network of faculty mentoring can be useful. Faculty mentoring across disciplines offers an opportunity for a faculty member to be exposed to a variety of perspectives that broaden thinking and potentially assist in enhancing online engagement, thus positively affecting student learning and motivation (Baker, 2010). Creating a culture where faculty analyze their own courses and pinpoint needed adjustments to benefit student learning can be effective. For example, between teaching terms, an online faculty member can examine the discussion thread student responses, noting which discussion prompts were responded to more often. Those that were not responded to frequently or with higher level thinking demonstrated, can be either reworded or eliminated. This process can be informal and a quick check or more formalized criteria for what constitutes a lengthy response and higher level thinking; more data can be examined when responses from more than one teaching term are considered for the same course. Continuing to build on this example, it is important to view every discussion question or prompt as a beginning point, rewording as needed to stimulate higher level thinking.

With all of the demands of teaching, it is easy to offer the same content in the same format term after term, rather than taking the time to evaluate the effectiveness of the presentation. When a teacher's efforts are rewarded through following a similar process with a colleague and sharing results, the effort may seem more rewarding.

FUTURE DIRECTIONS

Future research in the areas of student engagement and retention would contribute to the literature by focusing on a) the relationship between highly active faculty participation and student engagement and retention as well as b) the increase that occurs in faculty participation in online classes when the faculty have a support system within their institution including, but not limited to seminars, mentoring, and or professional learning communities.

1. Provide faculty with professional development opportunities related to best practices in online teaching, including the relationship between faculty participation in an online class, student engagement, and retention.
2. Provide institutional support for adjunct and full-time faculty teaching online, promoting the viewpoint that mentoring enrolled students, before, during, and after a course can promote student engagement and retention.
3. Create a culture that encourages faculty scholarship in conducting informal research related to instructional effectiveness of their own courses and making modifications, based on data, directed toward increasing student learning as related to established core learning outcomes.
4. Provide all faculty, adjunct and full-time, opportunities for mentoring and/or participation in a professional learning community.
5. Investigate desirable and effective institutional professional development infrastructure for online faculty that supports on-going development and sharing of online teaching skills and strategies.

CONCLUSION

Given that faculty have a pivotal role in student retention in online courses, institutions of higher education benefit from recognizing the process of change inherent in adapting to teaching online, providing on-going faculty support and developing a teaching culture inclusive of informal scholarly investigations related to instructional effectiveness.

"Times are changing for higher education.....
[From] using technology to expand distance education, to the recognition of the importance of sense of community, we are witnessing a transformation of higher education" (Rovai & Jordan, 2004, p. 1). The offering of online courses is a viable delivery mode for institutions of higher education; the U.S. Department of Education isolated 51 common factors across thousands of studies and concluded that, in general, online learning is more effective than face-to-face learning (U.S. Department of Education, 2009). Institutions of higher education are facing the challenge of how to retain students enrolled in an online course.

The premise of this chapter has been that faculty serve a pivotal role in student retention in online courses; faculty participation is key to student engagement and engaged students tend to finish courses in which they are enrolled. Engagement and retention can be promoted through providing a course infrastructure that supports students from enrollment in a course through course completion with numerous opportunities to engage with course content, peers, and a faculty member who serves as a facilitator for the course and a resource for institutional support. Teaching strategies that faculty can use to support student engagement an retention include implementing constructivist practices, building a sense of community among students, offering opportunities for critical thinking, and developing self-regulated learners. Learning to teach online requires on-going professional development opportunities for full-time and adjunct faculty. There is a need for an institutional systemic approach which recognizes the change process in moving from a face-to-face teaching pedagogy and skill base to best practices for teaching online. Institutionalizing a professional development structure inclusive of support for faculty to collect data on their own teaching and make modifications to course teaching and delivery that is based on data which support faculty in participating and sharing within their institution professional learning community.

REFERENCES

Allen, I. E., & Seaman, J. (2013). *Changing course: Ten years of tracking online education in the United States*. Retrieved October 11, 2014 from http://files.eric.ed.gov/fulltext/ED541571.pdf

Ally, M. (2004). Foundations of educational theory for online learning. In T. Anderson (Ed.), *The theory and practice of online learning* (pp. 15–44). Edmonton, CA: Athabasca University Press.

Almala, A. (2006). The community college leadership perspectives of quality e-learning. *Distance Learning*, *3*, 9–14.

Alwehaibi, H. (2012). Novel program to promote critical thinking among higher education students: Empirical Study from Saudi Arabia. *Asian Social Science*, *8*(11), 193–204.

American Psychological Association. (2010). *Publication manual of the American Psychological Association* (6th ed.). Washington, DC: Author.

Angelino, L. M., Williams, F. K., & Natvig, D. (2007). Strategies to engage online students and reduce attrition rates. *The Journal of Educators Online, 4*(2). Retrieved December 27, 2014 from http://www.thejo.com/

Baker, C. (2010). The impact of instructor immediacy and presence for online student affective learning, cognition, and motivation. *Journal of Educators Online, 7*(1), 1–30. Retrieved from http://www.thejeo.com/Archives/Volume7Number1/BakerPaper.pdf

Barr, R. B., & Tagg, J. (1995). From teaching to learning: A new paradigm for undergraduate education. *Change, 27*(6), 12–25. doi:10.1080/00091383.1995.10544672

Brookfield, S. D., & Preskill, S. (2005). *Discussion as a way of teaching*. San Francisco, CA: Jossey-Bass.

Browne, E. (2005). Structural and pedagogic change in further and higher education: A case study approach. *Journal of Further and Higher Education, 29*(1), 49–59. doi:10.1080/03098770500037754

Canton, M. E., & James, D. P. (2008). *Mentoring in higher education: Best practices* (2nd ed.). Robertson Publishing.

Cappola, N. W., Hiltz, S. R., & Rotter, N. (2002). Becoming a virtual professor: Pedagogical roles and ALN. *Journal of Management Information Systems, 18*(4), 169–190.

Chang, M. (2007). Enhancing web-based language learning through self-monitoring. *Journal of Computer Assisted Learning, 23*(3), 187–196. doi:10.1111/j.1365-2729.2006.00203.x

Chickering, A., & Ehrman, S. C. (1996). Implementing the seven principles: Technology as lever. *AAHE Bulletin, 49*(2), 3–6.

Chin, S. T. S., & Williams, J. B. (2006). A theoretical framework for effective online course design. *MERLOT Journal of Online Learning and Teaching, 2*(1), 12–21.

Collier, P., & Morgan, D. (2008). Is that paper really due today? Differences in first generation and traditional college students' understandings of faculty expectations. *Higher Education, 55*(4), 425–426. doi:10.1007/s10734-007-9065-5

Collison, G., Elbaum, B., Haavind, S., & Tinker, R. (2000). *Facilitating online learning: Effective strategies for moderators*. Madison, WI: Atwood Publishing.

Collom, G., Dallas, A., Jong, R., & Obexer, R. (2002). Six months in a leaky boat: Framing the knowledge and skills needed to teach well online. *Proceedings ASCILITE 2002*. Retrieved from http://www.ascilite.org.au/conferences/auckland02/proceedings/papers/181.pdf

Cueller, N. (2002). The transition from classroom to online teaching. *Nursing Forum, 37*(3), 5–13. doi:10.1111/j.1744-6198.2002.tb01005.x PMID:12430390

Dennen, V. P. (2005). From message posting to learning dialogs: Factors affecting learner participation in asynchronous discussion. *Distance Education, 26*(1), 127–148. doi:10.1080/01587910500081376

Digenti, D. (1998). Toward an understanding of the learning community. *Organization Development Journal, 16*(2), 91–96.

Evans, T. W. (2000). The new mentors. *Teachers College Record, 102*(1), 1–15. doi:10.1111/0161-4681.00053

Flottemesch, K. (2000). Building effective interaction in distance education. *Educational Technology, 4*(3), 46–51.

Goodyear, P., Salmon, G., Spector, J. M., Steeples, C., & Tickner, S. (2001). Competencies for online teaching: A special report. *Educational Technology Research and Development, 49*(1), 65–72. doi:10.1007/BF02504508

Grandzol, J., & Grandzol, C. (2006). Best practices for online business education. *International Review of Research in Open and Distance Learning, 7*(1), 1–18.

Grant, M. R., & Thornton, H. R. (2007). Best practices in undergraduate adult centered online learning: Mechanisms for course design and delivery. *Journal of Online Learning and Teaching, 3*(4).

Heisserer, D., & Parette, P. (2002). Advising at-risk students in college and university settings. *College Student Journal, 36*(1), 1–12.

Howell, S. L., Saba, F., Lindsay, N. K., & William, P. B. (2004). Seven strategies for enabling faculty success in distance education. *The Internet and Higher Education*, *7*(1), 33–49. doi:10.1016/j.iheduc.2003.11.005

Jairam, D., & Kiewra, K. A. (2010). Helping students soar to success on computers: An investigation of the SOAR study method for computer-based learning. *Journal of Educational Psychology*, *102*(3), 601–614. doi:10.1037/a0019137

Johnson, L., Smith, R., Willis, H., Levine, A., & Haywood, K. (2011). *The 2011 Horizon Report*. Austin, TX: The New Media Consortium.

Keengwe, J., & Kidd, T. T. (2010). Towards best practices in online learning and teaching in higher education. *MERLOT Journal of Online Learning and Teaching, 6*(2). Retrieved November 7, 2014 from http://jolt.merlot.org/vol6no2/keengwe_0610.htm

Kember, D. (1989). A longitudinal process model of drop-out from distance education. *The Journal of Higher Education*, *60*(3), 27–301. doi:10.2307/1982251

King, A. (1993). From sage on the stage to guide on the side. *College Teaching*, *41*(1), 30–35. doi:10.1080/87567555.1993.9926781

Kitsantas, A. (2013). Fostering college students' self-regulated learning with learning technologies. *Hellenic Journal of Psychology*, *10*, 235–252.

Kreijns, K., Kirschner, P. A., & Jochems, W. (2003). Identifying the pitfalls for social interactions in computer-supported collaborative learning environments: A review of the research. *Computers in Human Behavior*, *19*(3), 585–612. doi:10.1016/S0747-5632(02)00057-2

Lajoie, S. P., & Azevedo, R. (2006). Teaching and learning in technology-rich environments. In P. A. Alexander & P. H. Winne (Eds.), *Handbook of educational psychology* (2nd ed.; pp. 803–821). Mahwah, NJ: Erlbaum.

Lion, R. W. (2011). A study of performance support in higher education. *Performance Improvement Quarterly*, *24*(1), 49–67. doi:10.1002/piq.20101

Lovelock, C., & Wirtz, J. (2007). *Service marketing: People, technology and strategy* (6th ed.). Pearson Prentice Hall.

Mancuso-Murphy, J. (2007). Distance education in nursing: An integrated review of online nursing students' experience with technology-delivered education. *The Journal of Nursing Education*, *46*(5), 253–260. PMID:17580737

Mandernach, B. J. (2009). Three ways to improve student engagement in the online classroom. *Online Classroom,* 1-2.

Mandernach, B. J., Forrest, K. D., Babutzke, J. L., & Manker, L. R. (2009). The role of instructor, interactivity in promoting critical thinking in online and face-to-face classrooms. *MERLOT Journal of Online Learning and Teaching*, *5*(1), 49–62.

Marzano, R. J., Pickering, D. J., & Pollock, J. E. (2001). *Classroom instruction that works: Research-based strategies for increasing student achievement*. Alexandria, VA: Association for Supervision and Curriculum Development.

McLean, V. (1999). Becoming a teacher: The person in the process. In R. Lipka & T. Brinthhapupt (Eds.), *The role of self in teacher development*. Albany, NY: SUNY Press.

Moore, M. G. (1992). Distance education theory. *American Journal of Distance Education*, 5(3), 1–6. doi:10.1080/08923649109526758

Murphy, K., Smith, P., & Stacey, E. (2002). Teaching presence in computer conferencing: lessons from the United States and Australia. In *Proceedings of International conference on computers in education* (ICCE 2002), (pp. 694-698). IEEE Computer Society Press. doi:10.1109/CIE.2002.1186046

National Survey of Student Engagement. (2014). Center for Postsecondary Research, Indiana University School of Education, Bloomington, IND. Retrieved October 11, 2014 from http://nsse.iub.edu/NSSE_2014_Results/pdf/NSSE_2014_Annual_Results.pdf#page=8

Nicol, D. (2009). Assessment for learner self-regulation: Enhancing achievement in the first year using learning technologies. *Assessment & Evaluation in Higher Education*, 34(3), 335–352. doi:10.1080/02602930802255139

Nota, L., Soresi, S., & Zimmerman, B. J. (2004). Self-regulation and academic achievement and resilience: A longitudinal study. *International Journal of Educational Research*, 41(3), 198–215. doi:10.1016/j.ijer.2005.07.001

O'Brien, G. (2002). *Issues Paper 3: A sense of belonging*. Retrieved October 12, 2014 from http://www.fye.qut.edu.au/documents/FYIEissues&5Fpaper%5F3.pdf

Oblinger, D. G., & Oblinger, J. S. (Eds.). (2005). *Educating the Net generation*. Boulder, CO: EDUCAUSE.

Palloff, R. M., & Pratt, K. (2005). *Collaborating online: Learning together in community*. San Francisco, CA: Jossey-Bass.

Park, J., & Choi, H. J. (2009). Factors influencing adult learners' decision to drop out or persist in online learning. *Journal of Educational Technology & Society*, 12(4), 207–217.

Pate, A., Smaldino, S., Mayall, H. J., & Luetkehans, L. (2009). Questioning the necessity of nonacademic social discussion forums within online courses. *The Quarterly Review of Distance Education*, 10(1), 1–8.

Patterson, B., & McFadden, C. (2009). Attrition in online and campus degree programs. *Online Journal of Distance Learning Administration*, 12(2). Retrieved from http://www.westga.edu/~distance/ojdla/summer122/patterson112.html

Pearson, M. (2012). Building bridges: Higher degree student retention and counseling support. *Journal of Higher Education Policy and Management*, 34(2), 187–199. doi:10.1080/1360080X.2012.662743

Pittman, L. D., & Richmond, A. (2008). University belonging, friendship quality, and psychological adjustment during the transition to college. *Journal of Experimental Education*, 76(4), 343–361. doi:10.3200/JEXE.76.4.343-362

Robinson, B. (1998). A strategic perspective in staff development for open and distance learning. In C. Latchem & F. Lockwood (Eds.), *Staff development in open and flexible learning* (pp. 33–44). New York: Routledge.

Rogers, E. M. (2003). *Diffusion of innovations* (5th ed.). New York, NY: The Free Press.

Roman, T., Kelsey, K., & Lin, H. (2010). Enhancing online education through instructor skill development in higher education. *Online Journal of Distance Learning Administration*, 8(1). Retrieved from http://www.westga.edu/~distance/ojdla/winter134/roman_kelsey134.html

Rovai, A. P., & Jordan, H. (2004). Blended learning and sense of community: A comparative analysis with traditional and fully online graduate courses. *International Review of Research in Open and Distance Learning, 2*(5). Retrieved from http://www.irrodl.org/index.php/irrodl/article/view-Article/192/274

Ryman, S., Hardman, G., Richardson, B., & Ross, J. (2009). Creating and sustaining online learning communities: Designing for transformative learning. *International Journal of Pedagogies and Learning, 5*(3), 46–58. doi:10.5172/ijpl.5.3.46

Seaman, J. S. (2009). Online learning as a strategic asset. Volume II: The paradox of faculty voices--Views and experiences with online learning. Results of a National Faculty Survey, Part of the Online Education Benchmarking Study Conducted by the APLU-Sloan National Commission on Online Learning. Association of Public and Land Grant Universities.

Shea, P., Li, C. S., & Pickett, A. (2006). A study of teaching presence and student sense of learning community in fully online and web-enhanced college courses. *The Internet and Higher Education, 9*(3), 175–190. doi:10.1016/j.iheduc.2006.06.005

Shieh, R., Gummer, E., & Niess, M. (2008). The quality of a web-based course: Perspectives of the instructor and the students. *TechTrends: Linking Research & Practice to Improve Learning, 52*(6), 61–68. doi:10.1007/s11528-008-0220-3

Smith, G., Ferguson, D., & Caris, M. (2002). Teaching over the web versus in the classroom: Differences in the instructor experience. *International Journal of Instructional Media, 29*(1), 61–67.

Su, B. (2005). Examining instructional design development of a web-based course: A case study. *International Journal of Distance Education Technologies, 3*(4), 62–76. doi:10.4018/jdet.2005100106

Su, B., Bonk, C. J., Magjuka, R. J., Liu, X., & Lee, S. (2005). The importance of interaction in web-based education: A program level case study of online MBA courses. *Journal of Interactive Online Learning, 4*(1), 1–19.

Taylor, A., & McQuiggan, C. (2008). Faculty development programming: If we built it, will they come? *EDUCAUSE Quarterly, 3*, 29–37.

Terrion, J., & Leonard, D. (2010). A taxonomy of the characteristics of student peer mentors in higher education: Findings from a literature review. *Mentoring & Tutoring: Partnership in Learning, 15*(2), 149–164. doi:10.1080/13611260601086311

Tinto, V. (1975). Dropout from higher education: A theoretical synthesis of recent research. *Review of Educational Research, 45*(1), 89–125. doi:10.3102/00346543045001089

Tinto, V. (1993). Leaving college: Rethinking the causes and cures of student attrition (2nd ed.). Chicago, IL: The University of Chicago Press.

Umbach, P. D., & Wawrzynsli, M. R. (2005). Faculty do matter: The role of college faculty in student learning and engagement. *Research in Higher Education, 46*(2), 153–185. doi:10.1007/s11162-004-1598-1

U.S. Department of Education. (2009). *Evaluation of evidence-based practices in online learning: A meta-analysis and review of online learning studies.* Retrieved October 12, 2014 from http://www.gibill.va.gov/gi_bill_info/ch33/yellow_ribbon.htm

Varvel, V. (2007). Master online teacher competences. *Online Journal of Distance Learning Administration, 10*(1). Retrieved from http://www.westga.edu/~distance/ojdla/spring101/varvel101.htm

Vygotsky, L. (1986). *Thought and language.* Cambridge, MA: MIT Press.

Walker, S. C., & Taub, D. J. (2001). Variables correlated with satisfaction with a mentoring relationship in first-year college students and their mentors. *Journal of the First-Year Experience & Students in Transition, 13*(1), 47–67.

Wolf, P. (2006). Best practices in the training of faculty to teach online. *Journal of Computing in Higher Education, 17*(2), 47–78. doi:10.1007/BF03032698

Zimmerman, B. J. (2008). Investigating self-regulation and motivation: Historical background, methodological developments, and future prospects. *American Educational Research Journal, 45*(1), 166–183. doi:10.3102/0002831207312909

Zimmerman, B. J., & Kitsantas, A. (2005). Homework practices and academic achievement: The mediating role of self-efficacy and perceived responsibility beliefs. *Contemporary Educational Psychology, 30*(4), 397–417. doi:10.1016/j.cedpsych.2005.05.003

ADDITIONAL READING

Allen, I. E., & Seaman, J. (2011). *Going the distance: Online education in the USA*. Wellesley, MA: Babson Survey Research Group.

American Institutes for Research. (2010). Finishing the first lap: The cost of first year student attrition in America's four year colleges and universities. Retrieved October 12, 2014 from http://www.airorg/files/AIR%5FSchneider%5FFinishing

Betts, K. (2009). Online human touch (OHT) training & support: A conceptual framework to increase faculty engagement, connectivity, and retention in online education, part 2. MERLOT. *Journal of Online Learning and Teaching, 5*(1). http://jolt.merlot.org/vol4no3/betts_0908.htm Retrieved December 21, 2014

Chickering, A., & Gamson, Z. (1987). Seven principles for good practice in undergraduate education. *AAHE Bulletin, 39*(7), 3–6.

Diaz, D. P., & Botenbal, K. F. (2001). Learner preferences: Developing a learner-centered environment in the online or mediated classroom. *Ed at a Distance, 15(8)*. Retrieved from http://www.usdla.org/html/hournal/AUG01_Issue/article03.html

Fisher, M., & Baird, D. E. (2005). Online learning design that fosters student support, self-regulation, and retention. *Campus-Wide Information Systems, 22*(5), 88–107. doi:10.1108/10650740510587100

Lynch, R., & Dembo, M. (2004). The relationship between self-regulation and online learning in a blended learning context. *International Review of Research in Open and Distance Learning, 5*(2), 1–16.

Ryman, S., Vine, R., & Richardson, B. (2009). Creating and sustaining online learning communities: Designing environments for transformative learning Part III: Sustaining a learning community through constructive controversy. *International Journal of Pedagogies and Learning, 5*(3), 32–45. doi:10.5172/ijpl.5.3.32

Shea, P. L., Li, C. S., & Pickett, A. (2006). A study of teaching presence and student sense of learning community in fully online and web-enhanced courses. *The Internet and Higher Education, 9*(3), 175–190. doi:10.1016/j.iheduc.2006.06.005

Zimmerman, B. J. (2000). Attaining self-regulation: A social-cognitive perspective. In M. Boekaerts, P. Pintrich, & M. Zeidner (Eds.), *Self-regulation: Theory, research, and applications* (pp. 13–39). Orlando, FL: Academic Press. doi:10.1016/B978-012109890-2/50031-7

KEY TERMS AND DEFINITIONS

Attrition: In academia, attrition refers to the loss of student enrollment; a reduction in the number of enrolled students which results in a loss of revenue.

Faculty Participation: In the context of an online classroom, faculty participation is also referred to as teacher presence, teacher engagement, faculty visibility; in an asynchronous environment where students do not experience a face-to-face contact with faculty, students rely upon other modes of contact and communication.

Learning Management System (LMS): Institutions of higher education offering online courses, choose a software application company to administer, deliver, track and report the delivery of courses. Examples of LMS systems include, but are not limited to: Blackboard, E-College, D2L (Desire 2 Learn), Canvass.

Online Classroom: An online classroom is an environment created through use of a learning management system that allows students and teacher to connect either synchronously (real-time, with teacher and students meeting at the same time or asynchronously with interaction between teacher and students occurring intermittently with a time delay; teacher students are generally separated by location.

Online Learning: Online learning is a term that refers to the process of gaining informing through web-based, internet based sources. The term is also referred to as e-learning, virtual learning, net-based learning; a wide variety of technology is encompassed by the term online learning; in this chapter the term is used for whole course internet delivery.

Pedagogy: The theory and practice of teaching; what teachers do, based upon what they believe, when implementing their craft and assist student learning.

Professional Learning Communities: In the context of this chapter, a professional learning community can be formal or informal and serves the function of providing collaboration with colleagues for the purpose of discussing strategies of best practice for teaching online, examining one's own teaching outcomes through collection of data, and making decisions for teaching modifications based on collected data.

Self-Regulated Learning: Self-regulated learning (SRL) occurs when a student take responsibility for their own learning process, including setting goals and making a plan for taking steps toward meeting the established goals. Faculty teaching online can provide course infrastructure and teaching strategies to support students in the process of practicing self-regulation including self-monitoring and self-evaluation.

Student Engagement: Student engagement involves, not only active participation, but also critical thinking, synthesis, and application of content to real-life experiences. Highly engaged students tend to feel a connection to their institutions of higher education and remain committed to completion of individual courses within their degree plan.

Teaching as a Scholarly Endeavor: A process that involves faculty evaluating their own teaching and modifying instruction based on the evaluation data, for the purpose of on-going instructional improvement and maintaining a focus on student learning.

Chapter 4
Participation in Online Distance Learning Environments:
Proxy, Sign, or a Means to an End?

David Starr-Glass
University of New York in Prague, Czech Republic

ABSTRACT

Participation is actively encouraged and promoted in online distance learning environments because it is associated with effective learning behaviors and with overall learner satisfaction. Participation is easily observed and measured; indeed, it is often seen as "making visible" underlying behaviors and dynamics at both the individual and group level. The reality, however, is that the ease with which participation can be assessed is in stark contrast with the complexity that surrounds its role in the productive distance online learning environments. This chapter explores the multiplicity of meanings, definitions, and attributions associated with participation. It attempts to make sense of this complexity, to consider a broader framework that makes a connection between participation and learning outcomes, and to examine the ways in which individual learning styles and national culture assumptions impact and mediate student participation in online learning contexts.

INTRODUCTION

Participation has become a ubiquitous element in the assessment rubrics of online distance learning courses. There are two reasons for this – a good one and a bad one. The good reason is that participation is often, but not inevitably, the antecedent of effective learning behaviors – it can contribute to a growing sense of learner self-efficacy and empowerment. Participation is often a useful initiator and indicator of constructive dynamics within the online learning environment. As such, it should be recognized, monitored, and encouraged through formative and summative assessment, even although participation in itself may only be a distal factor in positive learning outcomes.

But there is a bad reason for assessing participation and unfortunately the bad reason is frequently confused and misunderstood in ways that make it the favored choice. The bad reason is that participation is simply so easy to measure in online distance learning contexts. Most modern online

DOI: 10.4018/978-1-4666-9582-5.ch004

platforms will automatically generate a plethora of participation statistics – the number of posts contributed to conference discussions, the total and average word counts associated with these contributions, the period of time that the learner was logged into discussion sites, and more. All of these statistics are easily derived and provide what can be understood as objective, quantitatively, and reliable measures of participation. Unfortunately, these measures ignore – and certainly do not assess – the quality, complexity, and consequences of online participation. Indeed, many online practitioners have come to acknowledge that although the number of comments posted and the length of discussion threads "may be common intuitive ways used by instructors to judge the 'health' of their discussion forums, it is far from clear… that they are useful measures to judge the quality of the learning taking place there" (Mazzolini & Maddison 2003, p. 252).

The measurement, interpretation, and implications of online participation are always tenuous; however, participation becomes even more challenging when we consider these parameters with the actual behavior and expectations of individual learners. The instructor's interpretation of participation may be at variance with the assumptions and behaviors of the learners who have actually participated, or who have been judged not to have participated. The learning styles of students, for example, may not favor social engagement and collaboration. The national and ethnic cultures of the learners involved may also not place a positive value on individualism, self-expression, and knowledge sharing – elements that are generally expected by instructors and which are linked with participatory behavior (Ardichvili, Maurer, Li, Wentling, & Stuedemann, 2006; Butler & Pinto-Zipp, 2006; Coldwell, Craig, Paterson, & Mustard, 2008; Zapalska & Brozik, 2006).

This chapter explores participation in online learning environments. It considers the ways in which participation might – or might not – serve to identify and promote successful learning outcomes. The first section provides background by examining the role of participation in different learning contexts, especially the context in which distance learning and online distance learning take place. This examination briefly reviews the understanding of participation in distance learning from a historical (and evolving) perspective. The second section explores the different meanings attached to "participation." It considers whether participation *per se* is of value, or whether it is regarded as a sign of, or as a proxy for, more distance but less easily determined behaviors that advance effective knowledge creation. This exploration invites an examination of participation and numerous related constructs such as social presence, learner-instructor and learner-learner interaction, engagement with content, communities of inquiry, and social and constructivist pedagogies. This section also considers participation from both instructor and learner perspectives, exploring the associated assumptions and anticipated end-results. This analysis of assumptions about, and requirements for, participation is conducted through the specific prisms of cultural norms and individual learning styles.

The third section reviews the challenges and opportunities presented by participation in online learning environments. It provides suggestions and recommendations that might contribute to understanding participation in more considered, flexible, and beneficial ways. The fourth section picks up on the issues proposed and suggests further research to provide a more comprehensive appreciation of the role that participation might play in online distance learning environments. Finally, the chapter sets out a concluding section that summarizes the main themes presented and suggests ways forward for instructional designers, online instructors, and learners involved in distance learning.

BACKGROUND: PRESENCE AND PARTICIPATION IN DISTANCE LEARNING

Before considering the assumed role and assumptions underlying presence and participation in online distance learning contexts, it will be useful examine participation in face-to-face instruction. This provides an opportunity to compare and contrast these two instructional modalities but, more importantly, it suggests reasons for the dominant position that participation has assumed in online distance learning environments.

The traditional face-to-face educational delivery mode is the lecture. It has a long history and is generally accepted as a significant learning technique. The traditional lecture, however, serves multiple cultural and social roles as well as educational ones. From a cultural perspective, the lecture makes manifest a number of underlying values, assumptions, and beliefs through drama and ritual. The face-to-face lecture is a cultural enactment that restates and displays institutional, professional, and disciplinary assumptions of power and authority. Indeed, many consider that the lecture is *the primary* ritual enactment in higher education (Benson, 1994; Thesen, 2007). As a cultural enactment, the traditional lecture effectively "freezes the hierarchy between lecturer and student, removing any responsibility on the students to respond" (Barnett, 2000, p. 159).

The lecture is grounded in an educational philosophy and pedagogy of transmission. There is an assumption that the "sage is on stage" and that he, or she, will be the active agent in transmitting knowledge. Whether the sage is brilliant – or less than adequate – is not a primary concern. Whether knowledge is an object, which can be passed around for review and accumulation, is not critically challenged. What is important – and what is accepted by lecturer and audience – is that learners have passive and receptive roles in the educational process. Learners are regarded metaphorically as vessels to be filled, sponges

to be soaked, or (perhaps more imaginatively) piles of wood waiting to be ignited. It is of little wonder that students often consider themselves the "passive consumers of knowledge, never fully engaging, thinking deeply, or truly understanding" (Ryan, 2013, p. 30). The assignment of a passive learner role in the traditional lecture-based approach has been criticized; indeed, many lecturers have attempted to provide a lecture experience that is engaging, interactive, and stimulating. At a disciplinary level, some areas of study have also evolved lecture models – such as the Sophist and the Socratic approaches – that demand more student participation and a prompt a more active exchange of ideas (Chaudhury, 2011; Di Leonardi, 2007; Larson & Lovelace, 2013; Pale, 2013).

Beginnings of Participation in Distance Learning: Dialogic Exchange

Many consider that we are presently in the *Fifth Generation* of distance learning, characterized by the specific technologies employed and the teaching and learning approaches used (Anderson & Dron, 2011; Taylor, 1995, 2001). Today, distance learning is almost inevitably mediated by computer technologies, enhanced by seamless connectivity to the Internet, supported by open educational resources, and linked to social media. Pedagogically, learners are generally viewed as knowledgeable, autonomous, and capable of accessing informational networks in order to explore, confirm, and augment their learning. Teaching and learning are predominantly understood and approached through constructivist and connectivist pedagogies (Hew & Cheung, 2011; Kanuka & Anderson, 1999; Saritas, 2008; Siemens, 2005a, 2005b).

However, in the period between (approximately) 1960 and 1980, distance learning employed quite different technologies and pedagogies. During that period, which has been called the *Second Generation* of distance learning, print (in the form of textbooks), audio (radio broadcasts), and visual (television programs) technologies dominated and cognitive-behavioralist pedagogies and transition models of instruction were in vogue. Although the Second Generation of distance learning may seem distant and somewhat remote, it was against this technological and pedagogic background that Moore's (1972, 1973) proposed his theory of transactional distance. It will be helpful to examine transactional distance theory because it made a significant contribution to our understanding of participation and knowledge exchange, particularly when the participants were physically and psychologically distanced.

Moore emphasized the critical need for *dialogue* in distance learning contexts. By *dialogue* he meant interaction – "an interaction or series of interactions having positive qualities that other interactions might not have" (Moore, 1997, p. 23). Dialogue was understood to be associated with the exchange of ideas, perspectives, and reflections. Dialogue was also considered necessary for constructing a common shared understanding – an understanding greater than might have been arrived at independently by students who elected not to participate in dialogic exchange.

Moore (1997) advised that dialogue, as a process of participative exchange, needed to be "purposeful, constructive and valued by each party" (p. 23). Constructive dialogue necessitated an appreciation of both the power and the purpose of exchange and required that "each party in a dialogue is a respectful and active listener; each is a contributor, and builds on the contributions of the other party or parties" (Moore, 1997, p. 23). Moore speculated that adult learners would work autonomously to restructure the initially imposed structure of the distanced experience if they perceived that there was a lack of dialogic engagement with their instructor. *Learner autonomy* was understood as the potential for learners to use "teaching materials and teaching programmes to achieve goals of their own, in their own way, under their own control" (Moore, 1997, p. 31).

Learner autonomy was also the extent "to which, in the teaching/ learning relationship, it is the *learner* rather than the teacher who determines the goals, the learning experiences, and the evaluation decisions of the learning programme" (p. 31, emphasis added).

Despite its somewhat distant origins in the Second Generation of distance learning, Moore's (1972, 1973) contribution is particularly valuable for understanding the challenges, opportunities, and trajectories of online distance learning today.

- **Altering Learning Dynamics and Behaviors:** Transactional distance recognizes that the dynamics and behaviors associated with face-to-face instruction (what Moore called *contiguous teaching*) are radically changed by the imposition of distance. Learners and instructors are physically separated, but more importantly they are also psychologically and socially separated. The ritualistic assumptions and dramaturgical enactments are challenged and ambiguous, and learners and instructors need to find new ways of approaching knowledge creation. They must find new roles and assume new responsibilities that recognize their spatial, social, and cognitive displacement. In the quest to cope with distance – where distance is recognized as a cluster of separations – all participants are at liberty to redistribute power and authority. It is clear that the problems of distancing learner and instructor cannot be solved by replicating approximations of face-to-face models. Distancing required new and relevant approaches.

- **Repositioning Value of Dialogue and Exchange:** Transactional distance repositions the form and value of dialogic exchange within learning – an exchange process that had often been overlooked, undervalued, or abandoned in traditional teaching modalities (Crawley, Curry,

Dumois-Sands, Tanner, & Wyker, 2008; Pang, 2008). In traditional face-to-face instruction, learners were all too often considered "passive consumers of knowledge, never fully engaging, thinking deeply, or truly understanding …. [expecting] knowledge to be passively transferred to them from their teacher with minimal input on their part" (Ryan, 2013, p. 30). The traditional face-to-face lecture system had become a highly ritualized and socially sanctioned enactment that effectively froze dialogic exchange.

- **Recognizing the Learner's Autonomy:** Moore appreciated the learning choices that adult, as autonomous learners, would make (Kilgore, 2001; Merriam, 2001). Appreciating distance learning as a *separation* of learner and instructor provokes recognition of the contributions that *each* of them makes to the outcome of the learning experience. Learner and instructor operate as a system in knowledge creation; however, considering them separately provides a better appreciation of how the system operates. Significantly, Moore recognized that learners might opt to *change* the learning dynamics – not simply as a *response* to the increased perception of transactional distance, but as a mature, considered, and personal expression of *preference* (Garrison, 2003; Hurd, 2005).

- **Conceptualizing Distance as a Distance in Understanding:** It is important to appreciate the kinds of distance learning contexts that Moore had in mind during the Second Generation of distance learning. His work (Moore, 1972, 1973) was set against a particular context: (a) distance learning courses were asynchronous; (b) dialogue flows were almost exclusively between learner and instructor, and rarely if ever between learners; and, (c) the norms

and expectations of traditional face-to-face instruction shaped and determined those in distance learning. Some have also noted that Moore's sense of *distance* was neither spatial nor even "the psychological and communication space between the two… [rather it was] the distance in understanding between teacher and learner… [where] understanding refers to mutual understanding (co-understanding)" (Giossos, Koutsouba, Lionarakis, & Skavantzos, 2009, p. 3). Within this context it is not surprising that participation – understood as engagement in constructive dialogic exchanges – should be given prime significance. It represented the only identifiable thread of connection and communication between the instructor and the learner: dialogue makes visible and it makes meaningful.

But participation and dialogue are *not synonymous* in Moore's consideration of transactional distance. Obviously, dialogue cannot take place without active, engaged, and respectful participation; however, constructive and empowering dialogue also requires active listening, mutual respect, and thoughtful consideration. In other words, it is the *quality* of the dialogue (participation) that is of key importance, not its *quantity*. As distance learning moved towards *online* distance learning – with both synchronous and asynchronous options – the role and the nature of participation, defined in terms of constructive dialogic exchange, would undergo reconsideration.

Moore's (1972, 1973) work was pivotal in appreciating and facilitating distance learning; accordingly, it was widely incorporated into the design, understanding, and facilitation of online distance learning environments. However, these learning environments were significantly different from those available in *Generation Two* distance learning. To reconsider the theory of transactional distance, the following section reviews the multiple definitions of participation and the behaviors that have been connected, or correlated, with demonstrations of participation.

A CONSTELLATION OF CONSIDERATIONS AND COMPLEXITY

Participation, understood and measured in different ways, has been a consistent and recurring aspect of learning environments, both face-to-face and virtual. The obvious thing about participation is just that: it *is* obvious. The fact that learners are present, physically in the lecture hall – or virtually in online environments – is evident and demonstrable. They are present and *part*-icipating in the sense that they are part of the event or experience. At one level, participation can be understood in an objective and neutral sense in which "participants" and their "participation" are simply part of a physical or virtual reality with no necessary or implied motivational engagement, behavioral intent, or consequential impact associated with their presence.

Participation as Inferred Behavior

Presence is demonstrable, but it is much more difficult to speculate on the consequences or the dynamics that may be associated with it. Equally, it is just as difficult to understand the final impact of participation as it is to understand the intermediate pathways, interactions, and moderating constructs involved. In online learning environments an active and discernible presence is frequently differentiated in a number of ways, each of which is considered to be associated with a different set of dynamics in the learning process.

This takes us to a second understanding of *participation*. Here, presence is not simply the act of being present, but is connected to a secondary behavior that is considered significant in the learning environment. This implied connection is

evident in the language that we use – participation and presence are commonly modified, or qualified, by adjectives such as *active*, *cognitive*, *social*, etc. In each instance, the modifier or qualifier *infers* – but it does not guarantee – that there is a connection between participation and subsequent learning behaviors.

- **Participation as Cognitive Presence:** Cognitive presence needs to be discernable to others and presumably can only happen if there is some form of interaction. Together with other participant "presences" – such as social presence and teacher presence – cognitive presence is central to constructivist pedagogies and to the Community of Inquiry framework in online distance learning (Lambert & Fisher, 2013; Swan, Garrison, & Richardson, 2009; Swan & Ice, 2010). In these contexts, *cognitive presence* is recognized as "the extent to which learners are able to construct meaning through sustained communication.... [it] is the key element in critical thinking, a necessary element for higher levels of thinking and learning" (Kanuka & Garrison, 2004, p. 24).

- **Participation as Social Presence:** Shen and Khalifa (2008, p. 729-730) recognized a hierarchy of social presence in online distance learning environments:
  - *Initial awareness*, which comes into existence when social actors believe that other social actors exist within the online environment and that they are capable of reacting;
  - *Affective social presence*, which comes into being when social actors sense an emotional connection and affective reciprocation with others who are located in the environment; and
  - *Cognitive social presence*, which materializes only when the partici-

pant in the online environment is able to "construct and confirm meaning about his or her relationship with the others and the social space" (p. 730).

Regarding social presence, Kanuka and Garrison (2004) have defined it as "the ability of the students to project their personal characteristics into the community…. [supporting] cognitive presence through indirect facilitation of critical thinking carried on by the community of learners" (p. 24).

- **Participation as Social and Community-Based Relationship:** Wenger (1998) considered participation to be a process "of taking part and also to the relations with others that reflect this process. It suggests both action and connection… the social experience of living in the world in terms of membership in social communities and active involvement in social enterprises" (pp. 55-56). In Wenger's sense, those who participate: (a) actively engage in the goals of their online community of learning; (b) contribute to the collective creation of knowledge; and (c) sense a strong and growing connection with their learning community. In online distance learning it is questionable whether full-blown communities of learning ever truly come into existence; however, it is certainly possible to create transient *bounded communities* that are "bounded by the expectations inducing participation, but also by the timeframe of a typical course" (Wilson, Ludwig-Hardman, Thornam, & Dunlap, 2004, p. 2).
- **Participation as Teaching Presence:** There is a marked asymmetry in the consequences of (a) the lack of instructor presence, and (b) the lack of learner presence (de la Varre, Keane, & Irvin, 2011; Shea,

Li, & Pickett, 2006). The instructor's active and engaged presence is understood by most theorists and practitioners as a critical element in productive online learning environments. Teaching presence "is comprised of two functions: the design of the educational experience and facilitation of the learning activities. This element reflects the creation, integration, and facilitation of both cognitive and social presence" (Kanuka & Garrison, 2004, p. 24). By contrast, *learner* presence and learner participation – or their absences – have a more complex and nuanced impact on online learning contexts.

- **Participation as Engagement and Quality of Engagement:** One of the problems associated with participation is that it can be easily quantified. Quantification, however, misses the underlying reasons for – or assumed connections of – participation. This has led many to underscore the significance of assessing the *quality* of participation. For example, participation has been defined as:
  ○ "Taking part and joining in a dialogue for engaged and active learning. Participation is *more* than the total number of student postings in a discussion forum" (Vonderwell & Zachariah, 2005, p. 214, emphasis added to original).
  ○ Similarly, following an analysis of the assessment measures associated with online distance learning participation, Hrastinski (2008a, 2008b) concluded that participation might be best defined as "a process of learning by taking part and maintaining relations with others…. a complex process comprising doing, communicating, feeling and belonging, which occurs both online and offline" (2008b, np.).

It might be inferred that participation (evidenced by the learner's presence) leads to active interaction, social exchange, involvement with learning content, and engagement in the learning process. It might be logically argued that none of these outcomes materialize *without* participation. Of course, it can also be argued that for some learners – in some circumstances, under some conditions, and in some cultures – learning is not recognized as a social, or shared, experience and that participation is therefore not expected, required, or productive.

Participation as Signs and Proxies

Just because a performance criterion can be easily measured does infer that it has reliability, validity, or that it necessarily correlates with underlying behavior that may be more difficult to determine (Austin & Villanova, 1992; Dimitrov, 2010; Kane, 2008; Messick, 1989). Participation is connected with underlying behaviors such as interaction, involvement, and engagement, all of which are difficult to measure directly. These underlying behaviors are themselves also positively associated with increased social presence, learner perceptions of success, learner satisfaction, and the creation of robust and dynamic online communities of inquiry (Anderson, Rourke, Garrison, & Archer, 2001; Croxton, 2014; Swan, 2001). Given the importance of these constructs and the problems of measuring them directly, it is not surprising that participation has been taken as a *sign* or *proxy* for them, even although their sign or proxy designation does not confer any robust statistical connection.

Simplistic *quantitative* measures of participation seem neither to be valid indicators of, nor efficient predictors for, behaviors that may be critical for effective learning. The richness and *quality* of constructs such as "dialogue" do seem to contribute positively to the learner's perception of success and satisfaction in online courses. Why this is so, how it impacts learner perceptions, and how it interacts with other aspects of the learner

and his or her online environment all remain unclear. The challenge for online facilitators is to differentiate between the proximal immediacy of participation and the more tenuous and distant (distal) consequences that it might produce.

Multiple Interpretations, Implicit Assumptions, and Implied Frameworks

Theorists and practitioners recognize the distant behaviors associated with online participation. In considering the effectiveness of online distance learning, for example, Swan (2003) noted that a review of the literature indicated two things: "[a] online environments support learning outcomes that are generally equivalent to those resulting from traditional, face-to-face instruction... [b] on the other hand, the research suggests that unique characteristics of the medium may afford and constrain particular kinds of learning" (p. 22). The "unique characteristics of the medium" are connected with the ability of participants to interact actively. In turn, these characteristics are set against a background of assumptions regarding social learning, constructivist pedagogies, and virtual communities of learning (Garrison, 2007; Swan & Shea, 2005).

This suggests that the perceived value of the online distance learning modality lies in engaging learners in environments that enrich *other-than-direct-learning outcomes* – such as social involvement and community membership – and not so much in delivering the same objective *learning outcomes* that are associated with face-to-face presentations. Such other-than-direct-learning outcomes may well be genuinely intended to enrich learners, and as such may have legitimate appeal for instructors, but to what extent should these agendas of enrichment be critically recognized by instructors and communicated to learners?

Participation has been connected with effective online discussion; however, the extent of the connection, and the actual role of participation in bringing about perceptions of learner success and vibrant learning communities, remains unclear – especially since many successful participants actually failed *to participate* in these learning contexts (Chang, Chen & Li, 2006; Guzdial & Turns, 2000; Yeh, 2010). Despite a lack of a clear understanding of the underlying mechanisms and pathways involved, many instructors might intuitively agree that "a commitment to imbuing social presence activities with encouragement and support that is timely and valued will both reinforce the instructor's social presence and also strengthen learners' opportunities for integrating learning more effectively" (Ley & Gannon-Cook, 2014, p. 30).

- **Philosophies and Pedagogies Shape Educational Experiences:** The values and vision of the learning experience are jointly created and reinforced by the instructional designer and instructor/facilitator of the learning experience, not the learner. It is the designer who suggests and the facilitator who implements the underlying pedagogical framework. This framework embodies four distinct conceptual values and pedagogic enactments (Steeples, Jones, & Goodyear, 2002):
  - *Philosophical Considerations:* These are the overarching institutional and instructor values regarding the purpose of learning and the value of creating and sharing knowledge. Deep philosophical considerations are often firmly held by online designers and facilitators and these considerations shape both educational and instructional efforts; however, these philosophical considerations are usually never explicitly revealed to the learners participating in the learning environment.
  - *High level Pedagogies:* These have been described as "a level of abstrac-

tion which is intermediate between philosophy and action" (Steeples, Jones, & Goodyear, 2002, p. 334). High level pedagogies are embedded in philosophical considerations about the purpose of education, preferred epistemological models, and in beliefs about how these higher level considerations should be employed. Once again, however, these perspectives and assumptions are often not explicitly acknowledged, explained, or communicated to learners and the learners themselves are not involved in their selection.
  - *Pedagogical Strategies:* These are the approaches planned and employed by the facilitating instructor to lead learners towards the stated learning goals and outcomes. Pedagogical strategies follow from both the philosophical considerations and high level pedagogies. The pedagogical framework is understood as a hierarchical structure. As the term *strategies* implies, these activities are focused on the long-term outcomes or expectations associated with the learning experience.
  - *Pedagogical Tactics:* These form the lowest level in the hierarchy of the pedagogical framework. They represent the "dynamic day-today activities of teaching" (Kehrwald, et al., 2005, p. 2). *Tactics* are short-term, instructor-initiated means through which the long-term pedagogical strategies are achieved. Pedagogical tactics are what the learners confront in the learning environment; however, tactics – and the ways in which the online distance environment is negotiated – are the direct consequence of the higher-level philosophies and

agendas that remain unshared, unchallenged, and unexplained with learners.

- **Widespread Presumptions of Social Learning:** In reviewing the design of many contemporary online environments – and in reading the guidelines and advice offered to the facilitators of these environments – it is clear that constructivist pedagogies and social learning models are the norm. In online environments, participation is thus an intended outcome based on implicit philosophical and educational considerations that may be clear to instructional designers and course facilitators, but which may well be different from those held by learners and which are generally never communicated to them (Keengwe, Onchawari, & Agamba, 2014; Parker, Maor, & Herrington, 2013).

Complexity of Construct: A Comparison with Motivation

The lack of an understanding – or rather the explicit lack of recognition and appreciation – of the mechanisms, moderating influences, and of pathways linking other constructs is not unique to participation. In many disciplinary areas it has been observed that "our understanding of behavior has been hindered by the very extent of our efforts" (Steele & Konig, 2006, p. 889). This can be seen in the ways that we have navigated other disciplinary constructs such as *motivation*.

In exploring motivation, we encounter a superabundance of theories and a fractured theoretical landscape in which "not only does each field have its particular interpretation, but there are ample subdivisions within each discipline…these subdivisions necessarily divide our efforts, limiting the extent to which insights can be shared" (Steele & Konig, 2006, p. 889). Divided efforts become apparent when motivation is viewed across disciplinary boundaries. Reviews in the psychology, applied psychology, and management literatures are all replete with different considerations of motivation, representing it as a constellation of connected constructs and suggested inter-linking pathways between them.

Motivational theories have evolved with their own distinctive association of intermediate constructs: intrinsic and extrinsic motivational factors, self-efficacy, personality dispositions, perceptions of achievement, and systems of cognition (Bandura & Locke, 2003; Cosmides & Tooby, 2013; Covington, 2000; Gagne & Deci, 2005; Judge & Ilies, 2002; Steele & Konig, 2006). This is true for motivation generically, but against such complexity what can be said specifically about participation as an indicator of learner motivation in distant online learning contexts?

- **Complexity of Constructs in Online Learning Environments:** For many there seems a clear positive connection between motivation and participation; however, there has often been a lack of complexity in the models proposed and in the linkages suggested. More recently, proposed models have accentuated the role of motivation and have sought to address the complexity of a participation-motivation linkage in ways that resonate with approaches of other disciplines. For example:
  - Motivation has been seen as a vehicle that can be used to prompt active participation and to facilitate sharing with others (Lampe, Walsh, Velasquez, & Ozkaya, 2010).
  - Motivation has been viewed as a driver to prompt richer content in participant contributions that are shared with other members of online communities (Tedjamulia, Olsen, Dean, & Albrecht, 2005).
  - Motivation has been considered as a mechanism to increase active participation in the delayed and punc-

tuated contexts of asynchronous environments (Dennen, 2005; Xie, Durrington, & Yen, 2011).

○ Motivation has been recognized as a factor in connecting individual learners (who are often isolated learners) within more inclusive socio-cultural systems of engagement and assessment (Hickey & Zuiker, 2005).

• **Understanding Models and Aligning Theory:** A lack of understanding of the operating mechanisms and construct-linkages has led many to question the traditional claims about the efficacy of participation in online distance learning. Following a rigorous examination of the quality of active listening and empathetic responses in asynchronous learning environments, with particular reference to the quality of learner-learner exchanges and dialogue, some have concluded that "while superficial listening *does not seem* to align with theoretical notions of meaningful participation in discussions, we *cannot clearly say* that concentrated or broad listening is preferable; there may also be other, more productive, ways to listen in an online discussion" (Wise, Speer, Marbouti, & Hsiao, 2013, p. 339, emphasis added).

Participation as a "pressing need to stimulate peer interaction" (Roberts, 2007, p. 2) may be a personal expectation of the online facilitator. However, the role and necessity of participation need to be reconsidered within relevant frameworks of social and cultural norms of learner behavior. This is critically important because online distance learning environments are increasingly diverse and facilitators are continually challenged to respond to difference through inclusive. In particular, two individual learner attributes deserve attention: (a) individual learning styles, and (b) national culture.

Participation and Learning Styles

In recent times, learning styles have received considerable attention in higher education and beyond. Dunn and Griggs (2000) defined a learning style as "a biologically and developmentally determined set of personal characteristics that make the identical instruction effective for some students and ineffective for others" (p. 9). Learning styles are individually adopted ways of creating new meaning and of acquiring new knowledge and "can be an expression, in the academic context, of more fundamental, and relatively stable, components of cognitive style and personality… [drawing] attention to the critical importance of intentionality in academic learning" (Entwhistle, 1987, p. 24).

Learning styles are often regarded as synonymous with a number of other constructs, even although these may be defined differently and place emphasis on different parameters:

• *Cognitive styles:* approaches to processing information that individuals habitually use when confronted with new cognitive tasks.
• *Learning preferences:* personally expressed preferences that individuals have for a particular learning environment or instructional approach.
• *Learner aptitudes:* the innate capacities and competencies that individual learners demonstrate in dealing with specific educational or learning content (Cassidy, 2004; Mayer, & Massa, 2003).

For many, there is an intuitive appreciation that individual learners possess different approaches to learning. Nevertheless, there is considerable debate as to the value in assessing individual learning styles, the degree to which instructors should accommodate them, and the extent to which instructional designers should incorporate them into learning spaces. Additionally, despite the institutional appeal of being seen to recognize them and the considerable commercial interest in assessing and measuring them, some remain concerned about the underlying validity of learning styles (Markham, 2004; Sternberg & Grigorenko, 1997; Towler & Dipboy, 2003). Indeed, some have noted that "the contrast between the enormous popularity of the learning-styles approach within education and the lack of credible evidence for its utility is, in our opinion, striking and disturbing" (Pashler, McDaniel, Rohrer, & Bjork, 2008, p. 117).

- **Learning Styles and Interpretations of Learning Behaviors:** Notwithstanding validity issues, many researchers and facilitators have suggested that learning styles do impact online distance learning participation, even although the extent of that impact remains contested. Different learner styles have been associated with online behavior including:
  - The frequency with which students connect with their online learning environments and the duration of their connections (Graf & Kinshuk, 2006)
  - Different observable approaches to the process of learning (Garcia, Amandi, Schiaffino, & Campo, 2007);
  - Different ways through which students approach learning outcomes, with participation seen as a mediating variable (Huang, Lin, & Huang, 2012).

Others have also found no clear linkage, in either face-to-face or online contexts, between participation and learner personality traits. However, these researchers have also argued that participation depends on the "the psychological impact of the two instructional environments" and have suggested that *social participation* is "a result of

educational context while individual differences play secondary role" (Caspi, Chajut, Saporta, & Beyth-Marom, 2006, p. 129).

- **Learning Styles and Interpretations of Non-Participation:** Participation is an expression of multiple factors: social norms established in learning environments, individual psychological dispositions, and preferred learning styles of those included in the environment. Instructor-centered expectations of participation and of its benefits may be at variance with the norms of the community of learners. This can lead to difficult questions for the instructor:
  - Should *non-participation* be thought of in a negative sense? Does non-participation violate what are considered to be the "real" socially constructed norms and embedded expectation of the online community? Should violators be legitimately considered to be *lurkers* (Beaudoin, 2002)? Should they even be characterized as *shirkers* (Taylor, 2002; Zhang, Perris, & Yeung, 2005)?
  - Should *non-participants* be reconsidered in a more positive light? Perhaps they are not exhibiting "deviant behavior," but are rather demonstrating personal choices and implementing individual learning strategies? Might it be more appropriate to regard them as *witness learners* (Fritsch, 1997), or as *vicarious learners* (Sutton, 2001)?

Further, how should late or deferred participation in online distance learning environments – or the decision not to participate at all – be interpreted or assessed?

- Should late or deferred participation be recognized, labelled, and subsequently assessed as *procrastination*? For many, such as classification carries with it an implied negativity and deviance from established social and collaborative norms of immediacy (Michinov, Brunot, Le Bohec, Juhel, & Delaval, 2011; Rakes, Dunn, & Rakes, 2013).

- Should such delayed or deferred behavior be more appropriately viewed in learner-centered terms? Might it better be construed as a legitimate expression of the autonomous learner behavior and learning strategy – is it really *active procrastination* (Chu & Choi, 2005), or a significant display of *functional delay* (Steele, 2007), or perhaps an important *self-regulatory skill* (Rakes & Dunn, 2010)?

Participation and National Culture Difference

The questions raised above suggest two reconsideration: (a) of the degree to which participation in online distance learning environments should be regarded as an essential and required ingredient of the educational mix; and (b) the extent to which the social, cultural, individual preferences of participants should be appreciated in setting participation expectations and outcomes.

The second point becomes more focused when the participation dichotomy – to participate, or not to participate – is considered from a perspective of national culture. Explorations of national culture have been greatly influenced by the work of Hofstede (1980, 1986), who considered that national culture was a commonly shared set of values and assumptions that operated as a *mental programming* or as the *software of the mind*. In Hofstede's extensive, but frequently contested, analysis different national groups possess distinctive cultural patterns that can be quantified and distinguished through a number of cultural-specific dimensions: power-distance, masculinity-femininity, individualism-collectivism, uncertainty and risk avoidance.

National cultural difference can be strikingly evident in traditional face-to-face instructional interactions, but it is perhaps even more apparent in online distance learning contexts (Bing & Ai-Ping, 2008; Liu, Liu, Lee, & Magjuka, 2010). At the outset, two reservations have to be kept in mind:

- **National Culture Recognition and Stereotyping:** Although it has been extensively recognized and employed, Hofestede's (1980, 1986) analysis and conclusions about the construct, nature, and measurement of national culture difference have been the subject of considerable criticism. The major areas of concern are his original research methodology and the inferences that have subsequently been made about national culture dimensions (Jones, 2007; McSweeney, 2002; Orr & Hauser, 2008). Additionally, many are concerned that although national culture profiles can provide valuable insights *all* national culture considerations need to recognize individual diversity within a population. National culture is a statistical construct, and the values associated with cultural dimensions are distributed around as a central representative value. There is considerable variation in cultural dimensions for sub-culture groups and individuals. Considering the extensive geographic range, immigration histories, and demographic shifts of America, for instance, what might "an American" be from a homogenous cultural perspective? It also seems wrong and disingenuous to use national culture dimensions and measurements to prejudge, restrictively classify, or stereotype individuals.

- **Online Participation and Power-Distance:** There is, however, considerable evidence to suggest that national culture difference plays a significant part in online distance learning environments, particularly in learner participation in asynchronous conferences, involvement in collaborative projects, and engagement in online team work (Olesova, Yang, & Richardson, 2011; Thongprasert & Cross, 2008; Yang, Olesova, & Richardson, 2010).

  ○ This is of particular importance in contemporary online learning environments, where there is often a great degree of national and ethnic diversity. Different national cultures have different assumptions regarding appropriate power-distance. Cultures with high power-distance are more likely to give credence to those considered to have higher rank or authority. The cultural recognition of power-distance can result in deferring to those with perceived higher status, failing to challenge those considered more authoritative, and feeling the need to respond to those considered more knowledgeable in online discussion conferences.

  ○ In considering Chinese learners – who generally possess a high power-distance sensitivity and behavior – Zhang (2013) explained that these learners were more instructor-centered, and that they viewing their instructors "as authorities, major sources of knowledge, and possessing high power… when encountering difficulties in learning, the Chinese learners were intimidated to interact with their instructors… [seeking] help from peers, particularly those who

shared similar cultural and linguistic backgrounds" (p. 250). Such attitudes inevitably impact the quantity and quality of interactions (participation) between their learners and their instructor, and between them and those that they perceive to have higher power in the online environment.

- **Quality and Nature of Online Participation:** Multiple national cultural dimensions often coexist to give the behavior and communications within culturally diverse online environments a rich and complex texture. This texture might not, however, be appreciated by learners or instructors of other cultures. For example, power-difference assumptions – and also individualism-collectivism differences – leads to different understandings of politeness, courtesy, and decorum that can impact the level and quality of participation.

  ○ Many Asian cultures – especially those with a Confucian heritage – prefer to make use of an indirect style of communication. These may be nuanced and differ significantly from the more direct approach and often pointed communication style that is commonly expected, and valued socially, in America and in some parts of Western Europe (Gunawardena, Wilson, & Nolla, 2003; Yang, Olesova, & Richardson, 2008). This cultural dependent perspective may lead to lower participation rates, or to online interactions that may seem disengaged, disinterested, or formulaic.

  ○ National difference can be quite striking in online learning environments, but it can also be under-appreciated or unobserved by the online facilitator or other members of the learning community who do not share that cultural perspective. For example, in reviewing the student satisfaction, performance, and knowledge construction of Chinese and Flemish online learners, Zhu (2012) observed that while both groups posted messages related to sharing and comparing of information, Flemish students posted *more* messages that explored dissonance and disagreement. Zhu (2012) believed that this might have been because "Chinese students did not want to openly disagree with their fellow group members…. dissonances and disagreements were expressed more subtly by Chinese students" (p. 133).

Solutions and Recommendations

When first encountered, participation seems a relatively straightforward issue. This perception is further strengthened because participation is easily demonstrated and simply measured. At best, however, participation should be regarded as a constellation of considerations and complexity. The nature, outcomes, and assessment of participation all deserve respect, both from those who facilitate distance learning environments and from those who participate in them.

The following suggestions are intended to raise the level of thought given to participation. Two perspectives are consideration: (a) the facilitator's personal approach to participation online; (b) the facilitator's perception of anticipated learner participation. Both are presented separately, but the effective online learning environment only comes into being when there is a complementary and synergistic fusion of both. Facilitators need to explain, demonstrate, and communicate their personal understanding of participation online to other online participants.

Online Facilitator's Personal Participation Approach

The facilitator of the online distance learning environment plays a pivotal role in shaping the environments and in managing it in ways that promote effective learning and enhance learner satisfaction. To accomplish this, the facilitator must design the environment beforehand, or have a collaborative involvement in its design, and needs to maintain an active and engaged presence in it as the learning experience progresses.

- **Maintain High Teacher Presence:** The instructor needs to be *visible* and actively present to all participants in the online distance learning environment. The instructor is central, in the same way that the conductor is central to the orchestral performance. Like the conductor, the online instructor needs to coordinate individual effort, inspire sustained performances, suggest different interpretations, and maintain the collective momentum of all participants. This coordinating performance requires considerable effort, conspicuous visibility, and persistent presence (Weaver & Albion, 2005). Having facilitated many hundreds of online learning environments, the present author wholeheartedly agrees with the premise that only "instructors who are present, attentive, and active in discussion boards can facilitate student participation in discussion forums" (Bliss & Lawrence, 2009, p. 29).

- **Communicate Participation Requirements:** Participation requirements for the online environment should be carefully established and unambiguously communicated to learners before learning commences. In formulating these requirements, facilitators should critically review the anticipated role that participation is to play. In communicating these requirements, facilitators should also explain the anticipated roles and benefits of participation. Requirements should indicate both quantitative measures (word count/ length of discussion conference threads) and qualitative expectations.

- **Explain Underlying Philosophies and Pedagogies:** Participation is often understood as a critical factor in the way that teaching and learning take place. All too often, however, the critical value of participation and the learning models employed are not communicated to learners. It is strongly recommended that facilitators explain the model upon which the online distance learning environment is constructed. In that explanation, the role of participation needs to be carefully outlined. Learners need to be aware not only of *what* is expected of them, but of *why* these expectations are in place and *how* they mesh with an underlying teaching-learner framework. This is important for learner and instructor. For instance, if a constructivist approach is being used "then becoming more aware of how our participation impacts our teaching will enable us to make the connections between our teaching practices and how this affects student learning" (Clarke & Bartholomew, 2014, p. 19). The same authors further believed that "by digging beneath the surface level of these interactions we can learn more about how this medium supports different types of discursive relationships and can help us create more effective online pedagogy" (p. 20). Commitment to a specific learning approach and digging beneath the surface are laudable enterprises; however, these efforts produce little unless the learner is included in them and informed about them.
- **Demonstrate through Participation Examples:** The simplest and most effective way for facilitators to communicate

what is desired through participation it to provide exemplars in their own contributions to online conferences. It should be clear that the facilitator's contribution is to stimulate discussion, prompt reconsideration of a particular opinion raised, or suggest alterative explanation and connections. Responses from the facilitator should be prompt, but they should also be considered because many participants will model their own responses on the facilitator's postings.

- **Use Participation to Achieve Objectives Directly:** As has been noted, participation is used for multiple purposes and with quite different objectives in mind. Sometimes, participation might be considered to add to the co-creation of knowledge. Sometimes, it might be used as an index of motivation. Because of this plurality of meanings and intended outcomes, it is always better to look at participation in a more direct and explicit manner. If the facilitator wants participation to generate a richer texture of ideas, then participants should be told that this is what is being considered. If participation is viewed as an index of motivation – or the lack of motivation and engagement – the facilitator should address the issue of motivation, preferably directly with the non-participating learners.

Online Facilitator's Perception of Learner's Participation

These following suggestions may provide constructive ways of viewing learner participation.

- **Appreciate Different Learning Styles:** Not all learners find participation and collaboration effective learning strategies. Some online instructor may believe that these learners are failing to use a valuable learning tool and may promote, encourage, and support the advantages of interactive learning approaches. Nevertheless, there will be some students who remain unconvinced. These students may participate if it is a requirement of the online course, but in doing so they will sense that they are fulfilling a facilitator-determined demand and not improving their own construction of knowledge. Instructors can *demand* and determine levels of participation in ways that *they* believe are necessary. It is suggested, however, that it is more productive to appreciate individual student learning preferences and to set course requirements that allow good grades to be earned based on other-than-participating measures. Although it may be considered that participation provides benefit and that it is a preferred feature of the learning experience, it is problematic to give it a dominant weighting in assessment.

- **If Participation is Required, Assess Quality not Quantity:** The online facilitator should approach the use of participation statistics with caution. The vital assessment question is: What do quantitative measures of participation indicate? As argued in this chapter the inevitable answer is: Not very much.
  - If mandated, learners will fulfill the quantitative participation requirements. They may do so enthusiastically, or grudgingly. They may use vague non-committal responses – "You are so right; that just what I think" – or they may employ more expanded, but equally vacuous variations. They may cut and paste stock responses to fill conference discussion space to meet quantitative requirements, adding nothing whatsoever to the richness of online discussion conferences.
  - Qualitative assessment is difficult, but if used it is important to standardize and communicate quality considerations by using an appropriate grading rubric with exemplars. Some instructors employ holistic appraisals. Others rely on a structured analysis of discussion scripts. Yet others turn to the informatics provided by the learning platform – sociograms that display learner connections, connection networks, and exchange intensity (Hrastinski, 2007; Nandi, Hamilton, Chang, & Balbo, 2012; Smith, 2008).
  - It may be useful to keep in mind the observation of Roberts (2007), after he had completed an extensive review of his research results: "[they are] arguably at odds with much of the literature advocating a pressing need to stimulate peer interaction. That is, the findings of this study indicate that it is the *nature* of contribution that is important, not the *volume* of contribution" (p. 902, emphasis added). Many of those who have attempted to objectively measure participation in online distant learning environments (including this present author) would agree.
- **Respect Different Cultural Orientations:** Similarly, participation orientations differ according the cultural understandings and assumptions. This is particularly obvious in many contemporary online distance learning environments that have considerable national culture diversity among participants. Facilitators should be sensitive to these differences and their impact on online discussion participation and collaborative projects. Assessment of participation should applied equally to all online participants; however, care and sensitivity should

be exercised in determining whether participation will be assessed, how it will be determined, and why it is considered a significant aspect of the online course that is convincingly associated with learning outcomes (Chen, Hsu, & Caropreso, 2006).

- **Avoid Unwarranted Conclusions about Non-Participation:** Against a preconceived framework of *why* participation is critical in the learning environment, it is all too easy for the facilitator to come to conclusions about why *a particular learner* fails to participate. These conclusions are usually unwarranted.

  ◦ The facilitator should avoid making these inferences by directly contacting the learner and finding out why participation is low or absent. Facilitators should not micro-manage the situation, or provide solutions based on unsubstantiated assumptions. First ask, then confirm, take time to consider, and finally advise (Starr-Glass, 2014).

  ◦ It is important to consider what the learner is *really* saying, or asking. It may be helpful to employ active listening techniques, or to use what has been called *humble inquiry*. In humble inquiry the facilitator does not respond immediately, but allows the student to explain the reason for the question. This may initially be done by silence and "if silence does not produce anything, you could say, 'Tell me a little more,' 'What is going on?' 'What is prompting you to ask this right now?'" (Lambrechts, Bouwen, Grieten, Huybrechts, & Schein, 2011, p. 134).

- **Respect Autonomous Decisions of Learners:** It is widely appreciated that learners select online distance learning because of its flexibility. Online distance

learning can be, and should be, "flexible and networked, bringing together formal and informal activities in a seamless environment that acknowledges that learning can occur anyplace, at any time, in either physical or virtual spaces"(Oblinger, 2006, p. 1.3). For many learners, participation is arduous, time-consuming, and – perhaps most importantly –perceived as providing little learning utility. This can lead adult learners to consider the anticipated learning payoff and their time budgets, and deciding to forego participation. Sometimes, this be seen as a perfectly reasonable autonomous decision; sometimes, it is simply the only outcome that seems available.

  ◦ For example, the present author has facilitated many hundreds of online distance learning courses populated exclusively by service members of the US military. In almost every course some participants will email to say that they have been assigned to active duty or to a training mission. They will have time to study, but they will not have computers or reliable Internet connectivity in the field. The will have limited opportunities to participate and recognize that they have a dilemma; the usual phrase that appears in their emails is "the mission comes first." Non-participation may be a result of an intervening technology failure or circumstance. Equally, it may be a considered decision made by a mature adult learner face with real and inalterable constrains.

FUTURE RESEARCH DIRECTIONS

A recurring issue in this chapter is lack of clear understanding of the pathways through which participation leads to desired learning outcomes.

This suggests a number of areas and directions for future research. First, although participation is afforded a key position in many learning approaches, its role still remains unclear. Research, which will undoubtedly be interdisciplinary in focus, is needed to develop models that show the place of participation in accomplishing successful learning outcomes. Participation, as a causal or moderating variable, needs to be more convincingly linked to key educational outcomes. There is currently a large body of research linking outcomes such as learner perceptions of success and learner satisfaction with participation. Most of this research, however, is observational with no long-term longitudinal studies pointing to causal relationships between the variables identified in the learning process.

Second, a strangely neglected reality of online distance learning is the construct of *distance*. Recently, considerable interest has been shown in the construal level theory of distance (Liberman, Sagristano, & Trope, 2002; Trope & Liberman, 2010). According to the construal level theory (CLT), an individual's *distance* from objects and events is "associated with how abstractly he or she will represent or construe them. Construing objects and events at lower versus higher levels of abstraction reflects conceptual differences (what information is brought to mind) as well as perceptual differences (how information is processed) (Henderson, Wakslak, Fujita, & Rohrbach, 2011, pp. 165-166). Although research grounded in CLT is in its infancy, findings have already "pointed to a range of implications of this relationship, suggesting that changes in construal are one way through which spatial distance broadly impacts judgment and behaviors" (Henderson et al, 2011, p. 171). Currently there seems to have been little or no research linking CLT and online distance learning, but it would seem that further research linking them might have significant benefits for both learners and online practitioners.

Third, an exceedingly exciting research avenue relates to participation in massive open online courses (MOOCs). MOOCs use a pedagogic approach that is sharply different from those generally considered to be the most successful in online distance learning; indeed, some have expressed the opinion that MOOCs represent a more regressive form of online distance teaching and learning (Starr-Glass, 2015). MOOCs are interesting because they generally do not accentuate participation. Research on learner participating in MOOCs has pointed to different individual learning strategies that seem to lead to course success learning outcomes and on how successful learners create and acquire new knowledge (Liyanagunawardena, Parslow, & Williams, 2014; Milligan, Littlejohn, & Margaryan, 2013; Saadatmand & Kumpulainen, 2014). Continuing research in these areas might shed light on the degree to which participation – particularly learner-learner interaction – contribution to learner success.

Fourth, in this chapter *participation* has been understood as the *part* – in a dramaturgical sense – which facilitators and learners take, or which they assume in the pre-existing online learning environment. There is, however, another aspect of participation – the extent to which individuals are personally engaged in *creating and designing* their own learning environment. There is considerable research on learner participation in the creation of physical and architectural learning spaces in order to produce environments that are conducive to effective teaching and learning (Blackmore et al. 2010; Oblinger, 2006). Similarly, research on how individuals create, interpret, and design their virtual learning spaces might be of particular value. Such research would provide a better understanding of how learners view participation and why they decide to participate in virtual environments and networks.

CONCLUSION

Participation in online distance learning environments is easily recognized and quantified.

As such, it is common to use participation as an index (of "something") with the general rule that "the more the better." Signs of participation are vital in online contexts because they make visible the activity of the distanced participants. They signal the possibilities of learner-instructor and learner-learner interaction, responsiveness, and communication. Nevertheless, although participation is visible and demonstrable, there are significant underlying questions associated with it: What does participation tell us? What can be inferred from it?

Participation in online distance learning environments can be regarded as neutral – a natural manifestation of behavior and expectations that have been specified in the online course requirements. From this perspective, learners are required to contribute a certain volume of responses to discussion conferences and learners prudently and dutifully provide those responses. Participation, in this context, is understood as simply fulfilling the role and requirements of the learning system. This begs the question: Why was participation mandated in the learning environment in the first place?

In most cases, participation is *not* regarded as a neutral response; it is understood as a sign, or proxy, for more distant (distal), invisible, and positive behavior. Participation has be seen as the primary factor in developing an online *presence* – social, cognitive, or teaching – that contributes to a more complex and successful learning dynamic. Participation is then understood to result in greater social presence, which then results in further participation; participation then come to be regarded either as an initiating factor, a desired outcome, or simply part of a virtuous circle. In the process, social presence is relegated to the status of the proverbial a Black Box – a mysterious and opaque process, the internal workings of which remain unconsidered and unknown.

To say that participation leads to social presence – or to any one of a cluster of different constructs such as involvement, engagement,

connection, or activity – may simply be tautology. Considering Moore's theory of transactional distance, for example, some have considered that the logic employed was flawed, because "when operationalized... the key dependent variable (transactional distance), by necessity becomes the inverse of the key independent variable (dialogue)" (Gorsky & Caspi, 2005, p. 4). Similar, when considering participation in higher education as involvement and inclusion, it has been observed that *participation* "cannot be assumed to be indicative of social inclusion, if we are to move beyond the tautology that participation constitutes social inclusion" (Fergusson, 2004, p. 315). Yet, in many of the ways in which "participation" is used in distance online learning, there is a very real sense that we are simply moving in tautological circles.

In online distance learning environments there are often many assumptions as to what participation is and how it operates. There is, however, all too often little understanding of whether participation: (a) operates as a dependent or independent variable; (b) initiates a sequence of reaction or it emerges as the result of it; (c) acts together with, moderates, or modifies other unspecified but presumably important variables; or (d) is distally or proximally involved with learning outcomes.

Richer, more detailed, and more complete models for understanding the connection between participation and effective online learning will hopefully be available in the future. As yet, however, they have not been constructed. Until then, it is better to consider participation as a constellation of considerations and complexity, and to treat it with the respect that it deserves. The paradox, which is evident in much online distance learning practice, is that although the role of participation remains questioned and questionable, many believe that its measurement is simple and decisive, leading to an assumption that the effects and result of participation must be equally straightforward.

It does seem that any advantages associated with participation are asymmetrically distributed:

the facilitator's participation is more critical than the learner's. This might encourage online practitioners to revisit their own participation efforts and purposes. If they believe that participation is a critical element of online learning – perhaps *the* critical element – then they may enjoy the challenge of enthusiastically promoting it within their learning environments. They may review the best practices for encouraging and sustaining participation; they may experiment and try new and different approaches. In doing so they will undoubtedly find that participation can be an exciting – perhaps even an electrifying – element in forming collaboration and a sense of community in their online environments.

In promoting participation, however, online instructor/ facilitators might also find that they become more sensitive to the ways that they measure participation and to the interpretations that they ascribe to their online learners. In particular, an increased sensitivity to participation might suggest a reconsideration of its dominance and its requirement in learner-centered environments, where it might be legitimately assumed that the individual learning styles and cultural values should be recognized and respected – even if they include non-participation.

REFERENCES

Anderson, T., & Dron, J. (2011). Three generations of distance education pedagogy. *International Review of Research in Open and Distance Learning, 12*(3), 80–97. Retrieved from http://www.irrodl.org/index.php/irrodl/article/view/890

Anderson, T., Rourke, L., Garrison, D. R., & Archer, W. (2001). Assessing teacher presence in computer conferencing context. *Journal of Asynchronous Learning Networks, 5*(2), 1–17.

Ardichvili, A., Maurer, M., Li, W., Wentling, T., & Stuedemann, R. (2006). Cultural influences on knowledge sharing through online communities of practice. *Journal of Knowledge Management, 10*(1), 94–107. doi:10.1108/13673270610650139

Austin, J. T., & Villanova, P. (1992). The criterion problem: 1917-1992. *The Journal of Applied Psychology, 77*(6), 836–874. doi:10.1037/0021-9010.77.6.836

Bandura, A., & Locke, E. A. (2003). Negative self-efficacy and goals revisited. [PubMed]. *The Journal of Applied Psychology, 88*(1), 87–99. doi:10.1037/0021-9010.88.1.87 PMID:12675397

Barnett, R. (2000). *Realizing the university in an age of supercomplexity*. Buckingham, UK: Society for Research in Higher Education, Open University Press.

Beaudoin, M. F. (2002). Learning or lurking? Tracking the "invisible" online student. *The Internet and Higher Education, 5*(2), 147–155. doi:10.1016/S1096-7516(02)00086-6

Benson, M. J. (1994). Lecture listening in an ethnographic perspective. In J. Flowerdew (Ed.), *Academic listening* (pp. 181–198). New York, NY: Cambridge University Press.

Bing, W., & Ai-Ping, T. (2008). The influence of national culture towards learners' interaction in the online learning environments: A comparative analysis of Shanghai TV University (China) and Wawasan Open University (Malaysia). *Quarterly Review of Distance Education, 9*(3), 327–339.

Blackmore, J., Bateman, D., Cloonan, A., Dixon, M., Loughlin, J., O'Mara, J., & Senior, K. (2010). Innovative learning environments research study. Melbourne, Australia: Deakin University; Retrieved from http://www.learningspaces.edu.au/docs/learningspaces-final-report.pdf

Bliss, C., & Lawrence, B. (2009). From posts to patterns: A metric to characterize discussion board activity in online courses. *Journal of Asynchronous Learning Networks, 13*(2), 15–32.

Butler, T. J., & Pinto-Zipp, G. (2006). Students' learning styles and their preferences for online instructional methods. *Journal of Educational Technology Systems, 34*(2), 199–221. doi:10.2190/8UD2-BHFU-4PXV-7ALW

Caspi, A., Chajut, E., Saporta, K., & Beyth-Marom, R. (2006). The influence of personality on social participation in learning environments. *Learning and Individual Differences, 16*(2), 129–144. doi:10.1016/j.lindif.2005.07.003

Cassidy, S. (2004). Learning styles: An overview of theories, models, and measures. *Educational Psychology, 24*(4), 419–444. doi:10.1080/0144341042000228834

Chang, C. K., Chen, G. D., & Li, L. Y. (2006). Constructing a community of practice to improve coursework activity. *Computers & Education, 50*(1), 235–247. doi:10.1016/j.compedu.2006.05.003

Chaudhury, S. R. (2011). The lecture. *New Directions for Teaching and Learning, 128*(128), 13–20. doi:10.1002/tl.464

Chen, S. J., Hsu, C. L., & Caropreso, E. J. (2006). Cross-cultural collaborative online learning: When the west meets the east. *International Journal of Technology in Teaching and Learning, 2*(1), 17–35.

Chu, A. H. C., & Choi, J. N. (2005). Rethinking procrastination: Positive effects of "active" procrastination behavior on attitudes and performance. [PubMed]. *The Journal of Social Psychology, 145*(3), 245–264. doi:10.3200/SOCP.145.3.245-264 PMID:15959999

Clarke, L. W., & Bartholomew, A. (2014). Digging beneath the surface: Analyzing the complexity of instructors' participation in asynchronous discussion. *Online Learning, 18*(4), 1-22. Retrieved from http://olj.onlinelearningconsortium.org/index.php/jaln/article/view/414/111

Coldwell, J., Craig, A., Paterson, T., & Mustard, J. (2008). Online students: Relationships between participation, demographics, and academic performance. *The Electronic Journal of e-Learning, 6*(1), 19-30. Retrieved from http://www.ejel.org/volume6/issue1

Cosmides, L., & Tooby, J. (2013). Evolutionary psychology: New perspectives on cognition and motivation. [PubMed]. *Annual Review of Psychology, 64*(1), 201–229. doi:10.1146/annurev.psych.121208.131628 PMID:23282055

Covington, M. V. (2000). Goal theory, motivation, and school achievement: An integrative review. [PubMed]. *Annual Review of Psychology, 51*(1), 171–200. doi:10.1146/annurev.psych.51.1.171 PMID:10751969

Crawley, S. L., Curry, H., Dumois-Sands, J., Tanner, C., & Wyker, C. (2008). Full-contact pedagogy: Lecturing with questions and student-centered assignment as methods for inciting self-reflexity for faculty and students. *Feminist Teacher, 19*(1), 13–30. doi:10.1353/ftr.0.0023

Croxton, R. A. (2014). The role of interactivity in student satisfaction and persistence in online learning. *Journal of Online Learning and Teaching, 10*(2), 314–324. Retrieved from http://jolt.merlot.org/vol10no2/croxton_0614.pdf

de la Varre, C., Keane, J., & Irvin, M. J. (2011). Dual perspectives on the contribution of on-site facilitators to teaching presence in a blended learning environment. *Journal of Distance Education, 25*(3). Retrieved from http://www.ijede.ca/index.php/jde/article/view/751

Dennen, V. P. (2005). From message posting to learning dialogues: Factors affecting learner participation in asynchronous discussion. *Distance Education, 26*(1), 127–148. doi:10.1080/01587910500081376

Di Leonardi, B. C. (2007). Tips for facilitating learning: The lecture deserves some respect. [PubMed]. *Journal of Continuing Education in Nursing, 38*(4), 154–175. doi:10.3928/00220124-20070701-09 PMID:17708114

Dimitrov, D. M. (2010). Contemporary treatment of reliability and validity in educational assessment. *Mid-Western Educational Researcher, 23*(1), 23–28.

Dunn, R., & Griggs, S. (Eds.). (2000). *Practical approaches to using learning styles in higher education*. Westport, CT: Bergin and Garvey.

Entwhistle, N. (1987). A model of the teaching-learning process. In T. E. Richardson, M. W. Eysenck, & D. W. Piper (Eds.), *Student learning: Research in education and cognitive psychology* (pp. 13–28). Milton Keynes, UK: SRHE and OUP.

Fergusson, R. (2004). Discourses of exclusion: Reconceptualising participation amongst young people. *Journal of Social Policy, 33*(2), 289–320. doi:10.1017/S0047279403007451

Fritsch, H. (1997). *Witness learning*. Hagen, Germany: Fern Universitat Central Institute for Distance Education Research.

Gagne, M., & Deci, E. L. (2005). Self-determination theory and work motivation. *Journal of Organizational Behavior, 26*(4), 331–362. doi:10.1002/job.322

Garcia, P., Amandi, A., Schiaffino, S., & Campo, M. (2007). Evaluating Bayesian networks' precision for detecting students' learning styles. *Computers & Education, 49*(3), 794–808. doi:10.1016/j.compedu.2005.11.017

Garrison, D. R. (2003). Self-directed learning and distance education. In M. G. Moore & W. G. Anderson (Eds.), *Handbook of distance education* (pp. 161–168). Mahwah, NJ: Lawrence Erlbaum.

Garrison, D. R. (2007). Online community of inquiry review: Social, cognitive, and teaching presence issues. *Journal of Asynchronous Learning Networks, 11*(1), 61–72.

Giossos, Y., Koutsouba, M., Lionarakis, A., & Skavantzos, K. (2009). Reconsidering Moore's transactional distance theory. *European Journal of Open, Distance and E-Learning, 2*, article 6. Retrieved from http://www.eurodl.org/materials/contrib/2009/Giossos_Koutsouba_Lionarakis_Skavantzos.pdf

Gorky, P., & Caspi, A. (2005). A critical analysis of transactional distance theory. *Quarterly Review of Distance Education, 6*(1), 1–11.

Graf, S., & Kinshuk. (2006). Considering learning styles in learning management systems: Investigating the behavior of students in an online course. In *Proceedings of the First IEEE International Workshop on Semantic Media Adaptation and Personalization* (SMAP 06). Athens, Greece: IEEE. doi:10.1109/SMAP.2006.13

Gunawardena, C., Wilson, P., & Nolla, A. (2003). Culture and online education. In M. Moore & W. Anderson (Eds.), *Handbook of distance education* (pp. 753–775). Mahwah, NJ: Lawrence Erlbaum Associates.

Guzdial, M., & Turns, J. (2000). Effective discussion through a computer-mediated anchored forum. *Journal of the Learning Sciences, 9*(4), 437–469. doi:10.1207/S15327809JLS0904_3

Henderson, M. D., Wakslak, C. J., Fujita, K., & Rohrbach, J. (2011). Construal Level Theory and spatial distance: Implications for mental representation, judgment, and behavior. *Social Psychology, 42*(3), 165–173. doi:10.1027/1864-9335/a000060

Hew, K. F., & Cheung, W. S. (2011). Student facilitators' habits of mind and their influences on higher-level knowledge construction occurrences in online discussions: A case study. *Innovations in Education and Teaching International, 48*(3), 275–285. doi:10.1080/14703297.2011.593704

Hickey, D. T., & Zuiker, S. J. (2005). Engaged participation: A sociocultural model of motivation with implications for educational assessment. *Educational Assessment, 10*(3), 277–305. doi:10.1207/s15326977ea1003_7

Hofstede, G. (1980). *Culture's consequence: International differences in work-related values.* Newbury Park, CA: Sage.

Hofstede, G. (1986). Cultural differences in teaching and learning. *International Journal of Intercultural Relations, 10*(3), 301–320. doi:10.1016/0147-1767(86)90015-5

Hrastinski, S. (2007). Participating in synchronous online education. Lund Studies in Informatics No. 6, Department of Informatics, School of Economics and Management. Lund, Sweden: University of Lund; Retrieved from https://lup.lub.lu.se/luur/download?func=downloadFile&recordOId=599311&fileOId=600490

Hrastinski, S. (2008a). What is online learner participation? A literature review. *Journal Computers & Education, 51*(4), 1755–1765. doi:10.1016/j.compedu.2008.05.005

Hrastinski, S. (2008b). What is online participation and how may it be studied in e-learning settings? In *Proceedings of the 16th European Conference on Information Systems.* Galway, Ireland: Academic Press.

Huang, E. Y., Lin, S. W., & Huang, T. K. (2012). What type of learning style leads to online participation in the mixed-mode e-learning environment? A study of software usage instruction. *Computers & Education, 58*(1), 338–349. doi:10.1016/j.compedu.2011.08.003

Hurd, S. (2005). Autonomy and the distance language learner. In B. Holmberg, M. Shelly, & C. White (Eds.), *Distance education and languages: Evolution and change* (pp. 1–19). Clevedon, UK: Multilingual Matters.

Jones, M. L. (2007). *Hofstede – culturally questionable?* Paper presented at the Oxford Business and Economics Conference, Oxford, UK.

Judge, T. A., & Ilies, R. (2002). Relationship of personality to performance motivation: A meta-analytic review. [PubMed]. *The Journal of Applied Psychology, 87*(4), 797–807. doi:10.1037/0021-9010.87.4.797 PMID:12184582

Kane, M. (2008). *Errors of measurement, theory, and public policy.* Paper presented at the 12th annual William H. Angoff Memorial Lecture, presented November 19, 2008 at the Educational Testing Service, Princeton NJ. Retrieved from http://www.ets.org/Media/Research/pdf/PICANG12.pdf

Kanuka, H., & Anderson, T. (1999). Using constructivism in technology-mediated learning: Constructing order out of the chaos in the literature. *Radical Pedagogy, 1*(2). Retrieved from http://www.radicalpedagogy.org/Radical_Pedagogy/Using_Constructivism_in_Technology-Mediated_Learning__Constructing_Order_out_of_the_Chaos_in_the_Literature.html

Kanuka, H., & Garrison, D. R. (2004). Cognitive presence in online learning. *Journal of Computing in Higher Education*, *15*(2), 21–39. doi:10.1007/BF02940928

Keengwe, J., Onchawari, G., & Agamba, J. (2014). Promoting effective e-learning practice through constructivist pedagogy. *Education and Information Technologies*, *19*(4), 887–898. doi:10.1007/s10639-013-9260-1

Kehrwald, B., Reushle, S., Redmond, P., Cleary, K., Albion, P., & Maroulis, J. (2005). *Online pedagogical practices in the faculty of education at the University of Southern Queensland*, Faculty Working Paper 05/01. Retrieved from http://eprints.usq.edu.au/archive/00000131/01/lfi_05_01.pdf

Kilgore, D. W. (2001). Critical and postmodern perspectives on adult learning. *New Directions for Adult and Continuing Education*, *89*, 3–13.

Lambert, J. L., & Fisher, J. L. (2013). Community of Inquiry Framework: Establishing community in an online course. *Journal of Interactive Online Learning*, *12*(1), 1–16. Retrieved from http://www.ncolr.org/jiol/issues/pdf/12.1.1.pdf

Lambrechts, F. J., Bouwen, R., Grieten, S., Huybrechts, J. P., & Schein, E. H. (2011). Learning to help through humble inquiry and implications for management research, practice, and education: An interview with Edgar H. Schein. *Academy of Management Learning & Education*, *10*(1), 131–147. doi:10.5465/AMLE.2011.59513279

Lampe, C., Walsh, R., Velasquez, A., & Ozkaya, E. (2010). *Motivations to participate in online communities*. *Proceedings of the SIGCHI Conference on Human Factors in Computing Systems*, Atlanta GA, 10-15 April, (pp. 1927-1936).

Larson, L. R., & Lovelace, M. D. (2013). Evaluating the efficacy of questioning strategies in lecture-based classroom environments: Are we asking the right questions? *Journal on Excellence in College Teaching*, *24*(1), 105–122.

Ley, K., & Gannon-Cook, R. (2014). Learner-valued interactions. *Quarterly Review of Distance Education*, *15*(1), 23–32.

Liberman, N., Sagristano, M. D., & Trope, Y. (2002). The effect of temporal distance on level of mental construal. *Journal of Experimental Social Psychology*, *38*(6), 523–534. doi:10.1016/S0022-1031(02)00535-8

Liu, X., Liu, S., Lee, S.-h., & Magjuka, R. J. (2010). Cultural differences in online learning: International student perceptions. *Journal of Educational Technology & Society*, *13*(3), 177–188.

Liyanagunawardena, T. R., Parslow, P., & Williams, S. A. (2014). Dropout: MOOC participants' perspective. In U. Cress & C. D. Kloos (Eds.), Proceedings of the European MOOC stakeholder summit 2014 (pp. 95–100)., Retrieved from http://www.emoocs2014.eu/sites/default/files/Proceedings-Moocs-Summit-2014.pdf

Markham, S. (2004). Learning styles measurement: A cause for concern. Technical Report (draft), Computing Educational Research Group. Melbourne, Australia: Monash University; Retrieved from http://www.csse.monash.edu.au/~ajh/research/cerg/techreps/learning_styles_review.pdf

Mayer, R. E., & Massa, L. J. (2003). Three facets of visual and verbal learners: Cognitive ability, cognitive style, and learning preference. *Journal of Educational Psychology*, *95*(4), 833–846. doi:10.1037/0022-0663.95.4.833

Mazzolini, M., & Maddison, S. (2003). Sage, guide or ghost? The effect of instructor intervention on student participation in online discussion forums. *Computers & Education, 40*(3), 237–253. doi:10.1016/S0360-1315(02)00129-X

McSweeney, B. (2002). Hofstede's model of national cultural differences and their consequences: A triumph of faith – a failure of analysis. *Human Relations, 55*(1), 89–118. doi:10.1177/0018726702055001602

Merriam, S. B. (2001). Andragogy and self-directed learning: Pillars of adult learning theory. *New Directions for Adult and Continuing Education, 89*, 53–63.

Messick, S. (1989). Validity. In R. L. Linn (Ed.), *Educational measurement* (3rd ed., pp. 13–103). New York, NY: Macmillan.

Michinov, N., Brunot, S., Le Bohec, O., Juhel, J., & Delaval, M. (2011). Procrastination, participation, and performance in online learning environments. *Computers & Education, 56*(1), 243–252. doi:10.1016/j.compedu.2010.07.025

Milligan, C., Littlejohn, A., & Margaryan, A. (2013). Patterns of engagement in connectivist MOOCs. *Journal of Online Learning and Teaching, 9*(2), 149–159. Retrieved from http://jolt.merlot.org/vol9no2/milligan_0613.pdf

Moore, M. G. (1972). Learner autonomy: The second dimension of independent learning. *Convergence, 5*(2), 76–88.

Moore, M. G. (1973). Towards a theory of independent learning and teaching. *The Journal of Higher Education, 44*(9), 661–679. doi:10.2307/1980599

Moore, M. G. (1997). Theory of transactional distance. In D. Keegan (Ed.), *Theoretical principles of distance education* (pp. 22–38). London, UK: Routledge.

Nandi, D., Hamilton, M., Chang, S., & Balbo, S. (2012). Evaluating quality in online asynchronous interactions between students and discussion facilitators. *Australasian Journal of Educational Technology, 28*(4), 684–702. Retrieved from http://www.ascilite.org.au/ajet/ajet28/nandi.pdf

Oblinger, D. G. (Ed.). (2006). *Learning spaces.* EDUCAUSE. Retrieved from http://net.educause.edu/ir/library/pdf/PUB7102.pdf

Olesova, L., Yang, D., & Richardson, J. C. (2011). Cross-cultural differences in undergraduate students' perceptions of online barriers. *Journal of Asynchronous Learning Networks, 15*(3), 68–80.

Orr, L. M., & Hauser, W. J. (2008). A re-inquiry of Hofstede's cultural dimensions: A call for 21st century cross-cultural research. *The Marketing Management Journal, 18*(2), 1–19.

Pale, P. (2013). Intrinsic deficiencies of lectures as a teaching method. [PubMed]. *Collegium Antropologicum, 37*(2), 551–559. Retrieved from http://www.collantropol.hr/antropo/article/view/70/30 PMID:23941004

Pang, K. (2008). Sophist or Socratic teaching methods in fostering learning in U.S. graduate education. *International Journal of Learning, 15*(6), 197–201.

Parker, J., Maor, D., & Herrington, J. (2013). Authentic online learning: Aligning learner needs, pedagogy, and technology. *Issues in Educational Research, 3*(2), 227–241. Retrieved from http://www.iier.org.au/iier23/parker.pdf

Pashler, H., McDaniel, M., Rohrer, D., & Bjork, R. (2008). Learning styles: Concepts and evidence. [PubMed]. *Psychological Science in the Public Interest, 9*(3), 105–119. PMID:26162104

Rakes, G. C., & Dunn, K. E. (2010). The impact of online graduate students' motivation and self-regulation on academic procrastination. *Journal of Interactive Online Learning*, 9(1), 78–93. Retrieved from http://www.ncolr.org/jiol/issues/pdf/9.1.5.pdf

Rakes, G. C., Dunn, K. E., & Rakes, T. A. (2013). Attribution as a predictor of procrastination in online graduate students. *Journal of Interactive Online Learning*, 12(3), 103–121. Retrieved from http://www.ncolr.org/jiol/issues/pdf/12.3.2.pdf

Roberts, A. G. (2007). Beyond a participation focus. In *Proceedings of the Australasian Society for Computers in Learning in Tertiary Education Conference*, (pp. 898-903). Retrieved from http://www.ascilite.org.au/conferences/singapore07/procs/roberts.pdf

Ryan, B. J. (2013). Flipping over: Student-centred learning and assessment. *Journal of Perspectives in Applied Academic Practice*, 1(2), 30–39. doi:10.14297/jpaap.v1i2.64

Saadatmand, M., & Kumpulainen, K. (2014). Participants' perceptions of learning and networking in connectivist MOOCs. *Journal of Online Learning and Teaching*, 10(1), 16–30. Retrieved from http://jolt.merlot.org/vol10no1/saadatmand_0314.pdf

Saritas, T. (2008). The construction of knowledge through social interaction via computer-mediated communication. *Quarterly Review of Distance Education*, 9(1), 35–49.

Shea, P., Li, C. S., & Pickett, A. (2006). A study of teaching presence and student sense of learning community in fully online and web-enhanced college courses. *The Internet and Higher Education*, 9(3), 175–190. doi:10.1016/j.iheduc.2006.06.005

Shen, K. N., & Khalifa, M. (2008). Exploring multidimensional conceptualization of social presence in the context of online communities. *International Journal of Human-Computer Interaction*, 24(7), 722–748. doi:10.1080/10447310802335789

Siemens, G. (2005a). Connectivism: Learning as network-creation. *ElearnSpace*. Retrieved from http://www.elearnspace.org/Articles/networks.htm

Siemens, G. (2005b). Connectivism: A learning theory for a digital age. *International Journal of Instructional Technology and Distance Learning*, 2(1), 3–10.

Smith, H. (2008). Assessing student contributions to online discussion boards. *Practitioner Research in Higher Education*, 2(1), 22-28. Retrieved from http://194.81.189.19/ojs/index.php/prhe/article/viewFile/18/18

Starr-Glass, D. (2014). Moderating the effective co-creation of knowledge in asynchronous online conferences. In C. N. Stevenson & J. C. Bauer (Eds.), *Building online communities in higher education institutions: Creating collaborative experience* (pp. 258–278). Hershey, PA: IGI-Global; doi:10.4018/978-1-4666-5178-4.ch014

Starr-Glass, D. (2015). Redemption through MOOCs? Valuing aggregation and pricing disaggregation in higher education markets. In A. Mesquita & P. Peres (Eds.), *Furthering higher education possibilities through massive open online courses*. Hershey, PA: IGI-Global; doi:10.4018/978-1-4666-8279-5.ch002

Steel, P. (2007). The nature of procrastination: A meta-analytic and theoretical review of quintessential self-regulatory failure. [PubMed]. *Psychological Bulletin*, 133(1), 65–94. doi:10.1037/0033-2909.133.1.65 PMID:17201571

Steel, P., & Konig, C. J. (2006). Integrating theories of motivation. *Academy of Management Review, 31*(4), 889–913. doi:10.5465/AMR.2006.22527462

Steeples, C., Jones, C., & Goodyear, P. (2002). Beyond e-learning: A future for networked learning. In C. Steeples & C. Jones (Eds.), *Networked learning: Perspectives and issues* (pp. 323–342). London, UK: Springer-Verlag; doi:10.1007/978-1-4471-0181-9_19

Sternberg, R. J., & Grigorenko, E. L. (1997). Are cognitive styles still in style? *The American Psychologist, 52*(7), 700–712. doi:10.1037/0003-066X.52.7.700

Sutton, L. (2001). The principle of vicarious interaction in computer-mediated communications. *International Journal of Educational Telecommunications, 7*(3), 223–242.

Swan, K. (2001). Virtual interaction: Design factors affecting student satisfaction and perceived learning in asynchronous online courses. *Distance Education, 22*(2), 306–333. doi:10.1080/0158791010220208

Swan, K. (2003). Learning effectiveness: What the research tells us. In J. Bourne & J. C. Moore (Eds.), *Elements of quality online education, practice and direction* (pp. 13–45). Needham, MA: Sloan Center for Online Education.

Swan, K., Garrison, D. R., & Richardson, J. C. (2009). A constructivist approach to online learning: The Community of Inquiry framework. In C. R. Payne (Ed.), *Information technology and constructivism in higher education: Progressive learning frameworks* (pp. 43–57). Hershey, PA: IGI Global; doi:10.4018/978-1-60566-654-9.ch004

Swan, K., & Ice, P. (2010). The Community of Inquiry framework ten years later: Introduction to the special issue. *The Internet and Higher Education, 13*(1-2), 1–4. doi:10.1016/j.iheduc.2009.11.003

Swan, K., & Shea, P. (2005). The development of virtual learning communities. In S. R. Hiltz & R. Goldman (Eds.), *Asynchronous learning networks: The research frontier* (pp. 239–260). New York, NY: Hampton Press.

Taylor, J. C. (1995). Distance education technologies: The fourth generation. *Australasian Journal of Educational Technology, 11*(2), 1–7.

Taylor, J. C. (2001). *Fifth generation distance education. Higher Education Series, Report 40.* Canberra, Australia: Australian Department of Education, Training and Youth Affairs.

Taylor, J. C. (2002). *Teaching and learning online: The workers, the lurkers and the shirkers.* Paper presented at Conference on Research in Distance and Adult Learning in Asia, Hong Kong, China. Retrieved from http://www.ouhk.edu.hk/CRIDAL/cridala2002/speeches/taylor.pdf

Tedjamulia, S. J. J., Olsen, D. R., Dean, D. L., & Albrecht, C. C. (2005). Motivating content contributions to online communities: Toward a more comprehensive theory. In *Proceedings of the 38th Hawaii International Conference on System Sciences,* (pp. 1-10). doi:10.1109/HICSS.2005.444

Thesen, L. (2007). Breaking the frame: Lectures, rituals, and academic literacies. *Journal of Applied Linguistics, 4*(1), 33–53.

Thongprasert, N., & Cross, J. M. (2008). Cross-cultural perspectives of knowledge sharing for different virtual classroom environments: A case study of Thai students in Thai and Australian universities. In *Proceedings of the EDU-COM 2008 International Conference.* Edith Cowan University. Retrieved from http://ro.ecu.edu.au/cgi/viewcontent.cgi?article=1050&context=ceducom

Towler, A. J., & Dipboy, R. L. (2003). Development of a learning style orientation measure. *Organizational Research Methods, 6*(2), 216–235. doi:10.1177/1094428103251572

Trope, Y., & Liberman, N. (2010). Construal-Level Theory of psychological distance. [PubMed]. *Psychological Review*, *117*(2), 440–463. doi:10.1037/a0018963 PMID:20438233

Vonderwell, S., & Zachariah, S. (2005). Factors that influence participation in online learning. *Journal of Research on Technology in Education*, *38*(2), 213–230. doi:10.1080/15391523.2005.10782457

Weaver, C. M., & Albion, P. R. (2005). Momentum in online discussions: The effect of social presence on motivation for participation. In *Proceedings of the Australasian Society for Computers in Learning in Tertiary Education Conference*, (pp. 703-706). Retrieved from http://www.ascilite.org.au/conferences/brisbane05/blogs/proceedings/81_Weaver.pdf

Wenger, E. (1998). *Communities of practice: Learning, meaning, and identity*. Cambridge, UK: Cambridge University Press; doi:10.1017/CBO9780511803932

Wilson, B. G., Ludwig-Hardman, S., Thornam, C. L., & Dunlap, J. C. (2004). Bounded communities: Design and facilitating learning communities in formal courses. *International Review of Research in Open and Distance Learning*, *5*(3). Retrieved from http://is2.lse.ac.uk/asp/aspecis/20080174.pdf

Wise, A., Speer, J., Marbouti, F., & Hsiao, Y.-T. (2013). Broadening the notion of participation in online discussions: Examining patterns in learners' online listening behaviors. *Instructional Science*, *41*(2), 323–343. doi:10.1007/s11251-012-9230-9

Xie, K., Durrington, V., & Yen, L. L. (2011). Relationship between students' motivation and their participation in asynchronous online discussions. *Journal of Online Learning and Teaching*, *17*(1), 17–29. Retrieved from http://jolt.merlot.org/vol7no1/xie_0311.pdf

Yang, D., Olesova, L., & Richardson, J. C. (2008). The impact of cross-cultural differences on learner participation and communication in asynchronous discussions. In K. McFerrin et al. (Eds.), *Proceedings of Society for Information Technology & Teacher Education International Conference 2008*, (pp. 825-829). Chesapeake, VA: AACE.

Yang, D., Olesova, L., & Richardson, J. C. (2010). Impact of cultural differences on students' participation, communication, and learning in an online environment. *Journal of Educational Computing Research*, *43*(2), 165–182. doi:10.2190/EC.43.2.b

Yeh, Y.-C. (2010). Analyzing online behaviors, roles, and learning communities via online discussions. *Journal of Educational Technology & Society*, *13*(1), 140–151.

Zapalska, A., & Brozik, D. (2006). Learning styles and online education. *Campus-Wide Information Systems*, *23*(5), 325–335. doi:10.1108/10650740610714080

Zhang, W.-y., Perris, K., & Yeung, L. (2005). Online tutorial support in open and distance learning: Students' perceptions. *British Journal of Educational Technology*, *36*(5), 789–804. doi:10.1111/j.1467-8535.2004.00492.x

Zhang, Y. (2013). Power distance in online learning: Experience of Chinese learners in U. S. higher education. *International Review of Research in Open and Distance Learning*, *14*(4), 238–254. Retrieved from http://www.irrodl.org/index.php/irrodl/article/view/1557

Zhu, C. (2012). Student satisfaction, performance, and knowledge construction in online collaborative learning. *Journal of Educational Technology & Society*, *15*(1), 127–136. Retrieved from http://www.ifets.info/journals/15_1/12.pdf

ADDITIONAL READING

Andresen, M. (2009). Asynchronous discussion forums: Success factors, outcomes, assessments, and limitations. Journal of Educational Technology & Society, 12(1), 249–257.

Bentley, J., Tinney, M., & Chia, B. (2005). Intercultural internet-based learning: Know your audience and what it values. Educational Technology Research and Development, 53(2), 117–127. doi:10.1007/BF02504870 doi:10.1007/BF02504870

Chiu, Y. (2009). Facilitating Asian students' critical thinking in online discussions. British Journal of Educational Technology, 40(1), 42–57. doi:10.1111/j.1467-8535.2008.00898.x doi:10.1111/j.1467-8535.2008.00898.x

Chung, J. E., Park, N., Wang, H., Fulk, J., & McLaughlin, M. (2010). Age differences in perceptions of online community participation among non-users: An extension of the Technology Acceptance model. Computers in Human Behavior, 26(6), 1674–1684. doi:10.1016/j.chb.2010.06.016 doi:10.1016/j.chb.2010.06.016

Coldwell, J., Craig, A., Paterson, T., & Mustard, J. (2008). Online students: Relationships between participation, demographics and academic performance. *The Electronic Journal of e-Learning*, 6(1), 10-30. Retrieved from http://www.ejel.org/volume6/issue1

Davies, J., & Graff, M. (2005). Performance in e-learning: Online participation and student grades. British Journal of Educational Technology, 36(4), 657–663. doi:10.1111/j.1467-8535.2005.00542.x doi:10.1111/j.1467-8535.2005.00542.x

Dennen, V. P. (2008). Pedagogical lurking: Student engagement in non-posting discussion behavior. Computers in Human Behavior, 24(4), 1624–1633. doi:10.1016/j.chb.2007.06.003 doi:10.1016/j.chb.2007.06.003

Hrastinski, S. (2009). A theory of online learning as online participation. Computers & Education, 52(1), 78–82. doi:10.1016/j.compedu.2008.06.009 doi:10.1016/j.compedu.2008.06.009

Kop, R., Fournier, H., & Mak, J. S. F. (2011). A pedagogy of abundance or a pedagogy to support human beings? Participant support on massive open online courses. International Review of Research in Open and Distance Learning, 12(7), 74–93. Retrieved from http://www.irrodl.org/index.php/irrodl/article/view/1041/2025

Lai, K. (2012). Assessing participation skills: Online discussions with peers. Assessment & Evaluation in Higher Education, 37(8), 933–947. doi:10.1080/02602938.2011.590878 doi:10.1080/02602938.2011.590878

Lee, J. (2012). Patterns of interaction and participation in a large online course: Strategies for fostering sustainable discussion. Journal of Educational Technology & Society, 15(1), 260–272.

Levy, D. (2010). Lessons learned from participating in a massive open online course. In Y. Eshet-Alkalai, A. Caspi, S. Eden, N. Geri, & Y. Yair (Eds.), *Learning in the technological era: Proceedings of the Chais Conference on Instructional Technologies Research 2011*(pp. 31-36). Ra'anana, Israel: The Open University of Israel. Retrieved from http://www.openu.ac.il/research_center/chais2011/download/f-levyd-94_eng.pdf

Lo, C. C., Johnson, E., & Tenorio, K. (2011). Promoting student learning by having college students participate in an online environment. Journal of the Scholarship of Teaching and Learning, 11(2), 1–15.

Masters, K., & Oberprieler, G. (2004). Encouraging equitable online participation through curriculum articulation. Computers & Education, 42(4), 319–332. doi:10.1016/j.compedu.2003.09.001 doi:10.1016/j.compedu.2003.09.001

Palmer, S., Holt, D., & Bray, S. (2008). Does the discussion help? The impact of a formally assessed online discussion on final student results. British Journal of Educational Technology, 39(5), 847–858. doi:10.1111/j.1467-8535.2007.00780.x doi:10.1111/j.1467-8535.2007.00780.x

Picciano, A. G. (2002). Beyond student perceptions: Issues of interaction, presence and performance in an online course. Journal of Asynchronous Learning Networks, 6(1), 21–38.

Rocca, K. A. (2010). Student participation in the college classroom: An extended multidisciplinary literature review. Communication Education, 59(2), 185–213. doi:10.1080/03634520903505936 doi:10.1080/03634520903505936

Wise, A. F., Marbouti, F., Speer, J., & Hsiao, Y. T. (2011). Towards an understanding of 'listening' in online discussions: A cluster analysis of learners' interaction patterns. In H. Spada, G. Stahl, N. Miyake, & N. Law (Eds.), *Connecting computer supported collaborative learning to policy and practice: CSCL2011 conference proceeding (Vol. I)*, (pp. 88-95), International Society of the Learning Sciences.

Wise, A. F., Speer, J., Marbouti, F., & Hsiao, Y.-T. (2013). Broadening the notion of participation in online discussions: Examining patterns in learners' online listening behaviors. Instructional Science, 41(2), 323–343. doi:10.1007/s11251-012-9230-9 doi:10.1007/s11251-012-9230-9

Yukselturk, E., & Top, E. (2013). Exploring the link among entry characteristics, participation behaviors and course outcomes of online learners: An examination of learner profile using cluster analysis. British Journal of Educational Technology, 44(5), 716–728. doi:10.1111/j.1467-8535.2012.01339.x doi:10.1111/j.1467-8535.2012.01339.x

KEY TERMS AND DEFINITIONS

Instructor/Facilitator: This is the role of most of those who manage distance learning environments. The term purposefully co-joins the two critical aspects of their role: (a) instructing and presenting a specific body of subject matter; and (b) facilitating the social, cognitive, and relational dynamics of the learning environment. Both of these roles are essential and the instructor/facilitator must be competent in each.

Learning Space: The dedicated place (real or virtual), purposefully designed by the instructor, in which learners are invited to meet and engage in knowledge creation. Through its design and affordances, the instructor suggests and encourages learners to create their own unique learning environment for optimal learning.

National Culture: A distinctive set of values and assumptions that are generally held by members of a national group. These can include attitudes towards power-distance, masculinity-femininity, individualism-collectivism, and uncertainty and risk avoidance. National culture dimensions can be quantified and expressed as country-specific indices; however, it is important to remember that this is a statistical average and that there is considerable individual variance and overlap with other national cultures. National culture dimensions should provide guidance when communicating and interacting with members of that group; they should not, however, be used to pre-judge or stereotype.

Pedagogical Framework: The integrated set of philosophical considerations, teaching preferences, and learning values that informs and motivates the instructor in designing and facilitating a learning experience. These considerations, preferences, and values – which are usually not articulated directly to the learner – are then translated into specific teaching strategies, tactics, and approaches that allow the instructor's broad philosophical considerations and specific educational objectives to be realized.

Power-Differential: The perceived difference between mentor and mentee in terms of status, authority, and self-efficacy. High power differentials limit the ways in which mentor and mentee regard one another, resulting in decreased mentee empowerment, creativity, and initiative.

Teaching Engagement: Teaching engagement begins with the teacher's recognition that the learner is an authentic party in the learning process. This leads to a flow of positive interest and active involvement in the learner's creation of knowledge and intellectual progress. Although teaching engagement originates with the instructor, it cannot be fully developed unless there is a reciprocal relationship, in which both instructor and learner recognize the benefits of cooperation, advantages of sharing, and the potential for synergism in the learning endeavor.

Validity: Perhaps the most precise and useful definition of validity was provided by Messick (1989), who understood it as: "an integrated evaluative judgment of the degree to which empirical evidence and theoretical rationales support the *adequacy* and *appropriateness* of *inferences* and *actions* based on test scores or other modes of assessment" (p. 13, emphasis in original).

Chapter 5
Building Interaction Online:
Reflective Blog Journals to link University Learning to Real World Practice

Arianne J Rourke
University of New South Wales

Annabelle Lewer-Fletcher
University of New South Wales

ABSTRACT

In higher education in recent years the educational value of blog journals for facilitating student engagement, reflection and learning has been emphasized (Chu, Kwan, & Warning, 2012; Ellison & Wu, 2008; Richardson, 2005; Yang, 2009). According to Williams and Jacobs (2004), blogs are seen as a 'transformative educational tool', which assists in the development of 'reflective and critical thinking skills' (Joshi & Chugh, 2009). This chapter critically analyzes the reflective and collaborative value of two different systems of blog journaling used by postgraduate student to reflect on their arts industry internships. Firstly Blogger (https://www.blogger.com), used between 2008 and 2012 and secondly, journal blogging in the Learning Management System (LMS) of Moodle (2014) are critiqued in terms their ability to promote student engagement, reflection, connection and collaboration. There is particular emphasis on how recent blog journals (2014) reflect how students' confidence, awareness and understandings evolve as they develop professional expertise.

INTRODUCTION

This chapter will discuss recent research that builds upon a previous study (Rourke & Coleman, 2009) that examined the effectiveness of digital diaries as a learning tool to encourage postgraduate students to share, reflect and capture their working and learning experiences, while undertaking internships in the arts industry. This study applied Bartlett-Bragg's (2003) model of the 5-stage blogging process to analyze the blog journals of ten randomly selected postgraduate students, which were created in Blogger (https://www.blogger.com). Rourke and Coleman (2009) devised a ten point evaluative system for thematically grouping and quantitatively analyzing students writing,

DOI: 10.4018/978-1-4666-9582-5.ch005

the results of this research (2008-2009) will be summarized for the purposes of comparison to the recent study (2014).

Recent research has focused on analyzing the reflective thinking processes students use while writing their Internship blog journals using adaptions of Moon's (1999) 'map of reflective writing' and Zarezadeh, Pearson and Dickinson (2009) 'Model of Reflection in Inter-professional Education'. Moon's (1999a) 'map of reflective writing', identifies five stages: noticing, making sense, making meaning and working with meaning and transformative learning. Zarezadeh, Pearson and Dickinson (2009) model "offers a structure for reflection in three personal, professional, and inter-professional levels, considering the organizational context and the culture of patient – centeredness" (p.2) in nursing education. In the case of postgraduate students writing journal blogs about their internship experiences, the 'centeredness' will be related to their relationship with other students and other professionals in their arts industry placements. Rourke and Coleman (2009) devised a ten-point evaluative system for thematically grouping and quantitatively analyzing students writing, which' will be employed as a tool for comparing the recent study to the previous study.

The recent study will analyze blog journals produced over two university Semesters by two different cohorts of postgraduate students within the Learning Management System (LMS) of Moodle. Here comparisons can be made between utilizing digital diaries (2008 to 2009) outside of the LMS compared to blog journals produced within the LMS (2014). It will critically analyze each systems effectiveness towards promoting student engagement, reflection, connection and collaboration and discuss how recent blog journals reflect how students' confidence, awareness and understandings have changed as the world of technology and learning has changed around them.

BACKGROUND

Recent literature in higher education has argued the advantages of using blogs in education for promoting active learning, stressing their usefulness as a tool for aiding critical reflection and encouraging reflective practice (Luca & McLoughlin, 2005; James, 2007; Yang, 2009; Yang, & Chang, 2012; Joyce, 2013). According to Efimova and Fiedler (2003) blogs are "personal diary-like-format websites enabled by easy to use tools and open for everyone to read" (p. 490). Stefanac (2006) taking a less personalized approach defines a blog as an "easy to update website characterized by dated entries displayed in reverse chronological order" (p. 230). Both refer to the 'easiness' of this online system, Efimova and Fiedler (2003) seeing blogs as 'diary-like' and Stefanac (2006) seeing blogs more in terms of a 'website' with organized entries. In education, blog journals are a popular means of engaging students in the process of reflective writing. As Crowe and Tonkin (2006) suggested blogs "enhance student learning in higher education through reflective journals for individual, collaborative learning activities, learning diaries during internships and postgraduate research and forums for debate" (p. 2).

In particular the benefits of reflective journal writing to student learning (Sockman, & Sharma, 2008; Burnett & Lingam, 2007; Brandt, 2007); for creating a strong sense of community (Efimova & Fiedler, 2003; Godwin-Jones, 2008) and encouraging peer collaborative reflection (Manouchehri, 2002) has been recognized. Blogs are interactive (Rodzvilla, 2002) and journalistic (Richardson, 2005) and are 'user-friendly', as they require only a simple interface that does not rely on having an understanding of HTML (HyperText Markup Language) or other web scripting. According to Alexander (2006) it is the simplicity and interactivity elements of blogs that has contributed to their popularity in education and other social settings.

Liaw, Chen and Huang (2008) have also expressed the important role that collaborative elearning can play towards promoting group knowledge sharing and individual knowledge construction and blog journals are one effective method it will be argued, to achieve these goals. William and Jacobs (2004) have stated that, "blogging has the potential to be a transformational technology for teaching and learning" (p. 242); especially when it provides a method for linking university learning to real world practice.

Here the connection between theory and practice can be fostered and within the immediacy of the blogging process students are able to reflect on these associations. Building empathy and being supportive of others in the online learning process while reflecting on one's practice, teaches students as future professionals to "embrace an awareness and appreciation of self and others" (Ghaye, 2004). Reflection in the learning process as Boud and Walker (1998) argue, is not a purely cognitive process as emotions are central to learning. The blogging process provides students with the opportunity to express their opinions and feelings in a more supportive often 'less judgmental' environment than the face-to-face (f2f) classroom. Educators have found that blogs were useful tools for promoting critical thinking skills and discovered that the use of blogs for student discussion was more effective than face-to-face discussion (Coutinho, 2007; Zeng & Harris, 2005). As Rourke and Coleman (2009), noted reflecting on the success of using digital diaries with internship students: "The blog journals provided an opportunity for these students to write reflective 'train of thought process' journals about their internship experiences in a supportive peer environment" (p.895).

The role blogs can play in developing a Community of Practice (CoP) (Levinsen, 2006; Bullen, 1998) is also a factor to consider when utilizing this learning method to enhance student engagement. Halic, Lee, Paulus, and Spence (2010), found that students believed that blogs created a 'sense of community', which in turn enhanced their learning. This is an important factor that needs nurturing for postgraduate students who often feel disenfranchised from university life. As many of these students study part-time at night, take fully online courses and come from varying educational backgrounds, this can result in some students experiencing difficulty 'connecting' with their peers. Blog journals where students share common experiences while undertaking professional practice can assist in promoting a 'sense of community' amongst the student body. As Collins, Harkins and Nind (2002) confer, "good learning is collaborative both because of the centrality of communication for learning and because thinking is, itself, a social practice" (p.110). Learning to work collaboratively within the university environment can also assist students to develop the coactive skills needed for future team and other workplace alliances.

There are however some less positive outcomes signaled in the literature about the worthiness of blog journals as a tool for promoting engagement, reflection and collaboration. For example Kerawalla, Minocha, Kirkup and Conole (2009), reported that some students chose not to engage with the course community through blogging and instead decided to blog mainly for themselves. Kerr (2006) also suggested that reverse chronological ordering of blog entries is counterproductive to good scholarship as academic writing usually starts from the past then move on to discuss and link to current themes, issues or concerns. Smith (2006) argues that because of the brevity of some students' blog posts there is limited real academic value to be found in their content, however there is merit in recording short blog entries over a period of time. Halic, Lee, Paulus, and Spence (2010) have commented that although blogs provide the opportunity for peer feedback, the value of this may not be apparent to some students.

In the case discussed here, postgraduate students are interacting in their blog journals in the final stages of their degree program. Many of these students have already had experience in the field so have a worthwhile contribution to make to their peers reflections regarding their arts industry placements. However as Hall and Davison (2007) have signalled, one disadvantage of blog journals is that they can leave learners feeling isolated as a result they limit the exchange of ideas and feel reticent about providing feedback. However, as Lam and Lawrence (2002) have claimed, one of the advantages of using technology in education is that it provides learners with a tool to regulate their own learning process. Chu, Kwan & Warning (2012), also found that undergraduate students writing blogs during their internship found the advantage of blogging being a positive knowledge sharing experience.

THE EDUCATIONAL VALUE OF BLOG JOURNALS

Recently there has been extensive discussion in the literature about the educational value of blog journaling for increasing students' engagement in their learning in higher education. Downes (2004) has suggested, that there were many learning advantages students can gain from actively participating in the process of blog journaling. Arguing that through the blogging process, students have the chance to reflect on their own writing and write more frequently, while engaging in lengthy dialogue with other students. There are however, some noted concerns about whether the blogging process actually encourages students to 'reflect' on their writing (Hall & Davidson, 2007). It is generally agreed upon, however that the processing of blogging can promote interaction and communication amongst students (Yang & Chang, 2012). An important aspect of the process of blog journal writing is that students are challenged to confront their beliefs and critically reflect on how their views might be interpreted by their audience (Williams & Jacobs, 2004). This has the

added bonus of encouraging students to be better communicators in the online environment. As according to Martindale and Wiley (2004), one of the advantages of blogs is that they can be read by a wide variety of people, which means that the 'blogger,' needs to present their thoughts in a way that perhaps more accurately reflects their personal views or arguments.

The process itself can promote further reflective writing and increase student interaction. This can lead to furthering students' ability to reflect and in doing so, develop more personal awareness, while gaining empathy and tolerance for others. Blogging provides students with a 'user-friendly' environment where they can discuss their common experiences, while practicing their ability to communicate through writing. Through this virtual platform students can connect, engage and learn from each other in an environment many find less confrontational than the f2f classroom. By interacting with each other through their blog journals, students have the opportunity to build 'trust' and become more comfortable sharing their knowledge and experience. This in turn can promote the social interaction of 'collaboration', an invaluable skill worth developing for any future role in a 'real-world' working environment.

Blogs are seen as 'transformational communicative technologies' (Papacharissi, 2006), as the process of writing, reflecting, reading and commenting on others experiences and points of view can assist students to move on in their understanding of themselves and others. There is also the claim that there is a metacognitive benefit to blogging as it encourages deep and continuous learning through frequent informational reflection and 'knowledge management' (O'Donnell, 2006). Through the blogging process, students not only learn to effectively monitor their own behavior in a social situation, they also learn to express more clearly their thoughts to others. Blogging as a process assists students to develop higher-order and associative thinking skills and to engage in authentic learning while participating as 'active' learners in an interactive learning environment (Farmer, 2006).

Some of the advantages of utilising the learning tool of blog journals, have been discussed by Fessakis, Tatsis, and Dimitracopoulou who stated:

Teachers can utilise blogs in order to increase the communication among the participants of the course as well as the level of their participation and the depth of engagement. Blogs support students' collaboration and enable teachers to monitor the evolution of students' interactions, intervene whenever needed (2008, p.202).

Blog journaling was chosen for the Internship class as a learning tool as it provided a mechanism where students could freely express their feelings, concerns and views with others while working in their internship placements. There is also the positive benefit that the actual process of blog journal writing can assist towards diminishing students' emotional stress (Brescis & Miller, 2006). It is also beneficial for students to publish their feelings and thought for a 'real' audience to read (Ferdig & Trammell, 2004), rather than keep them to themselves, which can exacerbate any feelings of isolation and loneliness. This 'sense of isolation' can be particularly concerning for students' working in an internship work placement where they often expressed feelings isolated from their student cohort, their course lecturer and the university environment. Blog journaling provides a mechanism to connect these, while providing an opportunity for support to be offered or for another person to listen to any problems or concerns.

The blog journaling process discussed in this chapter, took on the premise that the postgraduate student cohort were highly capable of monitoring their own as well as other's behaviour in this online learning environment. This was evidenced by the fact that on occasions the student cohort would pull up an individual who were being either over-opinionated or negative towards other students,

when commenting on other's blog journal entries. This provide the opportunity for the student cohort to learn to work together collaboratively in the online learning environment that encouraged a supportive, positive and active learning environment where respect for others was encouraged. The course tutor and Course Convenor did intervene if any problems arose that could not be appropriately dealt with within the student online community. As a group, postgraduate students have a lot of previous knowledge and experience to bring to the blog journaling process. To encourage reflection on this, it was necessary to limit teacher and student interaction in the journal blogging task, as it was decided that this could discourage students' from expressing their feelings about their internship experience. The next section of this chapter will discuss the use of Blogger (https://www.blogger.com) to write blog journals and their role towards promoting reflective practice and collaboration between postgraduate internship students outside the LMS.

OUT IN THE 'REAL WORLD': JOURNALING IN BLOGGER

An important aim in tertiary education that most universities embrace is the notion of promoting life-long learning. To achieve this objective, programs and course curriculums need to focus on providing students with opportunities to link their classroom learning to 'real world' experience. Kaptelinin, Nardi, and Macaulay (1999) have argued that, "the human mind emerges, exists, and can only be understood within the context of human interaction with the world" (p. 28). One method for facilitating this 'interaction' is through workplace internships. Blog journals or digital dairies can offer students the opportunity to record, reflect and collaborate with others while they experience this interconnection between their university learning and real world experience. Providing also the opportunity for developing peer-based learning, as Eisen (2001) discovered, 'relationally based' activities including peer conversations and feedback can ignite both individual and joint reflection.

The Internship course in the Master of Art Administration (MArt Admin.) at the University of New South Wales (UNSW), Australia, has since 2008 required students to write a reflective blog journal about their arts industry placement. For this course students are required to complete a 240-hour internship in an arts workplace of their choice. This could "include: gallery management in the public, private, commercial and not-for-profit sectors, community and public events management, curatorial practice, education and public programming and art writing" (Rourke & Coleman, 2009, p.891). This internship is completed in the final semester of the degree with the expectation that students have already acquired the necessary skills, knowledge and understanding to make a worthwhile contribution to an arts project while under supervision. The next section of this chapter will discuss previous research that examined postgraduate student blog journals role in promoting reflective and collaborative practice while completing an arts industry internship. The results from this study where Blogger (http://www.blogger.com) was used will be compared to a recent study of internship blog journals where the LMS of Moodle was utilized in order to access the value of both systems for promoting student engagement, reflection, connection and collaboration. It should be noted that at UNSW the main LMS at present that is supported for Technology Enhanced Learning and Teaching (TELT) is Moodle.

Between 2008 and 2012, the Internship students utilized Blogger (http://www.blogger.com) to write their twelve-blog entries. Only the Internship class, the Course Co-ordinator and the Course tutor had access to read these journals as it was decided that this would allow for more 'freedom of expression' as well as provide some privacy compared to an open blog that could distract from the purpose and direction of the journaling task. Hemmi, Bayne and Land (2009) argued that the advantage of keeping a private blog was that it provided a fairly secure environment which allowed students to feel safe to develop their ideas. As this is an ungraded course where the result received is either 'unsatisfactory' or 'satisfactory', students did not feel restricted to utilizing an academic style of writing. Which allows for both colloquial language and personal narrative stories, as the emphasis is less on supporting personal views or opinions with reference to the literature. This approach to course writing according to Heo (2004), allows students to "use narrative to express their thinking and learning, and to explore the connection between the self and the world" (p.374) while reflecting on their role within it. There is also the educational advantage as Hernandez-Serrano and Jonassen, (2003) discussed, that when a learner indirectly experiences another person's story, their skills and knowledge is both cognitively and morally increased. If this peer also provides the role of the "critical friend" as Moon (1999b) suggests, reflective thinking skills can be further promoted. As Moon states:

…working with others can facilitate learners to reflect and can deepen and broaden the quality of the reflection so long as all the learners are engaged in the process. Another person can provide the free attention that facilitates reflection; ask challenging questions, notice and challenge blocks and emotional barriers in reflection (1999b, p. 172).

The previous study by Rourke and Coleman (2009) studied the reflective nature of the MArt Admin. students' Internship blog journals written across four university semesters (between 2008 to 2009). This study gathered data from a sample size of ten randomly selecting blog journals from a student cohort of forty-four. They explained that: "The sample (n=10) was randomly selected with every fourth blog journal being selected from the

Blogger dashboard fixed at the beginning of the teaching sessions to represent a quarter of the cohort" (p.891). These digital diaries were analyzed using a ten-point evaluative system devised by Rourke and Coleman (2009) (Refer to Figure: 1), which identified students' ability to:

1. Reflect on the process: Evaluated for use of reflective language in relation to experiences and learning.
2. Describe their workload (Internship): Discussed their workloads and hours worked.
3. Describe their position (Internship) and what it entails: This included discussion about the various roles and responsibilities they undertook in the sector.
4. Post about personal/social life: Mentioned outside activities from academic studies and Internship placement activities.
5. Post apprehensively: Described apprehension involved in the creation or entry of posts.
6. Comment on their understanding/learning from the course (M. Art Admin): Indicated in posts issues arising from course subjects, learning process and relevance of the degree program to the industry based learning Internship.
7. Write posts that were socially supportive: Used social communication and writing style that indicate that they wanted to work as a social group.
8. Post collaboratively: Demonstrated knowledge of the contributor/reader presence in the writing style, suggesting an understanding of the collaborative process.
9. Supplement posts with video/photography: Linked their video and/or photographs to their diary entries, including curatorial practice evidence; hanging, presentation, exhibition spaces; invitations, graphic designs.
10. Number of posts over the Semester: The number of posts were analyzed for minimum

requirements: at least 1 mention of Internship in each post. (Rourke & Coleman, 2009, pp.893-894)

Rourke and Coleman (2009) provided a key to measure posts with each number representing the following: 1. Never; 2. Rarely; 3. Sometimes; 4. Usually; 5. Always (presented in Figure 1).

In this study Rourke and Coleman reported that:

In the sample (n=10) none of the students discussed being apprehensive or tentative about posting. Of the student participants 60% of the sample used language to discuss reflectively about their internship and the use of a digital journal. The majority of the participants (80% of the sample) reflected on their workload and described the nature of the position and the duties they performed daily. Only a minority used their blog diaries to discuss their life outside of academia and their Internship placement (30% of the sample). Just over half of the participants (60% of the sample) commented on how their industry placement had supplemented their coursework degree. Only 20% of the sample frequently used photographs and video to supplement their posts. The majority of the student participants (90% of the sample) described their Internship position and their roles and responsibilities (2009, p.894).

The results from the Rourke and Coleman (2009) study will be compared in the next section to the recent (2014) study, using the same ten point evaluative system devised by these researchers.

The Rourke and Coleman study (2009) analysed an engaged and technologically savvy cohort of students providing an example of best practice in regards to pedagogical strategies that help achieve high student outcomes. The blogging process was both "collaborative and self-directed" (Rourke & Coleman, 2009, p.896); the blogging task gave students the opportunity to discuss a

Figure 1. Graph of ten blog journals utilizing a ten-point evaluative system devised by Rourke & Coleman (2009). Note: Graph does not include number of posts (evaluative point number 10).

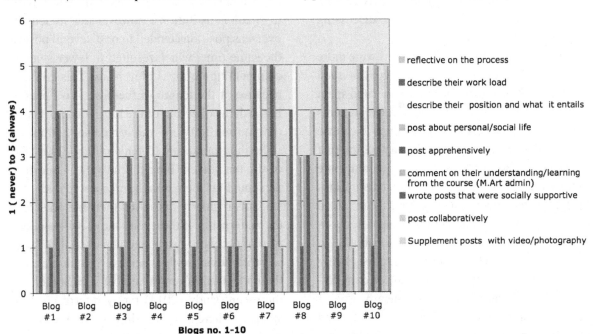

diverse range of arts based community activities using multiple platforms for their reflections. Their analysis of the blog journals showed that students were engaged in reflective thinking, committed to life-long learning and better prepared for their future career paths.

FACILITATING 'REAL WORLD' LEARNING: JOURNALING IN THE LMS

In recent years the Internship course has conducted all its learning activities including the digital journals in the LMS of Moodle. This has proven to be more convenient for the instructors but as this study will examine, has this system also proven to be worthwhile for the students? Using the ten-point evaluative system devised by Rourke and Coleman (2009) and an adaption of Moons (1999a) 'map of reflective writing' and Zareza-

deh, Pearson and Dickinson's (2009) 'Model of Reflection in Inter-professional Education'; this study will attempt to answer this question.

In order to compare the Rourke and Coleman study (2009) (Refer to Figure: 1) to the recent study (2014) a graph (Refer to Figure: 2) was produced using the same ten-point evaluative system. This graph is based on a selection of ten blog journals that were randomly selected from a total of thirty-three student blog journals using the selection method of taking every third blog. As with the Rourke and Coleman (2009) study, students were not overly apprehensive about blogging, as many had already created both personal and educational blogs in other MArt Admin. courses. In the recent study all the students used reflective language in their blogs, this varied from ten to twenty-six times across the twelve-blog entries. The Rourke and Coleman (2009) study identifies that only 60% of the sample (n=10) utilized language to discuss reflectively about their internship. Of the students' blogs that were selected the Rourke and Coleman study (2009), had eight out of ten students 'always' discussing their workloads (Figure 2).

In the recent study (2014) students were more concerned about discussing their work position and what this entailed than the amount of time spent in the workplace. This could be because students have more of a selection of internships to choose from, which allows them to select a position that really interested them and that could contribute to their future career paths. In more recent times postgraduate student interns have been given more responsibility and are more respected as a group that could make a valuable contribution to the arts industry. Hence students are less likely to complain about the requirement of completing a 240-hour internship. In fact nearly 75% of the thirty-three student cohort who completed the Internship blog journal task expressed that they were happy to stay on in the position after completing the required hours.

Student internship placements were from diverse arts organisations. Some observations can be made regarding the roles that students played in large public institutions compared to smaller private galleries and organisations. Students in smaller organisations were given more responsibility more quickly and did not report that they were given 'busy work', while students in large organisation typically had a 'settling in' period before they were given responsibilities. Those in smaller work places posted about relationships with colleagues, as did the larger work places, so it could be theorised that relationships remained similar across the board. Students were given the choice to choose in their blog journals to keep their workplace anonymous, using pseudonyms, or be more open if they desired. Students were asked to convey to their supervisors that in the internship course they were required to write twelve blog journal entries in an LMS about their industry placement. Students who chose to blog anonymously were often from smaller organisations that

were known by many of the students. Students in large institutions blogged at the same rate as those in smaller institutions, however the students in overseas positions tended to post several posts at the same time, which resulted in fewer students commenting on these blog posts. This could be because of the length of the post, it is apparent in the data collection of the blogs that posts over the required 250 words rarely received comments.

In the Rourke and Coleman study (2009) five of the ten student blog journals discussed their personal life whereas in the recent study very few students regularly discussed their life outside of their internship. In the recent study (2014) students were more work orientated and used their blogs as professional tools where they could separate their social life from their work life. Students in the recent study (2014) rarely referred to their studies, whereas in the Rourke and Coleman study (2009) seven out of 10 'mostly always' or 'always' discussed their degree program. In the recent study students expressed a more 'forward looking' approach seeing their internships leading towards a career path rather than just a job position, seeing the blog journal as a vocational tool rather than an assessable task.

At least five times during the required twelve journal blogs, the majority of students collaborated in the recent study (2014), however this was significantly higher in the Rourke and Coleman study (2009) where students produced their journals in Blogger. This is a key issue with using an LMS for creating blog journals, which had the disadvantage that: the students were not familiar with bogging in an LMS; the list format proved cumbersome and time consuming; it was difficult to personalize the space and the blogging process was limited to a university semester timeframe. The blogs in the LMS were also organized like a 'conversation' where posts from each student followed after each other similar to a discussion forum format. The disadvantage of this format is that it is difficult to follow one students' single narrative story throughout their entire internship.

Figure 2. Graph of ten blog journals (2014) utilizing the ten-point evaluative system from Rourke & Coleman (2009)

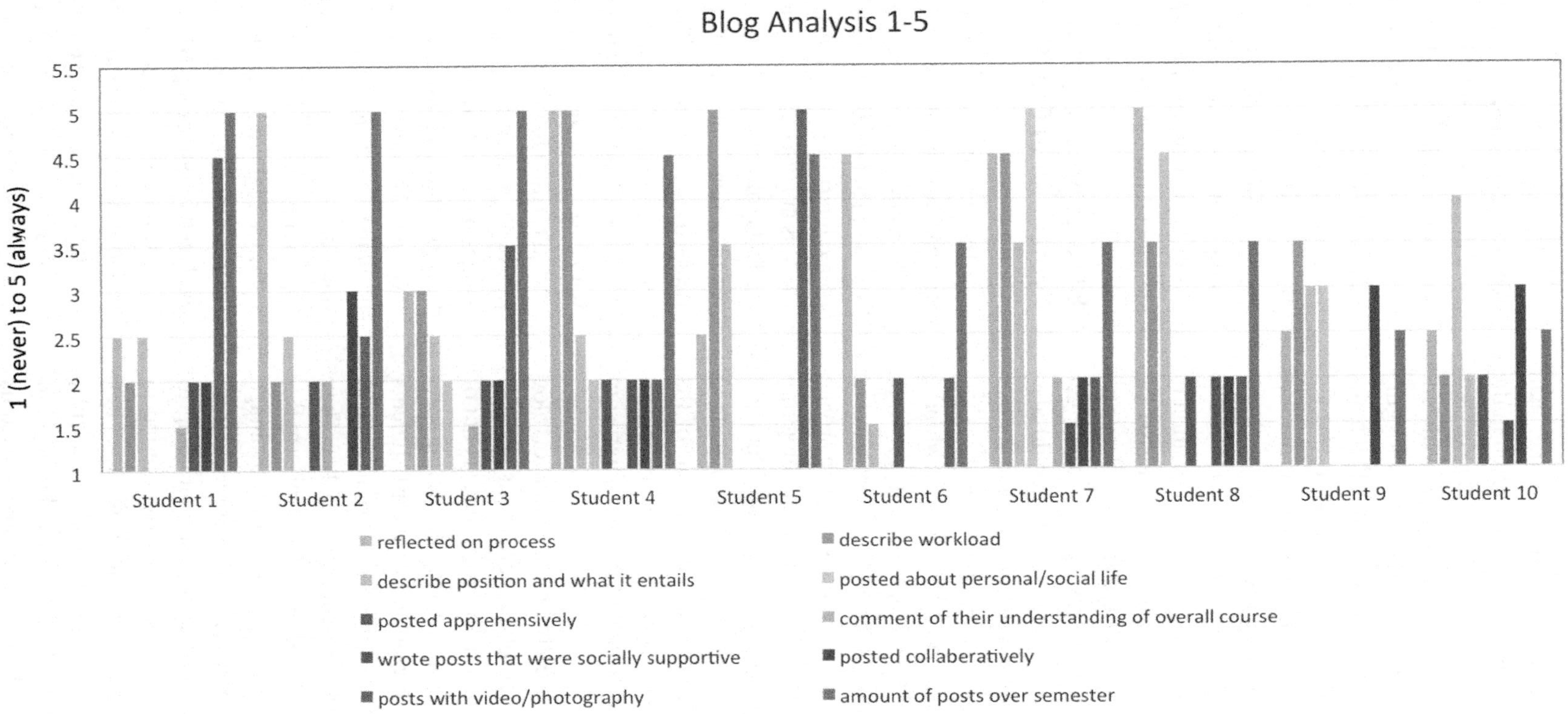

Blog Analysis 1-5

It was decided that the 'group mode' rather than individual blogging format would be used in the Moodle LMS as students could immediately view other student's posts, which hopefully would encourage more collaboration during the blogging process. Journaling in Blogger on the other hand, promoted more student collaboration as it provided a more flexible creative individualized format and it uses a 'dashboard' design rather than a textbook or forum format. Dashboard designs are seen as more 'user-friendly', they display information in a more logical readable format. According to Few (2006), they have "small concise and clear and intuitive display mechanisms" (p.36). As Blogger is not institutionally based, students could also feel 'more free' to express themselves and interact with other students on their own terms.

One student used both Blogger and Moodle and cut and pasted their blogs from Blogger into Moodle using simultaneously both systems at once, deciding to have a public as well as a private class blog. This student perceived the blogging journal task specifically as a vocational tool and soon after their internship gained employment at a large high profile arts institution. Four of the students gained employment through their internships, which they discussed in their internship blog journals.

As far as the creative presentation of blog journals and the use of supportive visuals, the Rourke and Coleman study (2009) had six out of ten student 'often' to 'always' supplementing posts with video or photography. In contrast students found it difficult to use visual support material in the LMS blogs in the recent study (2014). They preferred instead to include a URL (Uniform Resource Locator) link, which has the disadvantage of disengaging and disconnecting students from interacting with other students or continuing to read online posts. Students regularly referred to websites not related to their internships that they thought would be of interest to other students, which were occasionally about social events but mainly about events happening in other museums or galleries.

The below table (Refer to: Figure 3) compares the advantages and disadvantages of both online systems (Blogger & LMS) in their ability to provide an educational tool for creating blog journals.

As Figure 3 demonstrates, there are many advantages and disadvantages of both systems (Blogger & LMS) for writing blog journals. The Blogger system however, has the advantage over blogging in the LMS for art and design students as it provides a more creative and individualized visual layout that is more adaptable to be later developed into an eportfolio.

Blog Journaling and Professional Practice

For the recent study (2014) an adaption of the Zarezadeh, Pearson and Dickinson (2009) 'Model of Reflection in Inter-professional Education' has been used to further analyze the thirty-three completed internship blog journals (Refer to: Figure: 3). This analysis does not include the extra seven students' blogs who did not complete the twelve required diary entries. According to Zarezadeh, Pearson and Dickinson (2009), this model represents "an incessant cycle of reflection with self, profession, and others professions at the centre, with raised awareness being intended at each level and in relation to other levels" (p.9). This model has been implemented in a university nursing program not in a workplace setting. Zarezadeh, Pearson and Dickinson (2009), have stated that: "we would be enthusiastic to see the outcomes of implementing it in the real world" (p.9), which this study has attempted to do. In order to provide a clearer picture of how the adapted model works within a 'real world' context across arts industry internships all thirty-three students blogs will be analyzed as one group (Figure 4).

It was expected from the outset that students would write in a 'stream of consciousness' colloquial mode as they were given the freedom to move away from an academic style of writing. This proved not to be the case for the majority of students as most adopted a professional academic

Figure 3. Advantages and disadvantages of blog journaling in Blogger and the LMS

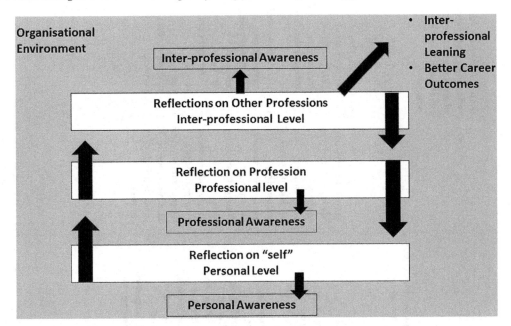

tone in their writing, using words such as: partnership divisions; creative development; cross-media marketing; putting theoretical studies to practical use; built partnerships, prestigious awards; curatorial master classes.

The student's internship blogs demonstrated both interpersonal as well as inter-professional awareness. Although they tended to focus on project-based work where professional relationships were between themselves and the team, they did consider their role within the institution and within the context of demonstrating both political and social awareness of the industry at large. In the study (2014) group there were two students interning at the same arts institution that debated about the politics and public outcry regarding a particular art event in their blog journals. These two students discussed openly and honestly the particulars of the argument demonstrating a deep level of reflection and understanding. This conversation was promptly picked up and discussed more broadly amongst the other students, which

created an engaging and lively dialogue. Here the beginnings of 'professional awareness' was demonstrated, where they expressed their understanding of the arts sector and arts culture; what role they wanted to have within this industry; daily workplace responsibilities; scope of employment opportunities and realistic ideas regarding limitations within the industry (such as financial, bureaucratic, political etc.). Here as Schön (1986, 1991) proposed student interns were beginning to act like 'professionals' who engage in "reflection-in-practice", where they have continuous dialogue with the changing situation of their practice.

Some blog journals demonstrate that they had developed some inter-professional skills, where they develop a shared understanding of the world (Karban & Smith, 2006). They discussed having workplace interactions with other professionals including: government officials; high school teachers; social workers; scientists and hospitality staff working outside of the arts industry. As well as their interactions with other student interns from

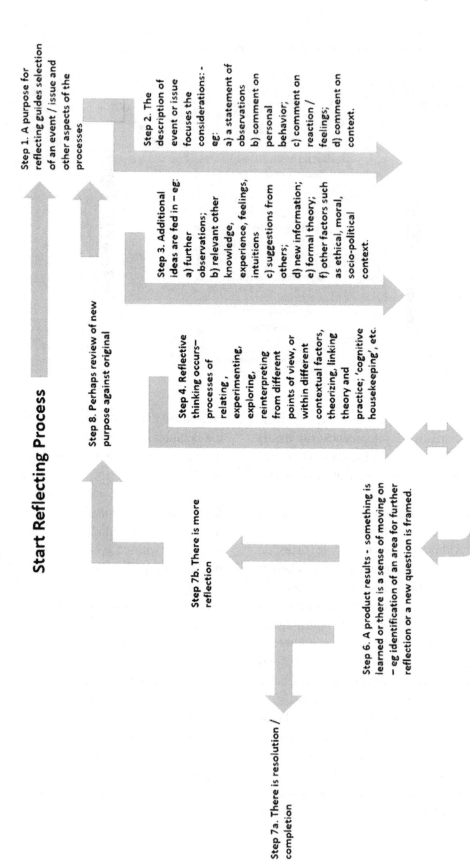

Figure 4. Reflective practice at the Service of Inter-professional education (Rourke & Lewer-Fletcher (2015) adaption of Zarezadeh, Pearson and Dickinson (2009) 'Model of Reflection in Inter-professional Education')

Start Reflecting Process

Step 1. A purpose for reflecting guides selection of an event / issue and other aspects of the processes

Step 2. The description of event or issue focuses the considerations: -
eg:
a) a statement of observations
b) comment on personal behavior;
c) comment on reaction / feelings;
d) comment on context.

Step 3. Additional ideas are fed in – eg:
a) further observations;
b) relevant other knowledge, experience, feelings, intuitions
c) suggestions from others;
d) new information;
e) formal theory;
f) other factors such as ethical, moral, socio-political context.

Step 4. Reflective thinking occurs– processes of relating, experimenting, exploring, reinterpreting from different points of view, or within different contextual factors, theorizing, linking theory and practice; 'cognitive housekeeping', etc.

Step 5. Other processing may occur such as testing of new ideas in practice and / or representation: eg in a first draft, or graphic form / in discussion etc.

Step 6. A product results - something is learned or there is a sense of moving on – eg identification of an area for further reflection or a new question is framed.

Step 7a. There is resolution / completion

Step 7b. There is more reflection

Step 8. Perhaps review of new purpose against original

other complementary professional practices such as graphic and interior design, marketing, tourism, personnel management and information technology. In these posts some interns demonstrated awareness of their own and others professional boundaries, roles and limitations (Torkington, Lymbery, Milward, Mufin & Richell, 2004), as they considered their future place within the arts industry. This in some cases was expressed as a sense of 'division' between themselves as only the 'intern' and other professionals either within or outside the arts profession. Many students discussed the limitations placed on them as interns even though in the majority of cases they felt supported and of value to the organization. The sense of having a 'professional identity' within the organization was important to interns who saw themselves as playing a vital role; some were even given major responsibility on large arts projects. Some blog journals would dwell on negative aspects of working on their internships including experiencing unprofessional behavior and a lack of respect and mutual trust, however the majority had positive experiences. Demonstrating some "awareness of one's assumptions, values and intentions embedded in practice and various social, cultural and psychological forces shaping these assumptions and values" (Tsang, 2007, p.682).

Many students discussed how during their internship, they felt that they were gaining valuable 'working' rather 'book' knowledge of the arts industry profession. Students reflected on the daily realities of working and the limitations placed on them as interns. Some students commented that they were surprised about the amount of paperwork they were required to do in terms of risk management and occupational health and safety. Another student commented on how they felt overwhelmed by administrative tasks (sorting, filing and digitising) they were expected to do, which were far more prevalent in a large organisation than they had originally considered. While

another student intern found that the amount of catering required for an art opening was surprising and resented having to wait on people.

As far as 'reflection of 'self' on a personal level', students discussed in their blog journals what role they thought they could play in the arts industry; what they felt comfortable doing; their sense of achievement and their feelings about having both positive and negative interactions with others. Here as Britton (1978) discussed, in the reflective process, the writer can change roles between being a participator as well as a spectator of their own thinking. Some blog journals were clearly written for an audience, others were introspective and more personal reflections of 'self'. Many articulated the worthiness of journaling, expressing that they looked forward to writing about their daily activities and sharing these experiences with their peers. The majority of students expressed that they found the blog journaling task a positive experience where they could feel 'connected' to their peers while on their industry placements. A blog is like a small learning community (Efimova & Fiedler, 2003) where students can interact with their peers in a relatively safe and positive environment.

The type of 'personal awareness' that was expressed in student's blog journals included that they felt more self-confidence, which particularly became apparent as they progressively wrote their blog journals. Many students blogged retrospectively, reflecting back on their feelings and thoughts about working in their internships. As Godwin-Jones (2003) has indicated, blogging is a system where people can record their reflections about things that are relevant to their daily life experiences. The blogging process in the LMS provided the advantage of students connecting with the support system of the tertiary institution, teachers and peers, as they 'revisited' their daily experiences in their reflective blog journals. It cannot be assumed that during the blogging process most students were 'reflectively learning' during their internships. It can however be argued that in the blogging process most students were progressively reflecting upon themselves, the institution, the profession and about others within and outside the arts industry.

One student while interning at a large national art gallery discussed in her blog journal how her confidence grew in regards to giving tours and acting as a tour guide. This student expressed towards the beginning of her blog journal her fear of public speaking, which was a large stumbling block for her to overcome in an internship that required taking large groups of the public on tours of the gallery. She also discussed in her blog that she did not feel she had enough knowledge or ability to effectively command the attention of a group of adults on a full day interstate tour, even under supervision of experienced gallery personnel. This student shared her trepidation about whether she had enough confidence or a high enough skill base to meet the expectations of her internship supervisor. She blogged on this topic several times throughout her internship, sharing with her student peers her experience of being mentored by the gallery staff. Slowly throughout her internship she was given more responsibility, had more opportunities to practice her presentation and people management skills, so that towards the end of her internship she was able on her own, to take a coach load of the public on a day long interstate gallery tour. In her final posts this student reflected on the success of the long day trip that she had full responsibility for and she commented on the positive encouraging feedback that she had received. This students' experience was not unusual, several other students communicated in their blog journals their apprehension in regards to the responsibility of guiding the public on tours around the gallery or other arts events.

If as Moon (1999b) suggests, that learning is a continuum that moves through the stages of "noticing," "making sense", "making meaning", "working-with-meaning" to "transformative learning" (p. 139). Specifically in the recent study (2014) as has been discussed, students' blog journals were more focused on the first four stages of Moon (1999b) 'Map of reflective writing', the final stage "transformative learning" was not apparent in the majority of the internship blogs. However this does not mean that this higher-level learning did not take place within the workplace context. The recognition of having moved on or expressing "transformative learning" in itself is a higher-order thinking skill that takes time and practice to master beyond the twelve blog entry requirement. The next section of this chapter will discuss the role reflective practice plays in the blog journaling process by examining this through the interpretive lens of an adaption of Moon's (1999a) 'Map of Reflective writing'.

Developing Reflective Practice Through Blog Journaling

According to Lester and Mayher (1987): "To be a professional is not to have all the answers. Rather, a professional is someone who can reflect on tentative solutions, collaborate with others on the possible avenues available, and risk making mistakes because mistakes are an inevitable part of building new roads" (p. 209). An important part of becoming a professional is having developed the ability to reflect on one's practice, which involves questioning as previously discussed, both 'self' and 'others'. The blog journal process provides an avenue where students can problem-solve, collaborate with their peers and make mistakes in a possibly less judgmental environment than the workplace.

Blog journaling in the LMS provides the opportunity to nurture the establishment of an evolving 'Community of Practice' (CoP) (Levinsen, 2006; Bullen, 1998) amongst the student cohort that extended into the workplace. In their blogs students invited each other to exhibitions they worked on, discussed job opportunities, provided mutual support and offered assistance where needed. At the end of the blogging process nearly half the student cohort congratulated each other for completing their degree and their 240-hour internships. Students collaboratively supported each other on their internships through the blogging process, while they develop their own self-expression and unique voices (Oravec, 2002) and self-esteem. The LMS provided students with an online environment where they could explore any issues of concern to an empathetic audience that could be possibly experiencing similar circumstances. Including the ethics of selling art and new artists commissions and the way new technologies were affecting art and the collecting, exhibiting and registration of art objects.

Reflective practice is according to Boyd and Fales (1983), "the process of internally examining and exploring an issue of concern, triggered by an experience, which reacts and clarifies meaning in terms of "self" and which results in a changed conceptual perspective" (p.100). An example of this was found in one blog journal, where a student expressed concern about leaving full-time employment to take up an unpaid internship after taking leave without pay. This students' blog journal initially expressed her apprehension about finding an appropriate internship that would suit what she originally perceived to be her 'limited set of professional skills'. Concern was also expressed about being overwhelmed by the responsibility of providing for her family as a mature aged non-paid intern and the perception this would have on other paid colleagues. Then throughout the blogging journey this student began to progressively communicate her 'sense of worth', put theory into practice, and re-invents herself by adjusting her views about her future career as an arts industry professional. As the student progressed in her blogs she also began to critically think about her future contribution to the profession. This example demonstrated the reflective practice process, which according to Bright (1996) is an "active, proactive, reactive

and action-based process" (p.167) that involves critically thinking about an experience.

Critical thinking according to Brookfield (1987), "involves calling into question the assumptions underlying our customary, habitual ways of thinking and acting and then being ready to think and act differently on the basis of this critical questioning" (p. 1). By the end of the blogging process this student had the confidence, knowledge and skill set to then mentor another student into this internship position. In the final blog entry this student discussed how she was planning to go back to her former employer with a 'new vision' and a more positive perspective. The student also provided a list of the positive changes that she was going to implement in this employment position.

The building of a CoP proved to be more difficult for the students who did their internships outside of Australia due to their lack of familiarity with their institutional workplace. These students spent longer than the local students discussing in detail the institutions they were working in to familiarize themselves with their surroundings and less time collaborating with other students. They felt that it was important to put their internships into context so that the other students could relate to their situation. Interestingly none of the four students who did overseas internships made any comparisons between the arts industry and their life in Australia and their overseas internship. This again reinforces the fact that the recent studies blogs journals were more about the student workplace experience and less about their personal lives.

Moon (1999b), believed that, "Reflection could be seen as a tool that facilitates personal learning towards the outcome of personal development, which ultimately leads towards empowerment and emancipation" (p.88). When reading the blog journals there was a sense that many students had progressed in the value they placed on themself as 'worthy' contributors to the arts industry. From being tentative at first about both the blogging process and their internships to concluding the journal in a more confident manner than which they started, where they appeared to have a better grasp of their future career directions. In order to explore the reflective nature of students' blog journals an adaption of Moon's (1999a) 'Map of Reflective writing' (Refer to Figure 5) will be utilized to examine more closely the different stages of their reflection.

Figure 5. Rourke & Lewer-Fletcher (2015) adaption of Moon's (1999a): 'Map of Reflective writing'

Advantages of blogger	Advantages of blogging in the LMS
• "professionally presented and visually interactive and engaging" (Rourke & Coleman, 2009, p.892). • "encourage shared and individual creative problem solving" (Rourke & Coleman, 2009, p.893). • Not limited to a semester timeframe. • Individual blogs. • Easier to instinctually navigate. • Can be continued after semester finishes. • Easy to url addresses. • Easily transferable to an eportfolio format.	• Continuous support from tutors during semester. • Other support material easily accessible. • Technical support from institution. • Private space. • Students concentrate on the writing task rather than the appearance of their blogs. • Easy to administer for staff. • More efficient system if assessing blogs. • Shows drafts and deleted content. • Easy to archive and access later.
Disadvantages of blogger	**Disadvantages of blogging in the LMS**
• No technical support from the institution if outside of LMS. • Requires setting up a gmail account. • Takes students away from the LMS. • Appears in reverse chronological order. • Requires more initial administrative effort to set-up as private. • Focuses on the 'look' of the blog so can distract students from the writing task. • Cumbersome to access blogs for assessment. • Does not show drafts or deleted content. • Difficult to archive.	• Limited to a university semester timeframe. • Students need to be enrolled in the course to have access. • Less flexible system. • Difficulty for posting photos and videos. • Students • Leave LMS when links are provided to other websites. • Less creative layout. • In reverse chronological order. • Students do not have their own space, it is set-up as a 'discussion forum'.

The reflective writing process according to Moon (1999b), begins with the selection of an event or issue then goes on to describe this by providing observations, personal behaviour, reactions, feelings or a comment on context. The writer then moves on to provide additional ideas including further observations and relevant other knowledge, experiences, feelings and intuitions or by providing suggestions for others. This then leads on to a 'reflective thinking' process, where the writer explores and reinterprets their stance from different viewpoints or contexts, while often linking theory to practice. They may then test new ideas in practice where something is learnt and there is then a sense of moving on, which could result in further reflection. This reflective process is cyclic, as one resolution results in more reflection then the process could begin again, where perhaps the writer reviews the new purpose against the original.

The following lists the reflective writing steps and the themes and issues students discussed in their internship blog journals (2014) using Moon's (1999b) Map of reflective writing':

Step 1: A purpose for reflecting guides selection of an event / issue and other aspects of the process

Observations: 100% of students used reflective writing in their blogs. The majority of student's had begun the reflective process by the 3rd or 4th blog, as they had become more familiar and more comfortable with the blogging process.

Step 2: The description of event or issue focuses the considerations: - eg:
   a.   a statement of observations;
   b.   comment on personal behavior;
   c.   comment on reaction / feelings;
   d.   comment on context.

Observations: Students mainly referred to each of the Step 2 criteria. Events and issues discussed included:
   ◦   the particulars involved in starting an internship;
   ◦   their feelings associated with interning;
   ◦   interactions with colleagues;
   ◦   daily responsibilities;
   ◦   events that were out of the ordinary;
   ◦   apprehension in regards unfamiliar activities.

Step 3: Additional ideas are fed in – eg:
   a.   further observations;
   b.   relevant other knowledge, experience, feelings, intuitions;
   c.   suggestions from others;
   d.   new information;
   e.   formal theory;
   f.   other factors such as ethical, moral, socio-political context.

Observations: 30% of student's blogged about the Stage 3 criteria. Student's blogs included:

• discussions regarding current discourse in the broader cultural sector;

• referring back to prior learning from the course. Putting theory into practice;

• students discussed being mentored by colleagues and the effectiveness of the advice.

Step 4: Reflective thinking occurs – processes of relating, experimenting, exploring, reinterpreting from different points of view, or within different contextual factors, theorizing, linking theory and practice; 'cognitive housekeeping', etc.

Observations: 20% of students reached this step of the reflective writing cycle. Students' writing included:

- perceiving experiences through different points of view;
- growth in the knowledge and cultural understanding of different people;
- a better understanding of their place in a broader arts community.

Step 5: Other processing may occur such as testing of new ideas in practice and / or representation: e.g. in a first draft, or graphic form/in discussion etc.

Observations: 10% of student's reached this step in the reflective writing map.

Students writing included:

- some evidence that they drafted ideas, as deleted drafts were saved by the LMS;
- some short reflective 'shared experience' conversations were had by students.

Step 6: A product results - something is learned or there is a sense of moving on – e.g. identification of an area for further reflection or a new question is framed.

Observations: Students were most likely to resolve the reflection on issues or events rather than to move onto more reflection on the same issue. The students tended to instead find a new issue or event to discuss rather than reflecting on the same issue on a deeper level.

Reflection according to Moon (1999b), "is a mental process with purpose and/or outcome that is applied to relatively complicated or unstructured ideas for which there is not an obvious solution" (p.152). To include 'reflective learning' in this process according to Garrison (1992), there should also be interaction with a critical other, as: "Meaning developed in isolation does not meet the criteria of critical or reflective learning. Critical discourse is essential for worthwhile and valid knowledge"

(p. 139). It was a requirement of the Internship course that students provided both supportive and constructive comments on other student blogs at least twelve times during the process of creating their own blog journals. An important learning objective of the internship blog journaling task was that student collaboratively interacted. As peer learning "offers the opportunity for students to teach and learn from each other", (Raadt, Toleman, & Watson, 2005, p.159), during the blogging process while they experience working in a 'real world' context outside the classroom. With the added bonus that as Ferdig & Trammell, (2004) argue, blog journaling can assist students' to feel a sense of ownership of their thinking and learning and also the premise that 'reflection' is an important factor for making learning more meaningful (Xie, Ke & Sharma, 2008).

According to Dewey (1933), reflective thinking is "the kind of thinking that consists of turning a subject over in the mind and giving it serious and consecutive consideration" (p. 3). This was apparent when students discussed their different approaches to dealing with problems such as: who to approach for advice on various workplace ethical issues or what was the demarcation in roles between the intern, employees and volunteers. Students discuss in their blogs their different approaches and different opinions within both the context of their internship placement and within the broader debates of the arts industry. Ennis (1987) stated that: "Critical thinking is reasonable reflective thinking that is focused on deciding what to believe or do" (p. 10) and that critical thinking has five key components: "practical, reflective, reasonable, belief, and action" (p. 10).

Moon (1999b) believes that the reflective writing process begins with the selection of an event or issue. The Internship students were advised to start their blogs by introducing themselves and describing their internship placement and to only include questions to other students when they wanted a response. However they were highly encouraged to include questions when they were reflecting on their own practice. Deng and Yuen (2009) discovered that when reflection was stressed as a learning outcome, students were more likely to take more responsibility for their role in this process. As the task was titled: 'Reflective journaling', students knew from the start that they were expected to 'reflect' on their internship experience. These postgraduate students had already had experience in their master coursework of writing reflectively so they were all aware of the expectations required of them in this learning task.

According to Xie, Ke and Sharma (2010), different blogging styles can affect interactivity and critical thinking. They conducted a study on the effect of peer-interaction styles on students' thinking, where they discovered that students were more likely to write longer posts when they started as a monologue than when they started with questions. Easing into the process of blogging by discussing factually a situation as the internship student discovered, allowed them to first become familiar with the process of blogging in an LMS, which differed from their previous experience of using weblog, Blogger or other social media.

In Moon's (1999b) 'reflective thinking' process, 'critical thinking' can evolve as writers explore and reinterpret their stance from different viewpoints or contexts, while often linking theory to practice. Students were encouraged in the blog journal task to link their university learning to their workplace practice. As previously mentioned, this did not frequently happen in the 2014 internship blog journals. They instead chose to critically reflect on their role in the workplace and their future career paths. As a result of the current competitive job market in Australia, these students chose to focus on professional skills and experiences rather than their past academic studies in their blog journals.

FUTURE RESEARCH DIRECTIONS

The literature has affirmed the usefulness of posing questions to promote reflective thinking (Brookfield, 1995; Driscol, 1994; Smyth, 1992). The authors are considering in the future adding question prompts at different stages of the blogging process to encourage students to reflect more deeply. The authors in the future will be considering moving the blog journals out of the LMS and into a more creative and flexible, non-institutional user-friendly web publishing service. Rourke and Coleman (2009) reported that Blogger provided the opportunity to create an "author designed creative space" (p.896), which the authors thought was one of the major disadvantages of using the LMS for blog journaling for future arts industry professionals. As there was also a low level of CoP developing between the students in this recent student group, further research needs to be conducted regarding student engagement in online groups, group size and blog post length. In the future the authors will also be trialling the idea of randomly placing students into a number of smaller groups if blogging remains in the LMS, to test out whether this approach promotes a higher level of student interaction and collaboration.

CONCLUSION

As this millenniums higher education institutions adapt to new learning technologies, tertiary students have progressively become more 'career' orientated in a increasingly competitive career market. In order to keep students in touch with this fast evolving world of inter-professional practice, workplace internships have become a vital component of both postgraduate as well as undergraduate programs. With the goal that this workplace learning provides the opportunity to link theory to practice while students acquire experience and work skills. To achieve this goal, educators need to provide authentic learning opportunities that facilitate collaboration, reflection and critical thinking. Workplace blog journals as has been argued, provides a tool where students can develop reflective writing and reflective practice skills that will help them to think more critically about their role in their future professions. Reflective blogs when developed in a creative, flexible and user-friendly environment as has been discussed, provides a space where students can be synergetic, emotive and build the confidence to make the leap between their university learning and 'real world' practice.

REFERENCES

Alexander, B. (2006). Web 2.0: A new wave of innovation for teaching and learning? *EDUCAUSE Review*, *41*(2), 32–44.

Barclay, K. H. (2001). *Humanizing learning-at-distance*. San Francisco: Saybrook Institute.

Bartlett-Bragg, A. (2003). Blogging to Learn, Knowledge Tree e-journal. Retrieved January 12, 2015, from: http://knowledgetree.flexiblelearning.net.au/edition04/pdf/Blogging_to_Learn.pdf

Beyer, B. K. (1985). Critical thinking: What is it. *Social Education, 49*(4), 270-276.

Boud, D., & Walker, D. (1998). Promoting reflection in professional courses: The challenge of context. *Studies in Higher Education, 23*(2), 191–206. doi:10.1080/03075079812331380384

Boyd, E., & Fales, A. (1983). Reflective learning key to learning from experience. *Journal of Humanistic Psychology, 23*(2), 99–117. doi:10.1177/0022167883232011

Brandt, C. (2008). Integrating feedback and reflection in teacher preparation. *ELT Journal, 62*(1), 37–46. doi:10.1093/elt/ccm076

Brescia, W. F. J., & Miller, M. T. (2006). What's it worth? The perceived benefits of instructional blogging. *Electronic Journal for the Integration of Technology in Education, 5*, 44–52.

Bright, B. (1996). Reflecting on "reflective practice.". *Studies in the Education of Adults, 28*(2), 162–184.

Britton, J. (1978). The composing processes and the functions of writing. In C. R. Cooper & L. Odell (Eds.), *Research on Composing: Points of Departure*. Urbana, IL: NCTE.

Brookfield, S. D. (1987). *Developing critical thinkers: Challenging adults to explore alternative ways of thinking and acting*. San Francisco, CA: Jossey-Bass.

Brookfield, S. D. (1995). *Becoming a critically reflective teacher*. San Francisco, CA: Jossey-Bass.

Bullen, M. (1998). Participation and critical thinking in on-line university distance education. *Canadian Journal of Distance Education, 13*(2), 1–32.

Burnett, G., & Lingam, G. I. (2007). Reflective teachers and teacher educators in the Pacific region: Conversations with us not about us. *Review of Education, 53*, 303–321.

Chu, S. K., Kwan, A. C., & Warning, P. (2012). Blogging for information management, learning and social support during internship. *Journal of Educational Technology & Society, 15*(2), 168–178.

Cisero, C. A. (2006). Does Reflective Journal Writing Improve Course Performance? *College Teaching, 54*(2), 231–236. doi:10.3200/CTCH.54.2.231-236

Collins, J., Harkin, J., & Nind, M. (2002). *Manifesto for Learning*. London, New York: Continuum.

Coutinho, C. P. (2007). Cooperative learning in higher education using weblogs: A study with undergraduate students of education in Portugal. *Proceedings of the 5th International Conference on Education and Information Systems, Technologies and Applications* (EISTA) (pp. 60-64). Orlando: EUA. Julho.

Crowe, C., & Tonkin, J. (2006). *Fifteen megabytes of fame: blogging, learning and assessment. Synergy, 24* (pp. 1–6). Sydney: University of Sydney.

De Raadt, M., Toleman, M., & Watson, R. (2005). Electronic peer review: a large cohort teaching themselves? *Proceedings of the 22nd Annual Conference of the Australasian Society for Computers in Learning in Tertiary Education*, 159-168.

Deng, L., & Yuen, A. H. K. (2009). Blogs in higher education: Implementation and issues. *TechTrends, 53*(3), 95–98.

Dewey, J. (1933). *How we think*. New York: DC Heath.

Dilworth, A. I. (2007). TECHNO ETHICS: Blogs: Online Practice Guides or Websites. *Electronic Rainmaking, 24*(8), 54–56.

Downes, S. (2004). Educational blogging. *EDUCAUSE Review*, (September/October): 14–26.

Driscoll, J. (1994). Reflective practice for practice. *Senior Nurse, 13*(7), 45–50. PMID:8303152

Efimova, L., & Fiedler, S. (2003). Learning webs: Learning in weblog networks. In P. Kommers, P. Isaias, & M. B. Nunes (Eds.), *Proceedings of the IADIS International Conference Web Based Communities*, (pp.490-494), Lisbon: IADIS Press.

Eisen, M. J. (2001). Peer-based professional development viewed through the lens of transformative learning. *Holistic Nursing Practice, 16*(1), 30–42. doi:10.1097/00004650-200110000-00008 PMID:15559045

Elbow, P. (1993). The war between reading and writing and how to end it. *Rhetoric Review, 12*(1), 94–113. doi:10.1080/07350199309389024

Ennis, R. H. (1987). A taxonomy of critical thinking dispositions and abilities. In J. B. Baron & R. J. Sternberg (Eds.), *Teaching thinking skills: Theory and practice* (pp. 9–26). New York: W.H. Freeman.

Farmer, J. (2006). Blogging to basics: How blogs are bringing online education back from the brink. In A. Bruns & J. Jacobs (Eds.), *Uses of blogs* (pp. 91–103). New York: Peter Lang.

Ferdig, R. E., & Trammell, K. D. (2004). Content delivery in the 'Blogosphere.'. *Technological Horizons in Education Journal, 31*(7), 12–20.

Fessakis, G., Tatsis, K., & Dimitracopoulou, A. (2008). Supporting 'learning by design' activities using group blogs. *Journal of Educational Technology & Society, 11*(4), 199–212.

Few, S. (2006). *Information Dashboard Design: The Effective Visual Communication of Data*. Burlingame, CA: Analytics.

Garrison, D. R. (1992). Critical thinking and self-directed learning in adult education: An analysis of responsibility and control issues. *Adult Education Quarterly, 42*(3), 136–148.

Ghaye, T. (2004). Editorial: Reflection for spiritual practice? *Reflective Practice, 5*(3), 291–295. doi:10.1080/1462394042000308699

Glogoff, S. (2005). Instructional blogging: Promoting Interactivity, student-centred learning, and peer input. Retrieved: May 10th, 2015, from: http://studentcenteredlearning.pbworks.com/f/Instructional+Blogging.pdf

Godwin-Jones, B. (2008). Emerging technologies: Web-writing 2.0: Enabling, documenting, and assessing writing online. *Language Learning & Technology, 12*(2), 7–13.

Halic, O., Lee, D., Paulus, T., & Spence, M. (2010). To blog or not to blog: Student perceptions of blog effectiveness for learning in a college-level course. *The Internet and Higher Education, 13*(4), 206–213. doi:10.1016/j.iheduc.2010.04.001

Hall, H., & Davison, B. (2007). Social software as support in hybrid learning environments: The value of the blog as a tool for reflective learning and peer support. *Library & Information Science Research, 29*(2), 163–187. doi:10.1016/j.lisr.2007.04.007

Hemmi, A., Bayne, S., & Land, R. (2009). The appropriation and repurposing of social technologies in higher education. *Journal of Computer Assisted Learning, 25*(1), 19–30. doi:10.1111/j.1365-2729.2008.00306.x

Heo, H. (2004). Story telling and retelling as narrative inquiry in cyber learning environments. In R. Atkinson, C. McBeath, D. Jonas-Dwyer & R. Phillips (Eds.), *Beyond the comfort zone: Proceedings of the 21st ASCILITE Conference* (pp. 374-378). Perth: ASCILITE.

Hernandez-Serrano, J., & Jonassen, D. H. (2003). The effects of case libraries on problem solving. *Journal of Computer Assisted Learning, 19*(1), 103–114. doi:10.1046/j.0266-4909.2002.00010.x

James, M. (2007). Blogging their way to Learning: Student perceptions of a reading Journal Blog Assessment task. Conference paper presented at: *International Symposium on eLearning*, Melbourne: RMIT.

Joyce, T. M. (2013). Reflective Practice through Blogging: An Alternative for Open and Distance Learning Context. *Journal of Communication, 4*(2), 123–130.

Kaptelinin, V., Nardi, B., & Macaulay, C. (1999). The activity checklist: A tool for representing the 'space' of context. *Interaction, 6*(4), 27–39. doi:10.1145/306412.306431

Karban, K., & Smith, S. (2006). Developing critical reflection within an interprofessional learning programme. Conference Paper presented at: *Professional lifelong learning: beyond reflective practice*, University of Leeds, UK.

Kerawalla, L., Minocha, S., Kirkup, G., & Conole, G. (2009). An empirically grounded framework to guide blogging in higher education. *Journal of Computer Assisted Learning, 25*(1), 31–42. doi:10.1111/j.1365-2729.2008.00286.x

Kerr, O. S. (2006). Blogs and the legal academy. *George Washington University Law School Publication*, Legal Research Paper No. 203, 7.

Lam, Y., & Lawrence, G. (2002). Teacher-student role redefinition during a computer-based second language project: Are computers catalysts for empowering change? *Computer Assisted Language Learning, 15*(3), 295–315. doi:10.1076/call.15.3.295.8185

Lang, P. (Ed.). (2009). Innovation in transformative Learning: Space, Culture and the Arts. Schapiro Source: Counterpoints, 341, 291-294.

Lasley, T. (1992). Promoting teacher reflection. *Journal of Staff Development, 13*(1), 24–29.

Lester, N. B., & Mayher, J. S. (1987). Critical professional inquiry. *English Education, 19*(4), 198–210.

Levinsen, T. K. (2006). Collaborative On-Line Teaching: The Inevitable Path to Deep Learning and Knowledge Sharing? *Electronic Journal of e-learning, 4*(1), 41-48.

Liaw, S. S., Chen, G. D., & Huang, H. M. (2008). Users' attitudes toward Web-based collaborative learning systems for knowledge management. *Computers & Education, 50*(3), 950–961. doi:10.1016/j.compedu.2006.09.007

Luca, J., & McLoughlin, C. (2005). Can blogs promote fair and equitable teamwork? In *Balance, fidelity, mobility: Maintaining the momentum?* Brisbane: ASCILITE.

Luskin, B. J. (2003). *Media psychology: A field whose time Is here, The California Psychologist.* May/June.

Manouchehri, A. (2002). Developing teaching knowledge through peer discourse. *Teaching and Teacher Education, 18*(6), 715–737. doi:10.1016/S0742-051X(02)00030-6

Martindale, T., & Wiley, D. A. (2005). Using weblogs in scholarship and teaching. *TechTrends, 49*(2), 55–61. doi:10.1007/BF02773972

Moon, J. (1999a). *Learning Journals: a Handbook for Academics, Students and Professional Development.* London: Kogan Page.

Moon, J. (1999b). *Reflection in Learning and Professional Development, Theory and Practice.* London: Kogan Page.

O'Donnell, M. (2006). Blogging as pedagogic practice: Artefact and ecology. *Asia Pacific Media Educator, 17*, 5–19.

Oravec, J. A. (2002). Bookmarking the world: Weblog applications in education. *Journal of Adolescent & Adult Literacy, 45*(7), 616–621.

Papacharissi, Z. (2006). Audiences as media producers: content analysis of 260 blogs. In M. Tremayne (Ed.), *Blogging, citizenship, and the future of media* (pp. 21–38). New York: Routledge.

Richardson, W. (2005). *Blogs, wikis, podcasts, and other powerful web tools for classrooms.* Thousand Oaks, CA: Corwin Press.

Rodzvilla, J. (2002). *We've got blog: How weblogs are changing our culture.* Cambridge, MA: Perseus Publishing.

Rogers, J. (2000). Communities of Practice: A framework for fostering coherence in virtual learning communities. *Journal of Educational Technology & Society, 3*(3), 384–392.

Rosen, L. S. (2006). Blogging to Inform, Educate, and Attract New Clients. *Family Advocate, 28*(3), 46–47.

Rourke, A. J., & Coleman, K. (2009). An emancipating space: reflective and collaborative blogging, Same places, Different spaces, Auckland, New Zealand: University of Auckland: ASCILITE, 888-897.

Schön, D. A. (1986). *Educating the reflective practitioner.* San Francisco, CA: Jossey-Bass.

Schön, D. A. (1991). *Educating the reflective practitioner: Toward a new design for teaching and learning in the professions.* San Francisco, CA: Jossey-Bass.

Smith, D. G. (2006). *Bit by Bit: A Case Study of Bloggership,* University of Wisconsin, Legal Studies Research Paper No. 1017, 4. Retrieved January 12th, 2015, from: http://papers.ssrn.com/sol3/papers.cfm?abstract_id=898178

Smyth, J. (1992). Teachers' works and the politics of reflection. *American Educational Research Journal, 29*(2), 267–300. doi:10.3102/00028312029002268

Sockman, B., & Sharma, P. (2008). Struggling toward a transformative model of instruction: It's not so easy! *Teaching and Teacher Education, 24*(4), 1070–1082. doi:10.1016/j.tate.2007.11.008

Stefanac, S. (2006). *Dispatches from blogistan: A travel guide for the modern blogger.* Berkeley, CA: New Riders.

Torkington, C., Lymbery, M., Milward, A., Mufin, M., & Richell, B. (2004). The impact of shared practice learning on the quality of assessment carried out by social work and district nurse students. *Learning in Health and Social Care*, *3*(1), 26–36. doi:10.1111/j.1473-6861.2004.00059.x

Tsang, N. M. (2007). Reflection as Dialogue. *British Journal of Social Work*, *37*(4), 681–694. doi:10.1093/bjsw/bch304

Williams, J. B., & Jacobs, J. (2004). Exploring the use of blogs as learning spaces in the higher education sector. *Australasian Journal of Educational Technology*, *20*(2), 232–247.

Xie, Y., Ke, F., & Sharma, P. (2010). The effect of peer-interaction styles in team blogging on students' cognitive thinking and blog participation. *Journal of Educational Computing Research*, *42*(4), 459–479. doi:10.2190/EC.42.4.f

Xie, Y., Ke, K., & Sharma, P. (2008). The effective peer feedback for blogging on college students' reflective learning processes. *The Internet and Higher Education*, *11*(1), 18–25. doi:10.1016/j.iheduc.2007.11.001

Yang, C., & Chang, Y. S. (2012). Assessing the effects of interactive blogging on student attitudes toward peer interaction, learning motivation, and academic achievements. *Journal of Computer Assisted Learning*, *28*(2), 126–135. doi:10.1111/j.1365-2729.2011.00423.x

Yang, S. H. (2009). Using Blogs to Enhance Critical Reflection and Community of Practice. *Journal of Educational Technology & Society*, *12*(2), 11–21.

Zarezadeh, Y., Pearson, P., & Dickinson, C. (2009). A model for reflection to enhance interprofessional education. *International Journal of Education*, *1*(1), 1–18. doi:10.5296/ije.v1i1.191

Zeng, X., & Harris, S. T. (2005). Blogging in an online health information technology class. *Perspectives in Health Information Management*, *2*(6). http://www.ncbi.nlm.nih.gov/pmc/articles/PMC2047310/ Retrieved October 14, 2014 PMID:18066374

ADDITIONAL READING

Bradbury, H., Frost, N., Kilminster, S., & Zukas, M. (2010) (Eds.). Beyond reflective practice: new approaches to professional lifelong learning, New York & London: Routledge.

Chu, S. K. W., Chan, C. K. K., & Tiwari, A. F. Y. (2012). Using blogs to support learning during internships. *Computers & Education*, *58*(3), 989–1000. doi:10.1016/j.compedu.2011.08.027

Ellison, N. B., & Wu, Y. (2008). Blogging in the classroom: A preliminary exploration of student attitudes and impact on comprehension. *Journal of Educational Multimedia and Hypermedia*, *17*(1), 99–122.

Freeman, W., & Brett, C. (2011). Prompting authentic blogging practice in an online graduate course. *Computers & Education*, *59*(3), 1032–1041. doi:10.1016/j.compedu.2012.03.019

Kun, L., Bado, N., Smith, J., & Moore, D. (2013). Blogging for teaching and learning: An examination of experience, attitude, and levels of thinking. *Contemporary Educational Technology*, *4*(3), 172–186.

Morrison, K. (1996). Developing reflective practice in higher degree students through a learning journal. *Studies in Higher Education*, *21*(3), 317–332. doi:10.1080/03075079612331381241

Rourke, A. J., & Coleman, K. S. (Eds.). (2011). *Pedagogy leads technology: Online Learning and Teaching in Higher Education: New Technologies, New Pedagogies*. Champaign, Illinois: Common Grounds.

KEY TERMS AND DEFINITIONS

Blog: A blog is an electronic medium used for posting journal style information, that also promotes interactive electronic replies and information sharing from readers. A blog has a reverse chronology format that is usually imbedded into a website. Blogs have a broad usage and are used by individuals, organisations and specifically educational institutions as an assessment tool that encourages personal reflection and group interaction. The contents page of a blog can list information that gives opportunities to add more layers of information than what is generally offered through a traditional electronic diary.

Blogging: Blogging is the process of writing and creating a blog. Blogging is an efficient and inexpensive way to broadcast to a broad audience, while also offering a platform for marketing and promoting businesses.

Community of Practice (CoP): A group of active supportive practitioners who interact regularly sharing experiences and common interests who have a passion for what they do. CoP's can be created with the goals of gaining further knowledge and understanding about a profession in order to improve practice or to support members.

Critical Thinking: This term refers to a process that involves clear, reasoned thinking involving critique and analysis. Its details vary amongst those who define it. According to Beyer (1995), critical thinking means making clear, reasoned judgements. During the process of critical thinking, ideas should be reasoned and well thought out/judged.

Dashboard Design: A digital dashboard is the digital page you see when you open up a web page. How a dash board is designed is crucial to the useability, effectiveness and accessibility of a web page. Dashboard design is the skill set behind designing and creating effective and accessible web pages.

Digital Diaries: A digital diary is very much the same as a traditional hand written diary. It differs however from a blog due to the chronological order and the interactivity with viewers (Rosen 2006). A digital diary is not interactive, readers are passive and do not partake in a dialogue with the author. Digital diaries are also often personal and not publically available.

eLearning: eLearning is the broad umbrella term that covers the use of electronic tools and technology in teaching and learning. ELearning incorporates many different aspects of technology in education and includes things such as information and communication technology (ICT), LMS's, MOOCS, VLE's, PLE's and multimedia learning. Barclay (2001) argues that elearning technologies have changed the way that both learning and teaching is being conducted across the broad educational landscape. It is Barclay's (2001) opinion that these changing educational paradigms are eroding the traditional dominance of instructional classroom learning and changing the way that people view educational pedagogies across the board. The origins of the term 'eLearning' according to Luskin (2003), is debatable. The 'e' in 'eLearning' could it is argued, stand for more than electronic. Luskin (2003) recommended that a broader perspective should be considered. The 'e' for example, could stand for other things such as: exciting, energetic, emotional or educational.

Inter-Professional Education: This refers to the occasions when students from two or more professions learn together during their professional training with the objective of fostering collaborative practice. The term is usually applied to student interns working in the health or social care professions.

Learning Management System (LMS): An LMS is a software programme used by educational institutions to document, track, report and deliver electronic educational technology. There are vast array of programmes designed for differing educational needs including courses that are primarily online or distance education as well as acting as accessible programmes that offer blended learning or augmented information for face-to-face courses.

Real Work Experience: In regards to this article 'real world experience' refers to the professional experiences that the students encounter during their internships. These experiences are broad and differ to the hypothetical experiences that have been discussed in the classroom. It is critical to the long-term work success for these students to encounter the broad experiences that only a professional internship can offer. Glogoff (2005) argues that in particular, blogging offers students a valuable way to share their real world experiences within an accessible online environment.

Reflective Practice: Learning from professional experience by consciously analyzing decisions and actions and drawing on relevant theories and the experience of others to assist with evaluating how to improve practice. According to Lasley (1992) reflective practice relies on the teacher's capacity to think creatively, and imaginatively as well as to think critically about their classroom practice.

Reflective Writing: According to Cisero (2006) reflective writing is the process of writing about personal experiences, while either analysing or critiquing information, synthesizing information, or creating a product based on that information. Reflective writing has been argued to be critical in the process of understanding contextualising new information and meaningful interactions (Elbow, 1993). Within tertiary education the process of reflective writing has been attributed to both helping students gain a deep level of understanding of their subjects and also promoting in-depth reflection outside their studies and into their broader lives.

Transformative Learning: This is when an individual becomes aware of having limitations in their views so through self-examination and critical reflection they explore alternatives and through this process they change their perspective and find new meaning. Reflective writing is a critical part of the process of transformative learning. It has been argued by Lang (2009) that 'transformative learning' should aim to explore different perspectives in a non-challenging and accessible manner.

Chapter 6
A Mixed Methods Examination of Instructor Social Presence in Accelerated Online Courses

Patrick Ryan Lowenthal
Boise State University, USA

ABSTRACT

Social Presence theory seeks to explain how people present themselves as being "there" and "real" while using a communication medium. Most studies on social presence focus on how students present themselves and/or are perceived as being "there" and "real" in computer-mediated environments. However, to date, very few studies have focused on how instructors establish and maintain their own social presence in online learning environments. The following study explored the phenomenon of instructor social presence in accelerated online courses. The results suggest that the construct of presence is more complicated than previously thought and that future studies should employ multiple methods to further explore the concept of instructor social presence.

INTRODUCTION

Many people, faculty included, remain skeptical of online learning (Jaschik & Lederman, 2014). While most of the critics of online learning focus on whether or not students learn as much in online courses as face-to-face courses, there is a deep seated fear that online learning will eventually replace the "teacher" and that students will end up taking teacherless courses online (Shank, 2008; Wilson & Christoper, 2008). Proponents of online learning, however, have been arguing for some time that there is a successful instructor behind every high quality online course (Dunlap, 2005; Wilson, Ludwig-Hardman, Thornam, & Dunlap, 2004). High quality online courses are designed and taught by real people. However, this is often overlooked because the role of an instructor changes in online courses (Kearsley, 2000; Palloff & Pratt, 1999, 2001, 2003). Online instructors are often no longer at the center of every interaction. Instead, they often find themselves intentionally acting more as a moderator or facilitator of learning (Dabbagh & Bannan-Ritland, 2005)--becoming more of a "guide-on-the-side." This approach, though, can become problematic when students

DOI: 10.4018/978-1-4666-9582-5.ch006

begin to question an instructor's presence in the online classroom (Smith & Taveras, 2005).

Previous research on online learning has shown that students can feel isolated and alone in the online classroom (Kilgore & Lowenthal, 2015; McInnerney & Roberts, 2004). Students need to get a firm sense that they are not alone and that there are other real people in the class with them; that is, students need to get a sense of social presence. Research on social presence has illustrated the importance of being perceived as being "there" and "real" in the online classroom (Lowenthal, 2009). For instance, researchers have shown that there is a relationship between social presence and student satisfaction (Gunawardena, 1995; Gunawardena & Zittle, 1997; Richardson & Swan, 2003; So & Brush, 2008), social presence and the development of a community of learners (Rourke, Anderson, Garrison, & Archer, 2001; Rovai, 2002), and social presence and perceived learning (Caspi & Blau, 2008; Richardson & Swan, 2003) to name a few. However, despite the growing body of research on social presence, very little research has focused specifically on the unique role of instructors and the arguably even greater need for instructors to establish their own social presence in the online classroom. Immediately establishing an instructor's presence can be challenging because it takes time to develop presence—especially in completely text-based environments (Tidwell & Walther, 2002; Venable, 2011; Walther, 1996). Establishing social presence then becomes even more challenging in accelerated online courses that are offered in abbreviated formats (e.g., an 8-week as opposed to 16-week format). As more and more institutions begin to offer accelerated online courses—whether during the fall and spring semesters or only during the summer—instructors and instructional designers need to better understand how instructors establish their own instructor social presence in accelerated online courses. Given this, the purpose of this study was to explore the construct of instructor social presence in accelerated online courses.

BACKGROUND

The theory of social presence was developed in the 1970s by Short, Williams, and Christie (1976). Short et al. were interested in how media influences how people communicate. They posited that some media have a higher social presence than others. However, they completed most of their work long before the rise of computer-mediated communication. Text-based computer-mediated communication (e.g., email and threaded discussion forums) did not begin to be used on a regular basis until the 1980s for business and then the 1990s for education (see Lowenthal, 2009). And while early research by Gunawardena and others (Gunawardena, 1995; Gunawardena & Zittle, 1997) began to explore the concept of social presence and text-based computer-mediated communication, Garrison, Anderson, and Archer's (2000) work on the Community of Inquiry (CoI) Framework is what ultimately pushed the concept of social presence in the forefront of the research and practice of online learning. Garrison et al. posited that a meaningful educational experience consists of three presences—social presence, teaching presence, and cognitive presence—that result in a community of inquiry.

Garrison's early work suggests that the CoI was ultimately an attempt to describe any learner-centered "constructivist" learning experience—not simply, those learning experiences that happen solely online (see Garrison, 1989; Garrison & Shale, 1990). The CoI clearly places the learner at the center of the educational experience. And while the CoI highlights the importance of teaching, through the inclusion of teaching presence as one of three core parts of a meaningful educational experience, Garrison and his colleagues did not see the act of teaching being done solely by instructors—which they explain is why it is called teaching presence and not teacher presence (Anderson, Rourke, Garrison, & Archer, 2001).

They defined teaching presence as,

the design, facilitation, and direction of cognitive and social processes for the purpose of realizing personally meaningful and educationally worthwhile outcomes. Teaching presence begins before the course commences as the teacher, acting as instructional designer, plans and prepares the course of studies, and it continues during the course, as the instructor facilitates the discourse and provides direct instruction when required. (p. 5)

Simply put, teaching presence involves instructional design and organization, direct instruction, and the facilitation of discourse in the goal of establishing social presence and cognitive presence. Research suggests that teaching presence—both when designing and facilitating online courses—is a key component of an effective online course and a meaningful educational experience (Anderson et al., 2001; Garrison et al., 2000; Shea, 2006; Shea, Fredericksen, Pickett, & Pelz, 2003; Shea, Li, & Pickett, 2006; Shea, Swan, & Pickett, 2005). However, I contend that how instructors establish their own social presence—not only through their instructional design, direct instruction, and facilitation of discourse—but also through their interactions with students, both within and outside of a learning management system as well as within and without of the discussion forums, is equally important (see Baker, 2010; Dennen, 2005; Mandermach, Gonzales, & Garrett, 2006; Richardson & Swan, 2003; Swan & Shih, 2005).

As an initial step into studying this larger phenomenon, this study explores how instructors establish their own social presence (i.e. "instructor social presence") through *facilitation* in asynchronous threaded discussions. While effective instructional design and direct instruction are key components of a meaningful and successful educational experience, these are components of a course that a growing number of faculty have little control over. At many universities, like the one where this study was conducted, faculty (especially adjuncts) teach courses designed by

others (see Lowenthal, 2012; McCluskey, 2006; Patton, 2014). So while effective instructional design and direct instruction are critical, more and more faculty find themselves teaching courses they did not design and cannot modify (Lowenthal, 2012). Therefore, it is important to investigate the nature of instructor social presence in situations likes these where facilitating discourse might be the primary method to establish and maintain an instructor's own social presence.

The design or format of an online course can influence how faculty and students develop and perceive social presence. For instance, having online faculty meet his/her students face-to-face before a course begins can effect a student's perception of presence (Lowenthal, 2009). In addition, whether or not a student is part of a cohort can also influence how presence is developed and perceived (Lowenthal, 2009). However, past research on social presence and teaching presence has not focused enough on how details like these can influence someone's perceptions of presence (Lowenthal, 2009, 2012; Lowenthal, Lowenthal, White & 2009). This study set out to explore instructor social presence in completely online asynchronous courses where students never meet face-to-face and are not part of a cohort.

The issue of time also needs to be considered when researching presence. Time, similar to course format, can and should influence an instructor's presence (Tu & Corry, 2004). For instance, whether faculty and students spend 5 weeks, 8 weeks, or 16 weeks communicating online should influence how social presence is developed, maintained, and perceived (see Walther, 1996). However, often these details are glossed over in research on presence (Lowenthal, 2009, 2012; Lowenthal, Lowenthal, & White, 2009). More and more institutions are beginning to offer accelerated online courses (i.e., courses that are less than a traditional 10 week quarter or 15 week semester) (Ross-Gordon, 2011; Tiley, 2014; Wlodkowski, 2003). For instance, in the state of Colorado, public institutions like Colorado

State University, non-profit private institutions like Regis University, and for-profit institutions like the University of Phoenix all offer accelerated online courses. More research needs to be conducted on how social presence and teaching presence develop in accelerated online courses.

METHODS

To study the nature of instructor social presence in accelerated asynchronous online courses, three accelerated, 8-week long, online courses were randomly selected from a pool of online graduate teacher education courses offered in a school of education at a private nonprofit university. I will refer to this university as Private University (P.U.). Students in these courses were predominantly fulltime working adults who were working on obtaining a teaching license. Following the work of Anderson et al. (2001), one week of each course was purposefully identified for analysis.

Previous research on social presence tends to either try to identify observable indicators of social presence by analyzing course discussions—usually with only one method of analysis—or survey students about their perceptions of social presence (Lowenthal & Leech, 2009). Researchers of online learning, and specifically those who focus on social presence, need to spend more time employing multiple methods of analysis (Lowenthal & Leech, 2009). Henceforth, multiple methods of analysis were used to explore the data in an effort to get a detailed understanding and an accurate depiction of instructor social presence in accelerated courses.

A mixed methods exploratory methodology (Miles & Huberman, 1994; Onwuegbuzie & Leech, 2005) utilizing both quantitative and qualitative methods was used in this study. Exploratory methods have traditionally been related to qualitative methods and confirmatory methods to quantitative methods. However, Onwuegbuzie and Teddlie (2003) illustrate that both quantita-

tive and qualitative data analyses can be used to understand a phenomena. In order to explore instructor social presence effectively, online course discussions were analyzed with multiple forms of data analysis—specifically, word count, content analysis, and constant comparative analysis.

The course discussions from all three courses were compiled and downloaded from the learning management system. Names were changed to protect anonymity. The transcripts were initially explored with word count to get an overall sense of the data. Then the online discussions were analyzed using content analysis. Finally, constant comparative analysis was used to search for themes and trends that did not emerge with the previous forms of analysis.

RESULTS AND DISCUSSION

Multiple methods of analysis were used to explore the data in an effort to develop a better understanding of how, if at all, instructors at P.U. establish their instructor social presence when teaching accelerated online courses. The first type of analysis used was a *type* of word count. Traditionally word count involves identifying deductively a word or words from the literature on a subject or inductively identifying from the data specific words that seem out of place or hold special meaning and then counting the frequency of these words (Onwuegbuzie, Leech, & Collins, 2012). Instead of counting the frequency of specific words, the total number of discussion postings and words posted by faculty and students were collected and compared. The numbers were collected and compiled from the discussion forums in the LMS for each course. Analyzing discussions posts in this manner was common in early research of online learning (Henri, 1992). However, over time researchers of online learning began to move beyond this basic level of inquiry. While simply counting words is limited in explanatory value, word count remains a helpful way to *initially* explore data when used in conjunction with other methods of analysis (Lowenthal & Leech, 2009).

Word count revealed that students were responsible for 88.78% of the postings and 94.45% of the words posted in these accelerated online courses (see Table 1 and Table 2). While these results do not address the quality of the postings, they do illustrate the quantity or frequency of participation of students compared to their instructors in the online discussion forums. While faculty had a higher frequency of postings (averaging 11.37 per faculty member) compared to students (averaging 7.69 per student), faculty posted fewer words in the discussion forum (1464 words used by faculty compared to 24,912 used by students), which coupled with the overall larger number of student postings, resulted in an overall perception that the discussions were student ran and student focused. These results show that students posted more as a whole than the faculty in the courses in this sample. While there has been some research on accelerated or intensive courses—most of which has focused on nursing programs (see Cangelosi & Whitt, 2005; Driessnack et al., 2011; Lindsey, 2009, Penprase, 2012; Penprase & Koczara, 2009; Rico, Beall, & Davies, 2010; Rafferty &

Lindell, 2001; Seamon, 2004), there has been very little research conducted specifically on accelerated online courses. In fact, in one of the only books on accelerated teaching, Wlodkowski and Ginsberg (2010) are quick to point out that their accelerated teaching principles only address face-to-face courses. This paucity of research on accelerated online courses only leaves previous research on non-accelerated online courses as a point of comparison. As a whole the breakdown of participation in this sample is similar to previous research on non-accelerated online courses (see, Hara, Bonk, & Angeli, 2000; Picciano, 2002; Rourke et al., 1999).

While this initial descriptive data could be interpreted as suggesting that these discussions were student centered, it could equally suggest that the instructors were relatively inactive or absent from the discussions. Further analysis, however, is needed to better understand the instructors' role in these discussions. For instance, the variation in the frequency of postings could be due to multiple students asking the same question, which in turn leads to the instructor posting one answer for the entire course. Further, instructors each have their own style of facilitating discourse. Some instructors like to be heavily involved from the beginning

Table 1. Total Number of postings

	Courses			Total
	ED 501	**ED 502**	**ED503**	**Total**
Number of students	13	14	8	35
Number of student postings	109	103	57	269
Number of words in student postings	11228	11712	1972	24912
Number of faculty	1	1	1	3
Number of faculty postings	12	15	7	34
Number of words in faculty postings	1009	299	156	1464
Total number of participants	14	15	9	38
Total number of postings	121	118	64	303
Total number of words	12237	12011	2128	26376

Table 2. Frequency of postings as an entire case

	Total participants	% of Postings	% of Words
Student	35	88.78%	94.45%
Faculty	3	11.22%	5.55%
Total	38	100%	100%

of each week, others like to wait until a certain point in the discussions to begin participating, while others focus on simply summarizing the discussion at the end of the week (see Anderson, et al., 2001). More research, though, is needed to see how facilitation styles might change in accelerated courses. Further, additional research needs to be conducted about how the amount and content of instructors' postings influence students' behavior in online courses. There is a fine line between being involved in discussions and facilitating discussions versus leading or dominating discussions (Mazzolini & Maddison, 2003, 2007).

Classical content analysis was then used to explore the data in an effort to better understand the content of the instructors' postings. Classical content analysis is similar to constant comparison analysis. However, instead of creating themes, the focus of classical content analysis is to identify the frequency of specific codes in the data. This type of analysis is helpful when there are a lot of codes. Classical content analysis helps identify which codes are used most often and it is complimentary to constant comparative analysis (Onwuegbuzie, Leech, & Collins, 2012).

To conduct classical content analysis, the data are partitioned into small chunks, as in Table 3. Each chunk is labeled with a code, or descriptive label; due to the unique nature of online postings, descriptive coding was used to capture the type of posting. For example, "post chart here" and "using REPLY post bulleted list of points here" were both coded as "directions," whereas the following was coded as "questioning": "Do you think that parents often do not want to accept or acknowledge the problems that their children might have?"

As shown in Table 4, the codes are then counted to assess which concepts (represented by codes) are used most frequently; for example, "closing remarks" were used most frequently (see Table 5 for the complete list and frequency of the data coded).

Table 3. Example of chunking the data

Data Chunked	Code
Post chart here	Directions
Using REPLY post bulleted list of points here.	Directions
Using REPLY post your discussion here.	Directions
Since *there are eight students in the class,*	Number of students
our groups	Inclusion
will really be pairs.	Groups of two
Melaine,	Greeting
I need	Teacher request
an email address for you.	Contact information
Elden	Closing remark
Are you accustomed	Questioning
to *writing assignment in APA format?*	Writing style
If not, *I would like* you	Teacher request
to learn to use the APA format for citations and are references. Here is a	Writing style
wonderful website	Resource
that *makes that easy to do.*	Make easier
Here is a website that is a great tool for	Resource
helping you get your reference page correct	Make easier
according to APA. http://www.citationmachine.net/index.php	Writing style
Elden	Closing remark

Table 4. Results from a classical content analysis

Code	Number of Times Used
Closing remark	14
Directions	12
Positive feedback	11
Greeting	8
Questioning	6
Answering question	5
Elaboration / clarification	5
Writing style Resource	3 3
Number of students Inclusive language Teacher request Colorado law Faculty seeking feedback Empathy	2 2 2 2 2 2
Welcoming Negotiation Accommodation Contact information	1 1 1 1

Classical content analysis revealed that "closing remarks" were used the most (14 times), followed by "Directions" (12 times), and "Positive feedback" (11 times). Table 4 illustrates the frequency of each descriptive code in the faculty postings. Greetings and closing remarks have been identified as an observable indicator of social presence (see Rourket et al., 1999). Working from the indicators of teaching presence developed by Anderson et al., (2001), giving directions is basically a form of instructional design and organization (i.e., Teaching Presence). The fact that faculty spent most of their time giving directions, giving positive feedback, questioning students, and answering questions is important. This suggests that faculty in this sample were focusing on direct instruction, instructional design, and facilitating discourse. This analysis also suggests that the faculty in this sample were spending very little time welcoming, negotiating, or accommodating students' needs online. In other words, they were spending more time on teaching presence than they were on social presence.

The final type of analysis conducted was Constant Comparative Analysis. Constant Comparative Analysis is useful when trying to explore and understand the big picture of a phenomenon like teaching online (Lowenthal & Leech, 2009). In constant comparative analysis, the researcher reads the data and partitions it into small chunks, as can be seen in Table 5. For example, the following post was chunked into six small chunks:

Hello everyone!

I love the educational environments you have created this week. Educators and students should always be the ones who create our schools. It is inspirational to see so many of you create from the schools you have been in or are currently in.

Thanks for your creativity!

Dr. Bob.

Table 5. Results from constant comparative analysis

Codes	Grouping of Codes
Closing remark	**Course logistics** Directions
Directions	Writing style Number of students
Positive feedback	Teacher request
Greeting	Colorado law
Questioning	**Greetings and Salutations** Welcoming
Answering question	Greeting
Elaboration / clarification	Closing remark
Writing style Resource	**Teaching / Facilitation** Questioning Answering questions
Number of students Inclusive language Teacher request Colorado law Faculty seeking feedback Empathy	Elaboration / clarification Positive feedback Resource **Caring teacher** Inclusive language Empathy Faculty seeking feedback
Welcoming Negotiation Accommodation Contact information	Negotiation Accommodation Contact information

Each chunk is then labeled with a code while constantly comparing new codes with previous ones. For instance, the previous example yielded the following six codes: (a) Greeting, (b) Positive feedback, (c) Elaboration / Clarification, (d) Positive feedback, (e) Positive feedback, and (f) Closing remark. The codes are then grouped together. Once the codes are grouped together, the researcher identifies a theme that has emerged from the data.

The most prevalent theme that emerged from the constant comparative analysis is the following:

While faculty at P.U. have to deal with day to day course logistics, such as directions on how to complete assignments and course expectations, they play more of a role as a facilitator through the use of questioning, elaborating/clarifying, and giving positive feedback than as a instructor or giver of knowledge.

All three types of analysis—the word count, the classical content analysis, and the constant comparative analysis—offered insight into how these instructors communicated online and the degree to which they strived to establish their own instructor social presence in the online course discussions. While all three types of analysis offered a different perspective or glimpse of the truth space, classical content analysis and constant comparative analysis did a better job of highlighting how these faculty communicated online. These two types of analysis illustrate that faculty in this sample spent some time establishing their own social presence. For example, greetings, positive feedback, questioning are all examples of social presence (Rourke et al., 1999). So even though these instructors are teaching accelerated 8-week courses designed by others, they show some evidence that even in an accelerated term faculty can begin to establish their own social presence. However, at the same time, they appear to be focused more on teaching presence and the goal of teaching students the content in a timely manner. I caution the reader from generalizing too much from these findings.

To date researchers have not identified what the appropriate amount of social presence is in an online course—let alone accelerated online courses. Further, research on accelerated learning (which predominantly focuses on face-to-face courses) suggests that a different type of student takes accelerated online courses as well that a different type of instructor might enjoy teaching this intense format. Therefore, more research is needed to support these findings.

Traditionally instructors' establish instructor social presence in online course discussion forums. Thus, it is important, significant, and commonplace to explore faculty behavior in online discussion forums. But instructors also establish their social presence in other ways (e.g., one-on-one emails and feedback on assignments) (Dunlap & Lowenthal, 2014). Therefore, one limitation of this study is the fact that it focused only on course discussions in three courses. Additional weeks as well as additional course sections need to be analyzed to support the findings of this study. Also more research needs to be done to triangulate the results in this study with other things such as student perceptions of online faculty as well as instructors' perceptions of their own social presence.

RECOMMENDATIONS AND DIRECTIONS FOR FUTURE RESEARCH

Past research on presence in the online classroom has predominantly focused on social presence. The majority of this research has specifically focused on students' perceptions of social presence within a community of inquiry (Dunlap & Lowenthal, 2014; Lowenthal, 2009, 2012). To date, very little research has focused on instructor social presence or how social presence is established in accelerated online courses.

Researchers have questioned for years whether or not there is a right amount of social presence; in other words, they have questioned whether there might be a tipping point in which there might be too much social presence (Lowenthal, 2012). The instructors in this study spent very little of their time intentionally establishing and maintain social presence in the online discussions. Instead, they focused more of their efforts, at least in the online discussion forums, on teaching presence and specifically on helping students successfully complete the course. It is impossible to discern from the data collected in this study whether or not this was an intentional move on the instructors or not. Previous research on accelerated programs suggests that students taking accelerated online courses tend to be non-traditional students, with lots of life experience, focused on learning skills that they can immediately apply in their day-to-day life. It is possible that these students care less about social presence than traditional students. However, at the same time, research on students in face-to-face accelerated programs does suggest that student's in these programs still want to build a relationship with their instructors and for their instructors to know who they are as students (Rico, Beal, & Davies, 2010); it is reasonable to suspect that students in accelerated online programs feel the same way. However, additional research needs to be conducted to confirm or deny this.

Additional research also needs to be conducted on whether or not students need for social presence is changing as they become more comfortable communicating online and taking online courses. It could be that as students get further along in their program of study online, they feel less of a need to spend time establishing a connection with their peers—especially in non-cohort-based programs where students might not see the relationships with other classmates persisting over time.

CONCLUSION

Three courses were randomly selected to explore the degree to which instructors establish their own instructor social presence in threaded discussions in accelerated fully online courses. Results suggest that while instructors did make attempts at establishing instructor social presence, most of their efforts focused on aspects of teaching presence such as instructional design and facilitating discourse. While the main purpose of this study was to investigate instructor social presence in accelerated online courses, a secondary purpose was to test a mixed methods approach of studying online discussions. Thus, the scholarly significance of this study lies not only in its investigation of an often overlooked area of study (i.e., instructor's social presence in accelerated online courses) but also and arguably more importantly in outlying a way in which other faculty can use word count, content analysis (whether with predefined codes or having the codes emerge from the discussions), and constant comparative analysis to study online discussions. Through using mixed method approaches of study, researchers can begin to get a better idea of what happens in online courses of all shapes and sizes.

REFERENCES

Anderson, T., Rourke, L., Garrison, D. R., & Archer, W. (2001). Assessing teaching presence in a computer conferencing context. *Journal of Asynchronous Learning Networks*, 5(2), 1–17.

Baker, C. (2010). The impact of instructor immediacy and presence for online student affective learning, cognition, and motivation. *The Journal of Educators Online*, 7(1), 1–30. Retrieved from http://www.thejeo.com/Archives/Volume7Number1/BakerPaper.pdf

Cangelosi, P. R., & Whitt, K. J. (2005). Accelerated nursing programs what do we know? *Nursing Education Perspectives*, 26(2), 113–116. PMID:15921128

Caspi, A., & Blau, I. (2008). Social presence in online discussion groups: Testing three conceptions and their relations to perceived learning. *Social Psychology of Education*, 11(3), 323–346. doi:10.1007/s11218-008-9054-2

Dabbagh, N., & Bannan-Ritland, B. (2005). *Online learning: Concepts, strategies, and application.* Upper Saddle River, NJ: Prentice Hall.

Dennen, V. P. (2005). From message posting to learning dialogues: Factors affecting learner participation in asynchronous discussion. *Distance Education, 26*(1), 127–148. doi:10.1080/01587910500081376

Driessnack, M., Mobily, P., Stineman, A., Montgomery, L. A., Clow, T., & Eisbach, S. (2011). We are different: Learning needs of accelerated second-degree nursing students. *Nurse Educator, 36*(5), 214–218. doi:10.1097/NNE.0b013e3182297c90 PMID:21857342

Dunlap, J. (2005). Workload reduction in online courses: Getting some shuteye. *Performance Improvement, 44*(5), 18–25. doi:10.1002/pfi.4140440507

Garrison, D. R. (1989). *Understanding distance education: A framework for the future.* London: Routledge.

Garrison, D. R., Anderson, T., & Archer, W. (2000). Critical inquiry in a text-based environment: Computer conferencing in higher education. *The Internet and Higher Education, 2*(2-3), 87–105. doi:10.1016/S1096-7516(00)00016-6

Garrison, D. R., & Shale, D. (Eds.). (1990). *Education at a distance: From issues to practice.* RE Krieger Publishing Company.

Gunawardena, C. N. (1995). Social presence theory and implications for interaction and collaborative learning in computer conferences. *International Journal of Educational Telecommunications, 1*(2/3), 147–166.

Gunawardena, C. N., & Zittle, F. J. (1997). Social presence as a predictor of satisfaction within a computer-mediated conferencing environment. *American Journal of Distance Education, 11*(3), 8–26. doi:10.1080/08923649709526970

Hara, N., Bonk, C. J., & Angeli, C. (2000). Content analysis of online discussion in an applied educational psychology course. *Instructional Science, 28*(2), 115–152. doi:10.1023/A:1003764722829

Henri, F. (1992). Computer conferencing and content analysis. In A. R. Kaye (Ed.), *Collaborative learning through computer conferencing* (pp. 117–136). Berlin, Germany: Springer. doi:10.1007/978-3-642-77684-7_8

Jaschik, S., & Lederman, D. (2014). The 2014 Inside Higher Ed Survey of Faculty Attitudes on Technology: A Study by Gallup and Inside Higher Ed. *Inside Higher Ed.* Retrieved from http://www.insidehighered.com/download/form.php?width=500&height=550&iframe=true&title=Survey%20of%20Faculty%20Attitudes%20on%20Technology&file=IHEFacTechSurvey2014%20final.pdf

Kearsley, G. (2000). *Online education: Learning and teaching in cyberspace.* Belmont, CA: Wadsworth.

Kilgore, W., & Lowenthal, P. R. (2015). The Human Element MOOC: An experiment in social presence. In R. D. Wright (Ed.), *Establishing an equitable and fair admissions system for an online* (pp. 389–407). Hershey, PA: IGI Global. doi:10.4018/978-1-4666-6461-6.ch017

Lindsey, P. (2009). Starting an accelerated baccalaureate nursing program: Challenges and opportunities for creative educational innovations. *The Journal of Nursing Education, 48*(5), 279–281. PMID:19476033

Mandermach, B. J., Gonzales, R. M., & Garrett, A. L. (2006). An examination of online instructor presence via threaded discussion participation. *Journal of Online Learning and Teaching, 2*(4), 248–260.

Mazzolini, M., & Maddison, S. (2003). Sage, guide or ghost? The effect of instructor intervention on student participation in online discussion forums. *Computers & Education, 40*(3), 237–253. doi:10.1016/S0360-1315(02)00129-X

Mazzolini, M., & Maddison, S. (2007). When to jump in: The role of the instructor in online discussion forums. *Computers & Education, 49*(2), 193–213. doi:10.1016/j.compedu.2005.06.011

McCluskey, M. (2006). Are canned courses impacting academic freedom? *Adjunct Nation*. Retrieved from http://www.adjunctnation.com/2006/01/01/50-are-canned-courses-impacting-academic-freedom/

McInnerney, J. M., & Roberts, T. S. (2004). Online learning: Social interaction and the creation of a sense of community. *Journal of Educational Technology & Society, 7*(3), 73–81.

Miles, M., & Huberman, A. M. (1994). *Qualitative data analysis: An expanded sourcebook* (2nd ed.). Thousand Oaks, CA: Sage.

Onwuegbuzie, A. J., & Leech, N. L. (2005). On becoming a pragmatic researcher: The importance of combining quantitative and qualitative research methodologies. *International Journal of Social Research Methodology, 8*(5), 375–387. doi:10.1080/13645570500402447

Onwuegbuzie, A. J., Leech, N. L., & Collins, K. M. (2012). Qualitative analysis techniques for the review of the literature. *Qualitative Report, 17*(56), 1–28.

Onwuegbuzie, A. J., & Teddlie, C. (2003). A framework for analyzing data in mixed methods research. In A. Tashakkori & C. Teddlie (Eds.), *Handbook of mixed methods in social and behavioral research* (pp. 351–383). Thousand Oaks, CA: Sage.

Palloff, R. N., & Pratt, K. (1999). *Building learning communities in cyberspace*. San Francisco: Jossey-Bass.

Palloff, R. N., & Pratt, K. (2001). *Lessons from the cyberspace classroom: The realties of online teaching*. San Francisco: Jossey-Bass.

Palloff, R. N., & Pratt, K. (2003). *The virtual student: A profile and guide to working with online learners*. San Francisco: Jossey-Bass.

Patton, S. (2014, October). On the Internet, nobody knows you're the 'wrong' professor. *Chronicle Vitae*. Retrieved from https://chroniclevitae.com/news/733-on-the-internet-nobody-knows-you-re-the-wrong-professor

Penprase, B. (2012). Perceptions, orientation, and transition into nursing practice of accelerated second-degree nursing program graduates. *Journal of Continuing Education in Nursing, 43*(1), 29–36. doi:10.3928/00220124-20110315-02 PMID:21425758

Penprase, B., & Koczara, S. (2009). Understanding the experiences of accelerated second-degree nursing students and graduates: A review of the literature. *Journal of Continuing Education in Nursing, 40*(2), 74–78. doi:10.3928/00220124-20090201-08 PMID:19263928

Picciano, A. G. (2002). Beyond student perceptions: Issues of interaction, presence, and performance in an online course. *Journal of Asynchronous Learning Networks, 6*(1), 21–40.

Rafferty, M., & Lindell, D. (2011). How nurse managers rate the clinical competencies of accelerated (second-degree) nursing graduates. *The Journal of Nursing Education, 50*(6), 355–358. doi:10.3928/01484834-20110228-07 PMID:21366163

Ragan, L. (1999). Good teaching is good teaching: An emerging set of guiding principles and practices for the design and development of distance education. *CAUSE/EFFECT, 22*(1).

Richardson, J. C., & Swan, K. (2003). Examining social presence in online courses in relation to students' perceived learning and satisfaction. *Journal of Asynchronous Learning Networks, 7*(1), 68–88.

Rico, J. S., Beal, J., & Davies, T. (2010). Promising practices for faculty in accelerated nursing programs. *The Journal of Nursing Education, 49*(3), 150–155. doi:10.3928/01484834-20100115-01 PMID:20143760

Ross-Gordon, J. M. (2011). Research on adult learners: Supporting the needs of a student population that is no longer nontraditional. *Peer Review, 13*(1), 26–29.

Rourke, L., Anderson, T., Garrison, D. R., & Archer, W. (1999). Assessing social presence in asynchronous text-based computer conferencing. *Journal of Distance Education, 14*. Retrieved from http://cade.athabascau.ca/vol14.2/ rourke_ et_al.html

Rovai, A. P. (2002). Building a sense of community at a distance. *International Review of Research in Open and Distance Learning, 3*(1). Retrieved from http://www.irrodl.org/index.php/ irrodl/article/view/79/153

Seamon, M. (2004). Short- and long-term differences in instructional effectiveness between intensive and semester-length courses. *Teachers College Record, 106*(4), 635–650. doi:10.1111/ j.1467-9620.2004.00360.x

Shank, P. (2008). Thinking critically to move e-Learning forward. In S. Carliner & P. Shank (Eds.), *The e-learning handbook: A comprehensive guide to online learning* (pp. 15–26). San Francisco, CA: Pfeiffer.

Shea, P., Li, C. S., & Pickett, A. (2006). A study of teaching presence and student sense of learning community in fully online and web-enhanced college courses. *The Internet and Higher Education, 9*(3), 175–190. doi:10.1016/j.iheduc.2006.06.005

Shea, P. J. (2006). A study of students' sense of learning community in online environments. *Journal of Asynchronous Learning Networks, 10*(1). Retrieved from http://www.sloan-c.org/ publications/JALN/v10n1/pdf/v10n1_4shea.pdf

Shea, P. J., Fredericksen, E. E., Pickett, A. M., & Pelz, W. E. (2003). A preliminary investigation of "Teaching Presence" in the SUNY Learning Network. In J. Bourne & J. C. Moore (Eds.), *Elements of quality online education: Practice and direction* (pp. 279–310). Needham, MA: Slocan-C.

Shea, P. J., Swan, K., & Pickett, A. M. (2005). Teaching presence and establishment of community in online learning environments. In J. C. Moore (Ed.), *Engaging communities, wisdom from the Sloan Consortium* (pp. 53–66). Needham, MA: Sloan-C.

Short, J., Williams, E., & Christie, B. (1976). *The social psychology of telecommunications*. London: John Wiley & Sons.

Smith, G. G., & Taveras, M. (2005, January). The missing instructor. *eLearn*. Retrieved from http:// elearnmag.acm.org/featured.cfm?aid=1070933

So, H.-Y., & Brush, T. (2008). Students perceptions of collaborative learning, social presence, and satisfaction in blended learning environment: Relationships and critical factors. *Computers & Education, 51*(1), 318–336. doi:10.1016/j. compedu.2007.05.009

Swan, K., & Shih, L. F. (n.d.). On the nature and development of social presence in online course discussions. *Journal of Asynchronous Learning Networks, 9*(3), 115–136.

Tidwell, L. C., & Walther, J. B. (2002). Computer-mediated communication effects on disclosure, impressions, and interpersonal evaluations: Getting to know one another a bit at a time. *Human Communication Research*, 28(3), 317–348. doi:10.1111/j.1468-2958.2002.tb00811.x

Tilley, B. P. (2014). What makes a student nontraditional? A comparison of students over and under age 25 in online, accelerated psychology courses. *Psychology Learning & Teaching*, 13(2), 95–106. doi:10.2304/plat.2014.13.2.95

Tu, C.-H., & Corry, M. (2004). Online discussion durations impact online social presence. C. C. In et al. (Eds.), *Proceedings of Society for Information Technology and Teacher Education International Conference 2004* (pp. 3073-3077). Chesapeake, VA: AACE.

Venable, M. (2011, December). Who is the instructor? Developing social presence in an online course. *Online College.org*. Retrieved from http://www.onlinecollege.org/2011/12/27/who-is-the-instructor-developing-social-presence-in-an-online-course/

Walther, J. B. (1996). Computer-mediated communication impersonal, interpersonal, and hyperpersonal interaction. *Communication Research*, 23(1), 3–43. doi:10.1177/009365096023001001

Wilson, B. G., & Christopher, L. (2008). Hype versus reality on campus: Why e-Learning isn't likely to replace a professor. In S. Carliner & P. Shank (Eds.), *The e-learning handbook: A comprehensive guide to online learning* (pp. 55–76). San Francisco, CA: Pfeiffer.

Wilson, B. G., Ludwig-Hardman, S., Thornam, C. L., & Dunlap, J. (2004). Bounded community: Designing and facilitating learning communities in formal courses. *International Review of Research in Open and Distance Learning*, 5(3). Retrieved from http://www.irrodl.org/index.php/irrodl/article/view/204/286

Wlodkowski, R. J. (2003, Spring). Accelerated learning in colleges and universities. *New Directions for Adult and Continuing Education*, 97(97), 5–16. doi:10.1002/ace.84

Wlodkowski, R. J., & Ginsberg, M. B. (2010). *Teaching intensive and accelerated courses: Instruction that motivates learning*. San Francisco, CA: John Wiley & Sons.

KEY TERMS AND DEFINITIONS

Accelerated Online Courses: Formal for-credit online courses offered in a compressed format (e.g., a 16-week semester course is offered in an abbreviated 8-week format).

Asynchronous Threaded Discussions: Online discussions that take place within a learning management system over time (e.g., over a given week).

Community of Inquiry: A framework that posits that a meaningful educational experience consists of teaching presence, social presence, and cognitive presence.

Instructor Social Presence: The way an instructor establishes oneself as a "real" person and "there" using communication media while teaching.

Mixed Methods Research: Research that employs quantitative and qualitative approaches to study a problem or phenomena.

Social Presence: Establishing oneself as "real" and "there" using a communication medium.

Teaching Presence: The design and facilitation of social and cognitive processes toward an educational goal.

Chapter 7

"I'm Not Simply Dealing with Some Heartless Computer":
Videoconferencing as Personalized Online Learning in a Graduate Literacy Course

Peggy Lynn Semingson
University of Texas at Arlington, USA

Pete Smith
The University of Texas at Arlington, USA

ABSTRACT

This chapter provides a case study example using cross-case analysis (Merriam, 2001) of digital mentoring within an online Master's level literacy course at a large public university in the Southwest United States. Two mentors provided individualized video conference sessions, using Blackboard Collaborate™ to 28 students (mentees). Data included written reflections from students as well as transcripts from selected videoconference sessions. Structured synchronous mentoring sessions provided a predictable framework for students and mentors alike. This chapter provides an analysis of the students' perceptions of the conferences, the types of discourse patterns and language analysis of the conferences, as well as description of themes and trends across the data. Suggestions on the usefulness of the conferences as well as the structure of mentoring sessions are described in the chapter. Established and emerging models of mentorship and e-development are outlined and utilized to frame the analyses and future research directions.

INTRODUCTION

This chapter reports on the results of an exploratory research study examining the uses, affordances, and constraints of individualized mentoring through desktop videoconferencing tools in an on-line graduate course in literacy studies. The study used real-time telecollaboration and synchronous digital mentoring to scaffold students' learning in an effort to bring the interpersonal aspects to an online-only teaching context. Both authors bring years of experience in working within online-only

DOI: 10.4018/978-1-4666-9582-5.ch007

or hybrid teaching contexts. The first author has been teaching online since 2008 and the second author is currently Vice President of the Division of Digital Teaching Learning at a large public university in the Southwest United States. In the summer of 2012 the university began a pilot project for a small group of selected faculty to integrate synchronous learning (Blackboard Collaborate™) into online teaching. The first author implemented regular use of Blackboard Collaborate for the purposes of individualized digital mentoring of students for this project.

A major purpose of implementing individualized synchronous learning sessions via regularly scheduled videoconferencing sessions was to increase the amount of personalized learning that took place in the course. Previous versions of the same course primarily relied on asynchronous discussion board conversations where students responded in writing to peers on the course readings. Therefore, digital mentoring was new to the two mentors (the lead instructor and a teaching assistant) on two levels. First, the mentoring component was new to the course and the regular use of the synchronous component was new to both mentors.

Throughout most of the chapter, the authors refer to graduate students in the class who participated in the mentoring sessions as "mentees". Nearly all of the mentees in the course reported that they had never engaged in any kind of synchronous learning activities as an online course requirement prior to this implementation in the summer 2012 course. However, several students indicated that they had engaged in synchronous learning as part of teacher professional development or in other contexts.

Following the summer 2012 course session, both authors wished to analyze the types of interactions and discussion topics that were taking place in the digital mentoring sessions. The authors also wished to know the students' perceptions of the sessions. Therefore, we used the case study format (Merriam, 2001) and qualitative analysis

(Miles & Huberman, 1994; Strauss & Corbin, 2008) to examine program effectiveness of the videoconferencing component of an online graduate course. Evaluation of program effectiveness is an aspect of teacher education research that Chris Dede and colleagues describe in the following way: "The purpose of this type of research is to immediately measure the perceived value of program design components and content as well as to assess learner satisfaction." (Dede et al., 2005, p. 11). Furthermore, online learning is becoming a primary learning context (Allen & Seaman, 2010), yet the research to keep up with this subject within teacher education, and literacy education in particular, is lacking. Very little research literature exists in the area of specifically using digital mentoring with synchronous tools in teacher education. The two research questions that guided this study are listed below.

Question 1: What is the perceived impact of increased teacher presence done via synchronous, 1-on-1 videoconference mentoring in a graduate online literacy course?

Question 2: What is the development of teachers via digital mentoring, as documented in the qualitative data of session transcripts?

BACKGROUND

This chapter draws on several writers who describe the mentoring of adults as well as the broader literature of best practices with online learning and synchronous real-time learning, in particular. Research into academic mentoring has covered informal and formal mentoring in both undergraduate and graduate academic settings (e.g., Jacobi, 1991). Theoretical frameworks for the mentoring process, according to Jacobi (1991), are varied and multi-faceted, and can include social learning theory, academic and social learning, social support, and developmental support. Additionally, the study draws upon the key components of effective mentoring for adult learners as identified in Cohen describing his *Adult Mentoring Inventory* (Cohen, 2003). These components, according to Cohen include: trust, advice, alternative, challenge, motivation, and initiative. Key ideas on mentoring of adults from Daloz (2012) inform the perspective of the researchers. Finally, we draw on seminal ideas from the multifaceted model of digital mentoring provided by Murphy et al. (2005) as well as the broader idea of teacher presence and the Community of Inquiry framework (e.g., Garrison, Anderson, & Archer, 2000; Garrison & Arbaugh, 2007).

The Many Definitions of Mentoring

Research into academic mentoring has covered informal and formal mentoring in both undergraduate and graduate academic settings (Jacobi, 1991). Daloz (2012) provides one of the most widely accepted definitions of mentorship--with the key elements of: providing support, challenge, and vision. Mentors engender empathy and trust, while supporting student learning and growth. Rather than traditional classroom-style instruction, mentors challenge their students with tasks that differ from traditional or direct instruction (e.g., exploration of and engagement with complex learning materials or contexts). According to Daloz, mentors help mentees to question tacit assumptions and more deeply reflect on their complex learning process; mentors also provide vision, offering the model to learn from. The research of Murphy et al. (2005) offers a concrete, three-part, established coding framework for discerning between the three related concepts of mentoring, coaching, and facilitation. Jacobi (1991) highlights the varied definitions of mentoring, where educational and other opportunities for psychosocial growth such as coaching or even technical facilitation are often conflated.

Sundii (2007) explores the linkage between reflection and mentoring. This work is backgrounded by the Norwegian educational context,

where mentorship is defined to include an active, reflective conversation between mentor and mentee. Although an educational "mentoring" session can easily focus on the practical such as planning or the classroom, Sundii argues that, at its best, mentoring links theory to practice and promotes reflective thinking in the service of professionalization She notes, too, Foucalt's distinction between the readily spoken language and the more socially distant written language, framing good mentoring sessions as an opportunity for oral reflection that is perhaps more approachable than written journaling or reflective assignments. And although the characterization of writing as a "socially distant" medium remains worrisome, research has begun into the impact of combining social media into settings with reflection and mentoring (Berg, 2010).

Synchronous Learning

The key component upon which this study rested was the use of synchronous or real-time learning. After several decades of investment in asynchronous online courses and degrees, college and university faculty are moving to include or feature significantly more synchronous teaching and learning opportunities into their online curricula. Although modern Learning Management Systems (LMSs) used as platforms for online learning provide for multiple forms of interaction, faculty designers and teachers still struggle to utilize such systems for deeper engagement and richer online pedagogies. More recently, LMS providers have begun to bundle synchronous tools, such as Blackboard Collaborate within the Blackboard Learn suite, and faculty usage of these higher-touch tools has skyrocketed. As a result, online course designers and teachers are in need of modern, desktop-based models, strategies, and best practices for this synchronous turn. The tool primarily used in this study was the use of Blackboard Collaborate.

Digital Mentoring

More recent exploration into virtual coaching and mentoring has pushed this definitional discussion into the realms of telephone and email-based mentoring, and most recently into domains of chat and videoconferencing (Clutterbuck & Hussain, 2010). Much of the early work in digital or e-mentoring focused on email-based approaches (e.g., as described in Murphy et al., 2005), with a particular concern that text-based mentoring may hinder or flatten the communication of emotion so critical in mentoring—emotional tone, intention, and intensity. Although research into the conveyance of emotion in email is mixed, the emergence of synchronous, web-based tools such as desktop videoconferencing now provides mentors and mentees the benefits of real-time learning conversations of depth and complexity, fostering creative thinking and the interactive flow of ideas (Clutterbuck & Hussain, 2010). The mentor model of Arthur and Kram (1985) has also emerged strongly in these recent discussions of digital mentoring.

Although not the focus here, it is extremely interesting to note that increased use of technology tools has also begun to move focus from the mentor-mentee relationship to that of "mentorship networks," where multiple individuals, now accessible via electronic means, might guide, support, and challenge the mentee (Goodyear, 2006). Also expansive is the work of Stokes, who labels the area broadly as "e-development" and frames online coaching and mentoring within the rapid growth of our use of electronic media to make social connections (Garvey, Stokes, Megginson, 2009).

Teacher Presence and Community of Inquiry

This study also examines definitions of mentoring and how practices of telementoring (via video-conferencing) map onto the theoretical concept of teacher presence as defined by Garrison, Anderson, and Archer (2000) in their Community of Inquiry (COI) model (see: https://coi.athabascau.ca/). The three types of elements that comprise a COI according to Garrison, Anderson, and Archer (2000) include the teacher presence, cognitive presence of the students, as well as the social presence of the students. Teacher presence can be characterized by design of the course, direct instruction, and facilitating discourse (Garrison, Anderson, & Archer, 2000). One challenge of online learning is the less personalized nature of courses and less interaction between professor and student(s). Increased teacher presence in a virtual learning environment helps to foster a community of inquiry in online settings (e.g., Garrison, Anderson, and Archer, 2000).

The learning construct of scaffolding comes from the framework of the gradual release of responsibility (Pearson and Gallagher, 1983) with use of explicit instructor modeling and guided practice by students built into the design of the course. This study also draws on Vygotsky's concept of scaffolding (1978), defined as learning in the presence of a more knowledgable other. For instance, by modeling through videoconferencing, students can be better prepared to apply course learning into their own teaching contexts and course projects and assignments. Scaffolding was built into the conference sessions through the modeling and guided practice components of the videoconferencing, highly structured initial design of the videoconference PowerPoints that guided the mentoring sessions, individualized instruction/mentoring for students in real time, and mentor guidance towards knowledge and information sharing. These theoretical components that focus on fostering a supportive and personalized online classroom guided the online learning context of this study.

METHODS

Data Collection and Context of the Study

This study is primarily a qualitative pilot study; data analysis is preliminary and exploratory. Using the theoretical models cited above (e.g., Garrison, Anderson, & Arbaugh, 2000) we used constant-comparative analysis (Corbin & Strauss, 2008) and discourse analysis (Gee, 2005) to look for emerging themes within and across the data set. Here we describe the context of the study, data collected, and participants in the study.

Description of the Course

The fully online course was 11 weeks in length and took place over the summer session in 2012. The graduate literacy course focused primarily on elementary literacy instruction and instructional methods across the PK-6th grade spectrum. The course material was geared towards Master's level students who were a mix of both pre-service graduate students seeking initial certification (with minimal to no teaching background) and students who were more experienced full-time practicing classroom teachers or literacy specialists at their schools. Course topics focused on a wide range of concepts; however, literacy learning methods from early childhood through sixth grade was a broad overarching curricular focus. The course covered diverse literacy topics such as phonics, beginning reading, vocabulary instruction, reading comprehension, writing instruction, developing fluency, and working with diverse learners. The course contained crucial and high-stakes content as students would eventually be tested on learning outcomes in their state level teacher certification test if they were seeking initial certification or, on the reading specialist state exam if they were seeking that certification in the state of Texas.

Structure of the Videoconference-Based Mentoring Sessions

The one-on-one individualized digital mentoring sessions were designed to take place for a total of five sessions across the duration of the 11-week online summer graduate course. The course consisted of a total of 31 graduate students (of whom three withdrew, resulting in a total of 28 students who participate in mentoring sessions) and represented a wide variety of experience and education in terms of teaching. The course was structured so that videoconference-based digital mentoring sessions were a required component of the course. Sessions took place approximately every other week and lasted in length from about 15 minutes to an hour in length, depending on the student's needs, schedule, and other variables unique to the student. Ultimately, mentoring sessions occurred with 28 students as three students withdrew from the course; 18 of the students were mentored by the lead professor and an additional mentor, who was also the course teaching assistant, mentored the remaining ten students in the course. Students were divided alphabetically by last name. That is, the first ten students in the roster were assigned to the second mentor, the teaching assistant, while the remaining 18 students worked with the lead professor, who was also the lead instructor and first author of this chapter.

Each of the five mentoring sessions were structured by a PowerPoint™, which was sent out ahead of time to students and posted on the learning management system, Blackboard. Sessions were structured in similar ways across the five sessions. For instance, students did an open-ended dialogue with the mentor in response to a structured opening prompt on the PowerPoint such as, "How's it going with the course and the readings?" and other questions. The PowerPoint used in the mentoring sessions included: open-ended questions posed to students relating to course concepts and applications to teaching, links to key curricular resources and literacy-focused websites, reminders of upcoming assignments, due dates, and success tips for doing well on work. The sessions also contained tutorials that focused on procedural knowledge such as how to access the University library's online research databases. New concepts and ideas were also introduced into the PowerPoint and the mentoring session, however, the overall focus was on course-related conversation and responding to the needs of each individual student. Appendix 3 describes in a summary table the overarching themes and questions that guided the five videoconference sessions across the course. This summary table was provided to students at the beginning of the course in the course syllabus.

Preparing for Synchronous Digital Mentoring Sessions

Digital mentoring has been previously described as occurring across asynchronous (non-real-time) formats, such as email (e.g., as described in Murphy et al., 2005). However, preparing to engage with graduate students via distance to engage in synchronous or real time sessions required a level of preparation that was "above and beyond" the typical course design. The first author consulted often with the second author prior to and during implementation of the required synchronous digital mentoring sessions as the second author had participated previously in a large international study that focused on synchronous learning connected to foreign language instruction (Smith & Marston, 2013). Both of the authors of the chapter frequently discussed key ideas of both mentoring of adults as well as best practices of synchronous learning within an online learning context.

Additionally, to prepare for the design of the sessions and to build knowledge capacity as a mentor, the lead mentor and the second mentor read Jonathan Finkelstein's *Learning in Real Time: Synchronous Teaching and Learning Online*

(2012). This text provided an overview of procedures and practices for synchronous learning. The book provied practical insights into how to engage students with active learning in an online session; however, a limitation of the text was that it focused more on group interactions rather than individual mentoring sessions. However, the book provided overall general guidance in getting started with digital mentoring. Another key resource for the first author in designing reflection-oriented mentoring sessions was Costa and Garmston's seminal text (2002), *Cognitive Coaching: A Foundation for Renaissance Schools.* This text, as well as Costa and Kallick's (2008) *Learning and Leading With Habits Of Mind: 16 Essential Characteristics for Success*, provided key insights into working with large overarching themes to prompt student reflection. That is, the goal of the sessions became to focus on coaching rather than entirely providing direction instruction.

In addition to planning conversations between the authors and establishment of a shared framework for understanding how reflection and mentoring could take place within synchronous sessions, the first author also wrote reflective analytical memos (e.g. as described by Miles & Huberman, 1994) during the planning stages of the project as well as during and after the project. These memos helped to set up goals and to focus on the researcher's strengths and weaknesses with synchronous mentoring. Through ongoing reflective memos, the first author determined, for instance, that intentional sharing of personal experiences, anecdotes, and vignettes from related prior teaching experience in elementary settings would be helpful to students in getting them to think about content in more applied ways.

Finally, overarching goals for the sessions were established such as sharing knowledge and expertise from the mentors, encouraging reflective learning by the students (mentees), fostering of knowledge development of the course content, and encouraging students to think ahead to their current or future teaching situations. The mentor was to focus on using probing questions to foster critical thinking of course content. It was also an intention to have the synchronous mentoring sessions function as a demonstration for students as to the uses and affordances of digital learning. Providing the synchronous sessions in the course in the first place provided a concrete example to students that the mentors were making a unique effort to personalize learning further beyond what was normally expected of an online course.

Participants

A total of 28 students participated in the digital mentoring sessions. Students represented a wide range of background experiences. The course consisted of both novices with no teaching experience and advanced practitioners seeking specialization. In addition to analyzing post-videoconference reflection documents from the 28 students in the course, we also chose to focus on a cross case analysis (Merriam, 2001) of four students as representative case examples to show more in-depth the nature of the mentoring sessions.

These four cases were chosen by the researchers for principled reasons for analysis in order to showcase representative instances of both veteran teachers and novice teachers. Veteran teachers were characterized as having more than three years of classroom experience while novice teachers were considered to be those who had three or less years of teaching experience. The primary

reasons for selecting these particular four case students were to showcase mentees across differing teaching contexts and years of experience. For instance, we selected a mentee in a primary grade classroom as well as a mentee in an upper grade elementary classroom setting. We wanted to show instances that represented students with differing background experiences and teaching contexts, as many online classes often contain students representing a wide range of background knowledge. Table 1 describes information about these four mentees. All names are pseudonyms. Although all mentees who were selected for a cross-case analysis participated in all five of the mentoring sessions, not all sessions were recorded (due to mentor omission in recording); however, most sessions were recorded. Sessions that were recorded were transcribed and analyzed.

Description of the Two Mentors

There were two mentors guiding the synchronous videoconference sessions; students (mentees) were divided equally across the lead instructor (the first author) and the second mentor, Jenna. Both mentors brought extensive experience as elementary classroom teachers, were formerly classroom teachers and literacy specialists in public schools, and had graduate training in literacy studies. The lead professor and mentor (the first author) has a PhD in language and literacy studies and the second mentor has a Master's degree in literacy studies.

Table 1. Background information of cross-case participants

Name (Pseudonym)	Experience Level	Comments	Number of Transcribed Sessions	Number of Written Reflections
Teresa	Veteran	Elementary-school teacher in upper grades	4	5
Krystal	Veteran	Elementary-school teacher; International teaching with ESL	5	5
Addison	Novice	Going into third year of teaching	5	5
Jessica	Novice	Not yet certified to teach; no full-time classroom teaching experience	3	5

Therefore, both mentors brought both advanced formal education and experience-based insight and advice about teaching to the mentoring sessions. For the course duration, both mentors met online on a regular basis to discuss digital mentoring strategies and a shared approach towards the digital mentoring sessions. Mentors met to also practice using the technology tools, as synchronous learning was fairly new as a teaching method to both mentors. The students' written reflections following the digital mentoring sessions were read by the first author throughout the semester as formative and ongoing feedback. Overall, the students were pleased with their interactions with the respective mentors based on their written feedback. The next section describes the types of data collection tools that informed the study.

Written Reflections

Following each of the videoconference sessions, students completed a required one to two-paged single-spaced written reflection and submitted it for feedback from the lead instructor in the learning management system. Students were to complete a total of five reflections. The reflections were in keeping with the robust literature in teacher education that suggests written reflections foster insight into learning (e.g., Zeichner & Liston, 1996). They also served as formative feedback on the mentoring sessions for the instructor on how the sessions were going. A copy of the written reflection template is in the appendices (Appendix 1) at the end of the chapter. A total of 186 written reflections were collected. The written reflection template that students used to compose their reflection remained the same across the course.

The first reflection question focused on providing an opportunity for the students to recap and synthesize the nature and content of the dialogue from the mentoring session. The second question helped students to identify practical resources

that were takeaways from this session; the third question concerned student feedback regarding technology related to the session; it was a chance to gauge and assess how the technology was working or not working in session. At times, the technology could be frustrating, for instance, when there was an audio delay.

Transcripts of Mentoring Sessions

Digital mentoring sessions were recorded and archived within the learning management system. For privacy reasons, only students in the mentoring session and the mentors had access to their archived mentoring session recordings. Not all recorded sessions were transcribed verbatim; however, the recorded sessions of four case students were transcribed for all of the recorded sessions that were available for them. A third-party transcription service was used to transcribe audio recordings of these case sessions. A total of 17 transcribed sessions were read and coded for the purposes of analysis for this aspect of the project. Appendix 2 of this chapter shares a brief excerpt of an interaction between the lead mentor (the first author) and a student in one of the mentoring sessions. This excerpt highlights the type of in-depth dialogue that took place within the sessions.

The purpose of transcribing the sessions was to examine the types of topics discussed (content) as well as the nature of the discourse and the interactions between mentor and mentee. We also wanted to examine the nature of the scaffolding (Vygotsky, 1978; Murphy et al., 2005) provided by the mentor in selected mentoring sessions. For the transcript sessions, only students who worked with the lead instructor (the first author) were selected for analysis. The rationale for this was that the first author had greater personal experience in terms of working closely with these selected students within the mentoring sessions; this would add greater context to the analysis.

Data Analysis

This study focused primarily on analysis of the written reflections. A total of 186 reflections were deidentified and compiled for the purposes of analysis. Each participant was assigned a standard number for tracking of reflections. In examining the data for emerging themes and trends, both researchers did an initial reading of the entire set of reflections. The researchers met in regular meetings to discuss themes and trends across the data set using a grounded theory approach (Corbin & Strauss, 2008). Data were read inductively, with initial themes being noted and summary description; constant-comparative analysis (Corbin & Strauss, 2008) of the 128 post-videoconference written student reflections (approximately five total reflections for 28 mentees) was used to locate emerging themes within and across the data set. Constant-comparative analysis of videoconference session transcripts (Corbin & Strauss, 2008) was also utilized. As previously stated, selected mentoring sessions were transcribed verbatim and analyzed to look for instances of personalization and types of instructor-student interaction and mentoring. The transcripts of the selected case sessions were read and reread iteratively by the researchers to look for and discuss emerging themes and trends in the transcripts. Additionally, analytical memos were written following the reading of the transcripts, drawing upon principles of writing memos from Miles and Huberman (1994).

To further investigate the discourse patterns within the transcript sessions, preliminary data analysis of video conference session transcripts utilized LIWC (Linguistics Inquiry and Word Count) (Tausczik & Pennebaker, 2009), a computer software research tool designed for the analysis of written and transcribed verbal texts. LIWC analysis is based on the belief that the words people use "provide important clues to their thought processes, emotional states, intentions, and motivations" (Tausczik & Pennebaker, 2009, p. 37). Additional analysis can be made of a speaker's or author's attentional focus, thinking styles, and individual differences. Although it is important to recall that language use is highly contextual and findings may not generalize to differing groups of people or across contexts, such analysis does offer a systematized look into these important areas (Tausczik & Pennebaker, 2009).

RESULTS

In this section, findings are presented of the two initial research questions about students' perceptions of personalized learning. We restate the first research question here:

Question 1: What is the perceived impact of increased teacher presence done via synchronous, 1-on-1 videoconference mentoring in a graduate online literacy course?

Preliminary analyses suggest several themes emerging across data examined so far.

First, students reported positive interactions in terms of perceived benefit of personalization in their interactions with their mentor in the videoconference. The second major theme that emerged, related to personalization, was the deepening of learning that took place within the videoconference sessions, as reported in students' written reflections and the transcript sessions. Preliminary analyses suggest that through participation in one-on-one synchronous videoconference teacher presence (Garrison & Arbaugh, 2007) led to an increase in student engagement at various levels of cognitive stages of inquiry while also developing student engagement with the course.

In conjunction with the increase in teacher presence, students reported an increase in personalized learning and overall feeling of support in the course. For instance, students reported the videoconferences afforded an increase in terms of helpfulness in working on current assignments as well as an increase in ability to learn more about online tools (e.g., the online library database) for both current and future classes. In written reflections, students also reported a lowering of anxiety, reporting such things as "feeling better"; "feeling more confident", "less overwhelming", "a sense of focus", "a sense of relief at end of conference"; and being thankful for synchronous learning tool during the videoconference. Students discussed in written reflections how they liked that they could see, hear, and interact with the mentors. Representative quotes here suggest that personalization and human support that were afforded through the digital mentoring sessions were appreciated by students. Each quote below is from a different student:

- "…I didn't feel like I was doing this alone and her [the mentor's] input was very valuable."
- "I'm beyond grateful that Dr. Semingson actually took time out to show me different websites, articles, and the ways that I could search for research articles."
- "This is the first time since I've taken online courses that I've been able to 'see' the professor…Everything went well and I enjoy being a part of this class!"
- "Reading about an assignment and actually talking about the assignment are two different things. It was good to hear Dr. Semingson's description of the assignment."

In terms of scaffolding, the anticipation of the videoconference assisted students in knowing that someone was available to support them. Students reported preparing for videoconferences with questions and reported appreciating the struc-

tured nature of the conferences. Many students reported they would have more questions for the second videoconference now that they understood how the digital mentoring worked. An additional personalized benefit was that students actively sought clarification from mentors on assignments. While the first conference created expectations for the structure and function of future conferences, subsequent conferences allowed students to participate in more of a dialogic session that focused on course content. One student in particular framed the personalized learning featured in the conference sessions as one that was unexpected. In the first videoconference reflection, the student stated:

Although I am highly trained in technology I prefer human interactions when dealing with stressful issues, like education. I can hone on visual clues as to how someone feels by their posture, facial expressions, and many other non-verbal cues. However, this video conference really gave me more confidence in my instructor and myself just from the visual and audio experience. And now I actually feel that I'm not simply dealing with some heartless computer. (Student 25, Transcript 1, First videoconference session)

In terms of student feedback about the supportive features of the conference tool, teacher presence, and mentoring, several findings emerged. Desktop sharing was especially useful to students as they could "see" their mentor thinking aloud about the procedures and intricacies of difficult topics such as navigating the library research databases. Students reported that the tools they learned about would potentially help save them time because they were previously using the library databases in inefficient ways. They liked the immediacy of this feedback and reported being excited about assignments now that concrete tools were provided to assist their learning goals. Overall, modeling and demonstration via the screen sharing tool, where the student could see demonstrations and modeling done on the mentor's own computer screen, was very popular with the students across the course.

Analysis of Transcripts of Sessions: Novices and Mentors

This section focuses on answering the second research question. The second research question is restated below:

Question 2: What is the development of teachers via digital mentoring, as documented in the qualitative data of session transcripts?

This question was examined through an exploratory analysis of the transcripts of four selected mentees. For principled reasons, we purposefully sampled four cases (mentees) from across the data set of the summer literacy course to look closer at the transcripts of their mentoring sessions. We intended to have a cross-case sampling (Merriam, 2001) of two novices, as defined by three or less years of classroom teaching experience, and two veterans, as defined by more than three years of classroom teaching experience. We present here qualitative summaries of these four cases using cross-case analysis (the two novices versus the two veterans), as well as computerized text analysis using the LIWC (Linguistics Inquiry and Word Count) software system.

Transcript sessions were read iteratively and inductively; emergent themes were coded and discussed among the researchers until we mutually agreed upon the codes and categories for each mentee's transcripts (Corbin & Strauss; 2008). Additionally, summaries of each conference were written for additional codes and categories. Following this iterative analysis, we examined the transcripts and summaries of the transcripts within cases (each individual mentee) and across cases (novices versus mentors). What follows is a qualitative summary of these analyses.

Jessica: Advanced Novice Teacher with Nuanced Perspectives

Recordings and transcripts were available for three sessions with Jessica, a novice teacher although all five conference sessions took place. This summary looks across the conference sessions analyzed. Jessica was termed a novice as she was about to enter her fourth year of teaching. As a primary grade elementary school teacher, she brought insight to the discussion that related to her experiences with elementary literacy learning. Despite being a novice, she brought nuanced response to questions relating to beginning reading that reflected genuine inquiry. Overall, Jessica was an enthusiastic learner across all-conference sessions. Throughout the conferences there was a certain amount of laughter, humor, and levity that facilitated an ease of conversation. Although interpersonal sharing beyond the course topics was minimal, the biggest connection between mentor and mentee related to prior teaching experiences in the elementary classroom. She also expressed a positive aspect for the technology tool Blackboard Collaborate, often commenting that she was impressed with the videoconference system and capabilities. Richer and more in-depth dialogue came from the following: discussion of the Habits of Mind topics (Costa & Kallick, 2008), connections to classroom practice, posing authentic questions to the instructor, and in-depth responses to the more open ended questions posed by the mentor.

Because Jessica already possessed good background knowledge about literacy teaching, mentor-student dialogue during the conference focused more on procedural knowledge about assignments, for instance, with the mentor modeling how to navigate the library databases as well as discussion of course concepts. Academically, there was reciprocity and knowledge sharing between mentor and mentee in terms of sharing teaching ideas. Across the conferences, the mentee's statements revealed some instances of confusion about concepts or procedures related to assignments. This allowed the mentor an opportunity to provide targeted and highly specific feedback to the mentee related to these confusing concepts. Throughout the transcripts, the mentor provided encouragement to Jessica and used facilitating language and regulating discourse. Regulating discourse is a concept used by Garrison & Arbaugh (2007) when describing the role of teacher presence. An example of regulating discourse within the transcript might include general reminders about assignments and direct instruction and feedback about draft work.

Addison: Novice Teacher Connecting to Prior Knowledge

As a beginning novice seeking initial teaching certification, Addison had zero years of full-time classroom teaching experience. However, she brought to the conversation her background knowledge as a parent, an observer and participant of her own children's experiences in elementary schooling, prior knowledge from related and concurrent coursework, her own personal explorations about education and literacy on the Internet, and insights gleaned from course readings and other structured materials and content provided from the mentor. Similar to Jessica, she responded more in depth to open-ended questions as opposed to direct advice from the mentor. Overall, she was more passive in terms of the interactions. For instance, there were many instances when her feedback was simply "okay", "yeah", and other one word utterances. However, there were instances of knowledge sharing on her part with the mentor, for example, when she explored ideas independently online on her own time and shared resources and activities related to the literacy learning topics on the agenda and course readings.

Additionally, Addison expressed a positive attitude for the course topic itself and her goal of becoming a teacher. In conference sessions, she often shared about herself as a learner, for instance, revealing information about her learning styles. This better helped the mentor to tailor feedback in response to her learning preferences and her background knowledge. She also expressed a preference for reminders about due dates. She was well prepared for sessions with lists of questions and actively took notes throughout the extended conversation. Overall, Addison was more focused on doing well on her assignments and driven to succeed in them as opposed to discussing her future students. She expressed some concerns in the conference sessions about being able to retain ideas and apply learning in future teaching scenarios. The mentor provided encouragement that the knowledge would one day become be useful to her practice.

Mentor feedback and input with Addison focused primarily on sharing and highlighting resources that connected to assignments and course concepts. Additionally, mentoring language provided encouragement, direct instruction about course concepts in which the student had little background knowledge, mentor thinking-aloud about ideas related to literacy learning, reminders about resources available on Blackboard, reminders and direction instruction about web-based resources, discussion of the textbook readings, and the mentor's previous teaching experiences. A challenge across the sessions included nudging Addison to think of applications towards feature teaching. Direct advice and feedback seemed to encourage more passivity in her responses to the mentor. The mentor helped Addison by naming and labeling positive aspects of Addison's idea, for instance, by naming her verbal and written reflections as indicative of becoming a reflective practitioner. Overall, the mentor provided scaffolding that was aimed at meeting Addison's needs as an inexperienced teacher who was coming to know how to become a classroom teacher.

Krystal: Experienced Teacher with a Student-Centered Focus

Krystal was an experienced teacher who taught in an international setting. The two-way conversations in the digital mentoring sessions had very little interpersonal remarks; however, the overall transcripts resembled what the researchers characterized as a "coffee-shop style conversation" between mentor and mentee. That is, there was a good deal of reciprocal communication, upon which a shared experience background in teaching was the basis of the conversation. Both mentor and the mentee shared experiences of ESL/bilingual teaching contexts. The mentor was a former bilingual/ESL elementary school teacher. Because of Krystal's interest in discussing ESL instruction and the shared background knowledge, much of the content of the mentoring sessions focused on the ESL-focused teaching context of the mentee.

A key theme with Krystal was the idea of reciprocity and knowledge sharing between mentor and mentee. Teaching ideas related to literacy learning were shared by the mentor, however, the mentee provided additional resources, teaching ideas, and insights that were appreciated by the mentor. Krystal made connections to resources on the learning management system, her own teaching experiences, texts and ideas from another related literacy course, websites she located and shared about, and her own goals as a teacher and informal teacher leader. She often introduced the concept of cultural context into the discussions. She primarily kept the needs of her students in the forefront of all conversations. She also spoke of wanting to share course ideas, concepts, and resources with her teaching colleagues when she returned to the classroom in the fall.

In terms of concepts shared and discussed by the mentor, the theme of practical advice and tips were ever-present across the sessions. The practitioner-oriented advice focused on ways to navigate complex teaching situations and included

ways to find shortcuts in teaching or ways to find resources that are commonly known. Krystal, also sought out advice about getting a PhD. Across the mentoring sessions, she asked quite a bit about what PhD programs were like and expressed her interest in pursuing a PhD in the future. In essence, her background and perspectives about ESL and international teaching scenarios gave more nuance to the conversation.

Teresa: Experienced Teacher with a Reflective Focus

Teresa had five years of teaching experience in the upper elementary grades and was thus considered an experienced teacher. She was a very enthusiastic learner. More interpersonal conversations occurred that were still within the course topic. Teresa was very responsive and positive to the mentor's ideas across all sessions. She brought prepared questions to each session. Her learning goals that connected to the course content related mostly to her student's needs. She could be characterized as a student-centered teacher. She was always ready with a progress update on assignments and expressed specific ways the mentor could help her to grow and progress in the class.

The conversation with Teresa was more substantive in her more extended responses to open-ended questions posed by the mentor. The shared experience of having taught in the upper-elementary grades was discussed. There was a deal of empathy and insight from the mentor about teaching fifth-grade and about teaching in general. Mentor language included empathy, encouragement, and facilitating language on the part of the mentor. There were some moments when the student was verbally more passive. However, overall, she shared about herself as a learner, herself as a teacher, and brought resources and ideas to the session. There was not as much reciprocal knowledge sharing as there was with Krystal. Overall, Teresa was an enthusiastic participant who brought to bear her teaching and learning experiences, a high level of preparedness, information about her professional interests, and concern for her students to the conference sessions.

Cross-Case Analysis: Comparing Two Novices versus Two Veterans

Continuing the cross-case analysis, this section compares the two novice mentees with the two veteran teacher mentees to look for trends within and across the transcript data set.

In looking within transcripts of both novice mentees, similarities included the following themes: both novice mentees expressed interest and enthusiasm regarding the discussion of course topics and content; both wanted to do well in the course and often spoke about their own learning styles, preferences, and interests; both revealed about themselves as learners and sought and appreciated specific feedback from the mentor on their course assignments. Overall, similarities across the novices also included a stronger focus on their own learning and coursework as opposed to connecting learning concepts to their current or future students.

Questions posed by the novice teacher mentees generally pertained to assignments within the course, such as assignment specifications or seeking of advice related to doing well on assignments. However, Addison posed more nuanced questions relating to course content and topics. For instance, her question about what constituted a miscue reflected an in-depth understanding of the subject of miscue analysis. This question was also possibly driven from her experiences as a primary-grade teacher. A transcript excerpt that demonstrates her thinking and posing of inquiry-based questions is below:

Mentor: Yeah, and so do you have any--to kind of wrap up--do you have any questions or thoughts about the readings, and have you thought about application to your future teaching?

Addison: Well, let's see, the reading has been really interesting, I mean, like I said...like the Self-Paced Phonics [textbook] and I think that will help me as, you know, eventually I would like to become a reading specialist. And, you know, I don't think that you can be a really good reading specialist unless you have the, you know, unless you're very aware and knowledgeable about phonics and how to teach it in, in the step, you know, in order, you know, and that kids will need to have in order to be successful. There was one part of the reading that I wasn't really clear about. (Addison, Transcript 1, first conferencing session)

Following this, she proceeded to ask a complex and technical question about miscue analysis. This generated in-depth dialogue about a complex literacy topic.

On the other hand, Jessica seldom posed nuanced questions regarding the course content. Additionally, of the four case students, Jessica was the most passive in terms of dialogue and interaction. Discussion was more in-depth for Addison in response to open-ended questions and whenever she brought to bear her prior knowledge to the conversation. For both mentees, more in-depth dialogue and two-way conversation emerged from the posing of an open-ended question on the part of the mentor.

Within the two veteran teacher mentees, both brought their teaching experiences into much of the dialogue. Similarities included enthusiasm towards connecting course content to improving the learning of their own students; both mentees reflected a desire to apply learning to specific instances of teaching with their students. Both sets of transcripts of the veteran teacher mentees included instances where specific teaching scenarios of learners were described and discussed with the mentor. For instance, Krystal spoke quite a bit about the cultural context of teaching in an international setting and explored what the teaching of reading meant for students in such a context. Conversations about gender, culture, bilingual learners, and other variables of teaching literacy were discussed between mentor and mentee. As well, Teresa also discussed instances of teaching goals as connected to course content.

For both of the veteran mentees, learning goals that were beyond the scope of the course content were discussed and brought up by the mentees. For instance, Krystal asked about PhD programs, while Teresa shared about wanting to branch out to teaching beyond the classroom such as private tutoring. Finally, both veteran teachers shared resources and insights that were useful to the mentor. This is not to say that the novice teacher mentees did not engage in reciprocal knowledge sharing, however, there were more instances of reciprocal knowledge sharing with the veteran teacher mentees.

Differences arose amongst the two veteran mentees. Krystal, in particular, required less direction in terms of assignment, and had fewer questions about class procedures. More time was spent discussing course content and teaching ideas and applications. Teresa took more notes during the session and was more passive in conversation than Krystal. Teresa spent more time describing herself as a learner and focused strongly on her learning goals.

To summarize across the cases, overall, all four mentees from the case examples demonstrated unique differences and idiosyncrasies in terms of their own individual background knowledge, teaching experiences, professional interests, interaction styles, and other learning differences. However, within the novices, there was more monologic (one-way) style of speech on the part of the mentor, with more passive conversation from the mentees. Within the veteran mentees, connections were strongly made on the part of the mentee to their own students and more applications were made towards improving the learning of their students as it connected to course content. This indicated a stronger tendency to prioritize their students' needs more so than the novices

did; the novices tended to focus more on their own identities as students while also bringing in background knowledge as it was appropriate to make sense of course content. With the veteran mentees, there was more reciprocity in terms of knowledge sharing with the mentor.

Data Analysis of Videoconference Session Transcripts with LIWC

We used the LIWC (Linguistics Inquiry and Word Count) software analysis program to conduct a computerized word count of the 17 transcript sessions of the four case students (Teresa, Krystal, Addison, and Jessica). A first stage of the LIWC analysis considered content and style words. Within English, content words are generally nouns, verbs, as well as many adjectives and adverbs, which convey the content of a communication. Style or function words, on the other hand, generally include pronouns, prepositions articles, conjunctions, and auxiliary verbs. Not surprisingly, according to the LIWC style guide, (Pennebaker, et al., 2007) style words reflect how an individual is communicating where content words express what they are saying. Overall, mentoring session transcript material utilized by teacher mentees in this case study registered between 60.69% and 61.55% style words, a percentage that is on the whole not dissimilar to spoken or transcript materials in various subdomains (Pennebaker, et. al, 2007). Style words typically represent 55% or more of transcript as well as print or written materials of a formal nature.

For content categories, transcript materials in this study were marked by LIWC as primarily occurring, not surprisingly, on social themes. LIWC output categories that were not represented by a significant percentage of words included: material about family or friends, general material about humans, the body, health, or other topics such as money, religion, home, leisure activities, or achievement. An important percentage was devoted to themes of work (3.24 - 4.16%) and time (4.15-6.52%). The topic of space was also present in a marked percentage of the combined transcripts, ranging from 3.51 to 4.92% of words in the transcript corpus.

The emotionality – positive and negative emotions – expressed within the transcripts showed a marked leaning toward the positive. This also connects with the results from examining the written reflections using qualitative analysis. Transcripts across the group of teachers range from 4.62 to 5.22% positively loaded, whereas negative emotion percentages clustered near 0.3% of words for all teacher sessions recorded and analyzed. This suggests a markedly positive environment was present for the sessions, even though troubling or complex situations faced by the teachers were discussed in multiple instances of the transcribed sessions. Interestingly, Tausczik & Pennebaker note that use of emotional words has also been seen as a proxy for degree of immersion. This suggests a positive sense of immersion on the half of these developing teachers (2009). For all four teacher subjects, extremely low levels of word choice expressing anxiety were recorded. Across subjects, these varied from 0.04 to 0.08% of total words. Similarly, low percentages of words expressing sadness and anger were also recorded.

Natural language also provides important information about how individuals process the environment around them and make sense of their situation. Thinking can vary in complexity and depth, and this is frequently reflected in the words people use to express and to connect their thoughts (Tausczik & Pennebaker, 2009). The relatively small set of transcribed sessions did allow for descriptive analysis of the teachers' thinking in depth and complexity. First and foremost, teacher-mentees uniformly increased their word counts noted as "cognitive mechanisms," but results in subsets such as words representing "insight" and "causation"—a marker for active mental processes or processes of appraisal—were

mixed, with more experienced teachers showing gains and at least one inexperienced teacher-mentee registering declines.

SOLUTIONS AND RECOMMENDATIONS

This exploratory qualitative analysis and case study (Merriam, 2001) highlights the value which the mentee-teachers clearly sensed and shows ways in which they benefitted from the mentoring sessions. Through qualitative analysis, researchers documented important elements such as teacher presence (Garrison & Arbaugh, 2007) and complex, intertwined discussions that were simultaneously tactical and strategic, social and technical, while providing self-insight for participants, behavioral change, and integrating of ideas and experiences (Megginson & Clutterback, 2005). Although quantitative tools such as LIWC can serve in a corroborating role, the numerical results provided little additional or unique insight into the given data set. Additionally, tools such as LIWC afford the researcher an opportunity to author dictionaries tailored to a given domain or environment, so latitude exists to compile such elements for more sophisticated activities such as coaching and mentoring, based on the recognized frameworks in the field.

It is no surprise, however, that complex activities such as mentoring are correspondingly challenging to define, document, and analyze. As new frameworks and tools for network-based learning and development emerge, it is hoped that researchers will be afforded a larger toolset to consider these sophisticated developmental acts and environments. Learning theories such as connectivism, although more frequently mapped onto instructional or subject matter learning, give promise to the emerging view of "e-development" that includes virtual mentoring (Siemens, 2008).

FUTURE RESEARCH DIRECTIONS

Importance of the Study and Implications for Practice

Within online learning contexts, there is a clear need for further research about complex learning and development activities such as mentoring, most especially within connective/constructivist learning contexts to accommodate the diverse learning needs of online students. Additionally, the content of phonics, beginning reading, and other technical course topics discussed in the sessions are complex linguistic topics (e.g., as described by Snow, Griffin, & Burns, 2005) and can be challenging to teach in an online-only context; this study helps to develop our understanding of the deepened and personalized ways online learning can facilitate such crucial and highly complex topics in teacher education. Additionally, it is crucial to have a better understanding of the nuanced ways that scaffolding (Vygotsky, 1978) supports digital mentoring. With the growth of online learning (Allen & Seaman, 2010) and greater use of synchronous learning across teaching contexts, we need to consider how more personalized approaches to online learning can apply to supporting a wide variety of novice and more experienced learners.

Knowledge gleaned from this study can also provide evidence of effectiveness of teleconferencing as a mentoring tool for online learning within online and/or hybrid/blended courses. Future research directions for the authors include continuing to look at discourse-based analysis of synchronous learning using both qualitative methods and computerized software (such as LIWC which we employed in this study). We also wish to examine the broader set of reflections to do more data analysis of the reflections across courses. Academic researchers need to further study the role of synchronous learning across online learning contexts and look for ways to support and personalize learning for students who come from a wide

range of backgrounds. Pre and post course surveys would also help to evaluate students' perceptions of synchronous learning and digital mentoring in particular. Complex, emerging theories of online learning and e-development such as connectivism are poised to inform a future where growth and potential is defined perhaps more online than off-line, in both educational as well as workplace settings (Boyce & Hernez-Broome, 2010).

CONCLUSION

In essence, this chapter represents a case study (Merriam, 2001) of one graduate online course and the implementation of digital mentoring via a synchronous learning tool—*Blackboard Collaborate*. Data analyses based on students' written reflection and transcripts of selected conference sessions reflected a more personalized learning approach that potentially can be tailored to students' background knowledge, experiences, and learning needs. The themes reflected in the findings of this study suggest that students approach synchronous learning and discussion with various levels of capacity versus engagement. Here, students brought a good level of preparedness to the session and readiness to talk and dialogue about the course. Overall, there was a positive affect across the written reflections as well as the transcripts. As a result of engaging in synchronous learning and digital mentoring, students gained in confidence, knowledge, and received advice that was useful towards course assignments, and understanding of course concepts and content. Sessions also allowed the mentors to gain insights and feedback from their mentees.

The role of teacher presence (e.g., as defined by Garrison & Arbaugh, 2007) in the digital mentoring sessions remains key to personalizing learning. Advice provided by the mentors drew upon the mentors' experiences and structured design of the sessions as well as the intentional use of facilitating and supportive discourse (Garrison & Arbaugh, 2007). While the technology was a mediating tool, it was merely a vehicle for learning and the broader goal became supporting students towards becoming reflective learners and practitioners. The Community of Inquiry model (e.g., Garrison & Arbaugh, 2007) as well as the broader literature on mentoring of adults (Daloz, 2012) provided promising components of a framework for approaching digital mentoring in synchronous contexts. Teacher presence (Garrison & Arbaugh, 2007) provided encouragement, facilitating discourse, direct instruction, external regulation towards the course and assignments, as well as scaffolding (Vygotsky, 1978). The amount of mentor support varied depending upon the student's level of experience and background knowledge.

This study identified that scaffolding from the teacher or mentor needs to take into consideration whether the learner is a novice or veteran. In this study students who were veterans were focused more on learning goals that applied to their teaching contexts. Novices, on the other hand were more focused on their identity as students within the course while also wanting to make and set goals for themselves in terms of their teaching. Ways to further personalize learning within synchronous digital mentoring are yet to be explored as the subject is new and emerging within new and future models of online learning and e-development.

REFERENCES

Allen, I. E., & Seaman, J. (2010). Learning on demand: Online education in the United States. Newburyport, MA: The Sloan Consortium. Retrieved from http://sloanconsortium.org/publications/survey/pdf/learningondemand.pdf

Arthur, M. B., & Kram, K. E. (1985). Mentoring at work: Developmental relationships in organizational life. *Administrative Science Quarterly*, *30*(3), 454. doi:10.2307/2392687

Berg, G. (2010). *Cases on online tutoring, mentoring, and educational services practices and applications*. Hershey, PA: Information Science Reference. doi:10.4018/978-1-60566-876-5

Boyce, L., & Clutterbuck, D. (2011). E-Coaching: Accept it, it's here, and it's evolving! In G. Hernez-Broome & L. Boyce (Eds.), *Advancing executive coaching: Setting the course for successful leadership coaching* (pp. 285–315). San Francisco: Jossey-Bass.

Clutterbuck, D., & Hussain, Z. (Eds.). (2010). *Virtual coach, virtual mentor*. Charlotte, NC: Information Age Publishing.

Cohen, N. H. (2003). The journey of the principles of the adult mentoring inventory. *Adult Learning*, *14*(1), 4–12.

Corbin, J., & Strauss, A. (2008). *Basics of qualitative research: Techniques to developing grounded theory* (3rd ed.). Thousand Oaks, CA: Sage.

Costa, A., & Garmston, R. (2002). *Cognitive coaching: a foundation for renaissance schools*. Norwood, MA: Christopher-Gordon.

Costa, A. L., & Kallick, B. (Eds.). (2008). *Learning and leading with habits of mind: 16 essential characteristics for success*. Alexandria, VA: ASCD.

Daloz, L. A. (2012). *Mentor: guiding the journey of adult learners* (2nd ed.). San Francisco, CA: Jossey-Bass.

Dede, C., Ketelhut, D. J., Whitehouse, P., Breit, L., & McCloskey, E. (2009). A research agenda for online teacher professional development. *Journal of Teacher Education*, *60*(1), 8–19. doi:10.1177/0022487108327554

Finkelstein, J. (2006). *Learning in real time: Synchronous teaching and learning online*. San Francisco: Jossey-Bass.

Garrison, D. R., Anderson, T., & Archer, W. (2000). Critical inquiry in a text-based environment: Computer conferencing in higher education. *The Internet and Higher Education, 2*(2/3), 87–105.

Garrison, D. R., & Arbaugh, J. B. (2007). Researching the community of inquiry framework: Review, issues, and future directions. *The Internet & Higher Education, 10*(3), 157-172. doi:10.1016/j.iheduc.2007.04.001

Garvey, B., Stokes, P., & Megginson, D. (2009). *Coaching & mentoring theory and practice.* London: Sage.

Goodyear, M. (2006). Mentoring: a learning collaboration. *EDUCAUSE Review Online.* Retrieved from: http://www.educause.edu/ero/article/mentoring-learning-collaboration

Megginson, D., & Clutterbuck, D. (2005). *Techniques for coaching and mentoring.* Oxford, UK: Elsevier Butterworth-Heinemann.

Merriam, S. B. (2001). *Qualitative research and case study applications in education.* San Francisco: Jossey-Bass.

Miles, M. B., & Huberman, A. M. (1994). *Qualitative data analysis: An expanded sourcebook* (2nd ed.). Thousand Oaks, CA: Sage.

Murphy, K. L., Mahoney, S. E., Chen, C. Y., Mendoza-Diaz, N. V., & Yang, X. (2005). A constructivist model of mentoring, coaching, and facilitating online discussions. *Distance Education, 26*(3), 341–366. doi:10.1080/01587910500291454

Pearson, P. D., & Gallagher, M. C. (1983). The instruction of reading comprehension. *Contemporary Educational Psychology, 8*(3), 317–344. doi:10.1016/0361-476X(83)90019-X

Pennebaker, J., Chung, C., Ireland, M., Gonzales, A., & Booth, R. (2007). *The development and psychometric properties of LIWC 2007.* Retrieved from: http://www.liwc.net/LIWC2007LanguageManual.pdf

Pennebaker, J. W., Chun, C. K., Frazee, J., Lavergne, G. M., & Beaver, D. I. (2014). When small words foretell academic success: The case of college admissions essays. *PLoS ONE, 9*(12), e115844. doi:10.1371/journal.pone.0115844 PMID:25551217

Shea, P., Sau Li, C., & Pickett, A. (2006). A study of teaching presence and student sense of learning community in fully online and web-enhanced college courses. *The Internet and Higher Education, 9*(3), 175–190. doi:10.1016/j.iheduc.2006.06.005

Siemens, G. (2008). Learning and knowing in networks: Changing roles for educators and designers. *ITFORUM for Discussion.* Retrieved from: http://itforum.coe.uga.edu/Paper105/Siemens.pdf

Smith, P., & Marston, J. (2013). Integrative language and culture learning: Connecting formal and non-formal learning in virtual language studies. In H. Yang & S. Wang (Eds.), *Cases on formal and informal E-learning environments: Opportunities and practices* (pp. 185–199). Hershey, PA: Information Science Reference. doi:10.4018/978-1-4666-1930-2.ch010

Snow, C., Griffin, P., & Burns, M. S. (2005). *Knowledge to support the teaching of reading: Preparing teachers for a changing world.* San Francisco, CA: Jossey-Bass.

Sundli, L. (2007). Mentoring—A new mantra for education? *Teaching and Teacher Education, 23*(2), 201–214. doi:10.1016/j.tate.2006.04.016

Tausczik, Y., & Pennebaker, J. (2009). The psychological meaning of words: LIWC and computerized text analysis methods. *Journal of Language and Social Psychology, 29*(1), 24–54. doi:10.1177/0261927X09351676

Vygotsky, L. S. (1978). *Mind in society: The development of higher psychological processes.* Cambridge, MA: Harvard University Press.

Zeichner, K. M., & Liston, D. P. (1996). *Reflective teaching: An introduction.* Mahwah, NJ: Lawrence Erlbaum.

ADDITIONAL READING

Allen, T. D., Eby, L. T., Poteet, M. L., Lentz, E., & Lima, L. (2004). Career Benefits Associated With Mentoring for Proteges: A Meta-Analysis. *The Journal of Applied Psychology, 89*(1), 127–136. doi:10.1037/0021-9010.89.1.127 PMID:14769125

Bullough, R. V. Jr. (2005). Being and becoming a mentor: School-based teacher educators and teacher educator identity. *Teaching and Teacher Education, 21*(2), 143–155. doi:10.1016/j.tate.2004.12.002

Cain, M. A. (1994). Mentoring as identity exchange: Conflicts and connections. *Feminist Teacher*, 112–118.

Cascio, T., & Gasker, J. (2001). Everyone has a shining side: Computer-mediated mentoring in social work education. *Journal of Social Work Education, 37*(2), 283–293.

Crocitto, M. M., Sullivan, S. E., & Carraher, S. M. (2005). Global mentoring as a means of career development and knowledge creation: A learning-based framework and agenda for future research. *Career Development International, 10*(6/7), 522–535. doi:10.1108/13620430510620593

Cullingford, C. (Ed.). (2012). *Mentoring in education: An international perspective.* Aldershot, England: Ashgate Publishing, Ltd.

de Janasz, S. C., Ensher, E. A., & Heun, C. (2008). Virtual relationships and real benefits: Using e-mentoring to connect business students with practicing managers. *Mentoring & Tutoring: Partnership in Learning, 16*(4), 394–411. doi:10.1080/13611260802433775

Devos, A. (2010). New teachers, mentoring and the discursive formation of professional identity. *Teaching and Teacher Education, 26*(5), 1219–1223. doi:10.1016/j.tate.2010.03.001

Dobrow, S. R., & Higgins, M. C. (2005). Developmental networks and professional identity: A longitudinal study. *Career Development International, 10*(6/7), 567–583. doi:10.1108/13620430510620629

Eby, L. T., Allen, T. D., Evans, S. C., Ng, T., & DuBois, D. L. (2008). Does mentoring matter? A multidisciplinary meta-analysis comparing mentored and non-mentored individuals. *Journal of Vocational Behavior, 72*(2), 254–267. doi:10.1016/j.jvb.2007.04.005 PMID:19343074

Ehrich, L., Tennent, L., & Hansford, B. (2002). A review of mentoring in education: Some lessons for nursing. *Contemporary Nurse, 12*(3), 253–264. doi:10.5172/conu.12.3.253 PMID:12219954

Ehrich, L. C., Hansford, B., & Tennent, L. (2004). Formal mentoring programs in education and other professions: A review of the literature. *Educational Administration Quarterly, 40*(4), 518–540. doi:10.1177/0013161X04267118

Ensher, E. A., & Murphy, S. E. (2007). E-mentoring. The Handbook of Mentoring at Work: Theory, Research and Practice, 299-322.

Fletcher, S., & Mullen, C. A. (Eds.). (2012). *SAGE handbook of mentoring and coaching in education.* Thousand Oaks, CA: Sage.

Garvey, B., & Alred, G. (2000). Educating mentors. *Mentoring & Tutoring, 8*(2), 113–126. doi:10.1080/713685525

Hagger, H., McIntyre, D., Wilkin, M., & Wilkin, M. (Eds.). (2013). *Mentoring: Perspectives on school-based teacher education*. London: Routledge.

Hall, L. A., & Burns, L. D. (2009). Identity development and mentoring in doctoral education. *Harvard Educational Review, 79*(1), 49–70. doi:10.17763/haer.79.1.wr25486891279345

Hargreaves, A., & Fullan, M. (2000). Mentoring in the new millennium. *Theory into Practice, 39*(1), 50–56. doi:10.1207/s15430421tip3901_8

Headlam-Wells, J., Gosland, J., & Craig, J. (2006). Beyond the organisation: The design and management of E-mentoring systems. *International Journal of Information Management, 26*(5), 372–385. doi:10.1016/j.ijinfomgt.2006.04.001

Homitz, D. J., & Berge, Z. L. (2008). Using e-mentoring to sustain distance training and education. *The Learning Organization, 15*(4), 326–335. doi:10.1108/09696470810879574

Johnson, K. A. (2003). "Every experience is a moving force": Identity and growth through mentoring. *Teaching and Teacher Education, 19*(8), 787–800. doi:10.1016/j.tate.2003.06.003

Johnson, W. B. (2007). *On being a mentor: A guide for higher education faculty*. Mahwah, NJ: Lawrence Erlbaum Associates Publishers.

Murphy, W. M. (2011). From e-mentoring to blended mentoring: Increasing students' developmental initiation and mentors' satisfaction. *Academy of Management Learning & Education, 10*(4), 606–622. doi:10.5465/amle.2010.0090

Nakamura, J., Shernoff, D. J., & Hooker, C. H. (2009). *Good mentoring: Fostering excellent practice in higher education*. San Francisco, CA: Jossey-Bass/John Wiley & Sons.

Perren, L. (2003). The role of e-mentoring in entrepreneurial education and support: a meta-review of academic literature. *Education+ Training, 45*(8/9), 517–525. doi:10.1108/00400910310508900

Ragins, B. R. (2009). Positive identities in action: A model of mentoring self-structures and the motivation to mentor. In L. M. Roberts & J. E. Dutton (Eds.), *Exploring positive identities and organizations: Building a theoretical and research foundation* (pp. 237–263). New York, NY: Routledge Press.

Rickard, K. (2004). E-mentoring and pedagogy: A useful nexus for evaluating online mentoring programs for small business? *Mentoring & Tutoring: Partnership in Learning, 12*(3), 383–401. doi:10.1080/0309100042000275972

Santos, S. J., & Reigadas, E. T. (2002). Latinos in higher education: An evaluation of a university faculty mentoring program. *Journal of Hispanic Higher Education, 1*(1), 40–50. doi:10.1177/1538192702001001004

Shrestha, C. H., May, S., Edirisingha, P., Burke, L., & Linsey, T. (2009). From face-to-face to e-mentoring: Does the "e" add any value for mentors? *International Journal of Teaching and Learning in Higher Education, 20*(2), 116–124.

Single, P. B., & Single, R. M. (2005). E-mentoring for social equity: Review of research to inform program development. *Mentoring & Tutoring: Partnership in Learning, 13*(2), 301–320. doi:10.1080/13611260500107481

Sundli, L. (2007). Mentoring—A new mantra for education? *Teaching and Teacher Education*, *23*(2), 201–214. doi:10.1016/j.tate.2006.04.016

KEY TERMS AND DEFINITIONS

Affective Learning: Learning that is characterized by factors such as motivation, emotions, and other individual psychological aspects of learning.

Asynchronous Learning: Learning that takes place at different places and times for different participants in a course; learning that does not take place in real time.

Digital Mentoring: Mentoring that occurs in an online format, whether it is in real time, such as videoconferencing, or asynchronously, for instance, through email.

Novice Teacher: A teacher who typically has zero to three years of teaching experience and is a newcomer to the teaching profession.

Open-Ended Question: A question that is intended to elicit a longer and more thoughtful response from a participant in dialogue, as opposed to a closed-ended question which is intended to elicit a very brief or short answer.

Personalized Learning: Learning that is targeted towards the unique needs of the individual learner for instance by taking into account background knowledge, interests, and/or individual learning goals.

Procedural Knowledge: The type of knowledge that focuses on knowing "how" to do something; it is focused on, for instance, knowledge of steps taken to accomplish a task.

Scaffolding: Support in a given context that provides knowledge from a formal or informal mentor; scaffolding can also occur via text search tools.

Social Presence: The supportive aspects of Community of Inquiry that foster the ability to feel connected within the course with others, willingness to take risks, and interaction with others in the course.

Synchronous Learning: Learning that takes place "live" in real time, for instance, videoconferencing or instant message messaging; this provides an opportunity for instant just-in-time feedback.

Teacher Presence: The aspect of Community of Inquiry where the teacher intentionally participates in structured interaction with a student or students as well as maintains a virtual presence within the course.

Veteran Teacher: A teacher who typically has more than three years of full-time classroom experience and is no longer a novice to the teaching profession.

APPENDIX 1: POST-VIDEOCONFERENCE WRITTEN REFLECTION TEMPLATE

Reflective practice and reflective writing are widely practiced within teacher education (e.g., Ziechner & Liston, 1996). A requirement of the individual videoconferences was for each student to submit a brief written reflection. The purpose of this activity was to deepen reflection as well as provide accountability for the student in fully preparing for each conference session. A structured format was used for each written reflection and a total of five reflections were required from each student for the overall assignment – one for each videoconference.

Post Video-Conference Reflection Form

Your Name:
Mentor's Name:
Topic of Session: (e.g. personal writing)

After each video-conference session with your mentor, post a 1-2 page (single-spaced; 12 font, standard margins) reflection here.

1.   What did you discuss with your mentor (recap and summarize)?
2.   What resources did you learn about that will be beneficial and how can you use them?
3.   How can the videoconference session help you with you this course in future sessions?

APPENDIX 2: EXCERPT OF DIGITAL MENTORING SESSION FROM TRANSCRIPT

The excerpt of dialogue between mentor and mentee represents turn-taking, active listening, and teacher support in a friendly, conversational, and supportive tone between mentor and student. The excerpt shared below is from a digital mentoring session that took place at a mid-way point during the summer semester, 2012.

The student is an experienced practicing teachers enrolled in the Master's course in literacy teacher education. The instructor (the first author) has eight years of teaching experience and brings that into the discussion along with more academic support.

Mentor: How has that been helping you in the class? [The topic being discussed is the notion of "persisting", which was last week's reflection topic for the mentoring session.]

Student: Um...Wow. This semester I'm taking two classes and it has been a little challenging even with summer break because in both of the classes I have like big projects and assignments due, and on top of that, like, I have other goals I'm trying to work on. And so....It's just a matter of just hanging in there.... sticking to....My goal is always to make an "A". I don't strive for anything less. If I don't make it I will at least make a "B". But I strive to make A's and to do everything with excellence. My mindset is to not to give up—to persist—in anything that I do. That's been since I was a little girl.

Mentor: Oh, good. That's awesome. That's good. Multi-tasking is challenging. What helps you.... juggle it? [Overlapping speech between mentor and mentee]

Student: Basically, I have to stay organized. I keep a schedule, like a calendar, and like basically the projects that are due I try to work on those and just try to keep some organization and set priorities and things like that and keep balance as well.

Mentor: Ok, good. We're going to touch briefly and I'm going to share, too, about...the next one is just to keep in mind as you continue reading in the class. And, also, these habits, you can teach these to your students is why I gave you that website. So these are all good to teach to your students when you teach. So I'm just kind of modeling them.

Student: Ok.

Mentor: The next one is just questioning and posing problems. Just kind of things you're wondering about the course content. Like, so this course is elementary literacy instruction and it kind of focuses more on reading so it's about the reading process. And then, so, questioning is just things you wonder. Curiosity. Things that push you forward in your learning. So, my first question is how has this helped you in this class? I wrote it down so I wouldn't forget.

Student: [Laughs]

Mentor: But, I wanted to share first [overlapping]. I know, a lot on our heads, right? I've always wondered how people learn to read. It just seemed like a big mystery. I don't know about you, but when I started my master's program I was like, "I want some answers!"

Student: Exactly! That's true.

Mentor: That's kind of motivated me. I'm still trying to figure out how to help kids who struggle. Some kids learn anyway by osmosis or whatever. But, it's those kids who can't read and I want to know how I can help them.

APPENDIX 3: DESCRIPTION OF CONTENT AND DESIGN OF VIDEOCONFERENCE SESSIONS

Table 2 describes the content and overarching goals of the five conference sessions that took place in the graduate level literacy course described in this chapter. The overview and the items in the table below were posted in the course syllabus for students to have an at-a-glance opportunity to see upcoming topics and discussion questions.

Table 2. Content and overarching goals

Videoconference Number	Discussion Questions to Embed	Outline of Session Content/Topics
Videoconference 1: Initial Professional Development Plan; be ready to discuss your tentative ideas with your mentor and selection of an initial topic.	• What are your initial thoughts for your Professional Development Handout plan? • What resources and assistance would be helpful to you in working on your PD Handout? • How is your understanding of the readings going for the recent weeks? • What applications are you thinking of for your current and future teaching?	1. "How's it going?" (open-ended introduction) 2. Selecting a topic for the Professional Development Handout 3. "What is considered a research article?" 4. Modeling of databases through desktop sharing feature (main focus of videoconference) 5. Sharing of other library resources 6. Recap about the assignment description 7. Applying past knowledge to new situations

Videoconference 2: Word Study Plan Draft	• What are your initial thoughts for your Word Study plan?
	• What resources and assistance would be helpful to you in working on your Word Study plan?
	• How is your understanding of the readings going for these recent weeks?
	• What applications are you thinking of for your current and future teaching?
		1. Touch base about overall course and assignments and readings
		2. Prior knowledge 2) Persistence
		3. Assignment: Word Study Plan
		    a. Your initial thoughts and background knowledge
		    b. Template
		    c. Examples (Smith and Read text)
		    d. Resources
		    e. Writing objectives
		    f. Hands-on phonics activities
		    g. Mobile apps/multi-media examples/sites
		    h. Assessment ideas for pre-and post-assessment
		4. Update about Professional Development Handout

Videoconference 3: Word Study Final Plan	• What are your initial thoughts for your Word Study plan? • What resources and assistance would be helpful to you in working on your Word Study plan? • How is your understanding of the readings going for these recent weeks? • What applications are you thinking of for your current and future teaching?	1. Questioning and Posing Problems 2. Assignment 1: Professional Development Handout 3. Assignment 2: Word Study Plan update. Please email your latest draft to your mentor before your videoconference. 4. General discussion of course readings so far.
Videoconference 4: Professional Development Handout	• How is your understanding of the readings going for the recent weeks? [This can include your readings for the PD Handout.] • What applications are you thinking of for your current and future teaching? [This can include your readings for the PD Handout.]	1. Thinking about thinking (Metacognition) 2. Professional Development Handout Check-in (facilitate assignment) 3. Key reminders for assignment 4. Application 5. Technology connections 6. Mobile apps
Videoconference 5: Closure/ Final thoughts on Professional Development Handout	• What are your current thoughts for your PD handout plan? • What resources and assistance would be helpful to you in finishing your PD Handout?	1. Professional Development Handout 2. Striving for accuracy 3. Applications of course ideas to teaching practice

Chapter 8
Building Interaction in Adults' Online Courses:
A Case Study on Training E-Educators of Adults

Maria Pavlis-Korres
General Secretariat for Lifelong Learning, Greece & Hellenic Open University, Greece

Piera Leftheriotou
General Secretariat for Lifelong Learning, Greece & Hellenic Open University, Greece

ABSTRACT

Integrating the principles of adult education in online environment -an environment which empowers the engagement of learners and their active participation, promotes interaction and immediacy between educator and learners, as well as between learners themselves, and improves learning outcomes- is a very important task. In this task the role of the educator is crucially important and simultaneously very complicated and demanding, as the integration of adult education principles in an online environment is not an easy issue and forms a big challenge for each online educator of adults. This chapter focuses on building interaction in adults' online courses by integrating the principles of adult education in an online environment, and presents one case study on training e-educators of adults. This case study concerns a one-month intensive seminar addressed to e-educators who teach adult courses, demonstrating that online interaction is both possible and effective by integrating the adult education principles in online educational environment.

INTRODUCTION

More and more adults attend educational programs online, taking advantage of the potentialities of learning technology in 21st century, overcoming time and space limits. Adults as learners have specific characteristics, which set them apart from children and must be taken into consideration for the successful creation and development of attractive and effective educational programs addressed to them.

Given that technology should not be considered a panacea for teaching and learning, but rather as a tool to be used appropriately and serve spe-

DOI: 10.4018/978-1-4666-9582-5.ch008

cific educational objectives within a pedagogical framework, adult education principles should be integrated in an online environment in order to maximize educational outcomes. An online environment – synchronous or asynchronous – which empowers engagement of learners, active participation and interaction and immediacy between educator and learners as well as between learners themselves, can promote learning satisfaction for participants and improve learning outcomes.

The role of the educator is crucially important and simultaneously very complicated and demanding, as the integration of adult education principles in an online environment is not an easy issue and forms a big challenge for each e-educator of adults. Educating adults' educators on how to integrate adult education principles in their training is a very effective way of providing quality training. By becoming learners themselves, educators will realize all the benefits of this kind of learning because they can, at a later stage, apply the same principles in their own teaching methods.

In the first part of this chapter we focus on the prerequisites of effective adult learning in online environment and on the role of the e-educator of adults. In the second part we present a case study on training adults' educators online, a one month intensive seminar addressed to adult educators who teach adults within the framework of general adult education courses, implemented by the General Secretariat for Lifelong Learning in Greece.

The chapter provides useful guidelines and proposals to designers, developers and educators involved in adult education on how they can integrate adult education principles in order to promote interaction in their online courses and programs.

ADULT EDUCATION

Theoretical approaches agree that adulthood is not based on the age criterion, which anyway differs from one society to another, even within the same society, overtime (Brookfield 1986; Knowles 1980; Rogers 2002, 2007; Jarvis 1995). The elements, facts and conditions by which each society considers a person to be an adult vary depending on cultural, social, and biological factors. Evidently any group of people in a specific time and place may not share all the elements by which a person is considered an adult, therefore from the educational point of view we have to establish general criteria by which the status of adult will be defined. Among the criteria accepted by theorists are maturity, responsibility and autonomy (Rogers 2002, 2007; Merriam & Caffarella, 1999).

Connecting the theme of adulthood with the educational process, Rogers (2007) supports that Adult Education consists of all those forms of education where learners are treated as adults – capable, experienced, responsible, mature and balanced people. He states that all forms of teaching adults should respect and enhance the adulthood of those who have voluntarily become students.

Adults' Learners Characteristics

Defining the specific characteristics which adults present as learners and which set them apart from children is very important, as the educator can use these useful elements for his teaching task. As one might expect these characteristics are varied.

Malcolm Knowles (1980, 1984), who is considered the father of Andragogy, worked on identifying the characteristics of adult learners that are different from the characteristics of children, on which traditional pedagogy is based. His five assumptions refer to Self-concept, Experience, Readiness to learn, Orientation to learning and Motivation to learn (Knowles 1984).

From the time of Knowles all the way to our days, the literature on adults' learning seems to exhibit a general consensus on some common characteristics that have an impact on adults' learning efficacy and the overall classroom experience (Knowles, 1980, 1984; Knowles, Holton, & Swanson, 1998; Cross, 1981; Brookfield, 1986, 1990; Jackson & Caffarella, 1994; Jarvis, 1995; Cranton, 2000; Rogers, 2002, 2007).

We can sum up the common grounds of many theorists and researchers who have focused on the special characteristics of adults as learners (Knowles, Holton III, & Swanson 1998; Kokkos, 2005; Leftheriotou, 2005; Pavlis-Korres, Karalis, Leftheriotou, & García Barriocanal, 2009) as follows:

1. *They participate in the learning process with concrete intents, goals and expectations.* Adult learners participating in educational programs are motivated by an internal feeling of "need". They come to the educational process with concrete and immediate goals (e.g. professional, social, personal development). In some cases the learners' "need feeling" could be inexplicit or abstract. In other cases their participation could be mandatory (e.g. imposed by their employers) or strictly for the subsidy in subsidized programs. Learners have specific expectations from the learning process, and when this process meets their expectations then their motivation for learning is empowered, their positive attitudes are enhanced and their negative attitudes are transformed to positive ones, contributing to the achievement of the educational goals.

2. *They already possess certain knowledge and experience as well as established perspectives.* Adults enter a learning situation having a specific spectrum of prior knowledge and a variety of life experiences – different for each individual. Adults would prefer this knowledge and experience to be both considered and exploited during their current educational process. Learning is facilitated when the instruction is related to these experiences. The rejection of learners' experience is often taken as a personal rejection which leads to negative reactions and attitudes in the context of the educational process.

3. *They have already developed personal styles of learning.* Each adult has already developed his own learning "model". In order to have an effective learning process, the learning style and personal pace of each learner has to be taken into consideration, leading to the adoption of the appropriate learning methods and techniques.

4. *They prefer self-directed learning and active involvement in the educational endeavor.* Adults desire and strive for self-directedness, emancipation and active participation in every situation in life in which they are involved. This fact affects their attitude towards active participation in the educational level. Usually, adults prefer to be self-directed learners. They wish to be asked for their opinion and to participate in all stages of an educational program (design, conditions of implementation, educational process and evaluation).

5. *They have to deal with certain barriers on their learning process.* The educational process of adults may face barriers which could render the whole procedure ineffective or cause its termination if not dealt with appropriately. Longworth (2003) summarizes the barriers which adults face as mental barriers, financial barriers, access barriers, learning design barriers and information barriers.

According to Cross (1981) and Rogers (2007) there are three main categories of barriers which adults face as learners:

- **Institutional Barriers:** Barriers related to the organization of educational programs.
- **Situational Barriers:** Barriers arising from the personal and social situation in which the learners are.

- **Dispositional Barriers:** Internal barriers related to the attitudes which adults may possess towards themselves or the program, such as existing experiences and knowledge as well as attitudes and principles in which the learners have emotionally invested in, hence are attached to, and psychological factors (stress related to the fear of failure or criticism, insecurity, uncertainty for standing up to the demands of education).

By studying the characteristics of adults as well as the barriers they face as learners, we realize that in the context of adult education the learning process is influenced by many interrelated factors with unpredictable results. All the characteristics of adults could have controversial effects in the learning process, operating either as catalysts for effective learning or as hindering factors (Rogers, 2007; Kokkos, 2005). Nevertheless variety is inevitable and the main characteristic of adult learners and adult learning processes (Rogers, 2002).

Additionally, all the barriers, no matter which categorization they are included in, can hinder access and participation of adults in educational programs. Laal (2011) supports that barriers to learning – whether situational, institutional and dispositional or cultural, structural and personal – are now seen as resolvable through the use of technology. Barriers which people might face differ from someone to another, therefore providers, administrative stuff, designers and educators have to find ways to help each one of the learners overcome these barriers.

Requirements for Effective Adult Learning

The main requirements for effective adult learning, as these are defined through the above mentioned characteristics and in the relative literature (Cross, 1981; Courau, 1994; Noyé & Piveteau, 1997;

Jaques, 2000; Leftheriotou, 2005; Rogers, 2007) are listed below:

1. Education is centered on the learners
   - The education meets the needs, interests and expectations of learners.
   - The ways of learning which learners prefer are seriously taken into consideration when instruction is organized.
   - The knowledge and experiences of adult learners should be used as much as possible in the educational process.
   - The orientation to learning should be life-centered; therefore the appropriate units for organizing adult learning are life situations, not subjects.
   - The barriers which the learners usually deal with are defined, and ways to overcome these are sought after.
2. The active participation of learners is both encouraged and intended
   - Learners are participating actively in the transformation of the learning process (curriculum, choice of educational material and methods, as well as the arrangement of many practical issues which rise during education e.g. time schedule of meetings, use of audiovisual media etc.).
   - In the learning process active educational practices are used (e.g. working in groups, exercises, discussion, case studies, role playing, brainstorming). Through these practices the development of a critical way of thinking is promoted, as well as the 'learning to learn' strategy, in order for learners to be able to continue their learning progress after the end of the educational process.
3. The creation of a learning environment based on communication, cooperation and mutual respect

◦ Bidirectional relations between educators and learners are cultivated, governed by sincerity, respect and acceptance.

◦ Relations of collaboration, mutual respect and trust are cultivated between learners functioning as a learning group.

The learning environment created by adherence to the above requirements results in a certain mode of operation of the educator, whose role is analyzed in the next section.

The Role of the Adult Educator

Because of the significance of the educator in the learning process, many specialists in adults' education have elaborated on the various qualities the educator must have in order to succeed in his task (reference to the educator using the masculine term "his" has been chosen for brevity reasons only and should be interpreted as containing the feminine term "her" too).

The educator of adults has to act as an exhorter, motivator, facilitator, inspirer, counselor, animator and adviser instead of adopting the monolithic teacher-authority model, in order to respond to the diverse individual or group learners' characteristics (Courau, 1994; Jarvis, 1995; Brookfield, 1995; Rogers, 2002, 2007). He must be open-minded and flexible in order to create the appropriate learning environment in which learners contribute, share and mutually participate in many of the decisions within the overall structure of the course. The resultant class structure is then intellectually functional for the learners and is more likely to meet their needs.

According to Knowles (1980, 1984) the educator of adults has to reorient from "educating people" to "helping them learn" (Knowles, 1980) and should serve as a facilitator of learning rather than content transmitter. The educator must also serve as a role model himself, demonstrating a willingness to learn and change (Cranton, 2006). He is often a co-learner and as such he is a participant in the process of learning-discovering, challenging and changing (Freire, 1970). Finally, the educator plays an important role in creating an environment which favors and promotes critical thinking. A good educator can listen and then ask the kinds of questions that help an individual critically reflect on his or her habits of mind. Critical questioning can be used to stimulate content, process, and premise reflection (Cranton, 2006).

Sisco (1984) has pointed out some of the personal attributes an adults' educator should possess. They are: empathy, use of reward, respect for the dignity and worth of each individual, a sense of fairness and objectivity, willingness to accept new things and ideas, patience, sensitivity, humility and commitment to their own lifetime learning. Genuineness (Brockett & Hiemstra, 1985) and unconditional acceptance of students (Billington, 1989) are also considered important. Fisher (1995) states that the abilities to instantly adapt to situations and be openly challenged without becoming intimidated are also extremely desirable.

Without underestimating the importance of the educator's knowledge on his domain, it must be stressed that the educator's attitudes towards adult education as well as his social competencies and skills are very important. Coordination and facilitation of a learning group requires developed personal and social skills and depends on his own assumptions on the notion of the group, while his personal and social skills define his interpersonal relations, allowing or not social contact and interaction, inspiration, persuasion, influence on others and the advancement of a comfortable feeling (Cranton, 2006).

THE E-LEARNING ENVIRONMENT FOR ADULTS

Taking into consideration the factors which affect adults' learning as they have been analyzed in the previous section of this chapter, the online learning environment within which an adult learner could learn effectively has to meet one's needs, expectations and interests, take advantage of one's existing knowledge and learning styles so as to promote active learning and participation, respect each learner's own pace in time, space and momentum and help overcome the barriers which an adult has to face during the educational process.

In the 90's researchers found out that web-courses have the potential to be equal to, or superior to traditional face-to-face courses (LaRose-Witten, 2000; Schutte, 1997; Hiltz & Wellman, 1997; LaRose, Gregg, & Eastin, 1998; Clark, 1994). Since then, the growing popularity of the World-Wide-Web and the improvement of learning technology have shown that the limitations of the web medium have been overcome and web courses can be effective on both cognitive and affective learning (Pavlis-Korres, 2010), whereas there has been intensive debate on whether web courses could become more immediate and interactive than conventional (classroom) courses (Szucs, Tait, Vidal, & Bernath, 2013).

Barriers for Adults in an Online Environment

Some of the barriers which adult learners face in conventional courses can be overcome through the appropriate use of new technologies. By exploiting new information and communication technologies (ICT), e-learning courses offer the potential of accessibility to everyone in any place, and can reduce dramatically the cost of attendance.

Besides the barriers which adult learners already tackle in face to face courses, in an online environment they have to deal with new barriers related to access to the courses, usability of technology, trust in and acceptance of ICTs in communication, sense of isolation and lack of immediacy with the educator and other learners,

as well as lack of social interaction (Waltonen-Moore, Stuart, Newton, Oswald, & Varonis, 2006; Gannon-Leary & Fontainha, 2007; Karalis & Koutsonikos, 2003).

In their survey trying to identify the barriers to online learning, Muilenburg and Berge (2005) point out among other factors (administrative issues, academic skills, technical skills, learner motivation, time and support for studies, cost and access to Internet, and technical problems), the single most important barrier to students learning online, i.e. lack of social interaction. This finding complies with the literature on online education, as many theorists and researchers of online education agree that the key for an effective online course is interaction (Palloff & Pratt, 2003; Kearsley 2000; Simonson, Smaldino, Albright, & Zvacek 2000; Conrad & Donalson 2004; Pavlis-Korres, 2012; Booher & Seiler, 1982; Thompson, 1990; Fulford & Zhang, 1993; Muirhead, 2001; Duck, 2005).

Conrad and Donalson (2004) support that the involvement of the learner in the course (whether one call it interaction, engagement, or building community), is critical if an online course is to provide much more than a lecture-oriented teaching.

Promotion of interaction and immediacy as well as the building and development of the learning group and the learning community seem to be very important in an online environment in order to minimize the isolation of learners and maximize the learning outcomes (Brown, 2001; Pavlis-Korres, 2010; Abdelmalak, 2013; Gamdi, Samarji, & Watt, 2016).

Consequently, an effective educational environment has to deal with all of the above mentioned barriers and promote interaction among participants, as this affects the nature and quality of communication and learning (Anderson, 2003; Pavlis-Korres, Karalis, Leftheriotou, & García Barriocanal, 2009; Grooms, 2003; Merlose & Bergeron, 2007; Garrison & Cleveland-Innes, 2005).

Interaction, Immediacy and Learning Group in an Online Environment

In this section we focus on the notion of interaction and immediacy, as both affect the nature and quality of communication and learning, and contribute to the building and development of the learning group and learning community in an online environment.

Interaction

Moore (1989) identified three kinds of interaction that support learning: learner-content, learner-instructor, and learner-learner. Learning group development does provide a framework within which these three types of interaction can be promoted effectively. Learners can interact with content, constructing knowledge through a process of personally accommodating information into previously existing cognitive structures and can communicate online in synchronous and asynchronous mode, interacting with the educator and other learners in the course. The fourth type of interaction, learner-interface interaction, added by Hilman, Willis and Gunawardena (1994), indicates the importance of technology in online learning. Additionally, other types of interaction, mainly associated with teacher, teacher-teacher interaction, teacher-content or content-content interaction have been added by Anderson and Garrison (1998). Teacher-teacher interaction can empower the professional development of teachers as it promotes and enhances their pedagogical abilities through participation in conferences, seminars, or through electronic communication. By promoting teacher-content interaction, the educational material can be adapted to the needs of each online classroom. The development of World Wide Web (www), Web.2.0 tools and the existence of learning objects repositories or other databases have increased the opportunities for teachers and educators to maximize the potential of teacher-teacher and teacher-content interaction.

It is evident that learner-interface interaction is an important intervening variable in all other types of interaction. A minimal level of self-efficacy must be present before learners even attempt Internet-based instruction (Nahl, 1996), while Hillman et al. (1994) argue that learners need to be fully literate with the interfaces which are used in communications technologies in an e-learning course or a program: "The learner must be skilled in using the delivery system in order to interact fully with the content, instructor and other learners" (p.40).

Lack of interaction appears to be a greater barrier in asynchronous communication modes as the communication between educator and learners and between learners themselves might have a significant delay in time. Synchronous communication modes made it possible for educators and learners to interact in real-time, although time lag and many technical problems may occur during online communication. Many studies have shown that high levels of interaction and collaboration with the educator and other learners can be a strong motivating force for learning (Johnson & Johnson, 1997), thus determining courses' quality (Roblyer & Ekhaml, 2000) and relating positively with cognitive learning (Gunawardena, 1995; Wegerif, 1998; Rovai, 2002) as well as with affective learning (Pavlis-Korres, 2010).

Immediacy

Many researchers have found a significant positive relationship between immediacy behaviors and higher ratings to the overall quality of instruction and value of a course, as well as students' online participation, satisfaction and learning outcomes (Moore, Masterson, Christophel, & Shea, 1996; Hackman & Zane, 1990; Christophel, 1990; Kelley & Gorham, 1988; Gorham & Zakahi, 1990; Gamdi, Samarji, & Watt, 2016).

Immediacy was first described by Mehrabian (1967) as the communicative behaviors that enhance physical or psychological closeness in interpersonal communication. Verbal and non-verbal immediacy can increase psychological closeness and interaction between teachers and students, and lessen the sense of isolation which an e-learning student might feel. Verbal immediacy would be a sense of psychological closeness produced by word selection, and includes the use of humor, frequent use of student name, encouragement of discussion and follow-up comments, and sharing of personal examples. Non-verbal immediacy would be a sense of psychological closeness produced by physical communicative behaviors and facial expression, smiling, eye contact, body movement and touch. Verbal immediacy seems to be more relevant to e-learning, as texting is the major means of communication in asynchronous mode. With the growth of learning technology this has changed, as in a synchronous communication mode the use of devices such as microphones and cameras has helped in establishing audio and optical contact between participants. Simultaneously the use of main chat or chat rooms can promote interaction and immediacy in plenary session or in smaller groups. Additionally, the use of video-lectures, and audio or video postings in forums or podcasts differentiates the non verbal communication.

Butland and Beebe (1992) find evidence that instructor immediacy in a synchronous e-learning environment, such as immediate verbal and non-verbal communications, including timely feedback and use of emoting in text (such as using a word or phrase enclosed in angle-brackets to express emotion, e.g. <sigh>, <grin>), as well as the frequency of response as variables of interaction. Thus, online educators need to manifest immediate behaviors when providing feedback to distant learners. Timely expressed immediacy is very crucial in order to overcome time and space barriers and promote interaction in online learning.

Furthermore, LaRose and Whitten (1998) suggest that perhaps the greatest potential for enhancing instructional immediacy lies in altering the behavior of the computer itself. Adaption of the computer's automatic response to students can contribute effectively to augment immediacy, e.g. personal greetings when users logs in, personal forms of address in all their communications with students, customization of a personal tutor that can help students with navigating the course site. They argue that this suggests one of the ways in which web courses could be made more immediate than conventional classroom instruction:

In live classrooms, few instructors can master the names of all of their students in classes of 20 or 30, let alone recognize them and greet them on sight with a salutation that lets the student know that the instructor recalls previous interactions. Web courses can do that, and from the very first day. Real instructors can give feedback and praise to the students they engage in class and the few more they may encounter at other times, but Web courses can do that for every student, all the time (Discussion, para. 4).

Learning Group and Learning Community

Woods and Baker (2004) support that interaction alone is insufficient to create a positive social dynamic in the online classroom. Educators have to understand the interaction and immediacy dynamics in order to avoid forms of negative communication, therefore greater isolation and alienation among distance learners and construct a positive social dynamic which affects positively the nature and quality of communication in the online learning environment.

In all models and studies of group development, interaction between its members is essential in order for the group to connect, grow, face up to challenges, tackle problems, find solutions, plan work and deliver results.

As educational technology increases rapidly, the potential of new communication tools (teleconferences, whiteboards, blogs and wikis) in group development must be evaluated and these tools should be integrated in the learning process. These tools are even more important for the maintenance of the learning group after the end of the course and/or the creation of a learning community (Pavlis-Korres, 2010).

Rovai (2002) includes interaction in the four dimensions -spirit, trust, interaction and learning- of the classroom community. If the aim is to create a strong sense of classroom community, educators should learn to enhance these dimensions, in order to rely on the communities to promote a sense of well-being, quality of the learning experience and effective learning.

Misanchuk and Anderson (2001) argue that richer learning takes place within the context of a learning community and they present instructional and non-instructional strategies in order to move from a cohort to a learning community. They support that one of the most important indicators of a strong learning community is when students communicate not only on an academic level but on a personal level. The evidence of a successful community is when a majority of the members feel they are in a safe enough space to "speak up" about things in the public forum, rather than in individual e-mail messages.

When they begin to talk about their personal lives (families, hobbies, jobs), their triumphs and trials with being a distance student (scheduling, technical problems, disagreement with pedagogy), when they seek each other's counsel for other areas of their life (job change, which elective course to take next, family issues), this is the point *at which we feel they are comfortable as a community* (Misanchuk & Anderson, 2001, p.7).

They propose the creation of an online café for off-topic discussions and as there may be a few members of the community who do not feel that the Online Café is an appropriate place to discuss non-academic subjects, it is the role of the mentor-educator and the community members to make the Café a welcoming place for this type of discussion. Their findings are aligned with the socio-cognitive literature (Vygotsky, 1978;

Harasim, 1990) which states that learning is a social activity and that social interaction is vital to cognitive development.

Finally, it must be stressed that neither interaction nor the group development itself are the primary goals. These should be considered means for helping learning groups achieve their educational goals.

The Role of the Educator in E-Learning

The role of educator of adults in an e-learning environment is even more critical than in traditional classes. On top of the task of "helping people to learn", the educator also has to help learners overcome potential barriers caused by various factors: technology; time; attitudes of learners towards the use of ICT; lastly, the way different types of interaction occur. In the literature a lot has been written about the critical role the educator plays in ensuring online courses are successful (Harasim, Hiltz, Teles, & Turoff, 1995; Minotti, 2002).

Shank (2004) delineates the competencies of the online educator and divides them into five competency areas: administrative, design, facilitation, evaluation, and technical. Administrative competencies aim to assure smooth course operations and reduce instructor and learner overload. Design competencies aim to assure adequate learning outcomes and satisfaction. This area of competencies includes plans activities that allow learners to attach personal meaning to content, the incorporation of social aspects to improve satisfaction and the provision of a realistic environment, while they also present multiple viewpoints and overcome anonymity. Facilitation competencies have as a primary goal to provide social benefits and enhance learning. Within this area the instructor sets or facilitates the formation of communication rules and group decision-making norms; provides compelling opportunities for online discussion, negotiation and debate; moderates discussion, contributes advanced content knowledge and insights; models desired methods of communication; fosters sharing of knowledge, questions, and expertise; contributes outside resources (online, print-based, others) and encourages learners to do so as well; responds adequately to discussion postings without "taking over"; acknowledges learners' contributions and moderates disagreements and group problems. In the evaluation area the primary goal is to assure that learners know how they will be evaluated, and help learners meet course objectives. Finally, in the technical area actions aim to overcome barriers associated with technical components. Shank's approach focuses on individual actions and applies mainly to asynchronous instruction. Some contexts may require additional or different actions. However, her approach satisfies the requirements of the adults' educator as these have been analyzed in the relevant section.

The same mentality underlies the "Making the Virtual Classroom a Reality" (MVCR) program, an online faculty development program which defines exactly the competencies required or at least recommended for a quality online instructor. The categories of competencies are administrative, personal, technological, pedagogical (subdivided into instructional design, instructional delivery, and assessment), plus social roles and abilities. Administrative roles involve the processes required to function within the given institutional and legal setting, as well as general institutionalized ethics. Competencies placed into the administrative roles category are institution specific, as the method of instructor evaluation, the policies regarding student management, the academic honesty policies etc. may differ by institution. Personal roles and abilities involve the overall physical and mental abilities of the instructor and the instructor's personality attributes. In most, but not all cases, these abilities function within an instructor's intrapersonal cognitive domain. Technological roles and abilities are specific to the utilization of technology

independent of pedagogy. They include the instructor's technical knowledge, the availability of that technology and his ability to actually use and help others in the use of a given form of technology. Pedagogical roles and abilities involve aspects of actual design and implementation of instruction. Finally, the social category entails to the social functions that an online instructor in a student-centered, social learning environment is expected to possess. Participation within a community of practice is probably the most general of the social roles that all instructors should possess, meaning that this category is valued somewhat independently of instructional context. However, some of these social roles may not be as highly valued in some paradigms of instruction, especially in a model based entirely on student-only self-paced instruction (Virgil & Varvel, 2007).

Furthermore, Kearsley (2000) points out that "the most important role of the instructor in online classes is to ensure a high degree of interactivity and participation. This means designing and conducting learning activities that result in engagement with the subject matter and with fellow students" (p. 78).

It is the educator in an online environment who, by asking questions, using humor, addressing individuals by name, initiating discussion, and sharing personal examples can produce immediacy and contribute to a sense of psychological closeness. Creating an online environment that promotes socio-emotional-driven interaction, such as exchanging empathetic messages, encouraging self-disclosure, and discussing the backgrounds and interests of learners will help promote feelings of friendship and connections to others, and consequently increase immediacy between learners, educator and content in a way that fits the requirements of effective online adult education.

Online educators must understand the nature and the ways group development works in web-based instructional settings, support group dynamics and facilitate the forming and function of the online group in order to promote real interaction, critical thinking, collaboration and immediacy with and between learners.

Summing up, in Figure 1 the role and the tasks of the educator in an E-learning education process is presented (Pavlis-Korres, 2010).

The above competencies of the online educator are not necessarily found in one person, therefore the various actions may be performed by more than one person acting as a team. Teaching as a whole requires a complex association of many skills, and the necessary associations may vary widely among contexts.

Training the E-Educators of Adults

Since, as stressed above, the e-educator's role is particularly complex and demanding, a prerequisite for its effective practice is the educator's appropriate training.

Figure 1. The role and the tasks of the online adult educator

Therefore, training the e-educators of adults is necessary, so that are able to integrate the adult education principles when teaching in an online environment in order to promote interaction.

The programs designed to train e-educators of adults should be implemented within an online environment. The training methods applied should be the same as those that the participants themselves will later apply in their own teaching. Educators who possess first-hand experience as learners in an online class can associate themselves easily with learner needs, if they have relevant personal student experience.

CASE STUDY: TRAINING E-EDUCATORS ON INTEGRATING ADULT EDUCATION PRINCIPLES IN ONLINE ENVIRONMENT

Historical Background: E-Learning Programs Provided in Greece by the General Secretariat for Lifelong Learning

The General Secretariat for Lifelong Learning (GSLLL) of the Hellenic Ministry of Education and Religious Affairs is a national agency responsible for the development of lifelong learning public policies and rules, as well as for the implementation and supervision of national educational programs. Among the responsibilities of GSLLL is the promotion of distance learning and training, including the use of new technologies and digital environments in lifelong learning programs for adults (Law 3879/2010, Greek Parliament).

In the period from 2006 to 2011, the GSLLL designed and implemented blended e-learning programs addressed to Greek citizens within the framework of non-formal general adult education. The Learning Management System (LMS) which was used for the program was a customized version of the Moodle platform. The programs aimed to provide free e-learning to any interested citizen over 18 years old, with the sole prerequisite of a certification on basic computer skills.

The learning model was a blended model, which combined traditional adult learning methods with distance learning methods. The courses included three face-to-face meetings which took place in the beginning, in the middle and in the end. The e-learning sessions included the use of educational materials, communication tools (mainly e-mail and forum), self-assessments and a graded test in each step.

A wide range of adult learners enrolled in these blended programs, making them very popular in Greece. The learners had the opportunity to participate in the entire learning process in a flexible manner because it was adapted to their backgrounds and personal, family and professional schedules. By the end of the second educational cycle 3.768 adult learners had successfully completed the program.

At the end of 2011 an external and an internal evaluation was conducted with the aim of assessing the successes and failures of the programs, taking into account the perspectives of learners and staff engaged. The results of the internal evaluation (Pavlis-Korres, 2013) showed that the vast majority of learners (82.3%) expressed a strong wish to attend another e-learning program. Again, when asked about their preference among the face-to-face, blended or online sessions, the majority (56.9%) reported that they preferred the blended model like the one that they had already attended, and 11.2% had chosen fully online courses. A worth mentioning percentage of 30.4% had chosen the use of a platform and the replacement of the face-to-face meetings by online meetings in synchronous mode. This information was the basis for the subsequent planning of Electronic Municipal Adult Education Centers (e-MAEC), which are currently running educational programs in Greece in cooperation with the GSLLL and are addressed to learners who live in remote and inaccessible areas such as small remote islands in the South Aegean Sea, increasing learners' participation and at the same time decreasing the functional cost of the program. In the first period of e-MAEC running, the educational model was based on a combination of synchronous and asynchronous mode of education, by the replacement of face-to-face meetings with online meetings and by the use of a customized version of the Moodle platform. This way, not only considerable benefits were achieved (reducing travel costs, overcoming spatial constraints), but also, owing to the synchronous mode of communication, there was a reduction of the negative effects associated with learner isolation which may occur in an asynchronous learning environment.

The e-MAEC centers are exercising a continuous effort to integrate the adult education principles and methods in programs using new technologies, to promote digital environments in lifelong learning and to develop educational material suitable for adults' e-learning. A specialist team has been assigned the task of adapting educational material for online purposes. Through the use of multimedia learners are engaged actively with content. Moreover, interactive and collaborative activities result in a considerable degree of interaction between learner and educator and among learners themselves.

The basic adult education principles have been integrated in the e-MAEC courses in a way that offers more than a simple transfer and adaptation of active educational techniques into an online environment.

Before starting the course, the learners have to attend a 25-hour face-to-face program, in order to become familiar with the on-line environment which they will be using in the e-courses.

The training of all e-educators on the implementation of the e-learning model used in the e-MAEC courses and on how to integrate the main principles of adult education in an on-line environment is considered a prerequisite, di-

rectly associated with the demanding role of the e-educator. For this purpose, GSLLL conducted two training seminars for 28 e-educators selected to teach in e-courses. The evaluation of the first seminar was taken into account for the design and implementation of the second one, which is presented hereafter.

Seminar for Training E-Educators of Adults

The integration of adult education principles in e-learning courses addressed to adults requires a different approach, taking into account the specific features of the learning process. Promoting interaction in combination with the development of the online group and community are the most important features to fight isolation in online environment and achieve better learning outcomes.

The main goals of the seminar were:

- Familiarizing trainees with the synchronous and asynchronous platform, which they will be using during their educational work
- Teaching how to integrate the principles of adult education in an online environment
- Practice on the above mentioned issues.

The training of e-educators was designed and implemented in collaboration with GSLLL trainers (three trainers), members of the technical support team and the scientific responsible persons of the project.

Fourteen e-educators of various specialties participated, (both male and female). Proven knowledge of basic computer usage skills (e.g. ECDL) was required for all the trainees.

The seminar was implemented fully online, with 8 synchronous three-hour meetings and several asynchronous activities which took place either before the synchronous meetings or in between. The duration of the seminar was one month. The Big Blue Button (BBB) synchronous open source platform was used together with a customized Moodle version.

Investigation of Educational Needs and Trainees Profile

In the beginning, the availability of trainees on attending the seminar was investigated with the use of Doodle, an internet calendar tool, which is very useful for time management and coordinating meetings. Then, with the use of an online questionnaire which was set on googledocs, the participants' training needs and expectations were investigated (Conrad & Donaldson, 2004; Hughes, 2004; Pavlis-Korres, 2010).

It was found that most of participants had teaching experience in adult education and had also received relevant training. Many had been trained on the subject of distance learning and had obtained relevant teaching experience which, however, was related to blended e-learning programs. It is important to notice that their experience was primarily on the asynchronous platform Moodle and only a few had any experience on synchronous platforms. However, in their everyday life, they were all frequent users of communication software such as Skype and social media applications such as Facebook. Regarding their expectations from the seminar, their main goal was to get familiarized with the platforms which they would be using, to acquire knowledge and skills on teaching methods in an online environment and to put in use the web and the various web 2.0 tools now available, contributing towards a more effective online teaching of their field of expertise.

Seminar Content

Taking into account the results of the assessment on the needs and expectations of trainees, the trainers of GSLLL developed the content for the

8 synchronous meetings (three hours each), as well as the content for the asynchronous activities related to the integration of the adult education principles and the promotion of interaction. The main topics included were the following:

1. The learner within an e-environment
   ◦ additional barriers and difficulties faced by adult learners in an online environment; ways to address them
   ◦ prerequisites for effective adult learning in an online environment
2. The educator of adults within an e-environment
   ◦ obstacles and difficulties the educator is facing and how to overcome them
   ◦ prerequisites of effective adult teaching in an online environment
   ◦ the role of the e-educator
3. Preparation and presentation of e-microteaching
   ◦ creation of interactive educational material
   ◦ using active techniques in educational process in order to promote interaction.

Depending on the trainees' needs, during the course there were constant adjustments on the sequence and the time schedule of the topics. All the GSLLL trainers worked as a team, collaborating constantly and closely with each other in order to achieve this goal (Cranton, 2000; Davis, 1995; Speer & Ryan, 1998; Partridge & Hallam, 2005).

Training Methodology and Implementation of the Seminar

Throughout the seminar there was an effort to promote the basic types of interaction described above (learner with content, learner with educator, between learners themselves, learner with interface). There was also an effort to make sure that the online learning group would work effectively, so that its members would be more involved in the learning process, would experience higher levels of satisfaction and would therefore obtain better learning outcomes.

For this purpose, various instructional techniques originating from the face-to-face adult classroom were applied (Caffarella, 2002), properly adapted to fulfill the demands of synchronous online environment. The GSLLL trainers also designed several activities; they either converted from face-to-face to online interactions, or developed from scratch in order to help trainees use the online communication tools and to promote the development of the online group. In order to implement these activities several communication tools were selected, according to the nature of each activity.

For the synchronous online meetings several activities were organized, which had to be completed either individually or in groups, with the use of the BBB and Moodle platform. These activities included:

- Brainstorming, where responses were typed by the learners in the chat room of the platform.
- Work in pairs, with "discussion" taking place between two learners in the "whisper in chat" part of the chat room; the results were announced in the whole group with the use of microphone and camera assigned to each speaker.
- Work in small groups, using the chat rooms provided by the asynchronous platform; these chat rooms had been made "open" before the beginning of each activity and had been updated with written instructions on teamwork required. The use of the asynchronous platform in order to create and manage chat rooms was a decision taken by the trainers because the BBB platform does not have such a feature. During this activity the trainers were "moving" from

group to group in order to facilitate their work, as it happens in a face-to-face classroom. The announcement of the results was made by a representative of each group in the synchronous platform (BBB) either via the microphone or camera, or combining those with live projection of the results of each group on the wallwisher (an internet application which allows learners to post their thoughts using electronic sticky notes on a shared digital wallscreen).

- "Voting and polls" on various issues, where the trainees could express their opinion by "raising a hand", using the relevant function of the synchronous communication platform.
- Discussion with other trainees in the plenary session, with the use of a microphone and web camera.
- Presentations made by trainers with the use of various online information sources and web 2.0 tools.

One fundamental aspect of meeting the needs of online learners is allowing adequate time for an activity to be accomplished. Owing to the fact that, in most cases, online communication takes longer than classroom communication, sufficient time had to be allowed in the course plan, for activities requiring online interaction among learners. Another factor which had to be considered was the frustration learners might experience due to various technical problems that might occur. In a synchronous activity, when technology fails and learners are unable to log in to a scheduled chat session, they feel that they have missed class; they have missed the opportunity to participate through no fault of their own. For that reason all synchronous meetings were recorded, so that those who could not attend could later, in retrospect, view the whole session (Conrad & Donaldson, 2004). Moreover, all members of the technical support team were present during the synchronous meetings, in order to provide their support to both trainers and trainees. This technical support provision proved to be very useful (Hughes, 2004).

Before the start of the seminar, as well as during its implementation, there were also different kinds of asynchronous activities, which were completed by trainees with the use of the forum in the training platform. Some of these were aimed at making trainees perform an initial processing of issues which would later be discussed in the synchronous meeting to follow. Moreover, trainees were asked to write down on a separate forum their views and thoughts on the synchronous meetings they had attended. In addition, there was an asynchronous group activity during which trainees were divided into 4 teams, allowed to select their own preferred means of communication among the synchronous BBB platform, the forum, the chat room or even phone-calls, so as to co-operate ideally and accomplish the assignment. As the course was intensive, it was not possible to run a bigger number of asynchronous activities, which would go deeper into the matters discussed and further develop critical thinking (Brookfield, 1995). However, the fact that all trainees managed to plan and present their own e-microteaching sessions, gave them the opportunity to test themselves in the role of an online adult educator, to put into practice knowledge gained from the seminar, to reflect critically on their own practice and to provide and receive feedback from instructors and fellow-trainees. During the preparation of the micro-teaching special forums were created to support trainees.

Particular care was taken in the development of the online learning group. Initially, trainers had adopted the roles of working as "social negotiators", providing activities that were interactive and would help learners get to know one another. Also trainers provided orientation to the course and kept learners on track by using ice-breaking activities, developing netiquette rules of the course etc. At a later stage they adopted the roles of facilitators, pairing dyads of learners, forming small groups and providing activities that require sharing of ideas, reflecting on experiences and collaboration to solve problems (Conrad & Donaldson, 2004). Special attention was paid to ice breaking activities, in order to facilitate the development of the online group (Pavlis-Korres, 2012). More specifically, before the start of the synchronous meetings, both trainees and their trainers posted a self-presentation by using various online resources and tools. In order to provide inspirational ideas to the trainees, trainers made use of different ways of self-presentation, e.g. forming an avatar, presenting a personal web-page, posting self-photos or creating a video. Similarly, the majority of trainees posted links of songs and personal pages on social networks, videos they created about themselves, photos etc. With this activity, trainees got to know each other better and their posts increased interaction with each-other. Additionally, during the first synchronous meeting, another ice-breaking activity took place which proved very effective, interactive and entertaining: the trainers took elements from trainees' self-presentations and created a puzzle with 17 images, each image reflecting a key personal characteristic of one trainee or trainer. The puzzle was gradually presented, image by image, on the whiteboard of the synchronous meeting; whenever one recognized a picture related to one's personal elements, one had to "raise hand" and address the group through a brief self-presentation. Some group members appeared to have common characteristics and interests, which resulted in the development of several sub-groups.

Evaluation of the Seminar

The evaluation of the seminar was conducted as an assessment in an engaged learning environment, focusing on whether the stated objectives of the course had been met and whether the students had been engaged in the learning process (Conrad & Donaldson, 2004).

At the end of the first synchronous meeting learners were asked to express anonymously their feelings about it on the wallwisher provided, in order to compose the "emotional map" of the group. It is important to note here that trainees mainly expressed satisfaction and increased interest; none reported any feelings of loneliness, isolation or alienation. Moreover, in the interval between synchronous online meetings, trainees were asked to provide feedback with regards to the content of each meeting, so that trainers could adapt the course content accordingly, in response to the individual needs of the participants.

In the last synchronous online meeting, trainees were asked to complete an online questionnaire for the evaluation of the seminar. Twelve out of fourteen participants completed the questionnaire. According to the results, all the trainees were very satisfied by their participation and believed that it helped them in exercising their future role as e-educators of adults. All of the trainees declared absolutely satisfied from their trainers. One, characteristically, commented that:

The seminar was something new for me... I fully realized its usefulness during its course, aided considerably by the trainers and the way they taught and presented material... they helped me use new technological means previously unknown to me... we were given the opportunity to learn and utilize new teaching methods, which lack nothing compared to traditional ones as they entail similar, if not more, potential ... we are grateful...

As to the duration of the seminar, the majority of participants (75%) stated that it was "exactly as long as was necessary", while 25% thought it was a little less than needed.

All trainees were satisfied with the content of the seminar. More specifically, the trainees' views on the usefulness of each thematic unit are presented in Table 1 below.

As is obvious in Table 1, all trainees appreciated the usefulness of the unit titled "communication tools in online environment", a unit focused primarily on promoting different types of interaction through these communicative tools.

Table 1. Usefulness of thematic units of the seminar for trainees

Unit \ Unit Usefulness	Not Useful	Slightly Useful	Moderately Useful	Very Useful	Extremely Useful
Overall presentation of program		8%	8%	50%	33%
Presentation on seminar content and modus operandi				8%	92%
Barriers and difficulties faced by adult learners in an online environment				33%	67%
Interaction in online environment				17%	83%
E-educator (e-trainer) role				8%	92%
Communication tools in online environment					100%
Optimum use of web tools				17%	83%
Online learning group				25%	75%
Netiquette				25%	75%
Familiarization with synchronous and asynchronous platform				17%	83%
E-Microteaching presentation				8%	92%
Tools to create and enrich educational material			8%	8%	84%

They also commented that they intend to apply all the instructional techniques they learned in practice in their own teaching. This was evident in their e-microteaching presentations, where they applied techniques such as work in small groups, writing on wallwishers, brainstorming, as well as several ice-breaking activities, a fact showing that they realized and valued the importance of activities promoting interaction, group building and development.

Table 2. depicts the intention of trainees to use, as educators, the communicative tools provided by the platform as well as activities, synchronous and asynchronous, similar to those conducted during the seminar.

As exhibited in Table 2, trainers do appreciate the effectiveness of active techniques and group work, since the percentages of pair work, group work and brainstorming are considerably high. Also, they feel comfortable with tools they already use, such as Power Point, which they wish to enrich with videos, but show some frustration towards new tools such as Prezi. As to the expression of their views in plenary meetings, they do value chat rooms and microphones, while they also favor the camera so as to see the speaker. It should be stressed here that at the beginning of the seminar most trainees avoided the camera, but gradually used it more and more as relations within the group developed more deeply. According to Table 2, trainees intended to use wallwisher writing in their future e-classes, as well as the synchronous warm-up activity since, as follows also from Table 3, they find them quite suitable for strengthening communication and interaction among participants.

Table 2. Intention of using communication tools and educational activities by the trainees

Communication Tools/Activities	None	Slight	Moderate	Strong	Absolute
Asynchronous self-presentation activity			17%	42%	42%
Typical forum			8%	67%	25%
Forum using web 2.0			17%	25%	58%
Pair work				17%	83%
Group work				25%	75%
Case-study in groups			8%	42%	50%
Brainstorming				25%	75%
View expression via microphone in plenary session				25%	75%
View expression through chat in plenary session			8%	8%	83%
View expression through camera in plenary session			8%	17%	75%
Power point presentations		8%		8%	83%
Prezi presentations		25%	25%	25%	25%
Presentations enriched with video				25%	75%
Word clouds (wordle)		8%	8%	25%	58%
Writing on wallwisher		8%		17%	75%
Glossary		8%	8%	42%	42%
Calendar		8%	25%	25%	42%
Announcements		8%		25%	58%
Synchronous ice breaking/self-presentation activity			8%	17%	75%

Table 3. Types of interaction achieved during the seminar, in relation to the activities implemented, according to trainees' views

Type of Interaction / Activity	Educator-Learner Interaction	Learner-Learner Interaction
Asynchronous Ice-Breaking Activity	59%	59%
Forum on the commons and differences between traditional educator and e-educator	50%	59%
Synchronous Ice-Breaking Activity	92%	75%
Pair work	84%	92%
Work in small groups	84%	92%
Group working on case studies	75%	84%
Brainstorming	84%	75%
Presentations by the trainers	59%	67%
Writing on wallwisher	84%	75%
Forum with the use of web 2.0 tools (e.g. use of avatars)	92%	75%
Discussion in plenary session by using the main chat	84%	92%
Discussion in plenary session by using the microphone	92%	75%
Use of camera by trainers and participants when they speak	100%	84%
Voting and polls	84%	84%
Use of video in presentations	84%	67%
Questionnaire before first meeting	67%	
Supporting Forum on e-microteaching	92%	75%
Critical reflective forum after e-microteaching	84%	92%
E-Microteaching support through synchronous BBB	84%	
Calendar	25%	
Announcements	33%	
Glossary	25%	
General questions forum	84%	
E-mail	100%	

It must be noted that trainees were satisfied by the fact that during the synchronous meetings all the GSLLL trainers were involved, working collaboratively. Moreover, team teaching was ex-

tensively applied, which kept the trainees' interest high and allowed them to take advantage of the knowledge and skills of all the different experts. (Davis, 1995; Speer & Ryan, 1998; Partridge & Hallam, 2005). Furthermore, their responses to the open questions of the questionnaire indicated that the seminar helped them overcome their reservations on the possibility of active participation and interaction between an educator and a learner, or among learners, within an online learning environment. They eventually reached the conclusion that this can indeed happen in an online course in the same way as in traditional face-to-face courses.

Table 3 shows the trainees' views on two types of interaction, educator-learner (trainer/trainee) and between learners (trainees), developed during the course of the seminar. For evaluation purposes, trainees completed a five-point Likert scale (1 = not at all, 2 = little, 3 = quite, 4 = much and 5 = very much), measuring the degree in which these two types of interaction were developed, in relation with each type of activity incorporated in the seminar. Table 3 summarizes the number of strong positive views expressed by the trainees (4 = very, and 5 = very much) towards each type of activity.

As shown in Table 3, according to the trainees' views, the activities which better promoted interaction between trainer and trainees were the use of camera by trainers and participants while speaking, e-mail, the synchronous ice-breaking activity, the forum with the use of web 2.0 tools, discussion in the plenary session with the use of a microphone and the forum on e-microteaching. Regarding the activities that better promoted interaction between learners, it is shown that trainees valued as most important the work in small groups, work in pairs, discussion in plenary session by using chat and the critical reflective forum on e-microteaching.

During the periods of asynchronous learning, trainees participated in forums on the educational platform. Among the most popular forums were: that on which they expressed and discussed general questions (17 posts); those related to e-microteaching (30 posts); the critical reflective ones after synchronous meetings (19 posts); finally, the one with the use of avatar (14 posts).

During the same periods, trainees were divided into 4 groups. They were asked to discuss within their own group some aspects of the e-educator role, and post their group views on the relevant forum. Groups discussed the following points: enrichment and adaptation of the educational material, promotion of participation and co-operation, synchronous and asynchronous trainer presence, trainer feedback and, finally, encouragement and facilitation of interaction.

In group results it is clear that trainees focus on ways to develop interaction and immediacy through the use of communication tools, and on ways to incorporate adult education principles in online environment. More specifically, they state:

The trainer should start "learning" his trainees at the very beginning, so as to discover interests and possible strengths or weaknesses, both individual and group, as well as the dynamics and expectations of the group etc. He should be in constant contact, synchronous and asynchronous, with trainees, investigating to what extent their needs and questions as to the content of his teachings are being met. (1st Group)

Enrichment of content must include the use of as many communicative tools as possible (chat, forum, BBB etc.), to compensate for the lack of physical contact and to enhance participation in the procedures (1st Group).

Central aims of the adult educator should be: a. Encouragement of participation b. strengthening of co-operation among trainees. Consequently, promoting the said aims should also be included in the agenda of an adult e-educator, all the more so as he, compared to the face-to-face educator, has to tackle the additional problem of possible isolation within a technical environment. Through the potential of technology, the e-trainer aims to create an educational environment infused

with true communication and a willingness to co-operate. To achieve this, he must himself be familiarized with and informed on his electronic working context to the highest possible degree, so as to minimize any reservations and uncertainties of trainees due to their probable lack of technological skills. Moreover, he must use and optimize as many technological tools as possible, so as to trigger his trainees' interest. (2nd Group)

The e-educator needs to organize his teaching based on his group's profile, and adapt the material to the trainees' interests. In addition to synchronous discussions, he must also promote a variety of asynchronous activities which can reinforce even more the good background feeling among participants. Finally, he must try to act as "facilitator" of learning and animator of the group through dialogue, assignments, setting discussion themes etc. (2nd Group)

The e-educator must use as much as possible adult education techniques adapted to electronic means: brainstorming, snowball, discussion, questions-answers, case-study, demonstration and role-play. He must also have a good sense of humour, and use word games or any other games tailored to suit his group's needs as well as the specific lesson so as to enliven interest, encourage participation and create a safe and comfortable background, in which trainees feel free to express views, questions, comments, personal experience etc. (2nd Group)

Elaboration of individual communication between trainer and each trainee through e-mail, and development of group communication through forums on selected issues (2nd Group).

In synchronous education mode, feedback between trainer and trainee is more direct and functional, as there is immediate interaction. It could be said that there is a sort of simulation of physical communication, so that the two end up bearing a considerable degree of similarity. To cope, an educator must possess, among other skills, those of clear speech and efficient use of oral communication. If a camera happens to be used, there is the additional advantage of body language, which is considered highly important for emphasis, illustration of points and comprehension of content. (3rd Group)

In asynchronous communication, knowledge of relevant codes of tools (e.g. emoticons, suitable punctuation, pictures etc.) is regarded as highly necessary, as it is an ideal way to compensate for a possible lack of body language (3rd Group).

To facilitate interaction and animation of the trainee group, the educator will need to consider thoroughly, from the very beginning of any activity, the characteristics of members, e.g. their age, experiences, expectations from the lesson, motives underlying their participation. Equally important is the framework within which the educational activity unfolds: environment, technology available, spare time, access to resources etc. (4th Group)

In an open question of the questionnaire, the trainees expressed their wish to maintain contact with their fellow-trainees as well as with their trainers, aiming at mutual support and the exchange of best practices (Anderson & Garrison, 1998). Indeed, after the completion of the seminar, trainees continued to participate in the forum of the platform, exchanging views, information, sources and experiences. The fact that their communication included several personal elements may be an indication that an online community had been created (Misanchuk & Anderson, 2001).

Limitations of the Case Study

The main limitation of the case study was its short duration. More time would be needed in order for the online learning group to operate as efficiently as possible and exploit the full potential of the asynchronous communication mode, especially

for the development of critical thinking through the use of the forum (Conrad & Donaldson, 2004; Pavlis-Korres, 2010).

Trainees also experienced several technical problems in relation to connecting with/logging on the platform. Finally, the BBB platform which was used, suffered a lack of the ability to create and manage chat rooms, thus hindering the possibility to work in small groups.

Solutions and Recommendations

Despite the limited duration of the seminar, which was primarily due to administrative reasons and dictated its intense character, it was proved necessary for the training of the trainees, as otherwise they would not be able to perform effectively as e-educators. The fact that most of the participants possessed knowledge and teaching experience in adult education allowed the designers of the seminar to focus on issues related to the integration of adult education principles in an online environment, rather than having to allocate precious time in teaching basic adult educational principles.

Seminars targeted at trainees who do not possess knowledge and experience in adult education should be designed accordingly, allowing the necessary time depending on the needs of each educational group. The same applies to trainees with lesser computer skills and/or missing knowledge and experience in e-learning. In all cases "design flexibility" should be applied both in content design and in seminar duration.

The training of the e-educators took place in the same online environment and with the same techniques and tools which they would be using later, in their own teaching, allowing them the opportunity to experience as learners the educational process they would be applying as e-educators of adults in the future.

Despite the short duration of the seminar, which did not allow for many critical thinking activities, the way the seminar content and its activities were constructed enhanced participants' critical thinking and promoted the formation of positive attitudes towards e-learning and the role of the e-educator of adults to a satisfactory level (Brookfield, 1995; Cranton, 2006).

Training seminars addressed to e-educators of adults should, therefore, take place in the online environment in which the trainees will later be teaching and with the techniques and tools they will be applying in their own teaching. In this way, e-educators will be better familiarized with online environments, and they will also develop a higher degree of empathy towards their learners, an element which is one of the basic personal attributes an educator of adults should possess (Sisco, 1984).

The course content was developed following a needs analysis of the trainees', in order to cover their specific needs and integrate the principles of adult education which should be followed regardless of whether the course was implemented face-to-face or online (Knowles, Holton III, & Swanson, 1998; Pavlis-Korres, 2010).

During the phase of course design, the GSLLL trainers cooperated closely with each other as well as with the technical supporting team and the scientifically responsible persons, exchanging views, ideas, information and sources on training materials, in order to develop the course content accordingly. During the implementation, they all engaged in collaborative teaching by working as a team. (Davis, 1995; Speer & Ryan, 1998; Partridge & Hallam, 2005).

The complex role of the online educator of adults, as well as the requirements on the design and implementation of an online program, dictate that collaborative processes and team work are required in order to achieve the best educational outcome (Pavlis-Korres, 2010).

The activities implemented during the course of the seminar aimed at the promotion of the main types of interaction (Moore, 1989; Hillman, Willis, & Gunawardena, 1994). The activities which enhanced collaborative learning, a process in which the teacher and student are partners in constructing knowledge and is consistent with the basic principles and methodology of adult education (Cross, 1981; Rogers, 2007), were either adapted from face-to-face learning, or designed from scratch with the use of appropriate communicative tools (Conrad & Donaldson, 2004; Pavlis-Korres, 2012). Throughout the seminar, particular attention was given to the development of the online learning group. The ice-breaking activities – both synchronous and asynchronous – as well as other activities during the seminar facilitated the operation of the online learning group in all its stages. Additionally, trainer-immediacy – both verbal and nonverbal – has been achieved through the quickness of trainers' response to trainees in e-mails and forum and through the use of humor, the use of inclusive pronouns (we, your, our) and the use of electronic gestures (smiles etc.) (Mehlenbacher, 2010; Mason & Rennie, 2008; Ghamdi, Samarji, & Watt, 2016).

A fundamental provision in online courses addressed to adults should be the design and implementation of educational activities through the use of the proper communication tools, in order to promote as many types of interaction as possible and empower the development and function of the online learning group and community, affecting positively the educational outcome (Anderson, 2003; Swan, 2002).

The implementation of e-microteaching is a great opportunity for practicing and developing teaching skills under controlled conditions and close supervision which provides useful feedback by the trainers as well as other trainees (Allen, 1967).

Continuous formative evaluation proved to be particularly useful to trainers, as it allowed them to adapt the sequence of topics and choose the appropriate educational activities in order to meet the learners' needs. The findings of the summative evaluation of the seminar will be used in the design of future training seminar addressed to e-educators of GSLLL.

Both types of evaluation – formative and summative – should be included in all online training programs addressed to e-educators of adults, so that all the elements deriving from the course experience and the trainees' active participation are taken into consideration to ensure the effectiveness of the program (Scriven, 1991; Cranton, 2000; Caffarella, 2002).

CONCLUSION AND FUTURE RESEARCH DIRECTIONS

Among the important prerequisites for effective adult learning one should include active participation in the educational process and the development of a learning environment which favors the creation of equal and collaborative relationships between all participants, including the educator. Successful e-learning in an online environment requires the promotion of various types of interaction and immediacy, as well as a satisfactory development of an online group and community. Integrating the principles of adult education in an online course creates a sound interactive environment in which adults will engage actively and learn effectively.

The role of the e-educator of adults is complex and demanding, and its optimum performance requires substantial training. The case study on training GSLLL e-educators in an online environment shows that integration of adult education principles is achievable and creates favorable conditions for effective interactive learning.

The model of e-learning replacing the face-to-face meetings with synchronous online ones, in combination with asynchronous e-learning, can be an important transitional stage for countries like Greece, where e-learning has not been widely applied in programs of general adult education. Also, a considerable number of adult learners in Greece – especially older ones – have some reservations regarding the degree in which e-learning

can improve communication and relationships between participants and can actually lead to better overall learning outcomes.

Taking into account the limitations of this case study, further research into the effectiveness of this model should be undertaken, focusing specifically on ways to promote the various types of interaction, critical thinking and development of online group and community in online environments. Furthermore, by designing and implementing training programs for e-educators of adults without the time limitations of the present case study, researchers could further explore the benefits arising from the integration of adult education principles into online training environments and the effective implementation of collaborative teaching.

REFERENCES

Abdelmalak, M. (2013). The Process of Building Learning Communities in an Online Course. In T. Bastiaens & G. Marks (Eds.), *Proceedings of World Conference on E-Learning in Corporate, Government, Healthcare, and Higher Education* 2013 (pp. 516-523). Chesapeake, VA: AACE. Retrieved November 16, 2014 from http://www.editlib.org/p/114885

Allen, D. (1967). *Microteaching: A Description.* Stanford University.

Anderson, T. (2003). Getting the Mix Right Again: An updated and theoretical rationale for interaction. *International Review of Research in Open and Distance Learning, 4*(2). Available at http://www.irrodl.org/index.php/irrodl/article/view/149/230

Anderson, T., & Garrison, D. R. (1998). Learning in a networked world: New roles and responsibilities. In C. Gibson (Ed.), *Distance Learners in Higher Education* (pp. 97–112). Madison, WI: Atwood Publishing.

Billington, D. D. (1989). *The role of education in stimulating human development*. Paper presented at the Annual Conference of the Western College Reading and Learning Association, Seattle, WA.

Booher, R. K., & Seiler, W. J. (1982). Speech communication anxiety: An impediment to academic achievement in the university classroom. *Journal of Classroom Interaction, 18*(1), 23–27.

Brockett, R. G., & Hiemstra, R. (1985). Bridging the theory-practice gap in self-directed learning. In S. Brookfield (Ed.), *Self-directed learning: From theory to practice* (pp. 31–40). San Francisco: Jossey-Bass Publishers. doi:10.1002/ace.36719852505

Brookfield, S. (1986). *Understanding and Facilitating Adult Learning*. Open University Press.

Brookfield, S. D. (1990). Discussion. In M. W. Galbraith (Ed.), *Adult learning methods: A guide to effective instruction* (pp. 187–204). Malabar, FL: Robert E. Krieger.

Brookfield, S. D. (1995). *Becoming a Critically Reflective Teacher*. San Francisco: Jossey-Bass Publishers.

Brown, R. E. (2001, September). The process of community-building in distance learning courses. *Journal of Asynchronous Learning Networks, 5*(2).

Butland, M. J., & Beebe, S. A. (1992). *A Study of the Application of Implicit Communication Theory to Teacher Immediacy and Student Learning*. Paper presented at the Annual Meeting of the International Communication Association, Miami, FL. Retrieved from ERIC database. ED 346 532.

Caffarella, R. (2002). *Planning programs for adult learners. A practical guide for educators, trainers and staff developers*. San Francisco: Jossey-Bass.

Christophel, D. (1990). The relationships among teacher immediacy behaviors, student motivation, and learning. *Communication Education, 39*(4), 323–340. doi:10.1080/03634529009378813

Clark, R. E. (1994). Media will never influence learning. *Educational Technology Research and Development, 47*(2), 21–29. doi:10.1007/BF02299088

Conrad, R. M., & Donalson, J. A. (2004). *Engaging the online learner, Activities and resources for creative instruction*. Jossey-Bass.

Courau, S. (1994). *Les outils d' excellence du formateur* (2nd ed.). Paris: ESF.

Cranton, P. (2000). *Planning Instruction for Adult Learners* (2nd ed.). Toronto: Wall & Emerson, Inc.

Cranton, P. (2006). *Understanding and promoting transformative learning: A guide for educators of Adults*. San Francisco, CA: Jossey-Bass.

Cross, K. P. (1981). *Adults as Learners*. San Francisco: Jossey-Bass.

Davis, J. R. (1995). *Interdisciplinary courses and team teaching*. Phoenix, AZ: American Council on Education and Oryx Press.

Duck, J. (2005). Creating Dynamic Interaction in a Virtual World: Add Value to Online Classrooms through Live Elearning and Collaboration: a Demonstration. *Developments in Business Simulation and Experiential Learning, 32*, 101–103.

Fisher, T. D. (1995). Self-directedness in adult vocational education students: its role in learning and implications for instruction, Kent State University. *Journal of Vocational and Technical Education, 12*(1). Available in http://scholar.lib.vt.edu/ejournals/JVTE/v12n1/fisher.html

Freire, P. (1970). *Pedagogy of the Oppressed*. New York: Herder and Herder.

Fulford, C., & Zhang, S. (1993). Perception of interaction: The critical predictor in distance learning. *American Journal of Distance Education, 7*(3), 8–12. doi:10.1080/08923649309526830

Gannon-Leary, P., & Fontainha, E. (2007). Communities of practice and virtual learning communities: benefits, barriers and success factors. *Elearning Papers, 5*, 20-29. Retrieved from http://nrl.northumbria.ac.uk/2147/)

Garrison, R., & Cleveland-Innes, M. (2005). Facilitating Cognitive Presence in Online Learning: Interaction Is Not Enough. *American Journal of Distance Education, 19*(3), 133–148. doi:10.1207/s15389286ajde1903_2

Ghamdi, A., Samrji, A., & Watt, A. (2016). Essential Considerations in Distance Education in KSA: Teacher Immediacy in a Virtual Teaching and Learning Environment. *International Journal of Information and Education Technology, 6*(1).

Gorham, J., & Zakahi, W. R. (1990). A comparison of teacher and student perceptions of immediacy and learning: Monitoring process and product. *Communication Education, 39*(4), 354–368. doi:10.1080/03634529009378815

Grooms, L. (2003). Computer-Mediated Communication: A vehicle for learning. *International Review of Research in Open and Distance Learning, 4*(2). Retrieved from http://www.irrodl.org/index.php/irrodl/article/view/148/709

Gunawardena, C. N. (1995). Social presence theory and implications for interaction and collaborative learning in computer conferences. *International Journal of Educational Telecommunications, 1*(2/3), 147–166.

Hackman, M. Z., & Walker, K. B. (1990). Instructional communication in the televised classroom: The effects of system design and teacher immediacy on student learning and satisfaction. *Communication Education, 39*(3), 196–206. doi:10.1080/03634529009378802

Harasim, L. M. (1990). *Online education: Perspectives on a new environment*. New York: Praeger.

Harasim, L. N., Hiltz, S. R., Teles, L., & Turoff, M. (1995). *Learning networks: A field guide to teaching and learning online*. Cambridge, MA: The MIT Press.

Hillman, D., Willis, D., & Gunawardena, C. (1994). Learner-Interface Interaction in Distance Education: An Extension of Contemporary Models and Strategies for Practitioners. *American Journal of Distance Education, 8*(2), 30–42. doi:10.1080/08923649409526853

Hiltz, S. R., & Wellman, B. (1997). Asynchronous learning networks as a virtual classroom. *Communications of the ACM, 40*(9), 44–48. doi:10.1145/260750.260764

Hughes, J. (2004). Supporting the Online Learner. In T. Anderson, & F. Elloumi (Eds.), *Theory and Practice of Online Learning* (pp. 367-384). Athabasca University. Retrieved from cde.athabascau.ca/online_book

Im, Y., & Lee, O. (2003-2004). Pedagogical implications of online discussion for preservice teacher training. *Journal of Research on Technology in Education, 36*(2), 155–170. doi:10.1080/15391523.2003.10782410

Jackson, L., & Caffarella, R. (1994). *Experiential learning: A new approach*. San Francisco: Jossey-Bass.

Jaques, D. (2000). *Learning in groups*. Kogan Page.

Jarvis, P. (1995). *Adult and continuing education. Theory and practice*. London: Routledge.

Johnson, D. W., & Johnson, F. P. (1997). *Joining together: Group theory and group skills*. Boston: Allyn & Bacon.

Karalis, T., & Koutsonikos, G. (2003). Issues and Challenges in Organising and Evaluating Web-based Courses for Adults. *Themes in education, 4*(2), 177-188.

Kearsley, G. (2000). *Online education: Learning and teaching in cyberspace*. Belmont, CA: Wadsworth/Thomson Learning.

Kelley, D., and, Gorham, J. (1988). Effects of immediacy on recall of information. *Communication Education, 37*(3), 198-207.

Knowles, M. (1980). *The modern practice of adult education*. Chicago: Follett.

Knowles, M. (1984). *Andragogy in Action. Applying modern principles of adult education*. San Francisco: Jossey Bass.

Knowles, M., Holton, E. III, & Swanson, R. (1998). *The Adult Learner*. Houston: Gulf Publishing Company.

Kokkos, A. (2005). *Εκπαίδευση Ενηλίκων: Ανιχνεύοντας το πεδίο (Adult Education: Scouting the field)*. Athens: Metaixmio. (In Greek)

Laal, M. (2011). Barriers to lifelong learning. *Procedia - Social and Behavioral Sciences, 28*, 612 – 615.

LaRose, R., Gregg, J., & Eastin, M. (1998). *Audiographic courses on the Web: An experiment*. Paper presented at the International Communication Association, Jerusalem, Israel. Available: www.telecommunication.msu.edu /faculty/larose/ica98.htm

LaRose, R., & Whitten, P. (1998). *October. Rethinking instructional immediacy for web courses: A social cognitive exploration*. Paper submitted to the International Communication Association, Instructional and Developmental Communication Division. Retrieved March 2014 from http://www.it.murdoch.edu.au/~sudweeks/papers/CBLS_Cyprus/larose.html

Leftheriotou, P. (2005). *Διερεύνηση των εκπαιδευτικών αναγκών των εκπαιδευτών ενηλίκων*. [Educational needs of adults' educators]. (Master Thesis). Hellenic Open University. (In Greek)

Longworth, N. (2003). *Lifelong Learning in Action: Transforming Education in the 21th Century*. London: Kogan Page.

Mason, R., & Rennie, F. (2008). *E- Learning and Social Networking Handbook: Resources for Higher Education*. Taylor and Francis.

Mehlenbacher, B. (2010). *Instruction and Technology: Designs for Everyday Learning*. The MIT Press. doi:10.7551/mitpress/9780262013949.001.0001

Mehrabian, A. (1967). Orientation behaviors and nonverbal attitude communication. *Journal of Communication, 17*(4), 324–332. doi:10.1111/j.1460-2466.1967.tb01190.x PMID:5588696

Merlose, Sh., & Bergeron, K. (2007). Instructor immediacy strategies to facilitate group work in online graduate study. *Australasian Journal of Educational Technology, 23*(1), 132–148.

Merriam, S., & Caffarella, R. (1999). *Learning in Adulthood*. San Francisco: Jossey Bass.

Misanchuk, M., & Anderson, T. (2001). Building Community in an Online Learning Environment: Communication, Cooperation and Collaboration. In *Proceedings of the Annual Mid-South Instructional Technology Conference*. Retrieved from http://www.mtsu.edu/-itconf/proceed01/19.pdf

Moore, A., Masterson, J. T., Christophel, D. M., & Shea, K. A. (1996). College teacher immediacy and student ratings of instruction. *Communication Education, 45*(1), 29–39. doi:10.1080/03634529609379030

Moore, M. G. (1989). Three types of interaction. *American Journal of Distance Education, 3*(2), 1–6. doi:10.1080/08923648909526659

Muilenburg, L., & Berge, Z. (2005). Student Barriers to Online Learning: A factor analytic study. *Distance Education, 26*(1), 29–48. doi:10.1080/01587910500081269

Muirhead, B. (2001). Interactivity research studies. *Journal of Educational Technology & Society, 4*(3).

Muirhead, B. (2002). Salmon's research. *USDLA Journal, 16*(5).

Nahl, D. (1996). Affective monitoring of Internet learners: Perceived self-efficacy and success. *Proceedings of the ASIS, 33*, 100–109.

Noyé, D., & Piveteau, J. (1997). *Guide pratique du formateur.* INSEP Editions.

Palloff, R. M., & Pratt, K. (2003). *Virtual student: A profile and guide to working with online learners.* San Francisco, CA: Jossey-Bass.

Partridge, H., & Hallam, G. (2005). New pathways to learning:The team teaching Approach. A library and Information Science Case Study. In E. Cohen (Ed.), *Issues in informing Science and Information Technology, v2* (pp. 103–118). Informing Science Press.

Pavlis-Korres, M. (2010). *Development of a framework for the e- education of educators of special groups aiming to improve their compatibility with their learners.* (PhD Thesis). University of Alcalá.

Pavlis-Korres, M. (2012). The Role of the Communication Tools in the Development of the Learning Group in an Online Environment. *International Journal of Engineering Education, 28*(6), 1360–1365.

Pavlis-Korres, M. (2013). Key Factors for Maximizing the Effectiveness of Blended E-Learning: The Outcome of the Internal Evaluation of a Distance Education Program for Adult Learning in Greece. In L. Kyei-Blankson & E. Ntuli (Eds.), *Practical Applications in Blended Learning Environments: Experiences in K-20 Education* (pp. 410–437). IGI Global.

Pavlis-Korres, M., Karalis, T., Leftheriotou, P., & García Barriocanal, E. (2009). Integrating Adults' Characteristics and the Requirements for their Effective Learning in an e-Learning Environment. In Lytras et al. (Eds.), *Best Practices for the Knowledge Society,* (pp. 570-584). Springer.

Roblyer, M. D., & Ekhaml, L. (2000). *How interactive are Your Distance Courses? A Rubric for Assessing Interaction in Distance Learning.* Paper presented at DLA 2000, Callaway, Georgia.

Rogers, A. (2002). Adult learners: characteristics, need, learning styles. In A. Kokkos (Ed.), *International conference for adults' learning.* Athens: Metaixmio. (In Greek)

Rogers, A. (2007). *Teaching Adults.* Open University Press.

Rovai, A. (2002). A preliminary look at the structural differences of higher education classroom communities in traditional and ALN courses. *Journal of Asynchronous Learning Networks, 6*(1). Retrieved from http://www.aln.org/publications/jaln/v6n1/pdf/v6n1_rovai.pdf

Salmon, G. (2004). *E-moderating: the key to teaching and learning online* (2nd ed.). London: Taylor and Francis.

Schutte, J. G. (1997). *Virtual teaching in higher education: The new intellectual superhighway or just another traffic jam?.* Available: http://www.csun.edu/sociology/virexp.htm

Scriven, M. S. (1991). *Evaluation Thesaurus.* Sage Publications.

Shank, P. (2004). Competencies for online instructors. In *Learning Peaks, LLC*. Retrieved in 22 February 2009, from http://www.insighted.com/instrcomp.pdf

Simonson, M., Smaldino, S., Albright, M., & Zvacek, S. (2000). *Teaching and Learning at a Distance: Foundations of Distance Education*. Upper Saddle River, NJ: Merrill.

Speer, T., & Ryan, B. (1998). Collaborative teaching in the de-centered classroom. *Teaching English in the Two-Year College, 26*(1), 39-49. ERIC Number: EJ573269.

Swan, K. (2002). Building Learning Communities in Online Courses: The importance of interaction. *Education Communication and Information, 2*(1), 23–49. doi:10.1080/1463631022000005016

Szucs, A., Tait, A., Vidal, M., & Bernath, U. (2013). *Distance and e-learning in transition: Learning Innovation, Technology and Social Challenges*. Wiley.

Thompson, G. (1990). How can correspondence-based distance education be improved? A survey of attitudes of students who are not well disposed toward correspondence study. *Journal of Distance Education, 5*(1), 53–65.

Tuckman, B. (1965). Developmental sequence in small groups. *Psychological Bulletin, 63*(6), 384–399. doi:10.1037/h0022100 PMID:14314073

Virgil,, E., & Varvel, Jr. (2007, Spring). Master Online Teacher Competencies. *Online Journal of Distance Learning Administration, 10*(1).

Vygotsky, L. (1978). *Mind in Society*. Cambridge, MA: Harvard University Press.

Waltonen-Moore, S., Stuart, D., Newton, E., Oswald, R., & Varonis, E. (2006). From Virtual Strangers to a Cohesive Online Learning Community: The Evolution of Online Group Development in a Professional Development Course. *Journal of Technology and Teacher Education, 14*(2), 287–311.

Wegerif, R. (1998). The Social Dimension of Asynchronous Learning Networks. *JALN, 2*(1), 34–49.

Woods, R., & Baker, J. (2004). Interaction and immediacy in online learning. *The International Review of Research in Open and Distance Learning, 5*(2). Retrieved 20-2-2009 from http://www.irrodl.org/index.php/irrodl/article/view/186/268

ADDITIONAL READING

Akyol, Z., & Garrison, D. R. (2008). The development of a community of inquiry over time in an online course: Understanding the progression and integration of social, cognitive and teaching presence. *Journal of Asynchronous Learning Networks, 12*(3), 3–22.

Baker, C. (2010). The Impact of Instructor Immediacy and Presence for Online Student Affective Learning, Cognition, and Motivation. *The Journal of Educators Online, 7*(1), 1–30.

Bonk, C., & Cunningham, D. (1998). Searching for learner-centred, constructivist, and sociocultural components of collaborative educational learning tools. In C. J. Bonk & K. S. King (Eds.), *Electronic collaborators: Learner-centred technologies for literacy, apprenticeship, and discourse* (pp. 25–50). Mahwah, NJ: Erlbaum.

Boston, W., Díaz, S., Gibson, A., Ice, P., Richardson, J., & Swan, K. (2014). An Exploration of the Relationship Between Indicators of the Community of Inquiry Framework and Retention in Online Programs. *Journal of Asynchronous Learning Networks, 13*(3), 67–83.

Ellis, A., & Phelps, R. (2000). Staff development for online delivery: A collaborative, team-based action learning model. *Australasian Journal of Educational Technology, 16*(1), 26–44. http://www.ascilite.org.au/ajet/ajet16/ellis.html

Flottenmesch, K. (2000). Building effective interaction in distance education: A review of the literature. *Educational Technology*, *40*(3), 46–51.

Garrison, D. R., Anderson, T., & Archer, W. (2000). Critical thinking in a text-based environment: Computer conferencing in higher education. *The Internet and Higher Education*, *11*(2), 1–14.

Garrison, D. R., Anderson, T., & Archer, W. (2001). Critical thinking, cognitive presence, and computer conferencing in distance education. *American Journal of Distance Education*, *15*(1), 7–23. doi:10.1080/08923640109527071

Goodyear, P., Salmon, G., Spector, J. M., Steeples, C., & Tickner, S. (2001). Competencies for online teaching: A special report. *Educational Technology Research and Development*, *49*(1), 65–72. doi:10.1007/BF02504508

Gunawardena, C. N., & Zittle, F. J. (1997). Social presence as a predictor of satisfaction within a computer-mediated conferencing environment. *American Journal of Distance Education*, *11*(3), 8–26. doi:10.1080/08923649709526970

Herrington, J., & Oliver, R. (2001). *Online learning: Professional development for the changing role of the lecturer.* Paper presented at the Moving Online Conference II (September 2-4, 2001).

Hewson, L., & Hughes, C. (1998). *On-line and on-demand: Staff development in the new university.* Paper presented at the Educause in Australasia Conference, 18-21 April. Sydney, New South Wales.

Ice, P., Curtis, R., Phillips, P., & Wells, J. (2007). Using asynchronous audio feedback to enhance teaching presence and student sense of community. *Journal of Asynchronous Learning Networks*, *11*(2), 3–25.

Leonard, J., & Guha, S. (2001). Education at the Crossroads: Online Teaching and Students' Perspectives on Distance Learning. *Journal of Research on Technology in Education*, *34*(1), 51–57. doi:10.1080/15391523.2001.10782333

Olson, S. J., & Werhan, C. (2005). Teacher Preparation Via Online Learning: A Growing Alternative for Many. *Action in Teacher Education*, *27*(4), 76–84. doi:10.1080/01626620.2005.10463392

Pavlis-Korres, M. (2014). Promoting interaction in an asynchronous e-learning environment. In Patricia Ordóñez de Pablos, Robert D. Tennyson and Miltiadis D. Lytras "Assessing the Role of Mobile Technologies and Distance Learning in Higher Education", pp. 154-175. IGI Global.

Picciano, A. G. (2002). Beyond student perceptions: Issues of interaction, presence and performance in an online course. *Journal of Asynchronous Learning Networks*, *6*(1). http://www.aln.org/publications/jaln/v6n1/pdf/v6n1_picciano.pdf

Richardson, J. C., & Swan, K. (2003). Examining social presence in online courses in relation to students' perceived learning and satisfaction. *Journal of Asynchronous Learning Networks*, *7*(1), 68–88.

Shea, P., & Bidjerano, T. (2009). Community of inquiry as a theoretical framework to foster "epistemic engagement" and "cognitive presence" in online education. *Computers & Education*, *52*(3), 543–553. doi:10.1016/j.compedu.2008.10.007

Shea, P., Li, C. S., Swan, K., & Pickett, A. (2005). Developing learning community in online asynchronous college courses: The role of teaching presence. *Journal of Asynchronous Learning Networks*, *9*(4), 59–82.

Sims, R. (2003). Promises of interactivity: Aligning learner perceptions and expectations with strategies for flexible and online learning. *Distance Education, 24*(1), 85–103. doi:10.1080/01587910303050

Stacey, E. (1999). Collaborative learning in an online environment. *Journal of Distance Education, 14*(2), 14–33.

Stacey, E. (2002). Learning links online: Establishing constructivist and collaborative learning environments. Available at http://dro.deakin.edu.au/eserv/DU:30004665/stacey-learninglinksonline-2002.pdf

Sutton, L. (2000). Vicarious interaction in a course enhanced through the use of computer-mediated communication. Unpublished doctoral dissertation, Arizona State University, Tempe.

Swan, K., & Shih, L. F. (2005). On the nature and development of social presence in online course discussions. *Journal of Asynchronous Learning Networks, 9*(3), 115–136.

Swan, K. J., Richardson, C., Ice, P., Garrison, D. R., Cleveland-Innes, M., & Arbaugh, J. B. (2008). *Validating a measurement tool of presence in online communities of inquiry. eMentor 241*(2) http://www.e-mentor.edu.pl/artykul_v2.php?numer=24&id=543

Tuovinen, J. (2000). Multimedia distance education interactions. *Educational Media International, 37*(1), 16–24. doi:10.1080/095239800361473

Willging, P. A., & Johnson, S. D. (2004). Factors that influence students' decision to dropout of online courses. *Journal of Asynchronous Learning Networks, 8*(4), 2–15. http://www.sloanconsortium.org/publications/jaln/v8n4/v8n4_willging_member.asp

Wilson, G., & Stacey, E. (2004). Online interaction impacts on learning: Teaching the teachers to teach online. *Australasian Journal of Educational Technology, 20*(1), 33–48.

KEY TERMS AND DEFINITIONS

Adult Education: Includes the entire body of educational processes, whatever their content, level or method, whereby persons regarded as adults by their society enhance abilities, enrich knowledge, improve technical or professional qualifications or turn them to a new direction. These educational processes –whether formal, non-formal or informal– are aimed at bringing about attitude changes and independent, full personal development as well as a balanced social, economic and cultural development.

Asynchronous and Synchronous Communication Mode: A synchronous refers to electronic bulletin boards, discussion boards, threaded discussions, forum, or electronic mail that participants can access at any time. Synchronous communication mode refers to "real time" interactions, in which participants communicate or "chat" at the same time.

Asynchronous: In online education, the term refers to educator-learner interaction and communication that does not take place at the same time and thus permits learners and educators to respond to each other at their own convenient time.

Educator/Educator of Adults: A teacher for adults. The term is used in order to define the different approach of the teacher, focusing on the dimensions of facilitation, co-learning, guiding and counseling.

E-Educator: A teacher for adults who teaches online (in synchronous or asynchronous mode or in combination of both).

E-Microteaching: Microteaching in an online environment.

General Adult Education: Includes all the organized learning activities that are addressed to adults and aim to enrich knowledge; develop and improve abilities and skills; develop an individual's personality and active citizenship, as well as mitigate education and social inequalities. It is provided mainly by non-formal or informal education institutions.

Interaction: A dynamic process of communication in a learning environment, between participants who modify their actions, behaviors and reactions owing to the actions, behaviors and reactions of the interaction partners.

Microteaching: A scaled-down teaching encounter which was developed at Stanford University in the mid-1960s to serve 3 purposes: (1) as preliminary experience and practice in teaching, (2) as a research vehicle to explore training effects under controlled conditions, and (3) as an in-service training instrument for experienced teachers.

Synchronous: In online education, the term refers to educator-learner interaction and communication that takes place at the same time through the use of technology, e.g. videoconferences, chats etc.

Web 2.0 Communication Tool: Any tool which allows and promotes communication between participants in an online educational environment, e.g. e-mail, forum, bulletin board, chat, blog, wiki, video conference.

Chapter 9
Preparing Online Learning Readiness with Learner–Content Interaction:
Design for Scaffolding Self–Regulated Learning

Juhong Christie Liu
James Madison University, USA

Elaine Roberts Kaye
James Madison University, USA

ABSTRACT

Online learning readiness is fundamental to student successful participation, presence, and interaction in online courses. Effective facilitation of these key components depends on sound instructional design. In self-directed online environments, learner-content interaction and scaffolding self-regulated learning have been found of primary importance to generate meaningful learning. To provide a solution to the challenges of interoperability of various functions in synchronous online learning environments, this chapter presents a case study about the design and development of a self-paced orientation to help students acquire online learning readiness. Learner-content interaction is strategically utilized in the design to scaffold self-regulated learning. The results of the case study demonstrate that this orientation positively prepares students to be ready for learning in a synchronous online environment. The approach can be of practical use to individuals and groups.

INTRODUCTION

As the enrollment in online courses continues to increase, higher education is faced with a paradigm shift in managing teaching and learning practices in immersed physical and online environments.

According to the Babson Survey Research Group's report, there were 7.1 million students enrolled in the universities and colleges in the United States taking at least one online course in the fall of 2012, which reached a historic peak with an increase of 411,000 (Allen & Seaman, 2014). To

DOI: 10.4018/978-1-4666-9582-5.ch009

meet the demand of rising enrollment in online learning, there is a need to provide training and support that are instrumental to student success in technology-mediated and self-directed online environments (Allen & Seaman, 2014). Thus, the preparation for student online learning readiness becomes an integral part of the strategic management of online programs and classes (Rufai, Alebiosu, & Adeakin, 2015).

In online learning, strategies are applied to manage a wide variety of resources, concepts, procedures, and techniques that are related to the access and needs of diverse stakeholders (Burgelman, Christensen, & Wheelwright, 2004; O'Neil, Fisher, & Rietschel, 2014; Sawyer & Howard, 2007). Grounded in sound instructional design, these strategies are integrated in online courses and programs to moderate the interaction, presence, and participation, which have been found closely associated with student satisfaction and learning experience (Alsharif & Roche, 2010; Baker, 2011; Salmon, 2011; Shea & Bidjerano, 2010).

Developing student readiness has been suggested to capitalize on the potential offered in online learning environments (Jones, 2013; Wozniak, Pizzica, & Mahony, 2012). Readiness manifests as a combination of basic technology skills, proactive access to and use of technology, attitude toward information and computer technologies, competency of online communication, formulating learning strategies, and capability of seeking help (Dray, Lowenthal, Miszkiewicz, Ruiz-Primo, & Marczynski, 2011; Hung, Chou, Chen, & Own, 2010). Lack of readiness preparation is found related to perceived barriers to success in online classes (Barbour & Reeves, 2009). Orientation programs that are focused on increasing students' readiness need to accommodate various technology competency levels and previous online learning experiences (Cho, 2012; Ullmann, 2009). In self-directed online environments, students are expected to have meaningful interaction with instructional content to generate learning (Moore & Kearsley, 2012).

The purpose of this chapter is to explore instructional design and development strategies in preparing students' online learning readiness with learner-content interaction. The exploration is based on the role that interaction plays in online courses, and designing the instructional product to scaffold student self-regulated learning. The presentation of a case study on designing an orientation for online learning readiness is intended to investigate strategies to facilitate learner-content interaction.

Participation, Presence, and Interaction in Online Courses

Participation, presence, and interaction are fundamental to engage students in online courses (Shea, Li, & Pickett, 2006). Strategic management of these core components consists of the analysis, decisions, and course of action that an organization or individual that operates online programs or classes needs to create and sustain to ensure the quality of learning (Nag, Hambrick, & Chen, 2007).

In online courses, instructors play important pedagogical, managerial, social, and technological roles (Liu, Bonk, Magjuka, Lee, & Su, 2005; O'Neil et al., 2014). To be able to effectively teach an online class, an instructor needs to first understand the transformation of pedagogy to online environments with concepts such as interaction and presence, and gain the ability of operating technologies. When managing an online class, an instructor monitors student-content interaction, models communication flow, mediates participation, creates collaborative opportunities, facilitates interaction with discussion prompts that are well-designed, focus on content, and evoke critical thinking, models online presence, and gauges the learning engagement with assessment strategies (Ertmer, Sadaf, & Ertmer, 2011; Salmon, 2011; Shea & Bidjerano, 2010; Shea et al., 2013). In the process, the instructor plays the roles of teacher, manager, supervisor, and leader to manage online learning behavior, articulate grading policies, operate various technologies, and guide the development of online learning community (Bigatel, Ragan, Kennan, May, & Redmond, 2012; Salmon, 2011). These competencies are usually acquired in the process of becoming aware of the technology capabilities (Burgelman et al., 2004), learning about and practicing in the online course platform (Bigatel et al., 2012), managing the time demand on online teaching (Parker & Howland, 2006), and understanding the types of interaction and presence in online learning environments (Bernard et al., 2009; Lehman & Conceição, 2010; Rodriguez & Armellini, 2014; Rufai et al., 2015).

How an online course is designed and delivered influences student participation (Connors, 2013). Michinov, Brunot, Le Bohec, Juhel, and Delaval (2011) studied procrastination patterns of eighty-three adult learners enrolled in a 10-week online course. They found that high procrastinators tended to push checking the online discussion forum toward the due time, and wrote briefer and fewer response entries than low procrastinators. The study findings had design implications for setting timing and reminders to encourage early participation in online discussion. The results also suggest that providing feedback or tutor mediation to model the flow of online discussion will increase meaningful participation. In a case study with 18 students taking a Blackboard-based online class about nutrition, Connors (2013) found that students liked to participate in online courses if they could keep up with the class pace, with scaffolding tools such as a class timetable that allowed them to plan for the course. Students expressed feeling fatigue when they were inundated with frequent and lengthy emails initiated by the instructor. They also suggested that online course sites have clear navigation and directions. Similar themes about enhancing participation in online courses were also found in other studies with diverse student populations (Oztok, Zingaro, Brett, & Hewitt, 2013; Shea et al., 2006).

Presence in online courses relates to both instructor and students, and how the course is designed. Perception of presence in online courses can be determined by the realism, immersion, and involvement that are usually enabled and mediated with technologies such as synchronous communication tools (Lehman & Conceição, 2010). For instance, synchronous video conferencing has a significant and positive impact on students' perception of instructor presence (Han, 2013). Essentially there are three types of presence in online classes, cognitive, social, and teaching presence (Lehman & Conceição, 2010; Swan et al., 2008). Perceived social presence in online classes was found associated with student perceived learning and course satisfaction (Richardson & Swan, 2003). Swan, Shea, Richardson, Garrison, Cleveland-Innes, and Arbaugh (2008) conducted a study to validate an instrument to measure perceived presence by students who took online courses in multiple institutions. They concluded that all three types of presence contributed to the community of inquiry. They also proposed the type of emotional presence in online learning for future research. With an increase in using social media and networking tools, social presence studies have expanded. Joyce and Brown (2009) proposed eight strategies to manage social presence with social media and tools, including organizing and archiving personal discussion entries, establishing immediacy, conducting synchronous live chat, personalizing emails, incorporating audio and video communication, providing feedback, facilitating group discussion, and allowing private space.

Mediated with technologies, learning performance in online courses is determined by effective interaction among students, instructional content, and instructors (Cho, 2011; Jowallah, 2014; Moore & Kearsley, 2012; Rufai et al., 2015). The four types of interaction proposed and studied were learner-content, learner-learner, learner-instructor, and learner-interface/technology interaction (Cho, 2011; Moore & Kearsley,

2012). The frequency and variety of interaction do not necessarily enhance the quality of learning (Garrison & Cleveland-Innes, 2005; Grandzol & Grandzol, 2010). At least one type of interaction that is carefully considered in instructional design will result in meaningful learning (Rodriguez & Armellini, 2014).

"Interaction by itself does not presume that one is engaged in a process of inquiry" (Garrison & Cleveland-Innes, 2005, p. 135). To generate useful interaction in an online course, instructional design needs to consider clear articulation of expectations, layout of manageable chunks of content, and alignment among content presentation, assessment methods and learning activities (Garrison & Cleveland-Innes, 2005; Murray, Pérez, Geist, & Hedrick, 2013). Types of questions designed for online discussion affect student cognitive responses and frequency of class interaction. Ertmer, Sadaf, and Ertmer (2011) examined 850 discussion responses from 10 different online courses. After studying the impact of types of questions on student-student and student-content interaction, they concluded that the "cognitive level of students' responses to instructors' questions matched the cognitive level of those questions" (p. 171). They suggested instructors select various types of questions to manage different types of interaction when facilitating the discussion in an online course. For instance, requiring students to generate new ideas would sustain learner-learner interaction; using a focal question or a case study and following with facilitating prompts would scaffold deep learning of the content.

Studies found that learner-content interaction directly influenced the learning outcome in online courses (Ekwunife-Orakwue & Teng, 2014; Rodriguez & Armellini, 2014; Rodriguez & Armellini, 2013). The time spent on content interaction had a statistically significant relationship with student grades (Zimmerman, 2012). Student interactions for learning in online environments were determined by their technological compe-

tencies and online learning readiness (Kaymak & Horzum, 2013). Technology access was found to affect learner-content interaction as well. Attebury (2010) presented and compared the use of synchronous features of web tour and application sharing for teaching library instruction sessions with Elluminate *Live!*. Both features offered the ability for instructors and students to share what were on their computer screens or share selected web content synchronously. These were used to facilitate student learning regarding how to search library databases. The study recognized that student interaction with the instructional content was affected by their ability of logging in proxy server, and their competency of selecting between alternative applications.

Instructional Design and Facilitation of Online Courses

Sound instructional design is the cornerstone for strategically managing participation, interaction, and presence in an online course (Lehman & Conceição, 2010; O'Neil et al., 2014; Rodriguez & Armellini, 2014). Defining objectives and aligning assessment methods with learning objectives are fundamental to the success of instruction. Learning objectives, when articulated clearly in the course syllabus and assessment policies, are closely associated with the administrative and managerial functions of the instructor in an online class (Bigatel et al., 2012; O'Neil et al., 2014). The analysis of needs, context, technology affordance, and learning tasks is the foundation for course development (Reeves, Herrington, & Oliver, 2005; Smith & Ragan, 2005). Selection of strategies in sequencing content presentation, formulating questions for reflection, determining assessment methods for learning, and scaffolding for transfer influences student participation and interaction in online courses (Ertmer et al., 2011; Morrison, Ross, Kemp, & Kalman, 2011). Planning for evaluation along with design prepares for revision and improvement of course design and implementation (Ohia, 2011; Richey & Klein, 2007; Smith & Ragan, 2005; Suskie, 2010).

Design for participation and interaction is important. This is related to decisions made on "when and where students will complete their work, interact with peers, link to outside resources, and extend the course in new directions" (Bonk, Kirkley, Hara, & Dennen, 2001, p. 84). As the critical components of instructional design, setting time parameters for learning activities, using media effectively, and facilitating various types of interaction create and model learning experiences in an online class (Bigatel et al., 2012; Rodriguez & Armellini, 2014). Types of questions designed for online discussion determine the sustainability of interaction and depth of learning (Ertmer et al., 2011).

Design for presence in online courses is associated with the sense of learning community (Joyce & Brown, 2009; Shea et al., 2006). Inclusion of expected etiquette for online class interaction, transparency of virtual classroom management policies, and scheduling of timely feedback at the design stage will help build social and cognitive presence in an online course (Connors, 2013; Lehman & Conceição, 2010; Salmon, 2011).

Instructional design is a "bricolage" (Cormier & Siemens, 2010, p.36) that links the affordance offered by online learning environments to strategic management of interaction, presence, and participation in online courses. In this linkage, asynchronous and synchronous technologies provide various approaches and access to the class communication for students and instructors (Burgelman et al., 2004; Rufai et al., 2015). Asynchronous online learning (AOL) technologies facilitate online presence of class members, presentation of content in text and media, and different types of interaction at time and location that are flexible and convenient to each individual in an online class (Hrastinski, 2008; Moore & Kearsley, 2012). Comparatively, synchronous online learning (SOL) platforms offer an assort-

ment of functions that enable members in a class to communicate at the same time, using features such as text chat, VoIP audio, video conferencing, whiteboard and presentation, break-out rooms for group work, and session recording. These features can support real-time communication, interaction, and collaboration for class members in distributed locations. These synchronous functions, when utilized appropriately, can enhance the quality of online learning (Blankson & Kyei-Blankson, 2008; Finkelstein, 2009; Yamagata-Lynch, 2014). The interoperability among different devices, synchronicity of time, and communication with text and media formats demand particular support and preparation to ensure student success (Bower, 2011).

Design with the intentional consideration of AOL and SOL features can optimize the management and facilitation of online classes (Giesbers, Rienties, Tempelaar, & Gijselaers, 2014; Yamagata-Lynch, 2014). This design process that is conscious of technology affordance influences the selection of technologies and techniques in teaching an online class, moderating class interactions, and mediating presence (Lehman & Conceição, 2010; Warden, Stanworth, Ren, & Warden, 2013).

SOL AND AOL CAPABILITIES FOR ONLINE LEARNING

Synchronous and asynchronous technologies can facilitate online interaction, presence, and participation with immediacy or delay in terms of timing and sequence. This flexibility can be used to support different formats of communication and mediate the completion of different types of learning tasks (Dabbagh & Kitsantas, 2005; Huang & Hsiao, 2012). Studies have demonstrated that the blending of AOL and SOL was correlated with enhanced interaction and course performance (Duncan, Kenworthy, & McNamara, 2012; Giesbers et al., 2014). Duncan, Kenworthy, and McNamara (2012) investigated the use of synchronous and asynchronous learning techniques in an online executive MBA accounting class. The course was taught with two one-hour synchronous sessions of lectures and weekly follow-ups that were mediated with satellite TV, and two hours of synchronous chat using SyncQuant. The class interaction was also supported with an ongoing asynchronous discussion board. The results indicated that the MBA students' synchronous engagement with the class significantly impacted their performance. The researchers suggested that blending synchronous and asynchronous tools for online class activities led to a higher level of learning. In particular, asynchronous tools were found to facilitate learner-learner interaction on course work for application and analysis; synchronous tools were very helpful for learner-instructor interaction and enhanced teaching presence. Oztok, Zingaro, Brett, and Hewitt (2013) found that asynchronous postings in nine online graduate education classes tended to be longer and more relevant to the course content; those students who frequently used private synchronous messaging tended to write and post longer asynchronous discussion entries. Giesbers, Rienties, Tempelaar, and Gijselaers (2014) studied undergraduates who majored in economics in an online program. In the six-week course, except for the first and last, each week started with synchronous videoconferencing facilitated with Adobe Connect, followed by asynchronous discussion forums. The problem-based AOL and SOL in this online class demonstrated that, "participants in a web-videoconference on the whole contributed more to the asynchronous discussions both in quality and quantity" (Giesbers et al., 2014, p. 43). Efficiency of logging in an online asynchronous system and its integrated synchronous platform with one single sign-on was explored to engage students in online learning (Er, Özden, & Arifoğlu, 2009; Ullmann, 2009).

Based on intentional design, blending AOL and SOL capabilities to facilitate and monitor participation, interaction and presence in online courses becomes possible. To ensure this, it is clear that relevant training, support and scaffolding for student readiness are needed (Kaymak & Horzum, 2013).

STUDENT SUPPORT AND SUCCESSFUL ONLNE LEARNING

Student support is a fundamental component in managing online learning (Bentley, Shegunshi, & Scannell, 2010; Simonson, Smaldino, Albright, & Zvacek, 2012). This is especially true for a student at the beginning of an online program or course (Salmon, 2011). At this stage, students need preparation to be aware of the technology capabilities and use them appropriately in communication and interaction for online courses (Bower, 2011; Epp, Green, Rahman, & Weaver, 2010; Heiser, Stickler, & Furnborough, 2013). "We cannot expect learners to be competent users of the new media who are aware of the affordances and how to use them constructively. Instead, we have to help them to develop 'electronic literacy'" (Hampel, 2006, p. 112). In designing learning tasks for a language class in a SOL environment, Hampel (2006) noted that even when capable tech support was available during class time, the time spent on troubleshooting and resolving technical issues for a remote student would deprive the individual of class participation. The researcher recommended familiarizing students with tools through training before online classes actually started. The study results also suggested encouraging student to use provided resources and gradually increasing the depth of training to meet the needs of applying more sophisticated features.

Student support can lead to the effective implementation of designed pedagogy in an online course. Epp, Green, Rahman, and Weaver (2010) conducted a study about synchronous scientific discourse in a distance general chemistry class. The text-based synchronous communication between instructor and students were intentionally facilitated with an IRE/IRF pattern, with I (Initiation) by instructor, R (Response) by students, E (Evaluation) or F (Follow-up) by instructor. The study proved this new pattern of synchronous online interaction in a science class had similar effect as the non-verbal cues in a traditional classroom. At the conclusion, the researchers recommended that training for students prior to starting a synchronous online class and information about technical support would improve success.

Using media such as audio and video in online learning environments demands extra training and support. Audio cues were found to be an advantageous feature of SOL technologies, as they enhanced student participation and satisfaction with online learning experiences (Blau & Barak, 2012). However, audio devices were often prone to causing technical difficulties (Bower, 2011; Martin, Parker, & Deale, 2012). Bower (2011) conducted a design-based research project when teaching introductory computer programming with Adobe Connect. The author found that the lack of technological preparation could prevent the use of usually effective online pedagogical strategies. Problems such as failure of audio setup could have been caused by factors unique to the user's computer settings, audio devices, operating system, or other hardware. The research results suggested that helping students to develop technical skills and build their operational and interactional competencies for online learning was essential; this could be accomplished through introductory tutorial sessions, planned practice opportunities, just-in-time support, and resources. Overall, the literature is clear on the necessity and importance of providing adequate and well-designed student support opportunities to ensure success in a SOL environment.

Preparation for readiness needs to be provided with easy access. Lee, Srinivasan, Trail, Lewis, and

Lopez (2011) reported that instructional, peer and technical support were identified by the students as being correlated to course satisfaction. Students suggested that the support should be provided with easy access. This request supported the use of a one-point of entry system, as in the Er, Özden, and Arifoğlu study (2009). Emphasizing the importance of easy access to support, Ullmann (2009) reported a series of support courses provided by Purdue University's School of Nursing, including a "Computer Tutor" course. The support course resided within the same learning management system that hosted the other online courses that the students were taking. Whenever students had a need for technological support, they had direct access within the same system, rather than having to search elsewhere for help.

When providing support for operating and interacting with SOL technologies, it is particularly crucial to facilitate student active engagement with the content in a real context. Bliesener (2006) reported the development of a training program to promote synchronous collaborative learning. Design choices were made such that conceptual awareness was promoted and behavioral experiences were created with simulation. These met the students' need for learning in a real-world context. Park and Bonk (2007) recommended providing practice sessions for synchronous classes, ideally within the real class context, to reduce potential technical issues and enhance the learning experience.

In an online learning environment, students interact with course content, communicate with teachers and peers, and present themselves through the mediation of technologies. The self-directed nature of online environments requires that the preparation of student online learning readiness is facilitated with scaffolding for self-regulated learning (SRL) (Delen, Liew, & Willson, 2014; Lawanto, Santoso, Lawanto, & Goodridge, 2014).

LEARNER-CONTENT INTERACTION AND SCAFFOLDING SRL IN ONLINE COURSES

Content is the essential component in building and managing an online course (Garrison & Cleveland-Innes, 2005; Rufai et al., 2015; Shea et al., 2006). Learner-content interaction has been identified as associated with student satisfaction in online learning and learning outcome (Cho, 2011; Ekwunife-Orakwue & Teng, 2014). Students tend to intentionally interact with the course content that directly leads to their grades in a class in online learning environments (Murray et al., 2013). More relevant to novice online learners, individualized support through learner-content interaction can alleviate the barriers or difficulties that students may perceive (Salmon, 2011).

Scaffolding in online learning environments is usually recommended to set up connections between learners and the content of study (Dabbagh & Bannan-Ritland, 2005; Dembo, Junge, & Lynch, 2006). Scaffolding includes strategies to support "novice learners by limiting the complexities of the learning context and gradually removing those limits as learners gain the knowledge, skills, and confidence to cope with the full complexity of the context" (Dabbagh, 2003, p. 39). In online classes where usually a teacher is not physically present, the support and guidance should be gradually adjusted to foster a student's ability to attain their learning objectives with assistance as needed (Dabbagh, 2003; Dabbagh & Bannan-Ritland, 2005). Some scaffolding strategies have been adopted from traditional classroom settings, such as modeling note-taking (Delen et al., 2014). Various web-based tools and technologies can support strategies to provide scaffolding for SRL (Dabbagh & Kitsantas, 2009). Examples include using Electronic Performance Support System (EPSS) (Kert & Kurt, 2012), supportive resources as linked content (Delen et al., 2014; Dowell & Small, 2011; Shih, 2010), web-based SRL training units (Azevedo & Hadwin, 2005; Tsai, Shen, & Tsai, 2011), and prompts (Azevedo & Hadwin, 2005; Lehmann, Hähnlein, & Ifenthaler, 2014). These scaffolding strategies are usually designed and developed as part of the online classes, and can be retrieved and utilized by students as just-in-need resources.

In online learning, scaffolding SRL is necessary for students, especially those who are new to such environments (Barnard, Paton, & Lan, 2008; Sun & Rueda, 2012; Tsai, Shen, & Fan, 2013; Tsai, 2013). Students with the SRL attributes are usually ready to construct learning goals. To achieve the goals, they actively adjust and monitor their behaviors, motivation, and engagement in learning. Their cognitive and behavioral regulation can minimize the constraints of personal and contextual factors in the learning environment (Pintrich & Zusho, 2002). Studies suggest that student SRL is correlated with course satisfaction, engagement level, and performance in online classes (Artino & Jones, 2012; Kuo, Walker, Belland, Schroder, & Kuo, 2014; Puzziferro, 2008; Sun & Rueda, 2012). A self-regulated student in an online class is active in goal-setting, environmental structuring, time management, help seeking, forming task strategies, and self-evaluation (Barnard-Brak, Lan, & Paton, 2010; Cheng, Liang, & Tsai, 2013). When scaffolding SRL, several phases are used to build the learning experience. These phases include planning, activation, monitoring, and controlling of presentation or fading of support, and providing opportunities for reflection (Lawanto et al., 2014; Pintrich & Zusho, 2002; Schunk & Mullen, 2013). Learner-content interaction can foster SRL with intentional design since minimal human intervention becomes possible with technology mechanisms in online environments (Kim, Olfman, Ryan, & Eryilmaz, 2014; Rodriguez & Armellini, 2014; Rowe & Rafferty, 2013; Rufai et al., 2015).

In the following section, a case study is presented about the design and development of an orientation to prepare student online learning readiness with learner-content interaction.

Blackboard Collaborate™ (Collaborate) is the synchronous platform that creates and supports real-time online class interaction and participation at the university in this case study. In order to support student online learning, professionals of instructional design and technology in this university have explored the design of a self-paced asynchronous online orientation for students to learn to use Collaborate. The research documents the design of the orientation program, its development and implementation strategies, and presents the formative evaluation results.

CASE STUDY: PREPARING ONLINE LEARNING READINESS WITH LEARNER-CONTENT INTERACTION

Theoretical Framework

Providing training and support for student readiness is essential to facilitate successful online courses (Quality Matters Program, 2013; 2014; Shelton, Saltsman, Holstrom, & Pederson, 2014; Simonson et al., 2012). This case study explores the design and development of an orientation program to prepare students for a SOL environment. The synchronous environment of Collaborate

entails a context with specific conceptual and procedural aspects that require student readiness. Students need to have sufficient interaction with the orientation content to be able to properly use the features in their online courses (Bower, 2011; Martin et al., 2012; Park & Bonk, 2007).

To optimize the conceptual and procedural preparation for student learning in an online environment, the instructional design framework is based on the system-oriented model proposed by Smith and Ragan (2005), as visualized in Figure 1. The framework consists of three major elements, 1) Analysis of Context and Learning Tasks; 2) Development and Implementation with Selected Instructional Strategies; 3) Evaluation (Smith & Ragan, 2005). Among these elements, the analysis of context and learning tasks is closely associated with technology affordance in an online learning environment (Reeves et al., 2005). The affordance has both the potential to enhance learning and to become a barrier that limits learning success. Sound instructional design accompanied by selective use of strategies in development and implementation can leverage the potential of enhancement and limitation (Benson & Whitworth, 2014; Liu et al., 2005; Shea et al., 2006). In developing readiness for online learning, the focus on learner-content interaction can prepare students with anticipated

Figure 1. Instructional design framework for scaffolding SRL with learner-content interaction

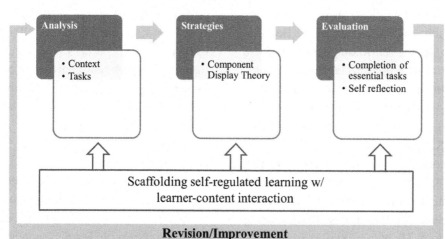

efficiency (Rodriguez & Armellini, 2014; Salmon, 2011). The evaluation provides data-driven suggestions for revision, from instructional design perspective; and for improvement, from the perspective of educational assessment (Ohia, 2011; Richey & Klein, 2007; Suskie, 2010).

Project Overview and Research Method

This research project intends to provide an instructional solution to developing student readiness to learn in a SOL environment. The context of this project is a large comprehensive university on the East Coast of the United States. Orientations were provided to the students enrolled in fully online for-credit courses in one-hour face-to-face or Elluminate *Live!* synchronous sessions. The previous iterations of the orientation revealed that the one-time experience did not transfer student readiness for their learning engagement in other online courses. This was especially challenging for synchronous functions. Students had unique issues associated to their own computers, including configurations, audio and video devices, and operating systems (Bower, 2011; Park & Bonk, 2007). There was a clear need to redesign a sustainable and more effective orientation program.

The orientation was also part of an educational assessment project (Ohia, 2011; Suskie, 2010). The university adopted the Quality Matters Higher Education Rubric (QM Rubric) (Quality Matters Program, 2013; 2014) and the Online Learning Consortium (OLC) Quality Scorecard for the Administration of Online Programs (OLC Quality Scorecard) (Shelton, Saltsman, Holstrom, & Pederson, 2013, 2014). Based on these criteria, an assessment plan was developed for the redesign of the orientation. The objectives of the redesign were mapped to the relevant student support standards in the QM Rubric and OLC Quality Scorecard. Two of the six mapped objectives addressed the need to support the SOL readiness, as the following:

- Demonstrate knowledge of online learning management system by successfully completing the essential tasks.
- Identify appropriate methods for contacting technical assistance and technical support staff.

Based on these objectives from the assessment plan and the technology affordance (Reeves et al., 2005), an asynchronous orientation was planned to scaffold students to learn the concepts and use of Collaborate, as well as develop awareness of how to locate support resources or personnel. Canvas, a learning management system (LMS) developed by Instructure, was adopted by the university a year ago. It was selected to manage and present the entire orientation course asynchronously. The course covered topics of conceptualization about online learning strategies and preparation for technology competencies. The topics were structured as a series of units in the Canvas course. Students enrolled in the summer 2014 for-credit online classes at the university were invited to participate in this orientation, on a voluntary basis. They accessed the course with the same log-in as their other classes in Canvas and could use it as a resource and guide when taking for-credit online courses in the summer. The design choice to use a self-paced course in Canvas was intended to decrease the cognitive demand on students and allow them convenient access to the orientation content in the same online learning environment that hosted their other online classes (Andrade, 2014; Bednall & Kehoe, 2011; Chen, Wang, & Chen, 2014; Cheng et al., 2013; Delen et al., 2014).

This case study is a design and development research, with the outcome of an instructional product (Richey & Klein, 2007). This type of research features "integrating design principles with technology affordance" (Reeves et al., 2005, p.105). In the technology context of integrating synchronous Collaborate within the asynchronous Canvas LMS, the research question for this study is:

- How can an orientation be designed to scaffold student self-regulated learning with learner-content interaction to develop their readiness for a synchronous online learning environment?

A case study is usually conducted in a bounded system that is defined by an individual or groups of people with unique characteristics or status, scenarios, factors of time and place, or a program (Creswell, Hanson, Plano, & Morales, 2007; Creswell, 2013; Merriam & Merriam, 2009). This case study was bounded by the following contextual parameters: 1) the *timeframe* required that the preparation for student readiness for the intensive online courses in summer sessions should be during the transition between the spring semester and beginning of summer sessions; 2) the *Canvas LMS* where the orientation course was managed might have responsive and directive implications to the instructional design of the orientation course (Benson & Whitworth, 2014); 3) the *learning activities* in the orientation course should be set up and monitored in such a way that students would be able to acquire the essential concepts, procedures, and skills that can enable their participation, interaction, and presence in the synchronous learning platform of Collaborate; 4) finally and most importantly, the *instructional design* needs to focus on learner-content interaction with minimal human intervention as this is a course for voluntary participation (Salmon, 2011).

Applied thematic analysis was conducted to analyze and interpret the formative evaluation results (Guest, MacQueen, & Namey, 2011; Vaismoradi, Turunen, & Bondas, 2013). Qualitative data of student reflection through online discussion posts and Collaborate session recordings were collected and analyzed in aggregate form; identifiers were replaced with index numbers before the analysis.

In the following sections, the components of this design and development research are presented, including the context and task analysis, development and implementation strategies, and formative evaluation.

Analysis of Context

Of primary importance in this design project was the analysis of context. From the research perspective, analyzing the context identified the bounded system of the case study, that is, individuals involved, time, place and status of the studied case or unit (Creswell et al., 2007; Creswell, 2013; Merriam & Merriam, 2009). From the instructional design perspective, the context analysis identified the concepts, tools, and features that the orientation would need to cover and support students to be successful in online learning (Smith & Ragan, 2005). Furthermore, detailed knowledge and experience with Collaborate and Canvas allowed the instructional designers to strategically utilize the technology affordance to develop student competencies, present instructional content, ensure easy and flexible access, facilitate reflection, as well as manage student participation in the course and their interaction with the instructional content (Benson & Whitworth, 2014; Burgelman et al., 2004; Reeves et al., 2005).

As a synchronous web-conferencing system, Collaborate is used to facilitate live participation in online courses when class members are located in physically distributed places and connected with various networked devices (Blackboard Collaborate, 2014; Tonsmann, 2014; Wdowik, 2014). The chat features offer text, audio and video options. Other features include user profile for virtual class attendance, whiteboard for presentation and interactive content posting, guided web tour to share web-based content, application sharing to display what is on an individual participant's computer screen, flexible user control of moderation and collaboration, group work with break-out rooms, and session recording for review or archival. All these features in Collaborate make it a robust SOL environment.

Setting up and using synchronous online conferencing tools are conceptual and procedural processes (Epp et al., 2010; Heiser et al., 2013). Students need to clearly understand the relevant concepts to be able to conduct the procedural tasks in SOL environments and use the tools in online courses. Practice with a simulation of the actual Collaborate web-conferencing sessions permits real experience of the procedure. Since students may also have previous SOL experiences, flexible access to the instructional content is important. The flexibility provides support and guides as scaffolding, which can fade or be skipped when needed (Dabbagh, 2003).

Managing online courses asynchronously, Canvas "centralizes course preparation; educational content and resources; the delivery and tracking of student activities, such as discussion and collaboration; the administration of assessment activities; and the accumulation and presentation of marks and grades" (Wright, Lopes, Montgomerie, Reju, & Schmoller, 2014). Canvas uses modules to organize course content (Instructure, 2014). A module is a content container in Canvas that can display and connect any existing materials internal and external to the system, including but not limited to wiki pages, discussion forums, and links to assignment submission, web resources, and multimedia content. The Canvas display and progress mechanism between and within modules helps manage the learner-content interaction that aids students' SRL progress.

Integrated within Canvas, Collaborate can be accessed through one single sign-on. After logging into a course in Canvas, locating Collaborate as a course menu item, and finding the session link, students can easily join a synchronous class meeting session. In a launched session, students can participate in a live online class by watch-

ing presentations on the whiteboard or through web tour or application sharing. They can also communicate with other class members with text, audio or video-based chat. The Collaborate auto-recording function can scaffold students' application of what they learn about setting up and launching a Collaborate session. With the function, students are able to pace themselves and experience the SOL environment from initial launching to testing basic tools. This also helps them to review and reflect on their practice results. The contextual factors analyzed above are essential to making decisions about strategies to manage learner-content interaction.

Task Analysis

The task analysis identified those tasks and related concepts that were essential for setting up a computer and launching a functioning Collaborate session. During the analysis, the categories of conceptual, procedural, and conditional knowledge were identified (Merrill, 2007; Parra, 2012). Then decisions were made as to which tasks students needed and should be included directly or indirectly in the module so as to provide scaffolding for students to develop the readiness for SOL (Dabbagh, 2003). The following tasks were identified:

1. **Install or Update Java:** This is essential to launching a Collaborate session in the versions prior to 2015. Diversified operating systems and types of web browsers need to be considered in the tutorials for acquainting students with configuring their computers by updating Java for the upcoming SOL tasks.

2. **Connect Headset with Microphone and Test Audio Setup:** This is important for audio-based communication and interactivity during real-time online meetings for a class. The inappropriate sequence of connecting hardware to a computer and launching a Collaborate session can cause

audio mal-functions in a Collaborate session. Students need to have this conceptual and procedural knowledge before they actually use audio in Collaborate for SOL.

3. **Launch a Collaborate Session:** Real-time simulation with the Collaborate self-recording feature situates the complexity of the task and allows for student control of the process (Merrill, 2007). After Task 1 and 2 are completed, students will be able to launch a Collaborate session, and practice essential features for class participation and interaction, including text chat, Audio Setup Wizard, tools for the whiteboard, and participation status icons.

Along with the procedural knowledge, conditional and conceptual or declarative knowledge needs to be analyzed and selected for use to facilitate scaffolding. These consist of best practice of using SOL, interactional competencies with SOL, resources, and support information (Bower, 2011; Martin, Parker, & Allred, 2013; Warden et al., 2013). Some of these can be collected from the literature and the product provider, Blackboard Collaborate™. Some can also come from open sources (Koohang & Harman, 2007). Other materials can be customized and created by the university that has contracted the system. The analysis of the content availability, simultaneously with the tasks, lays the foundation for the selection of development and implementation strategies.

Development and Implementation

The analysis of context and tasks further defined the module objectives and informed selection of strategies for developing instructional materials and managing learner-content interaction. At the completion of the module, students would be able to: 1) define the essential concepts and functions about using Collaborate, 2) identify the procedures to prepare and start a Collaborate session, 3) configure their computers for a Collaborate

session, 4) test basic tools with a practice session, 5) identify the support information and resources, 6) reflect on the learning experience.

The technology affordance in Canvas provides a general basis to allow descriptive and prescriptive methods for content delivery. Component Display Theory (CDT) is selected to guide the development, selection, use, and display of text and visual materials in order to capitalize on the potential of Canvas as an AOL environment. At a micro level, CDT describes the sequence and display of conceptual and procedural information (Glazatov, 2012; Merrill, 2007; Parra, 2012). With its prescriptive roles at a macro level, CDT allows learner control of access to the displayed content to scaffold student SRL through learner-content interaction (Chou & Liu, 2005).

The objectives and instructional strategies of CDT guided the development of the module content, as illustrated by Figure 2. The presentation of declarative, procedural, and conditional knowledge was intended to enable students' acquisition of concepts and procedures for SOL. Maintaining simplicity was the rationale for content presentation and selection of interaction strategies since students tended to not estimate possible technical issues (Bozarth, Chapman, & LaMonica, 2004; Salmon, 2011). Beginning to use a SOL tool needed sufficient preparation through interaction with the content of study, that is, the concepts and procedures to learn with Collaborate. In the duration, guidance was provided with direct or indirect (linked) display so that students can access them as needed. If they were proactive to seek help, they could choose to open the link; or if they felt confident in using the tool, the detailed instruction would stay hidden behind the link. Therefore, fading of assistance was achieved (Dabbagh, 2003). Students would be held accountable with SRL to access the externally linked tutorials or download sites that would open under a new tab, and then return to the Canvas tab in their web browser (Dabbagh, 2003; Driscoll, 2005; Merrill, 2007). In the entire process, learner-content interaction

Figure 2. Instructional development for scaffolding SRL with learner-content interaction

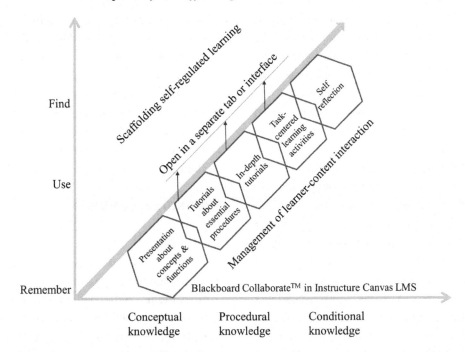

with minimal human intervention was utilized to scaffold SRL in order for students to participate on a voluntary basis without the concern of being treated as novice users (Salmon, 2011).

Following this approach to scaffolding SRL, one page for a discussion forum in Canvas was used to present declarative, procedural and conditional knowledge. The basic concepts and functions of Collaborate were presented succinctly in text. On the same page, students could find a link to a short screencast tutorial recorded with Adobe Captivate, which would open in a separate tab in the same web browser. The video tutorial explained how to install or update Java, and introduced the Collaborate support portal for first-time users. Returning to the same page in Canvas, students could find another link to a series of 19 clips of video. These clips were approximately one minute in length and adopted from open source screencasts provided by Collaborate via Brainshark (http://www.brainshark.com/). The use of existing open source materials substantially reduced the cost of instructional development for this module (Koo-

hang & Harman, 2007). Statements that would guide the students back to Canvas to continue the module always accompanied the externally linked instructional content. On the same page, the contact information of the institutional support entities and selected resources were provided. Students were also required to post their self-reflection to the online discussion, based on a simple and brief prompt.

In the module, students were expected to complete two major procedural tasks through learner-content interaction. The first task was to obtain or update the most current version of Java compatible to their computers, operating systems, and web browsers (i.e. if they used a laptop or desktop computer versus an iOS tablet). Failure of Java installation and updates were frequently the causes of inability to launch and use Collaborate. The completion of the task to obtain the updated Java would directly affect the launching of a simulation session with Collaborate, that is, the second procedural task. If a student had attempted to launch the practice session, she/he would initially receive an audio reminder that the session would begin recording. If a user chose to continue after the reminder, the session would be recorded and indexed under the Collaborate menu in the Canvas orientation course, with the time of recording in its native .jnlp format. However, it is important to note that the session could be closed at the alert, which would result in an un-recorded and un-indexed session.

The automatic recording for a practice session was decided as a development strategy for two purposes: 1) providing an indicator that a student was ready with her/his computer configuration and was able to launch a Collaborate session; 2) guiding students to perform audio setup which was the cause to the most common issues in SOL (Bower, 2011; Park & Bonk, 2007). Students could use the practice session as many times as they needed to test their computer configurations and become familiar with the tools in the environment. A recording session usually consists of several floating windows. The floating windows may include some or all of the following features: a recorder profile window with audio adjustment, a log of the participant's entries and exits in the session, feed of text chat, whiteboard (with trace of marking tools if a student tested any), options of display, and length of the session. If a student used the audio or video features, the recording would contain rich media in audio or video formats.

Three strategies of implementation were utilized to model learner-content interaction. First, concepts of learning with Collaborate and procedural guides with support information and resources were explained and then followed by the linked tutorials. This was intended for students to remember why these information were provided. Second, previous studies found that the perceived needs of support and training for technical skills between instructors and students might vary (Bozarth et al., 2004). Therefore, a simple interface was needed for students to interact with the presented conceptual and procedural information. In the process of using the information and practicing

with Collaborate, students would become aware of the gap between their previous perception and how the technology would work. Third, the management of the orientation within Canvas provided sustained access for students to find and continue to use the orientation course when they signed on to other for-credit online courses. This supported the previous study findings that "students often require reminding of how to use unfamiliar tools at the time of use" (Bower, 2011, p. 71).

Formative Evaluation

In April 2014, all the students enrolled in the summer online classes offered by the university were invited to the orientation course in Canvas. Among them, 1,820 accepted the course invitation. Between April and September of 2014 when the orientation was active, 515 students voluntarily completed the module to learn about using Collaborate.

Qualitative data collected from students' performance in the module served as the basis for the formative evaluation. For the conceptual readiness in SOL, students were prompted to provide self-reflection of the learning process. This reflection opportunity also provided transfer for students to actually use the SOL functions to present themselves, interact with other students, and participate in an online class (Driscoll, 2005; Merrill, 2007). For the procedural readiness, students were guided to configure their computers and launch a simulated synchronous session in the real context of Collaborate. Therefore, the two collections of data in aggregate form included 1) archived Collaborate recordings as indicators of practicing essential procedural tasks, and 2) text of online discussion post entries that were student self-reflection of their experience in setting up and using the synchronous platform. Identifiers were replaced with indexed numbers prior to the analysis. Applied thematic analysis (Guest et al., 2011; Vaismoradi et al., 2013) was used to analyze and interpret the data.

Findings from Practicing a Collaborate Session

The coding themes for the Collaborate recording sessions were developed based on the module objectives. In developing the themes, intercoder agreement (Guest et al., 2011) was reached by repeatedly reviewing the recordings with reference to the features offered by Collaborate. From this process a number of themes, as categories of functions, were identified based on what SOL procedures and tools were tested by the students. Then, the recordings were reviewed again to verify the categories. Based on the verification, all sessions were then coded in a spreadsheet with notes about emerging themes.

There were 168 sessions recorded between April 23 and September 9, 2014, including 25 duplicate attempts. Among them, two students had three repeated sessions; one individual had five repeated sessions. The rest of the individuals had two repeated sessions. Most individual students with duplicated sessions tried, or attempted to test different features. Excluding the duplicates, the sessions revealed that 144 unique individuals chose to launch and practice an automatically recorded Collaborate session. These counted as 28% of the students who completed the Collaborate orientation module. Since the purpose of this practice was to familiarize students with the tools and functions in a Collaborate session, the coding included all 168 sessions.

Among these sessions, three categories of functions, along with the associated tools were practiced. Of these functions and tools, multi-media-based communication with VoIP audio and live video was the most practiced, with 53% of the recorded sessions tested VoIP and 35% for video. Whiteboard interactivity was the next favored function that was tested in 33% of the recordings. The testing of the text chat function was not as popular. 12% of the recordings included the practice of this function. The low frequency of testing this tool may have been caused by the

influence of the prevalence of text chat in other social media platforms, which students interact with in their daily lives and are not as curious. Some participants tested multiple tools and functions, as displayed in the analysis results in Table 1.

With the remote presence and lack of face-to-face gestures in SOL, icons and indicators for class members to communicate about their presence and participation status would be important for an online class session. There were as many as 19% of the sessions that included the practice of raising hands, and 22% testing the Away indicator. The level of testing the SOL functions in Collaborate demonstrated that students did perform SRL with learner-content interaction.

Findings from Self Reflection

In evaluating the development of an instructional product, the perceived usefulness is an important measure of effective instructional design (Richey & Klein, 2007). There were 525 entries of self-reflection about the experience of learning to use Collaborate in the online discussion forum. These were analyzed to investigate the perceived usefulness of this orientation module as well as

Table 1. Functions and tools tested at Blackboard Collaborate practice sessions

Functions	Tools	Percentage of Sessions That Practiced the Tool
Multimedia-based communication	VoIP Audio	53%
	Live Video	35%
Interactivity	Whiteboard	33%
	Chat	12%
Awareness of class participation / presence	Away	22%
	Raise hand	19%
	Check mark	9%
	Emoticon (Smile, Applause, Thumbs down)	12%

other themes generated from the literature review. As introduced in the Development section, the module consisted of one single discussion forum in the orientation course in Canvas. The instruction, tutorials, resources, and support information were presented in the discussion forum prompt area. The participants were able to post without navigating away from the web page in the orientation module.

Applied thematic analysis was conducted to analyze these qualitative data both individually and collaboratively. Based on the repeated perusal of the data, review of the project purpose, and literature review, intercoder agreement was established through several iterations (Guest et al., 2011). After applying color codes to identified themes and comparing counterparts' coding line-by-line, the coders reached the consensus on a set of 10 themes.

Among these, five themes with nearly half of the entry excerpts demonstrated the perceived usefulness of the orientation module (Richey & Klein, 2007). These included 1) *perceived effective design*, 2) *perceived readiness for online classes*, 3) *perceived technology competency*, 4) *awareness of support,* and 5) *perceived possible*

use of Collaborate in online learning. These mirrored the module objectives and built the student readiness for SOL, as demonstrated with example excerpts in Table 2.

The repeated themes from the student reflection consisted of their perception of effective design of the tutorials, and how the orientation module provided scaffolding for them to gain confidence for online learning. The readiness for online learning was expressed as perceived technology competencies, and positive attitudes toward using technologies to learn, such as belief, confidence, and comfort (Dray, Lowenthal, Miszkiewicz, RuizPrimo, & Marczynski, 2011; Hung, Chou, Chen, & Own, 2010). It also correlated with student satisfaction with SOL and anticipated use in online courses (Puzziferro, 2008). Seeking help, an important aspect in online learning readiness, was identified in the theme of awareness of support and possible use of support information (Cheng et al., 2013; Heiser et al., 2013; Lawanto et al., 2014). This was demonstrated clearly with the theme of awareness of support.

Other themes confirmed the ease of using Collaborate or provided revision suggestions for future iterations of design. There were substantial

Table 2. Perceived usefulness and example excerpts

Perceived Usefulness	Example Excerpts
Perceived effective design	*...But these tutorials helped me setup my computer and gave me the confidence to know that I will participate in this online class to best of my abilities* *The tutorial was effective in explaining how to use this application. I was able to set up my microphone to the right volume.*
Perceived readiness for online classes	*I'm confident about using Blackboard online collaborate now. I learned to navigate and install the correct programs in order to use blackboard collaborate.*
Perceived technology competencies	*I have not previously done an online class so I will admit I was a little nervous that I wouldn't be able to figure out how to setup my computer. Especially in the area of video recordings, since I am not that tech savy. But these tutorials helped me setup.*
Awareness of support	*If I run into problems I think I'll be able to figure them out with the tutorials.*
Perceived possible use of Collaborate in online learning	*Collaborate is a very good meeting tool. Blackboard collaborate is an opportunity to actively interact with classmates through live-feed communication. Features such as hand raising, chats, and a whiteboard are great ways to allow us to actively participate. They allow for an in-class setting that is online.* *The incorporation of teachers into online "classrooms" is incredible! Blackboard Collaboration will be a very useful tool in the online learning experience. Communication among the participants looks to be organized and practical.*

entries about how easy Collaborate was. It might be an indicator of the effectiveness of orientation or of the robustness of Collaborate. Students also expressed concerns about possible issues when actually using it in real online classes. This might indicate that it took the student a certain amount of time and effort to get the Collaborate session working, since there were comments about encountered issues. Specific to SOL, some hardware and connection issues unique to individual computer operating systems or web browsers could create problems (Bower, 2011; Martin et al., 2012). This also indicated that training and support were clearly needed. The theme coincided with research-based recommendations, that is, to embed course-specific training and support for teaching and learning with synchronous technologies to prevent issues in specific class settings (Bliesener, 2006; Park & Bonk, 2007).

A few comments (<10 of the 525 reflection posts) were negative about this experience. Some expressed the fatigue of having to complete another orientation and some provided suggestions. These might be associated with perceived redundancy as resulted from previous experience with SOL. At a holistic view, however, these self-reflection entries demonstrated that the orientation module was useful in building the student readiness for SOL.

CONCLUSION AND DISCUSSION

The purpose of this research was to investigate how effective the learner-content interaction designed in an orientation module was in scaffolding SRL to develop student readiness for SOL. According to Richey and Klein (2007), the effectiveness of design and development research is mainly measured by the usefulness of the instructional product as perceived by users. Twenty eight percent of the students who completed the module successfully launched a simulated Collaborate session and tested the essential SOL procedures and functions. The reflection entries posted on the online discussion forum demonstrated that the students did perceive the orientation module useful. Students reported that the design of tutorials was effective; they gained technology competencies; they felt ready and confident for online classes; they were more aware of technical support and related information; and they anticipated using Collaborate in their online classes in a way that would positively impact their learning.

Another key outcome of the research includes "lessons learned from developing specific products and analyzing the conditions which facilitate their use" (Richey & Klein, 2007, p. 13). The lessons learned in this study are three-fold and closely related to the characteristics of design and development research, specifically the integration of design principles with technology potential (Reeves et al., 2005). The analysis of context and learning tasks enabled the design and development project to take advantage of the technology affordance. The analysis of context defined the possibilities that Collaborate could offer to enhance online learning. It also identified what mechanism Canvas could provide to present instructional content and how flexible it could permit learner-content interaction. With the capability of self-paced learning, students could use the orientation module conveniently and repeatedly if needed, and in the same system as their other summer online courses. The analysis of tasks ensured a clear step-by-step procedure for configuring and setting up computers to launch a Collaborate session. The identification of what would be of primary importance to launch and test a Collaborate session and to facilitate class participation and interaction in the SOL environment laid the foundation for selecting strategies to develop instructional content.

The selection of Component Display Theory (Merrill, 2007) for the development was effective in scaffolding SRL with learner-content interaction, which led to the achievement of the following outcomes:

- Acquainted students with the representative concepts and procedures of learning with Collaborate;
- Provided SRL scaffolding for students to complete essential learning tasks with practice in the real context;
- Built student awareness of available resources and how to access support;
- Fostered student awareness of SOL potential.

The analysis of the available training and support resources also made the development of this instructional product cost-effective. The instructional content was created and selected for use based on the analysis of existing content from internal and external sources. Internally, the institution facilitated technology support and related resources. Externally, the enterprise that provided the technology furnished with supportive information. The selection of content appropriate for the orientation, based on instructional design principles, made the integration practical and useful.

This study is not without limitation. Based in the context of one university and using Collaborate as the SOL platform in Canvas, the current results of the research are not ready for generalization. What other individuals or groups can use though, are the dynamic application of Component Display Theory, learner-content interaction as strategies for scaffolding SRL, and the cost-effective use of selected existing resources.

Suggestions for revision and improvement are also indicated by the findings of the formative evaluation (Ohia, 2011; Richey & Klein, 2007; Suskie, 2010). Suggestions include: 1) conducting a more in-depth needs analysis: this can reduce the comments of redundancy from those students who have had previous SOL experience; 2) providing a clearer statement of the purpose about practicing the automatically recorded Collaborate session so that students would be benefited better from the activity; 3) adding the training about etiquette and competencies for synchronous interaction, which have been identified as to enhance SOL (Bower, 2011; Gautreau, 2012; Warden et al., 2013).

Future research can include measuring student readiness for SOL prior to and after the participation in the orientation module. There are validated instruments that can be adapted to the synchronous environment (Cigdem & Yildirim, 2014; Dray, Lowenthal, Miszkiewicz, Ruiz-Primo, & Marczynski, 2011; Pennsylvania State University, 2014). The level of SRL can also be compared at the beginning and completion of the module, to detect whether there is an increase or not. This can contribute to the rising interest in SRL in online learning, specifically in SOL (Barnard, Lan, To, Paton, & Lai, 2009; Schraw, 2010).

To continue the design and development research in a more situated manner, orientation modules or units can be designed for subject-specific classes. Student training and support should be customized to different classes that utilize different functions of a synchronous system (Bower, 2011; Doggett, 2007; Epp et al., 2010). Furthermore, training and support available beyond an orientation and situated in individual classes are recommended for enhancing synchronous learning (Park & Bonk, 2007).

REFERENCES

Allen, I. E., & Seaman, J. (2014). *Grade change: Tracking online education in the United States.* Babson Survey Research Group & Online Learning Consortium. Retrieved from http://www.onlinelearningsurvey.com/reports/gradechange.pdf

Alsharif, N. Z., & Roche, V. F. (2010). Promoting key interactions in a distance medicinal chemistry course. *Currents in Pharmacy Teaching & Learning, 2*(2), 114–125. doi:10.1016/j.cptl.2010.01.003

Andrade, M. (2014). Course-embedded student support for online English language learners. *Open Praxis*, *6*(1), 65–73. doi:10.5944/openpraxis.6.1.90

Artino, A. R. Jr, & Jones, K. D. II. (2012). Exploring the complex relations between achievement emotions and self-regulated learning behaviors in online learning. *The Internet and Higher Education*, *15*(3), 170–175. doi:10.1016/j.iheduc.2012.01.006

Attebury, R. (2010). Elluminate *live!* and Jing: Instruction for synchronous and asynchronous online classes. *Journal of Library Administration*, *50*(7), 1027–1028.

Azevedo, R., & Hadwin, A. F. (2005). Scaffolding self-regulated learning and metacognition: Implications for the design of computer-based scaffolds. *Instructional Science*, *33*(5), 367–379. doi:10.1007/s11251-005-1272-9

Baker, D. L. (2011). Designing and orchestrating online discussions. *MERLOT Journal of Online Learning and Teaching*, *7*(3), 401–411.

Barbour, M. K., & Reeves, T. C. (2009). The reality of virtual schools: A review of the literature. *Computers & Education*, *52*(2), 402–416. doi:10.1016/j.compedu.2008.09.009

Barnard, L., Lan, W. Y., To, Y. M., Paton, V. O., & Lai, S. (2009). Measuring self-regulation in online and blended learning environments. *The Internet and Higher Education*, *12*(1), 1–6. doi:10.1016/j.iheduc.2008.10.005

Barnard, L., Paton, V., & Lan, W. (2008). Online self-regulatory learning behaviors as a mediator in the relationship between online course perceptions with achievement. *International Review of Research in Open and Distance Learning*, *9*(2), 1–11.

Barnard-Brak, L., Lan, W. Y., & Paton, V. O. (2010). Profiles in self-regulated learning in the online learning environment. *International Review of Research in Open and Distance Learning*, *11*(1), 61–80.

Bednall, T. C., & Kehoe, E. J. (2011). Effects of self-regulatory instructional aids on self-directed study. *Instructional Science*, *39*(2), 205–226. doi:10.1007/s11251-009-9125-6

Benson, A. D., & Whitworth, A. (Eds.). (2014). *Research on course management systems in higher education*. Charlotte, NC: Information Age Publishing, Inc.

Bentley, Y., Shegunshi, A., & Scannell, M. (2010). Evaluating the impact of distance learning support systems on the learning experience of MBA students in a global context. *Electronic Journal of E-Learning*, *8*(2), 51–62.

Bernard, R. M., Abrami, P. C., Borokhovski, E., Wade, C. A., Tamim, R. M., Surkes, M. A., & Bethel, E. C. (2009). A meta-analysis of three types of interaction treatments in distance education. *Review of Educational Research*, *79*(3), 1243–1289. doi:10.3102/0034654309333844

Bigatel, P. M., Ragan, L. C., Kennan, S., May, J., & Redmond, B. F. (2012). The identification of competencies for online teaching success. *Journal of Asynchronous Learning Networks*, *16*(1), 59–77.

Blackboard Collaborate. (2014). *Blackboard Collaborate web conferencing*. Retrieved from http://www.blackboard.com/Platforms/Collaborate/Products/Blackboard-Collaborate/Web-Conferencing/Features.aspx

Blankson, J., & Kyei-Blankson, L. (2008). Nontraditional students' perception of a blended course: Integrating synchronous online discussion and face-to-face instruction. *Journal of Interactive Learning Research*, *19*(3), 421–438.

Blau, I., & Barak, A. (2012). How do personality, synchronous media, and discussion topic affect participation? *Journal of Educational Technology & Society, 15*(2), 12–24.

Bliesener, T. (2006). Training synchronous collaborative E-learning. *International Journal on E-Learning, 5*(2), 185–196.

Bonk, C. J., Kirkley, J. R., Hara, N., & Dennen, N. (2001). *Finding the instructor in post-secondary online learning: Pedagogical, social, managerial, and technological locations*. London: Kogan Page Limited.

Bower, M. (2011). Synchronous collaboration competencies in web-conferencing environments - their impact on the learning process. *Distance Education, 32*(1), 63–83. doi:10.1080/0158791 9.2011.565502

Bozarth, J., Chapman, D. D., & LaMonica, L. (2004). Preparing for distance learning: Designing an online student orientation course. *Journal of Educational Technology & Society, 7*(1), 87–106.

Burgelman, R. A., Christensen, C. M., & Wheelwright, S. C. (2004). *Strategic management of technology and innovation* (4th ed.). New York, NY: McGraw-Hill Irwin.

Chen, C., Wang, J., & Chen, Y. (2014). Facilitating English-language reading performance by a digital reading annotation system with self-regulated learning mechanisms. *Journal of Educational Technology & Society, 17*(1), 102–114.

Cheng, K., Liang, J., & Tsai, C. (2013). University students' online academic help seeking: The role of self-regulation and information commitments. *The Internet and Higher Education, 16*, 70–77. doi:10.1016/j.iheduc.2012.02.002

Cho, M. (2012). Online student orientation in higher education: A developmental study. *Educational Technology Research and Development, 60*(6), 1051–1069. doi:10.1007/s11423-012-9271-4

Cho, T. (2011). The impact of types of interaction on student satisfaction in online courses. *International Journal on E-Learning, 10*(2), 109–125.

Chou, S., & Liu, C. (2005). Learning effectiveness in a web-based virtual learning environment: A learner control perspective. *Journal of Computer Assisted Learning, 21*(1), 65–76. doi:10.1111/j.1365-2729.2005.00114.x

Cigdem, H., & Yildirim, O. G. (2014). Effects of students' characteristics on online learning readiness: A vocational college example. *Turkish Online Journal of Distance Education, 15*(3), 80–93. doi:10.17718/tojde.69439

Connors, P. (2013). Delivery style moderates study habits in an online nutrition class. *Journal of Nutrition Education and Behavior, 45*(2), 171–175. doi:10.1016/j.jneb.2012.04.006 PMID:23041253

Cormier, D., & Siemens, G. (2010). The open course: Through the open door--open courses as research, learning, and engagement. *EDUCAUSE Review, 45*(4), 30.

Crawley, A. (2012). *Supporting online students: A practical guide to planning, implementing, and evaluating services*. Hoboken, NJ: John Wiley & Sons.

Creswell, J. W. (2013). *Research design: Qualitative, quantitative, and mixed methods approaches*. Thousand Oaks, CA: Sage.

Dabbagh, N. (2003). Scaffolding: An important teacher competency in online learning. *TechTrends, 47*(2), 39–44. doi:10.1007/BF02763424

Dabbagh, N., & Bannan-Ritland, B. (2005). *Online learning: Concepts, strategies, and application*. Hoboken, NJ: Prentice Hall.

Dabbagh, N., & Kitsantas, A. (2005). Using web-based pedagogical tools as scaffolds for self-regulated learning. *Instructional Science, 33*(5-6), 513–540. doi:10.1007/s11251-005-1278-3

Dabbagh, N., & Kitsantas, A. (2009). Exploring how experienced online instructors report using integrative technologies to support self-regulated learning. *International Journal of Technology in Teaching and Learning, 5*(2), 154–168.

Delen, E., Liew, J., & Willson, V. (2014). Effects of interactivity and instructional scaffolding on learning: Self-regulation in online video-based environments. *Computers & Education, 78,* 312–320. doi:10.1016/j.compedu.2014.06.018

Dembo, M. H., Junge, L., & Lynch, R. (2006). Becoming a self-regulated learner: Implications for web-based education. In H. F. O'Neil & R. S. Perez (Eds.), *Web-based learning: Theory, research, and practicepp* (pp. 185–202). Mahwah, NJ: Lawrence Erlbaum.

Doggett, A. M. (2007). The videoconferencing classroom: What do students think? *Journal of Industrial Teacher Education, 44*(4), 29–41.

Dowell, D. J., & Small, F. A. (2011). What is the impact of online resource materials on student self-learning strategies? *Journal of Marketing Education, 33*(2), 140–148. doi:10.1177/0273475311410846

Dray, B. J., Lowenthal, P. R., Miszkiewicz, M. J., Ruiz-Primo, M. A., & Marczynski, K. (2011). Developing an instrument to assess student readiness for online learning: A validation study. *Distance Education, 32*(1), 29–47. doi:10.1080/0158791 9.2011.565496

Driscoll, M. P. (2005). *Psychology of learning for instruction* (3rd ed.). Boston, MA: Allyn and Bacon.

Duncan, K., Kenworthy, A., & McNamara, R. (2012). The effect of synchronous and asynchronous participation on students' performance in online accounting courses. *Accounting Education, 21*(4), 431–449. doi:10.1080/09639284.2 012.673387

Ekwunife-Orakwue, K., & Teng, T. (2014). The impact of transactional distance dialogic interactions on student learning outcomes in online and blended environments. *Computers & Education, 78,* 414–427. doi:10.1016/j.compedu.2014.06.011

Epp, E. M., Green, K. F., Rahman, A. M., & Weaver, G. C. (2010). Analysis of student–instructor interaction patterns in real-time, scientific online discourse. *Journal of Science Education and Technology, 19*(1), 49–57. doi:10.1007/s10956-009-9177-z

Er, E., Özden, M. Y., & Arifoğlu, A. (2009). LIVELMS: A blended e-learning environment: A model proposition for integration of asynchronous and synchronous e-learning. *International Journal of Learning, 16*(2), 449–460.

Ertmer, P. A., Sadaf, A., & Ertmer, D. J. (2011). Student-content interactions in online courses: The role of question prompts in facilitating higher-level engagement with course content. *Journal of Computing in Higher Education, 23*(2-3), 157–186. doi:10.1007/s12528-011-9047-6

Finkelstein, J. E. (2009). *Learning in real time: Synchronous teaching and learning online*. Hoboken, NJ: John Wiley & Sons.

Garrison, D. R., & Cleveland-Innes, M. (2005). Facilitating cognitive presence in online learning: Interaction is not enough. *American Journal of Distance Education, 19*(3), 133–148. doi:10.1207/s15389286ajde1903_2

Gautreau, C. (2012). Video conferencing guidelines for faculty and students in graduate online courses. *MERLOT Journal of Online Learning and Teaching, 8*(4).

Giesbers, B., Rienties, B., Tempelaar, D., & Gijselaers, W. (2014). A dynamic analysis of the interplay between asynchronous and synchronous communication in online learning: The impact of motivation. *Journal of Computer Assisted Learning, 30*(1), 30–50. doi:10.1111/jcal.12020

Glazatov, T. R. (2012). Applying instructional design system theory to mobile learning environments. *Journal of Applied Learning Technology*, *2*(2), 29–35.

Grandzol, C. J., & Grandzol, J. R. (2010). Interaction in online courses: More is not always better. *Online Journal of Distance Learning Administration*, *13*(2), 1–18.

Guest, G., MacQueen, K. M., & Namey, E. E. (2011). *Applied thematic analysis*. Thousand Oaks, CA: Sage.

Hampel, R. (2006). Rethinking task design for the digital age: A framework for language teaching and learning in a synchronous online environment. *ReCALL*, *18*(1), 105–121. doi:10.1017/S0958344006000711

Han, H. (2013). Do nonverbal emotional cues matter? Effects of video casting in synchronous virtual classrooms. *American Journal of Distance Education*, *27*(4), 253–264. doi:10.1080/08923647.2013.837718

Hastie, M., Chen, N., & Kuo, Y. (2007). Instructional design for best practice in the synchronous cyber classroom. *Journal of Educational Technology & Society*, *10*(4), 281–294.

Heiser, S., Stickler, U., & Furnborough, C. (2013). Student training in the use of an online synchronous conferencing tool. *CALICO Journal*, *30*(2), 226–251. doi:10.11139/cj.30.2.226-251

Hrastinski, S. (2008). Asynchronous & synchronous e-learning. *EDUCAUSE Quarterly*, *31*(4), 51–55.

Huang, X., & Hsiao, E. (2012). Synchronous and asynchronous communication in an online environment: Faculty experiences and perceptions. *Quarterly Review of Distance Education*, *13*(1), 15–30.

Hung, M., Chou, C., Chen, C., & Own, Z. (2010). Learner readiness for online learning: Scale development and student perceptions. *Computers & Education*, *55*(3), 1080–1090. doi:10.1016/j.compedu.2010.05.004

Instructure, C. (2014). *Canvas help center*. Retrieved from http://guides.instructure.com/

Jones, K. R. (2013). Developing and implementing a mandatory online student orientation. *Journal of Asynchronous Learning Networks*, *17*(1), 43–45.

Jowallah, R. (2014). An investigation into the management of online teaching and learning spaces: A case study involving graduate research students. *International Review of Research in Open and Distance Learning*, *15*(4), 186–198.

Joyce, K. M., & Brown, A. (2009). Enhancing social presence in online learning: Mediation strategies applied to social networking tools. *Online Journal of Distance Learning Administration*, *12*(4).

Kaymak, Z. D., & Horzum, M. B. (2013). Relationship between online learning readiness and structure and interaction of online learning students. *Educational Sciences: Theory and Practice*, *13*(3), 1792–1797.

Kert, S. B., & Kurt, A. A. (2012). The effect of electronic performance support systems on self-regulated learning skills. *Interactive Learning Environments*, *20*(6), 485–500. doi:10.1080/10494820.2010.533683

Kim, R., Olfman, L., Ryan, T., & Eryilmaz, E. (2014). Leveraging a personalized system to improve self-directed learning in online educational environments. *Computers & Education*, *70*, 150–160. doi:10.1016/j.compedu.2013.08.006

Koohang, A., & Harman, K. (2007). Advancing sustainability of open educational resources. *Issues in Informing Science and Information Technology*, *4*, 535–544.

Kuo, Y., Walker, A. E., Belland, B. R., Schroder, K. E. E., & Kuo, Y. (2014). A case study of integrating interwise: Interaction, internet self-efficacy, and satisfaction in synchronous online learning environments. *International Review of Research in Open and Distance Learning*, *15*(1), 161–181.

Lawanto, O., Santoso, H. B., Lawanto, K. N., & Goodridge, W. (2014). Self-regulated learning skills and online activities between higher and lower performers on a web-intensive undergraduate engineering course. *Journal of Educators Online*, *11*(3), 1–32.

Lee, S. J., Srinivasan, S., Trail, T., Lewis, D., & Lopez, S. (2011). Examining the relationship among student perception of support, course satisfaction, and learning outcomes in online learning. *The Internet and Higher Education*, *14*(3), 158–163. doi:10.1016/j.iheduc.2011.04.001

Lehman, R. M., & Conceição, S. C. (2010). *Creating a sense of presence in online teaching: How to "be there" for distance learners*. San Francisco, CA: John Wiley & Sons.

Lehmann, T., Hähnlein, I., & Ifenthaler, D. (2014). Cognitive, metacognitive and motivational perspectives on preflection in self-regulated online learning. *Computers in Human Behavior*, *32*, 313–323. doi:10.1016/j.chb.2013.07.051

Liu, X., Bonk, C. J., Magjuka, R. J., Lee, S., & Su, B. (2005). Exploring four dimensions of online instructor roles: A program level case study. *Journal of Asynchronous Learning Networks*, *9*(4), 29–48.

Martin, F., Parker, M. A., & Deale, D. F. (2012). Examining interactivity in synchronous virtual classrooms. *International Review of Research in Open and Distance Learning*, *13*(3), 227–261.

Merrill, M. D. (2007). A task-centered instructional strategy. *Journal of Research on Technology in Education*, *40*(1), 5–22. doi:10.1080/15391523.2007.10782493

Michinov, N., Brunot, S., Le Bohec, O., Juhel, J., & Delaval, M. (2011). Procrastination, participation, and performance in online learning environments. *Computers & Education*, *56*(1), 243–252. doi:10.1016/j.compedu.2010.07.025

Moore, M. G., & Kearsley, G. (2012). *Distance education: A systems view of online learning* (3rd ed.). Belmont, VA: Wadsworth Cengage Learning.

Morrison, G. R., Ross, S. M., Kemp, J. E., & Kalman, H. (2011). *Designing effective instruction* (6th ed.). Hoboken, NJ: John Wiley & Sons.

Murray, M., Pérez, J., Geist, D., & Hedrick, A. (2013). Student interaction with content in online and hybrid courses: Leading horses to the proverbial water. *Informing Science*, *16*, 99–115.

Nag, R., Hambrick, D. C., & Chen, M. (2007). What is strategic management, really? Inductive derivation of a consensus definition of the field. *Strategic Management Journal*, *28*(9), 935–955. doi:10.1002/smj.615

O'Neil, C. A., Fisher, C. A., & Rietschel, M. J. (2014). *Developing online learning environments in nursing education*. New York, NY: Springer.

Ohia, U. O. (2011). A model for effectively assessing student learning outcomes. *Contemporary Issues in Education Research*, *4*(3), 25–32.

Oztok, M., Zingaro, D., Brett, C., & Hewitt, J. (2013). Exploring asynchronous and synchronous tool use in online courses. *Computers & Education, 60*(1), 87–94. doi:10.1016/j.compedu.2012.08.007

Park, J. Y., & Bonk, C. J. (2007). Synchronous learning experiences: Distance and residential learners' perspectives in a blended graduate course. *Journal of Interactive Online Learning, 6*(3), 245–254.

Parker, E. B., & Howland, L. C. (2006). Strategies to manage the time demands of online teaching. *Nurse Educator, 31*(6), 270–274. doi:10.1097/00006223-200611000-00012 PMID:17108792

Parra, S. (2012). Component display theory design in a foreign language unit. *Journal of Applied Learning Technology, 2*(3), 23–32.

Pennsylvania State University. (2014). *Student self-assessment for online learning readiness.* Retrieved from http://ets.tlt.psu.edu/learningdesign/assessment/onlinecontent/online_readiness

Pintrich, P. R., & Zusho, A. (2002). The development of academic self-regulation: The role of cognitive and motivational factors. In A. Wigfield & J. S. Eccles (Eds.), *Development of achievement motivation* (pp. 249–284). San Diego, CA: Academic Press. doi:10.1016/B978-012750053-9/50012-7

Puzziferro, M. (2008). Online technologies self-efficacy and self-regulated learning as predictors of final grade and satisfaction in college-level online courses. *American Journal of Distance Education, 22*(2), 72–89. doi:10.1080/08923640802039024

Quality Matters Program. (2013). *The Quality Matters higher education rubric.* Retrieved from https://www.qualitymatters.org/rubric

Quality Matters Program. (2014). *The Quality Matters higher education rubric.* Retrieved from https://www.qualitymatters.org/rubric

Reeves, T. C., Herrington, J., & Oliver, R. (2005). Design research: A socially responsible approach to instructional technology research in higher education. *Journal of Computing in Higher Education, 16*(2), 96–115. doi:10.1007/BF02961476

Richardson, J. C., & Swan, K. (2003). Examining social presence in online course in relation to students' perceived learning and satisfaction. *Journal of Asynchronous Learning Networks, 7*(1), 68–88.

Richey, R., & Klein, J. D. (Eds.). (2007). *Design and development research: Methods, strategies, and issues.* Mahwah, NJ: Lawrence Erlbaum Associates.

Rodriguez, B. C. P., & Armellini, A. (2013). Interaction and effectiveness of corporate e-learning programmes. *Human Resource Development International, 16*(4), 480–489. doi:10.1080/13678868.2013.803753

Rodriguez, B. C. P., & Armellini, A. (2014). Applying the interaction equivalency theorem to online courses in a large organization. *Journal of Interactive Online Learning, 13*(2), 51–66.

Rowe, F. A., & Rafferty, J. A. (2013). Instructional design interventions for supporting self-regulated learning: Enhancing academic outcomes in post-secondary E-learning environments. *Journal of Online Learning & Teaching, 9*(4), 590–601.

Rufai, M. M., Alebiosu, S. O., & Adeakin, O. A. S. (2015). A conceptual model for virtual classroom management. *International Journal of Computer Science. Engineering and Information Technology, 5*(1), 27–32. PMID:26029735

Salmon, G. (2011). *E-moderating: The key to online teaching and learning* (3rd ed.). New York, NY: Routledge.

Sawyer, E. A., & Howard, C. (2007). Online learning program strategic planning and execution: Considering goals, benefits, problems and communities of practice. *Journal of College Teaching & Learning*, *4*(8), 99–112.

Schraw, G. (2010). Measuring self-regulation in computer-based learning environments. *Educational Psychologist*, *45*(4), 258–266. doi:10.1080/00461520.2010.515936

Schunk, D. (2008). Metacognition, self-regulation, and self-regulated learning: Research recommendations. *Educational Psychology Review*, *20*(4), 463–467. doi:10.1007/s10648-008-9086-3

Schunk, D., & Mullen, C. (2013). Toward a conceptual model of mentoring research: Integration with self-regulated learning. *Educational Psychology Review*, *25*(3), 361–389. doi:10.1007/s10648-013-9233-3

Shea, P., & Bidjerano, T. (2010). Learning presence: Towards a theory of self-efficacy, self-regulation, and the development of a communities of inquiry in online and blended learning environments. *Computers & Education*, *55*(4), 1721–1731. doi:10.1016/j.compedu.2010.07.017

Shea, P., Li, C. S., & Pickett, A. (2006). A study of teaching presence and student sense of learning community in fully online and web-enhanced college courses. *The Internet and Higher Education*, *9*(3), 175–190. doi:10.1016/j.iheduc.2006.06.005

Shih, R. (2010). Blended learning using video-based blogs: Public speaking for English as a second language students. *Australasian Journal of Educational Technology*, *26*(6), 883–897.

Simonson, M., Smaldino, S., Albright, M., & Zvacek, S. (2012). *Teaching and learning at a distance* (5th ed.). Boston, MA: Pearson Education.

Smith, P. L., & Ragan, T. J. (2005). *Instructional design* (3rd ed.). Hoboken, NJ: John Wiley & Sons.

Sun, J. C., & Rueda, R. (2012). Situational interest, computer self-efficacy and self-regulation: Their impact on student engagement in distance education. *British Journal of Educational Technology*, *43*(2), 191–204. doi:10.1111/j.1467-8535.2010.01157.x

Suskie, L. (2010). *Assessing student learning: A common sense guide*. Hoboken, NJ: John Wiley & Sons.

Swan, K., Shea, P., Richardson, J., Ice, P., Garrison, D., Cleveland-Innes, M., & Arbaugh, J. (2008). Validating a measurement tool of presence in online communities of inquiry. *E-Mentor*, *2*(24), 1–12.

Tonsmann, G. (2014). A study of the effectiveness of blackboard collaborate for conducting synchronous courses at multiple locations. *InSight: A Journal of Scholarly Teaching, 9*, 54-63.

Tsai, C. (2013). How to involve students in an online course: A redesigned online pedagogy of collaborative learning and self-regulated learning. *International Journal of Distance Education Technologies*, *11*(3), 47–57. doi:10.4018/jdet.2013070104

Tsai, C., Shen, P., & Fan, Y. (2013). Research trends in self-regulated learning research in online learning environments: A review of studies published in selected journals from 2003 to 2012. *British Journal of Educational Technology*, *44*(5), 107–110. doi:10.1111/bjet.12017

Tsai, C., Shen, P., & Tsai, M. (2011). Developing an appropriate design of blended learning with web-enabled self-regulated learning to enhance students' learning and thoughts regarding online learning. *Behaviour & Information Technology*, *30*(2), 261–271. doi:10.1080/0144929X.2010.514359

Ullmann, J. (2009). Alternative uses for course management systems: They aren't just for classes any more. *Online Journal of Distance Learning Administration, 12*(3).

Vaismoradi, M., Turunen, H., & Bondas, T. (2013). Content analysis and thematic analysis: Implications for conducting a qualitative descriptive study. *Nursing & Health Sciences, 15*(3), 398–405. doi:10.1111/nhs.12048 PMID:23480423

Warden, C. A., Stanworth, J. O., Ren, J. B., & Warden, A. R. (2013). Synchronous learning best practices: An action research study. *Computers & Education, 63*, 197–207. doi:10.1016/j.compedu.2012.11.010

Wdowik, S. J. (2014). Using a synchronous online learning environment to promote and enhance transactional engagement beyond the classroom. *Campus-Wide Information Systems, 31*(4), 254–263.

Wozniak, H., Pizzica, J., & Mahony, M. J. (2012). Design-based research principles for student orientation to online study: Capturing the lessons learned. *Australasian Journal of Educational Technology, 28*(5), 896–911.

Wright, C. R., Lopes, V., Montgomerie, T. C., Reju, S. A., & Schmoller, S. (2014). Selecting a learning management system: Advice from an academic perspective. *EDUCAUSE Review Online,* November 3, 2014.

Yamagata-Lynch, L. (2014). Blending online asynchronous and synchronous learning. *International Review of Research in Open and Distance Learning, 15*(2), 189–212.

Zimmerman, T. D. (2012). Exploring learner to content interaction as a success factor in online courses. *International Review of Research in Open and Distance Learning, 13*(4), 152–165.

KEY TERMS AND DEFINITIONS

Asynchronous Online Learning (AOL): Learning activities in a web-based environment that allow communication between class members and interaction with content at time and location that are flexible and convenient to each individual in an online class. Technologies enabling AOL include emails, text-messaging, blogs, online discussion, wikis, streaming media, or a digital content management system.

Design and Development Research: A type of research that connects traditional research methodology with technology affordance, studying how to optimize the technology potential in solving instructional or non-instructional problems related to learning.

Learner-Content Interaction: The cognitive and/or perceptual contact between students and the materials of study that result in acquisition of meaning by students, such as reading text in print or digital formats, watching or listening to media, operating with equipment in labs, and finding information.

Online Learning Readiness: Cognitive awareness and maturity that a student develops for successful learning in a web-based environment. It manifests in the attributes of recognizing the self-directed nature, formulating learning strategies, obtaining technology competencies, adjusting to digital etiquettes, and being open for help-seeking.

Scaffolding: The direct and indirect support in instructional or non-instructional formats that aids students to learn complex or unfamiliar concepts, procedures or skills. It can be provided as explicit or implicit components in the learning process and gradually fade away or be available for use as needed.

Self-Regulated Learning: An active process where an individual takes responsibility to acquire knowledge and skills by setting goals, adjusting to the factors and conditions related to learning tasks, making decisions about when and how to seek help, and reflecting for transfer.

Strategic Management: a systematic process that analyzes needs, determines decisions and conducts course of action to maintain the competitive performance of an individual or organization, usually taking into consideration of long- and short-term goals, objectives, stakeholders, and outcomes.

Synchronous Online Learning (SOL): Learning activities in a web-based environment that allow real-time communication between class members and interaction with content. Technologies enabling SOL include text-, audio- and/or video-based chat, video conferencing, simultaneous presentations from physically distributed sites, and application sharing.

Technology Affordance: The contextual factors and conditions in a technology-mediated learning environment. These can be potential to enhance learning or barriers to limit learning success, which is usually leveraged for optimal integration in learning through sound instructional design.

Chapter 10

Web–Based Technologies for Ensuring Interaction in Online Courses:
Faculty Choice and Student Perception of Web–Based Technologies for Interaction in Online Economics

Olivia P. Morris
Online Learning, Chicago, USA

ABSTRACT

This chapter discusses findings from a study of five faculty and 33 students from micro- and macroeconomics sections of online economics courses over the course of a semester. The study investigated faculty choice of web-based technologies for interaction and students' perceptions of such technologies. The objectives of the study were twofold. First, the author investigated faculty choice of web-based technologies for three major types of online interactions (learner–instructor, learner–content, and learner–learner). Second, the author examined student perceptions of technologies and recorded recommendations. Results from two online surveys of faculty and students at 2- and 4-year colleges showed strong agreement with perceptions of Moore, Drouin, Rhode, and Gardner. Faculty and students reported learner–learner interactions as the least important of the three interaction types. Although the discussion board was most effective for all three types of interactions, students from this sample did not prefer more learner–learner discussions.

OVERVIEW

Innovations in web-based technologies continue to impact online courses and online interactions. Researchers showed that student satisfaction relates directly to their perceptions of interactions (Drouin, 2008). Knowing the ideal amount of interaction in online courses is of great significance to educators who address student satisfaction and retention. Acquiring such knowledge compels the need to discern whether online faculty's choice of web-based technologies has captured the di-

DOI: 10.4018/978-1-4666-9582-5.ch010

versity in student needs and perceptions of online interactions.

Studies confirmed that students' need for interaction varies and suggested that an ideal balance of interaction might exist (Anderson, 2003). Evidence from the studies supports the importance of achieving a balance between faculty choice of web-based technology and students' perceptions of the same web-based technologies used to promote learner–content, learner–instructor and learner–learner interaction in online courses. Although the discussion-board forum was cited as the most effective for all three types of interaction, students indicated it should not increase, but remain relevant to the subject area and needs of the class. In addition, a majority of students rated the technologies for learner–content interaction as having greater impact on their learning than the technology used for learner–instructor interaction. Most students in this sample recommended an increase in the use of online multimedia movie clips, podcasts, video lectures, and tutorials—that could be accessed through mobile/portable technologies such as iPhones, Kindles, Netbooks, and Laptops. Faculty and students perceived interactive homework tools, such as Aplia, as particularly suitable for interactive graphical and numerical aspects of economics, but cautioned about the purposes for which they were used. Online conferencing sessions such as Elluminate were scored as "Good for Learner–instructor" interaction, but not as important for learner–learner and learner–content interaction.

The focus of this chapter is to reinforce the inevitability of diverse preferences for web-based technologies and identify web-based technologies to ensure effective interaction in online courses. In pursuance, the author briefly explored the background surrounding interaction in online economics courses, the major theoretical perspectives on interaction, methodologies and variables, and here shares major findings, conclusions, and recommendations of the study.

BACKGROUND

Overall reviews suggest that teaching strategies in economics at 2- and 4-year colleges have gradually adjusted to the advent of new technologies. Instructors incorporate more interactive software and games to enhance student learning of concepts, and graphs and charts to develop analytical skills, thereby creating active student-learning environments. However, because technology tools are becoming vital teaching aids in online economics courses, it is important that instructors know how to assess a piece of technology. Faculty choice of technology may not correspond with students' needs for interaction. Drouin (2008) reported that "while some students enjoyed, needed, or desired social interaction, some students did not desire a sense of community (SOC) in an online course environment" (p. 267). Because students have different needs for online interaction, it is important to investigate whether faculty choices of technology consider the disparities in various learning settings, including economics, and meet students' expectations.

Consequently, technology resources can be wasted on providing interaction that does not necessarily enhance student learning. A particular level of social interaction may be ideal in online communities and care should be taken to avoid exceeding that level (Rourke, Anderson, Garrison, & Archer, 1999). Future research should focus on qualifying the "ideal amount of student–student and student–instructor interaction within different types of online interactive instructional environments so that educators are better able to construct effective social settings within the online classroom" (Drouin, 2008, p. 281). Though it might be unlikely to find the perfect mix between independent study and interactive learning strategies and activities that meet the needs of all students, it is advisable to aim for an ideal mixture (Anderson, 2003).

Reviewing the literature showed that it was still unclear which design principles actually guide the choice of technology for the three major types of interaction. "Designers and administrators must understand how the technology tool selected will aid interaction and which types of interaction it will promote" (Beldarrain, 2006, p. 144). Findings from this study determined the guiding forces behind faculty choices of technologies for the three types of interaction.

A lull exists in the research on online economic education. Arbaugh et al. (2009) stated,

considering that we have had peer-reviewed journals devoted to economics education for at least forty years and that the study of economics education has relatively high legitimacy compared to other business disciplines, the small number of studies of online and blended learning in economics is both surprising and disappointing. Beyond the previously discussed lack of transferability of the research questions and methods of their discipline, reasons for this lack of activity are unclear (p. 82).

These authors inferred that the lack of activity could have been due to the results of these studies, which showed that classroom sections of the economics classes were performing better (Arbaugh et al., 2009). Also, some researchers expressed concerns about whether quantitative content can be taught effectively online (Smith, Torres-Ayala, & Heindel, 2008). However, other disciplines with quantitative and technical subject matter have reported success in online courses (Arbaugh et al., 2009). Nevertheless, the few studies in online economics have focused more on creating online activities to support active student learning (Lee, Courtney, & Balassi, 2010) than on finding the "ideal amount" of interaction required for student engagement.

At some schools, the teaching of economics has changed to delivering the entire course, not only online, but completely divorced from online interaction with peers or instructors. According to Anderson (2003), as long as one of three primary forms of interaction (student–teacher, student–student, or student–content) is at high level, other forms may be minimized or eliminated without adversely affecting the learning experience. Greenlaw (1999) recommended the adoption of more active and collaborative learning methodologies. Likewise, Simkins (1999) stated that "teaching practices, which rely heavily on the lecture format, are not doing enough to develop students' cognitive learning skills, attract good students to economics, and motivate them to continue coursework in the discipline" (p. 278). Currently, no studies discerned how economics instructors are responding to recent developments in web-based technologies. The delivery of economics courses has undergone remarkable changes from the traditional lecture method to dissemination of course material through web-based teaching. However, the technologies that faculty choose to promote online interaction, and students' views of those technologies, are yet to be discussed.

Theory of Interaction

Moore (1989) revealed three types of learner interaction that are important for learning: learner–content, learner–instructor, and learner–learner. According to Moore, interaction is a component of distance education that has many meanings, often misunderstood by educators. Moore's theoretical position called for educators

to organize programs to ensure maximum effectiveness of each type of interaction, and ensure they provide the type of interaction that is most suitable for the various teaching tasks of different subject areas, and for learners at different stages of development. (p. 5)

This means that educators should plan for all three types of interaction because they are important and should be evident in all distance courses.

Learner–Content Interaction

The first type of interaction Moore (1989) described is interaction between the learner and the content or subject of study, the defining characteristic of education. Without learner–content interaction, no education will ensue because it is the process of intellectually interacting with content that results in changes in the learner's understanding, the learner's perspective, or the cognitive structures of the learner's mind. In that time period, Examples of this type of interaction were one-way communication such as written or printed material, content broadcast on radio and television programs, audiotape, videotape, and interactive computer software.

Nguyen and Trimarchi (2010) experimented with two popular learning technologies and course-management systems—MyEconLab and Aplia—to help students achieve learning objectives in spite of class-size increases. Participants for the experiment using MyEconLab included students from 12 introductory microeconomics classes of 2,629 students in 2 consecutive years, 2007–2008; participants for the experiment using the Aplia comprised 1,392 students studied over 3 consecutive years (2006–2008). Two classes used Aplia worth 10% in the marking scheme whereas the other four classes did not use Aplia at all. Using descriptive statistics, findings showed that for class sizes in the experiment, modern learning technology improved student grade only by a statistically significant 2%. Based on this article, the choice of technology was more teacher-centered because it brought relief to a previously labor-intensive style of teaching.

Learner–Instructor Interaction

Moore (1989) noted that the second type of interaction was learner–instructor. This type of interaction occurs between the learner and the designer who prepared the subject material or some other expert acting as instructor. Learner–instructor interac-

tions were essential and desirable, according to many educators and learners. In that era, examples of this type of interaction were teleconferences or presentations of recorded or videotaped materials that aimed to motivate and provide learner support, facilitate learner application of content, organize evaluation assignments, and provide feedback.

The role of the instructor in the learner–instructor interaction is to "organize evaluation to ascertain if learners are making progress and to help decide whether to change strategies" (Moore, 1989, p. 3). Self-directed learners can do several things to motivate themselves and interact with content presented, but they are quite vulnerable when it comes to application of subject matter. Further, learners are often unsure about whether they are applying the subject correctly or as intensively and extensively as possible or desirable; or if they have applied the content in all areas of application. Thus, the learner–instructor interaction becomes most valuable when for testing, application, and feedback (Moore, 1989).

O'Leary and Quinlan (2007) conducted a study on learner–instructor interactions that is also applicable to the present study because the instructor could have used Skype technology to make a phone call. Their study on learner–instructor telephone interaction measured the impact of telephone use on the satisfaction and achievement of online students. They noted that although online courses were often encouraged to construct environments that would support and engage students, those online course instructors were frequently criticized for failure to achieve adequate levels of interactivity (LaRose & Whitten, 1999, 2000). To investigate the relationship between student level of satisfaction with a telephone call from the instructor and their grade, these researchers administered a questionnaire to selected online students in a community-college setting (O'Leary & Quinlan, 2007). Participants were volunteers and not randomly selected. Therefore, the results of this study are limited to one group. This study used a pre-experimental one group pretest–post-test design. To measure satisfaction, researchers used the expectancy–disconfirmation paradigm. This study revealed that the telephone call had no significant effect on student satisfaction but also revealed a statistically significant effect between telephone calls and grade. The grades of students who received a telephone call were slightly lower than the grades of those who did not receive a call. The authors concluded that this might have been partly due to the call taking place at the beginning of the semester, when the students had few course-content questions. They further explained that "it takes more than one phone call to establish a meaningful and beneficial relationship between instructor and student" (O'Leary & Quinlan, 2007, p. 140).

Learner–Learner Interaction

Learner–learner interaction was Moore's (1989) third form of interaction and the latest dimension of distance education. This inter-learner interaction takes place between one learner and other learners, alone or in group settings, with or without the real-time presence of an instructor. Early examples of this type of learner–learner interaction were peer-group interactions by asynchronous e-mail and synchronous computer "chatting." Also two or more students shared a presentation followed by peer-group discussion, analysis in small groups, feedback, and further discussion. Also, teleconference groups were excellent for learner–learner interaction. Moore pointed out that inter-learner group interactions between students are not equally desirable by all students. For younger learners, peer-group interactions will assist the teaching task of stimulation and motivation will be assisted by peer-group interaction. However, for adults, peer-group interaction is not as important because they are advanced learners who tend to be self-motivated.

Learner–learner interaction, the discussion board was the means through which students interact with their peers. Another way to charac-

terize the advantages of electronic discussion is to consider the positive spillovers that can occur in a productive discussion, where students learn from other students and faculty input is leveraged (Greenlaw & DeLoach, 2003). In economics, educators often use the discussion board to develop critical-thinking skills. Students benefit from the opportunity to share their opinions and to respond to alternative viewpoints raised by classmates. The discussion board allows students to hear other perspectives, thereby forcing students to rethink their viewpoints and look at issues more analytically. Chizmar and Walbert (1999) used electronic discussion to help students clarify their thinking on difficult topics explained in class, and to implement 1-minute papers in which students identify what they see as the most important or least understood idea discussed in class that day. Vachris (1999) used electronic discussion as part of a strictly online principles course to have students comment on a reading assignment.

Very few studies on learner–learner interaction exist in economics. Navarro and Shoemaker (2000) conducted a survey study to examine course-design and research-design issues in online economics courses. Data collected from 200 undergraduate and 63 graduate students enrolled in online economics at the University of California revealed that both groups showed a high level of satisfaction with student–teacher interaction. Of graduate students, 88%, and of undergraduate students, 77% reported they had enough opportunities, through e-mail, online discussion group, and the class bulletin board, to ask questions of, or interact with, the professor. However, they reported dissatisfaction with the level of student-to-student interaction. Results suggested that the realm of student-to-student interaction appears to be an important area to consider in course design. Course design for online economics should include more opportunities for group assignments and mandatory group-chat sessions (Navarro & Shoemaker, 2000, p. 364).

Gardner (1983) developed the "theory of multiple intelligence" with the belief that one should not use the same methods and strategies for teaching and assessing all students. The question then becomes, does faculty choice of technology meet the diverse needs for varying levels and types of interaction among students and teachers in these settings?

Rhode (2009) explored the preferences of learners about various interactions during a self-paced online course. Rhode specifically investigated the forms of interaction adult learners' valued most in self-paced online courses and the forms of interaction adult learners identified as equivalent in self-paced online courses. Participants were online adult learners enrolled in a fully online one-year, self-paced professional-development certificate undergraduate program in educational technology offered by a private higher education institution for adult learners. Using an exploratory mixed-method study, Rhode required the students who participated in the study to use a learning-management system (Blackboard) and a social-networking system (Elgg), to examine students' interaction preferences for formal and informal situations (Rhode, 2009, pp. 235–244).

Rhode (2009) found that students valued interaction with the instructor and content most highly. Students also identified a nearly equal value for interaction between instructor and content but showed a lesser value for interaction with peers. Participants reported that informal blogging is as important as, or in some instances even more effective than asynchronous formal discussions on the discussion board in a learning-management system. Findings from this study showed that, depending on the specific circumstance, learners may not value all forms of interaction equally as effective. These findings did not support Anderson's (2003) Thesis 1, which postulated the possibility of eliminating or substituting one type of interaction for another. Results showed that this group of students reported the need to have all three types of interaction, but in varying

degrees. Rhode (2009) suggested that the forms of interaction valued by learners could be vary under different circumstances.

Drouin (2008) evaluated students' sense of community, satisfaction, achievement, and retention in three sections of the same online undergraduate psychology course. This study followed a survey design involving 71 students in three online sections of a middle-division undergraduate psychology course at a medium-sized Midwestern U.S. university. Drouin asked students to complete an online survey after taking their final exam, noting that student–student interaction connected more variables to sense of community than did student–instructor interaction. Also sense of community related to student satisfaction with a course and had no impact on student grade or retention. Sense of community refers to "the feeling of belonging that is established among learners who have common interests and goals and participate in joint activities" (Rovai, 2002a). Again, the need to find an ideal balance or mixture of the three forms of interaction in online courses influenced these study findings.

Study outcomes supported existing literature that encourages the use of asynchronous discussion threads to foster a sense of community in online learning environments (Swan, 2002). However, regarding the importance of student–student interaction vs. student–instructor interaction, only student–student interaction related to students' perceived sense of community. Drouin (2008) concluded that sense of community is fostered mainly through communication between students, and that instructor interactions may not necessarily foster students' sense of community in an online environment. Thus, sense of community might not be an essential component of online classes because not all students desired a sense of community. It is for this reason that a level of social interaction may exist that is ideal in online communities; instructors should that care to avoid exceeding that level (Drouin, 2008, p. 281).

The review of literature found several other studies that supported online interaction. Gosmire, Morrison, and Osdel (2009) examined the use of the synchronous video chat, Elluminate Live, in online graduate courses. The authors compared four types of instructor interaction with students in online courses: interacting with the instructor only asynchronously; instructor asynchronously plus a reader (coinstructor); instructor asynchronously plus synchronously through Elluminate Live; and instructor asynchronously, reader, and Elluminate Live. Data drawn from 150 graduate students in an online education-administration course revealed that graduate students in online courses perceived the use of Elluminate Live more positively than that of a reader and the instructor asynchronously. Gosmire et al. also reported that graduate students perceived the instructor interaction most positively when the instructor employed the methods of feedback and interaction on the discussion board, grade book, drop box, and e-mail features of the course-management system and used Elluminate Live (p. 615).

Osborne, Kriese, Tobey, and Johnson (2009) studied the differences between students' expectations for taking, and faculty perceptions about teaching, an online course. Findings suggested that potential "differences between student and faculty perceptions of online courses might create barriers that diminish the effectiveness of the teaching learning environment in such courses" (p. 171). These authors also noted that faculty and students come to the digital classroom from different realities: "digital natives" and "digital immigrants" (Prensky, 2009, p. 179). For example, faculty who are digital immigrants, that is, those who came to online teaching after having taught for a significant amount of time through more traditional methods, may construct an online-learning environment that is quite different from those who are digital natives, that is, faculty who have "grown up" teaching such courses (Prensky, 2009, p. 179).

WEB-BASED TECHNOLOGIES

The present study focused on online instructional tools using web-based technologies for asynchronous and synchronous communication. In distance learning, asynchronous communication most often takes the form of e-mail (e.g., the professor e-mails the student with feedback on an assignment), voice-mail (e.g., the student leaves a message for the instructor on an office phone), and discussion boards (e.g., the student posts a response to discussion questions and responds to peers' discussion posts). Whereas synchronous communication refers to live, real-time communication and voice communication delivered through standard telephone lines or Internet-based software (e.g., Elluminate and Skype), social-networking websites refers to online social networks (Web 2.0 technologies) for communities of people who share interests and activities, or who are interested in exploring the interests and activities of others (e.g., Facebook, MySpace, Twitter, YouTube, Blogs, and Wikis).

Widespread inventions of Web 2.0 technologies justify inquiries into their effective use in education to accomplish learning outcomes. Pollacia and McCallister (2009) discussed a quality-matters standard and rubric to demonstrate how Web 2.0 technologies may be used to meet set criteria they refer to as "standards." The authors demonstrated how Web 2.0 technologies could be used to meet the first "standard" course overview and introductions. Students could post their introductions to a discussion board using Blackboard or a Facebook page. Also, Pollacia and McCallister delineated the advantages and disadvantages of instructors and students using a Facebook page to introduce themselves to the class.

Another web-based application was the web log, or blog, identified as an effective tool to promote online interaction (Pollacia & McCallister, 2009). The blog allows all online participants to contribute ideas and comments in an ongoing conversational fashion. The online instructor could post questions or audio files on the blog to which students can respond in writing. The conversational structure encourages students to pursue deeper levels of thinking (Bartlett-Bragg, 2003). Pollacia and McCallister (2009) also noted the disadvantages of using blogs and some reasons why an instructor might prefer to use a discussion board to accomplish the same learning outcomes.

Likewise, Pollacia and McCallister (2009) demonstrated how other Web 2.0 technologies could be used to encourage student engagement in four major ways: inquiry, literacy, collaboration, and publication. For example, Wikiversity is a division of Wikipedia that supports educational research, PodCastSchool allows students to download and listen to podcasts, PBWorks provides forums where students can engage and collaborate, and Think Quest allows student to publish original work and collaborate with others around the world. Whether these are the motives behind the choice of web-based technologies or show respect for diverse talents and ways of learning remains unclear and calls for further research of online economics courses.

METHODOLOGY

Research Questions

This section describes the methodology and research design used to investigate faculty choice of technology for promoting the three types of interaction and students' perceptions of such technologies. The four research questions for this study follow:

1. Which web-based technologies does faculty choose to encourage types of interaction in online economics courses?
2. What are the reasons for choosing such technologies?

3. What are students' perceptions of the technologies used to encourage online interactions in economics?
4. What recommendations do students and faculty offer for technology to promote online interaction?

Research Design

Aligned with Creswell (2005), a survey research design collected descriptive data for this study. Survey research designs are "procedures in quantitative research in which investigators administer a survey to a sample from an entire population of people in order to describe the attitudes, opinions, behaviors or characteristics of the population" (Creswell, 2005, p. 354). In this procedure, survey researchers collect quantitative, numerical data using surveys, questionnaires, or interviews, and statistically analyze the data to describe trends about responses to questions and to test research questions or hypothesis.

For this study, survey research was applicable because the research did not involve a treatment given to participants. Because the purpose of this study was not to manipulate any conditions to explain cause and effect, descriptive research was most appropriate. This study described trends in the data and focused on learning about the online economics faculty and student population in Chicago. Survey research was relevant to this study because the intention was not to predict outcomes, as in the case of correlation research, but to generalize the findings from a sample of responses to a population (Creswell, 2005). This study sought to discern faculty choice of web-based technologies for interaction in online economics and students' perception of those technologies. Survey research was appropriate to identify students' preferences for web-based technologies used in online economics courses. Data collected during the fall semester, 2011 constituted cross-sectional research, most applicable for this study.

Prior to the data collection in fall 2011 semester, a pilot study was conducted during the summer 2011 to help determine that the individuals in the sample were capable of completing the survey, and that they understood the questions before the final version was administered (Creswell, 2005). Data-collection steps involved the design and administration of an online survey to a convenience sample of faculty and students from 2- and 4-year colleges in Chicago offering online economics.

Sites

This study targeted participants from 28 institutions in the Chicago area. Together these schools comprised over 100,000 students (see Tables 1 and 2 for demographic data). After identifying schools that offer undergraduate online economics courses, students and faculty in the following seven public postsecondary institutions participated in the survey: University of Illinois, Chicago; University

Table 1. Table of demographics for Chicago city colleges

College Name	Student Population	Student Ages	Student Ethnicities
Richard M. Daley	10,837 Total	12% 15–19	1% Asian
7500 S Pulaski Rd	62% female	26% 20–24	2% Native American
	39% male	19% 25–29	19% Black
	32% Full Time	26% 30–39	69% Hispanic
	68% Part Time	12% 40–49	9% White
	77% Day	4% 50–59	1% Other
	23% Evening	1% 60+	
Kennedy-King	7,073 Total	19% 15–19	4% Asian
6301 S Halsted St	63% female	27% 20–24	0.3% Native American
	37% male	16% 25–29	84% Black
	44% Full Time	18% 30–39	5% Hispanic
	56% Part Time	13% 40–49	6% White
	84% Day	6% 50–59	0.7% Other
	16% Evening	2% 60 +	
Malcolm X	7,771 Total	13% 15–19	4% Asian
1900 W Van Buren	63% female	23% 20–24	0.4% Native American
	37% male	17% 25–29	49% Black
	33% Full Time	23% 30–39	36% Hispanic
	67% Part Time	14% 40–49	9% White
	81% Day	8% 50–59	1% Other
	19% Evening	3% 60+	
Olive-Harvey	4,159 Total	20% 15–19	0.5% Asian
10001 S Woodlawn Ave	71% female	25% 20–24	0.3% Native American
	29% male	15% 25–29	79% Black
	42% Full Time	21% 30–39	18% Hispanic
	58% Part Time	12% 40–49	1% White
	82% Day	5% 50–59	0.7% Other
	18% Evening	2% 60+	

continued on following page

Table 1. Continued

College Name	Student Population	Student Ages	Student Ethnicities
Harry S. Truman	13,095 Total	10% 15–19	13% Asian
1345 W Wilson Ave	55% female	23% 20–24	0.4% Native American
	45% male	20% 25–29	19% Black
	20% Full Time	25% 30–39	44% Hispanic
	80% Part Time	14% 40–49	22% White
	79% Day	7% 50–59	3% Other
	21% Evening	3% 60+	
Harold Washington	8,937 Total	19% 15–19	17% Asian
30 East Lake St	55% female	35% 20–24	5% Native American
	40% male	16% 25–29	38% Black
	47% Full Time	14% 30–39	25% Hispanic
	53% Part Time	9% 40–49	21% White
	83% Day	5% 50–59	2% Other
	17% Evening	2% 60 +	
Wilber Wright	13,191 Total	21% 15–19	7% Asian
4300 N. Narragansett	59% female	30% 20–24	0.5% Native American
	41% male	15% 25–29	9% Black
	27% Full Time	16% 30–39	48% Hispanic
	73% Part Time	10% 40–49	35% White
	76% Day	6% 50–59	1% Other
	24% Evening	3% 60+	

Note. Adapted from *Fiscal Year 2011: Statistical Digest*, by City Colleges of Chicago, 2011. Retrieved from http://www.ccc.edu/menu/Documents/CCCFY2011StatisticalDigest.pd

Table 2. List of online schools offering economics

Name of College	Funding	Students Enrollment
University of Illinois Chicago	Public	26,245
University of Chicago	Public	15,600
Chicago State	Public	7,000
Northern Illinois University	Public	24,000
Governors State University	Public	7,788
DeVry University	Public	80,000
Northeastern Illinois University	Public	12,006
Loyola University	Private	15,951
National-Louis University	Private	11,905
Elmhurst College	Private	3,000
Roosevelt University	Private	7,306
St. Xavier University	Private	5,028
Benedictine University Online	Private	5,279
DePaul University	Private	80,000

of Chicago; Chicago State University; Northern Illinois University, College of Business and Management; Governors State University; DeVry University; Northeastern Illinois University. Additionally, students and faculty from the following seven private postsecondary institutions participated: DePaul University Chicago; Benedictine University Online; Loyola University; National Louis University, Chicago; Elmhurst College, Center for Business and Economics; Roosevelt University Walter E. Heller College of Business Administration; and St. Xavier University, Graham School of Management (see Table 2 for enrollment and funding data.)

Participants

Initially, this study targeted faculty and students attending seven 2-year colleges and 14 4-year colleges (seven public and seven private) from the Chicago area, identified using convenience sampling. Creswell (2005) stated that convenience sampling "is a quantitative sampling procedure in which the researcher selects participants because they are willing and available to be studied" (p. 149). Using convenience sampling, participants were to include 75 to 80 economics faculty and 800 to 1,000 online economics undergraduate students. All institutions included in the study offer online economics courses that take place 100% online. Participants accrued through e-mail sent from Survey Monkey. A researcher-generated e-mail described the project to all criteria-meeting faculty and students.

Materials

The survey, consisting of 16 items, asked students to assess the web-based technologies chosen by faculty. Because the reliability and validity of this instrument was not established, an additional objective of the current investigation was to assess the internal consistency reliability of the responses, as well as the validity of the instruments. Faculty

responded to questions about their choice of technologies for particular types of online interaction, and students answered questions on their perceptions of those technologies used for their online interaction.

Instrument

The faculty online survey consisted of 16 questions: 12 closed-ended questions, two with a 5-point Likert scale (1 = Strongly Disagree to 5 = Strongly Agree) aimed to ascertain responses from faculty regarding their choice of technology for specific types of online interaction; two open-ended questions aimed to identify faculty s' choices of technology and for them to state reasons for their choices. The data-collection instrument for students was an online survey consisting of 17 questions: 13 closed-ended questions, two with a 5-point Likert scale (1 = Strongly Disagree to 5 = Strongly Agree) and two open-ended questions for students to recommend technologies.

The two researcher-developed surveys used in this study contained three questions on demographic information. These were remodeled questions, taken from the Educause Center for Applied Research 2004 report. The Edu cause Center's study examined current students' experiences and skill using information technology.

Data Collection

Ethics Concerns

Creswell (2005) explained that ethical issues relate to "respecting the rights of participants, honoring research sites that you visit, and reporting research fully and honestly" (p. 11). Thus, individuals who participated in this study had certain rights that were respected. Before participating in this study, I informed faculty and students about the purpose and aims of the study, the use of the results, and the likely social consequences or impact the study would have on their lives. Also they had the right to refuse to participate in the study and the option to withdraw at any time. I took specific measures to protect identities of those who lent support to the study. For this purpose, I used an informed-consent process that not only emphasized and affirmed the voluntary nature of participants' engagement in the study and the right to suspend participation at any time, but also described the nature, scope, and purpose of the study (Creswell, 2005). I protected participants' identities and personal information by assigning an alphanumerical code to each participant, rather than using participants' names (Creswell, 2005).

Field Procedure

I contacted participants by e-mail about the likely risks involved in the research and of potential consequences for participants. The e-mail informed participants about the aims of the investigation and through e-mail; I kept participants updated about any significant changes in the research program. I took appropriate action to protect the confidentiality of participants and the data to the full extent provided by law. In this case, e-mail responses were coded and e-mailed surveys were assigned a special folder. Once informed consent was obtained, participants completed an online version of the Online Interaction Survey within a 2-week time frame, followed by a reminder at the end of each week for 5 weeks. The survey focused on the three types of online interaction defined by Moore (1993), conducted through Survey Monkey. The names and e-mail addresses of participants remain anonymous. Following data collection, the data I exported the data from Survey Monkey and analyzed the information with Microsoft Excel 2007.

Data Analysis and Statistical Procedure

The data analysis process used descriptive statistical procedures. Because this study was interested in faculty choice of web-based technologies for interaction in online economics and students' perception of those technologies, the results may be better presented by descriptive statistics. Resultant data addressed each of the research questions. Descriptive statistics such as mean, mode, and median helped summarize the overall trends or general tendencies in the data. I measured variability, or the spread of scores, by variance, standard deviation, and range. An internal-consistency reliability analysis using Cronbach's alpha (Creswell, 2005) assessed the survey's reliability in this population but is not reported.

Steps in preparing and analyzing the data for analysis in quantitative research consists of scoring the data and creating a codebook, determining the types of scores to use, selecting a computer program, inputting the data into the program for analysis, and clearing the data (Creswell, 2005). This researcher exported data from Survey Monkey into Microsoft Excel and created bar charts, pie charts, and line graphs to observe the results visually. The final report of the results comprised nine tables and accompanying narratives. However, responses to the two open-ended questions on the student survey were categorized into themes. I used the process of thematic coding (Creswell 2005) to analyze the data collected from the open-ended questions.

Reliability and Validity

I used Survey Monkey pretest pilot-survey functions to evaluate the competency of the survey questions, administering one version of the instrument once to two faculty s and three versions of the survey three times to the same student to obtain feedback and verify clarity of questions. A Cronbach's alpha analysis tested for internal-consistency reliability (Cronbach, 1984). Because a few items on the instrument were continuous variables, ranging from strongly agree to strongly disagree, the alpha provided a coefficient to estimate consistency of scores on the instrument.

Threats to Internal Validity

To address possible threats to validity, the following concerns seemed likely during this study:

1. Response bias may have occurred with the questionnaires. According to Creswell (2005), "response bias" occurs in survey research when responses do not accurately reflect the views of the sample and the population (p. 368). For example, students who return questionnaires may have been overly negative or positive.
2. Results from this study may be invalid for other populations of students. This study used convenience sampling, which is a quantitative sampling procedure in which the researcher selects participants because they are willing and available to be studied (Creswell, 2005). As a result, the researcher cannot say with confidence that the students were representative of the population.
3. Respondents replied to some open-ended questions. Open-ended questions in surveys consist of questions posed by the researcher to which participants provide their own responses. The researcher is therefore left to make meaningful inferences from their remarks. The remarks given by respondents can be influenced by emotion or by the time period in which the questions were asked (Creswell, 2005).

RESULTS

This study investigated faculty choice of web-based technologies for interaction in online economics and students' perception of those technologies. Using a survey research design, collected data helped answer these research questions. This study initially targeted seven 2-year colleges and 14 4-year colleges (seven public and seven private) from the Chicago area.

Initially, 75–80 faculty and 800 to 1,000 online economics undergraduate students comprised a convenience sampling. I dropped eight schools from the sample leaving a final sample size of 13 schools, which included six 4-year colleges (one private school and five public schools) and seven 2-year colleges. Of the remaining schools, only five faculty responded, 38%, and met the criteria of teaching economics 100% online (see Table 3). Of the eight schools deleted, one did not offer online economics during the fall 2011 semester, another offered online economics at the graduate level only, two discontinued the program, and four were online schools but never offered economics. As a result, the faculty sample size changed. The final target population became 10 to 12 faculty, and about 200 to 300 students. Students received their surveys through faculty; only 50 received

Table 3. Faculty demographics

Demographics	Percent Faculty
Gender	
Male	40
Female	60
Institution	
2-year	60
4-year	40
Employment	
Full time	20
Part time	80
Online teaching experience	
None	0
Experience	100
Courses taught	
Macroeconomics	50
Microeconomics	50
Levels taught	
Senior	50
Junior	0
Sophomore	25
Freshman	25

the survey. Of the 50 students, 28 responded, a response rate of 56%. Schools kept student e-mail listings private; as a result, students received survey links through faculty because school directories did not list students according to online courses (see Table 4).

Table 4. Student demographics

Demographics	Percent Students
Gender	
Male	40.0
Female	60.0
Student Location	
South Chicago	60.0
North Chicago	40.0
Institution	
2-year	85.7
4-year	14.3
Student Status	
Full time	70.0
Part time	30.0
Student employment per day	
Work less than 8 hours	30.0
Work more than 8 hours	70.0
Student majors	
Business	53.6
Economics	7.1
Non-business majors	28.6
Other	10.7
Student online experience	
First online course	10.7
1 to 2 courses	25.0
3 to 4 courses	28.6
More than 4 courses	35.7
Student year in school	
Senior	10.7
Junior	21.4
Sophomore	46.4
Freshman	10.7
Other	10.7

Faculty Demographics

Five faculty responded to the survey. Two were from 4-year colleges, whereas three were from 2-year colleges. Only one faculty taught at a private institution. The majority of faculty respondents were women; four taught online economics part time and all indicated that they were experienced in teaching online. Two taught at the senior level, 1 taught sophomores, and 1 taught at the freshman level. Two faculty taught microeconomics and two taught macroeconomics. Three faculty taught at least one online course per semester (see Table 3).

Student Demographics

The response rate on the student survey was 56%. The majority were female (60%), and a significant majority, 70%, reported they worked more than 8 hours per day. Only 10.7% of the sample had no online learning experience. Of these students, 60% lived on the south side of Chicago in neighborhoods where those with low socioeconomic status are located, whereas the remaining lived in downtown Chicago and north of Chicago (see Table 4).

The majority of students, 70.4%, attended college full time. Also 85.7% reported they attended 2-year colleges: 46.4% were sophomores. More than half the samples, 53.6%, were business majors and about 64.3% were taking online microeconomics courses (see Table 4). According to the results, the sample comprised mostly women working full time, attending school full time, and taking more than three online courses per semester.

This section is organized in order of the four research questions listed at the beginning of this chapter. The data that constitutes the results of this study follows each question, shown in tables and accompanied by a brief discussion of the results.

Research Question 1: Which web-based technologies do faculty choose to encourage types of interaction in online economics courses? The ensuing discussion centers on how faculty responded to each piece of technology use in promoting the three types of interaction.

For learner–instructor interaction, results showed that four faculty chose online conferencing sessions such as Elluminate or Skype from the technologies listed on the survey. From the technologies remaining on the list, only one chose online learning modules and interactive tools, one chose online multimedia and portable tools, and another one chose online discussion and group collaboration (see Table 5).

For learner–learner interactions, faculty chose online discussion and group-collaboration technologies such as threaded discussions, chats, blogs, and wikis, primarily for learner–learner interaction. All five faculty, indicated that technology considerations were least important when it came to learner–learner interaction (see Table 5). Only faculty at the private school reported using the Microsoft One Note program for numerical and graphical aspects of economics. Faculty primarily learned about such web-based technologies from distance-learning centers.

Research Question 2: What are the reasons for faculty choice of web-based technologies?

Data collected from faculty survey questions that asked about the order of importance when selecting web-based technologies, showed that all faculty sought features of functionality and design when choosing technologies for interaction, whereas accessibility over the Internet (4), flexibility (3), and download time (3) were the next important considerations. Three were neutral toward brand names (see Table 6).

In addition, data collected from faculty revealed several other reasons for selecting technologies (see Table 7): Faculty also chose technologies because they were highly effective and beneficial for student-learning and subject-matter outcomes. The following summarizes some specific reasons given for choosing different types of technologies:

1. Online conference sessions, used occasionally, are highly effective, helping students learn subject matter better.
2. Online interactive homework tools such as Aplia and EconLab are highly effective, helping students learned subject matter better.
3. Online multimedia and portable tools, which are accessible over the internet.
4. Online social-networking websites are easily accessible over the Internet, but are only moderately effective.

Table 5. Faculty choice of web-based technologies for interaction by percentage

Web-based technologies	Good for learner–instructor	Good for learner–learner	Good for learner–content	Good for all three types of interaction
Online conferencing sessions	80	0	0	20
Online interactive homework tools	0	20	40	20
Online learning modules and interactive tools	20	20	40	20
Online multimedia and portable tools	20	0	20	40
Online social networking websites	0	20	0	20
Online discussion and group collaboration	20	40	0	40
Online games	0	20	20	20
Other	0	0	0	0

Table 6. How faculty ranked importance of characteristics for their choice of technologies

Characteristics	Percent faculty
Quality	100
Access	80
Flexibility	60
Time	60
Cost	20
Quantity	20
Familiarity	20
Brand Name	0

5. Online-discussion and group-collaboration technologies were frequently, but are only moderately effective; faculty choose them primarily because they are easily accessible over the Internet and good for all three types of interaction.

6. Online games were ineffective for all student learning, but were beneficial in eliminating learner–instructor interaction.

7. The faculty from the private school reported satisfaction when using Microsoft's One Note program to teach economics online (see Table 7).

Research Question 3: What are students' perceptions of faculty choice of web-based technologies used to encourage online interactions in economics?

For learner–instructor interaction, 46.2% of students reported online conferencing sessions such as Elluminate or Skype were effective and improved their learning (see Table 9). Only 11.5% perceived online interactive homework tools and online multimedia and portable technologies relevant to learner–instructor interaction (see Table 8). Table 8 shows students' reaction to faculty choices of web-based technologies for interactions.

For learner–learner interaction, 40% of students rated discussion threads as highly effective. Students reported that the technologies used to promote learner–learner interaction, such as

Table 7. Additional reasons for faculty choice of web-based technologies by percentage

Additional reasons for choosing technologies	Online conferencing sessions	Online interactive homework tools	Online learning modules	Online multimedia and portable tools	Online social networking websites	Online discussion and group collaboration	Online games
Effects on learning outcomes							
Highly effective	60	60	40	0	0	0	20
Effective	20	20	40	60	0	40	0
Moderately effective	0	0	20	20	66.7	60	20
Lowly effective	20	0	0	0	0	0	20
Not effective at all	0	20	0	20	33.3	0	40
Benefits							
Helps ease my workload	0	20	40	0	0	0	0
Easily accessible over the internet	40	20	0	60	100	60	20
Helps students learn subject matter better	40	60	60	40	0	40	20
Benefits the school	0	0	0	0	0	0	40
Matches my teaching style	20	0	0	0	0	0	20

Table 8. Student reaction to web-based technologies for interaction by percentage

Web-based technologies	Good for learner–instructor	Good for learner–learner	Good for learner–content	Good for all three types of interactions
Online conferencing sessions	46.2	7.7	3.8	30.8
Online interactive homework tools	11.5	11.5	53.8	23.1
Online learning modules and interactive tools	8.0	20.0	40.0	28.0
Online Multimedia and portable tools	11.5	7.7	30.8	11.5
Online social networking websites	0.0	20.0	4.0	12.0
Online discussion and group collaboration	8.0	40.0	0.0	44.0
Online games	0.0	19.2	11.5	7.7
Other	0.0	0.0	0.0	0.0

discussion boards, blogs, and wikis were highly effective and kept them active and engaged (see Table 9). However, 100% of students also rated learner–learner interaction as the least important interaction.

For learner–content interaction, results show that 53.8% of students reported online interactive homework tools (Aplia or EconLab) as highly effective, improving their learning, and good for learner–content interaction (see Table 8). In addition, 40% indicated that online-learning modules and interactive tools (tutorials, PowerPoint notes, and quizzes) also improved their learning of subject matter (see Table 8). Also, 30.8% perceived online

Table 9. Student perception of faculty choice of web-based technologies by percentage

Student reaction to Faculty choice of technologies	Online conferencing sessions	Online interactive homework tools	Online learning modules	Online multimedia and portable tools	Online social networking websites	Online discussion and group collaboration	Online games
Effects on your performance							
Highly effective	25.9	51.9	37.	0	8.0	37.0	4.0
Effective	37.0	40.7	48.1	52.0	16.0	22.2	28.0
Moderately effective	25.9	3.7	14.8	20.0	4.0	22.2	20.0
Lowly effective	3.7	3.7	0.0	12.0	24.0	11.1	8.0
Not effective at all	7.4	0.0	0.0	16.0	48.0	7.4	40.0
Benefits							
Improves my learning	33.3	51.9	38.5	29.2	4.2	30.8	11.5
Matches my learning style	22.2	18.5	30.8	8.3	4.2	11.5	7.7
Helps me plan and manage my course activities better	11.1	14.8	19.2	8.3	4.2	7.7	3.8
Keeps me active and engaged	25.9	11.1	11.5	33.3	16.7	38.5	15.4
No benefits	7.4	3.7	0.0	20.8	70.8	11.5	61.5

multimedia and portable tools (video lectures, podcasts, movie clips, and iPhones) as being helpful when learning content (see Table 8). More than half of the students (61.5%) reported that games mostly benefited the school. For all three types of interaction, students perceived online conferencing sessions (30.8%), online learning modules (28%), discussion threads (44%), and online interactive homework tools (23.1%) as useful for all three types of interaction (see Table 8).

Table 9. shows student perceptions of faculty choice of web-based technologies for interaction in online economics courses. Results showed that 51.9% rated online interactive homework tools, 37.0% rated online learning modules, and 52.0% rated online multimedia and portable tools as highly effective, improving their learning. Only 25.9% stated that online conferencing sessions were highly effective and the majority stated that online games did not benefit them at all. Student rated web-based technologies used to promote learner–content interaction as having greater impact on their learning than web-based technologies used for learner–instructor interaction.

Research Question 4: What recommendations do students and faculty offer for web-based technologies to promote online interaction?

FACULTY RECOMMENDATIONS

When asked recommend the use of web-based technologies in online economics courses, faculty said technology could work as a barrier as well as a benefit in encouraging interaction, depending on how it is used.

Following are some specific faculty recommendations for the use of web-based technologies for interaction in online courses:

1. Faculty recommended that it was best to use a mix of tools to interact with students. Web-based technology should improve student interaction with content, thereby improving students' understanding of concepts in economics.

2. Faculty reported they occasionally used online conferencing sessions but recommended that online conferencing sessions, such as Elluminate, were best for learner–instructor interaction.

3. Faculty recommended the use of interactive homework tools (Aplia and EconLab) for the graphical and numerical aspects of online economics because they were best for learner–content interaction.

4. Regarding benefits from the use of faculty choice of technologies in improving student learning, data revealed strong preferences for online interactive homework tools.

5. Online learning modules and interactive tools (tutorials, PowerPoint notes, and quizzes) were best for a learner–content interface.

6. Although faculty occasionally used online multimedia and portable tools (video lectures, podcasts, movie clips, iPhones) these technologies were good for all three types of interaction.

7. Faculty indicated they very frequently used online discussion and group collaboration (threaded discussions, chats, blogs, and wikis), best for promoting learner–learner interaction. They recommended these kinds of technologies for all three types of interactions.

8. Faculty identified learner–learner interaction as the least important interaction. They suggested these types of technology should remain in use. Other technologies recommended for learner–learner interaction included online social-networking websites such as Facebook, but never for use in courses.

9. Twitter, Ning, online games, and simulations were hardly or never used by this faculty sample and were not part of the recommendations.

STUDENT RECOMMENDATIONS

The overall results for student recommendations for the use of web-based technologies in economics courses are presented in Table 8. Specific student recommendations for the use of web-based technologies for interaction in online courses follow.

1. Students recommended a need for more interactive sessions with professors and content. Students recommended an increase in faculty use of tutorials, video lectures, podcasts, and online conferencing sessions with the instructor.
2. Students indicated the need for more interactive content, accessible through portable technology.
3. Although students recommended interactive homework tools, such as Aplia, as best for interacting with graphs and numerical aspects of economics, they did not recommend an increase in their use.
4. Students recommended that multimedia and portable tool use should increase; however, the use of discussion boards should remain the same.
5. Students perceived that online discussion and group collaboration (threaded discussions, chats, blogs, and wikis) could be used for all three types of interaction, but were best for learner–learner interaction. Over 85.7% of students considered interaction with classmates least important, and although the discussion board was effective, did not recommend an increase in use.
6. Students recommended that online conferencing sessions (Elluminate and Skype) were best for learner–instructor interaction, whereas online interactive homework tools (Aplia and EconLab) were best for learner–content interaction.
7. Students suggested online learning modules and interactive tools (tutorials, PowerPoint notes, and quizzes) were also best to promote learner–content interaction.
8. Students reported that online multimedia and portable tools (video lectures, podcasts, movie clips, and iPhones) were rarely or never used in their economics course, but they need more use of these types of technologies because mobility and flexibility allows them to learn the content better.

DISCUSSION, CONCLUSIONS, AND RECOMMENDATIONS

The literature review of online interaction established the importance of learner–content, learner–instructor and learner–learner interaction in online courses (Moore, 1989). However, some studies confirmed that students' need for interaction varies and subsequently suggested that an ideal balance of interactions might exist (Anderson, 2003; Drouin, 2008; Rhode, 2009). As a consequence, this research investigated faculty choice of web-based technologies for interaction in online economics courses, and students' perceptions of those technologies.

Using a survey research design, I sent separate questionnaires to faculty and students to collect data to answer the research questions. Data showed that both faculty and students had online experience prior to the study. They shared the same perceptions about learner–learner interaction being least important. Respondents hailed mainly from 2-year colleges and students were mostly working adults, with most working more than 8 hours per day. Also students and faculty who completed the questionnaire were not always from the same class.

MAIN FINDINGS

Research Question 1: Which web-based technologies do faculty choose to encourage types of interaction in online economics courses? Learner–instructor, learner–learner, learner–content

The survey question used to answer this research question asked faculty to match technologies listed with each of the three types of interaction. Faculty chose online conference sessions such as Elluminate for learner–instructor interaction; online discussion and group collaboration such as discussion board threads for learner–learner interaction; and online interactive homework tools, online learning modules, and interactive tools for learner–content interaction in economics online courses. Although two of five faculty rated learner–learner interaction as least important, they also reported they could use discussion boards to accomplish all three levels of interaction. Faculty chose online multimedia and portable tools to engage students in all three types of interaction. Faculty considered web-based technology to be least helpful, whereas students thought online social-networking websites such as Facebook, Twitter, and Ning were least helpful. This sample of students did not use social-networking websites in their courses, as indicated in their responses to Survey Question 11, which asked them which technologies were used in their economics course. However, faculty rated social-networking sites as moderately effective, and easily accessible over the Internet.

Research Question 2: What are the reasons for faculty choice of web-based technologies?

The survey question used to answer this question asked faculty to rank what they looked for, in order of importance, when selecting web-based technologies. Based on the choices given, faculty ranked quality, then access, followed by flexibility as major considerations when choosing web-based technologies.

Faculty were neutral toward brand name or popular web-based technologies. However, results from the survey question that asked faculty why they used particular technologies in their courses could also add some insight into this question. Faculty reported they used technologies mostly because they were easily accessible over the Internet or helped students learn the subject matter better. They chose technologies primarily to benefit the students. This reason was supported by faculty not choosing simulation games that they thought benefited only the school.

Research Question 3: What are students' perceptions of faculty choice of web-based technologies used to encourage online interactions in economics?

The survey question used to answer this research question asked students the same question asked of faculty: match technologies given with each of the three types of interactions. Overall students had positively perceived web-based technologies used for interaction in online economics courses but showed greater preference for web-based technologies used for learner–content interaction. The sample of students considered learner–instructor interaction very important; however, because they were busy adults, most preferred an increase in the use of mobile technologies for learner–content interaction. Students also opted for greater interaction with content through video lectures and podcasts. A survey question that asked students how they benefited from the use of the technologies listed. Interpretation of their responses indicated students selected technologies such as online interactive homework tools and online learning modules because they had some impact on their learning.

Research Question 4: What recommendations do students and faculty offer for technology to promote online interaction?

Data collected revealed that faculty and students reported learner–learner interaction as least important of the three interactions, and indicated that use of the discussion-board forum, though effective, should be minimized. Also mobile technology should increase to promote more learner–content interaction, along with an increase in learner–instructor interaction.

DISCUSSION

Faculty Choice of Web-Based Technologies

Results from this study confirmed the results of a previous study conducted by Moore (1989), who established the theory of interaction. According to Moore, interaction occurs when instruction engages participants in learning. Moore classified interaction into three types: (a) interaction between learner and content, (b) interaction between learner and instructor, and (c) interaction between learner and learner. Moore noted that all three types of interaction were necessary components of distance-education instruction and were not listed in order of importance. Moore's definition of three types of interaction is the one used to describe interaction in this study. Other types of interaction, such as learner–interface and learner–management/feedback (Northrup, 2002) were not discussed in this study.

The results from this study paralleled some conclusions made by Moore (1989). For example, Moore stated that interaction between the learner and content describes the "process of intellectual interacting" (Moore, 1989, p. 2) with the subject matter, resulting in transformation of the learner's perspective, thought processes, or understanding. Moore (1989) stated that "this is the defining characteristics of education; without it there cannot be education" (p. 2). More than 50% of the students implied that technologies used for learner–content interaction did improve their learning more than technologies used for learner–instructor interaction.

Moore (1989) also stated that interaction between the learner and other learners teaches group-interaction skills, as well as motivates and stimulates learning through discussions and other forms of communication. Results from this current study alluded to the effectiveness of learner–learner interaction; however, because the questionnaire used in this study required students and faculty to state the least important of all interactions, unlike Moore (1989), results from this research revealed that learner–learner interaction was the least important of the three interactions. The studies differed in that the two studies are different in learner–learner. Moore (1989) described the importance of all three types of interaction, whereas this study required participants to identify the least importance of the three types of interactions.

Moore (1989) stated that interaction between learner and teacher describes the communication strategies employed by both parties, essential to a learning environment. Learner–teacher interaction is "regarded as essential by many educators and as highly desirable by many learners" (Moore, 1989, p. 2). Like Moore (1989), students in this study did support learner–teacher interaction as being highly desirable. However, two studies differ in learner–teacher interaction in that Moore (1989) dissected learner–teacher interaction into a two-way communication process with different strategies. Moore (1989) stated teacher–learner–instructor interaction includes stimulating;

motivating learning; presenting information; modeling attributes, skills, and values; organizing the learning; and counseling and supporting learners. Learner–instructor interaction includes clarifying course content and process understandings; exploring new connections between previous education, experience, and new concepts; seeking feedback regarding performance; and asking advice and counsel (Moore, 1989). In addition, "the instructor is especially valuable in responding to the learner's application of new knowledge" (p. 3). The current study primarily focused on the web-based technologies used and the general purposes of interaction between learner and teacher, and did not require a breakdown of the nature of the different forms of communication used by the two parties.

Student Perceptions of Faculty Choice of Web-Based Technologies

Results from this study also confirmed the results of a study conducted by Rhode (2009), who suggested that each student is different and requires a specific mix of interaction to fit specific preferences and needs. This study also arrived at similar conclusions to those of Drouin (2008) on learner–learner interaction. Drouin concluded the following:

Sense of Community, while not necessary to all for increased performance, satisfaction, or retention, appears to be desired by some students in the online learning environment. However, while Sense of Community is desirable to some, it is equally undesirable to others, as exemplified by student comments. (p. 281)

However, the study did not agree with Anderson's (2003) interaction-equivalency theorem in its entirety. Anderson stated that as long as one of the three forms of interaction is at a high level, the other two forms may be offered at minimal levels, or even eliminated without degrading the educational experience. Anderson's theory described the importance of aiming for an effective mix of interactions and implied that one form of interaction could be substituted for another without loss of educational value. Results from this study showed that the only interaction students are willing to minimize is learner–learner interaction.

Anderson (2003) also implied that simulation games easily could be substituted for any of the other forms of interaction. However, faculty and students in this sample did not support increased use of simulation games to teach economics. This outcome could have resulted from lack of experience with online games, considering students (70.4%) and faculty (40%) reported that games were never used in their economics courses. According to Anderson, a course designed as a game where learner–content interaction is at a high level, could directly impact school costs. Students may not accrue any benefits from games directly in student-learning outcomes, but could benefit from cost reductions.

Results of this study also confirmed the findings of Rhode (2009) in that adult learners did not value all forms of interaction, such as substituting blogging for discussion board. Drouin (2008), who found that some students did not desire sense of community, was supported by this current study, which revealed that students (85.7%) and faculty (100%) rated the discussion board as least important. Findings also supported Gardner's (1983) theory of multiple intelligences, which suggested different teaching strategies appeal to those with different learning styles. The sample studied comprised a diverse mix of full-time and part-time students working more than 8 hours per day, with diverse online experiences, living in diverse neighborhoods. Some students believed technology, such as Elluminate, video lectures, and podcasts, could increase their interaction with the online instructor. Others preferred interactive homework tools such as Aplia. This study also supported Wachenheim (2009), who stated that students showed preference for e-mail, grade book, and Elluminate live sessions. Wachenheim also suggested that faculty should post regular announcements to keep students motivated.

Some students enjoyed the flexibility of being able to log in from anywhere, access public WiFi services, and not have to adjust their work schedules. Although some reported the high costs of purchasing interactive homework tools, they nevertheless enjoyed the ability to use mobile technology to access textbook and materials online. They were able to use their iPhones, Kindle, net books, and laptops to complete assignments and to access student-support services from anywhere, using service centers throughout the day, night, and weekend. Others alluded to the cost savings associated with not traveling back and forth to campus, and not having to ask employers to reschedule their work hours to accommodate class schedules every semester. Others reported saving money on public transportation and fuel because they did not need to travel. These issues make online classes the most economical option for some students. The market that takes the most advantage of this are the older, professional, or experienced students who are working, have time constraints, or travel to conferences as part of their job assignments.

LIMITATIONS OF STUDY

This study was conducted only at 2- and 4-year colleges in Chicago offering online economics. The definition of online should have been restated in the survey because there some faculty taught blended courses. Also, there was no way of finding out if the students in the study were reacting exactly to their course instructor's choice of technologies or just responding to the choices given on the questionnaire. Another limitation was difficulty in obtaining access to students' e-mail addresses, even through campus technology-support centers.

In addition, no survey questions asked how much control faculty had over their choice of technology in their online economics courses. In other words, choices could have accrued from the school, from previous faculty, or from only full-time faculty.

It was evident that students responded to categories of technologies and not individual pieces of technologies; therefore, this study did not address if students preferred the Student Café more than the discussion forum or chat room. The Student Café is an open forum created for learner–learner interaction as well, allowing students to ask classmates questions pertaining to the course. Student participation is optional and ungraded. However, in this study, Student Café was categorized with the discussion board, indicating online discussions and group collaboration.

IMPLICATIONS

Because the general consensus was that interaction with classmates was the least important of interactions, discussion-board-thread assignments should be minimized. As a result of the low priority of that interaction, the researcher recommends an "ideal mix of technology" instead of an "ideal mix of interaction" to promote the other two types of interaction (Anderson, 2003). Therefore, if the class composition comprises busy adults, the teacher should provide several opportunities to use various web-based technologies to promote learner–instructor and learner–content interaction. Because learner–learner interaction is considered least important to faculty and students in these courses, no need exists for an "ideal mix of interaction." Educators should use various types of technology to encourage the other two types of interaction. Teacher immediacy could be improved through the use of audio files and video lectures that could be accessed "on the go" using mobile and portable technologies. Results this study could provide valuable feedback to instructional designers and faculty who want to stay current with improvements in those technologies that would improve student learning.

RECOMMENDATIONS

Faculty

Because faculty recommendations are based on a small sample, their suggestions varied significantly, and at times were unclear. Some faculty thought that technology could work as a barrier as well as a means to keep students engaged, depending on how it is used. Others opined that it was best to use a mix of tools (the more, the better) to encourage learner interaction at all three levels; whereas one faculty felt that web-based technologies should be used primarily to improve students' understanding of concepts in economics. Faculty's main recommendations were to focus web-based technologies on promoting two types of interaction: learner–instructor and learner–content. Based on the results of this study, faculty would prefer to use most technology resources to promote more learner–content interaction. Given the numerical and graphical components of economics, faculty recommended the use of online interactive homework tools improve student understanding of the numerical and graphical aspects of the course.

Student

Some students recommended more learner–instructor interaction via Elluminate sessions. Because the class comprises students with different intellects and levels of comprehension, discussion among students is often quite limited in value and scope. As a result, students preferred more interaction with the teacher to keep the discussion up to a certain level. A few others recommended

more interactive content such as tutorials and video lectures to keep them engaged. Therefore, discussion-board threads should be assigned a smaller weight in courses, but continue to accommodate those students who like to interact with classmates. Also, responding to classmates should be optional and bear no weight toward class grade. Activities planned for student orientations should outline the three types of interaction involved in online courses.

Because the nature of online learning removes face-to-face interaction with a teacher, students who need the physical presence of a teacher face decisions. They must be aware that an online class means choosing to relinquish the physical presence of a teacher in exchange for the flexibility of a class schedule, and rely on technology to enhance their learning. They must balance online learning requirements such as discipline, dedication, and self-motivation against the desire for classroom instruction. Students should remember that by having remote instruction, the material might not be as easily understandable as doing it themselves, studying on their own. Students who learn best independently, who are good self-learners, and who need very little teacher interaction, would do better at online learning. However, those students who require a teacher in front of them, taking them step by step through the class material, need to acquire independent learning skills to succeed at online education. Likewise, faculty making a decision to teach online courses should relinquish their role as chief disseminator of information, encouraging their class to become independent of face-to-face contact.

CONCLUSION

For Research Question 1, this chapter reveals that faculty should choose technology that satisfies the needs of their students. Faculty never or rarely used online social-networking sites, even though faculty identified them as easily accessible over the Internet. Online games were also not a choice for this group of faculty. This conclusion is supported by faculty who stated that online social-networking sites were moderately effective. It was unclear whether faculty might have had to choose from a list of web-based technologies provided by their colleges or they did not consider these technologies to sufficiently contribute to student learning.

For Research Question 2, the most important considerations given when choosing technology are type, access, and flexibility. However, it is important to evaluate how much freedom of choice faculty have when selecting web-based technologies. Some faculty might be allowed to choose only those web-technologies their school listed in the course-management system.

For Research Question 3, although students supported the use of Aplia, faculty and students cautioned that its use should remain the same. In some ways, students' and faculty's reaction to Aplia supported the findings of Lee et al. (2010), who stated that the impact of an online homework tool (Aplia) improved student performance by only 2%. This group of students was very favorable to online interactive homework tools and online multimedia and portable technologies, but believed increased use of portable technologies would be helpful.

For Research Question 4, faculty and student recommendations emphasized the importance of diversity in instruction. Faculty should ensure all parties are realizing instructional goals and are satisfied and highly motivated during the instructional process. When students have a positive perception of the tools used to accomplish their instructional goals, they are more inclined to study and interact with the instructor, their classmates, and the content. A positive perception of faculty choice of web-based technologies could encourage active learning and persistence to complete the course.

A final thought is that faculty should examine whether the utility of each piece of technology matches their reasons for choosing particular web technologies in online economics courses, and how the class would benefit. Students in this sample adapted the discussion board and portable technologies to their schedules and circumstances; however, if faculty help them connect technologies to learning outcomes, they might be able to see the relevance of web-based technologies to course objectives rather than to their individual circumstances. Also, faculty should pick topics of national economic interest for the discussion-board forum. This would be particularly helpful in courses where students from various backgrounds, multiple intelligences, and learning styles learn in a single forum. After 2 to 3 weeks of coursework, teachers should determine if they need to modify the nature and quantity of discussion-board topics. For example, each time they assign students a graded discussion-board topic, instructors should provide at least two or three topics for students to choose, rather than assigning only one discussion-board topic for the entire class.

Overall students have a positive perception of faculty choice of technologies for interaction in online economics courses. Faculty should aim for both an "ideal mix of technology" and an "ideal mix of interaction," thereby ensuring a satisfactory and efficient component of web-technologies to encourage interaction in online courses. Because the study revealed that faculty and students agreed that the discussion board is effective and good for all three types of interaction, but rated learner–learner interaction as the least important interaction in online economics courses, discussion-board forums should be purposeful. Also, faculty should conveniently share with students the rationale for using specific web-based technologies to promote interaction in online economics classes. The need exists not only for an "ideal mix of interaction" but also for an "ideal mix of technology" to ensure a balance among diverse groups of students in online courses.

FUTURE RESEARCH

Because the web-based technologies employed today will eventually become obsolete, it is worthwhile, given the findings from this study, to consistently investigate whether faculty choice of web-based technologies for interaction and student perception of those technologies are at satisfactory levels. Thus, it would be beneficial if future studies used various approaches to build on the findings of this study. This study could be replicated in universities of all types, sizes, and locations and as a case study of one online course, comprising one faculty and the students from the same online course. Also this study could be replicated in several online courses using the same research design and collecting data from two semesters. Additional recommendations for future research follow:

- A case study of faculty and students of the same online course
- A comparative study of different courses and students over 2 semesters
- A survey of a larger sample population at different locations across the country
- A qualitative study investigating whether an "ideal balance" of interaction exists when faculty choose web-based technologies for interaction and student perceptions of those choices synchronize.

REFERENCES

Anderson, T. (2003). Getting the mix right again: An updated and theoretical rationale for interaction. *The International Review of Research in Open and Distance Learning, 4*(2), Article 4.2.13. Retrieved from http://www.irrodl.org/index.php/irrodl/article/view/149/708

Arbaugh, J. B., Godfrey, M. R., Johnson, M., Pollack, B. L., Niendorf, B., & Wresch, W. (2009). Research in online and blended learning in the business discipline: Key findings and possible future decisions. *The Internet and Higher Education, 12*(2), 71–87. doi:10.1016/j.iheduc.2009.06.006

Bartlett-Bragg, A. (2003). Blogging to learn. *The Knowledge Tree e-Journal.* Retrieved from http://www.csus.edu/indiv/s/stonerm/blogging_to_learn.pdf

Beldarrain, Y. (2006). Distance education trends: Integrating new technologies to foster student interaction and collaboration. *Distance Education, 27*(2), 139–153. doi:10.1080/01587910600789498

Chizmar, J. F., & Walbert, M. S. (1999). Web-based learning environments guided by principles of good teaching practice. *The Journal of Economic Education, 30*(3), 248–264. doi:10.1080/00220489909595985

City Colleges of Chicago. (2011). *Fiscal year 2011: Statistical digest.* Retrieved from http://www.ccc.edu/menu/Documents/CCCFY2011Statistical Digest.pdf

Creswell, J. W. (2005). *Educational research: Planning, conducting, and evaluating quantitative and qualitative research* (2nd ed.). Berkeley, CA: Carlisle Communications.

Cronbach, L. J. (1984). *Essentials of psychological testing* (4th ed.). New York, NY: Harper Row.

Drouin, M. A. (2008). The relationship between students' perceived sense of community and satisfaction, achievement, and retention in online course. *The Quarterly Review of Distance Education, 9*, 267–284.

Gardner, H. (1983). *Multiple intelligences: The theory in practice.* New York, NY: Basic Books.

Gosmire, D., Morrison, M., & Osdel, J. V. (2009). Perceptions of interactions in online courses. *Journal of Online Learning and Teaching, 5,* 609–617. Retrieved from http://jolt.merlot.org/vol5no4/gosmire_1209.pdf

Greenlaw, S. A. (1999). Using groupware to enhance teaching and learning in undergraduate economics. *The Journal of Economic Education, 30*(1), 33–42. doi:10.1080/00220489909595936

Greenlaw, S. A., & DeLoach, S. B. (2003). Teaching critical thinking with electronic discussion. *The Journal of Economic Education, 34*(1), 36–52. doi:10.1080/00220480309595199

LaRose, R., & Whitten, P. (1999, June). Increasing the immediacy of web courses. *Proceedings of the Association for the Advancement of Computers in Education,* Seattle, Washington.

LaRose, R., & Whitten, P. (2000). Re-thinking instructional immediacy for web courses: A social cognitive exploration. *Communication Education, 40*(4), 320–338. doi:10.1080/03634520009379221

Lee, W., Courtney, R., & Balassi, S. J. (2010). Do online homework tools improve student results in microeconomics principles courses? *The American Economic Review, 100,* 283–286. doi:10.1257/aer.100.2.283

Moore, M. G. (1989). Three types of interaction. *American Journal of Distance Education, 3*(2), 1–6. doi:10.1080/08923648909526659

Moore, M. G. (1993). Theory of transactional distance. In D. Keegan (Ed.), *Theoretical principles of distance education* (pp. 22–38). London, UK: Routledge.

Navarro, P., & Shoemaker, J. (2000). Performance and perceptions of distance learners, in cyberspace. *American Journal of Distance Education, 14*(2), 15–35. doi:10.1080/08923640009527052

Nguyen, T. T., & Trimarchi, A. (2010). Active learning in introductory economics: Do MyEcon-Lab and Aplia make any difference? *International Journal for the Scholarship of Teaching and Learning, 4*(1), 10. Retrieved from http://digitalcommons.georgiasouthern.edu/cgi/viewcontent.cgi?article=1210&context=ij-sotl

Northrup, P. T. (2002). Online learners' preferences for interaction. *The Quarterly Review of Distance Education, 3,* 219–226.

O'Leary, P. F., & Quinlan, T. Jr. (2007). Learner–instructor telephone interaction: Effects on satisfaction and achievement of online students. *American Journal of Distance Education, 21*(3), 133–143. doi:10.1080/08923640701341661

Osborne, R. E., Kriese, P., Tobey, H., & Johnson, E. (2009). And never the two shall meet? Student vs. faculty perceptions of online courses. *Journal of Educational Computing Research, 40*(2), 171–182. doi:10.2190/EC.40.2.b

Pollacia, L., & McCallister, T. (2009). Using Web 2.0 technologies to meet Quality Matters requirements. *Journal of Information Systems Education, 20,* 155–164.

Prensky, M. (2009). Let's be digital multipliers. *Educational Technology.* Retrieved from http://www.marcprensky.com/writing/Prensky-Lets_Be_Digital_Multipliers-ET-01-09.pdf

Rhode, J. F. (2009). Interaction equivalency in self-paced online learning environments: An exploration of learner preferences. *International Review of Research in Open and Distance Learning, 10*(1), 11–23. Retrieved from http://www.irrodl.org/index.php/irrodl/article/view/603/1178

Rourke, L., Anderson, T., Garrison, D., & Archer, W. (1999). Assessing social presence in asynchronous text-based computer conferencing. *Journal of Distance Education, 14*(2), 51–70.

Rovai, A. (2002). Building sense of community at a distance. *International Review of Research in Open and Distance Learning*, *3*(1), 1–16. Retrieved from http://www.irrodl.org/index.php/irrodl/article/view/79/153

Simkins, S. P. (1999). Promoting active-student learning using the World Wide Web in economics courses. *The Journal of Economic Education*, *30*(3), 287–289. doi:10.1080/00220489909595990

Smith, G. G., Torres-Ayala, A. T., & Heindel, A. J. (2008). Disciplinary differences in e-learning instructional design. *Journal of Distance Education*, *22*(3), 63–88. Retrieved from http://files.eric.ed.gov/fulltext/EJ812564.pdf

Swan, K. (2002). Building learning communities in online courses: The importance of interaction. *Education Communication and Information*, *2*(1), 23–49. doi:10.1080/1463631022000005016

Vachris, M. A. (1999). Teaching principles of economics without "chalk and talk": The experience of CNU online. *The Journal of Economic Education*, *30*, 292–302. doi:10.2307/1183070

Wachenheim, C. J. (2009). Final exam scores in introductory economics courses: Effects of course delivery method and proctoring. *Review of Agricultural Economics*, *31*(3), 640–652. doi:10.1111/j.1467-9353.2009.01458.x

ADDITIONAL READING

Abrahamson, C. E. (1998). Issues in interactive communication in distance education. *College Student Journal*, *32*, 33–42. Retrieved from http://citeseerx.ist.psu.edu/viewdoc/download?doi=10.1.1.102.7929&rep=rep1&type=pdf

Agarwal, R., & Day, A. E. (1998). The impact of the Internet on economic education. *The Journal of Economic Education*, *29*(2), 99–110. doi:10.1080/00220489809597943

Ajjan, H., & Hartshorne, R. (2008). Investigating faculty decisions to adopt Web 2.0 technologies: Theory and empirical tests. *The Internet and Higher Education*, *11*(2), 71–86. doi:10.1016/j.iheduc.2008.05.002

Alavi, M. (1994). Computer-mediated collaborative learning: An empirical evaluation. *Management Information Systems Quarterly*, *18*(2), 159–174. doi:10.2307/249763

Allen, E., & Seaman, J. (2010). Class differences: Online education in the United States 2010. Newburyport, MA: Sloan Consortium; Retrieved from http://olc.onlinelearningconsortium.org/sites/default/files/class_differences.pdf

Angelino, L. M., Williams, F. K., & Natvig, D. (2007). Strategies to engage online students and reduce attrition rates. *The Journal of Educators Online*, *4*(2), 1–14. Retrieved from http://www.thejeo.com/Volume4Number2/Angelino%20Final.pdf

Atack, L., & Rankin, J. (2002). A descriptive study of registered nurses' experiences with web-based learning. *Journal of Advanced Nursing*, *40*(4), 457–465. doi:10.1046/j.1365-2648.2002.02394.x PMID:12421405

Barnes, S. (2000). What does electronic conferencing afford distance education? *Distance Education*, *21*(2), 236–247. doi:10.1080/0158791000210203

Batts, D. (2008). Comparison of student and instructor perceptions of best practice in online technology courses. *Journal of Online Learning and Teaching*, *4*, 477–489. Retrieved from http://jolt.merlot.org/vol4no4/batts_1208.pdf

Beard, L. A., & Harper, C. (2002). Student perceptions of online versus on campus instruction. *Education, 122*, 658–663.

Becker, W. E. (1997). Teaching economics to undergraduates. *Journal of Economic Literature, 35*, 1347–1373.

Becker, W. E., & Watts, M. (1996). Chalk and talk: A national survey on teaching undergraduate economics. *The American Economic Review, 86*, 448–453.

Becker, W. E., & Watts, M. (2001). Teaching economics at the start of the 21st century: Still chalk and talk. *The American Economic Review, 91*(2), 440–446. doi:10.1257/aer.91.2.446

Berge, Z. L. (2002). Active, interactive, and reflective e-learning. *Quarterly Review of Distance Education, 3*, 181–190. Retrieved from http://www.researchgate.net

Billings, D. M., Connors, H. R., & Skiba, D. J. (2001). Benchmarking best practices in Web-based nursing courses. *ANS. Advances in Nursing Science, 23*(3), 41–52. doi:10.1097/00012272-200103000-00005 PMID:11225049

Blair, J. (2002). The virtual teaching life. *Education Week, 21*(35), 1–6.

Blecha, B. (2000). *Economics technology project*. Retrieved from http://online.sfsu.edu/bjblecha/etp.htm

Bourne, J., & Moore, J. C. (2000). *Elements of quality online education: Into the mainstream* (Vol. 5). Newburyport, MA: Sloan Consortium.

Boyle, D. K., & Wambach, K. A. (2001). Interaction in graduate nursing Web-based instruction. *Journal of Professional Nursing, 17*(3), 128–134. doi:10.1053/jpnu.2001.23376 PMID:11391558

Brown, A., & Thompson, H. (1997). Course design for the WWW: Keeping online students onside. *Proceedings of the 14th Annual Conference of the Australian Society for Computers in Learning in Tertiary Education* (pp. 74–81). Perth, Australia: Curtin University of Technology.

Brown, M., & Kiriakidis, P. (2007). Learner empowerment in an online program. *College Teaching Methods & Styles Journal, 3*(3), 37–49.

Cao, Q., Griffin, T. E., & Bai, X. (2009). The importance of synchronous interaction for student satisfaction with course web sites. *Journal of Information Systems Education, 20*, 331–338.

Carr, N. G. (2004). *Does IT matter? Information technology and the corrosion of competitive advantage*. Boston, MA: Harvard Business School Press.

Carr, S. (2000). As distance education comes of age, the challenge is keeping the students. *The Chronicle of Higher Education, 46*, A39–A41. Retrieved from http://chronicle.com

Chen, G. D., Ou, K. L., Liu, C. C., & Liu, B. J. (2001). Intervention and strategy analysis for Web group-learning. *Journal of Computer Assisted Learning, 17*(1), 58–71. doi:10.1046/j.1365-2729.2001.00159.x

Chen, H. (2002). *Interaction In distance education*. Retrieved January 4, 2004, from http://seamonkey.ed.asu.edu/~mcisaac/disted/week2/7focushc.html

Chickering, A. W., & Ehrmann, S. C. (1996). *Implementing the seven principles: Technology as lever*. Retrieved January 3, 2004, from http://www.tltgroup.org/programs/seven.html

Chickering, A. W., & Gamson, Z. (1987). Seven principles for good practice in undergraduate education. *AAHE Bulletin, 39*(7), 3–7. Retrieved from http://www.lonestar.edu/multimedia/seven-principles.pdf

Collis, B., DeBoer, W., & Slotman, K. (2001). Feedback for Web-based assignments. *Journal of Computer Assisted Learning, 17*(3), 306–313. doi:10.1046/j.0266-4909.2001.00185.x

Conole, C. (2004, September). E-learning: The hype and the reality. *Journal of Interactive Media Education,* Art. 2. Retrieved from http://oro.open.ac.uk/6962/1/conole-2004-12.pdf

Crawford, M. W. (1999). *Students' perceptions of the interpersonal communication courses offered through distance education* (Doctoral dissertation). Available from ProQuest Dissertations and Theses database. (UMI No. 9929303)

Daley, B. J., Watkins, K., Watkins, K., Williams, S. W., Courtenay, B., & Davis, M. (2001). Exploring learning in a technology-enhanced environment. *Journal of Educational Technology & Society, 4*(3), 126–138. http://ifets.ieee.org/periodical/vol_3_2001/daley.html Retrieved January 4, 2004

DeBourgh, G. A. (1999). Technology is the tool, teaching is the task: Student satisfaction in distance learning. In J. Price et al. (Eds.), *Proceedings of Society for Information Technology & Teacher Education International Conference 1999* (pp. 131–137). Chesapeake, VA: Association for the Advancement of Computing in Education.

Dennen, V. P., Darabi, A. A., & Smith, L. J. (2007). Instructor–learner interaction in online courses: The relative perceived importance of particular instructor actions on performance and satisfaction. *Distance Education, 28*(1), 65–79. doi:10.1080/01587910701305319

Duffy, T. M., & Cunningham, D. J. (1996). Constructivism: Implications for the design and delivery of instruction. In D. H. Jonassen (Ed.), *Handbook of research for educational communication and technology* (pp. 170–199). New York, NY: Simon & Macmillan.

Ehrlich, D. B. (2002). Establishing connections: Interactivity factors for a distance education course. *Journal of Educational Technology & Society, 5*(1), 48–54. http://ifets.ieee.org/periodical/vol_1_2002/ehrlich.html Retrieved January 2, 2004

Emerson, T. L. N., & Taylor, B. A. (2004). Comparing student achievement across experimental and lecture-oriented sections of principles of microeconomics course. *Southern Economic Journal, 70*(3), 672–693. doi:10.2307/4135338

Faux, T. L., & Black-Hughes, C. (2000). A comparison of using the Internet versus lectures to teach social work history. *Research on Social Work Practice, 10*, 454–466.

Fredericksen, E., Pickett, A., Shea, P., Pelz, W., & Swan, K. (2000). Student satisfaction and perceived learning with on-line courses: Principles and examples from the SUNY learning network. *Journal of Asynchronous Learning Networks, 4*(2). http://www.aln.org/publications/jaln/v4n2/v4n2_fredericksen.asp Retrieved January 4, 2004

Fricker, D. (2007, November). *eLearning course design approaches & authorship to promote collaborative learning: Let the students create the course content.* Paper presented at the 24th Southeast Asia Regional Computer Conference, Bangkok, Thailand.

Gerald, D. E., & Hussar, W. J. (2010). *Projections of education statistics to 2010.* Washington, DC: U.S. Department of Education, National Center for Education Statistics.

Goffe, W. L., & Sosin, K. (2005). Teaching with technology: May you live in interesting times. *The Journal of Economic Education, 36*(3), 278–291. doi:10.3200/JECE.36.3.278-291

Grandzol, C. J., & Grandzol, J. R. (2010). Interaction in online courses: More is NOT always better. *Online Journal of Distance Learning Administration, 13*(2). Retrieved from http://www.westga.edu/~distance/ojdla/summer132/Grandzol_Grandzol132.html

Gunawardena, C. N. (1995). Social presence theory and implications for interaction and collaborative learning in computer conferences. *International Journal of Educational Telecommunications, 1,* 147–166.

Gutierrez, J. J. (2000). Instructor–student interaction. *USDLA Journal, 14*(3). Retrieved January 3, 2004, from http://www.usdla.org/html/journal/MAR00_Issue/Instructorstudent.htm

Hara, N., & Kling, R. (1999). Students' frustrations with a Web-based distance education course. *First Monday, 4*(12http://www.firstmonday.dk/issues/issue4_12/hara). RetrievedJanuary52004. doi:10.5210/fm.v4i12.710

Hartshorne, R., & Ajjan, H. (2009). Examining student decisions to adopt Web 2.0 technologies: Theory and empirical tests. *Journal of Computing in Higher Education, 21*(3), 183–198. doi:10.1007/s12528-009-9023-6

Hillman, D. C., Willis, D. J., & Gunawardena, C. N. (1994). Learner–interface interaction in distance education: An extension of contemporary models and strategies for parishioners. *American Journal of Distance Education, 8*(2), 30–42. doi:10.1080/08923649409526853

Instructional Technology Council. (2010). Distance education survey results: Trends in e-learning: Tracking the Impact of e-learning at Community Colleges. Washington, DC: ITC Annual Survey.

Jaffee, D. (1997). Asynchronous learning: Technology and pedagogical strategy in a computer-mediated distance learning course. *Teaching Sociology, 25,* 262–277. doi:10.2307/1319295

Jiang, M., & Ting, E. (1999, December). *A study of students' perceived learning in a Web-based online environment.* Paper presented at the WebNet 99 World Conference on the WWW and Internet, Honolulu, Hawaii.

Jonassen, D., Davidson, A., Collins, M., Campbell, J., & Haag, B. B. (1995). Constructivism and computer-mediated communication in distance education. *American Journal of Distance Education, 9*(2), 7–26. doi:10.1080/08923649509526885

Kartha, C. P. (2006). Learning business statistics: Online vs. traditional. *The Business Review, Cambridge, 5*(1), 27–32.

Katz, A., & Becker, W. E. (1999). Technology and the teaching of economics to undergraduates. *The Journal of Economic Education, 30*(3), 194–199. doi:10.1080/00220489909595979

Kearsley, G. (2000). *Online education: Learning and teaching in cyberspace.* Belmont, CA: Wadsworth.

Kearsley, G., & Shneiderman, B. (1999). *Engagement theory: A framework for technology based teaching and learning* (Working paper). Retrieved from http://home.sprynet.com/~gkearsley/engage.htm

Kellogg, D. L., & Smith, M. A. (2009). Student-to-student interaction revisited: A case study of working adult business students in online courses. *Decision Sciences Journal of Innovative Education, 7*(2), 433–456. doi:10.1111/j.1540-4609.2009.00224.x

Kenny, A. (2002). Online learning: Enhancing nurse education? *Journal of Advanced Nursing, 38*(2), 127–135. doi:10.1046/j.1365-2648.2002.02156.x PMID:11940125

King, J. C., & Doerfert, D. L. (2000). *Interaction in the distance education setting*. Retrieved January 5, 2004, from http://www.ssu.missouri.edu/ssu/aged/naerm/s-e-4.htm

Kirby, E. (1999). Building interaction in online and distance education courses. In J. Price etal. (Eds.), *Proceedings of the Society for Information Technology and Teacher Education Annual 1999* (pp. 199–205). Chesapeake, VA: Association for the Advancement of Computing in Education.

Kiriakidis, P. (2008). Online learner satisfaction: Learner–instructor interaction. *College Teaching Methods & Styles Journal, 14*(1), 11–18. Retrieved from http://etec.hawaii.edu/proceedings/2007/kiriakidis.pdf

Kiriakidis, P., & Parker, A. (2008). Faculty and learner interaction in online courses. *International Journal of Instructional Technology and Distance Learning, 5*(11), Art. 4. Retrieved from http://www.itdl.org/Journal/Nov_08/article03.htm

Larson, B. E., & Keiper, T. A. (2002). Classroom discussion and threaded electronic discussion: Learning in two arenas. *Contemporary Issues in Technology & Teacher Education, 2*(1). http://www.citejournal.org/vol2/iss1/socialstudies/article1.cfm Retrieved January 3, 2004

Leasure, A. R., Davis, L., & Thievon, S. L. (2000). Comparison of student outcomes and preferences in a traditional vs. World Wide Web-based baccalaureate nursing research course. *The Journal of Nursing Education, 39*, 149–154. PMID:10782758

Leong, P., Ho, C. P., & Saromines-Ganne, B. (2002). An empirical investigation of student satisfaction with Web-based courses. In M. Driscoll, & T. Reeves (Eds.), *Proceedings of the World Conference on E-Learning in Corporate, Government, Healthcare, & Higher Education 2002* (pp. 1792–1795). Chesapeake, VA: Association for the Advancement of Computing in Education.

Lombard, M., & Ditton, T. (1997). At the heart of it all: The concept of presence. *Journal of Computer-Mediated Communication, 3*(2). http://www.ascusc.org/jcmc/vol3/issue2/lombard.html Retrieved January 2, 2004

Lytle, J. S., Cross, C., & Lenhart, K. A. (2001). Analysis of large Web-based courses at the University of Central Florida. In J. Price etal. (Eds.), *Proceedings of the Society for Information Technology and Teacher Education International Conference 2001* (pp. 1117–1119). Chesapeake, VA: Association for the Advancement of Computing in Education.

Maloney, E. J. (2007). What Web 2.0 can teach us about learning. *The Chronicle of Higher Education, 53*(18), B26.

Manning, T., Algozzine, B., & Antonak, R. (2003). *Guide for preparing a thesis or dissertation*. Morgantown, WV: PNG.

McGinn, D. (2000, April 24). College online. *Newsweek, 135,* 54–58.

Merisotis, J. P. (2001). Quality and equality in Internet-based higher education: Benchmark for success. *Higher Education in Europe, 26*(4), 589–597. doi:10.1080/03797720220141924

Merisotis, J. P., & Phipps, R. A. (1999). What's the difference? Outcomes of distance vs. traditional classroom-based learning. *Change, 31*(3), 12–17. doi:10.1080/00091389909602685

Meyen, E., Lian, C. H. T., & Tangen, P. (1997). Developing online instruction: One model. *Focus on Autism and Other Developmental Disabilities, 12*(3), 159–165. doi:10.1177/108835769701200304

Mills, S. J., Yanes, M. J., & Casebeer, C. M. (2009). Perceptions of distance learning among faculty of a college of education. *Journal of Online Learning and Teaching, 5*, 19–28. Retrieved from http://jolt.merlot.org/vol5no1/mills_0309.htm

Moody, J. (2004). Distance education: Why are the attrition rates so high? *The Quarterly Review of Distance Education, 5*, 205–210.

Moore, M. G., & Kearsley, G. (1996). *Distance education: A systems view*. Belmont, CA: Wadsworth.

Morris, L. V., Finnegan, C., & Wu, S.-S. (2005). Tracking student behavior, persistence, and achievement in online courses. *The Internet and Higher Education, 8*(3), 221–231. doi:10.1016/j.iheduc.2005.06.009

Morris, N., Buck-Rolland, C., & Gagne, M. (2002). From bricks to bytes: Faculty and student perspectives of online graduate nursing courses. *Computers, Informatics, Nursing, 20*(3), 108–118. doi:10.1097/00024665-200205000-00010 PMID:12021609

Muirhead, B. (1999). *Attitudes toward interactivity in a graduate distance education program: A qualitative analysis* (Doctoral dissertation). Retrieved from http://www.bookpump.com/dps/pdf-b/1120710b.pdf

Muirhead, B. (2001a). Enhancing social interaction in computer-mediated distance education. *USDLA Journal, 15*(4). Retrieved January 4, 2004, from the World Wide Web: http://www.usdla.org/html/journal/APR01_Issue/article02.html

Muirhead, B. (2001b). Interactivity research studies. *Journal of Educational Technology & Society, 4*(3). http://ifets.ieee.org/periodical/vol_3_2001/muirhead.html Retrieved January 4, 2004

Nandi, D., Hamilton, M., & Harland, J. (2012). Evaluating the quality of interaction in asynchronous discussion forums in fully online courses. *Distance Education, 33*(1), 5–30. doi:10.1080/01587919.2012.667957

National Center for Education Statistics. (2002a). *Distance education instruction by postsecondary faculty and staff: Fall 1998*. Retrieved January 3, 2004, from http://www.ed.gov/about/bdscomm/list/acsfa/edlite-distance.html

National Center for Education Statistics. (2002b). *Teaching with technology: Use of telecommunications technology by postsecondary instructional faculty and staff*. Retrieved January 3, 2004, from http://nces.ed.gov/das/epubs/2002161/index.asp

National Governors Association. (2001). *The state of e-learning in the states*. Retrieved January 5, 2004, from http://www.nga.org/cda/files/060601ELEARNING.pdf

Otero, V., Peressini, D., Anderson-Meymaris, K., Ford, P., Garvin, T., Harlow, D., & Mears, C. etal. (2005). Integrating technology into teacher education: A critical framework for implementing reform. *Journal of Teacher Education, 56*(1), 8–23. doi:10.1177/0022487104272055

Palloff, R. M., & Pratt, K. (2001). *Lessons from the cyberspace classroom: The realities of online teaching*. San Francisco, CA: Jossey-Bass.

Payne, C. R. (2002). Good practice and motivation in online courses. *Virtual University Gazette.* Retrieved January 4, 2004, from http://www.geteducated.com/vug/aug02/vug0802.htm

Price, B. (1997). Defining quality student feedback in distance learning. *Journal of Advanced Nursing, 26*(1), 154–160. doi:10.1046/j.1365-2648.1997.1997026154.x PMID:9231290

Restauri, S. L., King, F. L., & Nelson, J. G. (2001). *Assessment of students' ratings for two methodologies of teaching via distance learning: An evaluative approach based on accreditation.* Retrieved from http://files.eric.ed.gov/fulltext/ED460148.pdf

Rich, L., Cowan, W., Herring, S., & Wilkes, W. (2009, March). *Collaborate, engage, and interact in online learning: Successes with wikis and synchronous virtual classrooms at Athens State University.* Paper presented at the 14th Annual Instructional Technology Conference. Murfreesboro, TN.

Richardson, J. C., & Swan, K. (2001). The role of social presence in online courses: How does it relate to students' perceived learning and satisfaction? In C. Montgomerie, & J. Viteli (Eds.), *Proceedings of the World Conference on Educational Multimedia and Technology 2001* (pp. 1545–1546). Chesapeake, VA: Association for the Advancement of Computing in Education.

Rovai, A. A. (2002). A preliminary look at the structural differences of higher education classroom communities in traditional and ALN courses. *Journal of Asynchronous Learning Networks, 6*(1). http://www.aln.org/publications/jaln/v6n1/v6n1_rovai.asp Retrieved February 19, 2003

Russell, M., Bebell, D., O'Dwyer, L. M., & O'Connor, K. M. (2003). Examining teacher technology use: Implications for pre-service and in-service teacher preparation. *Journal of Teacher Education, 54*(4), 297–310. doi:10.1177/0022487103255985

Schoenfeld-Tacher, R., McConnell, S., & Graham, M. (2001). Do no harm—A comparison of the effects of on-line vs. traditional delivery media on a science course. *Journal of Science Education and Technology, 10*(3), 257–265. doi:10.1023/A:1016690600795

Schrum, L., & Hong, S. (2002). Dimensions and strategies for online success: Voices from experienced educators. *Journal of Asynchronous Learning Networks, 6*(1). doi:10.1007/978-0-387-35596-2_2

Sciuto, G. T. (2002). Setting students up for success: The instructor's role in creating a positive, asynchronous, distance education experience. *Virtual University Gazette.* Retrieved January 2, 2004, from http://www.geteducated.com/vug/aug02/vug0802.htm

Sherry, A. C., Fulford, C. P., & Zhang, S. (1998). Assessing distance learners' satisfaction with instruction: A quantitative and a qualitative measure. *American Journal of Distance Education, 42*(3), 4–28. doi:10.1080/08923649809527002

Sherry, L. (1996). Issues in distance learning. *International Journal of Educational Telecommunications, 1,* 337–365. http://carbon.cudenver.edu/~lsherry/pubs/issues.html Retrieved January 5, 2004

Shin, M., & Lee, Y. (2009). Changing the landscape of teacher education via online teaching and learning. *Connecting Education & Careers, 84*(9), 32–38.

Shin, N. (2002). Beyond interaction: The relational construct of 'Transactional Presence.'. *Open Learning, 17*(2), 121–137. doi:10.1080/02680510220146887

Shuell, T. J. (1986). Cognitive conceptions theory. *Review of Educational Research, 56*(4), 411–438. doi:10.3102/00346543056004411

Smith, P. L., & Dillon, C. L. (1999). Comparing distance learning and classroom learning: Conceptual considerations. *American Journal of Distance Education, 13*(2), 6–23. doi:10.1080/08923649909527020

Sole, M. L., & Lindquist, M. (2001). Enhancing traditional, televised, and videotaped courses with Web-based technologies: A comparison of student satisfaction. *Nursing Outlook, 49*(3), 132–137. doi:10.1067/mno.2001.112111 PMID:11416815

Song, L., & McNary, S. W. (2011). Understanding students' online interaction: Analysis of discussion board postings. *Journal of Interactive Online Learning, 10*, 1–14. Retrieved from http://www.ncolr.org/jiol/issues/pdf/10.1.1.pdf

Song, L., Singleton, E. S., Hill, J. R., & Koh, M. H. (2004). Improving online learning: Student perceptions of useful and challenging characteristics. *The Internet and Higher Education, 7*(1), 59–70. doi:10.1016/j.iheduc.2003.11.003

Soo, K., & Bonk, C. J. (1998, June). *Interaction: What does it mean in online distance education?* Paper presented at the ED-MEDIA/ED-TELECOM 98 World Conference on Educational Multimedia and Hypermedia & 10th World Conference on Educational Telecommunications, Freiburg, Germany. Retrieved from http://files.eric.ed.gov/fulltext/ED428724.pdf

Soon, K. H., Sook, K. I., Jung, C. W., & Im, K. M. (2000). The effects of Internet-based distance learning in nursing. *Computers in Nursing, 18*, 19–25. PMID:10673813

Sosin, K., Blecha, B. J., Agarwal, R., Bartlett, R. L., & Daniel, J. I. (2004). Efficiency in the use of technology in economic education: Some preliminary results. *The American Economic Review, 94*(2), 253–258. doi:10.1257/0002828041301623

Stocks, J. T., & Freddolino, P. P. (1998). Evaluation of a World Wide Web-based graduate social work research methods course. *Computers in Human Services, 15*(2-3), 51–69. doi:10.1300/J407v15n02_05

Swan, K. (2001). Virtual interaction: Design factors affecting student satisfaction and perceived learning in asynchronous online courses. *Distance Education, 22*(2), 306–331. doi:10.1080/0158791010220208

Thurmond, V. A. (2003). *Examination of interaction variables as predictors of students' satisfaction and willingness to enroll in future Web-based courses while controlling for student characteristics* (Doctoral dissertation). Retrieved from http://www.bookpump.com/dps/pdf-b/1121814b.pdf

Thurmond, V. A., Wambach, K., Connors, H. R., & Frey, B. B. (2002). Evaluation of student satisfaction: Determining the impact of a Web-based environment by controlling for student characteristics. *American Journal of Distance Education, 16*(3), 169–189. doi:10.1207/S15389286AJDE1603_4

Tu, C., & Cory, M. (2003). Building active online interaction via a collaborative learning community. *Computers in the Schools, 20*(3), 51–59. doi:10.1300/J025v20n03_07

Tuovinen, J. E. (2000). Multimedia distance education interactions. *Educational Media International, 37*(1), 16–24. doi:10.1080/095239800361473

Turner, M. (2011). *Center for Distance Learning.* Chicago, IL: City Colleges of Chicago.

Volery, T. (2001). Online education: An exploratory study into success factors. *Journal of Educational Computing Research, 24*(1), 77–92. doi:10.2190/F0DY-BNYJ-18RB-NNNY

Vrasidas, C., & McIsaac, M. S. (1999). Factors influencing interaction in an online course. *American Journal of Distance Education, 13*(3), 22–36. doi:10.1080/08923649909527033

Wagner, E. D. (1994). In support of a functional definition of interaction. *American Journal of Distance Education, 8*(2), 6–29. doi:10.1080/08923649409526852

Wagner, E. D. (1997). Interactivity: From agents to outcomes. In T. E. Cyrs (Ed.), *Teaching and learning at a distance: What it takes to effectively design, deliver, and evaluate programs* (pp. 19–26). San Francisco, CA: Jossey-Bass.

Wilson, R. L., & Weiser, M. (2001). Adoption of asynchronous learning tools by traditional full-time students: A pilot study. *Information Technology Management, 2*(4), 363–375. doi:10.1023/A:1011446516889

Woodside, B. M., Wong, E. H., & Weist, D. J. (1999). The effect of student–faculty interaction on college students' academic achievement and self concept. *Education, 119*, 730–733.

Yucha, C., & Princen, T. (2000). Insights learned from teaching pathophysiology on the World Wide Web. *The Journal of Nursing Education, 39*, 68–72. PMID:10688464

Zafeiriou, G., Nunes, J. M., & Ford, N. (2001). Using students' perceptions of participation in collaborative learning activities in the design of online learning environments. *Education for Information, 19*, 83–106.

KEY TERMS AND DEFINITIONS

Faculty Choice: Faculty selection of web-based technologies used in course.

Ideal Mix of Interaction: A specific level of communication where the quantities and three main forms of interactions are most effective.

Ideal Mix of Technology: A: specific level of interface where the quantities and types of web-based technologies used for interaction is most effective.

Learner–Content Interaction: Students studying the subject matter and reviewing course materials.

Learner–Instructor Interaction: Any form of communication and collaboration between students and faculty.

Learner–Learner Interaction: Any form of communication and collaboration between one student and another or between several students.

Online Interaction: A mutual or reciprocal action or influence over the internet.

Student Perception: Student thoughts and beliefs about technology used in course.

Web-Based Technologies: Web-based technologies are network applications accessible over the internet (blogs, discussion boards, conferencing sessions tools, online multimedia and mobile technologies, online games etc.) that enable individuals to connect to each other.

Section 2
Practical Applications and Strategies for Ensuring Interaction, Presence, and Participation in Online Courses

Chapter 11
More Teaching in Less Time:
Leveraging Time to Maximize Teaching Presence

B. Jean Mandernach
Grand Canyon University, USA

Rick Holbeck
Grand Canyon University, USA

Ted Cross
Grand Canyon University, USA

ABSTRACT

There are a plethora of best practices highlighting strategies to personalize the online learning experience, promote interaction and establish teaching presence. Despite this knowledge, a gap remains between online instructors' pedagogical knowledge and teaching behaviors. This discrepancy is largely a function of time. With a wide range of instructional tasks to complete, faculty struggle to balance all the demands of the online classroom. To maximize student success and satisfaction, it is essential that faculty effectively manage their time to engage in instructional behaviors with the greatest impact. This chapter overviews strategies to help online instructors: 1) create an efficient online classroom; 2) manage teaching time more effectively; and 3) prioritize their time investment to promote interaction, presence and participation.

INTRODUCTION

Recent studies show that despite a leveling of the number of students enrolled in online programs, institutions increasingly highlight the importance of online education as an essential component of their strategic vision (Allen & Seaman, 2013). From community colleges to prestigious universities (Bowen & Lack, 2013; T. Johnson, 2013), online learning has become a mainstay of higher education. Yet, despite growing research on individualized pedagogical approaches relevant to the online classroom, a holistic approach to online teaching has received limited attention (D. Johnson, 2013). Research supports the value and relevance of creating an engaging, personalized,

DOI: 10.4018/978-1-4666-9582-5.ch011

interactive online learning experience, yet stops short of providing faculty with a comprehensive understanding of how to create this experience.

The value and importance of establishing a teaching presence, fostering a community of learners and promoting ongoing interaction in the online classroom is well established (Anderson, 2004; Anderson, Rourke, Garrison & Archer, 2001; Aragon, 2003; Garrison & Archer, 2000; Garrison, Anderson & Archer, 2000; Garrison & Anderson, 2003; Garrison & Cleveland-Innes, 2005; Gunawardena, 1995; Gunawardena & Zittle, 1997; Lowenthal & Parscal, 2008; Palloff & Pratt, 1999; Richardson & Swan, 2003; Rourke, Anderson, Garrison, Archer, 1999; Salmon, 2000; So, 2005; Swan, 2001; Swan, 2003; Tu, 2000); despite this knowledge, there is a gap between what online instructors *should* do and what online instructors *actually* do. This discrepancy between pedagogical knowledge and instructional behavior is largely a function of time (Cavanaugh, 2005; Concieção, 2006; Easton, 2003; Graham, Cagiltay, Craner, Lim & Duffy, 2000; Mandernach, Gonzales & Garrett, 2006; Mandernach, Hudson & Wise, 2013; Mandernach, 2013; Sheridan, 2006; Van De Vord, Pogue, 2012; Worley & Tesdell, 2009). Regardless of whether an online faculty member is fulltime or adjunct, each individual only has a limited amount of time available to devote to each class. This limited time must be divided between all associated tasks (including course development, technical challenges, interaction, course administration, grading and feedback, etc.); thus, more time spent in one area subtracts available time for other aspects of teaching.

In order to maximize student success and satisfaction in the online classroom, it is essential that online faculty prioritize their time investment to focus on high impact instructional activities that promote interaction, presence and participation (Mandernach, Forrest, Babuzke & Manaker, 2009). To maximize teaching time, faculty must do three things: 1) create an efficient online classroom; 2) manage teaching time more effectively; and 3) invest available time to the teaching activities with the greatest impact. Put simply, before an online instructor can implement best practice approaches to foster interaction and engagement, he/she must have the necessary time to do so. Once this time becomes available, it is essential to dedicate this time to targeted instructional activities that promote ongoing dialogue and engagement.

CREATING AN EFFICIENT ONLINE CLASSROOM

Online courses are driven by two, relatively distinct, components: course development and course delivery. Course development is typically completed prior to the beginning of an active course and generally involves chunking course content into modules or units along with the development of instructional material (text, videos, links, resources, etc.), interaction activities (discussion questions or group projects), and assignments (papers, projects, quizzes, tests, etc.). Course delivery is the active teaching and facilitation of the online course; this includes posting announcements, adding current material, facilitating discussions, grading assignments and providing feedback. Online course development and delivery may be completed by either the same individual, or online course development may be completed independently by instructors hired to teach existing course content. Regardless of which model is utilized, it is essential that online courses are created and developed with an explicit awareness of the time demands that each instructional design choice entails. With this in mind, the following guidelines are offered to maximize instructional efficiency through online course design:

1. Complete online course development prior to the start of the active course.

Ensuring adequate a priori course development time is essential to a successful online teaching experience (Sheridan, 2006). The reality for most faculty members is that they simply do not have sufficient time to simultaneously teach and develop an online course. Typically instructors that attempt to "stay just ahead of the students" in their online course design will be so busy preparing course material for the next module that they do not have sufficient time to interact with students in the active, current module. This over-scheduling of instructional activities results in dissatisfaction for both the instructor and students alike.

While all courses may be subject to minor modifications throughout an active teaching period, the basic components of the course (i.e., course structure, instructional content, activities and assignments) should all be completed prior to the start of the course. Full online course development prior to the active teaching period is essential to ensure instructional time during a live course is devoted overwhelmingly to course facilitation and teaching activities (i.e., posting announcements, facilitating discussions, grading and feedback).

2.   Identify support resources and services.

Just as the roles of course development and course delivery should be clearly delineated, it is equally important that instructors define the roles and expectations associated with online teaching. Because students in the online classroom are often geographically separated from the campus, they may be unaware of the range of supplemental services, resources and support available through the college or university. Compounding the issue, students' disconnect with the larger academic community translates into an increased reliance on the online instructor for all academic needs (Yu & Brandenburg, 2006). As a result of these converging factors, students often look to their online instructor as a one-stop source for holistic academic support including academic advising, technical support, skill development and career planning. While each faculty member likely has the knowledge to provide this type of comprehensive support, time invested helping students with these types of supplemental questions reduces the time available for interacting within the online classroom on issues pertaining to the course learning objectives. As such, to reduce the burden on individual instructors, it is useful to integrate guidance on these supplemental issues into the overall course design.

Within the online learning shell, courses should include dedicated information on the following:

- **Online Learning Guidance:** Many students simply do not know how to effectively learn online. Students' lack of knowledge in how to navigate the online course, interact asynchronously or utilize virtual resources can generate a host of questions and challenges. In order to reduce the demands on individual instructors, it is important to integrate generalized "how to" information to support students who are not familiar with online education. Online learning guidance may include topics such as: interacting in threaded discussions, evaluating online sources, time management, navigating the online classroom, accessing online resources, communicating effectively online, or collaborating asynchronously. The integration of this information within the online classroom allows students to more effectively help themselves and provides instructors with a quick, easy reference that they can direct struggling students toward.

- **Technical Support**: Technical support considerations include challenges with logging into the learning management system, difficulties posting or submitting, general computer issues, and/or downloading course content or software. While the online classroom does not need to contain *all* technical support information, it is useful to provide guidance on the most common topics and highlight how to contact university technical support for other issues or questions.

- **Library Resources:** Students should be provided not only with information on how to access the online library, but also on generalized information for utilizing the library portal. In addition to "how to" information for utilizing the online library, it is also beneficial to provide generalized information literacy resources to help students evaluate the value and utility of the information they will find online (from the library or otherwise).

- **Writing Resources:** Online courses involve a considerable amount of writing, thus students who struggle with writing (both native and non-native English writers) are at a particular disadvantage in the online format. Rather than invest extensive individualized instructional time providing feedback on general writing issues, it is useful to integrate generalized writing resources and guidance. In addition, if the university offers a writing center, course guidelines should provide clear guidance on how students should utilize available resources in relation to the expectations and assignments of the course. In addition, course developers should check with the university writing center to see if resources are available for inclusion in the online course shell.

- **Tutoring:** Increasingly, colleges and universities are providing dedicated tutoring services to support individual student needs. Course design should provide detailed information about available tutoring services and highlight circumstances under which students should actively seek tutoring support. As students are often unfamil-

iar with how traditional services work in the online environment, it is helpful to provide additional context on the timing, expectations, and format of online tutoring.

- **Academic Advising:** Students may have questions about future courses and/or the sequencing of courses in an online program. While it is not necessary to provide curriculum maps within each online course, it is essential to provide students with a point-of-contact that they can reach out to for questions that pertain beyond the scope of the current course. It is also useful to build basic curricular integration into the online course to highlight the relationship of current course knowledge to related areas in the program.

To be effective, course design must go beyond telling students what is available to showing students how to utilize the resources. Rather than simply providing a list of available resources and support, it is helpful to tell students when and how to utilize each resource. Likewise, students need clear and direct information that tells them when and how to utilize which support services. For example, information on technical support resources might say:

If you are experiencing technical challenges related to logging into the online classroom, posting in the discussion forums or submitting your assignments, please contact technical support for assistance. While you should notify your instructor if you are experiencing issues that prevent you from meeting course requirements, your instructor is not able to help you troubleshoot individual technical difficulties. There are three ways that you can contact technical support: 1) call xxx.xxx.xxxx Monday through Friday from 8:00am to 8:00pm CST; 2) email (insert link) at any time and expect a response within 24 hours; or 3) chat via (insert link) 7-days a week from 6:00am to

11:00pm CST. In addition, you can browse the technical support FAQ at (insert link) to look for answers to common questions and issues.

Providing guidance on resources and support will not eliminate all tangential questions to the instructor; the goal is simply to reduce the number of supplemental questions that the instructor receives. Decreasing time invested in responding to individual questions frees additional time to be dedicated toward instructional activities that have a greater impact on the overall student learning experience.

3. Ensure consistency in course design.

Just as instructors have limited time available to dedicate to each course, students also have limited time and cognitive energy that they can invest to mastering course requirements and learning objectives. Ideally, the goal is to have all cognitive time and energy focused on learning course material and NOT on navigating the online course or locating necessary course components. Within each module of the online course, information should be presented in a consistent format with consistent expectations (Lee, Dickerson & Winslow, 2012). For example, modules may be formatted in which information is always presented in the following order:

- Topic overview
- Learning objectives
- Required reading (textbook or additional external resources)
- Instructional content (text, videos, demonstrations, etc.)
- Summary
- Interaction activities or discussions
- Required assignments or deliverables
- Supplemental resources

Providing information and expectations in a consistent manner limits the amount of time each instructor must dedicate to course administration and related student questions. Consistency in the patterns of expectations and due dates (for example, assignments always due on Wednesday night or discussion posts always due by Monday at midnight) reduces student confusion and decreases the number of missed assignments that result as a function of schedule confusion. From an instructional perspective, this not only decreases student inquiries about the expectations, but also helps to ensure that all students are progressing through the course together. By promoting a cohesive flow, instructors are not required to split their time working with students who are behind schedule and can dedicate increased cognitive energy into the interactions and activities of the majority of students.

4. Limit supplemental technology.

Advances in educational technology are accelerating at a rapid pace; there are programs, websites and mobile apps available to support virtually every learning activity and pedagogical goal. While deliberate and intentional integration of instructional technology can be beneficial in enhancing the online learning experience, the potential gains associated with the integration of each new technology must be balanced with the increased time necessary to ensure effective utilization (Dailey, Mandernach & Donnelli, 2008; Dailey, Mandernach & Donnelli, 2010; Donnelli, Dailey & Mandernach, 2009; Mandernach, 2006). Not only is there a learning curve associated with mastering each technology (for both students and faculty), but each new technology raises a host of student questions concerning technical and functional usage. To minimize time investment in technology issues, course design should prioritize the use of existing LMS features prior to integration of supplemental technologies. When existing LMS features are insufficient to support learning objectives, select supplemental technologies with consideration of the time investment required for initial integration, maintenance and on-going use. In addition, technology integration decisions should consider factors such as longevity of the company, company-based technology support and customer service ratings to ensure that time invested in the integration of a supplemental technology is justified by the potential of both short- and long-term gains.

5.   Integrate automated activities with verification and feedback.

There is overwhelming evidence supporting the value of immediate, individualized feedback in fostering student learning, engagement and satisfaction with the online learning experience (Chickering & Ehrmann, 2008; Espasa & Meneses, 2010; Gibbs & Simpson, 2004; Mandernach, 2005; Mandernach & Garrett, 2014; Mandernach, 2013; Mason & Brunning, 2001; Nicol & Macfarlane-Dick, 2006). The challenge in providing this type of detailed, on-going feedback lies in the time investment required to do so. Simply put, there is one instructor and many students in each online course (in most cases 15-30 students; in extreme cases, 100+ students); in this one-on-many learning environment, it is not feasible for instructors to provide immediate, individualized feedback to each student on every learning activity. To address this challenge, online courses should integrate a range of activities and assignments that provide automated feedback in response to individual student submissions. For example:

- **Pretest Check:** Prior to each module, provide students a true/false based pretest that checks their baseline level of understanding of key course information. Answers can be provided as Java-script based roll-over images in which additional information pops up as a function of which answer is selected by the student.
- **Case Studies:** To promote application of course information, provide case studies (either text-based or video) in which students can select from a range of possible actions; based upon their selection, the system provides additional information on the implications of their choice in relation to the key issues or concepts in the course.
- **Mastery Quizzes:** Utilize the testing feature available in the system to provide mastery quizzes at the conclusion of each module in which students can self-test their knowledge of key course concepts. Set the quiz features to provide detailed feedback that not only verifies correct responses but provides elaborative information to help correct errors in understanding and point students toward textbook or instructional information that explains each error. In addition, is it valuable to set the quiz settings to allow the students to repeat the quiz activity until they are able to demonstrate mastery of course concepts.
- **Flashcards:** A range of automated flash-card programs are available to facilitate students' mastery of course-related terminology. Integrate a flash-card program directly into the LMS to provide students the opportunity to review key vocabulary and receive immediate feedback on the accuracy of their understanding.
- **Study Guides:** Automate study guides utilizing matching activities, crosswords, game-show formats and/or a host of other technology-mediated activities that encourage students to interact with course material in a manner that provides immediate feedback in response to student answers.

While it is common to integrate automated quizzes and tests into online courses as a component of graded work, it is equally important (if not *more* important) to seek out strategies that allow students to receive feedback on their understanding in a format that is not monitored or linked to course grades. Not only does the integration of automated feedback enhance student learning and satisfaction, but it does so in a manner that requires virtually no time from the course instructor. Further, the increased level of baseline knowledge that students can gain from these activities allows course discussions and interactions to focus on higher-order levels of learning.

6.   Provide opportunities for individualization.

One of the limitations of synchronous, one-on-many learning environments (typical in most face-to-face classrooms) is that all students are required to engage with course material at the same time, at the same pace and utilizing the same activities. The challenges associated with balancing the needs of diverse students in a synchronous classroom mandates that instructors target the average; as a result, instructors must then dedicate additional time to support students who deviate from this average in either pace or level of learning. In contrast, the online classroom can be designed to allow students the opportunity to select learning paths and activities that are individualized to their unique needs and preferences. By integrating different types of learning materials and variations in self-checks, mastery activities and supplemental resources, the online classroom can be more effectively tailored to support individual students. The result for instructors is a teaching environment in which the course material, as opposed to the instructor, provides variations in individual support. This type of online course design allows students who need additional resources, time or support to seek out necessary assistance without increasing the time demands placed on the instructor.

7.   Develop an instructor manual for each course.

Whether the online course is created by the instructor or by an independent course developer, it is important to create a support document that fosters efficient teaching. The reality in most courses is that there are similar goals, challenges and patterns of student interaction that occur from one section of a course to another and from one semester to the next. As such, one of the most effective ways to foster efficiency in online teaching is to provide faculty with tools, resources and materials that are tailored to each course. For example:

- **Lesson Plans:** Lesson plans should include a brief rationale highlighting the goal of each activity and assignment in relation to the learning objectives. The lesson plan is designed to provide a conceptual background so that instructors can facilitate interactions in a manner that ensures students gain the necessary knowledge, skills and abilities at the conclusion of each activity.
- **Concept Maps for Interaction:** Depending on the discussion question, the link between the initial discussion question and the ultimate learning objective may or may not be clear. In order to ensure effective and efficient facilitation of the discussions, it is important to provide instructors with a concept map that shows the connection between the discussion question, relevant course concepts and learning goals for that activity. In addition, it is helpful to include a list of relevant follow-up questions, links to related resources that may inform the discussion, and stock discussion thread posts that may be utilized depending on the flow and direction of the discussion.
- **Just-in-Time Teaching Resources:** In many cases, there is supplemental information that is not necessary to include in the overall course development, but may be useful depending on the nature of the student population and the dynamics of a given class. These types of "just-in-time" teaching resources may include announcements, case studies, resource links, discussion postings and other supplemental materials. It is helpful to provide instructors

with a bank of these stock resources (organized according to module and resource type) that can be customized and integrated as mandated by course needs.

- **Feedback Banks:** Research clearly highlights the importance of individual, customized feedback in the promotion of student learning and student satisfaction. To help ensure that instructors have the necessary time to provide individualized feedback, create a feedback bank of generalized comments that are widely applicable across student artifacts. Feedback banks may target issues such as grammar, formatting, writing style, or conceptual understanding (see Mandernach, Zafonte & Taylor, 2015, for an example of an APA style feedback bank). Instructors can then utilize these feedback banks (see Mandernach, 2014, for information on how to integrate feedback banks most efficiently) to save time on common feedback items so that there is additional time available to provide individualized comments in relation to students' work.

These materials are not designed to replace the individualized, custom contributions of each instructor; rather, providing instructors with a bank of information and resources that are tailored to their particular course prevents individual faculty from wasting time by repeatedly "reinventing the wheel." These course-specific resources can be customized, as necessary, by faculty to meet the needs of their students, but faculty save considerable time as they are not required to develop all supporting materials from scratch. As such, online instructors can invest the time saved to instructional activities that promote interaction, presence and participation.

8. Create a feedback loop for continuous course improvement.

Regardless of how well your online course is designed, there will always be areas that can be improved. To ensure that online course design is as current, effective and efficient as it can be, create formal feedback loop in which instructors can record challenges, ideas, technical issues (such as broken links) and resources that can be addressed in the course design for subsequent semesters. The value of the feedback loop lies in addressing issues on a system level to prevent individual instructors from repeatedly investing time to respond to student inquiries or difficulties.

Saving Time through Course Design

It is important to note that the course design recommendations provided here do not, in and of themselves, foster increased interaction or teaching presence. Rather, these recommendations provide the baseline for creating an efficient, high-quality course that allows instructors to streamline repetitive teaching activities to save time. Once the online course is in place, faculty must ensure that they are utilizing teaching time both effectively and efficiently. To do this, faculty need to manage their teaching time wisely and dedicate saved time toward instructional activities that have the greatest impact in fostering an interactive learning experience.

MANAGING ONLINE TEACHING TIME

All faculty bring a set of assumptions to their online teaching, many of these assumptions are grounded in the traditional, face-to-face environment. As faculty enter the online classroom, they attempt to apply traditional concepts of education to the novel context of the virtual classroom. But, these mental maps are often ineffective in the online environment (Black & Gregersen, 2008) and fail to provide faculty with an effective mindset from which to facilitate a quality learning experience. Complicating the issue further, one of the greatest barriers to successful managing online teaching time is the sheer ubiquity of the learning environment. The ever-present nature of the online classroom inhibits focused and effective teaching; with an endless list of possibilities and no naturally occurring boundaries to define the experience, it is challenging for online faculty to prioritize teaching tasks. In this ubiquitous environment, online instructors must differentiate between being busy and being effective. The key is not simple time-on-task; to create an effective online learning experience, faculty need to ensure adequate time investment to the teaching activities that foster the greatest student learning and satisfaction. Essential to this task is the need for online instructors to change their mindset, create boundaries, automate processes, and focus attention.

Change Your Mindset

Effective online teaching, teaching that prioritizes interaction, presence and participation, starts with a change in mindset. One of the biggest pitfalls instructors make as they begin teaching online is that they assume the practices they used in the face-to-face classroom will translate to the online environment. A key difference between online and face-to-face teaching is that online instruction can require considerable more time than its traditional, face-to-face counterpart (Mandernach, Forrest, Babuzke, & Manaker, 2009). From the need to type or record communications to monitoring discussion boards, many of the tasks that are often taken for granted in the traditional classroom become more overt and thus more time consuming; the one-on-many tasks of the face-to-face classroom shift to one-on-one in the online environment. This expansion of the time required to teach an online class challenges an instructor's ability to effectively complete all essential teaching tasks.

An online instructor's time and energy are limited. It is challenging in the online classroom, as it is in life, to realize that every choice is a trade-off; faculty must choose between many good things to focus on the most important (Friedman, 2008). The first step in doing so is realizing that attention, energy, and willpower are all subject to exhaustion. For instance, Baumeister et al. (1998) asked participants to sit in a room for five minutes with chocolate chip cookies and to not eat them, but to instead eat radishes. Later the participants were asked to solve a complex puzzle. Those in the group that did not have to resist the chocolate chip cookies and eat radishes (control group) persisted longer in trying to solve the puzzles than those that where in the "temptation group." In fact, results indicated that just five minutes of trying to resist chocolate chip cookies reduced the persistence time of the tempted participants from 21 minutes to eight minutes (Baumeister et al., 1998). This study illustrates that the cognitive demand of exerting simple self-control can lead to diminished energy available for other tasks.

Additional research reiterates the impact of cognitive load in decision-making. Iyengar and Lepper (2000) set up two tables of jams for taste testing; one table contained six choices while the other contained 24. As predicted, the table with 24 choices had many more taste testers; however, the table with only six choices resulted in more purchases. Three percent of participants made a purchase in the case of the table with 24 choices, while 30% made a purchase in the case of the limited choice table (Iyengar & Lepper, 2000).

Both of these studies illustrate the importance of cognitive overload; more decisions often result in decision fatigue in which individuals fail to make a choice or make a poor choice. The lessons learned from these studies can be applied to effective online teaching. Because there are so many available opportunities via the ubiquity of the online classroom it follows that decision fatigue can be a major problem in maintaining energy and effective teaching practices. The goal of an effective online teacher is not to find more to do, but rather to focus on what really matters by creating artificial constraints on pedagogical choices. There are several applicable ways to do this in the virtual classroom: 1) save energy by creating materials one time and reusing them; 2) create routines and procedures that can be followed on a daily, weekly, monthly, and course basis; and 3) focus on what you love first. These may seem like simple principles, but put into practice, each approach can help reduce cognitive overload and decision fatigue so that online instructors can maintain the energy levels necessary to teach effectively.

Create Boundaries

In the traditional classroom there are built-in limits, stops and parameters. For example, face-to-face classes last a specified length of time and are scheduled on specific days. In contrast, online classes, especially asynchronous ones, are potentially "in session" whenever a person is at the computer. This lack of boundaries challenges traditional views on time management; the result is disconnect between what instructors believe is important and where they actually spend their time. For example, research finds that while online instructors believe interaction in discussion forums has a greater impact on the online learning experience, they spend more of their time grading student work (Mandernach, Forrest, Babuzke, & Manaker, 2009). To overcome focus barriers and mismatched time allocation, online instructors should: 1) shift their mindset from what is "thought" to be important to what "is" important with more time spent on teaching and less on administrative tasks; 2) integrate technology to make administrative tasks efficient and meaningful to free up time for teaching; and 3) create time management structures that prioritize the most meaningful teaching tasks.

Many online instructors will contest that there just isn't enough time to get everything done. Parkinson (1955) put forth an earth-shattering proposition for time management. After studying civil servants in Britain, Parkinson noted that work would often fill the available time that was allotted (Parkinson, 1955). In short, the amount of time needed to complete a task contracts or expands depending on the time constraints. Applying this knowledge, self-imposed, artificial constraints can be implemented to make online teaching more efficient. For example, in the online classroom instructors can create heard stops and starts, batch similar tasks together, and utilize simultaneity in task management.

Friedman (2008) recommends creating hard boundaries between different activities in order to more effectively focus on each. In a physical classroom these boundaries already exist (i.e., when you leave the classroom, class is over and direct instruction ceases). But without these natural boundaries in the online classroom, it is important to create set times to start and stop each teaching task. If not, it is easy for instructors to fall into the mentality of always being "in" their online courses while accomplishing little. There are a number of technologies available to facilitate in time management and monitoring:

- Timers to monitor and give yourself deadlines for certain tasks (see http://www.orzeszek.org/dev/timer/ or https://itunes.apple.com/us/app/alinof-timer/id512464723?mt=12); or
- Applications that track where you spend your time on your computer or one that allows you to log where you spend your time elsewhere (see https://www.rescue-time.com/ and https://itunes.apple.com/us/app/my-minutes-simple-personal/id553366149?mt=8).

Similarly it is important to create barriers between tasks by grouping like tasks together for more efficient completion. This idea, often referred to as batching, is the simple concept of lumping similar tasks together rather than jumping from one type of task to a different one. For instance, it is helpful to batch respond to e-mails at specific times of the day (Ferris, 2009). Through batching, it is possible to efficiently move through your messages in a few sessions each day rather than jumping from task-to-task to individually respond to each one. Batching creates continuity by allowing instructors to focus on one task at a time. Creating blocks of time dedicated to one task, rather than dividing attention on many different tasks promotes focus and efficiency (Ferris, 2009) and reduces inefficiencies attributed to multitasking (Foroughi, Werner, Nelson, & Boehm-Davis, 2014). Effective tools for facilitating batching include:

- Robust e-mail filters that summarize unimportant e-mails on a set schedule (see www.sanebox.com);
- Task management software to schedule items for specific days or times (see https://trello.com or www.evernote.com);
- Repository of course announcements, discussion forum posts and replies, or other repetitive materials and/or resources and store them in a cloud storage service; or
- Comment banks or text expanding software to quickly insert comments when grading (see http://www.wavget.com/typeitin.html or https://www.trankynam.com/atext/).

While multitasking that jumps from one activity to the next is inefficient, Friedman (2008) advocates for simultaneity, a form of dual processing that is more efficient. This type of multitasking allows an individual to do two things at once but recognizes that performance on each task will be slightly decreased. For example, using a text-to-speech app to listen to course materials while exercising can be a good strategy. Albeit, your exercise regimen or your study will not be as focused as if you did either task independently. Other examples can include listening to audio books during a commute or grading if commuting by public transit. Recommended resources include:

- Text-to-speech applications for listening to course materials or articles for class (see http://www.voicedream.com); or
- Audio books (such as https://librivox.org/ or new ones on audible.com or summaries of books on http://www.getabstract.com/en/).

Automate Processes

Another important idea in saving energy is the notion of fast-thinking and slow-thinking (Khaneman, 2011). Nobel winning economist Daniel Kahneman (2011) persuasively argues that our brain processes information in two general ways: automatic and deliberate thinking. Automatic thinking, or fast thinking, is the type of thinking we do habitually. It is idea that our brains must process so much information at any given time that it relies on shortcuts or heuristics to be able to help us function. On the other hand slow thinking is the type of thinking we have to do when confronted with a complicated task for the first time. In a slow thinking situation there are no previous experiences, shortcuts, or generalizations to rely on so we have to think through it step-by-step (Khaneman, 2011). The goal is to move as many tasks or mental processes involved in the online teaching process from slow- to fast-thinking. In essence by creating routines and habits we are able to reduce the amount of deliberate slow thinking that taxes our mental reserves and use the excess energy for our most important tasks.

For example, having a number of templates for e-mails to students' redundant questions, not only saves time, but also reduces the amount of energy required to help students gain accurate information. Creating routines on the other hand can utilize the principal of frontloading to help classroom tasks become more effortless. For instance, having specific days during the week for grading or course material creation can allow for greater focus on current tasks because we know that we have specific times for specific things. There are several tools that can be helpful in moving things into a more systematic approach:

- Electronic to-do lists (see Apple's "Reminders" or "Tasks" in Microsoft Office);
- Template functions in e-mail applications that allowed for the creation of multiple e-mail templates; or
- Screen capture applications to record messages and/or give directions (see http://www.screencast-o-matic.com or http://www.techsmith.com/jing-features.html).

Focus Your Attention

Also, it can be helpful to focus on the teaching tasks one enjoys first before moving on to the less desirable teaching tasks. In this way online instructors can prioritize online discussion forum posting over grading. This helps create an artificial constraint where more time is spent on desirable activities and less time on necessary but less engaging tasks. Managing our energy in this way can help make the ubiquity of online classes more manageable and lead to better time management strategies.

While staying on one task at a time is theoretically feasible, it is challenging to do with multiple windows open on the computer (each of which is vying for attention). There are a number of technologies available that can help to limit your focus while working online:

- Applications that allow only one or select programs to be run at a time on your computer (see http://selfcontrolapp.com or http://www.getconcentrating.com); or

- Applications that block distracting websites and social media (see http://anti-social.cc).

Teaching More Efficiently

Inherent in these strategies toward more efficient online instruction is the application of the Pareto Principle (Pareto, 1971). In the early 1900s an economist, Vilfredo Pareto, noticed that 80% of the produce in his garden came from 20% of the plants. Later, investigating this idea further, Pareto found that roughly 80% of the wealth in his home country was held by 20% of the population (Pareto, 1971). Others have found this pattern in other places as well which has led to the Pareto Principle, the notion that 20% of inputs result in 80% of results (Pressman, 1982). Following this line of reasoning, it is important to identify the most important instructional strategies and tasks to focus on during online instruction and preparation as a dedicated amount of focused interaction can account for the greatest overall course impact.

Dedicated attention to strategies that promote efficiency in online teaching are essential to creating sufficient time for instructors to foster an interactive, engaging learning environment. As previously discussed, implementation of efficiency principles don't automatically translate into increased presence or participation. Teaching strategies that maximize presence do require intentional time and energy, thus it is essential that instructors create the necessary time and invest this saved time into pedagogical approaches that impact students in meaningful ways.

TEACHING ACTIVITIES TO FOSTER ENGAGEMENT, PRESENCE AND INTERACTION

Optimal student learning occurs during focused and engaging instruction; it is essential that online instructors focus their time on instructional strategies with the greatest potential impact to ensure that students receive the best learning experience. Online teaching takes considerable time inside and outside of the classroom (Van de Vord & Pogue, 2012). With this in mind, it is important to dedicate faculty time investment to effective teaching strategies with proven effectiveness. Research finds that student-teacher interaction is the most important aspect of online teaching, and also the most time consuming (Mandernach, Forrest, Babuzke, & Manaker, 2009). The increase in time commitment is due to high use of one-on-one interactions that are required for online instruction (Sword, 2012).

Faculty commit the most time to two teaching tasks: grading papers and assignments, as well as facilitating discussion threads (Mandernach, Hudson, & Wise, 2013). While grading is an important part of teaching and learning, it can be argued that in the online classroom grading provides summative feedback after learning should have already taken place. This feedback is useful for providing students with ideas for improvement of future assignments, but often the students are already moving on to the next topic before they receive this feedback. As such, online faculty are advised to shift their time to emphasize formative instructional activities that have a greater impact on the active learning process.

Online discussion forums provide an area where teaching can take place more quickly. It is important for instructors to use quality interactions in this area to provide students with the instruction they need to be successful, while keeping them engaged in the discussion. The discussion forum is not only a place where instructors are able to teach and reteach, students can also learn from each other by sharing and gaining knowledge (Nandi, Hamilton, & Harland, 2012). Online faculty can maximize the value and impact of online interactions by implementing strategies to focus students'

attention, address conceptual errors, personalize the online learning experience, and establishing teaching presence.

Focus Students' Attention

A major component of effective learning in both online and traditional face-to-face courses is student engagement. Piaget's constructivism theory posited that learning is most effective when meaningful participation that includes discourse is employed (Wadsworth, 2003). This learning can be most effective through engagement between all participants in an online class. One strategy to help in this area is to find ways to provide activities that are content related and provide the opportunity for students to interact with one another (Dixson, 2010). It is most important to find ways to connect students to the instructor and classmates through meaningful communications (Dixson, 2010). In adding this dynamic to the online classroom, instructor presence will be strengthened and the feelings of isolation will diminish among the students. This will in tune produce an environment of engagement and optimal learning. It is clear that online learning is only going to grow in popularity, so it is important to reflect on strategies that will engage learners in the online classroom. Online instructors must provide activities that are content related and provide the opportunity for students to interact with one another (Dixson, 2010). Increasing student participation and engagement in the online classroom will lead to a better learning and teaching experience for the group.

Address Conceptual Errors

Classroom Assessment Techniques (CATs) are a valuable formative assessment technique that can be used in online discussions to focus students' attention on key topics or conceptual errors. CATs are quick checks for understanding that were originally designed for the traditional face-to-face college classroom (Angelo & Cross, 1993). CATs have been found to be effective in the online classroom for increasing student success on assignments (Holbeck, Bergquist, & Lees, 2014) and increased participation in the discussion forum (Steele & Dyer, 2014). When added to the discussion forum in the classroom, CATs are able to provide students and instructors more opportunities to interact in a meaningful way with both peers and the instructor. Some CATs that are effective in the online classroom are:

- **Minute Paper:** In the minute paper, students write for 60 seconds about what they have learned about a topic.
- **Muddiest Point:** The muddiest point requires students to state what is least clear to them about a topic.
- **One Sentence Summary:** A one sentence summary asks students to summarize what they have learned using one sentence.
- **Background Knowledge Probe:** In the background knowledge probe, students reflect on what they have previously learned about a topic.
- **Misconception/Preconception Check:** This CAT asks students to share what they know about a topic and allows instructors to see where the gaps are in their background knowledge.

In each of these CATs, the instructor can post an additional content-related question in the discussion forum for student responses. These should be based on the objective of the current week. The student responses will identify gaps in the learning prior to the summative assessment. They can also provide an area where vibrant discussions can take place between students, instructor, and classmates. To maximize the value of CATs, it is essential to close the loop on all CATs (Angelo & Cross, 1993). In other words, when implementing a CAT

in the online classroom, it is extremely important to provide feedback to the students. This can be done for individual students, small groups, or as a single summary at the end of the week. The goal of the CAT is to provide students with additional support for their learning of the objectives.

One other strategy that works well in the online classroom discussion forum is the KWL chart. KWL was identified by Ogle (1986). This formative assessment identifies what students already know (K), what they want to learn (W), and finally what they have learned (L; Ogle, 1986). Due to the structure of most online classrooms, timing for the KWL is very important. The K and W portion must be delivered at the beginning of the week, while the L must be given toward the end without being too late for any teaching opportunities before the summative assessment. Much like CATs, this gives another opportunity for the entire class to interact while providing the instructor with more opportunities to redirect and reteach, as well as provide affirmation of student learning.

Personalize the Online Classroom

The nature of online classrooms can create feelings of isolation if the discussions and interactions are not adequate. When students are connected to the instructor and classmates, students feel that they are a part of a learning community (Young & Bruce, 2011) and are more likely to be satisfied with online education (Angelino, Williams, & Natvig, 2007). This interaction (both with classmates and the instructor) leads to increased learning and engagement (Handelsman, Briggs, Sullivan & Towler, 2005; Skinner, Wellborn & Connell, 1990; Young & Bruce, 2011). Student interaction is often more pronounced in an online class because there is not the opportunity to "hide in the back of the class" (Meyer & McNeal, 2011). In order to decrease the psychological distance and sense of isolation between students and instructors in the online classroom, instructors should consider a "narrative approach" to teaching, integrate technology to create a virtual class presence, and create mini-lessons to engage learners.

A useful strategy to create better presence and connection in the online classroom is to find ways to make the students feel persuaded that the instructor is close at hand. In line with this using the power of personal story or narrative can help decrease the psychological distance between students and the teacher and create empathy and persuade students to remember the information conveyed. One study found that when hearers or readers of the story are engrossed in a story they are transported into the plot; these researchers found that people in this state were more likely to have long-term changes in attitude in line with the story, leading the authors to argue that story may be one of the best vehicles for persuasion (Van, De, Wetzels, & Visconti, 2014). Zak (2013) found that watching a dramatic video greatly effected viewers in their subsequent giving behaviors. With those in the group who watched the dramatic video gave more than those that did not. This is all to say that it may be possible to evoke more presence via storytelling in the classroom. Several tools for doing this are:

- Screen capturing and video creation tools (see www.animoto.com and http://www.techsmith.com/jing.html);
- Avatar software (http://www.voki.com/); or
- Personalized mini-lessons (http://creately.com/, http://www.sliderocket.com/ or http://prezi.com/).

The Internet and Web 2.0 tools have made it easier to collaborate and find information than ever before. Online instructors can create a vibrant online learning community through the use of Web 2.0 tools, content repositories, and tools that foster increased collaboration.

Web 2.0 Tools

The number of available educational technologies continues to grow; this trend benefits online instructors and students by taking the engagement level to a higher level (Mandernach & Taylor, 2011; Revere & Kovach, 2011). With the power of these applications, students can interact with one another and the instructor from anywhere in the world. The number of Web 2.0 tools that are available to online instructors is immense, and they have a variety of utilizations to impact student learning in their power to allow students and instructors to collaborate, communicate, create, and share information (Kitsantas & Dabbagh, 2011).

Web 2.0 tools can be broken up into three categories: communication tools, experience- and resource-sharing tools, and social networking tools (Kitsantas & Dabbagh, 2011). Communication tools include email and web-conferencing tools. Communication tools can be used to build connections and relationships with classmates and instructors in the online classroom (Kitsantas & Dabbagh, 2011). Some effective applications in the area of communication tools are those that use audio and visual (Revere & Kovach, 2011), such as:

- Wimba (www.wimba.com)
- VoiceThread (http://voicethread.com/)
- Pow-Wow-Now (www.powwownow.com)
- Skype (www.skype.com)
- Join.Me (www.join.me)

These tools can be used for live dialogue between all members of an online class in the form of synchronous discussions, debates, and presentations. It also provides the opportunity for one-to-one tutoring or assistance when necessary. The synchronous nature of these tools allows for student and instructor trust formation and relationship building. In addition, it gives the instructors an opportunity to provide asynchronous audio feedback on an assignment (Revere & Kovach, 2011). Communication tools support both group learning as well as self-regulated learning (Kisantas & Dabbagh, 2011). They can also be useful for students when they want to seek support for a specific assignment or task (Kitsantas & Dabbagh, 2011).

Experience- and resource-sharing tools comprise the tools that can be used for collaboration with the benefit of fostering social interactions between students (Kitsantas & Dabbagh, 2011). Two examples of this kind of technology are weblogs (blogs) and wikis. Blogs are useful to both instructors and students in an online classroom by providing instructor feedback to students' self-reflections about topics (Kitsantas & Dabbagh, 2011). They may also serve the purpose of developing a digital portfolio for students. Further, blogs create a space for creative expression and learning of basic web design skills, as most blog platforms allow for the customization of templates etc. This freedom to personalize and experiment in the designing of ones own blog may inspire a greater level of ownership on the part of the student. Two web-based applications that work well for blogs (Kitsantas & Dabbagh, 2011) are:

- WordPress (https://wordpress.com/)
- Twitter (https://twitter.com/)

Wikis allow anyone with access to the Internet to create, access, and edit a Web site that can be shared with multiple people (Rosen & Nelson, 2008). Wikis may be used for collaborative projects in online classes, which may also allow instructors to give feedback during the project (Kitsantas & Dabbagh, 2011). It also allows peer feedback on the same project. Wikis may also be used to give added value to notes, lectures, and announcements, which could all benefit student learning and engagement in the classroom (Kitsantas & Dabbagh, 2011). Three examples of Wiki applications are:

- Wiki (www.wiki.com)
- PBWorks (www.pbworks.com)
- Wikispaces (https://www.wikispaces.com/)

The third category of Web 2.0 applications is social networking tools. In the traditional sense, social media is used to connect with friends and family, but it has great benefits for building a learning community. Leaners have reported that they feel that social media use in classes helps them in learning subject manner by extending their learning (Veletsianos & Navarette, 2012). In the same study, learners reported a strong social connection to their classmates and more connection to the course itself. This can become a community of practice that could lead to lifelong learning (Kitsantas & Dabbagh, 2011). In addition, social networking tools can be a great way to spur student initiated contextualized learning. In this way the social networking tools can allow students to collaboratively work on questions from class together on a platform that may be closer to "real life" than static content in a learning management system. Instructors can set up their own resource page on a social media platform where students can find extra resources as well as communicate with each other. Some of the social networking tools that may be used for teaching and learning are:

- Facebook (https://www.facebook.com/)
- LinkedIn (https://www.linkedin.com/)
- Ning (http://www.ning.com/)
- MySpace (https://myspace.com/)
- Pintrest (http://pinterest.com/)

Web 2.0 tools as discussed above can take some of the isolation feelings from students and add to social presence in the online classroom (Veletsiano & Navarette, 2012). These web-based applications not only connect students to one another, they also connect them to the world. Each has their own use in the online classroom to effectively connect students by giving them extra opportunities to communicate, collaborate, and cooperate. Web 2.0 tools also allow the instructor to integrate technologies that students may already be familiar with; .using relevant resources that students are currently using may ease the resistance of adoption of new learning activities. This is only a small snapshot of the available web-based tools that can enhance the teaching and learning in an online classroom. As new technologies emerge, new possibilities arise to foster student connection, contextualize learning, enhance communication, and support collaboration in creative ways.

Content Repositories

In the modern teaching era, there is an abundance of available resources for online instructors. A simple Google search of any topic will present an instructor with an abundance of ideas. Some of these web based tools are available for online instructors to post and share ideas with one another. The easiest of these to navigate is YouTube (Minguillon, Sicilia, & Lamb, 2011). Instructors are able to create videos and post them either publicly, or privately, online. These videos are also very easy to share with others through email and/or text message. A YouTube Education area is available for instructors that focuses completely on the area of teaching and learning.

MERLOT (Multimedia Educational Resources for Learning and Online Teaching; http://www.merlot.org) maintains a content repository that is useful for online instructors (Cervone, 2012). This resource gives online educators the opportunity to share ideas with others as well as keep an individual area that is private. It requires registration to get started. This is a great way to collaborate with other online instructors in similar content areas. Additional digital repositories include (Cervone, 2012):

- DOOR (http://door.sourceforge.net/)
- Ariadne (http://www.ariadne-cms.org/)
- Rhaptos (https://trac.cnx.org/)

Another way that faculty can share resources is through social media (Moran, Seaman, & Tinti-Kane, 2011). Many education areas have been set up in Facebook and LinkedIn. Twitter and Pinterest are also social networks that are used to share information and collaborate with other online educators. Social media has many applications for the online classroom, which should not be overlooked by instructors.

Establishing Teaching Presence

It is important that faculty members are present in the online classroom. Online students may feel disconnected from the rest of the class when they are alone at their computer (Veletsiano & Navarette, 2012). It is important to look at the different strategies that online instructors can utilize to minimize the transactional distance of the virtual classroom. The theory of constructivism posits that students learn best when actively engaged in their learning (Jones, 2011). Learners perceive a strong faculty presence in an online classroom when the instructor encourages students to interact with other classmates, interaction between students and the instructor, and active participation with the course materials (Jones, 2011).

Communication between students and faculty is not only a best practice in online teaching, it is also an expectation from students (Belair, 2012). Student satisfaction relies on the level of communication with the instructor as well as availability (Belair, 2012). Some strategies that can assure a high level of teacher presence through communication in an online classroom are:

- Personal introduction from the instructor at the beginning of the course

- Personalized weekly announcements
- Welcome calls and/or emails
- Prompt answers to student questions
- Virtual office hours
- Weekly wrap-ups
- Prompt and thorough assignment feedback
- Use of formative assessment in discussion forums
- Regular participation in discussion forums
- Adding additional resources, videos, CATs, and other instructional support

It is important to note that online classes do not teach themselves, which makes it important for instructors to show up and teach (Ragan, n.d.). The most important role of online teaching is to interact with the students in the classroom, as well as keeping a watch on the progress of all students (Ragan, n.d.).

Faculty engagement in the online classroom is perceived as very important to student learning experiences (Holzweiss, Joyner, Fuller, Henderson, & Young, 2014). Engagement requires more than someone who answers questions promptly or returns emails efficiently. Students also look for reassurance, encouragement, and guidance from their instructors (Holzweiss et al., 2014). Along with this engagement with the instructor, students also view the benefits of interacting with both their peers and the instructor. In fact, students see the most benefit through interacting with faculty regardless of purpose (Holzweiss et al., 2014).

FUTURE DIRECTIONS AND RECOMMENDATIONS

As online education continues to grow in popularity, it is important to create a pool of efficient, effective, capable online instructors. As a viable and popular modality of instructional delivery, online instructors strive to create the best learning experience as possible for their students. Future

research should focus on which instructional methods lead to the highest student learning outcomes with an inclusion of non-cognitive variables (i.e., engagement, satisfaction, retention). This research should include all instructor tasks such as course development and design strategies, strategies to bridge the distance between online learners and instructors, and implementation of technology to support student learning as well providing automated feedback for learning activities.

An integral piece of online education is in the rich, dynamic discussions created in the discussion forums. These discussions include instructor-student and student-student interactions. Forums are essential to the student experience and learning process in each class; as such, research should examine the most effective strategies for fostering learning, interaction and connection in the discussion forums. This should include the addition of formative assessments to check student understanding as well as techniques to foster increased critical thinking. In addition to being an area to implement formative assessments, the discussion forums also allow personalization of the online classroom and provide an efficient means for instructors to establish teaching presence. Further examination of the most effective strategies to maximize the value of discussion forums is necessary.

An important consideration for online teaching is time management for instructors. Online teaching takes a considerable amount of time; the quality of the experience is directly influenced by the degree to which instructors can dedicate time toward instructional tasks that have the greatest impact. Future research should focus on using instructional time efficiently. Specifically, instructional strategies that create a student-centered learning environment should be examined, which create a more student engagement with less instructor time commitments.

Finally, individual instructional tasks should be examined to show which are the most efficient and effective for creating positive student learning outcomes. For example, does it make more sense for instructors to spend a majority of time on grading, or actively participating in a discussion forum? Research is needed to examine the relative benefits of each instructional activity in relation to the time investment required to implement the instructional strategy.

Online learning is growing at a quick pace. In addition, new technologies and online teaching strategies are being developed at a high rate. As a collective community of online educators, it is important to document the successes and struggles of each new strategy. Student learning outcomes are the primary concern of online teaching. Ongoing research is necessary to examine the efficiency and efficacy of online teaching with the goal of improving the student learning experience.

CONCLUSION

In order to maximize student interaction and engagement, it is essential that instructors create an online environment with focused attention to instructional strategies that provide the greatest impact. While time is always a consideration in the selection of teaching approaches, online faculty should strive to create an efficient course and implement time management strategies that ensure they have adequate time to dedicate to creating an engaging, interactive online classroom. Available time should be dedicated to interacting with students in meaningful ways via integration of formative assessment strategies, technologies that foster personalization and development of meaningful teaching supplements. With this focus in mind online faculty members have the opportunity to not only add greater value in their virtual classrooms, but also create greater work/life balance that is particularly hard to establish within the ubiquitous online teaching environment.

REFERENCES

Allen, I. E., & Seaman. (2013). *Changing course ten years of tracking online education in the United States.* Babson Survey Research Group and Quahog Research Group. Retrieved from: http://www.onlinelearningsurvey.com/highered.html

Anderson, T. (2004). Teaching in an online learning context. In T. Anderson & F. Elloumi (Eds.), Theory and practice of online learning (pp. 273-294). Athabasca: Athabasca University.

Anderson, T., Rourke, L., Garrison, D. R., & Archer, W. (2001). Assessing teaching presence in a computer conferencing context. *Journal of Asynchronous Learning Networks, 5*(2), 1–17.

Angelino, L. M., Williams, F. K., & Natvig, D. (2007). Strategies to engage online students and reduce attrition rates. *Journal of Educators Online, 4,* 2.

Angelo, T. A., & Cross, P. K. (1993). *Classroom assessment techniques: A handbook for college teachers.* San Francisco: Jossey-Bass.

Aragon, S. R. (2003). Creating social presence in online environments. *New Directions for Adult and Continuing Education, 2003*(100), 57–68. doi:10.1002/ace.119

Baumeister, R. F. (1998). The self. In D. T. Gilbert, S. T. Fiske, & G. Lindzey (Eds.), *Handbook of social psychology* (4th ed.; pp. 680–740). New York: McGraw-Hill.

Belair, M. (2012). The investigation of virtual school communications. *Tech Trends: Linking Research & Practice to Improve Learning, 56*(4), 26–33. doi:10.1007/s11528-012-0584-2

Black, J. S., Gregersen, H. B., & Black, J. S. (2008). *It starts with one: Changing individuals changes organizations.* Upper Saddle River, NJ: Wharton School Pub.

Bowen, W. G., & Lack, K. A. (2013). Higher education in the digital age. Princeton, NJ: Princeton University Press.

Cavanaugh, J. (2005). Teaching online: A time comparison. *Journal of Distance Learning Administration Content, 8*(1).

Cervone, H. F. (2012). Managing digital libraries: The view from 30,000 feet. *OCLC Systems & Services: International Digital Library Perspectives, 28*(1), 14–16.

Chickering, A., & Ehrmann, S. C. (2008). *Implementing the seven principles: Technology as lever*. The TLT Group. Retrieved from: http://www. tltgroup.org/programs/seven.html

Conciêção, S. C. (2006). Faculty lived experiences in the online environment. *Adult Education Quarterly, 5*(1), 26–45. doi:10.1177/1059601106292247

Dailey, A., Mandernach, B., & Donnelli, E. (2008). The multimedia dilemma: Questioning beyond the what to the why. *Online Classroom*. Retrieved from http://www.magnapubs.com/issues/magnapubs_oc/8_12/news/602064-1.html

Dailey, A., Mandernach, B. J., & Donnelli, E. (2010). Teaching with technology: A more meaningful learning experience starts with two questions. *Faculty Focus*. Retrieved from http://www.facultyfocus.com/?p=11357

Dixson, M. D. (2010). Creating effective student engagement in online courses: What do students find engaging? *Journal of the Scholarship of Teaching and Learning, 10*(2), 1–13.

Donnelli, E., Dailey, A., & Mandernach, B. J. (2009). Toward a philosophy of multimedia inclusion. *Journal of Online Learning and Teaching, 5*(1), 149–154.

Easton, S. S. (2003). Clarifying the instructor's role in online distance learning. *Communication Education, 32*(2), 87–105. doi:10.1080/03634520302470

Espasa, A., & Meneses, J. (2010). Analyzing feedback processes in an online teaching and learning environment: An exploratory study. *Higher Education, 277*(3). doi:10.1007/s10734-009-9247-4

Ferriss, T. (2009). *The 4-hour workweek: Escape 9-5, live anywhere, and join the new rich*. New York: Crown Publishers.

Foroughi, C. K., Werner, N. E., Nelson, E. T., & Boehm-Davis, D. A. (2014). Do interruptions affect quality of work? *Human Factors, 56*(7), 1262–1271. doi:10.1177/0018720814531786

Friedman, S. D. (2008). *Total leadership: Be a better leader, have a richer life*. Boston: Harvard Business Press.

Garrison, D. R., & Anderson, T. (2003). *E-Learning in the 21st century: A framework for research and practice*. London: Routledge Falmer. doi:10.4324/9780203166093

Garrison, D. R., Anderson, T., & Archer, W. (2000). Critical inquiry in a text-based environment: Computer conferencing in higher education. *The Internet and Higher Education, 2*(2-3), 87–105. doi:10.1016/S1096-7516(00)00016-6

Garrison, D. R., & Archer, W. (2000). *A transactional perspective on teaching and learning: A framework for adult and higher education*. Oxford, UK: Pergamon.

Garrison, D. R., & Cleveland-Innes, M. (2005). Facilitating cognitive presence in online learning: Interaction is not enough. *American Journal of Distance Education, 19*(3), 133–148. doi:10.1207/s15389286ajde1903_2

Gibbs, G., & Simpson, C. (2004). Conditions under which assessment supports students' learning. *Learning and Teaching in Higher Education, 1*, 3–31.

Graham, C., Cagiltay, K., Craner, J., Lim, B., & Duffy, T. M. (2000). *Teaching in a web-based distance learning environment: An evaluation summary based on four courses.* Center for Research on Learning and Technology Technical Report No. 13-00. Indiana University Bloomington. Retrieved from: http://crlt.indiana.edu/publications/crlt00-13.pdf

Gunawardena, C. N. (1995). Social presence theory and implications for interaction and collaborative learning in computer conferences. *International Journal of Educational Telecommunications, 1*(2/3), 147–166.

Gunawardena, C. N., & Zittle, F. J. (1997). Social presence as a predictor of satisfaction within a computer-mediated conferencing environment. *American Journal of Distance Education, 11*(3), 8–26. doi:10.1080/08923649709526970

Handelsman, M. M., Briggs, W. L., Sullivan, N., & Towler, A. (2005). A measure of college student course engagement. *The Journal of Educational Research, 98*(3), 184–192. doi:10.3200/JOER.98.3.184-192

Holbeck, R., Bergquist, E., & Lees, S. (2014). Classroom assessment techniques: Checking for student understanding in an introductory university success course. *Journal of Instructional Research, 3*, 38–42.

Holzweiss, P. C., Joyner, S. A., Fuller, M. B., Henderson, S., & Young, R. (2014). Online graduate students' perceptions of best learning experiences. *Distance Education, 35*(3), 311–323. doi:10.1080/01587919.2015.955262

Iyengar, S. S., & Lepper, M. R. (2000). When choice is demotivating: Can one desire too much of a good thing? *Journal of Personality and Social Psychology, 79*(6), 995–1006. doi:10.1037/0022-3514.79.6.995 PMID:11138768

Johnson, D. R. (2013). Technological change and professional control in the professoriate. *Science, Technology & Human Values, 38*(1), 126–149. doi:10.1177/0162243911430236

Johnson, T. R. (2013). *Did I really go to Harvard if I got my degree taking online classes?* Retrieved from: http://www.theatlantic.com/education/archive/2013/09/did-i-really-go-to-harvard-if-i-got-my-degree-taking-online-classes/279644/

Jones, I. M. (2011). Can you see me now? Defining teaching presence in the online classroom through building a learning community. *Journal of Legal Studies Education, 28*(1), 67–116. doi:10.1111/j.1744-1722.2010.01085.x

Kahneman, D. (2011). *Thinking, fast and slow.* New York: Farrar, Straus and Giroux.

Kitsantas, A., & Dabbagh, N. (2011). The role of Web 2.0 technologies in self-regulated learning. *New Directions for Teaching and Learning, 126*(126), 99–106. doi:10.1002/tl.448

Lee, C.-Y., Dickerson, J., & Winslow, J. (2012). An analysis of organizational approaches to online course structures. *Online Journal of Distance Learning Administration, 15*(1). Retrieved from http://www.westga.edu/~distance/ojdla/spring151/lee_dickerson_winslow.html

Lowenthal, P. R., & Parscal, T. (2008). Teaching presence. *The Learning Curve, 3*(4), 1-2, 4.

Mandernach, B. J. (2005). Relative effectiveness of computer-based and human feedback for enhancing student learning. *Journal of Educators Online, 2*(1). Retrieved from www.thejeo.com

Mandernach, B. J. (2006). The evolution of online course development: From basics to bells and back again. *Online Classroom, 2*, 7–8.

Mandernach, B. J. (2013). Better feedback in less time. *Online Classroom, 13*(6), 1, 7.

Mandernach, B. J. (2014). Efficient and effective feedback in the online classroom. In J. Garrett (Ed.), *A Magna Publications White Paper*. Madison, WI: Magna Publications, Inc.

Mandernach, B. J., Forrest, K., Babuzke, J., & Manaker, L. (2009). The role of instructor interactivity in promoting critical thinking in online and face-to-face classrooms. *Online Journal of Learning and Teaching, 5*(1), 49–62.

Mandernach, B. J., & Garrett, J. (2014). Effective feedback strategies for the online classroom. *Faculty Focus*. Retrieved from: http://www.facultyfocus.com/articles/online-education/effective-feedback-strategies-online-classroom/

Mandernach, B. J., Gonzales, R. L., & Garrett, A. L. (2006). An examination of online instructor presence via threaded discussion participation. *Journal of Online Learning and Teaching, 2*(4), 248–260.

Mandernach, B. J., Hudson, S., & Wise, S. (2013). Where has the time gone? Faculty activities and time commitments in the online classroom. *Journal of Educators Online, 10*(2). Retrieved from http://www.thejeo.com/Archives/Volume10Number2/MandernachHudsonWise.pdf

Mandernach, B. J., & Taylor, S. S. (2011). Web 2.0 applications to foster student engagement. In R. L. Miller, E. Amsel, B. Kowalewski, B. Beins, K. Keith, & B. Peden (Eds.), *Promoting student engagement, volume 1: Programs, techniques and opportunities*. Syracuse, NY: Society for the Teaching of Psychology. Available from the STP web site: http://teachpsych.org/ebooks/pse2011/vol1/index.php

Mandernach, B. J., Zafonte, M., & Taylor, C. (in press). Instructional Strategies to Improve College Students' APA Style Writing. *International Journal of Teaching and Learning in Higher Education.*

Mason, J., & Brunning, R. (2001). *Providing feedback in computer-based instruction: What the research tell us*. Centre of Instructional Innovation, University of Nebraska-Lincoln. Retrieved from: http://dwb.unl.edu/Edit/MB/MasonBruning.html

Meyer, K. A., & McNeal, L. (2011). How online faculty improve student learning productivity. *Journal of Asynchronous Learning Networks, 15*(3), 37–53.

Minguillon, J., Sicilia, M., & Lamb, B. (2011). From content management to e-learning content repositories. *Content Management for E-Learning*. Retrieved from http://content.schweitzer-online.de/static/content/catalog/newbooks/978/144/196/9781441969583/9781441969583_Excerpt_001.pdf

Moran, M., Seaman, J., & Tinti-Kane, H. (2011). Teaching, learning, and sharing: How today's higher education faculty use social media. *Pearson Learning Solutions*. Retrieved from http://files.eric.ed.gov/fulltext/ED535130.pdf

Nandi, D., Hamilton, M., & Harland, J. (2012). Evaluating the quality of interaction in asynchronous discussion forums in fully online courses. *Distance Education, 33*(1), 5–30. doi:10.1080/01587919.2012.667957

Nicol, D., & Macfarlane-Dick, D. (2006). Formative assessment and self-regulated learning: A model and seven principles of good practice. *Studies in Higher Education, 31*(2), 199–218. doi:10.1080/03075070600572090

Ogle, D. M. (1986). K-W-L: A model that develops active reading of expository text. *The Reading Teacher, 39*(6), 564–570. doi:10.1598/RT.39.6.11

Palloff, R. N., & Pratt, K. (1999). *Building learning communities in cyberspace*. San Francisco: Jossey-Bass Inc.

Pareto, V. (1971). *Manual of political economy*. New York: A.M. Kelley.

Parkinson, C. (1955). *Parkinson's law*. Retrieved from: http://www.economist.com/node/14116121

Pressman, R. S. (1982). *Software engineering: A practitioner's approach*. New York: McGraw-Hill.

Ragan, L. C. (n.d.). 10 principles of effective online teaching: Best practices in distance education. *Faculty Focus*. Retrieved from http://www.facultyfocus.com/free-reports/principles-of-effective-online-teaching-best-practices-in-distance-education/

Richardson, J. C., & Swan, K. (2003). Examining social presence in online courses in relation to students' perceived learning and satisfaction. *Journal of Asynchronous Learning Networks, 7*(1), 68–88.

Rourke, L., Anderson, T., Garrison, D. R., & Archer, W. (1999). Assessing social presence in asynchronous, text-based computer conferencing. *Journal of Distance Education, 14*(3), 51–70.

Salmon, G. (2000). *E-moderating: The key to teaching and learning online*. London: Kogan Page. doi:10.4324/9780203465424

Sheridan, R. (2006). Reducing the online instructor's workload. *EDUCAUSE Quarterly, 29*(3), 65–67.

Skinner, E. A., Wellborn, J. G., & Connell, J. P. (1990). What it takes to do well in school and whether I've got it: A process model of perceived control and children's engagement and achievement in school. *Journal of Educational Psychology, 82*(1), 22–32. doi:10.1037/0022-0663.82.1.22

So, H. J. (2005). The content analysis of social presence and collaborative learning behavior patterns in a computer-mediated learning environment. In C.-K. Looi, D. Jonassen, & M. Ikeda (Eds.), *The 13th International Conference on Computers in Education* (pp. 413-419). Amsterdam: IOS Press.

Swan, K. (2001). Virtual interaction: Design factors affecting student satisfaction and perceived learning in asynchronous online courses. *Distance Education, 22*(2), 306–331. doi:10.1080/0158791010220208

Swan, K. (2003). Learning effectiveness online: What the research tells us. In J. Bourne & J. C. Moore (Eds.), *Elements of quality online education, practice and direction* (pp. 13–45). Needham, MA: Sloan Center for Online Education.

Tu, C.-H. (2000). On-line learning migration: From social learning theory to social presence theory in a CMC environment. *Journal of Network and Computer Applications, 2*(1), 27–37. doi:10.1006/jnca.1999.0099

Van, L. T., De, R. K., Wetzels, M., & Visconti, L. M. (2014). The extended transportation-imagery model: A meta-analysis of the antecedents and consequences of consumers' narrative transportation. *The Journal of Consumer Research, 40*(5), 797–817. doi:10.1086/673383

Van De Vord, R., & Pogue, K. (2012). Teaching time investment: Does online really take more time than face-to-face? *International Review of Research in Open and Distance Learning, 13*. Retrieved from http://www.irrodl.org/index.php /irrodl/article/view/1190/2212

Worley, W., & Tesdell, L. (2009). Instructor time and effort in online and face-to-face teaching: Lessons learned. *IEEE Transactions on Professional Communication, 52*(2), 138–151. doi:10.1109/ TPC.2009.2017990

Yu, C., & Brandenburg, T. (2006). I would have had more success if...: The reflections and tribulations of a first-time online instructor. *Journal of Technology Studies, 32*(1), 43–52.

Zak, P. J. (2013). *The moral molecule: The source of love and prosperity*. New York: Dutton.

KEY TERMS AND DEFINITIONS

Classroom Assessment Techniques (CATS): Short, informal, formative assessment activities that provide quick insight into student learning; results from CATS often used to guide teaching and learning activities.

Content Repository: A collection of online or digital content with management capabilities to store, organize or retrieve information.

Efficient Teaching: An approach to instruction that streamlines repetitive, administrative or supplemental instructional tasks to ensure adequate time for higher-order teaching activities.

Fast-Thinking Processes: Strategy for automatically processing information that produces quick, efficient decisions with minimal conscious attention.

Online Course Development: The process of creating the foundation of an online course that includes developing the course structure, format, learning materials, activities, and assignments.

Pareto Principle: The notion that 80% of effects can be attributed to 20% of causes.

Simultaneity: Engaging in two activities at the same time.

Student Engagement: The extent to which students are motivated, invested and interested in their learning experiences; reflects students' attitudes toward the learning process.

Web 2.0: Internet applications that go beyond static presentation of information; often allow users to create or edit multimedia, collaborate with other users or interact with content.

Chapter 12
Instructor–Driven Strategies for Establishing and Sustaining Social Presence

Michelle Kilburn
Southeast Missouri State University, USA

Martha Henckell
Southeast Missouri State University, USA

David Starrett
Southeast Missouri State University, USA

ABSTRACT

The purpose of this chapter is to provide readers with strategies and techniques to enhance social interaction/presence within the online learning environment. A discussion of current definitions and the importance of social media will be discussed, as well as examples for use in the online classroom. Proven effective and interactive instructional components (i.e., instructor response time, video lecturing, and pedagogical considerations) are included as best practices and quality assurance guidelines. Topics in this chapter include types of social media tools available, examples of appropriate use in higher education, and recommended strategies to assist faculty in identifying the best tool to match the pedagogical goal. With a wide variety of experiences and knowledge regarding the topic, the authors provide unique perspectives including: teaching in the online environment, instructional design, oversight of online programs, technology training/user services, quality assurance, and faculty/student support.

INTRODUCTION

In a face-to-face course, students are gathered together in one physical location with the instructor. It could be said that students experience a general sense of comfort from being near others. It could be further stated this sense of comfort develops as a result of being with peers who share similar experiences, common bonds, and/or desires. For whatever reason students take comfort being with others; people, by and large, are social beings.

DOI: 10.4018/978-1-4666-9582-5.ch012

Establishing a social presence in an online course helps meet the needs of students who may experience feelings of isolation when learning from a distance. The use of social media can help initiate a social presence, and, with proper usage, maintain the social presence throughout the course. Social media can be defined as any medium that enables connectivity and interaction among users and communities (Haenlein, 2010). Many formalized social media platforms exist, including Twitter, Facebook, Instagram, and You-Tube, among many others. With mobile devices being almost ubiquitous in society, the ease of participating in social interactions is as easy as a few taps on a smartphone. Instructors should take this opportunity to incorporate student expectations and experiences with the implementation of social media directly into the classroom.

Faculty have varying experiences with devices and social media tools. Instructional design plays a crucial role in the effective use of these tools. Faculty should avoid using a tool just because it is "cool" or the newest trend. With this in mind, proven effective and interactive instructional components (instructor response time, video lecturing, and pedagogical considerations) are included in the chapter to encourage instructors not only to incorporate, but to properly use these tools in their online classroom to promote social presence and constructivist pedagogy. Not only student-to-student engagement, but, also student-to-faculty interaction will be considered. With the increase in ownership, or easy access to mobile technology among students, instructors now have the means to take advantage of the many opportunities/tools available.

Technology continues to evolve with new types of devices. New ways of interacting are constantly appearing on the scene. The method by which people interact with each other continues to change, evidenced most prominently in younger generations, though even baby-boomers and older generations make use of these tools. Significant amounts of interaction can occur in the electronic environment. As a result, new cultures of social interaction have appeared, along with new social meeting and sharing places.

Like many tools, proper use can take some training, and inappropriate use can easily turn a good thing bad. Effective use can significantly enhance the learning environment while ineffective use can lead to many unintended and poor outcomes.

Social presence plays a crucial role in fostering student-teacher interaction in the online environment. The purpose of this chapter will be to provide readers with strategies and techniques to enhance the social interaction/presence within the online learning environment. Ideas for incorporating social media tools (wikis, blogs, Twitter, Facebook, digital media, etc.), will provide instructors with various channels for engaging students. Best practices will be discussed to assist faculty in identifying the best tool to match the pedagogical goal. It should be noted, though, that not all of the strategies mentioned in this chapter will work for all instructors in every class.

BACKGROUND

Social presence has many definitions but literature and recent research shows the lack of a consistent definition. Short, Williams, and Christie (1976), often considered the genitors of social presence theory, define social presence as the "degree of salience of the other person in the interaction and the consequent salience of the interpersonal relationships" (p.65). Tu (2000, 2001) states that in the online environment, social presence rests upon three dimensions: social context (task orientation, privacy, topics, social relationships and social process), online communication, and interactivity. In general, important aspects of social presence, as they relate to the current discussion, include sense of community, awareness of others in an interaction, immediacy and intimacy of social interactions (Gunawardena & Zittle, 1997; Rice, 1993; Tu & McIssac, 2002; Walther, 1992).

Social presence is not unique to the online environment, nor is it new. It has existed on college campuses and in classrooms long before the advent of technology and online learning environments. For effective online learning, it is an important aspect that needs to be recognized and embraced. The online learning environment, by its asynchronous and remote nature, does not immediately create an environment conducive to fostering social presence. Mechanisms need to be in place and environments need to be developed that will allow for, encourage, support and reward social presence. Interactions between student and instructor and student and student are enhanced with the proper tools and the proper use of those tools.

THE IMPORTANCE OF SOCIAL PRESENCE

In order to understand the importance of social presence, consideration must be given to the benefits it affords the educator and the student, or what could occur, if absent from the online course. First, social presence is a significant tool for improving instructional effectiveness, regardless of the medium, and is a very significant feature of online learning environments. According to the results of a study performed by Wei et al. (2012): "In online classrooms, improving learners' social presence can enhance their learning interaction, which would lead to improvement in their learning performance" (p. 540).

Second, social presence can create a learning environment in which participants are at ease with the instructor and other students. This environment is more conducive to effective learning and can play a significant role in the quality of learning and the learning environment. Kehrwald (2008) found that social presence defines how students relate to each other which can affect their ability to communicate effectively, and thus learn effectively. Wei, Chen and Kinshuk, (2012) add to this perspective and state that without social presence, learning interaction suffers and leads to negative effects on learning performance.

Third, a learning environment that is perceived as warm, collegial, and approachable for all involved - and the ability to instigate, sustain, and support cognitive and affective learning objectives by making group interactions appealing, engaging, and intrinsically rewarding - are further benefits of high levels of social presence (Rourke, et al., 1999). Finally, Gunawardena and Zittle (1997) found that social presence is a strong predictor of satisfaction in online environments and later suggested that social presence facilitates building of trust and self-disclosure in the same environments (Gunawardena, et al., 2001). Further evidence of student satisfaction, derived from high levels of social presence and positive correlation between social presence and degree of perceived learning outcomes, has been found (Shin, 2002; Gunawardena, et al., 2001).

An important consideration in creating opportunities for social presence is an understanding and comfort with the value of using it in the online classroom environment. There are many tools available for creating social presence. Appropriate use of those tools is important for creating effective learning opportunities. When reviewing tools and strategies for creating social presence, consider how each tool might allow for, encourage or promote social interaction. Identify the indicators of social presence, especially quality social presence. Building a community is key. Is there opportunity to encourage community development? What type of interactions can and do occur between student and instructor? How about between students in the class? What is the type or level of interaction? In the following sections, we discuss some of these tools and best practices for effective use, along with a brief discussion of quality assurance.

WEB 2.0

In the same manner as common practice in software, the web is assigned a version. And, as with software, the version number increases when functional advancements are added. Web 1.0 can be referred to and easily summed up as the passive Web version. Information was absorbed but interaction with the information didn't occur (Solomon & Schrum, 2007). While its arrival on the educational scene created change, Web 1.0 is now considered old news. When Web 2.0 arrived on the horizon, educators had cause to rejoice. Following the belief that learning is improved with student interactions (DePietro, 2013), Web 2.0 delivered the ability for students to collaborate, participate, interact, and build social networks (Solomon & Schrum, 2007).

In addition to websites, Web 2.0 offers the educator an entire toolbox to engage students. Among these tools, educators can choose from wikis, interactive forums, and applications (a.k.a. apps) available from mobile devices (DePietro, 2013). When used properly, these applications can facilitate social networking, as well as allow for easy digital file-sharing of photos, videos, and audio (Wilson, et. al., 2011). Along with the addition of numerous new tools, possibly the most exciting are the results that can be gained with proper use of them - an increase in the collective intellect of the class (Solomon & Schrum, 2007).

EDUCATION 3.0

Once education evolved into a design embraced by the industrial revolution, little change has occurred in the technique or practice of teaching (Kharbach, 2013). A star was born with the onset of Web 1.0, which then begot Education 1.0. With Education 1.0, the pedagogical process remained somewhat stagnant in nature. Teaching remained straightforward in manner, where the instructor continued to hold all of the knowledge, and imparted the knowledge to the passive student. While Web 1.0 was able to shake up the educational process somewhat, great strides in educational format failed to occur. This was through no fault of any one particular person or group of people, but rather the capabilities and purpose of the Web at that time.

In 2003-2004, the educational buzz focused on Web 2.0, and therefore, Education 2.0 (Keats & Schmidt, 2007). Web 2.0 resulted from the evolution of the World Wide Web, changing from "an *access* technology into a *participation* technology" (Keats & Schmidt, 2007, para. 2). Unfortunately, many instructors have been slow in adapting with a change to their teaching style, failing to take advantage of what Web 2.0 can offer. Institutions with instructors who are lagging behind on the use of Web 2.0 functionalities (and still practicing Education 1.0 pedagogy) will only fall further behind. Early adopters of Education 3.0 can influence the way students are taught and learn. This could then result in a change of student educational expectations.

Differences between Education 2.0 and 3.0 educators may be considered incremental by some who have embraced Education 2.0 but drastic by those still teaching in the Education 1.0. Education 3.0 educators can be characterized as clever planners of student collaborations that will result in knowledge construction. These educators encourage student creativity by using open, flexible learning activities. Moving away from the confines of the institution's learning management system, students are allowed to play a stronger role in the selection of applications in the learning environment. Social networking assignments have no discipline, institution, or national boundaries, and thereby promote higher level thinking in the broadest sense. Institutions that embrace and practice the doctrines of Education 3.0 can be expected to take the lead in moving education into a new and exciting frontier.

TOOLS OF THE TRADE

Decisions used to be simple, or at least they appeared to be simple. According to Siri, there are 49 types of sodas, yet according to ChaCha.com, there are over 100, just in the United States alone. The World Wide Web now offers so much more to the consumer, to the student and to the educator, that making choices is a significant component of surfing the Web. It is no wonder that students experience difficulty choosing which source to use for their course work. It is no wonder faculty struggle with choosing which technology to use in their classroom. Because there are so many options now available on the web, choosing the right technology for maximizing the learning outcomes can be confusing or simply overwhelming. With the information provided in this section, the goal is to assist faculty with making the right choices when developing strategic approaches for using social media in their courses.

Two of the most common complaints associated with online learning are student isolation and estrangement (Wei, et. al., 2012). With the advent of Web 2.0, instructors have a greater chance of not only combating these issues, but increasing the overall effectiveness of the course. Tools available through Web 2.0 can be incorporated into course design that will take advantage of constructivist teaching strategies and practices. Several tool options, which will be described in this section, can enhance and help sustain a social presence. According to Wei, et. al. "social presence has significant effect on learning interaction which in turn has significant effects on learning performance" (p. 529). Examples for tactically using some of the tools described are based on and demonstrate both cognitive and social constructivism strategies.

1. **Blogs:** Everybody's doing it. Companies like IBM, hospitals like Mayo Clinic, Hollywood movie stars, as well as universities. There are blogs on politics, sports, music; you name

a topic and you are likely going to find a blog related to that subject. According to *WPVirtuoso* (2013), an online blogging magazine, there are over 152,000,000 blogs on the Internet and a new blog is being created somewhere in the world every half second.

Some blogs are deemed useless or frivolous. Consider asking yourself exactly how many people would truly be interested in what you ate for breakfast. Other blogs are followed because they provide information people want and could use, such as to inform a purchase decision or to collect information on a particular topic in a field such as science. Regardless of the reasoning for blogging, blogs provide ways to form social connections. Blogs have been identified as changing the nature of human social interaction whether between people just down the hall or from another country (Guadagno, et. al., 2008). Because many of the bloggers are found to be young and better educated (Gaile, 2013), it only makes sense that educators should take advantage of this medium to create a social presence in their online courses.

2. **Microblogs:** The amount of information to be shared can help in the decision on which tool to use. Some microblogs, such as Twitter, have a limit as to how many characters can be used for each post. Only 140 characters are accommodated with a Twitter post. While Facebook now allows over 60,000 characters for status updates, group, or wall posts, it is generally used like a microblog, displaying only 200 characters with a "read more" link for longer posts. Although limitations may initially carry a negative connotation, blog character limits can train students to express their thoughts, hypothesis, or conclusion in a more concise manner (Tinti-Kane, 2013).

Teaching techniques that may have been used in past online courses can be enhanced and better meet student expectations when adding a tool that students use for social networking in their daily lives. Blogs can serve as the medium for easily updating current curriculum. For example, one instructor recommended using a blog to practice the just-in-time teaching methodology. A check for existing knowledge prior to an assignment could be performed by asking students to post what they know on particular topics. Another example would be collecting brief student responses to questions regarding a reading assignment. Higdon and Topaz (2009) proposed choosing two of the following three reading assignment questions: 1) what is the most difficult part of the material for you or for other students, 2) what is the most interesting part of the material, or 3) how is this material useful/relevant to your intellectual or career interests?

When using a tool, one should keep in mind that overuse can turn students off. Use blogs or any other social tool judicially and only when they add value to or enrich the learning environment. Dependent upon the class, one instructor reports the use of a blog assignment periodically in one class but weekly in another. To stimulate critical thinking, Wilson, et. al. (2011), shared a sample blog assignment that consisted of statements outlining two opposing views, Christopher Columbus and his belief the world is round and Thomas Friedman's (2005) book, *The World is Flat*. The students' charge was to identify and explain three events that led people to believe the world was flat.

As another example, "Current Events" was the headline for a weekly blog. Different media was used for this assignment, including possible choices of articles, vodcasts, or podcasts, which then required responding to a thought provoking question or statement. An example of a question posed: "Is the media unfairly biasing the American public in regards to the upcoming political election (Wilson, et. al., p.67)." Two examples were required from each student. Blogs have the potential to demonstrate whether or not students have mastered the material (Wynn, 2013) and Wilson's article provided prime examples.

3. **Facebook:** College students spend a great amount of personal time communicating. This communication may take place face-to-face, texting, talking on the phone, and/or using social networking sites (Hanson, et. al., 2011). Sturgeon and Walker (2009) found that some of the most effective faculty members were those who developed informal relationships with their students via Facebook. Facebook can serve as a means to network, communicate, recruit, share and generate knowledge (Davis, 2010), maintain existing relationships, form new relationships, aid academic purposes, and follow up on specific agendas (Mazman and Usleul, 2011). McCarthy's (2010) findings suggest that by emphasizing the use of social media to support learning and teaching in higher education, students were drawn into a university culture that encouraged social and academic interaction between peers.

Some faculty who have incorporated Facebook into their classroom have reported that Facebook and other social networks were helping to break down previous borders and barriers (Schaffhauser, 2009). After comparing students' use of Facebook groups with that of educational discussion forums, Schroeder and Greenbowe (2009) found that students at a particular state university used Facebook more dynamically than they used discussion forums in an online community for Organic Chemistry (Greebowe, 2009). In a review of current literature regarding the use of Facebook as an educational environment, Aydin (2012) found that Facebook increased learners' self-efficacy, motivation, self-esteem, positively changed perceptions and attitudes, reduced anxiety and improved foreign and second language writing skills in reading and writing.

In another example, a professor from the University of Kansas established a Facebook group for her class. Her instructions simply stated: Post examples of good or bad design from ads, magazines, books, blogs, websites, etc. Just about anything was "fair game" with the understanding that offensive content would not be tolerated. By Thanksgiving break, the students had posted more than 170 times, with 25 of those posts coming from a single student. Former students continue to revisit the site and continue to post even after their semester has ended (Holsted & Ward, 2013).

4. **Wiki:** When blogs or wikis are mentioned, it generally occurs synonymously, as if the tools are one and the same. In order to make a distinction between blogs and wikis, consider data used in blogs as entries, with a focus on reflections (Huber, 2010), whereas data placed in wikis can build articles, showing a complete record of learning (Huber). Another important distinction is that moderator settings can be established in both blogs and wikis but any member (if private) or anyone (if public, like Wikipedia) can edit or modify content in a wiki (DePietro, 2013).

When teaching in the online environment, instructors are often faced with the additional challenge of finding an efficient and effective means for promoting successful student collaboration. Wikis are websites that can bring students together for collaborative work while the instructor has the added benefit of being able to monitor the process and progress (Wilson, et. al., 2011). They also offer an efficient way to propagate information compiled by the students to the students.

An interesting wiki project, reportedly used by one instructor, involved assigning groups the role of a virtual explorer. This mission required the inclusion of the explorer's biography, results of the exploration, and its impact on the world (Wilson). Throughout the project, students worked communally, viewing and editing the content until a finished product emerged. While the example above may be considered a complete and finished assignment, the same instructor demonstrates how the project doesn't have to end there. Future

students can refer to the student generated articles or expand upon the existing information. An excellent illustration of this process is found in the instructor's government course wiki project.

In this wiki, students researched each candidate and wrote biographies and the position each candidate held on major issues. For future classes, the issues of the Obama administration could be tracked for any variance on his stance during the campaign. Future students may track recent political positions and current happenings of former candidates. Interactive components (e.g., comment postings) will allow students to share viewpoints, discuss positions, and build on ideas over time (Wilson, et. al., 2011, p. 70).

5. **Digital Media or Multimedia Sharing:** As long as it is applicable and interesting, students welcome the use of social media in courses (Wynn, 2013). Instructors are encouraged to include digital media when developing courses, in one form or another (McCabe & Meuter, 2011). Photographs, videos, podcasts, and music can facilitate learning assimilated in the course properly (DePietro, 2013).

We are probably all familiar with the popular saying, 'A picture paints a thousand words'. This statement speaks loudly to the suggestion that images, such as pictures/photographs, engage and provide meaning to their audiences. Using thought provoking questions in conjunction with a well-chosen photograph can aid in creating a social presence while also stimulating the learning process (Wei, et. al., 2012). The questions, as well as other responses to the question, equate with the premise that other people are interacting with or reacting to them while they are using technologies (Lei, et. al., 2011).

One prevalent social media technology that appears to work well with photos and short videos is Instagram. As a free mobile application, available for both iOS and Android systems, access is readily available to most students. In 2013, Instagram was reported to be the third most popular social networking tool used by college student in the United States, with approximately 130 million monthly active users (Salomon, 2013). Based on these statistics and its purported ease of use, Instagram is a likely technology choice for the following examples of engaging students in a learning activity.

One example of its use involved taking a photograph of a surgical tool kit. Placing the focus on one item, a small traveling saw used for amputations, the photo was posted with the question, "Can anyone guess what the saw was used for?" (Salomon, 2013, p. 409).

In a second example shared by Salomon, two phases of student engagement occurred. Phase one required photographing a beautiful old phrenology map used in the course. This time, the question posed was, "Does anyone know what this map of the head is?" (Salomon, 2013, p. 410) Phase two consisted of following up with posts of interesting facts about the history of phrenology.

Wilson, et. al. (2011), shared a course project that culminated in a digital media output. The assignments was to develop and include digital stories in a mock campaign advertisement for local or state political race. Requirements included extensive research on the political candidate, comprised of examining candidate voting records, previous employment, and current political agendas. At the conclusion of the assignment, the digital media projects were shared with classmates. As a result, all students gained a better understanding of the candidates and their issues.

YouTube is also a popular free digital media tool that instructors and students can make use of. For example, in a public speaking course, each group of students were charged with videotaping a 10 minute informative oral presentation consisting of an introduction, three main points, and a conclusion which were then loaded on YouTube. After reviewing the speeches, each group was tasked with posting one thing the other group did well, one area for improvement, one reference to the textbook, and one reference to an additional outside resource for the group's topic (Maybrey & Liu, 2013).

6. **Educational Games:** It's a chain reaction. The use of social media can positively influence the feelings of social presence that, in turn, increases learning interaction, and, in turn, impacts learning performance (Wei, et. al. 2012). Social media holds clout in the educational environment because of its interactive nature (Osterrieder, 2013). While several relatively new ways or approaches of creating an online social community have been discussed in this chapter, the final social media tool to be addresssed is educational games.

Games, while not new to the field of education, take on a social aspect when played in a networked environment. Online students get a sense of presence when connected in real-time with other students and the instructor (Lee, et. al., 2011). There are several other strong arguments for finding an appropriate networked educational game to augment learning: 1) depending upon the game context, student competition or collaboration can be stimulated, 2) overall gratification and memory retention can be improved, 3) teaching or coaching can be automatically customized by the actions taken, and 4) instant feedback (via scores, instant messaging, or chatting) can be gained (Lee).

Covertly teaching students while students enjoy themselves almost seems underhanded or sneaky but that is what can happen when educational games are employed. It's okay that the student enjoys the gaming activity, but the educator seeking a game for the purpose of educating should give credence to the following statement made by Lee, et.al.(2011).

"Education-focused educational games are developed mainly to maximize educational benefits by providing explicit educational contents. Educational effects of these games, therefore, are direct and overt. On the other hand, entertainment-focused games, therefore, are created primarily for entertainment with educational benefits as side effects" (p. 621).

In keeping with the times, educators should be teaching in the Education 3.0 mode and fully utilizing what can be gained by including social media in their online courses. While there are plenty of choices for Web 2.0 tools, instructors must match the correct tool to the assignment and expected outcomes. A brief summary of content, uses, and where to find the tools mentioned in this section, as well as additional tool options, has been provided in Table 1, Social Media Resources. While this is not an exhaustive list, it does contain the most popular and commonly recognized social media options.

The successful use of social media should provide multiple benefits to the learner. Just as with using tools of a particular trade, there are methods and techniques that must be used to ensure the best outcome. In the Quality Assurance section, different techniques are offered for the types of social media tools that were discussed above, as well as best practices and quality standards.

BEST PRACTICES

Research suggests that an instructor's verbal and nonverbal immediacy behaviors can lessen the perceived distance between themselves and their students. By attempting to address this disconnect between the instructor and the student, instructors have the ability to help facilitate (directly or indirectly) effective learning. Increasingly, social networks are being used in teaching (Joyce & Brown, 2009; Weekes, 2008). A pedagogical advantage of social networking applications is that they contribute to active learning (Virkus, 2008).

Pollard, et. al., (2013) have found a significant association between teacher presence and learner motivation in the online environment. Online courses should not be automatically assumed to be

Table 1. Social media resources

Content	Uses	URLs
Short Text Posts	Status updates; concise question posts and responses	http://www.twitter.com* http://www.blogger.com* http://www.edublogs.org* http://www.classblogmeister.com*
Long Text	Reports, research, papers, opinion pieces, and reflections	http://www.mediawiki.org* http://www.facebook.com* http://wordpress.com*
Photos	Photographs or snapshots of field trips, live research; topic related photos to provide context on content	http://www.flickr.com* http://www.instagram.com* http://www.facebook.com* http://www.pinterest.com*
Video	Short clips taken with a camera or smartphone; interviews, techniques, lectures, and talks	http://www.youtube.com* http://www.vimeo.com* http://www.vine.co* http://www.instagram.com*
Audio	Record, share, or save audio, interviews, talks, or podcasts	http://www.audioboom.com*
Publications, portfolio	Academic or professional online presence; build a portfolio to share work with future employers or graduate school	http://www.linkedin.com*

*Help Center, Demonstrations, or Frequently Asked Questions Available

interactive. The perception of instructor presence will depend on the nature, frequency and timeliness of discussions (Eastmond, 1995). In order to develop and maintain presence, instructors may find they must take on various roles including managerial, social and technical (Mupinga, et. al., 2006).

Specifically, interaction has been found to be an important expectation that will influence student satisfaction. Live chat sessions, instant messaging, participation in discussion boards, course announcements, grading feedback and timely response to e-mails are a few examples of ways that instructors can increase social presence in the online environment (Hunter, 2011). The upcoming section will discuss best practices and effective pedagogies that have been (a) identified through research, (b) experienced personally by the authors in their role as instructional designers and online program administrators, and (c) supported by the literature in the development of instructor presence in the online environment.

1. *Respond often and in detail.* The responsiveness of instructor emails and providing feedback affects students' perceptions of instructor presence (Russo & Campbell, 2004). It is important for faculty to communicate regularly with students. This communication should include such components as consistent feedback, responses to postings, and responses to student concerns (Vesely, Bloom & Sherlock, 2007). It should be noted that instructor and student perceptions of "quick feedback" may not be congruent. Faculty should clearly state in their syllabus the expected response time for e-mails (Kilburn, 2013).

It should be noted that although instructor-student interaction is important, instructor presence does not necessarily follow a "more is better" formula. Not all students feel as if a response to every discussion board posting by the instructor is necessary. The focus could be on proactive responses to the learners needs in course information and in quick responses to questions/emails on a case-by-case basis (Su, Bonk, Magjuka, Liu, & Lee, 2005). In one study conducted by Mazzolini and Maddison (2003), an increased number of instructor postings resulted in more infrequent and shorter student messages.

Faculty should strive to maintain a balance between responding often enough to meet the needs of the students and establish a personal presence in the classroom, but strive not to take on such an aggressive role in responding to forum discussions and posts that students are discouraged from interacting with each other.

2. *Add personal elements to the instructor's course.* Students have indicated that seeing a photo or hearing the instructor's voice can create a stronger feeling of instructor presence (Russo & Campbell, 2004). Other elements such as handwritten responses, detailed feedback, video announcements, and instructor introductions of family members may be considered positive interaction from a student perspective (Kilburn, 2013).

Students have better attitudes toward, and learn better in, classes where instructors share aspects of their personal lives (Cayanus, 2004). A social networking site, like Facebook, provides the opportunity for an instructor to quickly and informally share information. Mazer, Murphy, and Simonds (2007) found that students held significantly higher expectations for a course if the instructor shared personal information on Facebook as compared to a course where an instructor who provided only a photo and their academic background.

Using expressions of emotion (e.g., emoticons to indicate emphasis, surprise or confusion), humor, and informal tone have been identified as useful tools in establishing a positive social presence (Nunez, 2005; Scollins-Mantha, 2008).

3. *Utilize video technology.* "For faculty seeking to make a personal connection with their students, incorporating weekly video lectures and announcements appears to have an impact on students' perceptions of interaction and connection with the instructor" (Kilburn, 2013, p. 57). Instructor-created audio and video add an important element of individuality and social presence in the online environment (Lane, 2010).

One student descriptively summarized the benefits of weekly videos and announcements saying, "I have taken online courses, and this instructor is the only one that I actually feel like 'exists.' When you take an online course, it often seems like there is an 'invisible' person grading everything and we have no connection. By actually visually seeing this instructor and picking up pieces of her personality, I feel like there was a real teacher in the class" (Kilburn, 2013, p. 57).

In order to effectively utilize video technology to develop a social presence, faculty should consider the length, format and content of their videos. A 45 minute video of a face-to-face lecture would certainly not be perceived as "interactive" as three 15 minute videos that include some sort of activity (i.e., discussion, wiki post, video response, etc.) to reinforce the material.

4. *Utilize social media when applicable.* Using technology to communicate with students (i.e., Facebook, Twitter, Instagram, etc.) outside of the course management system removes a layer of formality and can allow students to increase their feeling of social presence (Kearns and Frey, 2010). According to Baird and Fisher (2005), today's students are active, wired "always on learners" who "Integrate social media technologies as a tool to support learning" (p. 10).

The use and purpose of the social media needs to be relevant personally, professionally and academically. The instructor should also make sure they are modeling effective use of the social media tool (Dunlap & Lowenthal, 2009). Pearson's "2013 Social Media in Higher Education Survey" collected data from nearly 8,000 instructors and found that the most commonly used social media tools for teaching and learning include: blogs & wikis, podcasts, LinkedIn, Facebook and Twitter. The upcoming section devotes best practices for common social media applications that assist in the development of a social presence in the online environment.

Blogs & Wikis. It is important that instructors provide detailed instructions, provide policies regarding student conduct and allow students time to practice adding content (Schroeder, 2008). Starting a blog/wiki off with at least one example post will help to clarify expectations and give the students a format to mimic (Waldo, 2013). According to Gathman and Talbut (2011) it is important to: (a) make sure the goal of the blog/wiki is clear, (b) decide who the audience will be (i.e., current class, future classes, outside "guests'), (c) identify a moderator/editor who will make sure the entries conform to the goal and format (usually the instructor), and (d) promote a culture of "friendly collaboration" (p. 90).

Make sure your students are engaged and developing/creating content as opposed to just merely consuming content. (Seaman & Tinti-Kane, 2013). Assigning meaningful and authentic activities will also establish an educational value to the blog/wiki for the students (Waldo, 2013). Students need to make the connection between the content generated from the wiki/blog and the learning objectives. Otherwise, the activity's value may be quickly lost and perceived as "busy work." Let your students know the benefits of the blog/wiki and how contributing to the content will assist them in mastering the course. Students often perceive value in points awarded for their efforts. If the blog/wiki is an integral component of the course, faculty should consider the value of the activity and assign points accordingly.

Podcasts & streaming videos. As mentioned above, instructors may be tempted to simply record their 50 minute lectures and post them as effective podcasts/streaming videos for their students. However, for maximum effectiveness it is recommended to keep recordings short, around 10-15 minutes long. Simply making a podcast does not promote learning. The student needs to be able to make the connection between the podcast, the objectives of the course, and the assigned activities.

From an access standpoint, it is important to include multiple output options and obtain copyright clearance for all content. (University of Kansas, 2011). Requiring students to perform a reflective task or asking students to create their own podcasts creates a learning environment where students teach and learn from one another (Dg'ambi & Lombe, 2011).

Facebook. Faculty have voiced concerns about "friending" students on Facebook. For privacy reasons, faculty may not want students having access to all information provided on a private Facebook page (i.e., family outings, recreational activities, etc.) Suggestions for setting parameters on interactions within Facebook include: creating groups instead of "friending" students; developing a professional profile; using public pages. These options allow you to share ideas with your students and they can share with each other without being "friends" on Facebook. If you (or your students) are concerned about privacy issues, groups or public pages may be a way to utilize Facebook while maintaining a high degree of privacy. As with many social media tools it is a good idea to post a clear set of rules of conduct (Gathman & Talbut, 2011).

Micro-blogging/Twitter. It should be noted that other microblogging tools can be used (i.e., Jaikku, Tumblr, MySay, Hictu and Edmodo). Twitter was chosen as the micro-blog of choice because it is well-established, the most easily recognized, has a large participant base and is easily accessible. In order to effectively incorporate Twitter in an online course, Dunlap & Lowenthal (2009) suggest instructors: (a) establish relevance for students, (b) define clear expectations for participation, (c) model effective Twitter use, (d) build twitter-derived results into assessment, and (e) continue to actively participate in Twitter. It is also important to be sure that students are aware of common Twitter language (i.e., hashtag, tweets, common texting language such as LOL, etc). Civility expectations must also be established. Too many unnecessary or irrelevant tweets can be too distracting unless expectations are set.

5. *Make expectations clear to learners.* Online instructors may feel at times they are overstating the obvious but providing clear expectations plays a role in establishing a social presence in an online course. Students often want detailed course information upfront, preferably before the course even begins (Conrad, 2002). In a face-to-face class instructors may hand out an assignment and then spend up to 5 minutes explaining the expectations of the project. It is important not to leave this critical step out of the online learning environment. Communicating clear and concise instructions lets students know the instructor is there and available to answer questions. Expectations such as (1) how attendance will be taken, (2) academic honesty policies, (3) no-tolerance policies for rudeness or incivility, (4) policies on homework submitted past the deadline and (5) grading policies are just a few example of expectations that communicate to an online learner that the instructor is present and active in the course (Kilburn, 2011).

6. *Consider students' access to technology and resources.* It is not the case that all participants enrolling in online courses are

tech-savvy or "digital natives". Even if they are relatively comfortable in the online environment, they may not be involved, or readily accept, social media outlets. Conversely, it is should not be assumed that all "older" students are less technologically capable. Caution should also be taken when generalizing about location, access and availability. Significant disparities continue to limit education opportunities in rural areas of the United States and other countries in the world (Beavis, 2013). Other considerations include bandwidth, mobile device access, computer access, and access to applications/software.

Often one of the most difficult, but necessary, commitments for students in the online environment is 24/7 support. Online students may often choose to complete coursework at odd hours (Institute for Higher Education Policy, 2000).

7. *Recognize the importance of instructional design and administrative support.* Although research indicates that technology can strengthen connections between students and the instructor, less than ¼ of instructors choose to use audio or video-based media on a regular basis in their online courses (Smith & Caruso, 2010). Working from experience as instructional designers, the authors feel that although faculty may see the benefit of incorporating new platforms and technology, they may be overwhelmed (a) by the choices available, (b) by the time it takes to develop new teaching tools in the online environment, (c) by the lack of expertise to utilize them and/or (d) a combination of all of the above. In an effort to address these issues, research suggests that faculty are more satisfied when provided release time for course development and when they

feel the institution values online teaching (Howell, Saba, Lindsay & Williams, 2004; Simonson, Smaldino, Albright & Zvacek, 2009; and Sloan Consortium, 2006).

An instructional designer is often instrumental in building the pedagogical bridge that connects the "cool" idea (i.e., Facebook group, Twitter, podcasts) to a measurable learning outcome. Simply using the newest gadget can quickly become a big distraction versus a learning enhancement. Instructional designers assist faculty in taking great ideas and making them work through the use of technology. It should be noted that technology is only a medium, the driving force should be pedagogy and the learning objectives of the course. An online course should maintain the same quality and integrity of the traditional face-to-face course.

QUALITY ASSURANCE

Hoffman (2010, p.x) notes "Teaching and learning in an online environment is not the same experience as a face-to-face class; professors cannot simply transfer lecture notes into an online environment and expect the same learning outcomes. Online teaching and learning are built from different pedagogical assumptions and require different pedagogical strategies." The upcoming section on quality assurance is devoted to providing guidelines and suggestions for incorporating quality, not only in an online course, but also into an online program.

1. **Quality Matters:** As detailed on the Quality Matters (QM) website (2013):

Quality Matters (QM) is a leader in quality assurance for online education and has received national recognition for its peer-based approach to continuous improvement in online education and student learning. The program features: (a) faculty-centered, continuous improvement models for assuring the quality of online courses through peer review; (b) professional development workshops and certification courses for instructors and online learning professionals and (c) rubrics for applying quality standards to course design.

QM touts they have trained more than 25,000 faculty and instructional design staff. QM looks at the course design and provides a process for peer-to-peer feedback in the continuous improvement of online courses. In order to meet QM standards, a course is not required to meet 100% of the criteria. A score of 85% is considered to be high quality. QM focuses on course design, as opposed to course delivery or academic content. There are eight general standards of course quality:

a. course overview and instruction, assisting the student on getting started in the course;

b. learning objectives, assuring course and module learning objectives are easy to understand;

c. assessment and measurement, measuring the learning objectives;

d. resource and materials, assuring instructional materials are prepared by qualified personnel and are sufficient to cover the learning objectives;

e. learner engagement, focusing on the encouragement of interaction between instructor and students, among students and between students and the course materials;

f. course technology, maintaining consistent navigation in the course;

g. learner support, addressing resources available to ensure student success; and

h. accessibility, ensuring all students have access to all components of the course (Pollacia, McCallister, 2009).

2. **International Association for K-12 Online Learning (iNACOL):** The INACOL group

has developed 11 National Standards for Quality Online Teaching (2011). These standards include:

a. The online teacher knows the primary concepts and structures of effective online instruction and is able to create learning experiences to enable student success

b. The online teacher understands and is able to use a range of technologies, both existing and emerging, that effectively support student learning and engagement in the online environment.

c. The online teacher plans, designs and incorporates strategies to encourage active learning, application, interaction, participation, and collaboration in the online environment.

d. The online teacher promotes student success through clear expectations, prompt responses, and regular feedback.

e. The online teacher, models, guides and encourages legal, ethical, and safe behavior related to technology use.

f. The online teacher is cognizant of the diversity of student academic needs and incorporates accommodations into the online environment.

g. The online teacher demonstrates competencies in creating and implementing assessments in the online learning environment in ways that ensure validity and reliability of the instruments and procedures.

h. The online teacher develops and delivers assessments, projects, and assignments that meet standards-based learning goals and assesses learning progress by measuring student achievement of the learning goals.

i. The online teacher demonstrates competency in using data from assessments and other data sources to modify content and guide student learning.

j. The online teacher interacts in a professional, effective manner with colleagues, parents and other members of the community to support students' success.

k. The online teacher arranges media and content to help students and teachers transfer knowledge more effectively in the online environment.

Assuring quality at the course level is most important for faculty intimately involved in teaching the course, however, best practices for online programs at a more systemic level within the institution is crucial to assure faculty have the support and policies in place to effectively develop a successful course and a positive social presence within the online environment. The upcoming section focuses on institutional best practices to developing quality online courses and programs.

3. **Sloan-C Framework:** The Sloan-C group (Moore, 2002) have outlined a scaffold consisting of five pillars of quality including: learning effectiveness, access, student satisfaction, faculty satisfaction and cost effectiveness. In regard to learning effectiveness, the goal for online courses should be equivalent or better than the institution's other delivery methods. Access consists of providing the means for all qualified and motivated students to complete the course or degree. Access includes three areas of support: academic, administrative and technical. Student satisfaction reflects the effectiveness of all aspects of the education experience. Faculty satisfaction should be considered in order to identify whether faculty find the online teaching experience professionally and personally beneficial. Finally, course

cost effectiveness enables the institution to offer their best educational value to learners (Wang, 2006)

4. **Council of Regional Accrediting Commissions (C-RAC):** The best practices developed by C-RAC include: (a) *institutional context and commitment,* consisting of the budgets, policies, and incorporating online into the institution's role and mission; (b) *curriculum and instruction,* assuring learning outcomes and appropriate rigor, academically quality persons for program oversight, appropriate interaction between instructor and students; (c) *faculty support,* addressing faculty workload, compensation, evaluation and ownership; (d) *student support,* comprising the institution's commitment to resources- administrative, financial and technical- to complete the program, proper communication and services in the areas of library, bookstore, academic advising, financial aid, tutoring, career counseling and technical support; and (e) *evaluation and assessment,* assuring the integrity of student work; improved retention rates, effective use of resources, and effective use of technology to improve pedagogy (Wang, 2006).

5. **Guidelines for Good Practices by the American Federation of Teachers (AFT):** The AFT (2000) recommends 14 strategies to assure quality of distance education (a) faculty must maintain academic control; (2) faculty must have the skill set necessary to teach at a distance; (c) course design should enhance the potential of the medium; (d) students should be fully aware of course requirements; (e) close personal interaction must be maintained; (f) class size should be set through normal faculty channels; (g) courses should cover all materials; (h) experimentation with a wide range of subjects should be encouraged; (i) equivalent

research opportunities must be provided; (j) student assessments should be comparable; (k) equivalent advising opportunities should be available; (l) faculty should maintain creative control over the use and re-use of materials; and (m) full undergraduate degree programs should include same-time same-place coursework; and (n) evaluation of distance coursework should be conducted at all levels (Wang, 2006).

6. **Council for Higher Education Accreditation (CHEA):** The CHEA (2002) identifies seven standards in assuring quality in distance education: (a) institutional mission; (b) institutional organizational structure; (c) institutional resources; (d) curriculum and instruction; (e) faculty support; (f) student support; and (g) student learning outcomes (Wang, 2006).

In summary, although many of the best practices may vary in benchmarks or assessments of quality many of them also contain similar elements including (a) strong institutional commitment; (b) curriculum and instruction that match the rigor of on-campus programs; (c) sufficient faculty support (d) student support and (e) consistent learning outcome assessment (Wang, 2006).

FUTURE RESEARCH DIRECTIONS

Current research regarding student use of social media is based on self-report studies. The authors anticipate that while students report an average daily use of 2.7 hours (Harvard, 2011), actual use might be higher. One area of suggested research is to study the actual use of social media used by students and to ascertain time spent in each platform. A second area for possible future research would be assessing actual student learning outcomes and seek correlation between them and the use of social presence or social media in an online course. Another area of interest might be

determining exactly what it is about Facebook that gives students a sense of belonging/community and if that can be truly replicated in other social media formats and or the learning environment. Finally, researching whether the use of social media removes the barriers of inequity, social class and economic opportunities or if it contributes to those barriers would be of interest to the researchers.

CONCLUSION

Social presence is essential in an online environment. When present, social presence helps create a community, which can then lead to greater student satisfaction, resulting in improved learning performance. With the number of social media tools now available, Education 3.0 online instructors are not asking themselves if social media should be incorporated in their course, but rather which tool can maximize the learning and social benefit of the assignment. Blogs, such as Twitter and Facebook, wikis, and digital media, such as video and podcasts, each offer social connectivity, as well as constructivist style methods (e.g., actively involved in creating/generating content, actively engaged in the learning process). When used appropriately, and not over abundantly, these tools can help faculty integrate social media effectively in their online courses. Students are coming to us as veteran users of multiple social media platforms and tools. Students expect that colleges and the classrooms will support interactions through social media. Perhaps it is our responsibility to take advantage of their familiarity with social media and use it to promote learning.

REFERENCES

Aragon, S. A. (2003). Creating Social Presence in Online Environments. *New Directions for Adult and Continuing Education*, 100.

Aydin, S. (2012). A review of research on Facebook as an educational environment. *Educational Technology Research and Development, 60*(6), 1093–1106. doi:10.1007/s11423-012-9260-7

Baird, D. E., & Fisher, M. (2005). Neomillennial user experience design strategies utilizing social networking media to support "always on" learning styles. *Journal of Educational Technology Systems, 34*(1), 5–32. doi:10.2190/6WMW-47L0-M81Q-12G1

Beavis, C. (2013). Young people, new media and education: Participation and possibilities. *Social Alternatives, 32*(2), 39–44.

Conrad, D. L. (2002). Engagement, excitement, anxiety and fear: Learners' experiences of starting an online course. *Distance Education, 76*(4), 205–226. doi:10.1207/S15389286AJDE1604_2

Davis, L. J. (2010). *Social networking sites as virtual communities of practice: A mixed method study.* (Ph.D. Dissertation). Capella University, Minneapolis, MN.

DePietro, P. (2013). Transforming education with new media: Participatory pedagogy, interactive learning and Web 2.0. *The International Journal of Technology Knowledge in Society, 8*, 1–11.

Diaz, O., Puente, G., Izquierdo, J., & Molina, J. (2013). Harvesting models from web 2.0 databases. *Software & Systems Modeling, 12*(1), 15–34. doi:10.1007/s10270-011-0194-z

Dunlap, J. C., & Lowenthal, P. R. (2009). Tweeting the night away: Using Twitter to enhance social presence. *Journal of Information Systems Education, 20*(2), 129–135.

Eastmond, D. V. (1995). *Alone but together: Adult distance study through computer conferencing.* Cresskill, NJ: Hampton Press.

Friedman, T. L. (2005). *The world is flat.* New York: Farrar, Straus and Giroux.

Gaile, B. (2013) *WPVirtuoso.* Retrieved 4/27/14 from http://www.wpvirtuoso.com/how-many-blogs-are-on-the-internet/

Gathman, A. C., & Talbut, M. H. (2011). Using social networking applications in online teaching. In S. Hoffman (Ed.), *Teaching the humanities online: A practical guide to the virtual classroom.* New York: M.E. Sharpe.

Gonzalez, M. D., Davis, B. P., Lopez, D., Munoz, C., & Soto, G. () Integration of social media in higher education environments. *Insights to a Changing World Journal*, 43-62.

Guadagno, R. E., Okdie, B. M., & Eno, C. A. (2008). Who blogs? Personality predictors of blogging. *Computers in Human Behavior, 24*(5), 1993–2004. doi:10.1016/j.chb.2007.09.001

Gunawardena, C. N., Nolla, A. C., Wilson, P. L., Lopez-Islas, J. R., Ramirez-Angel, N., & Megchun-Alpizar, R. M. (2001). A Cross-Cultural Study of Group Process and Development in Online Conferences. *Distance Education, 22*(1), 85–121. doi:10.1080/0158791010220106

Gunawardena, C. N., & Zittle, F. J. (1997). Social Presence as a Predictor of Satisfaction within a Computer-Mediated Conferencing Environment. *American Journal of Distance Education, 11*(3), 8–26. doi:10.1080/08923649709526970

Haenlein, M. (2010). Users of the world unite! The challenges and opportunities of social media. *Business Horizons, 1*, 59–68.

Hanson, T. L., Drumheller, K., Mallard, J. K., Mckee, C., & Schlegel, P. (2011). Cell phones, text messaging and Facebook: Competing time demands of today's college students. *College Teaching, 59*(1), 23–30. doi:10.1080/87567555.2010.489078

Harvard Institute On Politics. (2011). *IOP youth polling: Spring 2011 survey.* Cambridge, MA: Harvard University Kennedy School of Government.

Higdon, J., & Topaz, C. (2009). Blogs and wikis as instructional tools. *College Teaching*, *57*(2), 105–110. doi:10.3200/CTCH.57.2.105-110

Hoffman, S. (2011). Introduction. In S. Hoffman (Ed.), *Teaching the humanities online: A practical guide to the virtual classroom*. New York: M.E. Sharpe.

Holstead, C., & Ward, D. (2013). Using Facebook and Tumblr to engage students. *The Chronicle of Higher Education*. Retrieved May 1, 2014 from http://chronicle.com/blogs/profhacker/using-facebook-and-tumblr-to-engage-students/47221

Howell, S. L., Seba, F., Lindsay, N. K., & Williams, P. B. (2004). Seven strategies for enabling faculty success in distance education. *The Internet and Higher Education*, *7*(11), 33–49. doi:10.1016/j.iheduc.2003.11.005

Huber, C. (2010). Professional learning 2.0. *Educational Leadership*, *67*(8), 41–46.

Hunter, D. (2011). Who holds the pen? Strategies to student satisfaction scores in online learning environments. *The Business Review, Cambridge*, *18*(2), 75–81.

International Association for Online Learning. (2011). *National standards for quality online teaching*. Retrieved April 21, 2014 from http://www.inacol.org/cms/wp-content/uploads/2013/02/iNACOL_TeachingStandardsv2.pdf

Joyce, K. M., & Brown, A. (2009). *Enhancing social presence in online learning: mediation strategies applied to social networking tools*. Retrieved from www.westga.edu/~distance/ojdla/winter124/joyce124.html

Kearns, L. R., & Frey, I. (n.d.). How do students experiences differ in online LIS programs with and without a residency. *The Library Quarterly*, *77*(4), 359–363.

Keats, D., & Schmidt, J. P. (2007). The genesis and emergence of Education 3.0 in higher education and its potential for Africa. *First Monday*, *12*(3). Retrieved 4/23/14 from http://firstmonday.org/ojs/index.php/fm/article/view/1625/1540#k2

Kehrwald, B. (2008). Understanding Social Presence in Text-Based Online Learning Environments. *Distance Education*, *29*(1), 89–106. doi:10.1080/01587910802004860

Kharbach, M. (2013). *Education, Technology, and Mobile Learning*. Retrieved 4/23/14 from http://www.educatorstechnology.com/2013/11/education-10-vs-education-20-vs.html

Kilburn, M. (2011). Facilitating interaction in the online environment. In S. Hoffman (Ed.), *Teaching the humanities online: A practical guide to the virtual classroom*. New York: M.E. Sharpe.

Kilburn, M. (2013). Student perceptions of instructor interaction in the online environment. *International Journal of Research in Social Sciences*, *1*(1), 54-58.

Lane, L. M. (2011). Reducing distance in online classes. In S. Hoffman (Ed.), *Teaching the humanities online: A practical guide to the virtual classroom*. New York: M.E. Sharpe.

Mabrey, P. E., & Liu, J. (2013). Social media and public speaking: Student-produced multimedia informative presentations. In The plugged-in professor: Tips and techniques for teaching with social media. Oxford, UK: Chandos Publishing.

Mazer, J., Murphy, R., & Simonds, C. (2007). I'll see you on facebook: The effects of computer mediated teacher self-disclosure on student motivation, affective learning and classroom climate. *Communication Education*, *56*(1), 1–17. doi:10.1080/03634520601009710

Mazman, S. H., & Usleul, Y. K. (2011). Gender differences in using social networks. *Turkish Online Journal of Education Technology*, *10*(2), 133–139.

Mazzolini, M., & Maddison, S. (2003). Sage, guide or ghost? The effect of instructor intervention on student participation in online discussion forums. *Computers & Education*, *40*(3), 237–253. doi:10.1016/S0360-1315(02)00129-X

McCabe, D., & Meuter, M. (2011). A student view of technology in the classroom: Does it enhance the seven principles of good practice in undergraduate education? *Journal of Marketing Education*, *33*(2), 149–159. doi:10.1177/0273475311410847

McCarthy, J. (2010). Blended learning environments: Using social networking sites to enhance the first year experience. *Australasian Journal of Educational Technology*, *26*(6), 729–740.

Moore, J. C. (Ed.). (2002). *Elements of quality: The Sloan-C Framework*. Needham, MA: Sloan Center for Online Education.

Mupinga, D.M., Nora, R.T., & Yaw, D.C., (2006). The learning styles, expectations and needs of online students. *College Teaching, 54*(1), 185-189. Retrieved from Ebscohost on October 13, 2013.

Newberry, B. (2001). Raising Student Social Presence in Online Classes. In *WebNet 2001. Proceedings of the World Conference on the WWW and Internet*. Norfolk, VA: AACE.

Ng'ambi, D., & Lombe, A. (2011). Using podcasting to facilitate student learning: A constructivist perspective. *Journal of Educational Technology & Society*, *15*(4), 181–192.

Nunez, Y. S. (2005). Assessing faculty's social presence indicators in online courses. *Focus IV*, *I*, 47–49.

Pollacia, L., & McCallister, T. (2009). Using web 2.0 technologies to meet Quality Matters (QM) requirements. *Journal of Information Systems Education*, *20*(2), 155–164.

Pollard, H., Blevins, R., Connor, M., & McGovern, L. (2013). An examination of the relationship between teaching presence, social presence, learner motivation, and self-reported learning among online MBA students. Academy of Business, 18(2), 23-30.

Powell, K., & Kalina, C. (2009). Cognitive and social constructivism: Developing tools for an effective classroom. *Education*, *130*(2), 241–250.

Rice, R. E. (1993). Media appropriateness: Using social presence theory to compare traditional and new organization media. *Human Communication Research*, *19*(4), 451–484. doi:10.1111/j.1468-2958.1993.tb00309.x

Rourke, L., Anderson, T., Garrison, D. R., & Archer, W. (1999). Assessing Social Presence in Asynchronous Text-Based Computer Conferencing. *Journal of Distance Education*, *14*(2), 50–71.

Russo, T. C., & Campbell, S. W. (2004). Perceptions of mediated presence in an asynchronous online course: Interplay of communication behaviors and medium. *Distance Education*, *25*(2), 215–232. doi:10.1080/0158791042000262139

Saloman, D. (2013). Moving on from Facebook: Using Instagram to connect with undergraduates and engage in teaching and learning. *College & Research Libraries News*, *78*(8), 408–412.

Schaffhauser, D. (2009). Boundless opportunity. *T.H.E. Journal*, *36*(9), 13–18.

Schroeder, B. (2008). Ten best practices for using wikis in education. *Technology Teacher*. Retrieved April 21, 2014 from http://edtechtoday.wordpress.com/2008/05/21/10-best-practices-for-using-wikis-in-education/

Schroeder, J., & Greenbowe, T. J. (2009). The chemistry of Facebook: Using social networking to create an online community for the organic chemistry. *Innovate: Journal of Online Education*, *5*(4), 1–7.

Scollins-Mantha, B. (2008). Cultivating social presence in the online learning classroom: A literature review with recommendations for practice. *International Journal of Instructional Technology and Distance Education, 5*(3), 23–38.

Seaman, J. & Tinti-Kane, H. (n.d.). *Social media for teaching and learning.* Pearson Learning Solutions and Babson Survey Research Group.

Shin, N. (2002). Beyond Interaction: The Relational Construct of 'Transactional Presence.'. *Open Learning, 17*(2), 121–137. doi:10.1080/02680510220146887

Short, J. A., Williams, E., & Christie, B. (1976). *The social psychology of telecommunications.* London: Wiley.

Simonson, M., Smaldino, D., Albright, M., & Zvacek, S. (2009). *Teaching and learning at a distance: Foundations of distance education* (4th ed.). Boston: Allyn & Bacon.

Sloan Consortium (2006, August). *Faculty satisfaction.* Neeham, MA: Author.

Smith, S., & Caruso, J. (2010). *The ECAR study of undergraduate students and information technology.* Boulder, CO: CO EDUCAUSE Center for Applied Research.

Solomon, G., & Shrum, L. (2007). *Web 2.0 new tools, new schools.* Eugene, OR: ISTE.

Sturgeon, C. M., & Walker, C. (2009). *Faculty on Facebook: Confirm or deny?* Paper presented at the Annual Instructional Technology Conference, Murfreesboro, TN.

Su, B., Cong, C. J., Magjuka, R. J., Liu, X., & Lee, S. (2005). The importance of interaction in web-based education: A program-level study of online MBA courses. *Journal of Interactive Online Learning, 4*(1), 1–18.

The American Federation of Teachers. (2000). *Distance education, guidelines for good practice.* Retrieved April 20, 2014 from http://www.aft.org/higher_education/downloadable/distance.pdf

The Council of Higher Education Accreditation. (2002). *Accreditation and assuring quality in distance learning.* CHEA Monograph (1, Series 2002). Retrieved April 20, 2014 from http://www.chea.org/pdf/mono_1_accred_distance_02.pdf?pubID=246

The Institute for Higher Education Policy. (2000). *Quality on the line: Benchmarks for success in internet-based distance education.* Retrieved from http://www.ihep.com/pubs/pdf/quality.pdf

Tinti-Kane, H. (2013). Overcoming hurdles to social media in education. *EDUCAUSE Review Online.* Retrieved 4/21/14 from http://www.educause.edu/ero/article/overcoming-hurdles-social-media-eduation

Tu, C. H. (2000). On-Line learning migration: From social learning theory to social presence theory in CMC environment. *Journal of Network and Computer Applications, 23*(1), 27–37. doi:10.1006/jnca.1999.0099

Tu, C. H. (2001). How Chinese perceive social presence: An examination of an online learning environment. *Educational Media International, 38*(1), 45–60. doi:10.1080/09523980010021235

Tu, C. H., & McIssac, M. (2002). The relationship of social presence and interaction in online classes. *American Journal of Distance Education, 16*(3), 131–150. doi:10.1207/S15389286AJDE1603_2

University of Kansas Medical Center. (2011). *Best practices in educational podcasting. Teaching and Learning Technologies.* Retrieved 4/21/2013 from http://www.kumc.edu/Documents/TLT/KUMC%20Best%20Practices%20in%20Podcasting.pdf

Vesely, P., Bloom, L., & Sherlock, J. (2007). Key elements of building online community: Comparing faculty and student perceptions. *Journal of Online Learning and Teaching*, *3*, 234–246.

Virkus, S. (2008). Use of web 2.0 technologies in LIS education: Experiences at Tallinn University, Estonia. Program: Electronic Library and Information Systems, 42(3), 262-274.

Waldo, A. E. (2013). Cooperative study blog. In S. P. Ferris & H. A. Wilder (Eds.), *The plugged-in professor: tips and techniques for teaching with social media*. Cambridge, UK: Chandos Publishing. doi:10.1016/B978-1-84334-694-4.50013-2

Walther, J. B. (1992). Interpersonal effects in computer-mediated interaction: A relational perspective. *Communication Research*, *19*(1), 52–90. doi:10.1177/009365092019001003

Wang, Q. (2006). Quality assurance – best practices for assessing online programs. *International Journal on E-Learning*, *5*(2), 265–274.

Weekes, S. (2008, November-December). E-learning on the social. *Training & Coaching Today, 15*.

Wei, C., Chen, N., & Kinshuk, . (2012). A model for social presence in online classrooms. *Educational Technology Research and Development*, *60*(3), 529–545. doi:10.1007/s11423-012-9234-9

Whiteman, J.A.M. (2002) *Interpersonal Communication in Computer Mediated Learning*. (White/opinion paper).(ED 465 997).

Wilson, E. K., Wright, V. H., Inman, C. T., & Matherson, L. H. (2011). Retooling the social studies classroom for the current generation. *Social Studies*, *102*(2), 65–72. doi:10.1080/00377996.2010.484445

ADDITIONAL READING

Aidin, M., & Page, K. (2009). Podcasts and videostreaming: Useful tools to facilitate learning of pathophysiology in undergraduate nurse education. *Nurse Education in Practice*, *9*(6), 372–376. doi:10.1016/j.nepr.2008.11.003 PMID:19124275

Alman, S., Frey, B., & Tomer, C. (2012). Social and cognitive presence as factors in learning and student retention: An investigation of the cohort model in an ischool setting. *Journal of Education for Library and Information Science*, *53*(4), 290–302.

Aragon, S. R. (2003). Creating social presence in online environments. *New Directions for Adult and Continuing Education*, *2003*(100), 57–68. doi:10.1002/ace.119

Ariew, S. (2008). YouTube culture and the academic library: A guide to online open access educational videos. *Choice (Chicago, Ill.)*, *45*(12), 2057–2063. doi:10.5860/CHOICE.45.12.2057

Ascough, R. (2002). Designing for online distance education: Putting pedagogy before technology. *Teaching Theology and Religion*, *5*(1), 17–29. doi:10.1111/1467-9647.00114

Bolliger, D., & Wasilik, O. (2009). Factors influencing faculty satisfaction with online teaching and learning in higher education. *Distance Education*, *30*(1), 103–116. doi:10.1080/01587910902845949

Budden, C., & Budden, M. (2013). A look at an implementation of the Quality Matters program in a collegiate environment: Benefits and challenges. *Contemporary Issues in Education Research*, *6*(4), 381–384.

Copley, J. (2007). Audio and video podcast for lectures of campus-based students: Production and evaluation of student use. *Innovations in Education and Teaching International*, *44*(4), 387–399. doi:10.1080/14703290701602805

Dennen, V. (2007). Presence and positioning as components of online instructor persona. *Journal of Research on Technology in Education*, *40*(1), 95–108. doi:10.1080/15391523.2007.10782499

Dennen, V., Darabi, A., & Smith, L. (2007). Instructor-learner interaction in online courses: The relative perceived importance of particular instructor actions on performance and satisfaction. *Distance Education*, *28*(1), 65–79. doi:10.1080/01587910701305319

Ekmekci, O. (2013). Being there: Establishing instructor presence in an online learning environment. *Higher Education Studies*, *3*(1), 29–38. doi:10.5539/hes.v3n1p29

Hadjerrouit, S. (2011). Investigating technical and pedagogical usability issues of collaborative learning with wikis. *Informatics in Education*, *11*(1), 45–64.

Hastie, M., Chen, N., & Kuo, Y. (2007). Instructional design for best practice in the synchronous cyber classroom. *Journal of Educational Technology & Society*, *10*(4), 281–294.

Hayashi, Al, Chen, C., Ryan, T., & Wu, J. (2004). The role of social presence and moderating role of computer self efficacy in predicting the continuance usage of elearning systems. *Journal of Information Systems Education, 15*(2), 139-154.

Hoffman, E. S. (2014). Beyond the flipped classroom: Redesigning a research methods course for e³ instruction. *Contemporary Issues in Education Research*, *7*(1), 51–62.

Irlbeck, S. (2008). Implementation of best practices for online teaching and learning in an online institution. *Performance Improvement*, *47*(10), 25–29. doi:10.1002/pfi.20036

Lear, J., Isernhagen, J., LaCost, B., & King, J. (2009). Instructor presence for web-based classes. *Delta Pi Epsilon Journal*, *51*(2), 86–98.

Leong, P. (2011). Role of social presence and cognitive absorption in online learning environments. *Distance Education*, *32*(1), 5–28. doi:10.1080/01587919.2011.565495

Mullen, R., & Wedwick, L. (2008). Avoiding the digital abyss: Getting started in the classroom with YouTube, digital stories and blogs. *The Clearing House: A Journal of Educational Strategies, Issues and Ideas*, *82*(2), 66–69. doi:10.3200/TCHS.82.2.66-69

Mykota, D., & Duncan, R. (2007). Learner characteristics as predictors of online social presence. *Canadian Journal of Education*, *30*(1), 157–170. doi:10.2307/20466630

Nandi, D., Hamilton, M., & Harland, J. (2012). Evaluating the quality of interaction in asynchronous discussion forums in fully online courses. *Distance Education*, *33*(1), 5–30. doi:10.1080/01587919.2012.667957

Nevin, R. (2009). Supporting 21st century learning through Google apps. *Teacher Librarian*, *37*(2), 35–38.

Park, S. W. (2013). The potential of web 2.0 tools to promote reading engagement in a general education course. *TechTrends*, *57*(2), 48–53. doi:10.1007/s11528-013-0645-1

Peck, J. (2012). Keeping it social: Engaging students online and in class. *Asian Social Science*, *8*(14), 81–90. doi:10.5539/ass.v8n14p81

Russo, T., & Benson, S. (2005). Learning with invisible others: Perceptions of online presence and their relationship to cognitive and affective learning. *Journal of Educational Technology & Society*, *8*(1), 54–62.

Saeed, N., Yang, Y., & Sinnappan, S. (2009). Emerging web technologies in higher education: A case of incorporating blogs, podcasts and social bookmarks in a web programming course based on students' learning styles and technology preferences. *Journal of Educational Technology & Society*, *12*(4), 98–109.

Schmidt, K., & Brown, D. (2003). A model to integrate online teaching and learning tools into the classroom. *The Journal of Technology Studies*, *26*(1), 58–63.

Sims, R., & Graeme, D. (2002). Enhancing quality in online learning: Scaffolding planning and design through proactive evaluation. *Distance Education*, *23*(2), 135–148. doi:10.1080/0158791022000009169

Strickland, K., Gray, C., & Hill, G. (2012). The use of podcasts to enhance research-teaching linkages in undergraduate nursing students. *Nurse Education in Practice*, *12*(4), 210–214. doi:10.1016/j.nepr.2012.01.006 PMID:22321687

Turcxanyi-szabo, M. (2012). Aiming at sustainable innovation in teacher education - from theory to practice. *Informatics in Education*, *11*(1), 115–130.

Yang, S. H. (2009). Using blogs to enhance critical reflection and community of practice. *Journal of Educational Technology & Society*, *12*(2), 11–21.

KEY TERMS AND DEFINITIONS

Digital Media: Audio, video and images that exist in a computer-readable format, and can reside on a local device (CD, DVD, hard drive) or remote location (website) (https://www.uoguelph.ca/tss/pdfs/TBDigMedia.pdf).

Distance Learning: Learning that occurs when the instructor and students are separated by physical distance and technology is used to bridge the instructional bap (Boaz, et. al., 1999).

Microblogging: Posting short updates such as brief texts, photos, etc. on a personal blog, especially by using a mobile phone or instant messaging software.

Online Learning/Course: A context for learning in which students interact using technology and do not meet in a physical classroom with the instructor (http://www.macmillandictionary.com/).

Quality Assurance: The maintenance of a desired level of quality in a service or product, especially by means of attention to every stage of the process of delivery or production (http://www.oxforddictionaries.com/).

Social Media: Any medium that enables connectivity and interaction among users and communities (Haenlein, 2010).

Social Presence: The "degree of salience of the other person in the interaction and the consequent salience of the interpersonal relationships" (Short, Williams & Christie, p. 65).

Chapter 13
Engage Online Learners:
Design Considerations for Promoting Student Interactions

Sang Chan
Weber State University, USA

Devshikha Bose
Boise State University, USA

ABSTRACT

Online learning will continue to be one of the popular modes of instruction offered by higher education institutions to accommodate different learning needs. Student engagement is critical to the success of online learning. Students should be engaged cognitively, emotionally, and behaviorally. This chapter discusses design considerations for online courses to promote student-instructor, student-student, and student-content interactions to engage students cognitively, emotionally, and behaviorally. The chapter also discusses the application of flow theory, specifically, in the design of instruction to engage students during their interaction with course content.

INTRODUCTION

In order to make education accessible to diverse groups of people, many American colleges and universities offer fully online classes and degree programs (Parker, Lenhart, & Moore, 2011). Online course offerings will continue to grow. According to Allen and Seaman (2011), 65% of higher education institutions considered online learning as an important part of their long-term strategy. The growth rate for online enrollments was 10%, higher than the growth rate of only 2%

for the overall higher education enrollments. Over 6.1 million students took at least one online course during fall 2010, an increase of 560,000 students over the previous year. The number of students who took at least one online course increased to 6.7 million students during fall 2011 (Allen & Seaman, 2013) and 7.1 million students during fall 2012 (Allen & Seaman, 2014).

The importance of online learning is also reflected in efforts made by institutions to improve online teaching practices. Professional organizations such as the Online Learning Consortium

DOI: 10.4018/978-1-4666-9582-5.ch013

(formerly known as Sloan Consortium) offer many online teaching workshops. Other organizations (Quality Matters and Chico State) have developed a rubric to guide the design of quality online courses. Many colleges and universities offer their own in-house faculty development programs and workshops related to online teaching.

A popular topic that has frequently been addressed in the development programs, workshops, and course design rubrics is student engagement. The National Survey of Student Engagement (NSSE) defined student engagement as the amount of time and effort students devoted to their academic activities, and the resources the institution invests in curriculum and other opportunities to support student learning and to enhance student collegial experience (National Survey of Student Engagement, 2014a). Similarly, Kuh (2003) defined student engagement as "time and energy students devote to educationally sound activities inside and outside of the classroom, and policies and practices that institutions use to induce students to take part in these activities" (p. 25).

Student engagement has received a great deal of attention as a measure to assess the quality of student learning experiences (Kuh, 2003) and has been found to be a predictor of college completion (Price & Tovar, 2014). Kuh (2002) claimed student engagement was used as an indicator to differentiate high quality institutions from lower quality institutions. The institutions whose students were more fully engaged in activities that contributed to the college outcomes were considered higher quality institutions. Krause and Coates (2008) found a correlation between engagement and high quality learning outcomes. Engagement encompasses academic, non-academic, and social aspects of student experience and could be used as "a singularly sufficient means of determining whether students are engaging with their study and university learning community in ways likely to promote high-quality learning" (p. 493). In its own right, engagement plays more than a mediating

role in the prediction of outcomes and should be considered an independent educational outcome.

The literature categorizes student engagement as cognitive engagement, affective/emotional engagement, and behavioral/physical engagement. These three types of engagement are not isolated but dynamically interrelated (Bartko, 2005; Fredricks, Blumenfeld, & Paris, 2004). Fredricks et al. argued that engagement should be considered as a multidimensional construct, under which cognition, emotion, and behavior are united "to provide a richer characterization of children [students]" (p. 61) and to help us understand the complexity of educational experience, which allows the design of more specific and effective instructional interventions.

In a face-to-face course, students can interact with their peers and the instructor. Such interaction takes on a different dynamic for online learners (Hege, 2011). In an online environment, the instructor and students are not in the same physical location. Oftentimes, the interaction is asynchronous. Therefore, online courses require the use of different strategies for engaging students. This chapter discusses tips and strategies to increase student-instructor, student-student, and student-content interactions (Moore, 1989), as a way to enhance student engagement in online courses. Instructors and instructional designers may apply them to design an online course to engage students in the cognitive, affective, and behavioral areas. First, the chapter briefly discusses cognitive, affective, and behavioral engagement and, then, discusses student-instructor, student-student, and student-content interactions. Lastly, the authors review the literature on flow theory (Csikszentmihalyi, 2008) to derive common instructional components across the studies to inform the design of course content to promote flow experience in learning. However, it is not the authors' intention to conduct a comprehensive review of literature on student engagement and flow theory but to review only some of the relevant research. Readers who are interested in the theoretical aspects of these topics are advised to consult the original sources cited in the chapter.

COGNITIVE, AFFECTIVE, AND BEHAVIORAL ENGAGEMENT

Cognitive engagement is related to investment in learning and to self-regulation. The investment in learning includes willingness to put extra effort, preference for learning challenge, flexibility in problem solving, and positive coping with failure, all of which is to learn, understand, and master the required knowledge and skills (Fredricks, Blumenfeld, & Paris, 2004). Another aspect of cognitive engagement is self-regulation. Self-regulated students possess knowledge of learning strategies to rehearse, elaborate, and organize learning (Weinstein & Mayer, 1986) and of metacognitive strategies to plan, monitor, and regulate their learning and thinking (Pintrich, 2002). In addition, to make appropriate inferences, they also possess the problem-solving strategies (means-ends analysis and working backward from the goal) and the thinking strategies for deductive and inductive reasoning (Pintrich, 2002).

Affective engagement refers to students' positive and negative reactions to school, curriculum, teachers, and peers (Bartko, 2005). These include interest, boredom, happiness, sadness, anxiety, like, dislike, feeling of belonging, valuing of learning, appreciation of success in school, flexibility in problem solving, preference for hard work, and positive coping during failure (Fredricks, Blumenfeld, & Paris, 2004).

Behavioral engagement is concerned with participation and involvement in academic tasks and class social activities (Bartko, 2005). These activities include asking questions, contributing to class discussion, paying attention, putting effort to do the work, becoming a club member, or joining school governance (Fredricks, Blumenfeld, & Paris, 2004). Behaviorally engaged students

usually respond to instructors' questions and/or take initiative to participate in certain activities. They follow rules and policies and avoid disruptive behaviors. Natriello (1984) found students tended to be behaviorally disengaged when they perceived lack of fairness in enforcing rules and policies.

Previous research has investigated the effects of student engagement on school-related variables. Kuh et al. (2008) examined the relationship between student engagement, college GPA, and persistence and found engagement had a statistically significant positive effect on grades and persistence of the first and second year college students. Academic and social engagement behaviors were found to have significant impact on degree attainment in post-secondary education (Flynn, 2014). Fredricks, Blumenfeld, and Paris (2004) reviewed previous studies and concluded the following. Student engagement positively influenced student achievement. Behavioral disengagement was a precursor of school dropout. Students' emotional connections to their teachers (positive or supporting relationship) and their peers reduced student dropout rates.

Archambault, Janosz, Fallu, and Pagani (2009) found evidence to support cognitive, affective, and behavioral engagement together (global engagement) predicted school dropout. This result supports engagement as a multidimensional construct as proposed by Fredricks, Blumenfeld, and Paris (2004). Appleton, Christenson, Kim, and Reschly (2006) also acknowledged engagement as a multidimensional construct; however, their instrument only included items measuring cognitive and affective engagement. When analyzing separately, Archambault et al. (2009) found only behavioral engagement significantly predicted school dropout. Behavior problems (e.g., impoliteness, truancy, compliance, attendance) predicted school dropout better than other factors such as willingness and efforts to learn and level of pleasure students had with school-related activities. Archambault et al. explained behavioral engagement may be mediating the relationship between cognitive engagement and affective engagement and school dropout. It was also likely to account for the association between global engagement and school dropout. However, Archambault et al. argued cognitive engagement and affective engagement were still "important indicators of student alienation and this contribution, even if indirect, should not be neglected in our efforts to understand the problem. … it might be more beneficial to treat engagement as a multidimensional experience" (p. 667).

Although no research has shed light on how the three types of engagement exactly interact with one another, Fredricks, Blumenfeld, and Paris (2004) suggest examining them together as a multidimensional construct to gain better understanding of their impact. This could be an effective way to examine students at risks (school dropout) from different but related perspectives (Archambault, et al., 2009). For example, students may do the work and follow all rules and policies, but could feel disconnected from the instructor and their peers (Bartko, 2005). Therefore, instructors should try to engage students cognitively, emotionally, and behaviorally in class.

Student engagement in online classes can be enhanced through consistent student-instructor interaction, frequent peer interaction in a collaborative learning environment, and challenging tasks and activities (Robinson & Hullinger, 2008). In other words, student engagement is promoted through student-instructor interaction, student-student interaction, and student-content interaction (Moore, 1989), which are discussed next.

STUDENT INTERACTIONS

Student-Instructor Interaction

Student-instructor interaction is the interaction that the learner has with an expert who creates the content and/or with the instructor (Moore, 1989). According to Moore, this interaction aims to stimulate and maintain learning interest in the content, to motivate students to learn, and to promote self-directedness. During the interaction, the instructor would help students apply their knowledge and skills, evaluate learning progress, decide to use or change learning strategies, and provide counsel, support and encouragement on other aspects. On the other hand, learners would draw from the instructor's expertise and experience to help them understand the content and to apply the skills correctly. Student-instructor interaction can occur with or without the student's physical presence, for example, during class discussion or grading of student's work.

Fredricks, Blumenfeld, and Paris (2004) reviewed previous research and concluded teacher support and involvement (academic or interpersonal) was linked to behavioral, affective, and cognitive engagement. Variables such as age, GPA, participation in the program/course orientation, and participation in learning community were found to be significant predictors of student-instructor interaction (Wirt & Jaeger, 2014). Other variables such as reading remediation, study skills, and college orientation had a positive impact on student-instructor interaction (Wood, Ireland, & Mei-Yen, 2014). According to Tinto (1975), significant amounts of interaction with faculty was likely to enhance college persistence, grade performance, and intellectual development. Student-instructor interaction appeared to be more important in students' academic major areas than in other areas because it was related to students' particular intellectual interests as well as their future careers. Student-instructor interaction has often been associated with student success and persistence in both two and four year colleges (Wirt & Jaeger, 2014) and was a significant contributor to perceived learning (Fredericksen et al., 2000). Instructor's affective support was related to college students' academic enjoyment, academic hopelessness, behavioral engagement, and academic-help-seeking behaviors (Sakiz, 2011).

In high school settings, adolescent online learners rated student-instructor and student-content interactions higher in educational value than student-student interaction (Borup, Graham, & Davies, 2013). Most students expected instructors to provide feedback during and after assignments (Brinkerhoff & Koroghlanian, 2007), to communicate class expectations/requirements clearly, and to acknowledged assignment submissions (Mupinga, Nora, & Yaw, 2006). They were more behaviorally engaged when instructors communicated clear expectations and provided consistent responses (Fredricks, Blumenfeld, & Paris, 2004). Student-instructor interaction was most helpful when substantive contact encouraged students to devote more efforts to learning, to give feedback, and to discuss grades and assignments (Kuh, 2003). Robinson and Hullinger (2008) found most of student-instructor interaction was to discuss those issues (feedback on grades, assignments, class notes, and readings).

The authors' personal teaching experiences with undergraduate students also supported the benefits of having an open, honest, and encouraging conversations with students on a regular basis to obtain feedback on content, teaching methods, and other class-related issues to accommodate student learning needs. Through frequent communication and encouragement, students were willing to share their thought and express their concerns openly, which led to enhanced relationship between student and instructor and teaching practices.

Student-Student Interaction

The interaction between students, with or without instructor presence, is valuable and essential to learning (Moore, 1989). According to Moore, peer interaction may benefit younger learners more than adult learners because the latter group tends to be more self-motivated. The works from Jean Piaget also supported the importance of peer interaction in cognitive development (Wadsworth, 1988). Through social interaction, students may experience cognitive conflict, which forces them to assimilate and accommodate novelty into their existing cognitive structure. The process results in improvement of their cognitive functions. So, the world provides disequilibrium to provoke adjustment to one's behavior and thinking process such that the learner becomes less egocentric and capable of understanding the role of others.

Variables such as gender, familiarity between group members, ability level, ethnicity, and level of motivation play a role in the nature of the interaction between group members (Lei, Kuestermeyer, & Westmeyer, 2010). Tinto (1975) argued adequate social interaction with peers could assist college completion. Student-student interaction was one of the strong predictors of success and satisfaction in online courses (Moore, 2014). Online students wanted to stay connected with their peers (Mupinga, Nora, & Yaw, 2006). Bowman (2013) found frequent interaction between diverse groups of students was positively associated with growth in leadership skills, psychological well-being, and intellectual engagement. According to Kuh (2003), students who experienced more diversity (contact or conversation with other students from different racial backgrounds, religious beliefs, and personal values) tend to be more engaged in active and collaborative learning, achieve more gains in learning and personal development, and are more satisfied with college experience. Fredericksen et al. (2000) found interaction with peers was a significant contributor to perceived learning. Fredricks, Blumenfeld, and Paris (2004) reviewed previous studies and concluded: (a) peer interaction in active learning activities such as discussion, debate, and peer-review enhanced cognitive engagement, and (b) students were more behaviorally engaged in a respectful and socially-supportive learning environment.

Student-Content Interaction

Student-content interaction was found to be a significant predictor of student satisfaction (Kuo, 2014) and had a larger effect on achievement of learning outcomes when compared to the effects of student-student interaction and student-instructor interaction (Ekwunife-Orakwue & Tian-Lih, 2014). When students intellectually interact with the content, it produces change in their understanding, perspective, and cognitive structure (Moore, 1989). Course content includes recorded videos, audio lectures, PowerPoint slides, written documents, group discussion, role playing, peer review, reflection, and more. The course content should promote active learning. Active learning can be best facilitated when learners engage cognitively with the learning material (Lei, 2010). Students expected the course content to be challenging (Mupinga, Nora, & Yaw, 2006). They felt more engaged when their learning was challenging and authentic (Fredricks, Blumenfeld, & Paris, 2004) and when they learned at higher levels (analysis, application, evaluation) (Robinson & Hullinger, 2008). Students were highly engaged with coursework that required critical and analytical thinking.

Conrad (2002) found online students gave the first priority to interaction with course content, before considering the aspects of social presence. Students felt engaged with the course the moment they began reading and discussing class content. This may be due to anxiety, fear, excitement, apprehension, and eagerness at the beginning of a new online course. Therefore, students appreciate having access to the course one or two weeks prior to the start date to get familiar with and be prepared for the course.

In sum, all three interactions need to be addressed in class. According to Moore (1989), one weakness of an online course or program was a commitment to promoting only one type of interaction. The results of a meta-analysis study also supported the importance of these interactions

and their positive impacts on student learning in distance education (Bernard et al., 2009). Bernard et al. found stronger interactions were more effective than weaker interactions.

MEASURING STUDENT ENGAGEMENT

Researchers have suggested different ways to measure student engagement. Chickering and Gamson (1987) recommended seven principles for good practice to engage undergraduate students in general: (a) interaction between students and faculty, (b) interaction and cooperation among students, (d) active learning, (d) prompt feedback, (e) time on task, (f) high expectations for students, and (g) respect for diverse talents and ways of learning.

Krause and Coates (2008) also identified seven scales of student engagement for first year undergraduate students at public Australian universities. The seven engagement scales include: transition engagement (university life and experience during transition process), academic engagement (time management, study habit and strategies, self-initiated learning), peer engagement (peer collaboration in educationally purposeful activities), student-staff engagement (attitudes, behaviors, and skills of faculty and staff), intellectual engagement (challenging, stimulating, and meaningful learning), online engagement (web experience, computer software, access to resources, information and communication technology, online community), and beyond-class engagement (social, extracurricular, cultural activities for social connectedness and sense of belonging).

Another measure of engagement is the National Survey of Student Engagement (NSSE). This measurement is divided into four categories with the total of ten subcategories (National Survey of Student Engagement, 2014b). NSSE has been refined by many years of research and been widely used among higher education institutions to measure student engagement at the classroom and institution levels. Let's briefly discuss these engagement categories.

Academic challenges

- *Higher-order learning* is concerned with learning of challenging and complex cognitive tasks (e.g., apply, analyze, evaluate, and create) and coursework that requires critical and creative thinking.
- *Reflective and integrative learning* involves learning that is personally meaningful. Instructors should help students apply learning, reflect on their own beliefs, and consider issues from different perspectives.
- *Learning strategies* are related to active processing to enhance learning and retention using various strategies such as identifying key information in readings, reviewing notes after class, and summarizing course content.
- *Quantitative reasoning* is the ability to use and understand numerical and statistical information to evaluate, support, and critique issues and arguments during daily life.

Learning with peers

- *Collaborative learning* involves collaboration with peers in solving problems or mastering knowledge and skills. Collaboration includes group projects, peer tutoring, group study, group discussion, and exam preparation.
- *Discussions* involve interactions to learn from those with different backgrounds and life experiences, both inside and outside of the classroom.

Experiences with faculty

- *Student-faculty interaction* includes formal and informal interaction between student

and instructor inside and outside of class to discuss course content, academic performance, future career plan, and other projects.
- *Effective teaching practices* include organized instruction, clear explanations, and effective feedback on student work to promote student comprehension and learning.

Campus environment

- *Quality of interactions* includes positive interpersonal relations that promote student learning and success and supportive relationships with peers, faculty, and staff.
- *Supportive environment* includes institutional support in terms of services, activities, events, and opportunities to engage students cognitively, socially, and physically to enhance their performance and satisfaction.

Although the institutional services are essential for enhancing student engagement, this chapter only discusses engagement from instructional perspectives—how to design a course to engage students cognitively, affectively, and behaviorally. The following sections offer design suggestions to promote student interactions to engage student learning. These suggestions were drawn from the literature and the authors' professional experiences as instructional designers.

PROMOTING STUDENT-INSTRUCTOR INTERACTION

The lack of face-to-face meetings in an online class may create anxiety for some students. Therefore, student-instructor interaction is critical in an online environment. This interaction can be enhanced through frequent communication and feedback. Students may be interested in knowing who the instructor is and whether the instructor is supportive. This is especially relevant for international students who may have language barriers as well as a limited understanding and familiarity with a foreign educational environment. They are more likely to need extra assistance and attention. Student-instructor interaction may be enhanced in the following ways.

- The instructor may send an email(s) or announcement(s) in a learning management system (LMS) to welcome and/or remind students of important class issues or material (e.g., syllabus, schedule, deadline, etc.) at the beginning of and throughout the course. The goal is to create a supportive learning environment as well as a respectful and trustful relationship. Students were more behaviorally and affectively engaged in a respectful and supportive learning environment that promotes a sense of belonging, relatedness, and learning community (Fredricks, Blumenfeld, & Paris, 2004). When trust is built, students tend to share real concerns and offer authentic feedback.

- The instructor may create a short video (or host a synchronous meeting) to welcome and to introduce her/himself to students at the beginning of the class. The video may or may not discuss the course syllabus and other class materials. The first video should be short and welcoming so as not to overwhelm students. Different tools can be used to create a video such as Screencast-O-Matic, Jing, ScreenFlow (MAC), or a video-recording feature available in the LMS. A video helps create social presence, which has been found to have a significant impact on learning interaction (Wei, Chen, & Kinshuk, 2012). Use of videos also helps improve communication, makes instructors seem more real, present and familiar, and builds a closer relationship similar to that in a face-to-face classroom (Borup, West, Richard, & Graham, 2012).

- The instructor and students may meet to discuss the assignments, grades, and class content on a regular basis in real time via Skype, Google hangouts, Adobe Connect, GoToMeeting, GoToTraining, and other platforms in the LMS (e.g., Collaborate, BigBlueButton). Online students appreciate the instructor's feedback to improve their learning (Brinkerhoff & Koroghlanian, 2007; Robinson & Hullinger, 2008). The assignment and gradebook tools in the LMS can be used for feedback purposes. Other tools such as Google Drive may be used to provide pre-submission feedback on an assignment, to track learning progress, and to list the agenda for the next meeting between the instructor and student.

- Although the student-instructor discussion about class-related issues is important, conversations related to students' future career, community involvement, and research projects is also helpful and may occur via emails and/or the above communication technologies (e.g., Google hangouts, Skype, etc.).

PROMOTING STUDENT-STUDENT INTERACTION

Interaction between students is an important factor behind online students' achievement, motivation to learn, and persistence (Moore, 1989; Tinto, 1975). Student-student interaction in an online classroom can be enhanced through the use of various methods such as building online learning communities, peer instruction, and other collaborative learning activities (e.g., discussion, group presentation, etc.).

- Online discussion boards can be used to build communities of learners (Arkoudis et al., 2013) while Cloud technologies like

Google Drive enable real time online collaboration between users (Stevenson & Hedberg, 2013). Other social media platforms like Facebook, Twitter, or Google+ (YouTube, Hangouts, and Google Drive) may be used to help students interact with each other (Giebelhausen, 2015; Wilson, 2013). However, the use of social media, especially Facebook, should be given a serious consideration since research found an association between Facebook usage and narcissism (Miller, 2014). Student-student interaction and community building can be further facilitated through the use of video communication through which learners can engage synchronously in an online environment (Smyth, 2011). A simple class activity such as student-created videos to introduce themselves may help build a learning community in an online class.

- Other learning activities that promote collaboration and reflection such as team presentations, group project, group discussions, and group assignments may help further build and strengthen the learning community (Garrison & Vaughan, 2008). The interaction with peers helps students reflect and adjust their current belief and understanding as well as to assimilate and accommodate novelty into their existing cognitive structure, which leads to an improvement in their cognitive functions (Wadsworth, 1988). Some cloud based online tools can be used for online collaboration. Google Drive allows different users to create, edit, and share a document in real time. Users can work on a team presentation or write a group report online. Lucidchart (also available through Google Drive) functions in a similar manner. This tool allows students to build a diagram (e.g., concept map) online and share it for collaboration. Other tools such as Blogger, wiki page, discussion forum, Twitter, and

Facebook allow students to disseminate information and resources, ask questions, and share ideas.

- Peer instruction has been known to increase student motivation and engagement in class (Oliveira & Oliveira, 2013). Online web-based tutoring systems have been successfully used for peer instruction (Evans & Moore, 2013). Peer tutoring helps students confirm or deepen their own understanding. Different technologies may be used to assist peer tutoring. If face-to-face meeting is not possible, students can meet online synchronously via Adobe Connect, Collaborate, BigBlueButton, or GoToMeeting. These platforms allow students to communicate aurally and visually, share computer screens, send documents, and record the meeting session. Students can also use the built-in drawing board to demonstrate a procedure or explain other complex concepts.

PROMOTING STUDENT-CONTENT INTERACTION

Online students were found to place more emphasis on course content prior to considering the social aspects of the class (Conrad, 2002). Class content can be delivered to students via various media such as: radio and television (Özdemir, 2010), learning management system (LMS) (e.g., Canvas, Moodle, Blackboard, Desire2learn, Sakai, etc.), and/or smartphone and other mobile devices (Jain & Farley, 2012; Shin, Shin, Choo, & Beom, 2011). A decision about which technology to adopt for classroom purposes should be informed by pedagogy. Researchers suggest the use of student-generated content (Bolliger & Armier, 2013), cooperative learning (Herrmann, 2013), small group learning (Micari & Pazos, 2014), role-playing, case-based learning (Jalgaonkar, Sarkate, & Tripathi, 2012), and/or simulation (Skiba, 2009) as possible ways to enhance student-content interaction. Therefore, any adopted technology should support the implementation of the pedagogical best practices.

The last section of this chapter explores flow theory and its potential application to support the design of an engaging course. Previous research showed flow experience improved student learning experience, such as learning and course satisfactions (Clarke & Haworth, 1994). Flow was found to be correlated with course satisfaction, perceived skill development, and perceived learning (Rossin, Ro, Klein, & Guo, 2009). Klein, Rossin, Guo and Ro (2010) also found similar results. According to Esteban-Millat et al. (2014), flow was positively correlated with student learning and with positive effect (happiness, satisfaction, and cheerfulness). Flow also affected learning persistence of online students (Joo, Joung, & Sim, 2011), active procrastination (intentional decision to procrastinate), and achievement (Kim & Seo, 2013).

Although flow theory may also be relevant to the discussion of promoting student-student interaction and student-instructor interaction or to the discussion of increasing interaction in a group or teamwork setting, the authors argue the theory is more relevant to the discussion of increasing student-content interaction. Previous research on flow usually discussed how individuals or a group of people experienced flow when being engaged in a specific activity, such as "making music, rock climbing, dancing, sailing, chess, and so forth" (Csikszentmihalyi, 2008, p. 72). These activities are similar in nature to the activities students are usually engaged in class to learn the course content, such as: solving a math problem, analyzing a case study, watching a video lecture, reading a textbook, participating in a group discussion, debating over a topic, experimenting, role playing, reflecting on a concept, writing an essay, writing programing codes, interviewing an expert, installing an equipment, using machinery, or preparing for a class presentation. Therefore, it makes sense to use flow theory to inform the design of the course content.

Flow Theory

During the flow state or flow experience, the attention is focused on the task at hand such that the "[c]oncentration is so intense that there is no attention left over to think about anything irrelevant, or to worry about problems. Self-consciousness disappears, and the sense of time becomes distorted" (Csikszentmihalyi, 2008, p. 71). Flow experience may occur in an unplanned activity as well as a structured one. Some people have the natural ability to achieve flow easily. According to Csikszentmihalyi, every flow activity provides "a sense of discovery, a creative feeling of transporting the person into a new reality. It pushed the person to higher levels of performance" (p. 74). Konradt and Sulz (2001) found students in the flow state reported significantly higher levels of activation (alert, active, strong, excited), concentration, satisfaction, and motivation (wish to complete activity, sense of control, feeling involved). Ideally, this would be a type of learning students should experience when they interact with the course content. The authors' view of flow experience during content interaction is that students would enjoy learning, being persistent, and becoming motivated to complete the task at hand.

Pearce and Howard (2004) showed flow experience was a highly changeable state rather than an enduring one. The experience may fluctuate from time to time. Different students may experience different degrees of flow (Pearce, Ainley, & Howard, 2005). Flow is not an all-or-nothing phenomenon (van Schaik, Martin, & Vallance, 2012). Many previous studies examined flow as an overall state or overall experience; however, the authors of this chapter agree with Pearce, Ainley, and Howard (2005) that considering flow as a process offers more valuable insights to assist the design of instruction to better engage student learning. From this perspective, this chapter intends to identify instructional conditions, especially those that can be manipulated by the class instructor and instructional designers, to induce flow experience.

According to Csikszentmihalyi (2008), the conditions for flow include clear goals, balance between challenge and skill, immediate feedback, concentration, sense of control, loss of consciousness, time distortion, merging of action and awareness, clear rules, and intrinsically-rewarding experiences, most of which were used in Meyer and Jones' (2013) study to examine flow experience. According to Csikszentmihalyi, flow experience occurs when activities:

- are challenging to stretch the skill levels;
- are competitive that encourages people to focus on the task itself, rather than to beat the opponents or impress others;
- provide a sense of possible control of individual actions although the actuality of control may not exist;
- make people feel they could be more than what they actually are, through fantasy, pretense, and disguise;
- provide a sense of discovery; and
- are meaningful, relevant, and chosen freely.

In Ghani, Supnick, and Rooney's (1991) study, perceived control, skill, and perceived challenge were used as factors to affect flow experience, which was measured by enjoyment and concentration. The study results indicated perceived control, skill, and perceived challenge was significantly linked to flow. The higher the challenge students perceived, the higher the levels of concentration and enjoyment they experienced. In their experiment, Pearce, Ainley, and Howard (2005) studied the effect of the balance between challenge and skill on promoting flow in learning physics. They found different flow behaviors for different students and recommended tailored instruction based on the students' knowledge and skills to maximize the likelihood of promoting flow. Ghani, Supnick,

and Rooney (1991) also found variations in flow states students experienced when engaging in group decision making.

Shin (2006) examined the relationships among flow antecedents (challenge, skill, clear goal, gender, and concentration), flow experience (enjoyment, telepresence, focused attention, engagement, and time distortion), and flow consequences (course satisfaction) of online students and found flow was a significant predictor of course satisfaction. Clear goals and the ability to concentrate were strongly correlated with flow. The perceived balance between challenge and skill was important in determining the flow experience, which seemed to be in line with Chen (2000), who used clear goals, immediate feedback, sense of control, and merger of action and awareness as the flow antecedents. Rossin, Ro, Klein, and Guo (2009) found flow activities (clear goal, feedback, and perceived balance between challenge and skill) were correlated with different learning outcomes (student satisfaction, perceived skill development, perceived learning, and actual performance). To enhance course satisfaction and perceived learning, Rossin et al. suggested considering flow activities in the design and delivery of online classes. Klein, Rossin, Guo and Ro (2010) also found flow activities were correlated with perceived skill development. Joo, Lim, & Kim (2012) found self-efficacy (belief in one's ability), intrinsic value (enjoyment in doing a task), perceived usefulness (belief in using a system to enhance performance), and ease of use (a system helps free the effort) each had a significant effect on flow.

Kiili, Lainema, de Freitas, and Arnab (2014) used a flow framework to analyze the quality of educational games and argued the framework could also be used to design quality educational games. The framework consisted of nine flow conditions such as clear goals, balance between challenge and skill, immediate and cognitive feedback, sense of personal control, playability, rewarding experience, concentration, loss of self-consciousness, and time distortion. Esteban-Millat et al. (2014) found sense of control, learning interactivity, focused attention, and time distortion were positively associated with flow state. The challenge level, instructor's attitude, and learning content were in a direct positive correlation with focused attention and were indirectly correlated with flow. Skill and personalized learning were positively correlated with perceived control. Finneran and Zhang (2005) summarized common flow antecedents from previous research in computer-human interaction and web experience. The antecedents include clear goals, balance between challenge and skill, perceived control, telepresence, interactivity, vividness, attractiveness, immediate feedback, and previous experience. Finneran and Zhang also discussed the distinctions among artefact, activity, and task in flow, whereas Finneran and Zhang (2003) differentiated person, artefact, and task and their interactions in flow. However, these issues are not the focus of this chapter. Readers who are interested in the theoretical discussions may consult Finneran and Zhang (2003) on the Person-Artefact-Task model, Siekpe (2005) on the multidimensional construct of flow, and Pearce, Ainley, and Howard (2005) on measuring the flow process.

Instructional Conditions to Induce Flow Experience

Teaching and learning is a complex transaction. To increase the likelihood of promoting flow during student interaction with content, the authors offer the following design considerations.

- Have clear learning goals and learning objectives: Many courses only use learning objectives. Courses should have both goals and objectives. Students rely on the goals and objectives to learn more about a course. The goals give an overall picture of the course, set a boundary for the course

design process, and define learning objectives. The goals need to be well-written to clearly communicate the overall learning outcomes. The goals are broad, realistic, and achievable, but not usually measurable. On the other hand, learning objectives indicate specific learning outcomes. Objectives communicate clear course expectations to students and help them keep track of their learning progress. All objectives should be measurable to allow the instructor to easily observe successful and unsuccessful learning. A measurable learning objective consists of the performance statement (what students will be able to do), criterion (standard on which learning is assessed), and condition (situation under which learning is assessed) (Mager, 1984). Another guideline for writing measurable learning objectives was provided by Gagné, Briggs, and Wager (1992). Gagné et al. used five elements for writing an objective such as: situation (like Mager's condition), outcome verb, object (together like performance in Mager's), action verb (like criterion in Mager's), and tools or constrains (equipment or tools).

- Communicate clear expectations, rules and policies: Behavioral engagement involves participation and involvement in academic and social activities in class (Bartko, 2005), including paying attention, putting effort in completing the work, asking questions, contributing to class discussion, becoming a club member, or joining school governance (Fredricks, Blumenfeld, & Paris, 2004). Behaviorally engaged students follow rules and policies and avoid disruptive behaviors. The recommendations are straightforward: communicate clear expectations to students (e.g., required textbook, optional materials, prior knowledge and skills, required technology and tools, student responsibility, number of class meetings per week, face-to-face or online class, course LMS, etc.), provide clear instruction to complete an assessment (e.g., deadline, points, submission guideline, open-book test, proctored exam, testing center), communicate concise rules and policies (e.g., plagiarism, cheating, codes of conduct), and enforce the rules and policies fairly among students. Students should be treated equally and respectfully. Unfair treatments tend to disengage students behaviorally and emotionally.

- Promote active and meaningful learning: Learning should be relevant and personally meaningful. Ausubel suggests connecting new information with prior knowledge in a substantive and non-arbitrary way to make learning meaningful (Driscoll, 2005). Students should be able to use their learning to understand daily life events and to apply it to solve real-world problems. Teaching something which has practical applications is also supported by the constructivist principle (Brooks & Brooks, 1999). Reading the textbook or watching a video lecture and then taking an exam tends to focus more on passive learning. Students should be provided with opportunities to participate in more active learning such as: read and discuss content, build a concept map to synthesize a concept, write a one-minute summary of learned concepts, list clearest and muddiest points, tutor peers, present in class, collaborate on a group project, immerse in real-world experience through field trips or expert interviews, or conduct a case analysis of real-world problems. Learning activities should provide a sense of discovery and enjoyment and should transform the way students perceive reality and alter the consciousness (Csikszentmihalyi, 2008). This

can be done through role playing, simulation, and gaming to make students feel engaged and motivated.

- Balance between skill level and difficulty level: To stay in flow, students need to have sufficient skills to complete a task. If the skill level does not match the cognitive demand required by the task, they may experience anxiety and frustration. If the challenge level of the task is lower than the skill level, they tend to feel bored (Csikszentmihalyi, 2008). There needs to be a balance between challenge and skill levels. One way to achieve this is to increase the content difficulty levels based on the cognitive process levels in the revised Bloom's taxonomy when students progress throughout the course. The taxonomy consists of six cognitive process levels— remember, understand, apply, analyze, evaluate, and create (Krathwohl, 2002). Each level differs in its complexity. A higher level (understand) is more complex than a lower level (remember). It is recommended a course should have more high-level learning objectives than low-level ones. These learning objectives should be arranged based on their required cognitive process levels (and their prerequisites) to provide appropriate challenge for learning throughout the unit or course. For example: a low-level objective is listed first and then followed by higher-level objectives. The instructor, then, can design specific content to support each level. This process helps the instructor choose an appropriate difficulty level for course content as students acquire more skills to maintain flow experience (see Figure below). It is also important to note that the revised Bloom's taxonomy (Krathwohl, 2002) does not represent a cumulative hierarchy as rigid as its older version (Bloom et al., 1956) where students need to master lower-level thinking before they can master higher-level thinking. The revised version is less strict and allows overlapping among the levels. For example, understanding may require comprehension and application. To promote or maintain learning flow, instructors may use different activities that require the same level of cognitive processing or use a similar activity (in different contexts or with new prompts). Oftentimes, repetition is needed to master the skills properly before more difficult learning can occur (Figure 1).

- Provide frequent and effective feedback: Feedback is important for student learning. Students need feedback to correct misconceptions or mistakes and to improve

performance. Instructors are obligated to provide students with feedback. Feedback statements such as "Good job," "Wrong! Try again," or "Read my lecture notes on section 2.3" are not as effective to guide learning. According to Brookhart (2008) and Ovando (1992 as cited in Ovando, 1994), effective feedback needs to be immediate and frequent, respectful, confidential, encouraging and motivating, sensitive (including positive comments), tailored to student developmental level, relevant to learning goals and objectives, specific enough that students know their mistakes and why, and suggestive toward improvement. The feedback should not be too specific or detailed to give away the answer. The idea is to get students to think and reflect on their learning. It is noted that the

Figure 1. Adapted from Csikszentmihalyi (2008)

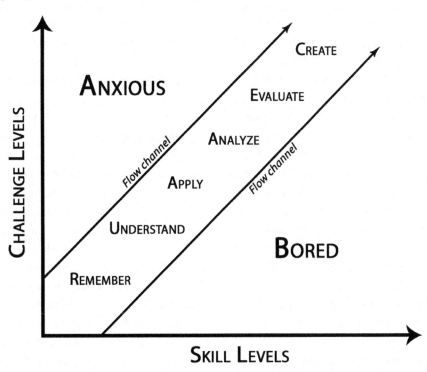

above feedback criteria contain the cognitive, affective, and behavioral components.

- Allow control of learning: Adults are self-directed, internally motivated, autonomous, and independent learners (Knowles, 1980; Merriam, Caffarella, & Baumgartner, 2007). Online students also need to be self-directed and independent to succeed. They need to take initiatives in planning and completing coursework. To facilitate this, instructors should allow students to take control over their learning. It could be as simple as making the pause, play, and rewind buttons available on the video lectures, making content available ahead of time, or providing students with choices to participate in an activity and/or assessment. Some activities or assessments may work well for students, but may create anxiety and frustration for others, given their individual and cultural differences. Instructors needs to be mindful of these issues. To allow more control, the instructors may work with students to decide on content that are personally meaningful and practical. One of the authors of this chapter has experienced this learning process as a student. The course instructor worked with students to select their preferred learning activities. Then, the instructor and each student signed a learning contract. They also scheduled one meeting to discuss the learning progress and/or remediation during the semester. Overall, it was an enjoyable and meaningful activity. Students had an opportunity to decide what was more relevant to their learning. However, this approach is time consuming and requires more effort and may not be suitable for some teaching situations.

In sum, although the instructor is responsible for providing the above instructional interventions to promote flow experience, to be in flow, students need to pay attention, to concentrate on the task at hand, and not to worry about irrelevant issues (other people's perceptions and criticism, wrong impression, or mistakes) (Csikszentmihalyi, 2008). The instructor can help students focus on the task at hand by making sure the learning content is relevant, meaningful, and practical. Tolerance for mistakes is another way to help students experience flow. The instructor may allow students to make mistakes and not to be punished for those mistakes. Instead, treat those mistakes as an opportunity to correct misconceptions, to promote creativity, and/or to encourage students to begin learning. Therefore, to promote flow experience, it requires efforts from both instructor and students. The role of the instructor is to provide an appropriate learning environment for students to strive.

CONCLUSION

The key to creating an online course that engages students cognitively, emotionally, and physically is to promote student-instructor, student-student, and student-content interactions. It is difficult to be motivated to learn in an environment that lacks support, encouragement, trust, respect, fairness, and clear expectations. Instructors need to create a welcoming, encouraging, collaborative, and respectful environment where students feel safe and motivated to contribute to learning. Course expectations and policies should be communicated clearly at the beginning of the class. Instructors need to make sure that students are treated fairly and equally. The class should allow students to build a learning community, where they can collaborate and reflect on learning. The role of the instructor is to provide constant support and guidance to help students succeed.

The culture of respect, support, and fairness contributes to the success of online classes. However, it may not be sufficient to engage students if the content is not challenging and meaningful. The student-instructor, student-student, and student-content interactions need to be promoted simultaneously in an online class.

To enhance student interaction with content, instructors may apply flow theory to assist the design of engaging content. Such content should communicate clear learning outcomes and expectations, promote active learning that assists real-world applications, match content difficulty levels with students' skill levels, contain frequent and constructive feedback to help students learn the correct concepts and skills, and allow students control over the process, pace, and/or choice in learning (e.g., material, activity, or assessment).

A final note is that although the pedagogical aspects are important to the success of online courses, instructors also need to consider the technical aspects of the course. These include making the course content easily accessible. This requires considering student access to technologies (e.g., internet bandwidth, software, hardware) as well as other campus resources such as the IT Helpdesk, disability resource center, writing center, tutoring center, library, testing center, etc. The goal is to help students engage in high levels of learning throughout the course, instead of being distracted and frustrated with technology-related problems, course navigation issues, and other technical errors. Instructors are advised to meet with instructional designers at their own institutions to discuss different ways to design effective online courses.

ACKNOWLEDGMENT

The authors wish to thank Dr. Charles Graham at Brigham Young University for many helpful suggestions and, especially, thank an anonymous reviewer for providing very thorough and valuable feedback to improve the chapter.

REFERENCES

Allen, E., & Seaman, J. (2011). *Going the distance: Online education in the United States, 2011*. Babson Survey Research Group. Retrieved from: http://www.onlinelearningsurvey.com/reports/goingthedistance.pdf

Allen, E., & Seaman, J. (2013). *Changing course: Ten years of tracking online education in the United States*. Babson Survey Research Group and Quahog Research Group. Retrieved from: http://www.onlinelearningsurvey.com/reports/changingcourse.pdf

Allen, E., & Seaman, J. (2014). *Grade change: Tracking online education in the United States*. Babson Survey Research Group and Quahog Research Group. Retrieved from: http://www.onlinelearningsurvey.com/reports/gradechange.pdf

Appleton, J. J., Christenson, S. L., Kim, D., & Reschly, A. L. (2006). Measuring cognitive and psychological engagement: Validation of the student engagement instrument. *Journal of School Psychology*, *44*(5), 427–445. doi:10.1016/j.jsp.2006.04.002

Archambault, I., Janosz, M., Fallu, J.-S., & Pagani, L. S. (2009). Student engagement and its relationship with early high school dropout. *Journal of Adolescence*, *32*(3), 651–670. doi:10.1016/j.adolescence.2008.06.007 PMID:18708246

Arkoudis, S., Watty, K., Baik, C., Yu, X., Borland, H., Chang, S., & Pearce, A. et al. (2013). Finding common ground: Enhancing interaction between domestic and international students in higher education. *Teaching in Higher Education*, *18*(3), 222–235. doi:10.1080/13562517.2012.719156

Bartko, W. T. (2005). The ABC of engagement in out-of-school-time programs. *New Directions for Youth Development*, *2005*(105), 109–120. doi:10.1002/yd.110 PMID:15943139

Bernard, R. M., Abrami, P. C., Borokhovski, E., Wade, C. A., Tamim, R. M., Surkes, M. A., & Bethel, E. C. (2009). A meta-analysis of three types of interaction treatments in distance education. *Review of Educational Research*, *79*(3), 1243–1289. doi:10.3102/0034654309333844

Bloom, B. S., Engelhart, M. D., Furst, E. J., Hill, W. H., & Krathwohl, D. R. (1956). *Taxonomy of educational objectives: The classification of educational goals. Handbook I: Cognitive domain.* New York: David McKay Company.

Bolliger, D. U., & Armier, D. D. (2013). Active learning in the online environment: The integration of student-generated audio files. *Active Learning in Higher Education*, *14*(3), 201–211. doi:10.1177/1469787413498032

Borup, J., Graham, C., & Davies, R. (2013). The nature of adolescent learner interaction in a virtual high school setting. *Journal of Computer Assisted Learning*, *29*(2), 153–167. doi:10.1111/j.1365-2729.2012.00479.x

Borup, J., West, R. E., & Graham, C. R. (2012). Improving online social presence through asynchronous video. *The Internet and Higher Education*, *15*(3), 195–203. doi:10.1016/j.iheduc.2011.11.001

Fredericksen, Pickett, Shea, Pelz, & Swan. (2000). Student satisfaction and perceived learning with online courses: Principles and examples from the SUNY learning network. In J. Bourne (Ed.), *Proceedings of the 1999 Sloan Summer Workshop on Asynchronous Learning Networks* (pp. 7-36). Sloan-Consortium.

Bowman, N. A. (2013). How much diversity is enough? The curvilinear relationship between college diversity interactions and first-year student outcomes. *Research in Higher Education*, *54*(8), 874–894. doi:10.1007/s11162-013-9300-0

Brinkerhoff, J., & Koroghlanian, C. M. (2007). Online students' expectations: Enhancing the fit between online students and course design. *Journal of Educational Computing Research*, *36*(4), 383–393. doi:10.2190/R728-28W1-332K-U115

Brookhart, S. M. (2008). *How to give effective feedback to your students.* Alexandria, VA: Association for Supervision and Curriculum Development.

Brooks, J. G., & Brooks, M. G. (1999). *In search of understanding: The case for constructivist classrooms.* Danvers, MA: Association for Supervision and Curriculum Development.

Chen, H. (2000). *Exploring web users' on-line optimal flow experiences.* (Unpublished Dissertation). Syracuse University, Syracuse, NY.

Chickering, A. W., & Gamson, Z. F. (1987). Seven principles for good practice in undergraduate education. *AAHE Bulletin*, 3-7. Retrieved from ERIC database. (ED 282491).

Clarke, S. G., & Haworth, J. T. (1994). 'Flow' experience in the daily lives of sixth-form college students. *British Journal of Psychology*, *85*(4), 511–523. doi:10.1111/j.2044-8295.1994.tb02538.x

Conrad, D. L. (2002). Engagement, excitement, anxiety, and fear: Learners' experiences of starting an online course. *American Journal of Distance Education*, *16*(4), 205–226. doi:10.1207/S15389286AJDE1604_2

Csikszentmihalyi, M. (2008). *Flow: The psychology of optimal experience.* New York, NY: HarperCollins.

Driscoll, M. P. (2005). *Psychology of learning for instruction* (3rd ed.). Boston, MA: Allyn and Bacon.

Ekwunife-Orakwue, K. V., & Tian-Lih, T. (2014). The impact of transactional distance dialogic interactions on student learning outcomes in online and blended environments. *Computers & Education*, *78*, 414–427. doi:10.1016/j.compedu.2014.06.011

Esteban-Millat, I., Martínez-López, F. J., Huertas-García, R., Meseguer, A., & Rodríguez-Ardura, I. (2014). Modelling students' flow experiences in an online learning environment. *Computers & Education*, *71*, 111–123. doi:10.1016/j.compedu.2013.09.012

Evans, M. J., & Moore, J. S. (2013). Peer tutoring with the aid of the Internet. *British Journal of Educational Technology*, *44*(1), 144–155. doi:10.1111/j.1467-8535.2011.01280.x

Finneran, C. M., & Zhang, P. (2003). A Person-Artefact-Task (PAT) model of flow antecedents in computer-mediated environments. *International Journal of Human-Computer Studies*, *59*(4), 475–496. doi:10.1016/S1071-5819(03)00112-5

Finneran, C. M., & Zhang, P. (2005). Flow in computer-mediated environments: Promises and challenges. *Communications of the Association for Information Systems*, *15*, 82–101.

Flynn, D. (2014). Baccalaureate attainment of college students at 4-Year institutions as a function of student engagement behaviors: Social and academic student engagement behaviors matter. *Research in Higher Education*, *55*(5), 467–493. doi:10.1007/s11162-013-9321-8

Fredricks, J. A., Blumenfeld, P. C., & Paris, A. H. (2004). School engagement: Potential of the concept, state of the evidence. *Review of Educational Research*, *74*(1), 59–109. doi:10.3102/00346543074001059

Gagné, R. M., Briggs, L. J., & Wager, W. M. (1992). *Principles of instructional design* (4th ed.). Orlando, FL: Harcourt Brace Jovanovich.

Garrison, D. R., & Vaughan, N. D. (2008). *Blended learning in higher education: Framework, principles, and guidelines*. San Francisco, CA: Jossey-Bass.

Ghani, J. A., Supnick, R., & Rooney, P. (1991). The experience of flow in computer mediated and in face-to-face groups. In J. I. DeGross, I. Benbasat, G. DeSanctis, & C. M. Beath (Eds), *Proceedings of the 20th International Conference on Information Systems* (pp. 229-237), New York: Academic Press.

Giebelhausen, R. (2015). What the tech is going on? Social media and your music classroom. *General Music Today*, *28*(2), 39–46. doi:10.1177/1048371314552523

Hege, B. A. R. (2011). The online theology classroom: Strategies for engaging a community of distance learners in a hybrid model of online education. *Teaching Theology and Religion*, *14*(1), 13–20. doi:10.1111/j.1467-9647.2010.00668.x

Herrmann, K. J. (2013). The impact of cooperative learning on student engagement: Results from an intervention. *Active Learning in Higher Education*, *14*(3), 175–187. doi:10.1177/1469787413498035

Jain, A., & Farley, A. (2012). Mobile phone-based audience response system and student engagement in large-group teaching. *Economic Papers*, *31*(4), 428–439. doi:10.1111/1759-3441.12002

Jalgaonkar, S. V., Sarkate, P. V., & Tripathi, R. K. (2012). Students' perception about small group teaching techniques: Role play method and case based learning in pharmacology. *Education in Medicine Journal*, *4*(2), 13–18. doi:10.5959/eimj.v4i2.21

Joo, Y. J., Joung, S., & Sim, W. J. (2011). Structural relationships among internal locus of control, institutional support, flow, and learner persistence in cyber universities. *Computers in Human Behavior*, *27*(2), 714–722. doi:10.1016/j.chb.2010.09.007

Joo, Y. J., Lim, K. Y., & Kim, S. M. (2012). A model for predicting learning flow and achievement in corporate e-learning. *Journal of Educational Technology & Society*, *15*(1), 313–325.

Kiili, K., Lainema, T., de Freitas, S., & Arnab, S. (2014). Flow framework for analyzing the quality of educational games. *Entertainment Computing*, *5*(4), 367–377. doi:10.1016/j.entcom.2014.08.002

Kim, E., & Seo, E. H. (2013). The relationship of flow and self-regulated learning to active procrastination. *Social Behavior and Personality*, *41*(7), 1099–1114. doi:10.2224/sbp.2013.41.7.1099

Klein, B. D., Rossin, D., Guo, Y. M., & Ro, Y. K. (2010). An examination of the effects of flow on learning in a graduate-level introductory operations management course. *Journal of Education for Business*, *85*(5), 292–298. doi:10.1080/08832320903449600

Knowles, M. S. (1980). *The modern practice of adult education: From pedagogy to andragogy (revised and updated)*. Englewood Cliffs, NJ: Cambridge Adult Education.

Konradt, U., & Sulz, K. (2001). The experience of flow in interacting with a hypermedia learning environment. *Journal of Educational Multimedia and Hypermedia*, *10*(1), 69–84.

Krathwohl, D. R. (2002). A revision of Bloom's taxonomy: An overview. *Theory into Practice*, *41*(4), 212–264. doi:10.1207/s15430421tip4104_2

Krause, K.-L., & Coates, H. (2008). Students' engagement in first-year university. *Assessment & Evaluation in Higher Education*, *33*(5), 493–505. doi:10.1080/02602930701698892

Kuh, G. D. (2002). *The National survey of student engagement: Conceptual framework and overview of psychometric properties*. Indiana University Center for Postsecondary Research and Planning. Retrieved from http://nsse.iub.edu/html/psychometric_framework_2002.cfm

Kuh, G. D. (2003). What's we are learning about student engagement from NSSE: Benchmarks for effective educational practices. *Change: The Magazine of Higher Learning*, *35*(2), 25–32. doi:10.1080/00091380309604090

Kuh, G. D., Cruce, T. M., Shoup, R., Kinzie, J., & Gonyea, R. M. (2008). Unmasking the effects of student engagement on first-year college grades and persistence. *The Journal of Higher Education*, *79*(5), 540–563. doi:10.1353/jhe.0.0019

Kuo, Y. (2014). Accelerated online learning: Perceptions of interaction and learning outcomes among African American students. *American Journal of Distance Education*, *28*(4), 241–252. doi:10.1080/08923647.2014.959334

Lei, S. A. (2010). Assessment practices of advanced field ecology course. *Education*, *130*(3), 404–415.

Lei, S. A., Kuestermeyer, B. N., & Westmeyer, K. A. (2010). Group composition affecting student interaction and achievement: Instructors' perspectives. *Journal of Instructional Psychology*, *37*(4), 317–325.

Mager, R. F. (1984). *Preparing instructional objectives* (2nd ed.). Belmont, CA: Lake Publishing.

Merriam, S. B., Caffarella, R. S., & Baumgartner, L. M. (2007). *Learning in adulthood: A comprehensive guide* (3rd ed.). San Francisco: Jossey-Bass.

Meyer, K. A., & Jones, S. J. (2013). Do students experience flow conditions online? *Journal of Asynchronous Learning Networks*, *17*(3), 137-148. Retrieved from ERIC database (EJ1018299)

Micari, M., & Pazos, P. (2014). Worrying about what others think: A social-comparison concern intervention in small learning groups. *Active Learning in Higher Education*, *15*(3), 249–262. doi:10.1177/1469787414544874

Miller, M. D. (2014). *Minds online: Teaching effectively with technology.* Cambridge, MA: Harvard University Press. doi:10.4159/harvard.9780674735996

Moore, J. (2014). Effects of online interaction and instructor presence on students' satisfaction and success with online undergraduate public relations courses. *Journalism & Mass Communication Educator, 69*(3), 271–288. doi:10.1177/1077695814536398

Moore, M. G. (1989). Editorial: Three types of interaction. *American Journal of Distance Education, 3*(2), 1–7. doi:10.1080/08923648909526659

Mupinga, D. M., Nora, R. T., & Yaw, D. C. (2006). The learning styles, expectations, and needs of online students. *College Teaching, 54*(1), 185–189. doi:10.3200/CTCH.54.1.185-189

National Survey of Student Engagement. (2014a). *What is student engagement?* Retrieved from http://nsse.iub.edu/html/about.cfm

National Survey of Student Engagement. (2014b). *Engagement indicators.* Retrieved from http://nsse.iub.edu/html/engagement_indicators.cfm

Natriello, G. (1984). Problems in the evaluation of students and student disengagement from secondary schools. *Journal of Research and Development in Education, 17*(4), 14–24.

Oliveira, P. C., & Oliveira, C. G. (2013). Using conceptual questions to promote motivation and learning in physics lectures. *European Journal of Engineering Education, 38*(4), 417–424. doi:10.1080/03043797.2013.780013

Ovando, M. N. (1994). Constructive feedback: A key to successful teaching and learning. *International Journal of Educational Management, 8*(6), 19–22. doi:10.1108/09513549410069185

Özdemir, S. (2010). Supporting printed books with multimedia: A new way to use mobile technology for learning. *British Journal of Educational Technology, 41*(6), 135–138. doi:10.1111/j.1467-8535.2010.01071.x

Parker, K., Lenhart, A., & Moore, K. (2011). *Digital revolution and higher education.* Pew Research Center. Retrieved from http://www.pewsocialtrends.org/files/2011/08/online-learning.pdf

Pearce, J. M., Ainley, M., & Howard, S. (2005). The ebb and flow of online learning. *Computers in Human Behavior, 21*(5), 745–771. doi:10.1016/S0747-5632(04)00036-6

Pearce, J. M., & Howard, S. (2004). *Designing for flow in a complex activity.* Paper presented at the 6th Asia-Pacific Conference on Computer-Human Interaction, New Zealand. doi:10.1007/978-3-540-27795-8_35

Pintrich, P. R. (2002). The role of metacognitive knowledge in learning, teaching, and assessing. *Theory into Practice, 41*(4), 219–225. doi:10.1207/s15430421tip4104_3

Price, D. V., & Tovar, E. (2014). Student engagement and institutional graduation rates: Identifying high-impact educational practices for community colleges. *Community College Journal of Research and Practice, 38*(9), 766–782. doi:10.1080/10668926.2012.719481

Robinson, C. C., & Hullinger, H. (2008). New benchmarks in higher education: Student engagement in online learning. *Journal of Education for Business, 84*(2), 101–109. doi:10.3200/JOEB.84.2.101-109

Rossin, D., Ro, Y. K., Klein, B. D., & Guo, Y. M. (2009). The effects of flow on learning outcomes in an online information management course. *Journal of Information Systems Education, 20*(1), 87–98.

Sakiz, G. (2012). Perceived instructor affective support in relation to academic emotions and motivation in college. *Educational Psychology*, *32*(1), 63–79. doi:10.1080/01443410.2011.625611

Shin, D., Shin, Y., Choo, H., & Beom, K. (2011). Smartphones as smart pedagogical tool: Implications for smartphones as u-learning devices. *Computers in Human Behavior*, *27*(6), 2207–2214. doi:10.1016/j.chb.2011.06.017

Shin, N. (2006). Online learner's 'flow' experience: An empirical study. *British Journal of Educational Technology*, *37*(5), 705–720. doi:10.1111/j.1467-8535.2006.00641.x

Siekpe, J. S. (2005). An examination of the multidimensionality of flow construct in a computer-mediated environment. *Journal of Electronic Commerce Research*, *6*(1), 31–43.

Skiba, D. J. (2009). Emerging technologies center nursing education 2.0: A second look at Second Life. *Nursing Education Perspectives*, *30*(2), 129–131. PMID:19476080

Smyth, R. (2011). Enhancing learner-learner interaction using video communications in higher education: Implications from theorising about a new model. *British Journal of Educational Technology*, *42*(1), 113–127. doi:10.1111/j.1467-8535.2009.00990.x

Stevenson, M., & Hedberg, J. G. (2013). Learning and design with online real-time collaboration. *Educational Media International*, *50*(2), 120–134. doi:10.1080/09523987.2013.795352

Tinto, V. (1975). Dropout from higher education: A theoretical synthesis of recent research. *Review of Educational Research*, *45*(1), 89–125. doi:10.3102/00346543045001089

van Schaik, P., Martin, S., & Vallance, M. (2012). Measuring flow experience in an immersive virtual environment for collaborative learning. *Journal of Computer Assisted Learning*, *28*(4), 350–365. doi:10.1111/j.1365-2729.2011.00455.x

Wadsworth, B. J. (1988). *Piaget's theory of cognitive and affective development* (4th ed.). New York: Longman.

Wei, C., Chen, N., & Kinshuk, . (2012). A model for social presence in online classrooms. *Educational Technology Research and Development*, *60*(3), 529–545. doi:10.1007/s11423-012-9234-9

Weinstein, C., & Mayer, R. (1986). The teaching of learning strategies. In M. C. Wittrock (Ed.), *Handbook of Research on Teaching and Learning* (3rd ed.; pp. 315–327). New York: Macmillan.

Wilson, C. D. (2013). Making connections: Higher education meets social media. *Change*, *45*(4), 51–57. doi:10.1080/00091383.2013.806201

Wirt, L. G., & Jaeger, A. J. (2014). Seeking to understand faculty-student interaction at community colleges. *Community College Journal of Research and Practice*, *38*(11), 980–994. doi:10.1080/10668926.2012.725388

Wood, J. L., & Ireland, S. M. (2014). Supporting black male community college success: Determinants of faculty–student engagement. *Community College Journal of Research and Practice*, *38*(2/3), 154–165. doi:10.1080/10668926.2014.851957

ADDITIONAL READING

Chickering, A. W., & Gamson, Z. F. (1987). Seven principles for good practice in undergraduate education. *AAHE Bulletin*, 3-7. Retrieved from ERIC database. (ED 282491).

Csikszentmihalyi, M. (2008). *Flow: The psychology of optimal experience*. New York, NY: HarperCollins.

Fredricks, J. A., Blumenfeld, P. C., & Paris, A. H. (2004). School engagement: Potential of the concept, state of the evidence. *Review of Educational Research*, *74*(1), 59–109. doi:10.3102/00346543074001059

National Survey of Student Engagement. (2014). *Engagement indicators*. Retrieved from http://nsse.iub.edu/html/engagement_indicators.cfm

Pearce, J. M., Ainley, M., & Howard, S. (2005). The ebb and flow of online learning. *Computers in Human Behavior, 21*(5), 745–771. doi:10.1016/S0747-5632(04)00036-6

KEY WORDS AND DEFINITIONS

Affective/Emotional Engagement: Students' positive and negative reactions and feeling toward the curriculum, instructor, and peer(s), including interest, boredom, happiness, sadness, anxiety, like, dislike, feeling of belonging, valuing of learning, appreciation of success in school, and so on.

Behavioral/Physical Engagement: Student's participation and involvement in class activities, including paying attention, asking questions, contributing to class discussion, putting effort to do the work, and so on.

Cognitive Engagement: Student's cognitive effort is invested to learn, understand, and master the intended knowledge and skills.

Flow Learning Experience: An intense engaging experience which occurs when students interact with the course materials in such a way that their concentration is focused on the task at hand, leaving less or no attention to think about irrelevant issues, and that the sense of time is distorted while completing the task.

Online Learners: Students who take a fully online course that does not require meeting in a physical classroom.

Student Engagement: Engagement at the course level is defined as the amount of time, cognitive effort, physical effort, and emotional effort students are willing to invest in learning content (e.g., video lecture, textbook), completing class activities (e.g., group discussion, peer-review, reflection), and participating in other activities relevant to the course topics (e.g., community presentation, internship, local event, volunteering).

Student Interaction: The interaction a student has with peers to collaborate on learning, with the class instructor to discuss learning materials and to obtain feedback, and with class content to learn the intended knowledge and skills.

Chapter 14
Ensuring Presence in Online Learning Environments

Eunice Luyegu
Nova Southeastern University, USA

ABSTRACT

Online learning in higher education has rapidly grown in recent years and has become the norm. However, pedagogical aspects on online learning environments are still developing. This chapter focuses on one foundational aspect of online and blended learning known as presence. First, the concept of presence in online learning is described i.e. teaching presence, social presence, and cognitive presence. Secondly, strategies for ensuring presence are discussed from different angles: course design, course instructors and course facilitators, and course participants. Thirdly, the implications for future research are outlined. This chapter enhances the research on the Community of Inquiry (CoI) framework a useful guide to the design of learning experiences that support learners' critical reflection and engagement within collaborative online learning environments.

INTRODUCTION

A central theme in research today is social, teaching, and cognitive presence in online and blended learning environments (Aragon, 2003; Garrison, Anderson, & Archer, 2000; Garrison & Vaughn, 2008; Shea & Bidjerano, 2012; Tu, 2002). Most research, as Swan, Garrison, and Richardson (2009) note, is focused on single presences of the Community of Inquiry (CoI) model, yet its theoretical strength lies in the dynamics of the whole community.

This chapter will look at the CoI framework wholistically and go beyond theory and jargon description by focusing on practical strategies for ensuring social, teaching, and cognitive presence in online learning environments. It will specifically examine strategies and tools for course design, teaching, and student participation. Tools and strategies will be gleaned from the literature and personal experience as an instructional designer and instructor in online and blended learning environments.

DOI: 10.4018/978-1-4666-9582-5.ch014

BACKGROUND

This chapter is based on the CoI framework (Garrison, Anderson, & Archer, 2000; Garrison & Vaughn, 2008). A literature review by Halverson et al. (2014) indicates that this model has been widely adapted and shows considerable promise in online learning. The CoI framework encompasses three core, interdependent elements: social presence, cognitive presence, and teaching presence. At the core of this model is the socio-constructivist view of learning – "construction of meaning may result from individual critical reflection but ideas are generated and knowledge constructed through collaborative and confirmatory process of sustained dialogue with a critical community of learners" (Garrison & Archer, 2000, p.91).

The three main, overlapping elements of the CoI framework are social presence, teaching presence, and cognitive presence as depicted in Figure 1.

Social presence is associated with how students and instructors interact online. According to the CoI framework, social presence is the degree to which students in an online learning environment are free to express themselves in a risk-free way. Gunawardena and Zittle (1997) define social presence as "the degree to which a person is perceived as 'real' in mediated communication" (p. 8). Social presence is conceptualized by open communication, group cohesion, and affective/personal connections (Garrison & Vaughan, 2008). Tu (2002) defines social presence as "a measure of the feeling of community that a learner experiences in an online environment" (p. 131). Social presence has been linked to students' satisfaction and perceived learning (Picciano, 2002; Richardson & Swan, 2003; Swan & Shih, 2005).

Cognitive presence is the extent to which students are able to construct meaning through sustained communication. Cognitive presence is "grounded in the critical thinking literature and is operationalized by the practical inquiry model" (Garrison, Anderson, & Archer, 2001, p.2). It is the element in the CoI that is the core to successful higher learning experiences (Kanuka & Harrison,

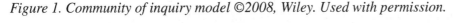

Figure 1. Community of inquiry model ©2008, Wiley. Used with permission.

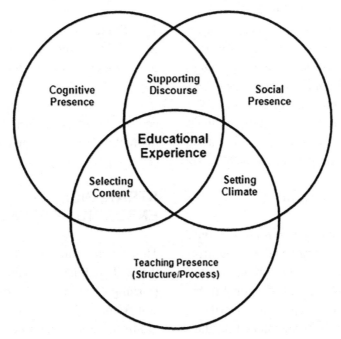

2004). There is evidence of positive significant relationship between a sense of community and cognitive learning (Rovai, 2002). The CoI framework has four phases of pragmatic inquiry: triggering, exploration, integration, and resolution.

Teaching presence in the CoI framework relates to course design and organization, facilitation, and direction. It is "the design, facilitation, and direction of cognitive and social processes for the purpose of realizing personally meaningful and educationally worthwhile learning outcomes" (Anderson, Rourke, Garrison, & Archer, 2001, p. 5). Successful social and cognitive presence is dependent on teaching presence. Ineffective online learning can be attributed to ineffective teaching presence with inadequate leadership and direction by the facilitator (Hiltz & Turoff, 1993). Teaching presence has been positively correlated with students' satisfaction and perceived learning (Shea, Pickett, & Pelz, 2003). Teaching presence is "important for the creation and sustainability of a community of inquiry focused on the exploration, integration, and testing of concepts and solutions" (Garrison & Cleveland-Innes, 2005, p. 135).

Naturally, there is student engagement in face-to-face courses; students meet in a physical location where they interact with one another and their instructor. Their meetings may include a lecture, discussions, lab sessions, team work, etc. Online learning provides a different learning environment. Meetings among students and their instructor in online learning are spread across different locations and times. Thus, creating a virtual community and establishing social, teaching, and cognitive presence is a strategic, conscious effort.

Interaction and Presence

Researchers agree that interaction is an essential component of online learning and that it significantly influences the success of an online course and its effectiveness (Bruning, 2005; Kim, Liu & Bonk, 2005; Sher, 2009). Picciano (2002) clarifies that there is a difference between interaction and presence. In a study involving 51 students enrolled in an online course, Tu and McIsaac (2002) explored the relationship between social presence and interaction in online learning environments. They concluded that social presence influences interaction. They cautioned that interaction may indicate presence but a student interacting with classmates is not necessarily engaged in a process of inquiry and cognitive presence may not even exist. Interaction and presence both influence student performance. Interaction is correlated with student satisfaction (Dziuban & Moskal, 2001) and online students' sense of community (Dawson, 2006). The CoI framework integrates cognitive, social, and teaching elements that are more than social exchanges and low-level cognitive interaction (Garrison & Anderson, 2003).

Interaction in online learning environments is very different from face-to-face environments. There is a physical distance in online environments and the lack of face-to-face interactions may create a sense of isolation (Blender, 2003) and a feeling of not being part of the community (Hrastinski, 2008). Interaction may lead to learner engagement in a course (Stein & Graham, 2014). There are three types of interaction in a course:

1. Student-instructor interaction
2. Student-student interaction
3. Student-content interaction

Stein and Graham recommend instructional activities with a mix of the different types of interaction for an engaging student experience.

STRATEGIES FOR ENSURING PRESENCE

This section will present and discuss strategies that will establish and maintain presence in online learning environments, the core of which is the CoI framework. Strategies for each of the three groups of people involved in the three functions of this environment – course designers (course design), instructors (delivery and management), and students (participation) (Aragon, 2003) – will be described. These three groups of people are the stakeholders that make for a successful learning experience (Swan, Garrison, & Richardson, 2009). Emerging findings from studies which use the CoI framework will be reported. The chapter will conclude with a summary and several directions for future research.

Course Design

Presence begins with course design. After a synthesis of literature, Garrison and Cleveland-Innes (2005) concluded that "if students are to reach a high level of critical thinking and knowledge construction, the interaction or discourse must be structured and cohesive" (p. 136). Designing, according to Lowyck and Poysa (2001), includes the "systematic choices and use of procedures, methods, prescriptions and devices in order to bring about effective, efficient and productive learning" (p. 507).

Tu and McIsaac (2002) have linked social presence to course design. Swan and Shi (2005), also linked course design to the development of social presence, based on a study of students enrolled in four online graduate courses. Swan and Shi concluded that social presence can be improved by selecting appropriated computer-mediated communication strategies and applying appropriate instructional elements to course design.

Tu (2000) has linked perceived presence and success in online courses and further associated the development of social presence in online courses to course design. He identified three dimensions of course design which influenced the development of social presence: social context including task orientation, perceptions of privacy, topics, and social processes; online communication referring to the language course participants use to com-

municate and express themselves; and interactivity including reciprocal communication patterns and timely responses.

Gasevic, Adesope, Joksimovic, and Kovanovic (2015) argue that a high level of cognitive presence can be achieved in student-student interactions through an effective instructional design, and that can compensate for facilitation and direct instruction, the two other components of teaching presence. One of the main problems with online courses is that they are very similar in design to existing face-to-face courses (Allen & Seaman, 2013). Online courses should be intentionally designed and may require learning various technologies used to connect to, participate in, and create meaningful learning artifacts (Arbaugh, 2000).

The following section explores course design strategies that establish presence in online learning environments.

Collaborative Learning

Early instructional design theories such as behaviorism focused on individual learners. However, there has been a rise in socio-constructivist theories of learning and design where learners collaboratively construct knowledge. Building on the foundations of constructivism, the social constructivist theory posits that interaction with others impacts and influences learning, and that learners socially negotiate meaning through reflection, collaboration, and articulation (Vygotsky, 1978). Collaborative learning involves students developing shared meaning while working together on problems, issues, or learning tasks (Stahl, Koschmann, & Suthers, 2006). Social learning does not just happen on its own. Rather, it occurs when the instructor creates a learning environment that makes it possible for it to take place (Michael, 2006).

Online collaborative learning refers to educational applications that emphasize collaborative discourse and knowledge building mediated by the Internet; learners work together online to identify and advance issues of understanding, and to apply their new understanding and analytical terms and tools to solving problems, constructing plans or developing explanations for phenomena (Harasim, 2012, pp. 88).

The online learning process includes three main elements: discourse, collaborative learning, and knowledge building (Harasim, 2012). Harasim (2002) theorizes online collaborative learning theory as a function of three intellectual phases:

1. Idea generating that involves brainstorming, verbalization, generating information, which leads to sharing of ideas and positions on a particular topic or problem
2. Idea organizing that marks the start of conceptual change and convergence. Students at this stage confront and clarify new or different ideas, select the strong and eliminate the weak ones. It's the phase of intellectual progress
3. Intellectual convergence, a phase of shared understanding. Students in this phase agree to disagree and/or co-produce a conclusion

The CoI framework theorizes online learning as a result of collaborative work among active participants – a collaborative constructivist view. Collaborative activities increase learner-to-learner interaction which in turn leads to social presence (Kim, Kwon, & Cho, 2011). Interaction of learners, as Garrison and Cleveland-Innes (2005) put it, is the *sine qua non* of higher education. It has to be structured and systematic. Success in collaborative learning is dependent on all participants' contribution to outcomes. The outcomes, therefore, should provide evidence of the nature of the collaborative endeavor. This requires systematic choices in course design. Reigeluth (1983) advices that the outcome of any design activity is a plan for

the format, content, and structure of the environment, the delivery systems, and implementation strategies.

Collaborative learning encompasses all group-based instructional methods (Prince, 2004). Students are likely to learn when they learn with others than when they learn alone. Approaches to students learning together include cooperative learning, peer learning, and problem-based learning (Michael, 2006). Collaborative learning may involve students working in pairs or teams to complete assignments, discussions, projects, debates, presentations, performances etc. Group size influences student participation in collaborative activities. Small groups tend to engage non-participating learners and supports a higher sense of engagement and presence (Hammond, 2000). Kesim and Agaoglu (2007) provide a list of tools that can be used to foster collaboration and social presence in online learning. They include messaging, text chat, discussion forums, blogs, weblogs, and wikis, among others.

Speaking of groups, Lowry, Roberts, Romano, and Cheney (2006) evaluated the impact of social presence on small-group communication. They examined the perceptions of the quality of group communication with varying small group sizes and levels of social presence. They found that the 3-person groups experienced better communication in regard to appropriateness, openness, and accuracy than did the 6-person groups. This research shows how the quality of discussion, communication appropriateness, communication richness, openness, and accuracy are correlated to social presence and group size.

Critical Thinking and Reflection

Critical thinking is characterized by the comprehensive exploration of issues, ideas, artifacts, and events before accepting or forming an opinion or conclusion (Rhodes, 2010). Critical thinking is an essential component of teaching and learning and its value is well-documented (Kim, Sharma, Land, & Furlong, 2013; Simpson & Courtney, 2002; Zakus, Malloy, & Edwards, 2007). However, questions remain about effective pedagogical strategies for incorporating critical thinking into learning. These questions are compounded when it comes to online learning environments where there is a physical distance among students and their instructor. This has led to a plethora of research on learning and instructional strategies that promote critical thinking (Jeong, 2003; MacKnight, 2000; Rovai, 2007).

Reflection is a key component to critical thinking. It is characterized by thoughtful mediation or contemplation that utilizes the power of the mind to form ideas and/or draw inferences that result in the expression of carefully considered thought expressed in critical dialogue (Kanuka & Garrison, 2004). Laurillard (2002) emphasizes the role of reflective deliberation in learning. According to this researcher, there are two ways in which knowledge is constructed. The first is through real life experience of a phenomena. The second way is through reflection on an abstract phenomena. It is not always easy or even possible to provide every learner with real-life experiences that are relevant to him or her. In online learning, it is typical for instructors to provide information through rhetorical discourse and text. Learners then reflect on the descriptive, abstract information and make it relevant to themselves. Learners articulate their reflections through writing. These reflections and then evaluated and feedback provided.

At the heart of practical inquiry model is the "rigorous and purposeful process of reflection and discourse to construct meaning and confirm knowledge" (Swan, Garrison, & Richardson, 2009, p.6). Cognitive presence is operationalized through the inquiry process. Course design should support the inquiry process by advancing discourse and reflection though the four phases of triggering event, exploration, integration, and resolution. Garrison and Cleveland-Innes (2005) warn that

high interaction of learners does not necessarily mean that they are cognitively engaged. These researchers add that cognitively rich interaction is characterized more by the quality than the quantity of the interaction. Quality of interaction, thus, must be specified in the design goal and the interaction should be facilitated and directed in a sustained manner. Learning activities that require students to complete low level tasks, e.g., define terms, will result in low levels of critical thinking than tasks that require learners to diagnose loosely-structured, authentic problems (Garrison & Cleveland-Innes).

Following a mixed-methods study of 73 students in a 15-week long online course, Darabi, Arrastia, Nelson, Cornille, and Liang. (2011) concluded that "discussion strategies requiring learners to take a perspective in an authentic scenario facilitate cognitive presence, and thus critical thinking and higher levels of learning" (p. 216).

To sum it up, learning environments should:

- Engage learners in activities authentic to the discipline in which they are learning;
- Provide for collaboration and the opportunity to engage multiple perspectives on what is being learned;
- Support learners in setting their own goals and regulating their own learning; and
- Encourage learners to reflect on what and how they are learning (Driscoll, 2012, p. 41).

Technology

Incorporating multimedia (graphics, audio, and video) in online learning can influence learners' motivation and improve learning. This is called the multimedia effect (Mayer, 2001). The multimedia principle is based on cognitive theory and research evidence. The rationale behind this principle is that use of multimedia creates active learning whereby learners engage in relevant cognitive processing by attending to relevant material, mentally organizing the material into coherent cognitive representation, and mentally integrating the material with existing knowledge (Clark & Mayer, 2011). Thus, multimedia helps create both cognitive and teaching presence. Ice, Bain, and Stewart's (2010) research shows that rich, technology-enhanced content, as opposed to static content, promotes higher order learning.

Greyling and Wentzel (2007) explored social presence in a large technology-assisted course of 3,000 students. They created a social space on the course website for social interaction to reduce the non-academic posts that cluttered the discussion board. As a result, "more students participated or read the discussion and started to associate positive feelings created by the social space with the subject of Economics" (p. 664). They add that these positive feelings led to a motivation for students to do better in Economics and encouraged the authors to take a more active role in facilitating and designing for social presence. The authors conclude that technology can facilitate online social presence which in turn promotes learning.

Technological tools maybe generic and include search engines such as Google, web browsers for accessing the web such as Chrome, email tools such as Gmail, productivity tools such as online calendars, document-creation tools such as Google docs and graphic presentation tools. Web 2.0 generic tools include blogs, wikis, podcast-authoring tools, web-authoring tools, social networking tools, and tools to enable social networking by user-generated content. Education-specific tools include websites or portals with resources specifically for teachers, students, or particular disciplines. This includes sites that offer lesson plans e.g. Planbook, Lesson builder; assessment tools e.g. Quizinator, Hot Potatoes; learner support or tutoring; and web portals that contain course materials and podcasts. (Harasim, 2012).

Table 1. Features related to social presence of web conference tools. ©2015, IGI Global. Used with permission.

Web Conferencing Tools						
Features	**Cisco WebEx**	**Adobe Connect**	**Fuze Meeting**	**Yugma**	**Elluminate**	**BigBlue-Button**
Whiteboard	√	√	√	√	√	√
Participant Annotation	√	√	√	√	√	√
Desktop Control	√	√	√	√	√	√
Screen Sharing	√	√	√	√	√	√
Call-in/Call-back	√	√	√	√	√	
Toll-free Calling	√	√	√	√	√	
VoIP	√	√	√		√	√
Webcam	√	√			√	√
File Transfer			√	√	√	
Public Chat	√	√	√	√	√	√
Private Chat	√	√	√	√	√	√
Mobile App	√	√	√		√	
User Profile Creation	√	√	√		√	
Polling		√	√		√	√
Quiz					√	
Maximum Participants	25	50	100	500	100	25

Web conference technologies provide opportunities for synchronous, multimodal communication among students or between students and their instructor. The web conference technologies have features that include audio, video, text chat, breakout rooms, presentation display, polling, white board collaboration, and application sharing. In online learning, web conferencing may improve students' perceptions of the course and could increase participation and motivation (Hudson, Knight, & Collins, 2012). Table 1 compares the basic features of different web conference tools in relation to social presence (Zhang, 2015, p. 167).

Web 2.0 Tools

Web 2.0 refers to "the social use of the Web which allow people to collaborate, to get actively involved in creating content, to generate knowledge and to share information online" Grosseck, 2009, p. 478). Web 2.0 tools are being used to establish teaching and social presence in online learning environments. The 2008 British Educational and Technology Communications Agency (Becta) report provides examples of Web 2.0 applications in education:

- Offer new opportunities for learners to take more control of their learning and access their own customized information, resources, tools, and services
- Encourage a wider range of expressive capability
- Facilitate more collaborative ways of working, community creation, dialogue and knowledge sharing
- Furnish a setting for learner achievements to attract authentic audience. (Crook & Harrison, 2008, p. 11)

Kaplan and Haenlein (2010) have defined six types of social media that people use to create and exchange information and ideas on the web. They are collaborative projects, blogs and microblogs, content communities, social networking sites, virtual game worlds, and virtual social worlds. These tools can also be used in online learning environments. Table 2 shows commonly used Web 2.0 tools and their examples.

Clark (1983, 1994) cautions that while using technology, the focus should be on the instructional methods and not the technology used.

Discussion Boards

When used effectively, discussion boards are known to create cognitive presence. Cognitive presence is a function of sustained communication over time on important content. To encourage this kind of sustained communication over time on a discussion board, posts should be substantial, concise, provocative, explanatory, timely, logical, and free of grammatical errors (Boettcher & Conrad, 2010). Research shows that most discussions do not move beyond the exploration phase (Davidson-Shivers, Luyegu, & Kimble, 2012; Murphy, 2004). The nature of assignments and facilitation are some of the reasons that have been given (Akyol & Garrison, 2008). That with good facilitation and challenge, integration and resolutions are possible (Murphy, 2004). Another explanation is that integration and resolution may be achieved in other parts of the course (Archer, 2010). Kanuka and Garrison (2004) note that to move online discussions from "sharing and comparing" of opinions to higher levels of learning, learners must be given an opportunity to apply what they have learned in addition to discussing it.

Social presence can be established in text-based courses. Based on Swan et. al.'s coding schema, Swan (2003) investigated how social presence developed in online discussions in a graduate course in Education. The three category indicators were affective (paralanguage, expressions of emotion, statements of values, humor, and self-disclosure), cohesive (greetings and salutations, use of vocatives, group reference, social sharing, and course reference), and interactive (acknowledgement,

Table 2. Web 2.0 applications for online learning

Tools	Description	Example
Blogs	A blog "can be considered as a special type of home page which has a time element, containing reverse-chronological entries of commentary, descriptions of proceedings, or other material such as graphics or video, depending on their purpose" (Chhabra & Sharma, 2013, p. 4).	Blogger, WordPress, Edublogs
Content syndication through RSS	Allows others to get updated ever-changing content without visiting the content website through RSS feed.	News sites syndicate their content as an RSS Feed to whoever wants it.
Mashups	"Web application which combines audio, video, text, etc. from multiple sources into an engaging and integrated experience" (Lal, 2015, p. 237).	Flappr, Buzzword
Microblogs	Microblogs are like blogs but shorter. Users exchange short content such as single sentences, individual images, or video links.	Twitter, Tumblr
Photos sharing	Sharing images by uploading to a website.	Flickr, Picasa
Podcasts	Podcasting "is the process of capturing an audio event, song, speech, or mix of sounds and then posting that digital sound object to a Web site or blog in a data structure called an RSS 2.0 envelope or feed" (Meng, 2005, p. 1).	TED Talks
Social bookmarking	Users add web documents to a collection and tag them with key words. The documents, tags, relationships, and other user-supplied information are compiled into a folksonomy. Users may browse or search the folksonomies for documents of interest (Gordon-Murnane, 2006).	Del.icio.us
Social networking	An online place or space where a user can create a profile and build a personal network that connects him or her to other users.	LinkedIn, Facebook
Video sharing	Sharing video by uploading to a website	YouTube, Vimeo, Edutopia, Teacher's TV, TeacherTube, SchoolTube
Wikis	A site for collaborative creation of content. A user can add, edit, or modify content.	Wikipedia

agreement, approval, invitation, and personal advice). Swan found an average of almost six indicators per posting in 235 postings. Brooks and Jeong (2006) found that pre-structured discussion threads in which the instructor scaffolds resulted in increased frequency of discussion posts that led to meaningful discourse.

The lack of verbal and visual cues in text-based discussion boards can hinder the exchange of information among students (Hew & Hara, 2007). Ching and Hsu (2013) investigated the use of multimodal communication for collaboration and knowledge sharing in a fully online graduate course. Out of 19 participants, more than half of them interacted with peers via audio, followed by text, and lastly via video. Approximately 70 percent of the contributions were by audio or video. Arbaugh and Benbunan-Fich (2006) emphasize that "communication facilities (such as discussion boards, chat rooms, etc.) should be brought to the forefront of the design and delivery of online courses, rather than being an 'add-on' activity" (p. 445).

Asking the right questions is key to an effective online discussion. Davis (1993) lists a range of question types including:

- Exploratory questions: probe facts and basic knowledge
- Challenge questions: interrogate assumptions, conclusions or interpretations
- Relational questions: ask for comparisons of themes, ideas, or issues
- Diagnostic questions: probe motives or causes
- Action questions: call for a conclusion or action

- Cause-and-effect questions: ask for causal relationships between ideas, actions, or events
- Extension questions: expand the discussion
- Hypothetical questions: pose a change in the facts or issues
- Priority questions: seek to identify the most important issue(s)
- Summary questions: elicit synthesis

Discussion Formats

There are several discussion formats that can be used in online learning (MacKnight, 2000). They include:

- Small group discussions that are typically led by the instructor or a group leader
- Buzz groups that consist of two people who discuss an issue or problem for a limited period of time
- Case discussions whereby real or simulated complex problems are analyzed thoroughly and a solution is offered
- Debate and argumentation teams in which students formulate ideas, identify evidence, defend positions, and counter the opposition's arguments
- Jigsaw groups where students are assigned to subgroups to discuss various parts of a topic. Each subgroup is responsible for presenting their topic to the rest of the class
- Mock trials occur when students assume the roles of individuals in a real life setting

Mobile Learning

Mobile learning, also known as m-learning, is "any type of learning that takes place in learning environments and spaces that take account of the mobility of technology, mobility of learners, and mobility of learning" (El-Hussein & Cronje, 2010, p. 20). Traxler (2005) defines mobile learning (m-learning) as:

...any educational provision where the sole or dominant technologies are handheld or palmtop devices. This definition may mean that mobile learning could include mobile phones, Smartphones, personal digital assistants (PDAs) and their peripherals, perhaps tablet PCs and perhaps laptop PCs, but not desktops in carts and other similar solutions. Perhaps the definition should address also the growing number of experiments with dedicated mobile devices such as games consoles and iPODs, and it should encompass both mainstream industrial technologies and one-off experimental technologies (p. 262 - 263).

Mobile learning has become a common tool that provides students with ubiquitous learning opportunities in higher education (Pastore, Land, & Jung, 2011; Zeng & Luyegu, 2012). Mobile learning has unique technology features that include social interactivity, context sensitivity, connectivity, individuality, and portability (Klopfer, Squire, & Jenkin, 2008), features that support social, cognitive, and teaching presence. Mobile learning includes handheld devices such as personal digital assistants, cell phones, iPod touch systems, portable gaming devices, global position systems (GPS), and iPod-like touch systems (Wagner, 2008). Each successive generation of these devices has added new features and applications, for example Wi-Fi, e-mail, productivity software, music player, and audio/video recording. Consequently, educators are adapting mobile technology for teaching and learning.

In learning, Short Messaging Service (SMS) and Multimedia Message Service (MMS) can be used for text and photo messaging for in class communication. They are suitable for that because they are robust, simple, affordable, and familiar to students (Lindquist et al., 2007). Handheld devices can be used as audience response systems for participation or real-time formative assessment (Evans & Johri, 2008). An example is the Multiple-choice Personal Response System (PRS) clickers.

Podcasting has become popular as a medium for accessing and assimilating information. There is evidence that podcasting is effective in reducing isolation-induced anxiety and promoting a sense of belonging to a community of learners (Lee & Chan, 2007). Podcasts have shown considerable promise as an effective learning tool. They have been used at some universities to distribute lectures to students with audio/video materials or distribute supplementary lectures for on-campus students (Concannon et al., 2005). Students use podcasts as review materials to prepare for quizzes and exams (Lonn & Teasley, 2009).

Below are overarching pedagogical steps for creating podcasts as proposed by the University of Wisconsin ("Podcasting – Resources for faculty," n.d.):

1. Select appropriate content
2. Determine your instructional goal
3. Design your content
4. Produce your content
5. Incorporate the podcast into your course

While discussing paradigms of learning app use, Dennen and Hao (2014) say that mobile apps can be used as a tutor to provide direct instruction and assessment, for example, flash cards, drill and practice, and quiz games. Mobile apps can be used as information source to present information, for example eBooks and animations. Mobile apps can also be used as a simulator by providing the environment, for example virtual worlds and role-play games. Lastly, mobile apps can be used as a collaboration enabler to connect students and/or instructor and help them work together, for example discussion forums and Web 2.0 tools.

Asynchronous Video

Synchronous communication is online learning is not always possible. It requires time commitment which is contrary to the flexibility that online learning is supposed to provide. In addition, syn-chronous video does not offer an opportunity for reflection prior to making comments and the technology can sometimes be unreliable (Griffiths & Graham, 2009). To remedy this, some researchers have suggested asynchronous video. That asynchronous video maintains the flexibility of online learning and at the same time establishes social, teaching, and cognitive presence (Borup, West, & Graham, 2012; Griffiths & Graham, 2009).

Borup, West, and Graham (2012) conducted a study to explore the impact of video-based strategies on students' perceptions of the instructor's social presence, and how video-based strategies influence students' perceptions of their own and their peers' social presence. They reported that students "indicated feeling that the video-based communication made their instructors seem more real, present, and familiar, and several students indicated that these relationships were similar to face-to-face instruction' (p. 2). They also reported that video communication impacted students' social presence and to a lesser degree instructor social presence.

Course Instructors

Course instructors have a role of facilitating discourse in online learning environments. They are the primary provider of teaching presence. This section explores strategies course instructors can implement to ensure presence.

Direction and Facilitation

It is the instructor's responsibility to direct and facilitate the course. Through research with 1067 online college students, Shea, Sauli, and Pickett (2006) found out that teachers' instructional design and direct facilitation was significantly correlated with students' sense of learning community. Research has shown that when the instructor directs and facilitates problem solving, students progress to resolution (Murphy, 2004). Shea and Bidjerano (2009) suggest that direction is centered around:

1. Providing valuable analogies
2. Offering useful illustration
3. Presenting helpful examples
4. Conducting supportive demonstrations
5. Supplying clarifying examples

Online students may need more guidance and additional faculty scaffolding. An online course should be a clear path through learning activities, resources, activities, and assessments with explicit guidance throughout (Graham & Stein, 2014).

Participation in Discussion Boards

Discussion boards have become central to online learning; they connect learners and the instructor. Therefore, instructors should be active in these discussions. The instructor demonstrates teaching presence by participating in online discussions, regulating the pace and content learned, and effectively moderating and redirecting discussions (Jefferies, Grodzinsky, & Griffin, 2003). Garrison and Cleveland-Innes (2005) recommend "structured discourse that facilitate clear discussion threads, avoid disjointed monologues, and move the discussion through the phases of inquiry" (p. 137). Instructors should challenge learners to resolve a problem, follow that by continual and effective facilitation for learners to progress toward integration and resolution (Murphy, 2004). Swan and Shih (2005) explain that discussion topics and grading rubrics that support sharing of personal experience promote social presence.

The role of the instructor is not just a facilitator of the discourse but rather a mediator of the students or discussion groups and the larger knowledge community that he or she represents (Harasim, 2012). For students to achieve higher order learning from discussions, instructors should possess knowledge and skills in educational methods and learning strategies, in addition to using information communication technology as a learning and teaching platform. For an effective discourse, the instructor should take an active role

of assisting and guiding the discussions. This can be accomplished by posing questions of emerging relevance (Kanuka & Garrison, 2004).

Synchronous Sessions

Synchronous sessions happen when students and the instructor meet at the same time. They are often referred to as live or real-time. These sessions may be optional or mandatory. The instructor can use these sessions to deliver presentations, clarify course material, provide guidelines, etc. (Arbaugh & Hwang, 2006).

Synchronous tools are no longer a new phenomenon in online learning. Synchronous sessions are made possible by web conferencing tools either in Learning Management Systems (LMS), for example Collaborate™, or outside of LMSs, for example, Cisco WebEx™ and Adobe Connect™. These web conferencing tools offer communication through audio, video, chat, presentation display, breakout rooms, white board collaboration, polling, and desktop/ application sharing. Synchronous learning increases both teaching and social presence, enables instant feedback from the instructor and peers, increases students' motivation to learn, and boosts their self-efficacy in online learning (Hudson, Knight, & Collins, 2012; Wang, Jaeger, Liu, & Xie, 2013). Synchronous communication in online learning can help reduce that sense of isolation that is common in online learners, assist in the formation of communities of practice, promote interaction, increase personal and cognitive participation, and facilitate student engagement (Falloon, 2011; McBrien, Jones, & Cheng, 2009; Pan & Sullivan, 2005; Schullo et al, 2007).

Instructor Contact Information and Availability

An online instructor should provide his/her contact information to students. This may include email address, phone number (if possible), skype name, and any other way students may reach him/her. The instructor should also specify when he/she can be reached and incase of email, when students should expect a response. Some instructors have virtual office hours. Specifying a time zone is also important.

Email communication is one of online learners' lifeline to their instructor. Prompt answers to email is thus critical. Email can be used to communicate with the whole class, subset of students, or individual students for announcements, clarifications, etc. (Svinicki & McKeachie, 2011). Instructors should provide students with a timeframe of when they should expect a response and what to do if they do not receive the response after that time frame.

Announcements

Instructors should create a message welcoming students to class. This can be in form of video, audio, or text. In this message, the instructor should welcome students, introduce himself or herself, and perhaps give an overview of the course (Aragon, 2003). This initial post creates social presence. As part of instructor introduction, Boettcher and Conrad (2010) recommend including a picture, short biography, link to a favorite publication, hobbies, etc.

Class-wide announcements may be made, once, twice, or three times a week depending on the course, students, and if there are other forms of communication being used in the online course. Boettcher and Conrad (2010), in their guide to online teaching, note that announcements contribute to teaching presence. They add that instructors do not use the announcement feature often enough. Overuse of the announcement feature, however, can be problematic – students may stop reading them. Announcements can be used "for general messages and reminders, such as the following (p.111):

- General schedule reminders such as holidays, assignments, and project deadlines
- Reminder's about the week's activities
- Announcements about special opportunities and events at the institution and online
- Reminders about general course processes, such as importance of making discussion postings early in the week

Announcements can be in the form of video, audio, or text. A study conducted by Borup, West, and Graham (2012) showed that the instructor's use of video increased social presence in the classroom.

Feedback

There are four major levels of feedback. First is the feedback that focuses on task or product, for example, is work correct or incorrect. Second, feedback that focuses on the process used to create a product or complete a task. Third, there is feedback that is focused at the self-regulation level. This is the feedback that influences a student's self-efficacy, self-regulation, and self-belief. Lastly, feedback that is focused on the individual, i.e. self, and is mostly unrelated to the task (Hattie & Timperley, 2007). Hattie and Timperley argue that the feedback focused on the individual is least effective.

Instructors should provide students with written feedback that is (Nicol, 2010, p. 512-3):

- **Understandable:** Expressed in a language that students will understand
- **Selective:** Commenting in reasonable detail on two or three things that the student can do something about
- **Specific:** Pointing to instances in the student's submission where the feedback applies

- **Timely:** Provided in time to improve the next assignment
- **Contextualized:** Framed with reference to the learning outcomes and/or assessment criteria
- **Non-Judgmental:** Descriptive rather than evaluative, focused on learning goals, not just performance goals
- **Balanced:** Pointing out the positive as well as areas in need of improvement
- **Forward-Looking:** Suggesting how students might improve subsequent assignments
- **Transferable:** Focused on process, skills, self-regulatory processes, not just on knowledge content
- **Personal:** Referring to what is already known about the student and her/his previous work

Feedback serves two purposes: to inform the learner of the correctness or adequacy of his or her response and to provide corrective information so that the learner for improvement (Driscoll, 2012). Feedback demonstrates cognitive and teaching presences. Some instructors have recently began using audio feedback. Students have found this kind of feedback to be more personal and humanizing than text (Kim, 2004). Although students on average prefer audio to text feedback, there is a lack of the instructor's facial expressions in audio feedback. Consequently, some instructors have begun using video feedback (Borup et al., 2014). Parton, Crain-Dorough, and Hancock's (2010) research revealed that the personal nature of video feedback helped students feel connected to their instructor. In conclusion, the use of audio and video feedback has been perceived by both students and instructors as effective in enhancing social presence.

Course Participants

Course participants refers to students enrolled in a course. These students have a role to play in creating presence in online learning environments. This section explores course participants' role in creating presence, especially social presence.

Student Profiles

Students should create their profiles that include their picture, bio, and any other information they choose to share, for example, interests, experience, etc. This information helps to build connection amongst students and the instructor (Aragon, 2003) which enhances social presence.

Discussion Board

Discussion boards in online learning environments are forums for communication and exchange of information. Discussion boards help to build a class community, therefore, students' active participation is just as important. Students who report interacting with fellow students in online courses describe higher levels of social presence (Kim, Kwon, & Cho, 2011). Schrire (2006) has found cognitive presence of students in student-student discussions to be higher than in student-instructor discussion.

For deep learning that supports critical thinking on discussion boards, online students must have a thorough understanding of the goal of the discussion. They should also have the skills to "ask the right questions, listen to each other, take turns to share work, help each other learn, respect each other's ideas, construct their own understanding, and think in new ways" (MacKnight, 2000, p. 39).

Instructor moderation of online discussions is an important factor in the success of the discussion. However, there are challenges to this moderation. For example, effective moderation of a large class may not be possible due to the time constraints (Rourke & Anderson, 2003). While the CoI model places the instructor at the center of moderation, Garrison, Anderson, and Archer (2000) acknowledge that teaching presence can also be achieved through meaningful student interaction. Consequently, facilitation of online discussions becomes a shared responsibility of the instructor and students.

Researchers are investigating the viability of having teacher-assigned or students self-select moderator roles. Baran and Correia (2009) found that peer-facilitation strategies can help generate innovative ideas, motivate students to participate actively in the discussions, and provide an atmosphere for involvement and commitment.

Course Participation

Course participation is not limited to the discussion board. The instructor should have an evaluation criteria for students' course participation, in addition to the general course assessment. Class participation points may be awarded at the end of a week, module, course, or at certain times in the course that the instructor deems as appropriate. Participation points should not be automatically give to students for just being there. Rather, these points should be awarded for students' active participation in class activities, discussions, teamwork, presentations, etc.

Things to consider for evaluation of students' course participation include (Patel, 2015, p. 362):

- How prepared was a student with his/her reflection on the weekly readings?
- How was the student able to promote dialogue based upon constructive discussion of others' works?

- Did the student advance ideas and actively listen to and reflected upon the ideas of others?
- Was the student present in the class most of the week?

Self-Assessment

Self-assessment promotes cognitive presence. Self-assessment includes "a range of different practices in which learners take responsibility for making their own judgments about their work" (Taylor, Marienau, & Fiddler, 2004, p. 64). It is a function of three components related in a cyclical, ongoing process: self-monitoring, self-evaluation, and identification and implementation of instructional correctives as needed. In this process, students identify their learning and performance strategies, provide themselves with feedback, and determine their next course of action to improve their performance. Instructors should maintain high standards and expectation as students set goals and progress through self-evaluations. Students' self-assessment should have clear objectives and evaluation criteria (McMillan & Hearns, 2008).

Self-assessment has been known to empower students to think critically and reflect on their learning processes, strategies, and outcomes (Dochy et al., 1999, Wang, 2013). Self-assessment can promote intrinsic motivation (McMillan & Hearn), is a key element of self-regulation (Panadero & Jesus, 2013), and promotes active learning (Roberts, 2006). After a review of literature, Falchikov (2005) identified seven types of benefits of self-assessment: improvement in cognitive and meta-cognitive competencies, development of a variety of skills, improved performance, enhanced personal or intellectual development or social competencies, improved 'affective dispositions', better assessments and benefits to teachers.

For self-assessment to be effective, instructors should provide students with the assessment criteria at the start of the activity so that they can strategically plan for their actions ((Andrade & Valtcheva, 2009). Self-assessment should not be limited to assessing the product of learning. The process of getting to the product should also be taken into consideration (Alonso-Tapia & Panadero, 2010).

Conditions that are necessary and promote self-assessment include (Panadero & Jesus, 2013, p. 564):

1. Awareness of the value of self-assessment. Unless students are aware of the usefulness of self-assessment, they will not self-assess their work, as it requires effort from them. For this reason, it is important that they understand that self-assessment is a crucial ability for learning.
2. Access to the criteria on which assessment is based. Students should know these criteria because it should be used to self-assess their work. It is recommended that students have access to these criteria from the beginning of the task, as it has been explained throughout this article (Andrade & Valtcheva, 2009).
3. The task to be assessed needs to be specific. If the task is too broad or it is not well defined, it can be complicated to self-assess its realization. For this reason, it is recommended that the teachers, having this fact in mind, try to choose tasks that are well defined and with steps clearly established, at least the first time they try to teach their students to self-assess their work.

Panadero and Jesus (2013) recommend instructional aids that promote self-assessment and facilitate the above conditions. They include:

1. Self-assessment modeling
2. Direct instruction and help in self-assessment

3. Cues that help to know when it is time to self-assess
4. Practice
5. Opportunities to review and improve the process of realizing a task as well as the final performance or product

There has been some concern over student self-assessment. Crowe (2000) points out three major ethical issues in this kind of assessment: (1) learner readiness, (2) evaluation credibility, and (3) power issues. To resolve these issues, Crowe suggests finding a balance between traditional assessment techniques with self-directed assessment techniques. There are also student-related issues with self-assessment. For example, students sometimes prefer to be assessed by their instructor – the expert.

CONCLUSION

This chapter presented strategies for establishing and maintaining social, teaching, and cognitive presence in online learning environments. The three key elements focused on are course design, course instructor, and course participants. There is a significant correlation between students' perceived and actual interactions with instructors and their perceived learning (Richardson & Swan, 2003). There also is evidence of a strong relationship between social, teaching, and cognitive presence and student satisfaction, retention, and perceived learning in online learning environments (Arbaugh, 2008; Garrison & Cleveland-Innes, 2005; Shea, Pickett, & Pelz, 2004).

The stakeholders of the CoI framework that encompasses social, teaching, and cognitive presence, are the student, instructor, and instructional designer. These stakeholders are responsible for a successful online or blended learning experience (Swan, Garrison, & Richardson, 2009). The social, teaching, and cognitive presence strategies provided offer practical benefits in terms of ensuring presence in online and blended learning environments. "The key to creating a cohesive, purposeful and worthwhile community of inquiry is the integration of social, teaching, and cognitive presence. Each of the three presences manifest themselves in different ways in a face-to-face or online context" (Vaughan & Garrison, 2006, p. 150).

Creating a sense of community is important in online learning. Learning community activities encourage students to explore, share, analyze, and refine their thinking and practice via social interaction. These activities target higher-level cognitive skills that are underlined by critical thinking and are based on the social aspect of being human (Stein & Graham, 2014). As more online courses and programs are offered, care should be taken to make sure that social, teaching, and cognitive presence is established and maintained, and that a vibrant community of learners exists. Educators in higher education should not be sidetracked by technology and lose sight of the importance of determining and using the most effective instructional best practices while delivering learning in online environments. Effective online teaching and learning should include approaches that are student-centered, developmentally responsive, and achievement oriented (Smith, 2009).

FUTURE RESEARCH DIRECTIONS

One of the challenges of online and blended learning is ensuring that there is social, cognitive, and teaching presence. While the CoI has shown considerable promise in online learning environments, more research is needed on the influence of motivational, metacognitive, and behavioral factors on the effectiveness of these presence strategies. The CoI is a dynamic framework with the presence and their categories shifting and interacting over time (Swan, Garrison, & Richardson, 2009). Thus, there is a need on research on how the social, teaching, and cognitive presence strategies interact with one another over time and across disciplines.

Equally important is how the CoI framework is linked to emerging technologies and how these technologies promote presence in online learning environments. Ice, Curtis, Phillips, and Wells (2007) investigated the effects of audio feedback from instructors in asynchronous courses to enhance teaching presence and students' sense of community. They found that audio feedback was related to perception on increased caring on the part of the instructor. Similar research that links the CoI framework elements and emerging technologies is important. The role of the cultural variables and its impact on social presence also needs further investigation.

REFERENCES

Akyol, Z., & Garrison, D. R. (2008). The development of a community of inquiry over time in an online course: Understanding the progression and integration of social, cognitive and teaching presence. *Journal of Asynchronous Learning Networks, 12*(3-4), 3–22.

Allen, E., & Seaman, J. (2010). *Class differences: Online education in the United States*. Needham, MA: Sloan Consortium.

Allen, I. E., & Seaman, J. (2013). *Changing course: Ten years of tracking online education in the United States*. Newburyport, MA: Sloan Consortium.

Alonso-Tapia, J., & Panadero, E. (2010). Effect of self-assessment scripts on self-regulation and learning. *Infancia y Aprendizaje, 33*(3), 385–397. doi:10.1174/021037010792215145

Anderson, T., Rourke, L., Garrison, D. R., & Archer, W. (2001). Assessing teaching presence in a computer conferencing context. *Journal of Asynchronous Learning Networks, 5*(2), 1–17.

Andrade, H., & Valtcheva, A. (2009). Promoting learning and achievement through self-assessment. *Theory into Practice, 48*(1), 12–19. doi:10.1080/00405840802577544

Aragon, S. R. (2003). Creating social presence in online environments. *New Directions for Adult and Continuing Education, 100*(100), 57–68. doi:10.1002/ace.119

Arbaugh, J. B. (2000). Virtual classroom characteristics and student satisfaction with internet-based MBA courses. *Journal of Management Education, 24*(1), 32–54. doi:10.1177/105256290002400104

Arbaugh, J. B. (2008). Does the community of inquiry framework predict outcomes in online MBA courses? *International Review of Research in Open and Distance Learning, 9*(2). Retrieved from http://www.irrodl.org/index.php/irrodl/article/view/490/1045

Arbaugh, J. B., & Benbunan-Fich, R. (2006). An investigation of epistemological and social dimensions of teaching in online learning environments. *Academy of Management Learning & Education, 5*(4), 435–447. doi:10.5465/AMLE.2006.23473204

Arbaugh, J. B., & Hwang, A. (2006). Does "teaching presence" exist in online MBA courses? *The Internet and Higher Education, 9*(1), 9–21. doi:10.1016/j.iheduc.2005.12.001

Archer, W. (2010). Beyond online discussion: Extending the community of inquiry framework to entire courses. *The Internet and Higher Education, 13*(1-2), 69. doi:10.1016/j.iheduc.2009.10.005

Baran, E., & Correia, A. (2009). Student-led facilitation strategies in online discussions. *Distance Education, 30*(3), 339–361. doi:10.1080/01587910903236510

Bender, T. (2003). *Discussion based online teaching to enhance student learning.* Sterling, VA: Stylus Publishing, LLC.

Bloch, J., & Spataro, S. E. (2014). Cultivating critical-thinking dispositions throughout the business curriculum. *Business and Professional Communication Quarterly, 77*(3), 249–265. doi:10.1177/2329490614538094

Boettcher, J. V., & Conrad, R. (2010). *The online survival teaching guide: Simple and practical pedagogical tips.* Jossey-Bass. Retrieved from http://www.myilibrary.com?ID=320339

Borup, J., West, R. E., & Graham, C. R. (2012). Improving online social interaction through asynchronous video. *The Internet and Higher Education, 15*(3), 195–203. doi:10.1016/j.iheduc.2011.11.001

Borup, J., West, R. E., Thomas, R. A., & Graham, C. R. (2014). Examining the impact of video feedback on instructor social presence in blended courses. *International Review of Research in Open and Distance Learning, 15*(3), 232–256.

Brooks, D., & Jeong, A. (2006). Effects of pre-structuring discussion threads on group interaction and group performance in computer-supported collaborative argumentation. *Distance Education, 27*(3), 371–390. doi:10.1080/01587910600940448

Bruning, K. (2005). The role of critical thinking in the online learning environment. *International Journal of Instructional Technology and Distance Learning, 2*(5), 21–31.

Chhabra, R., & Sharma, V. (2013). Application of blogging in problem-based learning. *Education and Information Technologies, 18*(1), 3–13. doi:10.1007/s10639-011-9168-6

Ching, Y.-H., & Hsu, Y.-C. (2013). Collaborative learning using VoiceThread in an online graduate course. *Knowledge Management & E-Learning*, *5*(3), 298–314.

Clark, R. C., & Mayer, R. E. (2011). *E-Learning and the science of instruction: Proven guidelines for consumers and designers of multimedia learning* (3rd ed.). San Francisco, CA: John Wiley & Sons. doi:10.1002/9781118255971

Clark, R. E. (1983). Reconsidering research on learning from media. *Review of Educational Research*, *53*(4), 445–459. doi:10.3102/00346543053004445

Clark, R. E. (1994). Media and method. *Educational Technology Research and Development*, *42*(3), 7–10. doi:10.1007/BF02298090

Cobb, S. C. (2009). Social presence and online learning: A current view from a research perspective. *Journal of Interactive Online Learning*, *8*(3), 241–254. Retrieved from http://anitacrawley.net/Articles/Social%20Presence%20and%20Online%20Learning%20A%20Current%20View%20from%20a%20Research.pdf

Collis, B., & Moonen, J. (2008). Web 2.0 tools and processes in higher education: Quality perspectives. *Educational Media International*, *45*(2), 93–106. doi:10.1080/09523980802107179

Concannon, F., Flynn, A., & Campbell, M. (2005). What campus-base students think about the quality of benefits of e-learning. *British Journal of Educational Technology*, *36*(3), 501–521. doi:10.1111/j.1467-8535.2005.00482.x

Crook, C., & Harrison, C. (2008). *Web 2.0 technologies for learning at Key State 3 and 4: Summary report*. London: BECTA. Retrieved from http://dera.ioe.ac.uk/1480/1/becta_2008_web2_summary.pdf

Crowe, J. L. (2000). Evaluation of adult learners: Ethical issues. *New Horizons in Adult Education*, *14*(3), 4–10. doi:10.1002/nha3.10117

Darabi, A., Arrastia, M. C., Nelson, D. W., Cornille, T., & Liang, X. (2011). Cognitive presence in asynchronous online learning: A comparison of four discussion strategies. *Journal of Computer Assisted Learning*, *27*(3), 216–227. doi:10.1111/j.1365-2729.2010.00392.x

Davidson-Shivers, G. V., Luyegu, E., & Kimble, B. E. (2012). An analysis of asynchronous discussions: A case study of graduate student participation in online debates. *Journal of Educational Media and Hypermedia*, *21*(1), 29–51.

Davis, B. G. (1993). *Tools for Teaching*. San Francisco: Jossey-Bass.

Dawson, S. (2006). A study of the relationship between student communication, interaction, and sense of community. *The Internet and Higher Education*, *9*(3), 153–162. doi:10.1016/j.iheduc.2006.06.007

Dennen, V. P., & Hao, S. (2014). Paradigms of use, learning theory, and app design. In C. Miller & A. Doering (Eds.), *The new landscape of mobile learning: Redesigning education in an app-based world* (pp. 20–40). Hershey, PA: IGI Global.

Dochy, F., Segers, M., & Sluijsmans, D. (1999). The use of self-, peer and co-assessment in higher education. *A review. Studies in Higher Education*, *24*(3), 331–350. doi:233137993510.1080/0307507991

Driscoll, M. P. (2012). Psychological foundations of instructional design. In R. A. Reiser & J. V. Dempsey (Eds.), *Trends and issues in instructional design and technology* (3rd ed., pp. 35–44). Saddlebrook, NJ: Merrill/Prentice-Hall.

Dziuban, C., & Moskal, P. (2001). *Emerging research issues in distributed learning*. Paper presented at the 7th SloanC International Conference on Asynchronous Learning Networks, Orlando, FL.

El-Hussein, M. O., & Cronje, J. C. (2010). Defining mobile learning in higher education landscape. *Journal of Educational Technology & Society*, *13*(3), 12–21.

Evans, M., & Johri, A. (2008). Facilitating guided participation through mobile technologies: Designing creative learning environments for self and others. *Journal of Computing in Higher Education*, *20*(2), 92–105. doi:10.1007/s12528-008-9004-1

Falchikov, N. (2005). *Improving assessment through student involvement: Practical solutions for aiding learning in higher and further education*. London: Routledge.

Falloon, G. (2011). Making the connection: Moore's theory of transactional distance and its relevance to the use of a virtual classroom in postgraduate online teacher education. *Journal of Research on Technology in Education*, *43*(3), 187–209. doi:10.1080/15391523.2011.10782569

Garrison, D. R., Anderson, T., & Archer, W. (2000). Critical inquiry in a text-based environment: Computer-conferencing in higher education. *The Internet and Higher Education*, *2*(2-3), 87–105. doi:10.1016/S1096-7516(00)00016-6

Garrison, D. R., Anderson, T., & Archer, W. (2001). Critical thinking, cognitive presence, and computer conferencing in distance education. *American Journal of Distance Education*, *15*(1), 7–23. doi:10.1080/08923640109527071

Garrison, D. R., & Archer, W. (2000). *A transactional perspective on teaching-learning: A framework for adult and higher education*. Oxford, UK: Pergamon.

Garrison, D. R., & Cleveland-Innes, M. (2005). Facilitating cognitive presence in online learning: Interaction is not enough. *American Journal of Distance Education*, *19*(3), 133–148. doi:10.1207/s15389286ajde1903_2

Garrison, D. R., & Vaughan, N. D. (2008). *Blended Learning in higher education: Framework, principles, and guidelines*. San Francisco: Jossey-Bass.

Gasevic, D., Adesope, O., Joksimovic, S., & Kovanovic, V. (2015). Externally-facilitated regulation scaffolding and role assignment to develop cognitive presence in asynchronous online discussion. *The Internet and Higher Education*, *24*, 53–65. doi:10.1016/j.iheduc.2014.09.006

Gordon-Murnane, L. (2006). Social bookmarking, folksonomies, and web 2.0 tools. *Searcher*, *14*(6), 26–38.

Greyling, F. C., & Wentzel, A. (2007). Humanising education through technology: Creating presence in large classes. *South Africa Journal of Higher Education*, *21*(4), 654–667.

Griffiths, M. E., & Graham, C. R. (2009a). Using asynchronous video in online classes: Results from a pilot study. *Instructional Technology & Distance Learning*, *6*(3), 65–76.

Grosseck, G. (2009). To use or not to use web 2.0 in higher education? *Procedia: Social and Behavioral Sciences,* *1*(1), 478–482. doi:. sbspro.2009.01.08710.1016/j

Gunawardena, C., & Zittle, F. (1997). Social presence as a predictor of satisfaction within a computer mediated conferencing environment. *American Journal of Distance Education*, *11*(3), 8–26. doi:10.1080/08923649709526970

Halverson, L. R., Graham, C. R., Spring, K. J., Drysdale, J. S., & Henrie, C. R. (2014). A thematic analysis of the most highly cited scholarship in the first decade of blended research. *The Internet and Higher Education*, *20*, 20–34.

Hammond, M. (2000). Communication within on-line forums: The opportunities, the constraints and the value of a communicative approach. *Computers & Education*, *35*(4), 251–262. doi:10.1016/S0360-1315(00)00037-3

Harasim, L. (2012). *Learning theory and online technologies*. New York: Routledge.

Hattie, J., & Timperley, H. (2007). The power of feedback. *Review of Educational Research, 77*(1), 81–112. doi:10.3102/003465430298487

Hew, K. F., & Hara, N. (2007). Empirical study of motivators and barriers of teacher online knowledge sharing. *Educational Technology Research and Development, 55*(6), 573–595. doi:10.1007/s11423-007-9049-2

Hiltz, S. R., & Turoff, M. (1993). *The Network Nation: Human communication via computer* (revised edition). Cambridge, MA: MIT Press.

Hrastinski, S. (2008). Asynchronous & synchronous e-learning. *EDUCAUSE Quarterly, 4*, 51–55.

Hudson, T. M., Knight, V., & Collins, B. C. (2012). Perceived effectiveness of Web conferencing software in the digital environment to deliver a graduate course in applied behavior analysis. *Rural Special Education Quarterly, 31*(2), 27–39.

Ice, P., Bain, B., & Stewart, M. (2010). Using the Community of inquiry survey instrument to inform online learning outcomes. In Z. Abas et al. (Eds.), Proceedings of Global Learn 2010 (p. 455). Association for the Advancement of Computing in Education (AACE).

Ice, P., Curtis, R., Phillips, P., & Wells, J. (2007). Using asynchronous audio feedback to enhance teaching presence and students' sense of community. *Journal of Asynchronous Learning Networks, 11*(2), 3–25.

Jefferies, P., Grodzinsky, F., & Griffin, J. (2003). Advantages and problems in using information communication technologies to support the teaching of a multi-institutional computer ethics course. *Journal of Educational Media, 28*(2–3), 191–202. doi:10.1080/1358165032000165644

Jeong, A. C. (2003). The sequential analysis of group interaction and critical thinking in online threaded discussions. *American Journal of Distance Education, 17*(1), 25–43. doi:10.1207/S15389286AJDE1701_3

Kaplan, A. M., & Haenlein, M. (2010). Users of the world, unite! The challenge and opportunities of social media. *Business Horizons, 53*(1), 59–68. doi:10.1016/j.bushor.2009.09.003

Kesim, A., & Agaoglu, E. (2007). A paradigm shift in distance education: Web 2.0 and social software. *Turkish Online Journal of Distance Education-TOJDE, 8*(3). Retrieved from: http://tojde.anadolu.edu.tr/tojde27/articles/article_4.htm

Kim, J. (2011). Developing an instrument to measure social presence in distance higher education. *British Journal of Educational Technology, 42*(5), 763–777. doi:10.1111/j.1467-8535.2010.01107.x

Kim, J., Kwon, Y., & Cho, D. (2011). Investigating factors that influence social presence and learning outcomes in distance higher education. *Computers & Education, 57*(2), 1512–1520. doi:10.1016/j.compedu.2011.02.005

Kim, K., Sharma, P., Land, S. M., & Furlong, K. P. (2013). Effects of active learning on enhancing student critical thinking in an undergraduate general science course. *Innovative Higher Education, 38*(3), 223–235. doi:10.1007/s10755-012-9236-x

Klopfer, E., Squire, K., & Jenkin, H. (2008). Environmental detectives - The development of an augmented reality platform for environmental simulations. *Educational Research Technology and Development, 56*(2), 1042–1629. doi:10.1007/s11423-007-9037-6

Lal, P. (2015). Leveraging Web 2.0 for online learning. In R. Wright (Ed.), Student-Teacher Interaction in Online Learning Environments (pp. 235–249). Hershey, PA: IGI Global. doi:10.4018/978-1-4666-6461-6.ch011

Laurillard, D. (2002). *Rethinking university teaching: A conversational framework for the effective use of learning technologies* (2nd ed.). RoutledgetFalmer. doi:10.4324/9780203304846

Lee, M. J. W., & Chan, A. (2007). Reducing the effects of isolation and promoting inclusivity for distance learners through podcasting. *Turkish Online Journal of Distance Education, 8*(1), 85–104. Retrieved from: http://tojde.anadolu.edu.tr/tojde25/ pdf/article_7.pdf

Lindquist, D., Denning, T., Kelly, M., Malani, R., Griswold, W. G., & Simon, B. (2007). Exploring the potential of mobile phones for active learning in the classroom. *ACM SIGCSE Bulletin, 39*(1), 384–388. doi:10.1145/1227504.1227445

Lonn, S., & Teasley, S. D. (2009). Podcasting in higher education: What are the implications for teaching and learning? *The Internet and Higher Education, 12*(2), 88–92. doi:10.1016/j.iheduc.2009.06.002

Lowry, P. B., Roberts, T. L., Romano, N. C., Cheney, D. P., & Hightower, P. D. (2006). The impact of group size and social presence on small-group communication. Does computer-mediated communication make a difference? *Small Group Research, 37*(6), 631–661. doi:10.1177/1046496406294322

Lowyck, J., & Poysa, J. (2001). Design of collaborative learning environments. *Computers in Human Behavior, 17*(5-6), 507–516. doi:10.1016/S0747-5632(01)00017-6

MacKnight, C. B. (2000). Teaching critical thinking through online discussion. *EDUCAUSE Quarterly, 4*, 38–41.

Mayer, R. E. (2001). *Multimedia learning*. New York: Cambridge University Press. doi:10.1017/CBO9781139164603

McBrien, J. L., Jones, P., & Cheng, R. (2009). Virtual spaces: Employing a synchronous online classroom to facilitate student engagement in online learning. *International Review of Research in Open and Distance Learning, 10*(3), 1–6.

McMillan, J. H., & Hearn, J. (2008). Student self-assessment: The key to stronger student motivation and higher achievement. *Education Digest, 74*, 39–44.

Michael, J. (2006). Where's the evidence that active learning works? *Advances in Physiology Education, 30*(4), 159–167. doi:10.1152/advan.00053.2006 PMID:17108243

Murphy, E. (2004). Identifying and measuring ill-structured problem formulation and resolution in online asynchronous discussions. *Canadian Journal of Learning and Technology, 30*(1), 5-20.

Nicol, D. (2010). From monologue to dialogue: Improving written feedback processes in mass higher education. *Assessment & Evaluation in Higher Education, 35*(5), 501–517. doi:10.1080/02602931003786559

Pan, C., & Sullivan, M. (2005). Promoting synchronous interaction in an eLearning environment. *Technical Horizons in Education, 33*(2), 27–30.

Panadero, E., & Jesus, A. (2013). Self-assessment: Theoretical and practical connotations. When it happens, how is it acquired, and what to do to develop it in our students. *Electronic Journal of Research in Educational Psychology, 11*(2), 551–576. doi:10.14204/ejrep.30.12200

Parton, B. S., Crain-Dorough, M., & Hancock, R. (2010). Using flip camcorders to create video feedback: Is it realistic for professors and beneficial to students? *International Journal of Instructional Technology and Distance Learning, 7*(1), 15–23.

Pastore, R. S., Land, S. M., & Jung, E. J. (2011). Mobile computing in higher education. In D. W. Surry, J. R. Stefurak, & R. M. Gray Jr., (Eds.), *Technology Integration in higher education: Social and organizational aspects* (pp. 160–173). Hershey, PA: IGI Global. doi:10.4018/978-1-60960-147-8.ch012

Patel, K. (2015). Planning, designing, implementing, and managing social presence in online programs and online classes. In R. D. Wright (Ed.), *Student-teacher interaction in online learning environments*. Hershey, PA: IGI Global. doi:10.4018/978-1-4666-6461-6.ch016

Picciano, A. G. (2002). Beyond student perceptions: Issues of interaction, presence, and performance in an online course. *Journal of Asynchronous Learning Networks*, 6(1), 21–40.

Podcasting – Resources for Faculty. (n.d.). Retrieved from http://engage.doit.wisc.edu/about/

Prince, M. (2004). Does active learning work? A Review of the Research. *The Journal of Engineering Education*, 93(3), 223–231. doi:10.1002/j.2168-9830.2004.tb00809.x

Reigeluth, C. M. (1983). Instructional design: What is it and why is it? In C. M. Reigeluth (Ed.), *Instructional-Design Theories and Models: An Overview of their Current Status*. Hillsdale, NJ: Erlbaum Associates.

Rhodes, T. (Ed.). (2010). *Assessing outcomes and improving education: Tips and tools for using rubrics*. Washington, DC: Association of American Colleges and Universities.

Richardson, J. C., & Swan, K. (2003). Examining social presence in online courses in relation to students' perceived learning and satisfaction. *Journal of Asynchronous Learning Networks*, 7(1), 68–88.

Roberts, T. (2006). Self, peer and group assessment in E-learning: An introduction. In T. Roberts (Ed.), *Self, peer and group assessment in E-learning* (pp. 1–16). Hershey, PA: Information Science. doi:10.4018/978-1-59140-965-6.ch001

Rovai, A. P. (2002). Sense of community, perceived cognitive learning, and persistence in asynchronous learning networks. *The Internet and Higher Education*, 5(4), 319–332. doi:10.1016/S1096-7516(02)00130-6

Rovai, A. P. (2007). Facilitating online discussions effectively. *The Internet and Higher Education*, 10(1), 77–88. doi:10.1016/j.iheduc.2006.10.001

Schullo, S., Hilbelink, A., Venable, M., & Barron, A. (2007). Selecting a virtual classroom system: Elluminate Live vs Macromedia Breeze (Adobe Connect Professional). *Journal of Online Learning and Teaching*, 3(4), 331–345. Retrieved from http://jolt.merlot.org/ documents/hilbelink.pdf

Shea, P., & Bidjerano, T. (2009). Community of inquiry as a theoretical framework to foster "epistemic engagement" and "cognitive presence" in online education. *Computers & Education*, 52(3), 543–553. doi:10.1016/j.compedu.2008.10.007

Shea, P., & Bidjerano, T. (2012). Learning presence as a moderator in the community of inquiry model. *Computers & Education*, 59(2), 316–326. doi:10.1016/j.compedu.2012.01.011

Shea, P., Sauli, C., & Pickett, A. (2006). A study of teaching presence and student sense of learning community in fully online and web-enhanced college courses. *The Internet and Higher Education*, 9(3), 175–190. doi:10.1016/j.iheduc.2006.06.005

Shea, P. J., Pickett, A. M., & Pelz, W. E. (2003). A follow-up investigation of "teaching presence" in the SUNY Learning network. *Journal of Asynchronous Learning Networks*, 7(2), 61–80.

Sher, A. (2009). Assessing the relationship of student-instructor and student-student interaction to student learning and satisfaction in Web-based online learning environment. *Journal of Interactive Online Learning*, *8*(2), 102–120. Retrieved from http://www.ncolr.org/jiol/issues/pdf/8.2.1.pdf

Simpson, E., & Courtney, M. (2002). Critical thinking in nursing education: Literature review. *International Journal of Nursing Practice*, *8*(2), 89–98. doi:10.1046/j.1440-172x.2002.00340.x PMID:11993582

Smith, D. (2009). *Using what we know: A practical guide to increasing student achievement*. Denver, CO: Outskirts Press.

Stahl, G., Koschmann, T., & Suthers, D. (2006). Computer-supported collaborative learning: An historical perspective. In R. K. Sawyer (Ed.), *Cambridge handbook of learning sciences* (pp. 409–426). Cambridge, UK: Cambridge University Press.

Stein, S., & Graham, C. R. (2014). *Essentials for blended learning: A standards-based guide*. New York: Routledge.

Svinicki, M. D., & McKeachie, W. J. (2011). *McKeachie's teaching tips: Strategies, research, and theory for college and university teachers*. New York: Routledge.

Swan, K. (2003). Developing social presence in online discussion. In S. Naidu (Ed.), *Learning and Teaching with Technology: Principles and Practices* (pp. 147–164). London: Kogan.

Swan, K., Garrison, D. R., & Richardson, J. C. (2009). A constructivist approach to online learning: The Community of Inquiry framework. In Information Technology and Constructivism in Higher Education: Progressive Learning Framework. Hershey, PA: IGI Global.

Swan, K., & Shih, L. F. (2005). On the nature and development of social presence in online course discussions. *Journal of Asynchronous Learning Networks*, *9*(3), 115–136.

Taylor, K., Marienau, C., & Fiddler, M. (2000). *Strategies for teachers and trainers: Developing adult learners*. San Francisco: Jossey-Bass.

Tu, C. H. (2000). On-line migration: From social learning theory to social presence in online course discussions. *Journal of Asynchronous Learning Networks*, *9*(3), 115–136.

Tu, C. H., & McIsaac, M. (2002). The relationship of social presence and interaction in online classes. *American Journal of Distance Education*, *16*(3), 131–150. doi:10.1207/S15389286AJDE1603_2

Tyson, T. (2006). It's a rap, but not as we know it…. *Times Higher Education Supplement*, *3*, 9.

Vygotsky, L. S. (1978). *Mind in society: The development of higher psychological processes*. Cambridge, MA: Harvard University Press.

Wang, C. X., Jaeger, D., Liu, J., & Xie, N. (2013). Using synchronous technology to enrich student learning. *TechTrends*, *57*(1), 20–25. doi:10.1007/s11528-012-0626-9

Zakus, D. H., Malloy, D. C., & Edwards, A. (2007). Critical and ethical thinking in sport management: Philosophical rationales and examples of methods. *Sport Management Review*, *10*(2), 133–158. doi:10.1016/S1441-3523(07)70008-6

Zeng, R., & Luyegu, E. (2012). Mobile Learning in Higher Education. In A. Olofsson & J. Lindberg (Eds.), *Informed Design of Educational Technologies in Higher Education: Enhanced Learning and Teaching* (pp. 292–306). Hershey, PA: Information Science Reference; doi:10.4018/978-1-61350-080-4.ch015

Zhang, B. (2015). Bridging the Social and Teaching Presence Gap in Online Learning. In R. Wright (Ed.), *Student-Teacher Interaction in Online Learning Environments* (pp. 158–182). Hershey, PA; doi:10.4018/978-1-4666-6461-6.ch008

ADDITIONAL READING

Baker, C. (2010). The impact of instructor immediacy and presence for online student affective learning, cognition and motivation. *The Journal of Educators Online, 7*(1).

Bangert, A. (2008). The Influence of social presence and teaching presence on the quality of online critical inquiry. *Journal of Computing in Higher Education, 20*(1), 34–61. doi:10.1007/BF03033431

Bender, T. (2012). *Discussion-based online teaching to enhance student learning: Theory, practice and assessment*. Sterling, VA: Stylus Publishing.

Boettcher, J., & Conrad, R. (2010). *The online teaching survival guide: Simple and practical pedagogical tips*. San Francisco, CA: Jossey-Bass.

Bonk, C. J. (2011). *The world is open: How Web technology is revolutionizing education*. San Francisco, CA: Jossey-Bass; doi:10.1002/9781118269381

Bransford, J. D., Brown, A. L., & Cocking, R. R. (2000). *How people learn: Brain, mind, experience, and school*. Washington, D.C.: National Academy Press.

Brown, R. E. (2001). The process of community building in distance learning classes. *Journal of Asynchronous Learning, 5*(2), 18–35.

Conrad, R. M., & Donaldson, J. A. (2011). *Engaging the online learner: Activities and resources for creative instruction* (Vol. 38). San Francisco, CA: John Wiley & Sons.

Dillenbourg, P. (1999). What do you mean by collaborative learning? In P. Dillenbourg (Ed.), *Collaborative-learning: Cognitive and computational approaches* (pp. 1–19). Oxford, UK: Elsevier.

Dirksen, J. (2012). *Design for how people learn*. Berkeley, CA: New Riders.

Fisher, M., & Baird, D. E. (2006). Making mlearning work: Utilizing mobile technology for active exploration, collaboration, assessment, and reflection in higher education. *Journal of Educational Technology Systems, 35*(1), 3–30. doi:10.2190/4T10-RX04-113N-8858

Franklin, T., Sun, Y., Yinger, N., Anderson, J., & Geist, E. (2013). The changing roles of faculty and students when mobile devices enter the higher education classroom. In J. Keengwe (Ed.), *Pedagogical applications and social effects of mobile technology integration* (pp. 238–257). Hershey, PA: IGI Global; doi:10.4018/978-1-4666-2985-1.ch014

Harasim, L. (2002). What makes online communities successful? The role of collaborative learning in social and intellectual development. In C. Vrasidas & G. Glass (Eds.), *Distance Education and Distributed Learning* (pp. 181–200). Greenwich, CT: Information Age Publishing.

Hosler, K., & Arend, B. (2012). Strategies and principles to develop cognitive presence in online discussions. In Z. Akyol & R. Garrison (Eds.), *Educational communities of inquiry: Theoretical framework, research and practice* (pp. 148–167). Hershey, PA: IGI Global; doi:10.4018/978-1-4666-2110-7.ch009

Kanuka, H., & Anderson, T. (1998). Online social interchange, discord, and knowledge construction. *Journal of Distance Education, 13*(1), 57–75.

Lemak, D., Shin, S., Reed, R., & Montgomery, J. (2005). Technology, transactional distance, and instructor effectiveness: An empirical investigation. *Academy of Management Learning & Education, 4*(2), 150–158. doi:10.5465/AMLE.2005.17268562

Moore, M. (1993). Theory of transactional distance. In D. Keegan (Ed.), *Theoretical principles of distance education* (pp. 22–38). New York, NY: Routledge.

Roschelle, J. (2003). Keynote paper: Unlocking the learning value of wireless mobile devices. *Journal of Computer Assisted Learning, 19*(3), 260–272. doi:10.1046/j.0266-4909.2003.00028.x

Saint-Jacques, A. (2012). Effective teaching practices to foster vibrant communities of inquiry in synchronous online learning. In Z. Akyol & R. Garrison (Eds.), *Educational communities of inquiry: Theoretical framework, research and practice* (pp. 84–108). Hershey, PA: IGI Global; doi:10.4018/978-1-4666-2110-7.ch006

Salmon, G. (2012). *E-moderating: The key to online teaching and learning.* London: Routledge.

Schutt, M., Allen, B. S., & Laumakis, M. A. (2009). The effects of instructor immediacy behaviors in online learning environments. *Quarterly Review of Distance Education, 10*(2), 135–148.

Shea, P., & Bidjerano, T. (2009). Measures of Quality in Online Education: An Investigation of the Community of Inquiry Model and the Net Generation. *Journal of Educational Computing Research, 39*(4), 339–361. doi:10.2190/EC.39.4.b

Shen, R., Wang, M., & Pan, X. (2008). Increasing interactivity in blended classrooms through a cutting-edge mobile learning system. *British Journal of Educational Technology, 39*(6), 1073–1086. doi:10.1111/j.1467-8535.2007.00778.x

Slagter Van Tryon, P. J., & Bishop, M. J. (2009). Theoretical foundations for enhancing social connectedness in online learning environments. *Distance Education, 30*(3), 291–315. doi:10.1080/01587910903236312

Smith, G. G., Ferguson, D., & Caris, M. (2001). Teaching college courses online versus face-to-face. *T.H.E. Journal, 28*(9), 18–22.

Stein, D., & Wanstreet, C. (2012). Coaching for cognitive presence: A model for enhancing online discussions. In Z. Akyol & R. Garrison (Eds.), *Educational communities of inquiry: Theoretical framework, research and practice* (pp. 133–147). Hershey, PA: IGI Global; doi:10.4018/978-1-4666-2110-7.ch008

Sung, E., & Mayer, R. E. (2012). Five facets of social presence in online distance education. *Computers in Human Behavior, 28*(5), 1738–1747. doi:10.1016/j.chb.2012.04.014

Traxler, J. (2005). Defining mobile learning. *IADIS International Conference Mobile Learning*. Retrieved from http://www.researchgate.net/profile/John_Traxler/publication/228637407_Defining_mobile_learning/links/0deec51c8a2b531259000000.pdf

Vaughan, N. D., Cleveland-Innes, M., & Garrison, D. R. (2013). *Teaching in blended learning environments: Creating and sustaining communities of inquiry*. Edmonton, Canada: AU Press, Athabasca University.

Vonderwell, S., & Zachariah, S. (2005). Factors that influence participation in online learning. *Journal of Research on Technology in Education, 38*(2), 213–230. doi:10.1080/15391523.2005.10782457

Wagner, E. D. (2008). Realizing the promises of mobile learning. *Journal of Computing in Higher Education, 20*(2), 4–14. doi:10.1007/s12528-008-9008-x

Wang, C. (2013). An exploratory study of student self-assessment in the online learning context. In M. S. Raisinghani (Ed.), *Curriculum, learning, and teaching advancements in online education* (pp. 123–135). Hershey, PA: IGI Global. doi:10.4018/978-1-4666-2949-3.ch009

Wang, F., & Bonk, C. J. (2001). A design framework for electronic cognitive apprenticeship. *Journal of Asynchronous Learning Networks*, 5(2), 131–151.

Wei, C.-W., Chen, N.-S., & Kinshuk, . (2012). A model for social presence in online classrooms. *Educational Technology Research and Development*, 60(3), 529–545. doi:10.1007/s11423-012-9234-9

York, C., & Richardson, J. C. (2013). Interpersonal interaction in online learning: Experienced online instructors' perceptions of influencing factors. *Journal of Asynchronous Learning Networks*, 16(4), 83–98.

Zach, L., & Agosto, D. E. (2009). Using the online learning environment to develop real-life collaboration and knowledge-sharing skills: A theoretical discussion and framework for online course design. *Journal of Online Learning and Teaching*, 5(4), 590–599.

KEY TERMS AND DEFINITIONS

Asynchronous Online Learning: A form of online learning where students access course materials and communicate with peers and instructor anytime per their convenience.

Blended Learning: A combination of different pedagogical theories in a face-to-face learning environment with or without technologically mediated interactions between students, teachers and learning resources.

Cognitive Presence: The extent to which learners are able to construct and confirm meaning through sustained personal reflection and discourse.

Community of Inquiry: A group of learners and instructors who share a technology-reliant environment, time-bound virtual space, course-dependent learning objectives, and rule-based interaction that results from the interaction of the perceptions of teaching, social, and cognitive presences.

Community of Inquiry (CoI) Framework: A model of online or blended learning that represents the learning experience as a result of the interaction of social, teaching, and cognitive presence.

Discourse: The use of words to exchange thoughts and ideas.

Instructional Design: A framework for organizing instructional content.

Learning Environment: A virtual or non-physical learning space that provides access to curriculum content, assessments, and communication and collaboration tools.

Online Learning: Learning via the web, internet, or other distance technologies.

Social Presence: The degree to which participants in computer-mediated communication feel affectively connected to one another.

Synchronous Online Learning: A form of online learning where students access course materials and communicate with peers and instructors at specific and pre-ordained times and locations.

Teaching Presence: An instructor's design, facilitation, and direction of cognitive and social processes.

Web Conferencing: A web-based service that allows people to meet in real time despite being in remote locations.

Chapter 15

Teaching and Learning Online:
An Examination of Effective Techniques, Practices, and Processes

Angelia Yount
Ball State University, USA

Kwesi Tandoh
Ball State University, USA

ABSTRACT

This chapter explores online learning and the pedagogical techniques needed to create an effective learning environment. In addition, it emphasizes the advances in contemporary online learning tracing its difficult beginning and the progress made due to advances made in technology especially the World Wide Web and the Internet. The chapter also discusses the importance of immediacy in online learning, and its ability to allow students to learn from anywhere and at any time. Student problems include lack of access to the technology, readiness to work online, and the erroneous impression that they know the technology more than the instructor. Interaction includes the effective application of scenarios of student and content, interaction between instructor and students, and the interaction between students which help promote social presence. We strongly believe the application of the afore-mentioned strategies will ensure successful development and implementations of an effective online course.

INTRODUCTION

The Internet and the World Wide Web has radically transformed the traditional practice of teaching and learning at a distance. Teaching online offers alternative instructional advantages for campus-based and locational-based non-traditional students the much needed flexibility and convenience. Pedagogically, online learning allows students

more control over the pace of their learning made possible by the asynchronous (learning environment where interaction between instructor and student occur at different times) nature of online learning (Meyen, Lian, & Tangen, 1997). This paper is written under the main principles of adult learning theory (Knowles, 1975), as well as constructivism, cognitivism, and behavioral learning theories. We believe that the principles

DOI: 10.4018/978-1-4666-9582-5.ch015

espoused in these theories are in line with the demands of online learning, which encourages the utilization of pedagogical procedures that are self-paced and student-centered. The literature shows that the continued growth in access to the Internet and the World Wide Web has spurred an increase in Internet-based learning (Picciano, 2002). According to Allen & Seaman (2013) there were between 6.7 million and 15 million (National Center for Education Statistics, 2012) individuals enrolled in online courses. The increase in popularity of online learning has motivated a critical mass of institutions to increase opportunities for students including non-traditional students to enroll in these courses (Shaw, Chametzky, Burrus, & Walters, 2013).

This chapter will analyze instructional best practices for online teaching and learning with the view to proposing helpful approaches to guide educators and courses designers. In the process, the authors will discuss the theoretical underpinnings and strategies needed to design effective online courses. In addition, this chapter will highlight a broader definition of pedagogy as encompassing andragogy as used in contemporary teaching and learning environment (Waterhouse, 2005). We will also discuss different strategies as illustrated in the literature that can be utilized in creating effective and engaging online courses. In order to do this, we will trace the history of distance learning and the evolving changes in definitions as indicated in the literature. We will also analyze the various strategies that contribute to make online teaching and learning a viable form of instruction in academia in the 21st Century.

Online learning has entrenched itself in recent years as part of our educational environment, specifically in higher education and business training centers (Anderson, 2008).

However, unlike most development trends, the increased interest in online learning has not been limited to developed countries only, colleges in developing countries have equally expressed interest in mediated learning for many reasons, including expanding access and flexibility to students' learning and training (Anderson, 2008). A closer look at the history of online or distance learning will help clarify why this method of learning continues to draw positive attention in academia.

HISTORY OF DISTANCE LEARNING

According to Anderson (2008), distance education is not an old discipline by academic standards though its theory and practice has evolved through five generations since its inception (Taylor, 2001). From its beginning, distance learning was viewed mostly as an individual pursuit interspersed with infrequent communication between learner and teacher (Anderson, 2008). However, the last part of the twentieth century witnessed a great transition and the emergence of three other generations of distance teaching and learning (Anderson, 2008). Of these three generations of distance learning, one was supported by the mass media of radio and television, next was the use of synchronous tools and audio teleconferencing, which was followed by computer conferencing (Anderson, 2008).

The rapid explosion of computer technology and the Internet in beginning of the 21st century has spurred emergence of a fifth generation of distance learning based on the autonomous agents and database assisted learning, which Anderson (2004) referred to in the literature as the educational "Semantic Web" and "Web 2.0." Though these generations have followed their predecessor more quickly than the previous ones, none of these has completely displaced the previous generations. This explains why we are currently dealing with different yet viable forms of distance education that use all five generations in combination. As a result, one can safely say that distance education can be described as complex, diverse, and rapidly evolving (Anderson, 2008).

The literature shows that online instruction has gained more popularity in higher education in recent years (Beatty & Ulasewicz, 2006). For instance, 89% of 4-year institutions offered distance education courses mediated by the Internet through Course Management Systems (CMS) during the 2000-2001 academic year (Tallent-Runnels, Thomas, Lan, Cooper, Ahern, Shaw, & Liu, 2006). Clearly, the increase in the power of the Internet is encouraging higher educational institutions to explore effective avenues of making education available to students of all ages anywhere and anytime (Chamberlain & Vrasidas. 2001).

The challenge for online educators, learners, administrators, and parents is to grapple with the choices concerning the pedagogical, economic, systemic, and political characteristics of the online education system within which to participate. In order to do that, stakeholders need to understand what online education means and its implication for teaching and learning.

WHAT IS ONLINE LEARNING?

In defining online learning, it is essential not only to describe what it entails but to show what it is not. Online learning is difficult to define because of the different terminologies it attracts (Moore & Kearsley, 2011). The literature shows there is no single accepted definition of online learning (Anderson, 2008). A closer look of Internet-based learning shows two distinct categories, with a large grey area. On one hand, there are courses that are mostly text-based which are often delivered online or by mail mostly mediated with computer enhancements. On the other hand, there are courses that are designed solely for the Internet setting which combines smaller components into a single course of study (Anderson, 2008). Presently, most of the courses delivered online are the former type, mostly text converted to electronic format often with multimedia enhancements (Anderson, 2008).

Keegan (1996) offered a variety of definitions of online learning. Among them he referred to distance education as a quasi-permanent separation of teacher and learner throughout the learning

process. Keegan (1996) also defined distance education as "the use of technical media-print, audio, video, or computer to unite teacher and learner and carry content of the course." In contemporary literature, online learning is often referred to as e-learning, distributed learning, web-based learning, tele-learning, computer-assisted learning, virtual learning, and distance teaching (Moore et al., 2011).

According to Shelton and Saltman (2005) the United States regional accreditation association defined distance education:

For the purposes of accreditation review, as a formal educational process in which the majority of the instruction occurs when student and instructor are not in the same place. Instruction may be synchronous or asynchronous. Distance education may employ correspondence study, or audio, video, or computer technologies. (The Commission on Colleges, 1997)

Similarly, Khan (1997) refers to online instruction as an innovative method of delivering instruction to a distant audience, using the web as the platform or "classroom." Carliner (1999) refers to online learning as presenting educational material through a computer with access to the internet. The different types of definitions in online learning show the diversity of methods and the associated technologies (Moore & Kearsley, 2011). However, Moore and Kearsley (2011) warn that online learning involves more than just delivering course materials on the web it involves a process where the main focus of attention is the learner and the learning process.

Shelton and Saltsman (2005) defined online learning as the delivery of education mediated by computers and the internet. It is a mode of instructional methodology in distance education. In this type of learning, both learner and instructor are in separate locations. It also indicates that some form of technology (normally a computer) is used as an intermediary to input and access course materials. During this process, instructors and learners use technology for interaction, and some form of administrative support is provided to both learner and instructor. All of these definitions show that the learner is always at a distance from the teacher, and the learning is mediated by some form of technology (usually a computer with internet access) used for interaction between the instructor and the learners and among the learners, and to access the learning materials (Ally, 2004).

In this chapter we define online learning as an innovative learning environment that utilizes the web and a course management system to deliver learning materials from a distance to remote learners. This environment allows the instructor to manage and facilitate the learning process. The student actively participates as a researcher performing authentic activities to acquire learning and transfer along with effective support systems for instructors and learners from administrators (Morrison, Lowther, & Demeneulle, 1999, Morrison, Ross, Kalman, & Kemp, 2011). Next, we will discuss the basic concepts needed to create effective online learning.

Basic Concepts of Teaching and Learning Online

According to Waterhouse, (2005), online learning is more impactful when the primary emphasis is on the basics of teaching and learning. In other words, teaching must focus on the basic principles of pedagogy not on the technology when teaching online. Thus, instructors teaching online should use the technology to help them achieve their stated instructional learning outcomes. Chizmar and Williams (2001) also emphasized the importance of making pedagogy the main determinant of the choice of technology in teaching and learning.

However, in making technology choices in education, instructors can take a cue from the suggested approaches from Bates' (as cited in Foley, 2003) 12 "golden rules" for the use of technology in education. Bates' (as cited in Foley, 2003)

suggestions show that effective teaching matters. That quality design of learning activities is crucial for all delivery methods (Foley, 2003). Bates (as cited in Foley, 2003) also emphasized that each unique medium has its own aesthetic value for teaching and must be recognized to highlight the importance of professionalism in online course design (Foley, 2003).

In addition, Bates (as cited in Foley, 2003) posited that teaching must be flexible to ensure inclusiveness (Foley, 2003). However, each teaching moment may have their own unique traits which can be exploited by instructors for successful teaching. Instructors must know that there is no "super-technology" out there (Foley, 2003). Each technology has its strengths and weaknesses; therefore, technologies need to be combined and used based on the instructional outcome. In addition, administration should make print, audio, television, and computers available to teachers and their students and let them decide which one best helps them achieve their instructional objectives at any given time (Foley, 2003).

Bates (as cited in Foley, 2003) also highlights the need to balance variety with economy. Using many technologies makes design more complex and expensive. Therefore, it is incumbent on stakeholders to limit the range of technologies in any given circumstance. In an online learning environment, Bates (as cited in Foley, 2003) also highlights the importance of interaction as well as the number of students in each course since the choice of a medium will depend greatly on the number of learners reached over the life of a course. The fact that a particular technology is new does not necessarily mean it is better than old ones. What instructors need is good training to use the technology more effectively. Bates (as cited in Foley, 2003) stresses technology will work well if it is based on a team effort because no one person has all the skills to develop and deliver an effective Web-based course. Therefore, subject matter experts, instructional designers, and media specialists are essential when it comes to creating a course online. Lastly, Bates (as cited in Foley, 2003) suggests technology is not the issue; rather it is what instructors want students to learn with the technology that matters.

In Online learning as in traditional face-to-face classroom, instructors need to make pedagogical decisions such as when to deliver a lecture, what to include in the lecture, and what kind of learning material and activities will best promote learning, and when to have students do group or individual activities like presentations, exams, written assignments to assess the effectiveness of the instruction (Waterhouse, 2005). These are some of the pedagogical principles instructors need to consider when preparing to teach online

However, it must be emphasized that using the web as a platform of education involves two major aspects, namely teaching and learning from a distance (Waterhouse, 2005). Teaching online also involves building a team that includes an instructional designer, subject matter expert, and a media specialist to ensure high quality materials, experiences, and a more effective teaching while learning involves a community of learners working together to achieve a learning outcome (Hirumi, 2000).

In online education, educational institutions design, develop, and deliver instructional material to the distant student through the internet to promote learning and application. To make teaching activities worthwhile instructors must follow general principles of good design. This will allow them to consider the target audience of their activities, content to be delivered, and the desired outcomes (Foley, 2003). The literature shows that online learning provides flexibility of access to material anywhere anytime, allowing learners to collapse time and space (Cole, 2000).

However, the rapid development in communication technologies has triggered a paradigm shift that calls for changes in the formats of teaching and learning. As a result, the learning material must be designed properly to allow learner en-

gagement and a better learning experience (Ally, 2004). There is the need for structural changes in teaching and the learning process. Thus the best way of creating an effective online learning environment is to identify the elements of quality instruction, accept the effectiveness of education at a distance, and the creation of an effective course on a viable education system (Wanstreet, 2009). According to Hirumi (2002), "A system is a set of interrelated components that work together to achieve a common purpose" (p. 90).

The components of this system include faculty, instructional designers, staff, administrators, and students working as a team. The team controls the creation of the courses which involves but not limited to the curriculum, instruction, management and logistics, academic services, professional development, and program evaluation (Wanstreet, 2009).

As the access and use of technology increases in academia, there is a need to explore whether the use of a specific technology or the systematic design of instruction improves learning (Clark, 2001; Kozma, 2001). Theorists such as Clark (1983) and Kozma (2001) have taken opposite positions on whether technology improves learning.

Does Technology Impact Learning?

There is an ongoing debate in academia on the impact of technology on learning. Clark (1983) for instance, argues that technology is just there to help the student, but plays no positive role in learner achievement. Clark emphasizes that the students learn more through instructional strategies.

On the other hand Kozma (2001) argues that the specific attributes of the technology are necessary to bring authentic models and simulations, thus the design of real life simulations in student interaction actually help students' achievement of stated learning outcomes. However, the choice to use technology and supporting material or not in online learning are not the only determinants of whether faculty will decide to teach online or not. There are deeper challenges that must be addressed as more and more courses are designed and taught online.

Though teaching online has progressed in quality and impact, it must be noted that the effectiveness of online learning does not come from the plethora of technology used alone. The power of online learning emerges when educators use the technology, and work in unison with instructional designers to create better instruction and learning environments (Waterhouse, 2005). Thus to make online learning more effective, instructors need to device effective means for making the learning experience more pragmatic and authentic. The first step in this process is to take a look at different theoretical schools of thought, and explore how they can be used to create effective online courses to promote learning.

LEARNING THEORIES

The literature shows that behaviorist thought underlined the development of early computer learning systems. Behaviorism as espoused by Thorndike, Skinner, and Pavlov, assumes the effects of external stimuli like reward and punishment shapes future behavior (Ally, 2004). To the behaviorists, the proof that an individual has learned depends on their observable external behavior and has nothing to do with the individual's thinking process (Ally, 2004). On the other hand, others believed that learning is more than change in external behavior. This challenge switched attention to cognitive learning theory, which postulates that learning is made possible by the triumvirate of memory, motivation, and thinking (Ally, 2004). Cognitive theorists believe that learning occurs when the learner is able to process and reflect on the amount of given information (Craik & Lockhart, 1972) with prior knowledge (Ausubel, 1974).

In recent years there has been a movement towards constructivism. This movement suggests that individuals construct their own meaning, and that we learn best when we bring our own reality to the learning environment and work with others to negotiate meaning (Ally, 2004, Morrison, et al, 2011).

A closer look at these theories shows an overlap in principle. Designing an effective online course can include the principles of the three schools of thought. In online learning behaviorist theory can be used to clarify the "what" (facts), while cognitive principles can be used to analyze the "how" (process), and constructivist theory to explore the "why" (critical thinking that triggers individual meaning in an authentic environment) (Ally, 2004). The question is how do these schools of thought affect online learning?

Behaviorism and Its Implication for Online Learning

Behaviorists believe learning can occur without any thought processes, because an individual's learning can be quantitatively measured by his/ her external behavior in response to stimulus. As a result, online learners must know the intended outcomes from the beginning so the learner can make a determination of achievement in the lesson. Learners must also be tested to see if they have met the intended outcome and have been given appropriate feedback (Ally, 2004). There is the need to sequence the learning material to promote student understanding, as well as provide feedback to allow learners to monitor their progress

Cognitivism and Online Learning

As stated earlier, cognitivists believe learning is an individual's ability to store and recall information. As a result, course developers of online learning must create structures that allow students to process the materials efficiently. The content must therefore be chunked and sequenced appropriately to allow easy information processing by learners (Ally, 2004). For instance, in online learning it is essential for important information to be highlighted to attract learner attention. Organized details for lesson headings allow learners to access and process the material with organized and informed thought (Ally, 2004). In addition, course materials should be structured to allow learners to connect long term memory with existing information. To do this, advanced organizers can be used to provide the information that comes with the details of the lesson to be learned (Ausubel, 1960). Instructors in online learning should provide conceptual models that allow students to create the strategy they will need to learn the lesson. Pre-instructional questions must also be used in online learning to set expectations and to trigger learners' existing knowledge structure. Chunking information and triggering the knowledge structure needed for learning the new material will not only avert information overload but allow students with different learning styles to choose their own path of learning (Ally, 2004). For instance, an effective online course should contain different forms of activities, be able to motivate students, allow learners to select activities that suit their unique learning styles, and help them choose their own path of learning. The question is what function does individual thinking play in this process? Constructivist theory will be discussed below to show how it can be structured to allow learners to create their own meaning in an online learning environment.

Constructivists Impact on Online Learning

Constructivist view learning as student-centered experience. It is a learning environment where the student is constantly engaged in authentic learning activities to create meaning. The instructor thus acts in multiple roles, as a designer, a manager, a coach, and a facilitator. In other words, the instructor is the "sage on the side" advising and guiding students' learning activities (Duffy & Cunningham, 1996). In online learning, having the students create their own meaning allows them to contextualize and personalize their learning and claim ownership of their experiences in this learning environment. The ability to negotiate meaning with their peers gives the student real world examples of collaborating in a group with others (Ally, 2004). Interacting with others and the materials in addition to creating their own meaning gives the student a sense of ownership. The literature shows that online instruction occurs when learners use the Web to go through a sequence of instruction provided by the instructor to complete an assigned learning activity to achieve certain outcomes (Ally, 2002, Ritchie & Hoffman, 1997). However, learning activities must be varied to accommodate different learning styles. Doing that allows students to choose the appropriate strategy to achieve learning outcomes. It is therefore incumbent on instructors to get learners prepared for the learning activity in order to achieve intended learning outcomes (Ally, 2002, Ritchie & Hoffman, 1997).

Preparing the Online Learner

Instructors can use a variety of pre-learning activities to prepare learners for intended lessons. Pre-learning activities should be designed to make connections and motivate students to learn online. There is also the need to provide a rationale to inform students about the importance of the lesson and its inherent benefits (Ally, 2004). For instance, a concept map can be used to reinforce existing cognitive structures, to add more details to the lesson, as well as activate learner prior knowledge to help them learn the details of the lesson. Using a concept map also helps students to have a more vivid idea of the big picture (Ally, 2004).

Instructors need to inform learners of intended outcomes, so that they can tailor their learning experience toward such goals and also measure their progress. Online course structures should have a structure that helps to organize the details, or provide a connection between students' prior knowledge and what they need to know. Course prerequisite requirements must be provided to help learners decide if they are ready to take the lesson, and help activate the required cognitive structures to help students learn the lessons (Ally, 2004). In addition, self-assessment should be provided in the beginning for students to determine if they have the necessary skill-sets to succeed in the lesson. As students get the necessary preparation for the details of the lesson, they will be ready to go on to complete the learning activities. To better understand these issues, we will take a look at interactions in courses and the challenges it brings in contemporary online learning.

INTERACTIONS IN AN ONLINE COURSE

Interaction in learning occurs in two different ways. One in which the student interacts individually with the content. The second type of interaction in learning is social (Berge, 1995). In this scenario the learner interacts with other students including the instructor about the course content and activities (Berge, 1995). Interaction has been defined many different ways in the literature. For instance, Vygotsky (1978) (as cited in Wanstreet, 2009) views interaction as "social and psychological connection that fosters learning as problem solving in collaboration with capable peers."

In other words, interaction is the act of sending and receiving messages between and sender and a recipient. According to Boyle & Wambach (2001) interaction can be synchronous in which communicants interact in real time, and asynchronous in which response is received at a later time. Most communication in online leaning is conducted asynchronously and it is sometimes done one-on-one or one-to-many and it is mostly

mediated by a computer. In this type of interaction, teacher and student interaction do not occur in real time (Berge, 1999).

The literature recognizes three kinds of Interactivity that support learning in an online environment. The first types of interaction deals with the learner's ability to access, interact, manipulate, synthesize, and communicate with the content. The second type of interaction in an online learning deals with the learner's ability to communicate with the instructor and receive timely informative feedback from the instructor. Thirdly, interaction in an online learning environment involves, the learners' ability to communicate effectively with each other through the content to create a learning community (Tu & McIsaac, 2002)

This section will discuss the importance of each type of interaction in the three dimensions of social presence namely social context, online communication, and interactivity (Tu & McIsaac, 2002). The literature shows that these dimensions help in establishing a sense of community in an online learning environment. In addition, improvements in social presence help increase interaction in an online interaction (Tu &McIsaac, 2002).

There are three types of interactions in online learning which include teacher to students, students to students, and students to content all of which are either synchronous or asynchronous. In teacher-student interaction as in online courses, instructors rely more on asynchronous communication, because synchronous communication often tends to defeat the purpose of online learning which is touted as being flexible and expedient (Meyen, Lian, & Tangen, 1997). In an attempt to clarify synchronous and asynchronous instructor-student interaction, Paulsen (1995) identified four pedagogical techniques namely one-to-one, one alone, one-to-many, and many to many (Berge, 1999).

One-to-one are normally asynchronous interaction mainly conducted through email. They help build one-to-one relationship and enhance individualized learning. This method of interaction is mainly written text and self-paced and done within specific time frame. On the other hand, one-alone interaction involves the retrieval of information or resources often done at learners' own pace with no direct involvement from the instructor or colleagues (Berge, 1999).

In many-to-many interaction all participants have the chance in the interaction. It can be synchronous or asynchronous depending on the instructor's instructional objective. This type of interaction includes electronic chat, threaded discussions, and debates. Electronic chats are synchronous and involve instructor and students being online in real time sometimes to exchange ideas, seek clarifications or listen to invited guest speakers. On the other hand, threaded discussions are asynchronous interactions that link messages by subject, making it easier for students to follow the conversational trends (Berge, 1999).

One-to-many interactions are usually asynchronous are used mainly on bulletin boards, blogs, Wikis, and email distribution list. Another example is the use of streaming media to deliver lectures and students' presentations to instructors (Berge, 1999).

Interaction with the Content

Online learning can often be overwhelming mainly because of the enormous amount of information that can be accessed on the World Wide Web. However, instructors must realize that information does not imply learning (Shank, 1998). According to Swan (2002) there are several ways to interact with content to promote learning in an online environment. For instance, using a variety of presentation styles help accommodate students' different learning styles. It also gives the learner control over the pace of the course. This technique ensures there is timely student interaction with the content. It is therefore important that instructors make sure the content is well organized within the course, and provide adequate support systems for the learner (Swan, 2002). Thus to facilitate effec-

tive student interaction with instructional content during the course design process, instructors must see themselves as facilitators, utilize a variety of presentation methods, create student-centered hands-on activities, provide frequent feedback, and utilize consistent course layout (Hannafin & Peck, 1988).

Interaction with the Instructor

Interaction between instructor and student is paramount not only in traditional classroom, but equally important in online learning environment. In traditional classrooms there is teacher immediacy as well as immediacy behaviors. Weiner and Mehrabian (1968) referred to "immediacy" as the 'psychological distance between communicators." In traditional face-to-face classroom instructors' immediacy behaviors such as verbal praise or asking for student clarification and non-verbal behaviors like eye contact, facial expressions can decrease the psychological distance between instructors and students leading to effective learning environment and student success (Swan, 2002).

As in the traditional classroom, interactions between instructors and students in online learning must receive equal attention. As a result, instructors can rely on asynchronous communication tools like emails, discussion threads to interact with course participants because it helps establish a social presence where individuals project their unique identities. In addition, it helps build a viable learning community through this application of verbal immediacy behaviors (Richardson & Swan, 2001).

As more and more classes continue to be delivered online so does the manner of interaction between instructor and students evolves. Coppola, Hiltz & Rotter (2001) identified three main roles of instructors in any given learning environment namely cognitive, affective, and managerial (Coppola et al., 2001). They found that the cognitive role of the instructor in an online course is more complex than in traditional classroom. The affective role of instructors in an online learning environment allows them more room to express emotion. In terms of being a manager in their classroom, the online instructor needs to pay more attention to detail, course structure, and more time on task to monitor student activities and progress (Coppola et al., 2001). In another study Anderson, Rourke, Garrison, & Archer (2001) observed similar categories. In what they termed as "teaching presence (will be discussed more in detail later) and described the roles of the instructor as that of providing direct instruction, facilitating, designing, and organizing course activities.

From the above we see the importance of instructor activity and interactive role in online as well as highlighting the link between content and interaction. In this learning environment instructors pay attention to structure, ensure student to student interaction and thus build a learning community (Swan, 2002). According to Swan, Shea, Fredericksen, Pickett, Pelz and Maher (2000) the social presence is actually greater than one may believe due to affective communication channels of the computer. The research study by Swan (2002) also showed student in online courses felt the instructor presence was imperative to online learning.

Student-to-Student Interaction

It is not enough initiate the interaction between student and instructor, but also of equal importance is interaction among students in online learning. The most used tools in online interactions among students are the discussion board and email features of the learning management system (Swan et al., 2000). According to Swan (2002) research showed students showed a need to interact among peers in the online course. Harasim (1990) also observed that student accept online discussion as more open and diverse than traditional face-to-face classroom discussions. This interaction allows the students to learn from each other. Online discussion allows students to reflect more

on their response as well as the contribution of their peers and helps students develop a sense of mindfulness and respect for their peers (Hiltz, 1994). In addition, students learn more from their peers in an online learning environment as they would have in a traditional classroom setting and sometimes better. Asynchronous student to student interactions in online learning also accounts for any lost channels of communication and allows the interactions to continue long after the class is over. Peer to peer communication allows students to make up for the lack of effective communication channels by engaging in a greater number of verbal immediacy behaviors (Swan, 2002). Interaction on the discussion board helps students experiment with their ideas, share information, and encourages collaborative thinking if the instructor creates a social milieu that encourages this type of interaction (Swan, 2002).

However, it must be noted that the availability of these communication tools in an online learning is not a panacea for success, but depends on the effectiveness of the instructor in making sure that students interact with these tools more frequently (Eastmond, 1995). The discussion posts within an online course are where students have the greatest chance to learn from other students. According to Swan (2002) the discussion boards do matter in an online course and are needed to create online learning communities. However, if the activities do not create a need to interact between students then the discussion board has not served its intended purpose. For example, if an instructor creates an assignment on the discussion board to answer simple short answer questions, and does not allow for analyzing the subject matter, the discussion posts are all going to be similar and may not foster creative interaction among learners.

From the above we see that student-to-student interaction in online learning is crucial. It is even more important if instructors encourage the development of social presence as well as the perceived interaction with others. In short, the close analysis of online interaction highlights the importance of the three types of interactivity discussed above in online learning and also reveals the significance of participants' use of verbal immediacy tools to build a viable online learning community (Swan, 2002). Using the interactive techniques discussed above can help address some of the perceived challenges of online learning.

CHALLENGES TO ONLINE TEACHING AND LEARNING

Although online teaching continues to grow in popularity, faculty participation remains prevalent challenge as institutions continue to increase the number of courses taught online (Matsom, 2006; Nelson & Thompson, 2005; Schifter, 2004). In recent years institutions have encouraged faculty to teach online as part of their regular faculty duties and often given stipends as added incentives (Kim & Bonk, 2006). Unfortunately, many faculty members still resist converting their traditional courses to an online format. This resistance is often an attribute of misconception about the effectiveness of teaching and learning online vis-à-vis traditional face-to-face teaching. These misconceptions are often compounded by inadequate training and support, and lack of clearly defined standards (Keengwe, Kidd, & Kyei-Blankson, 2009). Some faculty have the misconception that an online course cannot have the quality of interaction that a traditional classroom course offers.

Additional challenges in an online course may also hinge on whether the student gets the impact of interaction from an online course in comparison to a face-to-face course. This subject of collaboration in the classroom versus online is a topic worth discussing. According to the studies done by Clarke (2011) the majority of students after taking a survey felt they learned more through the discussion boards of an online course than the discussions in a face-to-face classroom. Experience shows that discussion boards in an online course can have a positive or negative impact.

For instance, if the discussion is not thought provoking and interesting, the student may find the discussion board monotonous. However, in the research done by Clarke (2011) the discussion boards were engaging. This type of engagement helps students to interact and make a positive contribution towards their cognitive development (Clarke, 2011).

The power of online learning emerges when educators use the technology, and work in unison with instructional designers to create better instruction and learning environments (Waterhouse, 2005). Thus, the success of teaching and learning online relies on the combination of the right instructional design strategies, and research-based values that promote systematic processes. These systematic processes include pedagogy and andragogy in online learning in educational practice (Waterhouse, 2005). Pedagogy in this chapter refers to the adaptation of effective instructional strategies related to teaching and learning, andragogy focuses more on effective instructional strategies to facilitate adult learning (Knowles, 1984). In other words, andragogy is more student-centered as opposed to pedagogy, which is teacher-centered. Thus teaching online must be authentic, allowing students to learn in the context of the workplace as well as being highly interactive and collaborative (Ally, 2004).

Research has shown effective online instruction can be just as good if not better than traditional or classroom instruction (Dixson, 2010). Effective online courses require strong methodology and interaction of students and the instructor (Dixson, 2010). Dixson (2010) expresses that the interaction of the learner with classmates and the instructor is what makes the student actually become more engaged than in the traditional classroom.

The problems encountered by Clarke (2011) were mainly related to technical issues in group project discussion boards. These technical issues include a student being registered late and not having their name added to a group. Another technical issue with the group discussions is the assignment of a student to more than one group (Clarke, 2011). Another finding with technology is when the assumption is that all students are confident with technology (Clarke, 2011). This assumption is not necessarily true. There are still students who are not self-confident with technological equipment (Clarke, 2011). Students may know how a technology works; however, they may not be able to apply it in educational setting without the help of an instructor. Despite the issues listed above, the positive advances of online outweigh the negative due to convenience and ease of access as well as the scope and reach of this method of teaching at any given period.

Similarly, the rapid influx of technology in education and the swiftness with which administrators adopt a new technology pose a unique challenge to educators. Stakeholders have to balance how to use these new technologies in order to achieve stated outcomes as well as dealing with students who sometimes are savvier with these technologies than they are. In addition, instructors often have to contend with lack of release time to develop these courses as well as lack of learner orientation to the online learning environment (Keengwe & Kidd, 2010). Then, there is the sourcing issue of funding to train the team of professionals like Instructional Designers and Technologists as well as purchasing the appropriate technology. There seems to be a dearth of funding for these positions and facilities to support the implementation. This exacerbated by recent steep cuts in government funds to institutions due to budget constraints.

In addition, some faculty members believe teaching online is too difficult, more labor intensive, and requires more preplanning. There is also the fear that they may lose control of the whole teaching process due to lack of technical expertise which may render their courses ineffective. Other instructors genuinely believe that online teaching is not as effective as traditional face-to-face teaching (Keengwe & Kidd, 2010).

Like instructors, students face a lot of hurdles in online learning environments. Students often complain that they do not have enough preparation time to move from one technology to another. Besides, instructors use the technology differently, thus students have to adapt to all these styles of applications and these are often problematic. In addition, whilst instructors are given training on how to use these technologies, students on the other hand are often given demonstrations at freshman seminars on how these technologies function often without hands-on activities or are directed to tutorials on a website. In most cases students get these directions when the class starts.

Another challenge in teaching online is the need to have a careful planning process that promotes a systematic design and implementation (Wanstreet, 2009). Educators must always contend with the fast changing workplace. In addition, educators must consider the issue of training students to perform efficiently in the fast changing work environment and be part of the workplace decision-making process. (Waterhouse, 2005).

However, online learning is an excellent alternative over the face-to-face classroom for some students. For instance, the mobile classroom gives students the ability to take their course at any time or place (Chaiprasurt & Esichaikul, 2013). Chaiprasurt and Esichaikul (2013) refer to the four strategic models of ARCS to enhance online learning which include attention, relevance, confidence and satisfaction. Attention is where the instructor is able to get the learners' attention throughout the course (Chaiprasurt and Esichaikul, 2013). Relevance is where the instructor knows what the learner needs to learn and uses tools or assessments to engage the learning of the student (Chaiprasurt & Esichaikul, 2013). Confidence is where the instructor is able to increase the confidence students in order to succeed (Chaiprasurt & Esichaikul, 2013). Satisfaction is the positive reinforcement needed from the instructor to reward students' efforts in the course (Chaiprasurt & Esichaikul, 2013). All these and be achieved through the development of effective online courses.

CREATING EFFECTIVE ONLINE COURSES

Online learning has increased both in presence and popularity. Unfortunately, there is a dearth in applying effective teaching practices in online learning. Fortunately, research shows that certain strategies enhance teaching and learning online in much the same ways certain instructional strategies in traditional learning environments (The Hanover Research Report, 2009). The literature shows what constitutes excellence in learning has shifted from the traditional perspective of what instructors provide in the classroom to a more pragmatic concern of what the student can actually do after taking a specific course (Frye, McKinney, & Trimble, 2007). There is also a paradigm shift in the way success and achievement is viewed in education and defined. There is a realization that in a learning-centered environment, learning success results from the interaction of good teaching, student engagement, and ongoing assessment (Frye et al., 2007).

In order for online learning to be effective, it must include a variety of learning activities to help students achieve intended learning outcomes. Learning activities like reading a text, watching a video, listening to audio lectures can support different learning styles and promote excess. In addition, learners can also use the Internet to search for supporting materials, or links to online library databases to access more information and to acquire needed knowledge (Ally, 2004).

Fortunately a number of scholars have created a list of best practices knowledge base about teaching and learning. According to Dick & Carey (2001), in order to achieve a specific learning goal, instructional best practices should be used to make the learning environment more student-centered.

The most notable among these sets of best teaching and learning principles is perhaps the "Seven Principles of Good Practice in Higher Education" (Chickering & Reisser, 1993). The best teaching and learning principles were in-troduced by Chickering and Gamson in 1987. These principles are instructional strategies that provide effective and concise guidelines for instructors, students, and administrators on ways to use instructional tools like computers, video, communication technologies to promote effective teaching and learning (Frye et al., 2007).

One of the best practices in online learning is to encourage contact between faculty and students (Chickering & Ehrmann, 1996). Maintaining a student-faculty contact in an online course increases student motivation and involvement. By using communications tools like email, twitter, blogs, discussion boards, and Wiki, participants in an online course can exchange resources. It also allows joint problem solving and lay foundations for future face-to-face collaborations. Communications in these media allow student especially shy students, who may be reluctant to challenge or ask questions of colleagues or faculty directly get involved in class activities. Using these tools also gives nontraditional student ample time for interactions not possible during class hours (Chickering & Ehrmann, 1996).

Instructors in time-delayed or asynchronous communication formerly posed questions in the form of assignments. The students then answered by handing in homework to which the instructor responded later by giving grades and comments (Chickering & Ehrmann, 1996).

In most cases the interaction ends, and quiet often by the time the comments come in, the course will be on the next topic, too late to be of use to the student. Fortunately, the advent of instant messaging, email, wikis, blogs, twitters increase the chances for faculty and students to communicate more speedily and thoughtfully, and in a less intimidating atmosphere (Chickering et al., 1996). The literature is also replete with stories of students in different cultures opening up to constructive and meaningful communications when these tools are placed at their disposal (Chickering & Ehrmann, 1996).

Using good practice promotes reciprocity and cooperation among students. It encourages to students to work more as a team than as individuals. The literature shows that interactions among students through course discussions are one of the most influential features of online courses (Swan, Shea, Fredericksen, Pickett, Pelz & Maher, 2000). However, instructors should provide clear guidelines for these interactions (Schlosser, 2004). When students work with others they are not only able to share ideas but respond to others. In addition, working in teams improves student thinking and understanding of the issues being discussed. According to Harasim, (1990) students perceive online discussion as more democratic and equitable than traditional face-to-face classroom discussion. The asynchronous nature of online discussion allows students to reflect more on their classmates while creating their own opinions (Hiltz, 1994). Students also benefit from increased interaction with each other as they do with faculty. Students working in groups are able to communicate with each other, solve problems, and discussion class activities more effectively with communication tools such as email, twitters, blogs, social media (Facebook), and Wikis. Working in groups allows students to size each other up, build work relationships, and forge acquaintanceship. This type of cooperative learning is only possible because of the technology tools students learn about and with (Chickering & Ehrmann, 1996).

Best practice also involves using authentic learning techniques. As the saying goes "Learning is not a spectator sport." The literature shows that students do not learn much when they just sit and absorb the material provided by the instructor and regurgitate answers. Learners must have the chance to discuss what they are learning, write diligently about it, connect it to past knowledge and experiences, and apply it to real life experiences. In other words, students should be able to make what they learn part of themselves (Chickering and Ehrmann, 1996). Technologies that promote authentic learning may include tools and resources for learning by doing, asynchronous exchange, and virtual conversation. These tools are supported with software like word processors, initially designed for other purposes but are now used effectively as instructional tool (Chickering & Ehrmann, 1996).

New technologies have emerge to enrich traditional apprentice-like (learn by doing) learning. For instance, students can use the Internet as a research tool to gather information that is not available in a local library. Students in a business class can use simulating software to mirror Wall Street financial management decision-making activities. In these environment students can experience the impact of their decision and instantly see the results. The purpose of these exercises is not to create management scenarios but to get a deeper understanding of financial management decision-making process (Chickering & Ehrmann, 1996).

Creating an effective course requires giving prompt informative and acknowledgement feedback to learners. The ability to focus what we do not know allows us to focus our learning. Students need help to assess their current knowledge base and ability. In addition, students need examples and frequent feedback on their work in class.

In an online learning environment, there are many ways in which technology can be used to provide feedback. As discussed earlier we have mentioned how email can be used to provide one-on-one feedback. Also, most simulation software has inherent instant feedback. Instructors can use the Internet to give students feedback. Instructors can observe students' performance on medium like YouTube or Skype and provide critical feedback. Videos can be used to provide critical information to nursing students or surgery simulations for potential surgeon trainees.

Instructors can also access student products and performances in portfolios to provide feedback to students which can be used preserved for future use. Furthermore, computers can be used to measure and store students' progress and students attributes like leadership skills, management, and multicultural activities for ongoing progress and critique (Chickering & Ehrmann, 1996).

One of the ways to make online course more effective is to emphasize time on task. In other words good practice online involves good time management as is done in the workplace. Online courses need deadlines and structure. It is therefore incumbent on instructors to allocate reasonable time for effective student learning and effective faculty teaching. Effective use of technology improves students and faculty time on task. The use of technology can increase time on task by making the student more efficient in learning. Students' homework assignments that include the use of technology save time otherwise spent going to and from campus. In addition, instructors and students work more efficiently when they have easy access to needed materials (Chickering & Ehrmann, 1996). Course management tools like Blackboard helps faculty measure students time on task by documenting student participation and interaction (Chickering & Ehrmann, 1996).

To placate faculty belief that online courses are not as effective as traditional face-to-face courses, it is always a good practice to communicate high expectations in online courses. For instance, challenging activities, case studies, and acknowledgement of good performance communicate higher expectations (Schlosser, 2004). It is good practice to invest time for good design and expect more from your online students as is done in face-to-face courses. Instructors can use technology to communicate explicit high expectations. Activities can be designed to sharpen students learning skills and elicit cognitive skills of analysis as well as application (Chickering & Ehrmann, 1996). According to Chickering and Ehrmann (1996), "Publishing" students work on the World Wide Web is an effective source of motivation for the student. Posting students work as good examples for their peers and also are a motivating factor for less performing student and an incentive for active

participation. This can also serve as a guide for learning, peer evaluation, so students can help each other (Chickering & Ehrmann, 1996).

Finally, an effective online course should respect diverse talents and different learning styles. As we continue to develop courses online, we must be aware that each student brings a unique talent and learning style to the learning environment. Some students may do well in lab studio; others may do well in hands-on activities and not so well in theory. It's therefore incumbent on faculty to create a dynamic learning environment that will support students' learning styles and help them achieve stated learning outcomes (Chickering & Ehrmann, 1996).

Technology tools like the computer with the appropriate software can be used to portray powerful visuals and well-organized print material. Technology can also be used as a tool to simulate real world activities. In this environment, the student becomes a researcher actively engaged in real world activities (Chickering & Ehrmann, 1996). Authentic activities can also encourage self-evaluation and reflection. It can motivate students to work together to solve real word problems. Using technology in online learning environment also help students adapt to different methods that suit their learning styles. Appropriate technologies can also provide a structure for students who may need it more open ended for those who do not. Technologies can also allow branching so that bright students take a shorter turn to learn the material than slower students but arrive at the same outcome in the end. With these technologies students with similar goals can work in cohort groups for success anywhere anytime (Chickering & Ehrmann, 1996).

Similarly, Pelz (2004) also suggested three Principles of Effective Online Pedagogy which reinforces Chickering and Erhmann. Pelz's first principle discusses the concept of letting the students do most of the work. In other words the more quality time the student spends with the content, the better the chance for the student learning the material or more learning less teaching. Activities like discussions, locating web resources, peer assistance and grading, and case study analysis should all have more students' presence and participation (Pelz, 2004).

Pelz also referenced interaction as the heart and soul of online learning. However, Pelz emphasized the need for social presence in online learning. In common parlance, Social presence is defined as "the degree of awareness of another person in an interaction and the consequent appreciation of an interpersonal relationship." (Short, Williams, & Christie, 1976). According to Pelz (2004), the most important forms of presence in online learning environment are Social Presence, Cognitive Presence, and Teaching Presence.

Social Presence helps online learners establish a sense of community as well as project the personalities. Social Presence allows learners to present themselves as "real people" in mediated communication (Gunawardena & Zittle, 1997). Social Presence in online learning comes in three forms. First there is the affective dimension which allows the students to show how they feel in this learning environment. Next, is interaction which is evidenced by students reading of course material, responding to others postings, and submitting assignments. The third form of Social Presence is the evidence of cohesiveness. In other words students reaction to material that builds on what others have already indicated as well as the pursuit of a common outcome (Pelz, 2004).

Once instructors have established a Social Presence in their online courses, the next form of presence is the Cognitive Presence. The objective for establishing a Cognitive presence is to explore how the material will be structured and sustained through a community of inquiry. This can be done with the introduction of factual, conceptual, and theoretical knowledge into the learning process. The responses to the material in the learning process can serve as a source of clarity, accuracy and understanding of the intended knowledge and also create a structure for the course (Pelz, 2004).

Pelz suggests it is essential for instructors to establish a Teaching Presence in their online courses. Thus, instructors can "wear many hats" depending on the situation in their online courses. They can be facilitators of the social and cognitive processes of the course. They can also act as coaches, designers, and managers of the learning process but must remember to be the "sage on the side" as opposed to "sage on the stage" to make the learning environment more student-centered (Pelz, 2004).

Finally online instructors need to be V.O.C.A.L in order to maximize their effectiveness in the online learning environment (Savery, 2005). The main characteristics of the acronym VOCAL according to Savery (2005) is Visible, Organized, Compassionate, Analytical, and Leader-by-example. The concepts espoused in the five components of VOCAL integrate existing best practices ideas discussed above with the development of learning environments that encourages learner ownership. The next section will take closer look at the five components of VOCAL.

Visible

Teaching online is different from the traditional face-to-face classroom because teaching in the former environment is mostly text-based. Unfortunately, this dynamic makes some student feel the instructor is not participating in the class, and thus stay passive in the course. If the students feel the instructor is not "visible" in the class they tend to doubt the instructor's competence (Savery, 2005).

Thus instructors can show visibility by using public and private communication by using part of the course website to give students personal and professional information. They can also give prompt informative feedback to assignments as well as distribute messages through email privately or to all participants. For instance, a private email can be sent to a student to complement him/her on a positive achievement or contribution. In short, the teacher can use private visibility or selective attention to individual students within the learning community to remove the anonymity that often occurs in online learning environments (Savery, 2005). Doing this allows students to know that the instructor is aware of what they are doing in the class and thus encourage their active participation. Instructors can also use banner notices on the Welcome page and update them regularly often to announce the addition of recent resources or additional course materials of interest. (Savery, 2005). They can also post regular course updates of shared calendar as well as use mass and personal email communication with the class. Instructors can also use small video clips to introduce course modules to increase visibility (Savery, 2005). In a situation where instructors use group as part of their instructional strategies, communication within the group can be constrained within just that group. Thus instructors need to organize their course in manner that will allow them to know when to send private message or other message that ensures that all students are included (Savery, 2005). To do this, instructors need to be very organized in this learning environment.

Organized

According to Simon, (2000) it is essential for instructors to ensure that all aspects of their courses are organized. The literature shows that most non-traditional students in the online learning environment often assume they will be able to fit online courses in their already crowded schedules. The same is also true of traditional students who may take an online class instead of the traditional face-to-face version to graduate. Students in an online learning always want to know what is expected of them and what they have to do so that they can organize their time to meet those expectations (Savery, 2005). Interestingly, most online courses are student-centered, which means students have to be better managers of their time (Smith, 2002).

It is therefore incumbent on instructors to create instructional materials that are clear, effectively organized, and straight to the point. For instance, instructors can use the shared calendar features of Course Management Systems(CMS) to provide due dates or schedule synchronous events such as chat sessions with influential subject matter experts (Savery, 2005).

Spontaneity is limited in online learning environment; therefore, in order to stay organized in their online courses they may have their students take online assessments surveys on the characteristics of a successful online learner. Instructors may also want to post their course material in a CMS so it is easily accessible and preempt any questions students may have (Savery, 2005).

Assignments due dates and must be provided early in a carefully created course schedule with reading activities, deliverable assignments, points possible, and due dates clearly stated. Class rules must be clearly stated in the syllabus as well as discussions netiquette. There is also the need to create a forum where students can meet and discuss class issues "Cyber Café" as well as an area where students can ask questions about the course (Savery, 2005). Instructional materials should be presented in different formats to promote accessibility and accommodate different learning styles. In some cases, instructors can use the CMS to organize the access to course material. For instance, the adoptive release feature of a CMS like Blackboard or Desire2Learn can be used to selectively release files so that new instructional material is only made available after the students shows a mastery of the present (Savery, 2005). This can be done if students know from the beginning that instructors are companionate about their work

Compassionate

The literature shows that most nontraditional students who are attempting to upgrade their skills face the enormous task of having to balance busy schedules. As a result they opt for a flexible learning environment which best suits their situations. Thus they come into the online learning environment already burdened with conflicting demands on their overcrowded schedules. In addition, most nontraditional students often come into an online learning environment with very little knowledge about the technology. As a result, when aspects of the online course do not work as anticipated they become discouraged and may often drop out. This shows that the success of students, especially nontraditional students in an online class depends mainly on the relationship between the instructor and the student which requires a careful attention and planning. If the instructor is visible and the course organization presents the material in an orderly manner, then attending to the emotional well-being of the student becomes much easier to manage (Savery, 2005).

Unlike face-to-face classrooms, the online situation is very intimate. Students of divulge personal information through emails to instructors which they may not do in a face-to-face classroom. Such personal student "revelation," calls for compassion on the part of the instructor than will be expected in a traditional classroom. What we see in the online learning environment is that there are no easy answers. However, instructors are can use sound judgment to deal with the situations as they come and make sure they treat their students fairly, especially when dealing with situations that have no written rules but must be viewed with compassion. Decisions on situations like family emergencies, illness, and death in the family are made from the heart of the instructor (Savery, 2005).

In view of the above, instructors must plan to have open lines of communications with students to communicate directly with him/her in case there is an unforeseen problem like a sick spouse or dead relative. For instance, a lost job or a sick child can impede a student's ability to complete assignments on time.

There is the need to create an "About Me "forum so students can get to know each other and share their experiences. Students can also be encouraged to share proud experiences with each other. However, it is always prudent to ask student permission before sharing intimate messages (example, sick child, divorce etc.) they share with you as an instructor with the class. It is also a good practice to keep reminding students about class rules and how you may respond to unforeseen problems and analyze issues in the class (Savery, 2005).

Analytical

In online courses instructors need to manage the online assignments to ensure that students are completing them and thus achieving the intended learning outcomes. To facilitate this process, instructors need to provide prompt feedback on student performance and progress toward attaining stated outcomes. Preparing and sharing material in an organized form with students in an online course is a very important aspect of teaching online. To achieve this goal, instructors can ask questions that test the students' ability to synthesize information and apply it to the specific concepts discussed in the course. Fortunately, CMS tools like Blackboard, Moodle, and Desire2Learn are designed to support a systematic organization of the course material to student. For instance, instructors can use a CMS to post assignments that contain detailed instructions, clearly stated rubrics and supporting resources. In addition, instructors can use a CMS to track student progress and provided needed feedback (Savery, 2005).

As a result, instructors in of online courses should provide small and frequent feedback and spread assessment activities across their courses to reduce student anxiety and offer students more opportunities to achieve course outcomes (Northedge, 2002). In addition they should consider face-to-face exams. A case in point is the University of Arkansas Global campus, Fayetteville where students in online courses go in person to designated libraries in the country to take exams to complete their courses.

There is also the need to specify the format for completed assignments to be submitted through course management systems as well as file naming convention students are to use. The chance for students to evaluate their performance both at midterm and end of the course also helps. Outlining clear expectations and guidelines for course activities is also an added incentive for student participation. This can be done effectively by an instructor who assumes a leadership role in his/her course (Savery, 2005).

Leader

Instructors should aspire to use best practices when teaching not only in a face-to-face class but in the online environment as well. As individuals, we always take our cues from our leaders. This is also true of online students. The literature shows that students always take their lead in the areas of visibility, organization, and compassion from their instructor (Savery, 2005). Instructors always set the tone in class and students follow their examples until the class ends. Gallimore and Tharp (1990) suggested instructors model offering non-verbal cues for imitation, reward good behavior through praise and encouragement, discourage inappropriate behaviors in the form of reprimand. In addition, instructors should respond to learner performance in relation to given criteria such as grades. Teachers should also model helping students to perform better in their courses and create meaningful activities to stimulate student critical thinking abilities. Finally, instructors should help student improve their cognitive structuring understanding of the material by providing opportunities for students' engagement in authentic activities.

As a result, instructors should share information about themselves with their students and follow through with promises. They should also give students ample time to adjust to new additions instructors may make to the course and share strategies for communicating in a mainly text-based learning environment (Savery, 2005). As leaders, instructors should plan closure activities, reinforce what is learned, and re-clarify some points, and recognize students contributions to the success of the class. In short, instructors who adopt the VOCAL concept in an online class will be more Visible, Organized, Compassionate, Analytical, as well as Leaders who strive to improve course effectiveness and through that ensure the success of their students in achieving stated learning outcomes.

CONCLUSION

The advent of the internet has the ability to give access to information anywhere anytime has revolutionized the way teachers teach and how students learn. The internet allows just-in-time learning, and it is designed to support active and independent learning (Lim, 2004).

However, to maximize the effectiveness of online courses stakeholders must emphasize three factors associated with success in learning in this learning environment. These include effective interaction with the course content, a more defined interaction between instructor and students, as well as students' interaction with each other within a well-developed social presence. In addition, instructors should aspire to be "vocal" as they navigate student success through interaction and other course activities. These activities must be closely monitored in order to create a vibrant learning community.

REFERENCES

Allen, I., & Seaman, J. (2013). Changing course: Ten years of tracking online education in the United States (pp. 1–26). Needham, MA: The Sloan Consortium. Retrieved from http://www.online-learningsurvey.com/reports/changingcourse.pdf

Ally, M. (2002). Designing and managing successful online distance education courses. *In Workshop presented at the 2002 World Computer Congress, Montreal, Canada.*

Ally, M. (2004). Foundations of educational theory for online learning. *Theory and Practice of Online Learning, 2,* 15-44.

Anderson, T. (2004). The educational semantic web: A vision for the next phase of educational computing. *Educational Technology, 44*(5), 5–9.

Anderson, T. (Ed.). (2008). *The theory and practice of online learning.* Athabasca University Press.

Anderson, T., Rourke, L., Garrison, D. R., & Archer, W. (2001). Assessing teaching presence in a computer conferencing context. Paper presented at the Annual Meeting of the American Educational Research Association, Seattle, WA.

Ausubel, D. P. (1960). The use of advance organizers in the learning and retention of meaningful verbal material. *Journal of Educational Psychology, 51*(5), 267–272. doi:10.1037/h0046669

Ausubel, D. P. (1974). *Educational psychology: A cognitive view.* New York, NY: Holt, Rinehart and Winston.

Beatty, B., & Ulasewicz, C. (2006). Faculty perspectives on moving from Blackboard to the Moodle learning management system. *TechTrends, 50*(4), 36–45. doi:10.1007/s11528-006-0036-y

Berge, Z. L (1995). Facilitating computer conferencing: Recommendations from the field. *Educational Technology, 35,* 22.

Berge, Z. L. (1999). Interaction in post-secondary web-based learning. *Educational Technology, 39,* 5–11.

Boyle, D. K., & Wambach, K. A. (2001). Interaction in graduate nursing Web-based instruction. *Journal of Professional Nursing, 17*(3), 128–134. doi:10.1053/jpnu.2001.23376 PMID:11391558

Carliner, S. (1999). *Overview of online learning.* Amherst, MA: Human Resource Development Press.

Chaiprasurt, C., & Esichaikul, V. (2013). Enhancing Motivation in Online Courses with Mobile communication tool support: A comparative study. *International Review of Research in Open and Distance Learning, 14*(3), 377–401.

Chamberlain, R., & Vrasidas, C. (2001). Creating engaging online instruction. In *Proceedings of the 17th Annual Conference on Distance Teaching and Learning.* Madison, WI: University of Wisconsin System.

Chickering, A. W., & Ehrmann, S. C. (1996). Implementing the seven principles: Technology as lever. *AAHE Bulletin, 49,* 3–6.

Chickering, A. W., & Reisser, L. (1993). *Education and identity* (2nd ed.). San Francisco: Jossey Bass.

Chizmar, J. F., & Williams, D. B. (2001). What do faculty want? *EDUCAUSE Quarterly, 24*(1), 18–24.

Clark, R. E. (1983). Reconsidering research on learning from media. *Review of Educational Research, 53*(4), 445–459. doi:10.3102/00346543053004445

Clark, R. E. (2001). A summary of disagreements with the "mere vehicles" argument. In *Learning from media: Arguments, analysis, and evidence* (pp. 125-136). Academic Press.

Clarke, S. (2011). *Peer Interaction and engagement through online discussion forums: A cautionary tale.* Springer Sciences Business Media; doi:10.1007/s10991-011-9092-2

Cole, R. A. (2000). *Issues in Web-based pedagogy: A critical primer.* Westport, CT: Greenwood Press.

Coppola, N. W., Hiltz, S. R., & Rotter, N. (2001). Becoming a virtual professor: Pedagogical roles and ALN. In *System Sciences, 2001. Proceedings of the 37th Annual Hawaii International Conference on System Sciences* (HICSS-34). Piscataway, NJ: Institute of Electrical and Electronics Engineers Press.

Craik, F. I. M., & Lockhart, R. S. (1972). Levels of processing: A framework for memory research. *Journal of Verbal Learning and Verbal Behavior, 11*(6), 671–684. doi:10.1016/S0022-5371(72)80001-X

Dick, W., Carey, L., & Carey, J. O. (2001). *The systematic design of instruction.* Addison-Wesley.

Dixon, M. D. (2010). Creating effective student engagement in online courses: What do students find engaging? *Journal of the Scholarship of Teaching and Learning, 10*(2), 1–13.

Duffy, T. M., & Cunningham, D. J. (1996). Constructivism: Implications for the design and delivery of instruction. In D. H. Jonassen (Ed.), *Handbook of research for educational communications and technology* (pp. 170–198). New York: Simon & Schuster Macmillan.

Eastmond, D. V. (1995). *Alone but together: Adult distance study through computer conferencing.* Cresskill, NJ: Hampton Press.

Fish, W. W., & Gill, P. B. (2009). Perceptions of Online Instruction. *Online Submission, 8*(1).

Foley, M. (2003). The global development learning network: A world bank initiative in distance learning for development. In M. G. Moore & W. G. Anderson (Eds.), *Handbook of distance education.* Mahwah, NJ: Erlbaum.

Frye, R., McKinney, G. R., & Trimble, J. E. (2007). *Tools and techniques for course improvement: A handbook of course review and assessment of student learning.* Retrieved 12/10/2014 from http://pandora.cii.wwu.edu/cii/resources/outcomes/course_handbook.pdf

Gallimore, R., & Tharp, R. (1990). Teaching mind in society: Teaching, schooling and literate discourse. In L. C. Moll (Ed.), *Instructional Implications and Applications of Sociohistorical Psychology* (pp. 175–205). New York: Cambridge University Press. doi:10.1017/CBO9781139173674.009

Gunawardena, C. N., & Zittle, F. J. (1997). Social presence as a predictor of satisfaction with a computer-mediated conferencing environment. *American Journal of Distance Education, 11*(3), 8–26. doi:10.1080/08923649709526970

Hannafin, M., & Peck, K. (1988). *The Design, Development, and Evaluation of Instructional Software.* New York, NY: Macmillan.

Harasim, L. (1990). On-line education: Perspectives on a new environment. New York: Praeger.

Hastie, M., Chen, N. S., & Kno, Y. H. (2007). Instructional Design for Best Practice in the Synchronous Cyber Classroom. *Journal of Educational Technology & Society, 10*(4), 281–294.

Hiltz, S. R. (1994). The virtual classroom: Learning without limits via computer networks. Norwood, NJ: Ablex, Intellect Books.

Hirumi, A. (2000). Chronicling the challenges of web-basing a degree program: A systems perspective. *The Quarterly Review of Distance Education*, *1*(2), 89–108.

Keegan, D. (1995). *Fundamentals of distance education* (3rd ed.). London: Routledge Press.

Keengwe, J., & Kidd, T. T. (2010). Towards best practices in online learning and teaching in higher education. *MERLOT Journal of Online Learning and Teaching*, *6*(2), 533–541.

Keengwe, J., Kidd, T. T., & Kyei-Blankson, L. (2009). Faculty and technology: Implications for faculty training and technology leadership. *Journal of Science Education and Technology*, *18*(1), 23–28. doi:10.1007/s10956-008-9126-2

Khan, B. (1997). Web-based instruction: What is it and why is it? In B. H. Khan (Ed.), *Web-based instruction*. Englewood Cliffs, NJ: Educational Technology Publications.

Kim, K. J., & Bonk, C. J. (2006). The future of online teaching and learning in higher education: The survey say. *EDUCAUSE Quarterly*, *29*(4), 22–30.

Knowles, M. (1975). *Self-directed learning: A guide for learners and teachers*. Chicago: Follett Publishing Company.

Knowles, M. S. (1984). *Andragogy in action*. San Francisco: Jossey-Bass.

Kozma, R. B. (2001). Counterpoint theory of "learning with media. In R. E. Clark (Ed.), *Learning from media: Arguments, analysis, and evidence* (pp. 137–178). Greenwich, CT: Information Age Publishing Inc.

Lim, C. P. (2004). Engaging learners in online learning environments. *TechTrends*, *48*(4), 16–23. doi:10.1007/BF02763440

Matsom, Y. (2006). A Model of a Decision Making Planning Strategy for the Development of Online Courses for Teacher Education Program. In C. Crawford et al. (Eds.), *Proceedings of Society for Information Technology and Teacher Education International Conference 2006* (pp. 1274-1278). Chesapeake, VA: AACE.

Meyen, E. L., Lian, C. H. T., & Tangen, P. (1997). Developing online instruction: One model. *Focus on Autism and Other Developmental Disabilities*, *12*(3), 159–165. doi:10.1177/108835769701200304

Moore, M. G., & Kearsley, G. (2011). *Distance education: A systems view of online learning*. Cengage Learning.

Morrison, G. R., Lowther, L. L., & Demeulle, L. (1999). *Integrating computer technology into the Classroom*. Upper Saddle River, NJ: Prentice Hall.

Morrison, G. R., Ross, S. M., Kemp, J. E., & Kalman, H. (2011). *Designing effective instruction* (6th ed.). John Wiley & Sons.

National Center for Education Statistics. (2012). *Distance education at degree-granting post-secondary institutions*. Retrieved from http://nces.ed.gov/pubsearch/pubsinfo.asp

Nelson, S. J., & Thompson, G. W. (2005). Barriers perceived by administrators and faculty regarding the use of distance education technologies in pre-service programs for secondary agricultural education teachers. *Journal of Agricultural Education*, *46*(4), 36–48. doi:10.5032/jae.2005.04036

Northedge, A. (2002). Teaching by Distance Education. In W. J. McKeachie (Ed.), *Teaching Tips* (11th ed.; pp. 258–267). Boston, MA: Houghton-Mifflin.

Paulsen, M. F. (1995). *The online report on pedagogical techniques for computer-mediated communication*. Retrieved from http://emoderators.com/wp-content/uploads/cmcped.html

Pelz, B. (2004). Three principles of effective online pedagogy. *Journal of Asynchronous Learning Networks, 14*(1), 103–116.

Picciano, A. G. (2002). Beyond student perceptions: Issues of interaction, presence, and performance in an online course. *Journal of Asynchronous Learning Networks, 6*(1), 21–40.

Richardson, J., & Swan, K. (2001). *An examination of social presence in online learning: Students' perceived learning and satisfaction*. Paper presented at the Annual Meeting of the American Educational Research Association, Seattle, WA.

Ritchie, D. C., & Hoffman, B. (1997). Incorporating instructional design principles with the World Wide Web. In B. H. Khan (Ed.), *Web-based Instruction* (pp. 135–138). Englewood Cliffs, NJ: Educational Technology Publications.

Rumble, G. (2001). Re-inventing distance education, 1971-2001. *International Journal of Lifelong Education, 20*(1/2), 31–43.

Savery, J. R. (2005). Be Vocal: Characteristics of successful online instructors. *Journal of Interactive Online Learning, 4*(2), 141–152.

Schifter. (2004). Faculty participation in distance education program: Practices and plans. In D. Monolescu, C. Schifte, & L. Greenwood (Eds.), *The distance education evaluation: issues and case studies* (pp. 22-39). Hershey, PA: Information Science.

Schlosser, C. (2004). We Need a Plan: An Instructional Design Approach for Distance Education Courses. *Distance Learn, 1*(4), 29–38.

Shank, R. (1998). Horses for courses. *Communications of the ACM, 41*(7), 23–25. doi:10.1145/278476.278482

Shaw, M., Chametzky, B., Burrus, S. W., & Walters, K. J. (2013). An evaluation of student outcomes by course duration in online higher education. *Online Journal of Distance Learning Administration, 16*(4).

Shelton, K., & Saltsman, G. (2005). *An administrators guide to online education*. Greenwich, CT: IAP- Information Age Publishing.

Short, J., Williams, E., & Christie, B. (1976). *The social psychology of telecommunications*. London: John Wiley & Sons.

Simon, M. (2000). Managing Time: Developing effective online organization. In K. White & B. Weight (Eds.), *The Online Teaching Guide* (pp. 73–82). Boston, MA: Allyn & Bacon.

Simonson, M., Smaldino, S., Albright, M., & Zvacek, S. (2003). *Teaching and learning at a distance* (2nd ed.). Upper Saddle River, NJ: Prentice Hall.

Smith, M. K. (2002). *Malcolm Knowles, informal adult education, self-direction and andragogy, the encyclopedia of informal education*. Retrieved December 22, 2014 from www.infed.org/thinkers/et-knowl.htm

Swan, K. (2002). Building learning communities in online courses: The importance of interaction. *Education Communication and Information, 2*(1), 23–49. doi:10.1080/1463631022000005016

Swan, K., Shea, P., Fredericksen, E., Pickett, A., Pelz, W., & Maher, G. (2000). Building knowledge building communities: Consistency, contact and communication in the virtual classroom. *Journal of Educational Computing Research, 23*(4), 359–384.

Tallent-Runnels, M. K., Thomas, J. A., Lan, W. Y., Cooper, S., Ahern, T. C., Shaw, S. M., & Liu, X. (2006). Teaching courses online: A review of the research. *Review of Educational Research, 76*(1), 93–135. doi:10.3102/00346543076001093

Taylor, J. (2001). The future of learning-learning for the future: Shaping the transition. *Open praxis: the bulleting of the International Council for Distance Education, 2,* 20-24. Retrieved from http://www.fernuni-hagen.de/ICDE/D-2001/final/keynote_speeches/wednesday/taylor_keynote.pdf

The Hanover Research Report. (2009). *Best practices in online teaching strategies.* Retrieved 12/4/2014 from http://www.uwec.edu/AcadAff/resources/edtech/upload/Best-Practices-in-Online-Teaching-Strategies-Membership.pdf

Tu, C. H., & McIsaac, M. (2002). The relationship of social presence and interaction in online classes. *American Journal of Distance Education, 16*(3), 131–150. doi:10.1207/S15389286AJDE1603_2

Wanstreet, C. E. (2009). Interaction in online learning environments. *The Perfect Online Course: Best Practices for Designing and Teaching,* 425.

Waterhouse, S. (2005). *The Power of eLearning: The Essential Guide for Teaching in the Digital Age.* Pearson/Allyn & Bacon.

Weiner, M., & Mehrabian, A. (1968). *Language within language: Immediacy, a channel in verbal communication.* New York: Appleton-Century-Crofts.

KEYWORDS AND DEFINITIONS

Distance Learning: Distance learning was viewed mostly as an individual pursuit interspersed with infrequent communication between learner and teacher (Anderson, 2008).

Impact of Learning: According to Waterhouse, (2005), online learning is more impactful when the primary emphasis is on the basics of teaching and learning. In other words, teaching must focus on the basic principles of pedagogy not on the technology when teaching online. Thus, instructors teaching online should use the technology to help them achieve their stated instructional learning outcomes. Chizmar and Williams (2001) also emphasized the importance of making pedagogy the main determinant of the choice of technology in teaching and learning.

Instructional Best Practices: These principles are instructional strategies that provide effective and concise recommendations for instructors, students, and administrators on ways to use technology like computers, video, communication technologies to promote effective teaching and learning (Frye et al., 2007).

Instructional Designers: "A systematic approach to creating a learning environment that promotes effective learning outcomes" (Hastie, Chen, & Kno, 2007).

Online Learning: The term online learning implies "that the learner is at a distance from the tutor or instructor, that the learner uses some form of technology to access learning materials" (Anderson, 2008).

Online Presence: "A sense of being in a place and belonging to group" (Picciano, 2002).

Social Presence: "The degree of awareness of another person in an interaction and the consequent appreciation of an interpersonal relationship." (Short, Williams, & Christie, 1976).

Chapter 16

Interacting at a Distance:
Creating Engagement in Online Learning Environments

Robert L. Moore
University of North Carolina at Chapel Hill, USA

ABSTRACT

Effective online instruction requires understanding not only interaction but also how to facilitate interaction through technology (Moore & Kearsley, 2012). Specifically, Moore and Kearsley (2012) categorize these types of interactions as "learner with content, interaction with instruction [or] interaction with other learners" (p. 132). This chapter examines each of these interaction types and suggests ways to incorporate them into online learning environments (OLEs). The chapter provides techniques and approaches that will be beneficial to both instructional design practitioners and online instructors. It seeks to assuage some of the concerns that faculty have about OLEs and provides ideas and activities that can be implemented by course designers or instructors in OLE projects.

INTRODUCTION

Interaction in an online course looks and feels different from interaction in a face-to-face classroom. In both environments students interact with the content, the instructor, and each other. One difference between these two learning environments is found in the third type of interaction—between learners and other learners (Moore & Kearsley, 2012). An online learning environment (OLE) that epitomizes this type of interaction can make a course engaging and enjoyable; the absence of this interaction can create feelings of isolation, ultimately causing students to become disenchanted

with online courses. To be successful in an OLE, both instructors and students must adjust their approaches. This chapter provides advice and suggestions for instructors, instructional designers, and administrators interested in improving online courses and creating successful OLEs.

This chapter is an outgrowth of the author's online education experience as both an instructional designer and support person for online instructors as well as an online student. This unique perspective has provided him with a better understanding of the types of challenges and difficulties faced by students in online learning environments and enabled him to provide useful

DOI: 10.4018/978-1-4666-9582-5.ch016

suggestions for making the learning environment a more engaging and enriching experience. To help illustrate the different components and challenges faced when developing engagement in online learning environments, this chapter makes use of three composite instructors (described below) who represent examples of different personality types and instructional approaches the author has encountered as an instructional designer.

- **Troy Henderson:** A new instructor who has just earned a master's degree in teaching. Troy is a big fan of technology and is always eager to use the newest technological tool.
- **Ruth Murray:** An experienced instructor with over eight years of instructional experience. Ruth enjoys teaching and is open to using technology but often becomes frustrated when she feels that the technology is too complicated or difficult to implement.
- **Charles Smith:** A tenured professor with more than twenty-five years of instructional experience. Charles has been teaching the same courses for the better part of his instructional career and is resistant to technology. He is not comfortable with new technology, considers it distracting and ineffective and strongly feels that in-class lecturing is by far the most effective way to deliver instruction.

Teaching in an online learning environment is very different from face-to-face, classroom instruction, and some teachers find the transition to the online environment quite challenging. These three instructors come from different perspectives but ultimately want to be successful as teachers. Throughout this chapter, their perspectives will be incorporated to help frame the discussion and to illustrate possible ways of addressing the challenges of creating an interactive and engaging online learning environment.

Online education affords new opportunities to leverage technology and create interactive and immersive learning environments for students. At the same time, instructors often struggle with striking an appropriate balance between instructor–learner interaction and learner–learner interaction (Moore & Kearsley, 2012). A common example of poor online instruction is when an instructor takes PowerPoint presentations used in a face-to-face classroom and posts them to a learning management system (LMS) as "lecture notes." An imbalance occurs because students are not given an opportunity to engage with the content or with each other; they are simply receiving passive instruction through PowerPoint slides. According to Vasu and Ozturk (2009), "any distance education course is enhanced if traditional lecture notes can be augmented with rich media." (p. 272). So how might the instructor in the above example achieve the balance of interaction needed for an effective online course? He or she could supplement the slides with a short screencast (a video that shows the viewer what is on the instructor's screen and is equipped with narration by the instructor that provides additional context) and then ask students to answer questions based on both the screencast and the slides. This is only one of many ways instructors can make online courses more interactive and create the type of engagement that makes an OLE successful for students.

This chapter is divided into three main sections, as follows:

- Section 1 ("Background") provides a brief background of online instruction and distance education and an explanation of the connectivist learning theory.
- Section 2 ("Creating Engagement in OLEs") outlines the importance of creating engagement in OLEs and explores the changing roles of instructors and students in OLEs and how these roles can create the kind of engagement and interaction that characterizes successful online courses.

- Section 3 ("Field of Dreams") offers solutions and recommendations that can help create the sense of community and interaction instructors should strive for in OLEs. The tools, strategies, techniques, and activities described will provide instructors with multiple options to support the type of engagement and interactive learning found in successful online courses.

The chapter concludes with suggestions for future research in this field of study.

Background

Before getting into the creation of an engaging online learning environment, it is helpful to understand why online learning environments are worth researching and understanding. For instructors such as Charles who are reluctant to teach in an online environment, this can be a helpful way of establishing the justification for the online instructional approach. Prior to 2008, a standard American college education would have been described as the completion of a face-to-face, two- or four-year program. This type of education is commonly referred to as residential education because students attend classes in the same physical location as their classmates and instructors. U.S. colleges and universities have traditionally built their infrastructure and support services around residential learners. Since 2008, however, this model has undergone significant changes. According to Allen and Seaman (2013), over 6.7 million students will take at least one online course during their higher education careers, and more than 30 percent of current higher education students have taken at least one course in an online format. Adkins (2013) predicts that by 2017, over 4 million U.S. students will be taking all of their classes online. What is more significant is that nearly 70 percent of higher education institutions have disclosed that online learning is now a critical part of their long-term strategy

(Allen & Seaman, 2013). Moreover, between fall 2010 and fall 2011, online enrollment increased by 9.3 percent while total enrollment decreased by .1 percent (Allen & Seaman, 2013).

Providing these numerical facts about the growth of online education is not usually enough justification for online instruction for an instructor such as Charles. His counterargument would be that he has been teaching face-to-face for years, that it has worked, and that students are not able to learn in online environments. This is a common rebuttal to online education but one that multiple research studies have demonstrated to be largely unfounded and incorrect. One such study, by Jahng, Krug, and Zhang (2007), showed that there was not a significant difference in student achievement between online courses and face-to-face courses. Moore (2014) found that when comparing students in an introductory Spanish course offered in a face-to-face model versus a hybrid model, there was not a statistical difference between the outcomes of the two classes. In other words, both studies found that students were not harmed by receiving instruction in online or hybrid formats.

Another reason for the explosion of online education has been in response to such concerns as the rising cost of education and the difficulty of balancing family life and school, both of which often preclude residential education as a viable option for a growing percentage of adult learners. Distance education, defined as instruction wherein learners and instructors are separated (Moller, 1998), may better fit the educational needs of these non-traditional students. Distance education can be delivered in a variety of ways—asynchronously, synchronously, or by a combination of the two in a hybrid model. Asynchronous instruction means that it is delivered in a self-paced format in which students have the ability to set their own schedules for completing the course and where interactions do not occur in real time (Croxton, 2014). A popular instructional site, lynda.com, is a good example of asynchronous instruction. Conversely, synchronous instruction follows a specific schedule for the interactions, such as web or video conferencing or online chat sessions (Croxton, 2014). A face-to-face environment is one in which students meet on specific days at a specific time and place for classroom instruction. An online course, in contrast, entails weekly virtual class meetings conducted by the instructor using such tools as GoToMeeting or Blackboard Collaborate.

Pence (2013) identifies three factors that have contributed to the increased acceptance of online education in recent years: (1) state and federal budget cuts in higher education funding, (2) the potential for high learner outcomes in online environments, and (3) the need for learners to develop new skills in order to succeed in a rapidly changing digital environment. Since the economic downturn in 2008, the demand for distance education options has grown. Colleges and universities have been forced to develop solutions to meet the needs of a larger number of adult students who have lost their jobs and gone back to school in search of new opportunities. Laitinen (2013) suggests that, generally speaking, "students today are more likely to be older, working, attending [school] part-time and learning outside of traditional credit-bearing classrooms than students in the past" (p. 63). For-profit schools have been able to identify this niche and need within higher education and have developed a model that seeks to fill that gap. Bonvillian and Singer (2013) report that the University of Phoenix had a total enrollment in 2012 of over 300,000 and that Kaplan University had more than 77,000 enrollees (p. 23). These are just two examples of the number of students seeking distance education options through the for-profit sector.

Educational institutions must pay attention to the different requirements of non-traditional students and develop support services that will allow these students to tackle the unique challenges inherent in distance education. Tschofen and Mackness (2012) describe four principles of learning—autonomy, connectedness, diversity, and openness—which they identify as components of "connectivism" (p. 124). Connectivism is a learning theory that values the connection between learning and real-life experiences, and it can have a significant impact on a learner's ability to meet a course's requirements. According to this theory, establishing and tapping into various connections is crucial to acquiring knowledge. Bell (2011) references Siemens's work in suggesting that connectivism be considered a "learning theory for the digital age," (p. 102) a nod to the growing reliance on technology in education and to the ease with which information is obtained from a multitude of sources. Thus, as students become more connected through technology, connectivism seeks to link that technology to their education. Distance education has evolved from the correspondence courses that offered little to no opportunity for interaction between instructors and students to the potentially dynamic and interactive courses that Web 2.0 and Web 3.0 technologies make possible. Connectivism requires students to take a more active role in their learning, but instructors must also create a learning environment that supports and enhances students' interaction with content, the instructor, and each other. This represents a transition for students from the traditional face-to-face classroom where they were more passive participants to the more active online environment (Hung & Chou, 2015).

Instructors can take several steps, outlined throughout this chapter, to promote more meaningful connections and create opportunities for interpersonal interactions. The resulting community of learners will be engaged and invested in the course and, consequently, will be more likely to succeed. One can see this evolution in alignment with the evolution of the Web. Currently, we are in the midst of a transition from Web 2.0 to Web 3.0, which focuses on mobile learning. In the earlier Web 2.0, learners had new opportunities to create Web pages, but typically these were built on centralized computers based in libraries or computer labs. The latter part of the Web 2.0 era saw more home computer use and better tools for developing interactive webpages. The Web 3.0 era, however, is lowering the barrier of entry for the creation of interactive online elements. One of these areas is through e-learning modules. Tools such as Articulate Storyline and Adobe Captivate enable even novice instructors to create engaging and interactive learning objects in a way that simply was not possible ten years ago without specialized training. This trend towards creating tools that provide for rapid development of learning objects will likely continue and further bolster the ability of instructors to create engaging online learning environments.

Notwithstanding the evidence that technology can help improve interaction in the classroom, emerging technologies can be a hindrance to some. Technology should always follow and support the instructional goals of the course. It is not uncommon for eager instructors such as Troy and Ruth to identify a new tool they have heard or read about and then try to simply add it to their course. Without aligning the technology tool to a specific learning objective, though, instructors run the risk of creating unnecessary headaches and challenges for students. If the tool is too complicated to use, requires significant training for students, or simply does not work as intended, frustration and anxiety will result and potentially contribute to a poor learning experience. Particularly in an online environment, instructors need to be mindful of the scaffolding they provide, and it is paramount that learning tools come equipped with adequate instructions and resources. One way to bolster these resources is by creating a short video screencast or digital recording of what is being shown on the computer screen. As instructors demonstrate how to download, set up an account with, and use the tool, students get a clear understanding of what is necessary and expected of them when completing a given assignment.

CREATING ENGAGEMENT IN ONLINE LEARNING ENVIRONMENTS (OLES)

The Importance of Engagement

In traditional face-to-face learning environments, the instructor manages course delivery and dictates the "scope of choices and learner control" (Tschofen & Mackness, 2012, p. 129). "Learner control" refers to the ability of students to determine their own instructional paths (Simsek, 2012). Simsek explains that giving learners control of their own learning will "accommodate their individual differences toward the purpose of maximizing their gains" (p. 1748). Learner control varies across learning environments. For example, if the instructor in a face-to-face classroom wants to show a short video at the start of class followed with a small group discussion, all of the students are engaged in that activity, at that specific time. Students cannot opt out of watching the video or watch it at a different time. In an online class environment, however, students have much more flexibility and control over when and how they complete assignments and thus must be more self-motivated. Pappano (2012) cites Ray Schroeder's three most important factors for online learning as "quality of material covered, engagement of the student, and interaction among students" (p. 3). A poorly designed online learning environment usually offers significantly less interaction between students and instructors than does a face-to-face course. This lack of interaction can cause students to feel isolated and disconnected from the course and can lead to a high rate of attrition, impacting overall course quality.

He, Xu, and Kruck (2014) designate social interaction as an important component in online learning environments, explaining that "online participation alone is not sufficient to achieve deep and meaningful learning" (p. 102). One way to achieve this "deep and meaningful learning" is by using the Community of Inquiry (CoI) framework developed by Garrison, Anderson, and Archer (2000). He et al. (2014) explain that this framework focuses on three elements: "social presence, teaching presence, and cognitive presence" (p. 102). A discussion of each follows.

Social Presence

Akyol and Garrison (2009) define social presence "in terms of affective expression, open communication and group cohesion" (p. 4). Boston et al. (2009) define affective expression as "the ability of online learners to project themselves through text-based verbal behaviors" and open communication as "the provision of a risk-free learning climate in which participants trust one another enough to reveal themselves" (p. 68). Finally, Boston et al. (2009) define group cohesion as "the development of a group identity and ability of participants in the learning community to collaborate meaningfully" (p. 68). Put another way, this is the concept of making personal connections between the students. Even in an online course, students should feel that they are dealing with actual people (Swan & Shih, 2005). Moore and Kearsley (2012) explain that the technique of creating an environment that supports learners by allowing them to build a rapport is called "humanizing" (p. 137). Akyrol et al. (2009) further explain that social presence provides the basis for a collaborative learning environment and a constructivist online learning environment. Gunawardena and Zittle (1997) found social presence to be "a strong predictor of satisfaction" in an online course (p. 23). Thus, it is important for instructors to work on developing this social presence if they hope to create the type of collaborative and interactive online learning environment that will make learning effective and efficient for students.

So what does social presence look like in an online learning environment? In the author's experience, it is created in the initial assignments. As explained in latter sections of this chapter, this assignment should be an ice-breaker activity that allows students to get to know both the instructor and each other on a personal level. Furthermore, Rourke et al. (2001) found that students who engage with social presence tend to demonstrate a high propensity for sustaining the content-related communications within the course because they find it more appealing and rewarding. When peers are equally engaged with the course content, they are more likely to comment and respond to more than the minimum required posts; they see an opportunity to connect with peers and to receive feedback and interactions that are both rewarding and encouraging for future projects.

Social presence is a powerful motivating factor for Troy, Ruth, and Charles. Ultimately these instructors are interested in having their students engage with the content, and understanding how a sense of community can lead to demonstrations of student engagement is a critical requisite in migrating to online learning environments. For Ruth, who is open to technology but also somewhat uneasy about its requirements, social presence will help ease her concerns about putting in the effort needed to integrate new tools like discussion forums and other interactive element requirements. Understanding that students with greater opportunities to engage with one another tend to see improved learning outcomes will help assuage her concern that implementing these tools is a waste of time. For Charles, the instructor least open to the use of online technology, the positive impact of social presence on student learning will help him see that it is worth his time to learn how to use these new tools.

Teaching Presence

Teaching presence is defined "in terms of design, facilitation and direct instruction" (Akyol & Garrison, 2008, p. 4). These are defined as instructor responsibilities by Borup, West, and Graham (2012), who assert that instructors need to "motivate, encourage and assess student performance and use direct instruction to scaffold student learning" (p.196). In combination with social presence, teaching presence can also lead to improved student learning (Borup et al., 2012). The role of the instructor in an online course cannot be overstated; it is a critical component for any online course because students tend to feed off the energy, or lack thereof, of the instructor. In the author's experience, courses that are highly interactive and engaging all involve a strong connection to the instructor. When the instructor is present and available to answer questions, students experience much less of the frustration that exists in courses where there is an ostensible disconnect between them and the instructor. In such courses, it feels as if the instructor is disinterested in the learning and overall educational experiences of the students.

Disconnection is often demonstrated through instructor feedback and responses to students. Baker (2011), explaining the importance of providing timely responses to email inquiries from students, suggests that a 12- to 24-hour turnaround is best. The author's experience bears this out; in courses where the author felt disconnected, instructors often took multiple days rather than several hours to respond to emails. When there is not a clear standard for when an instructor is expected to respond, students become frustrated because they expect a fairly immediate response as would occur in a face-to-face course. Such unmet expectations can result in students having negative feelings about a course.

All three of the instructors described in this chapter struggle with this concept. Each would benefit from establishing a set of standards, which is best done initially through the syllabus (Baker, 2011). Ruth and Charles tend to err on the side of not responding quickly enough, whereas Troy can be overzealous in replying and may become overwhelmed by the expectation to be constantly available. While providing this type of access may seem like a good approach, it can set unrealistic expectations that are difficult to maintain.

Answering a student email fifteen minutes after it is received may seem like a good demonstration of responsiveness, but in reality it creates an expectation that *all* emails will be responded to within the same time frame. By stating that he or she will try to reply to emails within 24 hours, the instructor elucidates the expectations of students while establishing an effective way to manage his or her time and obligations to students (Grant & Thornton, 2007). A common thread running throughout this discussion is the need for instructors to be clear and explicit with their students, whether in the form of course expectations or through evaluative feedback. Particularly in online learning environments, it is very important to set realistic standards. In the author's experience, instructors who fail to do so have the most challenges in managing and teaching their courses.

Cognitive Presence

Cognitive presence is defined as "the practical inquiry model and consisting of phases for triggering event, exploration, integration, and resolution" (Akyrol & Garrison, 2009, p. 4). Boston et al. (2009) describe it as the "extent to which learners are able to construct and confirm meaning through reflection and discourse" (p. 69). Borup et al. (2012) explain that the CoI framework provides "insight into ways that online interactions can improve students' and instructors' social presence and learning" (p. 195).

If students feel comfortable in the classroom—whether virtual or physical—they are more likely to excel and make the learning environment more enjoyable for everyone. One of the biggest complaints from students about online courses is that they are boring or lack the opportunity for interaction. For a majority of today's students, their entire education has taken place in a formal classroom setting where they have had frequent, if not daily, direct contact with both peers and the instructor; to these students, an online environment can feel foreign and devoid of this interaction. They do not feel connected to their peers or instructor and, without these connections, they struggle to understand the course material and fail to remain engaged. They can become frustrated and disillusioned and may ultimately drop the course. If they are unable to make interpersonal connections, a connectivist learning environment cannot exist.

The technique of creating an environment that supports learners by allowing them to build rapport is called "humanizing" (Moore & Kearsley, 2012, p. 137). A great way to facilitate such rapport in the beginning of a course is to implement an initial student introduction assignment. This allows students to become acquainted with one another and has the added benefit of introducing them to the course discussion forum. This assignment can be structured in many different ways, and instructors should experiment with different strategies to find the best option. In face-to-face classroom introductions, students typically take turns going around the room sharing information about themselves. This may be helpful for one or two students but does little to build an interactive community. In the online introduction assignment, pose a question that calls for discussion—such as "why are you taking the course?" or "what do you hope to learn?"—that also solicits the customary demographic information. Even more, ask students to include a picture of themselves with their posts. Then ask each student to reply to a specific number of classmates, perhaps two or three. Be explicit about the number of replies the students must make because, otherwise, they may not interact with many of their classmates. A good rule of thumb is to make the minimum requirements of replies equal to at least 10 percent of the total class enrollment. Having students reply to a specific minimum number of posts will help them make connections and find common interests. Likely they will have to read more than the required number of introductions to find enough posts to which they can meaningfully reply.

FlipGrid (http://www.flipgrid.com) is an example of a tool that enables video interaction between the instructor and the students of an online class. This Web-based tool requires the instructor to create an account and pose questions to which students respond via webcam and microphone (often built into the webcam). Since neither a download nor account creation is required for students to use this tool, it is very easy for them to use. Additionally, the 90-second response limit forces students to be concise and thoughtful. All three of the instructors discussed in this chapter would easily be able to use this tool. Troy and Ruth could use it to create their own videos and participate in the discussion along with their students. Even Charles would find this tool helpful as it would simplify grading. Instead of having to read discussion forum posts or track responses, he would simply click on a single URL to watch each of the students' video responses.

Online learning environments provide multiple methods and opportunities for the students and instructor to both engage in discourse and construct shared knowledge. Ultimately it is the instructor's responsibility to ensure that the OLE supports this type of learning (Moore & Kearsley, 2012). A majority of students in a research study by Borup, West, and Graham (2012) reported that "video communication helped them to develop an emotional connection with their instructor" (p. 199). Specifically, Swan and Shih (2005) identified the instructor's social presence as a significant factor in positive course outcomes for the students. In fact, when the author reflects on bad online learning experiences, one of the first aspects that comes to mind as a contributing factor is the perceived lack of interaction in that course, often evidenced by a feeling of isolation or disconnect from peers and/or their instructor. Thus the challenge for an instructor in an OLE is to identify ways to create the optimal amount of student engagement that facilitates learning and a sense of connectedness. One of the biggest challenges for online instructors—both experienced and new—is finding that right balance between interaction and autonomy. They must provide enough scaffolding for students to feel supported and comfortable but not so much that self-directed learning is inhibited. Instructors would be wise to approach the online learning environment as a fluid, dynamic setting that will evolve and develop over the course of a semester. Instructors should view each of their interactions as an opportunity to help shape and guide students, but should also limit restrictions that may hinder students' abilities to learn and develop their own skills. As instructors gain more experience, they will better understand how to maintain the right balance between interactive learning and self-directed learning.

A Sense of Community

Humans are social beings. We desire to be a part of a group and to feel connected to one another. It is not surprising that students seek this same feeling of connectedness in their instructional environments. Attrition is defined in large part as the absence of a sense of connection and community among learners (Dueber & Misanchuk, 2001), and avoiding it is one of the biggest challenges for distance education. Frydenberg (2007) found that attrition rates tend to be higher in online courses than those in face-to-face classes, and Carr (2000) found that the attrition rate for online courses could be as much as 10–15 percent higher than for face-to-face classes. According to Moller (1998), the number of dropouts "could be lessened through increasing the feelings of community among isolated learners" (p. 116).

One of the most powerful ways an instructor can mitigate feelings of isolation in online learners is to foster a sense of community in a course (Moore, 2014). Rovai and Wighting (2005) define this as "a sense of belonging, identity, emotional connection, and wellbeing" (p. 99). A strong sense of community is formed when "… the [learner's] contributions add to a common knowledge pool" and the "community spirit is fostered through social interactions facilitated by a skilled instructor" (p. 100). These interactions must include the

three types of interactions discussed above—social presence, teaching presence, and cognitive presence—between learners and content, learners and instructors, and learners and other learners. The content–learner interaction in which content is merely provided to the learner, as would be typical in a self-paced or correspondence-type course, is simply insufficient (Moller, 1998). Instead, students should frequently and dynamically interact with the content, demonstrate what they have learned, and apply it to real-life experiences. At the same time, they should be able to share their knowledge and insights with peers and receive input and feedback from both their peers and the instructor. Ultimately, increased interactions contribute to the creation of a collaborative learning environment, the foundation of which is a sense of community (Wegerif, 1998). Through this collaboration, students can expand their knowledge and add to the overall instructional value of the course.

The concept of community-building seems so simple yet, whether due to a lack of online instructional experience or an understanding of how to create a sense of community in this new instructional environment, online instructors continue to struggle with this aspect of effective OLEs. For an instructor like Charles, connecting with students he cannot see feels unnatural, which may make him hesitant to embrace the technological tools that can help foster adequate connections. Charles would need to understand that frequent interaction – either student to student or instructor to student – can contribute to a greater sense of community and satisfaction among learners (Dawson, 2006). A new instructor like Troy, on the other hand, may actually overdo the community development aspect of the course and incorporate too many different tools, leaving students feeling overwhelmed or confused. Meanwhile, the challenge for an instructor like Ruth might be determining which tool would best meet instructional needs, yielding a more cautious approach to the tools used in the course. But all of these instructors would benefit from taking a step back and understanding that developing an engaging, interactive learning environment is less about designing a complex system of communications and more about creating multiple opportunities for students to engage with each other. Activities that allow students to introduce themselves and learn from each other, such as the aforementioned introduction assignment or working in groups throughout the duration of the course, are excellent ways to encourage student interaction. Giving students an opportunity to develop into cohorts may facilitate learning and provide them with a support system as they proceed through the semester. Potentially useful examples of cohort-building activities include "discussion forum ice-breakers, orientation videos, and testimonials from past successful students" (Moore, 2014, p. 24). In addition, cohorts can help fill the feedback gap that results from having a less accessible instructor.

Active student participation is necessary for the development of community in an OLE. Students must interact with both the content and each other. Research shows that the most effective learning occurs between peers, and thus instructors should look for opportunities that allow learners to easily share their ideas and experiences.

The Role of Technology

Technology plays a central instructional role in an OLE. Most online courses use a learning management system, or LMS, such as Blackboard, Sakai, or Moodle. These Web-based systems provide a centralized location for course content, communication, and interactions. By using these systems, instructors can tap into ever-expanding technology resources to create and facilitate a myriad of instructional tools and activities. However, many instructors are either not familiar with or not sure how to implement and maximize instructional technology. An instructional design practitioner can assist a faculty member in creating an online

course, but whether or not an instructor is working with an instructional designer, all technology used in the course must support the course objectives. Technology should never be implemented for technology's sake. The instructor must first identify the specific learning objectives and align those with the appropriate technological tools. Ironically, this is often an area where an instructor who is keen on technology, such as Troy, will run into problems.

Although helpful for an instructional designer to work with instructors who understand technology, such collaborations can still present a challenge. In the author's experience, the tech-savvy instructors often need to take a step back and evaluate their options. These instructors often aim to implement every new tool they hear about without taking time to consider how it will be used in the context of their course or which learning objective it will help meet. As a student in an online course, the author can attest to the type of frustration that can ensue from being overly ambitious. When numerous tools are added to a course with little justification, students may find them to be overwhelming or ineffective, ultimately producing a feeling of disconnect from the course and confusion about the instructor's expectations.

One question to pose is, "How is this tool improving students' abilities to complete the assignment?" Instructors may find it easier to answer this question by completing the assignment themselves using the specific tool; by taking on the role of the student, they will be able to relate to the issues caused by the tool, such as an overly complicated process, difficulty understanding its use, and so on. This may reveal to the instructor that that the tool is not a good fit for the course; or, it may substantiate its use in the course and illustrate what type of documentation and support is needed in order for students to complete the assignment. Both outcomes provide useful information for the instructor and ultimately the students. For Troy, such an assignment will help him effectively evaluate tools in the future and at the same time identify ways they can be successfully implemented into his course. For Ruth, who prefers to focus on a few tools and become proficient using them, this process will help her narrow down the tools she decides to emphasize. She also may want to keep a running list of the desired functions the tool is not executing correctly to help evaluate other tools; if another tool is presented to her but does not address one of the limiting factors of an existing tool, she will know that she does not need to spend additional time evaluating it.

One of the most common tools used in OLEs is the discussion forum in which students respond to classmates' posts. Discussion forums and virtual class sessions, in which the instructor polls students to get immediate feedback, are just two ways to create a collaborative and engaging online experience. Ultimately, this engagement should help students participate in and demonstrate active learning while shaping and guiding class discussion.

Regardless of the specific tools employed, teaching online is fundamentally different from face-to-face instruction. Instructors will not be able to see their students in person, and the instruction is conducted using some type of technology (e.g., synchronous chat or video sessions, asynchronous reading assignments, or discussion forum postings, among many other methods). A classroom, whether face-to-face or online, should never be a one-way interaction. Instead, it should be a partnership where ideas and information are shared among students and with the instructor. In addition, as Moore and Kearsley (2012) suggest, "the best distance teachers are empathetic" (p. 127); instructors should understand the specific personalities of their students and find ways to engage and interact with them through various mediums. Some students will want a high level of instructor involvement while others will want more independence (Moore & Kearsley, 2012). A questionnaire given to students at the beginning of the course can help an instructor determine such preferences and expectations. As an instructor gains more experience in teaching in an online environment, he or she will be better able to identify individual student needs and tailor instruction to meet those needs.

The Changing Role of the Instructor

To be successful in an online learning environment, an online instructor must adapt his or her instructional approach. Where to devote time and effort, how to interact with students, and how to structure the course are considerations that may necessitate new skill sets for an online instructor.

Instructor Time and Effort

OLE instructors will likely spend more time teaching an online course than they would in a traditional face-to-face course (Gabriel & Kaufield, 2008). Online teaching involves more than simply taking all of the materials from a face-to-face course and putting them online. Additionally, how instructors spend their time will differ from how they spent it teaching a face-to-face course. In both environments the instructor must respond to emails and provide formative assessments and feedback. However, in the online environment, the instructor may spend additional time observing and commenting on activities in the discussion forum and creating videos or written tutorials and instructions for technological tools being used in the class.

The amount of time an instructor spends on assessment and evaluation may also be different in an online course. One of the first decisions an instructor must make is how to evaluate course participation. In a face-to-face class, he or she may base this evaluation on the number of questions asked and answered, but this approach might not be possible in an OLE. Instead, the instructor must quantify contributions and equate a grade to them. For instance, students might be expected to post four times to the course discussion forum each week.

Another difference between the two learning environments is the number of assessments. A face-to-face class would likely include several large assessments, such as a mid-term exam and one or two term papers along with quizzes or small homework assignments. In this environment instructors typically lecture two or three times a week and prepare lesson plans and class presentations. An instructor can generally assess student understanding of the material by virtue of the types and number of questions students ask during class. Because online instructors lack this opportunity, they should create a more structured learning environment that offers a higher number of attainable points and includes multiple smaller activities that build toward larger assignments.

Creating formative assessments requires additional work, but in doing so students will ultimately have a better grasp of the course subject matter. In addition, both the students and the instructor can accurately gauge course progress. If the assignment structure is such that the students watch a short video, complete a reading assignment, and then post their thoughts in the discussion forum, the instructor can quickly determine whether they have learned and understood the key concepts of the reading assignment. As smaller assignments build toward a larger one, the instructor can ensure that students have made the progress necessary to proceed.

Interaction with Students

Students learn by responding to various stimuli and interacting accordingly, so it is pivotal to consider the vast differences in instructor-student interaction between an online class and a face-to-face course. The challenge for instructors is identifying which stimuli are most conducive to a particular online learning environment. Students, meanwhile, must be more self-directed, particularly in an online course that is asynchronous. The freedom and flexibility of an online course may be appealing to students, but they must be more responsible for staying on task. As Tschofen and Mackness (2012) point out, a "potentially unfettered network environment may work best only for adults or the most experienced learners" and this type of environment may be best suited for "those with a large amount of traditional education as a background" (p. 129).

Understanding that students may not have experience with online learning places an even greater burden on the instructor to take proactive steps to support students and create an environment in which they feel safe and can see themselves excelling. For Charles, this will be particularly frustrating and another potential reason why he has doubts about the value of online education as an instructional tool. To help assuage his concerns, the author would provide more of a personal support approach as well as examples of existing syllabi or course assignments in the online environment. By creating a shell of the course in the learning management system and then generating assignments for him, the author would try to show Charles how the assignment itself is the same, just delivered in a different way. Creating sample sites and video demonstrations of how to use the different tools within the learning management system would be helpful also for Troy and Ruth, who are interested in technology but not always sure how to implement or utilize it. These sample sites would help establish a set of best practices that align not only to online learning environments but also to the specific learning management system being used.

Online instructors should take into account that students may not realize they need to approach online studies differently. Most online students, even experienced ones, will begin a course feeling apprehensive. They will be uncertain about what they must do to be successful in the course.

Perhaps they have previously had a poor instructional experience in an online class. Instructors cannot take anything for granted and should view each class as if all the students are new to online instruction. One way instructors can alleviate these concerns is to make themselves more accessible through multiple methods (such as by Skype, email, or telephone). Even if the students do not take advantage of these tools, making them available creates a sense of trust in and connection with the instructor. In a face-to-face class, a student knows exactly when to find the instructor because class meetings are always on a set schedule. This is not the case online. Knowing from the outset the instructor's availability during the semester will greatly reduce student feelings of isolation and disengagement.

An instructor in the traditional face-to-face environment may take an approach that resembles "sage on the stage," lecturing at the front of an auditorium, a setting in which students passively receive information and have no opportunity for interaction or engagement. While it is perhaps difficult to do, online instructors should take more of a coach or facilitator role and guide students through the curriculum instead of dictating their path (Cho & Cho, 2014; Anderson & Dron, 2011; Garrison, 2011; Moller 1998). This flexibility will allow different learning styles to develop and flourish.

The successful online instructor must also identify ways that students can support each other in the learning process. One way to accomplish this is by adapting and responding appropriately to student feedback. Just as it is important for learners to actively engage in the course, the instructor must support and guide exchanges among students without inserting him- or herself into the exchange. The instructor has a pivotal role in the discussion forum. He or she must model good posting behavior while keeping the conversation flowing in a way that encourages student participation and interaction (Garrison, 2011).

Course Creation and Modification

Creating an online course is not a simple process. A full transition from the classroom to an online environment could reasonably take several years. Online course design and instruction may be completely different from the way an instructor was trained to teach, so he or she may potentially have a steep learning curve. The author has found that one of the best ways to prepare to teach online is to take an online course as a student. Direct observation is helpful but nothing can compare to firsthand experience. Instructors often take the effectiveness of instruction for granted, so taking on the role of the student in an online course can provide an instructor with an entirely new perspective on what methods better enable students to learn.

For instance, Charles is resistant to teaching an online course primarily because he believes it is not an effective way to receive or provide instruction. Were he to enroll as a student in an effectively designed online course, it is likely that his perspective of online education would change. In addition, he would experience the feeling of success, and this feeling is key. The author has found that one of the underlying fears of an instructor like Charles, who has always taught and received instruction in face-to-face environments, is that students will not be as successful in this new environment. This fear of the unknown may be demonstrated or appear as resistance to the delivery method, but in reality it is it something completely different. Putting these instructors in an online environment so that they can experience what it is actually like to be a student and, more importantly, having them experience learning in that delivery method will be very effective in getting them to accept and adapt to an online learning environment. Being a student will also illustrate the types of interactions, communications, and issues that are important to this population and enable instructors to make changes that take student perspectives into account.

A thoughtful instructor will recognize and accept that not every student will be successful in an online environment and not all planned activities or tasks will be as effective as intended. Fortunately, creating online courses can be a dynamic, flexible process; an instructor can tweak a course and add content to it, shaping and reshaping it throughout the term of study if necessary. If the instructor notices that a specific unit of information has generated confusion, he or she might add supplemental content or resources, such as interactive lectures in the form of e-learning modules, to subsequent sections of the course.

An online instructor's attempts to reformulate his or her teaching approach to better suit online learning may be initially unsuccessful. A particular activity could fail to engage students or connect them with the material. Alternatively, students may not generate ideas that will keep a discussion thread going because the instructor did not provide a solid foundation for the discussion. Such setbacks could, justifiably, discourage an instructor, leading him or her to attribute these problems to an inability to fully engage and connect with students in the same way that was possible in the traditional classroom. These issues can and likely will occur, and instructors must focus their attention on ways to mitigate such challenges.

FIELD OF DREAMS (OF INTERACTION): IF I BUILD IT, WILL THEY COME? SOLUTIONS AND RECOMMENDATIONS

This section provides solutions and recommendations to help instructors create an online learning environment (OLE) in which students actively interact and engage with the content and each other. The connections and engagement established will result in a sense of community that ultimately is the foundation for a successful learning experience.

Course Design and Structure

To create opportunities for engagement in an online course, the instructor must design it to be conducive to engagement. The three specific areas in which this can be addressed are course navigation, the syllabus, and feedback.

Navigation

Problem: *My students are asking a lot of questions about where to find things. They don't seem to understand how to use the course site. How can I address this?*

In a face-to-face class, instructors can effectively teach without a learning management system (LMS). They can email the students the syllabus and accept assignments via email or in paper form. These are not all possible in an OLE. A successful online course must use an LMS. Of course, an online instructor could accept assignments and correspond with students through email. But, as discussed previously, communicating in this manner would not be conducive to an effective OLE because the students cannot interact with each other or feel engaged in any meaningful way. The specific LMS used by the instructor is not significant—they all allow posts of course content, discussion forums, and other tools that provide opportunities for student engagement and interaction.

Solution 1: *Make expectations consistent and design a navigation scheme that mirrors the course structure.*

Assume a semester is 16 weeks long. Within the LMS the instructor could create eight units and then explain the assignments within each unit. All of the units would be linked in the course site navigation, but the instructor would not release the unit content until the second week of the preceding unit. The syllabus would show and the students would see the links to all eight units. However, the content for unit three, for example, would not appear until the second week of unit two. Throughout the course and at any given time, students would understand exactly where they are. To foster communication, the instructor could email the students at the start of each unit, congratulating them on completing the previous unit and providing a brief overview of what to expect in the next unit.

The instructor would also want to have consistent assignment requirements and explain them in the course syllabus. For instance, discussion board postings would all be due on the same schedule within each given unit. In the two-week units described above, a particular unit assignment might be due at midnight on the Thursday of the second week. Students could always click on a link for a specific unit and know what to do without referring back to the syllabus. Structuring a course in this way sets clear expectations and allows students to focus on successfully completing assignments instead of trying to figure out what to expect from week to week.

Solution 2: *Make the course an interactive course rather than a "correspondence course."*

Structuring the course and navigation tools in the manner described above would prevent the class from becoming a correspondence course because students would have to progress through each unit together. Since everyone in the class is moving through the content at the same time and pace, they can share their knowledge, insights, and experiences with each other. In addition, the instructor will have more opportunities to gauge student progress and identify areas that need more discussion or explanation. If the instructor sees that the discussion forum posts are following an unintended path, he or she can redirect their focus. By concentrating on smaller chunks of content

at a time, students have a greater opportunity to familiarize themselves with individual concepts and reach deeper levels of understanding. They also will be able to demonstrate a more sophisticated application of the concepts using structured assignments and activities, leading to a greater level of success for the students and an enriching educational experience for the entire class.

Syllabus

Problem: *I don't think my online students even looked at the syllabus. They are always asking questions about assignments and submitting assignments in the wrong format. What should I do?*

The syllabus is the core document for any course regardless of the learning environment. It is even more important in an online course and should serve as its roadmap. It should include a course overview and expectations, a description of each of the assignments with due dates, and the instructor's contact information. Instructors should explicitly state their availability to answer questions (for instance, "Emails will be returned within 24 hours."). In addition, instructors should consider making themselves available via phone or an online tool, such as web conferencing software or Skype.

Solution: *Create a scavenger hunt quiz as an initial assignment.*

In the first day of a typical face-to-face class, the instructor usually reviews the syllabus and asks if there are any questions. In this situation the instructor can observe body language and get visual cues when there is confusion, neither of which is possible in an OLE. One way to address this is by creating a scavenger hunt in the form of a quiz. The quiz should be worth a nominal number of points (maybe two to five) and clearly presented as the students' initial assignment. Allow students to take the quiz as many times as they need in order to reach a score of 100 percent. The purpose of the assignment is not to assess the students; it is meant to expose them to the course design and navigation scheme and the format of the assignments. Each of the questions should address specific items within the syllabus, such as assignment due dates, the number of discussion forum postings required each week, and the location of other information. All of the answers should be found in the syllabus, and the quiz should randomize questions from a pool. The number of questions does not need to be extensive—between five and ten is sufficient—but the questions should cover the main points or parts of the syllabus. Administering this quiz will accomplish several things. First, it will ensure that students have actually read the syllabus. But more important, it will give the students a sense of accomplishment. Finally, if the instructor is planning on giving online tests or quizzes, this assignment will introduce students to the online quiz format. Remember, the assumption is that this is their first online course. Earning two to five points toward their grade for simply reading the syllabus and understanding the course structure demonstrates to them that success is possible in the course.

Feedback

Problem: *How can I evaluate students that I cannot "see" in class? How can I assess what they are learning?*

Usually a syllabus for a traditional face-to-face class describes a "course participation" grade. This grade is usually determined by the contributions made during class sessions. Determining course participation grades is a challenge in an online course, particularly an asynchronous course. In addition, an online course requires self-motivation. Because students in these courses are generally not required to attend class on a set schedule, they must meet some other quantifiable criteria to demonstrate they are actively engaging with the course content. This is the double-edged sword of distance education—the flexibility it offers is highly attractive for an adult learner who has a job and family, but students can very easily fall behind in the course work.

Solution 1: *Provide feedback on a unit basis.*

Frequent feedback serves multiple purposes. First, by providing feedback at the end of each unit, instructors give students the opportunity to take corrective action before they start the next unit. The instructor must be committed to providing timely feedback. If course units run from Monday to Sunday, students should be provided feedback and a grade on the Sunday before the start of the next unit. To make this goal more manageable, an instructor could provide feedback on smaller assignments throughout the specific unit. This formative feedback can be helpful to both the instructor and the student; each can evaluate a small course segment (in our example, two-week chunks) to evaluate progress. The feedback from the instructor should be constructive and offer suggestions for improvement. If points are deducted, the instructor should be explicit about why. This feedback will provide an opportunity for the student to take whatever action is necessary to improve in subsequent units. It may also motivate the student to reach out to the instructor if help is needed. Finally, feedback will help the instructor evaluate course structure and assignments. Low overall course grades for a specific unit might indicate that the instructor should make adjustments to subsequent units. Biweekly assessments of this nature can enhance the course as a whole.

A key tool for feedback is the use of rubrics. For every assignment, there should be a specific rubric. It should be shared with students before they complete a given assignment, and the instructor's grading should reference and reflect the rubric. Students will then understand explicitly the expectations for the assignment and the instructor can grade assignments consistently across the class.

Grade objections from students should decrease, as the students are provided with specific descriptions of how they will be evaluated and can work toward those standards.

Solution 2: *Provide video-based feedback.*

An instructor may also want to use screencast tools to provide feedback and assessment of an activity. For instance, if an assignment involves the submission of a Web-based module, the instructor may want to do a screencast that points out the things that were done well along with specific feedback for the parts that lost points based on the rubric. This type of feedback is helpful for an online course because it gives the instructor the benefit of explaining things in more detail. This feedback should align with the rubric to demonstrate to the student exactly how the instructor assessed the assignment. The video feedback can be more specific than a text response by allowing the instructor to go more in depth into areas for improvement.

Tools, Techniques, and Activities

This subsection will discuss how to leverage different tools to create interactive activities for learners in an online course.

Discussion Forums

Problem: *I've heard that discussion forums don't work in online courses because the students don't take them seriously and their posts are no more substantial than "good job." How can I make them more successful?*

Discussion forums can be the biggest source of frustration for both instructors and students in online courses. Students often complain that the discussion forum feels like busy work, and instructors get frustrated with superficial posts from students that neither engage their peers nor stimulate discussion. Consequently, many instructors will not include a discussion forum in their courses. This is a big mistake. As this chapter has shown, there are multiple ways to successfully integrate discussion forums into a course. They afford an opportunity to extend classroom discussion and may encourage students to participate in a more dynamic way than in the classroom; they provide an online instructor endless possibilities for motivating and inspiring students to interact and engage with each other and the course content. Every LMS, for example, Blackboard or Sakai, includes a discussion forum tool.

Solution: *Create guidelines for posting that allow students to demonstrate their understanding of course concepts.*

Clear guidelines for posting requirements and the rules of etiquette are key to a successful discussion forum. Simply asking students to post their comments to the forum is insufficient—give them specific instructions for how often to post and even consider providing them with specific questions or concepts to address. Do not make the students guess what is required in the posts; if a 500-word response is expected, state that in the guidelines. Modeling is a highly effective instructional tool, especially with discussion forums. Randomly select postings each week and comment on them. These model posts will demonstrate the desired format and style and show students that the instructor is in fact paying attention to their posts. Instructors should maintain their roles as facilitators and resist the urge to take over the discussion forum. Ultimately, the forum is intended for student interaction, and the instructor should remain on the sidelines, steering the conversations and providing additional points to consider. There should be a graded component to the discussion forum postings, as a percentage of students' participation grade or otherwise.

Once a discussion forum has been integrated into an online course, it can be used to support and employ many other activities. One way to use the discussion forum is to prompt students to demonstrate their understanding of a course concept. For instance, ask students to post videos from YouTube or other websites that relate to a specific topic and share their comments. Avoid making the assignment too passive by simply asking students to post a video. Create a rubric outlining what to include in the initial post and provide ample opportunities for learner-to-learner interaction by, among other things, requiring them to provide feedback and comments on their peers' postings. The discussion forum creates an opportunity for students to effectively share and engage with multimedia presentations. For example, students could create short videos and post them to the discussion forum. Because they would not be limited by the time or technology constraints of a traditional classroom, students could benefit greatly from this type of assignment, which offers almost unlimited means to express their creativity. In addition, the instructor can provide helpful and evaluative feedback.

Screencasts

Problem: *I've found software I want to use for an assignment, but the students seem confused about how to use it and are getting frustrated.*

An online course will likely use instructional technology tools that are new or unfamiliar to the students. In a face-to-face course, the instructor can devote the first class to showing students how to use a new tool and answering any questions. In an online course, an instructor must use other means to demonstrate new software or tools.

Solution: *Use screencasts to do mini-lectures, demonstrations, and training.*

Learning is best accomplished by both seeing *and* doing. Fortunately, current technology offers many educational tools that combine visual and kinesthetic activities to create optimal learning experiences. Screen capture videos, for example, are an excellent option for demonstrations. These videos are easy to create; can serve multiple audiences at once; and allow users to watch, pause, and stop them as needed. The creation of the video occurs in real time, since you are recording the steps as you complete them. . Once the target activity or lesson has been captured, the video may need additional editing. One benefit of making these videos short (two to four minutes, for example) is that if a mistake is made, the entire video can easily be redone. Several programs, such as Jing (http://www.techsmith.com/jing.html), CamStudio (http://www.camstudio.org), and Screencast-O-Matic (http://www.screencast-o-matic.com), facilitate the creation of screen-capture videos. These programs are free but have length limitations on recordings and add a watermark. Limiting recordings to five minutes or less, however, may make these programs beneficial to instructors, compelling them to make short and cogent videos. Instructors wishing to attempt more advanced screen captures, such as zoom and pan functions or embedded quizzing, should consider the licensed version of Camtasia Studio (http://www.techsmith.com/camtasia.html), a product of the same company that makes Jing.

Mini-Lectures

One way to integrate a screencast into your course is to introduce a unit with a two- to three-minute video that explains the lesson's objectives, reviews assignment due dates, and provides additional useful information. The video does not have to be complicated—it can be as simple as appearing before a webcam in the office while providing the information. Instructors can use "screen sharing" or "desktop sharing," recording what they are seeing on a screen or desktop and narrating the different steps of a new procedure. Students can then watch the video and see exactly where to click. These tools are particularly useful in describing a necessary sequence of steps (for example, logging into the LMS and clicking on the assignments link). Because the procedure has been recorded, students can start, pause, and stop the video as necessary and follow along on their own computers. The instructor also may want to consider giving a short quiz, worth one or two points, at the end of each screencast. The quiz will ensure that the students are both watching the video and beginning the unit with an understanding of all of its requirements and assignments.

Demonstrations and Training

Screencasts can also be used to demonstrate a new product, software, or application. Screencasting tools allow video and audio synchronization and zooming in for emphasis. They can also be used to create a more interactive "Frequently Asked Questions" section for the course or website. Instead of providing a list of written instructions for a new procedure or process, create a video companion that actively demonstrates those steps. This type of demonstration video is a highly effective resource and in many cases can actually reduce the number of questions students need to ask.

Imagine an assignment in which the students are asked to create an animated video using a website such as GoAnimate (http://www.goanimate.com) or Voki (http://www.voki.com). While these tools each provide tutorials, it may be helpful to create customized tutorials focused on the specific tasks the students should be able to complete. Providing these focused tutorials helps ensure th students are not overwhelmed by a tool's available options. Using one of the screen capture options, create a series of short training videos demonstrating how to use the tools. Students new to the tool can learn how to use it and can complete the assignment. Keep the videos as short as possible; six to eight minutes is the average attention span for someone watching a video. Also, keep the videos focused and simple; too much content will make learning

a task more difficult. Breaking a complicated concept into a series of videos benefits both the instructor and the students. First, the videos will be easier to edit—instead of making changes to a 15-minute video, the instructor can re-record the specific parts of the series that need correction. Also, the students can re-watch the specific video they want and more quickly find the answers they need instead of scrolling and searching through a longer video. Finally, an instructor can create a playlist that organizes a series of tutorials into content-related groups.

Web/Video Conferencing

Problem: *I'm teaching in an asynchronous course, but I want to interact with the students in real time. How can I do that?*

The biggest challenge in organizing any sort of meeting is getting everyone in the same place at the same time. Moving these meetings online provides flexibility and, in some cases, additional functionality.

Solution: *Use web/video conferencing to conduct virtual office hours, review sessions, or class sessions.*

Web conferencing tools, such as virtual office hours and online review sessions, are an additional resource for instructors who want to reach out to their students. These tools are easy to manage and, in many cases, free. Several, such as Blackboard Collaborate (formerly Elluminate!) (http://www.blackboardcollaborate.com) and BigBlueButton (http://www.bigbluebutton.org), provide free trial accounts that include a virtual room in which a certain number of people can meet. Instructors may also want to use Google+ (http://plus.google.com) for virtual meetings and course group pages. Meeting participants can communicate using webcams, microphones, phones, or text-based chat in the virtual rooms. Screen sharing will allow participants to share a desktop or an application, such as Word or PowerPoint, with everyone in the room.

Virtual Office Hours

Having regularly scheduled virtual office hours allows instructors to be more available to their students. An instructor can log into the room and check emails or do other work but still be accessible if needed. And even if students do not avail themselves of this resource, establishing reliable, predictable office hours will go a long way toward building student engagement and trust.

Review Sessions

Students are always interested in asking questions and getting help reviewing for a test, but finding a room and time for a review session that works for everyone is a daunting task. Web conferencing makes these sessions manageable and also enables an instructor to record and publish them for those students who are unable to attend.

Class Sessions

Web conferencing can also be used for an online class session (to offer additional course materials, for example). Most solutions allow the instructor to upload a PowerPoint presentation and then show it to participants in a synchronous Web-based environment.

FUTURE RESEARCH DIRECTIONS

Creating online learning environments that foster student engagement and interaction is a complicated endeavor, and many factors contribute to the success or failure of an online course. While Garrison, Anderson, and Archer (2000) present a fundamental framework with their Community of Inquiry, it was developed at a time when most online instruction was primarily text-based. With the advent of Web 2.0 and Web 3.0, some assumptions of this framework may not be as relevant.

Shea et al. (2010) identify two areas of potential research for better understanding online teaching and learning. First, they suggest the challenge of being able to "successfully utilize quantitative content analysis for research into online teaching and learning." They also propose the inability to "reliably [identify] affect in online courses" as another challenge and potential area for further investigation (p. 17).

Another area for future research will be how and what technology best supports distance education. Several technological solutions have been discussed in this chapter, but there are countless others. Bonvillian and Singer (2013) point out that universities that emphasize traditional, lecture-based instruction will likely need to make changes to their delivery methods in order to keep up with the changing landscape of higher education. They also assert that such universities will need to "develop a new blended model" in order to create "a new [and] more dynamic role for faculty" (30). Understanding that a new model is necessary is the first step; implementing the new model will probably be an even bigger challenge. It will be interesting to see how these universities address the change to more online instruction and what types of infrastructure and other developments will be needed to help them stay relevant and sustainable. With new tools being developed on a daily basis, additional research will be needed to enable them to identify ways that such tools can best be implemented to support and enhance instruction and create interactive learning environments.

One of the areas in which technology and education have begun to merge are Massive Open Online Courses (MOOCs), which represent another segment of online learning that merits future research. An especially big challenge for MOOCs has been integrating them into the existing higher education landscape (Bonvillian & Singer, 2013).

A contributing factor is what to do with the course credits that have been earned through a MOOC because, for the most part, these courses provide no tangible benefits for students. Some programs do connect completion of MOOC course work to a certificate or a grade, but this is an exception instead of the norm. High attrition rates and a lack of connection between students have been common complaints about MOOCs. This chapter has described how developing and encouraging community and engagement in online learning environments can create effective online courses and positive distance education experiences. Could these concepts be applicable to MOOCs, making them more successful in retaining and matriculating students? A MOOC, by definition, will have an extremely large enrollment, typically in the thousands. How are the concepts of creating connection and community translatable when the enrollment is so high? Changes would need to be made to make it more realistic. For instance, the best practice of responding to at least 10 percent of the enrolled students is not realistic when there are 10,000 students in a class. But what is that number? This is just one of many questions regarding MOOCs that merits future research.

Retention in online courses is a growing concern and another area deserving of additional research. Cochran et al. (2014) point out that while there has been research about retention in online programs, not much of that research has focused on retention within specific courses. It would be interesting to learn more about why students are dropping specific courses and identify possible trends. The course design, structure, and expectations (or respective lack thereof) of online courses that were dropped could be examined to see if any common trends or themes can be found. This information could then be used to develop more effective online courses.

Finally, as an increasing number of courses are delivered online and students have a wider variety of options to meet their education needs, more research should address exactly how students are making decisions about these educational opportunities and choices. What factors contribute to a student's decision to take a face-to-face class as opposed to an online course? Are there aspects or characteristics of face-to-face instruction that could be incorporated into an online program that would make the latter more attractive to students?

CONCLUSION

Online education is here to stay and will only become more prevalent and continue to evolve in the coming years. Higher education should examine what is effective and what is not and ensure that the same high quality of instruction found in face-to-face classrooms is made a part of the online environment. Too often students become disenchanted with online education because of poor instructional experiences or their own lack of preparation or apprehension about a course. While some of these poor experiences can be attributed to student lack of effort, it is necessary for instructors to do whatever they can to help students be successful in an online class. This chapter has examined specific tools that instructors can use to create an interactive and engaging learning environment, ranging from ice-breaker introduction assignments to technology applications such as screen captures for recording mini-lectures and demonstrations. This discussion has only scratched the surface but hopefully will help stimulate ideas and suggest directions instructors can take to create engaging and effective learning environments. Ultimately, the most powerful and effective way an online instructor can impact students and the learning experience is to foster a sense of community. Perhaps no other factor can have a more positive effect both in terms of current student success and future course effectiveness.

ACKNOWLEDGMENT

This chapter is dedicated to my beloved uncle, Larry H. Thompson, Sr. (1947–2015), a singularly great friend and supporter of my work in identifying ways to integrate technology into instruction.

REFERENCES

Adkins, S. (2013). Ambient insight whitepaper: The 2012 boom in learning technology investment. *Ambientinsight.com*. Retrieved from: http://www.ambientinsight.com/Resources/Documents/AmbientInsight-2012-Learning-Technology-Investment-Patterns.pdf

Akyol, Z., Arbaugh, J. B., Cleveland-Innes, M., Garrison, D. R., Ice, P., Richardson, J. C., & Swan, K. (2009). A response to the review of the community of inquiry framework. *International Journal of E-Learning & Distance Education*, *23*(2), 123–136.

Akyol, Z., & Garrison, D. R. (2008). The development of a community of inquiry over time in an online course: Understanding the progression and integration, social, cognitive, and teaching presence. *Journal of Asynchronous Learning Networks*, *12*(3-4), 3–22.

Allen, I. E., & Seaman, J. (2013). Changing course: Ten years of tracking online education in the United States. Babson Park, MA: Babson Survey Research Group and Quahog Research Group. Retrieved from http://www.onlinelearningsurvey.com/reports/changingcourse.pdf

Anderson, T., & Dron, J. (2011). Three generations of distance education pedagogy. *International Review of Research in Open and Distance Learning*, *12*(3), 80–97.

Baker, D. L. (2011). Designing and orchestrating online discussions. *MERLOT Journal of Online Learning and Teaching*, *7*(3), 401–411.

Bell, F. (2011). Connectivism: Its place in theory-informed research and innovation in technology-enabled learning. *International Review of Research in Open and Distance Learning*, *12*(3), 98–118.

Bonvillian, W. B., & Singer, S. R. (2013). The online challenge to higher education. *Issues in Science and Technology*, *29*(4), 23–30.

Borup, J., West, R. E., & Graham, C. R. (2012). Improving online social presence through asynchronous video. *The Internet and Higher Education*, *15*(3), 195–203. doi:10.1016/j.iheduc.2011.11.001

Boston, W., Díaz, S. R., Gibson, A. M., Ice, P., Richardson, J., & Swan, K. (2009). An exploration of the relationship between indicators of the community of inquiry framework and retention in online programs. *Journal of Asynchronous Learning Networks*, *13*(3), 67–83.

Carr, S. (2000). As distance education comes of age, the challenge is keeping the students. *The Chronicle of Higher Education*, *46*(23), A39–A-41.

Cho, M. H., & Cho, Y. J. (2014). Instructor scaffolding for interaction and students' academic engagement in online learning: Mediating roles of perceived online class goal structures. *The Internet and Higher Education*, *21*, 25–30. doi:10.1016/j.iheduc.2013.10.008

Cochran, J. D., Campbell, S. M., Baker, H. M., & Leeds, E. M. (2014). The role of student characteristics in predicting retention in online courses. *Research in Higher Education*, *55*(1), 27–48. doi:10.1007/s11162-013-9305-8

Croxton, R. A. (2014). The role of interactivity in student satisfaction and persistence in online learning. *MERLOT Journal of Online Learning and Teaching*, *10*(2), 314–326.

Dueber, B., & Misanchuk, M. (2001). Sense of community in a distance education course. In *Proceedings from Mid-South Instructional Technology Conference*. Murfreesboro, TN: Academic Press.

Frydenberg, J. (2007). Persistence in university continuing education online classes. *International Review of Research in Open and Distance Learning, 8*(3), 1–15.

Gabriel, M. A., & Kaufield, K. J. (2008). Reciprocal mentorship: An effective support for online instructors. *Mentoring & Tutoring: Partnership in Learning, 16*(3), 311–327. doi:10.1080/13611260802233480

Garrison, D. R. (2011). *E-learning in the 21st century: A framework for research and practice*. Taylor & Francis.

Garrison, D. R., Anderson, T., & Archer, W. (2000). Critical inquiry in a text-based environment: Computer conferencing in higher education. *The Internet and Higher Education, 2*(2), 87–105.

Gunawardena, C. N., & Zittle, F. J. (1997). Social presence as a predictor of satisfaction within a computer-mediated conferencing environment. *American Journal of Distance Education, 11*(3), 8–26. doi:10.1080/08923649709526970

He, W., Xu, G., & Kruck, S. E. (2014). Online is education for the 21st century. *Journal of Information Systems Education, 25*(2), 101–105.

Hung, M., & Chou, C. (2015). Students' perceptions of instructors' roles in blended and online learning environments: A comparative study. *Computers & Education, 81*, 315–325. doi:10.1016/j.compedu.2014.10.022

Jahng, N., Krug, D., & Zhang, Z. (2007). Student achievement in online distance education compared to face-to-face education. *European Journal of Open Distance and E-Learning, 1*, 19.

Laitinen, A. (2013). Changing the way we account for college credit. *Issues in Science and Technology, 29*(2), 62–68.

Moller, L. (1998). Designing communities of learners for asynchronous distance education. *Educational Technology Research and Development, 46*(4), 115–122. doi:10.1007/BF02299678

Moore, M. G., & Kearsley, G. (2012). *Distance education: A systems view of online learning*. Belmont, CA: Wadsworth, Cengage Learning.

Moore, R. L. (2014). Importance of developing community in distance education courses. *TechTrends, 58*(2), 20–24. doi:10.1007/s11528-014-0733-x

Pappano, L. (2012, November 2). Massive open online courses are multiplying at a rapid pace. *The New York Times*. Retrieved from: http://www.nytimes.com

Pence, H. (2013). When will college truly leave the building: If MOOCs are the answer, what is the question? *Journal of Educational Technology Systems, 41*(1), 25–33. doi:10.2190/ET.41.1.c

Rourke, L., Anderson, T., Garrison, D. R., & Archer, W. (2001). Assessing social presence in asynchronous text-based computer conferencing. *Journal of Distance Education, 14*(3), 51–70.

Rovai, A. P., & Wighting, M. J. (2005). Feelings of alienation and community among higher education students in a virtual classroom. *The Internet and Higher Education, 8*(2), 97–110. doi:10.1016/j.iheduc.2005.03.001

Shea, P., Hayes, S., Vickers, J., Gozza-Cohen, M., Uzuner, S., Mehta, R., & Rangan, P. et al. (2010). A re-examination of the community of inquiry framework: Social network and content analysis. *The Internet and Higher Education, 13*(1), 10–21. doi:10.1016/j.iheduc.2009.11.002

Simsek, A. (2012). Learner control. In N. Seel (Ed.), *Encyclopedia of the sciences of learning* (pp. 1748–1750). New York: Springer; doi:10.1007/978-1-4419-1428-6

Swan, K., & Shih, L. F. (2005). On the nature and development of social presence in online course discussions. *Journal of Asynchronous Learning Networks*, *9*(3), 115–136.

Tschofen, C., & Mackness, J. (2012). Connectivism and dimensions of individual experience. *International Review of Research in Open and Distance Learning*, *13*(1), 124–143.

Vasu, M. L., & Ozturk, A. O. (2009). Teaching methodology to distance education students using rich-media and computer simulation. *Social Science Computer Review*, *27*(2), 271–283. doi:10.1177/0894439308327129

Wegerif, R. (1998). The social dimension of asynchronous learning networks. *Journal of Asynchronous Learning Networks*, *2*(1), 34–49.

ADDITIONAL READING

Bailie, J. L. (2014). What online students want compared to what institutions expect. *Online Journal of Distance Learning Administration*, *17*(2).

Betts, K., & Heaston, A. (2014). Build it but will they teach?: Strategies for increasing faculty participation & retention in online & blended education. *Online Journal of Distance Learning Administration*, *17*(2).

Jeong, A. (2014). Quantitative analysis of interaction patterns in online distance education. *Online Distance Education: Towards a Research Agenda*, 403.

Kim, J., Kwon, Y., & Cho, D. (2011). Investigating factors that influence social presence and learning outcomes in distance higher education. *Computers & Education*, *57*(2), 1512–1520. doi:10.1016/j.compedu.2011.02.005

Kuo, Y., Walker, A. E., Schroder, K. E., & Belland, B. R. (2014). Interaction, internet self-efficacy, and self-regulated learning as predictors of student satisfaction in online education courses. *The Internet and Higher Education*, *20*, 35–50. doi:10.1016/j.iheduc.2013.10.001

Lion, R. W., & Stark, G. (2010). A glance at institutional support for faculty teaching in an online learning environment. *Small, 38*, 41.3.

Pallof, R., & Pratt, K. (2003). *The virtual student. A Profile and Guide to Working with Online Learners. San Franscisco*. Jossey-Bass.

Pallof, R., & Pratt, K. (2008). Effective course, faculty and program evaluation. Paper presented at the *Proceedings of the 24th Annual Conference on Distance Teaching and Learning*, 1–5.

Pallof, R. M., & Pratt, K. (2007). *Building online learning communities, effective strategies for the virtual classroom* (2nd ed.). San Francisco: Jossey-Bass.

Salmon, G., & Wright, P. (2014). Transforming future teaching through 'Carpe Diem' learning design. *Education Sciences*, *4*(1), 52–63. doi:10.3390/educsci4010052

Schulte, M. (2014). Online instructor excuses: What to look for and how to help. *The Journal of Continuing Higher Education*, *62*(3), 189–192. doi:10.1080/07377363.2014.953440

So, H., & Brush, T. A. (2008). Student perceptions of collaborative learning, social presence and satisfaction in a blended learning environment: Relationships and critical factors. *Computers & Education*, *51*(1), 318–336. doi:10.1016/j.compedu.2007.05.009

Sung, E., & Mayer, R. E. (2012). Five facets of social presence in online distance education. *Computers in Human Behavior*, *28*(5), 1738–1747. doi:10.1016/j.chb.2012.04.014

Williams, L., & Lahman, M. (2011). Online discussion, student engagement, and critical thinking. *Journal of Political Science Education*, 7(2), 143–162. doi:10.1080/15512169.2011.564919

Zheng, B., & Warschauer, M. (2015). Participation, interaction, and academic achievement in an online discussion environment. *Computers & Education*, *84*, 78–89. doi:10.1016/j.compedu.2015.01.008

KEY TERMS AND DEFINITIONS

Asynchronous: Not occurring in real-time; not live.

Connectivism: A learning theory that values connecting learning to real-life experiences.

Distance Education: Education in which learners and instructors are separated by time, space, or both.

Engagement: Having continuous interaction with an artifact or person.

Humanizing: A technique of creating a learning environment that feels personal for learners and facilitates their ability to build rapport.

Interaction: The ability to have an input on an artifact or with a person and receive an immediate output.

Learner Control: The ability of learners being able to determine their own instructional paths.

Online Learning Environment: A learning environment with no physical location and in which the instructors and students are separated by space.

Screen Capture: The capture, using either video or an image, of what appears on a screen.

Screen Sharing or Desktop Sharing: The use of a program, such as Camtasia Studio, to record what currently appears on a computer screen or desktop.

Synchronous: Occurring in real-time; live.

Chapter 17
Encouraging and Increasing Student Engagement and Participation in an Online Classroom

Kathryn Woods
Austin Peay State University, USA

ABSTRACT

Advances in technology have increased opportunities for students to participate in online courses. While some instructors are beginning their careers teaching only online courses, others are discovering a need to teach sections of courses online after they have enjoyed a long career teaching in a traditional classroom. In either situation, it is important for instructors to recognize that students in online learning environments require the use of different strategies for encouraging engagement and participation in class. In this chapter, the author describes the challenges that students and instructors face specifically in the online learning environment as well as strategies for success, including how to maximize the impact of students' experiences and prior knowledge, using multiple platforms to deliver information, discouraging procrastination, setting clear expectations, encouraging individuality, capitalizing on diversity, and providing and utilizing helpful resources.

INTRODUCTION

This chapter is intended to highlight some of the differences between learning that occurs in traditional face-to-face classrooms and online learning environments. Students in the online environment communicate with their peers and instructors dif-ferently than students in the traditional classroom. The main objectives for this chapter include providing insights to help instructors engage online students, increase their participation levels, and improve the overall experience of the online course for both instructors and students.

DOI: 10.4018/978-1-4666-9582-5.ch017

BACKGROUND

As technology continues to change the way we communicate, interact, innovate, and learn in most areas of life, distance education has become increasingly popular in the past decade. According to the U.S. Department of Education, National Center for Education Statistics (2011), about 4.3 million undergraduate students (20 percent of all undergraduates) took at least one distance education course in the 2007 – 2008 school year. About 800,000 students (4 percent of all undergraduates) took their entire degree program through distance education. The National Center for Education Statistics also reported that the percentage of undergraduates who took any distance education courses rose from 16 percent in 2003–04 to 20 percent in 2007–08. In addition to these undergraduate students, about 800,000, or 22 percent, of all post-baccalaureate students took distance education courses in 2007–08.

Measuring student participation in an online course can be quite similar to measuring participation in a traditional classroom setting. Instructors know which students contribute most often to discussions, turn in assignments on time, show up in class or log in to the course, and effectively display their knowledge of the course content. Student engagement may be more difficult to quantify. While some view participation and engagement as essentially the same concepts, Ingram (2005) proposed that true student engagement consists of, "deep attention to the learning tasks and activities at hand, activation of effective cognitive processes that improve both performance in the tasks and learning, and usually a social context, especially in collaborative learning activities" (p. 57). In order to improve the quality of instruction and levels of student engagement and participation, we must first understand what challenges students and instructors face when engaged in an online course.

As the body of research about online learning grows, many universities have trained their admissions departments and academic advisors to tell students that online learning is not for everyone. Bell (2007) asserts that many undergraduate students who have performed well in a traditional face-to-face class environment may not be ready to successfully complete a course in the online environment, because online courses "require more learner control and self-direction than traditional classroom-based instruction" (p. 523). Conrad and Donaldson (2004) suggest that successful online students must be comfortable with technology, communicating predominantly by text only, and maintaining a high level of self-direction. If a student is uncomfortable in even one of these areas, he or she could find the online classroom environment to be more frustrating than convenient.

Rao (2010) completed a study in which challenges and success factors for students in an online degree program were examined. The primary challenge students reported was finding time to do the coursework. Issues with technology (slow internet connections, lack of knowledge about basic computing skills, learning the course management system) took second place on the list.

So, why do online students find time management to be their main challenge? Radford (2011) examined whether 2007-08 undergraduates' reported participation in a distance education course or degree program differed by a number of factors including age, dependents, marital status, and work responsibilities. This researcher found that older undergraduates enrolled in distance education classes and degree programs at higher rates than younger students. Fifteen percent of undergraduates under the age of 24 participated in a distance education course, compared with 26 percent of those ages 24 - 29, and 30 percent of those 30 and older. The same study also found that 40 percent of all undergraduates in a distance education program were married and 55 percent of all undergraduates in a distance education degree program had at least one dependent. Lastly, Radford found that 45 percent of all undergraduates enrolled in a distance education class were employed full time, and 62 percent of all undergraduates enrolled in a distance education degree program were working full time. These increased responsibilities of online students likely contribute to their challenges in finding balance between work, home, and academics.

Online learning provides many opportunities for instructors, particularly to reach a greater number of students.

Wilson (2002) described differences between traditional and online learning by stating: Single path progression of information is replaced by multi-path progression, and the more traditional passive learning is replaced by active exploratory and inquiry-based learning. Factual, knowledge based learning will shift into critical thinking and informed decision-making for the student. Learning becomes customized, collaborative, communicative, and student centered (p. 638).

The opportunities for instructors to teach an increasing number of online courses also come with a specific set of challenges to achieve this ideal learning environment that Wilson described.

Instructors who have enjoyed a long career in a traditional classroom setting may find themselves transitioning to teaching at least one section of their courses in the online environment. Some of these instructors who have experience in both environments may carry some negative perceptions of online course delivery. Osborne, Kriese, Tobey, and Johnson (2009) found that online course instructors were more likely than online students to agree with the following negative generalizations about online courses: students learn less in online courses, online courses take up more time, internet courses have more problems, and that students take online courses because they believe that they will be easier than a traditional course. These results suggest that instructors of online courses may have to increase their efforts to overcome these negative assumptions about

online learning in order to be able to effectively engage students and fulfill the learning objectives that have been established for their course.

As instructors are teaching more online courses than ever before, they are forced to re-examine their pedagogical practices. Many elements of teaching online are the same or very similar to teaching in a classroom, but there are certainly other areas that create new opportunities and challenges.

Kong and Song (2013) contend: In the new learning environment, teachers are expected to be facilitators who monitor students' learning processes and provide them with timely support. Learners controls their own learning flow, not only in class but also out of class. This is different from the teacher-centered paradigm in which a teacher's role is to transmit knowledge in traditional classrooms (p. 209 - 210).

Since online courses are often marketed to students with an emphasis on convenience for the student, instructors of online courses should certainly consider how their role differs from that of the traditional teacher of a face-to-face course.

Perhaps that first step toward improvement of online course delivery methods is to recognize that these differences between a traditional classroom and an online classroom exist. Varvel (2007) reported that most online instructors have not received training specific to teaching online, other than the technical aspects of the course delivery system. This researcher proposes that instructors who are very effective in engaging students in a traditional classroom may not be equipped to engage students in an online classroom environment, and that the technology and expectations for online student engagement change so rapidly, that instructor readiness to teach online is increasingly difficult to assess.

In a typical face-to-face classroom, instructors can identify some characteristics of students with relative ease that may identify the student's strengths or weaknesses, or even their preferred learning styles. In an online environment, an instructor must seek out this information through different means. Mupinga, Nora, and Yaw (2006) suggest that instructors of online courses should put forth an extra effort to identify the strengths, weaknesses, and preferred learning styles of their students by administering a short survey in the beginning of the class by simply asking, "What are your needs and expectations as an online student?" By posing this question, instructors can gain a quick snapshot of the student's comfort level with online learning and their expectations for receiving feedback.

At many schools, instructors who will teach courses online receive formal training on how to effectively utilize the course management system from the Information Technology department as well as informal training from peers. Research from Hewett and Powers (2007) suggests that instructors who are transitioning from the traditional classroom setting should also receive training for the "practical and theoretical transfer of pedagogical principles and practices to online environments" (p. 1). These researchers suggests that universities offer this kind of training to instructors within the same course management system that their students use, in order to give the instructor first-hand experience with some of the challenges and opportunities of the system.

Faculty are charged with the responsibility of providing quality feedback in an online class environment, just as they are in an in-class setting. In the absence of face-to-face contact, instructors must place a great deal of importance on their written assignment feedback for students in online courses. Fernandez-Toro and Hurd (2014) found that the most effective model for providing feedback in an online environment is one in which the instructor gauges how far the study is from achieving the learning objective. Once they determine the distance between the student's current level and the desired level of knowledge, they should provide "just enough information to be able to work out a way for closing the gap

himself/herself" (p. 120). This type of feedback is said to encourage a deeper level of engagement in the learning, as the student will need to actively seek out the information needed to move toward meeting the learning objective. This researcher also advises faculty to provide encouragement in their feedback to stimulate positive emotions from students, and build their self-confidence in the learning process.

Moore (2014) found that students taking an online section of a course felt less of a sense of community than students taking the same course in an on-ground setting. However, the students in the online section of the course reported feeling a greater sense of community once they were placed into small groups for peer-led small group sessions. The researcher also found that students in the online courses reported that they experienced more frustration with the course material than their peers taking the course in the traditional classroom setting. They perceived that they had to learn more "on their own" than the students in the classroom environment, which negatively impacted their learning experience. In this situation, the instructors created a video in which a student who was very successful in the online course was interviewed about his thoughts on how to be successful in that particular course. In the subsequent sections of the course, the instructor posted the video for the students to watch at the beginning of the semester. The student's recipe for success reinforced the instructor's own advice that was listed for students in the syllabus.

Other research highlights the limitations of the course delivery systems that are currently in use at most universities (Mott, 2010). Mott reports that instructors utilize the content distribution and administrative tools most often, and the more interactive tools are often overlooked or under-utilized. Training for learning management systems is often conducted by members of a university's information technology department, who can instruct usage techniques from a functional perspective, but may not be aware of teaching and learning methods that have been proven to be effective for specific subject areas and student populations. As with on-ground teaching, online instructors may find that they will benefit from learning the best practices of more seasoned instructors who have experience teaching their specific subject online in order to utilize course management software to its fullest potential. Mott also criticizes learning management systems as being "teacher-centric", meaning that they are designed for teachers to create content, discussion topics, assignments, due dates, etc. Student-led assignments and discussions can be more difficult to create in this environment.

Another challenge for instructors teaching online is finding a balance for the appropriate amount of coursework to assign. In a face-to-face class setting, instructors can pick up on physical clues from students that they may be feeling overwhelmed or overworked. In an online environment, instructors must wait until they receive a written message from a student who feels overwhelmed. Students may be less likely to put this kind of message in writing to an instructor than to bring it up in conversation in a classroom. Vrasidas (1999) found that students who feel overworked or overwhelmed by too much coursework in an online course often decrease their participation in online asynchronous discussions because they feel that these discussions are less important than other assignments, which are often more heavily weighted in points than the discussions. In the same study, the students who admitted to feeling overwhelmed reported that they felt as if the discussions were "just busy work", because they were also completing more time-intensive projects on the same topics to meet course requirements.

Instructors of online courses may or may not be teaching in an online environment by choice. With the rise of online course offerings, some instructors who thrive in the traditional face-to-face classroom are asked (or persuaded, or sometimes even required) to begin teaching at least one online section of a course. In these situations, motivation levels may vary by instructor, according to their level of desire (or lack of desire) to teach the online course. Varvel (2007) developed several competencies for successful online instructors that cover administrative roles, personal roles, technical roles, instructional design roles, pedagogical roles, assessment roles, and social roles. While many may assume that technical knowledge, content knowledge, and time management/organizational skills are necessary to succeed as an online instructor, Varvel highlights the importance of an online instructor's recognition that creating a social presence in the online classroom is important for student engagement and satisfaction. He also asserts that effective online instructors are able to create a sense of community in an online classroom and displays appropriate levels of patience with students who are new to the online learning environment. These types of "soft skills" can be time-consuming for an instructor to develop, particularly when an online course is assigned to them only days (or worse – hours) prior to the start data.

Students may exhibit some "early warning signs" during the early stages of an online course that could indicate to the instructor that some action may be necessary to help the student understand how to be successful in the course. Iaonnou et al. (2014) found that students who provide low-quality postings on a discussion board should be encouraged and monitored carefully for improvements. The same study found that the contribution of too many low-quality postings in the beginning of the course can jeopardize collaborative knowledge construction for the course as a whole in online discussions.

Instructors generally do not have control over their class sizes and enrollments. When a course is larger in size, obviously there are more opportunities for students to find a discussion posting to respond to, or a classmate to connect with. In a very small course, instructors may find that their teaching methods or course requirements may need to be adjusted accordingly. Vrasidas (1999) conducted a study in which he found that students find it much more difficult to meet requirements for graded asynchronous discussions when class enrollments are low. The students reported that they were frustrated when they did not have many peers to interact with on the discussion boards, and of course found it more difficult to find opportunities to reply to others.

In a study by Rao (2010), students reported that factors that helped them succeed in a distance learning program included personal interactions during the course, organization/clarity of the course, and appreciation for course content. Students also noted that the opportunities to interact with each other in engaging online discussion forums were useful. In this study, students also expressed appreciation for a course that was well laid-out (in the course management system), instructors who stated instructions/expectations clearly, and when a course was well-organized.

McKinney et al. (2014) found that students' sense of community in their courses significantly predicted their classroom attitudes, perception of learning, and actual performance on course exams. In these courses, the sense of community was established by pairing high-achieving students with low-achieving students to complete assignments and by requiring that students provide a short reflection of their learning of each class topic, to be discussed by the group. These actions were directly linked with students feeling more engaged and performing at a higher level than peers who were not encouraged to complete these activities.

ENCOURAGING AND INCREASING STUDENT ENGAGEMENT AND PARTICIPATION IN AN ONLINE CLASSROOM

Leveraging the Introduction: Beyond the Bio

Research shows that students should be provided with a space within their online course that will

allow them to share information about themselves (Varvel, 2007). Many instructors choose to utilize a class discussion board to allow students to introduce themselves to their instructor and their peers. The information obtained in this biography can prove to be beneficial to the class as a whole in many ways, particularly if the instructor wishes to increase participation and engagement in the course.

Vrasidas (1999) found that students who did not have previous experience taking an online course participated less than students who had taken an online course before. Instructors should consider asking students to share whether they have taken online courses before in their biographical post. They can use this information to determine whether the class as a whole is very experienced with learning in an online environment, if they have a diverse mixture of experiences, or if most students are new to the online learning environment. Vrasidas suggests pairing students based on their experience level for an assignment. The more experienced student could have some helpful, practical advice for the less experienced student.

Other research has shown that students who have previous experience taking online courses show higher levels of motivation and utilize more effective learning strategies than students who have no previous experience taking online courses (Wang, Shannon, & Ross, 2013). This information could be helpful as instructors assist students who are new to the online learning environment. This knowledge could prevent these students from becoming discouraged if they find that moving from a traditional classroom environment to an online learning environment is more difficult or stressful than they had planned.

Lebow (1993) suggests that instructors must explore how they can better assess students' personal interests and goals, and try to support them in the learning environment. Information from student introductions can be used in a variety of ways to drive course discussion topics. If an instructor discovers that several students in class have work experience (or aspirations thereof) in a particularly applicable industry or type of business, this information can be applied to shape the discussion topics throughout the course, ensuring that students will find the topics interesting and relevant.

Other strategies recommended by the author of this chapter include asking students what they hope to learn in your course. This information can be gathered with the biographical post, and can provide insight for the instructor to determine whether any learning objectives should be added in future sections of the course. Instructors could also ask students why they are pursuing their degree. These reasons will vary by student, but can often be used to provide motivation for a student who might be at risk for dropping out of a course. Simply reminding a student why they are taking the course may provide them with a reason to continue when they feel like giving up. Finally, this author recommends commenting on each student's introduction individually, welcoming the student to your course. Finding even a minor point to connect with the student (perhaps you enjoyed your vacation to their hometown or your son also plays little league, etc.) can spark student engagement through the establishment of social presence.

Encouraging a Sense of Community

Dixon (2014) found that students will become more comfortable with and engaged in academic online discussions when instructors provide opportunities for them to establish a sense of community via the discussion boards. One method for encouraging students to get to know each other is to pair them up and "interview" each other to provide their initial post that describes their interests and academic goals. The students could introduce one another to the class on the introduction discussion board. The instructors should actively set the tone for discussions by providing guidelines for appropriate behaviors as well as modeling appropriate behaviors.

Further research contends that students must progress through five stages of online group development to fully realize the benefits of an online community in online course discussions. The first stage, Introduction, is simply one in which students tell others about their interests, academic goals, and professional experiences. In the next step, Identification, students and instructors become familiar with and begin to identify with or relate to one another. In this phase, students will agree with others about certain comments they have made or viewpoints they have offered. In the third stage, Interaction, students begin to discuss course content and develop cognitively with one another. While students may still feel a bit tentative about sharing their ideas, their trust level increases with each positive interaction that occurs within the discussion. The fourth stage, Involvement, is characterized by students engaging with one another and working collaboratively as colleagues. At this point, student comments show their knowledge of the course topics. In the final stage, Inquiry, students' comments consistently reflect students' comprehension of the course material and demonstrate their ability to analyze, apply, synthesize, and evaluate the material. (Waltonen-Moore, Stuart, and Newton, 2006).

Establishing a clear presence as an instructor is quite different in online courses when compared to face-to-face courses. In a traditional classroom environment, the instructor can be clearly identified as the person who stands in the front of the class to give instructions on what must happen that day, or the person who is passing out the syllabus, loading the presentation on the projection screen, or beginning a lecture. In an online environment, the students must actively seek to find the instructors' "presence" in the classroom. Many times they can click on link that simply states "Instructor Information" such as an email address and an office phone number/location. Research suggests that student engagement in an online course is increased when an instructor establishes a clear online presence by directly interacting with the students (Anderson, Rourke, Archer, & Garrison, 2001; Holzweiss, Joyner, Fuller, Henderson, and Young, 2014).

Utilizing Multiple Platforms to Deliver Information

Instructors in traditional face-to-face course settings may be used to utilizing lecture as the primary means to deliver information to students. Conrad and Donadson (2004) suggest that when instructors use lecture as the primary strategy to deliver course content in an online course environment, "the course becomes a digital correspondence course with potential problems of learner isolation and high dropout rate" (p. 6). Instructors of online courses must explore different methods of delivering course content to encourage students' engagement. Engaged learning occurs when students interact with their course content, instructor, and their peers.

Research suggests that students' levels of engagement increases when multiple channels of communication are made available in an online course, specifically when opportunities are created for students to interact with one another as well as with their instructor (Dixson, 2010). Many online courses are delivered in a standard format in which the instructor provides contact information such as an office phone number, an email address, and an "internal" email address that is used within the learning management system. Instructors should communicate to students what their preferred method of communication will be as well as an expectation for return messages. Students should also be made aware of the different platforms that are available for them to interact and communicate with one another. Some examples of these

platforms might be: a "water cooler" area for students to discuss casual or non-academic topics, discussion forums in which students should discuss relevant academic topics, various types of discussion groups for communication regarding assigned teamwork, course or subject-specific social media accounts that students can follow or join, etc.

Social Media Integration

Özmen and Atıcı (2014) found that students who were required to utilize social media platforms to engage with their instructors and classmates regarding course-related materials perceived that they had more positive communication and a greater level of interactions with their classmates and faculty than in classes in which they did not utilize social media platforms. Likewise, Kurtz (2014), found that incorporating a Facebook group into an online course was perceived by students to foster learner involvement, active contribution to the course, and frequent interaction with both peers and the course instructor.

Some organizations are utilizing open source frameworks that allow designers to create online social environments that are built on a custom basis for groups of learners. These frameworks can include discussions, file sharing, messaging, and status updates that can be seen by others in the pre-set group of peers. These social networking features can be integrated into many pre-existing learning management systems. Veletsianos et al. (2013) reported that some instructors find these type of systems to be valuable when learners share photos that can spark valuable discussions. For example, students in an online graduate education course could share photos of different ways they set up their classrooms, and then easily gather feedback from their peers and/or instructor.

Churchill and Lu (2012) found that utilizing social networks for course assignments increased student engagement on a social level, but not on a cognitive level. These researchers suggest that students bring a purely social mindset about social networking to class, and when they are asked to integrate a social network in an academic setting, it fees unnatural for them. Instructors could help students shift their thinking by setting an example for them of how to properly utilize social networking with an academic purpose. Instructors could create a professional account on Twitter or Facebook, on which they share course or subject-related research, news, and current events. If an instructor decides to incorporate social networking into course requirements, they should first ensure that they are comfortable with the medium and its practical uses.

Integrating Current Events

Rao (2010) reported that students in online courses appreciated the instances in which course content was made relevant to their local scenarios. This approach increased student engagement by bringing local topics and current events into play. Instructors can incorporate this practice most easily into discussion boards and written assignments. Students could be asked to answer the same set of questions about something that is going on now or has happened in the recent past in their area, and then provide links to related news coverage in their assignment, bringing online news sites into the course as an auxiliary platform for information. Another suggestion is to ask students to present information on a topic from multiple perspectives. For example, have them interview someone associated with an event, and also report on what was published in the local/national news, and to get a feel for the public's reaction to the event based on what they find when they search for the topic on various social media outlets. Comparing and contrasting the information from each of these platforms can encourage critical thinking while incorporating multiple platforms for content.

Planning Ahead: Battling Procrastination

Many online courses and programs are marketed to students based on the flexibility that students will enjoy in an asynchronous course. As previously discussed, the online course format often appeals to non-traditional students who may have many family and professional commitments in addition to their studies. These responsibilities could potentially cause students to procrastinate their coursework. While online courses still have as many due dates and deadlines as traditional face-to-face courses, the lack of physical course meetings may also make the course seem less tangible than a traditional course. Researchers have discovered that while procrastination is negatively correlated to exam performance and attitudes toward classes for online students, this correlation does not exist for traditional students (Elvers, Polzella, and Graetz, 2003). In this study, traditional students reported that they may have procrastinated studying for an exam until the last minute just as much as the online students, but their required attendance for the class lectures forced them to distribute their learning throughout the week. The online students were not required to listen to the lectures at a specific time, so they often waited until they studied for the test to listen to the lectures. This information highlights the need for instructors to encourage students not to procrastinate on assignments and studying for exams in online courses.

Vrasidas (1999) found that overall course participation was increased when students were required to evaluate their peers' assignments in online courses. Applying this concept toward the beginning of a course may be beneficial to students, as it would allow them to see how others interpreted the assignment instructions and course material. A suggestion from the author of this chapter is that instructors allow/require student groups to create exams as an assignment. The act of creating an exam ensures that students will be reviewing the information to be covered, and the instructor could certainly require that he/she approve the exam well in advance before it is administered.

Project Planning and Approval

One suggestion for instructors who wish to bolster engagement and stave off procrastination is to require that students submit ideas for large projects, papers, etc. due at the end of the course toward the beginning of course. Vrasidas (1999) found that online participation was increased throughout the course when students were required to discuss the final paper/project requirements with their instructor during the course. Students can then keep their selected topic in mind as they progress through the course modules, and apply the concepts as they go. This will also allow instructors to provide guidance to students who have selected a topic that will not be feasible for the project in plenty of time to select something else. Research shows that students benefit from early feedback that could prevent them from spending time on a project that may be headed in the wrong direction (Ebrahimi, 2011).

When students select their topics for class projects in the beginning of the term, the instructor could tailor the discussion questions to these projects. For example, a question could read, "Think about the company you selected for your project. Based on the readings this week and the research you have completed on this company, tell us how they have handled (insert relevant concept here)." If this method is used throughout the course, students and instructors will defend against procrastination on the projects, as the students will need to look up something about the company each week when they complete the discussion.

Setting Clear Expectations

Grading Rubrics

Setting clear expectations for students ensures that grades are not a complete surprise. Rovai (2001) suggests that providing a rubric for discussion standards can be quite useful in an online course. Since students taking online courses likely have had or will have multiple instructors for different courses, it is important to present expectations for participation in discussion in a rubric format in order to be sure the students know what is expected to earn an "A" grade in participation, and what the differences are between those expectations and those of a student who will earn a "B" or a "C" grade. Some instructors may tend to focus more on the grammar and formatting in each post, and some may be more concerned with how many posts the student read on each discussion board. Communicating the expectations for discussion requirements to students at the beginning of the course will allow them time to plan ahead as they prepare for a successful first week or module. Wyss, Freedman, and Siebert (2014) found that posting a rubric for students to be able to better assess their own discussion skills (and predict the grade that would be assigned) had a significant, positive effect on the grades the students received on the discussions. The researchers included timeliness of discussion posts, evidence of scholarship, and inclusion of personal/practical knowledge in the criteria for assessment on this rubric.

Establishing a Teaching Presence

To increase student success in a course, instructors in online environments must realize the value of establishing a teaching presence (Anderson, Rourke, Archer, & Garrison, 2001). These researchers found that some instructors put more effort into the design of an online course because they know it can be easily seen by their peers and superiors. They also contend that instructors must be deliberate as they think through the processes and design of the course from start to finish so that students will have a positive opinion of the instructor. Instructors of online courses are generally not afforded opportunities to make an impression on their students in person, and therefore must rely on their course materials to make the "first impression" for them. Similarly, Lebow (1993) and Dixson (2010) found that a firmly established teaching presence by the instructor enhances the overall effectiveness of a course for students, as well as their level of engagement. This researcher also concluded that students prefer for instructors to direct their activities and serve as a subject-matter expert, rather than to passively facilitate course content.

Anderson et al. (2001) also suggest that instructors can increase their teaching presence in online courses by setting curriculum, designing methods, establishing time parameters, utilizing their medium effectively, and establishing netiquette. Setting curriculum for students involves simply telling them what to expect. For example, weekly objectives could be posted to communicate the topics that will be covered in a given week in class. Designing methods refers to clearly communicating the ways in which students will be expected to complete their work. If the students are expected to complete a group project, tell them in plenty of time how the teams will be assigned and what the expectations are for how to write a group paper. Establishing time parameters refers to establishing, communicating, and enforcing specific due dates for assignments. Utilizing the medium effectively simply involves encouraging students to take advantage of the capabilities of the learning management system and the class structure. Finally, instructors are encouraged to establish netiquette, such as expectations for the length of discussion posts, the guidelines for maintaining academic tone, and how to respectfully communicate disagreement with their peers.

Anderson et al. found that these elements can all work together to improve an instructor's teaching presence in an online classroom, and therefore increase student engagement.

Creating Appropriate Assignments

Instructors of online courses must realize that a disorganized course can severely limit a student's comfort level in the course, and therefore limit their participation and engagement in the course. Heischmidt and Damoiseau (2012) surveyed students to discover what elements of an online course are most influential over the student's satisfaction with a course. With regard to content, the students said that the most important elements for them were that assignments were clearly explained, that the instructor's notes supplement the other course content, the course agenda was clear, the assignments were relevant to the course, and that course content was up to date.

The author of this chapter recommends that instructors consider creating a syllabus quiz in online courses. This quiz can be of a low point value, but should be administered within the first week of class to ensure that students are familiar with course requirements. The quiz can cover such topics as instructor contact information and preferred method of contact, assignment due dates, identification of the first assignment due, how to properly submit assignments, and the instructor's policy on accepting late work. This type of quiz ensures that students are familiar with the basic housekeeping items in the class that generally vary from instructor to instructor, and it could potentially reduce instances of missed assignment due dates and improperly submitted assignments, as well as providing motivation for students to read the syllabus thoroughly.

Research shows that students reported that application activities (in which they must apply the concepts covered in class to case studies or problem solving), research papers, and current events activities are more engaging than "passive" types of assignments such as answering end-of-chapter questions (Dixson, 2010). Even a slight revision to existing assignments in a course that instructors teach on a regular basis could prove to be beneficial as instructors strive to increase engagement within the course. Instructors should consider replacing even just one passive assignment with one that requires students to apply the concepts covered in the course.

Conrad and Donaldson (2004) suggest that instructors ask the following questions when incorporating an assignment from a traditional course into an online course in order to determine if the activity will encourage increased student engagement and participation: Will the activity help learners use the online tools? Does is assist in the social process needed to establish community? What type of interaction or collaboration with peers occurs? Is reflection required? Will a particular problem be resolved? These researchers also suggest assigning brainstorming and/or small group discussions via course discussion boards for all interactive online courses.

Teaching Students With No Previous Online Learning Experience

Wang, Shannon, and Ross (2013) found that students with previous experience taking online courses utilize more effective learning strategies and display higher levels of motivation than those who have no experience taking online courses. Vrasidas (1999) found that students who are less experienced taking online courses participate less than those who do have experience with online courses. Even when instructors are teaching upper-level courses, it should not be assumed that these students, who are presumably in their third or fourth year of their degree program, have taken online courses. These students may be taking an online course as an exception to their traditional, face-to-face course schedule due to course availability, etc. Instructors should include information

on the syllabus about where each assignment should be submitted (a course folder, via email, an assignment-specific area to upload documents, etc.), and all course materials should be prepared in a manner that clearly explains expectations and course procedures.

Instructors must model appropriate behavior for online students in attitude and academic tone. Instructors should identify instances in which students veer off topic by reading the discussion comments throughout the week, not just on the day they are grading them. Özmen and Atıcı (2014) found that students in a distance learning environment reported that the element of online learning that they find the most distracting is the overuse of chatting in discussion areas. Students can be sidetracked by one another as topics sometimes shift to a subject that is non-academic. In these cases, instructors find that they need to re-direct the conversation back to the intended topic. This can only occur if the instructor is carefully monitoring the discussions.

Some models for engaging online discussions (Dixon, 2014; Conrad and Donaldson, 2004) suggest that instructors should make an effort to assess students' skill level in online discussions and proactively encourage/engage those who show signs of discomfort or a lack of understanding in the beginning days and weeks of the course. If the instructor can get the students on the right track early, these students will likely be much more engaged throughout the duration of the course. Dixon suggests that this process does not have to take hours, but that evaluations can be made quickly as instructors review student's discussion comments for depth of understanding. This model also suggests that instructors participate in the course discussion frequently in the beginning weeks of a course, and that they should be able to gradually reduce their participation level as the students need less and less direction and redirection as the course ends. However, instructors must also consider that too much participation on their part will degrade the integrity of the discussion board as a place for students to exchange ideas, and can quickly become just another platform for lecture if they participate too much (Xin & Feenburg, 2006).

Creating Appropriate Discussion Questions

Just as instructors should carefully tailor assignments to the online environment, research suggests that instructors should consider the level of student proficiency regarding the course topic as they design the discussion questions to be used in an online course (Dixon, 2014). These questions should "reflect the appropriate level of difficulty while fostering students' participation and responses" (p. 6). As courses are developed, many times discussion questions are entered into the course at the beginning of the term. Instructors should consider entering these questions on a weekly basis instead, so that they level of difficulty can be adjusted. This also creates an opportunity for instructors to create questions that are timely, and can reference current events, the latest research on a topic, or even to build on an interesting topic presented in the previous week of discussion.

Xin and Feenburg (2006) suggest that instructors must place emphasis on the intellectual engagement of students in online discussions. These researchers suggest that instructors present examples of the class concepts in the course discussion. While most instructors are probably diligent about relating a weekly online discussion topic to the required reading and/or topic to be covered, students can benefit from reading additional examples and case studies in the discussion forums. These examples will allow students to apply what they have learned in a potential real-world setting. Instructors should also encourage students to elaborate on their arguments by providing sources that back up their

views, and constructively criticize students' posts, especially if incorrect information is presented as fact. Students can also benefit from being asked to define certain terms used in their posts, if they are not widely known.

Another strategy suggested for instructors who wish to create engaging discussion questions is to tailor each question to the student. For example, if a discussion question asks students to define a particular term and provide an example, students who respond in the latter half of the week or learning module may read through the other students' responses and then find it difficult to construct an original answer. If an end of course project or research paper has been assigned, instructors could require that students select the topic in the beginning weeks of the course, and then center the discussion questions on those selections. For example, instead of asking "What are some of best techniques for marketing a new menu item in a restaurant?", one could ask, "Tell us about how the restaurant you selected to write about in your project marketed their most recent menu addition. How effective was this strategy?" This technique encourages students to research their selected topic throughout the course, and makes the course seem more individualized.

Encouraging Appropriate Discussion Techniques

Research (Anderson et al., 2001; Dixon 2014; Xin and Feenburg, 2006) suggests that instructors in an online environment are responsible for the entire discussion board as a whole, due to its overall impact on student learning. If a few students are argumentative, post comments that do not maintain an academic tone, or post inaccurate information, this could certainly have a negative impact on the integrity of the discussion and cause the intended learning objectives to be compromised for the class as a whole. According to Anderson et al., "The teacher supports and encourages participation by modeling appropriate behaviors, commenting upon and encouraging student responses, drawing in the less active participants, and curtailing the effusive comments of those who tend to dominate the virtual space" (p. 7).

Research suggests that placing an emphasis on the discussion component of an online course by assigning a grade value of twenty percent or more of the total course grade to the discussion board can provide further motivation for students to increase their levels of participation (Rovai, 2001). Rovai suggests that online instructors can also achieve a greater sense of community in their classrooms by facilitating discussions with the intention of helping students avoid feelings of isolation and ensuring equity.

This researcher states: Online instructors should be sensitive to the different communication patterns used by their students and should adapt their teaching in ways that facilitate the interaction of diverse groups and accommodate individual and group differences without sacrificing or silencing other members of the learning community (p. 14).

There are many reasons that students may not feel entirely comfortable contributing their ideas to an online course discussion forum. Students who are uncomfortable with each other or the necessary technology used in an online discussion may require some extra encouragement from instructors as they get started. Instructors can provide discussion rubrics, model appropriate behavior on discussion boards, and provide examples of their expectations to students who are hesitant to post in a discussion forum. Churchill and Lu (2012) suggest that instructors should have a plan for "lurkers", or students who read comments but do not actively participate in the discussions, when a social network has been incorporated into the course requirements as well. Instructors can direct the more active students toward the activities of the more passive students by sharing their work, contributions, links, etc. that have been posted

within the medium, and by prompting two or more students to discuss similarities or differences in their opinions/information that has been presented.

Providing Timely Feedback

Dixson (2010) found that instructor-student communication is strongly correlated to higher student engagement in online courses. Instructors should clearly explain to students which methods of communication are preferred and will ensure the most rapid response. For example, if an instructor lists their office phone number under their contact information, but they are only in their office a few days each week to check voicemails, the instructor should share this information with students. If the internal messaging system in the course delivery system is preferable over traditional email, then instructors should clearly explain this to students. Setting students up for successful communications with their instructors could be considered the first step in encouraging strong student engagement in an online course.

Many instructors include a sentence in their syllabus that sets an expectation for students for how long it may take an instructor to respond to a message or request. Ley & Gannon-Cook (2014) researched which actions online students perceived to be the most valuable regarding increasing student engagement. The students reported that their top five observed actions for an instructor to increase classroom engagement by creating a social presence are as follows: check their messages/email often, frequently post to the discussion board, provide examples when communicating assignment expectations, provide timely feedback for assignments, and respond to all student inquiries quickly. Overall, responsiveness proved to be a significant factor in students' perception of an instructor's social presence in the course.

Vrasidas (1999) conducted a study to analyze factors that influence participation in online courses, and reported that students believed "lack of immediate feedback.....was discouraging and contributed to their limited participation in the online discussions" (p. 33). Based on these findings, instructors should be motivated to provide feedback as quickly as possible for online students, especially toward the beginning of class when the class climate and students' connections and motivation levels are still being established.

Heischmidt and Damoiseau (2012) surveyed students in an online course about what they believe instructors need to focus on regarding feedback to make a course more engaging. The students recommended that instructors facilitate an ease of communication between the instructor and student, provide quick feedback on assignments and exams, and provide comprehensive, individualized feedback (not blanket feedback to the entire course).

Further recommendations for instructors from the author of this chapter include communicating (and enforcing) the policy on accepting late work. Understandably, instructors will be able to provide more timely feedback if all assignments are received by a certain date. Instructors may also wish to adjust requirements when the course size is small. Students in a course with only a few students may not be able to participate in discussion as they could in a larger class, so expectations for participation may need to be scaled back.

Encouraging Individuality

Modeling Your Individuality

Instructors in an online environment sometimes struggle with how to incorporate their subject-matter expertise when interacting with students in a course that is not being delivered in a lecture format. Instructors can yield positive results from students by sharing their industry-based knowledge and wisdom earned through their years of professional experience. A study by Holzweiss et al. (2014) reported that students recognized the expertise of instructors as a contributor to their learning and level of course participation. When

instructors shared relevant professional experiences during discussions, students felt connected to them and their interest in the subject and course performance both increased.

Instructors could also make an effort to appeal to multiple generations by inviting students to follow your professional account on a social media platform such as Twitter. Instructors can essentially create a brand for themselves via the internet, and students can be a part of that experience. Instructors can create "professional" profiles (separate from their personal profiles) to interact with students, peers, and members of relevant industry communities. Instructors could provide subject-specific news and resources through their professional profile, connecting students with real-time information that appropriately supplements their required course materials.

Capitalizing on Diversity

Students in online courses, particularly adult learners, bring a wide range of experiences to class with them. The diversity of student experiences and beliefs should be leveraged to engage students of both the traditional and non-traditional varieties. Instructors should be willing to provide a flexible course that allows for changes to discussion questions and assignment topics that suit the specific students in a course. This customization can increase the level of student engagement, as students will feel a more personal connection with the course content as they draw on their experiences while completing their assigned tasks (Conrad and Donaldson, 2004).

Ingram (2005) advocates that to promote student engagement, instructors should encourage students to participate in more effective cognitive processes. According to Ingram, activating prior knowledge allows engaged students to connect what they already know to the new material they are learning, as well as to compare, question, and evaluate both sets of knowledge. Some of his other suggestions for enhancing students' cognitive processes include elaboration (providing examples, allowing students to draw conclusions, etc.), monitoring comprehension throughout the term (not just at test times), visual imagery, and enactment. Instructors can apply these suggestions in various ways based on the subjects they teach.

Reflective Assignments

Some instructors provide a summary-style discussion question in the last week (or module) of an online course for students to reflect on what they have learned during the semester. Others require students to write a narrative reflection of their experience. When requiring a reflective assignment, Conrad and Donaldson (2004) suggest that instructors ask themselves the following questions to ensure the assignment will serve its intended purpose: Does the activity ask for a synthesis of the learning experience? Does it require the learner to share his or her experiences? Does it require the learner to provide helpful feedback that will be useful to the instructor in future course development? Does it allow for honest and open responses? Does it require a person to be imaginative or to express genuine emotions or openness? Is the activity insightful and nonthreatening? These questions can help instructors create an engaging reflective assignment for students.

Providing Choices

Another strategy to allow students to highlight their individuality and at the same time accommodate their specific preferred learning style is to allow the students to choose a course project topic as well as the format. McCarthy (2012) suggests allowing students who learn best through reading and writing to write an essay, while giving students who feel they learn best through more visual or creative channels the opportunity to create an idea map or flow chart instead. This researcher

contends that students become more engaged with a course as the number of interactions increases. (These interactions could be with other students, the instructor, course content, or even with the student himself.) Assignments provide an interaction between the student and the course content, and they can be extended to other students when they are made into group work or included in the discussion topics.

An additional strategy for encouraging individuality is discouraging academic dishonesty. Simple technological advances in course management systems include randomizing test answers and utilizing plagiarism detection software. Telling students that plagiarism detection software will be used on assignment submissions could relieve them of the thought of attempting to "recycle" a research paper that was given to them from a friend who took the course in the past. Varying assignments each semester is another safeguard against cheating that will eliminate the possibility of this type of academic dishonesty.

Providing and Utilizing Resources

Online course systems generally provide ample opportunities for online course instructors to provide feedback for students on graded and non-graded items. In a study by Holzweiss et al. (2014) the researchers reported that while students appreciated timely feedback on assignments, "they also wanted a thoughtful evaluation of how they could improve. In addition, when the feedback contained positive encouragement, it motivated participants to continue learning" (p. 317). Even when a student's work does not meet the criteria that is set for the assignment, instructors should try to seek out some positive elements to bring to the student's attention when providing written feedback.

Wang, Shannon, and Ross (2013) reported that students with previous online learning experiences utilized more effective learning strategies and had higher levels of motivation than students who had no experience with online learning. Additionally, these researchers reported that students with higher levels of technological self-efficacy earned higher grades. Instructors should consider taking a quick assessment of students' technological self-efficacy in the beginning of a course, and distribute information on available resources that could help them succeed accordingly. For example, if a student feels confident in their ability to use the necessary word processing or spreadsheet software, but not as confident about their ability to navigate the course management system, the instructor could proactively send the student any information about where to find technical assistance and/or a refresher on the functions that will be most important for the specific course that being taught.

Being a Reliable, Positive Resource for Students

Instead of simply pointing out mistakes that students are making relative to the learning system itself (improper use of the 'reply' or 'quote' functions in a discussion board, submitting an assignment using email instead of the appropriate assignment folder, etc.) provide coaching for them on the proper way to use the system. Instructors should be prepared to direct students to student support resources, generally provided by technology administration, but they should also offer their own tips and advice. Anderson et al. (2001) found that instructors can also increase their teaching presence in an online environment by providing technical direction to students who are unfamiliar with the course management system. This research also found that increased teaching presence improves student engagement in an online environment. Instructors should also be specific

in their feedback when suggesting available labs, etc. that could help the students. For example, if a student's content knowledge is up to par, but they lack writing skills, instructors should send them a link to the hours and location of the writing center. If their writing skills are proficient, but their content knowledge is lacking, instructors should direct them to the pages in the textbook that they need to review again.

Lewis and Slapak-Barski (2014) conducted a study with instructors on creating a "learning community" for instructors to share their best practices with one another, and were not surprised to find that instructors were not always willing to share their hard work with others. They felt they were working hard to improve their courses and online learning environments, while other faculty were taking advantage of their skills and discoveries. To overcome this attitude, the university stressed to the instructors that improvement for any faculty performance is improvement for the university, and that learning by its very nature is sharing. It is important to recognize that any expert began as a novice, and that not all experts are willing to share their insights with novices. If you find yourself to be a novice online teacher (even if you are consider yourself to be an expert classroom teacher), you could still benefit from researching online teaching methods, best practices, and yes – having conversations with an instructor who has taught online to a similar student population. If you seek advice from such an instructor and they seem unwilling to share, take note of what you can do to try to change the culture of your learning environment.

Other research suggests that instructors of online courses take the time to create a professional development plan that lists attainable goals for the instructors to strive for in their lifelong learning plans (Varvel, 2007). While many instructors likely set goals for improvement based on feedback from supervisors, peers, and students, it is important for them to specifically consider what competencies could be improved with regard to online teaching.

Simpson and Benson (2013) recommend that all online faculty subscribe to a formal peer review process, as it has been linked to increased student satisfaction. Many universities require faculty to undergo frequent peer evaluations during the years leading up to tenure, but only annual evaluations after tenure is received. Likewise, many adjunct or part-time instructors only receive a review annually, and if they are teaching both online and face-to-face courses, the online course may not be selected for review at all. Online instructors can benefit from peer reviews, both from instructors who have taught online extensively, and from those who have not. Reviewers with little to no online teaching experience may provide insights as a "fresh audience", and could potentially bring any unclear expectations or processes to the instructor's attention.

Similarly, Hewett and Powers (2007) also recognize the positive impact of collaborating with other online instructors to improve specific methods of increasing student engagement and participation. These researchers encourage instructors who are new to the online learning environment to find an instructor within the same or a similar subject area to serve as a mentor to them. This mentor could be available to answer questions specifically about the complexities of online teaching.

Further research highlights the importance of instructors taking time to reflect on their courses in order to determine what could be improved the next time the course is taught (Kong and Song, 2013). Instructors should look for patterns of behavior in students who earned high grades, as well as those who earned low grades, or those who failed a course. As evidenced by all of the research presented in this chapter, it is likely that instructors will see patterns of high engagement and participation from the students who achieved the highest scores.

FUTURE RESEARCH DIRECTIONS

Online learning environments are still relatively new in the field of education, and therefore can still be considered to be in the beginning stages of implementation, observation, and research. While educators and students have provided feedback about online learning experiences for years that have enhanced course delivery systems as well as pedagogical practices, technology changes rapidly, and online course delivery as a whole will likely continue to evolve as time passes. This author recommends several paths for future research on this topic.

1. Creating quality discussion boards for online students.
2. Examining the impact of social media integration on learning for traditional and non-traditional students in online courses.
3. Effectively assisting students as they acclimate to online courses in an accelerated course environment.
4. Adapting pedagogical practices to a "convenience" mindset.
5. Developing competencies for online educators.

CONCLUSION

Online instructors and students alike come to class with varying degrees of knowledge about online learning and subject matter. Both parties should be made aware of the differences between online learning and the traditional classroom format prior to the course start date. Instructors can use various methods described in this chapter to increase student engagement and participation in online courses, which have both been linked to higher levels of student satisfaction as well as higher grades earned.

REFERENCES

Anderson, T., Rourke, L., Archer, W., & Garrison, R. (2001). Assessing teaching presence in a computer conferencing context. *Journal of Asynchronous Learning Networks*, 5(2), 1–17. Retrieved from http://go.galegroup.com.ezproxy. lib.apsu.edu/ps/paginate

Bell, P. D. (2007). Predictors of College Student Achievement in Undergraduate Asynchronous Web-Based Courses. *Education*, *127*(4), 523–533.

Churchill, D., & Lu, J. (2012). The effect of social interaction on learning engagement in a social networking environment. *Interactive Learning Environments*, *22*(4), 410–417. Retrieved from http://www.tandfonline.com

Conrad, R., & Donaldson, J. (2004). *Engaging the online learner: Activities and resources for creative instruction*. San Francisco, CA: Jossey-Bass.

Dixon, C. (2014). The three E's of online discussion. *Quarterly Review of Distance Education*, *15*(1), 1–8.

Dixson, M. (2010). Creating effective student engagement in online courses: What do students find engaging? *Journal of the Scholarship of Teaching and Learning*, *10*(2), 1–33. Retrieved from http:// josotl.indiana.edu/article/view/1744/1742

Ebrahimi, A. (2011). How Does Early Feedback in an Online Programming Course Change Problem Solving? *Journal of Educational Technology Systems*, *40*(4), 371–379. doi:10.2190/ET.40.4.c

Elvers, G., Polzella, D., & Graetz, K. (2003). Procrastination in Online Courses: Performance and Attitudinal Differences. *Teaching of Psychology*, *30*(2), 159–162. doi:10.1207/ S15328023TOP3002_13

Fernández-Toro, M., & Hurd, S. (2014). A model of factors affecting independent learners' engagement with feedback on language learning tasks. *Distance Education*, *35*(1), 106–125. doi:10.108 0/01587919.2014.891434

Heischmidt, K., & Damoiseau, Y. (2012). Dimensions of Quality in Online Business Course Offerings: Content, Format and Feedback. *Journal of Higher Education Theory & Practice*, *12*(2), 84–97.

Hewett, B., & Powers, C. (2007). Online Teaching and Learning: Preparation, Development, and Organizational Communication. *Technical Communication Quarterly*, *16*(1), 1–82. doi:10.1080/10572250709336574

Holzweiss, P., Joyner, S., Fuller, M., Henderson, S., & Young, R. (2014). Online graduate students' perceptions of best learning experiences. *Distance Education*, *35*(3), 311–323. doi:10.1080/015879 19.2015.955262

Ingram, A. (2005). Engagement in Online Learning Communities. In J. Bourne & J. C. Moore (Eds.), *Elements of quality online education: Engaging communities* (pp. 55–69). Needham, MA: Sloan Consortium.

Ioannou, A., Demetriou, S., & Mama, M. (2014). Exploring Factors Influencing Collaborative Knowledge Construction in Online Discussions: Student Facilitation and Quality of Initial Postings. *American Journal of Distance Education*, *28*(3), 183–195. doi:10.1080/08923647.2014.926780

Kong, S., & Song, Y. (2013). A principle-based pedagogical design framework for developing constructivist learning in a seamless learning environment: A teacher development model for learning and teaching in digital classrooms. *British Journal of Educational Technology*, *44*(6), E209–E212. doi:10.1111/bjet.12073

Kurtz, G. (2014). Integrating a Facebook Group and a Course Website: The Effect on Participation and Perceptions on Learning. *American Journal of Distance Education*, *28*(4), 253–263. doi:10.1 080/08923647.2014.957952

Lebow, D. (1993). Constructivist values for in-structional system design: Five principles toward a new mindset. *Educational Technology Research and Development*, *41*(3), 4–16. doi:10.1007/BF02297354

Lewis, D., & Slapak-Barski, J. (2014). "I'm not sharing my work!": An Approach to Community Building. *Quarterly Review of Distance Education*, *15*(2), 9–20.

Ley, K. l., & Gannon-Cook, R. r. (2014). Learner-valued interactions. *Quarterly Review Of Distance Education*, *15*(1), 23–32.

McCarthy, A. T. (2012). Designing Online Course Assignments for Student Engagement: Strategies and Best Practices. *Currents in Teaching & Learning*, *4*(2), 31–41.

McKinney, J. P., McKinney, K. G., Franiuk, R., & Schweitzer, J. (2006). The College Classroom as a Community: Impact on Student Attitudes and Learning. *College Teaching*, *54*(3), 281–284. doi:10.3200/CTCH.54.3.281-284

Moore, R. (2014). Importance of Developing Community in Distance Education Courses. *Techtrends: Linking Research & Practice to Improve Learning*, *58*(2), 20–24. doi:10.1007/s11528-014-0733-x

Mott, J. (2010). Envisioning the post LMS-era: The Open Learning Network. *EDUCAUSE Quarterly*, *33*, 1–9. Retrieved from http://www.educause.edu/ero/article/envisioning-post-lms-era-open-learning-network

Mupinga, D. M., Nora, R. T., & Yaw, D. C. (2006). The Learning Styles, Expectations, and Needs of Online Students. *College Teaching*, *54*(1), 185–189. doi:10.3200/CTCH.54.1.185-189

Osborne, R., Kriese, P., Tobey, H., & Johnson, E. (2009). And Never the Two Shall Meet?: Student vs. Faculty Perceptions of Online Courses. *Journal of Educational Computing Research*, *40*(2), 171–182. doi:10.2190/EC.40.2.b

Özmen, B., & Atıcı, B. (2014). Learners' Views Regarding the Use of Social Networking Sites in Distance Learning. *International Review of Research in Open and Distance Learning*, *15*(4), 21–42.

Radford, A. (2011). *Learning at a Distance: Undergraduate Enrollment in Distance Education Courses and Degree Programs. (NCES 2012-154)*. Washington, DC: National Center for Education Statistics, Institute of Education Sciences, U.S. Department of Education.

Rao. (2010). Reaching Remote Learners: Successes and Challenges for Students in an Online Graduate Degree Program in the Pacific Islands. *The International Review of Research in Open and Distance Learning, 11*(1), 141 – 160.

Rovai, A. P. (2001). Building classroom community at a distance: A case study. *Educational Technology Research and Development*, *49*(4), 33–48. doi:10.1007/BF02504946

Simpson, J., & Benson, A. (2013). Student perceptions of quality and satisfaction in online education. *Quarterly Review Of Distance Education*, *14*(4), 221–231.

U.S. Department of Education, National Center for Education Statistics. (2011). *The Condition of Education 2011* (NCES 2011-033). *Indicator (Minnesota Mining and Manfuacturing Company)*, 43.

Varvel, V. (2007). Master online teacher competencies. *Online Journal of Distance Learning Administration, 10*(1), 1 – 36. Retrieved from http://www.westga.edu/~distance/ojdla/spring101/varvel101.pdf

Veletsianos, G., Kimmons, R., & French, K. (2013). Instructor experiences with a social networking site in a higher education setting: Expectations, frustrations, appropriation, and compartmentalization. *Educational Technology Research and Development, 61*(2), 255–278. doi:10.1007/s11423-012-9284-z

Vrasidas, C., & McIsaac, S. M. (1999). Factors influencing interaction in an online course. *American Journal of Distance Education, 13*(3), 22–36. doi:10.1080/08923649909527033

Waltonen-Moore, S., Stuart, D., & Newton, E. (2006). From Virtual Strangers to a Cohesive Online Learning Community: The Evolution of Online Group Development in a Professional Development Course. *Journal of Technology and Teacher Education, 14*(2), 287–311.

Wang, C., Shannon, D., & Ross, M. (2013). Students' characteristics, self-regulated learning, technology self-efficacy, and course outcomes in online learning. *Distance Education, 34*(3), 302–323. doi:10.1080/01587919.2013.835779

Wilson, J. (2002). The power of distance learning. *Education, 122*(4), 638–673.

Wyss, V. v., Freedman, D., & Siebert, C. (2014). The Development of a Discussion Rubric for Online Courses: Standardizing Expectations of Graduate Students in Online Scholarly Discussions. *Techtrends: Linking Research & Practice to Improve Learning, 58*(2), 99-107. Retrieved from http://link.springer.com/article/10.1007/s11528-014-0741-x

Xin, C., & Feenberg, A. (2006). Pedagogy in Cyberspace: The Dynamics of Online Discourse. *Journal of Distance Education, 21*(2), 1–25.

ADDITIONAL READING

Arbaugh, J. B. (2014). System, scholar, or students? Which most influences online MBA course effectiveness? *Journal of Computer Assisted Learning, 30*(4), 349–362. doi:10.1111/jcal.12048

Artello, K. (2014). What they learned: Using multimedia to engage undergraduates in research. *Innovative Higher Education, 39*(2), 169–179. doi:10.1007/s10755-013-9266-z

Can, G., & Walker, A. (2014). Social science doctoral students' needs and preferences for written feedback. *Higher Education, 68*(2), 303–318. doi:10.1007/s10734-014-9713-5

Czerkawski, B. (2014). Designing Deeper Learning Experiences for Online Instruction. *Journal of Interactive Online Learning, 13*(2), 29–40.

Fitzgerald, R., & Carazzo, P. (2013). Out of sight, out of mind: Capturing the distance (online) learner experience. *Enhancing the Learner Experience in Higher Education., 5*(1), 58–64.

Friberg, J. C. (2008). The use of supplementary podcasting as an instructional tool in an online classroom setting. *Perspectives on Issues in Higher Education., 11*(2), 61–66. doi:10.1044/ihe11.2.61

Kezar, A. (2014). Higher education change and social networks: A review of research. *The Journal of Higher Education, 85*(1), 91–125. doi:10.1353/jhe.2014.0003

O'Neill, D., & Sai, T. (2014). Why not? Examining college students' reasons for avoiding an online course. *Higher Education, 68*(1), 1–14. doi:10.1007/s10734-013-9663-3

Prestridge, S. (2014). A focus on students' use of Twitter – their interactions with each other, content, and interface. *Active Learning in Higher Education, 15*(2), 101–115. doi:10.1177/1469787414527394

Rivera, B., & Rowland, G. (2008). Powerful e-learning: A preliminary study of learner experiences. *MERLOT Journal of Online Teaching and Learning*, 4(1), 14–23.

KEY TERMS AND DEFINITIONS

Asynchronous Discussion: Often used in online classrooms, asynchronous discussions are those in which students and instructors can interact with one another, providing input and responding to one another at no pre-set time of day.

Distance Education: A learning environment in which the student and instructor interact asynchronously from their own locations instead of in a traditional classroom setting. Classes in distance education programs often take place via the internet.

Online Group Development: The process in which a group of students in an online course get acquainted with one another and establish processes and norms with the intention of completing a group assignment.

Online Learning Community: Within an online course, a sense that students have developed a suitable comfort level with one another, as well as with their instructor. Students in a true online learning community effectively interact with and learn from one another.

Professional Development: Opportunities for instructors to enhance their skills carrying out a particular concept in their pedagogical practices or to increase their knowledge of their subject matter area.

Social Media Integration: Incorporating one or more social media outlets as a supplementary platform to deliver information in an online course environment.

Social Presence: The extent to which an instructor interacts with students in online courses with the intention of providing feedback, responding to messages, providing examples, and participating in discussions.

Teaching Presence: The extent to which an instructor in an online course makes himself/herself known as the instructor.

Chapter 18

Building Relationship Through Learning Communities and Participation in Online Learning Environments:
Building Interactions in Online Learning

Victoria Cardullo
Auburn University, USA

Megan Burton
Auburn University, USA

ABSTRACT

With the increase demand for distance education, institutions of higher education are actively exploring opportunities to weave self, subject and students for web based distance education. The pedagogical skills necessary to create effective active learning opportunities are explored throughout this chapter as well as lessons learned from research. The authors used vignettes to position effective course design and implementation aligned with both Bloom's Taxonomy and the SAMR (Substitution, Augmentation, Modification, Redefinition) model to enhance online learning environments. Learning objectives and course goals provided direction for developing task for social presence, cognitive presence and a collaborative stance in authentic online learning.

INTRODUCTION

Good teachers join self, subject, and students in the fabric of life... Palmer, 1999, p. 11

This quote is as true in an online learning environment as it is in the traditional brick and mortar classroom. In essence, "All education-face- to-face, distance mode, online- requires understanding the nature of the medium in order to conceptualize and design it as an educational environment" (Harasim, 1995, p 138). Due to the increase demand for distance education, institutions of higher education are actively exploring

DOI: 10.4018/978-1-4666-9582-5.ch018

opportunities to weave self, subject and students for web-based distance education. These institutions are often faced with challenges such as technological knowledge, pedagogical knowledge, student knowledge, and content knowledge (Wilson, Zygouris-Coe, Cardullo, & Fong, 2013). These challenges are often compounded by faculty members' busy schedules, lack of technology and preconceived notions and attitudes. Beyond simply offering online course work, instructors need to know how to set up the online format effectively to present opportunities for student involvement through collaborative discussion, video chats, Wiki pages, Twitter, and blogs to name a few. The pedagogical skills necessary to create effective active learning opportunities will be explored through this chapter. This chapter includes lessons learned from research, vignettes of effective course designs and implementations, and ideas about emerging technologies, and how they can enhance online learning environments.

SELECTING EMERGING TECHNOLOGY

When preparing to teach a course online, critical emphasis should be placed on the skills required for creating and facilitating effective online course work as well as the issues and ways the course may change for students. For example, it is important for instructors to implement activities that allow students to analyze and utilize critical thinking through emerging technologies such as blogs or Twitter. Often these emerging technologies require the user to assemble and analyze information differently, defying the typical notion of a static text. In a recent listserve discussion (EDUCAUSE, January, 2015) a faculty member was soliciting thoughts on a "good" cloud-based social network platforms that could facilitate substantive organic communication and collaboration amongst past,

present, and future students. Many faculty members offered descriptions of the platforms. Table 1 presents a snapshot of the suggestions.

While this list of resources is diverse, intuitive, and on target for what is needed to support substantive organic communication and collaboration amongst past, present, and future students, the key element that is being overlooked in the recommendations given is connection between the students and the technology and the students and the content (Cardullo, Zygouris-Coe & Wilson, 2014). When introducing a new platform in an online course the connection between all of these elements need to be in the forefront (Cardullo et al., 2014). Technology that doesn't connect to students and improve the way they experience the content misses the ultimate purpose of meeting learning goals (Arbaugh et al, 2010; Cohen & Hollebrands, 2011; Fey et al., 2010). Instead of implementing something new, instructors should consider surveying the students to find out what they are already using, and incorporating something, they are already familiar with using. This would alleviate the introduction of a new platform. It takes time to learn how to efficiently operate emerging technologies, and instructors must account for these elements in their coursework. If learning the new technology creates a benefit worthy of the time it will take away from other elements of the course, then it is worthwhile, but implementing something new simply for the sake of being "innovative" can cause students to miss important content related to the goals of the course.

Electronic technology in the age of new media creates a different type of literacy, developing a literacy stance that is no longer static. With each new tool or device comes a learning curve. Interactions between mode and media affect the discourse, design, production, and consumption of online courses. Technology rich activities can enhance high levels of student engagement and peer collaboration allowing students to connect,

Table 1. Snapshot of faculty choice of technology for communication and collaboration

Technology	Reason
Facebook Group	"Groups for Schools" feature today which will allow American colleges to create Group pages accessible only within the school community.
LinkedIn	LinkedIn is a business-oriented social networking service. Founded in December 2002 and launched on May 5, 2003, it is mainly used for professional networking.
K-12 Edmodo	Edmodo is a social networking site for teachers and students where over 46 million teachers, students, and parents are connecting to collaborate on assignments discover new resources. Edmodo is a web 2.0 social networking tool for educators to use to communicate with students and parents.
Microsoft OneDrive	A file hosting service that allows users to upload and synchronize files to a cloud storage and then access them from a Web browser or their local device.
12manage.com	A free management education and business education platform for management and organization of business or education.
Yammer	Yammer a private social network collaboration software and business applications that allows the user to connect to the right people, share information across teams and organize around projects.
Celly	Celly is a platform for ad-hoc social networks that is accessible via iPhone, Android, Web, SMS text and even email. Networks connect individuals and communities for instant and easy communication.
Jive	Jive is a communication and collaboration platform solution for business. Jive enables employees, partners and customers to work together.
Twitter	Twitter is a powerhouse for marketing, communication, business, and even education, letting people from around the world work together, share ideas, and gain exposure to concepts.
Google+ Communities	Google+ is a place to connect with friends and family, and explore interests. Google+ allows the user to share photos, send messages, and stay in touch with the people globally.
Hive Social	Hive Social is a specialist Social Media consultancy, which helps businesses and brands find, connect, build, and engage with their online audience through Social Media and Digital Marketing.
Enterprise Hive	HiveSocial for higher education is an enterprise social software, communication and collaboration platform with embedded game mechanics
Socialtext	Socialtext applies Web 2.0 technologies such as enterprise microblogging, enterprise social networking, and wikis to the critical challenges facing businesses. Socialtext's platform allows employees to share expertise, speed workflows, and get their jobs done faster.
Elgg	Elgg an open source social networking software that provides individuals and organizations with the components needed to create an online social environment. It offers blogging, microblogging, file sharing, networking, and groups.
Schoology	Schoology offers an LMS with a modern social media interface and integrations with Facebook, Microsoft OneDrive, etc...

communicate, collaborate and create content using rich digital resources (Ball & Stacey, 2005). Additional benefits of technology are the affordances of a more holistic learning experience that is student driven rather than teacher driven. Rather than trying to find ways to make an online course similar to a face-to-face course, instructors should find ways to maximize the benefits technology affords to explore the content in different, perhaps deeper levels (Palloff & Pratt, 1999).

In order to better prepare students for the demands of the 21st century college and career readiness expectations, emerging technologies must be integrated into instructional design and pedagogical practices. The purposeful integration of technologies will help support the skills that are needed for the global workforce. Active completion of these learning skills will foster critical thinking, the expression of ideas both orally and written as well as receiving and offering constructive feedback throughout the learning process. The greatest value of an active learning environment is the way it enables and supports social collaboration. Collaboration allows students to learn from each other and utilize their strengths, while growing and improving in weak areas through the expertise of their peers. The most engaging activities involve social interactions, collaboration, and creative components to an online learning environment (Shea, Li, & Pickett, 2006).

A well-crafted and captivating lecture presentation may seem like an effective way for instructors to cover material but it often does not promote deep and lasting learning. When students are actively involved in the learning task, they learn more (Cross, 1987). Effective classes are those that have students engaged in the learning community and content, taking ownership in their learning, with a clear understanding of the purpose of the course. This can seem daunting when creating an online course. However, there is a growing body of research (Christiansen & Anderson, 2004; Oblinger & Hawkins, 2006) to support the inclusion of specific practices and technologies in effective online course development and implementation. Effective instructors of online courses must create a space for students to be active participants who interact with the material, each other, technology, and the professor in ways that advance their learning.

In the following *Active Participation Vignette*, one can follow along as Maria negotiates first day jitters and the establishment of an online presence in Canvas, the Learning Management System used by her institution. This vignette is designed to illustrate the way students new to online courses can be set at ease and actively involved in interactions with the instructor and peers via a well-organized online learning environment. It provides a window into the apprehension many students experience when enrolled in their first online course. Instructors need to clearly communicate expectations for

the course and communication from the initial online introduction to foster an interactive, comfortable learning community.

Vignette # 1 Active Participation.

Maria, a junior at the university, is enrolled in her first online course. She is apprehensive, because she has never met the instructor or any of her classmates. She wonders: Will she be able to understand the assignments? What will she do if she has a question? How will she know if she is on track to accomplish the learning goals of the course? Maria is relieved when she logs on to Canvas for the first time. The first thing she sees is a homepage of her instructor introducing herself. This page contains photos, a brief introductory video, the professor's resume, and photos of her dogs. Seeing the personalized and detailed description of the professor makes Maria more comfortable, as she begins to feel she can relate to her. She also takes note of the contact information that the instructor has provided. She notes that the instructor seems approachable and shares a passion for the content and teaching of this course. Maria further explores the course material and sees a clearly organized syllabus with learning goals, assignments, a calendar, and expectations explicitly listed. There is a discussion board created for questions, comments, and concerns related to the course. She notices the first assignment involves creating a student homepage to introduce herself to the class using the same program her instructor used. She also realizes that she will view all of the other classmates' homepages and leave comments for her peers. This will be similar to the one the instructor created, but is a bit more basic in order to make it manageable for the student. There are directions on using the technology as well as the type of information she should share in the introduction that will guide her in the development of her introduction. She sees that they will be using a variety of technological tools to communicate not only with the professor, but also with each other and the content. There is contact information in order to receive university support with technical issues along with clear information about the technology being used. The detailed, organized information contained in the learning technology tool gives Maria a sense of ease about the expectations and excitement about the things she will learn throughout the semester.

Learning occurs when the student is actively engaged with the content and coursework in positive ways that promote deep understanding (NCTM, 2014; Shulman, 1987). In order to engage the student, the technology must be approachable, meaningful, and clear to the student. The opportunities that online environments offer are vast. Instructors must stay informed about emerging technology and consider how the technology can support the overarching goals of the course. Ultimately, the quality of online coursework is dependent upon the quality of planning and course design.

ELEMENTS OF A PEDAGOGICALLY SOUND COURSE

Course Development

Developing a course can be a daunting task, even for the most veteran instructors. Online course development has the added issue of not being able to immediately assess student reaction when material is being delivered, unlike in-person courses. Below is a vignette that follows the development of an online course for an experienced professor who is known for creating cognitively demanding, interactive, engaging, and meaningful face-to-face courses on campus. While technologically savvy, she struggled to find ways to make the online experience the same. Could she find a way to make the online experience as interactive, comfortable, meaningful, and content rich as her

campus courses? She did not want to lose the importance of relationships among all involved in the course, communication, and content. To prepare, she attended webinars, discussed experiences in online courses with colleagues and students, and researched ideas online. Through these experiences, she suddenly realized that her goal should not be to make the course the same. Instead, she should focus on ways technology can enhance the course relationships, communication, and content in a way that is unique to online learning. This vignette illustrates the planning and reflection required in course development when transitioning from an on campus course to an online format.

Vignette # 2 Course Development

Prior to developing her online course, Dr. Paige first developed ideas about ways to begin class so that students could grow comfortable with each other and with the content of the course. She created a web of ideas around the central goals of the course. This involved ideas such as personalized webpages, video conference discussions, discussion boards, etc... Each offer opportunities for students to share and learn about peer backgrounds and experiences that they bring to this course as well as expectations for the course. Dr. Paige decided to have students introduce themselves using the media aggregator, VoiceThread, which allows people to post media artifacts and receive feedback from others who view the artifacts. Dr. Paige created her own introduction to model the task for the students and help them grow more comfortable with her. She also planned to comment on each student's introductions in order to model the type of replies that students can make with each other.

Next Dr. Paige focused on the overall learning goals for the course. She created a list of possible assignments, information sources, activities, etc... under each goal. This included the information students would need to know to be able to ac-

complish each goal as well as how she might determine if the goals have been met. She planned opportunities for students to utilize the multiple modalities that online learning make possible. For example, students were involved in exploring content via video, Webquest, readings, discussion, and creating multi-media products. Each module built upon previous ones to create a cohesive, in-depth development of content knowledge. She then looked for patterns and possibilities of connecting goals and activities to build upon each other. Using ten design principles, listed later in the chapter, she created activities that have meaningful connections, involve student values, encourage collaboration, have multiple possibilities for a finished product, etc...

When she finished developing the course, Dr. Paige asked a colleague to look over it for advice. She added a place for student comments, questions, and suggestions to her and a place for students to discuss the course together online.

In the above vignette, Dr. Paige worked to ensure the overall goals and objectives remained the focus throughout the course. She utilized technological resources in ways that would support students achieving these goals, rather than simply for the experience of using technology. She looked for ways technology would support creating clear communication between students and herself. She also wanted to create an environment where students communicated with each other to foster in depth discussions about the content and varying perspectives.

In her introductory module, Dr. Paige videotaped herself introducing the course and acknowledged the challenge of creating community and interpreting information online. She encouraged students to communicate any questions or concerns they might have as she would not have the in-class advantage of watching student reactions for signs of confusion or worry. In addition, she detailed steps students could take if they were having dif-

ficulty with any of the technology, so this would not take away from time spent on the content of the course. However, she also expressed the positives of the various technological tools being used and the advantage of distance education allowing students from all over the world to participate. Having such a diverse student population with different perspectives, experiences, and knowledge adds immeasurably to the course. By acknowledging the differences between online and face-to-face courses and possible obstacles, she hoped these elements would establish a community feel and facilitate an understanding of the content goals of the course. This vignette illustrates the power of Dr. Paige's reflection in planning, implementing, and improving the course. While this is important in improving any course, it is especially necessary when creating an online course. Because instructors cannot physically observe the students as they would in a traditional setting, it is important to find many venues to allow students to ask questions, share confusions, and engage in content.

Course Structure

Vignette # 2 illustrated the need for a sound pedagogical framework, yet many teachers are not aware of the different pedagogical requirements for online teaching and learning. Course structures should provide a clear starting point for students just as Dr. Paige demonstrated through the use of a VoiceThread as an introduction. She provided modeling and tips for successful navigation. In Vignette # 1, student webpages and video introductions were used to enhance the course design and incorporate student profiles. The use of a VoiceThread or student homepages through the online learning platform in both vignettes demonstrated a few low cost options for instructors to utilize that incorporates both audio and video to increase student social presence in an online environment. Audio and video helped to create a social presence by incorporating a human element into the course and reflecting the emotions of the instructor as well as the students. If these technologies are not available, instructors can explore alternative ways to make virtual introductions. For example, having students create "Where I'm From" poems based off the poem by George Ella Lyon (1999) that describe things and memories that are important to the student as a way for students to get to know one another without video or audio.

Startup modules are critical in online courses as they often nurture a positive and inclusive online learning environment. Course syllabi, schedule, and protocols should be included in a sound pedagogical design as well. Dr. Paige shared where important information could be found in her introduction, but also worked to have it easily accessible on the course platform, as these are essential tools that provide students with directions on how to be successful with in an online course. Course content should be organized and all components of the course should be clear. In the case of Vignette # 2, Dr. Paige organized the course in sequential modules. This provided structure for the course so the content would build in an intentional way. Online learning environments require both strong communicative skills and interpersonal skills on the part of the instructor and students. Yet many students take online courses because they are attracted to the convenience, availability and flexibility of scheduling of these courses (Bocchi, Eastman & Swift, 2004). Finding ways to foster the communication, while maintaining the convenience and flexibility is an important element in course design.

Social Presence and Online Participation

It is vital to the success of instructors and students in online courses, that students perceive their instructor to be involved, knowledgeable, and concerned about the content and the student (Palloff & Pratt, 1999). Therefore, instructors must find ways to be visible and interact with

their students in online courses. If students believe the professor does not read posts or follow the online course, they may lose motivation to stay involved themselves. After all, if the professor does not seem to care, why should the student? In addition, successful online courses also foster participation and interaction among their students. Below is a vignette that follows an instructor, Dr. James, over three semesters as he reflects on and improves his online presence and the engagement level of students in his online business course. Dr. James reflected on and improved the course each semester to better accomplish his goal of creating an online environment where students share their ideas, experiences, and expertise with each other throughout the semester to foster an online presence. This vignette illustrates ways a professor can reflect and improve upon an online course to increase the social presence of the professor as well as ways students interact with each other during the course.

Vignette # 3 Developing a social presence

Dr. James wanted to foster meaningful interaction in his course that was organized into weekly modules. The first semester he required students to create four responses to others' posts as well as two original posts... He found that while some students engaged in discussions, many seemed to post as a requirement, rather than actually engaging in meaningful discourse. They also seemed to post all responses at one time in order to "get it over with."

The next semester he decided to do a few things to enhance his social presence and increase meaningful online participation. He added an element of video introduction intended to help students feel that they "knew" each other. He made a point of commenting on student posts daily and asking questions that would require students to respond. He also engaged in dialogue with multiple students who responded to one student post in an effort to promote discussion. Finally, he required the students to respond to posts at least two different times of the week to facilitate more dialogue.

While this showed improvement in student engagement, communication, and perception of the course, the following semester he added more collaborative work that required students to share their expertise and backgrounds, interactive elements (such as video chats) and dynamic elements for students to discuss (such as video and audio segments and vignettes). The assignments required students to interact more. By sharing more of himself, he was able to set an example for students to share more about themselves and learn more from each other. He also added in a rubric to assess interactive communication about the content that reflected the importance he placed upon this element of learning. Students received a grade based on their comments connecting peer comments to the content. He also added an assignment that required students to collaborate and create multimedia presentations to the class. By the third semester, he was extremely pleased with the course interaction and progress students made throughout the semester.

In Vignette # 3, each semester marked improvement from the past, due to the reflective nature of the instructor and the feedback given by peers and students. It also illustrates the struggles often experienced when creating a new course. Dr. James recognized the importance of his social presence. It was important that students saw he valued the course and what they had to say. Students needed to see him as an active facilitator with expertise to share, but also a desire to learn from the online community. Each semester Dr. James modified the course to support a facilitative stance. He continued to create opportunities for students to take charge of their learning without having to hover and control the learning environment.-

In addition to the instructor's social presence, it is important that students see their presence in the course as valued (Palloff & Pratt, 1999). Students need to feel that their thoughts, reactions, and beliefs add value to the course. In addition, online courses need to foster a community that encourages interactions among students. This can often be the most challenging element in an online teaching and learning environment. Online learning is often perceived as an independent endeavor, so encouraging students to interact with each other can be a struggle. In Vignette # 3, the course improved in this aspect each semester. What began as simply posting reactions to things read grew to students responding multiple times during the week, to students collaborating on products to present to the class, which then encourages and nurtures follow-up discussions. Dr. James added learning strategies such as a 5-minute video vignette of a situation that related to the topic of the week. This allowed students to have a common experience to discuss. In addition, groups met in video chats to discuss projects, which allowed students to interact as they would in an on campus course. Dr. James provided a detailed rubric that was used to score the communication between students regarding the content. This rubric allows students to understand the expectations and to see the importance of interacting with peers regarding the content being learned. Each of these strategies fostered a learning environment where students saw the benefit to the course. In addition, it allowed students to see value in listening, interacting, and learning from their peers.

Learning Community

Learning centered ideologies are founded in the constructivist view in which the process of learning encourages the learner to gain deeper understanding of content (Cardullo, 2013). Collaborative learning that emphasizes the constructivist view will enhance the individuals' potential to achieve the given objective. Learner centered environments require collaboration and discussion between all participants. Collaborative learning is a social process, which takes place through on going communication with others (Mead, 1934). In other words, learning is not only active but also interactive. Collaborative learning is learner centered not teacher centered, therefore the role of the instructor changes from a dispenser of information to a facilitator. This process encourages and supports students' construction of knowledge. Learning communities foster learning with and from one another, collaboratively. Faculty members or instructors structure topics, provide support, and expertize while working with students as they prepare their projects (Harasim et al., 1994).

Learning communities are built around the principles that all can learn from each other with a culture of collaboration (DuFour, 2004). Learning communities are effective ways to foster engagement and course satisfaction (Zhao & Kuh, 2004). In a study that looked at teaching presence and student sense of learning communities in online and web enhanced college courses Shea, Li, & Pickett (2006) investigated multi-institutions to determine if there was a significant link between students' sense of learning community and effective instructional design. Using random surveys in which 1067 respondents across 32 colleges participated; they found that there was a significant link between the two. Shea, Li, and Pickett found there is a clear connection between perceived teaching presence and students' sense of learning community. They position this research to gain insight into how to support the development of learners' sense of connectedness. Their research postulates the need for intellectual decisions about online course design, pedagogical and faculty development as well as the enhancement of online learning environment.

Learning communities are in essence a place to share and grow together (Palloff & Pratt, 1999). The vision of online learning communities is compelling. Introverts often struggle to find their voice in face-to-face classrooms, but virtual classrooms allow a space for them to construct their responses as they become more vocal (Palloff & Pratt, 1999). Although they may never meet, face-to-face intensive engagement in a collaborative environment can enhance a pedagogically sound course.

Developing an innovative online course that values strategic and planned use of interactive communication is often challenging. The options are vast and the learning curve is steep. However, when students and instructors interact in new social situations they create a social presence or a degree of interpersonal contact. These elements are critical and the level of success will depend on the ability to demonstrate strong communication skills both verbally and through writing. Social presence creates a learning environment perceived as warm, collegial, and approachable (Rourke et al., 1999). This social presence can foster a learning community in which students and instructor value the unique insights and experiences each bring to the learning environment. The focus is on results, but with the belief that working together with an openness about strengths and weaknesses accomplishes more than working in isolation (DuFour, 2004). Through openly sharing, listening, and learning together, student benefit not only from the knowledge of the professor, but also from the knowledge of their peers. In essence, social presence leads to inclusion or the need to establish an identity with others.

Learning Objectives and Course Goals

Learning objectives and course goals provide direction for creating tasks and course development. It is essential to understand and focus on what students need to know and be able to do by the end of the course in order to build a course that leads them to this end goal. When selecting tasks for a course, instructors should consider multiple strategies to encourage high-level thinking about the content in meaningful ways.

Bloom's Taxonomy

Educators have been using Bloom's Taxonomy (Bloom & Krathwohl, 1956) for years to promote higher order thinking skills. Bloom's Taxonomy provides educators with a systematic classification system for learning. In essence, Bloom's Taxonomy serves as a starting point for all instructional design, including online instruction. Interactions in an online course must incorporate a high level of learning using Bloom's Taxonomy. As instructors are developing course assignments, activities, and learning objectives a pedagogically sound course will align with both higher order thinking skills and the integration of technology. Bloom's taxonomy should be used for all aspects of the course development from design to topics for discussion. There are six levels in the hierarchy of cognitive development of mastery: *remembering, understanding, applying, analyzing, evaluating, and creating*. Remembering involves elements such as quick recall of information on fact-based multiple choice or matching quizzes. Understanding involves activities such as explaining and summarizing events and content. Students demonstrate application when they are able to utilize information learned to accomplish a task, such as being able effectively to use algorithm learned in class to solve a physics problem. Analysis is being able to break down complex material so it is easier to explain. This would involve activities such as identifying elements of a program based on a framework explored in class. Synthesis involves combining elements in a new or unique form. For example, students may use an imaginary budget to plan menu items that align with school nutrition guidelines. Evaluating includes making judgment calls about the value of materials and ideas. This can include persuasive writing or examining various economic investments to determine which would be most effective to meet the needs of a client. As instructors who

design, courses it is important to align learning objectives and assessment based on each level of cognitive development.

SAMR Model

Many instructors recognize that Bloom's Taxonomy can be a tool for developing and classifying quality tasks that challenge students to think critically about content, but they may be unaware that the *Substitution, Augmentation, Modification, Redefinition* model (SAMR) (Puentedura, 2006) can provide a framework for technology as instructors develop tasks to reach learning goals and objectives in online courses.

The SAMR model is further divided into two domains: transformation and enhancement. Enhancement includes the levels of *substitution* and *augmentation* whereas the transformation stage is inclusive of *modification* and *redefinition*. When developing online course modules substitution and augmentation phases often use technology to accomplish traditional tasks (discussion postings, summarization via online submission and mind mapping (see table 2)), with very little functional change in the task itself (Theisen, 2013). At the level of substitution the task is performed, but with a minimum use of technology. For example, the use of discussion postings offers very little change in the delivery using technology. At the augmentation level, the same type of technology may be used to perform a task, with some type of improvement (Israel & Lang, 2013). Mind mapping tool allows students to see connections between concepts using technology to facilitate this task often moving the task to the augmentation stage.

Modification and redefinition fall under the transformation domain of the SAMR model. In the transformation domain, technology begins to transform online active learning and students are often engaged beyond the classroom (WIX,

Table 2. Course outline of SAMR stages, tasks, and Bloom's Taxonomy

Online Module #	Application or Task Aligned With Learning Objective	Level of Integration SAMR Stages	Level of Integration Bloom's Taxonomy
2, 5	Discussion posting, summaries of readings and videos	Substitution	Remembering
3	Mind mapping	Augmentation	Applying & Understanding
3, 3, 4,5	Panopto recording, video segments of experts in the field, online observation, moderator discussion	Modification	Applying, Analyzing & Evaluating
1, 2, 5, **6**, 7, 8, 12	VoiceThread, synchronous meeting, Webquest, avatars to simulate students added to their class roster, podcast, **WIX**, PathBrite Portfolio, evaluation of observation	Redefinition	Evaluating & Creating

Webquest, Twitter, PathBrite, Podcast and other online tools (see table 2)). According to Puentedura (2013), modification allows for significant task redesign using technology. The final level in the transformation domain is redefinition. Redefinition is defined as the highest level of SAMR model in which technology is used in the creation of a new task (Israel & Lang, 2013). A task that was once inconceivable without technology (WIX homepage for student support (see table 2)).

Technology is another significant consideration when developing and delivering an online course. Awareness of levels of integration of technology can foster deeper understanding of content as instructors foster active student learning and the development of critical thinking skills. The SAMR model illustrates how instructors in an online course critically cultivate assignments when developing a pedagogically sound course. The following is an outline of the stages based on work from Puentedura (2006) and the alignment of Bloom's Taxonomy (Bloom et al., 1956).

- **Substitution**: Simply substituting one task for the other with no functional change.
  - Bloom's level of integration *Understanding*
- **Augmentation**: A direct substitution of the task with some functional improvement.
  - Bloom's level of integration *Understanding and Application*

- **Modification**: Allows for significant redesign of the task.
  - Bloom's level of integration *Application, Analysis, and Evaluation*
- **Redefinition**: Allows for the creation of a new task, previously inconceivable.
  - Bloom's level of integration *Evaluation and Creation*

As the author and developer of an online course, this researcher systematically evaluated and analyzed objectives, content, and the use of technology to facilitate knowledge and skills to enhance reading instruction in content area classrooms while enhancing the content knowledge of learning opportunities for English Learner (EL) students. The following outline of online modules (see Table 2) displays an active online classroom in which the students move systematically through all levels of the SAMR model (Puentedura, 2006) aligned closely with Bloom's taxonomy (Bloom et al., 1956) for learning.

Table 2. provides a snapshot of online content development using both the SAMR model and Bloom's Taxonomy. This process of integration is a fluid process that moves both forward and backward through the stages of development and taxonomy. In Module 6 of the instructor's online course (see table 2), she introduced the students to a WIX home page. This task offered real world application in which students could create a homepage for their future classroom to support student acquisition of reading strategies. The following assignment description outlines the process:

Student Objectives:

1. Students will understand why before-reading strategies that activate prior knowledge and raise interest in the subject prepare readers to approach a text in a critical frame of mind.
2. Students will understand the type of experiences that constitute meaningful learning activities.
3. Students will gain an appreciation for using strategies (before, during, and after) that motivate students to read text by arousing curiosity.
4. Students will be able to demonstrate the use of prediction strategies that help to facilitate reading comprehension.

During this module, students will develop a WIX class webpage for students to access anytime, anywhere to support their understanding of the teaching unit. Before, During, and After Reading Strategies will be developed to enhance reading comprehension and understanding of the teaching unit. Using your strategies selected in the previous module create a home page that student can access anywhere, anytime for additional support.

http://www.wix.com/website/templates/html/blank/1 this link will take you to is the website to start your class homepage; you must register and then log in to begin. Once you have registered, choose a template, and start working. Create an introduction page for your students, select a common theme that can be woven through your homepage, then develop a page for each reading strategy: Before, during, after reading strategy. Using your strategies identified in the previous module create a resource page for each with working links for students to use. Develop a conclusion page for your students giving further directions to guide them if they are stuck: (i.e., additional

resource pages, make an appointment to meet with you, ask a peer...). When you are finished, you should have FIVE tabs on your WIX page: Introduction, before reading strategies, during reading strategies, after reading strategies, and conclusion (additional support or resources for your students). You will need to save your file and send your working link in the assignment tab.

This assignment encouraged active learning that aligned with Bloom's taxonomy (evaluating and creating) as well as Puentedura's SAMR Model (Redefinition). The integration of Bloom's Taxonomy and the SAMR model adds fluidity to the online course assignments. In this above course models (see table 2) students often engage in activities and assignments that support critical thinking using the integration of technology.

The following vignette displays an active online learning environment in which students' progress through all levels of the SAMR model aligned with Bloom's Taxonomy for active learning.

Vignette # 4 Integrating Bloom's Taxonomy and SAMR Model

Students in a master's level elementary science education course watch a brief video [Augmentation] of a fifth grade class working in groups to explore and answer the question, "Can new substances be created by combining other substances?" The purpose of this video is for students in the course to see an effective teacher using the inquiry process to push elementary students to think deeply about content and take ownership in their learning.

The students in the online course are placed in groups [Modification], based on the grade level they teach, and challenged to discuss the teacher's role from the video [Substitution]. They are to share ways they observed the teacher facilitate the exploratory process and guide elementary students into developing new content knowledge. This discussion is meant to facilitate discussions about how to support elementary inquiry and the teacher's role in this process. Students of the course discuss things such as the teacher's use of group roles to foster collaboration and her questioning abilities to push student communication and thinking. Next, each group is charged with developing a science lesson that would involve some of the key pedagogical principles observed in the fifth grade lesson on the video. Groups post a summary [Redefinition] of the lessons they develop so the entire class can view them. A second grade group created a lesson based on the discovery of what plants need to grow. The summary describes a lesson where elementary students are able to design experiments with different elements to find which were essential.

The online students are challenged to respond with questions and comments regarding the pedagogy described in each lesson [Modification]. One person asked the second grade group what they would do if a plant with essential elements died. This allowed for a discussion on how to address experiments that don't demonstrate the principles they are designed to demonstrate.

Let us look at how this active learning in an online classroom used technology effectively to support the different stages of the SAMR model (Puentedura, 2006) as well as a strong alignment of Bloom's Taxonomy (Bloom et al., 1956) to activate student learning and the development of critical thinking (see Table 3).

This online lesson was able to move students through multiple layers of both Bloom's Taxonomy and the SAMR model. In order for this assignment to move into redefinition a simple refining of the assignment would be needed. To move this assignment into the redefinition stage of technology students could Blog or post comments for others outside of their classroom to respond creating a fluid discussion.

When converting face-to-face courses to an online platform it is important to adjust certain

presentations and delivery elements. Participants do not always have the benefit of body movements and facial expressions to communicate and communication is not always synchronous. For example, PowerPoints and recorded lectures can become stale and students often disengage when provided passive ways to understand content without interactions, meaning, and applications. Bloom's taxonomy has proven to be a practical tool in selecting, structuring, and communicating specific learning objectives. The alignment with the SAMR model helps to facilitate a deeper use of technology purposefully aligned with critical thinking skills (Puentedura, 2012)

CONNECTING STUDENTS TO SUBJECT MATTER

Active Learning in Online Environments

Active learning strategies in an online environment can be used to enhance online coursework. Learner participation is often self-directed and independent in online courses. Course management systems are being used to "put" face-to-face course content online. Many courses are simply a replication of the traditional classroom instructional practice such as a depository for lecture notes, readings, quizzes, term papers, exams, and

Table 3. Vignette # 4 Task outline of SAMR stages and Bloom's taxonomy

SAMR Stages	Application or Task	Bloom's Taxonomy
Substitution	Discussion of video	Remembering
Augmentation	Video	Applying & Understanding
Modification	Fluid groups	Applying, Analyzing & Evaluating
Redefinition	Create a lesson plan	Evaluating & Creating

other traditional "in-class" assignments. Oftentimes these strategies in traditional classrooms are seen by students as passively receiving information or using lower level thinking skills to share information the professor expects. The challenge of incorporating active learning, which is defined as any instructional method that engages students in the learning process (Cardullo et al., 2015), is not a technical issue but rather pedagogical innovation for all learning environments, traditional and online. Active learning requires the learner to be involved in the process of gaining new ideas, information, and insights. Active learning involves authentic, meaningful tasks and collaboration. Learning is heightened through active, meaningful, collaborative experiences. Herrington et al. (2003) defined ten design principles for developing authentic task based collaborative environments for active learning. The first design principle is the development of an authentic task that has real world relevance. In the following vignette, we will see how a graduate student negotiates an online presence, a cognitive presence, and a collaborative stance as she interacts with content to develop a task for real world submission. Active learning requires students to do meaningful learning activities and think about what they are doing (Bonwell & Eison, 1991). Active learning can empower students with skills and strategies for problem solving both inside and outside the walls of the classroom, or learning space (Cardullo et al., 2015). The following example of active learning illustrates the complexity of active learning in an online environment.

Vignette # 5 Authentic Task for Active Learning

Kim is a graduate student in reading education at the university. Her instructor designated her as the lead collaborator in an assignment for her group in an online Curriculum and Teaching Reading course. After reading through the module, her task is to work collaboratively to develop a manuscript for a local reading journal. Kim must

develop negotiation skills and communication skills to work with her group. During the five-week collaborative assignment, Kim took on a leadership role, encouraged, and motivated her team through online communication to prepare the manuscript submission. During this time, Kim refined her role as a facilitator and learned how to negotiate and articulate needs of the group in a professional tone. To do this she was in constant communication with the course instructor as she developed a facilitative stance. The outcome of the course lead to the article being published and the students presented their research at a local conference. As graduate students, these are real-world task with authentic implications.

The second design principle requires that the authentic task must be ill defined, requiring the students to define the task and subtask needed to complete the activity. Using the above vignette as an example, students were given the following task:

During this course, you will collaborate to develop a manuscript submission for The Reading Paradigm. You will do the following to complete the task 1) collaboratively research and write, 2) collaboratively develop a manuscript for submission and 3) individually and collectively develop a voice for graduate writing and future publications. We will write in teams of three or four and I will bring in my expertise with new literacy. Your topic of research will be: How is technology changing the way we teach reading. As a team, you will have five weeks to research, write, edit, and prepare your manuscript. Kim will be the team leader.

The directions were vague enough that students could interact with each other to develop a cognitive presence, a teaching presence, and a social presence in an online course through active learning. This element related to directions ties into the third design principle for active learning, which is the authentic task, must comprise complex activities to be investigated by students over a sustained period of time. Using the same vignette, students had to explore the submission requirements for both the manuscript and the local presentation in a five-week time span.

During this course, students researched and discussed their research findings as they formulated their cognitive and social presence in the online environment. The fourth design principle for developing an authentic task must provide the opportunities for students to examine the task from different perspectives, using a variety of resources. In the above task, students brought in different perspectives based on their current jobs. One student brought the perspective of an assistant principal, the other a higher education adjunct and the last a first grade teacher. Using these lenses each set out to develop a research agenda to support the collaborative writing process. The fifth design principle is to provide the opportunity to collaborate. This design principle requires the design of the task to be intentional and purposeful with collaboration as the focal point.

The sixth design principle calls for the authentic task to provide opportunity to reflect and involve students' beliefs and values. Allowing the learners to bring in their perspectives in a valued manner is an important element in any course design. In the vignette above, groups were given the opportunity to choose the topic for their manuscript. While it focused on the basic content of the course, reading education, the task allowed them to select something that was personally, meaningful to them.

The seventh design principle requires the authentic task to be integrated and applied across different subject areas and to extend beyond domain-specific outcomes. Using the various lenses the students were able to extend the research task to look at technological implications, content specific learning strategies, as well as technological strategies. One of the most difficult principles to incorporate for many educators developing online courses is design principle eight. This requires the

authentic task to be seamlessly integrated with assessment. For the collaborative vignette listed above, a rubric would need to be developed for both the authentic task and for peer collaboration. Although possible, it can be challenging to develop an authentic assessment and evaluation that accurately reflects the student's progress in meeting goals of the task and learning goals of the course. The final two design principles go hand and hand. Design principle nine requires that the authentic task must yield polished products valuable in their own right rather than as preparation for something else (the final submission of the manuscript and the proposal for the conference). Design principle ten outlines the need for the authentic task to allow for competing solutions and diversity of outcomes (presenting in front of a group of your peers at a local conference).

These design principles helped the designer realize the vision of powerful and effective active learning in online classrooms. Additionally, there is a strong understanding of the teaching techniques that build students' abilities and opportunities to create, evaluate, analyze, and apply knowledge (Cardullo et al., 2015). Instructional pedagogy must be enhanced to take advantage of the cognitive, social and teacher presence in online structures. The above scenario represents pedagogical innovation as delineated by the ten design principles (Herrington et al., 2003). These principles capitalize on the development of a rich online learning environment that simulates real world tasks that require collaboration and communication at a distance.

Student Expectations and Preferences

No matter how well one develops an online course, the bottom line is student satisfaction. Looking at student expectations and preferences can help gauge student satisfaction for online course development. There are several experiences that contribute to course satisfaction, clarity, and structure of course, including instructors' expertise in both content and e-learning, instructors' support and the level of support for group work. Additionally several items can negatively influence course satisfaction, including investment of time, difficulty with technology, and organization of course (Paechter & Maier, 2010). In a recent study on student satisfaction, Mupinga, Nora, and Yaw (2012) identified three critical expectations for online student satisfaction: Communication with the professor, instructor feedback, and challenging (i.e., demands of school, work, family, commitment, & balance) in regards to online courses.

These findings reported that students often expect instructors to be available 24/7 in online courses. They expect regular communication so they get the sense that: *a voice is on the other end of the screen.* Students reported that frequent communication puts them at ease. Students expect prompt feedback often within twenty-four hours for confirmation of assignment submission and they expect the assignment to be graded immediately and if that is not possible at least within two business days (Mupinga, Nora, & Yaw, 2012).

When focused on quality and rigor, students expect the online course to be comparable to the face-to-face course (Mupinga, Nora, & Yaw, 2012). This expectation is critical to the development of pedagogically sound courses. Often online teaching management systems are used to provide a place to "put" face-to-face classes' online providing access to material for students. Many instructors merely transport their course material without understanding the missed opportunities for interaction. For example adding hyperlinks does not create productive interaction in an online course. Online course development requires additional skills such as assembly, analysis, and adapting of material for online active learning. It often requires a depth of knowledge in which online content is broken into smaller or shorter

segments of learning. Online material can consist of both multimedia and multimodal. Each has the potential to represent and communicate information by the user or the constructor based on goals or outcomes.

One of the most important aspects to consider when developing online course work is related to academic information. Is the focus on the most recent academic information on the topic? For example, is the course content up to date? Are new, relevant topics or emerging issues included? Are current perspectives explored? The critical element is how students will interact with this material. Making learning objectives transparent is the first step to providing opportunities for self-regulated learning. This can help motivate students to invest the time needed for online course work (Paechter, Maier, & Macher, 2010). When developing assignments for an online course it is beneficial to keep in mind the following elements:

- Identify instructional objectives.
- Decide on what type of activity will suit the objective; consider factors such as grades, time, and complexity of assignment. A webpage creation will take considerable resources, time, and organization whereas a Prezi may not take as much time.
- Evaluate alternatives for the best fit for a platform. Will a blog or Twitter work better for this assignment?
- Evaluate alternatives for the best way to measure student outcomes. Options might include video, audio, presentation, collaborative submission…
- Develop instructions for the activity. Explain with a purpose. How does it align with the objective?

Below are examples of learning objectives for the course outlined in the introduction of an active learning assignment in an online module:

Moderator Discussion Introduction

For the New Literacies Module we will be working on the following objectives:

1. Students will articulate a rationale for using new literacies in content area classrooms.
2. Students will understand the meaning of the term *new literacies* and how those literacies affect content learning.
3. Students will understand that learning how to adapt to continuously changing technologies is more critical than knowing any particular information and communications technology (ICT).

As a graduate student, you will have the responsibility to moderate a weekly online discussions related to unit readings or voices in the field. Voices in the field are a section of the online module in which the instructor brings in perspectives from experts in the field. Below are the groups and the responsibilities for both the moderator and the participant. Moderator duties will rotate through the members of the graduate class. The purpose of moderating discussion is twofold: first to help you formulate and articulate your thoughts and second to consider alternate perspectives or viewpoints. Being able to accomplish both will allow you to engage in thoughtful dialogue and meaningful discussion about new literacies. Detailed responsibilities for both the moderator and the participant are listed below.

Moderator Responsibilities

1. Read given assignments for your moderation & clarify any concerns with the instructor *prior* to the posting of the initial discussion starter. Selections can be made based on personal interest in the articles or relationship(s) to weekly topics.

2. Post an initial "discussion starter" in Canvas no later than 5:00 pm Friday of each week *prior* to the due date for the reading.
3. Monitor *and participate* in the online discussion during the week, and lead the discussion in class, encouraging class members to participate, keeping track of trends in opinions, clarifying misunderstandings, and settling disputes as the week progresses. This means that you will have to function in two roles during the semester.
4. Compose and post a wrap-up/summary posting to the discussion prior to 8:00 pm of the date following the discussion for that reading.
5. The moderator's goal is to facilitate the class in the analysis and discussion of each reading as well as making sure that *dialogue* takes place between the participants rather than just random statements. Remember, there are seldom hard and fast right or wrong answers to problems that are presented.
6. A strong, engaging, discussion will focus on identifying the key aspects of the instructional design process that might inform your decision-making while solving problems or answering questions that are presented. It will also include a synthesis of information from a variety of sources (where appropriate). It might be that a member of the discussion sees similarities in another field of research, or recognizes how the presented problem is similar to one encountered in the work place. The moderator's job is to grow and maintain a rich, prolific garden of ideas and thoughts relating to the case at hand.

Participant Responsibilities

1. Read the announced discussion chapter or PDF article.

2. Respond to the initial discussion starter. Students should respond to the discussion starters and posted messages in such a way that provides evidence of having read the chapter and or article. While the discussions are reasonably informal, attention should still be paid to the posting of readable responses. Lapses in grammar, punctuation, or spelling that negatively impact the readability of a response and will negatively impact the poster's score for that discussion.

3. Critically respond to at least two classmate's posting during the week. This is a *minimum* level of participation. As graduate students, I expect more than simply minimum levels of participation. Lack of participation will be extra noticeable.

The purpose of this assignment is to engage in a *dialogue* (give & take) concerning the concepts and ideas that are presented in each case as well as those that are brought up in class. Each student will be evaluated on not only the number of their contributions to each discussion, but also the quality of their contributions. Students who respond, "yes, I agree," are not contributing to the online dialogue the same way that students who respond, "I agree with Suzie, and I think what she says relates to what Stan says in that..." Students should *strive to contribute something new to the knowledge/understanding of their classmates* when responding to prompts and other postings. New knowledge can be presented through statements, questions, and connections made with situations, experiences, and texts that are unique to each poster. Students should also remember that while healthy and scholarly disagreement and debate is something to be strived for, respect and honor in the formulation of written responses is vital to the development of a healthy academic atmosphere.

Once the due date for a particular chapter has passed, that discussion will be considered closed, and no further postings will be credited to students. However, students may refer to contributions made in weeks prior when developing their responses, or responding to their classmates' responses during later weeks.

Evaluation
Moderation Duties 50 points

Your moderation will be evaluated according to the following criteria:

1. Did the moderator post the initial start and final wrap-up of the discussion promptly?
2. Did the moderator facilitate rather than dominate the conversation?
3. Did the moderator encourage all members of the class to participate?
4. Did the moderator participate as a member of the online dialogue? See below for participation criteria.
5. Did the moderator keep the discussion "on track" in a reasonable fashion?
6. Did the moderator adequately prepare the class for the in-class discussion?
7. Did the moderator respect the opinions of all members of the class?
Discussion Participation- 20 points

Your weekly discussion participation will be evaluated according to the following criteria:

1. Did the participant fully participate in the discussion online?
2. Was the participation varied in time, length, depth, and other aspects of a dialogue as appropriate?
3. Did the participant participate in such a way as to encourage others also to participate?

4. Did the participant use respectful language and attitude when posting?
5. Did the participant help create a branching rather than a linear conversation through the inclusion of a variety of information?
6. Did the participant present ideas that are "outside the box" as appropriate (while staying "on track" with the topic of the online conversation)?

When developing assignments for an online course, identification of instructional objectives are needed for a clear alignment and purpose setting for students. The above active learning assignment positions learning objectives within the framework of new literacies. Student objectives were to articulate a rationale for new literacies while developing a deeper understanding of the effect of continuously changing technologies and content. The purpose of this assignment was to engage in a *dialogue* (give & take) concerning the concepts and ideas presented. Therefore, a discussion posting was a good fit for the assignment. A rubric with clear definers was used to evaluate student performances as well as student outcomes.

Effective Practices for Undergraduate Education

In 1987, Chickering and Gamson recommended seven principles for good practice in undergraduate education. Those seven principles are extremely important for online course development as well, nearly thirty years later. Best practice encourages interaction between students. Creating assignments as modeled in the moderator discussion above helps to create dialogue and new perspectives as students develop a visual presence in an online environment. The student is offering personalized feedback and communication. The shift has moved from the teacher to the student in regards to Chickering and Gamson's first principle: good practice encourages contact between students and faculty. Their second principle focuses on good practice, which develops reciprocity and cooperation among students. Activities that limit lecture and encourage more interaction between students, such as the moderator discussion posting, helps to facilitate reciprocity and collaboration among peers.

The third principle by Chickering and Gamson (1987) focuses on the ideal that good practice encourages active learning. Providing real world opportunities can help foster deeper authentic discussions. Providing multiple opportunities for students to develop a voice and a presence in an online course equates to active learning and opportunities for students to develop collaboration and communication skills, which are skills needed to join the global workforce. Principles four through seven focus on the development of pedagogy and are still applicable today. Principle four focuses on feedback and communication: Good practice gives prompt feedback. Feedback should be constructive, concrete feedback that focuses on both the positive and negative aspects of the submission. Feedback should also be completed within a quick time frame, often within twenty-four to forty-eight hours of submission. Principle five states that good practice emphasizes time on task, and is still relevant and extremely important in an online course. Set dates, develop a schedule for weekly readings, and clearly articulate policies for missed work. These details can be the difference between a well-developed course and a course that structured poorly. Clarifying expectations at the beginning of the semester, providing consequences, and providing learning opportunities to demonstrate growth round out principle number six: Good practice communicates high expectations. Principle number seven: Good practice respects diverse talents and ways of learning. Providing diversified learning opportunities will demonstrate that you value and respect differences and that student voice is important.

CONCLUSION

An instructional design that emphasizes knowledge construction, the development of critical thinking (Bloom's Taxonomy) and the thoughtful, purposeful integration of technology (SAMR model) should allow students to assume responsibility of their own learning. Knowledge construction is not a static function. Online threaded discussion boards merely function as a presentation and communication tool not as a cognitive and scaffold-learning tool (Tu, 2005). The need for tools to facilitate substantive organic communication and collaboration amongst past, present, and future students was discussed earlier in this chapter. Knowledge must be shared and disseminated throughout learning communities albeit online or face-to-face. Members of those learning communities must have opportunities to contribute to the common knowledge (Redefinition stage). Lastly, members of a knowledge construction community must be able to reconstruct the existing knowledge (Redefinition stage) (Tu, Sujo-Montes, Yen, Chan, & Blocher, 2012). These three processes ensure that knowledge acquisition is dynamic and learning is recursive-developing skills for critical thinking. The fluidity of facilitative substantive organic communication and collaboration amongst past, present, and future students brings the level of technology into the realm of redefinition/ creation. When developing online course material, it is important to think about the hierarchy of skills and knowledge aligned with student expectations and preferences.

How can quality be assured in online course development? The questions we should be asking is how can educators develop quality online courses and how do we measure the quality of these courses. The ultimate question is not whether online learning is as good as a face-to-face, but rather how can technology coupled with new learning centered pedagogies lead to improved student outcomes (Hitt & Hartan, 2002).

REFERENCES

Arbaugh, F., Erbel-Eisenmann, B., Ramirez, N., Kranendonk, H., Knuth, E., & Quander, J. R. (2010). *Linking research and practice: Practitioner community priorities for research in mathematics education.* Reston, VA: Report for the National Council of Teachers of Mathematics, Research Agenda Conference.

Ball, D. L., & Stacey, K. (2005). Teaching strategies for developing judicious technology use. In W. J. Masalski & P. C. Elliott (Eds.), *Technology-supported mathematics learning environments* (pp. 3–15). Reston, VA: NCTM.

Bloom, B. S., & Krathwohl, D. R. (1956). Taxonomy of educational objectives: The classification of educational goals by a committee of college and university examiners (H. I. C. Domain, Ed.). Academic Press.

Bocchi, J., Eastman, J. K., & Swift, C. O. (2004). Retaining the online learner: Profile of students in an online MBA program and implications for teaching them. *Journal of Education for Business*, 79(4), 245–253. doi:10.3200/JOEB.79.4.245-253

Cardullo, V., Wilson, N. S., & Zygouris-Coe, V. (2015). Enhanced Student Engagement through Active Learning and Emerging Technologies. In J. Keengwe (Ed.), *Handbook of Research on Educational Technology Integration and Active Learning. Edited by: Sagini Keengwe, Ph.D* (pp. 1–18). University of North Dakota.

Cardullo, V., Zygouris-Coe, V., & Wilson, N. S. (2014). The benefits and Challenges of Mobile Learning and Ubiquitous Technologies. In J. Keengwe (Ed.), Promoting Active Learning through the Integration of Mobile and Ubiquitous Technologies (pp. 185–196). Academic Press.

Cardullo, V. M. (2013). Cyber-place learning in an online teacher preparation program: Engaging learning opportunities through collaborations and facilitation of learning. In R. Hartshorne, T. Heafner, & T. Petty (Eds.), *Teacher education programs and online learning tools: Innovations in teacher prepration* (pp. 181–197). Hershey, PA: Information Science Reference. doi:10.4018/978-1-4666-1906-7.ch010

Chickering, A., & Gamson, Z. (1987). Seven principles of good practice in undergraduate education. *AAHE Bulletin, 39*, 3–7.

Christiansen, J., & Anderson, T. (2004). Feasibility of course development based on learning objects. *International Journal of Instructional Technology and Distance Learning, 1*(3).

Cohen, J., & Hollenbrands, K. F. (2011). Technology tools to support mathematics teaching. In T. P. Dick & K. F. Hollenbrands (Eds.), *Focus in high school mathematics: Technology to support reasoning and sense making* (pp. 105–122). Reston, VA: NCTM.

Cross, P. (1987). Teaching for learning. *AAHE Bulletin, 39*(8), 3–7.

Educause. (2015). *Thoughts on a "good" cloud-based social network platforms that could facilitate substantive organic communication and collaboration amongst past, present, and future students.* Retrieved from http://www.educause.edu/groups/

Fey, J. T., Hollenbeck, R. W., & Wray, J. A. (2010). Technology and the teaching of mathematics. In B. Reys, R. Reys, & R. Rubenstein (Eds.), *Curriculum: Issues, trends, and future directions (72nd Yearbook)*. Reston, VA: NCTM.

Harasim, L., Hiltz, S. R., Teles, L., & Turoff, M. (1995). *Learning Networks: A Field Guide to Teaching & Learning Online*. Cambridge, MA: MIT Press.

Herrington, J., Oliver, R., & Reeves, T. C. (2003). Patterns of engagement in authentic online learning environments. *Australasian Journal of Educational Technology, 19*(1), 59–71.

Hitt, J. C., & Hartman, J. L. (2002). *Distributed learning: New challenges and opportunities for institutional leadership (No. 3)*. American Council on Education.

Israel, M., & Lang, H. (2013). Redefining technology in libraries and schools. *Teacher Librarian*, 16–18.

Mead, G. H. (1934). *Mind, self and society*. Chicago: U. of Chicago Press.

Mupinga, D. M., Nora, R. T., & Yaw, D. C. (2006). The learning styles, expectations, and needs of online students. *College Teaching, 54*(1), 185–189. doi:10.3200/CTCH.54.1.185-189

Oblinger, D. G., & Hawkins, B. L. (2006). The myth about online course development:" A faculty member can individually develop and deliver an effective online course. *EDUCAUSE Review, 41*(1), 14–15.

Paechter, M., & Maier, B. (2010). Online or face-to-face? Students' experiences and preferences in e-learning. *The Internet and Higher Education, 13*(4), 292–297. doi:10.1016/j.iheduc.2010.09.004

Palloff, R. M., & Pratt, K. (1999). *Building learning communities in cyberspace* (Vol. 99). San Francisco: Jossey-Bass.

Puentedura, R. (2006). *Transformation, technology, and education*. Presentation given August 18, 2006 as part of the Strengthening Your District Through Technology Workshops. Retrieved from http://hippasus.com/resources/tte/part1.html

Puentedura, R. (2012). *SAMR: Guiding development.* Retrieved from http://www.hippasus.com/rrpweblog/archives/2012/01/19/SAMR_Guiding-Development.pdf

Rourke, L., Anderson, T., Garrison, D. R., & Archer, W. (2007). Assessing social presence in asynchronous text-based computer conferencing. *International Journal of E-Learning & Distance Education, 14*(2), 50–71.

Shea, P., Li, C. S., & Pickett, A. (2006). A study of teaching presence and student sense of learning community in fully online and web-enhanced college courses. *The Internet and Higher Education, 9*(3), 175–190. doi:10.1016/j.iheduc.2006.06.005

Shulman, L. S. (1987). Knowledge and teaching: Foundations of the new reform. *Harvard Educational Review, 57*(1), 1–23. doi:10.17763/haer.57.1.j463w79r56455411

Theisen, T. (2013). New spaces new realities: Expanding learning any time, any place. *Foreign Language Annals, 46*(4), 523–524. doi:10.1111/flan.12055

Tu, C. H., Sujo-Montes, L., Yen, C. J., Chan, J. Y., & Blocher, M. (2012). The integration of personal learning environments & open network learning environments. *TechTrends, 56*(3), 13–19. doi:10.1007/s11528-012-0571-7

Wilson, N., Zygouris-Coe, V., Cardullo, V., & Fong, J. (2013). Pedagogical frameworks of e-reader technologies in education. In S. Keengwe (Ed.), *Pedagogical Applications and Social Effects of Mobile Technology Integration* (pp. 1–24). doi:10.4018/978-1-4666-2985-1.ch001

ADDITIONAL READING

Aragon, S. R. (2003). Creating social presence in online environments. *New Directions for Adult and Continuing Education, 2003*(100), 57–68. doi:10.1002/ace.119

Azevedo, R. (2005). Using hypermedia as a metacognitive tool for enhancing student learning? The role of self-regulated learning. *Educational Psychologist, 40*(4), 199–209. doi:10.1207/s15326985ep4004_2

Beetham, H., & Sharpe, R. (Eds.). (2013). *Rethinking pedagogy for a digital age: Designing for 21st century learning.* New York, NY: Routledge.

Boettcher, J. V. 2003. The dangers and pitfalls of communicating with students or what not to do when communicating with students on the Internet, http://www.designingforlearning.info/services/writing/comm.htm

Bonwell, C. C., & Eison, J. A. (1991). ASHE ERIC Higher Education Report: Vol. 1. *Active learning: Creating excitement in the classroom.* Washington, DC: George Washington University.

Deed, C., & Edwards, A. (2011). Unrestricted student blogging: Implications for active learning in a virtual text-based environment. *Active Learning in Higher Education, 12*(1), 11–21. doi:10.1177/1469787410387725

DuFour, R. (2004). What is a "professional learning community"? *Educational Leadership, 61*(8), 6–11.

Ertmer, P. A., Ottenbreit-Leftwich, A. T., Sadik, O., Sendurur, E., & Sendurur, P. (2012). Teacher beliefs and technology integration practices: A critical relationship. *Computers & Education, 59*(2), 423–435. doi:10.1016/j.compedu.2012.02.001

Howland, J. L., & Moore, J. L. (2002). Student perceptions as distance learners in Internet-based courses. *Distance Education, 23*(2), 83–195. doi:10.1080/0158791022000009196

Jacobson, M. J., & Azevedo, R. (2008). Advances in scaffolding learning with hypertext and hypermedia: Theoretical, empirical, and design issues. *Educational Technology Research and Development, 56*(1), 1–3. doi:10.1007/s11423-007-9066-1

Laurillard, D. (2013). *Teaching as a design science: Building pedagogical patterns for learning and technology*. New York, NY: Routledge.

Leu, D. J. Jr. (2000). Literacy and technology: Deictic consequences for literacy education in an information age. In M. L. Kamil, P. Mosenthal, P. D. Pearson, & R. Barr (Eds.), *Handbook of Reading Research* (Vol. III, pp. 743–770). Mahwah, NJ: Erlbaum.

Liu, G. Z., & Hwang, G. J. (2010). A key step to understanding paradigm shifts in e-learning: Towards context-aware ubiquitous learning. *British Journal of Educational Technology*, *41*(2), E1–E9. doi:10.1111/j.1467-8535.2009.00976.x

Looi, C. K., Seow, P., Zhang, B., So, H. J., Chen, W., & Wong, L. H. (2010). Leveraging mobile technology for sustainable seamless learning: A research agenda. *British Journal of Educational Technology*, *41*(2), 154–169. doi:10.1111/j.1467-8535.2008.00912.x

Lyon, G. E. (1999). *Where I'm From: Where Poems Come from*. Spring, TX: Absey.

Moran, C., & Young, C. A. (2014). Active learning in the flipped English language arts classroom. *Promoting Active Learning Through the Flipped Classroom Model*, 163.

Mykota, D., & Duncan, R. (2007). Learner characteristics as predictors of online social presence. *Canadian Journal of Education*, *30*(1), 157–170. doi:10.2307/20466630

National Council of Teachers of Mathematice. (2014). *Principles to actions: Ensuring mathematical success for all*. Reston, VA: Author.

Palmer, P. J. (2010). *The courage to teach: Exploring the inner landscape of a teacher's life*. John Wiley & Sons.

Park, E. L., & Choi, B. K. (2014). Transformation of classroom spaces: Traditional versus active learning classroom in colleges. *Higher Education*, 1–23.

Powell, N. W., Cleveland, R., Thompson, S., & Forde, T. (2012). Using multi-instructional teaching and technology-supported active learning strategies to enhance student engagement. *Journal of Technological Integration in the Classroom*, *4*(2), 41–50.

Settles, B. (2010). Active learning literature survey. University of Wisconsin, Madison, 52, 55-66.

Sharples, M. (2000). The design of personal mobile technologies for lifelong learning. *Computers & Education*, *34*(3-4), 177–193. doi:10.1016/S0360-1315(99)00044-5

Sharples, M. (2005). *Re-thinking learning for the mobile age*. Retrieved from: http://www.noe-kaleidoscope.org/pub/lastnews/last-0-read159-display

Springer, L., Stanne, M. E., & Donovan, S. S. (1999). Effects of small-group learning on undergraduates in science, mathematics, engineering, and technology: A meta-analysis. *Review of Educational Research*, *69*(1), 21–51. doi:10.3102/00346543069001021

Swan, K. (2002). Building learning communities in online courses: The importance of interaction. *Education Communication and Information*, *2*(1), 23–49. doi:10.1080/1463631022000005016

Swan, K. (2003). Learning effectiveness online: What the research tells us. *Elements of Quality Online Education. Practice and Direction*, *4*, 13–47.

Swan, K., & Shea, P. (2005). The development of virtual learning communities. *Learning together online: Research on asynchronous learning networks*, 239-260.

U.S. Department of Education. Office of Planning, Evaluation, and Policy Development, Evaluation of Evidence-Based Practices in Online Learning: A Meta-Analysis and Review of Online Learning Studies, Washington, D.C., 2009.

Van Horne, S., Murniati, C., Gaffney, J. D., & Jesse, M. (2012). Promoting active learning in technology-infused TILE classrooms at the University of Iowa. *Journal of Learning Spaces, 1*(2).

Van Oostveen, R., Muirhead, W., & Goodman, W. M. (2011). Tablet PCs and reconceptualizing learning with technology: A case study in higher education. *Interactive Technology and Smart Education, 8*(2), 78–93. doi:10.1108/17415651111141803

Zhao, C. & Kuh, G. D. (2004). Adding value: Learning communities and student engagement. *Research in Higher Education, 45*(2), 115.138.

KEY TERMS AND DEFINITIONS

Active Learning: Defined as any instructional method that engages students in the learning process.

Bloom's Taxonomy: A tool used for classification of different levels of teaching and learning goals.

Emerging Technologies: Tools, concepts and advancements utilized in diverse educational settings to serve a variety of education related purposes.

Instructional Modules: An instructional module is a self-contained unit that focuses on a specific learning goal or instructional focus. It usually contains documents, multi-media experiences, discussion boards, and information for the student and groups to use.

Pedagogical Content Knowledge: The interaction between the teaching process and content knowledge.

SAMR Model: A model design used to help teachers align technology and learning.

Social Network Platforms: Technology that provides the ability to develop and manage social media sources, services, and resources.

Social Presence: The degree of interaction and visibility between oneself and others in a social network.

Chapter 19
Deepening Understanding of Multicultural Online Education:
Teaching Presence for English Language Learners

Alex Kumi-Yeboah
University at Albany (SUNY), USA

Guangji Yuan
University at Albany (SUNY), USA

Patriann Smith
University of Illinois at Urbana Champaign, USA

Christina Nash
University at Albany (SUNY), USA

ABSTRACT

In the 21st century, online education provides an alternative instructional medium for teachers and students in United States educational systems and the world at large. Technology transforms how, when, and where students can learn, as well as the trends and use of instructional tools by students and teachers in the teaching-learning process. Online learning has developed during the past two decades to support traditional face-to-face classroom instruction and provides an opportunity for students to "interact with faculty and peers about substantive matters" (National Survey of Student Engagement, 2007, p. 7). The increase in minority students within U.S. schools has created a rise in socio-cultural, personal histories, educational, religious, and language/linguistic differences within the virtual classroom, requiring online instructors who teach in these contexts to be prepared to meet students' diverse needs. Despite the increase in online instruction, many questions remain unanswered with regards to how one group of minorities, particularly, English learners, adjust to instructional processes and teacher presence in an online learning environment. This chapter addresses the role of teacher presence in multicultural and online education, potential challenges of online learning for English learners, and teacher presence in multicultural online education.

DOI: 10.4018/978-1-4666-9582-5.ch019

INTRODUCTION

The population of minority students, and particularly, students classified as English language learners (ELLs) or English learners (ELs) has grown steadily in the past three decades. About 8.7 million United States children have at least one-foreign-born parent, a figure which has doubled since 1990. A recent survey of over 50 United States online learning program directors who belong to a consortium of colleges and universities that offer fully online university degree programs responded to a survey in October 2002 in which they projected that the proportion of their students enrolled in totally online courses would increase from 20.2% to 36.6% in the next few years, but that those enrolled in "blended" courses would increase at an even faster rate, from 7.6% to 21.1% in the near future. In addition, the percentage of public school students who are ELLs in the U.S. has increased. For example, the percentage of ELLs increased from 8.7% in 2003 to 9.1% in 2011/2012. In contrast, during the latter part of this period, between 2009/2010 and 2011/2012, the overall percentage of ELLs remained about the same (National Center for Education Statistics, 2014). Reports show that foreign students enrolled in institutions of higher education in the United Stated increased from 547,873 in 2001 to 690,923 in 2009. This growing ELL population has drawn the attention of educators to offer suitable instructional strategies that meet ELLs' learning needs. The large number of ELLs in U.S. schools requires urgency in education reform if U.S. schools are to provide equitable learning opportunities and environments. The growth of diversity among students' population requires educators/institutions to seek and choose appropriate teaching methods and learning content in school, and to solve the cultural differences that exist between teachers and students who speak English as a second language (Taliaferro, 2011). During the past two decades, online instructors have attempted to teach to meet the needs of students in an increasingly diverse

and inequitable society and interconnected world (Merryfield, 2001), but the questions of how mainstream classroom teachers can teach effectively in a multicultural learning environment continue to remain unaddressed. Despite long existing calls for mainstream teachers to change their beliefs, values, and attitudes toward English as a second language students (Clair, 1995), the problem persists even in the wake of new modes of teaching and learning in online education.

If language pedagogy and multiculturalism are to be leveraged successfully in the teacher education curriculum, and specifically, in educational technology courses, teachers and educators in all content areas must begin to demonstrate the rigor and systematic reflective teaching that allows for re-examination of their own beliefs and practices (Major & Brock, 2003). Several researchers such as Bandura (1982), Gay (2000), and Nieto (2000) contend that the cross-cultural perceptions, beliefs and behaviors of classroom teachers can negatively affect the academic and social development of their students. Research indicates further that these beliefs and behaviors are instilled early in one's personal life (Richardson, 1996).

Technology educators responsible for inculcating the ideals of multicultural education can foster the kind of dedication necessary for facilitating educational experiences in which all students have equitable opportunities in a digital classroom. In this context, 'digital equity' is taken to mean ensuring that every student, regardless of socioeconomic status, language, race, geography, physical restrictions, cultural background, gender, or other attribute historically associated with inequities, has equitable access to advanced technologies, communication and information resources. Sufficient evidence is available (e.g., Beckett et al., 2003; Brown, 2004a; Damarin, 1998; Merryfield, 2001; Orly, 2007; Roblyer, et al., 1996; Sleeter & Tettagah, 2002; Wassell & Crouch, 2008) to reflect the ways in which technology is associated with multicultural education. Much of this literature indicates that professionals consists primarily of monolingual, middle-class European American females who may lack the requisite background knowledge, skills, and dispositions to teach effectively children from racially, ethnically, and linguistically diverse backgrounds in traditional classrooms (Cummins, 1994; Gay, 2010; Howard, 1999; Nieto, 1999), and by extension, in online instructional mediums.

So far, little research has been conducted around deepening understanding of multicultural online education for ELLs by considering teaching presence. This chapter will address minority students' roles in online learning participation, collaborative responsibilities, conflicts/challenges, multicultural understandings in online education, and the benefits of creating awareness among teachers and students, paying specific attention to the needs of ELLs in online education. The need for further research will be discussed.

LITERATURE REVIEW

Multicultural Education and Online Learning

The rapidly changing demographic landscape of the American population and growing advances in computer technologies require schools to re-conceptualize their instructional strategy and teaching content in preparation for online multicultural education. Multicultural education is defined as a field of study and an emerging discipline whose major goal is to create equal educational opportunities for students of different genders, diverse racial, ethnic, social-class, and cultural groups to achieve academically in school (Banks & Banks, 2009; Klein, 1985). Multicultural education is a critical framework that informs our understanding of diversity, and our belief that teacher educators need to prepare their students to become culturally responsive. While multicultural education has developed into various conceptual camps, we align ourselves most closely to multicultural education

as defined by Sleeter (1996) who describes it as a political movement that represented the larger sociopolitical struggle of minorities who wanted to receive equal "power and economic resources" (p. 137), and Nieto and Bode (2012) who state that it "challenges and rejects racism and other forms of discrimination in schools and society and accepts pluralism...that students, their communities, and their staff reflect" (p. 42). The fact that the majority of the teaching field continues to be comprised of European American pre-service and in-service teachers makes it more of an imperative for teacher educators to address how race, social class, and gender continue to provide unequal education to culturally and linguistically diverse students in schools, while advancing the interests of other groups that have more access to wealth and power (Sleeter, 1996). Nieto (2000) also argues that one critical aspect of multicultural education is its dedication to social justice for all students so they are receiving an equitable education. Multicultural education (a) recognizes the need to prepare students for an interdependent world and the important role schools can play in developing the requisite attitudes and values for a democratic society, (b) values cultural differences and affirms pluralism, (c) challenges all types of discrimination in schools and society by promoting social justice, (d) is a process that affects all aspects of a school's organization and policy so all students may achieve at the highest levels, (e) prepares students to work actively toward creating structural equality in organizations and institutions, and (f) encourages teachers and students to critically analyze relationships of power and oppression in their communities, society, and the world (NAME, 2003). The community of inquiry framework stipulates that social presence, teaching presence, and cognitive presence. Social presence relates to the idea that learners are free to express themselves as "real people" (p. 115) in an online community. Teaching presence relates to the idea that the instructor is thoughtful about course design, instructional strategies, and facilitating discussions that lead to "educationally worthwhile learning outcomes" (p. 116). Finally, cognitive presence refers to the inquiry process learners experience in an online course "[in] which learners are able to construct and confirm meaning through sustained reflection and discourse in a critical community of inquiry" (p. 115). The learner will explore and exchange new ideas that emanate with other learners (Garrison, 2007).

According to Gorski (2005), inequitable distribution of access to technology persists, despite an increase in the number of computers in schools. The National Center for Education Statistics (2006, 2014) contends that schools with the lowest level of minority enrollments had fewer students per computer than did schools with higher minority enrollments (NCES, 2006). Considering the inception and growth of online learning in the 21st century and the proliferation of technological innovations, and especially information and communication technologies, there is a rapidly increasing trend for universities to use computers in everyday teaching and learning. Since computing technology is mature enough to achieve distance communication for common daily uses, this innovation has been adopted in many educational circles to offer online courses in U.S. higher education (Lee, 2014; Licona & Gurung, 201). Using technology to examine issues of multiculturalism and diversity depicted within a framework designed by postcolonial theory and reflective inquiry, Merryfield (2001) asserts that online pedagogy can provide educators with a guide on how to approach curriculum development with a multicultural perspective. Merryfield (2001) used the World Wide Web to transform learning and teaching in an asynchronous threaded discussion, recognizing that the teachers felt more comfortable engaging in cross-cultural online discourse. The teachers in the multicultural course felt that technology acted as a barrier that kept them from "knowing one another or having real relationships" (p. 295).

Online Education or distance learning has been defined as "a planned teaching or learning experience that uses a wide spectrum of technologies to reach learners at a distance; it is designed to encourage learner interaction and certification of learning (Greenberg, 1998; Jung, Kudo & Choi et al., 2012). To explore the connection between classroom community and hybrid learning, Rovai (2002b) developed the Classroom Community Scale (CCS). Essential to a discussion about classroom community research in educational technology is an understanding of the CCS, because, since the development of this scale, a majority of the research conducted in hybrid learning has used it as a major data collection instrument. Rovai (2002) developed the CCS to measure student perceptions about their connectedness to other students in a classroom environment. Rovai (2002) defined classroom community as a feeling that members have of belonging, a feeling that members matter to one another and to the group, that they have duties and obligations to each other and to the school, and that they possess shared expectations that their educational needs will be met through their commitment to shared learning goals (p. 322). Building on this definition, the author suggests there are four components that give students a sense of connectedness to a classroom community: 1) spirit, 2) trust, 3) interaction, and 4) commonality of expectations and goals (Rovai, 2002b, p. 4). This collective provides students with the feeling of being connected to others in a classroom environment.

Online Education

According to Allen and Seaman (2010), online learning can be categorized based on content delivery. Online courses are those where majority or all of the content is delivered online. It is defined as at least 80 percent of seat time being replaced by online activities. Blended/hybrid courses are those that combine both online and face-to-face delivery methods. Thirty to 79 percent of the content is delivered online. Web-facilitated courses are those that use web-based technology to facilitate what is already being delivered in a face-to-face course (one to 29 percent of the content is delivered online). With the sudden increase in online learning, it is imperative to develop common language and similar definitions to collect accurate data.

Online Education, when functioning as a means of increasing accessibility to higher education (Hamdan, et al., 2014), provides numerous benefits such as no time zones, no location limitation, asynchronous lecturing methods enabling students to access online materials anytime and anywhere, and synchronous online learning that allows real-time interaction between students and instructors (Ally, 2004). Many students choose online education because it is flexible, accessible, convenient, cost-saving (low cost for commuting, relatively low cost for the tuition fee) and because course materials are easily updated and revised (Hopey & Ginsburg, 1996; Kilian, 1997; Owston, 1997). Due to these benefits, online learning is one of the fastest growing segments of community college offerings (Brown, 2013). The literature on online learning suggests that online courses require students to assume greater responsibility for their learning; thus, a successful online student may need high levels of self-regulation, self-discipline, and a related suite of metacognitive skills, which often fall under the broad umbrella of self-directed learning (Azevedo, Cromley, & Seibert, 2004; Corbeil, 2003; Guglielmino & Guglielmino, 2002; Hannafin & Land, 1997; Kearsley, 2002; Williams, 1996; Yen & Liu, 2009). As evident through these studies, much of the literature describes the features and demands of online learning, but fail to provide a special analysis of ELLs in an online learning multicultural environment, thus paying little attention to satisfaction levels and learning outcomes of ELLs.

Teacher Presence in Online Education

Teaching presence has been defined in terms of design, facilitation and direct instruction (Akyol & Garrison, 2014). According to Ware (2004), teaching presence in online learning involves organization, facilitating discourse, and direct instruction. Teaching presence is the process whereby online instructors actively engage students in critical conversation in online course management systems such as discussion board, chats, and/or drop box with the aim of extending their learning and reflection about important lecture topic (Grant & Lee, 2014; Rocco, 2010). Instructors also "offer guidance to students so they understand how to reflect meaningfully and critically within an online discussion form" (Grant & Lee, 2014). Ware (2004) found that "students who perceived higher levels of teaching presence also perceived higher levels of cognitive presence, learning and satisfaction" (p. 14), thus, associating a high quality of teaching presence in online learning with a guarantee for students' online learning outcomes. Another feature of teacher presence is that teachers' facilitation in online learning is a continuous process that involves replying to students' posts and asking challenging questions and encouraging students to clarify their understanding and make improvements because the instructor has "to diagnose misconceptions, to provide probing questions, comments, and additional information in an effort to ensure continuing development, and to model the critical thinking process" (Pawan, 2003. p. 10).

According to Lowes (2005), teacher instructional practices have transformed learning concerning how to teach online in developing new skills and pedagogical strategies using technology. The research study examined how online teachers serve as reform agents in the schools where they teach and found that online teaching improves practices in both virtual and face-to-face settings and that interaction between teachers and students was a major phenomenon in online learning. Teachers in the study reported that their interactions with students, parents, and colleagues more often were focused on teaching and learning in online courses than in traditional settings. Ferneding (2004) contends that teachers feel the inevitability of using technology and addresses the common misconception of technology as a neutral tool. Ferneding further postulates that administrators, teachers, parents, and students view technology as inevitable and as a tool with which students need as much experience and exposure as possible in order to prepare them for the future. For example, continued debates persist about the effectiveness of online instruction. Instructors who teach in higher education contexts believe that design factors (Lee, 2014, Nuangchalerm, Prachagool & Sriputta, 2011) play key roles in successful implementation of online learning.

Research indicates that students' satisfaction is closely related to clear guidelines on assignments, rubrics, and constructive feedback. In addition, students' satisfaction level is related to instructors' knowledge of materials (Lee, 2014). Zhu (2012) suggests that students' satisfaction level should be taken into consideration in designing online courses and building online environments. A high level of satisfaction is therefore thought to be related to the careful instructional design is also closely related to student's study outcomes. Other studies have shown that when teachers change from face-to-face to online interaction, some paradoxes emerge. For instance, teachers in an online environment were more open, frank, expansive, curious, and even confessional in their willingness to share and discuss "prickly" issues such as White privilege, racism, educational, inequities, injustice, and xenophobia than face-to-face teachers have been in the past. What's more, the interaction patterns online were more equitable and cross-cultural than those in the campus version (Merryfield, 2001). Some have

found that instructors may inadvertently enhance students' perception about the transactional presence of the lecturer in online settings such that when the lecturer responds in time to students' email or queries, students can increase their intrinsic motivation to learn (Belaja, Sai, & Lin, 2012). When teaching ELLs online, Clair (1995) foresees greater complexity, citing challenges in social, political and pedagogical assumptions that are context specific and dilemma ridden (Clair, 1995). As the ELL population continues to grow, considering ELLs in online course design will be necessary to fulfill the educational mission and reflect the spirit of equality.

Instructional providers must become more knowledgeable about the cultural differences existing among the learners they serve. With an unpredictable learner population in most settings, perhaps especially in open and distance learning settings, instructional providers can no longer make overarching judgments about the demographics of their learners before having the opportunity to interact with them (Lea & Goodfellow, 2003). Understanding the role of the advantages and disadvantages of online education in multicultural contexts for ELLs can enable educators to give due considerations to online instructional design and evaluation. An examination of online multicultural instruction and teaching strategies is needed for instructional designers to optimize their efforts to take care of ELLs and to become more involved in advocating for students from diverse backgrounds. Online instruction, in most cases, is a student-oriented and knowledge-centered learning process; the teacher's role has become a facilitator (Ellis, 2004). As such, this requires an instructor to recognize potential learning situations for ELLs and continuously create a free, safe, equal learning environment. Since learning outcomes are closely related to the collaborative responsibility of sharing and contributing online, how ELLs make unique contributions in this multicultural space, and the difficulties they face in a multicultural online learning setting requires serious discussion. The research that investigates teaching presence for ELLs in multicultural online education, though limited, provides useful information by way of improving online instructive quality. We now attend to the advantages of ELLs in online multicultural environments.

Advantages of Online Learning for English Language Learners

Online education has the potential to boost the academic progression and provide the best alternative instructional method for English language learners in the U.S. educational system. According to Lee (2012), online learning can increase ELLs' cultural understanding and diminish cultural gaps. Online learning makes it possible for ELLs students to communicate with both native students and students from other countries. Thus, online interaction can improve students' understanding of cultural differences and can provide the opportunity to contribute their diverse perspectives to the classroom conversation. Online learning has the potential to provide a platform upon which students can cross cultural boundaries and enter a new culture of learning, foster great appreciation for students of diverse backgrounds, offers a more comprehensive view of the world in which learners live and operate, and allows for a worldwide view, which is impossible to obtain in the traditional classroom settings. Online integrated discussion enables students to recognize diversity of perspectives among learners.

Online education is increasingly acknowledged by educators as encouraging students to take greater responsibility for their own learning. It provides students with greater control over the teaching-learning process, which includes setting goals, finding resources, selecting appropriate methods for learning, the ability to post feedback and assignments online, and to discuss points of interest from readings (Brookfield, 1995; Hamdan, 2014). Considering the above challenges faced by ELLs in the traditional classroom, online learning

can improve students' autonomous learning skills (Isiguzel, 2014) as well as enhance their learning motivation (Lee, 2012). Online asynchronous discussion offer many potentials for ELLs virtual environment, it is a reliable medium of exchange that promote a source of critical thinking and reflection through group discussions (Duffy, Dueber, & Hawley, 1998; Wells, 1999; Yang, 2008). The asynchronous online multicultural discussion serves as a constructive means to collaborate and engage students not only because "higher order thinking can and does occur" (Meyer, 2003, p. 5), but because it also motivates students "to take ownership of the discussion" (Chen, Wang, & Hung, 2009, p. 158). An asynchronous online multicultural discussion allows ELLs students to understand concepts in depth of content and equity of participation (Merryfield, 2001). Such discussions can provide multiple opportunities for critical emotional reflexivity via establishment of conversations on the learners' own feelings and experiences about difficult issues such as cultural diversity and discrimination that may not be possible in face-to-face environments (Zembylas, 2008).

Through online communication with classmates and instructors, ELLs not only improve their communication skills but also expand their understanding of the various issues under discussion. The Internet lends an attractive learning environment for English language learners to the typical traditional classroom environment by providing opportunities for engagement, and consequently, motivation and opportunities for ELLs to gather resources that enable them to do their class work with less difficulty (Sa'd, 2014), make the learning process visible; by recording every detail of students' thoughts and tracing the trajectory of their study patterns, online learning environments can demonstrate student learning in a very clear way. Through this avenue, ELLs have been known to obtain better results in writing and reading as compared to their traditional learner counterparts who performed better in speaking and sentence structure (Soleimani, Sarkhosh, & Gahhari, 2012). This may be attributed to students' writing; when students write posts, they have enough time to organize their thoughts, which enables them to express themselves more completely and clearly. Gradually their writing communication improves their writing skills and thinking abilities and eventually, the online setting sharpens students' thinking skills and broadens their horizons. According to Brookfield and Preskill (2005), "The privacy, relative isolation, and reflective space associated with asynchronous online learning enhance the development of genuinely individualistic, critical thought" (p. 232). Similarly, Tallent-Runnels et al. (2006) assert that online environments "may offer a unique social advantage as compared to the traditional classroom" (p. 97) including anonymity in the networked environment (Sullivan, 2002).

The "untiring, non-judgmental nature of the computer makes it an ideal tool to help second language learners feel sufficiently secure to make and correct their own errors without embarrassment or anxiety" (Ganesh & Middleton, 2006, p. 46). Also, since some English learners often fail to understand information as deeply as 'native' students, and may not read as quickly as do native English students, online learning may cause the study to seem more conducive to their needs since they are able to use their own pace, choose the times that they learn and contribute more readily to their learning outcomes.

Challenges of Online Learning for English Language Learners

Though online learning is known to facilitate effective instructional delivery and learning for students, and particularly ELLs, it is accompanied by certain deficits that tend to impede the teaching-learning process. According to Cole, Shelley and Swartz (2014) "lack of interaction" is the most cited reason for dissatisfaction in online learning. For example, when the learning environment has low frequency interaction, it decreases the motivation of students in learning participation. Another challenge for ELLs arises when an online discussion is designed as "post your thoughts in no less than two paragraphs according to the reading materials" or "reply to at least two post of others." Because the understanding of the language - grammar part will be different, as most ELLs may not understand the exact meaning of the statement. They may answer is in a different format which can lead to low score. According to Freeman and Bamford (2004), instructors face challenges in online learning environment regarding the identity and cultures of learners. For example, instructors will need to understand the strengths and constraints of diverse media that can support or impede learning and communication. Understanding the nature of the learner can have beneficial impacts on learning motivation and participation. Online learning environments, where students exist as identities in cyberspace, have given rise to some important questions in relation to the role of learner identities in the learning process.

Instructors often find it difficult to teach in ways that allow them to meet the needs of all students, and especially, ELLs. However, ELLs face an insurmountable amount of pressure both academically and psychologically. For example, Jung's (2012) study showed that for English learners, online learning activities could incur unnecessary excessive stress with a resultant adverse effect on learning. Another barrier to online learning is that students who have lower computer aptitude experience more barriers to learning online than those with high computer aptitude (Dolan, 2014). ELLs who come from developing countries or low-income families need extra time to deal with the technology issues, and this makes the learning process harder.

Furthermore, some students experience isolation in online learning classes (Dolan, 2014). They are not able to communicate with other students or instructors because of their language deficiency in English, and even when they are capable, they perceive their English as different and may often fail to be integrated into the classroom even in instances where an acceptable cultural climate is cultivated. For ELLs, online learning goals are doubled, because most often, in addition to learning academic content, they also need to improve their facility with English during the learning process. This increases the burden of learning and adjusting to the classroom environment via the virtual medium and may create a challenge for academic progression that is more pronounced than normal students. As a result, ELLs must expend greater effort and time in order to achieve learning outcomes similar to that of their native speaking-student counterparts. Palloff and Pratt (2001) argued that students are able to "achieve deeper levels of knowledge generation through the creation of shared goals, shared exploration, and a shared process of meaning-making" (p. 32) when they are engaged in learning collaboratively versus in isolation. The lack of real time interaction can make it harder for students to know their classmates on a more personal level. There are also questions about the quality of the learning experience for students who take a course focused on multicultural topics, and if online course have the potential to "trivialize cultural differences" (Hinton, 2007) without careful facilitation and planning. Furthermore, Licona (2011) raised the concern that when instructors choose not to participate in online discussions, students can project deficit perspectives and negative assumptions (p. 6) about race, class, disabilities, and gender, and other learners can be negatively impacted by those comments.

Best Practices for Online Education in Multicultural Settings

Several suggestions have been made to improve the facilitation of teacher presence in online learning for minority students, and particularly, ELLs. Pelz (2004) identified three forms of presence for which teachers can strive in online learning

environments. These are: (a) social presence; (b) cognitive presence; and (c) teaching presence. Pelz (2004) observes that social presence involves the process of establishing community of learning via discussions that include affective –expressions of emotions, feelings, and mood; interactive - evidence of reading, attending, understanding, thinking about other's response; and cohesive -- building and maintaining a sense of "belongingness" in online group goals and objectives. Through cognitive presence, the online instructor and students effectively construct and confirm meaning of the content through cordial discourse analysis in a community of inquiry (Pelz, 2004). Pelz (2004) recommends that online instructors promote teaching presence by facilitating discussion through a) identifying areas of agreement and disagreement; b) seeking to reach consensus/ understanding; c) encouraging, acknowledging and reinforcing student contributions; d) setting a climate for learning; e) drawing in participants/ prompting discussion; and f) assessing the efficacy of the process. With regards to direct instruction to be facilitated by online instructors, Pelz (2004) outlines the following best practices: a) presenting content and question; b) focusing the discussion; c) confirming understanding as well as diagnosing any misconceptions; and d) responding to all technical issues by students. Easton (2003), in studying the skills needed by distance learning instructors, extends this notion further to demonstrate that the online instructor must have a paradigm shift concerning instructional time and space, virtual management techniques and methods of engaging students through virtual communications. Pawan (2003) further suggests that instructors "participate regularly throughout the discussion and play a more visible role in guiding students toward the achievement of [those] learning objectives" (p.18). For students from different countries, cultural differences will unfold during the learning process. Teachers must therefore appreciate the student's individuality instead of blindly grouping students together and making assumptions about their background. It is the teacher's responsibility to continue learning about students' culture and religions as they progress interactively throughout the course (Grant & Lee, 2014. p. 9).

In responding to ELL students in online education, instructors can provide time for students to get to know group members because group projects are often "initiated before students have had time to assess other members of the class are likely to lead to homogenization" when students are allowed to choose their own groups (Strauss & Young, 2011, p. 826). Teachers might have students introduce themselves via discussion boards, and in other cases, by way of synchronous chat. Discussion boards allow students to respond at their convenience, compose and revise a quality response, and reread posts and replies from other students. The use of synchronous chat, on the other hand, has been found to create more positive feelings of belonging to a learning community (Lawrence, 2013; Zhu, Bazzoni, & Rolland 2005). Scheduling time for synchronous chats can be difficult, but offering several opportunities for students to chat with one another is one way to schedule around students' busy lives. The more informal the setting of the chat, the more inclined students will be to converse with one another in real time, without a predetermined topic, and to be open about topics that interest them. A whole-class chat can be difficult to execute as students will likely be "typing over" each other's conversations and ideas can easily be lost. By contrast, smaller group chats can be highly effective in simulating the more traditional face-to-face time to which students are accustomed.

Instructors in online learning environments should provide information and guidance on conflict resolution skills as cultural misunderstandings are likely to occur, especially in online environments where writing constitutes the primary means of communication (Zhu et al., 2005). One commonly cited area of conflict is the acceptable response time for emails and discussion boards. Unless new 'norms' of communication and ex-

pectations are explicitly negotiated, members are likely to project their norms implicitly onto others and judge accordingly (Lawrence, 2013, p. 306). The ability to develop understanding of how one's culture influences learning, as well as understanding and interpreting how other cultures approach learning is called "critical cultural awareness" (O'Dowd, 2003, p. 120) and can be particularly useful when students from different cultures are present and where differences in learning cultures are substantial. For example, students from individualistic cultures are typically more aggressive in their email communications and expect more a more active, student-centered pedagogy, versus students from collectivist cultures where communication is used to build consensus and a mutual agenda, and students expect a more passive, teacher-led pedagogy (Kelly, 2009; Popov, Brinkman, Biemans, Muldon, Kuznetsov, & Noroozi, 2012). Addressing these concerns adequately can enhance intercultural curiosity, awareness, discovery skills, "help minimize intercultural miscommunication" as well as address more general cultural stereotypes (Lawrence, 2013, pp. 308-9). To achieve this goal, language can be evaluated and the function of particular words and idiomatic expressions used in a particular culture explored, as these often cause the greatest language misunderstandings (O'Dowd, 2003). This process should be part of the overall introductory process for the groups in a learning environment. The use of narratives can further serve to assist students with building understanding and mutual respect. As students share their cultural learning stories, they use a familiar structure (that of narrative) to explore concepts, ideas, and beliefs that may be inherently different than their readers'. Narratives can help to correct prejudices and address incorrect cultural assumptions (O'Dowd, 2003).

The Pennsylvania State University's World Campus provides outlines guidelines for online instructors that can be used to facilitate instructor presence and student collaboration in a multicultural online learning environment:

1. Instructors must prepare their students for learning online such that they post a welcome message to help students get started, contact information where they can access technical help, and online office hours from which ELL students can benefit;

2. Online instructors should specify course goals, expectations, and policies in the syllabus;

3. Create a warm and friendly atmosphere for students to build a learning community via encouraging students to share their cultural backgrounds as well as personal introductions with an informal tone;

4. Promote and facilitate active learning; this could be accomplished by encouraging students to post constructive comments in learning, providing opportunities for active problem solving and team work, as well as including multiple discussion formats such as small group discussions, case studies, and "jigsaw groups" where student groups could discuss part of a topic and collaborate on their findings;

5. Model effective online interaction that includes providing feedback to the entire class about assignment, discussions or projects as well as general feedback on graded assignments, make suggestions for improvement where necessary;

6. Monitor students' progress and encourage struggling students; instructors should use all forms of educational technology tools, such as course management systems to track students' academic progress in online course activities because this can benefit ELLs;

7. Encourage students to regulate their own learning, that is by allowing students to become what is known as "process managers" in online course in order to become self-regulated learners and instructors could allow ELL students to take full responsibility for their peer's learning and their own via discussion forums;

8. Online instructors should deal with conflicts promptly by providing students access to web etiquette guidelines and communicating with students who happens to post what is considered inappropriate about the violation of academic integrity policies as well as providing peer evaluation mechanism for students functioning;

9. Instructors must understand the value and impact of multiculturalism. For example, they must avoid what is considered discriminatory language and must be aware of the cultural diversity that exists in the classroom (online). Instructors could join professional teaching communities to gain knowledge and exposure to the growing diversity in the global world.

In most cases online courses are designed and implemented by instructors with less knowledge about the cultures and ethnicities of their students (Rogers, Graham, & Mayes, 2007). We must recognize that Western approaches and assumptions may not prove useful in teaching across cultures (Rogers, et al., 2007; Tollman, 2003). Western institutions and instructors might reflect "educational and cultural imperialism" (Sadykova & Dautermann, 2009, p. 90), which is contrary to notions of a safe space. Yet given the current pace of globalization (Merriam, 2010) and the continuous movement towards international online education (Sadykova & Dautermann, 2009), understanding how to create social context for learning in a multinational environment is of great significance to educators and institutions. In addition, discussion questions should be specific and aligned to learning objectives, with clarity of due dates, expectations, participation policies, student responsibilities, and possible grades to be earned (Freeman & Bamford, 2004; Guldberg & Pilkington, 2007; Majeski & Stover, 2007). Equally important is the role of the instructor in facilitating online asynchronous discussions and knowing when to intervene or remain passive

(Andresen, 2009; Zhu, 2006). The instructor in online asynchronous discussions must be able to accomplish the following to include the ability to design and implement the discussion structures (Chen et al., 2009); to motivate student participation and take a role of cheerleading (Dysthe, 2002); to maintain the perceived presence (Swan & Shih, 2005); to engage in Socratic dialogues to deepen the ongoing inquiry of the discussions (Yang, 2008); and to identify critical points of discussions for intervention (Andresen, 2009).

FUTURE RESEARCH DIRECTIONS

The number of English language learners (ELLs), and by extension, minority students in U.S. school system continues to rise. Students who are English language learners (ELL) participate in appropriate programs of language assistance, such as English as a Second Language, High Intensity Language Training, and bilingual education have also increased in the public school system. According to a recent report from the National Center for Education Statistics (2014), the percentage of public school students in the United States who were English language learners was higher in the school years 2011/2012 (9.1%) than in 2002/2003 (8.7%). In eight states, Alaska, California, Colorado, Hawaii, Nevada, New Mexico, Oregon, and Texas, 10.0 percent or more of public school students were English language learners, with ELL students constituting 23.2 percent of public school enrollment in California. The percentages of ELL public school enrollment in the following states District of Columbia, Arizona, Arkansas, Florida, Illinois, Kansas, Maryland, Massachusetts, Minnesota, New York, Oklahoma, North Carolina, Rhode Island, Virginia, and Washington were between 6.0 and 9.9 percent.

Based on the above trend that demonstrates a continued increase in the ELL population, the authors propose that future studies utilize quantitative methods to examine the linguistic challenges of ELL in online learning environments in U.S. virtual schools. The results of such studies would add to the existing literature that English language learners' academic progression and dealing with language and literacy challenges in online education. Qualitative research may also be conducted to examine the influence of multiculturalism on ELLs in predominantly monolingual online learning environments. Longitudinal studies that investigate ELLs' academic performance and learning experiences in online learning environment over an extended duration of time may also help to identify factors that promote academic challenges and successes of ELLs students in online education.

CONCLUSION

The purpose of this chapter was to demonstrate how the field might deepen understanding of multicultural online education with respect to teaching presence for ELLs in the U.S. The chapter indicated that emerging technologies always [emphasis added] help to expand the tools and practices available to instructor (National Center for Educational Statistics 2003, p. 45) who plays an active role in not only keeping up pace with technology advancement, but also helping students specifically English language learners learn to utilize technology in their learning process. (p. 2). As indicated in the chapter, online education has the potential to promote the academic confidence of English language learners because they develop the urge to make contributions to online discussion as opposed to face-to-face traditional classrooms. The chapter also makes mention of some of the demerits of online learning for ELLs to include stress from experiencing challenges in online discussion because of their language deficit. In an online learning classroom, some ELLs feel a sense of isolation and/ or neglect (Dolan, 2014), particularly when they perceive that other course participants and/or the instructors are ignoring their contributions. Instructors in online learning who are engaged in the ideals of multicultural education must foster academic and instructional dedication that would be necessary for facilitating educational experiences in which all students will have equitable opportunities in an online environment. Teacher presence in online learning may play a significant role for ELL students because students' satisfaction level is highly related to instructors' knowledge of materials (Lee, 2014). It is evident that a high level of satisfaction is related to the careful instructional design, which is also closely related to student's study outcomes. We made recommendations about the best instructional strategies for instructors in online learning to help English language learners to succeed. Finally, we argue that there is the need for all instructors teaching in an online education paradigm should understand cultural, linguistic, educational, religious, and learning needs of their students since U.S. is a pluralistic society thus, the growth of minority students in online learning increases with the trend of student population in schools.

REFERENCES

Akyol, Z., & Garrison, D. R. (2014). The development of a community of inquiry over time in an online course: Understanding the progression and integration of social, cognitive and teaching presence. *Journal of Asynchronous Learning Networks*, *12*(3-4), 1–22.

Allen, E., & Seaman, J. (2010). *Class differences: Online education in the United States*. Newburyport, MA: Sloan Consortium.

Ally, M. (2004). Foundations of educational theory for online learning. *Theory and Practice of Online Learning*, *2*, 15–44.

Azevedo, R., Cromley, J. G., & Seibert, D. (2004). Does adaptive scaffolding facilitate students' ability to regulate their learning with hypermedia. *Contemporary Educational Psychology*, *29*(3), 344–370. doi:10.1016/j.cedpsych.2003.09.002

Bandura, S. A. (1982). Self-efficacy mechanism in human agency. *The American Psychologist*, *37*(2), 122–147. doi:10.1037/0003-066X.37.2.122

Banks, J. A. (2005). Multicultural education: Characteristics and goals. In J. A. Banks & C. A. M. Banks (Eds.), *Multicultural education: Issues and perspectives* (5th ed., pp. 1–30). New York, NY: John Wiley & Sons Inc.

Banks, J. A., & Banks, C. A. M. (Eds.). (2009). *Multicultural education: Issues and perspectives*. Hoboken, NJ: John Wiley & Sons.

Beckett, C., Wetzel, K., Chisholm, I., Zambo, R., Padgett, H., Williams, M. K., & Odom, M. (2003). Pre-service and in-service teachers collaborating with technology in K-8 multicultural classrooms: Year 2. *TechTrends*, *479*(5), 14–17. doi:10.1007/BF02763199

Belaja, K., Sai, G. T. B., & Lin, A. L. W. (2012). Effects of lecturer's transactional presence towards learners' intrinsic motivation in learning English as a second language through distance education. *Malaysian Journal of Distance Education*, *14*(1), 77–97.

Bennett, C. I. (2001). Genres of research in multicultural education. *Review of Educational Research*, *71*(2), 171–217. doi:10.3102/00346543071002171

Brown, E. L. (2004a). Overcoming the challenges of stand-alone multicultural courses: The possibilities of technology integration. *Journal of Technology and Teacher Education*, *12*(4), 535–559.

Brown, E. L. (2004b). What precipitates change in cultural diversity awareness during a multicultural course: The message or the method? *Journal of Teacher Education*.

Brookfield, S. D., & Preskill, S. (2005). *Discussion as a way of teaching: Tools and techniques for democratic classrooms* (2nd ed.). San Francisco, CA: Jossey-Bass.

Brookfield, S. (1995). Adult learning: An overview. In A. Tuinjman (Ed.), *International Encyclopedia of Education* (pp. 375–380). Oxford, UK: Pergamon.

Brown, J. W. (2013). Multicultural curriculum development in online classes: Practices from Washington State Community Colleges. Community College Journal of Research and Practices.

Chen, D.-T., Wang, Y.-M., & Hung, D. (2009). A journey on refining rules for online discussion: Implications for the design of learning management systems. *Journal of Interactive Learning Research, 20*(2), 157–173.

Clair, N. (1995). Mainstream Classroom Teachers and ESL students. *Teachers of English to Speakers of Other Languages, 29*(1).

Cole, M. T., Shelley, J. D., & Swartz, L. B. (2014). Online Instruction, E-learning, and student satisfaction: A three year study. *International Review of Research in Open and Distance Learning, 15*(6).

Corbeil, J. R. (2003). *Online technologies, self-efficacy, self-directed learning readiness, and locus of control of learners in a graduate-level web-based distance education program.* (Unpublished doctoral dissertation). University of Houston, Houston, TX.

Cummins, J. (1994). *Negotiating identities: Education for empowerment in a diverse society.* Los Angeles: California Association of Bilingual Education.

Damarin, S. K. (1998). Technology and multicultural education: The question of convergence. *Theory into Practice, 37*(1), 11–19. doi:10.1080/00405849809543781

Dolan, L. B. V. (2014). Massive Online Obsessive compulsion: What are they saying out there about the latest phenomenon in higher education? *International Review of Research in Open and Distance Learning, 15*(2).

Duffy, T. M., Dueber, B., & Hawley, C. (1998). Critical thinking in a distributed environment: A pedagogical base for the design of conferencing systems. In C. J. Bonk & K. S. King (Eds.), *Electronic collaborators: Learner-centered technologies for literacy, apprenticeship, and discourse* (pp. 51–78). Mahwah, NJ: Lawrence Erlbaum Associates.

Dysthe, O. (2002). The learning potential of a web-mediated discussion in a university course. *Studies in Higher Education, 27*(3), 339–352. doi:10.1080/03075070220000716

Easton, S. (2003). Clarifying the instructor's role in online distance learning. *Communication Education, 52*(2), 87–105. doi:10.1080/03634520302470

Ellis, A. (2004). *Exemplars of curriculum theory.* Larchmont, NY: Eye on Education.

Ferneding, K. A. (2004). The discourse of inevitability and the forging of an emergent social vision: Technology diffusion and the dialectic of educational reform discourse. In W. M. Reynolds & J. A. Webber (Eds.), *Expanding curriculum theory: Dis/positions and lines of flight* (pp. 47–63). Mahwah, NJ: Lawrence Erlbaum.

Freeman, M., & Bamford, A. (2004). Student choice of anonymity for learner identity in online learning discussion forums. *International Journal on E-Learning, 3*(3), 45–53.

Ganesh, T. G., & Middleton, J. A. (2006). Challenges in linguistically and culturally diverse elementary settings with math instruction using learning technologies. *The Urban Review, 38*(2), 101–143. doi:10.1007/s11256-006-0025-7

Gareis, Y. (2005). A collaborative online project between New Zealand and New York. *Business Communication Quarterly*, *68*(1), 81–96. doi:10.1177/1080569904273715

Garrison, D. R. (2007). Online community of inquiry review: Social, cognitive, and teaching presence issues. *Journal of Asynchronous Learning Networks*, *11*(1), 61–72.

Gay, G., & Howard, T. C. (2000). Multicultural education for the 21st century. *Teacher Educator*, *36*(1), 1–16. doi:10.1080/08878730009555246

Gorski, P. (2004). *Multicultural education and the Internet: Intersections and integrations* (2nd ed.). New York: McGraw-Hill Higher Education.

Gorski, P. (2005). Education equity and the digital divide. *Association for the Advancement of Computing in Education Journal*, *13*(1), 3–45.

Grant, K. S. L., & Lee, V. J. (2014). Teacher educators wrestling with issues of diversity in online courses. *Qualitative Report*, *19*(6), 1–25.

Greenberg, G. (1998). Distance education technologies: Best practices for K12 settings. *IEEE Technology and Society Magazine*, *17*(Winter), 36–40. doi:10.1109/44.735862

Guglielmino, L. M., & Guglielmino, P. J. (2002). Learner characteristics affecting success in electronic distance learning. In *H.B. Long & Associates, Twenty-First Century Advances in Self-Directed Leaning*. Boynton Beach, FL: Motorola University Press.

Guldberg, K., & Pilkington, R. M. (2007). Tutor roles in facilitating reflection on practice through online discussion. *Journal of Educational Technology & Society*, *10*(1), 61–72.

Hamdan, A. K. (2014). The reciprocal and correlative relationship between learning culture and online education: A case from Saudi Arabia. *International Review of Research in Open and Distance Learning*, *15*(1).

Hannafin, M. J., & Land, S. M. (1997). The foundations and assumptions of technology enhanced student-centered learning environments. *Instructional Science*, *25*(3), 167–202. doi:10.1023/A:1002997414652

Hinton, S. (2007, March). *Multicultural education online for graduate teachers: Some challenges*. Paper presented at the Annual Conference for the Comparative and International Education Society, Baltimore, MD.

Hopey, C. E., & Ginsburg, L. (1996). Distance learning and new technologies: You can't predict the future but you can plan for it. *Adult Learning*, *8*(1), 212–223.

Howard, G. R. (1999). *We can't teach what we don't know: White teachers, multiracial schools*. New York: Teachers College Press.

Isiguzel, B. (2014). The Blended Learning Environment on the foreign language learning process: A Balance for Motivation and Achievement. *Turkish Online Journal of Distance Education*, *15*(3).

Jung, I. M., Kudo, M., & Choi, S. (2012). Stress in Japanese learners engaged in online collaborative learning in English. *British Journal of Educational Technology*, *43*(6), 1016–1029. doi:10.1111/j.1467-8535.2011.01271.x

Kearsley, G. (2002). Is online learning for everybody. *Educational Technology*, *42*(1), 41–44.

Kelly, P. (2009). Group work and multicultural management education. *Journal of Teaching in International Business*, *20*(1), 80–102. doi:10.1080/08975930802671273

Kilian, C. (1997). Why Teach Online. *Educational Review*, *32*(4), 31–34.

Klein, S. S. (1985). *Handbook for achieving sex equity through education*. Baltimore, MD: Johns Hopkins University Press.

Lawrence, G. (2013). A working model for intercultural learning and engagement in collaborative online language learning environments. *Intercultural Education, 24*(4), 303–314. doi:10.1080/14 675986.2013.809247

Lea, M., & Goodfellow, R. (2003). *Supporting academic writing in a global online environment*. Paper presented at the European Association of Teachers of Academic Writing, Budapest, Hungary.

Lee, J. (2014). An exploratory study of effective online learning: Assessing satisfaction levels of graduate students of mathematics education associated with human and design factors of an online course. *International Review of Research in Open and Distance Learning, 15*(1).

Lee, S. M. (2012). Distance learning class model for teaching a foreign language in university-level education context. *Journal of Pan-Pacific Association of Applied Linguistics, 1.*

Licona, M. M., & Gurung, B. (2011). Asynchronous Discussions in Online Multicultural Education. *Multicultural Education, 19*(1), 2–8.

Lowes, S. (2005). *Online teaching and classroom change: The impact of virtual high school on its teachers and their schools*. Naperville, IL: Learning Point Associates.

Majeski, R., & Stover, M. (2007). Theoretically based pedagogical strategies leading to deep learning in asynchronous online gerontology courses. *Educational Gerontology, 33*(3), 171–185. doi:10.1080/03601270600850826

Major, E., & Brock, C. (2003). Fostering positive dispositions toward diversity: Dialogical explorations of a moral dilemma. *Teacher Education Quarterly, 30*(4), 7–26.

Mazyck, M. (2002). Integrated learning systems and students of color: Two decades of use in K-12 education. *TechTrends, 46*(2), 33–39. doi:10.1007/ BF02772074

Merriam, S. B. (2010). Globalization and the role of adult and continuing education. In C. E. Kasworm, A. D. Rose, & J. M. Ross-Gordon (Eds.), *Handbook of adult and continuing education* (pp. 401–409). Los Angeles, CA: Sage Publications, Inc.

Merryfield, M. M. (2001). The paradoxes of teaching a multicultural education course online. *Journal of Teacher Education, 52*(4), 283–299. doi:10.1177/0022487101052004003

Merryfield, M. M. (2001). Engaging with issues of cultural diversity and discrimination through critical emotional reflexivity in online learning. *Adult Education Quarterly, 59*, 61–82.

Meyer, K. A. (2003). Face-to-face versus threaded discussions: The role of time and higher order thinking. *Asynchronous Learning Networks, 7*(3), 55–65.

National Center for Education Statistics. (2006). *Internet Access in U.S. Public Schools and Classrooms: 1994–2005*. (NCES 2007-020). U.S. Department of Education. Retrieved January 30, 2015 from http://nces.ed.gov/pubsearch/pubsinfo. asp?pubid=2007020

National center for Education Statistics. (2011). *Open Doors: Report on International Educational Exchange, 1981 through 2010 (selected years)*. Institute of International Education.

National Center for Education Statistics. (2014). *The condition of education (NCES 2014-083), English Language Learners*. Department of Education.

National Center for Educational Statistics. (2003). *Distance education at degree granting post secondary institutions.* Retrieved January 20, 2015, from National Center for Educational Statistics: http://nces.ed.gov/pubsearch/pubsinfo

Nieto, S. (1999). *The light in their eyes: Creating multicultural learning communities.* New York: Teachers College Press.

Nieto, S. (2000). Placing equity front and center: Some thoughts on transforming teacher education for a new century. *Journal of Teacher Education, 51*(3), 180–187. doi:10.1177/0022487100051003004

Nieto, S., & Bode, P. (2012). *Affirming diversity: The sociopolitical context of multicultural education* (6th ed.). Boston, MA: Allyn and Bacon.

Nuangchalerm, P., Prachagool, V., & Sriputta, P. (2011). Online professional experiences in teacher preparation program: A pre-service teacher study. *Canadian Social Science, 7*(5), 116–120.

O'Dowd, R. (2003). Understanding the "other side": Intercultural learning in a Spanish-English e-mail exchange. *Language Learning & Technology, 7*(2), 118–144.

Orly, M. (2007). Multicultural e-learning project and comparison of teachers' student teacher' and pupils' perceptions about e-learning. *Multicultural Education & Technology Journal, 1*(3), 178–191. doi:10.1108/17504970710822377

Owston, R. D. (1997). The World Wide Web: A technology to enhance teaching and learning. *Educational Researcher,* 27–33.

Palloff, R. M., & Pratt, K. (2001). *Lessons from the cyberspace classroom: The realities of online teaching.* San Francisco, CA: Jossey-Bass.

Pawan, F., Paulus, T. M., Yalcin, S., & Chang, C. F. (2003). Online learning: Patterns of engagement and interaction among in-service teachers. *Language Learning & Technology, 7*(3), 119–140.

Pelz, B. (2004). Three principles of effective online pedagogy. *Journal of Asynchronous Learning Networks, 8*(3), 33–46.

Popov, V., Brinkman, D., Biemans, H. J. A., Muldon, M., Kuznetsov, A., & Noroozi, O. (2012). Multicultural student group work in higher education: A explorative case on challenges as perceived by students. *International Journal of Intercultural Relations, 36*(2), 302–317. doi:10.1016/j.ijintrel.2011.09.004

Richardson, V. (1996). The role of attitudes and beliefs in learning to teach. In J. Sikula (Ed.), *Handbook of research on teacher education* (2nd ed., pp. 102–119). New York: Simon & Schuster/ Macmillan.

Roblyer, M. D., Dozier-Henry, O., & Burnette, A. P. (1996). Technology and multicultural education: The 'uneasy alliance'. *Educational Technology, 36*(3), 5–12.

Rocco, S. (2010). Making reflection public: Using interactive online discussion board to enhance student learning. *Reflective Practice, 11*(3), 307–317. doi:10.1080/14623943.2010.487374

Rogers, P. C., Graham, C. R., & Mayes, C. T. (2007). Cultural competence and instructional design: Exploration research into the delivery of online instruction cross-culturally. *Educational Technology Research and Development, 55*(2), 197–217. doi:10.1007/s11423-007-9033-x

Rovai, A. (2002). Building a sense of community at a distance. *International Review of Research in Open and Distance Learning, 3*(1), 1–16.

Rovai, A. (2002b). Sense of community, perceived cognitive learning, and persistance in asynchronous learning networks. *The Internet and Higher Education, 5*(4), 319–332. doi:10.1016/S1096-7516(02)00130-6

Rovai, A., & Jordan, H. M. (2004). Blended learning and sense of community: A comparative analysis with traditional and fully online graduate courses. *International Review of Research in Open and Distance Learning, 5*(2), 2–13.

Sa'd, S. H. T. (2014). Implementing Internet-based EFL Teaching in Iran:(Dis) Advantages, Obstacles and Challenges from EFL Learners' Viewpoint. *Dil ve Edebiyat Eğitimi Dergisi Sayı, 10*, 24–40.

Sadykova, G., & Dautermann, J. (2009). Crossing cultures and borders in international online distance higher education. *Journal of Asynchronous Learning Networks, 13*(2), 89–114.

Sleeter, C., & Tettagah, S. (2002). Technology as a tool in multicultural teaching. *Multicultural Education, 10*(1), 28–30.

Sleeter, C. E. (1996). *Multicultural education as social activism.* Albany, NY: State University of New York Press.

Soleimani, M., Sarkhosh, M., & Gahhari, S. (2012). Computer assisted language testing: On the efficacy of web-based approach in the instruction of elementary learners of English. *English Language Teaching, 5*(9), 66–70. doi:10.5539/elt.v5n9p66

Strauss, P. U. A., & Young, S. (2011). 'I know the type of people I work well with: Student anxiety in multicultural group projects. *Studies in Higher Education, 36*(7), 815–829. doi:10.1080/03075079.2010.488720

Sullivan, P. (2002). It's easier to be yourself when you are invisible: Female college students discuss their online classroom experiences. *Innovative Higher Education, 27*(2), 129–143. doi:10.1023/A:1021109410893

Swan, K., & Shih, L. F. (2005). On the nature and development of social presence in online course discussions. *Journal of Asynchronous Learning Networks, 9*, 115–136.

Sweeney, A., Weaven, S., & Herington, C. (2008). Multicultural influences on group learning: A qualitative higher education study. *Assessment & Evaluation in Higher Education, 33*(2), 119–132. doi:10.1080/02602930601125665

Taliaferro, A. (2011). Developing culturally responsive leaders through online learning and teaching approaches. *Journal of Educational Technology, 8*(3).

Tallent-Runnels, M. K., Thomas, J. A., Lan, W. Y., Cooper, S., Ahern, T. C., Shaw, S. M., & Liu, X. (2006). Teaching courses online: A review of the research. *Review of Educational Research, 76*(1), 93–135. doi:10.3102/00346543076001093

Tollman, J. (2003). Classroom teaching in Botswana and online teaching from Georgia: Hard knocks and earned successes. *Journal of Education for Library and Information Science, 44*(1), 39–57. doi:10.2307/40323941

Villegas, A. M., & Lucas, T. (2002). *Educating culturally responsive teachers: A coherent approach.* Albany, NY: State University of New York Press.

Ware, P. D. (2004). Confidence and competition online: ESL student perspectives on web-based discussions in the classroom. *Computers and Composition, 21*(4), 451–468. doi:10.1016/S8755-4615(04)00041-6

Warschauer, M. (2013). Comparing face-to-face and electronic discussion in the second language classroom. *CALICO Journal*, *13*(2&3), 7–26.

Wassell, B., & Crouch, C. (2008). Fostering connections between multicultural education and technology: Incorporating weblogs into preservice teacher education. *Journal of Technology and Teacher Education*, *16*(2), 211–232.

Wells, G. (1999). *Dialogic inquiry: Toward a sociocultural practice and theory of education Cambridge*. UK: Cambridge University Press; doi:10.1017/CBO9780511605895

Williams, M. (1996). Learner control and instructional technologies. In D. Jonassen (Ed.), *Handbook of research on educational communications and technology* (pp. 957–983). Scholastic.

Yang, Y.-T. (2008). A catalyst for teaching critical thinking in a large university class in Taiwan: Asynchronous online discussions with the facilitation of teaching assistants. *Educational Technology Research and Development*, *56*(3), 241–264. doi:10.1007/s11423-007-9054-5

Yen, H. J., & Liu, S. (2009). Learner autonomy as a predictor of course success and final grades in community college online courses. *Journal of Educational Computing Research*, *41*(3), 347–367. doi:10.2190/EC.41.3.e

Zhu, C. (2012). Student satisfaction, performance, and knowledge construction in online collaborative learning. *Journal of Educational Technology & Society*, *15*(1), 127–136.

Zhu, E. (2006). Interaction and cognitive engagement: An analysis of four asynchronous online discussions. *Instructional Science*, *34*(6), 451–480. doi:10.1007/s11251-006-0004-0

ADDITIONAL READING

Anderson, M. (2000). Individual characteristics and web-based courses. In C. R. Wolfe (Ed.), *Learning and teaching on the World Wide Web* (pp. 47–73). San Diego, CA: Academic Press.

Angeli, C., Valanides, N., & Bonk, C. (2003). Communication in a web-based conferencing system. The quality of computer-mediated interactions. *British Journal of Educational Technology*, *34*(1), 31–43. doi:10.1111/1467-8535.00302

Banks, J. A. (2003). *Teaching strategies for ethnic studies* (7th ed.). Boston: Allyn and Bacon.

Banks, J. A. (Ed.). (2004a). *Diversity and citizenship education: Global perspectives*. San Francisco, CA: Jossey-Bass.

Banks, J. A. (2004b). Multicultural education: Historical development, dimensions, and practice. In J. A. Banks & C. A. M. Banks (Eds.), *Handbook of research on multicultural education* (2nd ed., pp. 3–29). San Francisco, CA: Jossey-Bass.

Banks, J. A. (2007). *Educating citizens in a multicultural society* (2nd ed.). New York: Teachers College Press.

Banks, J. A., & Banks, C. A. M. (Eds.). (2005). *Multicultural education: Issues and perspectives* (5th ed.). New York, NY: John Wiley & Sons, Inc. doi:10.4135/9781412952538.n178

Baron, J. (1998). Teaching on-line across cultures. In A. Gooley, C. Pearson, & S. Towers (Eds.), *Proceedings of the 3rd International Conference on Open Learning* (pp. 67–72). Brisbaine, Australia: Queensland Open Learning Network.

Bennett, C. I. (1995). Preparing teachers for cultural diversity and national standards of academic excellence. *Journal of Teacher Education*, *46*(4), 259–265. doi:10.1177/0022487195046004004

Bennett, C. I. (2001). Genres of research in multicultural education. *Review of Educational Research, 71*(2), 171–217. doi:10.3102/00346543071002171

Bond, M. H. (Ed.). (1996). *The handbook of Chinese psychology*. Hong Kong: Oxford University Press.

Caruthers, L., & Smith, D. (2006). Re-living dangerous memories: On-line journaling to interrogate spaces of "otherness" in a multicultural course. *Journal of Curriculum Theorizing, 22*(2), 123–137.

Chang, C. Y., & Tsai, C. C. (2005). The interplay between different forms of CAI and students' preferences of learning environment in the secondary science class. *Science Education, 89*(5), 707–724. doi:10.1002/sce.20072

Davis, N. E., & Cho, M. I. (2005). Intercultural competence for future leaders of educational technology. *Interactive Educational Multimedia, 10,* 1–22.

Dede, C. (2000). *Implications of emerging technologies for states' education policies*. Paper presented for the January, 2000 School Technology Leadership Conference of the Council of Chief State School Officers, Washington, D. C.

Gay, G. (1997). Multicultural infusion in teacher education: Foundations and applications. *Peabody Journal of Education, 72*(1), 150–177. doi:10.1207/s15327930pje7201_8

Gay, G. (2000). *Culturally responsive teaching: Theory, research and practice*. New York, London: Teachers College Press.

Gay, G., & Howard, T. C. (2000). Multicultural education for the 21st century. *Teacher Educator, 36*(1), 1–16. doi:10.1080/08878730009555246

Kay, R. (2007). A formative analysis of how preservice teachers learn to use technology. *Journal of Computer Assisted Learning, 23*(5), 366–383. doi:10.1111/j.1365-2729.2007.00222.x

Liang, A., & McQueen, R. (2000). Computer assisted adult interactive learning in a multi-cultural environment. *Adult Learning, 11*(1), 26–29.

Nieto, S. (2004). *Affirming diversity: The sociopolitical context of multicultural education* (4th ed.). Boston, MA: Pearson Allyn & Bacon.

Nieto, S., & Bode, P. (2008). *Affirming diversity: The sociopolitical context of multicultural education* (5th ed.). Boston, NY: Allyn & Bacon/ Longman.

Pittman, J. (2007). Converging instructional technology and critical intercultural pedagogy in teacher education. *Multicultural Education & Technology Journal, 1*(4), 200–222. doi:10.1108/17504970710832817

Scida, E. E., & Saury, R. E. (2006). Hybrid courses and their impact on student and classroom performance: A case study at the University of Virginia. *CALICO Journal, 23*(3), 517–531.

Sleeter, C. E. (1995). Reflections on my use of multicultural and critical pedagogy when students are white. In C. E. Sleeter & P. L. McLaren (Eds.), *Multicultural Education, Critical Pedagogy, and the Politics of Difference* (pp. 415–437). Albany, NY: State University of New York Press.

Sleeter, C. E. (1996). Multicultural education as a social movement. *Theory into Practice, 35*(4), 239–247. doi:10.1080/00405849609543730

Sleeter, C. E. (2000). *Critical multiculturalism and curriculum analysis*. Paper presented at the annual conference of the American Educational Research Association.

Sleeter, C. E. (2001). Preparing teachers for culturally diverse schools: Research and the overwhelming presence of whiteness. *Journal of Teacher Education, 52*(2), 94–106. doi:10.1177/0022487101052002002

Sleeter, C. E., & Grant, C. A. (2003). *Making choices for multicultural education: Five approaches to race, class and gender* (4th ed.). Englewood Cliffs, NJ: Merrill/Prentice Hall.

U.S. Department of Education Office of Planning, Evaluation, and Policy Development Policy and Program Studies Service (2010). Evaluation of Evidence-Based Practices in Online Learning: A Meta-Analysis and Review of Online Learning Studies. Washington, DC. Retrieved on August 4, 2014 from http://www2.ed.gov/rschstat/eval/tech/evidence-based-practices/finalreport.pdf

Walker, G. (2005). Critical thinking in asynchronous discussions. *International Journal of Instructional Technology and Distance Learning, 6*(2).

Wang, M. J. (2004). Correlational analysis of student visibility and learning outcomes in an online setting. *Journal of Asynchronous Learning Networks, 8*(4), 71–82.

Warschauer, M., Knobel, M., & Stone, L. (2004). Technology and equity in schooling: Deconstructing the digital divide. *Educational Policy, 18*(4), 562–588. doi:10.1177/0895904804266469

Watkins, D., & Biggs, J. (Eds.). (1996). *The Chinese learner: Cultural, psychological, and contextual influences*. Victoria: Comparative Education Research Centre, University of Hong Kong and the Australian Council for Educational Research Ltd.

Watson, J., Murin, A., Vashaw, L., Gemin, B., & Rapp, C. (2010). Keeping pace with K-12 online learning: A review of state-level policy and practice. Evergreen, CO: Evergreen Education Group. Retrieved on August 4, 2014 from http://www.kpk12.com/cms/wp-content/uploads/KeepingPaceK12_2010.pdf

Watson, J. F., & Kalmon, S. (2005). Keeping pace with K–12 online learning: A review of state-level policy and practice. Naperville, IL: Learning Point Associates. Retrieved on August 4, 2014 from http://www.learningpt.org/pdfs/tech/Keeping_Pace2.pdf

Whipp, J. L. (2003). Scaffolding critical reflection in online discussions: Helping prospective teachers think deeply about field experiences in urban schools. *Journal of Teacher Education, 54*(4), 321–333. doi:10.1177/0022487103255010

Wilhelm, J. D. (2013). Opening to possibility: Reflectivity and reflexivity in teaching. *Voices from the Middle, 20*(3), 57–59.

Young, A. (2008). Structuring asynchronous discussions to incorporate learning principles in an online class. One professor's course analysis. *Journal of Online Learning and Teaching, 4*(2), 217–225.

Zhao, Y., & Cziko, G. A. (2001). Teacher adoption of technology: A perceptual control theory perspective. *Journal of Technology and Teacher Education, 9*(1), 5–30.

Zhu, C., Valcke, M., & Schellens, T. (2008a). The relationship between epistemological beliefs, learning conceptions, and approaches to study: A cross-cultural structural model? *Asia Pacific Journal of Education, 28*(4), 411–423. doi:10.1080/02188790802468823

Zhu, C., Valcke, M., & Schellens, T. (2008b). Collaborative learning in a social constructivist e-learning environment: A cross-cultural study. *Proceedings of the 13th Annual Conference of the European Learning Styles Information Network*.

Zydney, J., deNoyelles, A., & Seo, K. K.-J. (2012). Creating a community of inquiry in online environments: An exploratory study on the effect of a protocol on interactions within asynchronous discussions. *Computers & Education, 58*(1), 77–87. doi:10.1016/j.compedu.2011.07.009

KEY TERMS AND DEFINITIONS

Distance Education: General term for any type of educational activity in which the participants are at a distance from each other--in other words, are separated in space. They may or may not be separated in time (asynchronous vs. synchronous).

Distance Education Course: Any course offered at a distance. See "Distance education."

Distributed Learning: Any learning that allows instructor, students, and content to be located in different locations so that instruction and learning occur independent of time and place; often used synonymously with the term "Distance learning."

Diversity: Used to communicate a term inclusive of historically marginalized sociocultural educational discrepancies associated with race, ethnicity, social class, gender, religion, languages (other than English), and sexual orientation.

English Language Learners or ELLs: Students who are unable to communicate fluently or learn effectively in English, who often come from non-English-speaking homes and backgrounds, and who typically require specialized or modified instruction in both the English language and in their academic courses.

Multicultural Education: A progressive approach for transforming education that holistically critiques and addresses current shortcomings, failings, and discriminatory practices in education. It is grounded in ideals of social justice, education equity, and a dedication to facilitating educational experiences in which all students reach their full potential as learners and as socially aware and active beings, locally, nationally, and globally. Multicultural education acknowledges that schools are essential to laying the foundation for the transformation of society and the elimination of oppression and injustice (Banks, 2004)

Online Learning: Education in which instruction and content are delivered primarily over the Internet. (Watson & Kalmon, 2005) The term does not include printed-based correspondence education, broadcast television or radio, videocassettes, and stand-alone educational software programs that do not have a significant Internet-based instructional component. (U.S. Department of Education Office of Planning, Evaluation, and Policy Development Policy and Program Studies Service, 2010) Used interchangeably with Virtual learning, Cyber learning, e-learning.

Online Learning Program: An online learning program is an organized offering of courses delivered primarily over the Internet.

Online Learning Resources: Any digital material used for supporting student learning that is delivered in multiple delivery models.

Synchronous Learning: Online learning in which the participants interact at the same time and in the same space.

Chapter 20
Stylized Moments:
Creating Student Engagement and Participation in an Asynchronous Online University Film Course

William Thomas McBride
Illinois State University, USA

ABSTRACT

This chapter provides academic researchers and teachers with access to a unique pedagogical approach to teaching film online with a detailed exhibition of strategies and technological tools that have proven to encourage and ensure interaction, presence, and participation in an asynchronous online setting. With a persistent comparative eye toward both F2F and asynchronous online versions of the course, the chapter reveals both the content and the infrastructure as it is currently delivered to 100 students, detailing how each component works, and the advantages and disadvantages of delivering such a course online.

INTRODUCTION

This chapter provides academic researchers and teachers with access to a unique pedagogical approach to teaching film style 100% online along with a detailed exhibition of the strategies and technological tools that have proven to encourage and ensure interaction, presence, and participation in an asynchronous online setting. It is drawn from twenty years of experience teaching face-to-face (f2f) various iterations of the author's English Department film course in both small and large lecture classroom settings as well as five subsequent years of teaching an online version. What

follows is, first, a general introduction to the field of cinema studies entitled "Background," then a zeroing in on the course's unique approach to film style and its hermeneutic project in "What is a Stylized Moment." Then "Turning Film Style Into Meaning" shares with readers the infrastructure of the course as currently delivered with a class size of 100 students with the collaboration of two graduate student Teaching Assistants (TAs), detailing how each component works, with a perusal of the required eTextbook and syllabus. The "Nuts & Bolts" section details the day-to-day operation of the course arguing for the effectiveness of Discussion Forum groupings. With a persistent

DOI: 10.4018/978-1-4666-9582-5.ch020

comparative eye toward the traditional and electronic versions of the course, readers follow a discussion of the quantity and quality of learning, how instructor and student interaction, presence, and participation can be guaranteed, and the advantages and disadvantages of delivering such a course 100% online. The chapter openly confronts questions of online classroom instructional quality, academic rigor, and parity with f2f instruction, and concludes with an assessment of how each of its components potentially contributes to an enjoyable yet rigorous pedagogical experience.

BACKGROUND

Pundits of the post-MTV/Internet generation(s) are fond of claiming how a new visual acuity in young people is replacing the literary-based knowledge systems of yore, often citing the massive hours spent in front of TV and computer/device screens rather than between the pages of books. However, most of us are "babes in the woods" when it comes to acknowledging and articulately responding to this more visual way of knowing. In fact as a human enterprise, we have yet to quite recover from the astounding invention of the photograph over 150 years ago. Anthropological reports abound documenting first nation and aboriginal tribal suspicion over having one's picture taken, based on the belief that part of one's soul or spirit is also taken when "captured" on film: "There was never a photograph taken or a likeness made from first hand witness of Crazy Horse;" so claims Mari Sandoz in the 1942 biography, *Crazy Horse the Strange Man of the Oglala* (p. 424). The Oglala Lakota leader allegedly resisted being photographed as defense from "shadow catching" or soul stealing. In his illuminating and challenging book, *La Chambre claire* (1980), translated into English as *Camera Lucida*, Roland Barthes calls photography "unclassifiable," a "disturbance (to civilization)" and a "wound" (pp. 6,13, 26). This last characterization

bears witness to the inherent violence embedded in the filmic language of "aiming," "shooting'" and "taking" of photographs and movies. In fact early cameras were often mounted on the stocks of modified rifles. The pioneering photographer Henri Cartier-Bresson (1908-2004), quoted by Michael Kimmelman in the *New York Times* 2004 obituary, once remarked: "I adore shooting photographs. It's like being a hunter." In his introduction to a rare interview granted to Charlie Rose for PBS (7/6/00), Rose described Cartier-Bresson as both a "sharpshooter" and a "marksman." Weaponry metaphors prevailed throughout the interview by both interlocutor and subject. Students read in my eTextbook, *Stylized Moments. Turning Film Style Into Meaning* (2013), how this violence of looking, gazing, photographing, and filming, as well as its penetrative logic, are thematized by several American films, most notably under discussion in the course are Hitchcock's *Rear Window* (1954), David Lynch's *Blue Velvet* (1986), and as a sort of progressive antidote, Sam Mendes' *American Beauty* (1999).

Students are immediately attracted to the University film course because they have a lifetime of experience watching and analyzing films. A big part of film's uncanny power over humans, and one must include recorded sound, is undoubtedly due to the spectacular realism it captures, what Barthes calls photography's "ethnological knowledge," and the cognitive illusion of life-like movement achieved by the technology of the movie camera and projector. (*Camera Lucida*, p.12) As rehearsed in Martin Scorsese's recent love letter to early cinema (and excellent condensed history of film origins), *Hugo* (2011), when the Lumière brothers first publically screened *The Arrival of a Train at La Ciotat* (1896), some audience members ducked their heads while others ran from the screen hysterically. We at times still duck from oncoming objects or involuntarily cry out warnings to on-screen characters despite our sophisticated, jaded cinematic palates. Students are introduced to the proposition that cinema not only does a seemingly picture-perfect job of capturing reality, it also has the power to change it. There remains the undigested impact of this technology's ability to manipulate and contaminate said reality. The Heisenberg Principle explains precisely this phenomenon of the observer and her instruments intervening in the perception of the data. With the advent of photography and then moving images, the reality it so brilliantly records, or better, mimics necessarily must incorporate that technology's simulacra experience into our everyday impression of the real.

By granting 1) the ubiquity of the moving image, 2) its ideological juices that course through our brains and veins, and 3) the ramifications of such a study for an engaged and responsible citizenry, the grander goal of the course Film Style & Literature is to serve as a step toward better reading our "movied" selves as well as our movies. To this end students are introduced to the practice of "hermeneutics." So named from Hermes, the Greek messenger and herald to the Gods, hermeneutics is the science of interpretation. This search for meaning in texts originated as Biblical exegesis and soon branched out to legal, philosophical and literary hermeneutics, marked by a concern with the relation between interpretive subject and text. In this chapter the all-important pedagogical heart of the course content must precede the setting up of the "nuts and bolts" of the structure and moving parts of delivering a course online that ensures engagement and participation.

What Is a Stylized Moment?

This Film Style & Literature online course and my accompanying eTextbook (Figure 1) are designed to show students how to concretely discover meaning in film by logically decoding the simple, but often invisible, stylistic choices made by directors, directors of photography, set designers, costumers, soundtrack composers, actors, and the rest of the creative collaborators of cinema. What is endemic to film, clearly, is its

visual aspect above all. Film Style & Literature is unlike most university film "appreciation" courses, which typically target narrative critique and genre study. Film Style & Literature argues the only authentic way to interpret a film, and its story is first and foremost to attend to its *visual* style, otherwise one may as well be analyzing a novel, play, or short story. This attention to the form of the object of study begins by identifying, defining, and explaining individual "stylized moments," and then applying those insights toward an interpretation of each film as a whole. What we do in analyzing these moments is we articulate and interpret *choices* that are made by the artists who created the film. Students begin to see the logic that they can produce a convincing reading of a film by targeting for analysis particular moments where the director has gently or not so gently nudged the audience with stylized cinematic gestures that, when decoded, unlock significance. After these moments have been identified and analyzed in isolation, the interpretive results can be integrated into the film's entire system of signs in order to reach conclusions with extraordinary explanatory power about the film as a whole. The basic premise by which this formalistic approach operates is known as structuralism, a linguistic and anthropological procedure of understanding social phenomena as part of a system of signs whose meaning resides in their interrelationships. This structuralist approach to film claims that each stylized moment carries meaning based on the generally accepted conventions of mainstream moviemaking language which students acquire by reading the eTextbook and teacher feedback, and that, like beginning with the embedded code of a tiny sample of DNA, the entire organism, or film, can be convincingly explicated. Students learn that the only way to succeed in this formal analysis is to first distinguish stylistic choices that bear meaning from merely functional elements.

One of the best ways to make this distinction and develop a grasp of the concept behind the stylized moment is to begin by describing it by

Figure 1. Cover Art for eTextbook Stylized Moments: Turning Film Style Into Meaning illustrating a "stylized moment"

what it is not. In order to do so, I ask my students to examine the typical shot/reverse shot as exclusively functional. A shot/reverse shot consists of a series of connected over-the-shoulder shots or one-shot close-ups of each speaker pointed approximately180-degrees opposite of each other and used to portray a conversation between two characters. Such camera placement is utterly conventional and rather transparent; it does not call attention to itself. Within the conventions of Hollywood style this is the most efficient and widespread way to film a conversation. The shot/reverse shot *functions* to effortlessly and transparently convey dialogue between two characters carrying no grander symbols or meaning based on camera placement or lighting or editing.

On the other hand, a pronounced stylized moment occurs at the conclusion of one of the earliest films I teach, *The Maltese Falcon* (Huston 1941). After the film's protagonist, Sam Spade (Humphrey Bogart), in typical hard-boiled fashion

denies his emotional feelings for the femme fatale, Brigid O'Shaunessey (Mary Astor), and exposes her as a murderer, there is a medium close-up of the elevator gate closing upon her face. Students are encouraged to note how the lighting design ensures that the gate casts an unmistakable shadow in the shape of a downward pointing arrow on her face just before the elevator descends. The gate certainly stands for the prison bars through which the murderess will gaze for many years to come, if she isn't hung for her crime, and the arrow invokes the Christian notion of hell and her descent there. An insightful student once pointed out in a Discussion Forum that the shadow also resembles a falcon's claw. This image is so illustrative of a stylized moment, it constitutes the cover art of the eTextbook *Stylized Moments: Turning Film Style Into Meaning*. A stylized moment, therefore, is any formal cinematic element not reproducible on the stage or page that bears meaning by way of metaphor.

Turning Film Style Into Meaning

Containing over one hundred explanatory film stills, I assign to students the richly illustrated eTextbook *Stylized Moments* whose distillation and amplification of lectures and learning points are taken from over twenty years of weekly f2f meetings and is dedicated to Alan Spiegel, my film professor at the University of Buffalo, who taught me how to look at film in a new way and who first introduced to me the concept of the "stylized moment."

There are several fine film textbooks on the market—some of them quite good, for example, at rehearsing the history of narrative cinema from magic lanterns to CGI, or at providing descriptions of film's various genres like the Western and Film Noir, some even include sample student essays, but very few stress the importance of style as *Stylized Moments* does, nor do any provide insight into the meaning of films by delivering workable strategies and detailed formal analyses. These traditional textbooks reflect the content and approach of most University film classes. The first chapter of *Stylized Moments* explores many of the stylistic conventions of modern cinema, what to call them, how to describe them, what they usually mean, and how then students can apply that knowledge as a descriptive and interpretive tool. After reading this first chapter students, who have been assigned to a Discussion group with four other classmates, are asked to identify and discuss in a 350 word minimum post two examples of cinematically stylized moments— those moments only achievable in films—and two examples of significant moments not dependent on the language of film but still meaningful. The remaining chapters present detailed readings of eleven assigned films, introducing new terms and concepts each week. For each ensuing week, members of each Discussion group identify and discuss in a 250 word minimum post one example of a cinematically stylized moment and one example of a significant moment. Students who screen

these films, read this book, and participate in the dedicated online community learn this language of film along with several interpretive strategies and hence, most films (and TV shows, music videos, filmed commercials) begin to signify in a more meaningful way, and in turn, student responses become clearer and more persuasive as well. My approach to teaching fiction, drama, and film seeks to demonstrate how to describe and interpret stylized structural and linguistic choices. Film students analyze titles, word choices, character's names, and, armed with technical film terms and concepts employed from the eTextbook, they read closely the use of camera (graphic match, spatial relationships, canted angles, point of view), editing, lighting, set, soundtrack, and costume design. For example, students are introduced to the concept of the graphic match, which consists of two or more shots linked by similar visual elements. The significance of this stylistic choice visually links the meaning of the two objects—they are a pair of parallel signifiers contributing meaning to each other.

Early on in John Ford's *Stagecoach* (1939), the Calvary Scout (Yakima Canutt) assures the telegraph operator not to fear the collaborating Cheyenne Indian Scout (Chief John Big Tree) standing in his office, stating: "They [the Cheyenne] hate the Apaches worse than we do." As we hear that line we see an insert shot close-up that is held for several seconds of the Cheyenne Scout scowling wordlessly. Like most elements of a stylized moment, this shot sticks out like a sore thumb. An insert shot is often a medium or close-up shot that clarifies detail and punctuates meaning from a previous master shot. Several minutes and scenes later in the film we are introduced to a distinguished looking bank officer named Henry Gatewood (Berton Churchill) who, after self-righteously pronouncing "What's good for the banks is good for the country," is then placed for a few seconds in a near identical insert close-up, like the Cheyenne, wordless and scowling. Again, after being hen-pecked by his wife with the threat that the members of the Ladies' Law and Justice League are coming over for lunch, we see the same wordless insert close-up of Gatewood. Gatewood then proceeds to stuff $50,000 of his depositors' money into his black bag and heads out on the stagecoach with his embezzled funds. The logic of the graphic match is undeniable. A relation between the Indian who is betraying his "red"-skinned brethren is established visually with the banker who is betraying his stakeholders, not to mention his wife. The graphic match italicizes this relationship, presented in Figure 2.

Symbolically linking the content of analogous images within a film via the graphic match is one of cinema's most pervasive stylistic practices. Once introduced to this concept, students begin to discover other graphic matches throughout the semester, and hopefully continue to do so regarding all of these stylized elements for many years to come.

The eTextbook

A perusal of the eTextbook's Table of Contents explicitly reveals the content of the course.

Stylized Moments: Turning Film Style Into Meaning
William McBride, Illinois State University
Contents

Figure 2. Two betrayers connected via the graphic match

Chapter Fourteen
Blue Velvet (Lynch 1986)
opening and closing montages
film noir inside a film noir
Chekhov's dictum
the ear of Denmark
garden hose and artery conceptually matched
industrial soundscapes
two primal scenes
Booth and Lincoln
the voyeur caught in the act
slow motion or over cranking
shock cut/lightning mix
shifting tone
beneath the surface/various vegetation shots
stairs lead to knowledge and danger
three beer analysis
masochism's theatricality
pop songs turned upside down
authorial distance
the throwaway test
the tyranny of the ending
soft or shallow focus
rack focus
deep focus
two diseases
Glossary

A few days before the beginning of the online class I send out a welcoming email to all registerees. Most students are already familiar with the workings of Illinois State University's collaborative web-based learning environment "Reggienet" managed by the Sakai system which features communication tools, accommodates assignment submission and grading, and "houses" film links to the University's streaming server. The email also provides a link to the eTextbook website at Smashwords. The advantage of students reading this text electronically is that each insight and accompanying screen shot exemplar is right in front of them on their screen to be dwelled upon at their own pace rather than projected in a classroom momentarily. In a f2f configuration students listening to a lecture do have the immediate opportunity to ask for clarification, for another example, or for another way of expressing the same point, while asynchronous online students do not. Online students certainly have the option to electronically request clarification on any point contained in the eTextbook, and such requests do occur, although they require more effort on the student's part than merely raising one's hand. Since turning this augmented version of my weekly lectures into an eBook, I have opted to deliver the course exclusively online since a f2f iteration in a lecture hall would be unproductively redundant. Students begin the class by reading the eTextbook's introductory chapter which answers two targeted questions addressed above: what is a "stylized moment" and how does one differ from a merely "significant moment"?

The age-old wisdom about Hollywood style is that it strives to be *invisible*. This is evident in the title of the 2004 PBS documentary *Masters of Production: The Hidden Art of Hollywood*. Unlike so-called "foreign films," those selected "art" films university film professors invariably assign that are not produced in North America and that self-consciously use style, most American films traditionally stick to an invisible, rather neutral, functional approach. As President of The Art Directors Guild, Jackson Degovia, explains in the *Hidden Art* documentary, films work "because they look real, they don't make you stop and think." While all the films considered in my film course are American and mainstream, each one constitutes a significant exception to Degovia's rule about which I do encourage my students to stop and think. The course homepage describes Film Style & Literature ENG 124 this way:

Think of this course as an intensive English Department literature course in which you write essays in a "foreign" language—the language of film. The theory of Film Style & Literature argues that style can be described, analyzed, and turned into meaning via metaphor. Your goal is to acquire adequate film vocabulary and skill to convert your observations of camera placement and movement, lighting, spatial relationships, soundtrack, etc. into an analysis of the meaning of a "stylized moment" and, from that, of the film as a whole. Do not be misled by the fact that this is a 100 level General Education course—it is nonetheless challenging. It is essential to distinguish between style and significance: all stylized moments carry meaning, not all significant moments are stylized—see "Guide to Writing Essays" and eTextbook.

In a first-chapter-dedicated Discussion Forum students are asked to demonstrate their comprehension of this distinction for their discussion group to share, and are awarded points. After this introductory reading and assignment have been completed during the first week, students are instructed to screen the first assigned film, the hugely popular screwball comedy *Caddyshack* (1980), read the accompanying eTextbook chapter, and demonstrate their grasp of the material by composing an entry in the dedicated Discussion Forum.

Discussion Forum Groups

Since there are a limited number of stylized and significant moments in each film, a population of 100 would inevitably begin repeating what their classmates had written and thereby necessitates the setting up of smaller groups for each weekly discussion forum. This step limits access so students only see what their group, comprised of five students, posts. This way I can realistically require students to submit original content for each forum since their feedback loop contains only four other responders and there are certainly at least five unique moments in each film. *This stipulation of originality guarantees a kind of engagement and interaction within each group.* Students are instructed that they may write on the same moment as has a classmate if their interpretation differs significantly. Setting up individual fora for each student group for each of the eleven

assigned films and chapters is initially daunting, repetitive work, but once established within the Reggienet site, those fora are transferrable to each future semester. At the beginning of the semester students are told,

Each of you has been assigned to a group of five. You will only view four other posts each week in the Discussion Fora. Your assignment each week is to describe and discuss stylized and significant moments from that week's film. You may not repeat the same moments discussed by one of your classmates. In order to avoid such repetition it is paramount that you read all posts that precede yours and provide recognizably different content. You may describe and discuss the same moment if your description and interpretation is different from that of your classmate. You may also respond to classmates' posts as you describe and interpret your two moments.

Organizing students into discussion groups of five, and prohibiting the repetition of similar material previously posted by classmates ensures presence, interaction, and engagement with each other's work. Students must read what classmates have already posted in order not to repeat that content. Each student *must* post an analysis of weekly assigned films and readings in a discussion forum, which serves as a kind of chat room where students and teachers engage in feedback loops available for all within dedicated groups to witness and in which to participate for credit. Once that forum is closed my TAs and I read and post responses to interesting points made, correct imprecise descriptions, point out unconvincing interpretations, and answer questions raised. These responses are available for everyone in the dedicated cohort to read, allowing another level of engagement, interaction, and learning to occur. Although points for each weekly post are minimal, combined they constitute more than a third of a student's overall grade. Students with questions are urged to contact the instructor or TA during virtual office hours and via email at any time. To best strategically manage correspondences between students and teachers the TAs and I cc each other on all of our email replies to students' inquiries, ensuring we are "all on the same page."

Since there is a word count minimum for these posts, the most effective way to grade them is to copy and paste each post into an open word document for easy word count and visibility. The best practice is to not grade these submissions until that Forum is closed and then assess an entire group of five in one sitting in order to track "originality" within that group. Each week the forum opens Monday 8am and closes Thursday 11:59 pm.

The instructions for each week's Discussion Forum assignment stipulates:

Identify (plot wise and w/ time stamp) and discuss 1 example of a cinematically stylized moment—a moment only achievable in films—and 1 example of a significant moment not dependent on the language of film. Your entry may not repeat material covered by classmates who have posted before you. 250-word minimum.

To insure weekly student/teacher and student/student presence, interaction and participation in the course material students are presented on the course website with the following stipulation, "Students may not choose those assignments (regardless of the point value) they wish to complete." All students necessarily must participate weekly in the class and interact with their teachers and classmates. All responses to films and eTextbook sections and the two assigned essays must be submitted on time. Students are encouraged to post well before the due date and time. After three missed assignments points are deducted from the final grade. Extra credit opportunities and a curve are also extended. Participants in the Discussion forum are presented with the reactions of their classmate group, and when removed from a physical classroom setting, all voices receive "equal time."

The pedagogical goal is to show how to apply these skills to each film and text studied. After students read the long first chapter, complete the expanded Discussion Forum assignment by reading posts by fellow group members and identifying, describing, and interpreting stylized and significant moments, they receive and review detailed feedback from the instructors. Students then launch into the weekly schedule of an assigned film, chapter, and Discussion post in four "Phases," comprised of "Genres," "Hitchcock," "Theater on Film," and "American Independents."

Genres, Hitchcock, Theater on Film, American Independents

"Genres" begins, as does the class, with the screwball comedy *Caddyshack*, then comes the film noir *Maltese Falcon*, and we conclude with the Western and Social Drama, *Stagecoach*. The "Hitchcock" phase is comprised of *Notorious* and *Vertigo*, and concludes with the mid term essay on *Psycho* (discussed below). Following the mid term we turn to studying the filming of stage plays, namely *Death of a Salesman, Who's Afraid of Virginia Woolf?, Dutchman*, and *Miss Julie*, the latter comprising one of two extra credit assignments. The final phase is an examination of American Independents," specifically David Lynch's *Blue Velvet* and Martin Scorsese's *Taxi Driver*, and as the final extra credit assignment, Scorsese's *Life Lessons*. Each week's Discussion Forum requires the student to "identify (plot wise and time stamp) and discuss 1 example of a cinematically stylized moments—those moments only achievable in films—and 1 example of a significant moment not dependent on the language of film. 250 word minimum."

As one can see, the schedule of films begins with a hugely popular, albeit 35 year old, cult screwball comedy classic, *Caddyshack*—a film that critics have yet to appreciate, beyond its near universal popularity, or acknowledge as important. This curricular choice immediately establishes a populist principle that goes against the grain of University art film/foreign film studies prevalent throughout American universities and as practiced in other departments at my university. It also demonstrates to students, particularly those who seem to know the film "by heart," how these stylized filmic gestures can be discovered in the most unexpected places. Students see potential meaning, for example, behind what seems to be a run of the mill slow motion (over cranked) sequence of a lifeguard tower being toppled. Slow motion or over cranking is so called because more than 24 frames per second—the ideal, standardized speed at which to capture the illusion of movement—are taken by the camera (i.e., over cranking) so that when they are projected back at 24 frames per second (each frame exposed twice per second), the movement appears slower than real time. The common effect of slow motion is a dreamlike experience and often it allows the viewer to savor the moment. Just as when I first introduce the stylized moment concept by explaining what it is not with the functional shot/reverse shot, the eTextbook exhibits a functional use of slow motion before analyzing a stylized one. As the yacht of

the newly rich "slob," Al Czervik (Rodney Dangerfield), engages in violent piloting, a fisherman catches his hook on one of its masts and is taken for a brief stuntman ride of excitement, and we see a pair of jet skiers breach over Al's wake that is filmed in slow motion. As discussed throughout *Stylized Moments*, slow motion is almost always a stylized choice as it is during the scene to which I will return when the caddies take over the pool, but the slow motion here is *not stylized*. This shot of the jet skiers is in slow motion perhaps to lend it an "instant replay" feel to this sportsman blooper reel with no other deep meaning and is therefore merely functional (Figure 3).

The film's director, Harold Ramis, shows a stylized use of slow motion and angles however when depicting the lifeguard (Marcus Breece) during the chaotic pool scene. This enforcer of the rules of decent pool society blows his whistle on Angie D'Annunzio (Peter Berkot), ordering him to put back on his swimsuit. The first close up of the lifeguard in midshot is taken from an extreme low angle which students learn stylistically depicts his power and height as we look up at him (Figure 4). He immediately has a wet

Figure 3. A typically stylized gesture, slow motion, is here empty of meaning as if part of a blooper reel

towel thrown in his face foreshadowing the next element of the stylized moment to come. Once the caddies push over the lifeguard's tower, the audience witnesses this icon of rules and regulations come tumbling down in slow motion from his position of strength and authority, breaking the fictive reality of the scene as it breaks "the fourth wall." Readers of *Stylized Moments* learn that in the theater the fourth wall is that invisible line between actors and audience. Everything that happens behind that imaginary line is virtually real for the duration of the performance. It is the social convention we all accept when consuming narrative art as explained by Coleridge's dictum: "the willing suspension of disbelief" (p. 308). In traditional proscenium arch theatrical productions, that fourth wall that separates actors from audience is never to be crossed in order to maintain the illusion that what happens behind it, on stage, is "real. " Out of a fear of breaking this "fictive reality," one of the cardinal rules of stage acting prohibits the actor from looking directly into the eyes of the audience members or walking off stage into the audience, and film acting continues that tradition by forbidding direct eye contact with the camera or calling attention to the filmmaking. This breaking of the fourth wall however was a practice preached by the Marxist theorist and playwright Berthold Brecht as a way to prompt critical thinking by the audience, which he saw lacking, for example, at Nazi rallies. Many filmmakers strategically have adopted this strategy, as does Ramis

here. The stylization of this over cranking allows the audience to savor this emblematic moment and have its meaning of overturning hierarchical power punctuated. Interestingly enough, once in the pool the lifeguard joins the fun and raises on his shoulders a voluptuous woman who removes her bikini top.

What follows in Film Style & Literature from analyzing this screwball comedy is a genre-based exploration of the history of cinema by addressing both film noir (*The Maltese Falcon*) and the Western (*Stagecoach*). John Huston's *The Maltese Falcon* exhibits, in addition to the aforementioned shadow on the face of the *femme fatale* and other stylized shadows, a stylized tilt down, and an extreme low angle of the powerful "heavy" Casper Gutman (Sydney Greenstreet), as well as Dashiell Hammett's existential investigation into the hard-boiled tradition. John Ford's *Stagecoach* introduces students to the practice of the aforementioned stylized graphic match, the zoom in, "mickey-mousing," deep focus photography, and a cinematic mistake. Then comes Alfred Hitchcock.

In *Notorious* students study split point of view, extreme oblique angles, a merging of two characters' shadows, global image patterns, and a stylized use of props. *Vertigo* introduces students to the infamous "vertigo shot" as it is compared to the "Mickey Finn" shot and its use of blue screen, the stylized opening title sequence, global image patterns, and the reading of repeated stylized poses. No director deploys stylized moments as

Figure 4. Low angle signifies power & authority. Slo-mo savors and punctuates meaning of the descent

consistently and effectively as Alfred Hitchcock. I recently taught a tremendously rewarding graduate seminar consisting entirely of his stylized films, and just published "Hitchcock's Stylized Capture of Post-Adolescent Fatheads" in the volume *Children in the Films of Alfred Hitchcock* from Palgrave-McMillan.

Midterm Essay

Once students complete their assignments on *Notorious* and *Vertigo*, they begin work on their first essay. It is an investigation of the stylized sequence that immediately follows the infamous stabbing sequence in *Psycho* that requires students to deploy all of the vocabulary and tools learned thus far. A detailed grading rubric, *unavailable to students prior to composing their essays*, is applied to each submitted essay. I reproduce it here (see Table 1) with the fervent hope that no industrious undergraduate reads this chapter!

I personally grade half of the *Psycho* midterm essays and TAs each grade a quarter each of those remaining. The same grading distribution applies to the final *Into The Wild* essay ensuring that throughout the semester I have the opportunity to grade at least one of each of the student's two major exam essays, and the TAs swap the

Midterm essay population for the final. Prior to writing, students read a version of the following information in the digitized "Guide to Writing Essays," which includes detailed prompts for both the *Psycho* post-stabbing Midterm (but not the grading rubric) and the *Into the Wild* Final essay as well as a section entitled "Frequently Made Mistakes."

I explain that their essays should provide a working definition of what a stylized moment is, justify those moments chosen as stylized, and argue what these selected moments signify. To insure that the meanings they assign do not seem arbitrary, they must argue the logic of these meanings, while answering the question, "What is the internal logic established within the film that authorizes these meanings and not others?" I remind them to keep in mind the difference between plot significance ("This is when we find out Judge Smails is dishonest") and stylistic significance ("This scene uses a canted angle and point of view shots to convey Radio Raheem's brewing anger and frustration.") Most casual viewers can talk about plot, but my film students will attend to style. They know that should be their field of inquiry.

I also seek to demonstrate for students the difference between a shot that is just filmed in a "cool" manner (i.e. the drug sequences in *The Big*

Table 1. Elements-all authorial camera

	Description	Interpretation
Water/Blood r to l pan zoom in/counterclockwise into drain	/3	/2
Diegetic sound water/drain--Lap Dissolve to Eye graphic match	/3	/2
Camera counter clock matches drain zoom out--Face Tableau Showerhead edit	/3	/2
Pan l to r to nightstand/zoom/push in newspaper	/2	/1
Pan l to r past vine pattern wallpaper	/2	/1
To window/internal frame/Bates House-storm clouds Tableau. "Mother!"-runs	/3	/2
Edit camera outside cabin/Non-diegetic sndtk heard before	/3	/2
Edit cabin r to l pan/back to camera/no music/bird pix	/4	/3
Film as a whole	/23	/4 /19 Your grade: /30 Out of possible 42

Lebowski [1998] and most other such sequences) and scenes that use style to convey an explicit meaning (i.e. the use of tracking back and forth tight close-ups in *Who's Afraid of Virginia Woolf?* [1966] to portray Martha as a trapped animal). The drug sequences may be fun to look at, but don't really have anything substantive to say via style other than the transparent message that the main character is under the influence of drugs. It is much more productive to analyze the second kind of cinematic moment than the first.

Regarding academic honesty I explain that they may be working in groups or dealing with ideas from the eTextbook and that in their essays they must be extremely careful to develop their own unique and insightful ideas and to give credit to every idea and language that is not their own. For example, if they are writing an essay with another person or persons, they must make sure their essay makes its own unique points, and that they write in parentheses at the end of the shared sentence the last name of the person in their cohort whose idea or words they used. It is up to each member of a study group to agree upon consistently and accurately assigning credit for ideas, words, etc. When using ideas brought up in the eTextbook, students should use them only to advance their own points, and then write the word "eTextbook" in parentheses following their appearance. Students are required to always discuss sources and place quotation marks around any words that are not their own, and provide page numbers or a full web address and a works cited page. The Midterm and Final essays are designed to be "plagiarism-proof," and in The Guide to Writing Essays I warn students away from consulting film summaries found in texts and on websites, and stick to discovering, describing and interpreting stylized moments. Students are encouraged to consult MLA documentation rules and visit the University's Student Conduct & Conflict Resolution Website. If one is caught plagiarizing, even if it is "unintentional," a student is assigned an "F" for the course.

Students who do poorly on these essays often simply 'list' shots, such as several cuts in a row, but never say anything about the effect, the significance of those moments. They are instructed to avoid just listing shots, to have patience, and to spend time discussing what every choice confers in the sequence, and what it contributes to the film as a whole. Some "Frequently Made Mistakes" are presented:

- It is not effective to claim that a stylized moment "draws the audience in," "creates interest," "grabs our attention," etc. These shots are almost always functional and carry no deeper meaning.
- It is essential to distinguish between style and significance: all stylized moments carry meaning, are significant, not all meaningful/signficant moments (such as meaningful soundtrack lyrics, character's names) are stylized.
- Reserve the word "focus" for describing actual soft focus, deep focus, rack focus, etc. Avoid using it as a metaphor. Replace "This zoom in focuses on his sister" with "This zoom in results in a close up of his sister" or "targets his sister" or "centers on his sister" etc. Incidentally, zooms and close ups are rarely stylized in and of themselves because they merely "grab our attention."
- Title your essay! The absence of an original title is a missed opportunity to further advance your thesis.
- Some readings are stronger than others and some ways of analyzing lead to better essays than others. The best arguments are those that are well supported with specific evidence accompanied by an insightful discussion of that evidence.

The assignment for the Midterm *Psycho* essay explains the three-step process for composing a successful essay:

Midterm Essay-*Psycho* (minimum 900 words. 30 points)

Your analysis of the scene will consist of three parts—be sure to *combine* 1 and 2:

1. The scene you need to analyze shot by shot begins with the blood traveling down the tub basin and ends with Norman inadvertently knocking down the picture from the wall. Describe the scene in film terms employing the technical language of cinema - camera technique, mise en scene, lighting, soundtrack, props, editing, etc. Read the eTextbook carefully and appropriately use as many of these terms as you can, such as close-up, lap dissolve, etc. Remember to discuss all aspects of the scene;

2. Discuss what meaning these film techniques reasonably confer via style. You should employ the eTextbook to support your points. For example "This scene is shot in a canted angle, meaning that the camera is off of its vertical axis giving us a slanted view of the scene. Typically, this angle implies 'a world off kilter (Stylized Moments)." Then go beyond this to provide your own unique and keen insight to what this may mean in the scene. For example "The canted angle here tells us that Radio Raheem is an "off kilter" character about to explode."

3. Analyze this scene in terms of the entire movie. Discuss both large themes in the movie - coming of age, sexuality, evil, etc. - and specific parts of the movie - the opening, the climax, the ending - in order to ground your ideas in the movie itself. Make sure you discuss the entire movie with a consideration of how the film ends.

Your grade will be based upon how accurately and consistently you use film terms to analyze the scene, how thoroughly you attend to all aspects of the scene, how specifically your interpretation fol-

lows from the film terms, and finally how insightful and smart your overall interpretation is. You should go point by point through the scene analyzing the techniques in turn, combining parts 1 and 2 as you write. Students often feel overwhelmed that they cannot possibly 'read' all of the deep meanings in the scene, but if you concentrate on analyzing specific stylistic techniques, you will do well. We will tend to be more lenient grading this first essay, as we understand this is your first extended attempt at analyzing style. You should be creative and speculative, but be specific and prove your interpretations by discussing the scene in film language.

TAs or I typically insert over 20 comments in the margin of the student's submitted word file. Midterm essays are typically graded and returned within 10 days and on occasion a student may request an in-person meeting usually in hopes of clarification and an enhanced grade. I direct such students whose essays I did not grade to first meet with the TA whose initials appear on their graded work, and if they still wish to meet with me following that I will schedule a time. In preparation to respond to such emails, I reread their graded essay and summarize again for them the elements they neglected or ineffectively described/interpreted which have been explicitly detailed in the grading rubric. I also encourage all struggling students requesting a meeting to be sure to complete the optional extra credit postings and to begin work on their final essay. I explain in preparation for composing the final essay that they first need to finish reading the eTextbook, then the non-fiction text *Into the Wild* by Jon Krakauer, which is a free eBook, stored as a pdf in Resources & Materials. They are then to screen Sean Penn's film version of the same name taking notes before composing their descriptions and interpretations of the required three stylized moments and send them to us (either me or the TA assigned to grade that essay) via email to which we will provide detailed feedback, indicating what seems effective description and analysis and where they might improve. I indicate this is just a starting point and we will respond to a series of drafts as students wish until the deadline passes. Upon receiving this email, most students realize meeting in person is not necessary and do not request such a meeting. Following the grading of the Mid Term *Psycho* Essay, a compendium of particularly well-described and analyzed moments along with oft-committed missteps is usually posted online in the "Announcements" section for the entire class to review.

A unit on films of classic American plays follows the Midterm essay, fostering a discussion of film/theater connections and an examination of the ontological differences between the two. In their study of Schlondorff's *Death of a Salesman* (1986) students are again exposed to a "breaking of the fourth wall" and learn about the crane shot, as they encounter Arthur Miller's incisive critique of the "American Dream." Nichols' *Who's Afraid of Virginia Woolf?* (1966) exposes students to stylized lap dissolves, canted frames, tracking in, and Albee's witty and devastating puzzle making. Finally Harvey's *Dutchman* (1966) introduces students to stylized sets, splitting of point of view, and Leroi Jones'/Amiri Baraka's brilliant diatribe on race in America. Insights I have developed in that chapter are about to be published as "*Dutchman* Heaped in Modern Cinema" in the widely used *MLA Approaches to Teaching* series, this one on *Amiri Baraka's Dutchman*.

Students then turn to the work of two iconic auteur American directors, Martin Scorsese and David Lynch. They examine Scorsese's widely recognized masterpiece *Taxi Driver* (1976) with its stylized *faux raccord*, jump cut, and Bernard Herrmann's stylized split soundtrack. Their last assigned film before the final is the controversial *Blue Velvet* (1986) by David Lynch. Students are exposed again to Chekhov's Dictum, voyeurism, shock cut/lightning mix, and authorial distance.

Final Essay

Students are then given two weeks to study *Into the Wild*, both the 1996 non-fiction book by Jon Krakauer and the 2007 film by Sean Penn and compose their final essay. The end of the course presents to students the opportunity to demonstrate their proficiency at identifying, accurately describing, and delivering convincing interpretations of a number of stylized moments in the film. Ending the semester with the story of the questioning college grad Chris McCandless (Emile Hirsch) nicely bookends with the similar questioning of the semester's first film's protagonist, *Caddyshack*'s Danny Noonan (Michael O'Keefe). In the first film a young man asks the existential questions about the meaning of life as the High School grad anticipates entering college, and in the final film a young man asks those same questions having finished his degree at Emory University. The following instructions for the final essay explain the requirements and how to compose a successful final:

Final Essay-*Into The Wild* (35 points)

This essay asks you to write a longer and more detailed analysis than the Midterm did, and requires you to include a literary component in order to address the "Literature" part of the course's title as the eTextbook has been all semester. Identify, describe and interpret 3 stylized sequences from Sean Penn's film just as you did with the shower scene in Psycho. Be specific, prove your points with film language, and demonstrate that you have learned something from the course. We will certainly grade this essay more rigorously than the first, as we will expect that you have become proficient at analyzing style by this point. Use the literary component as additional support for your argument; this is not a book report, you should use the book to analyze the movie—a minimum of four consecutive words quoted in your essay from Jon Krakauer's book not used in the film.

Extra Credit

Penn's film provides a wealth of stylized moments from split screens to jump cuts to rack focus to global image patterns. During the course of the semester, as already indicated, students have the opportunity to screen, read eTextbook chapters about, and post on two additional films for extra credit, Scorsese's short film *Life Lessons* (1989) and an adaptation of Strindberg's *Miss Julie* (1999) directed by Mike Figgis. *Life Lessons* introduces students to double point of view, iris fades, set framing of characters, and a stylized application of a pop song. *Miss Julie* allows them to witness and analyze the use of split screen. Although these are extra credit posts, students are required to read the corresponding chapters nonetheless, particularly since their final film, *Into the Wild*, stylistically uses the split screen technique covered in the eTextbook chapter on *Miss Julie*.

The Nuts and Bolts of Online Instructional Quality, Rigor, and Asynchronous/f2f Contrasts

Films lend themselves particularly well to asynchronous online instruction and analysis since a semester's curriculum of films can be streamed on a password-protected university server. Traditional f2f film courses already inaugurate technology's integration within education by extending the classification of the canon to these audio/visual "texts". An asynchronous pedagogical approach is useful in distance learning whereby the instruction and student participation and performance is not limited by time and place. Some key advantages are indeed lost when viewing a feature film on one's own in front of a computer screen or even smaller 4 to 6 inch smart device screen. One can

no longer experience the dynamic of a public crowd of strangers nor monitor those reactions of laughter, gasps, tears, and odd silences. The relative enormity of the movie house screen (roughly 20 feet wide by 50 feet tall but this varies) and the sumptuousness of its professional sound system (or typical university lecture hall equivalent), are sacrificed when viewed on a 16" or smaller computer screen and listened to via the inferior sound reproduction of desktop speakers (somewhat mitigated by a good pair of headphones). Many advantages are nonetheless also gained.

Digital age students are comfortable and adept at viewing visual narratives on individual smaller screens. Individual screening affords students multiple ways to study a film. Online film students can asynchronically watch, rewatch and manipulate at will their primary resource, the assigned film. Viewing a film repeatedly, like reading and rereading any text, is a prime technique for successfully identifying a stylized moment or for grasping a particular nuance in a film, and with frame-by-frame advance even closer scrutiny is possible. Cueing an entire film or section via fast-forward and/or rewind may also reveal certain previously undetected visual patterns such as graphic matches established over a period of time in separate scenes. Other defamiliarizing techniques such as turning down the audio may open other unexpected, fruitful passageways into meaningful stylistic aspects of a film.

All Illinois State University undergraduates must complete the General Education Program. Film Style & Literature has successfully received its designation as a Language in the Humanities "Middle Core" General Education course. The student population each semester is extremely diverse representing all majors from Accountancy and Acting to Technology & Engineering Education. This is not the place to launch a comparative analysis of the benefits and challenges of teaching classes limited to students within one's college or department versus general education classes open to the entire university, however, suffice it to say that the notion of educating a representative sampling of *all* majors provides a certain kind of empowering teacher satisfaction.

Asynchronous/f2f Contrasts

As any teacher of a f2f class knows, certain students invariably dominate discussions, often with superb insights that at times may be expressed with untrained enthusiasm, but nonetheless good will. Since f2f class time is limited, other voices are inevitably drowned out. The necessary f2f restricting of such exuberance can have the unintended effect of tamping down a motivated student's love for the subject matter and learning. Once physically present bodies and voices are removed, along with the brick and mortar classroom, certain elements such as in-person spontaneous humor, passion, and immediacy are inevitably sacrificed. This is one of online education's greatest losses. Individual, personalized attention to the everyday output of each student, however, and a different kind of immediacy are gained via online instruction, because only such interaction is available online. TAs read and respond to student posts and award successful submissions a maximum of 3 points each week. I monitor a representative sampling of these exchanges and respond to any error-filled or inflammatory (rare) entries flagged by the TAs. Students are encouraged to read TA responses as well since this is where a second order of learning occurs. This opportunity for students to witness both the work of their classmates and the responses of their teachers creates a collaborative working group and is a decided advantage to online instruction, although I use discussion groups in my f2f classes as well. In a positive way, 100% online instruction's removal of physically present bodies and voices prevents the often-unrecognized discriminatory practice commonly know as "lookism." This prejudicial practice of perhaps favoring those who's body types

and ethnicities match one's cultural expectations could lead, however unintended, to preferential treatment toward one student over another. Just as online students are necessarily afforded equal time, they can also receive evaluation potentially unbiased by lookism as well. It is nonetheless important to note most online instructors do use University-generated rosters replete with student identification photos, and of course one can never perfectly eradicate every possible degree of unintentional prejudicial practice.

Students who struggle in my 100% online delivery of Film Style & Literature find themselves confronted with certain obstacles. Any successful online student must be "computer literate," self-monitoring and self-motivated. While it may appear as a "given" for any academic success, online students who lack certain traditional literacy skills are immediately confronted with stumbling blocks. No matter how simple or detailed an instructor's syllabus and other pedagogical components may be, there are those students who either do not, nor cannot, effectively read these materials. Some students who do not thrive in the asynchronous online community are those who require repeated in-person contact and feedback, despite the appearance of electronic reminders on the website or in their email inbox. The efficacy of redundancy in all pedagogical approaches is well known. Studies of rhetoric and information theory stress the importance of repeating a message as an antidote to noise in any communication system. Students with communication difficulties often wrestle with translating written instructions, assignments, and prompts into meaningful guidelines. The relationships between learner and instructor, and between individual learners are changed dramatically in the online iteration of Film Style & Literature, as is the interaction between learner and content. It may at first sound counterintuitive to claim there is a more intimate learner-instructor connection in an online course, but my experience has shown that attention to each student's weekly posts and electronic essay submissions requires a more comprehensive response to that written work since those are my only grading parameters. When the immediate instructor-learner presence of f2f configurations is absent, greater focus is given to each student's output. It is important to note that online students read each week a chapter dedicated to that week's film in the *Stylized Moments* textbook in lieu of a f2f lecture. So much more detailed material is packed into these individual chapters than I could ever cover in the limited weekly class time.

My experience with scheduled voluntary live or synchronous chat rooms has shown that only a handful of committed and active students participate along with a few of those who are troubled about participation and think they *must* log on, and those who suspect it may garner extra points. I have thereby discontinued scheduled voluntary synchronous chat rooms since requiring them would be counter-productive. Part of the charm and advantage of asynchronous online instruction is the student can engage and participate on her or his own timetable within the strictures of assigned deadlines There are already enough extra credit opportunities that negate the efficacy of assigning potential points to required synchronous chat room participation, however much it might approximate the spontaneity of the f2f classroom experience.

FUTURE RESEARCH DIRECTIONS

Millennials will continue to push universities to adapt to ever improving technology and AI (Artificial Intelligence) applications and capabilities; universities welcome the cost savings on instructional facilities and related staff. Subsequent investigations of technology-based pedagogical models must and most likely will continue to develop innovations in individualized learning. The field will also require research and development of strategies that mitigate the potential of online education to isolate both teachers and students. If the charge of the educational system is to foster life-long learning, we must also be vigilant in creating innovative and effective ways to monitor the quality of instructional outcomes.

CONCLUSION

The current push for online instruction can cynically be ascribed to a financial consideration of the bottom line which is served by not having to illuminate, maintain, nor control the temperature of a brick and mortar building, but things are not that simple. The liberation students *and* teachers who engage in asynchronous online education is undeniable. They can participate and interact with the material on a laptop in the comfort of one's own home or dorm room, apartment, remote coffee shop, or on smart devices as they travel by train or car, or as they lounge on the quad. An asynchronous pedagogical approach allows instruction and student participation and performance anytime anywhere within the limits of deadlines. Traditional f2f film courses already inaugurate technology's integration within education by extending the classification of the canon to these audio/visual "texts". Films in particular lend themselves well to asynchronous online instruction and interpretation since they can be accessed on a password-protected university streaming-server at anytime and from anywhere with an Internet connection.

Film Style & Literature is unlike most university film "appreciation" courses that typically teach narrative critique and genre study. This film course and accompanying eTextbook seek to demonstrate that the only legitimately objective way to interpret a film and its narrative is to attend to its cinematic stylized moments, otherwise one may as well be analyzing a novel, play, or short story. This approach provides interpretive strategies that analyze entire films by means of identifying, defining, and explaining their stylized moments, and then applying those insights toward an interpretation of each film as a whole. What we do in analyzing these moments is we articulate and interpret *choices* that are made by the artists who created the film. The logic operating here states that interpreters can produce a convincing reading of a film by targeting for analysis particular moments where the director has gently or not so gently nudged the audience with stylized cinematic gestures that, when decoded, unlock significance. After these moments have been identified and analyzed in isolation, the interpretive results can be integrated into the film's entire system of signs in order to reach conclusions with extraordinary explanatory power about the film as a whole. The basic premise by which this approach operates is known as structuralism, a linguistic and anthropological procedure of understanding social phenomena as part of a system of signs whose meaning resides in their interrelationships. This structuralist approach to film claims that each stylized moment carries meaning based on the generally accepted conventions of mainstream moviemaking language and that, like beginning with the imbedded code of a tiny sample of DNA, the entire organism, or film, can be convincingly and thoroughly explicated.

While the bulk of American popular films do not contain stylized moments, examples do abound: The downward pointed shadow caused by the elevator cage cast across Brigid O'Shaughnessy's face at the end of *The Maltese Falcon*, the simultaneously tracking in/zooming out pov shots in *Vertigo*, the *faux raccord* transition from Sport and Iris slow dancing to Travis Bickle firing at the shooting range in *Taxi Driver*, the jump cuts during Alex Supertramp's apple monologue from *Into the Wild* all speak the "foreign" language of film. Arguing that film style can be described, analyzed, and translated into meaning via metaphor, this asynchronous 100% online course and accompanying eTextbook deploy film vocabulary and skill in order to convert observations of camera placement and movement,

lighting, spatial relationships, editing, soundtrack, costuming, prop arrangement, set design, etc. into an analysis of the meaning of "stylized moments" and, from that, of the film as a whole. Film Style & Literature grants the ubiquity of the moving image and the ideological juices that it sends coursing through our brains and veins, while it considers the ramifications of such a study for an engaged and responsible citizenry. The grander goal of this course is to serve as a step toward better reading our "movied" selves as well as our movies. Students are thereby introduced to the practice of "hermeneutics," or the science of interpretation. This search for meaning in texts is marked by a concern with the relation between interpretive subject and text. This interpretive strategy is invaluable in all aspects of life. The sumptuous and immediate, interactive film-going experience in the movie theater or university lecture hall is no doubt surrendered in online iterations of the film class, but in its place appears the manipulability of the original film source with all of its attendant benefits for study along with its mobility and availability at any time.

Limiting discussion groups to five allows the instructor and TAs to effectively require that students create unique content while it ensures presence, interaction, and engagement with each other's work since they must read what classmates have already posted in order not to repeat that content. The opportunity for students to witness both the work of their classmates and the responses of their teachers creates a collaborative working group and is a decided advantage over f2f instruction. Online discussion groups also guarantee all voices receive "equal time." Students who are connected virtually with access to the same online platform and resources are able to experience a kind of equality not available in the physical world. Personal elements such as spontaneous humor, passion, and immediacy that characterize the synchronous brick and mortar classroom experience are inevitably sacrificed. Individual, personalized attention to the everyday output of each student, however, and a different kind of immediacy are gained via online instruction, because only such individualized interaction is available online. Just as online students are necessarily afforded equal time, so online students can receive evaluation unbiased by lookism as well. Attention to each student's weekly posts and electronic essay submissions requires a more comprehensive response to that written work since those are the only grading parameters. When the immediate instructor-learner presence of f2f configurations is absent, greater focus can be given to each student's output.

The transmission of knowledge and learning skills remains the charter of all educational institutions, something we have been doing since Plato's Academy. The ramifications of fewer f2f university experiences within brick and mortar establishments inevitably raise questions that pertain to our ever-increasingly technology-determined lives in general. The advent of such "smart" technology has the potential to isolate us as it obviates physical social interaction, a concern I expressed in a paper delivered at the 2015 American Comparative Literature Association Annual Meeting entitled "'She's Not There': Shallow Focus on Emerging Techno-Mediated Modes of Being in Spike Jonze's *Her*." One of the rich but, in the end, unassessable outcomes of the traditional brick and mortar pedagogical experience whether in primary or graduate school is the socializing maturity that can result. Despite online instruction's attempts at integration and participation, aspects of the flesh-and-blood presence and synchronous immediacy of traditional schooling is unreproducible and irreplaceable. On the other hand, with the democratizing effect of online education as it continues to morph and grow, students will increasingly have better access to a variety of teachers, cohorts, and resources, as a single pocketed smart device replaces the backpack filled with 25-60 pounds of textbooks.

REFERENCES

Barthes, R. (1980). *La Chambre claire*trans (R. Howard, Trans.). Hill and Wang.

Bevan, T. (Producer) & Coen, J. & Coen, E. (Directors). (1998). *The Big Lebowski*. [Motion Picture]. United States: Polygram.

Caruso, F. (Producer) & Lynch, D. (Director). (1986). *Blue Velvet*. [Motion Picture]. United States: MGM.

Cohen, B. (Producer) & Mendes, S. (Director). (1999). *American Beauty*. [Motion Picture]. United States: DreamWorks.

Coleridge, S. T. (1985). Biographia Literaria. In The Collected Works of Samuel Taylor Coleridge, Biographical Sketches of my Literary Life & Opinions (Vol. 7). Princeton University Press.

Colesberry, R. (Producer) & Schlondorff, V. (Director). (1985) Death of a Salesman. [TV Motion Picture]. United States: Roxbury Production.

DeFina, B. (Producer) & Scorsese, M. (Director). (1989). *Life Lessons*. [Motion Picture]. United States: Touchstone.

Ford, J. (Producer & Director). (1939). *Stagecoach*. [Motion Picture]. United States: Walter Wanger Productions.

Hitchcock, A. (Producer & Director). (1946). *Notorious*. [Motion Picture]. United States: RKO Radio Pictures.

Hitchcock, A. (Producer & Director). (1954). *Rear Window*. [Motion Picture]. United States: *Paramount.*

Hitchcock, A. (Producer & Director). (1958). *Vertigo*. [Motion Picture]. United States: *Paramount.*

Hitchcock, A. (Producer & Director). (1960). *Psycho*. [Motion Picture]. United States: *Shamley Productions.*

Keith, L. (Producer) & Flynn, J. J. (Director). (2004, August 25). *Masters of Production: The Hidden Art of Hollywood*. [Television Broadcast]. Public Broadcasting Service.

Kimmelman, M. (2004, August 6). *Cartier-Bresson, Artist Who Used Lens, Dies at 95*. New York Times.

Lehman, E. (Producer) & Nichols, M. (Director). (1966). *Who's Afraid of Virginia Woolf?* [Motion Picture]. United States: Warner Brothers.

Lumière, A., & Lumière, L. (Producers & Directors). (1896). *The Arrival of a Train at La Ciotat*. [Motion Picture]. France: Lumiere.

McBride, W. T. (2014). Hitchcock's Stylized Capture of Post-Adolescent Fatheads. In *Children in the Films of Alfred Hitchcock*. McMillan-Palgrave.

McBride, W. T. (2015). *Dutchman Heaped in Modern Cinema. MLA Approaches to Teaching Amiri Baraka's Dutchman*. MLA.

McBride, W. T. (2013). *Stylized Moments: Turning Film Style Into Meaning*. Smashwords.

McBride, W. T. (2015, March). *She's Not There: Shallow Focus on Emerging Techno-Mediated Modes of Being in Spike Jonze's Her*. Paper presented at the meeting of the American Comparative Literature Association Annual Meeting, Seattle, WA.

Penn, S. (Producer & Director). (2007). *Into The Wild*. [Motion Picture]. United States: Paramount Vantage.

Persson, E. (Producer) & Harvey, A. (Director). (1967). *Dutchman*. [Motion Picture]. United Kingdom: Dutchman Film Company.

Peters, J. (Producer) & (Director) Ramis, H. (1980). *Caddyshack*. [Motion Picture]. United States: Orion.

Phillips, J., & Phillips, M. (Producers) & Scorsese, M. (Director). (1976). *Taxi Driver*. [Motion Picture]. United States: Paramount.

Sandoz, M. (2008). Crazy Horse the Strange Man of the Oglala (3rd ed.). Knopf.

Scorsese, M. (Producer & Director). (2011). *Hugo*. [Motion Picture]. United States: Paramount.

Wallis, H. B. (Producer) & Huston, J. (Director). (n.d.). *Maltese Falcon*. [Motion Picture]. United States: Warner Brothers.

Weissman, A. (Executive Producer). (2000, July 6). Interview of Henri Cartier-Bresson. In *The Charlie Rose Show*. PBS.

ADDITIONAL READING

Brecht, B. (1949). A Short Organum for the Theatre. In Brecht on Theatre: The Development of an Aesthetic. John Willett (Translator & Editor). (1964). Methuen.

Collom, G., Dallas, A., Jong, R., & Obexer, R. (2002). Six months in a leaky boat: Framing the knowledge and skills needed to teach well online. *Proceedings ASCILITE 2002,* December 8-11. Auckland, New Zealand [24 Jan 2004] http://www.ascilite.org.au/conferences/auckland02/proceedings/papers/181.pdf

Fine, D., & Jacobs, K. "Online Education: Best Practices to Promote Learning." *Proceedings of the Human Factors and Ergonomics Society Annual Meeting* September 1, 2012 *56:* 546-550.

Larreamendy-Joerns, J., & Leinhardt, D. (2006, January 1). Going the Distance With Online Education. *Review of Educational Research*, 76(4), 567–605. doi:10.3102/00346543076004567

Screen Research. http://www.scoop.it/t/screen-research. Where the moving image is, and where it's going. Curated by Luke McKernan

Wilson, G., & Stacey, E. (2004). Online interaction impacts on learning: Teaching the teachers to teach online. *Australasian Journal of Educational Technology*, 20(1), 33–48.

KEY TERMS AND DEFINITIONS

Asynchronous Learning: A pedagogical approach useful in distance learning whereby the instruction and student participation and performance is not limited by time and place.

Auteur: 1950's French film critics writing in the *Cahier du Cinema* advanced the auteur theory that certain powerful directors, like literary authors, manage to impose a kind of unified sensibility upon this most collaborative of arts.

Authorial Camera: An authorial camera is a particularly Hitchcockian flourish whereby a seemingly subjective camera takes you on a journey to reveal information, however no one can plausibly be assigned the viewing perspective other than the film itself. In narrative theory, this perspective would be assigned to an omniscient narrator, although in Hitchcock films the authorial camera is at times (such as the camera work immediately following the murder of Marion Crane in *Psycho*) much more fluid than the rote stationary establishing shots of most films' omniscient perspectives. Whose viewpoint is seeing this odd tableau of Scotty and the mirrored reflection of false Madeleine? It is the author of the film, and as with all stylized moments, the director is nudging us to receive some meaning.

Blue Screen: A blue screen or green screen effect depends on technology that combines a foreground image (such as a meteorologist) with a background image (such as a weather map). The foreground subject is filmed in front of a vividly colored solid background, often blue or green, then everything blue is replaced by a background plate (image or footage) to form a composite image.

Canted Frame: The canted frame is achieved by tilting the camera on its axis resulting in a framed shot at an oblique angle. A canted frame usually depicts a world askew or off-kilter. Also known as a "dutch angle" or "German angle."

Chekhov's Dictum: Russian playwright Anton Chekhov dictated his "Dictum" to all would-be narrative artists: "If in the first act you have hung a pistol on the wall, then in the following one it should be fired. Otherwise don't put it there. "From over one hundred years ago this strict economy of props serves well as a principle for all well made films, as it supports the kind of analysis this book advocates: read everything on the screen as necessary and meaningful.

Crane Shot: A crane shot is achieved by a camera mounted on a mechanism adapted from farm and building construction machinery known as a crane, which can extend vertically several feet to several stories. Helicopter or other air flight-mounted cameras can accomplish "super-crane" effects as well. In general an ascending crane shot away from an object, person, or scene can confer to viewers a sense of effortless, privileged superiority, escape, or alienation. It often serves as closure or poignant commentary inviting contemplation at the ends of films. A descending crane shot toward an object, person, or scene can confer to viewers a sense of increasing observation and interest accompanied, nonetheless, by a certain detachment.

Deep Focus: Soft focus photography is the opposite of deep focus photography whereby a specific lens and necessary lighting is employed to keep fore, middle, and background all in focus in a single shot. Pioneered by directors such as John Ford, Orson Welles, and the cinematographer they shared, Gregg Toland, deep focus photography delivers a kind of three dimensional image that seems to mimic the ability of human sight, although in actuality humans must imperceptibly refocus in order to see this way. Deep focus enables directors to arrange material on all three visual planes, creating tableaux where associations with props and other characters may be pondered in terms of spatial relationships.

Faux Raccord: From the French, literally "false echo," *faux raccord* describes a moment when sound from the scene we are about to see echoes back into the scene we are watching. We hear the upcoming scene's sound "bleed" back, causing a discrepancy with the image, and as with all stylized moments, we are challenged to make sense of it.

Femme Fatale: The femme fatale is film noir's stereotypical fatal woman to whom the male hero is attracted, yet she must be resisted and defeated. The Western male-dominated notion of the fatal temptress goes back at least as far as Eve in the Hebrew Bible and the Sirens and Circe in Homer's *Odyssey*.

Film Noir: French film critics writing in *Les cahiers du cinéma* codified the genre-linked features of this particularly American creation, including the femme fatale, the existential perspective on the individual and fate, the hard-boiled tradition, and the stylistic use of light and shadow, dubbing the genre "black film" or *film noir*.

Fourth Wall: In the theater the fourth wall is that invisible line between actors and audience. Everything that happens behind that imaginary line is virtually real for the duration of the performance. It is the social convention we all accept as explained by Coleridge's dictum: "the willing suspension of disbelief." In traditional proscenium arch theatrical productions, that line is never to be crossed in order to maintain the illusion that what happens behind it, on stage, is "real." Out of a fear of breaking this "fictive reality," one of the cardinal rules of stage acting prohibits the actor from looking directly into the eyes of the audience members, and film acting continues that tradition by forbidding direct eye contact with the camera.

Functional Shot: Any shot, such as the shot/reverse shot that *functions* effortlessly and transparently and carries no grander symbols, metaphor, nor meaning.

Global Image Pattern: An iconic schema of similarly stylized shots, montages, gestures, detectable globally across the entire film.

Graphic Match: Two or more shots linked by similar visual elements. The significance of this stylistic choice visually links the meaning of the two objects—they are a pair of parallel signifiers contributing meaning to each other.

Hardboiled: Deflecting emotion is the key motivation for hardboiled language and demeanor.

Heisenberg Principle: The phenomenon of the observer and her instruments intervening in the perception of the data.

Hermeneutics: So named from Hermes, the Greek messenger and herald to the Gods, hermeneutics is the science of interpretation. This search for meaning in texts originated as Biblical exegesis and soon branched out to legal, philosophical and literary hermeneutics, marked by a concern with the relation between interpretive subject and text.

Iris Effect: Sometimes called an iris fade or an iris wipe, consists of two choices: the iris in and the iris out. The iris out usually begins as a black screen and then opens up and out like the iris in the human eye or in a camera to reveal an image. This effect was often used in the beginning of cinema as a point of view shot to imitate the opening of the eye upon a new scene. The iris in places the circle around the frame and closes it around the image with blackness surrounding the circle. This effect literally gave closure to a scene and served as just such a transition.

Jump Cut: An artificial interruption of a chronological sequence via missing footage. It is necessarily a breaking of the fourth wall and calls attention to the fact that one is watching a film because it disrupts the continuity of either time or space or both. An image unexpectedly appears, disappears or the mise en scene is altered by time, jerking the audience out of the habitual reality the film has constructed thus far.

Lap Dissolve: An editing technique whereby one image is gradually substituted by another image that immediately follows, the two overlapping for a brief moment before the second image is alone on the screen and the first image has disappeared. A lap dissolve often confers the passing of time while forging a strong connection between the two momentarily co-existing images.

Lookism: An often unrecognized discriminatory practice of favoring those whose body types and ethnicities match one's cultural expectations.

Mickey-Mousing: When the on-screen action matches the beat and movement of the non-diegetic music of the soundtrack, so named because it mimics the way Disney choreographed his animated characters and synchronized them to the accompanying music.

The Mickey Finn Shot: From the code slang word for a drug-laced drink, this shot is more than likely a functional shot revealing the distorted vision of a character. In *Maltese Falcon* Gutman "slips" Spade "a Mickey," or a Mickey Finn which is the hard boiled term for a spiked drink with "knock-out" drops—any drink laced with chloral hydrate or other sedative that renders the drinker unconscious. We witness Spade getting drowsy as he raises his eyebrows and slurs his speech. He attempts to compose himself as he glances at Gutman and then Huston inserts Spade's pov shot, which is severely out of focus. There is no question that this unfocused shot conveys Spade's drug-induced wooziness just prior to his swooning unconscious, but it is functional rather than stylized. Similar moments in *The Big Lebowski* (Joel & Ethan Coen 1998) and *Fear and Loathing in Las Vegas* (Gilliam 1998) are not stylized because they simply depict drug-induced states in a functional way, such as the addled experiences of Jeff Lebowski and Hunter Thompson respectively and carry no metaphoric meaning beyond a drugged state of consciousness.

Point Of View or POV Shot: A shot from a particular character's subjective perspective as if seen through that character's eyes. A director grants a particular privilege to any character afforded such a shot since the audience is being let in on that character's view of the world. Most POV shots indicate that the subject is the center or protagonist of the film.

Rack Focus: When the focus puller shifts sharp shallow focus from one plane to the other.

Set Designer/Set Decorator: Artists in charge of all items visible within the indoor or outdoor set such as furniture, wall hangings, etc.

Shot/Reverse Shot: A series of connected over-the-shoulder shots or one-shot close-ups of each speaker pointed approximately 180-degrees opposite of each other and used to functionally portray a conversation between two characters.

Slow Motion/Over Cranking: So called because more than 24 frames per second—the ideal, standardized speed at which to capture the illusion of movement—are taken by the camera so that when they are projected back at 24 frames per second (each frame exposed twice per second), the movement appears slower than real time. The common effect of slow motion is a dream-like experience and often it allows the viewer to savor the moment.

Soft Focus or Shallow Focus Photography: Shot with a specific lens that concentrates the depth of field to objects targeted by the camera which appear in sharp, clear focus, while everything else remains out of focus. Soft focus photography is used to isolate certain images for inspection, granting a heightened interest in those objects in sharp focus. A meaningful distance or isolation can be indicated among two or more characters and/or objects when sharing a frame but only one is in focus at a time.

Spatial Relationships: A technique often arranged as "blocking" on stage whereby significant relationships of power and intimacy are developed by means of the placement of actors and objects in a kind of tableau.

Split Screen: Typically two or more separate shots (separate camera takes) divided by a thin black line placed on the screen simultaneously. Edwin S. Porter's *Life of an American Fireman* (1903) is often credited with being the first film to use multiple screens, while Abel Gance sought to announce a new art form with his "polyvision"—a three screen presentation in his 1927 film *Napoléon*. The effect is used to depict Rock Hudson's and Doris Day's characters on the phone in *Pillow Talk* (Gordon 1959), which is taken to extreme with multiple conversationalists on screen in *Bye, Bye Birdie* (Sidney 1963). Richard Fleischer's *The Boston Strangler* (1968) seems to split the screen in a vague attempt to reproduce Albert DeSalvo's split personality. In the case of a documentary film like Wadleigh's 1970 *Woodstock* (with fledgling editors Martin Scorsese and Thelma Schoonmaker), at times two separate screens produce discrete, asynchronous footage that the viewer is encouraged to integrate, while during live musical performances, such as by the Who, multiple images of lead singer Roger Daltrey and separate images of Daltrey and guitarist/singer Pete Townsend invite viewers to inspect and savor multiple perspectives of a single event.

Structuralism: A linguistic and anthropological procedure of understanding social phenomena as part of a system of signs whose meaning resides in their interrelationships.

Stylized Moment: Any formal filmic element not reproducible on the stage or page that bears meaning by way of metaphor.

Tilt: A vertical movement of the camera and, depending on the speed of the tilt and from whose perspective we are seeing it, can give the impression of hope, inquisitiveness, or dread (tilt up), or meekness, melancholy, or at times, a search for hidden meaning (tilt down).

Vertigo Shot: Hitchcock's famous vertigo shot—a tracking in one direction while simultaneously zooming in the opposite direction. Irmin Roberts, the second-unit director of photography/cameraman, is credited (though not in the film) for having developed this photographic "trick" done with miniatures placed horizontally. Also called a contra-zoom shot or a trombone shot, by zooming the lens, in this case, *in* on the subject, while simultaneously tracking out, the subject, according to all accounts, allegedly remains the

same size as the background changes through compression. This is an accurate description of later vertigo shots for example in *Jaws* (Spielberg 1975) and *Indochine* (Wargnier 1992) etc., however it is not an accurate description of the effect in *Vertigo* where the subject is minimized as the "sides" of the image expand, creating an unusual three dimensional effect. Rather, the result is that the foreground remains relatively constant, if a bit elongated, as the background recedes.

Voyeurism: (From the Fr. *Voir*, to see)—the gazing upon someone without the awareness or permission of the object of the gaze, often motivated by sexual or otherwise devious desires—is a notion as old as human history. King Claudius calls Polonius and himself "lawful espials" as they hide in order to watch young Hamlet "seeing, unseen" (III. i). Voyeurism also describes the active/passive dynamic every moviegoer experiences. While the stage experience allows the audience to look anywhere at the theatrical spectacle, films place us in a passive position by specifically directing our gaze, dictating every angle and object. The active element of cinematic voyeurism is evident with regard to the fourth wall rule, whereby the audience gazes upon characters who do not look directly into the camera and at least pretend to not know they are being watched.

Zoom: Achieved by a lens or lenses whose focal length can be increased thereby magnifying the size of the subject—zoom in, or decreased thereby minimizing the size of the subject—zoom out. A zoom in (as well as push in, dolly in, track or truck in) often confers an invitation to look closer at a character or object. The opposite movement of zooming out, like the ascending crane shot discussed earlier, produces a feeling of escape, alienation, and abandonment.

Compilation of References

Abdelmalak, M. (2013). The Process of Building Learning Communities in an Online Course. In T. Bastiaens & G. Marks (Eds.), *Proceedings of World Conference on E-Learning in Corporate, Government, Healthcare, and Higher Education* 2013 (pp. 516-523). Chesapeake, VA: AACE. Retrieved November 16, 2014 from http://www.editlib.org/p/114885

Abramson, L. Y., Seligman, M. E., & Teasdale, J. D. (1978). Learned helplessness in humans: Critique and reformulation. *Journal of Abnormal Psychology, 87*(1), 49–74. doi:10.1037/0021-843X.87.1.49 PMID:649856

Adelman, C. (2006). *The toolbox revisited: Paths to degree completion from high school through college.* (U.S. Department of Education, Office of Policy, Research, and Evaluation). Retrieved from: http://www.ed.gov/pubs/edpubs.html

Adeyinka, T., & Mutula, S. (2010). A proposed model for evaluating the success of WebCT course content management system. *Computers in Human Behavior, 26*(6), 1795–1805. doi:10.1016/j.chb.2010.07.007

Adkins, S. (2013). Ambient insight whitepaper: The 2012 boom in learning technology investment. *Ambientinsight.com*. Retrieved from: http://www.ambientinsight.com/Resources/Documents/AmbientInsight-2012-Learning-Technology-Investment-Patterns.pdf

Akyol, Z., Arbaugh, J. B., Cleveland-Innes, M., Garrison, D. R., Ice, P., Richardson, J. C., & Swan, K. (2009). A response to the review of the community of inquiry framework. *International Journal of E-Learning & Distance Education, 23*(2), 123–136.

Akyol, Z., & Garrison, D. R. (2008). The development of a community of inquiry over time in an online course: Understanding the progression and integration of social, cognitive and teaching presence. *Journal of Asynchronous Learning Networks, 12*(3-4), 3–22.

Akyol, Z., & Garrison, D. R. (2008). The development of a community of inquiry over time in an online course: Understanding the progression and integration, social, cognitive, and teaching presence. *Journal of Asynchronous Learning Networks, 12*(3-4), 3–22.

Alexander, B. (2006). Web 2.0: A new wave of innovation for teaching and learning? *EDUCAUSE Review, 41*(2), 32–44.

Allen, E. I., & Seaman, J. (2007). *Blending in the extent and promise of blended education in the United States.* (Research Report No. 6). Retrieved from http://sloanconsortium.org/sites/default/files/Blending_In.pdf

Allen, E. I., & Seaman, J. (2010). *Learning on demand: Online education in the United States, 2009* (Research Report No. 7). Retrieved from: http://www.sloan-c.org/publications/survey/pdf/learningondemand.pdf

Allen, E. I., & Seaman, J. (2011). *Going the distance: Online education in the United States, 2011* (Research Report No. 8). Retrieved from: http://www.babson.edu/Academics/centers/blank-center/global-research/Documents/going-the-distance.pdf

Allen, E. I., & Seaman, J. (2013). *Changing course: Ten years of tracking online education in the United States* (Research Report No. 10). Retrieved from: http://www.onlinelearningsurvey.com/reports/changingcourse.pdf

Allen, E., & Seaman, J. (2011). *Going the distance: Online education in the United States, 2011*. Babson Survey Research Group. Retrieved from: http://www.onlinelearningsurvey.com/reports/goingthedistance.pdf

Allen, E., & Seaman, J. (2013). *Changing course: Ten years of tracking online education in the United States.* Babson Survey Research Group and Quahog Research Group. Retrieved from http://www.onlinelearningsurvey.com/reports/changingcourse.pdf

Allen, E., & Seaman, J. (2013). *Changing course: Ten years of tracking online education in the United States.* Babson Survey Research Group and Quahog Research Group. Retrieved from: http://www.onlinelearningsurvey.com/reports/changingcourse.pdf

Allen, E., & Seaman, J. (2014). *Grade change: Tracking online education in the United States.* Babson Survey Research Group and Quahog Research Group. Retrieved from: http://www.onlinelearningsurvey.com/reports/gradechange.pdf

Allen, I. E., & Seaman, J. (2010). Learning on demand: Online education in the United States. Newburyport, MA: The Sloan Consortium. Retrieved from http://sloanconsortium.org/publications/survey/pdf/learningondemand.pdf

Allen, I. E., & Seaman, J. (2013). Changing course: Ten years of tracking online education in the United States. Babson Park, MA: Babson Survey Research Group and Quahog Research Group. Retrieved from http://www.onlinelearningsurvey.com/reports/changingcourse.pdf

Allen, I. E., & Seaman, J. (2013). *Changing course: Ten years of tracking online education in the United States.* Retrieved October 11, 2014 from http://files.eric.ed.gov/fulltext/ED541571.pdf

Allen, I. E., & Seaman, J. (2014). *Grade change: Tracking online education in the United States.* Babson Survey Research Group & Online Learning Consortium. Retrieved from http://www.onlinelearningsurvey.com/reports/gradechange.pdf

Allen, I. E., & Seaman. (2013). *Changing course ten years of tracking online education in the United States.* Babson Survey Research Group and Quahog Research Group. Retrieved from: http://www.onlinelearningsurvey.com/highered.html

Allen, I., & Seaman, J. (2013). Changing course: Ten years of tracking online education in the United States (pp. 1–26). Needham, MA: The Sloan Consortium. Retrieved from http://www.onlinelearningsurvey.com/reports/changingcourse.pdf

Allen, D. (1967). *Microteaching: A Description.* Stanford University.

Allen, E., & Seaman, J. (2010). *Class differences: Online education in the United States.* Needham, MA: Sloan Consortium.

Allen, I. E., & Seaman, J. (2013). *Changing course: Ten years of tracking online education in the United States.* Newburyport, MA: Sloan Consortium.

Ally, M. (2004). Foundations of educational theory for online learning. *Theory and Practice of Online Learning, 2*, 15-44.

Ally, M. (2002). Designing and managing successful online distance education courses. *In Workshop presented at the 2002 World Computer Congress, Montreal, Canada.*

Ally, M. (2004). Foundations of educational theory for online learning. In T. Anderson (Ed.), *The theory and practice of online learning* (pp. 15–44). Edmonton, CA: Athabasca University Press.

Ally, M. (2004). Foundations of educational theory for online learning. *Theory and Practice of Online Learning, 2*, 15–44.

Almala, A. (2006). The community college leadership perspectives of quality e-learning. *Distance Learning, 3*, 9–14.

Alonso-Tapia, J., & Panadero, E. (2010). Effect of self-assessment scripts on self-regulation and learning. *Infancia y Aprendizaje, 33*(3), 385–397. doi:10.1174/021037010792215145

Alport, G. W. (1937). *Personality: A psychological interpretation.* New York, NY: Holt.

Alsharif, N. Z., & Roche, V. F. (2010). Promoting key interactions in a distance medicinal chemistry course. *Currents in Pharmacy Teaching & Learning, 2*(2), 114–125. doi:10.1016/j.cptl.2010.01.003

Alwehaibi, H. (2012). Novel program to promote critical thinking among higher education students: Empirical Study from Saudi Arabia. *Asian Social Science*, *8*(11), 193–204.

American Psychological Association. (2010). *Publication manual of the American Psychological Association* (6th ed.). Washington, DC: Author.

Ames, C. (1992). Classrooms: Goals, structures, and student motivation. *Journal of Educational Psychology*, *84*(3), 262–274. doi:10.1037/0022-0663.84.3.261

Ames, C., & Archer, J. (1988). Achievement goals in the classroom: Students' learning strategies and motivation processes. *Journal of Educational Psychology*, *80*(3), 260–267. doi:10.1037/0022-0663.80.3.260

Anderson, T. (2003). Getting the mix right again: An updated and theoretical rationale for interaction. *The International Review of Research in Open and Distance Learning, 4*(2), Article 4.2.13. Retrieved from http://www.irrodl.org/index.php/irrodl/article/view/149/708

Anderson, T. (2003a). Getting the right mix again: An updated and theoretical rationale for interaction. *International Review of Open and Distance Learning, 4*. Retrieved from http://www.irrodl.org/content/v4.2/anderson.html

Anderson, T. (2004). Teaching in an online learning context. In T. Anderson & F. Elloumi (Eds.), Theory and practice of online learning (pp. 273-294). Athabasca: Athabasca University.

Anderson, T., Rourke, L., Garrison, D. R., & Archer, W. (2001). Assessing teaching presence in a computer conferencing context. Paper presented at the Annual Meeting of the American Educational Research Association, Seattle, WA.

Anderson, L. W., & Krathwohl, D. R. (Eds.). (2001). *A taxonomy for learning, teaching, and assessing: A revision of Bloom's taxonomy of educational objectives*. New York: Longman.

Anderson, T. (2003). Getting the Mix Right Again: An updated and theoretical rationale for interaction. *International Review of Research in Open and Distance Learning*, *4*(2). Available at http://www.irrodl.org/index.php/irrodl/article/view/149/230

Anderson, T. (2003b). Modes of interaction in distance education: Recent developments and research questions. In M. G. Moore & W. G. Anderson (Eds.), *Handbook of distance education* (pp. 129–144). Mahwah, NJ: Lawrence Erlbaum.

Anderson, T. (2004). The educational semantic web: A vision for the next phase of educational computing. *Educational Technology*, *44*(5), 5–9.

Anderson, T. (Ed.). (2008). *The theory and practice of online learning*. Athabasca University Press.

Anderson, T., & Dron, J. (2011). Three generations of distance education pedagogy. *International Review of Research in Open and Distance Learning*, *12*(3), 80–97. Retrieved from http://www.irrodl.org/index.php/irrodl/article/view/890

Anderson, T., & Garrison, D. R. (1998). Learning in a networked world: New roles and responsibilities. In C. Gibson (Ed.), *Distance Learners in Higher Education* (pp. 97–112). Madison, WI: Atwood Publishing.

Anderson, T., Rourke, L., Garrison, D. R., & Archer, W. (2001). Assessing teacher presence in computer conferencing context. *Journal of Asynchronous Learning Networks*, *5*(2), 1–17.

Anderson, T., Rourke, L., Garrison, D. R., & Archer, W. (2001). Assessing teaching presence in a computer conferencing context. *Journal of Asynchronous Learning Networks*, *5*(2), 1–17.

Andrade, H., & Valtcheva, A. (2009). Promoting learning and achievement through self-assessment. *Theory into Practice*, *48*(1), 12–19. doi:10.1080/00405840802577544

Andrade, M. (2014). Course-embedded student support for online English language learners. *Open Praxis*, *6*(1), 65–73. doi:10.5944/openpraxis.6.1.90

Angelino, L. M., Williams, F. K., & Natvig, D. (2007). Strategies to engage online students and reduce attrition rates. *The Journal of Educators Online, 4(2)*. Retrieved December 27, 2014 from http://www.thejo.com/

Angelino, L. M., Williams, F. K., & Natvig, D. (2007). Strategies to engage online students and reduce attrition rates. *Journal of Educators Online, 4*, 2.

Angelo, T. A., & Cross, P. K. (1993). *Classroom assessment techniques: A handbook for college teachers*. San Francisco: Jossey-Bass.

Appleton, J. J., Christenson, S. L., Kim, D., & Reschly, A. L. (2006). Measuring cognitive and psychological engagement: Validation of the student engagement instrument. *Journal of School Psychology*, *44*(5), 427–445. doi:10.1016/j.jsp.2006.04.002

Aragon, S. A. (2003). Creating Social Presence in Online Environments. *New Directions for Adult and Continuing Education*, 100.

Aragon, S. R. (2003). Creating social presence in online environments. *New Directions for Adult and Continuing Education*, *2003*(100), 57–68. doi:10.1002/ace.119

Aragon, S., & Johnson, R. (2008). Factors influencing completion and non-completion of community college online courses. *American Journal of Distance Education*, *22*(3), 146–158. doi:10.1080/08923640802239962

Arbaugh, F., Erbel-Eisenmann, B., Ramirez, N., Kranendonk, H., Knuth, E., & Quander, J. R. (2010). *Linking research and practice: Practitioner community priorities for research in mathematics education*. Reston, VA: Report for the National Council of Teachers of Mathematics, Research Agenda Conference.

Arbaugh, J. B. (2000). Virtual classroom characteristics and student satisfaction with internet-based MBA courses. *Journal of Management Education*, *24*(1), 32–54. doi:10.1177/105256290002400104

Arbaugh, J. B. (2008). Does the community of inquiry framework predict outcomes in online MBA courses? *International Review of Research in Open and Distance Learning*, *9*(2). Retrieved from http://www.irrodl.org/index.php/irrodl/article/view/490/1045

Arbaugh, J. B., & Benbunan-Fich, R. (2006). An investigation of epistemological and social dimensions of teaching in online learning environments. *Academy of Management Learning & Education*, *5*(4), 435–447. doi:10.5465/AMLE.2006.23473204

Arbaugh, J. B., Godfrey, M. R., Johnson, M., Pollack, B. L., Niendorf, B., & Wresch, W. (2009). Research in online and blended learning in the business discipline: Key findings and possible future decisions. *The Internet and Higher Education*, *12*(2), 71–87. doi:10.1016/j.iheduc.2009.06.006

Arbaugh, J. B., & Hwang, A. (2006). Does "teaching presence" exist in online MBA courses? *The Internet and Higher Education*, *9*(1), 9–21. doi:10.1016/j.iheduc.2005.12.001

Archambault, I., Janosz, M., Fallu, J.-S., & Pagani, L. S. (2009). Student engagement and its relationship with early high school dropout. *Journal of Adolescence*, *32*(3), 651–670. doi:10.1016/j.adolescence.2008.06.007 PMID:18708246

Archer, W. (2010). Beyond online discussion: Extending the community of inquiry framework to entire courses. *The Internet and Higher Education*, *13*(1-2), 69. doi:10.1016/j.iheduc.2009.10.005

Ardichvili, A., Maurer, M., Li, W., Wentling, T., & Stuedemann, R. (2006). Cultural influences on knowledge sharing through online communities of practice. *Journal of Knowledge Management*, *10*(1), 94–107. doi:10.1108/13673270610650139

Arkoudis, S., Watty, K., Baik, C., Yu, X., Borland, H., Chang, S., & Pearce, A. et al. (2013). Finding common ground: Enhancing interaction between domestic and international students in higher education. *Teaching in Higher Education*, *18*(3), 222–235. doi:10.1080/13562517.2012.719156

Arthur, M. B., & Kram, K. E. (1985). Mentoring at work: Developmental relationships in organizational life. *Administrative Science Quarterly*, *30*(3), 454. doi:10.2307/2392687

Artino, A. R. Jr, & Jones, K. D. II. (2012). Exploring the complex relations between achievement emotions and self-regulated learning behaviors in online learning. *The Internet and Higher Education*, *15*(3), 170–175. doi:10.1016/j.iheduc.2012.01.006

Atkinson, J. W. (1957). Motivational determinants of risk taking behavior. *Psychological Review, 64*(6, Pt.1), 359–372. doi:10.1037/h0043445 PMID:13505972

Attebury, R. (2010). Elluminate *live!* and Jing: Instruction for synchronous and asynchronous online classes. *Journal of Library Administration, 50*(7), 1027–1028.

Attewell, P., Heil, S., & Reisel, L. (2012). What is academic momentum? And does it matter? *Educational Evaluation and Policy Analysis, 34*(1), 27–44. doi:10.3102/0162373711421958

Aud, S., Hussar, W., Kena, G., Bianco, K., Frolich, L., Kemp, J., & Tahan, K. (2011). *The condition of education. (U.S. Department of Education, National Center for Educational Statistics, NCES 2011-033)*. Washington, DC: U.S. Government Printing Office.

Austin, J. T., & Villanova, P. (1992). The criterion problem: 1917-1992. *The Journal of Applied Psychology, 77*(6), 836–874. doi:10.1037/0021-9010.77.6.836

Ausubel, D. P. (1960). The use of advance organizers in the learning and retention of meaningful verbal material. *Journal of Educational Psychology, 51*(5), 267–272. doi:10.1037/h0046669

Ausubel, D. P. (1974). *Educational psychology: A cognitive view*. New York, NY: Holt, Rinehart and Winston.

Aydin, S. (2012). A review of research on Facebook as an educational environment. *Educational Technology Research and Development, 60*(6), 1093–1106. doi:10.1007/s11423-012-9260-7

Azevedo, R., Cromley, J. G., & Seibert, D. (2004). Does adaptive scaffolding facilitate students' ability to regulate their learning with hypermedia. *Contemporary Educational Psychology, 29*(3), 344–370. doi:10.1016/j.cedpsych.2003.09.002

Azevedo, R., & Hadwin, A. F. (2005). Scaffolding self-regulated learning and metacognition: Implications for the design of computer-based scaffolds. *Instructional Science, 33*(5), 367–379. doi:10.1007/s11251-005-1272-9

Babb, S., Stewart, C., & Bachman, C. (2010). Constructing communication in blended learning environments: Students' perceptions of good practice in hybrid courses. *Journal of Online Learning and Teaching, 6*, 735–753.

Babb, S., Stewart, C., & Johnson, R. (2013). Applying the seven principles for good practice in undergraduate education to blended learning environments. In L. Kyei-Blankson & E. Ntuli (Eds.), *Practical applications and experiences in K-20 blended learning environments*. Hershey, PA: IGI Global.

Bachman, C., & Stewart, C. (2011). Self-determination theory and web-enhanced course template development. *Teaching of Psychology, 38*(3), 180–188. doi:10.1177/0098628311411798

Baird, D. E., & Fisher, M. (2005). Neomillennial user experience design strategies utilizing social networking media to support "always on" learning styles. *Journal of Educational Technology Systems, 34*(1), 5–32. doi:10.2190/6WMW-47L0-M81Q-12G1

Baker, C. (2010). The impact of instructor immediacy and presence for online student affective learning, cognition, and motivation. *Journal of Educators Online, 7*(1), 1–30. Retrieved from http://www.thejeo.com/Archives/Volume7Number1/BakerPaper.pdf

Baker, C. (2010). The impact of instructor immediacy and presence for online student affective learning, cognition, and motivation. *The Journal of Educators Online, 7*(1), 1–30. Retrieved from http://www.thejeo.com/Archives/Volume7Number1/BakerPaper.pdf

Baker, D. L. (2011). Designing and orchestrating online discussions. *MERLOT Journal of Online Learning and Teaching, 7*(3), 401–411.

Ball, D. L., & Stacey, K. (2005). Teaching strategies for developing judicious technology use. In W. J. Masalski & P. C. Elliott (Eds.), *Technology-supported mathematics learning environments* (pp. 3–15). Reston, VA: NCTM.

Bandura, A. (1986). *Social foundation of thought and action: A social cognitive theory*. Upper Saddle River, NJ: Prentice Hall.

Bandura, A. (1989). Human agency in social cognitive theory. *The American Psychologist, 44*(9), 1175–1184. doi:10.1037/0003-066X.44.9.1175 PMID:2782727

Bandura, A. (1997). *Self-efficacy: the exercise of control*. New York, NY: Freeman.

Bandura, A. (2001). Social-cognitive theory: An agentic perspective. *Annual Review of Psychology, 52*(1), 1–26. doi:10.1146/annurev.psych.52.1.1 PMID:11148297

Bandura, A., & Cervone, D. (1986). Differential engagement of self-reactive influences in cognitive motivation. *Organizational Behavior and Human Decision Processes, 38*(1), 92–113. doi:10.1016/0749-5978(86)90028-2

Bandura, A., & Locke, E. A. (2003). Negative self-efficacy and goals revisited.[PubMed]. *The Journal of Applied Psychology, 88*(1), 87–99. doi:10.1037/0021-9010.88.1.87 PMID:12675397

Bandura, A., & Schunk, D. H. (1981). Cultivating competence, self-efficacy, and intrinsic interest through proximal self-motivation. *Journal of Personality and Social Psychology, 41*(3), 586–598. doi:10.1037/0022-3514.41.3.586

Bandura, S. A. (1982). Self-efficacy mechanism in human agency. *The American Psychologist, 37*(2), 122–147. doi:10.1037/0003-066X.37.2.122

Banks, J. A. (2005). Multicultural education: Characteristics and goals. In J. A. Banks & C. A. M. Banks (Eds.), *Multicultural education: Issues and perspectives* (5th ed., pp. 1–30). New York, NY: John Wiley & Sons Inc.

Banks, J. A., & Banks, C. A. M. (Eds.). (2009). *Multicultural education: Issues and perspectives*. Hoboken, NJ: John Wiley & Sons.

Baran, E., & Correia, A. (2009). Student-led facilitation strategies in online discussions. *Distance Education, 30*(3), 339–361. doi:10.1080/01587910903236510

Barbour, M. K., & Reeves, T. C. (2009). The reality of virtual schools: A review of the literature. *Computers & Education, 52*(2), 402–416. doi:10.1016/j.compedu.2008.09.009

Barclay, K. H. (2001). *Humanizing learning-at-distance*. San Francisco: Saybrook Institute.

Barnard-Brak, L., Lan, W. Y., & Paton, V. O. (2010). Profiles in self-regulated learning in the online learning environment. *International Review of Research in Open and Distance Learning, 11*(1), 61–80.

Barnard, L., Lan, W. Y., To, Y. M., Paton, V. O., & Lai, S. (2009). Measuring self-regulation in online and blended learning environments. *The Internet and Higher Education, 12*(1), 1–6. doi:10.1016/j.iheduc.2008.10.005

Barnard, L., Paton, V., & Lan, W. (2008). Online self-regulatory learning behaviors as a mediator in the relationship between online course perceptions with achievement. *International Review of Research in Open and Distance Learning, 9*(2), 1–11.

Barnett, R. (2000). *Realizing the university in an age of supercomplexity*. Buckingham, UK: Society for Research in Higher Education, Open University Press.

Baron, D. E. (2009). *A better pencil: Readers, writers, and the digital revolution*. New York: Oxford University Press.

Barrie, S. C. (2007). A conceptual framework for the teaching and learning of generic graduate attributes. *Studies in Higher Education, 32*(4), 439–458. doi:10.1080/03075070701476100

Barr, R. B., & Tagg, J. (1995). From teaching to learning: A new paradigm for undergraduate education. *Change, 27*(6), 12–25. doi:10.1080/00091383.1995.10544672

Barthes, R. (1980). *La Chambre claire*trans (R. Howard, Trans.). Hill and Wang.

Bartko, W. T. (2005). The ABC of engagement in out-of-school-time programs. *New Directions for Youth Development, 2005*(105), 109–120. doi:10.1002/yd.110 PMID:15943139

Bartlett-Bragg, A. (2003). Blogging to Learn, Knowledge Tree e-journal. Retrieved January 12, 2015, from: http://knowledgetree.flexiblelearning.net.au/edition04/pdf/Blogging_to_Learn.pdf

Bartlett-Bragg, A. (2003). Blogging to learn. *The Knowledge Tree e-Journal*. Retrieved from http://www.csus.edu/indiv/s/stonerm/blogging_to_learn.pdf

Battle, E. (1965). Motivational determinants of academic task persistence. *Journal of Personality and Social Psychology, 4*, 534–632. PMID:14316982

Baumeister, R. F. (1998). The self. In D. T. Gilbert, S. T. Fiske, & G. Lindzey (Eds.), *Handbook of social psychology* (4th ed.; pp. 680–740). New York: McGraw-Hill.

Baumeister, R. F., Heatherton, T. F., & Tice, D. (1994). *Losing control: How and why people fail at self-regulation.* San Diego, CA: Academic Press.

Beatty, B., & Ulasewicz, C. (2006). Faculty perspectives on moving from Blackboard to the Moodle learning management system. *TechTrends, 50*(4), 36–45. doi:10.1007/s11528-006-0036-y

Beaudoin, M. F. (2002). Learning or lurking? Tracking the "invisible" online student. *The Internet and Higher Education, 5*(2), 147–155. doi:10.1016/S1096-7516(02)00086-6

Beaudoin, M. F. (2013). The evolving role of the instructor in the digital age. In Y. Kats (Ed.), *Learning Management Systems and Instructional Design: Best Practices in Online Education* (pp. 233–247). Hershey, PA: IGI Global. doi:10.4018/978-1-4666-3930-0.ch012

Beavis, C. (2013). Young people, new media and education: Participation and possibilities. *Social Alternatives, 32*(2), 39–44.

Beckett, C., Wetzel, K., Chisholm, I., Zambo, R., Padgett, H., Williams, M. K., & Odom, M. (2003). Pre-service and in-service teachers collaborating with technology in K-8 multicultural classrooms: Year 2. *TechTrends, 479*(5), 14–17. doi:10.1007/BF02763199

Bednall, T. C., & Kehoe, E. J. (2011). Effects of self-regulatory instructional aids on self-directed study. *Instructional Science, 39*(2), 205–226. doi:10.1007/s11251-009-9125-6

Behrmann, M., Geng, J. J., & Shomstein, S. (2004). Parietal cortex and attention. *Current Opinion in Neurobiology, 14*(2), 112–217. doi:10.1016/j.conb.2004.03.012 PMID:15082327

Bejjar, M. A., & Boujelbene, Y. (2014). E-Learning and Web 2.0: A couple of the 21st Century advancements in higher education. In J. Pelet (Ed.), *E-learning 2.0 technologies and web applications in higher education* (pp. 1–21). Hershey, PA: IGI Global.

Belair, M. (2012). The investigation of virtual school communications. *Tech Trends: Linking Research & Practice to Improve Learning, 56*(4), 26–33. doi:10.1007/s11528-012-0584-2

Belaja, K., Sai, G. T. B., & Lin, A. L. W. (2012). Effects of lecturer's transactional presence towards learners' intrinsic motivation in learning English as a second language through distance education. *Malaysian Journal of Distance Education, 14*(1), 77–97.

Beldarrain, Y. (2006). Distance education trends: Integrating new technologies to foster student interaction and collaboration. *Distance Education, 27*(2), 139–153. doi:10.1080/01587910600789498

Bell, S. (2012). Nontraditional students are the new majority. *Library Journal*. Retrieved from http://lj.libraryjournal.com/2012/03/opinion/nontraditional-students-are-the-new-majority-from-the-bell-tower/

Bell, F. (2011). Connectivism: Its place in theory-informed research and innovation in technology-enabled learning. *International Review of Research in Open and Distance Learning, 12*(3), 98–118.

Bell, P. D. (2007). Predictors of College Student Achievement in Undergraduate Asynchronous Web-Based Courses. *Education, 127*(4), 523–533.

Bembenutty, H. (2000). Sustaining motivation and academic goals: The role of academic delay of gratification. *Learning and Individual Differences, 11*(3), 233–257. doi:10.1016/S1041-6080(99)80002-8

Bender, T. (2003). *Discussion based online teaching to enhance student learning.* Sterling, VA: Stylus Publishing, LLC.

Bennett, C. I. (2001). Genres of research in multicultural education. *Review of Educational Research, 71*(2), 171–217. doi:10.3102/00346543071002171

Bennett, S., Bishop, A., Dalgarno, B., Waycott, J., & Kennedy, G. (2012). Implementing Web 2.0 technologies in higher education: A collective case study. *Computers & Education, 59*(2), 524–534. doi:10.1016/j.compedu.2011.12.022

Bennett, S., & Lockyer, L. (2004). Becoming an online teacher: Adapting to a changed environment for teaching and learning in higher education. *Educational Media International*, *41*(3), 231–248. doi:10.1080/09523980 410001680842

Benson, A. D., & Whitworth, A. (Eds.). (2014). *Research on course management systems in higher education.* Charlotte, NC: Information Age Publishing, Inc.

Benson, M. J. (1994). Lecture listening in an ethnographic perspective. In J. Flowerdew (Ed.), *Academic listening* (pp. 181–198). New York, NY: Cambridge University Press.

Bentley, Y., Shegunshi, A., & Scannell, M. (2010). Evaluating the impact of distance learning support systems on the learning experience of MBA students in a global context. *Electronic Journal of E-Learning*, *8*(2), 51–62.

Berge, Z. L (1995). Facilitating computer conferencing: Recommendations from the field. *Educational Technology*, *35*, 22.

Berge, Z. L. (1999). Interaction in post-secondary web-based learning. *Educational Technology*, *39*, 5–11.

Berg, G. (2010). *Cases on online tutoring, mentoring, and educational services practices and applications.* Hershey, PA: Information Science Reference. doi:10.4018/978-1-60566-876-5

Berglas, S., & Jones, E. E. (1978). Drug choice s a self-handicapping strategy in response to non-contingent success. *Journal of Personality and Social Psychology*, *36*(4), 405–417. doi:10.1037/0022-3514.36.4.405 PMID:650387

Bernard, R. M., Abrami, P. C., Borokhovski, E., Wade, C. A., Tamim, R. M., Surkes, M. A., & Bethel, E. C. (2009). A meta-analysis of three types of interaction treatments in distance education. *Review of Educational Research*, *79*(3), 1243–1289. doi:10.3102/0034654309333844

Bernard, R. M., Abrami, P. C., Lou, Y., Evgueni, B., Wade, A., Wozney, L., & Huang, B. et al. (2004). How does distance education compare to classroom instruction? A meta-analysis of the empirical literature. *Meta-Analysis of Distance Education Studies*, *10*, 63–96.

Bernard, R. M., Borokhovski, E., & Tamim, R. M. (2014). Detecting bias in meta-analyses of distance education research: Big pictures we can rely on. *Distance Education*, *35*(3), 271–293. doi:10.1080/01587919.2015.957433

Bevan, T. (Producer) & Coen, J. & Coen, E. (Directors). (1998). *The Big Lebowski.* [Motion Picture]. United States: Polygram.

Beyer, B. K. (1985). Critical thinking: What is it. *Social Education*, *49*(4), 270-276.

Bigatel, P. M., Ragan, L. C., Kennan, S., May, J., & Redmond, B. F. (2012). The identification of competencies for online teaching success. *Journal of Asynchronous Learning Networks*, *16*(1), 59–77.

Billington, D. D. (1989). *The role of education in stimulating human development.* Paper presented at the Annual Conference of the Western College Reading and Learning Association, Seattle, WA.

Bing, W., & Ai-Ping, T. (2008). The influence of national culture towards learners' interaction in the online learning environments: A comparative analysis of Shanghai TV University (China) and Wawasan Open University (Malaysia). *Quarterly Review of Distance Education*, *9*(3), 327–339.

Blackboard Collaborate. (2014). *Blackboard Collaborate web conferencing.* Retrieved from http://www.blackboard.com/Platforms/Collaborate/Products/Blackboard-Collaborate/Web-Conferencing/Features.aspx

Black, J. S., Gregersen, H. B., & Black, J. S. (2008). *It starts with one: Changing individuals changes organizations.* Upper Saddle River, NJ: Wharton School Pub.

Blackmore, J., Bateman, D., Cloonan, A., Dixon, M., Loughlin, J., O'Mara, J., & Senior, K. (2010). Innovative learning environments research study. Melbourne, Australia: Deakin University; Retrieved from http://www.learningspaces.edu.au/docs/learningspaces-final-report.pdf

Blankson, J., & Kyei-Blankson, L. (2008). Nontraditional students' perception of a blended course: Integrating synchronous online discussion and face-to-face instruction. *Journal of Interactive Learning Research*, *19*(3), 421–438.

Blau, I., & Barak, A. (2012). How do personality, synchronous media, and discussion topic affect participation? *Journal of Educational Technology & Society*, *15*(2), 12–24.

Bliesener, T. (2006). Training synchronous collaborative E-learning. *International Journal on E-Learning*, *5*(2), 185–196.

Bliss, C., & Lawrence, B. (2009). From posts to patterns: A metric to characterize discussion board activity in online courses. *Journal of Asynchronous Learning Networks*, *13*(2), 15–32.

Bloch, J., & Spataro, S. E. (2014). Cultivating critical-thinking dispositions throughout the business curriculum. *Business and Professional Communication Quarterly*, *77*(3), 249–265. doi:10.1177/2329490614538094

Bloom, B. S., & Krathwohl, D. R. (1956). Taxonomy of educational objectives: The classification of educational goals by a committee of college and university examiners (H. I. C. Domain, Ed.). Academic Press.

Bloom, B. S., Engelhart, M. D., Furst, E. J., Hill, W. H., & Krathwohl, D. R. (1956). *Taxonomy of educational objectives: The classification of educational goals. Handbook I: Cognitive domain*. New York: David McKay Company.

Bloom, B., Englehard, M. D., Furst, E. J., Hill, W. H., & Kraftwohl, D. R. (1956). *Taxonomy of educational objectives: The classification of educational goals: Handbook 1. Cognitive domain* (B. Bloom, Ed.). New York, NY: David McKay.

Bocchi, J., Eastman, J. K., & Swift, C. O. (2004). Retaining the online learner: Profile of students in an online MBA program and implications for teaching them. *Journal of Education for Business*, *79*(4), 245–253. doi:10.3200/JOEB.79.4.245-253

Boettcher, J. V., & Conrad, R. (2010). *The online survival teaching guide: Simple and practical pedagogical tips*. Jossey-Bass. Retrieved from http://www.myilibrary.com?ID=320339

Bolliger, D. U., & Armier, D. D. (2013). Active learning in the online environment: The integration of student-generated audio files. *Active Learning in Higher Education*, *14*(3), 201–211. doi:10.1177/1469787413498032

Bonk, C. J., Kirkley, J. R., Hara, N., & Dennen, N. (2001). *Finding the instructor in post-secondary online learning: Pedagogical, social, managerial, and technological locations*. London: Kogan Page Limited.

Bonnel, W., Ludwig, C., & Smith, J. (2008). Providing feedback in online courses: What do students want? How do we do that? In M. H. Oermann (Ed.), *Annual review of nursing education*. New York, NY: Springer.

Bonvillian, W. B., & Singer, S. R. (2013). The online challenge to higher education. *Issues in Science and Technology*, *29*(4), 23–30.

Booher, R. K., & Seiler, W. J. (1982). Speech communication anxiety: An impediment to academic achievement in the university classroom. *Journal of Classroom Interaction*, *18*(1), 23–27.

Borup, J., Graham, C., & Davies, R. (2013). The nature of adolescent learner interaction in a virtual high school setting. *Journal of Computer Assisted Learning*, *29*(2), 153–167. doi:10.1111/j.1365-2729.2012.00479.x

Borup, J., West, R. E., & Graham, C. R. (2012). Improving online social presence through asynchronous video. *The Internet and Higher Education*, *15*(3), 195–203. doi:10.1016/j.iheduc.2011.11.001

Borup, J., West, R. E., Thomas, R. A., & Graham, C. R. (2014). Examining the impact of video feedback on instructor social presence in blended courses. *International Review of Research in Open and Distance Learning*, *15*(3), 232–256.

Boston, W., Díaz, S. R., Gibson, A. M., Ice, P., Richardson, J., & Swan, K. (2009). An exploration of the relationship between indicators of the community of inquiry framework and retention in online programs. *Journal of Asynchronous Learning Networks*, *13*(3), 67–83.

Boston, W., Ice, P., & Gibson, A. (2011). Comprehensive assessment of student retention in online learning environments. *Online Journal of Distance Learning Administration, 4*(1).

Boud, D., & Walker, D. (1998). Promoting reflection in professional courses: The challenge of context. *Studies in Higher Education, 23*(2), 191–206. doi:10.1080/030 75079812331380384

Bowden, J. (2008). Improving feedback to students in online courses. *Nurse Researcher, 15,* 253–270.

Bowen, W. G., & Lack, K. A. (2013). Higher education in the digital age. Princeton, NJ: Princeton University Press.

Bowen, W. G., Chingos, M. M., Lack, K. A., & Nygren, T. I. (2012, May). *Interactive learning online at public universities: Evidence from randomized trials.* Retrieved from http://www.sr.ithaka.org/research-publications/ interactive-learning-online-public-universities-evidence-randomized-trials

Bower, M. (2011). Synchronous collaboration competencies in web-conferencing environments - their impact on the learning process. *Distance Education, 32*(1), 63–83. doi:10.1080/01587919.2011.565502

Bowman, N. A. (2013). How much diversity is enough? The curvilinear relationship between college diversity interactions and first-year student outcomes. *Research in Higher Education, 54*(8), 874–894. doi:10.1007/ s11162-013-9300-0

Boyce, L., & Clutterbuck, D. (2011). E-Coaching: Accept it, it's here, and it's evolving! In G. Hernez-Broome & L. Boyce (Eds.), *Advancing executive coaching: Setting the course for successful leadership coaching* (pp. 285–315). San Francisco: Jossey-Bass.

Boyd, E., & Fales, A. (1983). Reflective learning key to learning from experience. *Journal of Humanistic Psychology, 23*(2), 99–117. doi:10.1177/0022167883232011

Boyle, D. K., & Wambach, K. A. (2001). Interaction in graduate nursing Web-based instruction. *Journal of Professional Nursing, 17*(3), 128–134. doi:10.1053/ jpnu.2001.23376 PMID:11391558

Bozarth, J., Chapman, D. D., & LaMonica, L. (2004). Preparing for distance learning: Designing an online student orientation course. *Journal of Educational Technology & Society, 7*(1), 87–106.

Brandt, C. (2008). Integrating feedback and reflection in teacher preparation. *ELT Journal, 62*(1), 37–46. doi:10.1093/elt/ccm076

Bransford, J. D., Vye, N., Kinzer, C., & Risko, V. (1990). Teaching thinking and content knowledge: Toward an integrated approach. In B. Jones & L. Idol (Eds.), *Dimensions of thinking and cognitive instruction.* Hillsdale, NJ: Lawrence Erlbaum Associates.

Brescia, W. F. J., & Miller, M. T. (2006). What's it worth? The perceived benefits of instructional blogging. *Electronic Journal for the Integration of Technology in Education, 5,* 44–52.

Bright, B. (1996). Reflecting on "reflective practice.". *Studies in the Education of Adults, 28*(2), 162–184.

Brinkerhoff, J., & Koroghlanian, C. M. (2007). Online students' expectations: Enhancing the fit between online students and course design. *Journal of Educational Computing Research, 36*(4), 383–393. doi:10.2190/R728-28W1-332K-U115

Britton, J. (1978). The composing processes and the functions of writing. In C. R. Cooper & L. Odell (Eds.), *Research on Composing: Points of Departure.* Urbana, IL: NCTE.

Broadbent, B. (2002). *ABCs of e-learning: Repeating the benefits and avoiding the pitfalls.* San Francisco, CA: Jossey-Bass.

Brockett, R. G., & Hiemstra, R. (1985). Bridging the theory-practice gap in self-directed learning. In S. Brookfield (Ed.), *Self-directed learning: From theory to practice* (pp. 31–40). San Francisco: Jossey-Bass Publishers. doi:10.1002/ace.36719852505

Bronfenbrenner, U. (1977). Toward an experimental ecology of human development. *The American Psychologist, 32*(7), 513–531. doi:10.1037/0003-066X.32.7.513

Bronfenbrenner, U. (1979). *The ecology of human development: Experiments by nature and design*. Cambridge, MA: Harvard University Press.

Bronfenbrenner, U. (1989). Ecological systems theory. *Annals of Child Development, 6*, 187–24.

Bronfenbrenner, U. (1995). Developmental ecology through space and time: A future perspective. In P. Moen & G. H. Elder Jr., (Eds.), *Examining lives in context: Perspectives on the ecology of human development* (pp. 619–647). Washington, DC: American Psychological Association. doi:10.1037/10176-018

Bronfenbrenner, U. (2005). *Making human beings human: Bioecological perspectives of human development*. Thousand Oaks, CA: Sage.

Brookfield, S. (1986). *Understanding and Facilitating Adult Learning*. Open University Press.

Brookfield, S. (1995). Adult learning: An overview. In A. Tuinjman (Ed.), *International Encyclopedia of Education* (pp. 375–380). Oxford, UK: Pergamon.

Brookfield, S. D. (1987). *Developing critical thinkers: Challenging adults to explore alternative ways of thinking and acting*. San Francisco, CA: Jossey-Bass.

Brookfield, S. D. (1990). Discussion. In M. W. Galbraith (Ed.), *Adult learning methods: A guide to effective instruction* (pp. 187–204). Malabar, FL: Robert E. Krieger.

Brookfield, S. D. (1995). *Becoming a critically reflective teacher*. San Francisco, CA: Jossey-Bass.

Brookfield, S. D. (1995). *Becoming a Critically Reflective Teacher*. San Francisco: Jossey-Bass Publishers.

Brookfield, S. D., & Preskill, S. (2005). *Discussion as a way of teaching*. San Francisco, CA: Jossey-Bass.

Brookfield, S. D., & Preskill, S. (2005). *Discussion as a way of teaching: Tools and techniques for democratic classrooms* (2nd ed.). San Francisco, CA: Jossey-Bass.

Brookhart, S. M. (2008). *How to give effective feedback to your students*. Alexandria, VA: Association for Supervision and Curriculum Development.

Brooks, D., & Jeong, A. (2006). Effects of pre-structuring discussion threads on group interaction and group performance in computer-supported collaborative argumentation. *Distance Education, 27*(3), 371–390. doi:10.1080/01587910600940448

Brooks, J. G., & Brooks, M. G. (1999). *In search of understanding: The case for constructivist classrooms*. Danvers, MA: Association for Supervision and Curriculum Development.

Brown, J. W. (2013). Multicultural curriculum development in online classes: Practices from Washington State Community Colleges. Community College Journal of Research and Practices.

Brown, E. L. (2004a). Overcoming the challenges of stand-alone multicultural courses: The possibilities of technology integration. *Journal of Technology and Teacher Education, 12*(4), 535–559.

Brown, E. L. (2004b). What precipitates change in cultural diversity awareness during a multicultural course: The message or the method? *Journal of Teacher Education*.

Browne, E. (2005). Structural and pedagogic change in further and higher education: A case study approach. *Journal of Further and Higher Education, 29*(1), 49–59. doi:10.1080/03098770500037754

Brown, R. E. (2001, September). The process of community-building in distance learning courses. *Journal of Asynchronous Learning Networks, 5*(2).

Bruning, K. (2005). The role of critical thinking in the online learning environment. *International Journal of Instructional Technology and Distance Learning, 2*(5), 21–31.

Bullen, M., Morgan, T., Belfer, K., & Qayyum, A. (2008). The digital learner at BCIT and implications for an e-strategy. In *Proceedings of the 2008 Research Workshop of the European Distance Education Network (EDEN) Researching and promoting access to education and training: The role of distance education and e-learning in technology-enhanced environment*. Retrieved from http://www.box.net/shared/fxqyutottt

Bullen, M. (1998). Participation and critical thinking in on-line university distance education. *Canadian Journal of Distance Education, 13*(2), 1–32.

Burgelman, R. A., Christensen, C. M., & Wheelwright, S. C. (2004). *Strategic management of technology and innovation* (4th ed.). New York, NY: McGraw-Hill Irwin.

Burnett, G., & Lingam, G. I. (2007). Reflective teachers and teacher educators in the Pacific region: Conversations with us not about us. *Review of Education, 53*, 303–321.

Burruss, N. M., Billings, D. M., Brownrigg, V., Skiba, D. J., & Connors, H. R. (2009). Class size as related to the sue of technology, educational practices, and outcomes in web-based nursing courses. *Journal of Professional Nursing, 25*(1), 33–41. doi:10.1016/j.profnurs.2008.06.002 PMID:19161961

Butland, M. J., & Beebe, S. A. (1992). *A Study of the Application of Implicit Communication Theory to Teacher Immediacy and Student Learning*. Paper presented at the Annual Meeting of the International Communication Association, Miami, FL. Retrieved from ERIC database. ED 346 532.

Butler, T. J., & Pinto-Zipp, G. (2006). Students' learning styles and their preferences for online instructional methods. *Journal of Educational Technology Systems, 34*(2), 199–221. doi:10.2190/8UD2-BHFU-4PXV-7ALW

Caffarella, R. (2002). *Planning programs for adult learners. A practical guide for educators, trainers and staff developers*. San Francisco: Jossey-Bass.

Campbell, D. T., & Fehr, B. (1990). Self-esteem and perceptions of conveyed impressions: Is negative affectivity associated with greater realism? *Journal of Personality and Social Psychology, 58*(1), 122–133. doi:10.1037/0022-3514.58.1.122 PMID:2308069

Cangelosi, P. R., & Whitt, K. J. (2005). Accelerated nursing programs what do we know? *Nursing Education Perspectives, 26*(2), 113–116. PMID:15921128

Canton, M. E., & James, D. P. (2008). *Mentoring in higher education: Best practices* (2nd ed.). Robertson Publishing.

Cappola, N. W., Hiltz, S. R., & Rotter, N. (2002). Becoming a virtual professor: Pedagogical roles and ALN. *Journal of Management Information Systems, 18*(4), 169–190.

Cardullo, V., Zygouris-Coe, V., & Wilson, N. S. (2014). The benefits and Challenges of Mobile Learning and Ubiquitous Technologies. In J. Keengwe (Ed.), Promoting Active Learning through the Integration of Mobile and Ubiquitous Technologies (pp. 185–196). Academic Press.

Cardullo, V. M. (2013). Cyber-place learning in an online teacher preparation program: Engaging learning opportunities through collaborations and facilitation of learning. In R. Hartshorne, T. Heafner, & T. Petty (Eds.), *Teacher education programs and online learning tools: Innovations in teacher prepration* (pp. 181–197). Hershey, PA: Information Science Reference. doi:10.4018/978-1-4666-1906-7.ch010

Cardullo, V., Wilson, N. S., & Zygouris-Coe, V. (2015). Enhanced Student Engagement through Active Learning and Emerging Technologies. In J. Keengwe (Ed.), *Handbook of Research on Educational Technology Integration and Active Learning. Edited by: Sagini Keengwe, Ph.D* (pp. 1–18). University of North Dakota.

Carey, K. B., Scott-Sheldon, L. A., Elliott, J. C., Bolles, J. R., & Carey, M. P. (2009). Computer delivered interventions to reduce college student drinking: A meta-analysis. *Addiction (Abingdon, England), 104*(11), 1807–1819. doi:10.1111/j.1360-0443.2009.02691.x PMID:19744139

Carliner, S. (1999). *Overview of online learning*. Amherst, MA: Human Resource Development Press.

Carr, S. (2000). As distance education comes of age, the challenge is keeping the students. *The Chronicle of Higher Education, 46*, A39–A41.

Caruso, F. (Producer) & Lynch, D. (Director). (1986). *Blue Velvet*. [Motion Picture]. United States: MGM.

Caspi, A., & Blau, I. (2008). Social presence in online discussion groups: Testing three conceptions and their relations to perceived learning. *Social Psychology of Education, 11*(3), 323–346. doi:10.1007/s11218-008-9054-2

Caspi, A., Chajut, E., Saporta, K., & Beyth-Marom, R. (2006). The influence of personality on social participation in learning environments. *Learning and Individual Differences, 16*(2), 129–144. doi:10.1016/j.lindif.2005.07.003

Cassidy, S. (2004). Learning styles: An overview of theories, models, and measures. *Educational Psychology, 24*(4), 419–444. doi:10.1080/0144341042000228834

Cavanaugh, J. (2005). Teaching online: A time comparison. *Journal of Distance Learning Administration Content, 8*(1).

Cervone, D., Jiwani, N., & Wood, R. (1991). Goal setting and the differential influence of self-regulatory processes on complex decision-making performance. *Journal of Personality and Social Psychology, 61*(2), 257–266. doi:10.1037/0022-3514.61.2.257 PMID:1920065

Cervone, H. F. (2012). Managing digital libraries: The view from 30,000 feet. *OCLC Systems & Services: International Digital Library Perspectives, 28*(1), 14–16.

Chaiprasurt, C., & Esichaikul, V. (2013). Enhancing Motivation in Online Courses with Mobile communication tool support: A comparative study. *International Review of Research in Open and Distance Learning, 14*(3), 377–401.

Chamberlain, R., & Vrasidas, C. (2001). Creating engaging online instruction. In *Proceedings of the 17th Annual Conference on Distance Teaching and Learning*. Madison, WI: University of Wisconsin System.

Champaign, J., & Cohen, R. (2010). A model for content sequencing in intelligent tutoring systems based on the ecological approach and its validation through simulated students. In *Proceedings of the Ninth Florida Artificial Intelligence Research Symposium*. Daytona Beach, FL: Academic Press.

Chang, C. K., Chen, G. D., & Li, L. Y. (2006). Constructing a community of practice to improve coursework activity. *Computers & Education, 50*(1), 235–247. doi:10.1016/j.compedu.2006.05.003

Chang, M. (2007). Enhancing web-based language learning through self-monitoring. *Journal of Computer Assisted Learning, 23*(3), 187–196. doi:10.1111/j.1365-2729.2006.00203.x

Chang, M. M., & Lehman, J. (2002). Learning foreign language through an interactive multimedia program: An experimental student of the effects of the relevance components of the ARCS model. *CALICO Journal, 20*, 81–98.

Chatzisarantis, N. D., Hagger, M. S., Smith, B., & Sage, L. D. (2006). The influence of intrinsic motivation on execution of social behavior within the theory of planned behavior. *European Journal of Social Psychology, 36*(2), 229–237. doi:10.1002/ejsp.299

Chaudhury, S. R. (2011). The lecture. *New Directions for Teaching and Learning, 128*(128), 13–20. doi:10.1002/tl.464

Chemers, M. M., Hu, L., & Garcia, B. F. (2001). Academic self-efficacy and first-year college student performance and adjustment. *Journal of Educational Psychology, 93*(1), 55–64. doi:10.1037/0022-0663.93.1.55

Chen, H. (2000). *Exploring web users' on-line optimal flow experiences*. (Unpublished Dissertation). Syracuse University, Syracuse, NY.

Chen, C.-M., Liu, C.-Y., & Chang, M.-H. (2006). Personalized curriculum sequencing utilizing modified item response theory for web-based instruction. *Expert Systems with Applications, 30*(2), 378–396. doi:10.1016/j.eswa.2005.07.029

Chen, C., Wang, J., & Chen, Y. (2014). Facilitating English-language reading performance by a digital reading annotation system with self-regulated learning mechanisms. *Journal of Educational Technology & Society, 17*(1), 102–114.

Chen, D.-T., Wang, Y.-M., & Hung, D. (2009). A journey on refining rules for online discussion: Implications for the design of learning management systems. *Journal of Interactive Learning Research, 20*(2), 157–173.

Cheng, C. K., Paré, D. E., Collimore, L. M., & Joordens, S. (2011). Assessing the effectiveness of a voluntary online discussion forum on improving students' course performance. *Computers & Education, 56*(1), 253–261. doi:10.1016/j.compedu.2010.07.024

Cheng, K., Liang, J., & Tsai, C. (2013). University students' online academic help seeking: The role of self-regulation and information commitments. *The Internet and Higher Education, 16*, 70–77. doi:10.1016/j.iheduc.2012.02.002

Cheng, Y. C., & Yeh, H. T. (2009). From concepts of motivation to its application in instructional design: Reconsidering motivation from an instructional design perspective. *British Journal of Educational Technology, 40*(4), 597–605. doi:10.1111/j.1467-8535.2008.00857.x

Chen, H. R. (2012). Assessment of learners' attention to e-learning by monitoring facial expressions for computer network courses. *Journal of Educational Computing, 47*, 3710385.

Chen, S. J., Hsu, C. L., & Caropreso, E. J. (2006). Cross-cultural collaborative online learning: When the west meets the east. *International Journal of Technology in Teaching and Learning*, 2(1), 17–35.

Chhabra, R., & Sharma, V. (2013). Application of blogging in problem-based learning. *Education and Information Technologies*, 18(1), 3–13. doi:10.1007/s10639-011-9168-6

Chickering, A. W., & Gamson, Z. F. (1987). Seven principles for good practice in undergraduate education. *AAHE Bulletin*, 3-7. Retrieved from ERIC database. (ED 282491).

Chickering, A., & Ehrmann, S. C. (2008). *Implementing the seven principles: Technology as lever*. The TLT Group. Retrieved from: http://www.tltgroup.org/programs/seven.html

Chickering, A. W., & Reisser, L. (1993). *Education and identity* (2nd ed.). San Francisco: Jossey Bass.

Chickering, A., & Ehrman, S. C. (1996). Implementing the seven principles: Technology as lever. *AAHE Bulletin*, 49(2), 3–6.

Chickering, A., & Gamson, Z. (1987). Seven principles of good practice in undergraduate education. *AAHE Bulletin*, 39, 3–7.

Ching, Y.-H., & Hsu, Y.-C. (2013). Collaborative learning using VoiceThread in an online graduate course. *Knowledge Management & E-Learning*, 5(3), 298–314.

Chin, S. T. S., & Williams, J. B. (2006). A theoretical framework for effective online course design. *MERLOT Journal of Online Learning and Teaching*, 2(1), 12–21.

Chi, Y. L. (2009). Ontology-based curriculum content sequencing system with semantic rules. *Expert Systems with Applications*, 36(4), 7838–7847. doi:10.1016/j.eswa.2008.11.048

Chizmar, J. F., & Walbert, M. S. (1999). Web-based learning environments guided by principles of good teaching practice. *The Journal of Economic Education*, 30(3), 248–264. doi:10.1080/00220489909595985

Chizmar, J. F., & Williams, D. B. (2001). What do faculty want? *EDUCAUSE Quarterly*, 24(1), 18–24.

Choi, W. (2013). The effects of self-efficacy and internal locus of control on academic performance of students: The moderating role of class satisfaction. *Journal of Convergence Information Technology*, 8(12), 391–396. doi:10.4156/jcit.vol8.issue12.47

Cho, M. (2012). Online student orientation in higher education: A developmental study. *Educational Technology Research and Development*, 60(6), 1051–1069. doi:10.1007/s11423-012-9271-4

Cho, M. H., & Cho, Y. J. (2014). Instructor scaffolding for interaction and students' academic engagement in online learning: Mediating roles of perceived online class goal structures. *The Internet and Higher Education*, 21, 25–30. doi:10.1016/j.iheduc.2013.10.008

Cho, T. (2011). The impact of types of interaction on student satisfaction in online courses. *International Journal on E-Learning*, 10(2), 109–125.

Chou, S., & Liu, C. (2005). Learning effectiveness in a web-based virtual learning environment: A learner control perspective. *Journal of Computer Assisted Learning*, 21(1), 65–76. doi:10.1111/j.1365-2729.2005.00114.x

Choy, S. (2002). *Nontraditional undergraduates. (U.S. Department of Education, National Center for Education Statistics, NCES 2002-012)*. Washington, DC: U.S. Government Printing Office.

Christiansen, J., & Anderson, T. (2004). Feasibility of course development based on learning objects. *International Journal of Instructional Technology and Distance Learning*, 1(3).

Christophel, D. (1990). The relationships among teacher immediacy behaviors, student motivation, and learning. *Communication Education*, 39(4), 323–340. doi:10.1080/03634529009378813

Chu, A. H. C., & Choi, J. N. (2005). Rethinking procrastination: Positive effects of "active" procrastination behavior on attitudes and performance.[PubMed]. *The Journal of Social Psychology*, 145(3), 245–264. doi:10.3200/SOCP.145.3.245-264 PMID:15959999

Churchill, D., & Lu, J. (2012). The effect of social interaction on learning engagement in a social networking environment. *Interactive Learning Environments*, 22(4), 410–417. Retrieved from http://www.tandfonline.com

Chu, S. K., Kwan, A. C., & Warning, P. (2012). Blogging for information management, learning and social support during internship. *Journal of Educational Technology & Society*, *15*(2), 168–178.

Cigdem, H., & Yildirim, O. G. (2014). Effects of students' characteristics on online learning readiness: A vocational college example. *Turkish Online Journal of Distance Education*, *15*(3), 80–93. doi:10.17718/tojde.69439

Cisero, C. A. (2006). Does Reflective Journal Writing Improve Course Performance? *College Teaching*, *54*(2), 231–236. doi:10.3200/CTCH.54.2.231-236

City Colleges of Chicago. (2011). *Fiscal year 2011: Statistical digest*. Retrieved from http://www.ccc.edu/menu/Documents/CCCFY2011Statistical Digest.pdf

Clair, N. (1995). Mainstream Classroom Teachers and ESL students. *Teachers of English to Speakers of Other Languages, 29*(1).

Clark, R. E. (2001). A summary of disagreements with the "mere vehicles" argument. In *Learning from media: Arguments, analysis, and evidence* (pp. 125-136). Academic Press.

Clarke, L. W., & Bartholomew, A. (2014). Digging beneath the surface: Analyzing the complexity of instructors' participation in asynchronous discussion. *Online Learning*, *18*(4), 1-22. Retrieved from http://olj.onlinelearningconsortium.org/index.php/jaln/article/view/414/111

Clarke, S. (2011). *Peer Interaction and engagement through online discussion forums: A cautionary tale.* Springer Sciences Business Media; doi:10.1007/s10991-011-9092-2

Clarke, S. G., & Haworth, J. T. (1994). 'Flow' experience in the daily lives of sixth-form college students. *British Journal of Psychology*, *85*(4), 511–523. doi:10.1111/j.2044-8295.1994.tb02538.x

Clark, R. C., & Mayer, R. E. (2011). *E-Learning and the science of instruction: Proven guidelines for consumers and designers of multimedia learning* (3rd ed.). San Francisco, CA: John Wiley & Sons. doi:10.1002/9781118255971

Clark, R. E. (1983). Reconsidering research on learning from media. *Review of Educational Research*, *53*(4), 445–459. doi:10.3102/00346543053004445

Clark, R. E. (1994). Media and method. *Educational Technology Research and Development*, *42*(3), 7–10. doi:10.1007/BF02298090

Clark, R. E. (1994). Media will never influence learning. *Educational Technology Research and Development*, *47*(2), 21–29. doi:10.1007/BF02299088

Clutterbuck, D., & Hussain, Z. (Eds.). (2010). *Virtual coach, virtual mentor*. Charlotte, NC: Information Age Publishing.

Cobb, S. C. (2009). Social presence and online learning: A current view from a research perspective. *Journal of Interactive Online Learning*, *8*(3), 241–254.

Cochrane, T., & Bateman, R. (2010). Smartphones give you wings: Pedagogical affordances of mobile 2.0. *Australasian Journal of Educational Technology*, *26*(1), 1–14.

Cochran, J. D., Campbell, S. M., Baker, H. M., & Leeds, E. M. (2014). The role of student characteristics in predicting retention in online courses. *Research in Higher Education*, *55*(1), 27–48. doi:10.1007/s11162-013-9305-8

Cohen, B. (Producer) & Mendes, S. (Director). (1999). *American Beauty*. [Motion Picture]. United States: DreamWorks.

Cohen, J., & Hollenbrands, K. F. (2011). Technology tools to support mathematics teaching. In T. P. Dick & K. F. Hollenbrands (Eds.), *Focus in high school mathematics: Technology to support reasoning and sense making* (pp. 105–122). Reston, VA: NCTM.

Cohen, N. H. (2003). The journey of the principles of the adult mentoring inventory. *Adult Learning*, *14*(1), 4–12.

Coldwell, J., Craig, A., Paterson, T., & Mustard, J. (2008). Online students: Relationships between participation, demographics, and academic performance. *The Electronic Journal of e-Learning*, *6*(1), 19-30. Retrieved from http://www.ejel.org/volume6/issue1

Cole, M. T., Shelley, J. D., & Swartz, L. B. (2014). Online Instruction, E-learning, and student satisfaction: A three year study. *International Review of Research in Open and Distance Learning*, *15*(6).

Cole, R. A. (2000). *Issues in Web-based pedagogy: A critical primer*. Westport, CT: Greenwood Press.

Coleridge, S. T. (1985). Biographia Literaria. In The Collected Works of Samuel Taylor Coleridge, Biographical Sketches of my Literary Life & Opinions (Vol. 7). Princeton University Press.

Colesberry, R. (Producer) & Schlondorff, V. (Director). (1985) Death of a Salesman. [TV Motion Picture]. United States: Roxbury Production.

Collier, P., & Morgan, D. (2008). Is that paper really due today? Differences in first generation and traditional college students' understandings of faculty expectations. *Higher Education*, *55*(4), 425–426. doi:10.1007/s10734-007-9065-5

Collins, J., Harkin, J., & Nind, M. (2002). *Manifesto for Learning*. London, New York: Continuum.

Collins, W. J. (1913). The place of volition in education. *International Journal of Ethics*, *23*, 379–396.

Collis, B., & Moonen, J. (2008). Web 2.0 tools and processes in higher education: Quality perspectives. *Educational Media International*, *45*(2), 93–106. doi:10.1080/09523980802107179

Collison, G., Elbaum, B., Haavind, S., & Tinker, R. (2000). *Facilitating online learning: Effective strategies for moderators*. Madison, WI: Atwood Publishing.

Collom, G., Dallas, A., Jong, R., & Obexer, R. (2002). Six months in a leaky boat: Framing the knowledge and skills needed to teach well online. *Proceedings ASCILITE 2002*. Retrieved from http://www.ascilite.org.au/conferences/auckland02/proceedings/papers/181.pdf

Concannon, F., Flynn, A., & Campbell, M. (2005). What campus-base students think about the quality of benefits of e-learning. *British Journal of Educational Technology*, *36*(3), 501–521. doi:10.1111/j.1467-8535.2005.00482.x

Concieção, S. C. (2006). Faculty lived experiences in the online environment. *Adult Education Quarterly*, *5*(1), 26–45. doi:10.1177/1059601106292247

Connell, J. P., & Wellborn, J. G. (1991). Competence, autonomy and relatedness: A motivational analysis of the self-system processes. In M. R. Gunnar, & L. A. Sroufe (Eds.), *Minnesota Symposium on Child Psychology*. Hillsdale, NJ: Lawrence Erlbaum.

Connors, P. (2013). Delivery style moderates study habits in an online nutrition class. *Journal of Nutrition Education and Behavior*, *45*(2), 171–175. doi:10.1016/j.jneb.2012.04.006 PMID:23041253

Conrad, D. L. (2002). Engagement, excitement, anxiety and fear: Learners' experiences of starting an online course. *Distance Education*, *76*(4), 205–226. doi:10.1207/S15389286AJDE1604_2

Conrad, R. M., & Donalson, J. A. (2004). *Engaging the online learner, Activities and resources for creative instruction*. Jossey-Bass.

Conrad, R., & Donaldson, J. (2004). *Engaging the online learner: Activities and resources for creative instruction*. San Francisco, CA: Jossey-Bass.

Coppola, N. W., Hiltz, S. R., & Rotter, N. (2001). Becoming a virtual professor: Pedagogical roles and ALN. In *System Sciences, 2001. Proceedings of the 37th Annual Hawaii International Conference on System Sciences* (HICSS-34). Piscataway, NJ: Institute of Electrical and Electronics Engineers Press.

Corbeil, J. R. (2003). *Online technologies, self-efficacy, self-directed learning readiness, and locus of control of learners in a graduate-level web-based distance education program*. (Unpublished doctoral dissertation). University of Houston, Houston, TX.

Corbin, J., & Strauss, A. (2008). *Basics of qualitative research: Techniques to developing grounded theory* (3rd ed.). Thousand Oaks, CA: Sage.

Cormier, D., & Siemens, G. (2010). The open course: Through the open door--open courses as research, learning, and engagement. *EDUCAUSE Review*, *45*(4), 30.

Cosmides, L., & Tooby, J. (2013). Evolutionary psychology: New perspectives on cognition and motivation.[PubMed]. *Annual Review of Psychology*, *64*(1), 201–229. doi:10.1146/annurev.psych.121208.131628 PMID:23282055

Costa, A. L., & Kallick, B. (Eds.). (2008). *Learning and leading with habits of mind: 16 essential characteristics for success*. Alexandria, VA: ASCD.

Costa, A., & Garmston, R. (2002). *Cognitive coaching: a foundation for renaissance schools*. Norwood, MA: Christopher-Gordon.

Courau, S. (1994). *Les outils d' excellence du formateur* (2nd ed.). Paris: ESF.

Coutinho, C. P. (2007). Cooperative learning in higher education using weblogs: A study with undergraduate students of education in Portugal. *Proceedings of the 5th International Conference on Education and Information Systems, Technologies and Applications* (EISTA) (pp. 60-64). Orlando: EUA. Julho.

Covington, M. V. (2000). Goal theory, motivation, and school achievement: An integrative review. *Annual Review of Psychology, 51*(1), 171–2000. doi:10.1146/annurev.psych.51.1.171 PMID:10751969

Craik, F. I. M., & Lockhart, R. S. (1972). Levels of processing: A framework for memory research. *Journal of Verbal Learning and Verbal Behavior, 11*(6), 671–684. doi:10.1016/S0022-5371(72)80001-X

Cranton, P. (2000). *Planning Instruction for Adult Learners* (2nd ed.). Toronto: Wall & Emerson, Inc.

Cranton, P. (2006). *Understanding and promoting transformative learning: A guide for educators of Adults*. San Francisco, CA: Jossey-Bass.

Crawley, A. (2012). *Supporting online students: A practical guide to planning, implementing, and evaluating services*. San Francisco: John Wiley & Sons.

Crawley, S. L., Curry, H., Dumois-Sands, J., Tanner, C., & Wyker, C. (2008). Full-contact pedagogy: Lecturing with questions and student-centered assignment as methods for inciting self-reflexity for faculty and students. *Feminist Teacher, 19*(1), 13–30. doi:10.1353/ftr.0.0023

Creswell, J. W. (2005). *Educational research: Planning, conducting, and evaluating quantitative and qualitative research* (2nd ed.). Berkeley, CA: Carlisle Communications.

Creswell, J. W. (2013). *Research design: Qualitative, quantitative, and mixed methods approaches*. Thousand Oaks, CA: Sage.

Cronbach, L. J. (1984). *Essentials of psychological testing* (4th ed.). New York, NY: Harper Row.

Crook, C., & Harrison, C. (2008). *Web 2.0 technologies for learning at Key State 3 and 4: Summary report*. London: BECTA. Retrieved from http://dera.ioe.ac.uk/1480/1/becta_2008_web2_summary.pdf

Crosling, G., & Heagney, M., & Thomas. (2009). Improving student retention in higher education: Improving teaching and learning. *Australian Universities Review, 51*, 9–18.

Cross, K. P. (1981). *Adults as Learners*. San Francisco: Jossey-Bass.

Cross, P. (1987). Teaching for learning. *AAHE Bulletin, 39*(8), 3–7.

Crowe, C., & Tonkin, J. (2006). *Fifteen megabytes of fame: blogging, learning and assessment. Synergy, 24* (pp. 1–6). Sydney: University of Sydney.

Crowe, J. L. (2000). Evaluation of adult learners: Ethical issues. *New Horizons in Adult Education, 14*(3), 4–10. doi:10.1002/nha3.10117

Croxton, R. A. (2014). The role of interactivity in student satisfaction and persistence in online learning. *Journal of Online Learning and Teaching, 10*(2), 314–324. Retrieved from http://jolt.merlot.org/vol10no2/croxton_0614.pdf

Croxton, R. A. (2014). The role of interactivity in student satisfaction and persistence in online learning. *MERLOT Journal of Online Learning and Teaching, 10*(2), 314–326.

Csikszentmihalyi, M. (2008). *Flow: The psychology of optimal experience*. New York, NY: HarperCollins.

Cueller, N. (2002). The transition from classroom to online teaching. *Nursing Forum, 37*(3), 5–13. doi:10.1111/j.1744-6198.2002.tb01005.x PMID:12430390

Cummins, J. (1994). *Negotiating identities: Education for empowerment in a diverse society*. Los Angeles: California Association of Bilingual Education.

Cunningham, S. J., Brebner, J. L., Quinn, F., & Turk, D. J. (2014). The self-reference effect on memory in early childhood. *Child Development, 85*(2), 808–823. doi:10.1111/cdev.12144 PMID:23888928

Dabbagh, N. (2003). Scaffolding: An important teacher competency in online learning. *TechTrends, 47*(2), 39–44. doi:10.1007/BF02763424

Dabbagh, N., & Bannan-Ritland, B. (2005). *Online learning: Concepts, strategies, and application*. Upper Saddle River, NJ: Prentice Hall.

Dabbagh, N., & Kitsantas, A. (2005). Using web-based pedagogical tools as scaffolds for self-regulated learning. *Instructional Science*, *33*(5-6), 513–540. doi:10.1007/s11251-005-1278-3

Dabbagh, N., & Kitsantas, A. (2009). Exploring how experienced online instructors report using integrative technologies to support self-regulated learning. *International Journal of Technology in Teaching and Learning*, *5*(2), 154–168.

Daffner, K. R., Mesulam, M. M., Scinto, L. F., Acar, D., Calvo, V., Faust, R., & Holcomb, P. et al. (2000). The central role of the prefrontal cortex in directing attention to novel events. *Brain*, *123*(5), 927–939. doi:10.1093/brain/123.5.927 PMID:10775538

Dailey, A., Mandernach, B. J., & Donnelli, E. (2010). Teaching with technology: A more meaningful learning experience starts with two questions. *Faculty Focus*. Retrieved from http://www.facultyfocus.com/?p=11357

Dailey, A., Mandernach, B., & Donnelli, E. (2008). The multimedia dilemma: Questioning beyond the what to the why. *Online Classroom*. Retrieved from http://www.magnapubs.com/issues/magnapubs_oc/8_12/news/602064-1.html

Daloz, L. A. (2012). *Mentor: guiding the journey of adult learners* (2nd ed.). San Francisco, CA: Jossey-Bass.

Damarin, S. K. (1998). Technology and multicultural education: The question of convergence. *Theory into Practice*, *37*(1), 11–19. doi:10.1080/00405849809543781

Darabi, A., Arrastia, M. C., Nelson, D. W., Cornille, T., & Liang, X. (2011). Cognitive presence in asynchronous online learning: A comparison of four discussion strategies. *Journal of Computer Assisted Learning*, *27*(3), 216–227. doi:10.1111/j.1365-2729.2010.00392.x

Daughenbaugh, R., Daughenbaugh, D., Surry, D., & Islam, M. (2002). Personality type and online versus in-class course satisfaction. *EDUCAUSE Quarterly*, *3*, 71–72.

Davidson-Shivers, G. V., Luyegu, E., & Kimble, B. E. (2012). An analysis of asynchronous discussions: A case study of graduate student participation in online debates. *Journal of Educational Media and Hypermedia*, *21*(1), 29–51.

Davies, A., Little, P., & Stewart, B. (2008). Developing and infrastructure for online learning. In T. Anderson (Ed.), *The theory and practice of online learning* (pp. 121–142). Athabasca University Press.

Davis, L. J. (2010). *Social networking sites as virtual communities of practice: A mixed method study.* (Ph.D. Dissertation). Capella University, Minneapolis, MN.

Davis, B. G. (1993). *Tools for Teaching*. San Francisco: Jossey-Bass.

Davis, F. D. (1989). Perceived usefulness, perceived ease of use, and user acceptance of information technology. *Management Information Systems Quarterly*, *13*(3), 319–339. doi:10.2307/249008

Davis, J. R. (1995). *Interdisciplinary courses and team teaching*. Phoenix, AZ: American Council on Education and Oryx Press.

Dawson, S. (2006). A study of the relationship between student communication, interaction, and sense of community. *The Internet and Higher Education*, *9*(3), 153–162. doi:10.1016/j.iheduc.2006.06.007

de la Varre, C., Keane, J., & Irvin, M. J. (2011). Dual perspectives on the contribution of on-site facilitators to teaching presence in a blended learning environment. *Journal of Distance Education*, *25*(3). Retrieved from http://www.ijede.ca/index.php/jde/article/view/751

De Raadt, M., Toleman, M., & Watson, R. (2005). Electronic peer review: a large cohort teaching themselves? *Proceedings of the 22nd Annual Conference of the Australasian Society for Computers in Learning in Tertiary Education*, 159-168.

Deci, E. L., & Ryan, R. M. (1991). A motivational approach to self: Integration of personality. In R. Dienstbier (Ed.), Nebraska Symposium on Motivation: Vol. 38. *Perspectives on motivation*. Lincoln, NE: University of Nebraska Press.

Deci, E. L., & Ryan, R. M. (1992). The initiation and regulation of intrinsically motivated learning and achievement. In A. K. Boggiano & T. S. Pittman (Eds.), *Achievement and Motivation. A social developmental perspective*. New York, NY: Cambridge University Press.

Deci, E. L., & Ryan, R. M. (2008). Self-determination theory: A macro-theory of human motivation, development, and health. *Canadian Psychology, 40*(3), 182–185. doi:10.1037/a0012801

Deci, E. L., Vallerand, R. J., Pelletier, L. G., & Ryan, R. M. (1991). Motivation and education: The self-determination perspective. *Educational Psychologist, 26*(3-4), 325–346. doi:10.1080/00461520.1991.9653137

Dede, C. (2005). Planning for neomillennial learning styles. *EDUCAUSE Quarterly, 28*(1), 7–12.

Dede, C., Ketelhut, D. J., Whitehouse, P., Breit, L., & Mc-Closkey, E. (2009). A research agenda for online teacher professional development. *Journal of Teacher Education, 60*(1), 8–19. doi:10.1177/0022487108327554

DeFina, B. (Producer) & Scorsese, M. (Director). (1989). *Life Lessons*. [Motion Picture]. United States: Touchstone.

Deimann, M., & Keller, J. M. (2006). Volitional aspects of multimedia learning. *Journal of Educational Multimedia and Hypermedia, 15*, 137–158.

Delen, E., Liew, J., & Willson, V. (2014). Effects of interactivity and instructional scaffolding on learning: Self-regulation in online video-based environments. *Computers & Education, 78*, 312–320. doi:10.1016/j.compedu.2014.06.018

Dembo, M. H., Junge, L., & Lynch, R. (2006). Becoming a self-regulated learner: Implications for web-based education. In H. F. O'Neil & R. S. Perez (Eds.), *Web-based learning: Theory, research, and practicepp* (pp. 185–202). Mahwah, NJ: Lawrence Erlbaum.

Deng, L., & Yuen, A. H. K. (2009). Blogs in higher education: Implementation and issues. *TechTrends, 53*(3), 95–98.

Dennen, V. P. (2005). From message posting to learning dialogs: Factors affecting learner participation in asynchronous discussion. *Distance Education, 26*(1), 127–148. doi:10.1080/01587910500081376

Dennen, V. P., & Hao, S. (2014). Paradigms of use, learning theory, and app design. In C. Miller & A. Doering (Eds.), *The new landscape of mobile learning: Redesigning education in an app-based world* (pp. 20–40). Hershey, PA: IGI Global.

DePietro, P. (2013). Transforming education with new media: Participatory pedagogy, interactive learning and Web 2.0. *The International Journal of Technology Knowledge in Society, 8*, 1–11.

Dewey, J. (1933). *How we think*. New York: DC Heath.

Dewitte, S., & Lens, W. (2000). Procrastinators lack a broad action perspective. *European Journal of Personality, 27*(2), 121–140. doi:10.1002/(SICI)1099-0984(200003/04)14:2<121::AID-PER368>3.0.CO;2-#

Dewitte, S., Siegfried, R., Lens, W., & Willy, A. (1999). Volition: Use with measure. *Learning and Individual Differences, 11*(3), 321–334. doi:10.1016/S1041-6080(99)80006-5

Di Leonardi, B. C. (2007). Tips for facilitating learning: The lecture deserves some respect.[PubMed]. *Journal of Continuing Education in Nursing, 38*(4), 154–175. doi:10.3928/00220124-20070701-09 PMID:17708114

Diaz, O., Puente, G., Izquierdo, J., & Molina, J. (2013). Harvesting models from web 2.0 databases. *Software & Systems Modeling, 12*(1), 15–34. doi:10.1007/s10270-011-0194-z

Dick, W., Carey, L., & Carey, J. O. (2001). *The systematic design of instruction*. Addison-Wesley.

Digenti, D. (1998). Toward an understanding of the learning community. *Organization Development Journal, 16*(2), 91–96.

Dilworth, A. I. (2007). TECHNO ETHICS: Blogs: Online Practice Guides or Websites. *Electronic Rainmaking, 24*(8), 54–56.

Dimitrov, D. M. (2010). Contemporary treatment of reliability and validity in educational assessment. *Mid-Western Educational Researcher, 23*(1), 23–28.

Dixon, C. (2014). The three E's of online discussion. *Quarterly Review of Distance Education, 15*(1), 1–8.

Dixson, M. D. (2010). Creating effective student engagement in online courses: What do students find engaging? *Journal of the Scholarship of Teaching and Learning, 10*(2), 1–13.

Dochy, F., Segers, M., & Sluijsmans, D. (1999). The use of self-, peer and co-assessment in higher education. *A review. Studies in Higher Education, 24*(3), 331–350. doi: 233137993510.1080/0307507991

Dochy, F., Segers, M., van den Bossche, P., & Gijbels, D. (2003). Effects of problem based learning: A meta-analysis. *Learning and Instruction, 13*(5), 533–568. doi:10.1016/S0959-4752(02)00025-7

Doggett, A. M. (2007). The videoconferencing classroom: What do students think? *Journal of Industrial Teacher Education, 44*(4), 29–41.

Dolan, L. B. V. (2014). Massive Online Obsessive compulsion: What are they saying out there about the latest phenomenon in higher education? *International Review of Research in Open and Distance Learning, 15*(2).

Dollinger, S. J. (2000). Locus of control and incidental learning: An application to college student success. *College Student Journal, 34*, 537–540.

Domyei, Z. (2001). *Motivational strategies in the language classroom*. Cambridge University Press.

Donnelli, E., Dailey, A., & Mandernach, B. J. (2009). Toward a philosophy of multimedia inclusion. *Journal of Online Learning and Teaching, 5*(1), 149–154.

Donovan, J. J., & Williams, K. J. (2003). Missing the mark: Effects of time and causal attributions on goal revision in response to goal performance discrepancies. *The Journal of Applied Psychology, 89*, 1035–1056. PMID:12814288

Dowell, D. J., & Small, F. A. (2011). What is the impact of online resource materials on student self-learning strategies? *Journal of Marketing Education, 33*(2), 140–148. doi:10.1177/0273475311410846

Downes, S. (2004). Educational blogging. *EDUCAUSE Review*, (September/October): 14–26.

Dray, B. J., Lowenthal, P. R., Miszkiewicz, M. J., Ruiz-Primo, M. A., & Marczynski, K. (2011). Developing an instrument to assess student readiness for online learning: A validation study. *Distance Education, 32*(1), 29–47. doi:10.1080/01587919.2011.565496

Driessnack, M., Mobily, P., Stineman, A., Montgomery, L. A., Clow, T., & Eisbach, S. (2011). We are different: Learning needs of accelerated second-degree nursing students. *Nurse Educator, 36*(5), 214–218. doi:10.1097/NNE.0b013e3182297c90 PMID:21857342

Driscoll, J. (1994). Reflective practice for practice. *Senior Nurse, 13*(7), 45–50. PMID:8303152

Driscoll, M. P. (2005). *Psychology of learning for instruction* (3rd ed.). Boston, MA: Allyn and Bacon.

Driscoll, M. P. (2012). Psychological foundations of instructional design. In R. A. Reiser & J. V. Dempsey (Eds.), *Trends and issues in instructional design and technology* (3rd ed., pp. 35–44). Saddlebrook, NJ: Merrill/Prentice-Hall.

Drouin, M. A. (2008). The relationship between students' perceived sense of community and satisfaction, achievement, and retention in online course. *The Quarterly Review of Distance Education, 9*, 267–284.

Duck, J. (2005). Creating Dynamic Interaction in a Virtual World: Add Value to Online Classrooms through Live Elearning and Collaboration: a Demonstration. *Developments in Business Simulation and Experiential Learning, 32*, 101–103.

Dueber, B., & Misanchuk, M. (2001). Sense of community in a distance education course. In *Proceedings from Mid-South Instructional Technology Conference*. Murfreesboro, TN: Academic Press.

Duffy, T. M., & Cunningham, D. J. (1996). Constructivism: Implications for the design and delivery of instruction. In D. H. Jonassen (Ed.), *Handbook of research for educational communications and technology* (pp. 170–198). New York: Simon & Schuster Macmillan.

Duffy, T. M., Dueber, B., & Hawley, C. (1998). Critical thinking in a distributed environment: A pedagogical base for the design of conferencing systems. In C. J. Bonk & K. S. King (Eds.), *Electronic collaborators: Learner-centered technologies for literacy, apprenticeship, and discourse* (pp. 51–78). Mahwah, NJ: Lawrence Erlbaum Associates.

Duncan, K., Kenworthy, A., & McNamara, R. (2012). The effect of synchronous and asynchronous participation on students' performance in online accounting courses. *Accounting Education, 21*(4), 431–449. doi:10.1080/09639284.2012.673387

Dunlap, J. (2005). Workload reduction in online courses: Getting some shuteye. *Performance Improvement, 44*(5), 18–25. doi:10.1002/pfi.4140440507

Dunlap, J. C., & Lowenthal, P. R. (2009). Tweeting the night away: Using Twitter to enhance social presence. *Journal of Information Systems Education, 20*(2), 129–135.

Dunn, R., & Griggs, S. (Eds.). (2000). *Practical approaches to using learning styles in higher education.* Westport, CT: Bergin and Garvey.

Dutton, J., Dutton, M., & Perry, J. (2002). How do online student differ from lecture students? *Journal of Asynchronous Learning Networks, 6*, 1–20.

Dweck, C. S. (1986). Motivaitonal processes affecting learning. *The American Psychologist, 41*(10), 1040–1048. doi:10.1037/0003-066X.41.10.1040

Dysthe, O. (2002). The learning potential of a web-mediated discussion in a university course. *Studies in Higher Education, 27*(3), 339–352. doi:10.1080/03075070220000716

Dziuban, C., & Moskal, P. (2001). *Emerging research issues in distributed learning.* Paper presented at the 7th SloanC International Conference on Asynchronous Learning Networks, Orlando, FL.

Eastmond, D. V. (1995). *Alone but together: Adult distance study through computer conferencing.* Cresskill, NJ: Hampton Press.

Easton, S. S. (2003). Clarifying the instructor's role in online distance learning. *Communication Education, 32*(2), 87–105. doi:10.1080/03634520302470

Ebrahimi, A. (2011). How Does Early Feedback in an Online Programming Course Change Problem Solving? *Journal of Educational Technology Systems, 40*(4), 371–379. doi:10.2190/ET.40.4.c

Eccles, J. S., Adler, T. F., Fullerman, R., Goff, S. B., Kaczala, C. M., Meece, J., & Midgley, C. (1983). Expectancies, values and academic behaviors. In J. T. Spence (Ed.), *Achievement and Achievement Motives.* San Francisco, CA: W. H. Freeman.

Eccles, J. S., & Wigfield, A. (2002). Motivational beliefs, values and goals. *Annual Review of Psychology, 53*(1), 109–132. doi:10.1146/annurev.psych.53.100901.135153 PMID:11752481

Educause. (2015). *Thoughts on a "good" cloud-based social network platforms that could facilitate substantive organic communication and collaboration amongst past, present, and future students.* Retrieved from http://www.educause.edu/groups/

Efimova, L., & Fiedler, S. (2003). Learning webs: Learning in weblog networks. In P. Kommers, P. Isaias, & M. B. Nunes (Eds.), *Proceedings of the IADIS International Conference Web Based Communities,* (pp.490-494), Lisbon: IADIS Press.

Eisen, M. J. (2001). Peer-based professional development viewed through the lens of transformative learning. *Holistic Nursing Practice, 16*(1), 30–42. doi:10.1097/00004650-200110000-00008 PMID:15559045

Ekwunife-Orakwue, K., & Teng, T. (2014). The impact of transactional distance dialogic interactions on student learning outcomes in online and blended environments. *Computers & Education, 78*, 414–427. doi:10.1016/j.compedu.2014.06.011

Elbow, P. (1993). The war between reading and writing and how to end it. *Rhetoric Review, 12*(1), 94–113. doi:10.1080/07350199309389024

El-Hussein, M. O., & Cronje, J. C. (2010). Defining mobile learning in higher education landscape. *Journal of Educational Technology & Society, 13*(3), 12–21.

Ellis, A. (2004). *Exemplars of curriculum theory.* Larchmont, NY: Eye on Education.

Elvers, G., Polzella, D., & Graetz, K. (2003). Procrastination in Online Courses: Performance and Attitudinal Differences. *Teaching of Psychology*, *30*(2), 159–162. doi:10.1207/S15328023TOP3002_13

Ennis, R. H. (1987). A taxonomy of critical thinking dispositions and abilities. In J. B. Baron & R. J. Sternberg (Eds.), *Teaching thinking skills: Theory and practice* (pp. 9–26). New York: W.H. Freeman.

Entwhistle, N. (1987). A model of the teaching-learning process. In T. E. Richardson, M. W. Eysenck, & D. W. Piper (Eds.), *Student learning: Research in education and cognitive psychology* (pp. 13–28). Milton Keynes, UK: SRHE and OUP.

Epp, E. M., Green, K. F., Rahman, A. M., & Weaver, G. C. (2010). Analysis of student–instructor interaction patterns in real-time, scientific online discourse. *Journal of Science Education and Technology*, *19*(1), 49–57. doi:10.1007/s10956-009-9177-z

Er, E., Özden, M. Y., & Arifoğlu, A. (2009). LIVELMS: A blended e-learning environment: A model proposition for integration of asynchronous and synchronous e-learning. *International Journal of Learning*, *16*(2), 449–460.

Ertmer, P. A., Sadaf, A., & Ertmer, D. J. (2011). Student-content interactions in online courses: The role of question prompts in facilitating higher-level engagement with course content. *Journal of Computing in Higher Education*, *23*(2-3), 157–186. doi:10.1007/s12528-011-9047-6

Espasa, A., & Meneses, J. (2010). Analyzing feedback processes in an online teaching and learning environment: An exploratory study. *Higher Education*, *277*(3). doi:10.1007/s10734-009-9247-4

Esteban-Millat, I., Martínez-López, F. J., Huertas-García, R., Meseguer, A., & Rodríguez-Ardura, I. (2014). Modelling students' flow experiences in an online learning environment. *Computers & Education*, *71*, 111–123. doi:10.1016/j.compedu.2013.09.012

Evans, M. J., & Moore, J. S. (2013). Peer tutoring with the aid of the Internet. *British Journal of Educational Technology*, *44*(1), 144–155. doi:10.1111/j.1467-8535.2011.01280.x

Evans, M., & Johri, A. (2008). Facilitating guided participation through mobile technologies: Designing creative learning environments for self and others. *Journal of Computing in Higher Education*, *20*(2), 92–105. doi:10.1007/s12528-008-9004-1

Evans, T. W. (2000). The new mentors. *Teachers College Record*, *102*(1), 1–15. doi:10.1111/0161-4681.00053

Falchikov, N. (2005). *Improving assessment through student involvement: Practical solutions for aiding learning in higher and further education*. London: Routledge.

Falloon, G. (2011). Making the connection: Moore's theory of transactional distance and its relevance to the use of a virtual classroom in postgraduate online teacher education. *Journal of Research on Technology in Education*, *43*(3), 187–209. doi:10.1080/15391523.2011.10782569

Fan, J., McCandliss, B. D., Sommer, T., Raz, M., & Posner, M. I. (2002). Testing the efficiency and independence of attentional networks. *Journal of Cognitive Neuroscience*, *14*(3), 340–347. doi:10.1162/089892902317361886 PMID:11970796

Farmer, J. (2006). Blogging to basics: How blogs are bringing online education back from the brink. In A. Bruns & J. Jacobs (Eds.), *Uses of blogs* (pp. 91–103). New York: Peter Lang.

Fazio, R. H., & Dunton, B. C. (1997). Categorization by race: The impact of automatic and controlled components of racial prejudice. *Journal of Experimental Social Psychology*, *33*(5), 451–470. doi:10.1006/jesp.1997.1330

Felder, R. M., & Brent, R. (2005). Understanding student differences. *The Journal of Engineering Education*, *94*(1), 57–72. doi:10.1002/j.2168-9830.2005.tb00829.x

Ferdig, R. E., & Trammell, K. D. (2004). Content delivery in the 'Blogosphere.'. *Technological Horizons in Education Journal*, *31*(7), 12–20.

Fergusson, R. (2004). Discourses of exclusion: Reconceptualising participation amongst young people. *Journal of Social Policy*, *33*(2), 289–320. doi:10.1017/S0047279403007451

Fernández-Toro, M., & Hurd, S. (2014). A model of factors affecting independent learners' engagement with feedback on language learning tasks. *Distance Education, 35*(1), 106–125. doi:10.1080/01587919.2014.891434

Ferneding, K. A. (2004). The discourse of inevitability and the forging of an emergent social vision: Technology diffusion and the dialectic of educational reform discourse. In W. M. Reynolds & J. A. Webber (Eds.), *Expanding curriculum theory: Dis/positions and lines of flight* (pp. 47–63). Mahwah, NJ: Lawrence Erlbaum.

Ferriss, T. (2009). *The 4-hour workweek: Escape 9-5, live anywhere, and join the new rich.* New York: Crown Publishers.

Fessakis, G., Tatsis, K., & Dimitracopoulou, A. (2008). Supporting 'learning by design' activities using group blogs. *Journal of Educational Technology & Society, 11*(4), 199–212.

Few, S. (2006). *Information Dashboard Design: The Effective Visual Communication of Data.* Burlingame, CA: Analytics.

Fey, J. T., Hollenbeck, R. W., & Wray, J. A. (2010). Technology and the teaching of mathematics. In B. Reys, R. Reys, & R. Rubenstein (Eds.), *Curriculum: Issues, trends, and future directions (72nd Yearbook).* Reston, VA: NCTM.

Finkelstein, J. (2006). *Learning in real time: Synchronous teaching and learning online.* San Francisco: Jossey-Bass.

Finneran, C. M., & Zhang, P. (2003). A Person-Artefact-Task (PAT) model of flow antecedents in computer-mediated environments. *International Journal of Human-Computer Studies, 59*(4), 475–496. doi:10.1016/S1071-5819(03)00112-5

Finneran, C. M., & Zhang, P. (2005). Flow in computer-mediated environments: Promises and challenges. *Communications of the Association for Information Systems, 15,* 82–101.

Fish, W. W., & Gill, P. B. (2009). Perceptions of Online Instruction. *Online Submission, 8*(1).

Fishbein, M., & Azjen, I. (1975). *Belief, attitude, intention, and behavior: An introduction to theory and research.* Reading, MA: Addison-Wesley.

Fisher, T. D. (1995). Self-directedness in adult vocational education students: its role in learning and implications for instruction, Kent State University. *Journal of Vocational and Technical Education, 12*(1). Available in http://scholar.lib.vt.edu/ejournals/JVTE/v12n1/fisher.html

Flottemesch, K. (2000). Building effective interaction in distance education. *Educational Technology, 4*(3), 46–51.

Flynn, D. (2014). Baccalaureate attainment of college students at 4-Year institutions as a function of student engagement behaviors: Social and academic student engagement behaviors matter. *Research in Higher Education, 55*(5), 467–493. doi:10.1007/s11162-013-9321-8

Foley, M. (2003). The global development learning network: A world bank initiative in distance learning for development. In M. G. Moore & W. G. Anderson (Eds.), *Handbook of distance education.* Mahwah, NJ: Erlbaum.

Ford, J. (Producer & Director). (1939). *Stagecoach.* [Motion Picture]. United States: Walter Wanger Productions.

Foroughi, C. K., Werner, N. E., Nelson, E. T., & Boehm-Davis, D. A. (2014). Do interruptions affect quality of work? *Human Factors, 56*(7), 1262–1271. doi:10.1177/0018720814531786

Fredericksen, Pickett, Shea, Pelz, & Swan. (2000). Student satisfaction and perceived learning with online courses: Principles and examples from the SUNY learning network. In J. Bourne (Ed.), *Proceedings of the 1999 Sloan Summer Workshop on Asynchronous Learning Networks* (pp. 7-36). Sloan-Consortium.

Fredricks, J. A., Blumenfeld, P. C., & Paris, A. H. (2004). School engagement: Potential of the concept, state of the evidence. *Review of Educational Research, 74*(1), 59–109. doi:10.3102/00346543074001059

Freeman, M., & Bamford, A. (2004). Student choice of anonymity for learner identity in online learning discussion forums. *International Journal on E-Learning, 3*(3), 45–53.

Freire, P. (1970). *Pedagogy of the Oppressed.* New York: Herder and Herder.

Friedman, S. D. (2008). *Total leadership: Be a better leader, have a richer life.* Boston: Harvard Business Press.

Friedman, T. L. (2005). *The world is flat*. New York: Farrar, Straus and Giroux.

Fritsch, H. (1997). *Witness learning*. Hagen, Germany: Fern Universitat Central Institute for Distance Education Research.

Frydenberg, J. (2007). Persistence in university continuing education online classes. *International Review of Research in Open and Distance Learning, 8*(3), 1–15.

Frye, R., McKinney, G. R., & Trimble, J. E. (2007). *Tools and techniques for course improvement: A handbook of course review and assessment of student learning*. Retrieved 12/10/2014 from http://pandora.cii.wwu.edu/cii/resources/outcomes/course_handbook.pdf

Fryer, J. W., & Elliot, A. J. (2007). Stability and change in achievement goals. *Journal of Educational Psychology, 99*(4), 700–714. doi:10.1037/0022-0663.99.4.700

Fulford, C., & Zhang, S. (1993). Perception of interaction: The critical predictor in distance learning. *American Journal of Distance Education, 7*(3), 8–12. doi:10.1080/08923649309526830

Gabriel, M. A., & Kaufield, K. J. (2008). Reciprocal mentorship: An effective support for online instructors. *Mentoring & Tutoring: Partnership in Learning, 16*(3), 311–327. doi:10.1080/13611260802233480

Gagne, M., & Deci, E. L. (2005). Self-determination theory and work motivation. *Journal of Organizational Behavior, 26*(4), 331–362. doi:10.1002/job.322

Gagné, R. M., Briggs, L. J., & Wager, W. M. (1992). *Principles of instructional design* (4th ed.). Orlando, FL: Harcourt Brace Jovanovich.

Gaile, B. (2013) *WPVirtuoso*. Retrieved 4/27/14 from http://www.wpvirtuoso.com/how-many-blogs-are-on-the-internet/

Gallimore, R., & Tharp, R. (1990). Teaching mind in society: Teaching, schooling and literate discourse. In L. C. Moll (Ed.), *Instructional Implications and Applications of Sociohistorical Psychology* (pp. 175–205). New York: Cambridge University Press. doi:10.1017/CBO9781139173674.009

Ganesh, T. G., & Middleton, J. A. (2006). Challenges in linguistically and culturally diverse elementary settings with math instruction using learning technologies. *The Urban Review, 38*(2), 101–143. doi:10.1007/s11256-006-0025-7

Gannon-Leary, P., & Fontainha, E. (2007). Communities of practice and virtual learning communities: benefits, barriers and success factors. *Elearning Papers, 5*, 20-29. Retrieved from http://nrl.northumbria.ac.uk/2147/)

García, E., Romero, C., Ventura, S., & de Castro, C. (2006). Using rules discovery for the continuous improvement of e-learning courses. In *Intelligent Data Engineering and Automated Learning–IDEAL 2006* (pp. 887–895). Berlin: Springer. doi:10.1007/11875581_106

Garcia, P., Amandi, A., Schiaffino, S., & Campo, M. (2007). Evaluating Bayesian networks' precision for detecting students' learning styles. *Computers & Education, 49*(3), 794–808. doi:10.1016/j.compedu.2005.11.017

Garcia-Valcarcel, A. (2010). Integrating ICT into the teaching-learning process. *British Journal of Educational Technology, 41*(5), E75–E77. doi:10.1111/j.1467-8535.2009.00988.x

Gardner, H. (1983). *Multiple intelligences: The theory in practice*. New York, NY: Basic Books.

Gareis, Y. (2005). A collaborative online project between New Zealand and New York. *Business Communication Quarterly, 68*(1), 81–96. doi:10.1177/1080569904273715

Garrison, D. R. (2011). *E-learning in the 21st century: A framework for research and practice*. Taylor & Francis.

Garrison, D. R., & Arbaugh, J. B. (2007). Researching the community of inquiry framework: Review, issues, and future directions. *The Internet & Higher Education, 10*(3), 157-172. doi:10.1016/j.iheduc.2007.04.001

Garrison, D. R. (1989). *Understanding distance education: A framework for the future*. London: Routledge.

Garrison, D. R. (1992). Critical thinking and self-directed learning in adult education: An analysis of responsibility and control issues. *Adult Education Quarterly, 42*(3), 136–148.

Garrison, D. R. (2003). Self-directed learning and distance education. In M. G. Moore & W. G. Anderson (Eds.), *Handbook of distance education* (pp. 161–168). Mahwah, NJ: Lawrence Erlbaum.

Garrison, D. R. (2007). Online community of inquiry review: Social, cognitive, and teaching presence issues. *Journal of Asynchronous Learning Networks, 11*(1), 61–72.

Garrison, D. R. (2011). *E-learning in the 21st century: A framework for research and practice.* New York: Taylor and Francis.

Garrison, D. R., & Anderson, T. (2003). *E-Learning in the 21st century: A framework for research and practice.* London: Routledge Falmer. doi:10.4324/9780203166093

Garrison, D. R., Anderson, T., & Archer, W. (2000). Critical inquiry in a text-based environment: Computer conferencing in higher education. *The Internet and Higher Education, 2*(2-3), 87–105. doi:10.1016/S1096-7516(00)00016-6

Garrison, D. R., Anderson, T., & Archer, W. (2001). Critical thinking, cognitive presence, and computer conferencing in distance education. *American Journal of Distance Education, 15*(1), 7–23. doi:10.1080/08923640109527071

Garrison, D. R., & Archer, W. (2000). *A transactional perspective on teaching and learning: A framework for adult and higher education.* Oxford, UK: Pergamon.

Garrison, D. R., & Archer, W. (2000). *A transactional perspective on teaching-learning: A framework for adult and higher education.* Oxford, UK: Pergamon.

Garrison, D. R., & Shale, D. (Eds.). (1990). *Education at a distance: From issues to practice.* RE Krieger Publishing Company.

Garrison, D. R., & Vaughan, N. D. (2008). *Blended learning in higher education: Framework, principles, and guidelines.* San Francisco, CA: Jossey-Bass.

Garrison, D. R., & Vaughan, N. D. (2008). *Blended Learning in higher education: Framework, principles, and guidelines.* San Francisco: Jossey-Bass.

Garrison, R., & Cleveland-Innes, M. (2005). Facilitating Cognitive Presence in Online Learning: Interaction Is Not Enough. *American Journal of Distance Education, 19*(3), 133–148. doi:10.1207/s15389286ajde1903_2

Garvey, B., Stokes, P., & Megginson, D. (2009). *Coaching & mentoring theory and practice.* London: Sage.

Gasevic, D., Adesope, O., Joksimovic, S., & Kovanovic, V. (2015). Externally-facilitated regulation scaffolding and role assignment to develop cognitive presence in asynchronous online discussion. *The Internet and Higher Education, 24,* 53–65. doi:10.1016/j.iheduc.2014.09.006

Gathman, A. C., & Talbut, M. H. (2011). Using social networking applications in online teaching. In S. Hoffman (Ed.), *Teaching the humanities online: A practical guide to the virtual classroom.* New York: M.E. Sharpe.

Gautreau, C. (2012). Video conferencing guidelines for faculty and students in graduate online courses. *MERLOT Journal of Online Learning and Teaching, 8*(4).

Gay, G., & Howard, T. C. (2000). Multicultural education for the 21st century. *Teacher Educator, 36*(1), 1–16. doi:10.1080/08878730009555246

Gaytan, J., & McEwen, B. C. (2007). Effective online instructional and assessment strategies. *American Journal of Distance Education, 21*(3), 117–132. doi:10.1080/08923640701341653

Ghamdi, A., Samrji, A., & Watt, A. (2016). Essential Considerations in Distance Education in KSA: Teacher Immediacy in a Virtual Teaching and Learning Environment. *International Journal of Information and Education Technology, 6*(1).

Ghani, J. A., Supnick, R., & Rooney, P. (1991). The experience of flow in computer mediated and in face-to-face groups. In J. I. DeGross, I. Benbasat, G. DeSanctis, & C. M. Beath (Eds), *Proceedings of the 20th International Conference on Information Systems* (pp. 229-237), New York: Academic Press.

Ghaye, T. (2004). Editorial: Reflection for spiritual practice? *Reflective Practice, 5*(3), 291–295. doi:10.1080/1462394042000308699

Gibbs, G., & Simpson, C. (2004). Conditions under which assessment supports students' learning. *Learning and Teaching in Higher Education, 1*, 3–31.

Gibson, S. G., Harris, M. L., & Colaric, S. M. (2008). Technology acceptance in an academic context: Faculty acceptance of online education. *Journal of Education for Business, 4*(6), 355–359. doi:10.3200/JOEB.83.6.355-359

Giebelhausen, R. (2015). What the tech is going on? Social media and your music classroom. *General Music Today, 28*(2), 39–46. doi:10.1177/1048371314552523

Giesbers, B., Rienties, B., Tempelaar, D., & Gijselaers, W. (2014). A dynamic analysis of the interplay between asynchronous and synchronous communication in online learning: The impact of motivation. *Journal of Computer Assisted Learning, 30*(1), 30–50. doi:10.1111/jcal.12020

Giossos, Y., Koutsouba, M., Lionarakis, A., & Skavantzos, K. (2009). Reconsidering Moore's transactional distance theory. *European Journal of Open, Distance and E-Learning, 2*, article 6. Retrieved from http://www.eurodl.org/materials/contrib/2009/Giossos_Koutsouba_Lionarakis_Skavantzos.pdf

Glazatov, T. R. (2012). Applying instructional design system theory to mobile learning environments. *Journal of Applied Learning Technology, 2*(2), 29–35.

Glogoff, S. (2005). Instructional blogging: Promoting Interactivity, student-centred learning, and peer input. Retrieved: May 10th, 2015, from: http://studentcenteredlearning.pbworks.com/f/Instructional+Blogging.pdf

Godwin-Jones, B. (2008). Emerging technologies: Web-writing 2.0: Enabling, documenting, and assessing writing online. *Language Learning & Technology, 12*(2), 7–13.

Gollwitzer, P. M. (1999). Implementation intentions: Strong effects of simple plans. *The American Psychologist, 54*(7), 493–503. doi:10.1037/0003-066X.54.7.493

Gonzalez, M. D., Davis, B. P., Lopez, D., Munoz, C., & Soto, G. () Integration of social media in higher education environments. *Insights to a Changing World Journal*, 43-62.

Goodyear, M. (2006). Mentoring: a learning collaboration. *EDUCAUSE Review Online*. Retrieved from: http://www.educause.edu/ero/article/mentoring-learning-collaboration

Goodyear, P., Salmon, G., Spector, J. M., Steeples, C., & Tickner, S. (2001). Competencies for online teaching: A special report. *Educational Technology Research and Development, 49*(1), 65–72. doi:10.1007/BF02504508

Goold, A., Coldwell, J., & Craig, A. (2010). An examination of the role of the e-tutor. *Australasian Journal of Educational Technology, 26*(5), 704–716.

Gordon-Murnane, L. (2006). Social bookmarking, folksonomies, and web 2.0 tools. *Searcher, 14*(6), 26–38.

Gorham, J., & Zakahi, W. R. (1990). A comparison of teacher and student perceptions of immediacy and learning: Monitoring process and product. *Communication Education, 39*(4), 354–368. doi:10.1080/03634529009378815

Gorky, P., & Caspi, A. (2005). A critical analysis of transactional distance theory. *Quarterly Review of Distance Education, 6*(1), 1–11.

Gorski, P. (2004). *Multicultural education and the Internet: Intersections and integrations* (2nd ed.). New York: McGraw-Hill Higher Education.

Gorski, P. (2005). Education equity and the digital divide. *Association for the Advancement of Computing in Education Journal, 13*(1), 3–45.

Gosmire, D., Morrison, M., & Osdel, J. V. (2009). Perceptions of interactions in online courses. *Journal of Online Learning and Teaching, 5*, 609–617. Retrieved from http://jolt.merlot.org/vol5no4/gosmire_1209.pdf

Graf, S., & Kinshuk. (2006). Considering learning styles in learning management systems: Investigating the behavior of students in an online course. In *Proceedings of the First IEEE International Workshop on Semantic Media Adaptation and Personalization* (SMAP 06). Athens, Greece: IEEE. doi:10.1109/SMAP.2006.13

Graham, C., Cagiltay, K., Craner, J., Lim, B., & Duffy, T. M. (2000). *Teaching in a web-based distance learning environment: An evaluation summary based on four courses*. Center for Research on Learning and Technology Technical Report No. 13-00. Indiana University Bloomington. Retrieved from: http://crlt.indiana.edu/publications/crlt00-13.pdf

Graham, S., & Weiner, B. (1996). Theories and principles of motivation. In D. C. Berliner & R. C. Calfee (Eds.), *Handbook of educational psychology*. New York, NY: Macmillan.

Grandzol, C. J., & Grandzol, J. R. (2010). Interaction in online courses: More is not always better. *Online Journal of Distance Learning Administration*, *13*(2), 1–18.

Grandzol, J., & Grandzol, C. (2006). Best practices for online business education. *International Review of Research in Open and Distance Learning*, *7*(1), 1–18.

Grant, K. S. L., & Lee, V. J. (2014). Teacher educators wrestling with issues of diversity in online courses. *Qualitative Report*, *19*(6), 1–25.

Grant, M. R., & Thornton, H. R. (2007). Best practices in undergraduate adult centered online learning: Mechanisms for course design and delivery. *Journal of Online Learning and Teaching*, *3*(4).

Gray, H. M., Ambady, N., Lowenthal, W. T., & Deldin, P. (2004). P300 as an index of attention to self-relevant stimuli. *Journal of Experimental Social Psychology*, *40*(2), 216–224. doi:10.1016/S0022-1031(03)00092-1

Greenberg, G. (1998). Distance education technologies: Best practices for K12 settings. *IEEE Technology and Society Magazine*, *17*(Winter), 36–40. doi:10.1109/44.735862

Greenlaw, S. A. (1999). Using groupware to enhance teaching and learning in undergraduate economics. *The Journal of Economic Education*, *30*(1), 33–42. doi:10.1080/00220489909595936

Greenlaw, S. A., & DeLoach, S. B. (2003). Teaching critical thinking with electronic discussion. *The Journal of Economic Education*, *34*(1), 36–52. doi:10.1080/00220480309595199

Greyling, F. C., & Wentzel, A. (2007). Humanising education through technology: Creating presence in large classes. *South Africa Journal of Higher Education*, *21*(4), 654–667.

Griffiths, M. E., & Graham, C. R. (2009a). Using asynchronous video in online classes: Results from a pilot study. *Instructional Technology & Distance Learning*, *6*(3), 65–76.

Grimes, P., Milea, M., & Woodruff, T. (2004). Grades--Who's to blame? Students' evaluation of teaching and locus of control. *The Journal of Economic Education*, *35*(2), 125–147. doi:10.3200/JECE.35.2.129-147

Grolnick, W. S., & Ryan, R. M. (1987). Autonomy in children's learning: An experimental and individual difference investigation. *Journal of Personality and Social Psychology*, *52*(5), 890–898. doi:10.1037/0022-3514.52.5.890 PMID:3585701

Grooms, L. (2003). Computer-Mediated Communication: A vehicle for learning. *International Review of Research in Open and Distance Learning*, *4*(2). Retrieved from http://www.irrodl.org/index.php/irrodl/article/view/148/709

Grosseck, G. (2009). To use or not to use web 2.0 in higher education? *Procedia: Social and Behavioral Sciences*, *1*(1), 478–482. doi:.sbspro.2009.01.08710.1016/j

Guadagno, R. E., Okdie, B. M., & Eno, C. A. (2008). Who blogs? Personality predictors of blogging. *Computers in Human Behavior*, *24*(5), 1993–2004. doi:10.1016/j.chb.2007.09.001

Guest, G., MacQueen, K. M., & Namey, E. E. (2011). *Applied thematic analysis*. Thousand Oaks, CA: Sage.

Guglielmino, L. M., & Guglielmino, P. J. (2002). Learner characteristics affecting success in electronic distance learning. In *H.B. Long & Associates, Twenty-First Century Advances in Self-Directed Leaning*. Boynton Beach, FL: Motorola University Press.

Guldberg, K., & Pilkington, R. M. (2007). Tutor roles in facilitating reflection on practice through online discussion. *Journal of Educational Technology & Society*, *10*(1), 61–72.

Gunawardena, C. N. (1995). Social presence theory and implications for interaction and collaborative learning in computer conferences. *International Journal of Educational Telecommunications*, *1*(2/3), 147–166.

Gunawardena, C. N., Nolla, A. C., Wilson, P. L., Lopez-Islas, J. R., Ramirez-Angel, N., & Megchun-Alpizar, R. M. (2001). A Cross-Cultural Study of Group Process and Development in Online Conferences. *Distance Education*, *22*(1), 85–121. doi:10.1080/0158791010220106

Gunawardena, C. N., & Zittle, F. J. (1997). Social presence as a predictor of satisfaction within a computer-mediated conferencing environment. *American Journal of Distance Education, 11*(3), 8–26. doi:10.1080/08923649709526970

Gunawardena, C., Wilson, P., & Nolla, A. (2003). Culture and online education. In M. Moore & W. Anderson (Eds.), *Handbook of distance education* (pp. 753–775). Mahwah, NJ: Lawrence Erlbaum Associates.

Guzdial, M., & Turns, J. (2000). Effective discussion through a computer-mediated anchored forum. *Journal of the Learning Sciences, 9*(4), 437–469. doi:10.1207/S15327809JLS0904_3

Hackman, M. Z., & Walker, K. B. (1990). Instructional communication in the televised classroom: The effects of system design and teacher immediacy on student learning and satisfaction. *Communication Education, 39*(3), 196–206. doi:10.1080/03634529009378802

Haenlein, M. (2010). Users of the world unite! The challenges and opportunities of social media. *Business Horizons, 1*, 59–68.

Halic, O., Lee, D., Paulus, T., & Spence, M. (2010). To blog or not to blog: Student perceptions of blog effectiveness for learning in a college-level course. *The Internet and Higher Education, 13*(4), 206–213. doi:10.1016/j.iheduc.2010.04.001

Hall, H., & Davison, B. (2007). Social software as support in hybrid learning environments: The value of the blog as a tool for reflective learning and peer support. *Library & Information Science Research, 29*(2), 163–187. doi:10.1016/j.lisr.2007.04.007

Halverson, L. R., Graham, C. R., Spring, K. J., Drysdale, J. S., & Henrie, C. R. (2014). A thematic analysis of the most highly cited scholarship in the first decade of blended research. *The Internet and Higher Education, 20*, 20–34.

Hamdan, A. K. (2014). The reciprocal and correlative relationship between learning culture and online education: A case from Saudi Arabia. *International Review of Research in Open and Distance Learning, 15*(1).

Hammond, M. (2000). Communication within on-line forums: The opportunities, the constraints and the value of a communicative approach. *Computers & Education, 35*(4), 251–262. doi:10.1016/S0360-1315(00)00037-3

Hampel, R. (2006). Rethinking task design for the digital age: A framework for language teaching and learning in a synchronous online environment. *ReCALL, 18*(1), 105–121. doi:10.1017/S0958344006000711

Handelsman, M. M., Briggs, W. L., Sullivan, N., & Towler, A. (2005). A measure of college student course engagement. *The Journal of Educational Research, 98*(3), 184–192. doi:10.3200/JOER.98.3.184-192

Han, H. (2013). Do nonverbal emotional cues matter? Effects of video casting in synchronous virtual classrooms. *American Journal of Distance Education, 27*(4), 253–264. doi:10.1080/08923647.2013.837718

Hannafin, M. J., Hill, J. R., Land, S. M., & Lee, E. (2014). Student-centered, open learning environments: Research, theory, and practice. In J. M. Spector, M. D. Merrill, J. Elen, & M. J. Bishop (Eds.), *Handbook of Research on Educational Communications and Technology* (pp. 641–651). New York: Springer. doi:10.1007/978-1-4614-3185-5_51

Hannafin, M. J., & Land, S. M. (1997). The foundations and assumptions of technology enhanced student-centered learning environments. *Instructional Science, 25*(3), 167–202. doi:10.1023/A:1002997414652

Hannafin, M., & Peck, K. (1988). *The Design, Development, and Evaluation of Instructional Software*. New York, NY: Macmillan.

Hanson, T. L., Drumheller, K., Mallard, J. K., Mckee, C., & Schlegel, P. (2011). Cell phones, text messaging and Facebook: Competing time demands of today's college students. *College Teaching, 59*(1), 23–30. doi:10.1080/87567555.2010.489078

Hara, N., Bonk, C. J., & Angeli, C. (2000). Content analysis of online discussion in an applied educational psychology course. *Instructional Science, 28*(2), 115–152. doi:10.1023/A:1003764722829

Harasim, L. (1990). On-line education: Perspectives on a new environment. New York: Praeger.

Harasim, L. (2012). *Learning theory and online technologies*. New York: Routledge.

Harasim, L. M. (1990). *Online education: Perspectives on a new environment*. New York: Praeger.

Harasim, L. N., Hiltz, S. R., Teles, L., & Turoff, M. (1995). *Learning networks: A field guide to teaching and learning online*. Cambridge, MA: The MIT Press.

Harasim, L., Hiltz, S. R., Teles, L., & Turoff, M. (1995). *Learning Networks: A Field Guide to Teaching & Learning Online*. Cambridge, MA: MIT Press.

Hargittai, E. (2010). Digital na(t)ives? Variation in internet skills and uses among members of the "Net Generation.". *Sociological Inquiry*, *80*(1), 92–113. doi:10.1111/j.1475-682X.2009.00317.x

Hart, C. (2012). Factors associated with student persistence in an online program of study: A review of the literature. *Journal of Interactive Online Learning*, *11*(1), 19–42.

Harter, J., & Szurminski, M. (2001). *PASS program (Project Assuring Student Success)*. Mercy College of Northwest Ohio. Unpublished paper. Retrieved from: http://www.eric.ed.gov/ERICWebPortal/custom/portlets/record-Details/detailmini.jsp?_nfpb=true&ERICExtSearch_SearchValue_0=ED453887&ERICExtSearch_SearchType_0=no&accno=ED453887

Harvard Institute On Politics. (2011). *IOP youth polling: Spring 2011 survey*. Cambridge, MA: Harvard University Kennedy School of Government.

Hastie, M., Chen, N. S., & Kno, Y. H. (2007). Instructional Design for Best Practice in the Synchronous Cyber Classroom. *Journal of Educational Technology & Society*, *10*(4), 281–294.

Hastie, M., Chen, N., & Kuo, Y. (2007). Instructional design for best practice in the synchronous cyber classroom. *Journal of Educational Technology & Society*, *10*(4), 281–294.

Hattie, J., & Timperley, H. (2007). The power of feedback. *Review of Educational Research*, *77*(1), 81–112. doi:10.3102/003465430298487

Hege, B. A. R. (2011). The online theology classroom: Strategies for engaging a community of distance learners in a hybrid model of online education. *Teaching Theology and Religion*, *14*(1), 13–20. doi:10.1111/j.1467-9647.2010.00668.x

Heischmidt, K., & Damoiseau, Y. (2012). Dimensions of Quality in Online Business Course Offerings: Content, Format and Feedback. *Journal of Higher Education Theory & Practice*, *12*(2), 84–97.

Heiser, S., Stickler, U., & Furnborough, C. (2013). Student training in the use of an online synchronous conferencing tool. *CALICO Journal*, *30*(2), 226–251. doi:10.11139/cj.30.2.226-251

Heisserer, D., & Parette, P. (2002). Advising at-risk students in college and university settings. *College Student Journal*, *36*(1), 1–12.

Hemmi, A., Bayne, S., & Land, R. (2009). The appropriation and repurposing of social technologies in higher education. *Journal of Computer Assisted Learning*, *25*(1), 19–30. doi:10.1111/j.1365-2729.2008.00306.x

Henderson, M. D., Wakslak, C. J., Fujita, K., & Rohrbach, J. (2011). Construal Level Theory and spatial distance: Implications for mental representation, judgment, and behavior. *Social Psychology*, *42*(3), 165–173. doi:10.1027/1864-9335/a000060

Henri, F. (1992). Computer conferencing and content analysis. In A. R. Kaye (Ed.), *Collaborative learning through computer conferencing* (pp. 117–136). Berlin, Germany: Springer. doi:10.1007/978-3-642-77684-7_8

Heo, H. (2004). Story telling and retelling as narrative inquiry in cyber learning environments. In R. Atkinson, C. McBeath, D. Jonas-Dwyer & R. Phillips (Eds.), *Beyond the comfort zone: Proceedings of the 21st ASCILITE Conference* (pp. 374-378). Perth: ASCILITE.

Hernandez-Serrano, J., & Jonassen, D. H. (2003). The effects of case libraries on problem solving. *Journal of Computer Assisted Learning*, *19*(1), 103–114. doi:10.1046/j.0266-4909.2002.00010.x

Herrington, J., Oliver, R., & Reeves, T. C. (2003). Patterns of engagement in authentic online learning environments. *Australasian Journal of Educational Technology*, *19*, 59–71.

Herrington, J., Reeves, T. C., & Oliver, R. (2006). Authentic tasks online: A synergy among learner, task, and technology. *Distance Education*, *27*(2), 233–247. doi:10.1080/01587910600789639

Herrington, J., Reeves, T., & Oliver, R. (2014). Authentic learning environments. In J. M. Spector, M. D. Merrill, J. Ellen, & M. J. Bishop (Eds.), *Handbook of research on educational communications and technology* (4th ed., pp. 401–412). New York: Springer. doi:10.1007/978-1-4614-3185-5_32

Herrmann, K. J. (2013). The impact of cooperative learning on student engagement: Results from an intervention. *Active Learning in Higher Education, 14*(3), 175–187. doi:10.1177/1469787413498035

He, W., Xu, G., & Kruck, S. E. (2014). Online is education for the 21st century. *Journal of Information Systems Education, 25*(2), 101–105.

Hewett, B., & Powers, C. (2007). Online Teaching and Learning: Preparation, Development, and Organizational Communication. *Technical Communication Quarterly, 16*(1), 1–82. doi:10.1080/10572250709336574

Hewitt, P. L., & Flett, G. L. (1991). Perfectionism in the self and social contexts: Conceptualization, assessment and association with psychopathology. *Journal of Personality and Social Psychology, 60*(3), 456–470. doi:10.1037/0022-3514.60.3.456 PMID:2027080

Hew, K. F., & Cheung, W. S. (2011). Student facilitators' habits of mind and their influences on higher-level knowledge construction occurrences in online discussions: A case study. *Innovations in Education and Teaching International, 48*(3), 275–285. doi:10.1080/14703297.2011.593704

Hew, K. F., & Hara, N. (2007). Empirical study of motivators and barriers of teacher online knowledge sharing. *Educational Technology Research and Development, 55*(6), 573–595. doi:10.1007/s11423-007-9049-2

Hickey, D. T., & Zuiker, S. J. (2005). Engaged participation: A sociocultural model of motivation with implications for educational assessment. *Educational Assessment, 10*(3), 277–305. doi:10.1207/s15326977ea1003_7

Higdon, J., & Topaz, C. (2009). Blogs and wikis as instructional tools. *College Teaching, 57*(2), 105–110. doi:10.3200/CTCH.57.2.105-110

Hillman, D. C., Willis, D. J., & Gunawardena, C. N. (1994). Learner-interface in distance education: An extension of contemporary models and strategies for practitioners. *American Journal of Distance Education, 8*(2), 31–42. doi:10.1080/08923649409526853

Hiltz, S. R. (1994). The virtual classroom: Learning without limits via computer networks. Norwood, NJ: Ablex, Intellect Books.

Hiltz, S. R., & Turoff, M. (1993). *The Network Nation: Human communication via computer* (revised edition). Cambridge, MA: MIT Press.

Hiltz, S. R., & Wellman, B. (1997). Asynchronous learning networks as a virtual classroom. *Communications of the ACM, 40*(9), 44–48. doi:10.1145/260750.260764

Hinton, S. (2007, March). *Multicultural education online for graduate teachers: Some challenges.* Paper presented at the Annual Conference for the Comparative and International Education Society, Baltimore, MD.

Hirumi, A. (2000). Chronicling the challenges of web-basing a degree program: A systems perspective. *The Quarterly Review of Distance Education, 1*(2), 89–108.

Hitchcock, A. (Producer & Director). (1946). *Notorious.* [Motion Picture]. United States: RKO Radio Pictures.

Hitchcock, A. (Producer & Director). (1954). *Rear Window.* [Motion Picture]. United States: Paramount.

Hitchcock, A. (Producer & Director). (1958). *Vertigo.* [Motion Picture]. United States: Paramount.

Hitchcock, A. (Producer & Director). (1960). *Psycho.* [Motion Picture]. United States: Shamley Productions.

Hitt, J. C., & Hartman, J. L. (2002). *Distributed learning: New challenges and opportunities for institutional leadership (No. 3).* American Council on Education.

Hodgkinson-Williams, C. (2014, June). *Degrees of ease: Adoption of OER, Open Textbooks and MOOCs in the Global South.* Paper presented at the 2nd Regional Symposium on Open Educational Resources: Beyond Advocacy, Research and Policy, Penang. Retrieved from https://open.uct.ac.za/handle/11427/1188

Hoffman, S. (2011). Introduction. In S. Hoffman (Ed.), *Teaching the humanities online: A practical guide to the virtual classroom.* New York: M.E. Sharpe.

Hofstede, G. (1980). *Culture's consequence: International differences in work-related values.* Newbury Park, CA: Sage.

Hofstede, G. (1986). Cultural differences in teaching and learning. *International Journal of Intercultural Relations, 10*(3), 301–320. doi:10.1016/0147-1767(86)90015-5

Holbeck, R., Bergquist, E., & Lees, S. (2014). Classroom assessment techniques: Checking for student understanding in an introductory university success course. *Journal of Instructional Research*, *3*, 38–42.

Holstead, C., & Ward, D. (2013). Using Facebook and Tumblr to engage students. *The Chronicle of Higher Education*. Retrieved May 1, 2014 from http://chronicle.com/blogs/profhacker/using-facebook-and-tumblr-to-engage-students/47221

Holzweiss, P. C., Joyner, S. A., Fuller, M. B., Henderson, S., & Young, R. (2014). Online graduate students' perceptions of best learning experiences. *Distance Education*, *35*(3), 311–323. doi:10.1080/01587919.2015.955262

Hopey, C. E., & Ginsburg, L. (1996). Distance learning and new technologies: You can't predict the future but you can plan for it. *Adult Learning*, *8*(1), 212–223.

Horn, L., Cataldi, E., & Skilor, A. (2005). *Waiting to attend college: Undergraduates who delay their postsecondary enrollment. (U.S. Department of Education, National Center for Education Statistics, NCES 2005-152)*. Washington, DC: U.S. Government Printing Office.

Howard, G. R. (1999). *We can't teach what we don't know: White teachers, multiracial schools*. New York: Teachers College Press.

Howell, S. L., Saba, F., Lindsay, N. K., & William, P. B. (2004). Seven strategies for enabling faculty success in distance education. *The Internet and Higher Education*, *7*(1), 33–49. doi:10.1016/j.iheduc.2003.11.005

Hrastinski, S. (2007). Participating in synchronous online education. Lund Studies in Informatics No. 6, Department of Informatics, School of Economics and Management. Lund, Sweden: University of Lund; Retrieved from https://lup.lub.lu.se/luur/download?func=downloadFile&recordOId=599311&fileOId=600490

Hrastinski, S. (2008). Asynchronous & synchronous e-learning. *EDUCAUSE Quarterly*, *31*(4), 51–55.

Hrastinski, S. (2008a). What is online learner participation? A literature review. *Journal Computers & Education*, *51*(4), 1755–1765. doi:10.1016/j.compedu.2008.05.005

Hrastinski, S. (2008b). What is online participation and how may it be studied in e-learning settings? In *Proceedings of the 16th European Conference on Information Systems*. Galway, Ireland: Academic Press.

Huang, R., & Yang, J. (2014). The framework and method for understanding the new generation of learners. In R. Huang, Kinshuk, & N. Chen (Eds.), The new development of technology enhanced learning (pp. 3-25). Berlin: Springer. doi:10.1007/978-3-642-38291-8_1

Huang, E. Y., Lin, S. W., & Huang, T. K. (2012). What type of learning style leads to online participation in the mixed-mode e-learning environment? A study of software usage instruction. *Computers & Education*, *58*(1), 338–349. doi:10.1016/j.compedu.2011.08.003

Huang, X., & Hsiao, E. (2012). Synchronous and asynchronous communication in an online environment: Faculty experiences and perceptions. *Quarterly Review of Distance Education*, *13*(1), 15–30.

Huber, C. (2010). Professional learning 2.0. *Educational Leadership*, *67*(8), 41–46.

Hudson, T. M., Knight, V., & Collins, B. C. (2012). Perceived effectiveness of Web conferencing software in the digital environment to deliver a graduate course in applied behavior analysis. *Rural Special Education Quarterly*, *31*(2), 27–39.

Huett, J. B., Young, J., Huett, K. C., Moller, L., & Bray, M. (2008b). Supporting the distant student: The effect of ARCS-based strategies on confidence and performance. *Quarterly Review of Distance Education*, *9*, 113–126.

Huett, J., Kalinowski, K., Moholer, L., & Huett, K. (2008a). Improving motivation and retention of online students through the use of the ARCS-V based emails. *American Journal of Distance Education*, *22*(3), 159–176. doi:10.1080/08923640802224451

Hughes, J. (2004). Supporting the Online Learner. In T. Anderson, & F. Elloumi (Eds.), *Theory and Practice of Online Learning* (pp. 367-384). Athabasca University. Retrieved from cde.athabascau.ca/online_book

Hung, M., & Chou, C. (2015). Students' perceptions of instructors' roles in blended and online learning environments: A comparative study. *Computers & Education, 81,* 315–325. doi:10.1016/j.compedu.2014.10.022

Hung, M., Chou, C., Chen, C., & Own, Z. (2010). Learner readiness for online learning: Scale development and student perceptions. *Computers & Education, 55*(3), 1080–1090. doi:10.1016/j.compedu.2010.05.004

Hung, W., Jonassen, D. H., & Liu, R. (2007). Problem based learning. In J. Spector, J. van Merrienboer, M. Merrill, & M. Driscoll (Eds.), *Handbook of research on education communications and technology.* Mahwah, NJ: Lawrence Erlbaum.

Hunter, D. (2011). Who holds the pen? Strategies to student satisfaction scores in online learning environments. *The Business Review, Cambridge, 18*(2), 75–81.

Hunter, S. B., Ober, A. J., Paddock, S. M., Hunt, P. E., & Levan, D. (2014). Continuous Quality Improvement (CQI) in addiction treatment settings: Design and intervention protocol of a group randomized pilot study. *Addiction Science and Clinical Practice, 9*(4), 1–11. PMID:24467770

Hurd, S. (2005). Autonomy and the distance language learner. In B. Holmberg, M. Shelly, & C. White (Eds.), *Distance education and languages: Evolution and change* (pp. 1–19). Clevedon, UK: Multilingual Matters.

Ice, P., Bain, B., & Stewart, M. (2010). Using the Community of inquiry survey instrument to inform online learning outcomes. In Z. Abas et al. (Eds.), Proceedings of Global Learn 2010 (p. 455). Association for the Advancement of Computing in Education (AACE).

Ice, P., Curtis, R., Phillips, P., & Wells, J. (2007). Using asynchronous audio feedback to enhance teaching presence and students' sense of community. *Journal of Asynchronous Learning Networks, 11*(2), 3–25.

Im, Y., & Lee, O. (2003-2004). Pedagogical implications of online discussion for preservice teacher training. *Journal of Research on Technology in Education, 36*(2), 155–170. doi:10.1080/15391523.2003.10782410

Inghilterra, X., & Ravatua-Smith, W. S. (2014). Online learning communities: Use of micro blogging for knowledge construction. In J. Pelet (Ed.), *E-learning 2.0 technologies and web applications in higher education* (pp. 107–128). Hershey, PA: IGI Global. doi:10.4018/978-1-4666-4876-0.ch006

Ingram, A. (2005). Engagement in Online Learning Communities. In J. Bourne & J. C. Moore (Eds.), *Elements of quality online education: Engaging communities* (pp. 55–69). Needham, MA: Sloan Consortium.

Instructure, C. (2014). *Canvas help center.* Retrieved from http://guides.instructure.com/

International Association for Online Learning. (2011). *National standards for quality online teaching.* Retrieved April 21, 2014 from http://www.inacol.org/cms/wp-content/uploads/2013/02/iNACOL_TeachingStandardsv2.pdf

Ioannou, A., Demetriou, S., & Mama, M. (2014). Exploring Factors Influencing Collaborative Knowledge Construction in Online Discussions: Student Facilitation and Quality of Initial Postings. *American Journal of Distance Education, 28*(3), 183–195. doi:10.1080/08923647.2014.926780

Isiguzel, B. (2014). The Blended Learning Environment on the foreign language learning process: A Balance for Motivation and Achievement. *Turkish Online Journal of Distance Education, 15*(3).

Israel, M., & Lang, H. (2013). Redefining technology in libraries and schools. *Teacher Librarian,* 16–18.

iTunes. (2014). *Blackboard Mobile Learn™ by Blackboard Inc.* Retrieved from https://itunes.apple.com/au/app/blackboard-mobile-learn/id376413870?mt=8

Iyengar, S. S., & Lepper, M. R. (2000). When choice is demotivating: Can one desire too much of a good thing? *Journal of Personality and Social Psychology, 79*(6), 995–1006. doi:10.1037/0022-3514.79.6.995 PMID:11138768

Jackson, L., & Caffarella, R. (1994). *Experiential learning: A new approach.* San Francisco: Jossey-Bass.

Jaggars, S., & Xu, D. (2010) *Online learning in the Virginia community college system*. Community College Research Center, Teachers College, Columbia University. Retrieved from: http://ccrc.tc.columbia.edu/publications/online-learning-virginai.html

Jahng, N., Krug, D., & Zhang, Z. (2007). Student achievement in online distance education compared to face-to-face education. *European Journal of Open Distance and E-Learning, 1*, 19.

Jain, A., & Farley, A. (2012). Mobile phone-based audience response system and student engagement in large-group teaching. *Economic Papers, 31*(4), 428–439. doi:10.1111/1759-3441.12002

Jairam, D., & Kiewra, K. A. (2010). Helping students soar to success on computers: An investigation of the SOAR study method for computer-based learning. *Journal of Educational Psychology, 102*(3), 601–614. doi:10.1037/a0019137

Jalgaonkar, S. V., Sarkate, P. V., & Tripathi, R. K. (2012). Students' perception about small group teaching techniques: Role play method and case based learning in pharmacology. *Education in Medicine Journal, 4*(2), 13–18. doi:10.5959/eimj.v4i2.21

James, M. (2007). Blogging their way to Learning: Student perceptions of a reading Journal Blog Assessment task. Conference paper presented at: *International Symposium on eLearning*, Melbourne: RMIT.

James, W. (1902). *The principles of psychology*. New York, NY: Holt.

Jaques, D. (2000). *Learning in groups*. Kogan Page.

Jarvis, P. (1995). *Adult and continuing education. Theory and practice*. London: Routledge.

Jaschik, S., & Lederman, D. (2014). The 2014 Inside Higher Ed Survey of Faculty Attitudes onTechnology: A Study by Gallup and Inside Higher Ed. *Inside Higher Ed*. Retrieved from http://www.insidehighered.com/download/form.php?width=500&height=550&iframe=true&title=Survey%20of%20Faculty%20Attitudes%20on%20Technology&file=IHEFacTechSurvey2014%20final.pdf

Jefferies, P., Grodzinsky, F., & Griffin, J. (2003). Advantages and problems in using information communication technologies to support the teaching of a multi-institutional computer ethics course. *Journal of Educational Media, 28*(2–3), 191–202. doi:10.1080/1358165032000165644

Jeong, A. C. (2003). The sequential analysis of group interaction and critical thinking in online threaded discussions. *American Journal of Distance Education, 17*(1), 25–43. doi:10.1207/S15389286AJDE1701_3

John, M. (2011). Going to Harvard from your bedroom. *BBC News Business*. Retrieved from http://www.bbc.co.uk/news/business-12766562

John, O. P., & Robins, R. W. (1994). Accuracy and bias in self-perception: Individual differences in self-enhancement and the role of narcissism. *Journal of Personality and Social Psychology, 66*(1), 206–219. doi:10.1037/0022-3514.66.1.206 PMID:8126650

Johnson, G. M., & Broadley, T. (2012). Web-based active learning and frequent feedback: Engaging first-year university students. In A. Herrington, J. Schrape, & K. Singh (Eds.), *Engaging students with learning technologies* (pp. 77-96). Perth, Australia: Curtin University. Available at http://espace.library.curtin.edu.au/R/?func=dbin-jumpfull&object_id=187378&local_base=GEN01-ERA02

Johnson, G. M., & Johnson, J. A. (2006). *Personality, internet experience, and e-communication preference*. Paper presented at the Annual Conference of the International Association for Development of the Information Society, Murcia, Spain. (ERIC Document Reproduction No. ED494002). Available at http://files.eric.ed.gov/fulltext/ED494002.pdf

Johnson, G., & Davies, S. (2012). Unsupervised online constructed-response tests: Maximising student learning and results integrity. In M. Brown, M. Harnett, & T. Steward (Eds.), Future challenges, sustainable futures. Proceedings ascillite Wellington 2012 (pp. 400–408). Available at http://www.ascilite2012.org/images/custom/johnson,_genevieve_-_unsupervised_online_constructed_response.pdf

Johnson, T. R. (2013). *Did I really go to Harvard if I got my degree taking online classes?* Retrieved from: http://www.theatlantic.com/education/archive/2013/09/did-i-really-go-to-harvard-if-i-got-my-degree-taking-online-classes/279644/

Johnson, D. R. (2013). Technological change and professional control in the professoriate. *Science, Technology & Human Values, 38*(1), 126–149. doi:10.1177/0162243911430236

Johnson, D. W., & Johnson, F. P. (1997). *Joining together: Group theory and group skills.* Boston: Allyn & Bacon.

Johnson, E. S. (2008). Ecological systems and complexity theory: Toward an alternative model of accountability in education. *Complicity: An International Journal of Complexity and Education, 5*(1), 1–10.

Johnson, G. (2011). Learning style and interaction preference: Application of Moore's typology. In S.-M. Barton, J. Hedberg, & K. Suzuki (Eds.), *Proceedings of global learn asia pacific* (pp. 1445–1450). AACE.

Johnson, G. (2012). Internet use among first-year university students: Computer versus mobile phone activities across home, school and community contexts. In *Proceedings of World Conference on Educational Multimedia, Hypermedia and Telecommunications 2012* (pp. 2637–2642). Chesapeake, VA: AACE.

Johnson, G. M. (2005). Student alienation, academic achievement, and WebCT use. *Journal of Educational Technology & Society, 8*, 179–189.

Johnson, G. M. (2006a). College student psycho-educational functioning and satisfaction with online study groups. *Educational Psychology, 26*(5), 677–688. doi:10.1080/01443410500390848

Johnson, G. M. (2006b). Perception of classroom climate, use of WebCT, and academic achievement. *Journal of Computing in Higher Education, 17*(2), 25–46. doi:10.1007/BF03032697

Johnson, G. M. (2006c). Optional online quizzes: College student use and relationship to achievement. *Canadian Journal of Learning & Technology, 32*, 105–118.

Johnson, G. M. (2007a). Learning style under two web-based study conditions. *Educational Psychology, 27*(5), 617–634. doi:10.1080/01443410701309159

Johnson, G. M. (2007b). Restricted versus unrestricted learning: Synthesis of recent meta-analyses. *AACE Journal, 15*, 267–278.

Johnson, G. M. (2008a). Online study tools: College student preference versus impact on achievement. *Computers in Human Behavior, 24*(3), 930–939. doi:10.1016/j.chb.2007.02.012

Johnson, G. M. (2008b). Cognitive processing differences between frequent and infrequent Internet users. *Computers in Human Behavior, 24*(5), 2094–2106. doi:10.1016/j.chb.2007.10.001

Johnson, G. M. (2008c). The relative learning benefits of synchronous and asynchronous text-based discussion. *British Journal of Educational Technology, 39*, 166–169.

Johnson, G. M. (2010a). Internet use and child development: The techno-microsystem. [ASB]. *Australian Journal of Educational and Developmental Psychology, 10*, 32–43.

Johnson, G. M. (2010b). Internet use and child development: Validation of the ecological techno-subsystem. *Journal of Educational Technology & Society, 13*, 176–185.

Johnson, G. M. (2014). The ecology of interactive learning environments: Situating traditional theory. *Interactive Learning Environments, 22*(3), 298–308. doi:10.1080/10494820.2011.649768

Johnson, G. M., & Davies, S. M. (2014). Self-regulated learning in digital environments: Theory, research, praxis. *British Journal of Research, 1*(2), 1–14.

Johnson, G. M., & Howell, A. J. (2005). Attitude toward instructional technology following required vs. optional WebCT usage. *Journal of Technology and Teacher Education, 13*, 643–654.

Johnson, G. M., & Oliver, R. (2014). Small screen technology use among Indigenous boarding school adolescents from remote regions of Western Australia. *Australian Journal of Indigenous Education, 43*(2), 75–84. doi:10.1017/jie.2014.15

Johnson, G. M., & Puplampu, P. (2008). Internet use during childhood and the ecological techno-subsystem. *Canadian Journal of Learning and Technology, 34*, 19–28.

Johnson, L., Smith, R., Willis, H., Levine, A., & Haywood, K. (2011). *The 2011 Horizon Report*. Austin, TX: The New Media Consortium.

Johnson, R., Stewart, C., & Bachman, C. (2013). What drives students to complete online courses? What drives faculty to teach online? Validating a measure of motivation orientation in university students and faculty. *Interactive Learning Environments*. doi:10.1080/10494820.2013.788037

Joiner, R., Gavin, J., Duffield, J., Brosnan, M., Crook, C., Durndell, A., & Lovatt, P. et al. (2005). Gender, internet identification, and Internet anxiety: Correlates of internet use. *Cyberpsychology & Behavior, 8*(4), 371–378. doi:10.1089/cpb.2005.8.371 PMID:16092894

Jones, M. L. (2007). *Hofstede – culturally questionable?* Paper presented at the Oxford Business and Economics Conference, Oxford, UK.

Jones, C., & Goodfellow, R. (2012). The digital university: Discourse, theory, and evidence. *International Journal of Learning and Media, 4*(3-4), 59–63. doi:10.1162/IJLM_a_00103

Jones, C., Ramanau, R., Cross, S., & Healing, G. (2010). Net generation or digital natives: Is there a distinct new generation entering university? *Computers & Education, 54*(3), 722–732. doi:10.1016/j.compedu.2009.09.022

Jones, C., Reichard, C., & Mokhtari, K. (2003). Are students' learning styles discipline specific? *Community College Journal of Research and Practice, 27*(5), 363–375. doi:10.1080/713838162

Jones, I. M. (2011). Can you see me now? Defining teaching presence in the online classroom through building a learning community. *Journal of Legal Studies Education, 28*(1), 67–116. doi:10.1111/j.1744-1722.2010.01085.x

Jones, K. R. (2013). Developing and implementing a mandatory online student orientation. *Journal of Asynchronous Learning Networks, 17*(1), 43–45.

Joo, Y. J., Joung, S., & Sim, W. J. (2011). Structural relationships among internal locus of control, institutional support, flow, and learner persistence in cyber universities. *Computers in Human Behavior, 27*(2), 714–722. doi:10.1016/j.chb.2010.09.007

Joo, Y. J., Lim, K. Y., & Kim, S. M. (2012). A model for predicting learning flow and achievement in corporate e-learning. *Journal of Educational Technology & Society, 15*(1), 313–325.

Jowallah, R. (2014). An investigation into the management of online teaching and learning spaces: A case study involving graduate research students. *International Review of Research in Open and Distance Learning, 15*(4), 186–198.

Joyce, K. M., & Brown, A. (2009). *Enhancing social presence in online learning: mediation strategies applied to social networking tools.* Retrieved from www.westga.edu/~distance/ojdla/winter124/joyce124.html

Joyce, K. M., & Brown, A. (2009). Enhancing social presence in online learning: Mediation strategies applied to social networking tools. *Online Journal of Distance Learning Administration, 12*(4).

Joyce, T. M. (2013). Reflective Practice through Blogging: An Alternative for Open and Distance Learning Context. *Journal of Communication, 4*(2), 123–130.

Judge, T. A., & Bono, J. E. (2001). Relations of core self-evaluations traits-self-esteem, generalized self-efficacy, locus of control, and emotional stability-with job satisfaction and job performance: A meta-analysis. *The Journal of Applied Psychology, 86*(1), 80–92. doi:10.1037/0021-9010.86.1.80 PMID:11302235

Judge, T. A., & Ilies, R. (2002). Relationship of personality to performance motivation: A meta-analytic review. [PubMed]. *The Journal of Applied Psychology, 87*(4), 797–807. doi:10.1037/0021-9010.87.4.797 PMID:12184582

Jung, I. M., Kudo, M., & Choi, S. (2012). Stress in Japanese learners engaged in online collaborative learning in English. *British Journal of Educational Technology, 43*(6), 1016–1029. doi:10.1111/j.1467-8535.2011.01271.x

Kahneman, D. (2011). *Thinking, fast and slow*. New York: Farrar, Straus and Giroux.

Kahu, E. R., Stephens, C., Leach, L., & Zepke, N. (2013). The engagement of mature distance students. *Higher Education Research & Development*, *32*(5), 1–14. doi:1 0.1080/07294360.2013.777036

Kane, M. (2008). *Errors of measurement, theory, and public policy*. Paper presented at the 12th annual William H. Angoff Memorial Lecture, presented November 19, 2008 at the Educational Testing Service, Princeton NJ. Retrieved from http://www.ets.org/Media/Research/pdf/PICANG12.pdf

Kanuka, H., & Anderson, T. (1999). Using constructivism in technology-mediated learning: Constructing order out of the chaos in the literature. *Radical Pedagogy*, *1*(2). Retrieved from http://www.radicalpedagogy.org/Radical_Pedagogy/Using_Constructivism_in_Technology-Mediated_Learning__Constructing_Order_out_of_the_Chaos_in_the_Literature.html

Kanuka, H., & Garrison, D. R. (2004). Cognitive presence in online learning. *Journal of Computing in Higher Education*, *15*(2), 21–39. doi:10.1007/BF02940928

Kaplan, A. M., & Haenlein, M. (2010). Users of the world, unite! The challenge and opportunities of social media. *Business Horizons*, *53*(1), 59–68. doi:10.1016/j.bushor.2009.09.003

Kaplan, A., & Maehr, M. L. (2007). Achievement goals and student well-being. *Educational Psychology Review*, *19*, 141–187. doi:10.1007/s10648-006-9012-5

Kaptelinin, V., Nardi, B., & Macaulay, C. (1999). The activity checklist: A tool for representing the 'space' of context. *Interaction*, *6*(4), 27–39. doi:10.1145/306412.306431

Karalis, T., & Koutsonikos, G. (2003). Issues and Challenges in Organising and Evaluating Web-based Courses for Adults. *Themes in education*, *4*(2), 177-188.

Karban, K., & Smith, S. (2006). Developing critical reflection within an interprofessional learning programme. Conference Paper presented at: *Professional lifelong learning: beyond reflective practice*, University of Leeds, UK.

Kaymak, Z. D., & Horzum, M. B. (2013). Relationship between online learning readiness and structure and interaction of online learning students. *Educational Sciences: Theory and Practice*, *13*(3), 1792–1797.

Kearns, L. R., & Frey, I. (n.d.). How do students experiences differ in online LIS programs with and without a residency. *The Library Quarterly*, *77*(4), 359–363.

Kearsley, G. (2000). *Online education: Learning and teaching in cyberspace*. Belmont, CA: Wadsworth.

Kearsley, G. (2002). Is online learning for everybody. *Educational Technology*, *42*(1), 41–44.

Keats, D., & Schmidt, J. P. (2007). The genesis and emergence of Education 3.0 in higher education and its potential for Africa. *First Monday*, *12*(3). Retrieved 4/23/14 from http://firstmonday.org/ojs/index.php/fm/article/view/1625/1540#k2

Keefe, J. W. (1979). Learning style: An overview. In J. W. Keefe (Ed.), *Student learning styles: Diagnosing and prescribing programs* (pp. 1–17). Reston, VA: National Association of Secondary School Principals.

Keegan, D. (1995). *Fundamentals of distance education* (3rd ed.). London: Routledge Press.

Keengwe, J., & Kidd, T. T. (2010). Towards best practices in online learning and teaching in higher education. *MERLOT Journal of Online Learning and Teaching, 6*(2). Retrieved November 7, 2014 from http://jolt.merlot.org/vol6no2/keengwe_0610.htm

Keengwe, J., & Kidd, T. T. (2010). Towards best practices in online learning and teaching in higher education. *MERLOT Journal of Online Learning and Teaching*, *6*(2), 533–541.

Keengwe, J., Kidd, T. T., & Kyei-Blankson, L. (2009). Faculty and technology: Implications for faculty training and technology leadership. *Journal of Science Education and Technology*, *18*(1), 23–28. doi:10.1007/s10956-008-9126-2

Keengwe, J., Onchawari, G., & Agamba, J. (2014). Promoting effective e-learning practice through constructivist pedagogy. *Education and Information Technologies*, *19*(4), 887–898. doi:10.1007/s10639-013-9260-1

Kehrwald, B., Reushle, S., Redmond, P., Cleary, K., Albion, P., & Maroulis, J. (2005). *Online pedagogical practices in the faculty of education at the University of Southern Queensland,* Faculty Working Paper 05/01. Retrieved from http://eprints.usq.edu.au/archive/00000131/01/lfi_05_01.pdf

Kehrwald, B. (2008). Understanding Social Presence in Text-Based Online Learning Environments. *Distance Education, 29*(1), 89–106. doi:10.1080/01587910802004860

Keith, L. (Producer) & Flynn, J. J. (Director). (2004, August 25). *Masters of Production: The Hidden Art of Hollywood*. [Television Broadcast]. Public Broadcasting Service.

Keller, J. M. (2008a). An integrative theory of motivation, volition, and performance. *Technology, Instruction, Cognition, and Learning, 6*.

Keller, J. M. (1983). Motivational design of instruction. In C. M. Reigeluth (Ed.), *Instructional design theories and models: An overview of their current status*. Hillsdale, NJ: Lawrence Erlbaum.

Keller, J. M. (1984). The use of ARCS model of motivation in teacher training. In K. E. Shaw (Ed.), *Aspects of educational technology* (Vol. 17). London: Kogan Page.

Keller, J. M. (1987). Development and use of the ARCS model of motivational design. *Performance and Instruction, 26*, 1–8.

Keller, J. M. (1999). Motivational systems. In H. D. Stolovitch & E. J. Keeps (Eds.), *Handbook of human performance technology*. San Francisco, CA: Jossey-Bass.

Keller, J. M. (2005). *Course interest survey: Short form*. Florida State University, Department of Educational Psychology and Learning Systems.

Keller, J. M. (2008b). First principles of motivation to learn and e³-learning. *Distance Education, 29*(2), 175–185. doi:10.1080/01587910802154970

Keller, J. M., & Kopp, T. W. (1987). An application of the ARCS model of motivational design. In C. M. Reigeluth (Ed.), *Instructional theories in action: Lessons illustrating selected theories and models*. Hillsdale, NJ: Lawrence Erlbaum.

Kelley, D., and, Gorham, J. (1988). Effects of immediacy on recall of information. *Communication Education, 37*(3), 198-207.

Kelly, G. A. (1995). *The psychology of personal constructs*. New York, NY: Norton.

Kelly, P. (2009). Group work and multicultural management education. *Journal of Teaching in International Business, 20*(1), 80–102. doi:10.1080/08975930802671273

Kember, D. (1989). A longitudinal process model of drop-out from distance education. *The Journal of Higher Education, 60*(3), 27–301. doi:10.2307/1982251

Kemp, J. E. (1985). *The instructional design process*. New York: Harper and Row.

Kennedy, G. E., Judd, T. S., Churchward, A., Gray, K., & Krause, K.-L. (2008). First year students' experiences with technology: Are they really digital natives? *Australasian Journal of Educational Technology, 24*(1), 108–122.

Kerawalla, L., Minocha, S., Kirkup, G., & Conole, G. (2009). An empirically grounded framework to guide blogging in higher education. *Journal of Computer Assisted Learning, 25*(1), 31–42. doi:10.1111/j.1365-2729.2008.00286.x

Kerr, O. S. (2006). Blogs and the legal academy. *George Washington University Law School Publication*, Legal Research Paper No. 203, 7.

Kert, S. B., & Kurt, A. A. (2012). The effect of electronic performance support systems on self-regulated learning skills. *Interactive Learning Environments, 20*(6), 485–500. doi:10.1080/10494820.2010.533683

Kesim, A., & Agaoglu, E. (2007). A paradigm shift in distance education: Web 2.0 and social software. *Turkish Online Journal of Distance Education-TOJDE, 8*(3). Retrieved from: http://tojde.anadolu.edu.tr/tojde27/articles/article_4.htm

Khan, B. (1997). Web-based instruction: What is it and why is it? In B. H. Khan (Ed.), *Web-based instruction*. Englewood Cliffs, NJ: Educational Technology Publications.

Kharbach, M. (2013). *Education, Technology, and Mobile Learning*. Retrieved 4/23/14 from http://www.educatorstechnology.com/2013/11/education-10-vs-education-20-vs.html

Kiili, K., Lainema, T., de Freitas, S., & Arnab, S. (2014). Flow framework for analyzing the quality of educational games. *Entertainment Computing, 5*(4), 367–377. doi:10.1016/j.entcom.2014.08.002

Kilburn, M. (2013). Student perceptions of instructor interaction in the online environment. *International Journal of Research in Social Sciences, 1*(1), 54-58.

Kilburn, M. (2011). Facilitating interaction in the online environment. In S. Hoffman (Ed.), *Teaching the humanities online: A practical guide to the virtual classroom.* New York: M.E. Sharpe.

Kilgore, D. W. (2001). Critical and postmodern perspectives on adult learning. *New Directions for Adult and Continuing Education, 89*, 3–13.

Kilgore, W., & Lowenthal, P. R. (2015). The Human Element MOOC: An experiment in social presence. In R. D. Wright (Ed.), *Establishing an equitable and fair admissions system for an online* (pp. 389–407). Hershey, PA: IGI Global. doi:10.4018/978-1-4666-6461-6.ch017

Kilian, C. (1997). Why Teach Online. *Educational Review, 32*(4), 31–34.

Kim, C., & Keller, J. M. (2008). Effects of motivational and volitional email messages (MVEM) with personal messages on undergraduate students' motivation, study habits and achievement. *British Journal of Educational Technology, 39*, 36–51.

Kim, C., & Keller, J. M. (2011). Towards technology integration: The impact of motivational and volitional email messages. *Educational Technology Research and Development, 59*(1), 91–111. doi:10.1007/s11423-010-9174-1

Kim, E., & Seo, E. H. (2013). The relationship of flow and self-regulated learning to active procrastination. *Social Behavior and Personality, 41*(7), 1099–1114. doi:10.2224/sbp.2013.41.7.1099

Kim, J. (2011). Developing an instrument to measure social presence in distance higher education. *British Journal of Educational Technology, 42*(5), 763–777. doi:10.1111/j.1467-8535.2010.01107.x

Kim, J., Kwon, Y., & Cho, D. (2011). Investigating factors that influence social presence and learning outcomes in distance higher education. *Computers & Education, 57*(2), 1512–1520. doi:10.1016/j.compedu.2011.02.005

Kim, K. J., & Bonk, C. J. (2006). The future of online teaching and learning in higher education: The survey say. *EDUCAUSE Quarterly, 29*(4), 22–30.

Kim, K., Sharma, P., Land, S. M., & Furlong, K. P. (2013). Effects of active learning on enhancing student critical thinking in an undergraduate general science course. *Innovative Higher Education, 38*(3), 223–235. doi:10.1007/s10755-012-9236-x

Kimmelman, M. (2004, August 6). *Cartier-Bresson, Artist Who Used Lens, Dies at 95.* New York Times.

Kim, R., Olfman, L., Ryan, T., & Eryilmaz, E. (2014). Leveraging a personalized system to improve self-directed learning in online educational environments. *Computers & Education, 70*, 150–160. doi:10.1016/j.compedu.2013.08.006

King, A. (1993). From sage on the stage to guide on the side. *College Teaching, 41*(1), 30–35. doi:10.1080/87567555.1993.9926781

Kirkpatrick, M. A., Stant, K., Downes, S., & Gaither, L. (2008). Perceived locus of control and academic performance: Broadening the construct's applicability. *Journal of College Student Development, 49*(5), 486–496. doi:10.1353/csd.0.0032

Kitsantas, A. (2013). Fostering college students' self-regulated learning with learning technologies. *Hellenic Journal of Psychology, 10*, 235–252.

Kitsantas, A., & Dabbagh, N. (2011). The role of Web 2.0 technologies in self-regulated learning. *New Directions for Teaching and Learning, 126*(126), 99–106. doi:10.1002/tl.448

Kitsantas, A., & Zimmerman, B. J. (2009). College students' homework and academic achievement: The mediating role of self-regulatory beliefs. *Metacognition and Learning, 4*(2), 97–110. doi:10.1007/s11409-008-9028-y

Klein, B. D., Rossin, D., Guo, Y. M., & Ro, Y. K. (2010). An examination of the effects of flow on learning in a graduate-level introductory operations management course. *Journal of Education for Business, 85*(5), 292–298. doi:10.1080/08832320903449600

Klein, S. B. (2012). A role for the self-referential processing tasks requiring participants to imagine survival in the Savannah. *Journal of Experimental Psychology. Learning, Memory, and Cognition, 38*(5), 1234–1242. doi:10.1037/a0027636 PMID:22409181

Klein, S. B., & Loftus, E. M. (1988). The nature of self-referent encoding: The contribution of elaborative and organizational processes. *Journal of Personality and Social Psychology*, *55*(1), 5–11. doi:10.1037/0022-3514.55.1.5

Klein, S. S. (1985). *Handbook for achieving sex equity through education*. Baltimore, MD: Johns Hopkins University Press.

Klenowski, V. (2011). Assessment for learning in the accountability era: Queensland, Australia. *Studies in Educational Evaluation*, *37*(1), 78–83. doi:10.1016/j.stueduc.2011.03.003

Klopfer, E., Squire, K., & Jenkin, H. (2008). Environmental detectives - The development of an augmented reality platform for environmental simulations. *Educational Research Technology and Development*, *56*(2), 1042–1629. doi:10.1007/s11423-007-9037-6

Knowles, M. (1975). *Self-directed learning: A guide for learners and teachers*. Chicago: Follett Publishing Company.

Knowles, M. (1980). *The modern practice of adult education*. Chicago: Follett.

Knowles, M. (1984). *Andragogy in Action. Applying modern principles of adult education*. San Francisco: Jossey Bass.

Knowles, M. S. (1980). *The modern practice of adult education: From pedagogy to andragogy (revised and updated)*. Englewood Cliffs, NJ: Cambridge Adult Education.

Knowles, M. S. (1984). *Andragogy in action*. San Francisco: Jossey-Bass.

Knowles, M., Holton, E. III, & Swanson, R. (1998). *The Adult Learner*. Houston: Gulf Publishing Company.

Kokkos, A. (2005). *Εκπαίδευση Ενηλίκων: Ανιχνεύοντας το πεδίο (Adult Education: Scouting the field)*. Athens: Metaixmio. (In Greek)

Komarraju, M., & Nadler, D. (2013). Self-efficacy and academic achievement: Why do implicit beliefs, goals, and effort regulation matter? *Learning and Individual Differences*, *25*, 67–72. doi:10.1016/j.lindif.2013.01.005

Kong, S., & Song, Y. (2013). A principle-based pedagogical design framework for developing constructivist learning in a seamless learning environment: A teacher development model for learning and teaching in digital classrooms. *British Journal of Educational Technology*, *44*(6), E209–E212. doi:10.1111/bjet.12073

Konradt, U., & Sulz, K. (2001). The experience of flow in interacting with a hypermedia learning environment. *Journal of Educational Multimedia and Hypermedia*, *10*(1), 69–84.

Koohang, A., & Harman, K. (2007). Advancing sustainability of open educational resources. *Issues in Informing Science and Information Technology*, *4*, 535–544.

Kozma, R. B. (2001). Counterpoint theory of "learning with media. In R. E. Clark (Ed.), *Learning from media: Arguments, analysis, and evidence* (pp. 137–178). Greenwich, CT: Information Age Publishing Inc.

Krathwohl, D. R. (2002). A revision of Bloom's taxonomy: An overview. *Theory into Practice*, *41*(4), 212–264. doi:10.1207/s15430421tip4104_2

Krause, K.-L., & Coates, H. (2008). Students' engagement in first-year university. *Assessment & Evaluation in Higher Education*, *33*(5), 493–505. doi:10.1080/02602930701698892

Kreijns, K., Kirschner, P. A., & Jochems, W. (2003). Identifying the pitfalls for social interactions in computer-supported collaborative learning environments: A review of the research. *Computers in Human Behavior*, *19*(3), 585–612. doi:10.1016/S0747-5632(02)00057-2

Kuh, G. D. (2002). *The National survey of student engagement: Conceptual framework and overview of psychometric properties*. Indiana University Center for Postsecondary Research and Planning. Retrieved from http://nsse.iub.edu/html/psychometric_framework_2002.cfm

Kuh, G. D. (2003). What's we are learning about student engagement from NSSE: Benchmarks for effective educational practices. *Change: The Magazine of Higher Learning*, *35*(2), 25–32. doi:10.1080/00091380309604090

Kuh, G. D., Cruce, T. M., Shoup, R., Kinzie, J., & Gonyea, R. M. (2008). Unmasking the effects of student engagement on first-year college grades and persistence. *The Journal of Higher Education, 79*(5), 540–563. doi:10.1353/jhe.0.0019

Kuhl, J. (1984). Volitional aspects of achievement motivation and learned helplessness: Toward a comprehensive theory of action control. In B. A. Maher & W. B. Maher (Eds.), *Progress in experimental personality research.* Orlando, FL: Academic Press.

Kuhl, J. (1985). Volitional mediation of cognitive behavior consistency: Self-regulatory processes and actions versus state-orientation. In J. Kuhl & J. Beckman (Eds.), *Action control: From cognition to behavior.* Berlin, Germany: Springer-Verlag. doi:10.1007/978-3-642-69746-3_6

Kuhl, J., & Furhman, A. (1998). Decomposing self-regulation and self-control: The volitional components inventory. In J. Heckhausen & S. Dweck (Eds.), *Motivation and self-regulation across the life span.* New York, NY: Cambridge University Press. doi:10.1017/CBO9780511527869.003

Kuo, Y. (2014). Accelerated online learning: Perceptions of interaction and learning outcomes among African American students. *American Journal of Distance Education, 28*(4), 241–252. doi:10.1080/08923647.2014.959334

Kuo, Y., Walker, A. E., Belland, B. R., Schroder, K. E. E., & Kuo, Y. (2014). A case study of integrating interwise: Interaction, internet self-efficacy, and satisfaction in synchronous online learning environments. *International Review of Research in Open and Distance Learning, 15*(1), 161–181.

Kurtz, G. (2014). Integrating a Facebook Group and a Course Website: The Effect on Participation and Perceptions on Learning. *American Journal of Distance Education, 28*(4), 253–263. doi:10.1080/08923647.2014.957952

Kyndt, E., Dochy, F., Struyven, K., & Cascallar, E. (2011). The perception of workload and task complexity and its influence on students' approaches to learning: A study in higher education. *European Journal of Education, 26*, 393–415.

Laal, M. (2011). Barriers to lifelong learning. *Procedia - Social and Behavioral Sciences, 28*, 612 – 615.

Laitinen, A. (2013). Changing the way we account for college credit. *Issues in Science and Technology, 29*(2), 62–68.

Lajoie, S. P., & Azevedo, R. (2006). Teaching and learning in technology-rich environments. In P. A. Alexander & P. H. Winne (Eds.), *Handbook of educational psychology* (2nd ed.; pp. 803–821). Mahwah, NJ: Erlbaum.

Lal, P. (2015). Leveraging Web 2.0 for online learning. In R. Wright (Ed.), Student-Teacher Interaction in Online Learning Environments (pp. 235–249). Hershey, PA: IGI Global. doi:10.4018/978-1-4666-6461-6.ch011

Lambert, J. L., & Fisher, J. L. (2013). Community of Inquiry Framework: Establishing community in an online course. *Journal of Interactive Online Learning, 12*(1), 1–16. Retrieved from http://www.ncolr.org/jiol/issues/pdf/12.1.1.pdf

Lambrechts, F. J., Bouwen, R., Grieten, S., Huybrechts, J. P., & Schein, E. H. (2011). Learning to help through humble inquiry and implications for management research, practice, and education: An interview with Edgar H. Schein. *Academy of Management Learning & Education, 10*(1), 131–147. doi:10.5465/AMLE.2011.59513279

Lampe, C., Walsh, R., Velasquez, A., & Ozkaya, E. (2010). *Motivations to participate in online communities.Proceedings of the SIGCHI Conference on Human Factors in Computing Systems*, Atlanta GA, 10-15 April, (pp. 1927-1936).

Lam, Y., & Lawrence, G. (2002). Teacher-student role redefinition during a computer-based second language project: Are computers catalysts for empowering change? *Computer Assisted Language Learning, 15*(3), 295–315. doi:10.1076/call.15.3.295.8185

Lane, L. M. (2011). Reducing distance in online classes. In S. Hoffman (Ed.), *Teaching the humanities online: A practical guide to the virtual classroom.* New York: M.E. Sharpe.

Lang, P. (Ed.). (2009). Innovation in transformative Learning: Space, Culture and the Arts. Schapiro Source: Counterpoints, 341, 291-294.

LaPadula, M. (2003). A comprehensive look at online student support services for distance learners. *American Journal of Distance Education, 17*(2), 119–128. doi:10.1207/S15389286AJDE1702_4

LaRose, R., & Whitten, P. (1998). *October. Rethinking instructional immediacy for web courses: A social cognitive exploration.* Paper submitted to the International Communication Association, Instructional and Developmental Communication Division. Retrieved March 2014 from http://www.it.murdoch.edu.au/~sudweeks/papers/CBLS_Cyprus/larose.html

LaRose, R., Gregg, J., & Eastin, M. (1998). *Audiographic courses on the Web: An experiment.* Paper presented at the International Communication Association, Jerusalem, Israel. Available: www.telecommunication.msu.edu / faculty/larose/ica98.htm

LaRose, R., & Whitten, P. (1999, June). Increasing the immediacy of web courses.*Proceedings of the Association for the Advancement of Computers in Education,* Seattle, Washington.

LaRose, R., & Whitten, P. (2000). Re-thinking instructional immediacy for web courses: A social cognitive exploration. *Communication Education, 40*(4), 320–338. doi:10.1080/03634520009379221

Larson, L. R., & Lovelace, M. D. (2013). Evaluating the efficacy of questioning strategies in lecture-based classroom environments: Are we asking the right questions? *Journal on Excellence in College Teaching, 24*(1), 105–122.

Lasley, T. (1992). Promoting teacher reflection. *Journal of Staff Development, 13*(1), 24–29.

Latham, G. P., & Brown, T. C. (2006). The effect of learning, distal, and proximal goals on MBA self-efficacy and satisfaction. *Applied Psychology, 55,* 606–623. doi:10.1111/j.1464-0597.2006.00246.x

Laurillard, D. (2002). *Rethinking university teaching: A conversational framework for the effective use of learning technologies* (2nd ed.). RoutledgetFalmer. doi:10.4324/9780203304846

Lavendar, R., Nguyen-Rodriguez, S. T., & Spruijt-Metz, D. (2010). Teaching the whole student: Perceived academic control in college art instruction. *Studies in Art Education, 51,* 198–218.

Lawanto, O., Santoso, H. B., Lawanto, K. N., & Goodridge, W. (2014). Self-regulated learning skills and online activities between higher and lower performers on a web-intensive undergraduate engineering course. *Journal of Educators Online, 11*(3), 1–32.

Lawrence, G. (2013). A working model for intercultural learning and engagement in collaborative online language learning environments. *Intercultural Education, 24*(4), 303–314. doi:10.1080/14675986.2013.809247

Lea, M., & Goodfellow, R. (2003). *Supporting academic writing in a global online environment.* Paper presented at the European Association of Teachers of Academic Writing, Budapest, Hungary.

Leary, M. R. (1995). *Self-presentation: Impression management and interpersonal behavior. Social psychology series.* Madison, WI: Brown and Benchmark Publishers.

Lebow, D. (1993). Constructivist values for instructional system design: Five principles toward a new mindset. *Educational Technology Research and Development, 41*(3), 4–16. doi:10.1007/BF02297354

Lebow, D., & Wager, W. W. (1994). Authentic activity as a model for appropriate learning activity: Implications for emerging instructional technologies. *Canadian Journal of Educational Communication, 23,* 231–244.

Lederman, D. (2013). Growth for online learning. *Inside Higher Ed.* Retrieved from http://www.insidehighered.com/news/2013/01/08/survey-finds-online-enrollments-slow-continue-grow

Lee, M. J. W., & Chan, A. (2007). Reducing the effects of isolation and promoting inclusivity for distance learners through podcasting. *Turkish Online Journal of Distance Education, 8*(1), 85–104. Retrieved from: http://tojde.anadolu.edu.tr/tojde25/ pdf/article_7.pdf

Lee, S. M. (2012). Distance learning class model for teaching a foreign language in university-level education context. *Journal of Pan-Pacific Association of Applied Linguistics, 1.*

Lee, C.-Y., Dickerson, J., & Winslow, J. (2012). An analysis of organizational approaches to online course structures. *Online Journal of Distance Learning Administration, 15*(1). Retrieved from http://www.westga.edu/~distance/ojdla/spring151/lee_dickerson_winslow.html

Lee, J. (2014). An exploratory study of effective online learning: Assessing satisfaction levels of graduate students of mathematics education associated with human and design factors of an online course. *International Review of Research in Open and Distance Learning, 15*(1).

Lee, S. J., Srinivasan, S., Trail, T., Lewis, D., & Lopez, S. (2011). Examining the relationship among student perception of support, course satisfaction, and learning outcomes in online learning. *The Internet and Higher Education, 14*(3), 158–163. doi:10.1016/j.iheduc.2011.04.001

Lee, W., Courtney, R., & Balassi, S. J. (2010). Do online homework tools improve student results in microeconomics principles courses? *The American Economic Review, 100*, 283–286. doi:10.1257/aer.100.2.283

Leftheriotou, P. (2005). Διερεύνηση των εκπαιδευτικών αναγκών των εκπαιδευτών ενηλίκων. [Educational needs of adults' educators]. (Master Thesis). Hellenic Open University. (In Greek)

Lehman, E. (Producer) & Nichols, M. (Director). (1966). *Who's Afraid of Virginia Woolf?* [Motion Picture]. United States: Warner Brothers.

Lehmann, T., Hähnlein, I., & Ifenthaler, D. (2014). Cognitive, metacognitive and motivational perspectives on preflection in self-regulated online learning. *Computers in Human Behavior, 32*, 313–323. doi:10.1016/j.chb.2013.07.051

Lehman, R. M., & Conceição, S. C. (2010). *Creating a sense of presence in online teaching: How to "be there" for distance learners.* San Francisco, CA: John Wiley & Sons.

Lei, S. A. (2010). Assessment practices of advanced field ecology course. *Education, 130*(3), 404–415.

Lei, S. A., Kuestermeyer, B. N., & Westmeyer, K. A. (2010). Group composition affecting student interaction and achievement: Instructors' perspectives. *Journal of Instructional Psychology, 37*(4), 317–325.

Lepper, M. R., & Henderlong, J. (2000). Turnign play into work and work into play: Twenty-five years of research on intrinsic versus extrinsic motivation. In C. Sansone & J. M. Harackiewicz (Eds.), *Intrinsic and extrinsic motivation: The search for optimal motivation and performance.* San Diego, CA: Academic Press.

Lester, N. B., & Mayher, J. S. (1987). Critical professional inquiry. *English Education, 19*(4), 198–210.

Levinsen, T. K. (2006). Collaborative On-Line Teaching: The Inevitable Path to Deep Learning and Knowledge Sharing? *Electronic Journal of e-learning, 4*(1), 41-48.

Lewis, D., & Slapak-Barski, J. (2014). "I'm not sharing my work!": An Approach to Community Building. *Quarterly Review of Distance Education, 15*(2), 9–20.

Lewis, P. A., & Price, S. (2007). Distance education and the integration of e-learning in a graduate program. *Journal of Continuing Education in Nursing, 38*(3), 139–143. doi:10.3928/00220124-20070501-08 PMID:17542173

Ley, K. l., & Gannon-Cook, R. r. (2014). Learner-valued interactions. *Quarterly Review Of Distance Education, 15*(1), 23–32.

Ley, K., & Gannon-Cook, R. (2014). Learner-valued interactions. *Quarterly Review of Distance Education, 15*(1), 23–32.

Liaw, S. S., Chen, G. D., & Huang, H. M. (2008). Users' attitudes toward Web-based collaborative learning systems for knowledge management. *Computers & Education, 50*(3), 950–961. doi:10.1016/j.compedu.2006.09.007

Liberman, N., Sagristano, M. D., & Trope, Y. (2002). The effect of temporal distance on level of mental construal. *Journal of Experimental Social Psychology, 38*(6), 523–534. doi:10.1016/S0022-1031(02)00535-8

Licona, M. M., & Gurung, B. (2011). Asynchronous Discussions in Online Multicultural Education. *Multicultural Education, 19*(1), 2–8.

Lim, C. P. (2004). Engaging learners in online learning environments. *TechTrends, 48*(4), 16–23. doi:10.1007/BF02763440

Lindquist, D., Denning, T., Kelly, M., Malani, R., Griswold, W. G., & Simon, B. (2007). Exploring the potential of mobile phones for active learning in the classroom. *ACM SIGCSE Bulletin, 39*(1), 384–388. doi:10.1145/1227504.1227445

Lindsey, P. (2009). Starting an accelerated baccalaureate nursing program: Challenges and opportunities for creative educational innovations. *The Journal of Nursing Education, 48*(5), 279–281. PMID:19476033

Linnenbrink-Garcia, L., Middleton, M. J., Ciani, K. D., Easter, M. A., O'Keefe, P. A., & Zusho, A. (2012). The strength of the relation between performance-approach and performance-avoidance goal orientations: Theoretical, methodological and instructional implications. *Educational Psychologist, 47*(4), 281–301. doi:10.1080/00461520.2012.722515

Lion, R. W. (2011). A study of performance support in higher education. *Performance Improvement Quarterly, 24*(1), 49–67. doi:10.1002/piq.20101

Lips, D. (2010, January). *How to make higher education more affordable.* The Heritage Foundation: Leadership for America, 2785. Retrieved from: http://www.heritage.org/research/education/wm2785.cfm

Litchfield, A., Dyson, L., Lawrence, E., & Zmijewska, A. (2007). Directions for m-learning research to enhance active learning. In ICT: Providing choices for learners and learning. *Proceedings Ascilite Singapore 2007.* Retrieved from http://www.ascilite.org.au/conferences/singapore07/procs/litchfield.pd

Littlejohn, A., Falconer, I., & McGill, L. (2008). Characterising effective eLearning resources. *Computers & Education, 50*(3), 757–771. doi:10.1016/j.compedu.2006.08.004

Liu, X., Bonk, C. J., Magjuka, R. J., Lee, S., & Su, B. (2005). Exploring four dimensions of online instructor roles: A program level case study. *Journal of Asynchronous Learning Networks, 9*(4), 29–48.

Liu, X., Liu, S., Lee, S.-h., & Magjuka, R. J. (2010). Cultural differences in online learning: International student perceptions. *Journal of Educational Technology & Society, 13*(3), 177–188.

Liyanagunawardena, T. R., Parslow, P., & Williams, S. A. (2014). Dropout: MOOC participants' perspective. In U. Cress & C. D. Kloos (Eds.), Proceedings of the European MOOC stakeholder summit 2014 (pp. 95–100)., Retrieved from http://www.emoocs2014.eu/sites/default/files/Proceedings-Moocs-Summit-2014.pdf

Locke, E. A., & Latham, G. P. (1990). *A theory of goal setting and task performance.* Englewood Cliffs, NJ: Prentice Hall.

Locke, E. A., & Latham, G. P. (2002). Building a practically useful theory of goal setting and task motivation: A 35-year odyssey. *The American Psychologist, 57*(9), 705–717. doi:10.1037/0003-066X.57.9.705 PMID:12237980

Locke, E. A., & Latham, G. P. (2006). New directions in goal-setting theory. *Current Directions in Psychological Science, 15*(5), 265–268. doi:10.1111/j.1467-8721.2006.00449.x

Locke, E. A., McClear, K., & Knight, D. (1996). Self-esteem and work. *International Review of Industrial and Organizational Psychology, 11*, 1–32.

Lohman, M. C., & Finkelstein, M. (2000). Designing groups in problem based learning to promote problem solving skills and self-directedness. *Instructional Science, 28*(4), 291–307. doi:10.1023/A:1003927228005

Longworth, N. (2003). *Lifelong Learning in Action: Transforming Education in the 21th Century.* London: Kogan Page.

Lonn, S., & Teasley, S. D. (2009). Podcasting in higher education: What are the implications for teaching and learning? *The Internet and Higher Education, 12*(2), 88–92. doi:10.1016/j.iheduc.2009.06.002

Lovelock, C., & Wirtz, J. (2007). *Service marketing: People, technology and strategy* (6th ed.). Pearson Prentice Hall.

Lowenthal, P. R., & Parscal, T. (2008). Teaching presence. *The Learning Curve, 3*(4), 1-2, 4.

Lowes, S. (2005). *Online teaching and classroom change: The impact of virtual high school on its teachers and their schools.* Naperville, IL: Learning Point Associates.

Lowry, P. B., Roberts, T. L., Romano, N. C., Cheney, D. P., & Hightower, P. D. (2006). The impact of group size and social presence on small-group communication. Does computer-mediated communication make a difference? *Small Group Research*, *37*(6), 631–661. doi:10.1177/1046496406294322

Lowyck, J., & Poysa, J. (2001). Design of collaborative learning environments. *Computers in Human Behavior*, *17*(5-6), 507–516. doi:10.1016/S0747-5632(01)00017-6

Luca, J., & McLoughlin, C. (2005). Can blogs promote fair and equitable teamwork? In *Balance, fidelity, mobility: Maintaining the momentum?* Brisbane: ASCILITE.

Lumière, A., & Lumière, L. (Producers & Directors). (1896). *The Arrival of a Train at La Ciotat*. [Motion Picture]. France: Lumiere.

Luskin, B. J. (2003). *Media psychology: A field whose time Is here, The California Psychologist*. May/June.

Lust, G., Elen, J., & Clarebout, G. (2013). Students' tool-use within a web enhanced course: Explanatory mechanisms of students' tool-use pattern. *Computers in Human Behavior*, *29*(5), 2013–2021. doi:10.1016/j.chb.2013.03.014

Lust, G., Juarez Collazo, N. A., Elen, J., & Clarebout, G. (2012). Content management systems: Enriched learning opportunities for all? *Computers in Human Behavior*, *28*(3), 795–808. doi:10.1016/j.chb.2011.12.009

Luszczynska, A., & Schwarzer, R. (2003). Planning and self-efficacy in the adoption and maintenance of breast self-examination: A longitudinal study on self-regulatory cognitions. *Psychology & Health*, *18*(1), 93–108. doi:10.1080/0887044021000019358

Ma, W. W., & Chan, C. K. (2014, December). Online knowledge sharing and psychological well-being among Chinese college students. In C. K. Chan, K. M. Chan, W. L. Chan, H. L. Chui, C. W. Fong, H. Fung, . . . Tong, K. W. (Eds.), Communication and education: New media, knowledge practices, and multiliteracies. Hong Kong: HKAECT. Retrieved from http://stu.hksyu.edu/~wkma/ref/Ma_Chan_2014_hkaect_pp77-86.pdf

Mabrey, P. E., & Liu, J. (2013). Social media and public speaking: Student-produced multimedia informative presentations. In The plugged-in professor: Tips and techniques for teaching with social media. Oxford, UK: Chandos Publishing.

MacGregor, C. J. (2002). Personality differences between online and face-to-face students. *Journal of Continuing Higher Education*, *50*(3), 14–23. doi:10.1080/0737736 6.2002.10401201

MacKnight, C. B. (2000). Teaching critical thinking through online discussion. *EDUCAUSE Quarterly*, *4*, 38–41.

Madden, T. J., Ellen, P. S., & Azjen, I. (1992). A comparison for the theory of planned behavior and the theory of reasoned action. *Journal of Personality and Social Psychology*, *18*(1), 3–9. doi:10.1177/0146167292181001

Maehr, M. L. (2001). Goal theory is not dead-not yet anyway: A reflection on a special issue. *Educational Psychology Review*, *13*(2), 177–185. doi:10.1023/A:1009065404123

Mager, R. F. (1984). *Preparing instructional objectives* (2nd ed.). Belmont, CA: Lake Publishing.

Majeski, R., & Stover, M. (2007). Theoretically based pedagogical strategies leading to deep learning in asynchronous online gerontology courses. *Educational Gerontology*, *33*(3), 171–185. doi:10.1080/03601270600850826

Major, E., & Brock, C. (2003). Fostering positive dispositions toward diversity: Dialogical explorations of a moral dilemma. *Teacher Education Quarterly*, *30*(4), 7–26.

Malone, D. M. (2011). Forward. In B. Göransson & C. Brundenius (Eds.), *Universities in transition: The changing role and challenges for academic institutions* (pp. v–vi). Ottawa: Springer.

Mancuso-Murphy, J. (2007). Distance education in nursing: An integrated review of online nursing students' experience with technology-delivered education. *The Journal of Nursing Education*, *46*(5), 253–260. PMID:17580737

Mandermach, B. J., Gonzales, R. M., & Garrett, A. L. (2006). An examination of online instructor presence via threaded discussion participation. *Journal of Online Learning and Teaching, 2*(4), 248–260.

Mandernach, B. J. (2009). Three ways to improve student engagement in the online classroom. *Online Classroom,* 1-2.

Mandernach, B. J. (2013). Better feedback in less time. *Online Classroom, 13*(6), 1, 7.

Mandernach, B. J., & Garrett, J. (2014). Effective feedback strategies for the online classroom. *Faculty Focus.* Retrieved from: http://www.facultyfocus.com/articles/online-education/effective-feedback-strategies-online-classroom/

Mandernach, B. J., & Taylor, S. S. (2011). Web 2.0 applications to foster student engagement. In R. L. Miller, E. Amsel, B. Kowalewski, B. Beins, K. Keith, & B. Peden (Eds.), *Promoting student engagement, volume 1: Programs, techniques and opportunities.* Syracuse, NY: Society for the Teaching of Psychology. Available from the STP web site: http://teachpsych.org/ebooks/pse2011/vol1/index.php

Mandernach, B. J. (2005). Relative effectiveness of computer-based and human feedback for enhancing student learning. *Journal of Educators Online, 2*(1). Retrieved from www.thejeo.com

Mandernach, B. J. (2006). The evolution of online course development: From basics to bells and back again. *Online Classroom, 2,* 7–8.

Mandernach, B. J. (2014). Efficient and effective feedback in the online classroom. In J. Garrett (Ed.), *A Magna Publications White Paper.* Madison, WI: Magna Publications, Inc.

Mandernach, B. J., Forrest, K. D., Babutzke, J. L., & Manker, L. R. (2009). The role of instructor, interactivity in promoting critical thinking in online and face-to-face classrooms. *MERLOT Journal of Online Learning and Teaching, 5*(1), 49–62.

Mandernach, B. J., Forrest, K., Babuzke, J., & Manaker, L. (2009). The role of instructor interactivity in promoting critical thinking in online and face-to-face classrooms. *Online Journal of Learning and Teaching, 5*(1), 49–62.

Mandernach, B. J., Hudson, S., & Wise, S. (2013). Where has the time gone? Faculty activities and time commitments in the online classroom. *Journal of Educators Online, 10*(2). Retrieved from http://www.thejeo.com/Archives/Volume10Number2/MandernachHudsonWise.pdf

Mandernach, B. J., Zafonte, M., & Taylor, C. (in press). Instructional Strategies to Improve College Students' APA Style Writing. *International Journal of Teaching and Learning in Higher Education.*

Manouchehri, A. (2002). Developing teaching knowledge through peer discourse. *Teaching and Teacher Education, 18*(6), 715–737. doi:10.1016/S0742-051X(02)00030-6

Markham, S. (2004). Learning styles measurement: A cause for concern. Technical Report (draft), Computing Educational Research Group. Melbourne, Australia: Monash University; Retrieved from http://www.csse.monash.edu.au/~ajh/research/cerg/techreps/learning_styles_review.pdf

Martindale, T., & Wiley, D. A. (2005). Using weblogs in scholarship and teaching. *TechTrends, 49*(2), 55–61. doi:10.1007/BF02773972

Martínez-Torres, M. R., Toral, S. L., & Barrero, F. (2011). Identification of the design variables of eLearning tools. *Interacting with Computers, 23*(3), 279–288. doi:10.1016/j.intcom.2011.04.004

Martin, F., Parker, M. A., & Deale, D. F. (2012). Examining interactivity in synchronous virtual classrooms. *International Review of Research in Open and Distance Learning, 13*(3), 227–261.

Marzano, R. J., Pickering, D. J., & Pollock, J. E. (2001). *Classroom instruction that works: Research-based strategies for increasing student achievement.* Alexandria, VA: Association for Supervision and Curriculum Development.

Maslen, G. (2012). Digital campus changes the game. *The AGE National*. Retrieved from http://www.theage.com.au/national/education/digital-campus-changes-the-game-20120604-1zrtd.html

Mason, J., & Brunning, R. (2001). *Providing feedback in computer-based instruction: What the research tell us*. Centre of Instructional Innovation, University of Nebraska-Lincoln. Retrieved from: http://dwb.unl.edu/Edit/MB/MasonBruning.html

Mason, R., & Rennie, F. (2008). *E- Learning and Social Networking Handbook: Resources for Higher Education*. Taylor and Francis.

Matsom, Y. (2006). A Model of a Decision Making Planning Strategy for the Development of Online Courses for Teacher Education Program. In C. Crawford et al. (Eds.), *Proceedings of Society for Information Technology and Teacher Education International Conference 2006* (pp. 1274-1278). Chesapeake, VA: AACE.

Ma, W. W., & Yuen, A. H. (2011). Understanding online knowledge sharing: An interpersonal relationship perspective. *Computers & Education*, 56(1), 210–219. doi:10.1016/j.compedu.2010.08.004

Mayer, R. E. (2001). *Multimedia learning*. New York: Cambridge University Press. doi:10.1017/CBO9781139164603

Mayer, R. E., & Massa, L. J. (2003). Three facets of visual and verbal learners: Cognitive ability, cognitive style, and learning preference. *Journal of Educational Psychology*, 95(4), 833–846. doi:10.1037/0022-0663.95.4.833

Mazer, J., Murphy, R., & Simonds, C. (2007). I'll see you on facebook: The effects of computer mediated teacher self-disclosure on student motivation, affective learning and classroom climate. *Communication Education*, 56(1), 1–17. doi:10.1080/03634520601009710

Mazman, S. H., & Usleul, Y. K. (2011). Gender differences in using social networks. *Turkish Online Journal of Education Technology*, 10(2), 133–139.

Mazyck, M. (2002). Integrated learning systems and students of color: Two decades of use in K-12 education. *TechTrends*, 46(2), 33–39. doi:10.1007/BF02772074

Mazzolini, M., & Maddison, S. (2003). Sage, guide or ghost? The effect of instructor intervention on student participation in online discussion forums. *Computers & Education*, 40(3), 237–253. doi:10.1016/S0360-1315(02)00129-X

Mazzolini, M., & Maddison, S. (2007). When to jump in: The role of the instructor in online discussion forums. *Computers & Education*, 49(2), 193–213. doi:10.1016/j.compedu.2005.06.011

McBride, W. T. (2014). Hitchcock's Stylized Capture of Post-Adolescent Fatheads. In *Children in the Films of Alfred Hitchcock*. McMillan-Palgrave.

McBride, W. T. (2015). *Dutchman Heaped in Modern Cinema. MLA Approaches to Teaching Amiri Baraka's Dutchman*. MLA.

McBride, W. T. (2015, March). *She's Not There: Shallow Focus on Emerging Techno-Mediated Modes of Being in Spike Jonze's Her*. Paper presented at the meeting of the American Comparative Literature Association Annual Meeting, Seattle, WA.

McBride, W. T. (2013). *Stylized Moments: Turning Film Style Into Meaning*. Smashwords.

McBrien, J. L., Jones, P., & Cheng, R. (2009). Virtual spaces: Employing a synchronous online classroom to facilitate student engagement in online learning. *International Review of Research in Open and Distance Learning*, 10(3), 1–6.

McCabe, D., & Meuter, M. (2011). A student view of technology in the classroom: Does it enhance the seven principles of good practice in undergraduate education? *Journal of Marketing Education*, 33(2), 149–159. doi:10.1177/0273475311410847

McCalla, G. (2004). The ecological approach to the design of e-learning environments: Purpose-based capture and use of information about learners. *Journal of Interactive Media in Education*, 7(1), 1–23.

McCarthy, A. T. (2012). Designing Online Course Assignments for Student Engagement: Strategies and Best Practices. *Currents in Teaching & Learning*, 4(2), 31–41.

McCarthy, J. (2010). Blended learning environments: Using social networking sites to enhance the first year experience. *Australasian Journal of Educational Technology, 26*(6), 729–740.

McCluskey, M. (2006). Are canned courses impacting academic freedom? *Adjunct Nation*. Retrieved from http://www.adjunctnation.com/2006/01/01/50-are-canned-courses-impacting-academic-freedom/

McInnerney, J. M., & Roberts, T. S. (2004). Online learning: Social interaction and the creation of a sense of community. *Journal of Educational Technology & Society, 7*(3), 73–81.

McKimm, J., & Swanwick, T. (2009). Setting learning objectives. *British Journal of Hospital Medicine, 70*(7), 406–409. doi:10.12968/hmed.2009.70.7.43125 PMID:19584784

McKinney, J. P., McKinney, K. G., Franiuk, R., & Schweitzer, J. (2006). The College Classroom as a Community: Impact on Student Attitudes and Learning. *College Teaching, 54*(3), 281–284. doi:10.3200/CTCH.54.3.281-284

McLean, V. (1999). Becoming a teacher: The person in the process. In R. Lipka & T. Brinthhaupt (Eds.), *The role of self in teacher development*. Albany, NY: SUNY Press.

McMillan, J. H., & Hearn, J. (2008). Student self-assessment: The key to stronger student motivation and higher achievement. *Education Digest, 74*, 39–44.

McPherson, M. A., & Nunes, J. M. B. (2004). The role of tutors as an integral part of online learning support. *European Journal of Open and Distance Learning*. Retrieved from http://www.eurodl.org/materials/contrib/2004/Maggie_MsP.html

McSweeney, B. (2002). Hofstede's model of national cultural differences and their consequences: A triumph of faith – a failure of analysis. *Human Relations, 55*(1), 89–118. doi:10.1177/0018726702055001602

Mead, G. H. (1934). *Mind, self and society*. Chicago: U. of Chicago Press.

Mead, G. H. (1934). *Mind, self, and society*. Chicago, IL: University of Chicago Press.

Means, B., Toyama, Y., Murphy, R., Bakia, M., & Jones, K. (2010). *Evaluation of evidence-based practices in online learning: A meta-analysis and review of online learning studies*. Retrieved from the Department of Education: http://www.ed.gov/about/offices/list/opepd/ppss/reports.html

Means, B., Toyama, Y., Murphy, R., & Baki, M. (2013). The effectiveness of online and blended learning: A meta-analysis of the empirical literature. *Teachers College Record, 115*, 47–69.

Means, T., Johnson, D., & Graff, R. (2013). Lessons learned from a course management system review at the University of Florida. In Y. Kats (Ed.), *Learning Management Systems and Instructional Design: Best Practices in Online Education* (pp. 55–71). Hershey, PA: IGI Global. doi:10.4018/978-1-4666-3930-0.ch004

Megginson, D., & Clutterbuck, D. (2005). *Techniques for coaching and mentoring*. Oxford, UK: Elsevier Butterworth-Heinemann.

Mehlenbacher, B. (2010). *Instruction and Technology: Designs for Everyday Learning*. The MIT Press. doi:10.7551/mitpress/9780262013949.001.0001

Mehrabian, A. (1967). Orientation behaviors and nonverbal attitude communication. *Journal of Communication, 17*(4), 324–332. doi:10.1111/j.1460-2466.1967.tb01190.x PMID:5588696

Merlose, Sh., & Bergeron, K. (2007). Instructor immediacy strategies to facilitate group work in online graduate study. *Australasian Journal of Educational Technology, 23*(1), 132–148.

Merriam, S. B. (2001). Andragogy and self-directed learning: Pillars of adult learning theory. *New Directions for Adult and Continuing Education, 89*, 53–63.

Merriam, S. B. (2001). *Qualitative research and case study applications in education*. San Francisco: Jossey-Bass.

Merriam, S. B. (2010). Globalization and the role of adult and continuing education. In C. E. Kasworm, A. D. Rose, & J. M. Ross-Gordon (Eds.), *Handbook of adult and continuing education* (pp. 401–409). Los Angeles, CA: Sage Publications, Inc.

Merriam, S. B., Caffarella, R. S., & Baumgartner, L. M. (2007). *Learning in adulthood: A comprehensive guide* (3rd ed.). San Francisco: Jossey-Bass.

Merriam, S., & Caffarella, R. (1999). *Learning in Adulthood*. San Francisco: Jossey Bass.

Merrill, M. D. (2007). A task-centered instructional strategy. *Journal of Research on Technology in Education, 40*(1), 5–22. doi:10.1080/15391523.2007.10782493

Merryfield, M. M. (2001). Engaging with issues of cultural diversity and discrimination through critical emotional reflexivity in online learning. *Adult Education Quarterly, 59*, 61–82.

Merryfield, M. M. (2001). The paradoxes of teaching a multicultural education course online. *Journal of Teacher Education, 52*(4), 283–299. doi:10.1177/0022487101052004003

Messick, S. (1989). Validity. In R. L. Linn (Ed.), *Educational measurement* (3rd ed., pp. 13–103). New York, NY: Macmillan.

Meyen, E. L., Lian, C. H. T., & Tangen, P. (1997). Developing online instruction: One model. *Focus on Autism and Other Developmental Disabilities, 12*(3), 159–165. doi:10.1177/108835769701200304

Meyer, K. A., & Jones, S. J. (2013). Do students experience flow conditions online? *Journal of Asynchronous Learning Networks, 17*(3), 137-148. Retrieved from ERIC database (EJ1018299)

Meyer, K. A. (2003). Face-to-face versus threaded discussions: The role of time and higher order thinking. *Asynchronous Learning Networks, 7*(3), 55–65.

Meyer, K. A., & McNeal, L. (2011). How online faculty improve student learning productivity. *Journal of Asynchronous Learning Networks, 15*(3), 37–53.

Micari, M., & Pazos, P. (2014). Worrying about what others think: A social-comparison concern intervention in small learning groups. *Active Learning in Higher Education, 15*(3), 249–262. doi:10.1177/1469787414544874

Michael, J. (2006). Where's the evidence that active learning works? *Advances in Physiology Education, 30*(4), 159–167. doi:10.1152/advan.00053.2006 PMID:17108243

Michinov, N., Brunot, S., Le Bohec, O., Juhel, J., & Delaval, M. (2011). Procrastination, participation, and performance in online learning environments. *Computers & Education, 56*(1), 243–252. doi:10.1016/j.compedu.2010.07.025

Miles, M., & Huberman, A. M. (1994). *Qualitative data analysis: An expanded sourcebook* (2nd ed.). Thousand Oaks, CA: Sage.

Miller, M. D. (2014). *Minds online: Teaching effectively with technology*. Cambridge, MA: Harvard University Press. doi:10.4159/harvard.9780674735996

Milligan, C., Littlejohn, A., & Margaryan, A. (2013). Patterns of engagement in connectivist MOOCs. *Journal of Online Learning and Teaching, 9*(2), 149–159. Retrieved from http://jolt.merlot.org/vol9no2/milligan_0613.pdf

Milne, S., Orbell, S., & Sheeran, P. (2002). Combining motivational and volitional interventions to promote exercise participation: Protection motivation theory and implementation intentions. *British Journal of Health Psychology, 7*(2), 163–184. doi:10.1348/135910702169420 PMID:14596707

Miltiadou, M., & Savenye, W. C. (2003). Applying social cognitive constructs of motivation to enhance student success in online distance education. *AACE Journal, 11*, 78–95.

Minguillon, J., Sicilia, M., & Lamb, B. (2011). From content management to e-learning content repositories. *Content Management for E-Learning*. Retrieved from http://content.schweitzer-online.de/static/content/catalog/newbooks/978/144/196/9781441969583/9781441969583_Excerpt_001.pdf

Misanchuk, M., & Anderson, T. (2001). Building Community in an Online Learning Environment: Communication, Cooperation and Collaboration. In *Proceedings of the Annual Mid-South Instructional Technology Conference*. Retrieved from http://www.mtsu.edu/-itconf/proceed01/19.pdf

Mischel, W. (1974). In L. Berkowitz (Ed.), Advances in experimental social psychology: Vol. 7. *Processes in delay of gratification*. New York, NY: Academic Press.

Miserandino, M. (1996). Children who do well in school: Individual differences in perceived competence and autonomy in above-average children. *Journal of Educational Psychology, 88*(2), 203–214. doi:10.1037/0022-0663.88.2.203

Mitchell, R. L. (2010). Approaching common ground: Defining quality in online education. *New Directions for Community Colleges, 150*(150), 89–94. doi:10.1002/cc.408

Miyazoe, T., & Anderson, T. (2010). Learning outcomes and students' perceptions of online writing: Simultaneous implementation of a forum, blog, and wiki in an EFL blended learning setting. *System, 38*(2), 185–199. doi:10.1016/j.system.2010.03.006

Moller, L. (1998). Designing communities of learners for asynchronous distance education. *Educational Technology Research and Development, 46*(4), 115–122. doi:10.1007/BF02299678

Moon, J. (1999a). *Learning Journals: a Handbook for Academics, Students and Professional Development*. London: Kogan Page.

Moon, J. (1999b). *Reflection in Learning and Professional Development, Theory and Practice*. London: Kogan Page.

Moore, A., Masterson, J. T., Christophel, D. M., & Shea, K. A. (1996). College teacher immediacy and student ratings of instruction. *Communication Education, 45*(1), 29–39. doi:10.1080/03634529609379030

Moore, J. (2014). Effects of online interaction and instructor presence on students' satisfaction and success with online undergraduate public relations courses. *Journalism & Mass Communication Educator, 69*(3), 271–288. doi:10.1177/1077695814536398

Moore, J. C. (Ed.). (2002). *Elements of quality: The Sloan-C Framework*. Needham, MA: Sloan Center for Online Education.

Moore, M. G. (1972). Learner autonomy: The second dimension of independent learning. *Convergence, 5*(2), 76–88.

Moore, M. G. (1973). Towards a theory of independent learning and teaching. *The Journal of Higher Education, 44*(9), 661–679. doi:10.2307/1980599

Moore, M. G. (1989). Three types of interaction. *American Journal of Distance Education, 3*(2), 1–6. doi:10.1080/08923648909526659

Moore, M. G. (1992). Distance education theory. *American Journal of Distance Education, 5*(3), 1–6. doi:10.1080/08923649109526758

Moore, M. G. (1997). Theory of transactional distance. In D. Keegan (Ed.), *Theoretical principles of distance education* (pp. 22–38). London, UK: Routledge.

Moore, M. G., & Kearsley, G. (2012). *Distance education: A systems view of online learning* (3rd ed.). Belmont, VA: Wadsworth Cengage Learning.

Moore, R. L. (2014). Importance of developing community in distance education courses. *TechTrends, 58*(2), 20–24. doi:10.1007/s11528-014-0733-x

Moran, M., Seaman, J., & Tinti-Kane, H. (2011). Teaching, learning, and sharing: How today's higher education faculty use social media. *Pearson Learning Solutions*. Retrieved from http://files.eric.ed.gov/fulltext/ED535130.pdf

Moray, N. (1959). Attention in dichotic listening: Affective cues and the influence of instructions. *The Quarterly Journal of Experimental Psychology, 34*, 740–754.

Morrison, G. R., Lowther, L. L., & Demeulle, L. (1999). *Integrating computer technology into the Classroom*. Upper Saddle River, NJ: Prentice Hall.

Morrison, G. R., Ross, S. M., Kemp, J. E., & Kalman, H. (2010). *Designing effective instruction*. Hoboken, NJ: John Wiley & Sons.

Mott, J. (2010). Envisioning the post LMS-era: The Open Learning Network. *EDUCAUSE Quarterly, 33*, 1–9. Retrieved from http://www.educause.edu/ero/article/envisioning-post-lms-era-open-learning-network

Muilenburg, L., & Berge, Z. (2005). Student Barriers to Online Learning: A factor analytic study. *Distance Education, 26*(1), 29–48. doi:10.1080/01587910500081269

Muirhead, B. (2002). Salmon's research. *USDLA Journal, 16*(5).

Muirhead, B. (2001). Interactivity research studies. *Journal of Educational Technology & Society, 4*(3).

Mullenberg, L. Y., & Berge, Z. L. (2001). Barriers to distance education: A factor analytic study. *American Journal of Distance Education, 15*(2), 7–22. doi:10.1080/08923640109527081

Mupinga, D.M., Nora, R.T., & Yaw, D.C., (2006). The learning styles, expectations and needs of online students. *College Teaching, 54*(1), 185-189. Retrieved from Ebscohost on October 13, 2013.

Mupinga, D. M., Nora, R. T., & Yaw, D. C. (2006). The learning styles, expectations, and needs of online students. *College Teaching, 54*(1), 185–189. doi:10.3200/CTCH.54.1.185-189

Murphy, E. (2004). Identifying and measuring ill-structured problem formulation and resolution in online asynchronous discussions. *Canadian Journal of Learning and Technology, 30*(1), 5-20.

Murphy, K., Smith, P., & Stacey, E. (2002). Teaching presence in computer conferencing: lessons from the United States and Australia. In *Proceedings of International conference on computers in education* (ICCE 2002), (pp. 694-698). IEEE Computer Society Press. doi:10.1109/CIE.2002.1186046

Murphy, K. L., Mahoney, S. E., Chen, C. Y., Mendoza-Diaz, N. V., & Yang, X. (2005). A constructivist model of mentoring, coaching, and facilitating online discussions. *Distance Education, 26*(3), 341–366. doi:10.1080/01587910500291454

Murray, M., Pérez, J., Geist, D., & Hedrick, A. (2013). Student interaction with content in online and hybrid courses: Leading horses to the proverbial water. *Informing Science, 16*, 99–115.

Myers, I. B. (1993). *Introduction to type.* Palo Alto, CA: Consulting Psychologists Press.

Nagler, W., & Ebner, M. (2009). Is your university ready for the Ne(x)t-Generation? In J. Luca, & E. Weippl (Eds.), *Proceedings of 21st world conference on educational multimedia, hypermedia and telecommunications* (pp. 4344–4351). Honolulu, HI: Academic Press.

Nag, R., Hambrick, D. C., & Chen, M. (2007). What is strategic management, really? Inductive derivation of a consensus definition of the field. *Strategic Management Journal, 28*(9), 935–955. doi:10.1002/smj.615

Nahl, D. (1996). Affective monitoring of Internet learners: Perceived self-efficacy and success. *Proceedings of the ASIS, 33*, 100–109.

Nandi, D., Hamilton, M., Chang, S., & Balbo, S. (2012). Evaluating quality in online asynchronous interactions between students and discussion facilitators. *Australasian Journal of Educational Technology, 28*(4), 684–702. Retrieved from http://www.ascilite.org.au/ajet/ajet28/nandi.pdf

Nandi, D., Hamilton, M., & Harland, J. (2012). Evaluating the quality of interaction in asynchronous discussion forums in fully online courses. *Distance Education, 33*(1), 5–30. doi:10.1080/01587919.2012.667957

Nash, R. (2005). Course completion rates among distance learners: Identifying possible methods to improve retention. *Online Journal of Distance Learning Administration, 8.* Retrieved from http://www.westga.edu/%7Edistance/ojdla/winter84/nash84.htm

National Center for Education Statistics. (2006). *Internet Access in U.S. Public Schools and Classrooms: 1994–2005.* (NCES 2007-020). U.S. Department of Education. Retrieved January 30, 2015 from http://nces.ed.gov/pubsearch/pubsinfo.asp?pubid=2007020

National center for Education Statistics. (2011). *Open Doors: Report on International Educational Exchange, 1981 through 2010 (selected years).* Institute of International Education.

National Center for Education Statistics. (2012). *Distance education at degree-granting post-secondary institutions.* Retrieved from http://nces.ed.gov/pubsearch/pubsinfo.asp

National Center for Education Statistics. (2014). *The condition of education (NCES 2014-083), English Language Learners.* Department of Education.

National Center for Educational Statistics. (2003). *Distance education at degree granting post secondary institutions.* Retrieved January 20, 2015, from National Center for Educational Statistics: http://nces.ed.gov/pubsearch/pubsinfo

National Survey of Student Engagement. (2014). Center for Postsecondary Research, Indiana University School of Education, Bloomington, IND. Retrieved October 11, 2014 from http://nsse.iub.edu/NSSE_2014_Results/pdf/NSSE_2014_Annual_Results.pdf#page=8

National Survey of Student Engagement. (2014a). *What is student engagement?* Retrieved from http://nsse.iub.edu/html/about.cfm

National Survey of Student Engagement. (2014b). *Engagement indicators.* Retrieved from http://nsse.iub.edu/html/engagement_indicators.cfm

Natriello, G. (1984). Problems in the evaluation of students and student disengagement from secondary schools. *Journal of Research and Development in Education, 17*(4), 14–24.

Navarro, P., & Shoemaker, J. (2000). Performance and perceptions of distance learners, in cyberspace. *American Journal of Distance Education, 14*(2), 15–35. doi:10.1080/08923640009527052

Nawaz, A., & Khan, M. Z. (2012). Issues of technical support for e-learning systems in higher education institutions. *International Journal of Modern Education and Computer Science, 4*(2), 38–44. doi:10.5815/ijmecs.2012.02.06

Nelson, S. J., & Thompson, G. W. (2005). Barriers perceived by administrators and faculty regarding the use of distance education technologies in pre-service programs for secondary agricultural education teachers. *Journal of Agricultural Education, 46*(4), 36–48. doi:10.5032/jae.2005.04036

Newberry, B. (2001). Raising Student Social Presence in Online Classes. In *WebNet 2001.Proceedings of the World Conference on the WWW and Internet.* Norfolk, VA: AACE.

Ng'ambi, D., & Lombe, A. (2011). Using podcasting to facilitate student learning: A constructivist perspective. *Journal of Educational Technology & Society, 15*(4), 181–192.

Nguyen, T. T., & Trimarchi, A. (2010). Active learning in introductory economics: Do MyEconLab and Aplia make any difference? *International Journal for the Scholarship of Teaching and Learning, 4*(1), 10. Retrieved from http://digitalcommons.georgiasouthern.edu/cgi/viewcontent.cgi?article=1210&context=ij-sotl

Nicol, D. (2009). Assessment for learner self-regulation: Enhancing achievement in the first year using learning technologies. *Assessment & Evaluation in Higher Education, 34*(3), 335–352. doi:10.1080/02602930802255139

Nicol, D. (2010). From monologue to dialogue: Improving written feedback processes in mass higher education. *Assessment & Evaluation in Higher Education, 35*(5), 501–517. doi:10.1080/02602931003786559

Nicol, D., & Macfarlane-Dick, D. (2006). Formative assessment and self-regulated learning: A model and seven principles of good practice. *Studies in Higher Education, 31*(2), 199–218. doi:10.1080/03075070600572090

Nieto, S. (1999). *The light in their eyes: Creating multicultural learning communities.* New York: Teachers College Press.

Nieto, S. (2000). Placing equity front and center: Some thoughts on transforming teacher education for a new century. *Journal of Teacher Education, 51*(3), 180–187. doi:10.1177/0022487100051003004

Nieto, S., & Bode, P. (2012). *Affirming diversity: The sociopolitical context of multicultural education* (6th ed.). Boston, MA: Allyn and Bacon.

Noel, J. G., Forsythe, D. R., & Kelly, K. N. (1987). Improving performance of failing students by overcoming their self-serving attributional biases. *Basic and Applied Psychology, 8*(1-2), 151–162. doi:10.1080/01973533.1987.9645882

Northedge, A. (2002). Teaching by Distance Education. In W. J. McKeachie (Ed.), *Teaching Tips* (11th ed.; pp. 258–267). Boston, MA: Houghton-Mifflin.

Northrup, P. T. (2002). Online learners' preferences for interaction. *The Quarterly Review of Distance Education, 3*, 219–226.

Nota, L., Soresi, S., & Zimmerman, B. J. (2004). Self-regulation and academic achievement and resilience: A longitudinal study. *International Journal of Educational Research, 41*(3), 198–215. doi:10.1016/j.ijer.2005.07.001

Noyé, D., & Piveteau, J. (1997). *Guide pratique du formateur.* INSEP Editions.

Ntoumanis, N. (2001). A prospective study of participation in optional school physical education based on self-determination theory. *Journal of Educational Psychology, 97*(3), 444–453. doi:10.1037/0022-0663.97.3.444

Nuangchalerm, P., Prachagool, V., & Sriputta, P. (2011). Online professional experiences in teacher preparation program: A pre-service teacher study. *Canadian Social Science, 7*(5), 116–120.

Nunez, Y. S. (2005). Assessing faculty's social presence indicators in online courses. *Focus IV, I*, 47–49.

O'Brien, G. (2002). *Issues Paper 3: A sense of belonging.* Retrieved October 12, 2014 from http://www.fye.qut.edu.au/documents/FYIEissues&5Fpaper%5F3.pdf

O'Keefe, P. A., Ben-Eliyahu, A., & Linnenbrink-Garcia, L. (2013). Shaping achievement goal orientations in a mastery-structured environment and concomitant changes in related contingencies of self-worth. *Motivation and Emotion, 37*(1), 50–64. doi:10.1007/s11031-012-9293-6

O'Leary, P. F., & Quinlan, T. Jr. (2007). Learner–instructor telephone interaction: Effects on satisfaction and achievement of online students. *American Journal of Distance Education, 21*(3), 133–143. doi:10.1080/08923640701341661

Oblinger, D. G. (Ed.). (2006). *Learning spaces.* EDUCAUSE. Retrieved from http://net.educause.edu/ir/library/pdf/PUB7102.pdf

Oblinger, D. G., & Hawkins, B. L. (2006). The myth about online course development:" A faculty member can individually develop and deliver an effective online course. *EDUCAUSE Review, 41*(1), 14–15.

Oblinger, D. G., & Oblinger, J. S. (Eds.). (2005). *Educating the Net generation.* Boulder, CO: EDUCAUSE.

O'Donnell, M. (2006). Blogging as pedagogic practice: Artefact and ecology. *Asia Pacific Media Educator, 17*, 5–19.

O'Dowd, R. (2003). Understanding the "other side": Intercultural learning in a Spanish-English e-mail exchange. *Language Learning & Technology, 7*(2), 118–144.

Ogle, D. M. (1986). K-W-L: A model that develops active reading of expository text. *The Reading Teacher, 39*(6), 564–570. doi:10.1598/RT.39.6.11

Ohia, U. O. (2011). A model for effectively assessing student learning outcomes. *Contemporary Issues in Education Research, 4*(3), 25–32.

Olesova, L., Yang, D., & Richardson, J. C. (2011). Cross-cultural differences in undergraduate students' perceptions of online barriers. *Journal of Asynchronous Learning Networks, 15*(3), 68–80.

Oliveira, P. C., & Oliveira, C. G. (2013). Using conceptual questions to promote motivation and learning in physics lectures. *European Journal of Engineering Education, 38*(4), 417–424. doi:10.1080/03043797.2013.780013

Oliver, R., & Omari, A. (1999). Using online technologies to support problem-based learning: Learners responses and perceptions. *Australasian Journal of Educational Technology, 15*, 158–179.

O'Neil, C. A., Fisher, C. A., & Rietschel, M. J. (2014). *Developing online learning environments in nursing education.* New York, NY: Springer.

Onwuegbuzie, A. J., & Leech, N. L. (2005). On becoming a pragmatic researcher: The importance of combining quantitative and qualitative research methodologies. *International Journal of Social Research Methodology, 8*(5), 375–387. doi:10.1080/13645570500402447

Onwuegbuzie, A. J., Leech, N. L., & Collins, K. M. (2012). Qualitative analysis techniques for the review of the literature. *Qualitative Report, 17*(56), 1–28.

Onwuegbuzie, A. J., & Teddlie, C. (2003). A framework for analyzing data in mixed methods research. In A. Tashakkori & C. Teddlie (Eds.), *Handbook of mixed methods in social and behavioral research* (pp. 351–383). Thousand Oaks, CA: Sage.

Oravec, J. A. (2002). Bookmarking the world: Weblog applications in education. *Journal of Adolescent & Adult Literacy, 45*(7), 616–621.

Orly, M. (2007). Multicultural e-learning project and comparison of teachers' student teacher' and pupils' perceptions about e-learning. *Multicultural Education & Technology Journal*, *1*(3), 178–191. doi:10.1108/17504970710822377

Orr, L. M., & Hauser, W. J. (2008). A re-inquiry of Hofstede's cultural dimensions: A call for 21st century cross-cultural research. *The Marketing Management Journal*, *18*(2), 1–19.

Osborne, R. E., Kriese, P., Tobey, H., & Johnson, E. (2009). And never the two shall meet? Student vs. faculty perceptions of online courses. *Journal of Educational Computing Research*, *40*(2), 171–182. doi:10.2190/EC.40.2.b

Ovando, M. N. (1994). Constructive feedback: A key to successful teaching and learning. *International Journal of Educational Management*, *8*(6), 19–22. doi:10.1108/09513549410069185

Owston, R. D. (1997). The World Wide Web: A technology to enhance teaching and learning. *Educational Researcher*, 27–33.

Özdemir, S. (2010). Supporting printed books with multimedia: A new way to use mobile technology for learning. *British Journal of Educational Technology*, *41*(6), 135–138. doi:10.1111/j.1467-8535.2010.01071.x

Özmen, B., & Atıcı, B. (2014). Learners' Views Regarding the Use of Social Networking Sites in Distance Learning. *International Review of Research in Open and Distance Learning*, *15*(4), 21–42.

Oztok, M., Zingaro, D., Brett, C., & Hewitt, J. (2013). Exploring asynchronous and synchronous tool use in online courses. *Computers & Education*, *60*(1), 87–94. doi:10.1016/j.compedu.2012.08.007

Ozturk, E. O. (2012). Contemporary motivation theories in educational psychology and language learning: An overview. *The International Journal of Social Sciences*, *3*, 33–46.

Paechter, M., & Maier, B. (2010). Online or face-to-face? Students' experiences and preferences in e-learning. *The Internet and Higher Education*, *13*(4), 292–297. doi:10.1016/j.iheduc.2010.09.004

Paechter, M., Maier, B., & Macher, D. (2010). Students' expectations of and experiences in e-learning: Their relation to learning achievements and course satisfaction. *Computers & Education*, *54*(1), 222–229. doi:10.1016/j.compedu.2009.08.005

Pale, P. (2013). Intrinsic deficiencies of lectures as a teaching method.[PubMed]. *Collegium Antropologicum*, *37*(2), 551–559. Retrieved from http://www.collantropol.hr/antropo/article/view/70/30 PMID:23941004

Palloff, R. M., & Pratt, K. (2001). *Lessons from the cyberspace classroom: The realities of online teaching*. San Francisco, CA: Jossey-Bass.

Palloff, R. M., & Pratt, K. (2003). *Virtual student: A profile and guide to working with online learners*. San Francisco, CA: Jossey-Bass.

Palloff, R. M., & Pratt, K. (2005). *Collaborating online: Learning together in community*. San Francisco, CA: Jossey-Bass.

Palloff, R. N., & Pratt, K. (1999). *Building learning communities in cyberspace*. San Francisco: Jossey-Bass.

Palloff, R. N., & Pratt, K. (2001). *Lessons from the cyberspace classroom: The realties of online teaching*. San Francisco: Jossey-Bass.

Palloff, R. N., & Pratt, K. (2003). *The virtual student: A profile and guide to working with online learners*. San Francisco: Jossey-Bass.

Panadero, E., & Jesus, A. (2013). Self-assessment: Theoretical and practical connotations. When it happens, how is it acquired, and what to do to develop it in our students. *Electronic Journal of Research in Educational Psychology*, *11*(2), 551–576. doi:10.14204/ejrep.30.12200

Pan, C., & Sullivan, M. (2005). Promoting synchronous interaction in an eLearning environment. *Technical Horizons in Education*, *33*(2), 27–30.

Pang, K. (2008). Sophist or Socratic teaching methods in fostering learning in U.S. graduate education. *International Journal of Learning*, *15*(6), 197–201.

Pankowski, P. (2004). Faculty training for online teaching. *THE Journal*. Retrieved from: http://thejournal.com/Articles/2004/09/01/Faculty-Training-for-Online-Teaching.aspx

Pan, Y., Xu, Y. C., Wang, X., Zhang, C., Ling, H., & Lin, J. (2014). Integrating social networking support for dyadic knowledge exchange: A study in a virtual community of practice. *Information & Management, 52*(1), 61–70. doi:10.1016/j.im.2014.10.001

Papacharissi, Z. (2006). Audiences as media producers: content analysis of 260 blogs. In M. Tremayne (Ed.), *Blogging, citizenship, and the future of media* (pp. 21–38). New York: Routledge.

Pappano, L. (2012, November 2). Massive open online courses are multiplying at a rapid pace. *The New York Times*. Retrieved from: http://www.nytimes.com

Pareto, V. (1971). *Manual of political economy*. New York: A.M. Kelley.

Park, C. L., Perry, B., & Edwards, M. (2011). Minimizing attrition: Strategies for assisting students who are at risk of withdrawal. *Innovations in Education and Teaching International, 48*(1), 37–47. doi:10.1080/14703297.2010.543769

Parker, K., Lenhart, A., & Moore, K. (2011). *Digital revolution and higher education*. Pew Research Center. Retrieved from http://www.pewsocialtrends.org/files/2011/08/online-learning.pdf

Parker, E. B., & Howland, L. C. (2006). Strategies to manage the time demands of online teaching. *Nurse Educator, 31*(6), 270–274. doi:10.1097/00006223-200611000-00012 PMID:17108792

Parker, J., Maor, D., & Herrington, J. (2013). Authentic online learning: Aligning learner needs, pedagogy, and technology. *Issues in Educational Research, 3*(2), 227–241. Retrieved from http://www.iier.org.au/iier23/parker.pdf

Parkinson, C. (1955). *Parkinson's law*. Retrieved from: http://www.economist.com/node/14116121

Park, J. Y., & Bonk, C. J. (2007). Synchronous learning experiences: Distance and residential learners' perspectives in a blended graduate course. *Journal of Interactive Online Learning, 6*(3), 245–254.

Park, J., & Choi, H. J. (2009). Factors influencing adult learners' decision to drop out or persist in online learning. *Journal of Educational Technology & Society, 12*(4), 207–217.

Parra, S. (2012). Component display theory design in a foreign language unit. *Journal of Applied Learning Technology, 2*(3), 23–32.

Parsad, B., & Lewis, L. (2008). *Distance education at degree-granting postsecondary institutions: 2006-2007 (U.S. Department of Education, National Center for Education Statistics, NCES 2009-044)*. Washington, DC: U.S. Government Printing Office.

Parton, B. S., Crain-Dorough, M., & Hancock, R. (2010). Using flip camcorders to create video feedback: Is it realistic for professors and beneficial to students? *International Journal of Instructional Technology and Distance Learning, 7*(1), 15–23.

Partridge, H., & Hallam, G. (2005). New pathways to learning:The team teaching Approach. A library and Information Science Case Study. In E. Cohen (Ed.), *Issues in informing Science and Information Technology, v2* (pp. 103–118). Informing Science Press.

Pashler, H., McDaniel, M., Rohrer, D., & Bjork, R. (2008). Learning styles: Concepts and evidence.[PubMed]. *Psychological Science in the Public Interest, 9*(3), 105–119. PMID:26162104

Pastore, R. S., Land, S. M., & Jung, E. J. (2011). Mobile computing in higher education. In D. W. Surry, J. R. Stefurak, & R. M. Gray Jr., (Eds.), *Technology Integration in higher education: Social and organizational aspects* (pp. 160–173). Hershey, PA: IGI Global. doi:10.4018/978-1-60960-147-8.ch012

Pate, A., Smaldino, S., Mayall, H. J., & Luetkehans, L. (2009). Questioning the necessity of nonacademic social discussion forums within online courses. *The Quarterly Review of Distance Education, 10*(1), 1–8.

Patel, K. (2015). Planning, designing, implementing, and managing social presence in online programs and online classes. In R. D. Wright (Ed.), *Student-teacher interaction in online learning environments*. Hershey, PA: IGI Global. doi:10.4018/978-1-4666-6461-6.ch016

Patrick, H., Kaplan, A., & Ryan, A. M. (2011). Positive classroom motivational environments: Convergence between mastery goal structure and the classroom social climate. *Journal of Educational Psychology, 103*(2), 367–382. doi:10.1037/a0023311

Patron, H., & Lopez, S. (2011). Student effort, consistency, and online performance. *Journal of Educators Online, 8*, 1–11.

Patterson, B., & McFadden, C. (2009). Attrition in online and campus degree programs. *Online Journal of Distance Learning Administration, 12*(2). Retrieved from http://www.westga.edu/~distance/ojdla/summer122/patterson112.html

Patton, S. (2014, October). On the Internet, nobody knows you're the 'wrong' professor. *Chronicle Vitae.* Retrieved from https://chroniclevitae.com/news/733-on-the-internet-nobody-knows-you-re-the-wrong-professor

Paul, G., & Verhulst, S. (2010). Improving reading comprehension skills of minority adults from educationally disadvantaged backgrounds. *Journal of Adolescent & Adult Literacy, 54*(2), 131–140. doi:10.1598/JAAL.54.2.5

Paulsen, M. F. (1995). *The online report on pedagogical techniques for computer-mediated communication.* Retrieved from http://emoderators.com/wp-content/uploads/cmcped.html

Pavlis-Korres, M. (2010). *Development of a framework for the e- education of educators of special groups aiming to improve their compatibility with their learners.* (PhD Thesis). University of Alcalá.

Pavlis-Korres, M., Karalis, T., Leftheriotou, P., & García Barriocanal, E. (2009). Integrating Adults' Characteristics and the Requirements for their Effective Learning in an e-Learning Environment. In Lytras et al. (Eds.), *Best Practices for the Knowledge Society,* (pp. 570-584). Springer.

Pavlis-Korres, M. (2012). The Role of the Communication Tools in the Development of the Learning Group in an Online Environment. *International Journal of Engineering Education, 28*(6), 1360–1365.

Pavlis-Korres, M. (2013). Key Factors for Maximizing the Effectiveness of Blended E-Learning: The Outcome of the Internal Evaluation of a Distance Education Program for Adult Learning in Greece. In L. Kyei-Blankson & E. Ntuli (Eds.), *Practical Applications in Blended Learning Environments: Experiences in K-20 Education* (pp. 410–437). IGI Global.

Pawan, F., Paulus, T. M., Yalcin, S., & Chang, C. F. (2003). Online learning: Patterns of engagement and interaction among in-service teachers. *Language Learning & Technology, 7*(3), 119–140.

Pearce, J. M., & Howard, S. (2004). *Designing for flow in a complex activity.* Paper presented at the 6th Asia-Pacific Conference on Computer-Human Interaction, New Zealand. doi:10.1007/978-3-540-27795-8_35

Pearce, J. M., Ainley, M., & Howard, S. (2005). The ebb and flow of online learning. *Computers in Human Behavior, 21*(5), 745–771. doi:10.1016/S0747-5632(04)00036-6

Pearson, M. (2012). Building bridges: Higher degree student retention and counseling support. *Journal of Higher Education Policy and Management, 34*(2), 187–199. doi:10.1080/1360080X.2012.662743

Pearson, P. D., & Gallagher, M. C. (1983). The instruction of reading comprehension. *Contemporary Educational Psychology, 8*(3), 317–344. doi:10.1016/0361-476X(83)90019-X

Pelz, B. (2004). Three principles of effective online pedagogy. *Journal of Asynchronous Learning Networks, 14*(1), 103–116.

Pence, H. (2013). When will college truly leave the building: If MOOCs are the answer, what is the question? *Journal of Educational Technology Systems, 41*(1), 25–33. doi:10.2190/ET.41.1.c

Penn, S. (Producer & Director). (2007). *Into The Wild.* [Motion Picture]. United States: Paramount Vantage.

Pennebaker, J., Chung, C., Ireland, M., Gonzales, A., & Booth, R. (2007). *The development and psychometric properties of LIWC 2007*. Retrieved from: http://www. liwc.net/LIWC2007LanguageManual.pdf

Pennebaker, J. W., Chun, C. K., Frazee, J., Lavergne, G. M., & Beaver, D. I. (2014). When small words foretell academic success: The case of college admissions essays. *PLoS ONE*, *9*(12), e115844. doi:10.1371/journal. pone.0115844 PMID:25551217

Pennsylvania State University. (2014). *Student self-assessment for online learning readiness*. Retrieved from http://ets.tlt.psu.edu/learningdesign/assessment/onlinecontent/online_readiness

Penprase, B. (2012). Perceptions, orientation, and transition into nursing practice of accelerated second-degree nursing program graduates. *Journal of Continuing Education in Nursing*, *43*(1), 29–36. doi:10.3928/00220124-20110315-02 PMID:21425758

Penprase, B., & Koczara, S. (2009). Understanding the experiences of accelerated second-degree nursing students and graduates: A review of the literature. *Journal of Continuing Education in Nursing*, *40*(2), 74–78. doi:10.3928/00220124-20090201-08 PMID:19263928

Perry, R. (2003). Perceived (academic) control and causal thinking in achievement settings. *Canadian Psychology*, *44*(4), 312–331. doi:10.1037/h0086956

Persson, E. (Producer) & Harvey, A. (Director). (1967). *Dutchman*. [Motion Picture]. United Kingdom: Dutchman Film Company.

Peters, J. (Producer) & (Director) Ramis, H. (1980). *Caddyshack*. [Motion Picture]. United States: Orion.

Phillips, J., & Phillips, M. (Producers) & Scorsese, M. (Director). (1976). *Taxi Driver*. [Motion Picture]. United States: Paramount.

Piaget, J. (2003). Development and thinking. *Journal of Research in Science Teaching*, *40*, 8–18.

Picciano, A. G., & Seaman, J. (2007). K-12 online learning. A survey of U.S. school district administrators. Boston: Sloan Consortium. Retrieved from http://www.sloan-c.org/publications/survey/K-12_06.asp

Picciano, A. G. (2002). Beyond student perceptions: Issues of interaction, presence, and performance in an online course. *Journal of Asynchronous Learning Networks*, *6*(1), 21–40.

Pintrich, P. R. (2000). An achievement goal theory perspective on issues in motivation terminology, theory, and research. *Contemporary Educational Psychology*, *25*(1), 92–104. doi:10.1006/ceps.1999.1017 PMID:10620384

Pintrich, P. R. (2002). The role of metacognitive knowledge in learning, teaching, and assessing. *Theory into Practice*, *41*(4), 219–225. doi:10.1207/s15430421tip4104_3

Pintrich, P. R. (2003). A motivational science perspective on the role of student motivation in learning and teaching contexts. *Journal of Educational Psychology*, *95*(4), 667–686. doi:10.1037/0022-0663.95.4.667

Pintrich, P. R. (2004). A conceptual framework for assessing motivation and self-regulated learning in college students. *Educational Psychology Review*, *16*(4), 385–407. doi:10.1007/s10648-004-0006-x

Pintrich, P. R., & De Groot, V. (1990). Motivational and self-regulated learning components of classroom academic performance. *Journal of Educational Psychology*, *82*(1), 33–40. doi:10.1037/0022-0663.82.1.33

Pintrich, P. R., & Garcia, T. (1994). Taking control of research on volitional control: Challenges for the future theory and research. *Learning and Individual Differences*, *11*(3), 335–351. doi:10.1016/S1041-6080(99)80007-7

Pintrich, P. R., Smith, D. A., Garcia, T., & McKeachie, W. J. (1993). Reliability and predictive validity of the motivated strategies for learning questionnaire (MLSQ). *Educational and Psychological Measurement*, *53*(3), 801–813. doi:10.1177/0013164493053003024

Pintrich, P. R., & Zusho, A. (2002). The development of academic self-regulation: The role of cognitive and motivational factors. In A. Wigfield & J. S. Eccles (Eds.), *Development of achievement motivation* (pp. 249–284). San Diego, CA: Academic Press. doi:10.1016/B978-012750053-9/50012-7

Pittman, L. D., & Richmond, A. (2008). University belonging, friendship quality, and psychological adjustment during the transition to college. *Journal of Experimental Education, 76*(4), 343–361. doi:10.3200/JEXE.76.4.343-362

Plante, I., O'Keefe, P. A., & Theoret, M. (2013). The relation between achievement goal and expectancy-value theories in predicting achievement-related outcomes: A test of four theoretical conceptions. *Motivation and Emotion, 37*(1), 65–78. doi:10.1007/s11031-012-9282-9

Podcasting – Resources for Faculty. (n.d.). Retrieved from http://engage.doit.wisc.edu/about/

Polanco, R., Calderon, P., & Delgado, F. (2004). Effects of a problem based learning program on engineering students' academic achievements in a Mexican university. *Innovations in Education, Teaching, and Instruction, 41*(2), 145–155. doi:10.1080/1470329042000208675

Pollacia, L., & McCallister, T. (2009). Using web 2.0 technologies to meet Quality Matters (QM) requirements. *Journal of Information Systems Education, 20*(2), 155–164.

Pollacia, L., & McCallister, T. (2009). Using Web 2.0 technologies to meet Quality Matters requirements. *Journal of Information Systems Education, 20*, 155–164.

Pollard, H., Blevins, R., Connor, M., & McGovern, L. (2013). An examination of the relationship between teaching presence, social presence, learner motivation, and self-reported learning among online MBA students. Academy of Business, 18(2), 23-30.

Pollard, C., Gupta, D., & Satzinger, J. (2010). Teaching systems development: A compelling case for integrating the SDLC with the ITSM lifecycle. *Information Systems Management, 27*(2), 113–122. doi:10.1080/10580531003684959

Pontes, M., Hasit, C., Pontes, N., Lewis, P., & Siefring, K. (2010). Variables related to undergraduate students preference for distance education classes. *Online Journal of Distance Learning Administration, 13*, 8–22.

Popov, V., Brinkman, D., Biemans, H. J. A., Muldon, M., Kuznetsov, A., & Noroozi, O. (2012). Multicultural student group work in higher education: A explorative case on challenges as perceived by students. *International Journal of Intercultural Relations, 36*(2), 302–317. doi:10.1016/j.ijintrel.2011.09.004

Postman, L., Bruner, J. S., & McGinnies, E. (1948). Personal values as selective factors in perception. *Journal of Abnormal and Social Psychology, 43*(2), 142–154. doi:10.1037/h0059765 PMID:18861376

Powell, K., & Kalina, C. (2009). Cognitive and social constructivism: Developing tools for an effective classroom. *Education, 130*(2), 241–250.

Prensky, M. (2009). Let's be digital multipliers. *Educational Technology*. Retrieved from http://www.marcprensky.com/writing/Prensky-Lets_Be_Digital_Multipliers-ET-01-09.pdf

Pressman, R. S. (1982). *Software engineering: A practitioner's approach*. New York: McGraw-Hill.

Price, D. V., & Tovar, E. (2014). Student engagement and institutional graduation rates: Identifying high-impact educational practices for community colleges. *Community College Journal of Research and Practice, 38*(9), 766–782. doi:10.1080/10668926.2012.719481

Prince, M. (2004). Does active learning work? A Review of the Research. *The Journal of Engineering Education, 93*(3), 223–231. doi:10.1002/j.2168-9830.2004.tb00809.x

Provansnik, S., & Planty, M. (2008). *Community colleges: Supplemental to the condition of education. (U.S. Department of Education, National Center for Educational Statistics, NCES 2008-033)*. Washington, DC: U.S. Government Printing Office.

Puentedura, R. (2006). *Transformation, technology, and education*. Presentation given August 18, 2006 as part of the Strengthening Your District Through Technology Workshops. Retrieved from http://hippasus.com/resources/tte/part1.html

Puentedura, R. (2012). *SAMR: Guiding development.* Retrieved from http://www.hippasus.com/rrpweblog/archives/2012/01/19/SAMR_GuidingDevelopment.pdf

Pursell, D. P. (2009). Adapting to student learning styles: Engaging students with cell phone technology in organic chemistry instruction. *Journal of Chemical Education, 86*(10), 1219–1222. doi:10.1021/ed086p1219

Puzziferro, M. (2008). Online technologies self-efficacy and self-regulated learning as predictors of final grade and satisfaction in college-level online courses. *American Journal of Distance Education, 22*(2), 72–89. doi:10.1080/08923640802039024

Quality Matters Program. (2013). *The Quality Matters higher education rubric.* Retrieved from https://www.qualitymatters.org/rubric

Quality Matters Program. (2014). *The Quality Matters higher education rubric.* Retrieved from https://www.qualitymatters.org/rubric

Radford, A. (2011). *Learning at a Distance: Undergraduate Enrollment in Distance Education Courses and Degree Programs. (NCES 2012-154).* Washington, DC: National Center for Education Statistics, Institute of Education Sciences, U.S. Department of Education.

Rafferty, M., & Lindell, D. (2011). How nurse managers rate the clinical competencies of accelerated (second-degree) nursing graduates. *The Journal of Nursing Education, 50*(6), 355–358. doi:10.3928/01484834-20110228-07 PMID:21366163

Ragan, L. (1999). Good teaching is good teaching: An emerging set of guiding principles and practices for the design and development of distance education. *CAUSE/EFFECT, 22*(1).

Ragan, L. C. (n.d.). 10 principles of effective online teaching: Best practices in distance education. *Faculty Focus.* Retrieved from http://www.facultyfocus.com/free-reports/principles-of-effective-online-teaching-best-practices-in-distance-education/

Rakes, G. C., & Dunn, K. E. (2010). The impact of online graduate students' motivation and self-regulation on academic procrastination. *Journal of Interactive Online Learning, 9*(1), 78–93. Retrieved from http://www.ncolr.org/jiol/issues/pdf/9.1.5.pdf

Rakes, G. C., Dunn, K. E., & Rakes, T. A. (2013). Attribution as a predictor of procrastination in online graduate students. *Journal of Interactive Online Learning, 12*(3), 103–121. Retrieved from http://www.ncolr.org/jiol/issues/pdf/12.3.2.pdf

Rao. (2010). Reaching Remote Learners: Successes and Challenges for Students in an Online Graduate Degree Program in the Pacific Islands. *The International Review of Research in Open and Distance Learning, 11*(1), 141–160.

Reddy, P. (2011). The evolving role of universities in economic development: The case of university–industry linkages. In B. Göransson & C. Brundenius (Eds.), *Universities in transition: The changing role and challenges for academic institutions* (pp. 25–51). Ottawa: Springer. doi:10.1007/978-1-4419-7509-6_3

Reeve, J., Deci, E. L., & Ryan, R. M. (2004). Self-determination theory: A dialectical framework for understanding socio-cultural influences on student motivation. In D. M. McInemey & S. Van Etten (Eds.), *Big theories revisited.* Greenwich, CT: Information Age.

Reeves, T. C., Herrington, J., & Oliver, R. (2005). Design research: A socially responsible approach to instructional technology research in higher education. *Journal of Computing in Higher Education, 16*(2), 96–115. doi:10.1007/BF02961476

Reigeluth, C. M. (1983). Instructional design: What is it and why is it? In C. M. Reigeluth (Ed.), *Instructional-Design Theories and Models: An Overview of their Current Status.* Hillsdale, NJ: Erlbaum Associates.

Reiser, R. A., & Dempsey, J. V. (2012). *Trends and issues in instructional design and technology.* Boston: Pearson.

Reznick, C. B., & Werner, E. (2001). *Integrating technology into problem based learning small groups in a medical education setting.* Paper presented at the annual meeting of the American Educational Research Association, Seattle, WA.

Rhode, J. F. (2009). Interaction equivalency in self-paced online learning environments: An exploration of learner preferences. *International Review of Research in Open and Distance Learning, 10*(1), 11–23. Retrieved from http://www.irrodl.org/index.php/irrodl/article/view/603/1178

Rhodes, T. (Ed.). (2010). *Assessing outcomes and improving education: Tips and tools for using rubrics.* Washington, DC: Association of American Colleges and Universities.

Rice, R. E. (1993). Media appropriateness: Using social presence theory to compare traditional and new organization media. *Human Communication Research, 19*(4), 451–484. doi:10.1111/j.1468-2958.1993.tb00309.x

Richardson, J., & Swan, K. (2001). *An examination of social presence in online learning: Students' perceived learning and satisfaction.* Paper presented at the Annual Meeting of the American Educational Research Association, Seattle, WA.

Richardson, J. C., & Swan, K. (2003). Examining social presence in online course in relation to students' perceived learning and satisfaction. *Journal of Asynchronous Learning Networks, 7*(1), 68–88.

Richardson, J. C., & Swan, K. (2003). Examining social presence in online courses in relation to students' perceived learning and satisfaction. *Journal of Asynchronous Learning Networks, 7*(1), 68–88.

Richardson, J. C., & Swan, K. (2003). Examining social presence in online courses in relation to students' perceived learning and satisfaction. *Journal of Asynchronous Learning Networks, 7*(1), 68–88.

Richardson, V. (1996). The role of attitudes and beliefs in learning to teach. In J. Sikula (Ed.), *Handbook of research on teacher education* (2nd ed., pp. 102–119). New York: Simon & Schuster/Macmillan.

Richardson, W. W. H. (2010). *Blogs, wikis, podcasts, and other powerful web tools for classrooms.* Thousand Oaks, CA: Corwin Press.

Richey, R., & Klein, J. D. (Eds.). (2007). *Design and development research: Methods, strategies, and issues.* Mahwah, NJ: Lawrence Erlbaum Associates.

Rickard, W. (2010). *The efficacy (an inevitability) of online learning in higher education.* Retrieved from http://chronicle.com/items/biz/pdf/Pearson_WP_EfficacyOfOnlineLearning.pdf

Rico, J. S., Beal, J., & Davies, T. (2010). Promising practices for faculty in accelerated nursing programs. *The Journal of Nursing Education, 49*(3), 150–155. doi:10.3928/01484834-20100115-01 PMID:20143760

Riding, R., & Rayner, S. (1998). *Cognitive styles and learning strategies: Understanding style differences in learning and behaviour.* London: David Fulton.

Rismark, M., Sølvberg, A. M., Strømme, A., & Hokstad, L. M. (2007). Using mobile phones to prepare for university lectures: Student's experiences. *The Turkish Online Journal of Educational Technology, 6*(4), Article 9. Retrieved from http://www.tojet.net/articles/649.pdf

Ritchie, D. C., & Hoffman, B. (1997). Incorporating instructional design principles with the World Wide Web. In B. H. Khan (Ed.), *Web-based Instruction* (pp. 135–138). Englewood Cliffs, NJ: Educational Technology Publications.

Roberts, A. G. (2007). Beyond a participation focus. In *Proceedings of the Australasian Society for Computers in Learning in Tertiary Education Conference,* (pp. 898-903). Retrieved from http://www.ascilite.org.au/conferences/singapore07/procs/roberts.pdf

Roberts, T. (2006). Self, peer and group assessment in E-learning: An introduction. In T. Roberts (Ed.), *Self, peer and group assessment in E-learning* (pp. 1–16). Hershey, PA: Information Science. doi:10.4018/978-1-59140-965-6.ch001

Robinson, B. (1998). A strategic perspective in staff development for open and distance learning. In C. Latchem & F. Lockwood (Eds.), *Staff development in open and flexible learning* (pp. 33–44). New York: Routledge.

Robinson, C. C., & Hullinger, H. (2008). New benchmarks in higher education: Student engagement in online learning. *Journal of Education for Business, 84*(2), 101–109. doi:10.3200/JOEB.84.2.101-109

Roblyer, M. D., & Ekhaml, L. (2000). *How interactive are Your Distance Courses? A Rubric for Assessing Interaction in Distance Learning.* Paper presented at DLA 2000, Callaway, Georgia.

Roblyer, M. D., Dozier-Henry, O., & Burnette, A. P. (1996). Technology and multicultural education: The 'uneasy alliance'. *Educational Technology, 36*(3), 5–12.

Roca, J. C., & Gagne, M. (2008). Understanding e-learning continuance intention in the workplace: A self-determination theory perspective. *Computers in Human Behavior, 24*(4), 1585–1604. doi:10.1016/j.chb.2007.06.001

Rocco, S. (2010). Making reflection public: Using interactive online discussion board to enhance student learning. *Reflective Practice, 11*(3), 307–317. doi:10.1080/14623 943.2010.487374

Rochford, R. (2003). Assessing learning styles to improve the quality of performance of community college students in developmental writing programs: A pilot study. *Community College Journal of Research and Practice, 27*(8), 665–677. doi:10.1080/713838240

Rodriguez, B. C. P., & Armellini, A. (2013). Interaction and effectiveness of corporate e-learning programmes. *Human Resource Development International, 16*(4), 480–489. doi:10.1080/13678868.2013.803753

Rodriguez, B. C. P., & Armellini, A. (2014). Applying the interaction equivalency theorem to online courses in a large organization. *Journal of Interactive Online Learning, 13*(2), 51–66.

Rodriquez, M. C., Ooms, A., Montanez, M., & Yan, Y. L. (2005). *Perceptions of online learning quality given comfort with technology, motivation to learn technology skills, satisfaction, and online learning experience.* Paper presented at the Annual Meeting of the American Educational Research Association. Montreal, Canada. (ERIC Document Reproduction Service No. ED491688).

Rodzvilla, J. (2002). *We've got blog: How weblogs are changing our culture.* Cambridge, MA: Perseus Publishing.

Rogers, A. (2002). Adult learners: characteristics, need, learning styles. In A. Kokkos (Ed.), *International conference for adults' learning.* Athens: Metaixmio. (In Greek)

Rogers, A. (2007). *Teaching Adults.* Open University Press.

Rogers, C. R. (1959). A theory of therapy, personality, and interpersonal relations, developed in the client-centered framework. In S. Koch (Ed.), *Psychology: A study of a science.* New York, NY: McGraw-Hill.

Rogers, E. M. (2003). *Diffusion of innovations* (5th ed.). New York, NY: The Free Press.

Rogers, J. (2000). Communities of Practice: A framework for fostering coherence in virtual learning communities. *Journal of Educational Technology & Society, 3*(3), 384–392.

Rogers, P. C., Graham, C. R., & Mayes, C. T. (2007). Cultural competence and instructional design: Exploration research into the delivery of online instruction cross-culturally. *Educational Technology Research and Development, 55*(2), 197–217. doi:10.1007/s11423-007-9033-x

Rogers, T. B., Kuiper, N. A., & Kirker, W. S. (1977). Self-reference and the encoding of personal information. *Journal of Personality and Social Psychology, 35*(9), 677–688. doi:10.1037/0022-3514.35.9.677 PMID:909043

Roman, T., Kelsey, K., & Lin, H. (2010). Enhancing online education through instructor skill development in higher education. *Online Journal of Distance Learning Administration, 8*(1). Retrieved from http://www.westga.edu/~distance/ojdla/winter134/roman_kelsey134.html

Romero, M., Guitert, M., Sangrà, A., & Bullen, M. (2013). Do UOC students fit in the Net Generation profile? An approach to their habits in ICT use. *International Review of Research in Open and Distance Learning, 14*(3), 158–181.

Rosen, L. S. (2006). Blogging to Inform, Educate, and Attract New Clients. *Family Advocate, 28*(3), 46–47.

Ross-Gordon, J. M. (2011). Research on adult learners: Supporting the needs of a student population that is no longer nontraditional. *Peer Review, 13*(1), 26–29.

Rossin, D., Ro, Y. K., Klein, B. D., & Guo, Y. M. (2009). The effects of flow on learning outcomes in an online information management course. *Journal of Information Systems Education, 20*(1), 87–98.

Rotter, J. B. (1966). Generalized expectancies for internal versus external control of reinforcement. *Psychological Monographs, 80*(1), 1–28. doi:10.1037/h0092976 PMID:5340840

Rourke, A. J., & Coleman, K. (2009). An emancipating space: reflective and collaborative blogging, Same places, Different spaces, Auckland, New Zealand: University of Auckland: ASCILITE, 888-897.

Rourke, L., Anderson, T., Garrison, D. R., & Archer, W. (1999). Assessing Social Presence in Asynchronous Text-Based Computer Conferencing. *Journal of Distance Education*, *14*(2), 50–71.

Rourke, L., Anderson, T., Garrison, D. R., & Archer, W. (1999). Assessing social presence in asynchronous text-based computer conferencing. *Journal of Distance Education*, *14*. Retrieved from http://cade.athabascau.ca/vol14.2/ rourke_et_al.html

Rourke, L., Anderson, T., Garrison, D. R., & Archer, W. (1999). Assessing social presence in asynchronous, text-based computer conferencing. *Journal of Distance Education*, *14*(3), 51–70.

Rourke, L., Anderson, T., Garrison, D. R., & Archer, W. (2007). Assessing social presence in asynchronous text-based computer conferencing. *International Journal of E-Learning & Distance Education*, *14*(2), 50–71.

Rovai, A. (2002). A preliminary look at the structural differences of higher education classroom communities in traditional and ALN courses. *Journal of Asynchronous Learning Networks*, *6*(1). Retrieved from http://www.aln.org/publications/jaln/v6n1/pdf/v6n1_rovai.pdf

Rovai, A. (2002). Building sense of community at a distance. *International Review of Research in Open and Distance Learning*, *3*(1), 1–16. Retrieved from http://www.irrodl.org/index.php/irrodl/article/view/79/153

Rovai, A. P. (2001). Building classroom community at a distance: A case study. *Educational Technology Research and Development*, *49*(4), 33–48. doi:10.1007/BF02504946

Rovai, A. P. (2002). Building a sense of community at a distance. *International Review of Research in Open and Distance Learning*, *3*(1). Retrieved from http://www.irrodl.org/index.php/irrodl/article/view/79/153

Rovai, A. P. (2002). Sense of community, perceived cognitive learning, and persistence in asynchronous learning networks. *The Internet and Higher Education*, *5*(4), 319–332. doi:10.1016/S1096-7516(02)00130-6

Rovai, A. P. (2003). In search of higher persistence rates in distance education online programs. *Internet and Education*, *6*(1), 1–16. doi:10.1016/S1096-7516(02)00158-6

Rovai, A. P. (2007). Facilitating online discussions effectively. *The Internet and Higher Education*, *10*(1), 77–88. doi:10.1016/j.iheduc.2006.10.001

Rovai, A. P., & Jordan, H. (2004). Blended learning and sense of community: A comparative analysis with traditional and fully online graduate courses. *International Review of Research in Open and Distance Learning*, *2*(5). Retrieved from http://www.irrodl.org/index.php/irrodl/article/viewArticle/192/274

Rovai, A. P., & Wighting, M. J. (2005). Feelings of alienation and community among higher education students in a virtual classroom. *The Internet and Higher Education*, *8*(2), 97–110. doi:10.1016/j.iheduc.2005.03.001

Rowe, F. A., & Rafferty, J. A. (2013). Instructional design interventions for supporting self-regulated learning: Enhancing academic outcomes in postsecondary E-learning environments. *Journal of Online Learning & Teaching*, *9*(4), 590–601.

Rubenstein, L., Khodyakov, D., Hempel, S., Danz, M., Salem-Schatz, M., Foy, R., & Shekelle, P. et al. (2014). How can we recognize continuous quality improvement? *International Journal for Quality in Health Care*, *26*(1), 6–15. doi:10.1093/intqhc/mzt085 PMID:24311732

Rufai, M. M., Alebiosu, S. O., & Adeakin, O. A. S. (2015). A conceptual model for virtual classroom management. *International Journal of Computer Science. Engineering and Information Technology*, *5*(1), 27–32. PMID:26029735

Rufer, R., & Adams, R. H. (2013). Deep learning through Reusable Learning Objects in an MBA Program. *Journal of Educational Technology Systems*, *42*(2), 107–120. doi:10.2190/ET.42.2.c

Rumble, G. (2001). Re-inventing distance education, 1971-2001. *International Journal of Lifelong Education*, *20*(1/2), 31–43.

Russell, G. (2005). The distancing question in online education. *Innovate, 1*(4).

Russo, T. C., & Campbell, S. W. (2004). Perceptions of mediated presence in an asynchronous online course: Interplay of communication behaviors and medium. *Distance Education, 25*(2), 215–232. doi:10.1080/0158791042000262139

Ryan, B. J. (2013). Flipping over: Student-centred learning and assessment. *Journal of Perspectives in Applied Academic Practice, 1*(2), 30–39. doi:10.14297/jpaap.v1i2.64

Ryan, G. (1993). Student perceptions about self-directed learning in a professional course implementing problem-based learning. *Studies in Higher Education, 18*(1), 53–63. doi:10.1080/03075079312331382458

Ryan, R. M. (1995). Psychological needs and the facilitation of integrative processes. *Journal of Personality, 63*(3), 397–427. doi:10.1111/j.1467-6494.1995.tb00501.x PMID:7562360

Ryan, R. M., & Deci, E. L. (2000a). Self-determination theory and the facilitation of intrinsic motivation, social development and well-being. *The American Psychologist, 55*(1), 68–78. doi:10.1037/0003-066X.55.1.68 PMID:11392867

Ryan, R. M., & Deci, E. L. (2000b). Intrinsic and extrinsic motivations: Classic definitions and new directions. *Contemporary Educational Psychology, 25*(1), 54–67. doi:10.1006/ceps.1999.1020 PMID:10620381

Ryan, R. M., & Deci, E. L. (2003). On assimilating identities to the self: A self-determination theory perspective on internalization and integrity within cultures. In M. R. Leary & J. P. Tangney (Eds.), *Handbook on self and identity*. New York, NY: The Guilford Press.

Ryan, R. M., & Niemiec, C. P. (2009). Self-determination theory in schools of education: Can empirically supported framework also be critical and liberating? *Theory and Research in Education, 7*(2), 263–272. doi:10.1177/1477878509104331

Ryman, S., Hardman, G., Richardson, B., & Ross, J. (2009). Creating and sustaining online learning communities: Designing for transformative learning. *International Journal of Pedagogies and Learning, 5*(3), 46–58. doi:10.5172/ijpl.5.3.46

Sa'd, S. H. T. (2014). Implementing Internet-based EFL Teaching in Iran:(Dis) Advantages, Obstacles and Challenges from EFL Learners' Viewpoint. *Dil ve Edebiyat Eğitimi Dergisi Sayı, 10*, 24–40.

Saadatmand, M., & Kumpulainen, K. (2014). Participants' perceptions of learning and networking in connectivist MOOCs. *Journal of Online Learning and Teaching, 10*(1), 16–30. Retrieved from http://jolt.merlot.org/vol10no1/saadatmand_0314.pdf

Sadykova, G., & Dautermann, J. (2009). Crossing cultures and borders in international online distance higher education. *Journal of Asynchronous Learning Networks, 13*(2), 89–114.

Sagone, E., & De Caroli, M. E. (2014). Locus of control and academic self-efficacy in university students: The effects of self-concepts. *Procedia: Social and Behavioral Sciences, 114*, 222–228. doi:10.1016/j.sbspro.2013.12.689

Sakiz, G. (2012). Perceived instructor affective support in relation to academic emotions and motivation in college. *Educational Psychology, 32*(1), 63–79. doi:10.1080/01443410.2011.625611

Salmon, G. (2000). *E-moderating: The key to teaching and learning online*. London: Kogan Page. doi:10.4324/9780203465424

Salmon, G. (2004). *E-moderating: the key to teaching and learning online* (2nd ed.). London: Taylor and Francis.

Salmon, G. (2011). *E-moderating: The key to online teaching and learning* (3rd ed.). New York, NY: Routledge.

Saloman, D. (2013). Moving on from Facebook: Using Instagram to connect with undergraduates and engage in teaching and learning. *College & Research Libraries News, 78*(8), 408–412.

Sanders, R. H. (2012). E-Tutor. *The Computer Assisted Language Instruction Consortium, 29*(3), 580–587.

Sandoz, M. (2008). Crazy Horse the Strange Man of the Oglala (3rd ed.). Knopf.

Saritas, T. (2008). The construction of knowledge through social interaction via computer-mediated communication. *Quarterly Review of Distance Education, 9*(1), 35–49.

Savery, J. R. (2005). Be Vocal: Characteristics of successful online instructors. *Journal of Interactive Online Learning, 4*(2), 141–152.

Sawyer, E. A., & Howard, C. (2007). Online learning program strategic planning and execution: Considering goals, benefits, problems and communities of practice. *Journal of College Teaching & Learning, 4*(8), 99–112.

Schaffhauser, D. (2009). Boundless opportunity. *T.H.E. Journal, 36*(9), 13–18.

Scheg, A. G. (2014). *Reforming teacher education for online pedagogy development*. Hershey, PA: IGI Global. doi:10.4018/978-1-4666-5055-8

Schiaffino, S., Garcia, P., & Amandi, A. (2008). eTeacher: Providing personalised assistance to e-learning students. *Computers & Education, 51*(4), 1744–1754. doi:10.1016/j.compedu.2008.05.008

Schifter. (2004). Faculty participation in distance education program: Practices and plans. In D. Monolescu, C. Schifte, & L. Greenwood (Eds.), *The distance education evaluation: issues and case studies* (pp. 22-39). Hershey, PA: Information Science.

Schlosser, C. (2004). We Need a Plan: An Instructional Design Approach for Distance Education Courses. *Distance Learn, 1*(4), 29–38.

Schmidt, H. G., Vermelen, L., & van der Molen, H. T. (2006). Long-term effects of problem based learning: A comparison of competencies acquired by graduate of problem based and conventional medical schools. *Medical Education, 40*(6), 562–567. doi:10.1111/j.1365-2929.2006.02483.x PMID:16700772

Schneider, W., & Shiffrin, R. M. (1977). Controlled and automatic human information processing: Detection, search, and attention. *Psychological Review, 84*(1), 1–66. doi:10.1037/0033-295X.84.1.1

Schön, D. A. (1986). *Educating the reflective practitioner*. San Francisco, CA: Jossey-Bass.

Schön, D. A. (1991). *Educating the reflective practitioner: Toward a new design for teaching and learning in the professions*. San Francisco, CA: Jossey-Bass.

Schraw, G. (2010). Measuring self-regulation in computer-based learning environments. *Educational Psychologist, 45*(4), 258–266. doi:10.1080/00461520.2010.515936

Schroeder, B. (2008). Ten best practices for using wikis in education. *Technology Teacher*. Retrieved April 21, 2014 from http://edtechtoday.wordpress.com/2008/05/21/10-best-practices-for-using-wikis-in-education/

Schroeder, J., & Greenbowe, T. J. (2009). The chemistry of Facebook: Using social networking to create an online community for the organic chemistry. *Innovate: Journal of Online Education, 5*(4), 1–7.

Schullo, S., Hilbelink, A., Venable, M., & Barron, A. (2007). Selecting a virtual classroom system: Elluminate Live vs Macromedia Breeze (Adobe Connect Professional). *Journal of Online Learning and Teaching, 3*(4), 331–345. Retrieved from http://jolt.merlot.org/ documents/hilbelink.pdf

Schunk, D. (2008). Metacognition, self-regulation, and self-regulated learning: Research recommendations. *Educational Psychology Review, 20*(4), 463–467. doi:10.1007/s10648-008-9086-3

Schunk, D., & Mullen, C. (2013). Toward a conceptual model of mentoring research: Integration with self-regulated learning. *Educational Psychology Review, 25*(3), 361–389. doi:10.1007/s10648-013-9233-3

Schutte, J. G. (1997). *Virtual teaching in higher education: The new intellectual superhighway or just another traffic jam?*. Available: http://www.csun.edu/sociology/virexp.htm

Schutt, M., Allen, B. S., & Laumakis, M. A. (2009). The effects of instructor immediacy behavior in online learning environments. *Quarterly Review of Distance Education, 10*, 135–148.

Schwinger, M., Wirthwein, L., Lemmer, G., & Steinmayr, R. (2014). Academic self-handicapping and achievement: A meta-analysis. *Journal of Educational Psychology, 106*(3), 744–761. doi:10.1037/a0035832

Scollins-Mantha, B. (2008). Cultivating social presence in the online learning classroom: A literature review with recommendations for practice. *International Journal of Instructional Technology and Distance Education, 5*(3), 23–38.

Scorsese, M. (Producer & Director). (2011). *Hugo*. [Motion Picture]. United States: Paramount.

Scriven, M. S. (1991). *Evaluation Thesaurus*. Sage Publications.

Seaman, J. & Tinti-Kane, H. (n.d.). *Social media for teaching and learning*. Pearson Learning Solutions and Babson Survey Research Group.

Seaman, J. S. (2009). Online learning as a strategic asset. Volume II: The paradox of faculty voices--Views and experiences with online learning. Results of a National Faculty Survey, Part of the Online Education Benchmarking Study Conducted by the APLU-Sloan National Commission on Online Learning. Association of Public and Land Grant Universities.

Seamon, M. (2004). Short-and long-term differences in instructional effectiveness between intensive and semester-length courses. *Teachers College Record*, *106*(4), 635–650. doi:10.1111/j.1467-9620.2004.00360.x

Shank, P. (2004). Competencies for online instructors. In *Learning Peaks, LLC*. Retrieved in 22 February 2009, from http://www.insighted.com/instrcomp.pdf

Shank, P. (2008). Thinking critically to move e-Learning forward. In S. Carliner & P. Shank (Eds.), *The e-learning handbook: A comprehensive guide to online learning* (pp. 15–26). San Francisco, CA: Pfeiffer.

Shank, R. (1998). Horses for courses. *Communications of the ACM*, *41*(7), 23–25. doi:10.1145/278476.278482

Sharpe, R., & Greg, B. (2005). The student experience of e-learning in higher education: A review of the literature. *Brookes eJournal of Learning and Teaching, 1*. Retrieved from http://www.brookes.ac.uk/publications/bejlt/volume1issue3/academic/sharpe_benfield.html

Shaw, M., Chametzky, B., Burrus, S. W., & Walters, K. J. (2013). An evaluation of student outcomes by course duration in online higher education. *Online Journal of Distance Learning Administration*, *16*(4).

Shea, P. (2007b). *Study unearths what motivated RIT faculty to teach online*. RIT Online Learning. Retrieved from: http://online.rit.edu/about/newsletter/one_article.cfm?which=99

Shea, P. (2007a). Bridges and barriers to teaching online college courses: A study of experienced faculty in thirty-six colleges. *Journal of Asynchronous Learning Networks*, *11*, 73–128.

Shea, P. J. (2006). A study of students' sense of learning community in online environments. *Journal of Asynchronous Learning Networks*, *10*(1). Retrieved from http://www.sloan-c.org/publications/JALN/v10n1/pdf/v10n1_4shea.pdf

Shea, P. J., Fredericksen, E. E., Pickett, A. M., & Pelz, W. E. (2003). A preliminary investigation of "Teaching Presence" in the SUNY Learning Network. In J. Bourne & J. C. Moore (Eds.), *Elements of quality online education: Practice and direction* (pp. 279–310). Needham, MA: Slocan-C.

Shea, P. J., Pickett, A. M., & Pelz, W. E. (2003). A follow-up investigation of "teaching presence" in the SUNY Learning network. *Journal of Asynchronous Learning Networks*, *7*(2), 61–80.

Shea, P. J., Swan, K., & Pickett, A. M. (2005). Teaching presence and establishment of community in online learning environments. In J. C. Moore (Ed.), *Engaging communities, wisdom from the Sloan Consortium* (pp. 53–66). Needham, MA: Sloan-C.

Shea, P., & Bidjerano, T. (2009). Community of inquiry as a theoretical framework to foster "epistemic engagement" and "cognitive presence" in online education. *Computers & Education*, *52*(3), 543–553. doi:10.1016/j.compedu.2008.10.007

Shea, P., & Bidjerano, T. (2010). Learning presence: Towards a theory of self-efficacy, self-regulation, and the development of a communities of inquiry in online and blended learning environments. *Computers & Education*, *55*(4), 1721–1731. doi:10.1016/j.compedu.2010.07.017

Shea, P., & Bidjerano, T. (2012). Learning presence as a moderator in the community of inquiry model. *Computers & Education*, *59*(2), 316–326. doi:10.1016/j.compedu.2012.01.011

Shea, P., Hayes, S., Vickers, J., Gozza-Cohen, M., Uzuner, S., Mehta, R., & Rangan, P. et al. (2010). A re-examination of the community of inquiry framework: Social network and content analysis. *The Internet and Higher Education*, *13*(1), 10–21. doi:10.1016/j.iheduc.2009.11.002

Shea, P., Li, C. S., & Pickett, A. (2006). A study of teaching presence and student sense of learning community in fully online and web-enhanced college courses. *The Internet and Higher Education*, *9*(3), 175–190. doi:10.1016/j.iheduc.2006.06.005

Sheldon, K. M., Ryan, R. M., Rawsthorne, L., & Ilardi, B. (1997). Trait self and true self: Cross-role variation in the big five traits and its relations with authenticity and subjective well-being. *Journal of Personality and Social Psychology*, *73*, 1380–1393. doi:10.1037/0022-3514.73.6.1380

Shelton, K., & Saltsman, G. (2005). *An administrators guide to online education*. Greenwich, CT: IAP- Information Age Publishing.

Shen, K. N., & Khalifa, M. (2008). Exploring multidimensional conceptualization of social presence in the context of online communities. *International Journal of Human-Computer Interaction*, *24*(7), 722–748. doi:10.1080/10447310802335789

Sher, A. (2009). Assessing the relationship of student-instructor and student-student interaction to student learning and satisfaction in Web-based online learning environment. *Journal of Interactive Online Learning*, *8*(2), 102–120. Retrieved from http://www.ncolr.org/jiol/issues/ pdf/8.2.1.pdf

Sheridan, R. (2006). Reducing the online instructor's workload. *EDUCAUSE Quarterly*, *29*(3), 65–67.

Shieh, R., Gummer, E., & Niess, M. (2008). The quality of a web-based course: Perspectives of the instructor and the students. *TechTrends: Linking Research & Practice to Improve Learning*, *52*(6), 61–68. doi:10.1007/s11528-008-0220-3

Shih, R. (2010). Blended learning using video-based blogs: Public speaking for English as a second language students. *Australasian Journal of Educational Technology*, *26*(6), 883–897.

Shin, D., Shin, Y., Choo, H., & Beom, K. (2011). Smartphones as smart pedagogical tool: Implications for smartphones as u-learning devices. *Computers in Human Behavior*, *27*(6), 2207–2214. doi:10.1016/j.chb.2011.06.017

Shin, N. (2002). Beyond Interaction: The Relational Construct of 'Transactional Presence.'. *Open Learning*, *17*(2), 121–137. doi:10.1080/02680510220146887

Shin, N. (2006). Online learner's 'flow' experience: An empirical study. *British Journal of Educational Technology*, *37*(5), 705–720. doi:10.1111/j.1467-8535.2006.00641.x

Short, J., Williams, E., & Christie, B. (1976). *The social psychology of telecommunications*. London: John Wiley & Sons.

Shulman, L. S. (1987). Knowledge and teaching: Foundations of the new reform. *Harvard Educational Review*, *57*(1), 1–23. doi:10.17763/haer.57.1.j463w79r56455411

Siekpe, J. S. (2005). An examination of the multidimensionality of flow construct in a computer-mediated environment. *Journal of Electronic Commerce Research*, *6*(1), 31–43.

Siemens, G. (2005a). Connectivism: Learning as network-creation. *ElearnSpace*. Retrieved from http://www.elearnspace.org/Articles/networks.htm

Siemens, G. (2008). Learning and knowing in networks: Changing roles for educators and designers. *ITFORUM for Discussion*. Retrieved from: http://itforum.coe.uga.edu/Paper105/Siemens.pdf

Siemens, G. (2005b). Connectivism: A learning theory for a digital age. *International Journal of Instructional Technology and Distance Learning*, *2*(1), 3–10.

Simkins, S. P. (1999). Promoting active-student learning using the World Wide Web in economics courses. *The Journal of Economic Education*, *30*(3), 287–289. doi:10.1080/00220489909595990

Simon, M. (2000). Managing Time: Developing effective online organization. In K. White & B. Weight (Eds.), *The Online Teaching Guide* (pp. 73–82). Boston, MA: Allyn & Bacon.

Simonson, M., Smaldino, D., Albright, M., & Zvacek, S. (2009). *Teaching and learning at a distance: Foundations of distance education* (4th ed.). Boston: Allyn & Bacon.

Simonson, M., Smaldino, S., Albright, M., & Zvacek, S. (2000). *Teaching and Learning at a Distance: Foundations of Distance Education*. Upper Saddle River, NJ: Merrill.

Simonson, M., Smaldino, S., Albright, M., & Zvacek, S. (2012). *Teaching and learning at a distance* (5th ed.). Boston, MA: Pearson Education.

Simpson, E., & Courtney, M. (2002). Critical thinking in nursing education: Literature review. *International Journal of Nursing Practice, 8*(2), 89–98. doi:10.1046/j.1440-172x.2002.00340.x PMID:11993582

Simpson, J., & Benson, A. (2013). Student perceptions of quality and satisfaction in online education. *Quarterly Review Of Distance Education, 14*(4), 221–231.

Simpson, O. (2013). *Supporting students in online, open and distance learning*. New York: Routledge.

Simsek, A. (2012). Learner control. In N. Seel (Ed.), *Encyclopedia of the sciences of learning* (pp. 1748–1750). New York: Springer; doi:10.1007/978-1-4419-1428-6

Skiba, D. J. (2009). Emerging technologies center nursing education 2.0: A second look at Second Life. *Nursing Education Perspectives, 30*(2), 129–131. PMID:19476080

Skinner, E. A., Wellborn, J. G., & Connell, J. P. (1990). What it takes to do well in school and whether I've got it: A process model of perceived control and children's engagement and achievement in school. *Journal of Educational Psychology, 82*(1), 22–32. doi:10.1037/0022-0663.82.1.22

Sleeter, C. E. (1996). *Multicultural education as social activism*. Albany, NY: State University of New York Press.

Sleeter, C., & Tettagah, S. (2002). Technology as a tool in multicultural teaching. *Multicultural Education, 10*(1), 28–30.

Sloan Consortium (2006, August). *Faculty satisfaction*. Neeham, MA: Author.

Smith, D. G. (2006). *Bit by Bit: A Case Study of Bloggership*, University of Wisconsin, Legal Studies Research Paper No. 1017, 4. Retrieved January 12th, 2015, from: http://papers.ssrn.com/sol3/papers.cfm?abstract_id=898178

Smith, G. G., & Taveras, M. (2005, January). The missing instructor. *eLearn*. Retrieved from http://elearnmag.acm.org/featured.cfm?aid=1070933

Smith, H. (2008). Assessing student contributions to online discussion boards. *Practitioner Research in Higher Education, 2*(1), 22-28. Retrieved from http://194.81.189.19/ojs/index.php/prhe/article/viewFile/18/18

Smith, M. K. (2002). *Malcolm Knowles, informal adult education, self-direction and andragogy, the encyclopedia of informal education*. Retrieved December 22, 2014 from www.infed.org/thinkers/et-knowl.htm

Smith, D. (2009). *Using what we know: A practical guide to increasing student achievement*. Denver, CO: Outskirts Press.

Smith, G. G., Torres-Ayala, A. T., & Heindel, A. J. (2008). Disciplinary differences in e-learning instructional design. *Journal of Distance Education, 22*(3), 63–88. Retrieved from http://files.eric.ed.gov/fulltext/EJ812564.pdf

Smith, G., Ferguson, D., & Caris, M. (2002). Teaching over the web versus in the classroom: Differences in the instructor experience. *International Journal of Instructional Media, 29*(1), 61–67.

Smith, P. L., & Ragan, T. J. (2005). *Instructional design* (3rd ed.). Hoboken, NJ: John Wiley & Sons.

Smith, P., & Marston, J. (2013). Integrative language and culture learning: Connecting formal and non-formal learning in virtual language studies. In H. Yang & S. Wang (Eds.), *Cases on formal and informal E-learning environments: Opportunities and practices* (pp. 185–199). Hershey, PA: Information Science Reference. doi:10.4018/978-1-4666-1930-2.ch010

Smith, S., & Caruso, J. (2010). *The ECAR study of undergraduate students and information technology*. Boulder, CO: CO EDUCAUSE Center for Applied Research.

Smyth, J. (1992). Teachers' works and the politics of reflection. *American Educational Research Journal, 29*(2), 267–300. doi:10.3102/00028312029002268

Smyth, R. (2011). Enhancing learner-learner interaction using video communications in higher education: Implications from theorising about a new model. *British Journal of Educational Technology, 42*(1), 113–127. doi:10.1111/j.1467-8535.2009.00990.x

Sniehotta, F. F., Scholz, U., & Schwarzer, R. (2005). Bridging the intention-behavior gap: Planning, self-efficacy, and action control in the adoption and maintenance of physical exercise. *Psychology & Health, 20*(2), 143–160. doi:10.1080/08870440512331317670

Snow, C., Griffin, P., & Burns, M. S. (2005). *Knowledge to support the teaching of reading: Preparing teachers for a changing world.* San Francisco, CA: Jossey-Bass.

So, H. J. (2005). The content analysis of social presence and collaborative learning behavior patterns in a computer-mediated learning environment. In C.-K. Looi, D. Jonassen, & M. Ikeda (Eds.), *The 13th International Conference on Computers in Education* (pp. 413-419). Amsterdam: IOS Press.

Sockman, B., & Sharma, P. (2008). Struggling toward a transformative model of instruction: It's not so easy! *Teaching and Teacher Education, 24*(4), 1070–1082. doi:10.1016/j.tate.2007.11.008

So, H.-Y., & Brush, T. (2008). Students perceptions of collaborative learning, social presence, and satisfaction in blended learning environment: Relationships and critical factors. *Computers & Education, 51*(1), 318–336. doi:10.1016/j.compedu.2007.05.009

Soleimani, M., Sarkhosh, M., & Gahhari, S. (2012). Computer assisted language testing: On the efficacy of web-based approach in the instruction of elementary learners of English. *English Language Teaching, 5*(9), 66–70. doi:10.5539/elt.v5n9p66

Soles, C., & Moller, L. (2002). Myers Briggs type preferences in distance learning education. *International Journal of Educational Technology, 2*. Retrieved from http://education.illinois.edu/ijet/v2n2/soles/index.html

Solomon, G., & Shrum, L. (2007). *Web 2.0 new tools, new schools.* Eugene, OR: ISTE.

Speer, T., & Ryan, B. (1998). Collaborative teaching in the de-centered classroom. *Teaching English in the Two-Year College, 26*(1), 39-49. ERIC Number: EJ573269.

Stahl, G., Koschmann, T., & Suthers, D. (2006). Computer-supported collaborative learning: An historical perspective. In R. K. Sawyer (Ed.), *Cambridge handbook of learning sciences* (pp. 409–426). Cambridge, UK: Cambridge University Press.

Standage, M., Duda, J. L., & Ntoumanis, M. (2005). A test of self-determination theory in school physical education. *The British Journal of Educational Psychology, 75*(3), 411–433. doi:10.1348/000709904X22359 PMID:16238874

Starr-Glass, D. (2014). Moderating the effective co-creation of knowledge in asynchronous online conferences. In C. N. Stevenson & J. C. Bauer (Eds.), *Building online communities in higher education institutions: Creating collaborative experience* (pp. 258–278). Hershey, PA: IGI-Global; doi:10.4018/978-1-4666-5178-4.ch014

Starr-Glass, D. (2015). Redemption through MOOCs? Valuing aggregation and pricing disaggregation in higher education markets. In A. Mesquita & P. Peres (Eds.), *Furthering higher education possibilities through massive open online courses.* Hershey, PA: IGI-Global; doi:10.4018/978-1-4666-8279-5.ch002

Steel, P. (2007). The nature of procrastination: A meta-analytic and theoretical review of quintessential self-regulatory failure.[PubMed]. *Psychological Bulletin, 133*(1), 65–94. doi:10.1037/0033-2909.133.1.65 PMID:17201571

Steel, P., & Konig, C. J. (2006). Integrating theories of motivation. *Academy of Management Review, 31*(4), 889–913. doi:10.5465/AMR.2006.22527462

Steeples, C., Jones, C., & Goodyear, P. (2002). Beyond e-learning: A future for networked learning. In C. Steeples & C. Jones (Eds.), *Networked learning: Perspectives and issues* (pp. 323–342). London, UK: Springer-Verlag; doi:10.1007/978-1-4471-0181-9_19

Stefanac, S. (2006). *Dispatches from blogistan: A travel guide for the modern blogger.* Berkeley, CA: New Riders.

Stein, S., & Graham, C. R. (2014). *Essentials for blended learning: A standards-based guide.* New York: Routledge.

Sternberg, R. J., & Grigorenko, E. L. (1997). Are cognitive styles still in style? *The American Psychologist, 52*(7), 700–712. doi:10.1037/0003-066X.52.7.700

Stevenson, M., & Hedberg, J. G. (2013). Learning and design with online real-time collaboration. *Educational Media International, 50*(2), 120–134. doi:10.1080/09523987.2013.795352

Stewart, C., & Crone, T. (2014). *Examining the effectiveness of the ARCS-V motivational design model on non-traditional online students performance and persistence.* Unpublished raw data.

Stewart, C., Bachman, C., & Johnson, R. (2010a). Students' characteristics and motivation orientations for online and traditional degree programs. *Journal of Online Learning and Teaching, 6.* Retrieved from: http://jolt.merlot.org/vol6no2/stewart_0610.htm

Stewart, C., Bachman, C., & Babb, S. (2009). Replacing professor monologues with online dialogues: A constructivist approach to online course template design. *Journal of Online Learning and Teaching, 5,* 511–521.

Stewart, C., Bachman, C., & Johnson, R. (2010b). Predictors of faculty acceptance of online education. *Journal of Online Learning and Teaching, 6,* 597–616.

Stewart, M. A., & De George-Walker, L. (2014). Self-handicapping, perfectionism, locus of control and self-efficacy: A path model. *Personality and Individual Differences, 66,* 160–164. doi:10.1016/j.paid.2014.03.038

Stone, D. N., Deci, E. L., & Ryan, R. M. (2009). Beyond talk: Creating autonomous motivation through self-determination theory. *Journal of General Management, 34,* 75–91.

Strauss, P. U. A., & Young, S. (2011). 'I know the type of people I work well with: Student anxiety in multicultural group projects. *Studies in Higher Education, 36*(7), 815–829. doi:10.1080/03075079.2010.488720

Sturgeon, C. M., & Walker, C. (2009). *Faculty on Facebook: Confirm or deny?* Paper presented at the Annual Instructional Technology Conference, Murfreesboro, TN.

Su, B. (2005). Examining instructional design development of a web-based course: A case study. *International Journal of Distance Education Technologies, 3*(4), 62–76. doi:10.4018/jdet.2005100106

Su, B., Bonk, C. J., Magjuka, R. J., Liu, X., & Lee, S. (2005). The importance of interaction in web-based education: A program level case study of online MBA courses. *Journal of Interactive Online Learning, 4*(1), 1–19.

Su, B., Cong, C. J., Magjuka, R. J., Liu, X., & Lee, S. (2005). The importance of interaction in web-based education: A program-level study of online MBA courses. *Journal of Interactive Online Learning, 4*(1), 1–18.

Suddarth, B. H., & Slaney, R. B. (2001). An investigation of the dimensions of perfectionism in college students. *Measurement & Evaluation in Counseling & Development, 34,* 157–165.

Sullivan, P. (2002). It's easier to be yourself when you are invisible: Female college students discuss their online classroom experiences. *Innovative Higher Education, 27*(2), 129–143. doi:10.1023/A:1021109410893

Sundli, L. (2007). Mentoring—A new mantra for education? *Teaching and Teacher Education, 23*(2), 201–214. doi:10.1016/j.tate.2006.04.016

Sun, J. C., & Rueda, R. (2012). Situational interest, computer self-efficacy and self-regulation: Their impact on student engagement in distance education. *British Journal of Educational Technology, 43*(2), 191–204. doi:10.1111/j.1467-8535.2010.01157.x

Suskie, L. (2010). *Assessing student learning: A common sense guide.* Hoboken, NJ: John Wiley & Sons.

Sutton, L. (2001). The principle of vicarious interaction in computer-mediated communications. *International Journal of Educational Telecommunications, 7*(3), 223–242.

Svetkey, L. P., Stevens, V. J., Brantley, P. J., Appel, L., Hollis, J., & Vollmer, W. (2008). Comparison of strategies for sustaining weight loss: The weight loss maintenance randomized controlled trial. *Journal of the American Medical Association, 299,* 1139–1148. doi:10.1001/jama.299.10.1139 PMID:18334689

Svinicki, M. D., & McKeachie, W. J. (2011). *McKeachie's teaching tips: Strategies, research, and theory for college and university teachers.* New York: Routledge.

Swan, K., Garrison, D. R., & Richardson, J. C. (2009). A constructivist approach to online learning: The Community of Inquiry framework. In Information Technology and Constructivism in Higher Education: Progressive Learning Framework. Hershey, PA: IGI Global.

Swan, K. (2001). Virtual interaction: Design factors affecting student satisfaction and perceived learning in asynchronous online courses. *Distance Education, 22*(2), 306–333. doi:10.1080/0158791010220208

Swan, K. (2002). Building Learning Communities in Online Courses: The importance of interaction. *Education Communication and Information, 2*(1), 23–49. doi:10.1080/1463631022000005016

Swan, K. (2003). Developing social presence in online discussion. In S. Naidu (Ed.), *Learning and Teaching with Technology: Principles and Practices* (pp. 147–164). London: Kogan.

Swan, K. (2003). Learning effectiveness online: What the research tells us. In J. Bourne & J. C. Moore (Eds.), *Elements of quality online education, practice and direction* (pp. 13–45). Needham, MA: Sloan Center for Online Education.

Swan, K. (2003). Learning effectiveness: What the research tells us. In J. Bourne & J. C. Moore (Eds.), *Elements of quality online education, practice and direction* (pp. 13–45). Needham, MA: Sloan Center for Online Education.

Swan, K., Garrison, D. R., & Richardson, J. C. (2009). A constructivist approach to online learning: The Community of Inquiry framework. In C. R. Payne (Ed.), *Information technology and constructivism in higher education: Progressive learning frameworks* (pp. 43–57). Hershey, PA: IGI Global; doi:10.4018/978-1-60566-654-9.ch004

Swan, K., & Ice, P. (2010). The Community of Inquiry framework ten years later: Introduction to the special issue. *The Internet and Higher Education, 13*(1-2), 1–4. doi:10.1016/j.iheduc.2009.11.003

Swan, K., & Shea, P. (2005). The development of virtual learning communities. In S. R. Hiltz & R. Goldman (Eds.), *Asynchronous learning networks: The research frontier* (pp. 239–260). New York, NY: Hampton Press.

Swan, K., Shea, P., Fredericksen, E., Pickett, A., Pelz, W., & Maher, G. (2000). Building knowledge building communities: Consistency, contact and communication in the virtual classroom. *Journal of Educational Computing Research, 23*(4), 359–384.

Swan, K., Shea, P., Richardson, J., Ice, P., Garrison, D., Cleveland-Innes, M., & Arbaugh, J. (2008). Validating a measurement tool of presence in online communities of inquiry. *E-Mentor, 2*(24), 1–12.

Swan, K., & Shih, L. F. (2005). On the nature and development of social presence in online course discussions. *Journal of Asynchronous Learning Networks, 9*(3), 115–136.

Sweeney, A., Weaven, S., & Herington, C. (2008). Multicultural influences on group learning: A qualitative higher education study. *Assessment & Evaluation in Higher Education, 33*(2), 119–132. doi:10.1080/02602930601125665

Symons, C. S., & Johnson, B. T. (1997). The self-reference effect in memory: A meta-analysis. *Psychological Bulletin, 121*(3), 371–394. doi:10.1037/0033-2909.121.3.371 PMID:9136641

Szucs, A., Tait, A., Vidal, M., & Bernath, U. (2013). *Distance and e-learning in transition: Learning Innovation, Technology and Social Challenges*. Wiley.

Taft, S. H., Perkowski, T., & Martin, L. S. (2011). A framework for evaluating class size in online education. *The Quarterly Review of Distance Education, 12*, 181–197.

Taliaferro, A. (2011). Developing culturally responsive leaders through online learning and teaching approaches. *Journal of Educational Technology, 8*(3).

Tallent-Runnels, M. K., Thomas, J. A., Lan, W. Y., Cooper, S., Ahern, T. C., Shaw, S. M., & Liu, X. (2006). Teaching courses online: A review of the research. *Review of Educational Research, 76*(1), 93–135. doi:10.3102/00346543076001093

Tausczik, Y., & Pennebaker, J. (2009). The psychological meaning of words: LIWC and computerized text analysis methods. *Journal of Language and Social Psychology, 29*(1), 24–54. doi:10.1177/0261927X09351676

Taylor, J. (2001). The future of learning-learning for the future: Shaping the transition. *Open praxis: the bulleting of the International Council for Distance Education, 2*, 20-24. Retrieved from http://www.fernuni-hagen.de/ICDE/D-2001/final/keynote_speeches/wednesday/taylor_keynote.pdf

Taylor, J. C. (2002). *Teaching and learning online: The workers, the lurkers and the shirkers*. Paper presented at Conference on Research in Distance and Adult Learning in Asia, Hong Kong, China. Retrieved from http://www.ouhk.edu.hk/CRIDAL/cridala2002/speeches/taylor.pdf

Taylor, A., & McQuiggan, C. (2008). Faculty development programming: If we built it, will they come? *EDUCAUSE Quarterly, 3*, 29–37.

Taylor, J. C. (1995). Distance education technologies: The fourth generation. *Australasian Journal of Educational Technology, 11*(2), 1–7.

Taylor, J. C. (2001). *Fifth generation distance education. Higher Education Series, Report 40*. Canberra, Australia: Australian Department of Education, Training and Youth Affairs.

Taylor, K., Marienau, C., & Fiddler, M. (2000). *Strategies for teachers and trainers: Developing adult learners*. San Francisco: Jossey-Bass.

Taylor, S. E., & Brown, J. (1988). Illusion and well-being: A social psychological perspective on mental health. *Psychological Bulletin, 103*(2), 193–210. doi:10.1037/0033-2909.103.2.193 PMID:3283814

Tedjamulia, S. J. J., Olsen, D. R., Dean, D. L., & Albrecht, C. C. (2005). Motivating content contributions to online communities: Toward a more comprehensive theory. In *Proceedings of the 38th Hawaii International Conference on System Sciences*, (pp. 1-10). doi:10.1109/HICSS.2005.444

Terrion, J., & Leonard, D. (2010). A taxonomy of the characteristics of student peer mentors in higher education: Findings from a literature review. *Mentoring & Tutoring: Partnership in Learning, 15*(2), 149–164. doi:10.1080/13611260601086311

The American Federation of Teachers. (2000). *Distance education, guidelines for good practice*. Retrieved April 20, 2014 from http://www.aft.org/higher_education/downloadable/distance.pdf

The Council of Higher Education Accreditation. (2002). *Accreditation and assuring quality in distance learning*. CHEA Monograph (1, Series 2002). Retrieved April 20, 2014 from http://www.chea.org/pdf/mono_1_accred_distance_02.pdf?pubID=246

The Hanover Research Report. (2009). *Best practices in online teaching strategies*. Retrieved 12/4/2014 from http://www.uwec.edu/AcadAff/resources/edtech/upload/Best-Practices-in-Online-Teaching-Strategies-Membership.pdf

The Institute for Higher Education Policy. (2000). *Quality on the line: Benchmarks for success in internet-based distance education*. Retrieved from http://www.ihep.com/pubs/pdf/quality.pdf

Theisen, T. (2013). New spaces new realities: Expanding learning any time, any place. *Foreign Language Annals, 46*(4), 523–524. doi:10.1111/flan.12055

Thesen, L. (2007). Breaking the frame: Lectures, rituals, and academic literacies. *Journal of Applied Linguistics, 4*(1), 33–53.

Thompson, G. (1990). How can correspondence-based distance education be improved? A survey of attitudes of students who are not well disposed toward correspondence study. *Journal of Distance Education, 5*(1), 53–65.

Thongprasert, N., & Cross, J. M. (2008). Cross-cultural perspectives of knowledge sharing for different virtual classroom environments: A case study of Thai students in Thai and Australian universities. In *Proceedings of the EDU-COM 2008 International Conference*. Edith Cowan University. Retrieved from http://ro.ecu.edu.au/cgi/viewcontent.cgi?article=1050&context=ceducom

Tidwell, L. C., & Walther, J. B. (2002). Computer-mediated communication effects on disclosure, impressions, and interpersonal evaluations: Getting to know one another a bit at a time. *Human Communication Research, 28*(3), 317–348. doi:10.1111/j.1468-2958.2002.tb00811.x

Tilley, B. P. (2014). What makes a student non-traditional? A comparison of students over and under age 25 in online, accelerated psychology courses. *Psychology Learning & Teaching*, *13*(2), 95–106. doi:10.2304/plat.2014.13.2.95

Tinti-Kane, H. (2013). Overcoming hurdles to social media in education. *EDUCAUSE Review Online*. Retrieved 4/21/14 from http://www.educause.edu/ero/article/overcoming-hurdles-social-media-eduation

Tinto, V. (1993). Leaving college: Rethinking the causes and cures of student attrition (2nd ed.). Chicago, IL: The University of Chicago Press.

Tinto, V. (1975). Dropout from higher education: A theoretical synthesis of recent research. *Review of Educational Research*, *45*(1), 89–125. doi:10.3102/00346543045001089

Tinto, V. (2007). Research and practice of student retention: What next? *Journal of College Student Retention*, *8*(1), 1–20. doi:10.2190/4YNU-4TMB-22DJ-AN4W

Tollman, J. (2003). Classroom teaching in Botswana and online teaching from Georgia: Hard knocks and earned successes. *Journal of Education for Library and Information Science*, *44*(1), 39–57. doi:10.2307/40323941

Tonsmann, G. (2014). A study of the effectiveness of blackboard collaborate for conducting synchronous courses at multiple locations. *InSight: A Journal of Scholarly Teaching, 9*, 54-63.

Torkington, C., Lymbery, M., Milward, A., Mufin, M., & Richell, B. (2004). The impact of shared practice learning on the quality of assessment carried out by social work and district nurse students. *Learning in Health and Social Care*, *3*(1), 26–36. doi:10.1111/j.1473-6861.2004.00059.x

Towler, A. J., & Dipboy, R. L. (2003). Development of a learning style orientation measure. *Organizational Research Methods*, *6*(2), 216–235. doi:10.1177/1094428103251572

Trope, Y., & Liberman, N. (2010). Construal-Level Theory of psychological distance.[PubMed]. *Psychological Review*, *117*(2), 440–463. doi:10.1037/a0018963 PMID:20438233

Tsai, C. (2013). How to involve students in an online course: A redesigned online pedagogy of collaborative learning and self-regulated learning. *International Journal of Distance Education Technologies*, *11*(3), 47–57. doi:10.4018/jdet.2013070104

Tsai, C., Shen, P., & Fan, Y. (2013). Research trends in self-regulated learning research in online learning environments: A review of studies published in selected journals from 2003 to 2012. *British Journal of Educational Technology*, *44*(5), 107–110. doi:10.1111/bjet.12017

Tsai, C., Shen, P., & Tsai, M. (2011). Developing an appropriate design of blended learning with web-enabled self-regulated learning to enhance students' learning and thoughts regarding online learning. *Behaviour & Information Technology*, *30*(2), 261–271. doi:10.1080/0144929X.2010.514359

Tsai, Y., Kunter, M., Ludtke, O., Trautwein, U., & Ryan, R. M. (2008). What makes lessons interesting? The role of situational and individual factors in three school subjects. *Journal of Educational Psychology*, *100*(2), 460–472. doi:10.1037/0022-0663.100.2.460

Tsang, N. M. (2007). Reflection as Dialogue. *British Journal of Social Work*, *37*(4), 681–694. doi:10.1093/bjsw/bch304

Tschofen, C., & Mackness, J. (2012). Connectivism and dimensions of individual experience. *International Review of Research in Open and Distance Learning*, *13*(1), 124–143.

Tu, C. H. (2000). On-line migration: From social learning theory to social presence in online course discussions. *Journal of Asynchronous Learning Networks*, *9*(3), 115–136.

Tu, C. H. (2001). How Chinese perceive social presence: An examination of an online learning environment. *Educational Media International*, *38*(1), 45–60. doi:10.1080/09523980010021235

Tu, C. H., & McIssac, M. (2002). The relationship of social presence and interaction in online classes. *American Journal of Distance Education*, *16*(3), 131–150. doi:10.1207/S15389286AJDE1603_2

Tu, C. H., Sujo-Montes, L., Yen, C. J., Chan, J. Y., & Blocher, M. (2012). The integration of personal learning environments & open network learning environments. *TechTrends*, *56*(3), 13–19. doi:10.1007/s11528-012-0571-7

Tu, C.-H. (2000). On-line learning migration: From social learning theory to social presence theory in a CMC environment. *Journal of Network and Computer Applications*, *2*(1), 27–37. doi:10.1006/jnca.1999.0099

Tu, C.-H., & Corry, M. (2004). Online discussion durations impact online social presence.C. C. In et al. (Eds.), *Proceedings of Society for Information Technology and Teacher Education International Conference 2004* (pp. 3073-3077). Chesapeake, VA: AACE.

Tuckman, B. (1965). Developmental sequence in small groups. *Psychological Bulletin*, *63*(6), 384–399. doi:10.1037/h0022100 PMID:14314073

Turk, D. J., Cunningham, S. J., & Macrae, C. N. (2008). Self-memory biases in explicit and incidental encoding of trait adjectives. *Consciousness and Cognition*, *17*(3), 1040–1045. doi:10.1016/j.concog.2008.02.004 PMID:18395467

Tyson, T. (2006). It's a rap, but not as we know it.... *Times Higher Education Supplement*, *3*, 9.

U.S. Department of Education, National Center for Education Statistics. (2011). *The Condition of Education 2011* (NCES 2011-033). *Indicator (Minnesota Mining and Manfuacturing Company)*, 43.

U.S. Department of Education. (2009). *Evaluation of evidence-based practices in online learning: A meta-analysis and review of online learning studies*. Retrieved October 12, 2014 from http://www.gibill.va.gov/gi_bill_info/ch33/yellow_ribbon.htm

Ullmann, J. (2009). Alternative uses for course management systems: They aren't just for classes any more. *Online Journal of Distance Learning Administration*, *12*(3).

Umbach, P. D., & Wawrzynsli, M. R. (2005). Faculty do matter: The role of college faculty in student learning and engagement. *Research in Higher Education*, *46*(2), 153–185. doi:10.1007/s11162-004-1598-1

University of Kansas Medical Center. (2011). *Best practices in educational podcasting. Teaching and Learning Technologies*. Retrieved 4/21/2013 from http://www.kumc.edu/Documents/TLT/KUMC%20Best%20Practices%20in%20Podcasting.pdf

Urdan, T., & Midgley, C. (2001). Predictors of academic self-handicapping and achievement: Examining achievement goals, classroom goal structures, and culture. *Journal of Educational Psychology*, *96*(2), 251–264. doi:10.1037/0022-0663.96.2.251

Vachris, M. A. (1999). Teaching principles of economics without "chalk and talk": The experience of CNU online. *The Journal of Economic Education*, *30*, 292–302. doi:10.2307/1183070

Vaismoradi, M., Turunen, H., & Bondas, T. (2013). Content analysis and thematic analysis: Implications for conducting a qualitative descriptive study. *Nursing & Health Sciences*, *15*(3), 398–405. doi:10.1111/nhs.12048 PMID:23480423

Vallacher, R. R., & Wegner, D. M. (1985). *A theory of action identification*. Erlbaum Hillsdale.

Vallerand, R. J., & Bissonnette, R. (1992). Intrinsic, extrinsic, and amotivational styles as predictors of behavior: A prospective study. *Journal of Personality*, *60*(3), 599–620. doi:10.1111/j.1467-6494.1992.tb00922.x

Van De Vord, R., & Pogue, K. (2012). Teaching time investment: Does online really take more time than face-to-face? *International Review of Research in Open and Distance Learning*, *13*. Retrieved from http://www.irrodl.org/index.php/irrodl/article/view/1190/2212

Van den Bos, M., Cunningham, S. J., & Turk, D. J. (2010). Mine to remember: The effects of minimal ownership on remembering and knowing. *Quarterly Journal of Experimental Psychology*, *63*, 1065–1071. doi:10.1080/17470211003770938

van Schaik, P., Martin, S., & Vallance, M. (2012). Measuring flow experience in an immersive virtual environment for collaborative learning. *Journal of Computer Assisted Learning*, *28*(4), 350–365. doi:10.1111/j.1365-2729.2011.00455.x

Vankatesh, V., & Davis, F. D. (2000). A theoretical extension of the technology acceptance model: Four longitudinal field studies. *Management Science, 2*(2), 186–204. doi:10.1287/mnsc.46.2.186.11926

Van, L. T., De, R. K., Wetzels, M., & Visconti, L. M. (2014). The extended transportation-imagery model: A meta-analysis of the antecedents and consequences of consumers' narrative transportation. *The Journal of Consumer Research, 40*(5), 797–817. doi:10.1086/673383

Vansteenkiste, M., Lens, W., & Deci, E. L. (2006). Intrinsic versus extrinsic goal contents in self-determination theory: Another look at the quality of academic motivation. *Educational Psychologist, 4*(1), 19–31. doi:10.1207/s15326985ep4101_4

Vansteenkiste, M., Simons, J., Lens, W., Sheldon, K. M., & Deci, E. L. (2004). Motivating learning, performance, and persistence: The synergistic role of intrinsic goals and autonomy-support. *Journal of Personality and Social Psychology, 87*, 246–260. doi:10.1037/0022-3514.87.2.246 PMID:15301630

Varvel, V. (2007). Master online teacher competencies. *Online Journal of Distance Learning Administration, 10*(1), 1–36. Retrieved from http://www.westga.edu/~distance/ojdla/spring101/varvel101.pdf

Varvel, V. (2007). Master online teacher competences. *Online Journal of Distance Learning Administration, 10*(1). Retrieved from http://www.westga.edu/~distance/ojdla/spring101/varvel101.htm

Vasu, M. L., & Ozturk, A. O. (2009). Teaching methodology to distance education students using rich-media and computer simulation. *Social Science Computer Review, 27*(2), 271–283. doi:10.1177/0894439308327129

Veletsianos, G., Kimmons, R., & French, K. (2013). Instructor experiences with a social networking site in a higher education setting: Expectations, frustrations, appropriation, and compartmentalization. *Educational Technology Research and Development, 61*(2), 255–278. doi:10.1007/s11423-012-9284-z

Venable, M. (2011, December). Who is the instructor? Developing social presence in an online course. *Online College.org*. Retrieved from http://www.onlinecollege.org/2011/12/27/who-is-the-instructor-developing-social-presence-in-an-online-course/

Vesely, P., Bloom, L., & Sherlock, J. (2007). Key elements of building online community: Comparing faculty and student perceptions. *Journal of Online Learning and Teaching, 3*, 234–246.

Villegas, A. M., & Lucas, T. (2002). *Educating culturally responsive teachers: A coherent approach*. Albany, NY: State University of New York Press.

Virgil,, E., & Varvel, Jr. (2007, Spring). Master Online Teacher Competencies. *Online Journal of Distance Learning Administration, 10*(1).

Virkus, S. (2008). Use of web 2.0 technologies in LIS education: Experiences at Tallinn University, Estonia. Program: Electronic Library and Information Systems, 42(3), 262-274.

Visser, J., & Keller, J. M. (1990). The clinical use of motivational messages: An inquiry into the validity of the ARCS model of motivational design. *Instructional Science, 19*(6), 467–500. doi:10.1007/BF00119391

Visser, J., Plomp, T., Amirault, R. J., & Kuiper, R. W. (2002). Motivating students at a distance: The case of an international audience. *Educational Technology Research and Development, 50*(2), 94–110. doi:10.1007/BF02504998

Vonderwell, S., & Zachariah, S. (2005). Factors that influence participation in online learning. *Journal of Research on Technology in Education, 38*(2), 213–230. doi:10.1080/15391523.2005.10782457

Vrasidas, C., & McIsaac, S. M. (1999). Factors influencing interaction in an online course. *American Journal of Distance Education, 13*(3), 22–36. doi:10.1080/08923649909527033

Vygotsky, L. S. (1997). The collected works of L. S. Vygotsky, Vol. 4: The history of the development of higher mental functions (M. J. Hall, Translator; R. W. Reiber, Ed.). New York: Plenum Press.

Vygotsky, L. (1978). *Mind in Society*. Cambridge, MA: Harvard University Press.

Vygotsky, L. (1986). *Thought and language*. Cambridge, MA: MIT Press.

Vygotsky, L. S. (1978). *Mind in society: The development of higher psychological processes*. Cambridge, MA: Harvard University Press.

Vygotsky, L. S. (1987). Thought and word. In R. Rieber & A. Carton (Eds.), *The collected works of L. S. Vygotsky* (Vol. 1). New York, NY: Plenum Press.

Wachenheim, C. J. (2009). Final exam scores in introductory economics courses: Effects of course delivery method and proctoring. *Review of Agricultural Economics, 31*(3), 640–652. doi:10.1111/j.1467-9353.2009.01458.x

Wadsworth, B. J. (1988). *Piaget's theory of cognitive and affective development* (4th ed.). New York: Longman.

Waldo, A. E. (2013). Cooperative study blog. In S. P. Ferris & H. A. Wilder (Eds.), *The plugged-in professor: tips and techniques for teaching with social media*. Cambridge, UK: Chandos Publishing. doi:10.1016/B978-1-84334-694-4.50013-2

Walker, S. C., & Taub, D. J. (2001). Variables correlated with satisfaction with a mentoring relationship in first-year college students and their mentors. *Journal of the First-Year Experience & Students in Transition, 13*(1), 47–67.

Wallis, H. B. (Producer) & Huston, J. (Director). (n.d.). *Maltese Falcon*. [Motion Picture]. United States: Warner Brothers.

Walther, J. B. (1992). Interpersonal effects in computer-mediated interaction: A relational perspective. *Communication Research, 19*(1), 52–90. doi:10.1177/009365092019001003

Walther, J. B. (1996). Computer-mediated communication impersonal, interpersonal, and hyperpersonal interaction. *Communication Research, 23*(1), 3–43. doi:10.1177/009365096023001001

Waltonen-Moore, S., Stuart, D., Newton, E., Oswald, R., & Varonis, E. (2006). From Virtual Strangers to a Cohesive Online Learning Community: The Evolution of Online Group Development in a Professional Development Course. *Journal of Technology and Teacher Education, 14*(2), 287–311.

Wang, C. X., Jaeger, D., Liu, J., & Xie, N. (2013). Using synchronous technology to enrich student learning. *TechTrends, 57*(1), 20–25. doi:10.1007/s11528-012-0626-9

Wang, C., Shannon, D., & Ross, M. (2013). Students' characteristics, self-regulated learning, technology self-efficacy, and course outcomes in online learning. *Distance Education, 34*(3), 302–323. doi:10.1080/01587919.2013.835779

Wang, Q. (2006). Quality assurance – best practices for assessing online programs. *International Journal on E-Learning, 5*(2), 265–274.

Wanstreet, C. E. (2009). Interaction in online learning environments. *The Perfect Online Course: Best Practices for Designing and Teaching*, 425.

Warden, C. A., Stanworth, J. O., Ren, J. B., & Warden, A. R. (2013). Synchronous learning best practices: An action research study. *Computers & Education, 63*, 197–207. doi:10.1016/j.compedu.2012.11.010

Ware, P. D. (2004). Confidence and competition online: ESL student perspectives on web-based discussions in the classroom. *Computers and Composition, 21*(4), 451–468. doi:10.1016/S8755-4615(04)00041-6

Warschauer, M. (2013). Comparing face-to-face and electronic discussion in the second language classroom. *CALICO Journal, 13*(2&3), 7–26.

Wassell, B., & Crouch, C. (2008). Fostering connections between multicultural education and technology: Incorporating weblogs into preservice teacher education. *Journal of Technology and Teacher Education, 16*(2), 211–232.

Waterhouse, S. (2005). *The Power of eLearning: The Essential Guide for Teaching in the Digital Age*. Pearson/Allyn & Bacon.

Watson, G. (2002). Using technology to promote success in problem based learning courses. *Technology Source*. Retrieved from: http://technology-source.org/article/using_technology_to_promote_success_in_pbl_courses/

Watson, W. R., & Watson, S. L. (2007). What are Learning Management Systems, What are they not, and what should they become? *TechTrends, 51*(2), 28–34. doi:10.1007/s11528-007-0023-y

Wdowik, S. J. (2014). Using a synchronous online learning environment to promote and enhance transactional engagement beyond the classroom. *Campus-Wide Information Systems, 31*(4), 254–263.

Weaver, C. M., & Albion, P. R. (2005). Momentum in online discussions: The effect of social presence on motivation for participation. In *Proceedings of the Australasian Society for Computers in Learning in Tertiary Education Conference*, (pp. 703-706). Retrieved from http://www.ascilite.org.au/conferences/brisbane05/blogs/proceedings/81_Weaver.pdf

Weekes, S. (2008, November-December). E-learning on the social. *Training & Coaching Today, 15*.

Wegerif, R. (1998). The Social Dimension of Asynchronous Learning Networks. *JALN, 2*(1), 34–49.

Wegerif, R. (1998). The social dimension of asynchronous learning networks. *Journal of Asynchronous Learning Networks, 2*(1), 34–49.

Wei, C., Chen, N., & Kinshuk, . (2012). A model for social presence in online classrooms. *Educational Technology Research and Development, 60*(3), 529–545. doi:10.1007/s11423-012-9234-9

Weiner, M., & Mehrabian, A. (1968). *Language within language: Immediacy, a channel in verbal communication*. New York: Appleton-Century-Crofts.

Weinstein, C., & Mayer, R. (1986). The teaching of learning strategies. In M. C. Wittrock (Ed.), *Handbook of Research on Teaching and Learning* (3rd ed.; pp. 315–327). New York: Macmillan.

Weissman, A. (Executive Producer). (2000, July 6). Interview of Henri Cartier-Bresson. In *The Charlie Rose Show*. PBS.

Wells, G. (1999). *Dialogic inquiry: Toward a sociocultural practice and theory of education Cambridge*. UK: Cambridge University Press; doi:10.1017/CBO9780511605895

Wenger, E. (1998). *Communities of practice: Learning, meaning, and identity*. Cambridge, UK: Cambridge University Press; doi:10.1017/CBO9780511803932

White, B. Y., Collins, A., & Frederiksen, J. R. (2011). The nature of scientific meta-knowledge. In M. S. Khine & I. Saleh (Eds.), *Dynamic modeling: Cognitive tool for scientific enquiry* (pp. 41–76). London: Springer.

Whiteman, J.A.M. (2002) *Interpersonal Communication in Computer Mediated Learning*. (White/opinion paper). (ED 465 997).

Wigfield, A. (1984). *Relations between ability perceptions, other achievement-related beliefs, and school performance*. Paper presented at the Annual Meeting of the American Educational Research Association, New Orleans, LA.

Wigfield, A. (1994). Expectancy-value of achievement motivation: A developmental perspective. *Educational Psychology Review, 6*(1), 49–78. doi:10.1007/BF02209024

Wigfield, A., & Cambia, J. (2010). Students' achievement values, goal orientations, and interest: Definitions, development, and relations to achievement outcomes. *Developmental Review, 30*(1), 1–35. doi:10.1016/j.dr.2009.12.001

Wigfield, A., & Eccles, J. (1992). The development of achievement task values: A theoretical analysis. *Developmental Review, 12*(3), 265–310. doi:10.1016/0273-2297(92)90011-P

Wigfield, A., & Eccles, J. (2000). Expectancy-value theory of achievement motivation. *Contemporary Educational Psychology, 25*(1), 68–81. doi:10.1006/ceps.1999.1015 PMID:10620382

Wigfield, A., Eccles, J. S., Roeser, R., & Schiefele, U. (2009). Development of achievement motivation. In W. Damon & R. M. Lerner (Eds.), *Developmental psychology: An advanced course book*. New York, NY: Wiley.

Wiggins, G. (1990). *The case for authentic assessment. (Clearinghouse on Tests, Measurement, and Evaluation, American Institutes for Research, ED328611 1990-12-00)*. Washington, DC: Government Printing Office.

Williams, J. B., & Jacobs, J. (2004). Exploring the use of blogs as learning spaces in the higher education sector. *Australasian Journal of Educational Technology, 20*(2), 232–247.

Williams, M. (1996). Learner control and instructional technologies. In D. Jonassen (Ed.), *Handbook of research on educational communications and technology* (pp. 957–983). Scholastic.

Wilson, B. G., & Christopher, L. (2008). Hype versus reality on campus: Why e-Learning isn't likely to replace a professor. In S. Carliner & P. Shank (Eds.), *The e-learning handbook: A comprehensive guide to online learning* (pp. 55–76). San Francisco, CA: Pfeiffer.

Wilson, B. G., Ludwig-Hardman, S., Thornam, C. L., & Dunlap, J. (2004). Bounded community: Designing and facilitating learning communities in formal courses. *International Review of Research in Open and Distance Learning, 5*(3). Retrieved from http://www.irrodl.org/index.php/irrodl/article/view/204/286

Wilson, B. G., Ludwig-Hardman, S., Thornam, C. L., & Dunlap, J. C. (2004). Bounded communities: Design and facilitating learning communities in formal courses. *International Review of Research in Open and Distance Learning, 5*(3). Retrieved from http://is2.lse.ac.uk/asp/aspecis/20080174.pdf

Wilson, C. D. (2013). Making connections: Higher education meets social media. *Change, 45*(4), 51–57. doi:10.1080/00091383.2013.806201

Wilson, E. K., Wright, V. H., Inman, C. T., & Matherson, L. H. (2011). Retooling the social studies classroom for the current generation. *Social Studies, 102*(2), 65–72. doi:10.1080/00377996.2010.484445

Wilson, J. (2002). The power of distance learning. *Education, 122*(4), 638–673.

Wilson, N., Zygouris-Coe, V., Cardullo, V., & Fong, J. (2013). Pedagogical frameworks of e-reader technologies in education. In S. Keengwe (Ed.), *Pedagogical Applications and Social Effects of Mobile Technology Integration* (pp. 1–24). doi:10.4018/978-1-4666-2985-1.ch001

Winn, W. (1993). Instructional design and situated learning: Paradox or partnership. *Educational Technology, 33*, 16–21.

Wirt, L. G., & Jaeger, A. J. (2014). Seeking to understand faculty-student interaction at community colleges. *Community College Journal of Research and Practice, 38*(11), 980–994. doi:10.1080/10668926.2012.725388

Wise, A., Speer, J., Marbouti, F., & Hsiao, Y.-T. (2013). Broadening the notion of participation in online discussions: Examining patterns in learners' online listening behaviors. *Instructional Science, 41*(2), 323–343. doi:10.1007/s11251-012-9230-9

Wladis, C., Hachey, A. C., & Conway, K. M. (2015). The representation of minority, female, and non-traditional STEM majors in the online environment at community colleges: A nationally representative study. *Community College Review, 43*(1), 89–114. doi:10.1177/0091552114555904

Wlodkowski, R. J. (2003, Spring). Accelerated learning in colleges and universities. *New Directions for Adult and Continuing Education, 97*(97), 5–16. doi:10.1002/ace.84

Wlodkowski, R. J., & Ginsberg, M. B. (2010). *Teaching intensive and accelerated courses: Instruction that motivates learning.* San Francisco, CA: John Wiley & Sons.

Wolf, P. (2006). Best practices in the training of faculty to teach online. *Journal of Computing in Higher Education, 17*(2), 47–78. doi:10.1007/BF03032698

Wolters, C. (2003). Regulation of motivation: Evaluating an underemphasized aspect of self-regulated learning. *Educational Psychologist, 38*(4), 189–205. doi:10.1207/S15326985EP3804_1

Wood, D. F. (2003). ABC of learning and teaching in medicine: Problem based learning. *BMJ (Clinical Research Ed.), 326*(7384), 328–330. doi:10.1136/bmj.326.7384.328 PMID:12574050

Wood, J. L., & Ireland, S. M. (2014). Supporting black male community college success: Determinants of faculty–student engagement. *Community College Journal of Research and Practice, 38*(2/3), 154–165. doi:10.1080/10668926.2014.851957

Woods, R., & Baker, J. (2004). Interaction and immediacy in online learning. *The International Review of Research in Open and Distance Learning, 5*(2). Retrieved 20-2-2009 from http://www.irrodl.org/index.php/irrodl/article/view/186/268

Worley, W., & Tesdell, L. (2009). Instructor time and effort in online and face-to-face teaching: Lessons learned. *IEEE Transactions on Professional Communication*, *52*(2), 138–151. doi:10.1109/TPC.2009.2017990

Wozniak, H., Pizzica, J., & Mahony, M. J. (2012). Design-based research principles for student orientation to online study: Capturing the lessons learned. *Australasian Journal of Educational Technology*, *28*(5), 896–911.

Wright, C. R., Lopes, V., Montgomerie, T. C., Reju, S. A., & Schmoller, S. (2014). Selecting a learning management system: Advice from an academic perspective. *EDUCAUSE Review Online,* November 3, 2014.

Wyss, V. v., Freedman, D., & Siebert, C. (2014). The Development of a Discussion Rubric for Online Courses: Standardizing Expectations of Graduate Students in Online Scholarly Discussions. *Techtrends: Linking Research & Practice to Improve Learning, 58*(2), 99-107. Retrieved from http://link.springer.com/article/10.1007/s11528-014-0741-x

Xie, K., Durrington, V., & Yen, L. L. (2011). Relationship between students' motivation and their participation in asynchronous online discussions. *Journal of Online Learning and Teaching*, *17*(1), 17–29. Retrieved from http://jolt.merlot.org/vol7no1/xie_0311.pdf

Xie, Y., Ke, F., & Sharma, P. (2010). The effect of peer-interaction styles in team blogging on students' cognitive thinking and blog participation. *Journal of Educational Computing Research*, *42*(4), 459–479. doi:10.2190/EC.42.4.f

Xie, Y., Ke, K., & Sharma, P. (2008). The effective peer feedback for blogging on college students' reflective learning processes. *The Internet and Higher Education*, *11*(1), 18–25. doi:10.1016/j.iheduc.2007.11.001

Xin, C., & Feenberg, A. (2006). Pedagogy in Cyberspace: The Dynamics of Online Discourse. *Journal of Distance Education*, *21*(2), 1–25.

Yamagata-Lynch, L. (2014). Blending online asynchronous and synchronous learning. *International Review of Research in Open and Distance Learning*, *15*(2), 189–212.

Yang, D., Olesova, L., & Richardson, J. C. (2008). The impact of cross-cultural differences on learner participation and communication in asynchronous discussions. In K. McFerrin et al. (Eds.), *Proceedings of Society for Information Technology & Teacher Education International Conference 2008,* (pp. 825-829). Chesapeake, VA: AACE.

Yang, C., & Chang, Y. S. (2012). Assessing the effects of interactive blogging on student attitudes toward peer interaction, learning motivation, and academic achievements. *Journal of Computer Assisted Learning*, *28*(2), 126–135. doi:10.1111/j.1365-2729.2011.00423.x

Yang, D., Olesova, L., & Richardson, J. C. (2010). Impact of cultural differences on students' participation, communication, and learning in an online environment. *Journal of Educational Computing Research*, *43*(2), 165–182. doi:10.2190/EC.43.2.b

Yang, S. H. (2009). Using Blogs to Enhance Critical Reflection and Community of Practice. *Journal of Educational Technology & Society*, *12*(2), 11–21.

Yang, Y., & Cornelius, L. F. (2005). Preparing instructors for quality online instruction. *Online Journal of Distance Learning Administration*, *8*, 12–31.

Yang, Y.-T. (2008). A catalyst for teaching critical thinking in a large university class in Taiwan: Asynchronous online discussions with the facilitation of teaching assistants. *Educational Technology Research and Development*, *56*(3), 241–264. doi:10.1007/s11423-007-9054-5

Yeh, Y.-C. (2010). Analyzing online behaviors, roles, and learning communities via online discussions. *Journal of Educational Technology & Society*, *13*(1), 140–151.

Yen, H. J., & Liu, S. (2009). Learner autonomy as a predictor of course success and final grades in community college online courses. *Journal of Educational Computing Research*, *41*(3), 347–367. doi:10.2190/EC.41.3.e

Yen, Y. S., Hu, S. C., & Ke, T. S. (2011). The impact of learning attention on learning performance in e-learning. *T & D Journal, 112*, 1–21.

Young, M. F. (1993). Instructional design for situated learning. *Educational Technology Research and Development*, *41*(1), 43–58. doi:10.1007/BF02297091

Young, S. (2006). Student views of effective online teaching in higher education. *American Journal of Distance Education*, *20*(2), 65–77. doi:10.1207/s15389286ajde2002_2

Yu, C., & Brandenburg, T. (2006). I would have had more success if...: The reflections and tribulations of a first-time online instructor. *Journal of Technology Studies*, *32*(1), 43–52.

Zak, P. J. (2013). *The moral molecule: The source of love and prosperity*. New York: Dutton.

Zakus, D. H., Malloy, D. C., & Edwards, A. (2007). Critical and ethical thinking in sport management: Philosophical rationales and examples of methods. *Sport Management Review*, *10*(2), 133–158. doi:10.1016/S1441-3523(07)70008-6

Zandberg, I., & Lewis, L. (2008). *Technology-based distance education courses for public elementary and secondary school students*. Retrieved from the National Center for Education Statistics: http://nces.ed.gov/pubs2008/2008008.pdf

Zapalska, A., & Brozik, D. (2006). Learning styles and online education. *Campus-Wide Information Systems*, *23*(5), 325–335. doi:10.1108/10650740610714080

Zarezadeh, Y., Pearson, P., & Dickinson, C. (2009). A model for reflection to enhance interprofessional education. *International Journal of Education*, *1*(1), 1–18. doi:10.5296/ije.v1i1.191

Zeichner, K. M., & Liston, D. P. (1996). *Reflective teaching: An introduction*. Mahwah, NJ: Lawrence Erlbaum.

Zeng, R., & Luyegu, E. (2012). Mobile Learning in Higher Education. In A. Olofsson & J. Lindberg (Eds.), *Informed Design of Educational Technologies in Higher Education: Enhanced Learning and Teaching* (pp. 292–306). Hershey, PA: Information Science Reference; doi:10.4018/978-1-61350-080-4.ch015

Zeng, X., & Harris, S. T. (2005). Blogging in an online health information technology class. *Perspectives in Health Information Management*, *2*(6). http://www.ncbi.nlm.nih.gov/pmc/articles/PMC2047310/ Retrieved October 14, 2014 PMID:18066374

Zhang, B. (2015). Bridging the Social and Teaching Presence Gap in Online Learning. In R. Wright (Ed.), *Student-Teacher Interaction in Online Learning Environments* (pp. 158–182). Hershey, PA; doi:10.4018/978-1-4666-6461-6.ch008

Zhang, W.-y., Perris, K., & Yeung, L. (2005). Online tutorial support in open and distance learning: Students' perceptions. *British Journal of Educational Technology*, *36*(5), 789–804. doi:10.1111/j.1467-8535.2004.00492.x

Zhang, Y. (2013). Power distance in online learning: Experience of Chinese learners in U. S. higher education. *International Review of Research in Open and Distance Learning*, *14*(4), 238–254. Retrieved from http://www.irrodl.org/index.php/irrodl/article/view/1557

Zhao, P., & Johnson, G. (2012). A theoretical framework of self-regulated learning with web-based technologies. In Proceedings of Global TIME 2012 (pp. 163–168). AACE. Retrieved from http://www.editlib.org/p/39417

Zhu, C. (2012). Student satisfaction, performance, and knowledge construction in online collaborative learning. *Journal of Educational Technology & Society*, *15*(1), 127–136. Retrieved from http://www.ifets.info/journals/15_1/12.pdf

Zhu, E. (2006). Interaction and cognitive engagement: An analysis of four asynchronous online discussions. *Instructional Science*, *34*(6), 451–480. doi:10.1007/s11251-006-0004-0

Zimmerman, B. J. (1986). Development of self-regulated learning: Which are the key sub-processes? *Contemporary Educational Psychology*, *11*(4), 307–313. doi:10.1016/0361-476X(86)90027-5

Zimmerman, B. J. (1989). Self-regulated learning and academic achievement: An overview. *Educational Psychologist, 25*(1), 3–17. doi:10.1207/s15326985ep2501_2

Zimmerman, B. J. (2000). Attainment of self-regulation: A social-cognitive perspective. In M. Boekaerts, P. Pintrich, & M. Zeidner (Eds.), *Handbook of self-regulation, research, and applications.* Orlando, FL: Academic Press.

Zimmerman, B. J. (2006). Enhancing students' academic responsibility and achievement: A social-cognitive self-regulatory account. In R. J. Sternberg & R. Subotnick (Eds.), *Optimizing student success in school with the other three Rs: Reasoning, resilience, and responsibility.* Greenwich, CT: Information Age.

Zimmerman, B. J. (2008). Investigating self-regulation and motivation: Historical background, methodological developments, and future prospects. *American Educational Research Journal, 45*(1), 166–183. doi:10.3102/0002831207312909

Zimmerman, B. J., Bandura, A., & Martinez-Pons, M. (1992). Self-motivation for academic attainment: The role of self-efficacy beliefs and personal goal setting. *American Educational Research Journal, 29*(3), 663–676. doi:10.3102/00028312029003663

Zimmerman, B. J., & Kitsantas, A. (2005). Homework practices and academic achievement: The mediating role of self-efficacy and perceived responsibility beliefs. *Contemporary Educational Psychology, 30*(4), 397–417. doi:10.1016/j.cedpsych.2005.05.003

Zimmerman, B. J., & Schunk, D. H. (2001). *Self-regulated learning and academic achievement: Theoretical perspectives* (2nd ed.). Mahway, NJ: Lawrence Erlbaum.

Zimmerman, T. D. (2012). Exploring learner to content interaction as a success factor in online courses. *International Review of Research in Open and Distance Learning, 13*(4), 152–165.

About the Contributors

Lydia Kyei-Blankson is an Associate Professor in the Educational Administration and Foundations Department at Illinois State University. Her expertise and training is in research methods, applied statistics, and psychometrics. Her assignment at ISU includes teaching research methods and statistics graduate courses. Dr. Kyei-Blankson's research agenda focuses on the scholarship of teaching and learning, online education, and effective technology integration in teaching and learning.

Joseph Blankson, is the Educational Technology Manager at Ohio Northern University in Ada, Ohio. Dr. Blankson has extensive experience in supporting innovative curriculum development, including integration of technologies into higher education programs. He has designed and facilitated numerous professional development activities in the use of educational technologies, online/hybrid course design and provided instructional development services particularly with Learning Management Systems for faculty, staff and students. He has also taught educational technology courses at the undergraduate and graduate levels. Joseph has particular interest in using emerging technologies to promote excellence in teaching and learning, the design of web-based instruction and faculty development in the use of technology for teaching and learning.

Esther Ntuli is an Assistant Professor in the Department of Teaching and Educational Studies at Idaho State University (ISU). Her expertise and training is in curriculum and instruction, early childhood education, instructional technology, children's literature and writing. Dr. Ntuli teaches undergraduate instructional technology courses, foundational undergraduate and graduate courses at ISU. Her research interest focuses on technology use and practice in the classroom, teacher education, assessment, and culturally responsive education.

Cynthia Agyeman has a doctorate degree in Instructional Technology and a background in Visual Arts. Her research centers on visual arts and new digital media with a special focus on the integration of emergent technologies and the aesthetic and design elements and principles to create new art forms. Dr. Agyeman also has experience teaching online courses.

* * *

Devshikha Bose, Ph.D., is an Instructional Designer at the Boise State University, Instructional Design and Educational Assessment (IDEA) shop. Her research interests include mobile learning, just-in-time learning, flipped learning, hybrid learning, digital learning objects, communities of learning, educational uses of 3D printing, and social media.

Megan Burton received her Ph.D. in Elementary Education with an emphasis in mathematics in 2006 from the University of Alabama. She is currently an Associate Professor at Auburn University. Her research interests include innovational instructional strategies, mathematics teacher empowerment, and rural education.

Victoria Cardullo is an Assistant Professor of Reading in the College of Education and the Department of Curriculum and Teaching at Auburn University. She received her Master's Degree in Reading from the University of Central Florida. Her Ed.D was awarded in Curriculum and Instruction-Reading at the University of Central Florida. Dr. Cardullo is actively involved in publications and presentations related to her research. Her research interests are in digital literacies, specifically New Literacies. She is particularly interested in exploring how to support adolescent readers' reading and comprehension skills to prepare them for 21st century learning. Many of these skills will require a new pedagogical framework for classroom teachers as they prepare students for the digital literacies of the 21st century. In addition to New Literacies, teacher preparation is of particular interest to her, specifically co-teaching as part of the internship process, using collaboration and mentoring within partnership programs.

Sang Chan is an instructional designer at Weber State University.

Audrey Cooke has worked with pre-service teachers since 2008. Her passions for technology and mathematics have combined in her work with pre-service teachers. Her beliefs that everyone should have the opportunity to engage with technology and to enjoy mathematics and their mathematical experiences, have driven her scholarship and research at university. Her work with pre-service teachers, many of who will work with children from birth through to 12 years of age, focuses on creating experiences that enable pre-service teachers to fully embrace the opportunities that teaching will provide. She uses technology to help pre-service teachers re-vision how they see and engage with mathematics. These experiences include pre-service teachers finding out personal mathematical strengths and areas needing development, their disposition towards mathematics, ways of sharing their investigations of and solutions for mathematical problems, accessing resources that provide different mathematical different to those in their past, interacting with new technology-driven ways of engaging with mathematics, and opportunities to reflect on what they know about mathematics.

Travis Crone is an Assistant Professor of Psychology at the University of Houston-Downtown. His research examines social cognition with an emphasis on conscious and nonconscious goals, perceptions of the divine, and the effects of academic best practices on student attitudes.

Ted Cross is a University Innovation Fellow at Arizona State University, in the Office of University initiatives (a Special Projects Unit of the Office of the President). He is passionate about innovation in higher education and works on projects aimed at leveraging technology and human capital to reach more students via both digital and traditional means. Ted holds a bachelors degree from Brigham Young University, an MA from Arizona State University, an MSed from The University of Pennsylvania, an EdD from Pepperdine University, and a Post Graduate Certificate from The Wharton School of Business.

Ted has also served as a Teach for America Corps Member where he taught 8th grade English. Before coming to ASU, Ted was the Director of Dissertation Research at Grand Canyon University where he also served as one of the first full-time online faculty members.

Judi Simmons Estes is an Associate Professor and Chair of the Department of Elementary and Secondary Teacher Preparation at Park University, USA. Dr. Estes has taught courses through a variety of distance education modes since 1996 and has developed courses for online delivery at two institutions. In addition to teaching face-to-face with web-based support, she has used both hybrid and fully online formats for course delivery during the past seven years. Her particular research interests are student engagement, student retention, and instructional effectiveness.

Martha Henckell is the Information Technology (IT) Director of User Services and an adjunct faculty member at Southeast Missouri State University for both the College of Business and College of Education. In her role as IT Director, Martha is responsible for the IT training program, comprised of both online and face-to-face courses and presentations. Martha has published a number of articles, book chapters, and book, Evaluation of Distance Education: The Student Perspective.

Rick Holbeck earned a Bachelor's Degree in Secondary Music Education from Bemidji State University (Minnesota) and a Master's Degree in Educational Leadership from Southwest Minnesota State University and a Master's Degree in Curriculum and Instruction with an emphasis on Technology from Grand Canyon University. He has also finished the coursework for a PhD in Educational Leadership at Walden University and is currently in a doctoral program at Grand Canyon University in Higher Education Leadership. Rick began teaching adjunct classes for Grand Canyon University in February of 2010 and moved to a Full Time Online Faculty position in August, 2010. Rick held the position of Manager of Online Full Time Faculty for about two years and has recently transitioned to the role of Director of Online Full Time Faculty.

Genevieve Marie Johnson received a doctoral degree from the University of Alberta (Canada) in 1990 and a Graduate Diploma in Distance Education Technology from Athabasca University (Canada) in 2007. Having been actively involved in university and college teaching for more than 20 years, she is currently associate professor in the School of Education at Curtin University in Western Australia.

Michelle Kilburn is an assistant professor at Southeast Missouri State University. Kilburn's teaching focuses on crime and human behavior, juvenile justice, statistics and criminal justice administration. Her areas of focus include student perceptions of online learning, student percpetions of critical issues in criminal justice, social media influence in criminal justice and innovative strategies teaching criminal justice.

Alex Kumi-Yeboah, PhD is an assistant professor of education at the University at Albany, State University University of New York. His research interests are multicultural online education and educational experiences of Black immigrants.

Piera Leftheriotou obtained one bachelor's degree in French Literature and one in Early Childhood Education in Athens. In 2005 she obtained a Master's degree and in 2014 a PhD from the Hellenic Open

University. The subject of her PhD is "Planning adult education programs in Greece: the case of General Secretariat for Lifelong Learning". She has been working on Adult Education in the Greek Ministry of Education since 1984. She is a member of the scientific staff of Hellenic Open University and she has been assigned to teach Adult Education in postgraduate courses for the present academic year. She has published articles and chapters on adult education and e-learning. Her research interests mainly focus on topics related to adult education and educators' training in conventional and e-learning environments.

Annabelle Lewer-Fletcher, before beginning on an academic path Annabelle Lewer-Fletcher began her working career in the lively arts sector in Canberra, running her own theatre company and while also working as a media spokesperson for prominent lobbying organisations. She has been working at UNSW for 4 years and has been a course convener at UNSW for 3 years, she is currently delivering the DVC-A Introduction to Global Citizenship course within the Diploma of Professional Practice and tutoring in the UNSW Art & Design, design history program. Annabelle is passionate about online delivery methods and utilising the visual in the delivery of course content and prides herself on creating engaging and accessible resources for students. Her unique mix of tertiary qualifications (BA, ANU; MA, UNSW; GDip Ed, MQ) and industry experience gives her insight into both the academic understanding of her areas of interest but also the practical implications of topics in the daily lives of her students. Lewer-Fletcher areas of interest include: global citizenship theory, e-learning, education, art history, design history and educational design.

Juhong Christie Liu is an Instructional Technologist/Assistant Professor, Professional Faculty, in the Center for Instructional Technology at James Madison University. She has taught undergraduate and graduate classes in face-to-face, online asynchronous and synchronous environments. Her research interest focuses on student support in technology-mediated learning environments, impact of teaching and learning with evolving and emerging technologies, and collaborative teaching and learning in distributed environments. Christie received a Ph.D. in Instructional Design and Technology from Virginia Polytechnic Institute and State University. She published in TechTrends and HETL, and presented at AECT, Online Learning Consortium, Mid-Atlantic EDUCAUSE, SITE, E-Learn and ASCD conferences. Her presentation at the Online Learning Consortium 10th Annual Blended Learning Conference was awarded as the "Best-in-Track" Student Support session.

Patrick R. Lowenthal is an assistant professor in the Department of Educational Technology at Boise State University where he teaches in a fully online graduate program. Prior to joining the faculty full-time, he spent two years as an instructional designer at Boise State. Before moving to Idaho, Patrick worked as an Academic Technology Coordinator at the University of Colorado Denver as well an assistant professor at Regis University. Patrick is interested in problems of practice with teaching and learning online. He researches how faculty and students communicate using emerging technologies and, specifically, how they establish presence and community online.

Eunice Luyegu is a faculty member and Instructional Design Specialist in the College of Healthcare Sciences at Nova Southeastern University – Tampa Campus. She consults with faculty to create engaging learning environments. Dr. Luyegu holds a PhD in Instructional Design and Technology from the University of South Alabama. She is also a Certified Performance Technologist. She facilitates faculty training workshops on the pedagogy and technology of teaching and learning. Her research interests include blended learning and the integration of learning, emerging, and open technologies in course design.

B. Jean Mandernach, Ph.D. is Research Professor and Director of the Center for Innovation in Research and Teaching at Grand Canyon University. Her research focuses on enhancing student learning through assessment and innovative online instructional strategies. In addition, she has interests in examining the perception of online degrees, the quality of online course offerings and the development of effective faculty evaluation models. Jean received her B.S. in comprehensive psychology from the University of Nebraska at Kearney, an M.S. in experimental psychology from Western Illinois University and Ph.D. in social psychology from the University of Nebraska at Lincoln.

William Thomas McBride teaches film, drama, cultural studies, and hermeneutics at Illinois State University and is the author of Stylized Moments: Turning Film Style Into Meaning. He has published, among other topics, on the "fathead" shot in Hitchcock, circumcision and midrash, apocalyptic fun in the paintings of Kenny Scharf, chiasm, lex talio and money in the Book of Esther, pedagogical approaches to the film of Leroi Jones' Dutchman, Samuel Beckett's homo mensura, Indian masking and native funk, shyster vampires, and Bahktin's Marxist formalism.

Robert L. Moore has been an instructional designer with the University of North Carolina at Chapel Hill School of Government since 2010 and has worked at UNC since 2004. In his current position, he collaborates with faculty on integrating innovative technology to support their instruction in face-to-face, blended, and online instructional environments. Moore is currently pursuing a PhD in Curriculum and Instruction from North Carolina State University. He holds a Masters of Project Management from Western Carolina University, an M.S. in instructional technology from East Carolina University, and a B.A. in political science from UNC-Chapel Hill. He is also a UNC-Chapel Hill Center for Faculty Excellence Future Faculty Fellow and has attained the LEARN NC Online Instructor certification and the East Carolina University Distance Learning and Administration certificate.

Olivia P. Morris (Graduate Illinois State University 2012, Ed.D Curriculum & Instruction) Online Professor Macroeconomics Online Learning (May, 2009 - Present) Masters of Science Economics 1995 Illinois State University, Bachelors of Science Economics 1980 University of Guyana.

Christina M. Nash is a doctoral candidate in the Department of Educational Theory and Practice at the University at Albany, SUNY. Her dissertation is a metaphorical analysis of educational standards. Other areas of research and publication include multicultural education and online learning.

Maria Pavlis Korres obtained a university degree in Political Sciences in Athens (1981). From 1983 until today she works on Adult Education in the Greek Ministry of Education. She has participated as an expert in the first research on Roma Education conducted by the European Council (1985-1986) and she has participated in educational and research projects on Roma Education implemented by the E.E, the General Secretariat for Lifelong Learning in Greece, the University of Ioannina and the University of Athens, Greece). Since 2005 her research interests are focused on e-learning and she became PhD student in the University of Alcalá, Spain. In 2008 she obtained her Advance Studies Degree from the Computer Science Department of the University of Alcalá and in 2010 she obtained her PhD with honors.

The subject of her PhD is "Development of an e-education framework for the education of educators of special groups in order to improve their compatibility with their learners". Since 2012 she is a member of the scientific staff of Hellenic Open University and she has been assigned to teach Adult Education in postgraduate courses. She has published several articles, chapters and books on Roma, adult education and e-learning. Her current interests are focused on design, development and evaluation of educational projects for adults, face to face and e-learning, as well as the group dynamics in an online environment and the appropriate use of communication tools in order to promote interaction in an online environment.

Elaine Roberts Kaye is an Instructional Technologist/Professional Faculty in the Center for Instructional Technology, as well as a Faculty member in the College of Education at James Madison University.

Arianne Rourke is an academic in the Faculty of Art and Design, the University of New South Wales, Sydney, Australia. She has over 23 years of experience of university teaching. During this time Dr Rourke has Co-ordinated and taught design history and theory in the Bachelor of Design and the Internship and Research paper courses in the Master of Art Administration. Her research is in Cognitive load theory, visual literacy, learning style modalities, prototype theory, expert/novice differences and online teaching and learning examining ways of improving instructional design towards the long-term retention of learning. Dr Rourke has published widely her experimental research into teaching and learning in higher education and has co-edited a book with Kathryn Coleman titled: 'Pedagogy Leads Technology, Online Learning and Teaching in Higher Education: New Pedagogies, New Technologies' (2011) with Common grounds publishing. She has also co-authored a book with Dr Zena O'Connor titled: 'Effective use of visuals in higher education' (2012) published by Nova Science. More recently Dr Rourke has co-edited a books with Dr Vaughan Rees titled: 'Building minds, forging bridges: teaching in a visually littered world' (2013) and another book titled: 'Researching the Visual: Demystifying 'the picture that's worth a thousand words' (2014), published by Common grounds publishing. She holds the following degrees: BA(Vis.Arts), AMCAE; BEd(Art), SCAE; MA(History), UNSW; MA(Hons) Macq; MHEd, UNSW; MPhil(HE), UNSW and EdD, UNSW.

Peggy Semingson is an Associate Professor of Curriculum and Instruction at The University of Texas at Arlington where she teaches courses in Literacy Studies. Dr. Semingson has experience as a classroom teacher and reading specialist in both Southern California and Texas. She received her M.Ed. in Reading Education from Texas State University, San Marcos in 2004 and her Ph.D. in Curriculum and Instruction with a specialization in Language and Literacy Studies from The University of Texas at Austin in 2008. Her research interests include social contexts of literacy learning, digital pedagogies, and students who face challenges in reading. She has published in Teachers College Record and other peer-reviewed journals. She was awarded the Jeanne S. Chall Research Grant from Harvard University during 2009-2010 and received the Platinum level--Best Practices Award for Excellence in Distance Learning Teaching from the United States Distance Learning Association in 2013.

Patriann Smith serves as a faculty member in the Department of Curriculum and Instruction at the University of Illinois at Urbana-Champaign. Patriann teaches courses in reading and literacy and conducts research on cross-cultural language and literacy teaching, considering specifically the intercultural experiences of international multilingual students and teachers. She is an International Reading Association

(IRA) Hall of Fame Young Scholar (2013-2016) and a Literacy Research Association (LRA) Scholar of color Transitioning into Academic Research Institutions (STAR) (2015-2017).

Pete Smith is Vice Provost for Digital Teaching and Learning at the University of Texas Arlington, where he oversees UTA's Center for Distance Education, Classroom Technology Support Services, and the Learning Innovation and Networked Knowledge Laboratory. Dr. Smith is an active teacher of German and Russian language and culture and a participating faculty member in the Center for Post-Soviet and East European Studies. He earned his B.A. and B.S. degrees from the Pennsylvania State University, and his Master's in Slavic Languages and Doctorate in Second Language Acquisition at the University of Texas at Austin. Dr. Smith served as a coordinator and telementor in the Drake University Language Acquisition Program, an evaluator and coordinator in Drake's Virtual Language Studies (federal grant initiative for teaching Russian and Chinese online), and a program officer in the Network for Effective Language Learning (a national network of Liberal Arts colleges exploring critical languages and technologies). He also advises initiatives statewide which include the Teacher Quality Federal Grants Program in Texas. His recent presentations and publications have centered on the role of the Internet and network-based tools in teaching of language, culture, and the potential of online communities of practice to foster teachers' professional development and growth.

David Starr-Glass is a faculty member of the University of New York in Prague, Czech Republic, and a senior mentor with the International Programs (Prague Unit) of the State University of New York, Empire State College. He teaches a wide range of business related areas at the undergraduate level, in both blended and online distance learning formats. He also serves as the supervisor for undergraduate dissertations, mentoring final year students in designing and writing their work. David has a wide range of managerial and educational experience and has earned three master's degrees: business administration (Notre Dame de Namur University, California), organizational psychology (Birkbeck College, University of London), and flexible education and online learning (University of Southern Queensland, Australia). David has contributed more than a dozen chapters to edited books and published about sixty peer-reviewed journal articles in the international business, online distance learning, and mentoring literature. When not in Prague, he lives in Jerusalem where he teaches economic and business related courses with a number of local colleges.

David Starrett is Dean of Academic Information Services, Director of Kent Library, Director of Institutional and Programmatic Accreditations, and Accreditation Liaison Officer at Southeast Missouri State University. Dave has directed the Center for Scholarship in Teaching and Learning and established Southeast Online Programs. He has served as a reviewer for Educause and ELI, has served on conference program committees for regional Educause conferences, is an Educause FRYE Fellow, and currently serves on the Senior Leadership Roundtable Council with Educause. Dave has served as a Research Associate with the TLT Group, Executive Director of the Council for Administration of General and Liberal Studies, board member of the Association of General and Liberal Studies, and member of the Educause Advisory Committee on Teaching and Learning.

Cindy Stewart is an Associate Professor of Psychology at the University of Houston-Downtown. Her research examines applications of constructivist and motivation theory to online education.

Kwesi Tandoh has a doctorate degree in Instructional Technology and Design and currently working as an Instructional Designer at Ball State. His primary responsibilities include designing and preparing faculty to teach online as well as mentoring faculty on instructional best practices and the integration of technology in face-to-face, and hybrid courses using Blackboard Learn. Prior to coming to Ball State University, he worked as an instructional designer at the University of Arkansas, Fayetteville and the Appalachian State University. He has also worked as an adjunct professor and Instructional Technology specialist at the Southwest Minnesota State University. Academically, he extensive course work in educational technology and instructional design at the Ohio University and work experiences at the University of Arkansas Global Campus, Appalachian State University, and Southwest Minnesota State University has allowed him to gain an understanding and appreciation for the academic processes which are exhibited. This rewarding experience not only sharpened his desire to make a positive contribution in this field, but provided me the opportunity to cross train with other educators. His experience has further strengthened my interest in academic support and instructional design. Today, he is an active member of Ball State University's dynamic instructional design team. I assist team members, design course layouts and graphics for Blackboard Learn 9.1 SP 13, and work with instructors to design effective face-to-face, hybrid, and online courses in Blackboard to promote learning.

Kathryn Woods is an Assistant Professor in the Professional Studies department at Austin Peay State University. Dr. Woods has significant work experience in the fields of healthcare administration and financial services. Her research interests include marketing, social media, employee turnover, corporate culture, and online learning.

Angelia Yount is an instructional designer at Ball State with a passion for education and training individuals both face-to-face and online. Yount has trained in the corporate setting, K-12, and in higher education. She was an administrator for online education at Ivy Tech Community College Northwest, and was a department chair for the School of Business online for ITT-Tech. Yount is currently working toward a doctorate degree in organizational leadership, maintaining a 3.89 GPA while working full time. She earned a master's degree in business administration management from Indiana Wesleyan University. She has a bachelor's degree in visual communications from Ball State. Yount brings more than 15 years of experience and expertise in training and developing curriculum, both regionally and nationally. She takes pride in constantly analyzing how to make a course online more dynamic than the face-to-face course. She recognizes that online teaching can sometimes be more challenging due to the learning format and the need to incorporate media and technology in place of the face-to-face lecture. Yount also draws upon her previous experience of writing training manuals and training individuals in the manufacturing environment to continue to enhance her analysis of courses.

Guangji Yuan is a doctoral student in curriculum development and instructional technology at the department of educational theory and practice, school of education, University at Albany New York. Her research interest are instructional technology, bet practices in online learning, and creativity and research in instructional technology.

Index

INTERNATIONAL

Information Resources Management Association

Become an IRMA Member

Members of the **Information Resources Management Association (IRMA)** understand the importance of community within their field of study. The Information Resources Management Association is an ideal venue through which professionals, students, and academicians can convene and share the latest industry innovations and scholarly research that is changing the field of information science and technology. Become a member today and enjoy the benefits of membership as well as the opportunity to collaborate and network with fellow experts in the field.

IRMA Membership Benefits:

- **One FREE Journal Subscription**
- **30% Off Additional Journal Subscriptions**
- **20% Off Book Purchases**
- Updates on the latest events and research on Information Resources Management through the IRMA-L listserv.
- Updates on new open access and downloadable content added to Research IRM.
- A copy of the Information Technology Management Newsletter twice a year.
- A certificate of membership.

IRMA Membership $195

Scan code to visit irma-international.org and begin by selecting your free journal subscription.

Membership is good for one full year.

www.irma-international.org

CPSIA information can be obtained
at www.ICGtesting.com
Printed in the USA
LVOW03*1531070616

491587LV00022B/285/P